GREAT COOKING IDEAS

by HATTIE CARTER

illustrated by
ARTHUR FRIEDMAN
MARC MALLIN
and
BILL SILBERT

MOBY BOOKS

PLAYMORE, INC. Publishers
Under arrangement with I. WALDMAN AND SON, INC.
New York, New York

cover design by Al Leiner

CONTENTS

INTRODUCTION

RECIPES

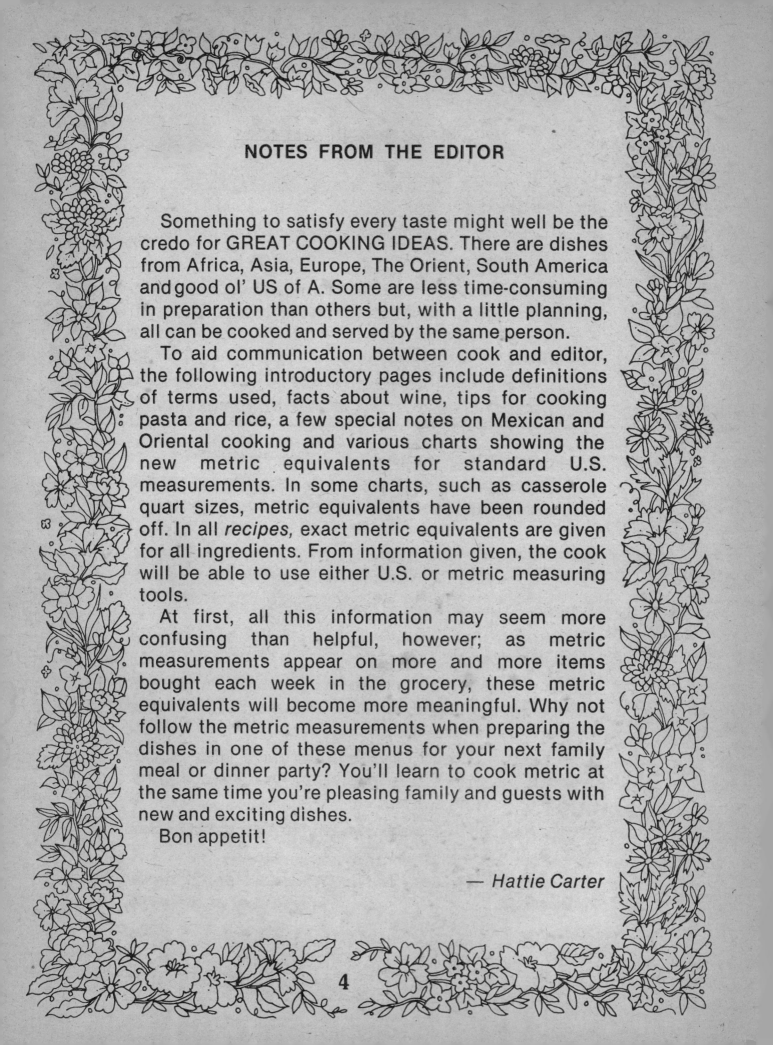

NOTES FROM THE EDITOR

Something to satisfy every taste might well be the credo for GREAT COOKING IDEAS. There are dishes from Africa, Asia, Europe, The Orient, South America and good ol' US of A. Some are less time-consuming in preparation than others but, with a little planning, all can be cooked and served by the same person.

To aid communication between cook and editor, the following introductory pages include definitions of terms used, facts about wine, tips for cooking pasta and rice, a few special notes on Mexican and Oriental cooking and various charts showing the new metric equivalents for standard U.S. measurements. In some charts, such as casserole quart sizes, metric equivalents have been rounded off. In all *recipes,* exact metric equivalents are given for all ingredients. From information given, the cook will be able to use either U.S. or metric measuring tools.

At first, all this information may seem more confusing than helpful, however; as metric measurements appear on more and more items bought each week in the grocery, these metric equivalents will become more meaningful. Why not follow the metric measurements when preparing the dishes in one of these menus for your next family meal or dinner party? You'll learn to cook metric at the same time you're pleasing family and guests with new and exciting dishes.

Bon appetit!

— *Hattie Carter*

COOKING TERMS DEFINED

Baste — Spoon or brush liquid or melted fat over food as it cooks.

Beat — Stir thoroughly with a spoon or egg beater.

Blend — Mix thoroughly.

Bouillon — A clear broth made by cooking meat, fish or vegetables in liquid and then straining the liquid. Packaged bouillon cubes may be used as a substitute.

Bouquet Garni — A selection of herbs placed in a small bag of cheesecloth and put in a broth or stock to flavor it while cooking.

Bread (To Bread) — Roll meat or fish in crumbs.

Bread Crumbs — *Soft* are made with day-old bread; *fine* with bread that is dried out and rolled or grated.

Broth — Liquid left after simmering vegetables, meat, fish or other foods. Also used to mean a thin soup.

Brown — To cook in a little fat until brown.

Buttered Crumbs — Fine bread crumbs cooked with melted butter until saturated.

Chop — Cut into small pieces. Use food chopper or sharp, heavy knife. A large French knife with a triangular blade is the best tool.

Chowder — A thick, hearty soup made with fish or seafood, or sometimes vegetables, that are cooked in a seasoned milk liquid.

Coat — Cover thoroughly, as in coating meat or fish with crumbs before cooking.

Consommé — Clear, highly seasoned broth made from meat.

(continued on next page)

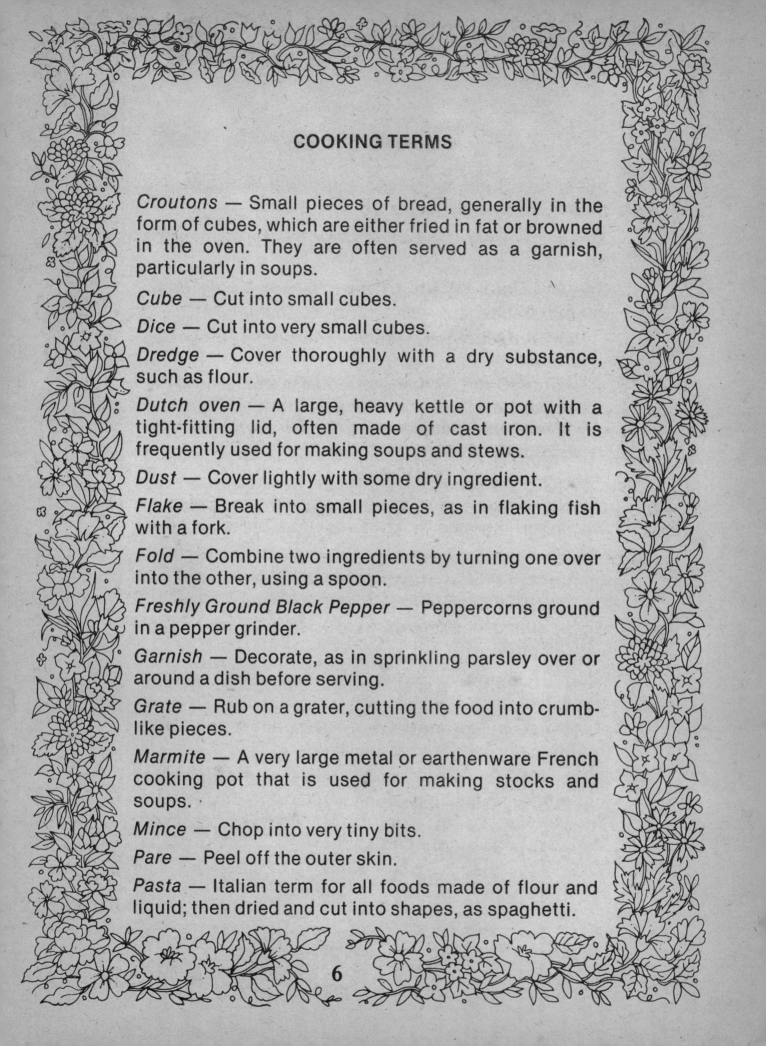

COOKING TERMS

Croutons — Small pieces of bread, generally in the form of cubes, which are either fried in fat or browned in the oven. They are often served as a garnish, particularly in soups.

Cube — Cut into small cubes.

Dice — Cut into very small cubes.

Dredge — Cover thoroughly with a dry substance, such as flour.

Dutch oven — A large, heavy kettle or pot with a tight-fitting lid, often made of cast iron. It is frequently used for making soups and stews.

Dust — Cover lightly with some dry ingredient.

Flake — Break into small pieces, as in flaking fish with a fork.

Fold — Combine two ingredients by turning one over into the other, using a spoon.

Freshly Ground Black Pepper — Peppercorns ground in a pepper grinder.

Garnish — Decorate, as in sprinkling parsley over or around a dish before serving.

Grate — Rub on a grater, cutting the food into crumb-like pieces.

Marmite — A very large metal or earthenware French cooking pot that is used for making stocks and soups.

Mince — Chop into very tiny bits.

Pare — Peel off the outer skin.

Pasta — Italian term for all foods made of flour and liquid; then dried and cut into shapes, as spaghetti.

COOKING TERMS

Pinch — As much as you can hold between the thumb and first finger, as a pinch of salt.

Preheat — Heat the pan or oven before placing the food in it.

Sauté — Cook on top of the stove in a very small amount of fat.

Until brown means gently until golden brown on all sides.

Until just soft means until tender but not necessarily brown.

Until transparent means until the food, such as onion, has turned slightly clear.

Shred — Cut into thin slivers.

Soufflé — Made with beaten egg whites, folded in with other ingredients so the mixture puffs up when baked.

Stiff But Not Dry — Egg whites are beaten "stiff but not dry" when used to make a mixture light and airy.

Stir — Blend ingredients by a wide, circular motion with a spoon.

Stock — Liquid in which food has been cooked: meat, fish or vegetables.

Tureen — A covered deep oval or round dish traditionally used for serving soup.

Whip — Beat an ingredient quickly and thoroughly until puffy. This can be done with an egg beater, wire whisk, fork or electric mixer. The utensil used depends on the ingredients.

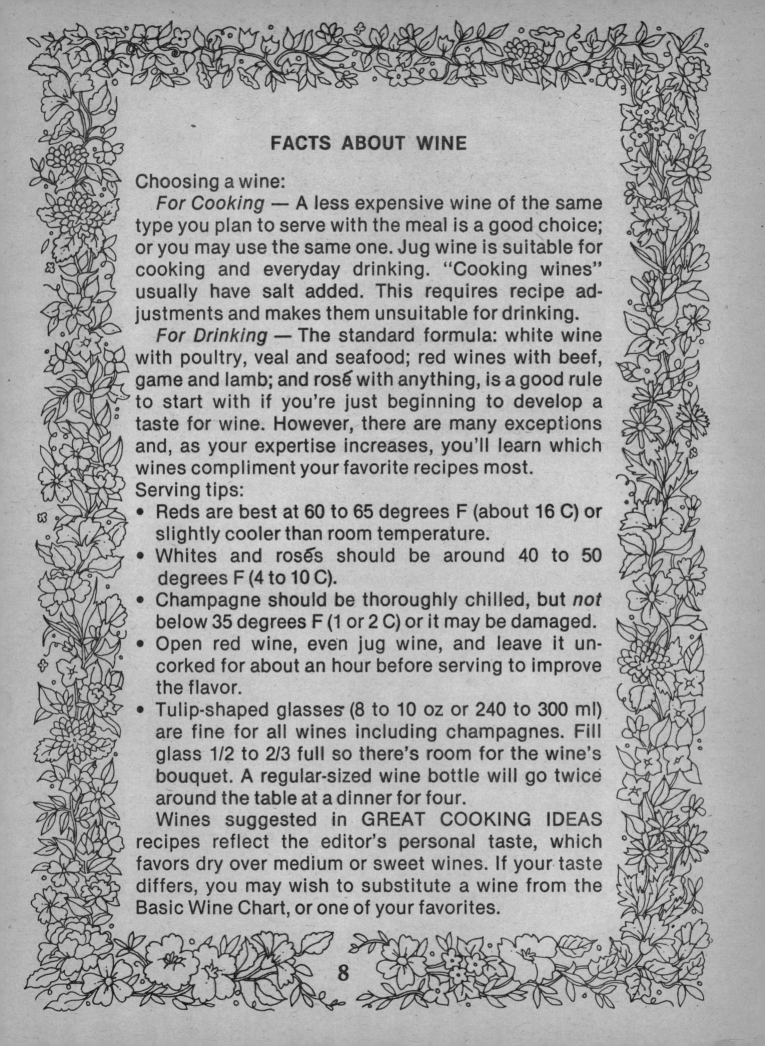

FACTS ABOUT WINE

Choosing a wine:

For Cooking — A less expensive wine of the same type you plan to serve with the meal is a good choice; or you may use the same one. Jug wine is suitable for cooking and everyday drinking. "Cooking wines" usually have salt added. This requires recipe adjustments and makes them unsuitable for drinking.

For Drinking — The standard formula: white wine with poultry, veal and seafood; red wines with beef, game and lamb; and rosé with anything, is a good rule to start with if you're just beginning to develop a taste for wine. However, there are many exceptions and, as your expertise increases, you'll learn which wines compliment your favorite recipes most.

Serving tips:

- Reds are best at 60 to 65 degrees F (about 16 C) or slightly cooler than room temperature.
- Whites and rosés should be around 40 to 50 degrees F (4 to 10 C).
- Champagne should be thoroughly chilled, but *not* below 35 degrees F (1 or 2 C) or it may be damaged.
- Open red wine, even jug wine, and leave it uncorked for about an hour before serving to improve the flavor.
- Tulip-shaped glasses (8 to 10 oz or 240 to 300 ml) are fine for all wines including champagnes. Fill glass 1/2 to 2/3 full so there's room for the wine's bouquet. A regular-sized wine bottle will go twice around the table at a dinner for four.

Wines suggested in GREAT COOKING IDEAS recipes reflect the editor's personal taste, which favors dry over medium or sweet wines. If your taste differs, you may wish to substitute a wine from the Basic Wine Chart, or one of your favorites.

You will note that an alternative is given in each recipe where wine is used for those who do not wish to imbibe. However, even a tee-totaler can cook with wine as the alcoholic content evaporates when the wine is heated. Only the "essence" of the wine remains to impart its subtle flavor to the dish.

BASIC WINE CHART

	Dry	Medium	Sweet
Red	Bordeaux	Grenache Rosé	Kosher Concord
	Burgundy	Lake Country Red	Malaga
	Cabernet Sauvignon	Medium-Dry Sherry	Port (Ruby or Tawny)
	Chianti	Rosé d'Anjou	Sweet (Red) Vermouth
	Claret		
	Côtes du Rhône Reds		
	Gamay Beaujolais		
	Grignolino Rosé		
	Pinot Noir		
	Zinfandel		
	Zinfandel Rosé		
White	Burgundy	Lake Country White	Cream Sherry
	Chablis	Liebfraumilch	Haut (Sweet) Sauterne
	Chenin Blanc	Rhine Wine	Marsala
	Dry Rhine Wine	Riesling	Muscatel
	Dry Sherry	Vouvray	Sauternes
	Dry (White) Vermouth		Tokay
	Grey Riesling		
	Muscadet		White Kosher Wines
	Pinot Blanc		
	Pinot Chardonnay		
	Soave		

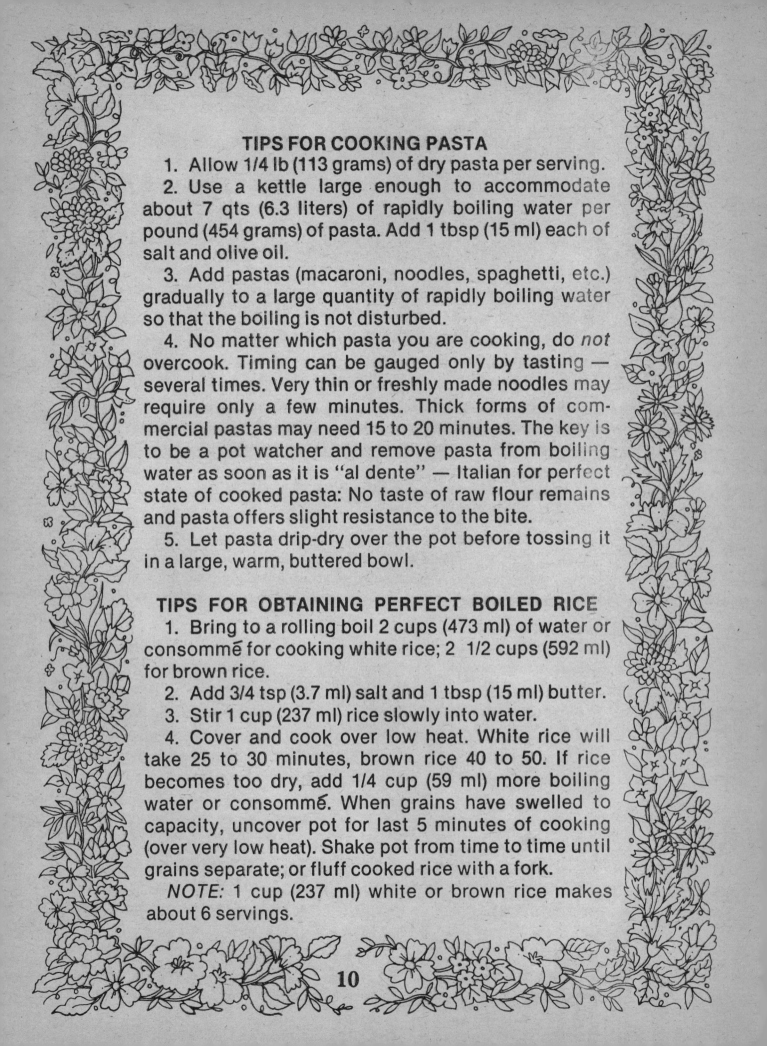

TIPS FOR COOKING PASTA
1. Allow 1/4 lb (113 grams) of dry pasta per serving.
2. Use a kettle large enough to accommodate about 7 qts (6.3 liters) of rapidly boiling water per pound (454 grams) of pasta. Add 1 tbsp (15 ml) each of salt and olive oil.
3. Add pastas (macaroni, noodles, spaghetti, etc.) gradually to a large quantity of rapidly boiling water so that the boiling is not disturbed.
4. No matter which pasta you are cooking, do *not* overcook. Timing can be gauged only by tasting — several times. Very thin or freshly made noodles may require only a few minutes. Thick forms of commercial pastas may need 15 to 20 minutes. The key is to be a pot watcher and remove pasta from boiling water as soon as it is "al dente" — Italian for perfect state of cooked pasta: No taste of raw flour remains and pasta offers slight resistance to the bite.
5. Let pasta drip-dry over the pot before tossing it in a large, warm, buttered bowl.

TIPS FOR OBTAINING PERFECT BOILED RICE
1. Bring to a rolling boil 2 cups (473 ml) of water or consommé for cooking white rice; 2 1/2 cups (592 ml) for brown rice.
2. Add 3/4 tsp (3.7 ml) salt and 1 tbsp (15 ml) butter.
3. Stir 1 cup (237 ml) rice slowly into water.
4. Cover and cook over low heat. White rice will take 25 to 30 minutes, brown rice 40 to 50. If rice becomes too dry, add 1/4 cup (59 ml) more boiling water or consommé. When grains have swelled to capacity, uncover pot for last 5 minutes of cooking (over very low heat). Shake pot from time to time until grains separate; or fluff cooked rice with a fork.
NOTE: 1 cup (237 ml) white or brown rice makes about 6 servings.

INTRODUCTION TO PASTA

Making Egg-Noodle Dough:
- 4 large eggs
- 4 tbsp (60 ml) cold water
- 1 lb (454 grams) all-purpose flour

1. In a large mixing bowl, break the eggs.
2. Add the water and about 1/4 of the flour. Beat this mixture with a wire whisk until very smooth.
3. Add nearly all of the remaining flour and work mixture with hands into a soft dough. If dough seems sticky, work in rest of flour.
4. Turn dough out on kneading surface and knead well 10 minutes. This gives the dough its elasticity.
5. Return dough to bowl, cover and leave at least 20 minutes.
6. Roll out dough to a thickness of 1/8 (.3 cm) inch.

Note: The dough will be more manageable if it is divided into two pieces before rolling is done.

Shaping Pasta:

This is the fun part. The easiest and most popular shapes to make at home are those cut from flat sheets of pasta, which are then called noodles.

Roll the flat sheet of dough up from one side to the other, like a jelly-roll and cut slices off with a sharp knife. Unroll the slices and lay the noodles flat on pieces of well-floured waxed paper. Leave them dry 10 - 15 minutes before cooking.

For tagliatelle: cut roll into 1/2-inch (1-cm) thick slices.

For fettuccine: cut roll into 1/4-inch (.6-cm) slices.

For fettucce: cut roll into 1/2 - 3/4-inch (1-cm-2-cm) slices.

(continued on next page)

The following shapes are also cut from flat sheets:

Manicotti: cut into 3-inch (8-cm) squares.

Lasagna: cut dough into 4 x 10-inch (10 x 25-cm) rectangles.

Cannelloni: cut into 4-inch (10-cm) squares.

Don't dry any of these; cook them as soon as possible.

Any left-over pasta dough can be gathered into a ball and rolled out again to be cut into noodles, or it can be cut into small squares and used in soups.

Storing Pasta:

Noodles which are not cooked immediately after the specified drying time should be left out on floured waxed paper until they are completely dry — at least one day. They will resemble commercially produced pasta and should be stored as such — in paper bags or cardboard boxes to allow the air to circulate.

Filled pastas such as ravioli and tortellini cannot be dried; however, they can be frozen. Place on floured waxed paper in rows, not touching or they will stick together. Roll in waxed paper, then wrap roll in foil and freeze.

Cooking Pasta:

For cooking commercial pastas, refer to p 10.

For homemade fresh pasta:

Egg noodles, yellow	5-6 minutes
Lasagna	2 minutes
Manicotti	2 minutes
Cannelloni	2 minutes
Tortellini	5-8 minutes
Ravioli	5-8 minutes

At best, these are rough guides. As a general rule homemade pasta is cooked when it rises to the top of the pot.

NOTES ON MEXICAN COOKING

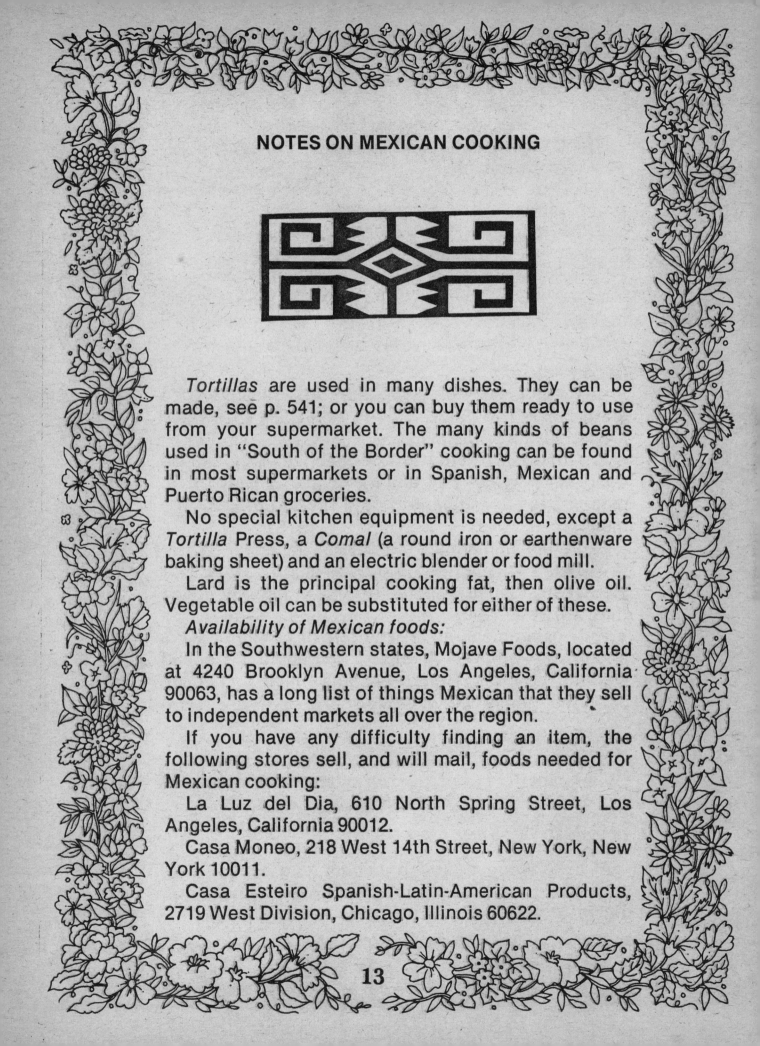

Tortillas are used in many dishes. They can be made, see p. 541; or you can buy them ready to use from your supermarket. The many kinds of beans used in "South of the Border" cooking can be found in most supermarkets or in Spanish, Mexican and Puerto Rican groceries.

No special kitchen equipment is needed, except a *Tortilla* Press, a *Comal* (a round iron or earthenware baking sheet) and an electric blender or food mill.

Lard is the principal cooking fat, then olive oil. Vegetable oil can be substituted for either of these.

Availability of Mexican foods:

In the Southwestern states, Mojave Foods, located at 4240 Brooklyn Avenue, Los Angeles, California 90063, has a long list of things Mexican that they sell to independent markets all over the region.

If you have any difficulty finding an item, the following stores sell, and will mail, foods needed for Mexican cooking:

La Luz del Dia, 610 North Spring Street, Los Angeles, California 90012.

Casa Moneo, 218 West 14th Street, New York, New York 10011.

Casa Esteiro Spanish-Latin-American Products, 2719 West Division, Chicago, Illinois 60622.

INTRODUCTION TO ORIENTAL COOKING

Food Preparation:

1. Prepare everything ahead of time because once started, you can't stop. This is especially true when preparing stir-fry dishes.

2. Chop ingredients to uniform size. This can be done early in the day and items can be stored in plastic bags in refrigerator until time to prepare the meal.

3. Parboil or marinate ingredients, if necessary.

4. Place all chopped ingredients on a board or plate ready for use. Assemble all other ingredients so they will be at hand.

5. If using meat, all fat and bits of gristle or bone should be removed. If sliced, it should be sliced against the grain. Before cooking, meat should be dried thoroughly with paper towels.

Cooking Methods (4 basic ones):

1. *Deep-frying* — ingredients are chopped in large bite-sized pieces, often marinated, and rolled in batter or cornstarch, then added piece by piece to hot, deep fat. They are cooked until golden brown. When oil bubbles it is ready for fish, kidneys or poultry. When it smokes it's ready for beef or pork. Be sure ingredients are *dry* or they will spatter and become soggy. When done, drain on paper towels.

2. *Steaming* — set a rack in a pan of boiling water. Set a Pyrex dish on rack. Water should come about 2/3 up side of dish. Place food to be steamed in dish, cover and steam as long as recipe requires.

3. *Stewing* — use a heavy Dutch oven. There are two types of stew: red is with soy sauce and is used for lamb, pork or beef; white is with clear broth and is used for fish and chicken.

4. *Stir-frying* — ingredients are chopped into bite-sized pieces. Heat a heavy skillet or wok and add oil. When it is hot, add garlic, ginger and salt. Fry about 30 seconds. Add other ingredients and fry 2-3 minutes, tossing food constantly with two spoons. Timing is the key factor: going too fast, ingredients will start to burn. Remove from heat and keep tossing. Reduce heat slightly and return to heat, if necessary. Serve dish immediately. Do not start stir-frying until diners are seated at table; otherwise, food will be soggy.

Ingredients:

The items listed are necessary to Oriental cooking and should be on hand. In cases where an item is not readily available in stores, an alternative is given.

Allspice
Anise seeds and powder
Bamboo shoots (canned)
Bay leaves
Bean sprouts (canned)
Black Beans (canned or dried)
Broth (canned chicken)
Celery (fresh)
Chicken stock (homemade, then refrigerated)

Chives (dried)
Cinnamon (sticks and grated)
Cornstarch
Curry powder
Dried mushrooms
Flour (wheat)
Garlic (fresh)
Ginger (powdered)
Ginger root
(list continued on next page)

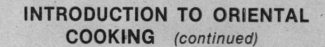

INTRODUCTION TO ORIENTAL
COOKING *(continued)*

Hot pepper sauce
Mustard (Chinese hot)
Noodles (cellophane)*
Noodles (large, flat)
Oil (peanut and sesame)
Onions
Parsley (fresh)
Peppercorns (black and
  white)
Potatoes
Rice
Rice wine**
Rosemary
Salt (kosher or rock)
Scallions
Snow peas (frozen)

Soy sauce (China
  Beauty — thin and
  sweet; La Choy —
  medium; Kikkoman —
  Japanese, heavy and
  strong)
Spaghetti
Sugar (brown and
  white)
Tea
Thyme
Tomato purée
Turmeric
Vermicelli
Vinegar (red and
  white wine)

*Transparent (cellophane) Chinese noodles are found in Chinese food shops, where they are known as *sai fun*.

**Sherry may be substituted for rice wine, but it must be dry. (Dry white wine, Japanese sake, or cognac can also be used).

Note: Monosodium glutamate has not been included in any of the recipes, even though it is often used in Oriental restaurants, because it causes adverse physical side-effects in some people.

Ingredients (additional):

The following bottled sauces are handy to have stored in the refrigerator:

Brown	Sweet and Sour
Chili	Hoisin
Dark or Plum	Oyster

Beverages include tea, *sake* (rice wine) and beer. In Japan, a fine grade of beer is made, including stout or black beer, but the native alcoholic beverages are: *sake*, made from the best rice; and *shochu*, distilled from inferior rice or sweet potatoes. There are two kinds of *sake*: *mirin*, used in cooking and drunk with everyday meals; and *toso*, served on ceremonial and holiday occasions.

About Tea:

Chinese tea is drunk from tiny bowls, without either sugar or milk. It has a very subtle flavor.

To make tea properly: the water must boil (use cold tap water or bottled water); use one rounded tsp tea for each person and one for the pot. The tea should not go on brewing indefinitely, but be drunk at once.

The teapot should never be washed with soap or the flavor of the tea will be ruined. Simply rinse it out with very hot water.

Preparation of Japanese Green Tea:

A scant tsp of leaves is used per cup. If tea is very delicate, water should not be quite boiling; if less delicate, water may be boiling rapidly. Tea is placed in pot, water added, allowed to rest a moment, swirled gently to dampen all the leaves, and then poured. Extra water is not added until more tea is wanted. This preserves the fragrance of the liquid and prevents tea from becoming bitter.

(continued on next page)

INTRODUCTION TO ORIENTAL
COOKING *(continued)*

About Wine:

A Basic Wine Chart (European), p. 9, has been included in this introductory material for your convenience; however, Chinese food is traditionally served with rice wine. *Shaoshing* wine is milder and drier than dry sherry and is fermented from rice. It is the best Chinese wine for Chinese food and should be served warm (or hot) from a porcelain or pewter wine pot. Small special wine cups are used instead of glasses. Another Chinese wine is *kaoling,* which is made from sorghum. It is very strong and good in cold weather. Rose petals and various kinds of fruit are used to enhance the flavor and color. Other fruit-flavored wines include lychee, orange and green plum.

Preparation of Japanese Rice:

In Japan, rice is cooked in a special pot called a *kama*; however, similar results can be obtained by cooking rice in the top of a double boiler.

The grains should be carefully washed. Then place 1 cup (237 ml) rice and 1 1/4 cups (296 ml) water in top of double boiler. Watered rice should be brought to boiling over a high flame. Then reduce heat and cook 10 to 15 minutes; reduce heat again, to very low, and cook 10 minutes longer. Finally, turn off flame and let cooked rice stand, lid on pot, another 10 or 15 minutes. This will prevent sticky or gummy rice.

Rice is eaten plain, hot or cold, white and fluffy. It is also eaten soaked in Japanese tea in a style called *chazuke,* p. 429.

18

SPELLING AND SYMBOLS
FOR MEASURING UNITS

The spelling of names of units, as adopted by the National Bureau of Standards, is given in the list below. Following the name of each unit the corresponding symbol (abbreviation) is given. No periods are used with symbols; however, inch, gram, liter and meter are spelled out. The same symbol is used for both singular and plural to avoid any confusion.

Unit Name	Symbol	As Used In COOK PAD
Celsius, degree	°C	C
centimeter	cm	cm
Fahrenheit, degree	°F	degree F
gram	g	gram(s)
inch	in	inch
kilogram	kg	kg
liter	liter	liter
meter	m	meter
milligram	mg	mg
milliliter	ml	ml
ounce	oz	oz
pint, liquid	liq pt	pt
pound	lb	lb
quart, liquid	liq qt	qt
tablespoon	tbsp	tbsp
teaspoon	tsp	tsp

OVEN TEMPERATURE CHART

Recipe Calls For	Fahrenheit Degrees	Centigrade Degrees
Warm	200 — 225	93 — 107
Very Low	250 — 275	121 — 135
Low	300 — 325	149 — 163
Medium	350 — 375	177 — 191
High	400 — 425	204 — 218
Very High	450 — 475	232 — 246
Extremely High	500 — 525	260 — 274
Broil	600	316

Note: Throughout this COOK PAD "degrees F" is used to represent Fahrenheit and "C" is used for Centigrade.

Formula for converting from Fahrenheit to Centigrade:

Start with F temperature.
Subtract 32.
Multiply by 5.
Divide by 9.
Result is C temperature equivalent.

Formula for converting from Centigrade to Fahrenheit:

Start with C temperature.
Multiply by 9.
Divide by 5.
Add 32.
Result is F temperature equivalent.

CONVERSION TABLE FOR VOLUME MEASUREMENTS

Teaspoons to Milliliters

tsp	ml	tsp	ml
1/8	.6	1 3/4	8.7
1/4	1.2	2	10.0
1/2	2.5	2 1/4	11.2
3/4	3.7	2 1/2	12.5
1	5.0	2 3/4	13.7
1 1/4	6.2	3	15.0
1 1/2	7.5		

Tablespoons to Milliliters

tbsp	ml	tbsp	ml
1/2	7.5	2 1/2	37.5
1	15.0	3	45.0
1 1/2	22.5	3 1/2	52.5
2	30.0	4	60.0

Cups and Pints to Milliliters

cups	ml	cups	ml
1/8	29.6 = 30	1 1/2	354.8 = 355
1/4	59.2 = 59	1 3/4	414.0 = 414
1/3	78.9 = 79	2 (1 pint)	473.2 = 473
3/8	88.7 = 89	2 1/4	532.3 = 532
1/2	118.3 = 118	2 1/2	591.5 = 592
5/8	147.9 = 148	2 3/4	650.6 = 651
2/3	157.7 = 158	3	709.8 = 710
3/4	177.4 = 177	3 1/4	768.9 = 769
7/8	207.0 = 207	3 1/2	828.1 = 828
1	236.6 = 237	3 3/4	887.2 = 887
1 1/4	295.7 = 296	4 (or 2 pints)	946.4 = 946

Quarts to Liters

quarts	liters	quarts	liters
1	1.0	3	3.0
1 1/2	1.5	3 1/2	3.5
2	2.0	4 (or	
2 1/2	2.5	1 gallon)	4.0

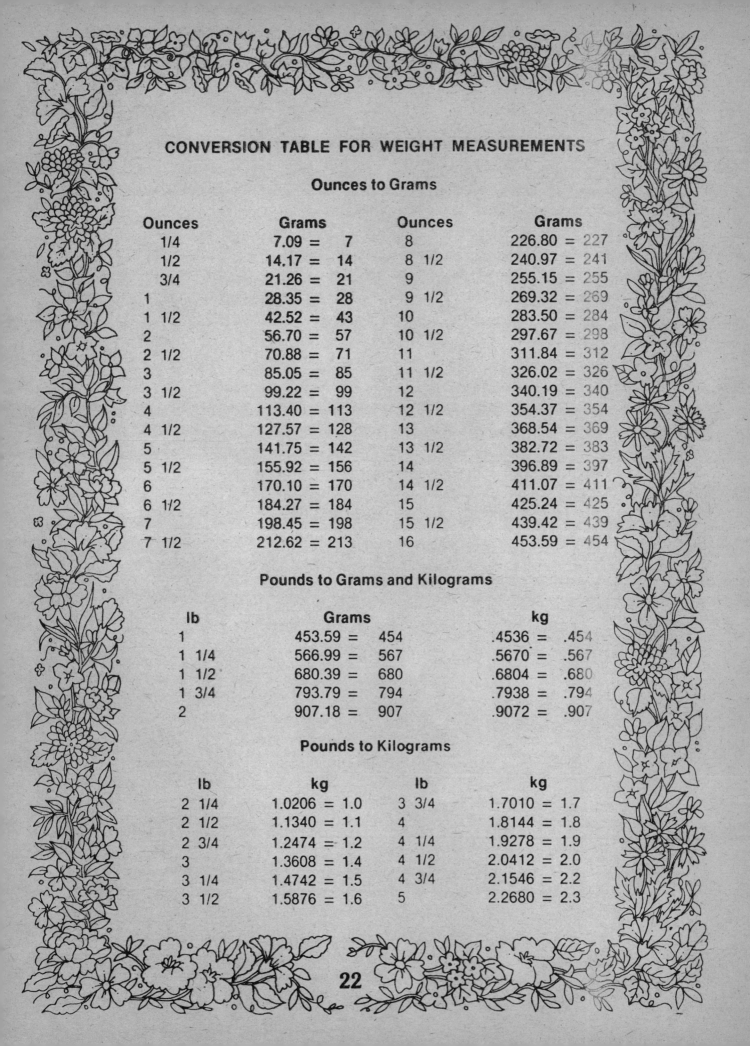

CONVERSION TABLE FOR WEIGHT MEASUREMENTS

Ounces to Grams

Ounces	Grams		Ounces	Grams	
1/4	7.09 =	7	8	226.80 =	227
1/2	14.17 =	14	8 1/2	240.97 =	241
3/4	21.26 =	21	9	255.15 =	255
1	28.35 =	28	9 1/2	269.32 =	269
1 1/2	42.52 =	43	10	283.50 =	284
2	56.70 =	57	10 1/2	297.67 =	298
2 1/2	70.88 =	71	11	311.84 =	312
3	85.05 =	85	11 1/2	326.02 =	326
3 1/2	99.22 =	99	12	340.19 =	340
4	113.40 =	113	12 1/2	354.37 =	354
4 1/2	127.57 =	128	13	368.54 =	369
5	141.75 =	142	13 1/2	382.72 =	383
5 1/2	155.92 =	156	14	396.89 =	397
6	170.10 =	170	14 1/2	411.07 =	411
6 1/2	184.27 =	184	15	425.24 =	425
7	198.45 =	198	15 1/2	439.42 =	439
7 1/2	212.62 =	213	16	453.59 =	454

Pounds to Grams and Kilograms

lb	Grams		kg	
1	453.59 =	454	.4536 =	.454
1 1/4	566.99 =	567	.5670 =	.567
1 1/2	680.39 =	680	.6804 =	.680
1 3/4	793.79 =	794	.7938 =	.794
2	907.18 =	907	.9072 =	.907

Pounds to Kilograms

lb	kg		lb	kg	
2 1/4	1.0206 =	1.0	3 3/4	1.7010 =	1.7
2 1/2	1.1340 =	1.1	4	1.8144 =	1.8
2 3/4	1.2474 =	1.2	4 1/4	1.9278 =	1.9
3	1.3608 =	1.4	4 1/2	2.0412 =	2.0
3 1/4	1.4742 =	1.5	4 3/4	2.1546 =	2.2
3 1/2	1.5876 =	1.6	5	2.2680 =	2.3

CONVERSION TABLE FOR LENGTH MEASUREMENTS

Inches to Centimeters

Inches	Exact cm	Rounded cm	Inches	Exact cm	Rounded cm
1/8	.318	.3	2	5.080	5
1/4	.635	.6	2 1/4	5.715	6
1/2	1.270	1.0	2 1/2	6.350	6
3/4	1.905	2	2 3/4	6.985	7
1	2.540	3	3	7.620	8
1 1/4	3.175	3	3 1/2	8.890	9
1 1/2	3.810	4	4	10.160	10
1 3/4	4.445	4			

COMMON CASSEROLE DISH AND PAN SIZES

Casseroles (quarts to liters)

U.S. (quarts)	Exact Metric (liters)	Rounded Metric (liters)
1	.9465	1.0
1 1/2	1.4195	1.5
2	1.8927	2.0
2 1/2	2.3659	2.5
3	2.8391	2.8 or 3
3 1/2	3.3122	3.0
4	3.7854	3.8 or 4

Pans (inches to centimeters)

U.S. (inches)	Exact Metric (cm)	Rounded Metric (cm)
8 x 8 x 2	20.3 x 20.3 x 5.1	20 x 20 x 5
9 x 9 x 2	22.9 x 22.9 x 5.1	23 x 23 x 5
10 x 6 x 1 1/2	25.4 x 15.2 x 3.8	25 x 15 x 4
12 x 7 1/2 x 2	30.5 x 19.1 x 5.1	30 x 19 x 5
13 x 9 x 2	33.0 x 22.9 x 5.1	33 x 23 x 5
18 x 12 x 2 1/2	45.7 x 30.5 x 6.4	46 x 30 x 6

EDAM CHEESE BALLS

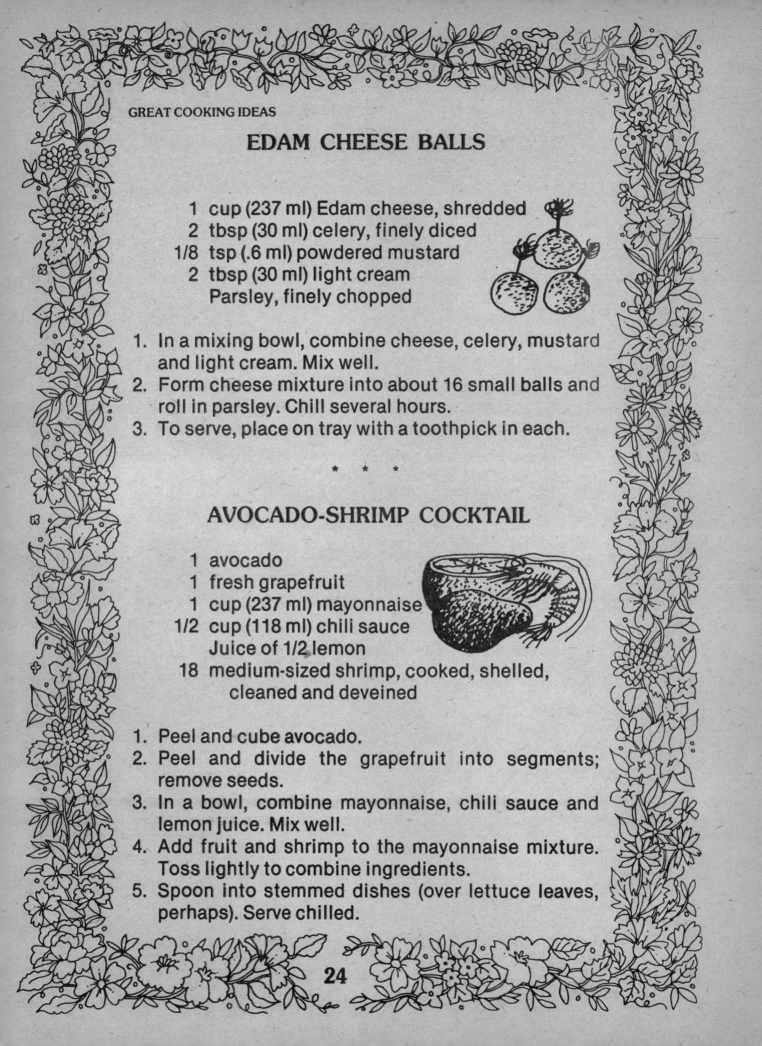

1 cup (237 ml) Edam cheese, shredded
2 tbsp (30 ml) celery, finely diced
1/8 tsp (.6 ml) powdered mustard
2 tbsp (30 ml) light cream
Parsley, finely chopped

1. In a mixing bowl, combine cheese, celery, mustard and light cream. Mix well.
2. Form cheese mixture into about 16 small balls and roll in parsley. Chill several hours.
3. To serve, place on tray with a toothpick in each.

* * *

AVOCADO-SHRIMP COCKTAIL

1 avocado
1 fresh grapefruit
1 cup (237 ml) mayonnaise
1/2 cup (118 ml) chili sauce
Juice of 1/2 lemon
18 medium-sized shrimp, cooked, shelled, cleaned and deveined

1. Peel and cube avocado.
2. Peel and divide the grapefruit into segments; remove seeds.
3. In a bowl, combine mayonnaise, chili sauce and lemon juice. Mix well.
4. Add fruit and shrimp to the mayonnaise mixture. Toss lightly to combine ingredients.
5. Spoon into stemmed dishes (over lettuce leaves, perhaps). Serve chilled.

AVOCADOS WITH SAGE DRESSING

Makes 4 servings.

2 large avocados
Boston lettuce
2 fresh sage leaves or 4 dried sage leaves
2 tbsp (30 ml) white wine vinegar
6 tbsp (90 ml) olive oil
1/4 tsp (1.2 ml) salt
Grating of fresh white pepper
Juice of 1/2 lemon
1 clove garlic, minced
1 tsp (5 ml) Worcestershire sauce

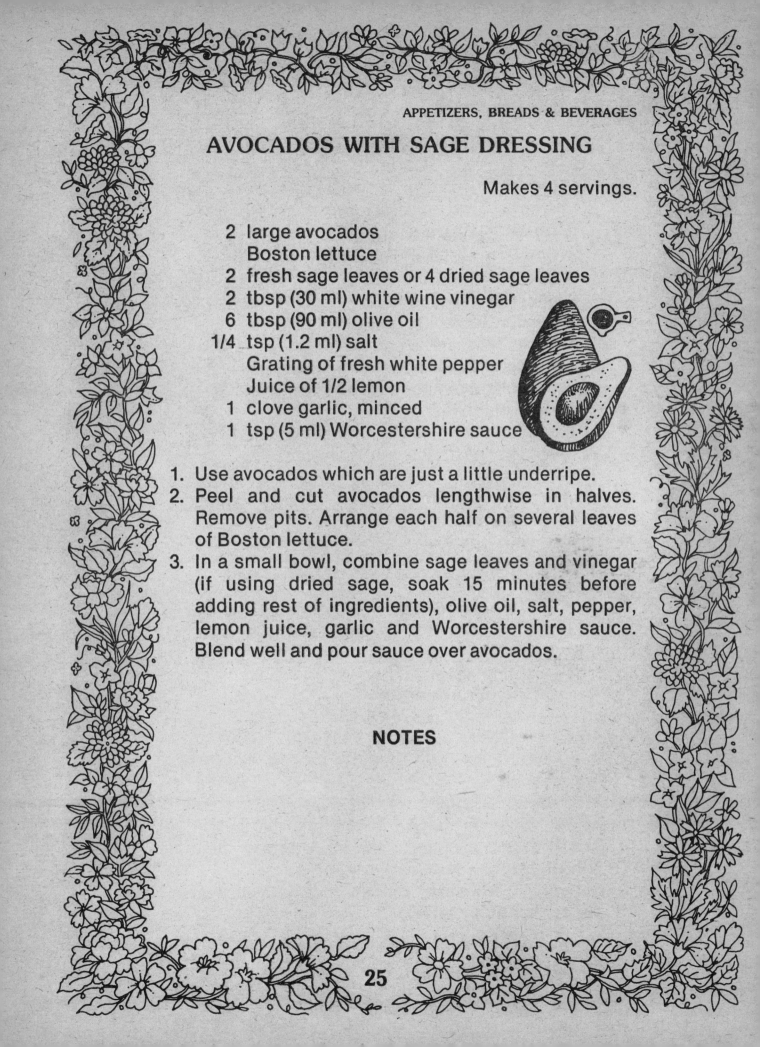

1. Use avocados which are just a little underripe.
2. Peel and cut avocados lengthwise in halves. Remove pits. Arrange each half on several leaves of Boston lettuce.
3. In a small bowl, combine sage leaves and vinegar (if using dried sage, soak 15 minutes before adding rest of ingredients), olive oil, salt, pepper, lemon juice, garlic and Worcestershire sauce. Blend well and pour sauce over avocados.

NOTES

COLD ANTIPASTO

Makes 4 servings.

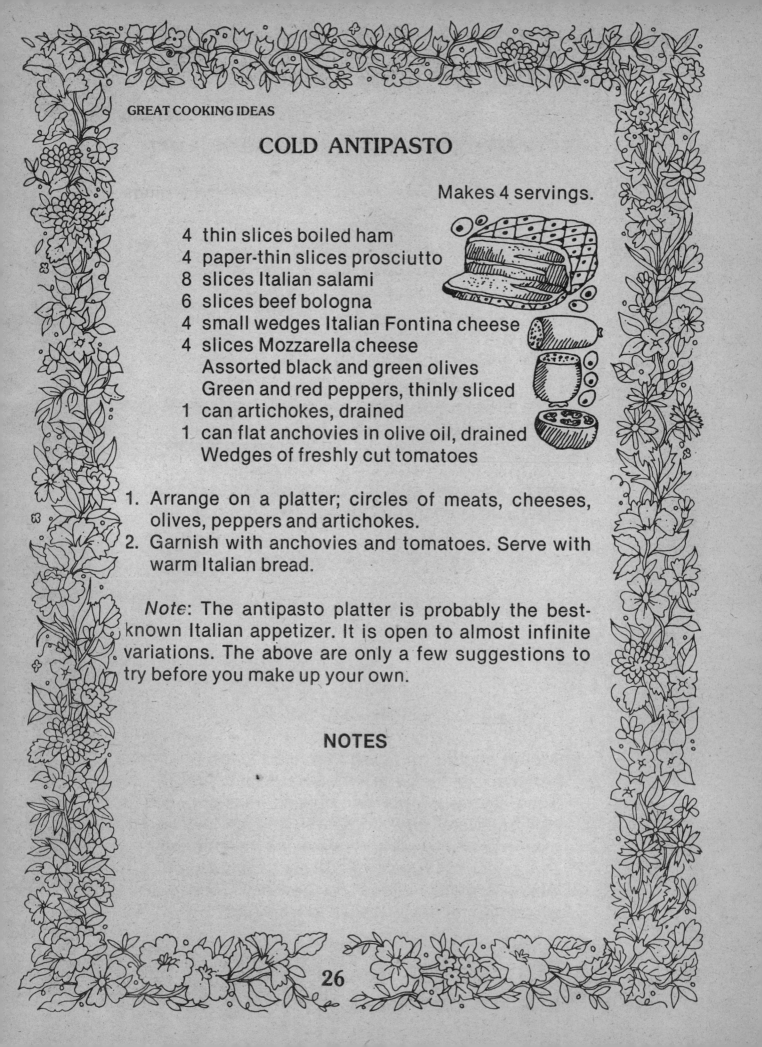

4   thin slices boiled ham
4   paper-thin slices prosciutto
8   slices Italian salami
6   slices beef bologna
4   small wedges Italian Fontina cheese
4   slices Mozzarella cheese
    Assorted black and green olives
    Green and red peppers, thinly sliced
1   can artichokes, drained
1   can flat anchovies in olive oil, drained
    Wedges of freshly cut tomatoes

1. Arrange on a platter; circles of meats, cheeses, olives, peppers and artichokes.
2. Garnish with anchovies and tomatoes. Serve with warm Italian bread.

Note: The antipasto platter is probably the best-known Italian appetizer. It is open to almost infinite variations. The above are only a few suggestions to try before you make up your own.

NOTES

CELERY STUFFED WITH ROQUEFORT

Makes 10 - 15 servings.

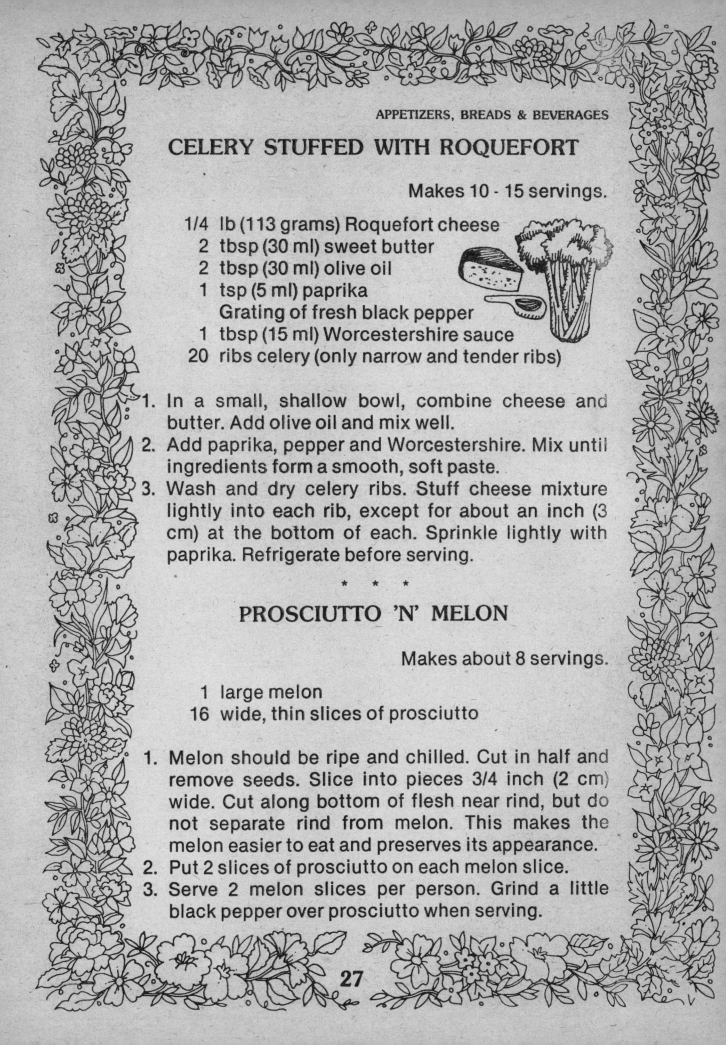

1/4 lb (113 grams) Roquefort cheese
2 tbsp (30 ml) sweet butter
2 tbsp (30 ml) olive oil
1 tsp (5 ml) paprika
Grating of fresh black pepper
1 tbsp (15 ml) Worcestershire sauce
20 ribs celery (only narrow and tender ribs)

1. In a small, shallow bowl, combine cheese and butter. Add olive oil and mix well.
2. Add paprika, pepper and Worcestershire. Mix until ingredients form a smooth, soft paste.
3. Wash and dry celery ribs. Stuff cheese mixture lightly into each rib, except for about an inch (3 cm) at the bottom of each. Sprinkle lightly with paprika. Refrigerate before serving.

* * *

PROSCIUTTO 'N' MELON

Makes about 8 servings.

1 large melon
16 wide, thin slices of prosciutto

1. Melon should be ripe and chilled. Cut in half and remove seeds. Slice into pieces 3/4 inch (2 cm) wide. Cut along bottom of flesh near rind, but do not separate rind from melon. This makes the melon easier to eat and preserves its appearance.
2. Put 2 slices of prosciutto on each melon slice.
3. Serve 2 melon slices per person. Grind a little black pepper over prosciutto when serving.

GUACAMOLE 'N' FRESH VEGETABLES

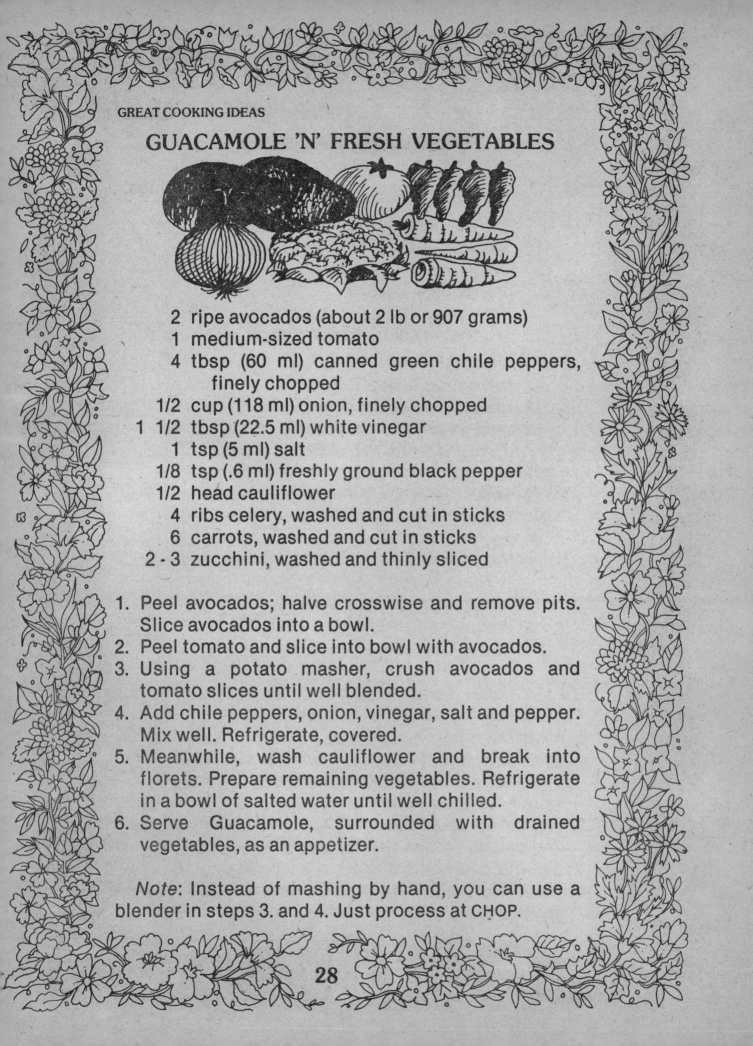

2 ripe avocados (about 2 lb or 907 grams)
1 medium-sized tomato
4 tbsp (60 ml) canned green chile peppers, finely chopped
1/2 cup (118 ml) onion, finely chopped
1 1/2 tbsp (22.5 ml) white vinegar
1 tsp (5 ml) salt
1/8 tsp (.6 ml) freshly ground black pepper
1/2 head cauliflower
4 ribs celery, washed and cut in sticks
6 carrots, washed and cut in sticks
2 - 3 zucchini, washed and thinly sliced

1. Peel avocados; halve crosswise and remove pits. Slice avocados into a bowl.
2. Peel tomato and slice into bowl with avocados.
3. Using a potato masher, crush avocados and tomato slices until well blended.
4. Add chile peppers, onion, vinegar, salt and pepper. Mix well. Refrigerate, covered.
5. Meanwhile, wash cauliflower and break into florets. Prepare remaining vegetables. Refrigerate in a bowl of salted water until well chilled.
6. Serve Guacamole, surrounded with drained vegetables, as an appetizer.

Note: Instead of mashing by hand, you can use a blender in steps 3. and 4. Just process at CHOP.

VEGETABLE COCKTAIL

Makes 6 - 8 servings.

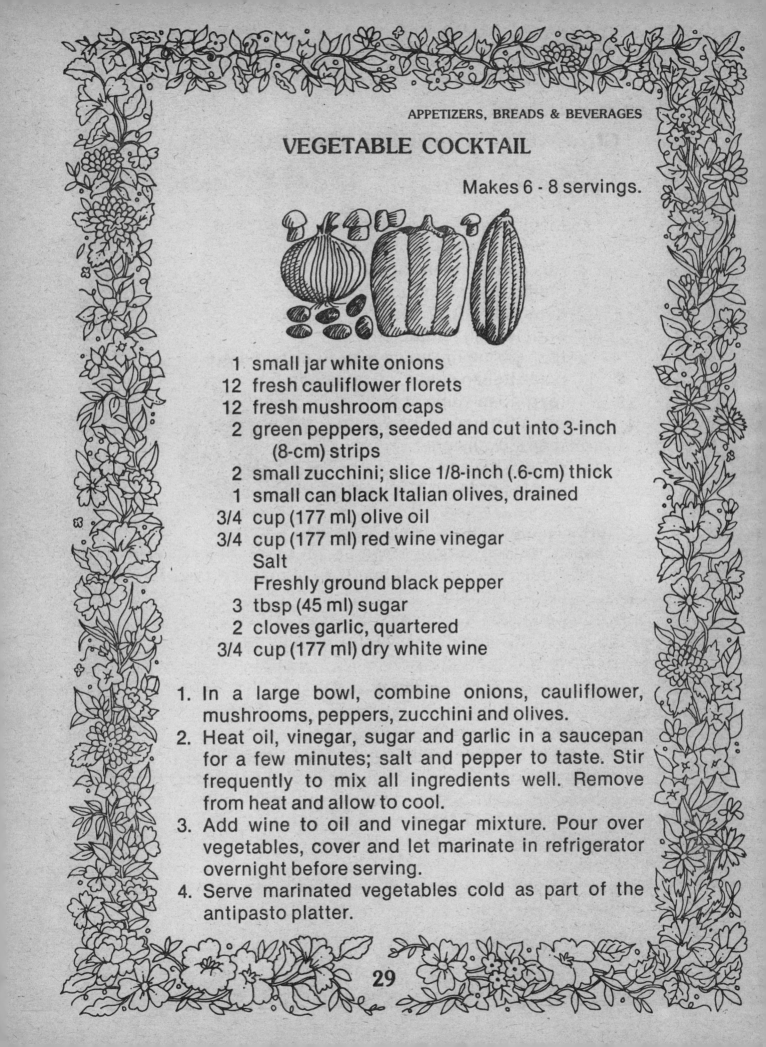

1	small jar white onions
12	fresh cauliflower florets
12	fresh mushroom caps
2	green peppers, seeded and cut into 3-inch (8-cm) strips
2	small zucchini; slice 1/8-inch (.6-cm) thick
1	small can black Italian olives, drained
3/4	cup (177 ml) olive oil
3/4	cup (177 ml) red wine vinegar
	Salt
	Freshly ground black pepper
3	tbsp (45 ml) sugar
2	cloves garlic, quartered
3/4	cup (177 ml) dry white wine

1. In a large bowl, combine onions, cauliflower, mushrooms, peppers, zucchini and olives.
2. Heat oil, vinegar, sugar and garlic in a saucepan for a few minutes; salt and pepper to taste. Stir frequently to mix all ingredients well. Remove from heat and allow to cool.
3. Add wine to oil and vinegar mixture. Pour over vegetables, cover and let marinate in refrigerator overnight before serving.
4. Serve marinated vegetables cold as part of the antipasto platter.

SWEET 'N' SOUR EGGPLANT

Makes 6 - 8 servings.

2 medium-sized eggplants, peeled and cut into 1-inch (3- cm) square pieces
4 ribs celery, finely diced
3 medium-sized onions, thinly sliced
1 1/2 cups (355 ml) olive oil
3/4 cup (177 ml) tomato purée
2 tbsp (30 ml) Italian capers; rinse and drain
12 black Italian olives; pit and chop fine
1 tbsp (15 ml) pine nuts
1/4 cup (59 ml) red wine vinegar
2 tbsp (30 ml) sugar
1/2 tsp (2.5 ml) salt
Grating of fresh black pepper

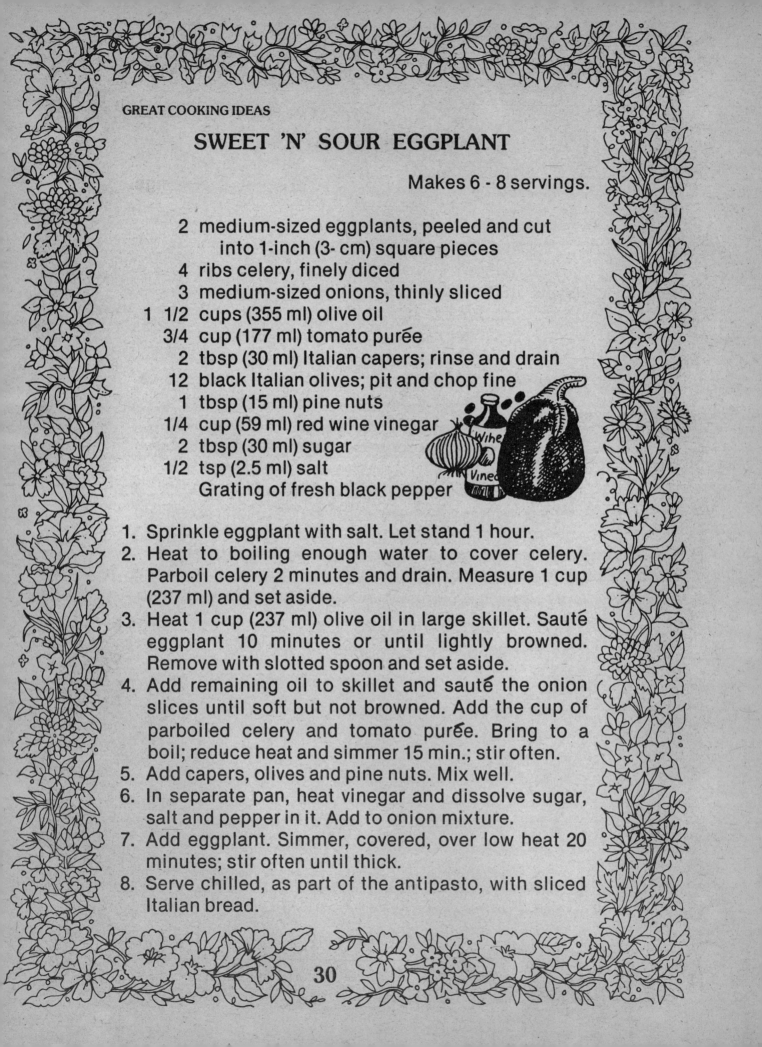

1. Sprinkle eggplant with salt. Let stand 1 hour.
2. Heat to boiling enough water to cover celery. Parboil celery 2 minutes and drain. Measure 1 cup (237 ml) and set aside.
3. Heat 1 cup (237 ml) olive oil in large skillet. Sauté eggplant 10 minutes or until lightly browned. Remove with slotted spoon and set aside.
4. Add remaining oil to skillet and sauté the onion slices until soft but not browned. Add the cup of parboiled celery and tomato purée. Bring to a boil; reduce heat and simmer 15 min.; stir often.
5. Add capers, olives and pine nuts. Mix well.
6. In separate pan, heat vinegar and dissolve sugar, salt and pepper in it. Add to onion mixture.
7. Add eggplant. Simmer, covered, over low heat 20 minutes; stir often until thick.
8. Serve chilled, as part of the antipasto, with sliced Italian bread.

SPICY MUSHROOMS

Makes 4 - 6 servings.

Preparing mushrooms:

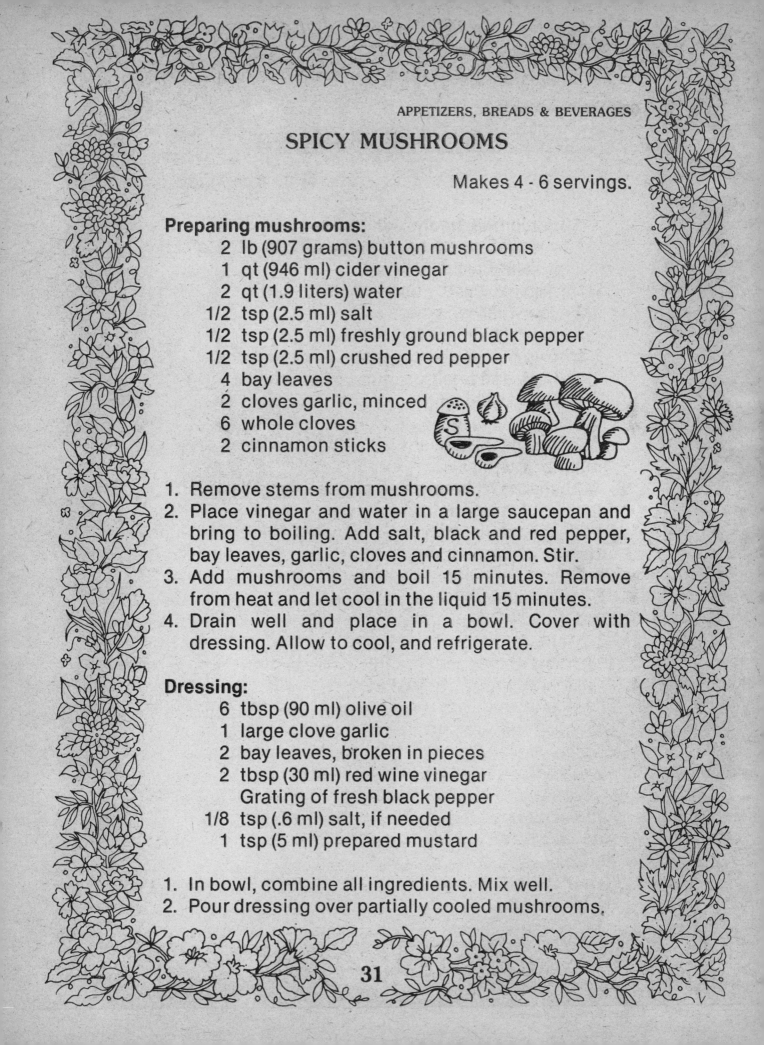

2 lb (907 grams) button mushrooms
1 qt (946 ml) cider vinegar
2 qt (1.9 liters) water
1/2 tsp (2.5 ml) salt
1/2 tsp (2.5 ml) freshly ground black pepper
1/2 tsp (2.5 ml) crushed red pepper
4 bay leaves
2 cloves garlic, minced
6 whole cloves
2 cinnamon sticks

1. Remove stems from mushrooms.
2. Place vinegar and water in a large saucepan and bring to boiling. Add salt, black and red pepper, bay leaves, garlic, cloves and cinnamon. Stir.
3. Add mushrooms and boil 15 minutes. Remove from heat and let cool in the liquid 15 minutes.
4. Drain well and place in a bowl. Cover with dressing. Allow to cool, and refrigerate.

Dressing:

6 tbsp (90 ml) olive oil
1 large clove garlic
2 bay leaves, broken in pieces
2 tbsp (30 ml) red wine vinegar
Grating of fresh black pepper
1/8 tsp (.6 ml) salt, if needed
1 tsp (5 ml) prepared mustard

1. In bowl, combine all ingredients. Mix well.
2. Pour dressing over partially cooled mushrooms.

DEVILED EGGS

9 hard-boiled eggs
3 scallions, finely chopped
1 can (12 oz or 340 grams) crab meat, drained
   and flaked
1 1/2 tsp (7.5 ml) dry mustard
3/4 cup (177 ml) soy sauce
1 tbsp (15 ml) sesame or peanut oil
1 1/2 tsp (7.5 ml) lemon juice
Salt and freshly ground black pepper
Paprika

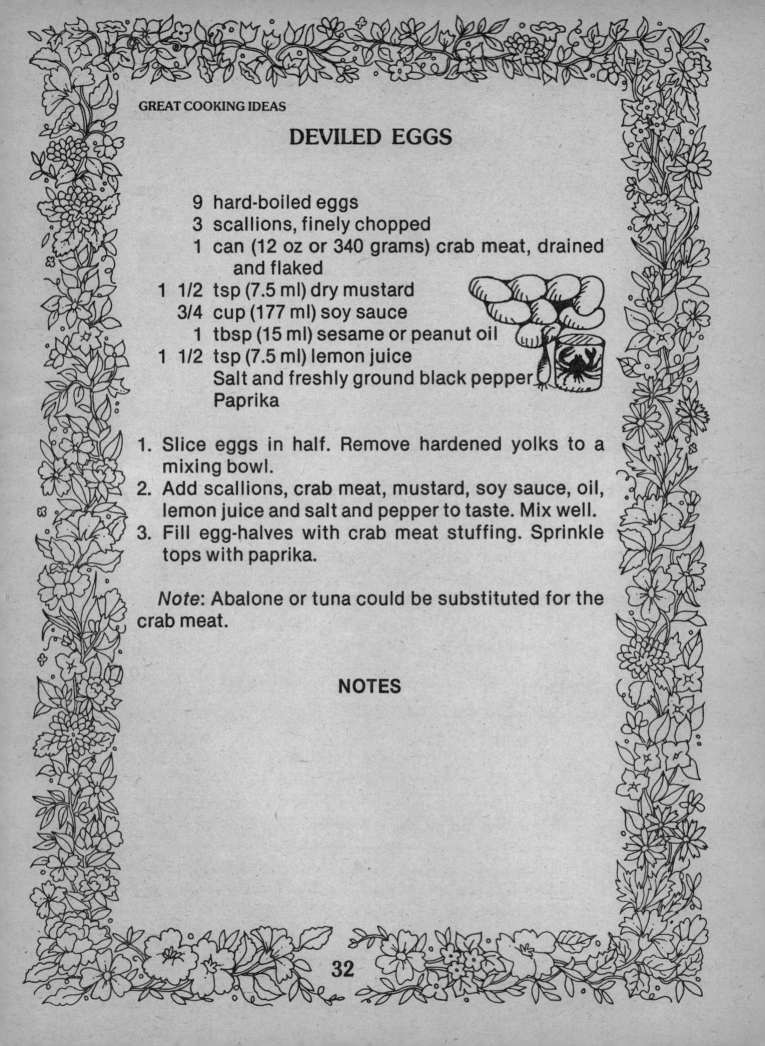

1. Slice eggs in half. Remove hardened yolks to a mixing bowl.
2. Add scallions, crab meat, mustard, soy sauce, oil, lemon juice and salt and pepper to taste. Mix well.
3. Fill egg-halves with crab meat stuffing. Sprinkle tops with paprika.

Note: Abalone or tuna could be substituted for the crab meat.

NOTES

CHICKEN LIVER PÂTÉ

Makes 15 - 20 servings.

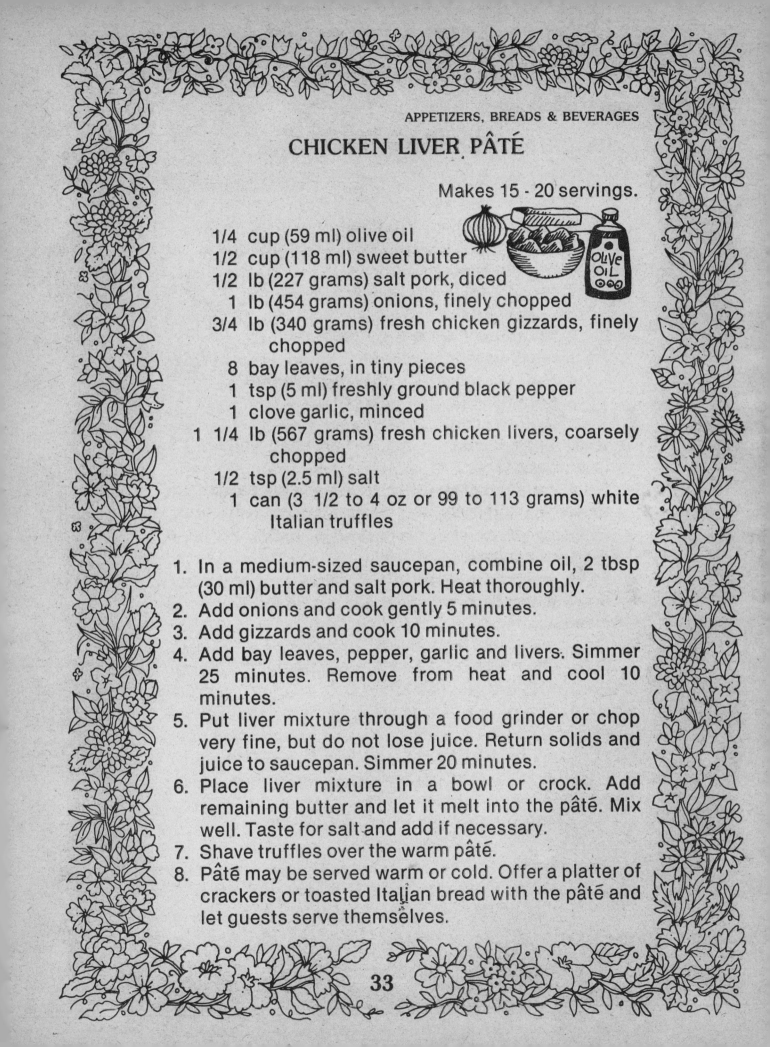

1/4 cup (59 ml) olive oil
1/2 cup (118 ml) sweet butter
1/2 lb (227 grams) salt pork, diced
1 lb (454 grams) onions, finely chopped
3/4 lb (340 grams) fresh chicken gizzards, finely chopped
8 bay leaves, in tiny pieces
1 tsp (5 ml) freshly ground black pepper
1 clove garlic, minced
1 1/4 lb (567 grams) fresh chicken livers, coarsely chopped
1/2 tsp (2.5 ml) salt
1 can (3 1/2 to 4 oz or 99 to 113 grams) white Italian truffles

1. In a medium-sized saucepan, combine oil, 2 tbsp (30 ml) butter and salt pork. Heat thoroughly.
2. Add onions and cook gently 5 minutes.
3. Add gizzards and cook 10 minutes.
4. Add bay leaves, pepper, garlic and livers. Simmer 25 minutes. Remove from heat and cool 10 minutes.
5. Put liver mixture through a food grinder or chop very fine, but do not lose juice. Return solids and juice to saucepan. Simmer 20 minutes.
6. Place liver mixture in a bowl or crock. Add remaining butter and let it melt into the pâté. Mix well. Taste for salt and add if necessary.
7. Shave truffles over the warm pâté.
8. Pâté may be served warm or cold. Offer a platter of crackers or toasted Italian bread with the pâté and let guests serve themselves.

CHICKEN TIDBITS

Makes 9 - 10 servings.

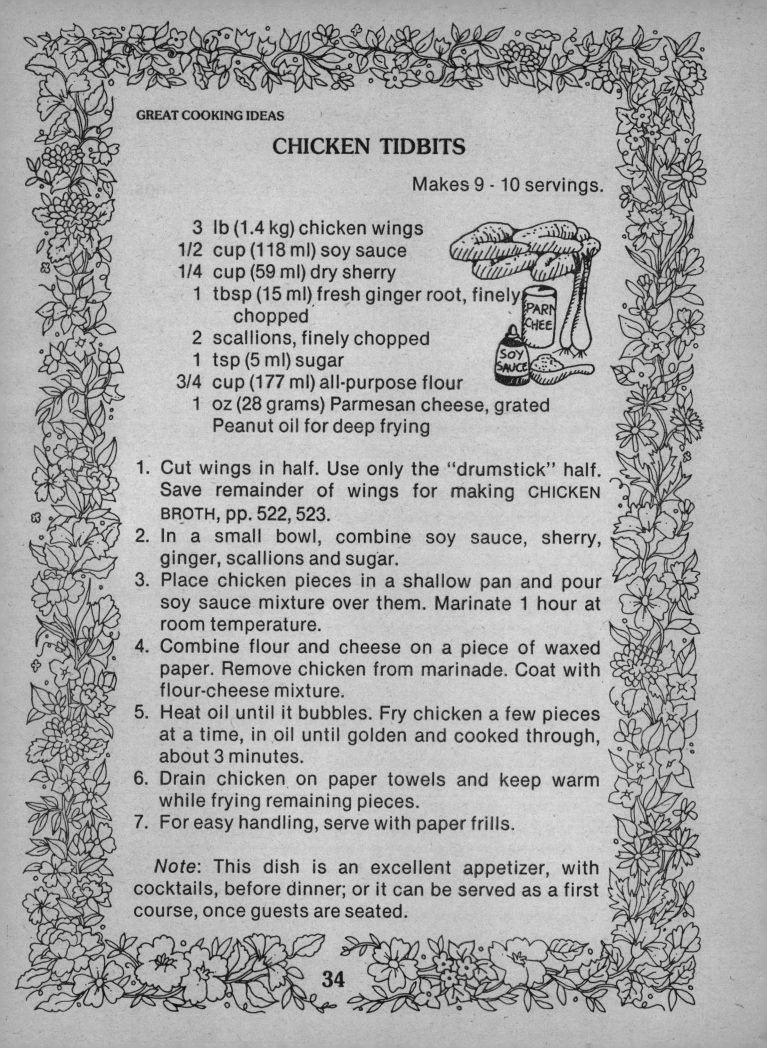

- 3 lb (1.4 kg) chicken wings
- 1/2 cup (118 ml) soy sauce
- 1/4 cup (59 ml) dry sherry
- 1 tbsp (15 ml) fresh ginger root, finely chopped
- 2 scallions, finely chopped
- 1 tsp (5 ml) sugar
- 3/4 cup (177 ml) all-purpose flour
- 1 oz (28 grams) Parmesan cheese, grated
- Peanut oil for deep frying

1. Cut wings in half. Use only the "drumstick" half. Save remainder of wings for making CHICKEN BROTH, pp. 522, 523.
2. In a small bowl, combine soy sauce, sherry, ginger, scallions and sugar.
3. Place chicken pieces in a shallow pan and pour soy sauce mixture over them. Marinate 1 hour at room temperature.
4. Combine flour and cheese on a piece of waxed paper. Remove chicken from marinade. Coat with flour-cheese mixture.
5. Heat oil until it bubbles. Fry chicken a few pieces at a time, in oil until golden and cooked through, about 3 minutes.
6. Drain chicken on paper towels and keep warm while frying remaining pieces.
7. For easy handling, serve with paper frills.

Note: This dish is an excellent appetizer, with cocktails, before dinner; or it can be served as a first course, once guests are seated.

CHINESE MEATBALLS

Makes 6 servings.

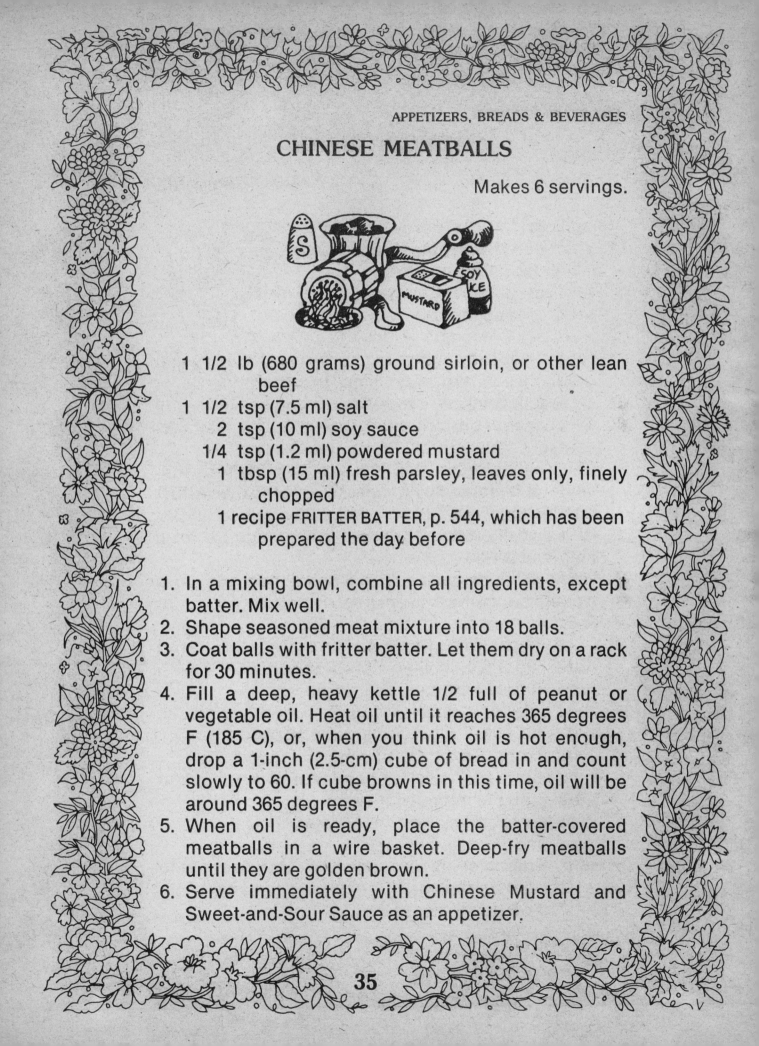

1 1/2 lb (680 grams) ground sirloin, or other lean beef
1 1/2 tsp (7.5 ml) salt
2 tsp (10 ml) soy sauce
1/4 tsp (1.2 ml) powdered mustard
1 tbsp (15 ml) fresh parsley, leaves only, finely chopped
1 recipe FRITTER BATTER, p. 544, which has been prepared the day before

1. In a mixing bowl, combine all ingredients, except batter. Mix well.
2. Shape seasoned meat mixture into 18 balls.
3. Coat balls with fritter batter. Let them dry on a rack for 30 minutes.
4. Fill a deep, heavy kettle 1/2 full of peanut or vegetable oil. Heat oil until it reaches 365 degrees F (185 C), or, when you think oil is hot enough, drop a 1-inch (2.5-cm) cube of bread in and count slowly to 60. If cube browns in this time, oil will be around 365 degrees F.
5. When oil is ready, place the batter-covered meatballs in a wire basket. Deep-fry meatballs until they are golden brown.
6. Serve immediately with Chinese Mustard and Sweet-and-Sour Sauce as an appetizer.

EGG ROLLS

Makes 12.

Pancakes:

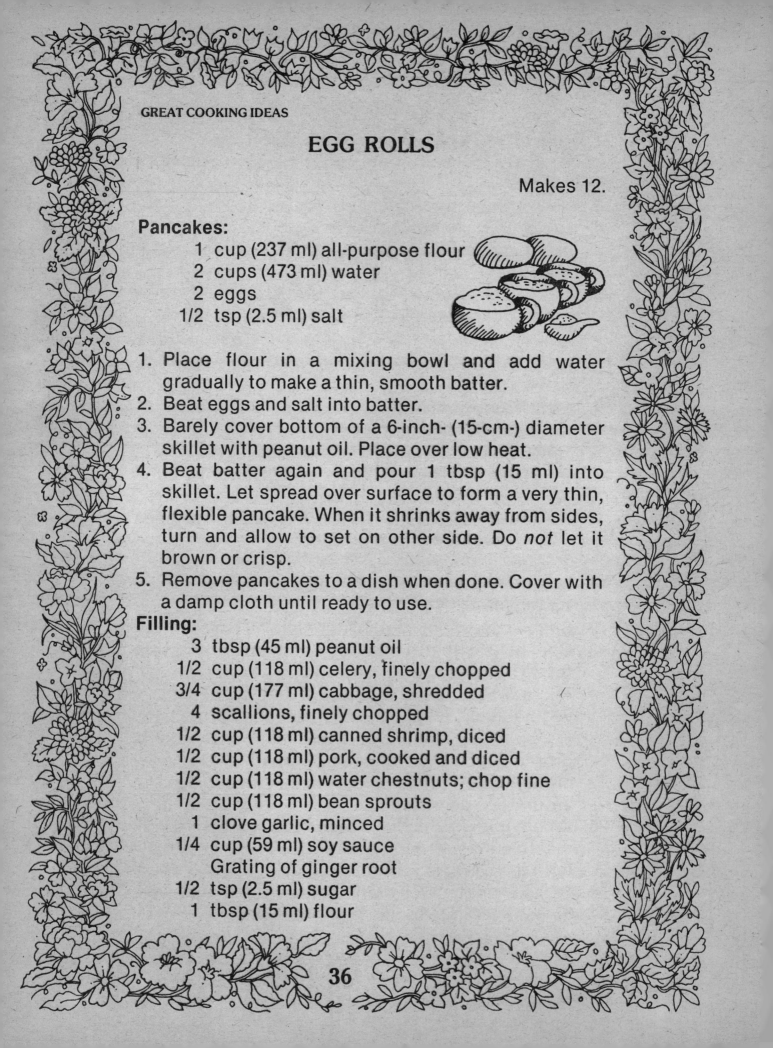

   1   cup (237 ml) all-purpose flour
   2   cups (473 ml) water
   2   eggs
 1/2   tsp (2.5 ml) salt

1. Place flour in a mixing bowl and add water gradually to make a thin, smooth batter.
2. Beat eggs and salt into batter.
3. Barely cover bottom of a 6-inch- (15-cm-) diameter skillet with peanut oil. Place over low heat.
4. Beat batter again and pour 1 tbsp (15 ml) into skillet. Let spread over surface to form a very thin, flexible pancake. When it shrinks away from sides, turn and allow to set on other side. Do *not* let it brown or crisp.
5. Remove pancakes to a dish when done. Cover with a damp cloth until ready to use.

Filling:

   3   tbsp (45 ml) peanut oil
 1/2   cup (118 ml) celery, finely chopped
 3/4   cup (177 ml) cabbage, shredded
   4   scallions, finely chopped
 1/2   cup (118 ml) canned shrimp, diced
 1/2   cup (118 ml) pork, cooked and diced
 1/2   cup (118 ml) water chestnuts; chop fine
 1/2   cup (118 ml) bean sprouts
   1   clove garlic, minced
 1/4   cup (59 ml) soy sauce
     Grating of ginger root
 1/2   tsp (2.5 ml) sugar
   1   tbsp (15 ml) flour

1. Heat oil in a wok or large, heavy skillet.
2. In oil, stir-fry celery, cabbage and scallions about 1 minute.
3. Add shrimp and pork and stir-fry 3 minutes.
4. Add water chestnuts, bean sprouts, garlic, soy sauce, ginger and sugar. Stir-fry 5 minutes longer. Set aside to cool.
5. When filling is cooled, place 4 tbsp (60 ml) in a rectangular shape in the center of each pancake. Fold up envelope-style, sealing the last flap with a paste made of 1 tbsp flour and 2 tbsp (15 ml) cold water.
6. Heat peanut oil about 1 inch deep in skillet. Fry egg rolls until golden brown.
7. Serve egg rolls with Chinese mustard, soy sauce and sweet-and-sour sauce.

Note: Although frequently used for appetizers, egg rolls may be served as the main dish for lunch.

NOTES

FRIED BEEF TREATS

2 lb (907 grams) round steak, cut in 1/4-inch
(.6-cm) strips
1 1/2 tsp (7.5 ml) each of the following: turmeric,
salt, freshly ground black pepper, garlic
powder, onion powder
1 1/2 tbsp (22.5 ml) sugar
1 cup (237 ml) vegetable oil

1. Layer meat strips in a shallow baking pan.
2. In a small bowl, combine turmeric, pepper, garlic
powder, onion powder, salt and sugar. Sprinkle on
meat. Allow to stand 1 hour, turning occasionally
to coat all pieces.
3. Heat oil in skillet. Put all meat in hot oil and cook
until brown, stirring and turning so each piece
browns. Drain well and serve as hot appetizers
with Sweet and Sour Sauce.

* * *

FRUIT COCKTAIL

2 ripe bananas
2 ripe oranges
2 ripe mangoes
1/4 section of pawpaw
1/4 section of pineapple
Sugar (optional)

1. Wash all fruits thoroughly before peeling. Cut
each fruit in cubes. Reserve juices.
2. Place cubed fruits in a pottery or ironstone bowl
and add sugar to taste, if desired. Add reserved
fruit juices and stir to combine all ingredients well.
Chill.

BAKED OYSTERS

Makes 6 servings.

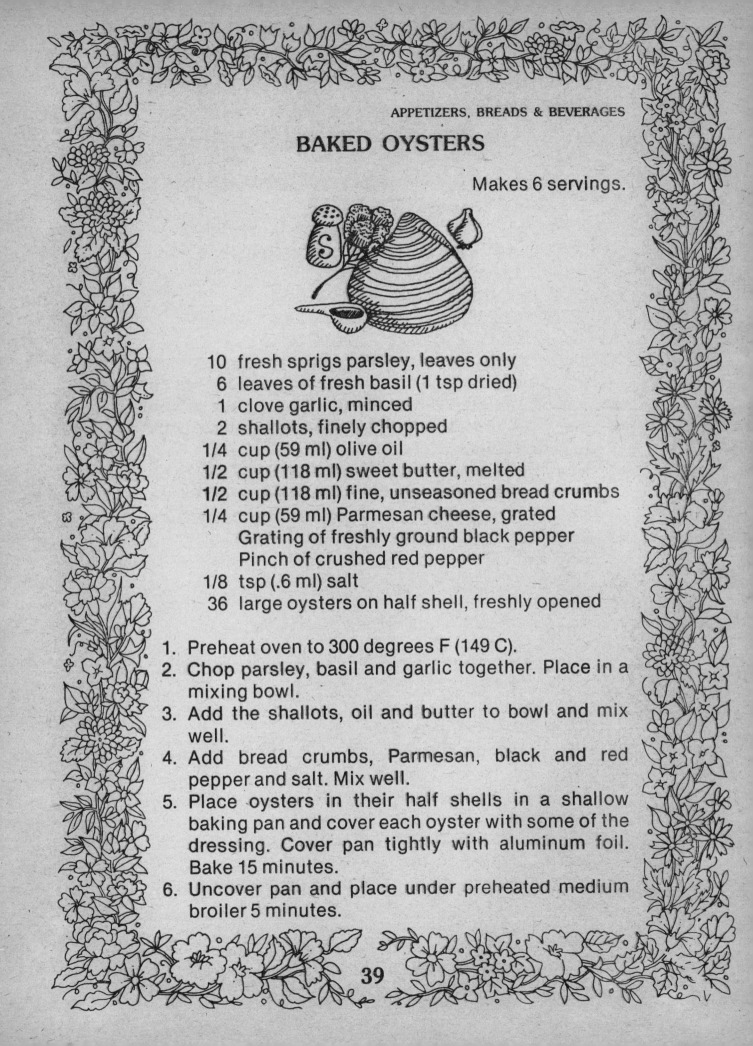

10 fresh sprigs parsley, leaves only
6 leaves of fresh basil (1 tsp dried)
1 clove garlic, minced
2 shallots, finely chopped
1/4 cup (59 ml) olive oil
1/2 cup (118 ml) sweet butter, melted
1/2 cup (118 ml) fine, unseasoned bread crumbs
1/4 cup (59 ml) Parmesan cheese, grated
    Grating of freshly ground black pepper
    Pinch of crushed red pepper
1/8 tsp (.6 ml) salt
36 large oysters on half shell, freshly opened

1. Preheat oven to 300 degrees F (149 C).
2. Chop parsley, basil and garlic together. Place in a mixing bowl.
3. Add the shallots, oil and butter to bowl and mix well.
4. Add bread crumbs, Parmesan, black and red pepper and salt. Mix well.
5. Place oysters in their half shells in a shallow baking pan and cover each oyster with some of the dressing. Cover pan tightly with aluminum foil. Bake 15 minutes.
6. Uncover pan and place under preheated medium broiler 5 minutes.

CLAMS STEAMED IN SHERRY

Makes 4 servings.

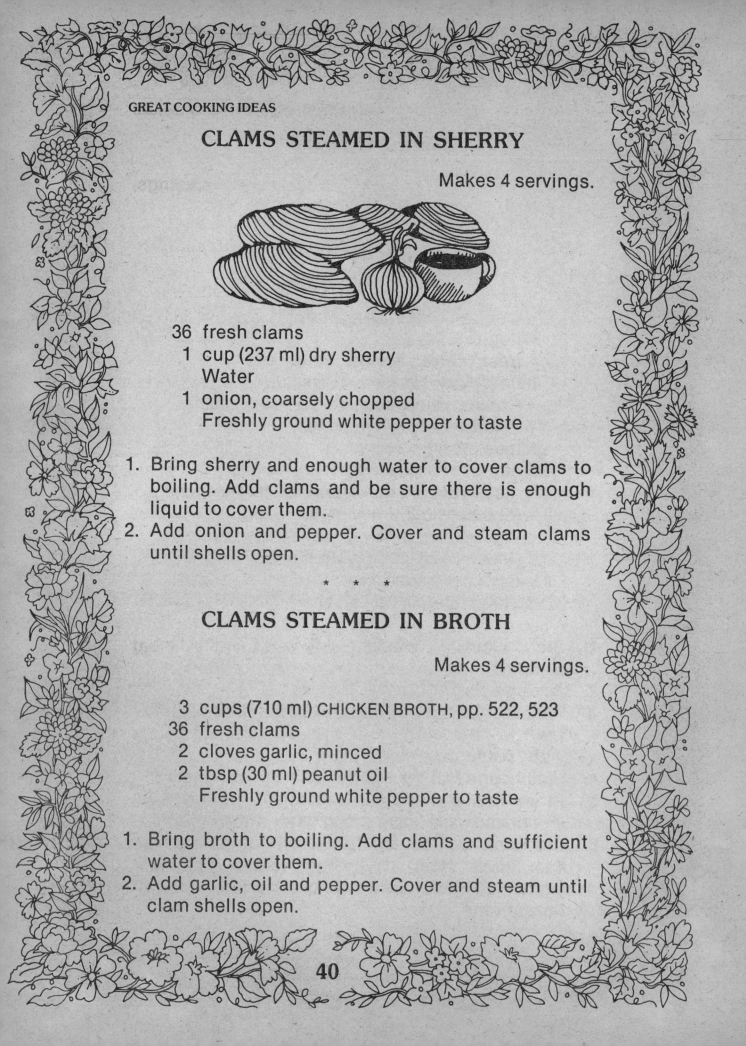

36 fresh clams
 1 cup (237 ml) dry sherry
    Water
 1 onion, coarsely chopped
    Freshly ground white pepper to taste

1. Bring sherry and enough water to cover clams to boiling. Add clams and be sure there is enough liquid to cover them.
2. Add onion and pepper. Cover and steam clams until shells open.

*   *   *

CLAMS STEAMED IN BROTH

Makes 4 servings.

 3 cups (710 ml) CHICKEN BROTH, pp. 522, 523
36 fresh clams
 2 cloves garlic, minced
 2 tbsp (30 ml) peanut oil
    Freshly ground white pepper to taste

1. Bring broth to boiling. Add clams and sufficient water to cover them.
2. Add garlic, oil and pepper. Cover and steam until clam shells open.

HOT CLAM DIP

Makes 4 - 6 servings.

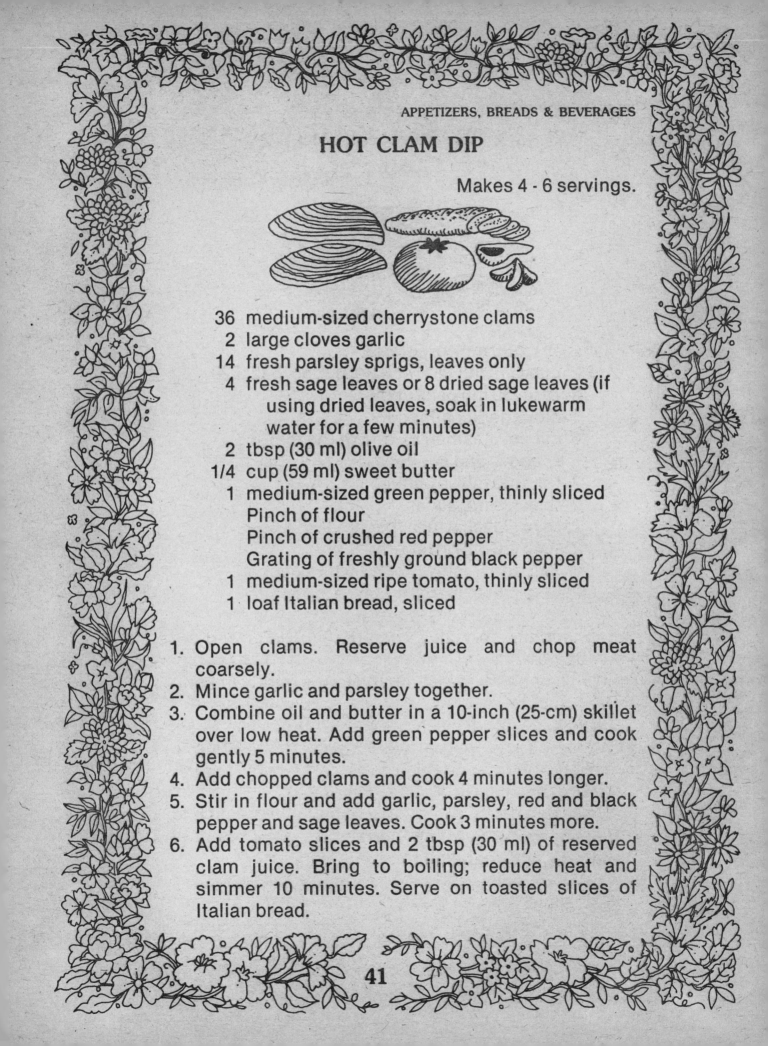

36 medium-sized cherrystone clams
 2 large cloves garlic
14 fresh parsley sprigs, leaves only
 4 fresh sage leaves or 8 dried sage leaves (if
      using dried leaves, soak in lukewarm
      water for a few minutes)
 2 tbsp (30 ml) olive oil
1/4 cup (59 ml) sweet butter
 1 medium-sized green pepper, thinly sliced
      Pinch of flour
      Pinch of crushed red pepper
      Grating of freshly ground black pepper
 1 medium-sized ripe tomato, thinly sliced
 1 loaf Italian bread, sliced

1. Open clams. Reserve juice and chop meat coarsely.
2. Mince garlic and parsley together.
3. Combine oil and butter in a 10-inch (25-cm) skillet over low heat. Add green pepper slices and cook gently 5 minutes.
4. Add chopped clams and cook 4 minutes longer.
5. Stir in flour and add garlic, parsley, red and black pepper and sage leaves. Cook 3 minutes more.
6. Add tomato slices and 2 tbsp (30 ml) of reserved clam juice. Bring to boiling; reduce heat and simmer 10 minutes. Serve on toasted slices of Italian bread.

STIR-FRIED CLAMS

Makes 4 - 6 servings.

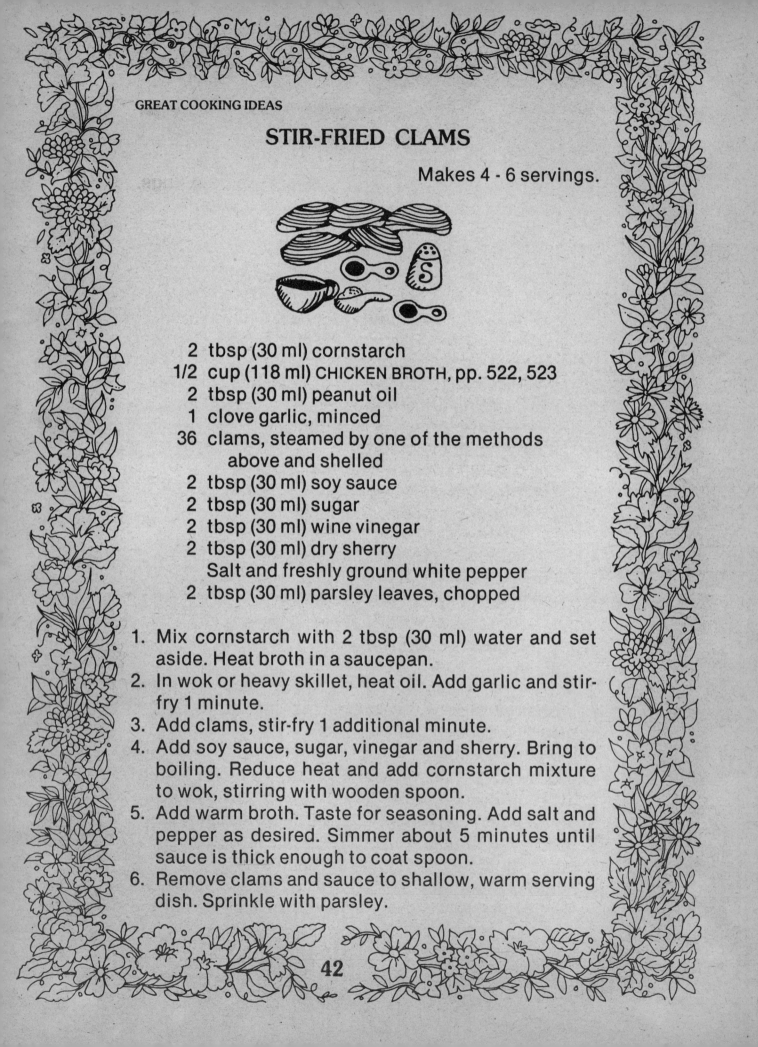

   2 tbsp (30 ml) cornstarch
1/2 cup (118 ml) CHICKEN BROTH, pp. 522, 523
   2 tbsp (30 ml) peanut oil
   1 clove garlic, minced
 36 clams, steamed by one of the methods
      above and shelled
   2 tbsp (30 ml) soy sauce
   2 tbsp (30 ml) sugar
   2 tbsp (30 ml) wine vinegar
   2 tbsp (30 ml) dry sherry
      Salt and freshly ground white pepper
   2 tbsp (30 ml) parsley leaves, chopped

1. Mix cornstarch with 2 tbsp (30 ml) water and set aside. Heat broth in a saucepan.
2. In wok or heavy skillet, heat oil. Add garlic and stir-fry 1 minute.
3. Add clams, stir-fry 1 additional minute.
4. Add soy sauce, sugar, vinegar and sherry. Bring to boiling. Reduce heat and add cornstarch mixture to wok, stirring with wooden spoon.
5. Add warm broth. Taste for seasoning. Add salt and pepper as desired. Simmer about 5 minutes until sauce is thick enough to coat spoon.
6. Remove clams and sauce to shallow, warm serving dish. Sprinkle with parsley.

CHILLED CRABMEAT

Makes 4 - 6 servings.

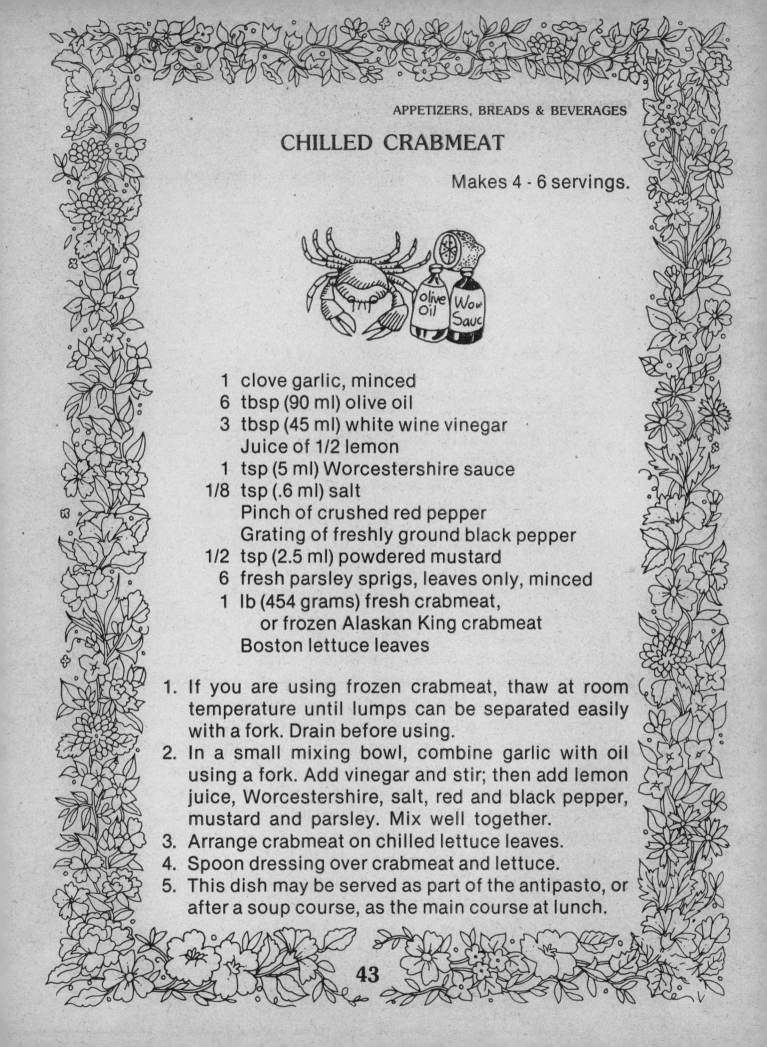

1 clove garlic, minced
6 tbsp (90 ml) olive oil
3 tbsp (45 ml) white wine vinegar
Juice of 1/2 lemon
1 tsp (5 ml) Worcestershire sauce
1/8 tsp (.6 ml) salt
Pinch of crushed red pepper
Grating of freshly ground black pepper
1/2 tsp (2.5 ml) powdered mustard
6 fresh parsley sprigs, leaves only, minced
1 lb (454 grams) fresh crabmeat,
    or frozen Alaskan King crabmeat
Boston lettuce leaves

1. If you are using frozen crabmeat, thaw at room temperature until lumps can be separated easily with a fork. Drain before using.
2. In a small mixing bowl, combine garlic with oil using a fork. Add vinegar and stir; then add lemon juice, Worcestershire, salt, red and black pepper, mustard and parsley. Mix well together.
3. Arrange crabmeat on chilled lettuce leaves.
4. Spoon dressing over crabmeat and lettuce.
5. This dish may be served as part of the antipasto, or after a soup course, as the main course at lunch.

CRABMEAT STUFFED MUSHROOMS

Makes 12.

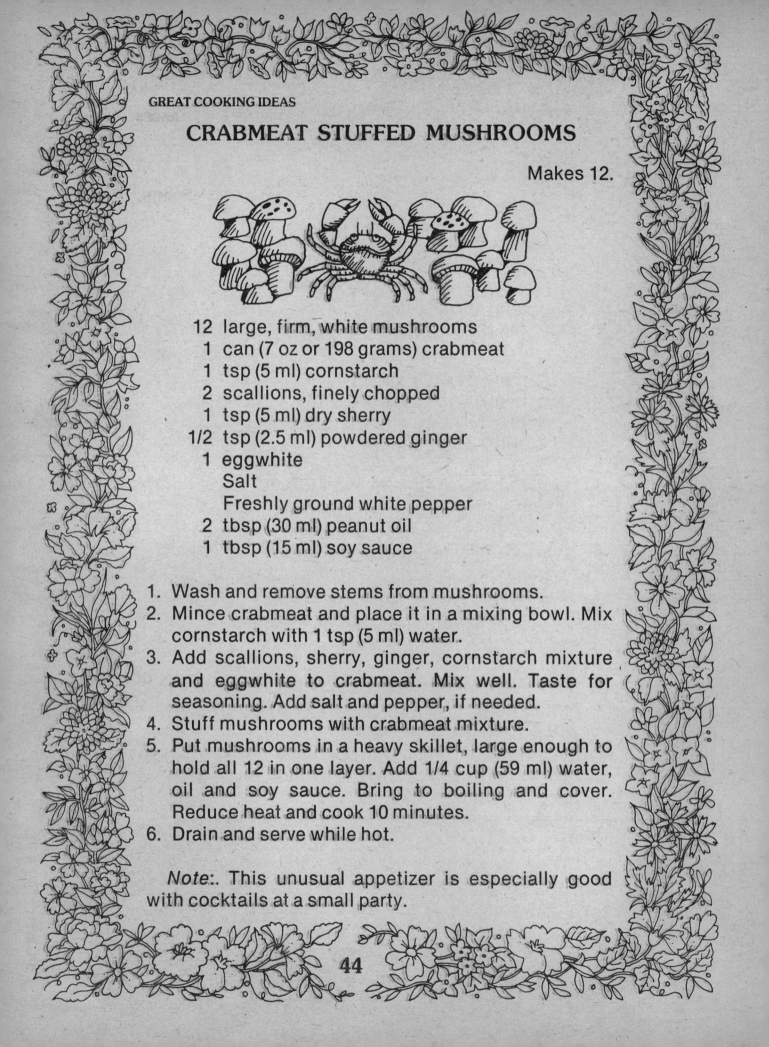

12   large, firm, white mushrooms
 1   can (7 oz or 198 grams) crabmeat
 1   tsp (5 ml) cornstarch
 2   scallions, finely chopped
 1   tsp (5 ml) dry sherry
1/2   tsp (2.5 ml) powdered ginger
 1   eggwhite
     Salt
     Freshly ground white pepper
 2   tbsp (30 ml) peanut oil
 1   tbsp (15 ml) soy sauce

1. Wash and remove stems from mushrooms.
2. Mince crabmeat and place it in a mixing bowl. Mix cornstarch with 1 tsp (5 ml) water.
3. Add scallions, sherry, ginger, cornstarch mixture and eggwhite to crabmeat. Mix well. Taste for seasoning. Add salt and pepper, if needed.
4. Stuff mushrooms with crabmeat mixture.
5. Put mushrooms in a heavy skillet, large enough to hold all 12 in one layer. Add 1/4 cup (59 ml) water, oil and soy sauce. Bring to boiling and cover. Reduce heat and cook 10 minutes.
6. Drain and serve while hot.

Note:. This unusual appetizer is especially good with cocktails at a small party.

SAUTEED CRABMEAT

Makes 4 servings.

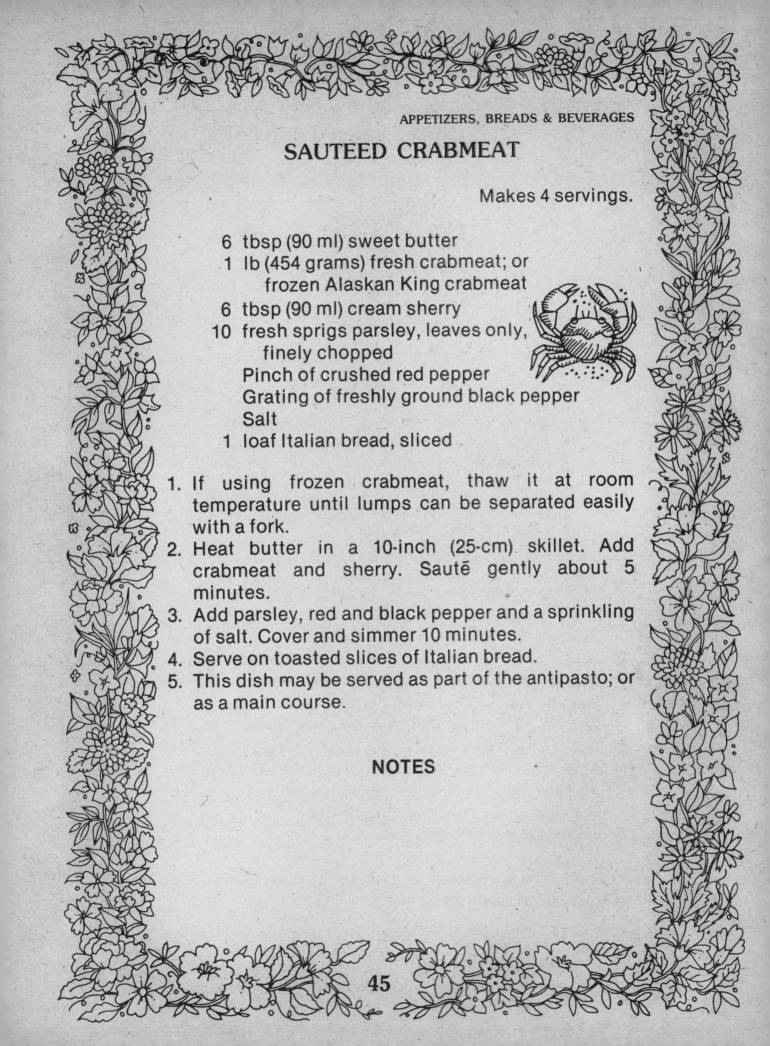

- 6 tbsp (90 ml) sweet butter
- 1 lb (454 grams) fresh crabmeat; or frozen Alaskan King crabmeat
- 6 tbsp (90 ml) cream sherry
- 10 fresh sprigs parsley, leaves only, finely chopped
- Pinch of crushed red pepper
- Grating of freshly ground black pepper
- Salt
- 1 loaf Italian bread, sliced

1. If using frozen crabmeat, thaw it at room temperature until lumps can be separated easily with a fork.
2. Heat butter in a 10-inch (25-cm) skillet. Add crabmeat and sherry. Sauté gently about 5 minutes.
3. Add parsley, red and black pepper and a sprinkling of salt. Cover and simmer 10 minutes.
4. Serve on toasted slices of Italian bread.
5. This dish may be served as part of the antipasto; or as a main course.

NOTES

SHRIMP TOAST

Makes 6 servings.

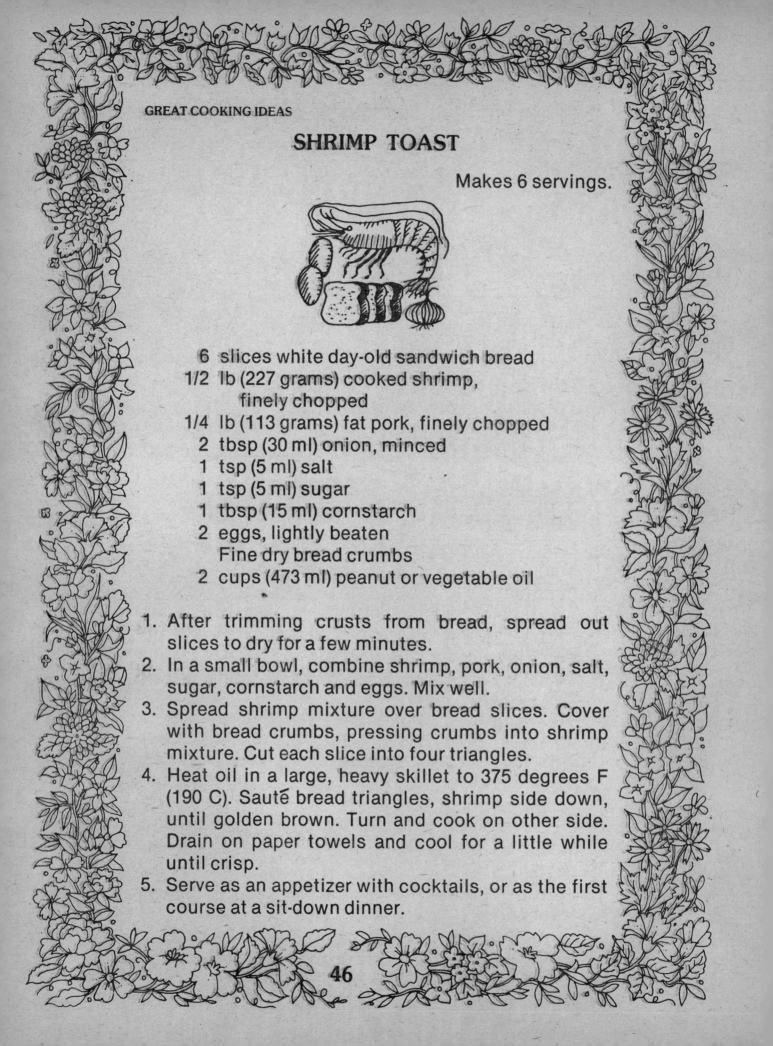

6 slices white day-old sandwich bread
1/2 lb (227 grams) cooked shrimp,
    finely chopped
1/4 lb (113 grams) fat pork, finely chopped
2 tbsp (30 ml) onion, minced
1 tsp (5 ml) salt
1 tsp (5 ml) sugar
1 tbsp (15 ml) cornstarch
2 eggs, lightly beaten
    Fine dry bread crumbs
2 cups (473 ml) peanut or vegetable oil

1. After trimming crusts from bread, spread out slices to dry for a few minutes.
2. In a small bowl, combine shrimp, pork, onion, salt, sugar, cornstarch and eggs. Mix well.
3. Spread shrimp mixture over bread slices. Cover with bread crumbs, pressing crumbs into shrimp mixture. Cut each slice into four triangles.
4. Heat oil in a large, heavy skillet to 375 degrees F (190 C). Sauté bread triangles, shrimp side down, until golden brown. Turn and cook on other side. Drain on paper towels and cool for a little while until crisp.
5. Serve as an appetizer with cocktails, or as the first course at a sit-down dinner.

SHRIMP PUFFS

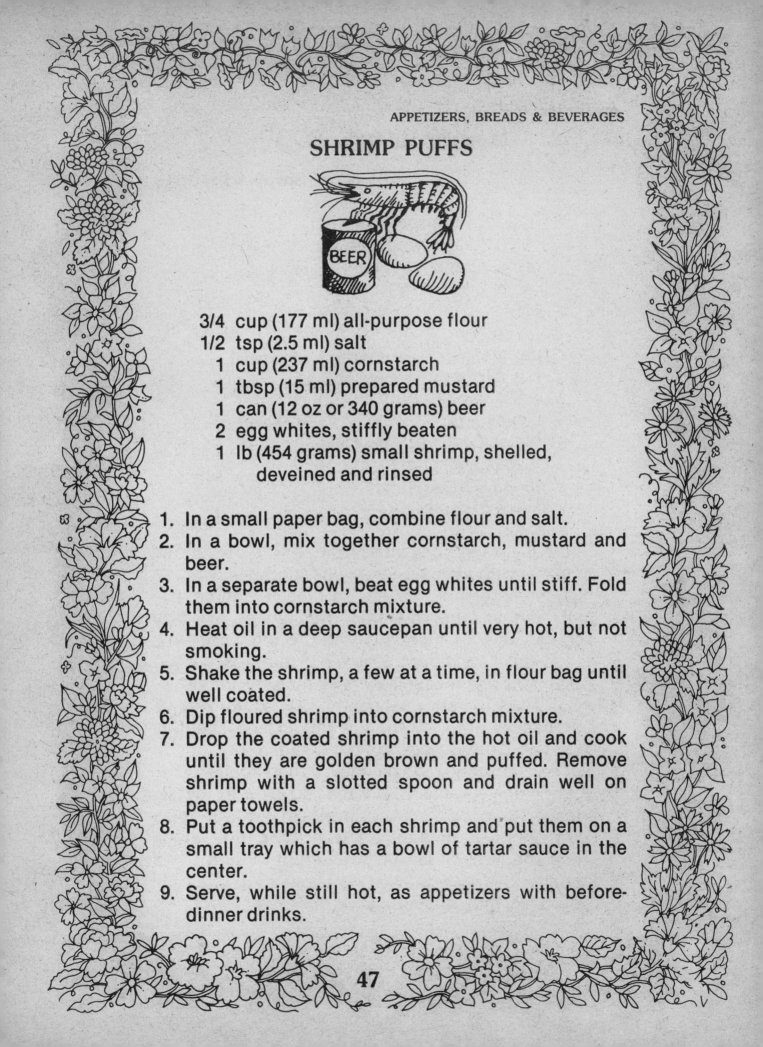

3/4 cup (177 ml) all-purpose flour
1/2 tsp (2.5 ml) salt
1 cup (237 ml) cornstarch
1 tbsp (15 ml) prepared mustard
1 can (12 oz or 340 grams) beer
2 egg whites, stiffly beaten
1 lb (454 grams) small shrimp, shelled, deveined and rinsed

1. In a small paper bag, combine flour and salt.
2. In a bowl, mix together cornstarch, mustard and beer.
3. In a separate bowl, beat egg whites until stiff. Fold them into cornstarch mixture.
4. Heat oil in a deep saucepan until very hot, but not smoking.
5. Shake the shrimp, a few at a time, in flour bag until well coated.
6. Dip floured shrimp into cornstarch mixture.
7. Drop the coated shrimp into the hot oil and cook until they are golden brown and puffed. Remove shrimp with a slotted spoon and drain well on paper towels.
8. Put a toothpick in each shrimp and put them on a small tray which has a bowl of tartar sauce in the center.
9. Serve, while still hot, as appetizers with before-dinner drinks.

MARINATED SEAFOOD

Makes 8 servings.

1 lb (454 grams) small shrimp
1/2 lb (227 grams) baby cherrystone clams
1 lb (454 grams) mussels
1 carrot
1 rib celery
1 onion
1 bay leaf
1 tsp (5 ml) salt
6 white peppercorns
1/2 clove garlic
2 tbsp (30 ml) fresh parsley leaves, chopped
1 tbsp (15 ml) capers, chopped
6 tbsp (90 ml) olive oil
Juice of 1 lemon

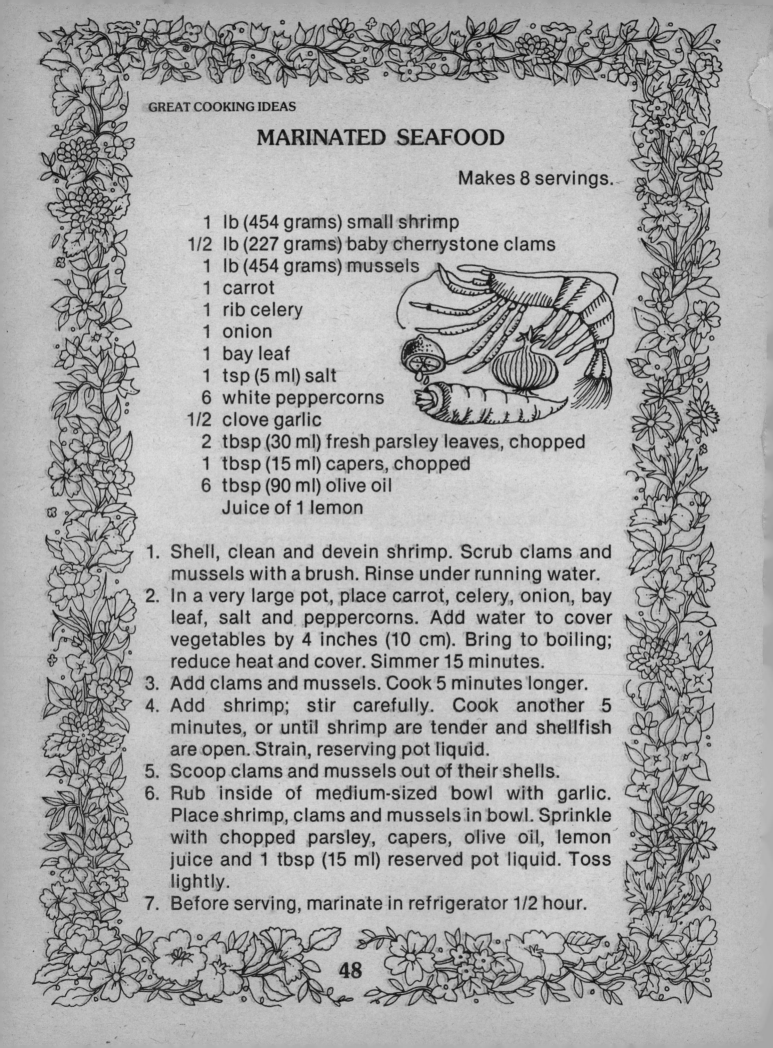

1. Shell, clean and devein shrimp. Scrub clams and mussels with a brush. Rinse under running water.
2. In a very large pot, place carrot, celery, onion, bay leaf, salt and peppercorns. Add water to cover vegetables by 4 inches (10 cm). Bring to boiling; reduce heat and cover. Simmer 15 minutes.
3. Add clams and mussels. Cook 5 minutes longer.
4. Add shrimp; stir carefully. Cook another 5 minutes, or until shrimp are tender and shellfish are open. Strain, reserving pot liquid.
5. Scoop clams and mussels out of their shells.
6. Rub inside of medium-sized bowl with garlic. Place shrimp, clams and mussels in bowl. Sprinkle with chopped parsley, capers, olive oil, lemon juice and 1 tbsp (15 ml) reserved pot liquid. Toss lightly.
7. Before serving, marinate in refrigerator 1/2 hour.

INDIAN-STYLE APPETIZERS

Makes 8 servings.

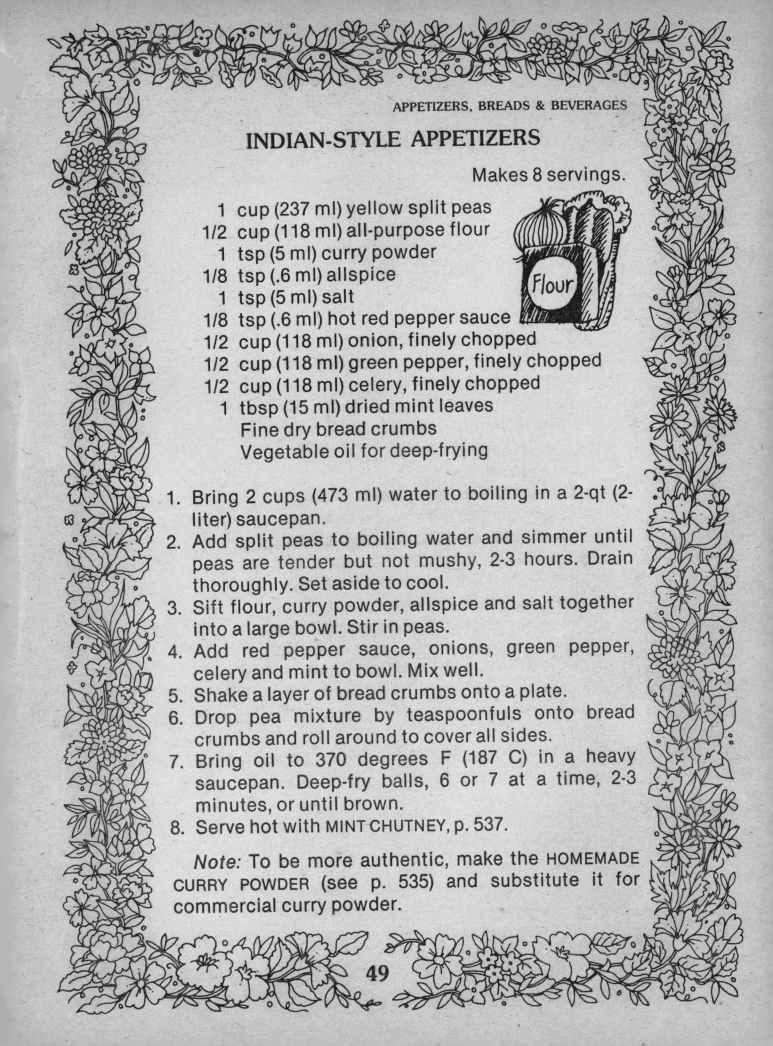

1 cup (237 ml) yellow split peas
1/2 cup (118 ml) all-purpose flour
1 tsp (5 ml) curry powder
1/8 tsp (.6 ml) allspice
1 tsp (5 ml) salt
1/8 tsp (.6 ml) hot red pepper sauce
1/2 cup (118 ml) onion, finely chopped
1/2 cup (118 ml) green pepper, finely chopped
1/2 cup (118 ml) celery, finely chopped
1 tbsp (15 ml) dried mint leaves
Fine dry bread crumbs
Vegetable oil for deep-frying

1. Bring 2 cups (473 ml) water to boiling in a 2-qt (2-liter) saucepan.
2. Add split peas to boiling water and simmer until peas are tender but not mushy, 2-3 hours. Drain thoroughly. Set aside to cool.
3. Sift flour, curry powder, allspice and salt together into a large bowl. Stir in peas.
4. Add red pepper sauce, onions, green pepper, celery and mint to bowl. Mix well.
5. Shake a layer of bread crumbs onto a plate.
6. Drop pea mixture by teaspoonfuls onto bread crumbs and roll around to cover all sides.
7. Bring oil to 370 degrees F (187 C) in a heavy saucepan. Deep-fry balls, 6 or 7 at a time, 2-3 minutes, or until brown.
8. Serve hot with MINT CHUTNEY, p. 537.

Note: To be more authentic, make the HOMEMADE CURRY POWDER (see p. 535) and substitute it for commercial curry powder.

DILL BREAD

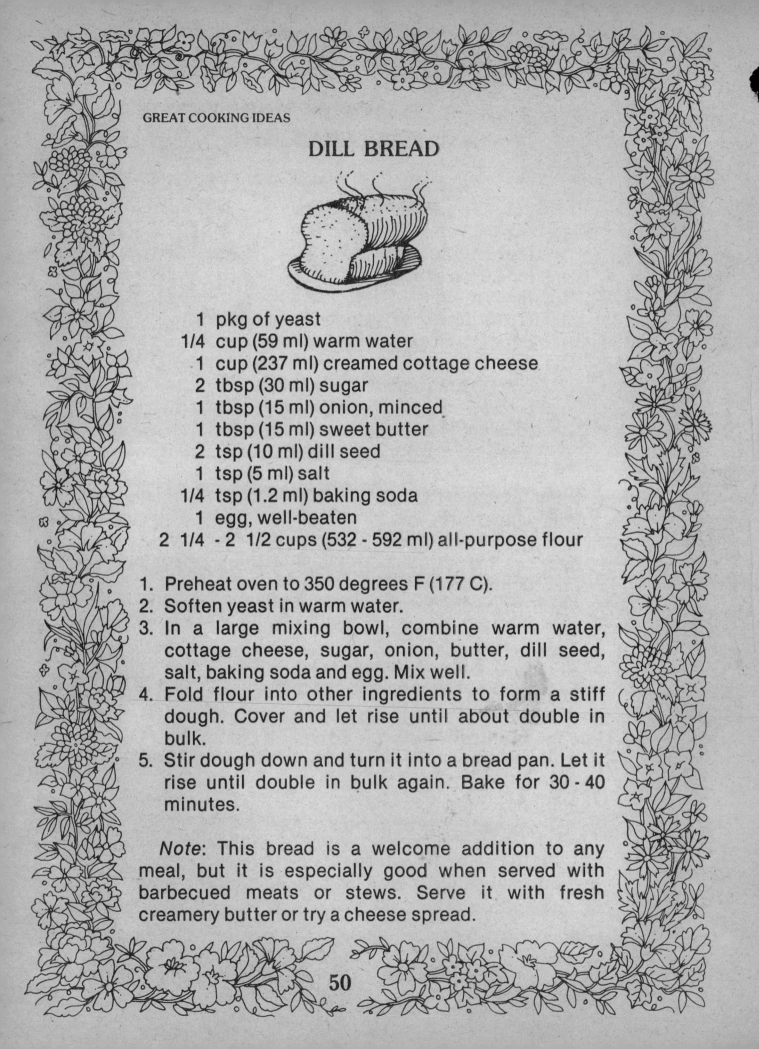

1 pkg of yeast
1/4 cup (59 ml) warm water
1 cup (237 ml) creamed cottage cheese
2 tbsp (30 ml) sugar
1 tbsp (15 ml) onion, minced
1 tbsp (15 ml) sweet butter
2 tsp (10 ml) dill seed
1 tsp (5 ml) salt
1/4 tsp (1.2 ml) baking soda
1 egg, well-beaten
2 1/4 - 2 1/2 cups (532 - 592 ml) all-purpose flour

1. Preheat oven to 350 degrees F (177 C).
2. Soften yeast in warm water.
3. In a large mixing bowl, combine warm water, cottage cheese, sugar, onion, butter, dill seed, salt, baking soda and egg. Mix well.
4. Fold flour into other ingredients to form a stiff dough. Cover and let rise until about double in bulk.
5. Stir dough down and turn it into a bread pan. Let it rise until double in bulk again. Bake for 30 - 40 minutes.

Note: This bread is a welcome addition to any meal, but it is especially good when served with barbecued meats or stews. Serve it with fresh creamery butter or try a cheese spread.

WHEAT BREAD

Makes about 24 pieces.

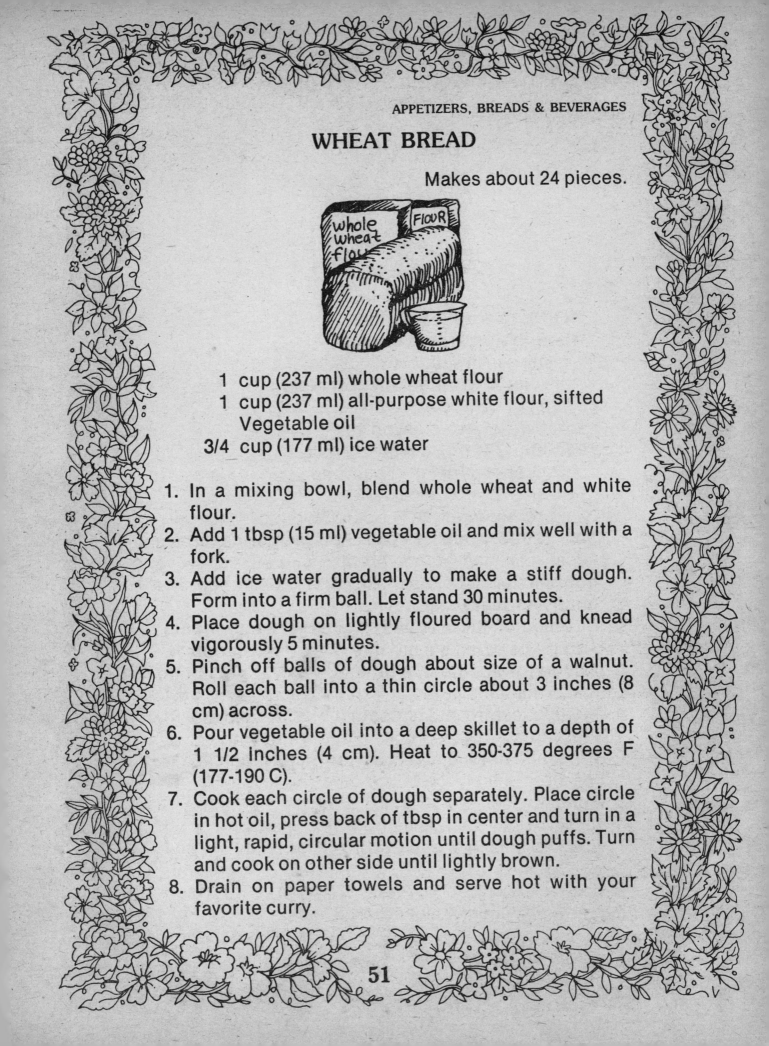

1 cup (237 ml) whole wheat flour
1 cup (237 ml) all-purpose white flour, sifted
Vegetable oil
3/4 cup (177 ml) ice water

1. In a mixing bowl, blend whole wheat and white flour.
2. Add 1 tbsp (15 ml) vegetable oil and mix well with a fork.
3. Add ice water gradually to make a stiff dough. Form into a firm ball. Let stand 30 minutes.
4. Place dough on lightly floured board and knead vigorously 5 minutes.
5. Pinch off balls of dough about size of a walnut. Roll each ball into a thin circle about 3 inches (8 cm) across.
6. Pour vegetable oil into a deep skillet to a depth of 1 1/2 inches (4 cm). Heat to 350-375 degrees F (177-190 C).
7. Cook each circle of dough separately. Place circle in hot oil, press back of tbsp in center and turn in a light, rapid, circular motion until dough puffs. Turn and cook on other side until lightly brown.
8. Drain on paper towels and serve hot with your favorite curry.

CORNBREAD ROLLS

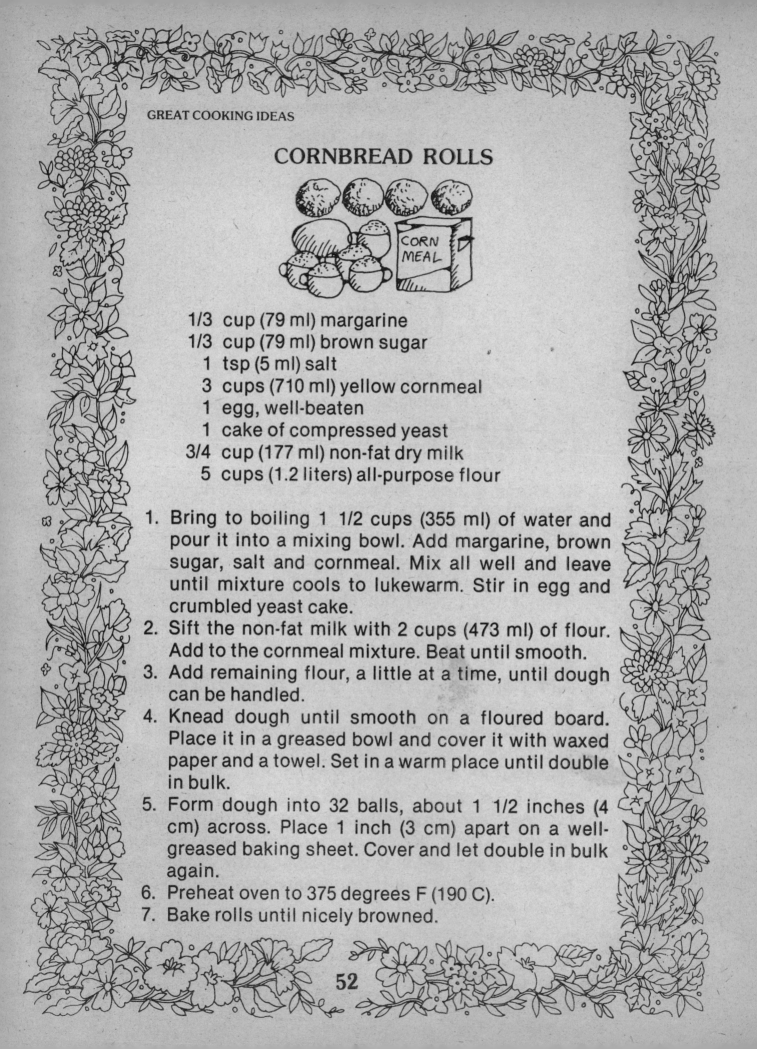

1/3 cup (79 ml) margarine
1/3 cup (79 ml) brown sugar
1 tsp (5 ml) salt
3 cups (710 ml) yellow cornmeal
1 egg, well-beaten
1 cake of compressed yeast
3/4 cup (177 ml) non-fat dry milk
5 cups (1.2 liters) all-purpose flour

1. Bring to boiling 1 1/2 cups (355 ml) of water and pour it into a mixing bowl. Add margarine, brown sugar, salt and cornmeal. Mix all well and leave until mixture cools to lukewarm. Stir in egg and crumbled yeast cake.
2. Sift the non-fat milk with 2 cups (473 ml) of flour. Add to the cornmeal mixture. Beat until smooth.
3. Add remaining flour, a little at a time, until dough can be handled.
4. Knead dough until smooth on a floured board. Place it in a greased bowl and cover it with waxed paper and a towel. Set in a warm place until double in bulk.
5. Form dough into 32 balls, about 1 1/2 inches (4 cm) across. Place 1 inch (3 cm) apart on a well-greased baking sheet. Cover and let double in bulk again.
6. Preheat oven to 375 degrees F (190 C).
7. Bake rolls until nicely browned.

MILK BISCUITS

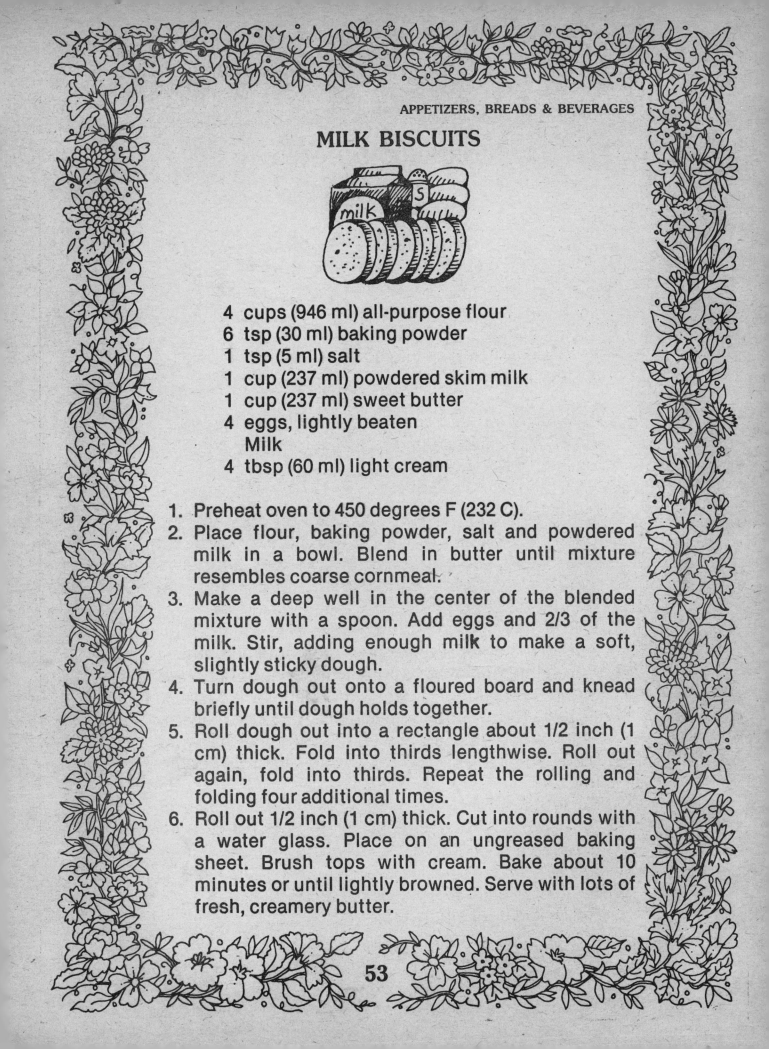

4 cups (946 ml) all-purpose flour
6 tsp (30 ml) baking powder
1 tsp (5 ml) salt
1 cup (237 ml) powdered skim milk
1 cup (237 ml) sweet butter
4 eggs, lightly beaten
  Milk
4 tbsp (60 ml) light cream

1. Preheat oven to 450 degrees F (232 C).
2. Place flour, baking powder, salt and powdered milk in a bowl. Blend in butter until mixture resembles coarse cornmeal.
3. Make a deep well in the center of the blended mixture with a spoon. Add eggs and 2/3 of the milk. Stir, adding enough milk to make a soft, slightly sticky dough.
4. Turn dough out onto a floured board and knead briefly until dough holds together.
5. Roll dough out into a rectangle about 1/2 inch (1 cm) thick. Fold into thirds lengthwise. Roll out again, fold into thirds. Repeat the rolling and folding four additional times.
6. Roll out 1/2 inch (1 cm) thick. Cut into rounds with a water glass. Place on an ungreased baking sheet. Brush tops with cream. Bake about 10 minutes or until lightly browned. Serve with lots of fresh, creamery butter.

BUTTERMILK SPOON BREAD

Makes 8 servings.

3 cups (710 ml) water
2 cups (473 ml) white cornmeal
2 eggs
2 tbsps (30 ml) butter
2 cups (473 ml) buttermilk
2 tsps (10 ml) baking soda
1 1/2 tsps (7.5 ml) salt

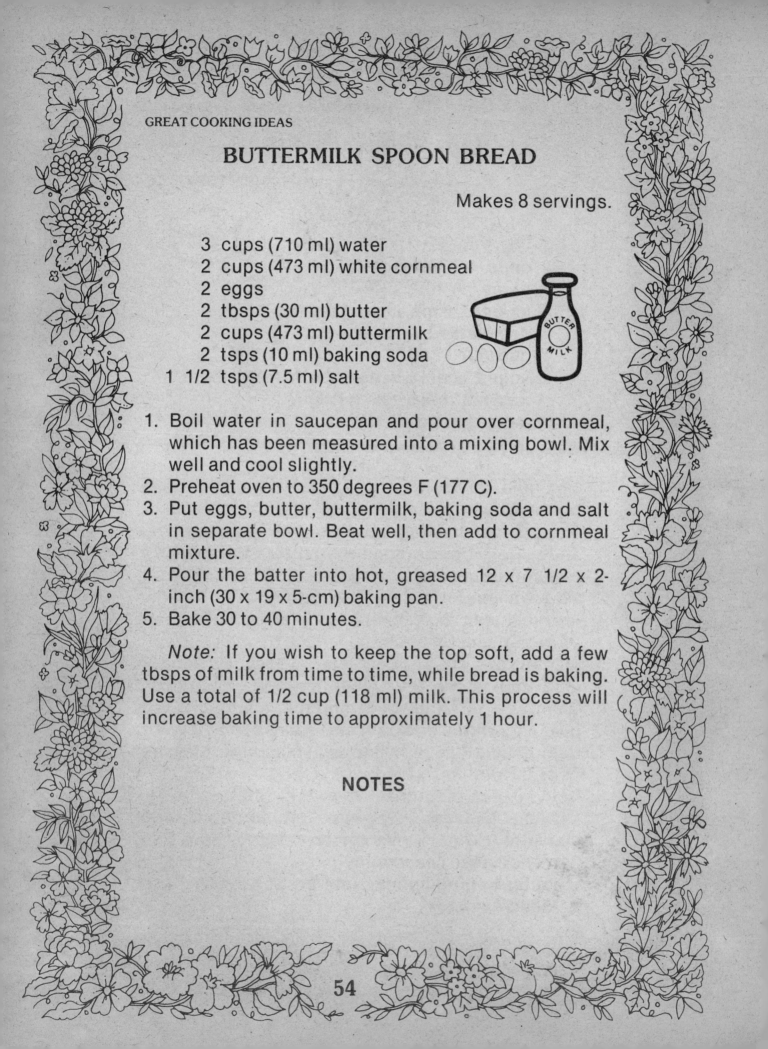

1. Boil water in saucepan and pour over cornmeal, which has been measured into a mixing bowl. Mix well and cool slightly.
2. Preheat oven to 350 degrees F (177 C).
3. Put eggs, butter, buttermilk, baking soda and salt in separate bowl. Beat well, then add to cornmeal mixture.
4. Pour the batter into hot, greased 12 x 7 1/2 x 2-inch (30 x 19 x 5-cm) baking pan.
5. Bake 30 to 40 minutes.

Note: If you wish to keep the top soft, add a few tbsps of milk from time to time, while bread is baking. Use a total of 1/2 cup (118 ml) milk. This process will increase baking time to approximately 1 hour.

NOTES

CHEDDAR SPOON BREAD

Makes 8 servings.

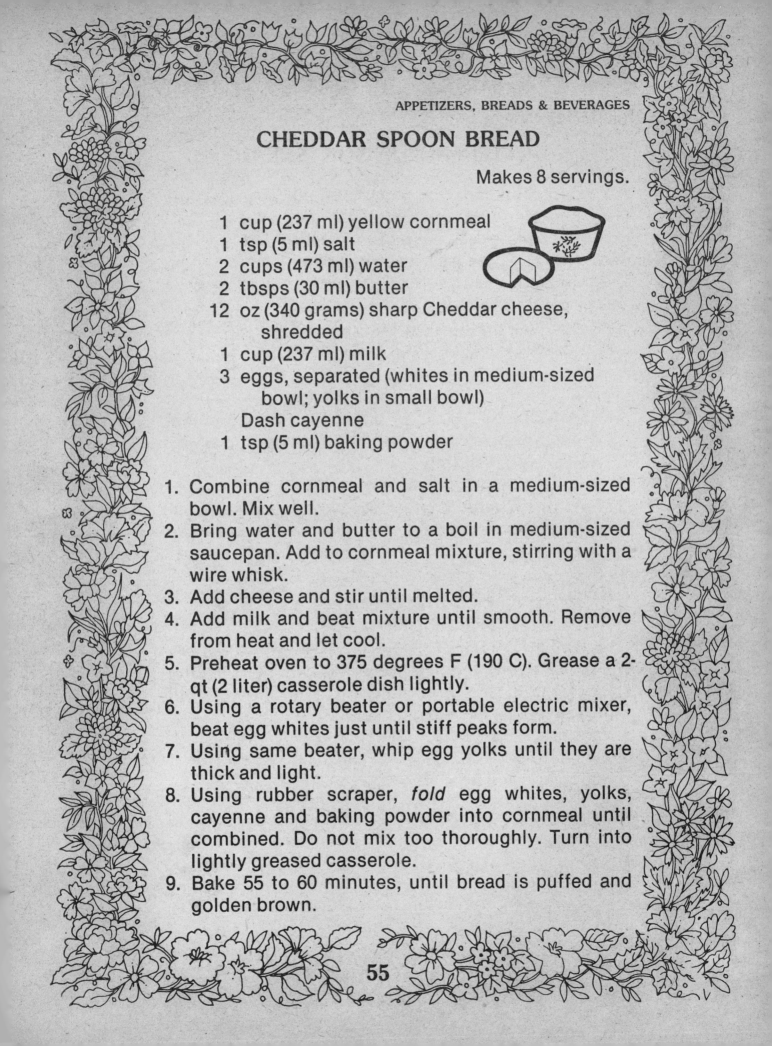

1 cup (237 ml) yellow cornmeal
1 tsp (5 ml) salt
2 cups (473 ml) water
2 tbsps (30 ml) butter
12 oz (340 grams) sharp Cheddar cheese, shredded
1 cup (237 ml) milk
3 eggs, separated (whites in medium-sized bowl; yolks in small bowl)
Dash cayenne
1 tsp (5 ml) baking powder

1. Combine cornmeal and salt in a medium-sized bowl. Mix well.
2. Bring water and butter to a boil in medium-sized saucepan. Add to cornmeal mixture, stirring with a wire whisk.
3. Add cheese and stir until melted.
4. Add milk and beat mixture until smooth. Remove from heat and let cool.
5. Preheat oven to 375 degrees F (190 C). Grease a 2-qt (2 liter) casserole dish lightly.
6. Using a rotary beater or portable electric mixer, beat egg whites just until stiff peaks form.
7. Using same beater, whip egg yolks until they are thick and light.
8. Using rubber scraper, *fold* egg whites, yolks, cayenne and baking powder into cornmeal until combined. Do not mix too thoroughly. Turn into lightly greased casserole.
9. Bake 55 to 60 minutes, until bread is puffed and golden brown.

Tips For Making Good Cornbread

For a rich brown crust and a light but slightly gritty bite, use stone-ground cornmeal and a heavy, hot pan. To obtain a very crisp crust, grease pan well and heat it in a 425 degree F (218 C) oven before filling. The corn and wheat proportion may be varied within a 2-cup (473 ml) limit, to suit individual taste. A generally accepted proportion is 1 1/4 cups (296 ml) cornmeal to 3/4 cup (177 ml) all-purpose flour.

* * *

CORN SPOON BREAD

Makes 6 servings.

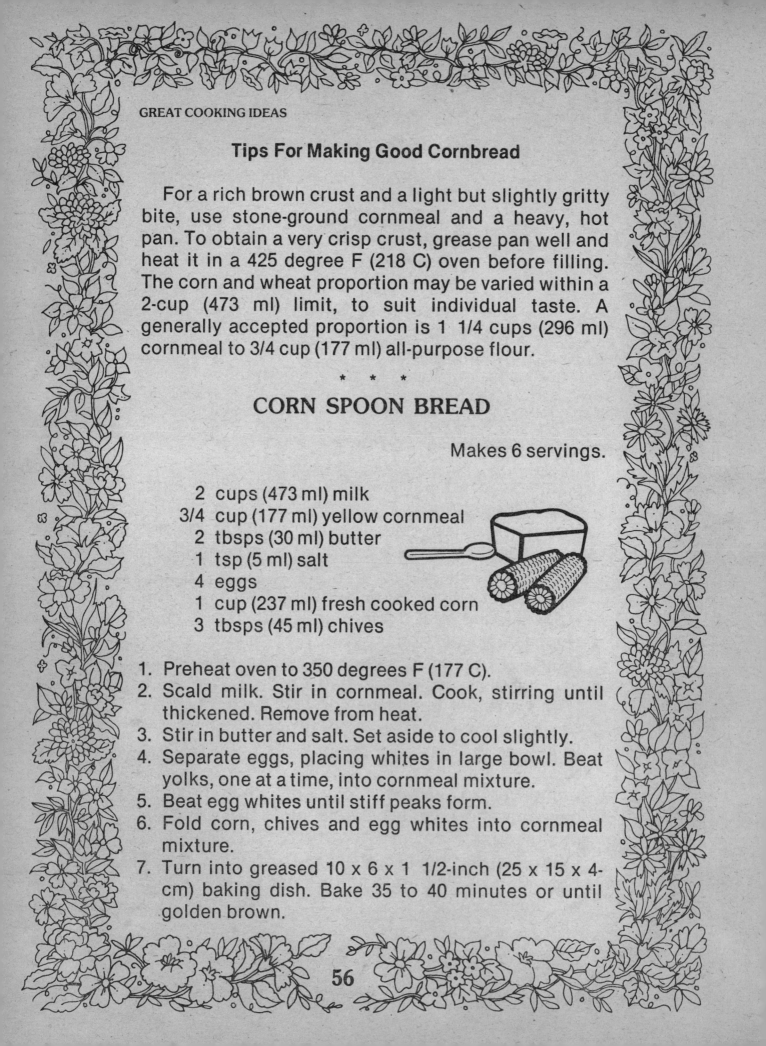

2 cups (473 ml) milk
3/4 cup (177 ml) yellow cornmeal
2 tbsps (30 ml) butter
1 tsp (5 ml) salt
4 eggs
1 cup (237 ml) fresh cooked corn
3 tbsps (45 ml) chives

1. Preheat oven to 350 degrees F (177 C).
2. Scald milk. Stir in cornmeal. Cook, stirring until thickened. Remove from heat.
3. Stir in butter and salt. Set aside to cool slightly.
4. Separate eggs, placing whites in large bowl. Beat yolks, one at a time, into cornmeal mixture.
5. Beat egg whites until stiff peaks form.
6. Fold corn, chives and egg whites into cornmeal mixture.
7. Turn into greased 10 x 6 x 1 1/2-inch (25 x 15 x 4-cm) baking dish. Bake 35 to 40 minutes or until golden brown.

RICE SPOON BREAD

Makes 6 servings.

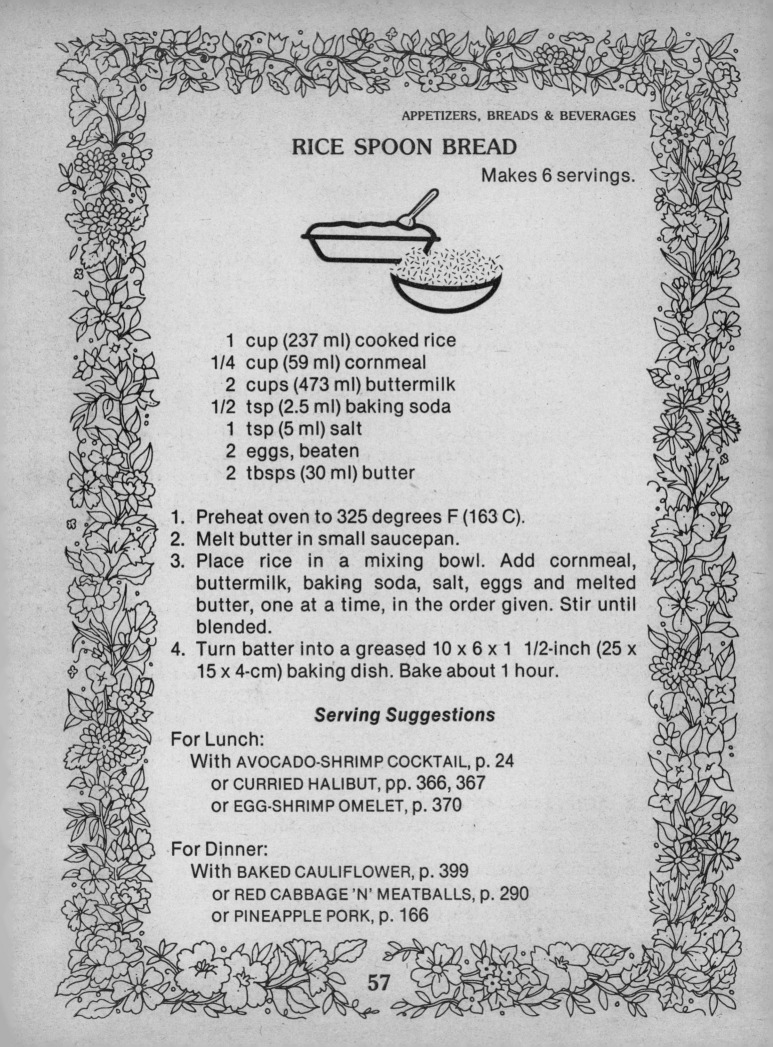

1 cup (237 ml) cooked rice
1/4 cup (59 ml) cornmeal
2 cups (473 ml) buttermilk
1/2 tsp (2.5 ml) baking soda
1 tsp (5 ml) salt
2 eggs, beaten
2 tbsps (30 ml) butter

1. Preheat oven to 325 degrees F (163 C).
2. Melt butter in small saucepan.
3. Place rice in a mixing bowl. Add cornmeal, buttermilk, baking soda, salt, eggs and melted butter, one at a time, in the order given. Stir until blended.
4. Turn batter into a greased 10 x 6 x 1 1/2-inch (25 x 15 x 4-cm) baking dish. Bake about 1 hour.

Serving Suggestions

For Lunch:
   With AVOCADO-SHRIMP COCKTAIL, p. 24
      or CURRIED HALIBUT, pp. 366, 367
      or EGG-SHRIMP OMELET, p. 370

For Dinner:
   With BAKED CAULIFLOWER, p. 399
      or RED CABBAGE 'N' MEATBALLS, p. 290
      or PINEAPPLE PORK, p. 166

CAFFE ESPRESSO

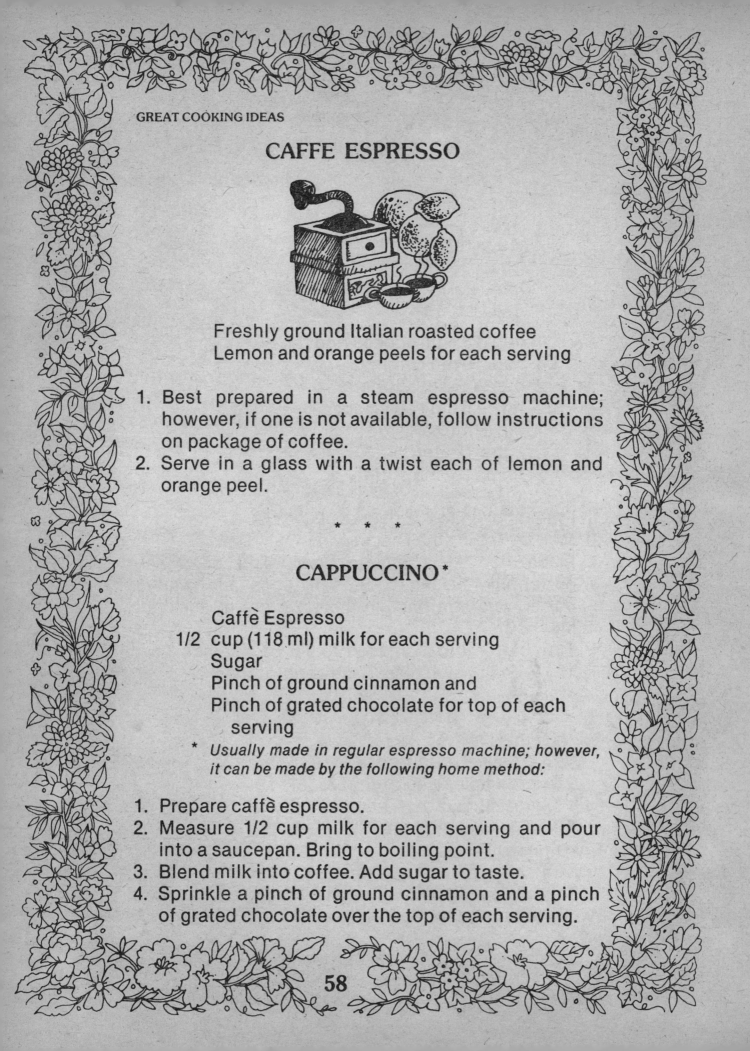

Freshly ground Italian roasted coffee
Lemon and orange peels for each serving

1. Best prepared in a steam espresso machine; however, if one is not available, follow instructions on package of coffee.
2. Serve in a glass with a twist each of lemon and orange peel.

* * *

CAPPUCCINO *

Caffè Espresso
1/2 cup (118 ml) milk for each serving
Sugar
Pinch of ground cinnamon and
Pinch of grated chocolate for top of each
serving

* *Usually made in regular espresso machine; however, it can be made by the following home method:*

1. Prepare caffè espresso.
2. Measure 1/2 cup milk for each serving and pour into a saucepan. Bring to boiling point.
3. Blend milk into coffee. Add sugar to taste.
4. Sprinkle a pinch of ground cinnamon and a pinch of grated chocolate over the top of each serving.

MOCHA

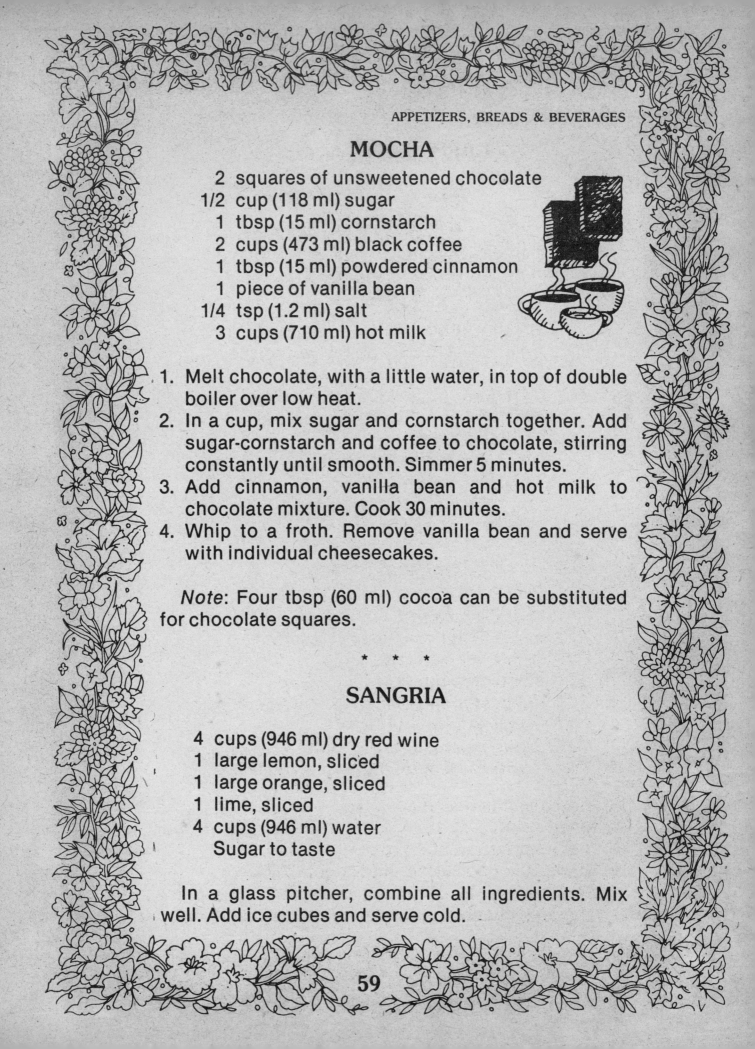

2 squares of unsweetened chocolate
1/2 cup (118 ml) sugar
1 tbsp (15 ml) cornstarch
2 cups (473 ml) black coffee
1 tbsp (15 ml) powdered cinnamon
1 piece of vanilla bean
1/4 tsp (1.2 ml) salt
3 cups (710 ml) hot milk

1. Melt chocolate, with a little water, in top of double boiler over low heat.
2. In a cup, mix sugar and cornstarch together. Add sugar-cornstarch and coffee to chocolate, stirring constantly until smooth. Simmer 5 minutes.
3. Add cinnamon, vanilla bean and hot milk to chocolate mixture. Cook 30 minutes.
4. Whip to a froth. Remove vanilla bean and serve with individual cheesecakes.

Note: Four tbsp (60 ml) cocoa can be substituted for chocolate squares.

* * *

SANGRIA

4 cups (946 ml) dry red wine
1 large lemon, sliced
1 large orange, sliced
1 lime, sliced
4 cups (946 ml) water
Sugar to taste

In a glass pitcher, combine all ingredients. Mix well. Add ice cubes and serve cold.

SPICY ESPRESSO

Makes 8 servings.

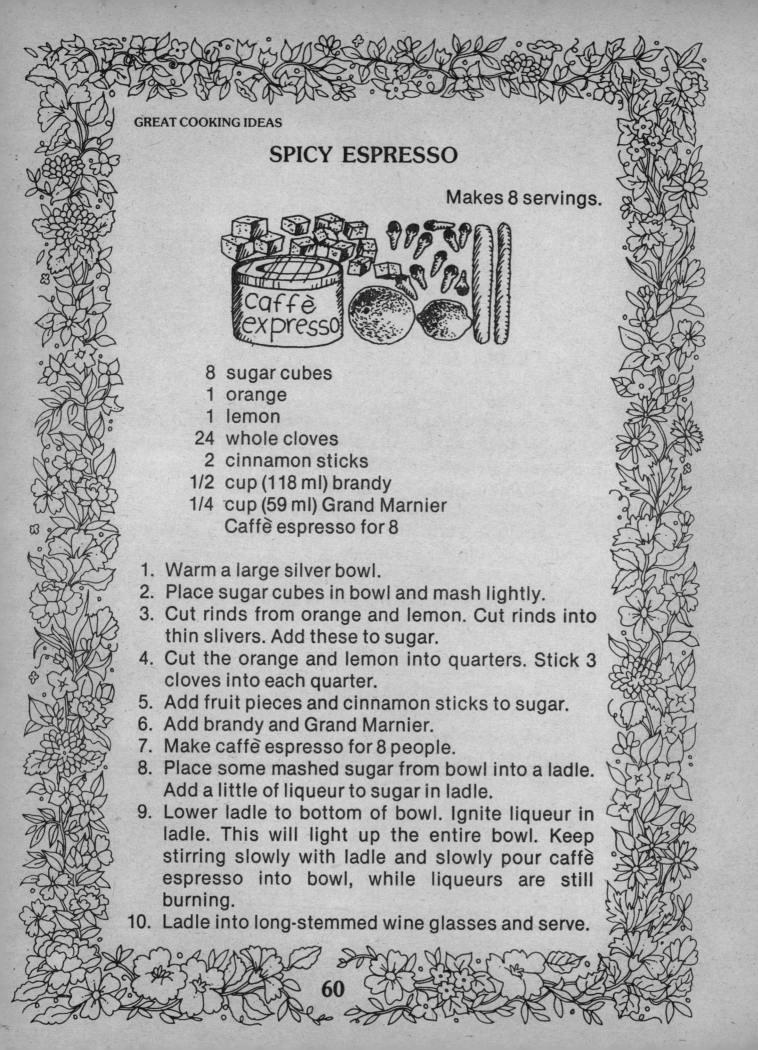

8	sugar cubes
1	orange
1	lemon
24	whole cloves
2	cinnamon sticks
1/2	cup (118 ml) brandy
1/4	cup (59 ml) Grand Marnier
	Caffè espresso for 8

1. Warm a large silver bowl.
2. Place sugar cubes in bowl and mash lightly.
3. Cut rinds from orange and lemon. Cut rinds into thin slivers. Add these to sugar.
4. Cut the orange and lemon into quarters. Stick 3 cloves into each quarter.
5. Add fruit pieces and cinnamon sticks to sugar.
6. Add brandy and Grand Marnier.
7. Make caffè espresso for 8 people.
8. Place some mashed sugar from bowl into a ladle. Add a little of liqueur to sugar in ladle.
9. Lower ladle to bottom of bowl. Ignite liqueur in ladle. This will light up the entire bowl. Keep stirring slowly with ladle and slowly pour caffè espresso into bowl, while liqueurs are still burning.
10. Ladle into long-stemmed wine glasses and serve.

TEQUILA COCKTAIL BOWL

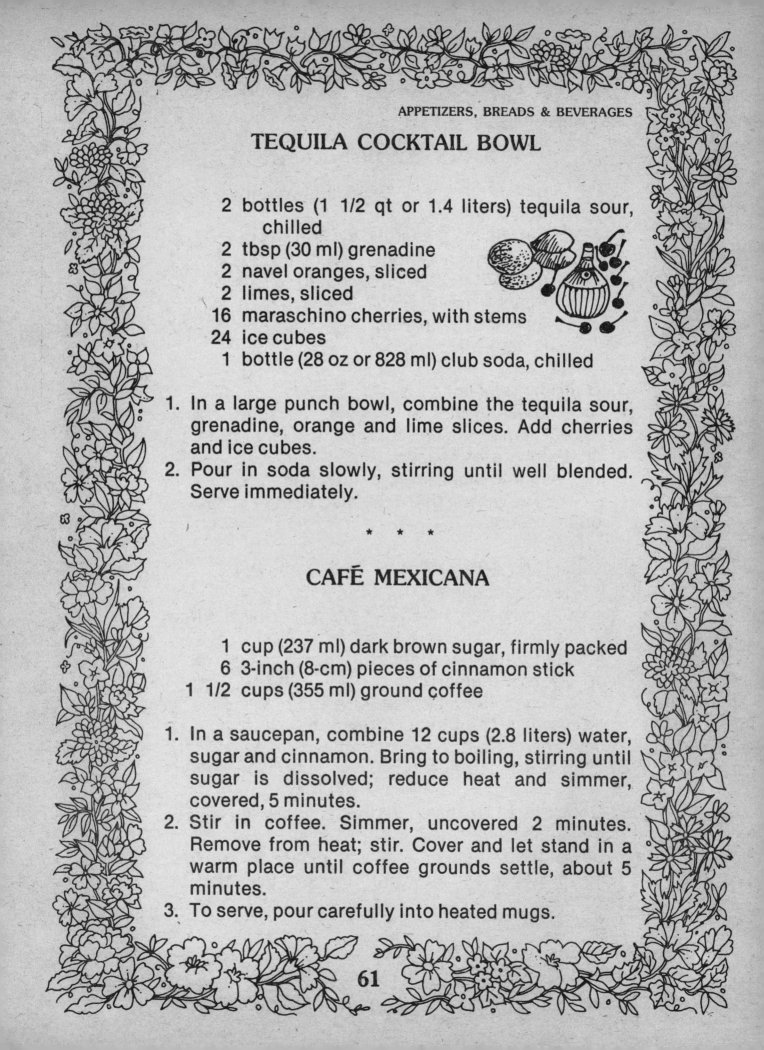

2 bottles (1 1/2 qt or 1.4 liters) tequila sour, chilled
2 tbsp (30 ml) grenadine
2 navel oranges, sliced
2 limes, sliced
16 maraschino cherries, with stems
24 ice cubes
1 bottle (28 oz or 828 ml) club soda, chilled

1. In a large punch bowl, combine the tequila sour, grenadine, orange and lime slices. Add cherries and ice cubes.
2. Pour in soda slowly, stirring until well blended. Serve immediately.

* * *

CAFÉ MEXICANA

1 cup (237 ml) dark brown sugar, firmly packed
6 3-inch (8-cm) pieces of cinnamon stick
1 1/2 cups (355 ml) ground coffee

1. In a saucepan, combine 12 cups (2.8 liters) water, sugar and cinnamon. Bring to boiling, stirring until sugar is dissolved; reduce heat and simmer, covered, 5 minutes.
2. Stir in coffee. Simmer, uncovered 2 minutes. Remove from heat; stir. Cover and let stand in a warm place until coffee grounds settle, about 5 minutes.
3. To serve, pour carefully into heated mugs.

BOURBON SOUR PUNCH

   1 qt (946 ml) orange juice, unsweetened
   1 qt (946 ml) lemon juice
   1/4 cup (59 ml) grenadine syrup
   1 qt (946 ml) bourbon
   3 qt (2.8 liters) sparkling water
      Sugar to taste
      Maraschino cherries
      Orange slices

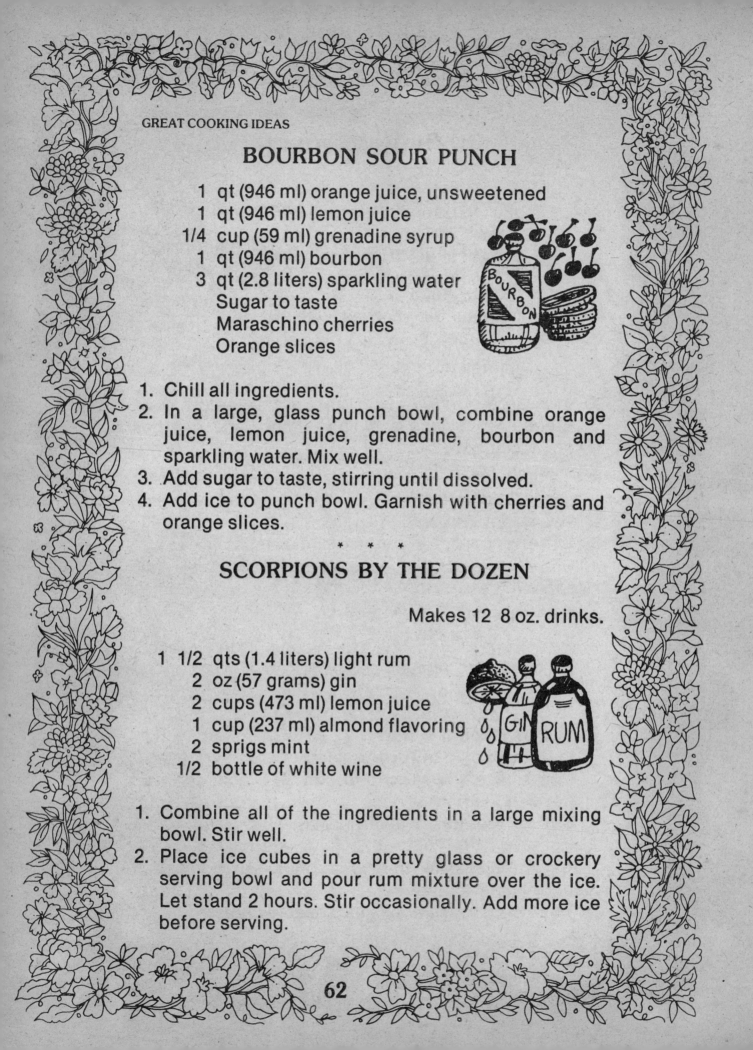

1. Chill all ingredients.
2. In a large, glass punch bowl, combine orange juice, lemon juice, grenadine, bourbon and sparkling water. Mix well.
3. Add sugar to taste, stirring until dissolved.
4. Add ice to punch bowl. Garnish with cherries and orange slices.

* * *

SCORPIONS BY THE DOZEN

Makes 12 8 oz. drinks.

   1 1/2 qts (1.4 liters) light rum
      2 oz (57 grams) gin
      2 cups (473 ml) lemon juice
      1 cup (237 ml) almond flavoring
      2 sprigs mint
   1/2 bottle of white wine

1. Combine all of the ingredients in a large mixing bowl. Stir well.
2. Place ice cubes in a pretty glass or crockery serving bowl and pour rum mixture over the ice. Let stand 2 hours. Stir occasionally. Add more ice before serving.

LUAU (RUM) PUNCH

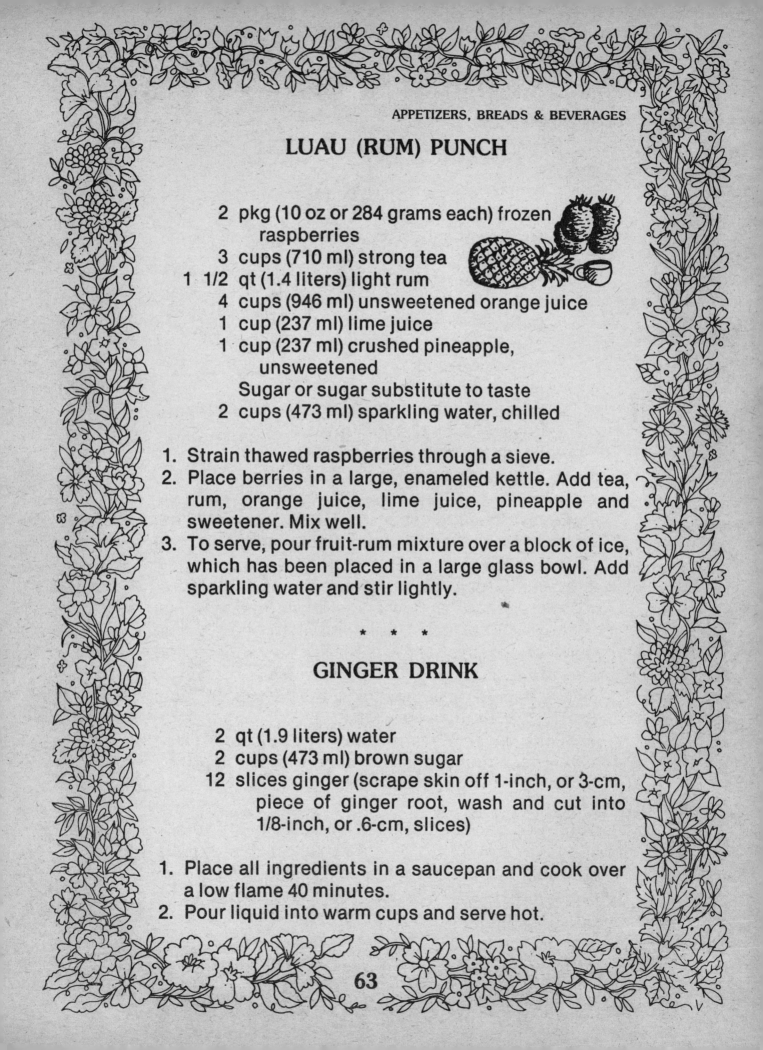

  2 pkg (10 oz or 284 grams each) frozen
       raspberries
  3 cups (710 ml) strong tea
1 1/2 qt (1.4 liters) light rum
  4 cups (946 ml) unsweetened orange juice
  1 cup (237 ml) lime juice
  1 cup (237 ml) crushed pineapple,
       unsweetened
     Sugar or sugar substitute to taste
  2 cups (473 ml) sparkling water, chilled

1. Strain thawed raspberries through a sieve.
2. Place berries in a large, enameled kettle. Add tea,
    rum, orange juice, lime juice, pineapple and
    sweetener. Mix well.
3. To serve, pour fruit-rum mixture over a block of ice,
    which has been placed in a large glass bowl. Add
    sparkling water and stir lightly.

* * *

GINGER DRINK

  2 qt (1.9 liters) water
  2 cups (473 ml) brown sugar
 12 slices ginger (scrape skin off 1-inch, or 3-cm,
       piece of ginger root, wash and cut into
       1/8-inch, or .6-cm, slices)

1. Place all ingredients in a saucepan and cook over
    a low flame 40 minutes.
2. Pour liquid into warm cups and serve hot.

HOLIDAY FRUIT PUNCH

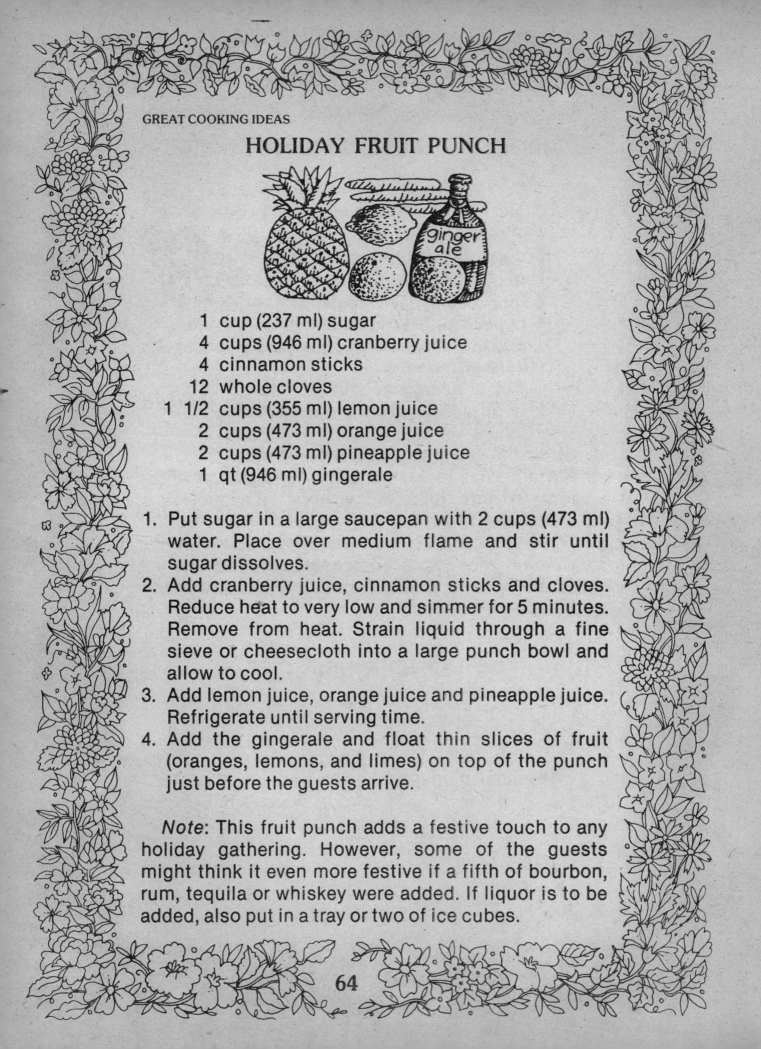

- 1 cup (237 ml) sugar
- 4 cups (946 ml) cranberry juice
- 4 cinnamon sticks
- 12 whole cloves
- 1 1/2 cups (355 ml) lemon juice
- 2 cups (473 ml) orange juice
- 2 cups (473 ml) pineapple juice
- 1 qt (946 ml) gingerale

1. Put sugar in a large saucepan with 2 cups (473 ml) water. Place over medium flame and stir until sugar dissolves.
2. Add cranberry juice, cinnamon sticks and cloves. Reduce heat to very low and simmer for 5 minutes. Remove from heat. Strain liquid through a fine sieve or cheesecloth into a large punch bowl and allow to cool.
3. Add lemon juice, orange juice and pineapple juice. Refrigerate until serving time.
4. Add the gingerale and float thin slices of fruit (oranges, lemons, and limes) on top of the punch just before the guests arrive.

Note: This fruit punch adds a festive touch to any holiday gathering. However, some of the guests might think it even more festive if a fifth of bourbon, rum, tequila or whiskey were added. If liquor is to be added, also put in a tray or two of ice cubes.

BROCCOLI SALAD WITH WALNUTS

Makes 4 servings.

1 lb (454 grams) fresh young broccoli
1 tsp (5 ml) powdered mustard
1 tbsp (15 ml) mayonnaise
2 tbsp (30 ml) rice vinegar*
1/4 cup (59 ml) walnut meats, finely chopped

   * *Available in Japanese grocery markets; or substitute distilled cider vinegar.*

1. Wash broccoli and cut off tough bottom stems. Separate into florets. Place florets in saucepan with small amount of water and salt. Cook broccoli until tender, but not mushy. Drain and allow to cool, then cut in bite-sized pieces.
2. In a cup, combine mustard, mayonnaise and rice vinegar. Mix well and season to taste with salt.
3. Pour sauce over cooled broccoli. Toss lightly.
4. Serve broccoli in individual bowls sprinkled with chopped walnuts.

Note: Delicious with STEAK HAWAIIAN, p. 296
      or MARINATED LAMB CURRY, p. 356.

CAULIFLOWER SALAD

Makes 6 servings.

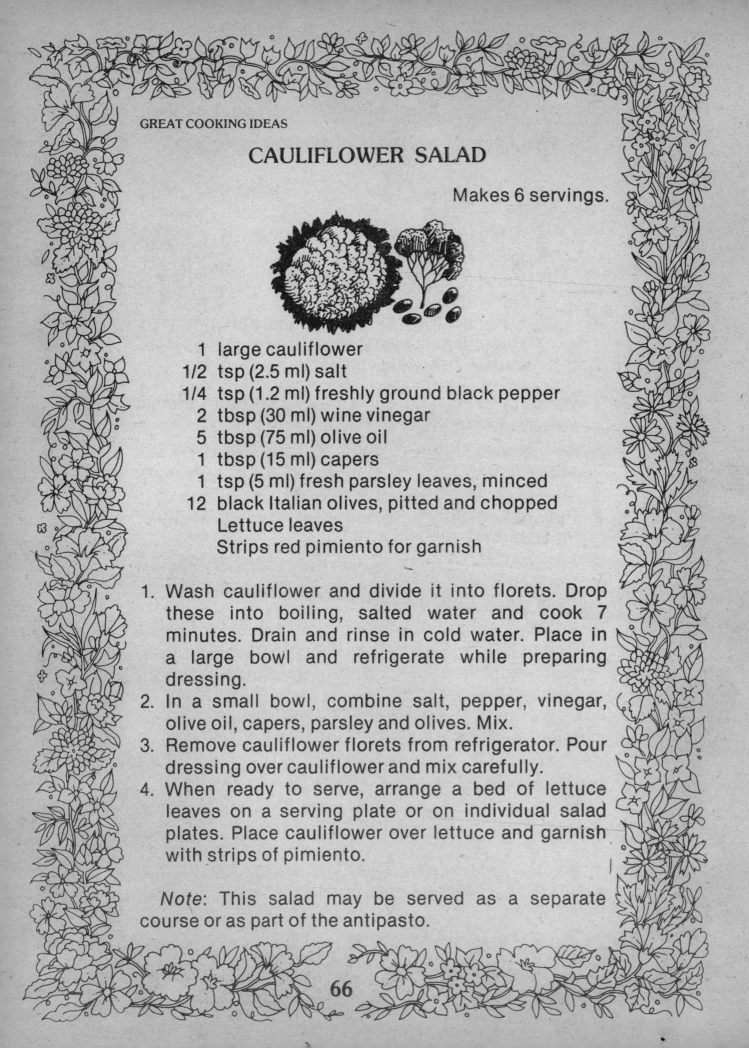

1 large cauliflower
1/2 tsp (2.5 ml) salt
1/4 tsp (1.2 ml) freshly ground black pepper
2 tbsp (30 ml) wine vinegar
5 tbsp (75 ml) olive oil
1 tbsp (15 ml) capers
1 tsp (5 ml) fresh parsley leaves, minced
12 black Italian olives, pitted and chopped
Lettuce leaves
Strips red pimiento for garnish

1. Wash cauliflower and divide it into florets. Drop these into boiling, salted water and cook 7 minutes. Drain and rinse in cold water. Place in a large bowl and refrigerate while preparing dressing.
2. In a small bowl, combine salt, pepper, vinegar, olive oil, capers, parsley and olives. Mix.
3. Remove cauliflower florets from refrigerator. Pour dressing over cauliflower and mix carefully.
4. When ready to serve, arrange a bed of lettuce leaves on a serving plate or on individual salad plates. Place cauliflower over lettuce and garnish with strips of pimiento.

Note: This salad may be served as a separate course or as part of the antipasto.

CELERY CABBAGE-CARROT SALAD

Makes 8 servings.

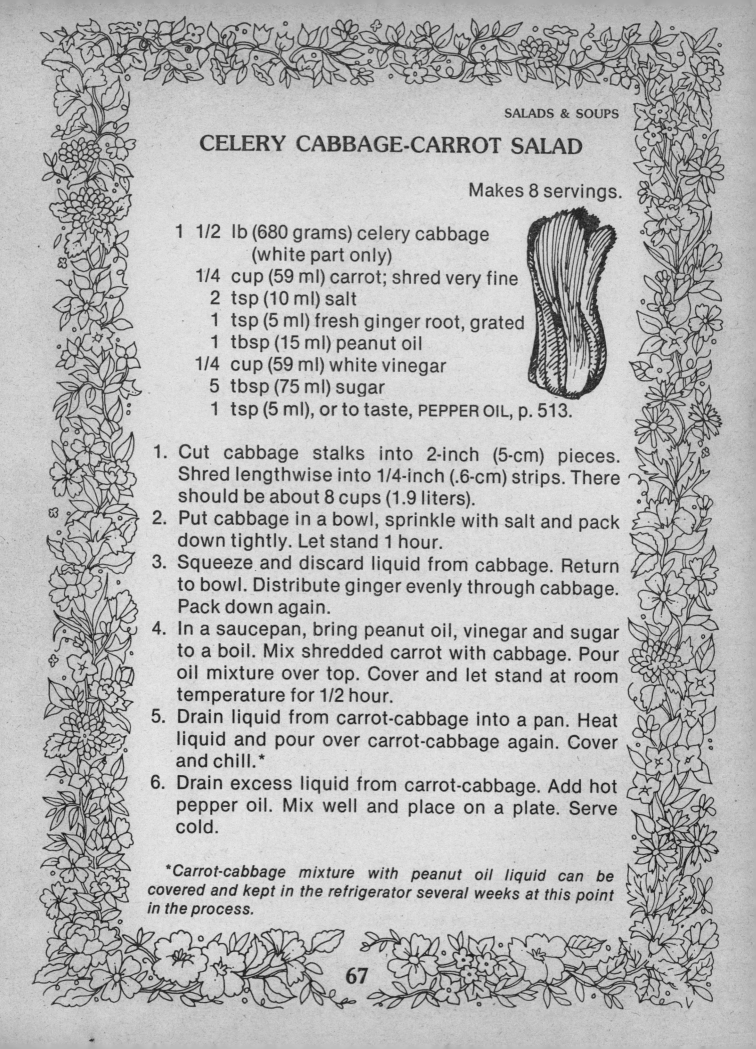

1 1/2 lb (680 grams) celery cabbage
       (white part only)
1/4   cup (59 ml) carrot; shred very fine
2   tsp (10 ml) salt
1   tsp (5 ml) fresh ginger root, grated
1   tbsp (15 ml) peanut oil
1/4   cup (59 ml) white vinegar
5   tbsp (75 ml) sugar
1   tsp (5 ml), or to taste, PEPPER OIL, p. 513.

1. Cut cabbage stalks into 2-inch (5-cm) pieces. Shred lengthwise into 1/4-inch (.6-cm) strips. There should be about 8 cups (1.9 liters).
2. Put cabbage in a bowl, sprinkle with salt and pack down tightly. Let stand 1 hour.
3. Squeeze and discard liquid from cabbage. Return to bowl. Distribute ginger evenly through cabbage. Pack down again.
4. In a saucepan, bring peanut oil, vinegar and sugar to a boil. Mix shredded carrot with cabbage. Pour oil mixture over top. Cover and let stand at room temperature for 1/2 hour.
5. Drain liquid from carrot-cabbage into a pan. Heat liquid and pour over carrot-cabbage again. Cover and chill.*
6. Drain excess liquid from carrot-cabbage. Add hot pepper oil. Mix well and place on a plate. Serve cold.

*Carrot-cabbage mixture with peanut oil liquid can be covered and kept in the refrigerator several weeks at this point in the process.

COUNTRY COLESLAW

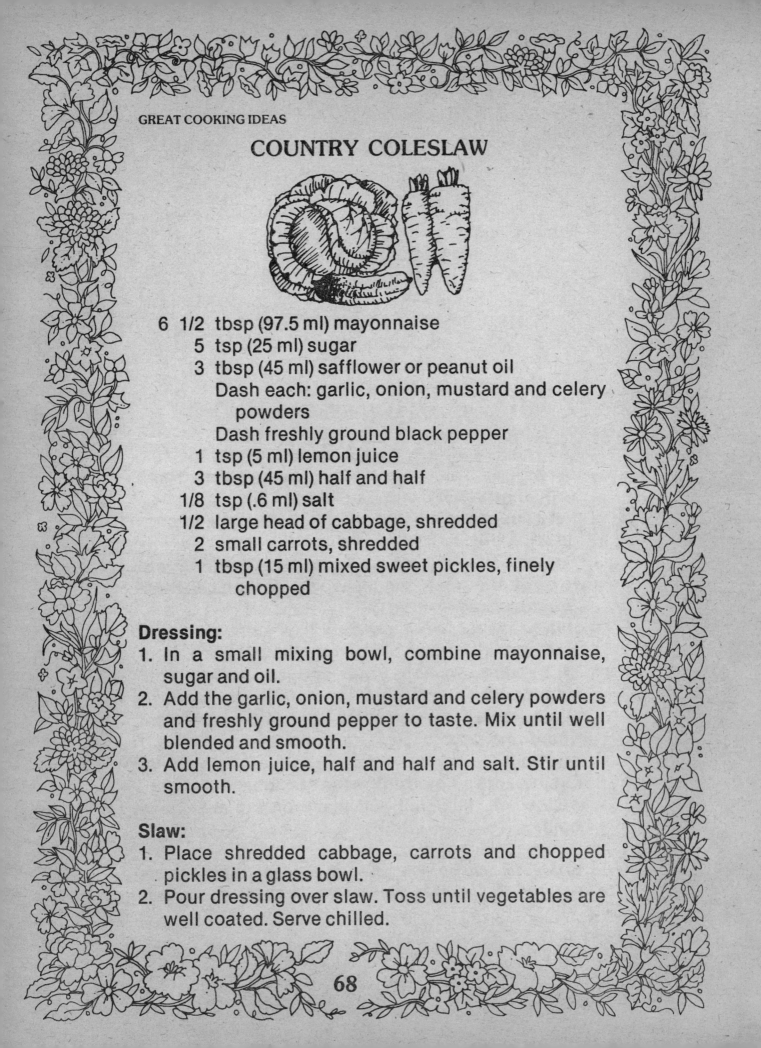

6 1/2 tbsp (97.5 ml) mayonnaise
    5 tsp (25 ml) sugar
    3 tbsp (45 ml) safflower or peanut oil
       Dash each: garlic, onion, mustard and celery
          powders
       Dash freshly ground black pepper
    1 tsp (5 ml) lemon juice
    3 tbsp (45 ml) half and half
  1/8 tsp (.6 ml) salt
  1/2 large head of cabbage, shredded
    2 small carrots, shredded
    1 tbsp (15 ml) mixed sweet pickles, finely
          chopped

Dressing:

1. In a small mixing bowl, combine mayonnaise, sugar and oil.
2. Add the garlic, onion, mustard and celery powders and freshly ground pepper to taste. Mix until well blended and smooth.
3. Add lemon juice, half and half and salt. Stir until smooth.

Slaw:

1. Place shredded cabbage, carrots and chopped pickles in a glass bowl.
2. Pour dressing over slaw. Toss until vegetables are well coated. Serve chilled.

KIMCH'I
(Celery-Cabbage Salad)

Makes 6 servings.

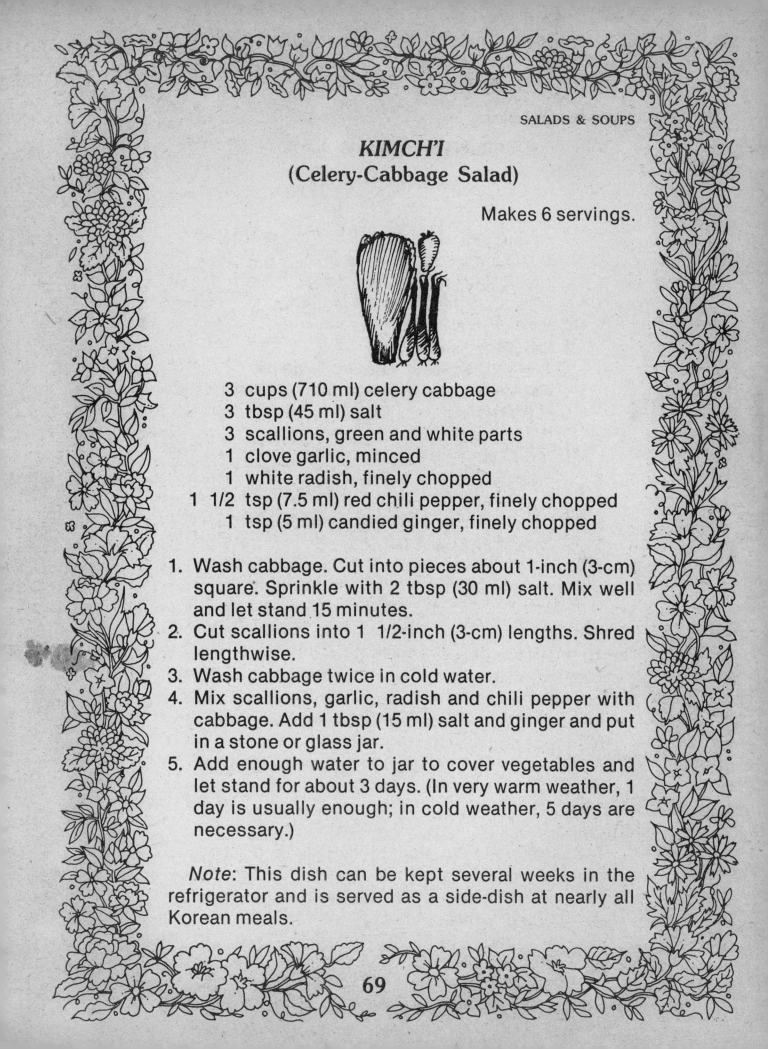

    3   cups (710 ml) celery cabbage
    3   tbsp (45 ml) salt
    3   scallions, green and white parts
    1   clove garlic, minced
    1   white radish, finely chopped
1 1/2   tsp (7.5 ml) red chili pepper, finely chopped
    1   tsp (5 ml) candied ginger, finely chopped

1. Wash cabbage. Cut into pieces about 1-inch (3-cm) square. Sprinkle with 2 tbsp (30 ml) salt. Mix well and let stand 15 minutes.
2. Cut scallions into 1 1/2-inch (3-cm) lengths. Shred lengthwise.
3. Wash cabbage twice in cold water.
4. Mix scallions, garlic, radish and chili pepper with cabbage. Add 1 tbsp (15 ml) salt and ginger and put in a stone or glass jar.
5. Add enough water to jar to cover vegetables and let stand for about 3 days. (In very warm weather, 1 day is usually enough; in cold weather, 5 days are necessary.)

Note: This dish can be kept several weeks in the refrigerator and is served as a side-dish at nearly all Korean meals.

CUCUMBER SALAD

Makes 4 servings.

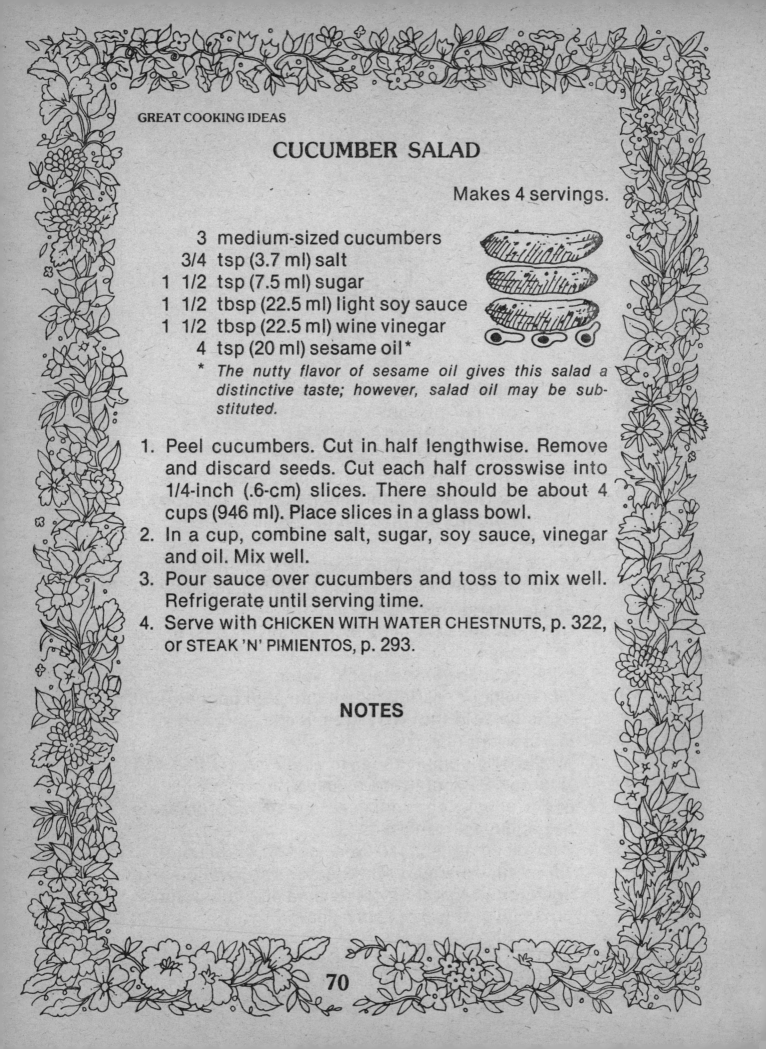

3 medium-sized cucumbers
3/4 tsp (3.7 ml) salt
1 1/2 tsp (7.5 ml) sugar
1 1/2 tbsp (22.5 ml) light soy sauce
1 1/2 tbsp (22.5 ml) wine vinegar
4 tsp (20 ml) sesame oil*

* *The nutty flavor of sesame oil gives this salad a distinctive taste; however, salad oil may be substituted.*

1. Peel cucumbers. Cut in half lengthwise. Remove and discard seeds. Cut each half crosswise into 1/4-inch (.6-cm) slices. There should be about 4 cups (946 ml). Place slices in a glass bowl.
2. In a cup, combine salt, sugar, soy sauce, vinegar and oil. Mix well.
3. Pour sauce over cucumbers and toss to mix well. Refrigerate until serving time.
4. Serve with CHICKEN WITH WATER CHESTNUTS, p. 322, or STEAK 'N' PIMIENTOS, p. 293.

NOTES

ENDIVE AND RADISH SALAD

Makes 4 - 6 servings.

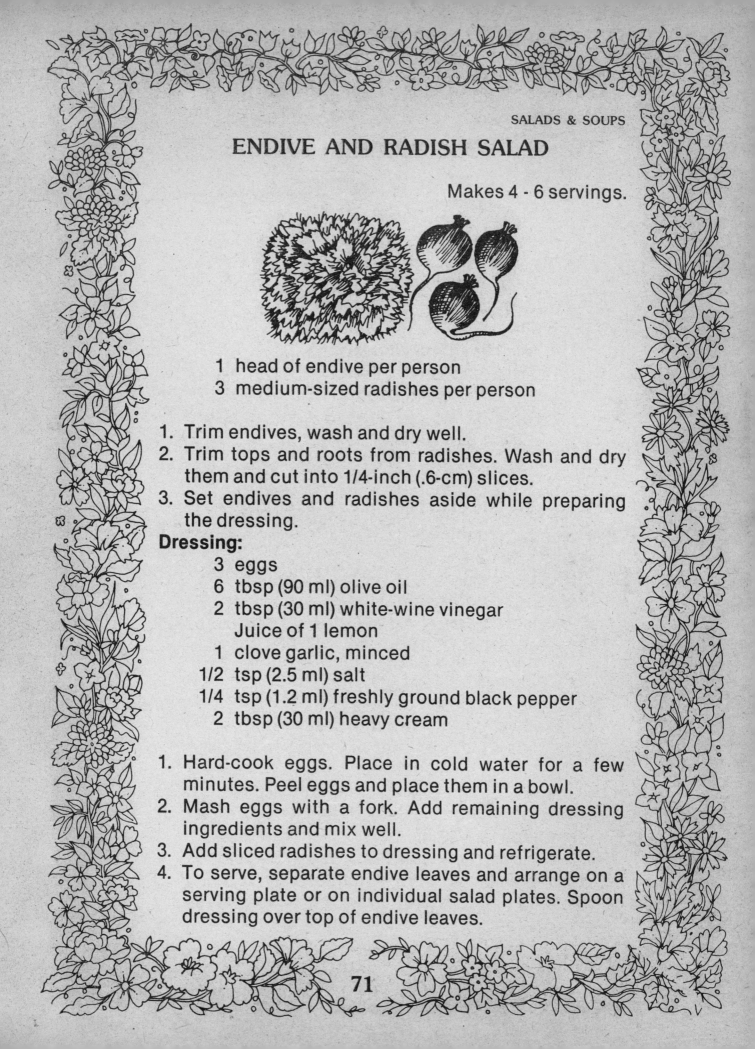

1 head of endive per person
3 medium-sized radishes per person

1. Trim endives, wash and dry well.
2. Trim tops and roots from radishes. Wash and dry them and cut into 1/4-inch (.6-cm) slices.
3. Set endives and radishes aside while preparing the dressing.

Dressing:

3 eggs
6 tbsp (90 ml) olive oil
2 tbsp (30 ml) white-wine vinegar
   Juice of 1 lemon
1 clove garlic, minced
1/2 tsp (2.5 ml) salt
1/4 tsp (1.2 ml) freshly ground black pepper
2 tbsp (30 ml) heavy cream

1. Hard-cook eggs. Place in cold water for a few minutes. Peel eggs and place them in a bowl.
2. Mash eggs with a fork. Add remaining dressing ingredients and mix well.
3. Add sliced radishes to dressing and refrigerate.
4. To serve, separate endive leaves and arrange on a serving plate or on individual salad plates. Spoon dressing over top of endive leaves.

LETTUCE-ZUCCHINI SALAD

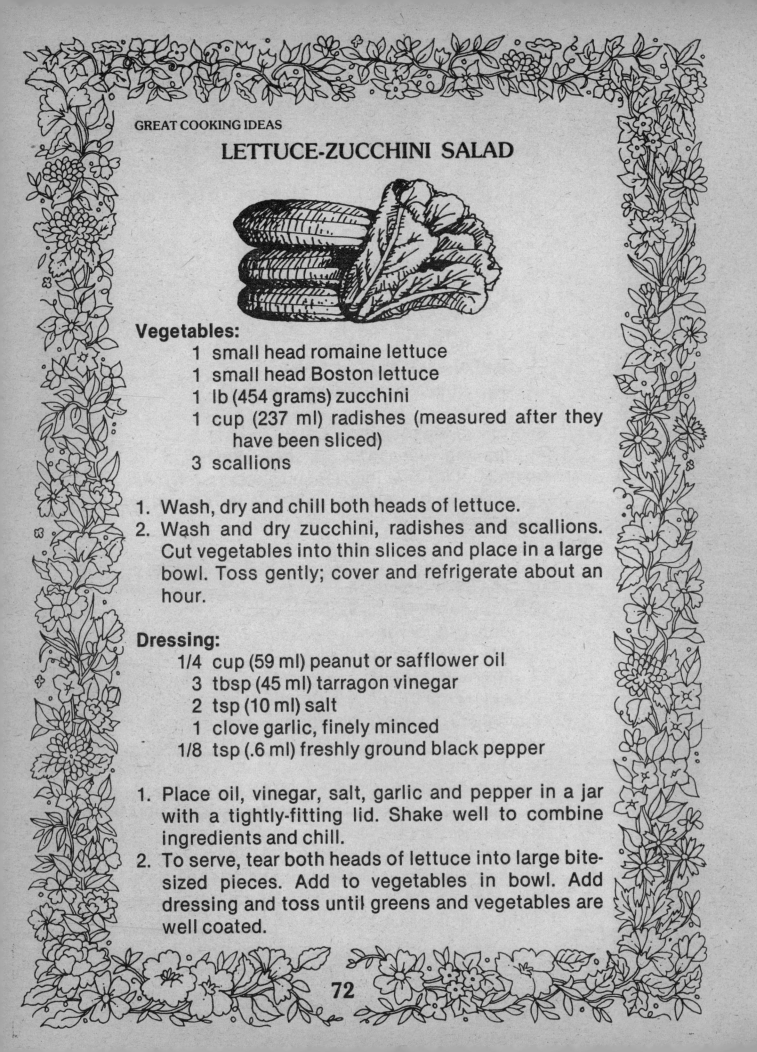

Vegetables:

- 1 small head romaine lettuce
- 1 small head Boston lettuce
- 1 lb (454 grams) zucchini
- 1 cup (237 ml) radishes (measured after they have been sliced)
- 3 scallions

1. Wash, dry and chill both heads of lettuce.
2. Wash and dry zucchini, radishes and scallions. Cut vegetables into thin slices and place in a large bowl. Toss gently; cover and refrigerate about an hour.

Dressing:

- 1/4 cup (59 ml) peanut or safflower oil
- 3 tbsp (45 ml) tarragon vinegar
- 2 tsp (10 ml) salt
- 1 clove garlic, finely minced
- 1/8 tsp (.6 ml) freshly ground black pepper

1. Place oil, vinegar, salt, garlic and pepper in a jar with a tightly-fitting lid. Shake well to combine ingredients and chill.
2. To serve, tear both heads of lettuce into large bite-sized pieces. Add to vegetables in bowl. Add dressing and toss until greens and vegetables are well coated.

ZUCCHINI WITH OIL AND LEMON

Makes 4 - 6 servings.

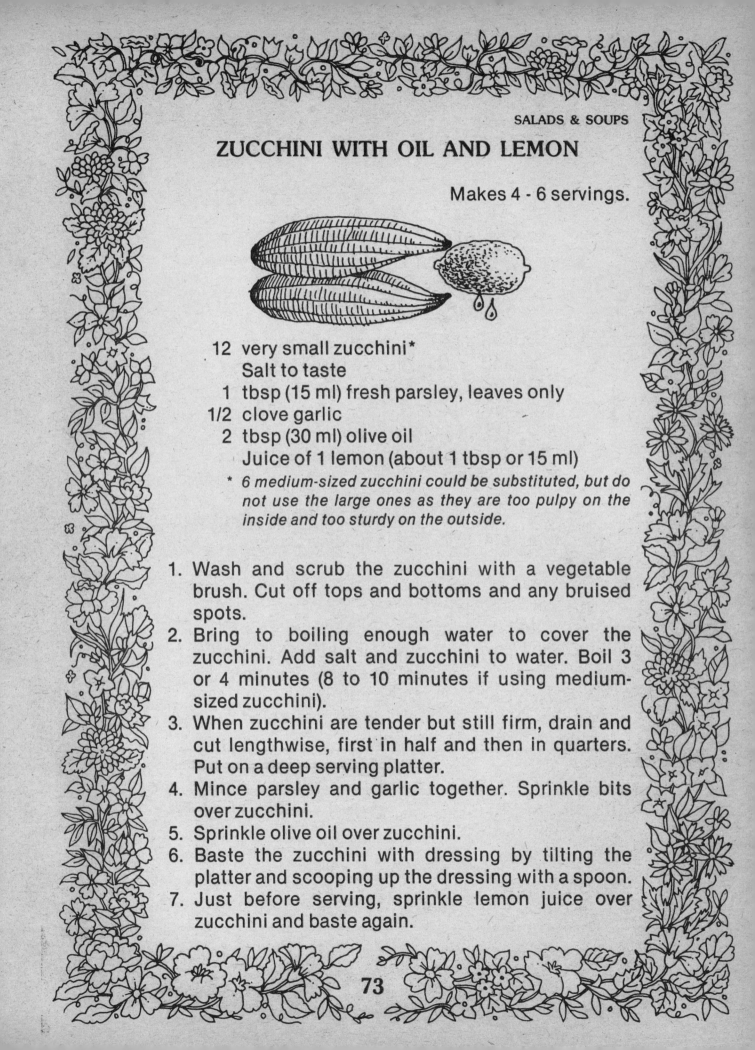

12 very small zucchini*
    Salt to taste
 1 tbsp (15 ml) fresh parsley, leaves only
1/2 clove garlic
 2 tbsp (30 ml) olive oil
    Juice of 1 lemon (about 1 tbsp or 15 ml)

 * *6 medium-sized zucchini could be substituted, but do not use the large ones as they are too pulpy on the inside and too sturdy on the outside.*

1. Wash and scrub the zucchini with a vegetable brush. Cut off tops and bottoms and any bruised spots.
2. Bring to boiling enough water to cover the zucchini. Add salt and zucchini to water. Boil 3 or 4 minutes (8 to 10 minutes if using medium-sized zucchini).
3. When zucchini are tender but still firm, drain and cut lengthwise, first in half and then in quarters. Put on a deep serving platter.
4. Mince parsley and garlic together. Sprinkle bits over zucchini.
5. Sprinkle olive oil over zucchini.
6. Baste the zucchini with dressing by tilting the platter and scooping up the dressing with a spoon.
7. Just before serving, sprinkle lemon juice over zucchini and baste again.

POTATO AND ONION SALAD

Makes 4 servings.

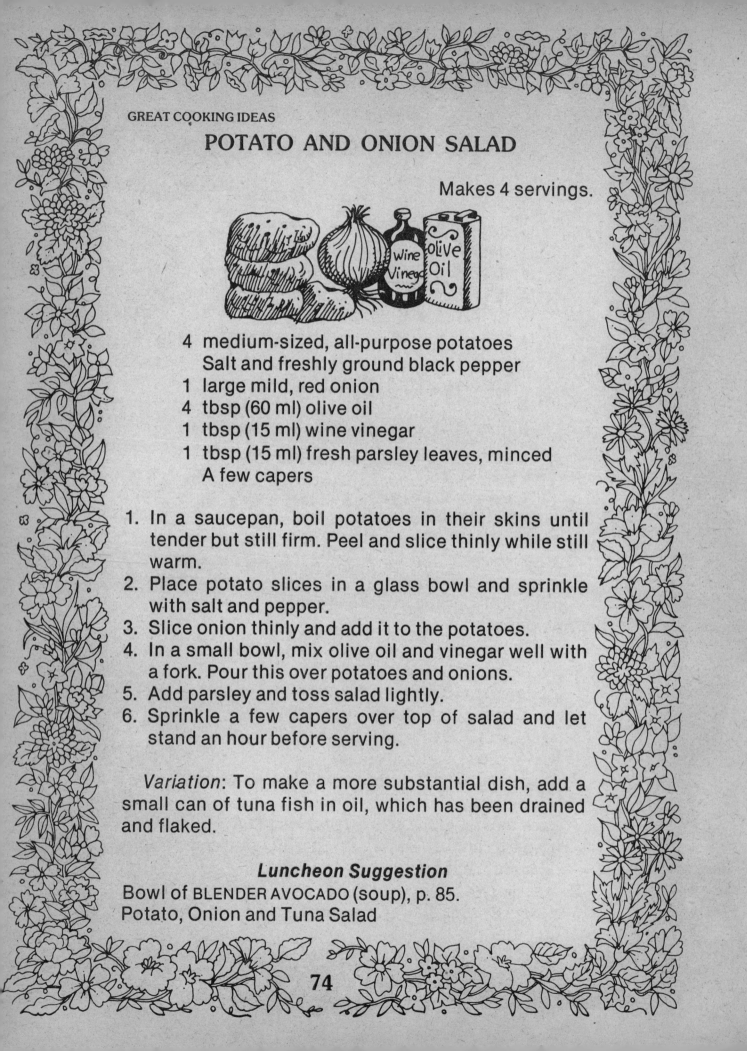

4 medium-sized, all-purpose potatoes
   Salt and freshly ground black pepper
1 large mild, red onion
4 tbsp (60 ml) olive oil
1 tbsp (15 ml) wine vinegar
1 tbsp (15 ml) fresh parsley leaves, minced
   A few capers

1. In a saucepan, boil potatoes in their skins until tender but still firm. Peel and slice thinly while still warm.
2. Place potato slices in a glass bowl and sprinkle with salt and pepper.
3. Slice onion thinly and add it to the potatoes.
4. In a small bowl, mix olive oil and vinegar well with a fork. Pour this over potatoes and onions.
5. Add parsley and toss salad lightly.
6. Sprinkle a few capers over top of salad and let stand an hour before serving.

Variation: To make a more substantial dish, add a small can of tuna fish in oil, which has been drained and flaked.

Luncheon Suggestion
Bowl of BLENDER AVOCADO (soup), p. 85.
Potato, Onion and Tuna Salad

RED AND GREEN SALAD

Makes 8 servings.

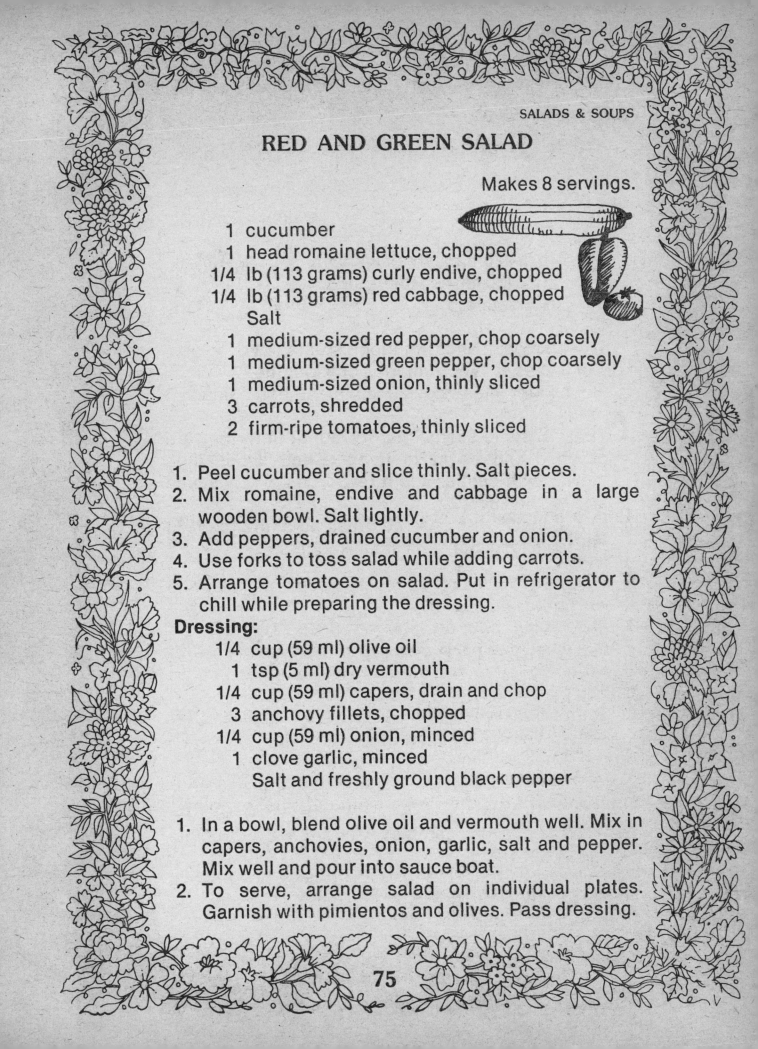

1 cucumber
1 head romaine lettuce, chopped
1/4 lb (113 grams) curly endive, chopped
1/4 lb (113 grams) red cabbage, chopped
Salt
1 medium-sized red pepper, chop coarsely
1 medium-sized green pepper, chop coarsely
1 medium-sized onion, thinly sliced
3 carrots, shredded
2 firm-ripe tomatoes, thinly sliced

1. Peel cucumber and slice thinly. Salt pieces.
2. Mix romaine, endive and cabbage in a large wooden bowl. Salt lightly.
3. Add peppers, drained cucumber and onion.
4. Use forks to toss salad while adding carrots.
5. Arrange tomatoes on salad. Put in refrigerator to chill while preparing the dressing.

Dressing:

1/4 cup (59 ml) olive oil
1 tsp (5 ml) dry vermouth
1/4 cup (59 ml) capers, drain and chop
3 anchovy fillets, chopped
1/4 cup (59 ml) onion, minced
1 clove garlic, minced
Salt and freshly ground black pepper

1. In a bowl, blend olive oil and vermouth well. Mix in capers, anchovies, onion, garlic, salt and pepper. Mix well and pour into sauce boat.
2. To serve, arrange salad on individual plates. Garnish with pimientos and olives. Pass dressing.

ORIENTAL SPINACH SALAD

Makes 4 servings.

3/4 lb (340 grams) fresh spinach
2 tbsp (30 ml) sesame seeds
Soy sauce

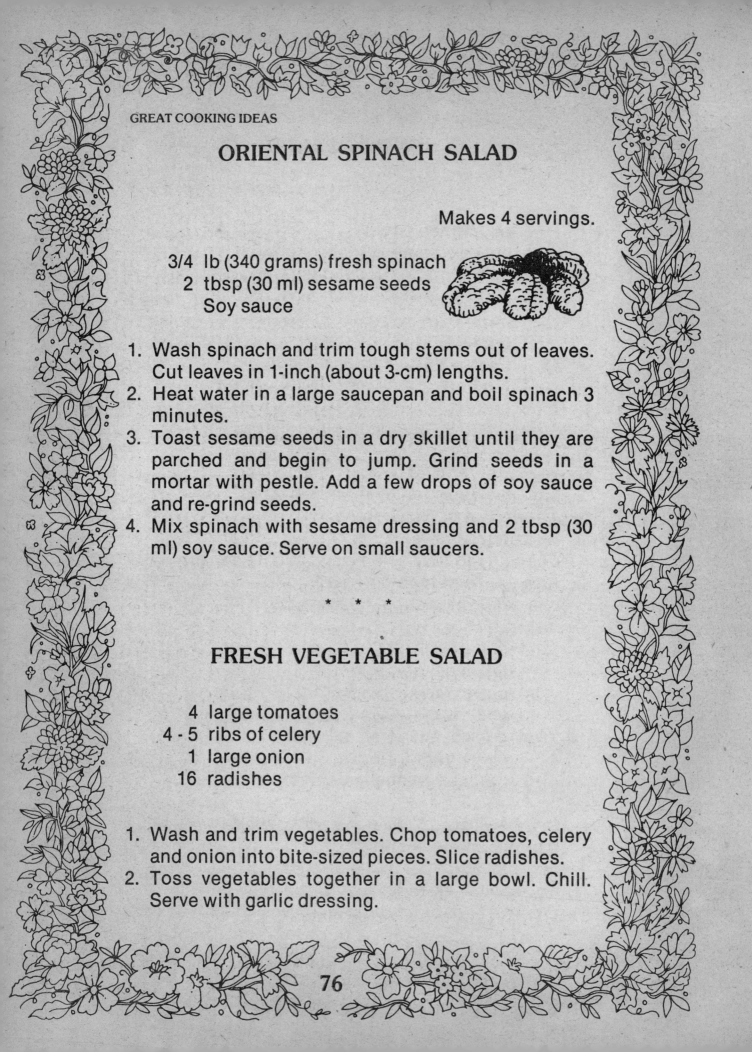

1. Wash spinach and trim tough stems out of leaves. Cut leaves in 1-inch (about 3-cm) lengths.
2. Heat water in a large saucepan and boil spinach 3 minutes.
3. Toast sesame seeds in a dry skillet until they are parched and begin to jump. Grind seeds in a mortar with pestle. Add a few drops of soy sauce and re-grind seeds.
4. Mix spinach with sesame dressing and 2 tbsp (30 ml) soy sauce. Serve on small saucers.

* * *

FRESH VEGETABLE SALAD

4 large tomatoes
4 - 5 ribs of celery
1 large onion
16 radishes

1. Wash and trim vegetables. Chop tomatoes, celery and onion into bite-sized pieces. Slice radishes.
2. Toss vegetables together in a large bowl. Chill. Serve with garlic dressing.

SPINACH SALAD

Makes 6 servings.

1 head romaine lettuce, separated into leaves, washed and drained
1 small bunch watercress, separated, washed and drained
2 sprigs parsley leaves, washed and drained
1 lb (454 grams) fresh spinach, separated into leaves, washed and drained

1. Break romaine leaves in halves and place in a large wooden salad bowl. Add watercress and parsley.
2. Pick over spinach. Discard any old or tough leaves. Mix spinach with other greens. Set aside while preparing dressing.

Dressing:

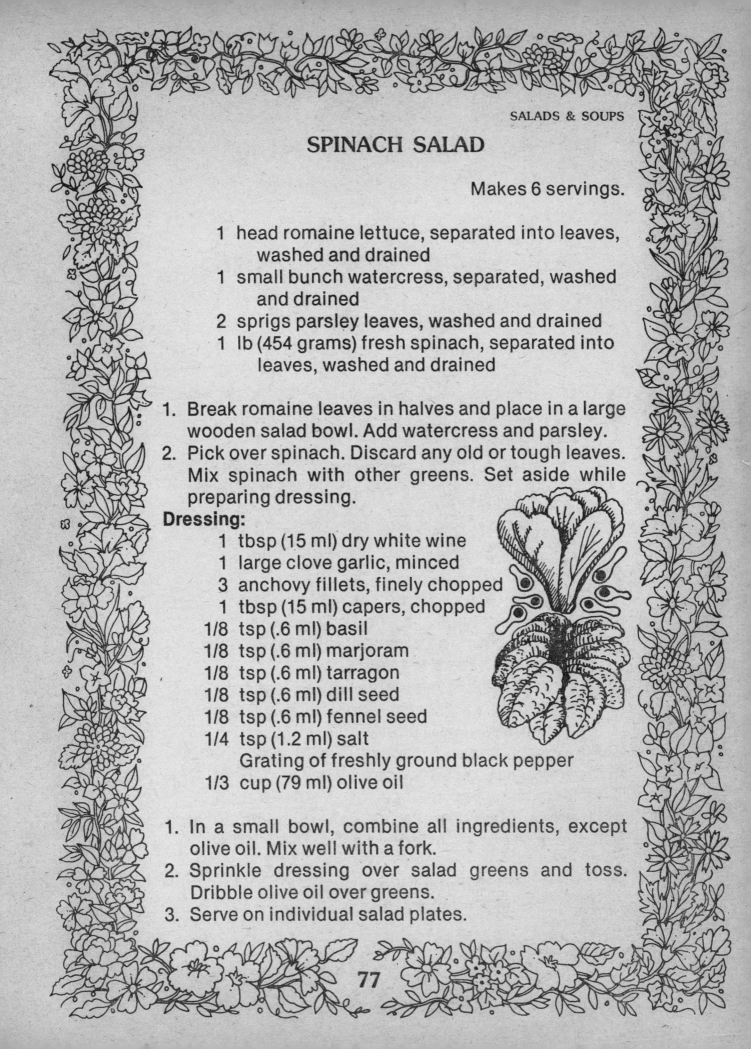

1 tbsp (15 ml) dry white wine
1 large clove garlic, minced
3 anchovy fillets, finely chopped
1 tbsp (15 ml) capers, chopped
1/8 tsp (.6 ml) basil
1/8 tsp (.6 ml) marjoram
1/8 tsp (.6 ml) tarragon
1/8 tsp (.6 ml) dill seed
1/8 tsp (.6 ml) fennel seed
1/4 tsp (1.2 ml) salt
    Grating of freshly ground black pepper
1/3 cup (79 ml) olive oil

1. In a small bowl, combine all ingredients, except olive oil. Mix well with a fork.
2. Sprinkle dressing over salad greens and toss. Dribble olive oil over greens.
3. Serve on individual salad plates.

STUFFED TOMATOES

Makes 4 servings.

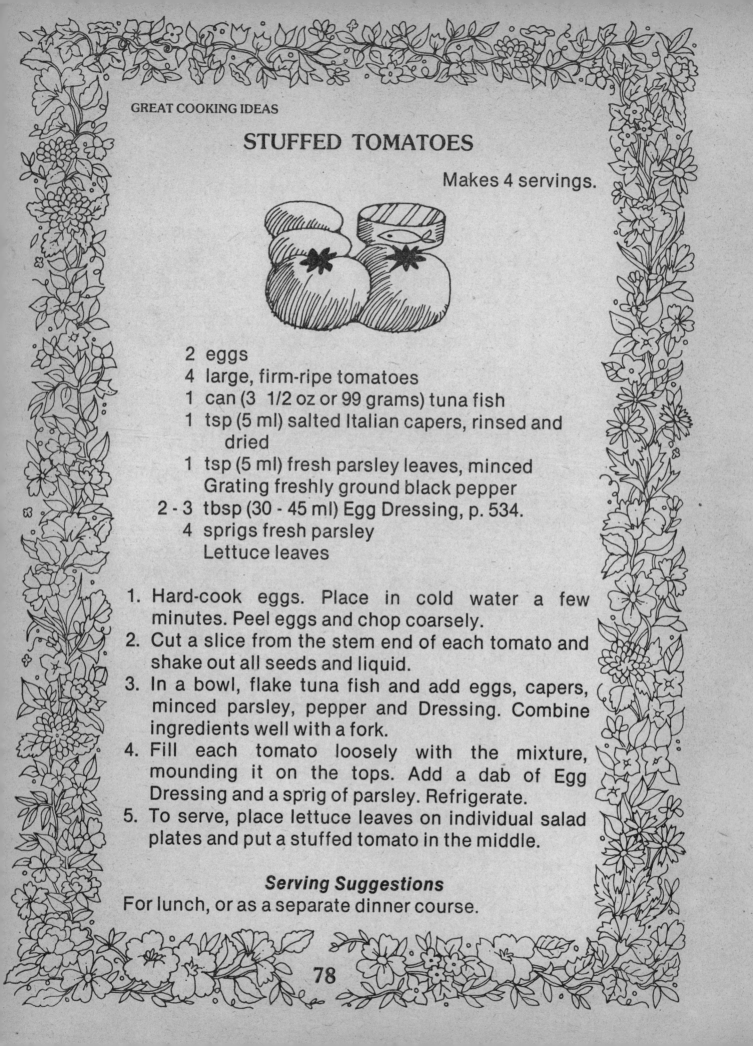

2 eggs
4 large, firm-ripe tomatoes
1 can (3 1/2 oz or 99 grams) tuna fish
1 tsp (5 ml) salted Italian capers, rinsed and
    dried
1 tsp (5 ml) fresh parsley leaves, minced
    Grating freshly ground black pepper
2 - 3 tbsp (30 - 45 ml) Egg Dressing, p. 534.
4 sprigs fresh parsley
    Lettuce leaves

1. Hard-cook eggs. Place in cold water a few minutes. Peel eggs and chop coarsely.
2. Cut a slice from the stem end of each tomato and shake out all seeds and liquid.
3. In a bowl, flake tuna fish and add eggs, capers, minced parsley, pepper and Dressing. Combine ingredients well with a fork.
4. Fill each tomato loosely with the mixture, mounding it on the tops. Add a dab of Egg Dressing and a sprig of parsley. Refrigerate.
5. To serve, place lettuce leaves on individual salad plates and put a stuffed tomato in the middle.

Serving Suggestions
For lunch, or as a separate dinner course.

TOMATOES WITH FRESH BASIL

Makes 4 servings.

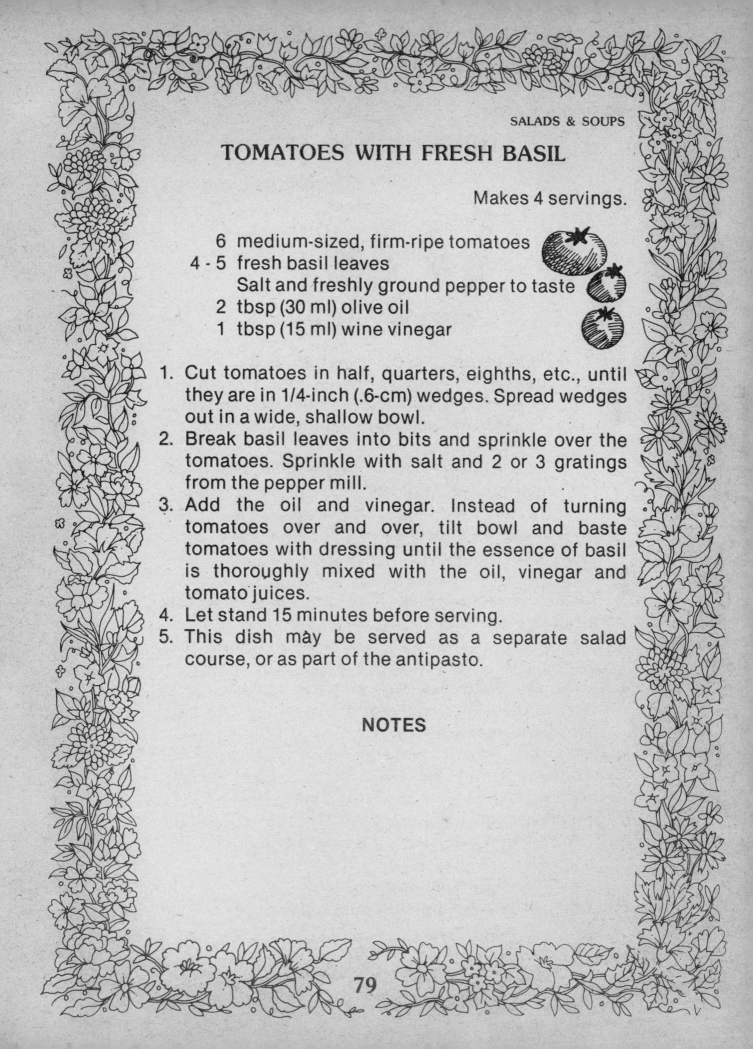

    6   medium-sized, firm-ripe tomatoes
 4 - 5   fresh basil leaves
         Salt and freshly ground pepper to taste
    2   tbsp (30 ml) olive oil
    1   tbsp (15 ml) wine vinegar

1. Cut tomatoes in half, quarters, eighths, etc., until they are in 1/4-inch (.6-cm) wedges. Spread wedges out in a wide, shallow bowl.
2. Break basil leaves into bits and sprinkle over the tomatoes. Sprinkle with salt and 2 or 3 gratings from the pepper mill.
3. Add the oil and vinegar. Instead of turning tomatoes over and over, tilt bowl and baste tomatoes with dressing until the essence of basil is thoroughly mixed with the oil, vinegar and tomato juices.
4. Let stand 15 minutes before serving.
5. This dish may be served as a separate salad course, or as part of the antipasto.

NOTES

THREE-BEAN SALAD

Makes 6 - 8 servings.

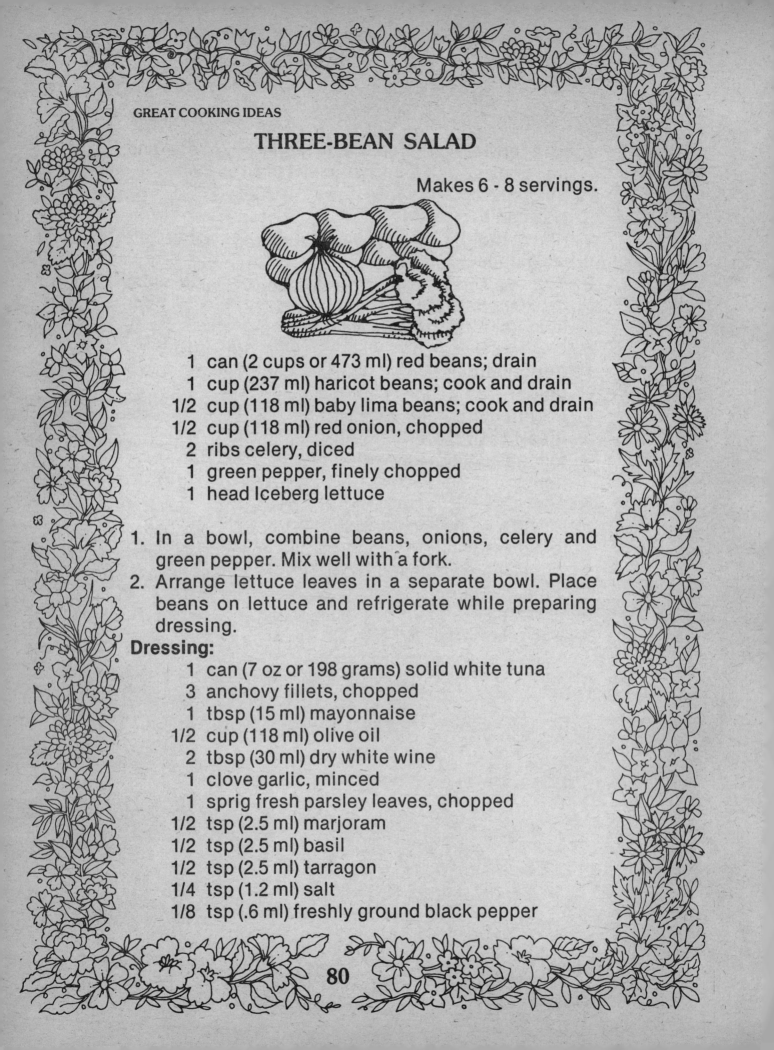

1 can (2 cups or 473 ml) red beans; drain
1 cup (237 ml) haricot beans; cook and drain
1/2 cup (118 ml) baby lima beans; cook and drain
1/2 cup (118 ml) red onion, chopped
2 ribs celery, diced
1 green pepper, finely chopped
1 head Iceberg lettuce

1. In a bowl, combine beans, onions, celery and green pepper. Mix well with a fork.
2. Arrange lettuce leaves in a separate bowl. Place beans on lettuce and refrigerate while preparing dressing.

Dressing:

1 can (7 oz or 198 grams) solid white tuna
3 anchovy fillets, chopped
1 tbsp (15 ml) mayonnaise
1/2 cup (118 ml) olive oil
2 tbsp (30 ml) dry white wine
1 clove garlic, minced
1 sprig fresh parsley leaves, chopped
1/2 tsp (2.5 ml) marjoram
1/2 tsp (2.5 ml) basil
1/2 tsp (2.5 ml) tarragon
1/4 tsp (1.2 ml) salt
1/8 tsp (.6 ml) freshly ground black pepper

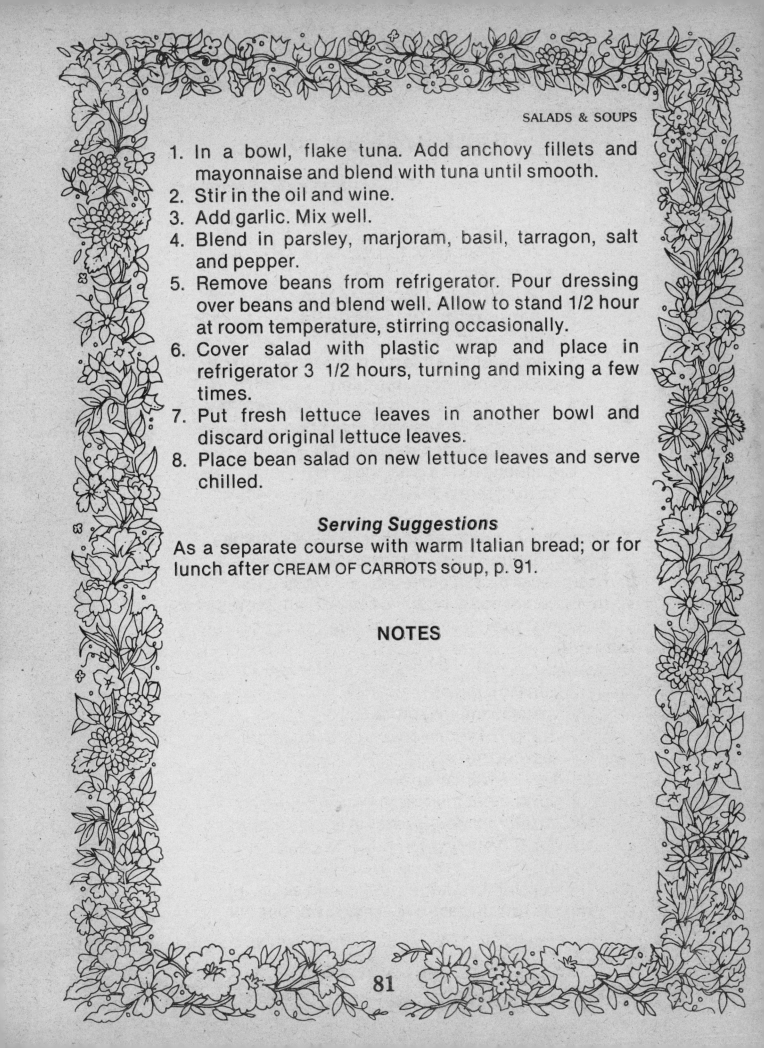

1. In a bowl, flake tuna. Add anchovy fillets and mayonnaise and blend with tuna until smooth.
2. Stir in the oil and wine.
3. Add garlic. Mix well.
4. Blend in parsley, marjoram, basil, tarragon, salt and pepper.
5. Remove beans from refrigerator. Pour dressing over beans and blend well. Allow to stand 1/2 hour at room temperature, stirring occasionally.
6. Cover salad with plastic wrap and place in refrigerator 3 1/2 hours, turning and mixing a few times.
7. Put fresh lettuce leaves in another bowl and discard original lettuce leaves.
8. Place bean salad on new lettuce leaves and serve chilled.

Serving Suggestions

As a separate course with warm Italian bread; or for lunch after CREAM OF CARROTS soup, p. 91.

NOTES

VEGETABLE SALAD

Makes 6 - 8 servings.

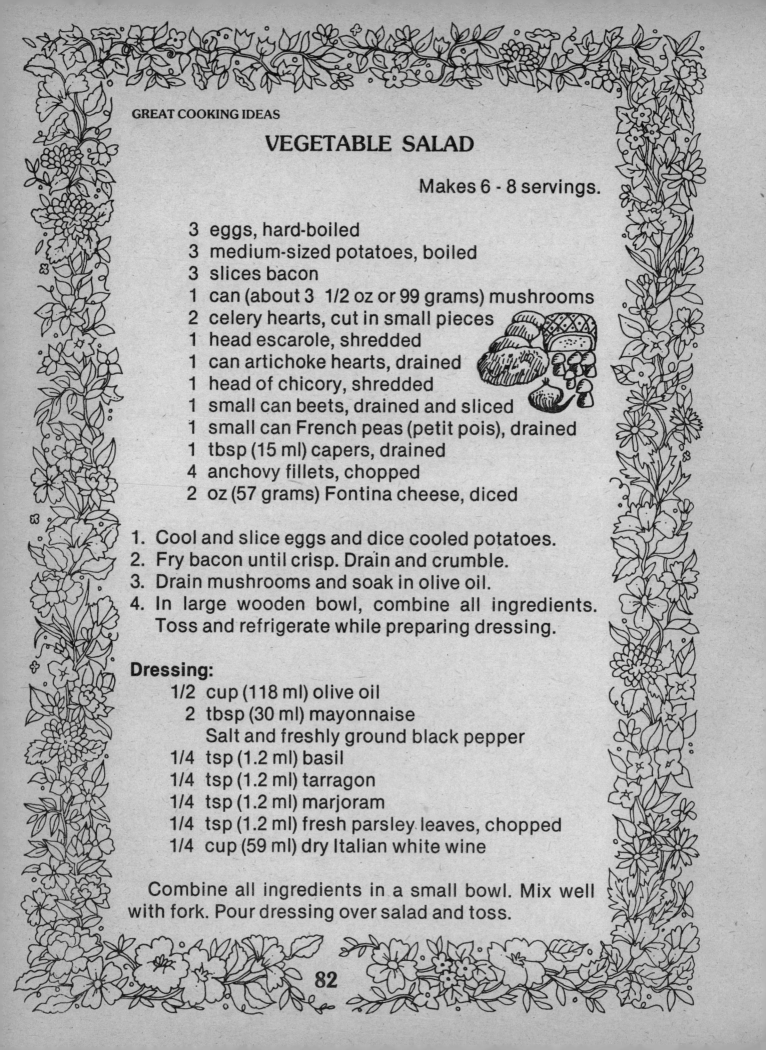

- 3 eggs, hard-boiled
- 3 medium-sized potatoes, boiled
- 3 slices bacon
- 1 can (about 3 1/2 oz or 99 grams) mushrooms
- 2 celery hearts, cut in small pieces
- 1 head escarole, shredded
- 1 can artichoke hearts, drained
- 1 head of chicory, shredded
- 1 small can beets, drained and sliced
- 1 small can French peas (petit pois), drained
- 1 tbsp (15 ml) capers, drained
- 4 anchovy fillets, chopped
- 2 oz (57 grams) Fontina cheese, diced

1. Cool and slice eggs and dice cooled potatoes.
2. Fry bacon until crisp. Drain and crumble.
3. Drain mushrooms and soak in olive oil.
4. In large wooden bowl, combine all ingredients. Toss and refrigerate while preparing dressing.

Dressing:
- 1/2 cup (118 ml) olive oil
- 2 tbsp (30 ml) mayonnaise
- Salt and freshly ground black pepper
- 1/4 tsp (1.2 ml) basil
- 1/4 tsp (1.2 ml) tarragon
- 1/4 tsp (1.2 ml) marjoram
- 1/4 tsp (1.2 ml) fresh parsley leaves, chopped
- 1/4 cup (59 ml) dry Italian white wine

Combine all ingredients in a small bowl. Mix well with fork. Pour dressing over salad and toss.

ABALONE SALAD

Makes 4 servings.

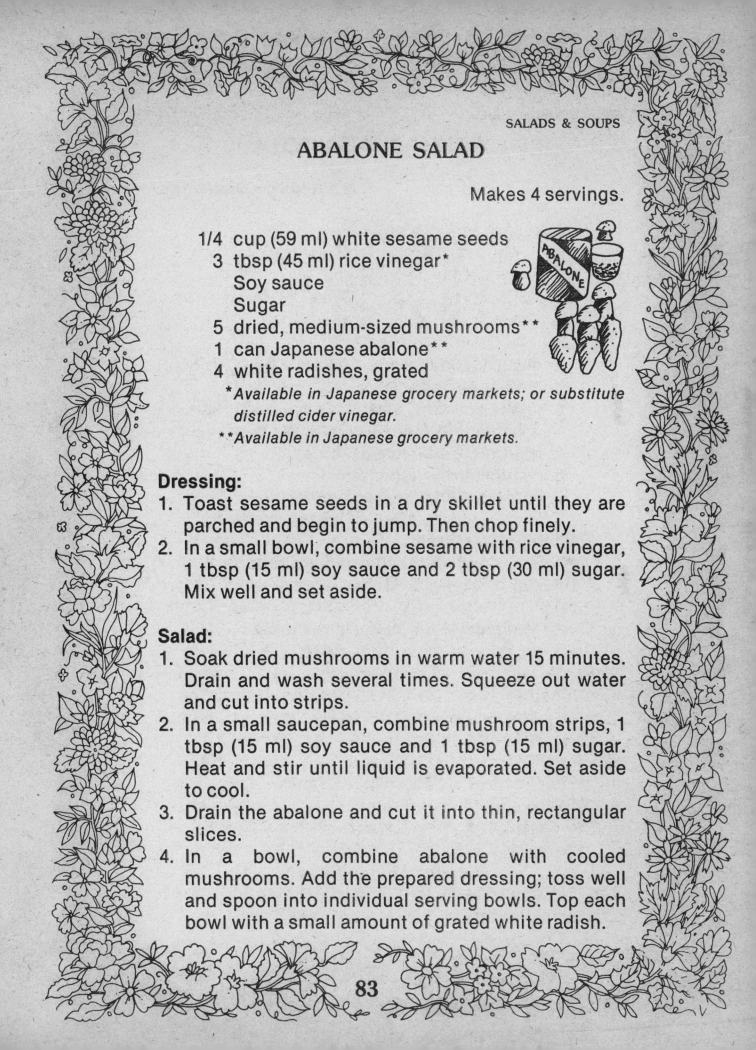

- 1/4 cup (59 ml) white sesame seeds
- 3 tbsp (45 ml) rice vinegar*
- Soy sauce
- Sugar
- 5 dried, medium-sized mushrooms**
- 1 can Japanese abalone**
- 4 white radishes, grated

*Available in Japanese grocery markets; or substitute distilled cider vinegar.

**Available in Japanese grocery markets.

Dressing:
1. Toast sesame seeds in a dry skillet until they are parched and begin to jump. Then chop finely.
2. In a small bowl, combine sesame with rice vinegar, 1 tbsp (15 ml) soy sauce and 2 tbsp (30 ml) sugar. Mix well and set aside.

Salad:
1. Soak dried mushrooms in warm water 15 minutes. Drain and wash several times. Squeeze out water and cut into strips.
2. In a small saucepan, combine mushroom strips, 1 tbsp (15 ml) soy sauce and 1 tbsp (15 ml) sugar. Heat and stir until liquid is evaporated. Set aside to cool.
3. Drain the abalone and cut it into thin, rectangular slices.
4. In a bowl, combine abalone with cooled mushrooms. Add the prepared dressing; toss well and spoon into individual serving bowls. Top each bowl with a small amount of grated white radish.

SALAMI 'N' SHRIMP SALAD

Makes 4 servings.

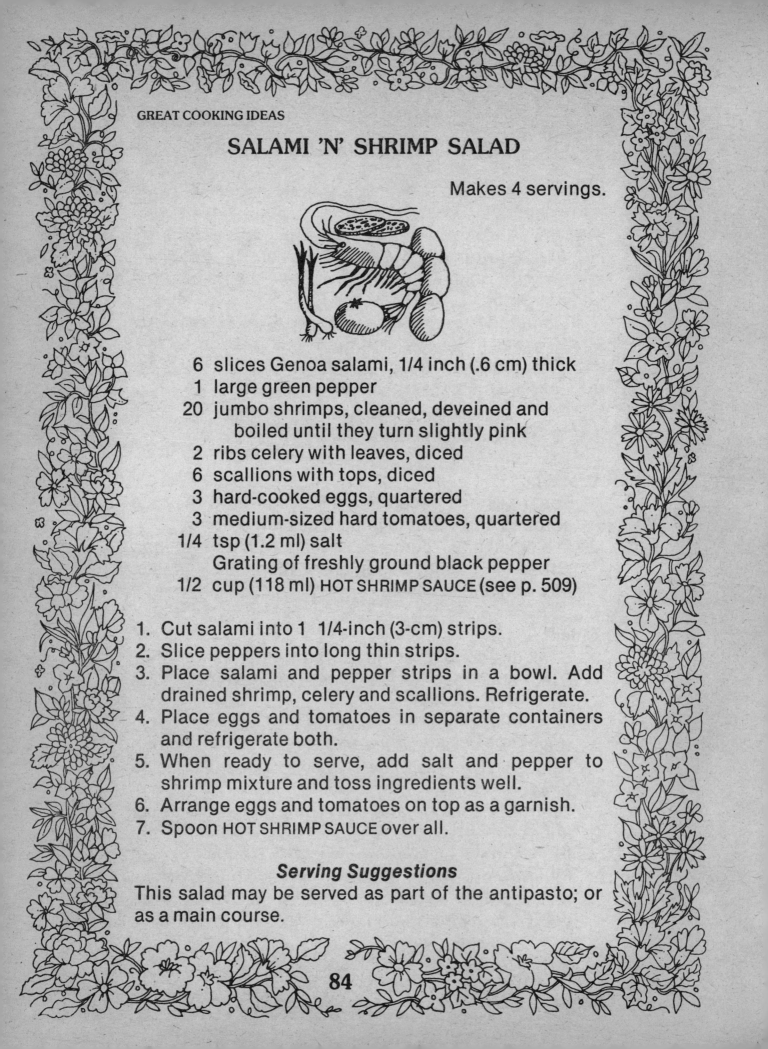

6	slices Genoa salami, 1/4 inch (.6 cm) thick
1	large green pepper
20	jumbo shrimps, cleaned, deveined and boiled until they turn slightly pink
2	ribs celery with leaves, diced
6	scallions with tops, diced
3	hard-cooked eggs, quartered
3	medium-sized hard tomatoes, quartered
1/4	tsp (1.2 ml) salt
	Grating of freshly ground black pepper
1/2	cup (118 ml) HOT SHRIMP SAUCE (see p. 509)

1. Cut salami into 1 1/4-inch (3-cm) strips.
2. Slice peppers into long thin strips.
3. Place salami and pepper strips in a bowl. Add drained shrimp, celery and scallions. Refrigerate.
4. Place eggs and tomatoes in separate containers and refrigerate both.
5. When ready to serve, add salt and pepper to shrimp mixture and toss ingredients well.
6. Arrange eggs and tomatoes on top as a garnish.
7. Spoon HOT SHRIMP SAUCE over all.

Serving Suggestions

This salad may be served as part of the antipasto; or as a main course.

ABOUT BLENDER SOUPS

Blender soups can be made quickly and easily from leftover vegetables by adding 1/2 cup (118 ml) cooked vegetables to 1 cup (237 ml) of thin white sauce in blender. Cover and process at *Purée* until vegetables are smooth. Heat and serve. Broth or consommé may be substituted for white sauce.

Note about type of blender and speeds: If you have a multi-speed blender, use the lower speeds to the left if the recipe calls for LO, and the higher speeds to the right if it calls for HI.

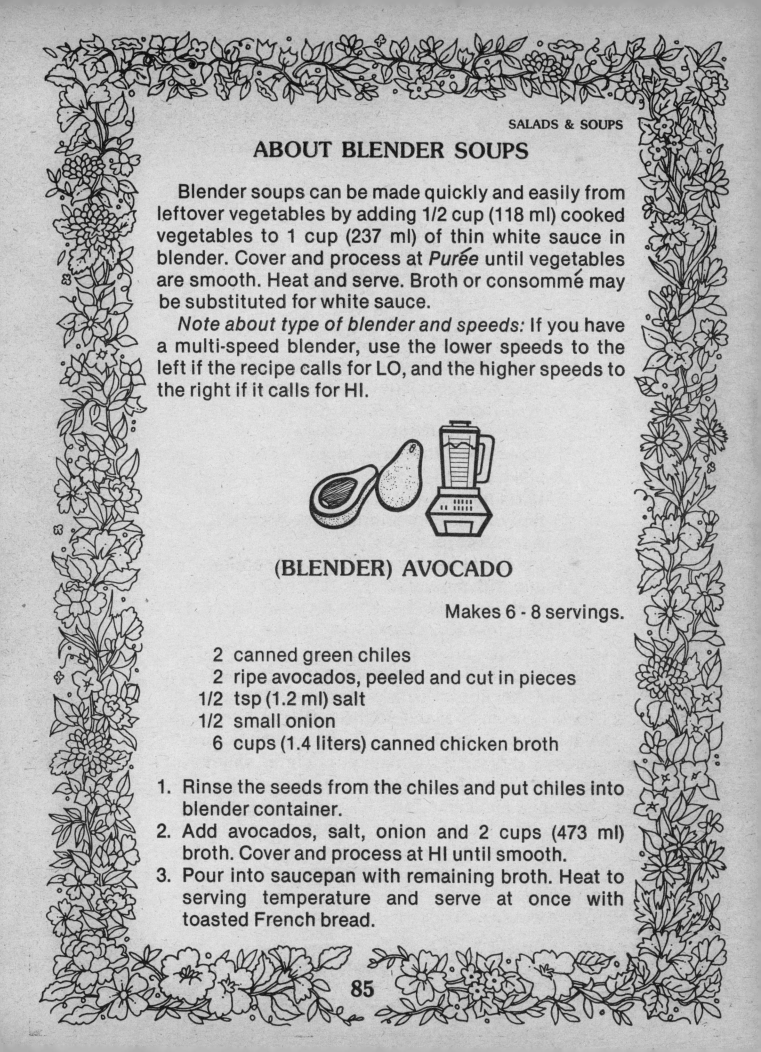

(BLENDER) AVOCADO

Makes 6 - 8 servings.

    2 canned green chiles
    2 ripe avocados, peeled and cut in pieces
1/2 tsp (1.2 ml) salt
1/2 small onion
    6 cups (1.4 liters) canned chicken broth

1. Rinse the seeds from the chiles and put chiles into blender container.
2. Add avocados, salt, onion and 2 cups (473 ml) broth. Cover and process at HI until smooth.
3. Pour into saucepan with remaining broth. Heat to serving temperature and serve at once with toasted French bread.

(BLENDER) PEA SOUP WITH SAUSAGE

Makes 5 servings.

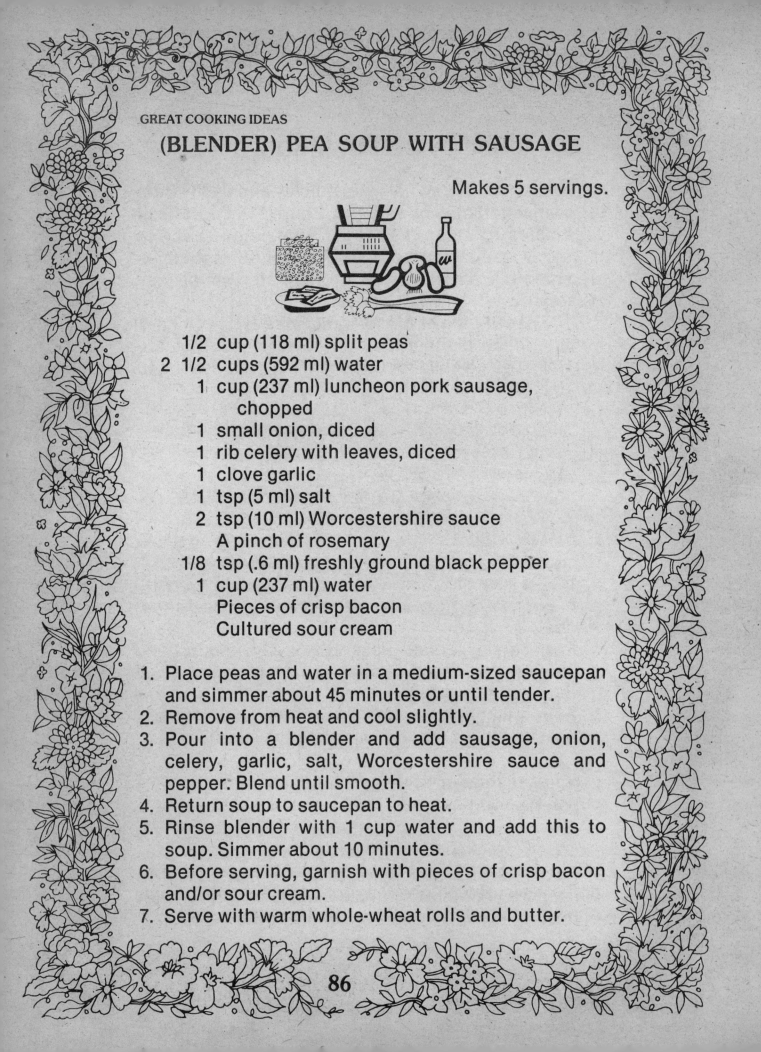

- 1/2 cup (118 ml) split peas
- 2 1/2 cups (592 ml) water
- 1 cup (237 ml) luncheon pork sausage, chopped
- 1 small onion, diced
- 1 rib celery with leaves, diced
- 1 clove garlic
- 1 tsp (5 ml) salt
- 2 tsp (10 ml) Worcestershire sauce
- A pinch of rosemary
- 1/8 tsp (.6 ml) freshly ground black pepper
- 1 cup (237 ml) water
- Pieces of crisp bacon
- Cultured sour cream

1. Place peas and water in a medium-sized saucepan and simmer about 45 minutes or until tender.
2. Remove from heat and cool slightly.
3. Pour into a blender and add sausage, onion, celery, garlic, salt, Worcestershire sauce and pepper. Blend until smooth.
4. Return soup to saucepan to heat.
5. Rinse blender with 1 cup water and add this to soup. Simmer about 10 minutes.
6. Before serving, garnish with pieces of crisp bacon and/or sour cream.
7. Serve with warm whole-wheat rolls and butter.

(BLENDER) TUNA CHOWDER

Makes 6 - 8 servings.

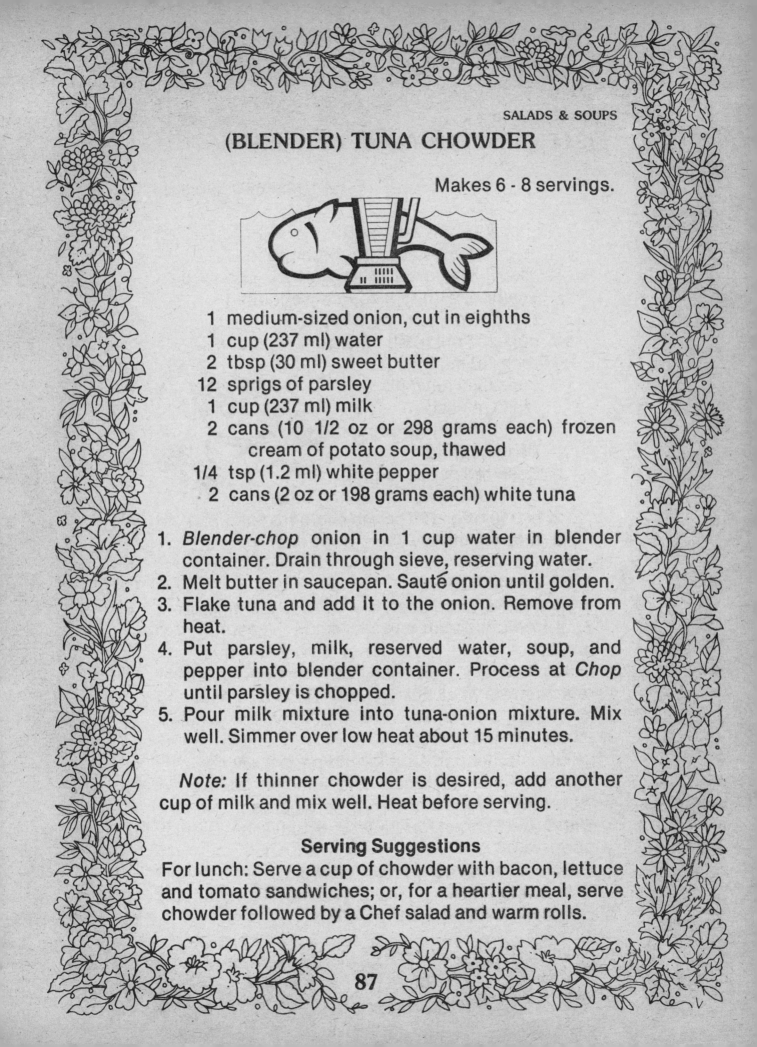

1 medium-sized onion, cut in eighths
1 cup (237 ml) water
2 tbsp (30 ml) sweet butter
12 sprigs of parsley
1 cup (237 ml) milk
2 cans (10 1/2 oz or 298 grams each) frozen cream of potato soup, thawed
1/4 tsp (1.2 ml) white pepper
2 cans (2 oz or 198 grams each) white tuna

1. *Blender-chop* onion in 1 cup water in blender container. Drain through sieve, reserving water.
2. Melt butter in saucepan. Sauté onion until golden.
3. Flake tuna and add it to the onion. Remove from heat.
4. Put parsley, milk, reserved water, soup, and pepper into blender container. Process at *Chop* until parsley is chopped.
5. Pour milk mixture into tuna-onion mixture. Mix well. Simmer over low heat about 15 minutes.

Note: If thinner chowder is desired, add another cup of milk and mix well. Heat before serving.

Serving Suggestions

For lunch: Serve a cup of chowder with bacon, lettuce and tomato sandwiches; or, for a heartier meal, serve chowder followed by a Chef salad and warm rolls.

BISQUE OF CRABMEAT 'N' MUSHROOMS

Makes 4 servings.

6 tbsp (90 ml) sweet butter
4 tbsp (60 ml) onion, finely chopped
4 tbsp (60 ml) green pepper, finely chopped
1 scallion, with top, coarsely chopped
2 tbsp (30 ml) parsley, chopped
1 cup (237 ml) fresh mushrooms, sliced
2 tbsp (30 ml) flour
1 1/2 cups (355 ml) milk
1 tsp (5 ml) salt
1/8 tsp (.6 ml) white pepper
Dash paprika
Dash red pepper sauce
1 cup (237 ml) half milk, half cream
2 pkg (6 oz or 170 grams each) frozen crabmeat
3 tbsp (45 ml) dry sherry (optional)

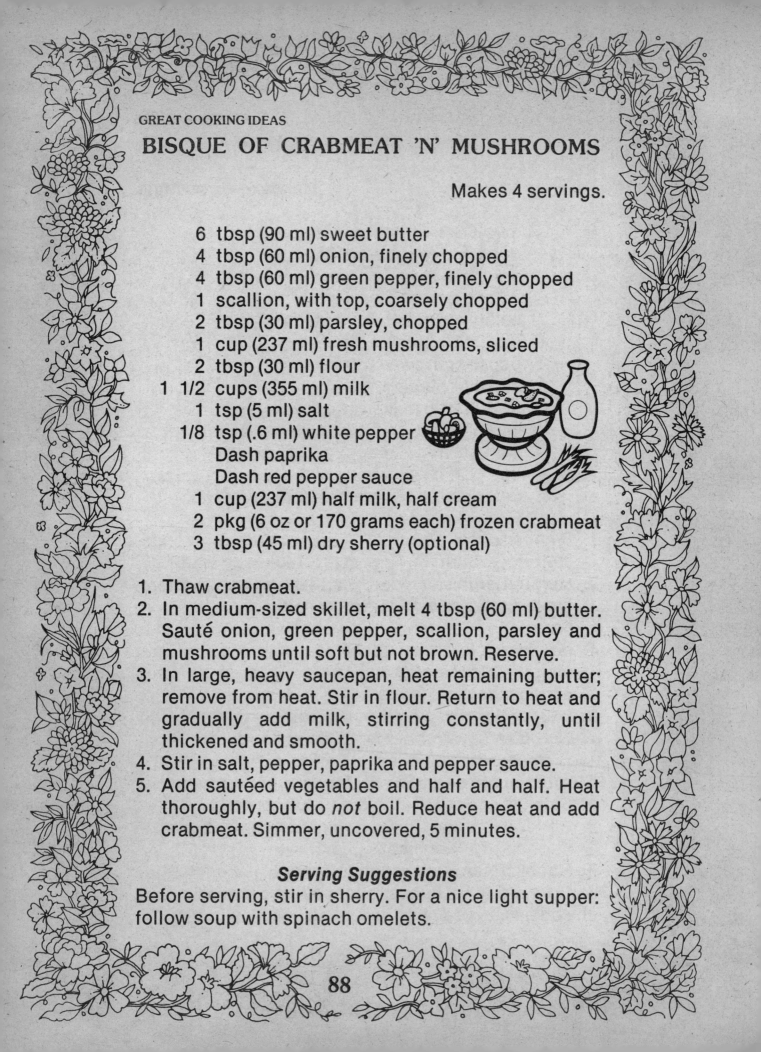

1. Thaw crabmeat.
2. In medium-sized skillet, melt 4 tbsp (60 ml) butter. Sauté onion, green pepper, scallion, parsley and mushrooms until soft but not brown. Reserve.
3. In large, heavy saucepan, heat remaining butter; remove from heat. Stir in flour. Return to heat and gradually add milk, stirring constantly, until thickened and smooth.
4. Stir in salt, pepper, paprika and pepper sauce.
5. Add sautéed vegetables and half and half. Heat thoroughly, but do *not* boil. Reduce heat and add crabmeat. Simmer, uncovered, 5 minutes.

Serving Suggestions
Before serving, stir in sherry. For a nice light supper: follow soup with spinach omelets.

BISQUE OF LOBSTER

Makes 8 servings.

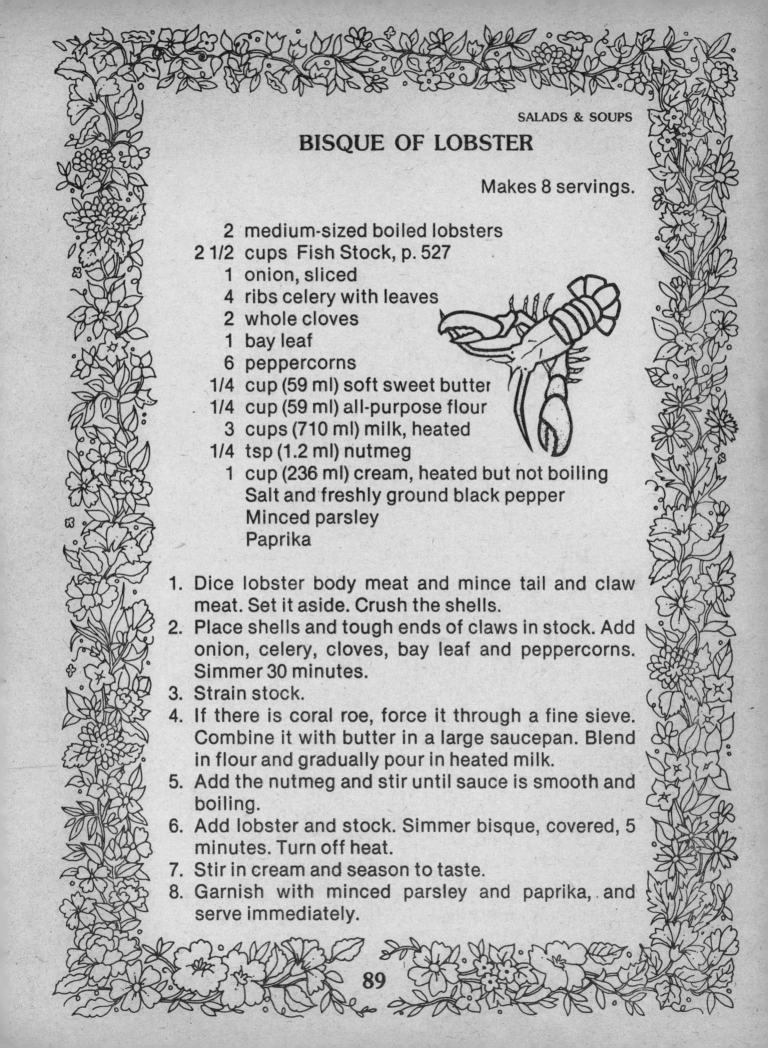

2   medium-sized boiled lobsters
2 1/2   cups Fish Stock, p. 527
1   onion, sliced
4   ribs celery with leaves
2   whole cloves
1   bay leaf
6   peppercorns
1/4   cup (59 ml) soft sweet butter
1/4   cup (59 ml) all-purpose flour
3   cups (710 ml) milk, heated
1/4   tsp (1.2 ml) nutmeg
1   cup (236 ml) cream, heated but not boiling
     Salt and freshly ground black pepper
     Minced parsley
     Paprika

1. Dice lobster body meat and mince tail and claw meat. Set it aside. Crush the shells.
2. Place shells and tough ends of claws in stock. Add onion, celery, cloves, bay leaf and peppercorns. Simmer 30 minutes.
3. Strain stock.
4. If there is coral roe, force it through a fine sieve. Combine it with butter in a large saucepan. Blend in flour and gradually pour in heated milk.
5. Add the nutmeg and stir until sauce is smooth and boiling.
6. Add lobster and stock. Simmer bisque, covered, 5 minutes. Turn off heat.
7. Stir in cream and season to taste.
8. Garnish with minced parsley and paprika, and serve immediately.

POACHED SHRIMP BISQUE

Makes 4 - 5 servings.

Poaching the Shrimp:

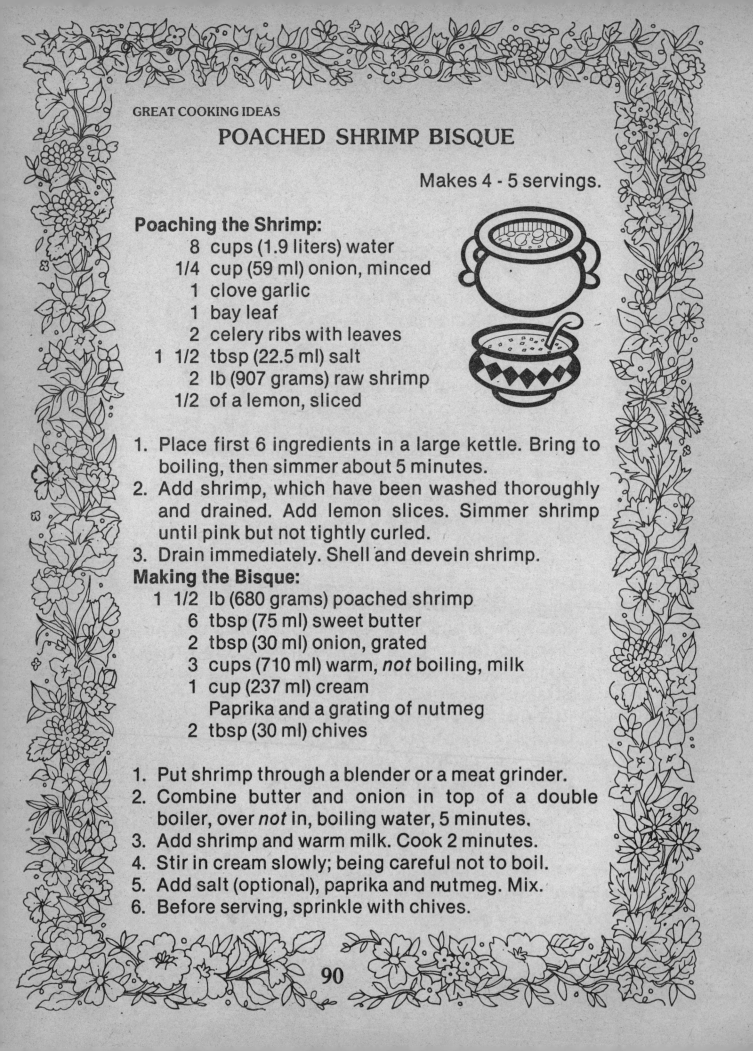

    8 cups (1.9 liters) water
  1/4 cup (59 ml) onion, minced
    1 clove garlic
    1 bay leaf
    2 celery ribs with leaves
1 1/2 tbsp (22.5 ml) salt
    2 lb (907 grams) raw shrimp
  1/2 of a lemon, sliced

1. Place first 6 ingredients in a large kettle. Bring to boiling, then simmer about 5 minutes.
2. Add shrimp, which have been washed thoroughly and drained. Add lemon slices. Simmer shrimp until pink but not tightly curled.
3. Drain immediately. Shell and devein shrimp.

Making the Bisque:

1 1/2 lb (680 grams) poached shrimp
    6 tbsp (75 ml) sweet butter
    2 tbsp (30 ml) onion, grated
    3 cups (710 ml) warm, *not* boiling, milk
    1 cup (237 ml) cream
        Paprika and a grating of nutmeg
    2 tbsp (30 ml) chives

1. Put shrimp through a blender or a meat grinder.
2. Combine butter and onion in top of a double boiler, over *not* in, boiling water, 5 minutes.
3. Add shrimp and warm milk. Cook 2 minutes.
4. Stir in cream slowly; being careful not to boil.
5. Add salt (optional), paprika and nutmeg. Mix.
6. Before serving, sprinkle with chives.

CREAM OF CARROTS

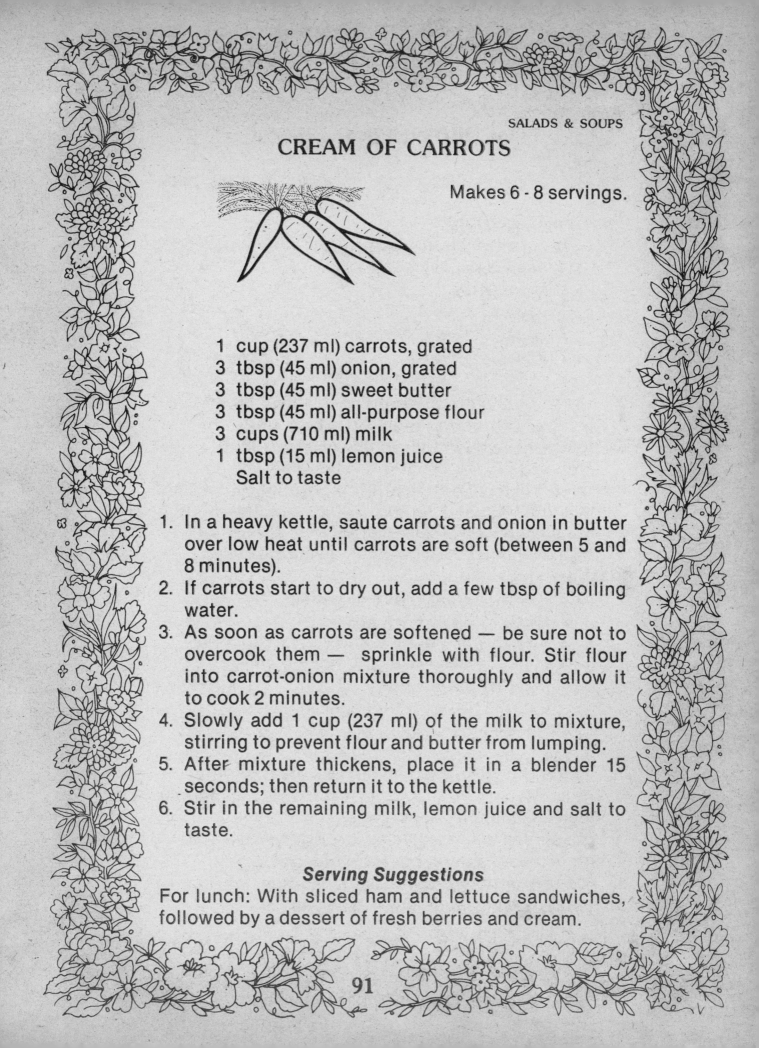

Makes 6 - 8 servings.

1 cup (237 ml) carrots, grated
3 tbsp (45 ml) onion, grated
3 tbsp (45 ml) sweet butter
3 tbsp (45 ml) all-purpose flour
3 cups (710 ml) milk
1 tbsp (15 ml) lemon juice
Salt to taste

1. In a heavy kettle, saute carrots and onion in butter over low heat until carrots are soft (between 5 and 8 minutes).
2. If carrots start to dry out, add a few tbsp of boiling water.
3. As soon as carrots are softened — be sure not to overcook them — sprinkle with flour. Stir flour into carrot-onion mixture thoroughly and allow it to cook 2 minutes.
4. Slowly add 1 cup (237 ml) of the milk to mixture, stirring to prevent flour and butter from lumping.
5. After mixture thickens, place it in a blender 15 seconds; then return it to the kettle.
6. Stir in the remaining milk, lemon juice and salt to taste.

Serving Suggestions

For lunch: With sliced ham and lettuce sandwiches, followed by a dessert of fresh berries and cream.

CREAM OF LEEK

Makes 6 - 8 servings.

4 large leeks
3/4 cup (177 ml) sweet butter
8 tbsp (118 ml) all-purpose flour
Boiling water
Milk
Salt
Lemon juice

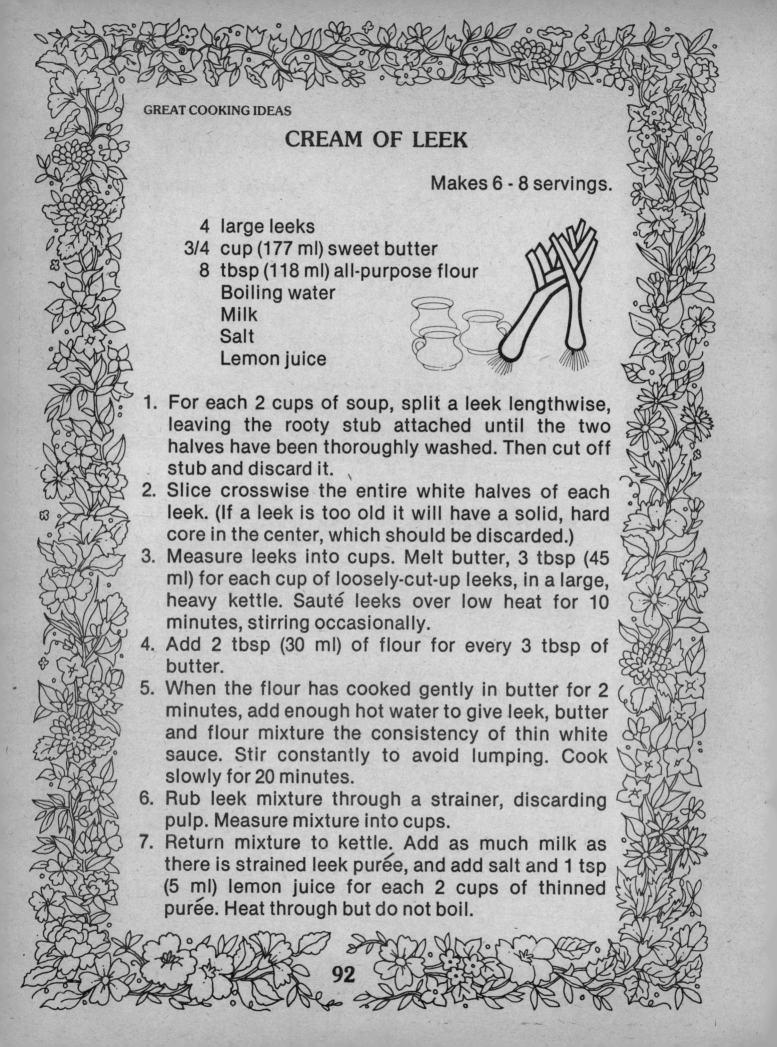

1. For each 2 cups of soup, split a leek lengthwise, leaving the rooty stub attached until the two halves have been thoroughly washed. Then cut off stub and discard it.
2. Slice crosswise the entire white halves of each leek. (If a leek is too old it will have a solid, hard core in the center, which should be discarded.)
3. Measure leeks into cups. Melt butter, 3 tbsp (45 ml) for each cup of loosely-cut-up leeks, in a large, heavy kettle. Sauté leeks over low heat for 10 minutes, stirring occasionally.
4. Add 2 tbsp (30 ml) of flour for every 3 tbsp of butter.
5. When the flour has cooked gently in butter for 2 minutes, add enough hot water to give leek, butter and flour mixture the consistency of thin white sauce. Stir constantly to avoid lumping. Cook slowly for 20 minutes.
6. Rub leek mixture through a strainer, discarding pulp. Measure mixture into cups.
7. Return mixture to kettle. Add as much milk as there is strained leek purée, and add salt and 1 tsp (5 ml) lemon juice for each 2 cups of thinned purée. Heat through but do not boil.

CHEESY VEGETABLE CHOWDER

Makes 6 - 8 servings.

4 tbsp (60 ml) sweet butter
1/4 cup (59 ml) onion, chopped
1 cup (237 ml) green pepper, chopped
1 cup (237 ml) carrot, scraped and diced
1 cup (237 ml) potato, peeled and diced
1 pkg (10 oz or 284 grams) frozen peas
5 tbsp (75 ml) all-purpose flour
2 1/2 - 3 cups (592 - 710 ml) Poultry Stock, p. 528
12 oz (340 grams) Cheddar cheese, grated
2 cups (473 ml) milk
1/4 tsp (1.2 ml) salt
Dash freshly ground black pepper
Chopped parsley

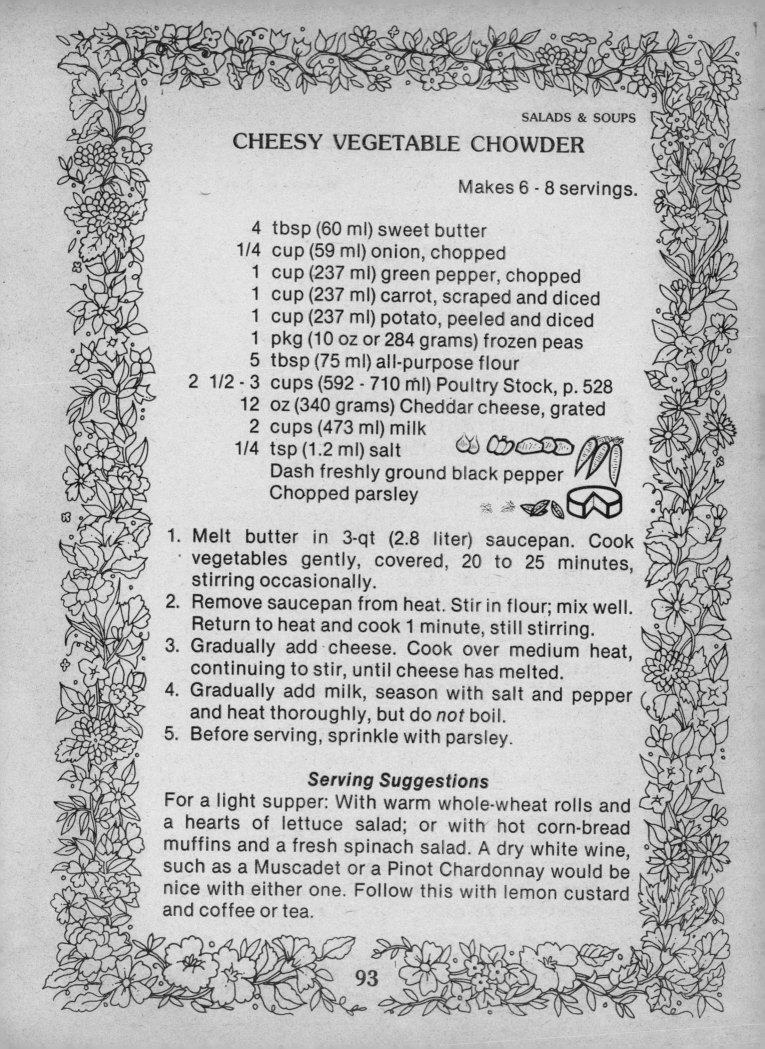

1. Melt butter in 3-qt (2.8 liter) saucepan. Cook vegetables gently, covered, 20 to 25 minutes, stirring occasionally.
2. Remove saucepan from heat. Stir in flour; mix well. Return to heat and cook 1 minute, still stirring.
3. Gradually add cheese. Cook over medium heat, continuing to stir, until cheese has melted.
4. Gradually add milk, season with salt and pepper and heat thoroughly, but do *not* boil.
5. Before serving, sprinkle with parsley.

Serving Suggestions

For a light supper: With warm whole-wheat rolls and a hearts of lettuce salad; or with hot corn-bread muffins and a fresh spinach salad. A dry white wine, such as a Muscadet or a Pinot Chardonnay would be nice with either one. Follow this with lemon custard and coffee or tea.

CHILLED SPANISH VEGETABLE

Makes 4 - 6 servings.

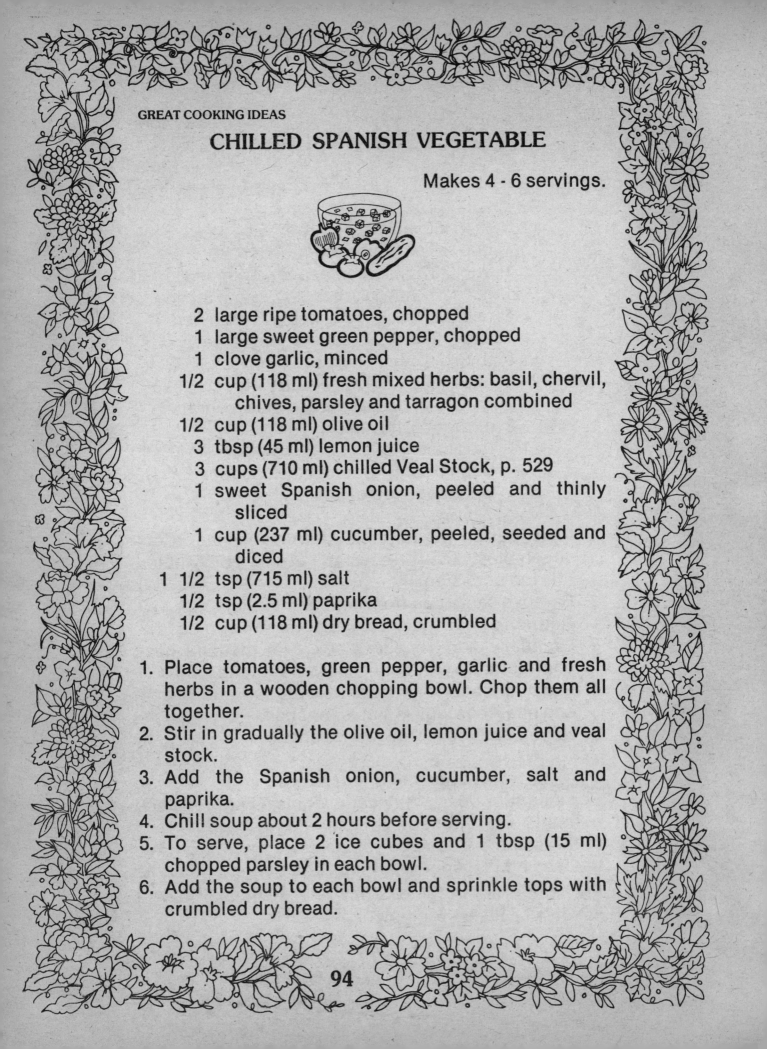

2 large ripe tomatoes, chopped
1 large sweet green pepper, chopped
1 clove garlic, minced
1/2 cup (118 ml) fresh mixed herbs: basil, chervil, chives, parsley and tarragon combined
1/2 cup (118 ml) olive oil
3 tbsp (45 ml) lemon juice
3 cups (710 ml) chilled Veal Stock, p. 529
1 sweet Spanish onion, peeled and thinly sliced
1 cup (237 ml) cucumber, peeled, seeded and diced
1 1/2 tsp (715 ml) salt
1/2 tsp (2.5 ml) paprika
1/2 cup (118 ml) dry bread, crumbled

1. Place tomatoes, green pepper, garlic and fresh herbs in a wooden chopping bowl. Chop them all together.
2. Stir in gradually the olive oil, lemon juice and veal stock.
3. Add the Spanish onion, cucumber, salt and paprika.
4. Chill soup about 2 hours before serving.
5. To serve, place 2 ice cubes and 1 tbsp (15 ml) chopped parsley in each bowl.
6. Add the soup to each bowl and sprinkle tops with crumbled dry bread.

CORNY POTATO CHOWDER

Makes 6 servings.

- 3 slices bacon
- 1/2 cup (118 ml) onion, chopped
- 1 1/2 cups (355 ml) celery, diced
- 2 cups (473 ml) boiling water
- 2 cups (473 ml) raw potatoes, diced
- 4 cups (946 ml) milk
- 2 cups (473 ml) fresh corn
- 2 tsp (10 ml) salt
- 1 1/2 tsp (7.5 ml) white pepper
- 3/4 tsp (3.7 ml) fresh lemon juice

1. Fry bacon in Dutch oven until crisp. Place on paper towels to drain and set aside.
2. Sauté onion and celery in bacon fat remaining in Dutch oven until onion is limp and transparent.
3. Add the water and potatoes. Cook, covered, 20 minutes or until potatoes are tender.
4. Add milk, corn, salt and pepper. Cook 5 or 6 minutes until corn is just tender.
5. Add lemon juice.
6. Serve the soup in individual bowls. Garnish each bowl with a sprinkling of crumbled bacon.

Serving Suggestions

For lunch: With grilled bacon and American cheese sandwiches and cole slaw.

DUTCH VEGETABLE

Makes 8 - 10 servings.

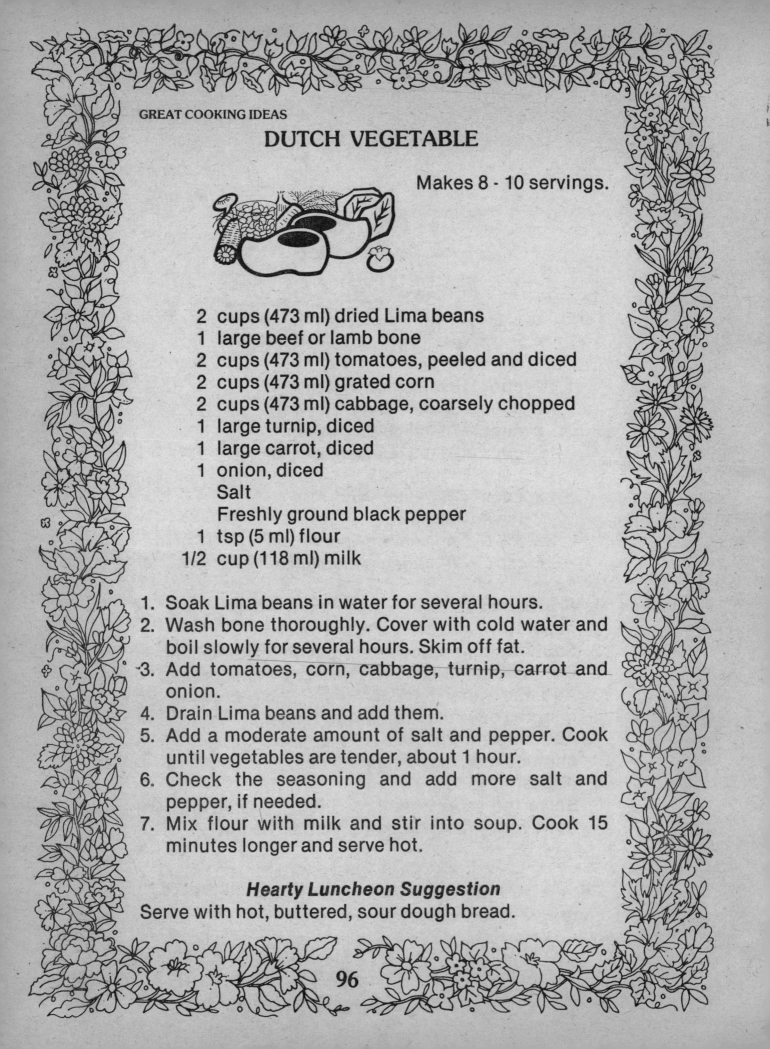

2 cups (473 ml) dried Lima beans
1 large beef or lamb bone
2 cups (473 ml) tomatoes, peeled and diced
2 cups (473 ml) grated corn
2 cups (473 ml) cabbage, coarsely chopped
1 large turnip, diced
1 large carrot, diced
1 onion, diced
  Salt
  Freshly ground black pepper
1 tsp (5 ml) flour
1/2 cup (118 ml) milk

1. Soak Lima beans in water for several hours.
2. Wash bone thoroughly. Cover with cold water and boil slowly for several hours. Skim off fat.
3. Add tomatoes, corn, cabbage, turnip, carrot and onion.
4. Drain Lima beans and add them.
5. Add a moderate amount of salt and pepper. Cook until vegetables are tender, about 1 hour.
6. Check the seasoning and add more salt and pepper, if needed.
7. Mix flour with milk and stir into soup. Cook 15 minutes longer and serve hot.

Hearty Luncheon Suggestion
Serve with hot, buttered, sour dough bread.

FRESH SPINACH

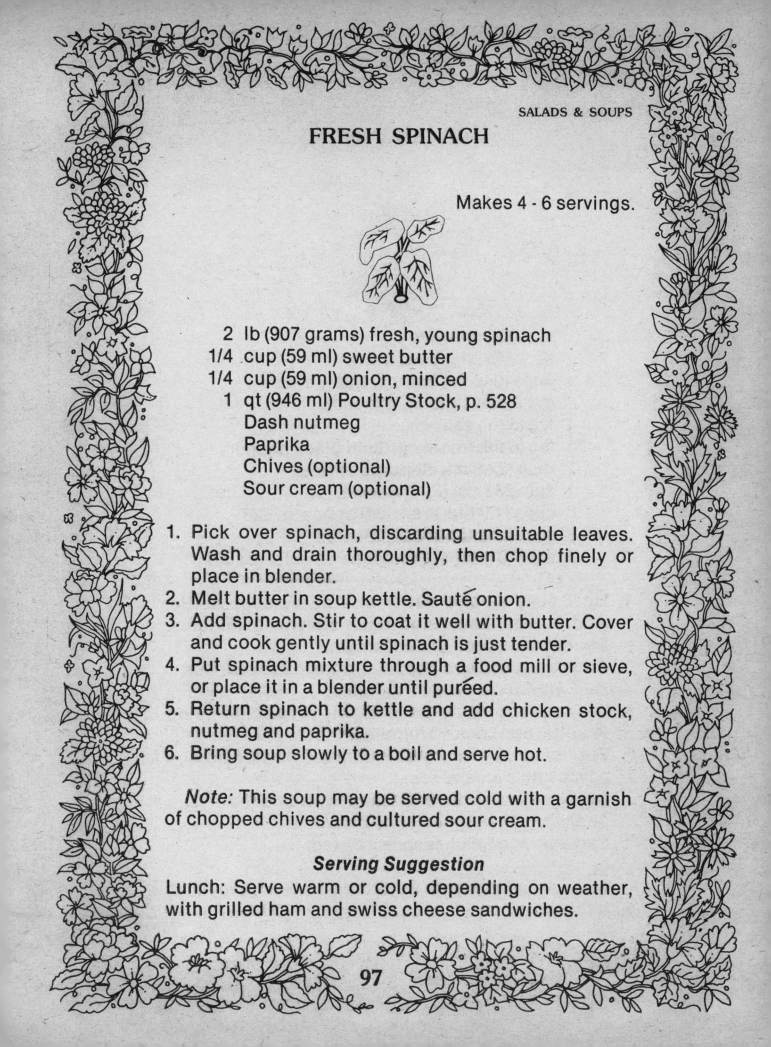

Makes 4 - 6 servings.

2 lb (907 grams) fresh, young spinach
1/4 cup (59 ml) sweet butter
1/4 cup (59 ml) onion, minced
1 qt (946 ml) Poultry Stock, p. 528
Dash nutmeg
Paprika
Chives (optional)
Sour cream (optional)

1. Pick over spinach, discarding unsuitable leaves. Wash and drain thoroughly, then chop finely or place in blender.
2. Melt butter in soup kettle. Sauté onion.
3. Add spinach. Stir to coat it well with butter. Cover and cook gently until spinach is just tender.
4. Put spinach mixture through a food mill or sieve, or place it in a blender until puréed.
5. Return spinach to kettle and add chicken stock, nutmeg and paprika.
6. Bring soup slowly to a boil and serve hot.

Note: This soup may be served cold with a garnish of chopped chives and cultured sour cream.

Serving Suggestion

Lunch: Serve warm or cold, depending on weather, with grilled ham and swiss cheese sandwiches.

ITALIAN ONION

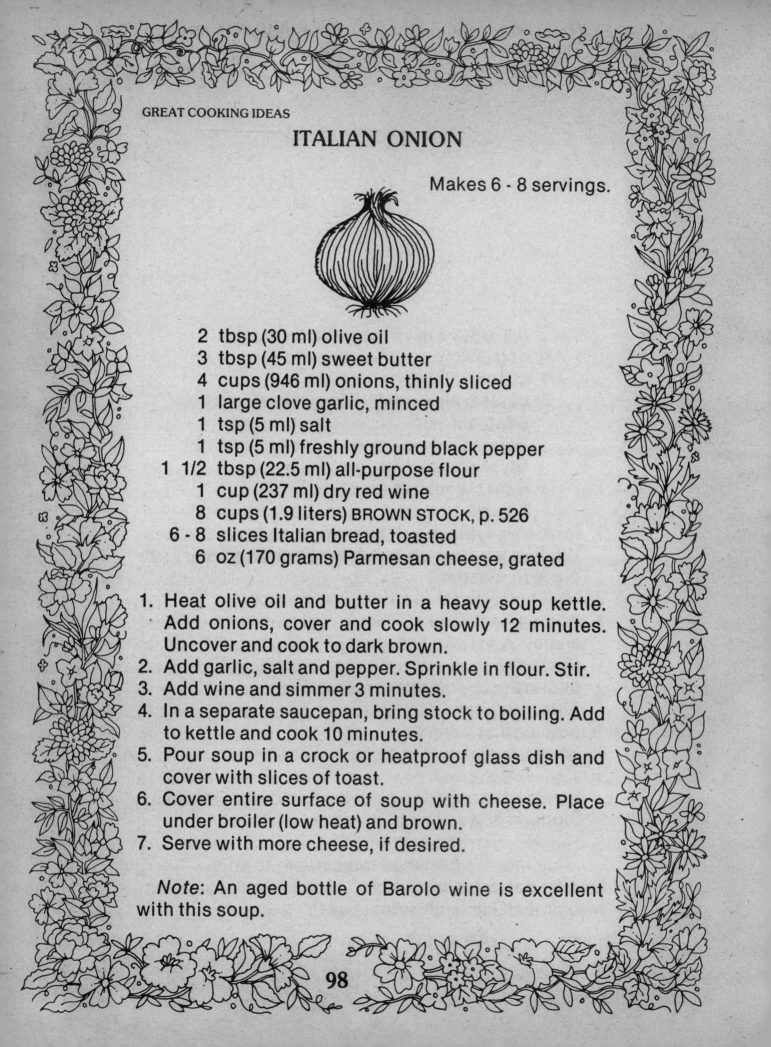

Makes 6 - 8 servings.

```
    2    tbsp (30 ml) olive oil
    3    tbsp (45 ml) sweet butter
    4    cups (946 ml) onions, thinly sliced
    1    large clove garlic, minced
    1    tsp (5 ml) salt
    1    tsp (5 ml) freshly ground black pepper
1   1/2  tbsp (22.5 ml) all-purpose flour
    1    cup (237 ml) dry red wine
    8    cups (1.9 liters) BROWN STOCK, p. 526
 6 - 8   slices Italian bread, toasted
    6    oz (170 grams) Parmesan cheese, grated
```

1. Heat olive oil and butter in a heavy soup kettle. Add onions, cover and cook slowly 12 minutes. Uncover and cook to dark brown.
2. Add garlic, salt and pepper. Sprinkle in flour. Stir.
3. Add wine and simmer 3 minutes.
4. In a separate saucepan, bring stock to boiling. Add to kettle and cook 10 minutes.
5. Pour soup in a crock or heatproof glass dish and cover with slices of toast.
6. Cover entire surface of soup with cheese. Place under broiler (low heat) and brown.
7. Serve with more cheese, if desired.

Note: An aged bottle of Barolo wine is excellent with this soup.

LETTUCE

Makes 8 servings.

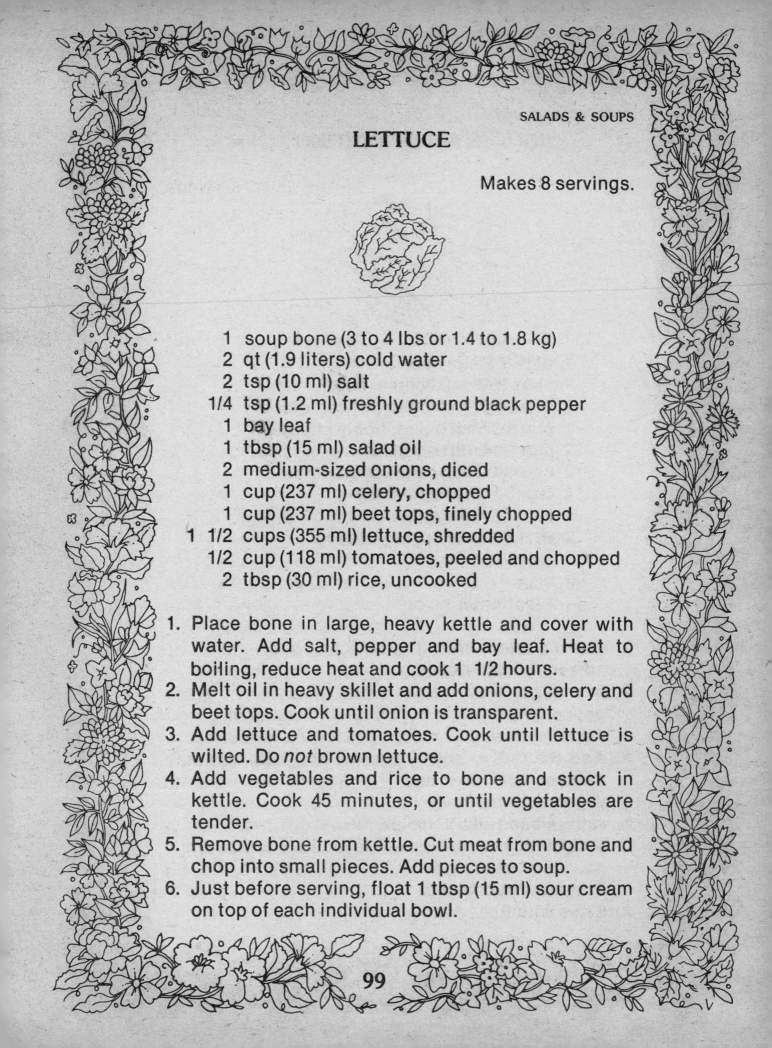

```
1    soup bone (3 to 4 lbs or 1.4 to 1.8 kg)
2    qt (1.9 liters) cold water
2    tsp (10 ml) salt
1/4  tsp (1.2 ml) freshly ground black pepper
1    bay leaf
1    tbsp (15 ml) salad oil
2    medium-sized onions, diced
1    cup (237 ml) celery, chopped
1    cup (237 ml) beet tops, finely chopped
1 1/2 cups (355 ml) lettuce, shredded
1/2  cup (118 ml) tomatoes, peeled and chopped
2    tbsp (30 ml) rice, uncooked
```

1. Place bone in large, heavy kettle and cover with water. Add salt, pepper and bay leaf. Heat to boiling, reduce heat and cook 1 1/2 hours.
2. Melt oil in heavy skillet and add onions, celery and beet tops. Cook until onion is transparent.
3. Add lettuce and tomatoes. Cook until lettuce is wilted. Do *not* brown lettuce.
4. Add vegetables and rice to bone and stock in kettle. Cook 45 minutes, or until vegetables are tender.
5. Remove bone from kettle. Cut meat from bone and chop into small pieces. Add pieces to soup.
6. Just before serving, float 1 tbsp (15 ml) sour cream on top of each individual bowl.

OKRA 'N' TOMATO CHOWDER

Makes 10 - 12 servings.

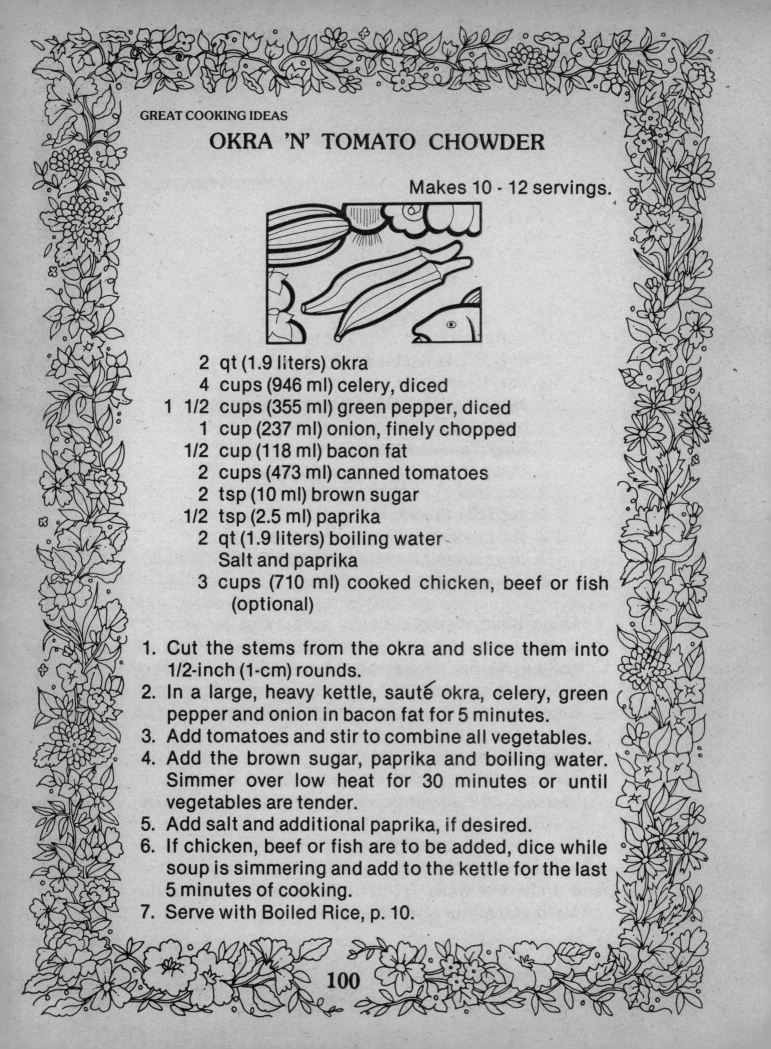

2	qt (1.9 liters)	okra

2 qt (1.9 liters) okra
4 cups (946 ml) celery, diced
1 1/2 cups (355 ml) green pepper, diced
1 cup (237 ml) onion, finely chopped
1/2 cup (118 ml) bacon fat
2 cups (473 ml) canned tomatoes
2 tsp (10 ml) brown sugar
1/2 tsp (2.5 ml) paprika
2 qt (1.9 liters) boiling water
Salt and paprika
3 cups (710 ml) cooked chicken, beef or fish (optional)

1. Cut the stems from the okra and slice them into 1/2-inch (1-cm) rounds.
2. In a large, heavy kettle, sauté okra, celery, green pepper and onion in bacon fat for 5 minutes.
3. Add tomatoes and stir to combine all vegetables.
4. Add the brown sugar, paprika and boiling water. Simmer over low heat for 30 minutes or until vegetables are tender.
5. Add salt and additional paprika, if desired.
6. If chicken, beef or fish are to be added, dice while soup is simmering and add to the kettle for the last 5 minutes of cooking.
7. Serve with Boiled Rice, p. 10.

RUSSIAN CABBAGE

Makes 4 servings.

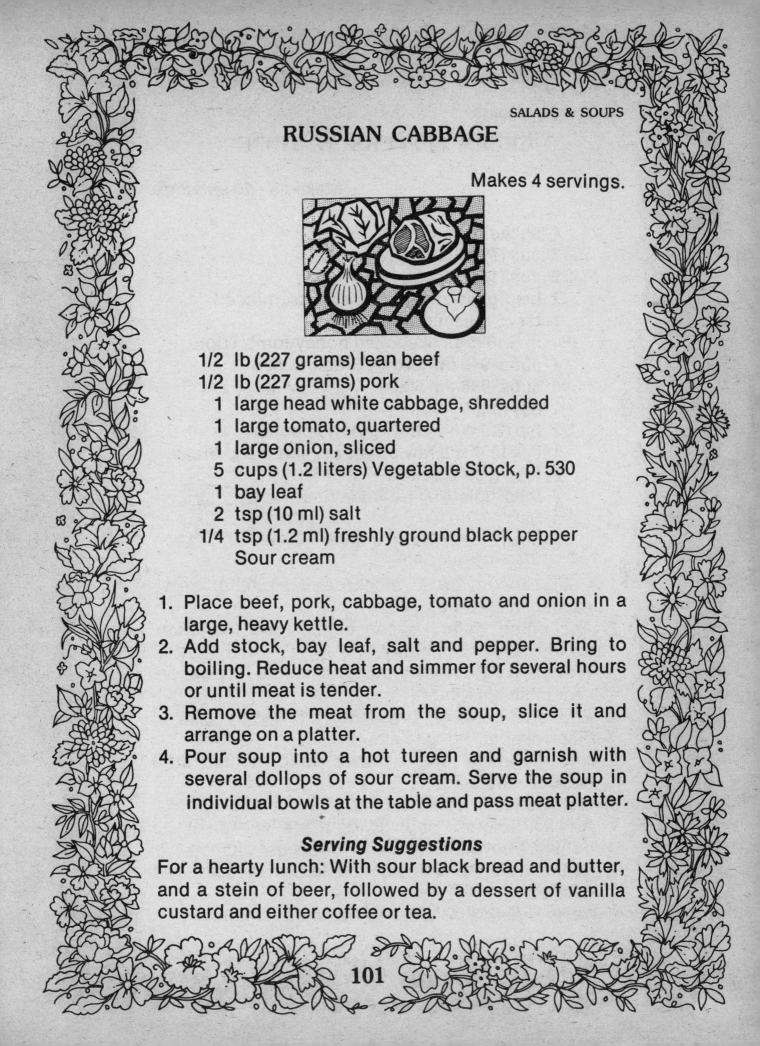

1/2 lb (227 grams) lean beef
1/2 lb (227 grams) pork
   1 large head white cabbage, shredded
   1 large tomato, quartered
   1 large onion, sliced
   5 cups (1.2 liters) Vegetable Stock, p. 530
   1 bay leaf
   2 tsp (10 ml) salt
1/4 tsp (1.2 ml) freshly ground black pepper
      Sour cream

1. Place beef, pork, cabbage, tomato and onion in a large, heavy kettle.
2. Add stock, bay leaf, salt and pepper. Bring to boiling. Reduce heat and simmer for several hours or until meat is tender.
3. Remove the meat from the soup, slice it and arrange on a platter.
4. Pour soup into a hot tureen and garnish with several dollops of sour cream. Serve the soup in individual bowls at the table and pass meat platter.

Serving Suggestions

For a hearty lunch: With sour black bread and butter, and a stein of beer, followed by a dessert of vanilla custard and either coffee or tea.

GREEN PEPPERS 'N' TRIPE

Makes 8 - 10 servings.

- 4 slices bacon
- 1/3 cup (79 ml) onion, minced
- 1/2 cup (118 ml) celery, minced
- 2 medium-sized green peppers, minced
- 1 tsp (5 ml) marjoram
- 3/4 lb (340 grams) cooked honeycomb Tripe
- 4 cups (946 ml) Brown Stock, p. 526
- 4 cups (946 ml) water
- 1 bay leaf
- 1/2 tsp (2.5 ml) freshly ground pepper
- 1 cup (237 ml) raw potatoes, pared and diced
- 2 tbsp (30 ml) butter
- 2 tbsp (30 ml) all-purpose flour
- Salt
- 1/2 cup (118 ml) warm cream

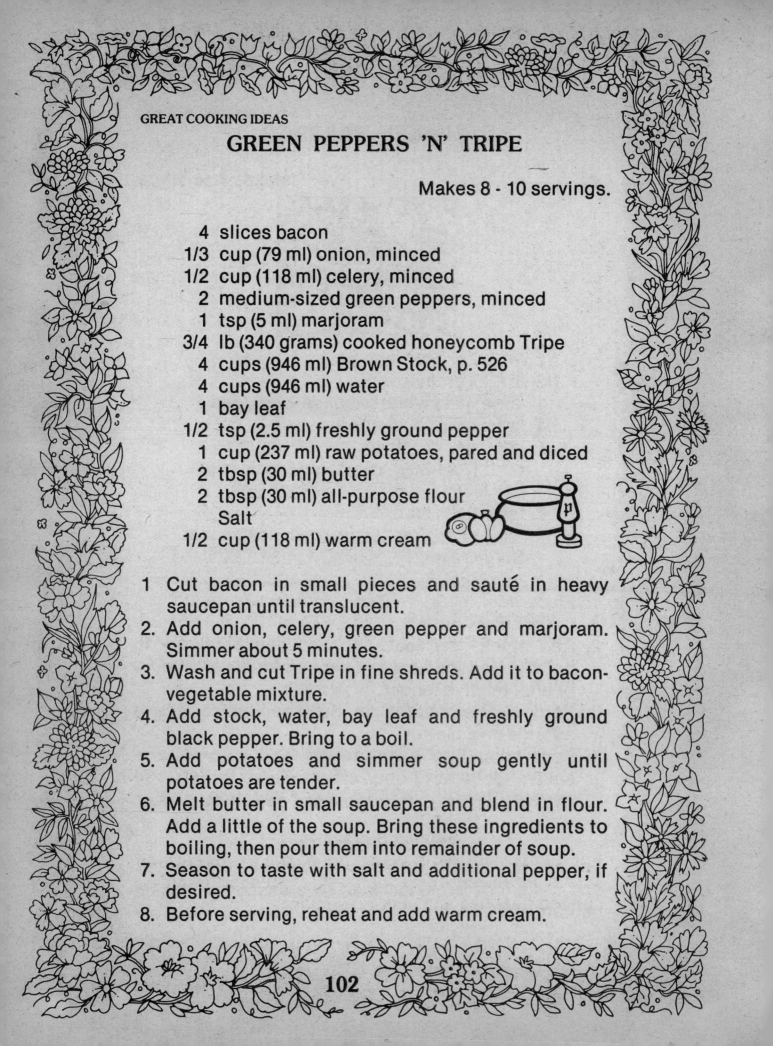

1. Cut bacon in small pieces and sauté in heavy saucepan until translucent.
2. Add onion, celery, green pepper and marjoram. Simmer about 5 minutes.
3. Wash and cut Tripe in fine shreds. Add it to bacon-vegetable mixture.
4. Add stock, water, bay leaf and freshly ground black pepper. Bring to a boil.
5. Add potatoes and simmer soup gently until potatoes are tender.
6. Melt butter in small saucepan and blend in flour. Add a little of the soup. Bring these ingredients to boiling, then pour them into remainder of soup.
7. Season to taste with salt and additional pepper, if desired.
8. Before serving, reheat and add warm cream.

CHINESE MEATBALL

Makes 4 - 6 servings.

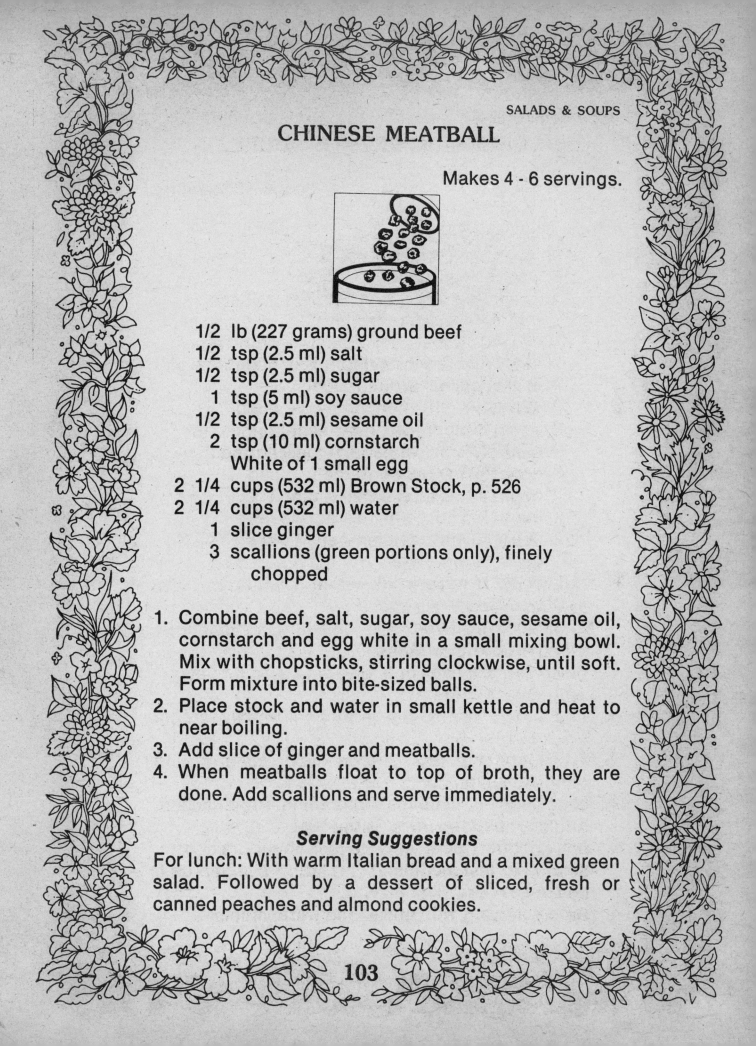

1/2 lb (227 grams) ground beef
1/2 tsp (2.5 ml) salt
1/2 tsp (2.5 ml) sugar
1 tsp (5 ml) soy sauce
1/2 tsp (2.5 ml) sesame oil
2 tsp (10 ml) cornstarch
White of 1 small egg
2 1/4 cups (532 ml) Brown Stock, p. 526
2 1/4 cups (532 ml) water
1 slice ginger
3 scallions (green portions only), finely chopped

1. Combine beef, salt, sugar, soy sauce, sesame oil, cornstarch and egg white in a small mixing bowl. Mix with chopsticks, stirring clockwise, until soft. Form mixture into bite-sized balls.
2. Place stock and water in small kettle and heat to near boiling.
3. Add slice of ginger and meatballs.
4. When meatballs float to top of broth, they are done. Add scallions and serve immediately.

Serving Suggestions

For lunch: With warm Italian bread and a mixed green salad. Followed by a dessert of sliced, fresh or canned peaches and almond cookies.

HAMBURGER-MINESTRONE SOUP

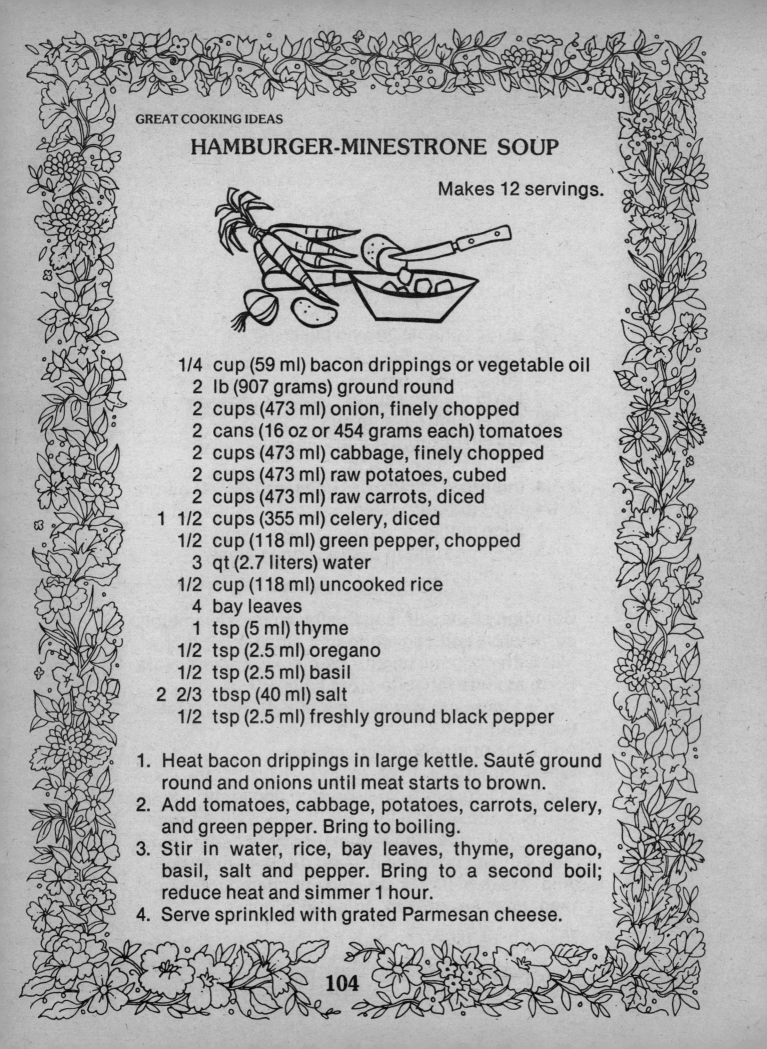

Makes 12 servings.

1/4 cup (59 ml) bacon drippings or vegetable oil
2 lb (907 grams) ground round
2 cups (473 ml) onion, finely chopped
2 cans (16 oz or 454 grams each) tomatoes
2 cups (473 ml) cabbage, finely chopped
2 cups (473 ml) raw potatoes, cubed
2 cups (473 ml) raw carrots, diced
1 1/2 cups (355 ml) celery, diced
1/2 cup (118 ml) green pepper, chopped
3 qt (2.7 liters) water
1/2 cup (118 ml) uncooked rice
4 bay leaves
1 tsp (5 ml) thyme
1/2 tsp (2.5 ml) oregano
1/2 tsp (2.5 ml) basil
2 2/3 tbsp (40 ml) salt
1/2 tsp (2.5 ml) freshly ground black pepper

1. Heat bacon drippings in large kettle. Sauté ground round and onions until meat starts to brown.
2. Add tomatoes, cabbage, potatoes, carrots, celery, and green pepper. Bring to boiling.
3. Stir in water, rice, bay leaves, thyme, oregano, basil, salt and pepper. Bring to a second boil; reduce heat and simmer 1 hour.
4. Serve sprinkled with grated Parmesan cheese.

TIJUANA MEAT BALL SOUP

Makes 6 servings.

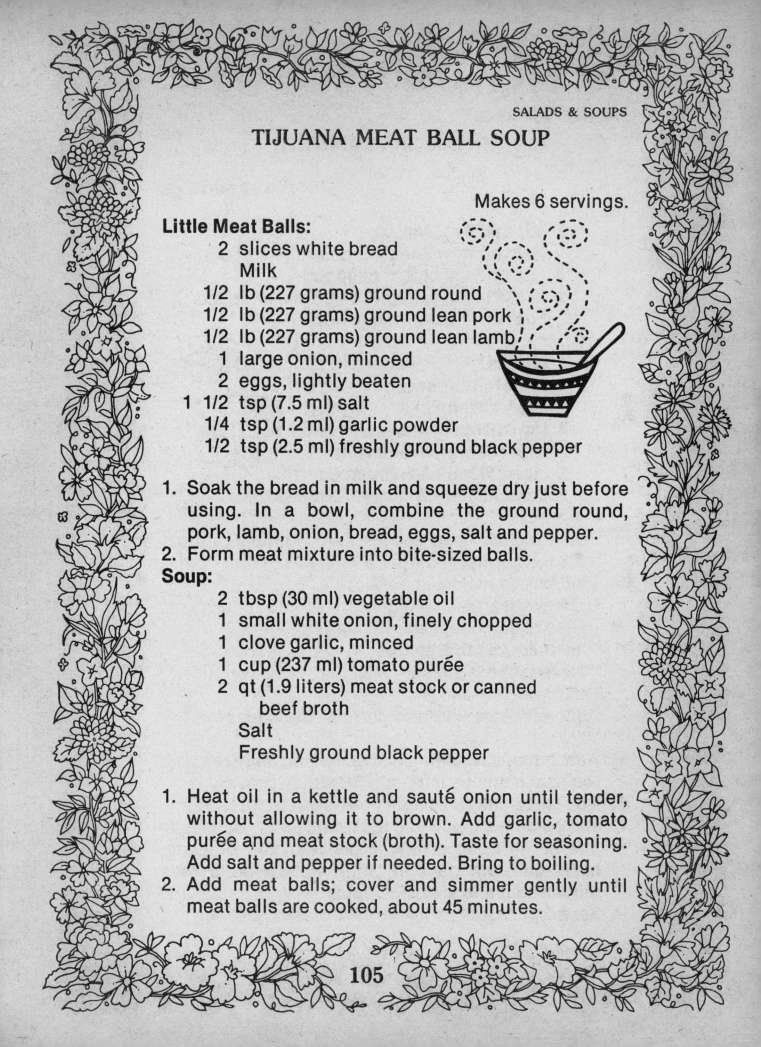

Little Meat Balls:

- 2 slices white bread
- Milk
- 1/2 lb (227 grams) ground round
- 1/2 lb (227 grams) ground lean pork
- 1/2 lb (227 grams) ground lean lamb
- 1 large onion, minced
- 2 eggs, lightly beaten
- 1 1/2 tsp (7.5 ml) salt
- 1/4 tsp (1.2 ml) garlic powder
- 1/2 tsp (2.5 ml) freshly ground black pepper

1. Soak the bread in milk and squeeze dry just before using. In a bowl, combine the ground round, pork, lamb, onion, bread, eggs, salt and pepper.
2. Form meat mixture into bite-sized balls.

Soup:

- 2 tbsp (30 ml) vegetable oil
- 1 small white onion, finely chopped
- 1 clove garlic, minced
- 1 cup (237 ml) tomato purée
- 2 qt (1.9 liters) meat stock or canned beef broth
- Salt
- Freshly ground black pepper

1. Heat oil in a kettle and sauté onion until tender, without allowing it to brown. Add garlic, tomato purée and meat stock (broth). Taste for seasoning. Add salt and pepper if needed. Bring to boiling.
2. Add meat balls; cover and simmer gently until meat balls are cooked, about 45 minutes.

HAM 'N' LENTIL

Makes 6 - 8 servings.

2 cups (473 ml) lentils
Ham bone or 2-inch (5-cm) cube salt pork
1/2 cup (118 ml) onion, chopped
1 cup (237 ml) celery with leaves, chopped
1/2 cup (118 ml) carrots, chopped
1 clove garlic
1 bay leaf
1 tsp (5ml) sugar
Dash cayenne
1/4 tsp (1.2 ml) thyme
2 tbsp (30 ml) sweet butter
2 tbsp (30 ml) all-purpose flour
Salt and freshly ground black pepper

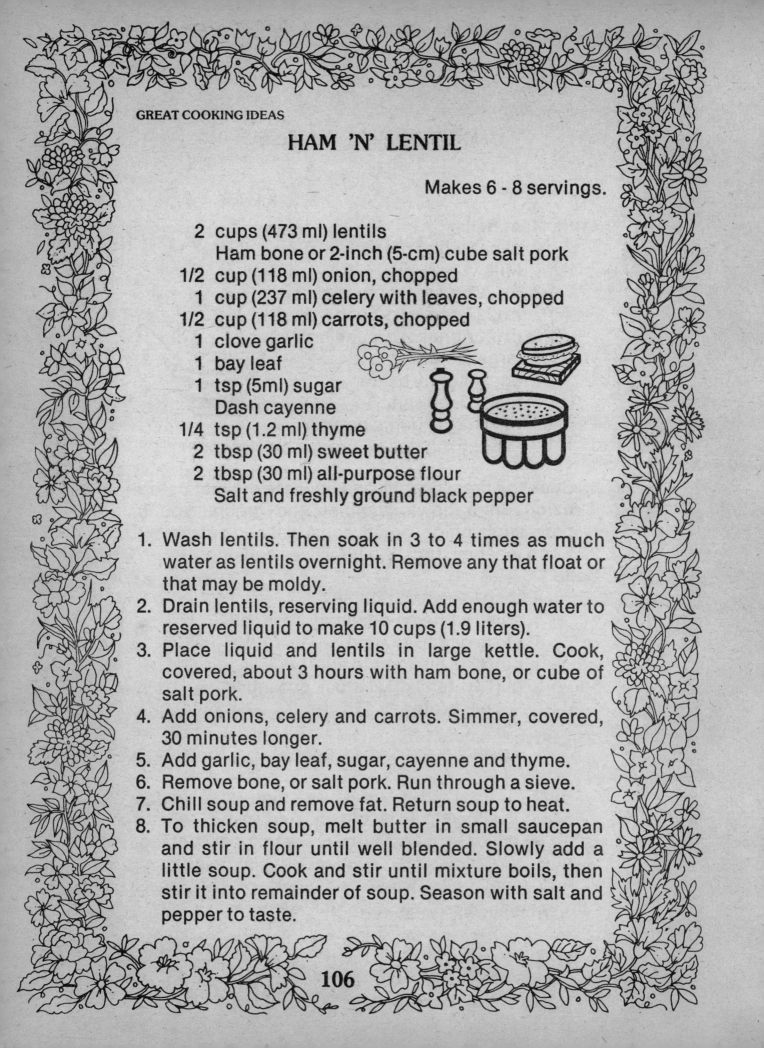

1. Wash lentils. Then soak in 3 to 4 times as much water as lentils overnight. Remove any that float or that may be moldy.
2. Drain lentils, reserving liquid. Add enough water to reserved liquid to make 10 cups (1.9 liters).
3. Place liquid and lentils in large kettle. Cook, covered, about 3 hours with ham bone, or cube of salt pork.
4. Add onions, celery and carrots. Simmer, covered, 30 minutes longer.
5. Add garlic, bay leaf, sugar, cayenne and thyme.
6. Remove bone, or salt pork. Run through a sieve.
7. Chill soup and remove fat. Return soup to heat.
8. To thicken soup, melt butter in small saucepan and stir in flour until well blended. Slowly add a little soup. Cook and stir until mixture boils, then stir it into remainder of soup. Season with salt and pepper to taste.

HOT 'N' SOUR SOUP

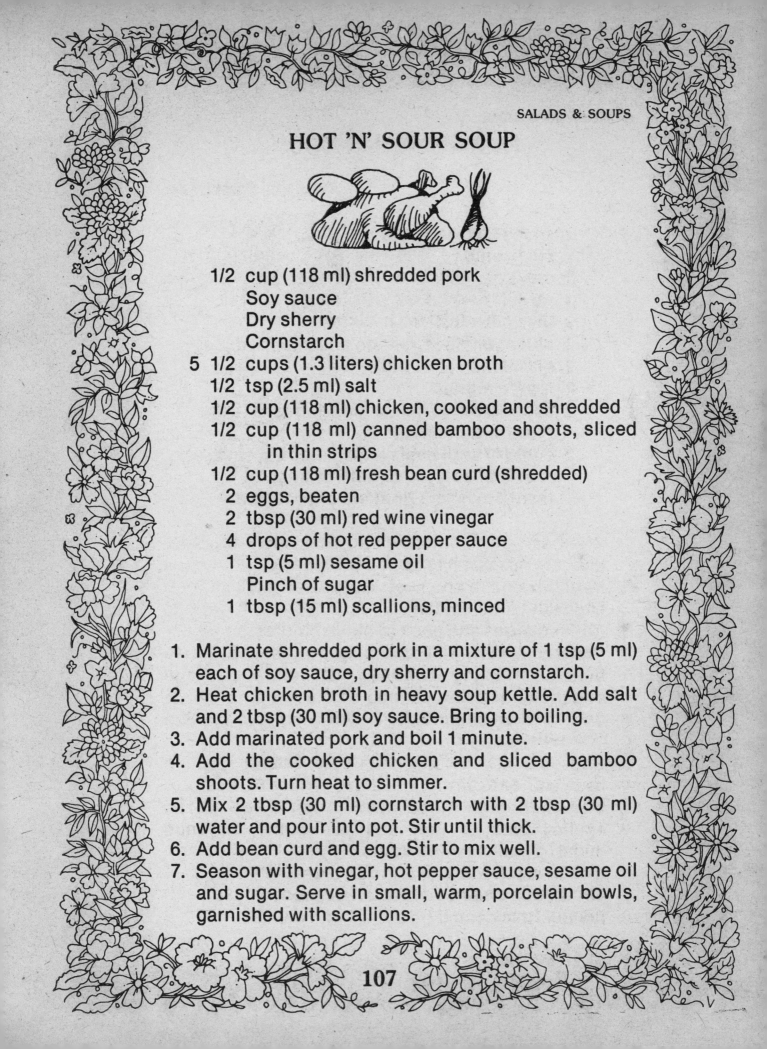

1/2 cup (118 ml) shredded pork
     Soy sauce
     Dry sherry
     Cornstarch
5 1/2 cups (1.3 liters) chicken broth
1/2 tsp (2.5 ml) salt
1/2 cup (118 ml) chicken, cooked and shredded
1/2 cup (118 ml) canned bamboo shoots, sliced
       in thin strips
1/2 cup (118 ml) fresh bean curd (shredded)
  2 eggs, beaten
  2 tbsp (30 ml) red wine vinegar
  4 drops of hot red pepper sauce
  1 tsp (5 ml) sesame oil
     Pinch of sugar
  1 tbsp (15 ml) scallions, minced

1. Marinate shredded pork in a mixture of 1 tsp (5 ml) each of soy sauce, dry sherry and cornstarch.
2. Heat chicken broth in heavy soup kettle. Add salt and 2 tbsp (30 ml) soy sauce. Bring to boiling.
3. Add marinated pork and boil 1 minute.
4. Add the cooked chicken and sliced bamboo shoots. Turn heat to simmer.
5. Mix 2 tbsp (30 ml) cornstarch with 2 tbsp (30 ml) water and pour into pot. Stir until thick.
6. Add bean curd and egg. Stir to mix well.
7. Season with vinegar, hot pepper sauce, sesame oil and sugar. Serve in small, warm, porcelain bowls, garnished with scallions.

PASTA 'N' BEAN SOUP

Makes 8 servings.

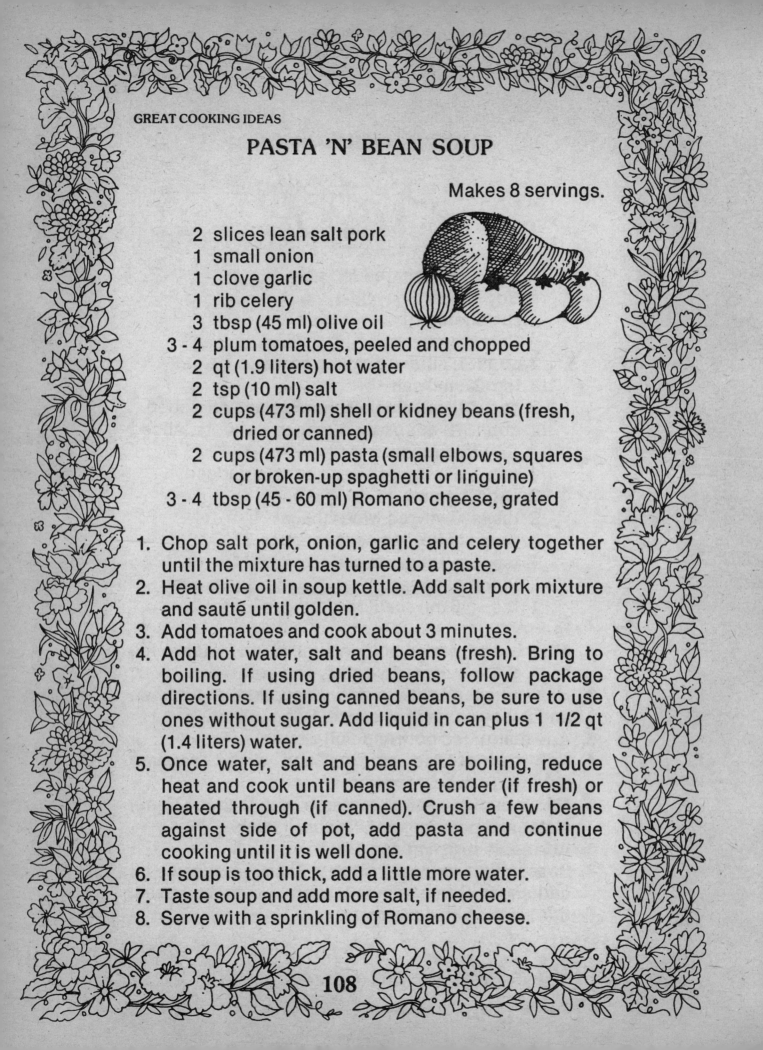

2 slices lean salt pork
1 small onion
1 clove garlic
1 rib celery
3 tbsp (45 ml) olive oil
3 - 4 plum tomatoes, peeled and chopped
2 qt (1.9 liters) hot water
2 tsp (10 ml) salt
2 cups (473 ml) shell or kidney beans (fresh, dried or canned)
2 cups (473 ml) pasta (small elbows, squares or broken-up spaghetti or linguine)
3 - 4 tbsp (45 - 60 ml) Romano cheese, grated

1. Chop salt pork, onion, garlic and celery together until the mixture has turned to a paste.
2. Heat olive oil in soup kettle. Add salt pork mixture and sauté until golden.
3. Add tomatoes and cook about 3 minutes.
4. Add hot water, salt and beans (fresh). Bring to boiling. If using dried beans, follow package directions. If using canned beans, be sure to use ones without sugar. Add liquid in can plus 1 1/2 qt (1.4 liters) water.
5. Once water, salt and beans are boiling, reduce heat and cook until beans are tender (if fresh) or heated through (if canned). Crush a few beans against side of pot, add pasta and continue cooking until it is well done.
6. If soup is too thick, add a little more water.
7. Taste soup and add more salt, if needed.
8. Serve with a sprinkling of Romano cheese.

CHICKEN-SHRIMP SOUP

Makes 8 servings.

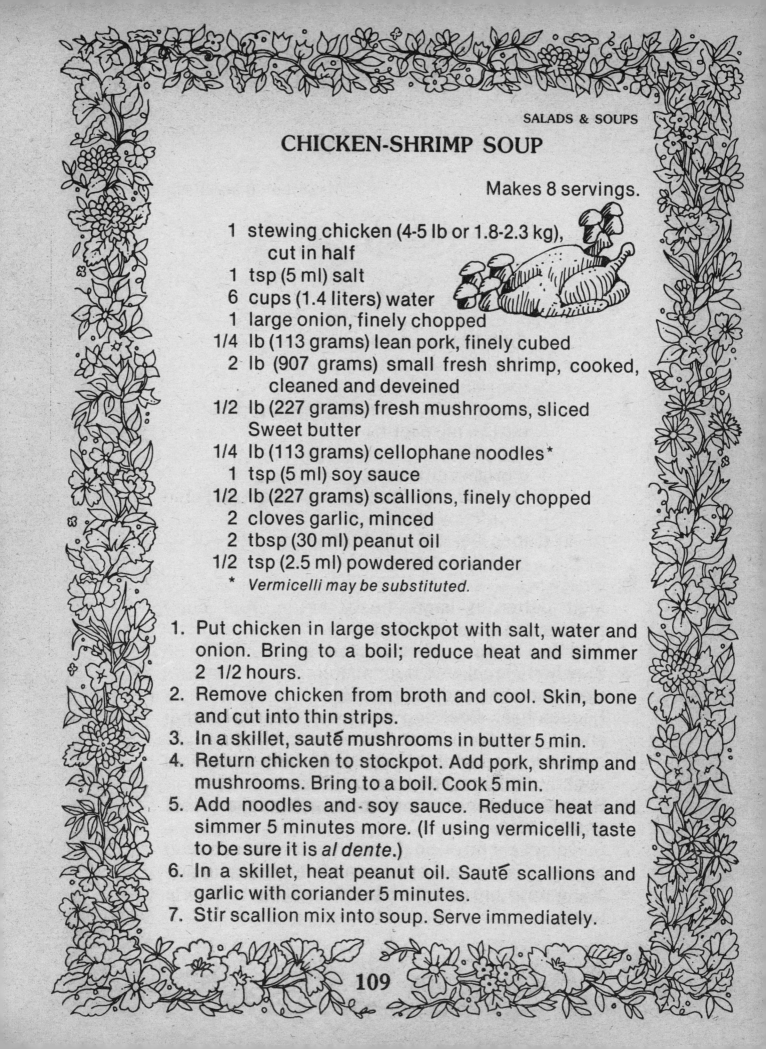

1 stewing chicken (4-5 lb or 1.8-2.3 kg), cut in half
1 tsp (5 ml) salt
6 cups (1.4 liters) water
1 large onion, finely chopped
1/4 lb (113 grams) lean pork, finely cubed
2 lb (907 grams) small fresh shrimp, cooked, cleaned and deveined
1/2 lb (227 grams) fresh mushrooms, sliced
Sweet butter
1/4 lb (113 grams) cellophane noodles*
1 tsp (5 ml) soy sauce
1/2 lb (227 grams) scallions, finely chopped
2 cloves garlic, minced
2 tbsp (30 ml) peanut oil
1/2 tsp (2.5 ml) powdered coriander

* *Vermicelli may be substituted.*

1. Put chicken in large stockpot with salt, water and onion. Bring to a boil; reduce heat and simmer 2 1/2 hours.
2. Remove chicken from broth and cool. Skin, bone and cut into thin strips.
3. In a skillet, sauté mushrooms in butter 5 min.
4. Return chicken to stockpot. Add pork, shrimp and mushrooms. Bring to a boil. Cook 5 min.
5. Add noodles and soy sauce. Reduce heat and simmer 5 minutes more. (If using vermicelli, taste to be sure it is *al dente*.)
6. In a skillet, heat peanut oil. Sauté scallions and garlic with coriander 5 minutes.
7. Stir scallion mix into soup. Serve immediately.

CURRIED CHICKEN

Makes 6 - 8 servings.

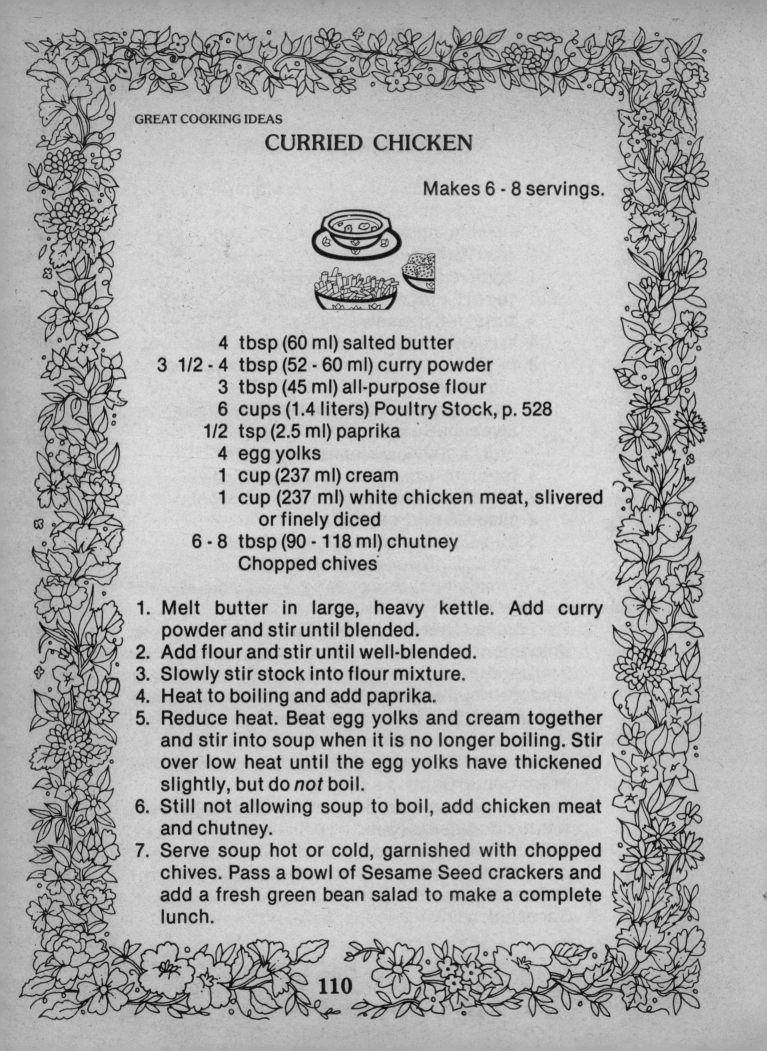

```
       4   tbsp (60 ml) salted butter
3  1/2 - 4  tbsp (52 - 60 ml) curry powder
       3   tbsp (45 ml) all-purpose flour
       6   cups (1.4 liters) Poultry Stock, p. 528
     1/2   tsp (2.5 ml) paprika
       4   egg yolks
       1   cup (237 ml) cream
       1   cup (237 ml) white chicken meat, slivered
           or finely diced
   6 - 8   tbsp (90 - 118 ml) chutney
           Chopped chives
```

1. Melt butter in large, heavy kettle. Add curry powder and stir until blended.
2. Add flour and stir until well-blended.
3. Slowly stir stock into flour mixture.
4. Heat to boiling and add paprika.
5. Reduce heat. Beat egg yolks and cream together and stir into soup when it is no longer boiling. Stir over low heat until the egg yolks have thickened slightly, but do *not* boil.
6. Still not allowing soup to boil, add chicken meat and chutney.
7. Serve soup hot or cold, garnished with chopped chives. Pass a bowl of Sesame Seed crackers and add a fresh green bean salad to make a complete lunch.

SPICY CHICKEN SOUP

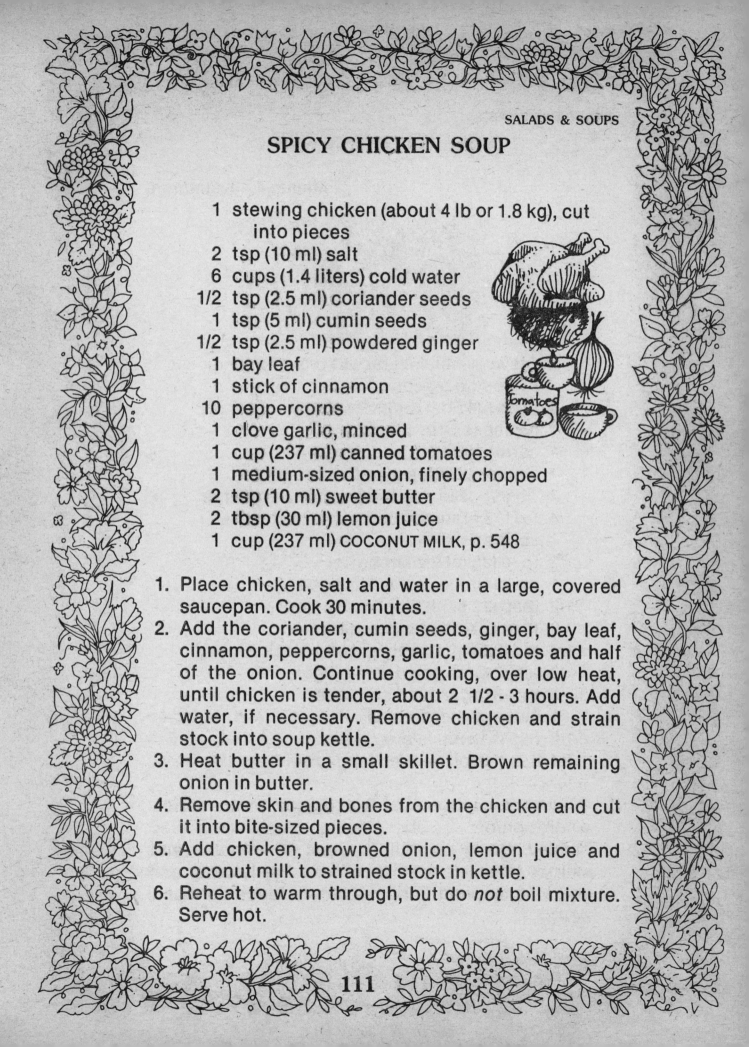

1 stewing chicken (about 4 lb or 1.8 kg), cut into pieces
2 tsp (10 ml) salt
6 cups (1.4 liters) cold water
1/2 tsp (2.5 ml) coriander seeds
1 tsp (5 ml) cumin seeds
1/2 tsp (2.5 ml) powdered ginger
1 bay leaf
1 stick of cinnamon
10 peppercorns
1 clove garlic, minced
1 cup (237 ml) canned tomatoes
1 medium-sized onion, finely chopped
2 tsp (10 ml) sweet butter
2 tbsp (30 ml) lemon juice
1 cup (237 ml) COCONUT MILK, p. 548

1. Place chicken, salt and water in a large, covered saucepan. Cook 30 minutes.
2. Add the coriander, cumin seeds, ginger, bay leaf, cinnamon, peppercorns, garlic, tomatoes and half of the onion. Continue cooking, over low heat, until chicken is tender, about 2 1/2 - 3 hours. Add water, if necessary. Remove chicken and strain stock into soup kettle.
3. Heat butter in a small skillet. Brown remaining onion in butter.
4. Remove skin and bones from the chicken and cut it into bite-sized pieces.
5. Add chicken, browned onion, lemon juice and coconut milk to strained stock in kettle.
6. Reheat to warm through, but do *not* boil mixture. Serve hot.

MULLIGATAWNY SOUP

Makes 4 - 6 servings.

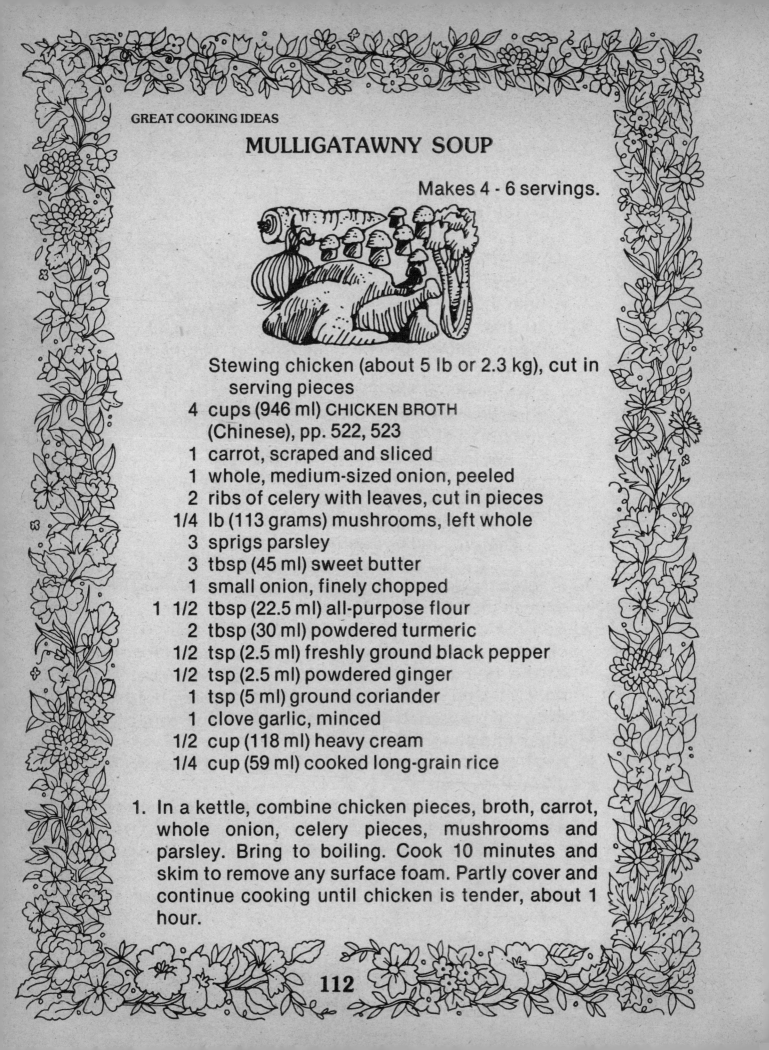

Stewing chicken (about 5 lb or 2.3 kg), cut in
    serving pieces
4 cups (946 ml) CHICKEN BROTH
  (Chinese), pp. 522, 523
1 carrot, scraped and sliced
1 whole, medium-sized onion, peeled
2 ribs of celery with leaves, cut in pieces
1/4 lb (113 grams) mushrooms, left whole
3 sprigs parsley
3 tbsp (45 ml) sweet butter
1 small onion, finely chopped
1 1/2 tbsp (22.5 ml) all-purpose flour
2 tbsp (30 ml) powdered turmeric
1/2 tsp (2.5 ml) freshly ground black pepper
1/2 tsp (2.5 ml) powdered ginger
1 tsp (5 ml) ground coriander
1 clove garlic, minced
1/2 cup (118 ml) heavy cream
1/4 cup (59 ml) cooked long-grain rice

1. In a kettle, combine chicken pieces, broth, carrot, whole onion, celery pieces, mushrooms and parsley. Bring to boiling. Cook 10 minutes and skim to remove any surface foam. Partly cover and continue cooking until chicken is tender, about 1 hour.

2. Remove chicken pieces from broth. Set aside half of breast, remove bone and cut it into very thin strips. Refrigerate remaining chicken for another purpose. Strain broth and set aside.
3. Melt butter in kettle. Add chopped onion and sauté, stirring, until golden but *not* brown.
4. Stir flour into butter-onion mixture. Add turmeric, pepper, ginger, coriander and garlic. Mix well.
5. Add strained broth gradually, stirring constantly. Bring to boiling, skimming as needed. Simmer 10 minutes.
6. Taste and adjust seasoning, if necessary.
7. Stir in cream and rice. Heat through, stirring, but do *not* boil.
8. Serve hot in hot bowls. Garnish each with strips of chicken breast.

Luncheon Suggestion

Bowls of Mulligatawny Soup with WHEAT BREAD, p. 51 and a mixed green salad. Followed by KARACHI PINEAPPLE p. 498, for dessert.

NOTES

CRABBY SHRIMP

Makes 6-8 servings.

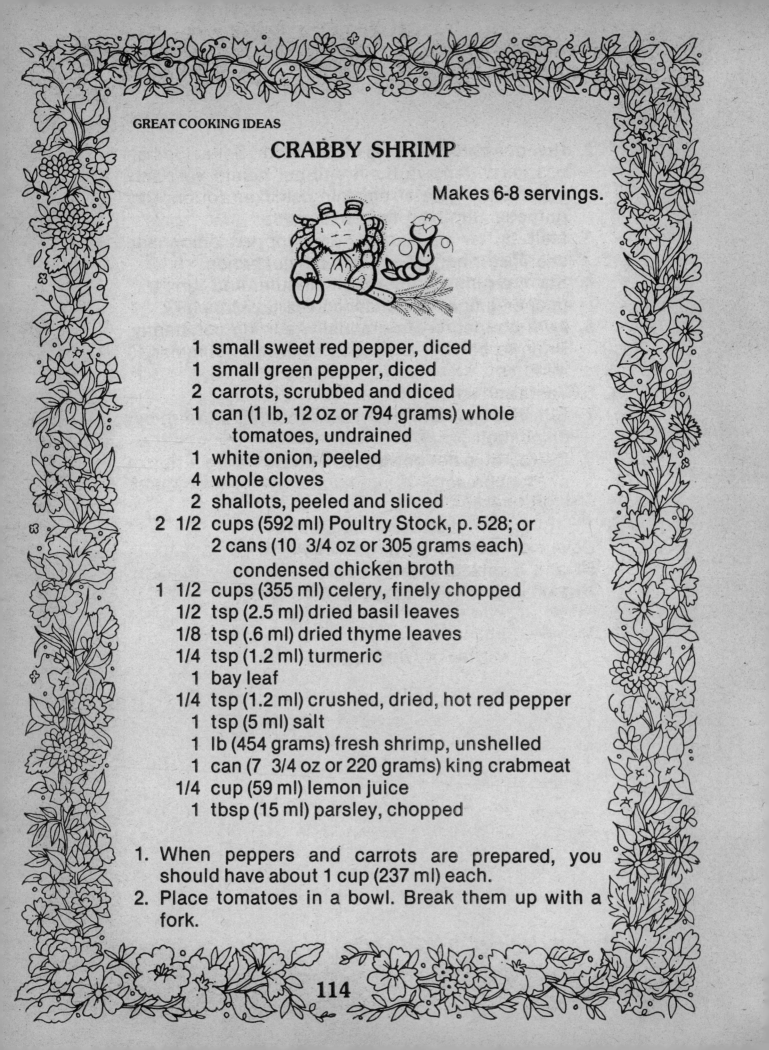

- 1 small sweet red pepper, diced
- 1 small green pepper, diced
- 2 carrots, scrubbed and diced
- 1 can (1 lb, 12 oz or 794 grams) whole tomatoes, undrained
- 1 white onion, peeled
- 4 whole cloves
- 2 shallots, peeled and sliced
- 2 1/2 cups (592 ml) Poultry Stock, p. 528; or 2 cans (10 3/4 oz or 305 grams each) condensed chicken broth
- 1 1/2 cups (355 ml) celery, finely chopped
- 1/2 tsp (2.5 ml) dried basil leaves
- 1/8 tsp (.6 ml) dried thyme leaves
- 1/4 tsp (1.2 ml) turmeric
- 1 bay leaf
- 1/4 tsp (1.2 ml) crushed, dried, hot red pepper
- 1 tsp (5 ml) salt
- 1 lb (454 grams) fresh shrimp, unshelled
- 1 can (7 3/4 oz or 220 grams) king crabmeat
- 1/4 cup (59 ml) lemon juice
- 1 tbsp (15 ml) parsley, chopped

1. When peppers and carrots are prepared, you should have about 1 cup (237 ml) each.
2. Place tomatoes in a bowl. Break them up with a fork.

114

3. Stud onion with cloves.
4. In a kettle or Dutch oven, bring 3 cups (710 ml) water and stock or chicken broth to a boil. Add peppers, carrots, tomatoes, onion with cloves, shallots, celery, basil, thyme, turmeric, bay leaf and dried red pepper. Return to boiling; reduce heat and simmer, uncovered, 30 minutes.
5. In a medium-sized saucepan, bring 2 cups (473 ml) water and 1/2 tsp (2.5 ml) salt to a boil. Add shrimp. Reduce heat and simmer, uncovered, 10 minutes. Drain and set aside 1 cup (237 ml) liquid. Cool shrimp; shell and devein.
6. Add shrimp, reserved cooking liquid, crabmeat and lemon juice to other ingredients in kettle. Cook gently, uncovered, 10 minutes more.
7. Add parsley at end of cooking time. If desired, add additional salt.

Elegant Luncheon Suggestion
Soup: Crabby Shrimp
Bread: Warm Croissants and butter
Wine: Pinot-Chardonnay-Macon
Dessert: Pecan Pie
          Coffee or Tea

NOTES

FISH 'N' SHELLFISH

Makes 8 - 10 servings.

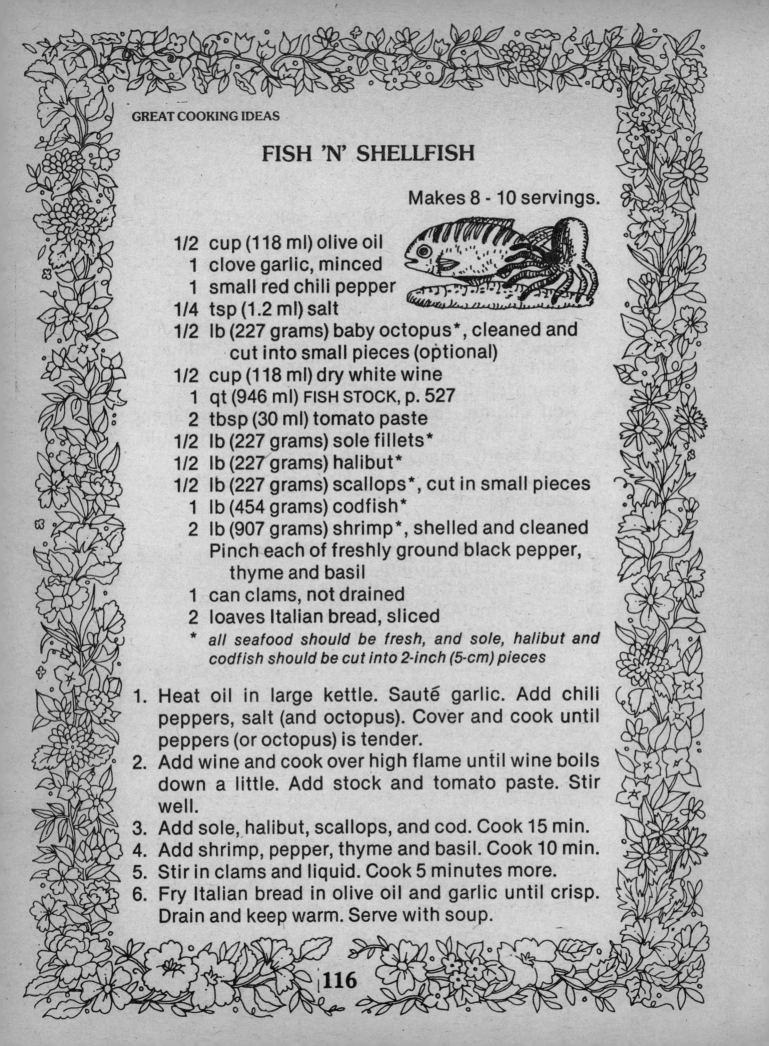

- 1/2 cup (118 ml) olive oil
- 1 clove garlic, minced
- 1 small red chili pepper
- 1/4 tsp (1.2 ml) salt
- 1/2 lb (227 grams) baby octopus*, cleaned and cut into small pieces (optional)
- 1/2 cup (118 ml) dry white wine
- 1 qt (946 ml) FISH STOCK, p. 527
- 2 tbsp (30 ml) tomato paste
- 1/2 lb (227 grams) sole fillets*
- 1/2 lb (227 grams) halibut*
- 1/2 lb (227 grams) scallops*, cut in small pieces
- 1 lb (454 grams) codfish*
- 2 lb (907 grams) shrimp*, shelled and cleaned
  Pinch each of freshly ground black pepper, thyme and basil
- 1 can clams, not drained
- 2 loaves Italian bread, sliced
- * *all seafood should be fresh, and sole, halibut and codfish should be cut into 2-inch (5-cm) pieces*

1. Heat oil in large kettle. Sauté garlic. Add chili peppers, salt (and octopus). Cover and cook until peppers (or octopus) is tender.
2. Add wine and cook over high flame until wine boils down a little. Add stock and tomato paste. Stir well.
3. Add sole, halibut, scallops, and cod. Cook 15 min.
4. Add shrimp, pepper, thyme and basil. Cook 10 min.
5. Stir in clams and liquid. Cook 5 minutes more.
6. Fry Italian bread in olive oil and garlic until crisp. Drain and keep warm. Serve with soup.

FRENCH-STYLE CLAM

Makes 4 servings.

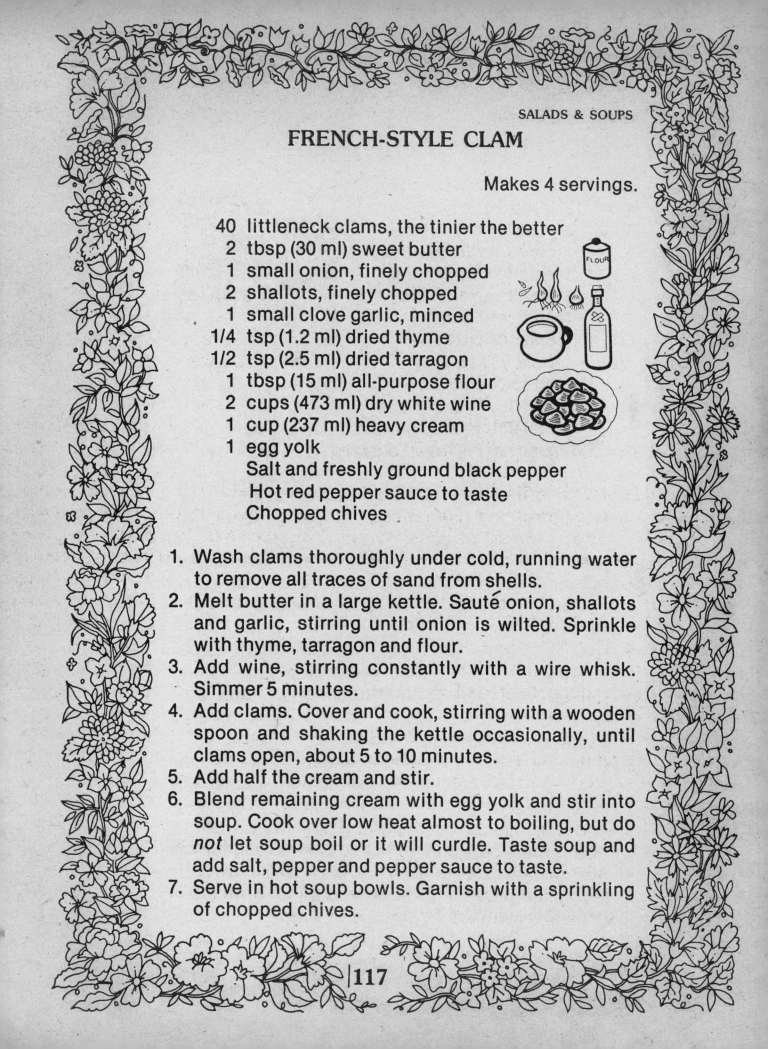

40 littleneck clams, the tinier the better
2 tbsp (30 ml) sweet butter
1 small onion, finely chopped
2 shallots, finely chopped
1 small clove garlic, minced
1/4 tsp (1.2 ml) dried thyme
1/2 tsp (2.5 ml) dried tarragon
1 tbsp (15 ml) all-purpose flour
2 cups (473 ml) dry white wine
1 cup (237 ml) heavy cream
1 egg yolk
Salt and freshly ground black pepper
Hot red pepper sauce to taste
Chopped chives

1. Wash clams thoroughly under cold, running water to remove all traces of sand from shells.
2. Melt butter in a large kettle. Sauté onion, shallots and garlic, stirring until onion is wilted. Sprinkle with thyme, tarragon and flour.
3. Add wine, stirring constantly with a wire whisk. Simmer 5 minutes.
4. Add clams. Cover and cook, stirring with a wooden spoon and shaking the kettle occasionally, until clams open, about 5 to 10 minutes.
5. Add half the cream and stir.
6. Blend remaining cream with egg yolk and stir into soup. Cook over low heat almost to boiling, but do *not* let soup boil or it will curdle. Taste soup and add salt, pepper and pepper sauce to taste.
7. Serve in hot soup bowls. Garnish with a sprinkling of chopped chives.

FROG SOUP

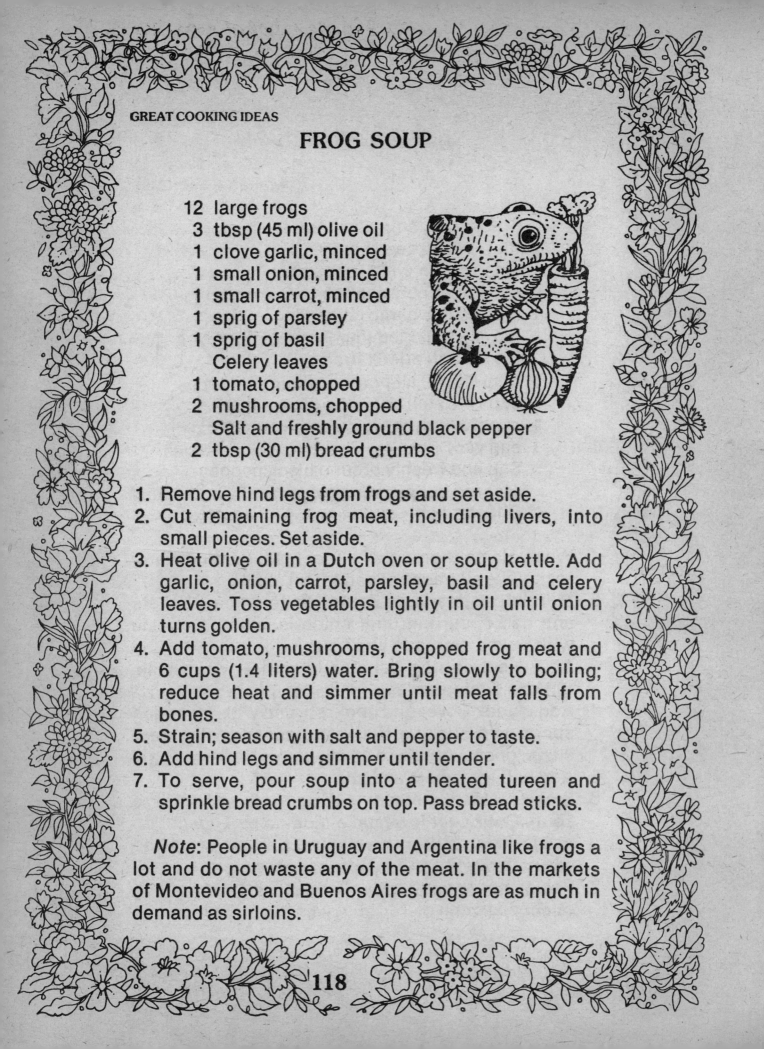

12 large frogs
3 tbsp (45 ml) olive oil
1 clove garlic, minced
1 small onion, minced
1 small carrot, minced
1 sprig of parsley
1 sprig of basil
  Celery leaves
1 tomato, chopped
2 mushrooms, chopped
  Salt and freshly ground black pepper
2 tbsp (30 ml) bread crumbs

1. Remove hind legs from frogs and set aside.
2. Cut remaining frog meat, including livers, into small pieces. Set aside.
3. Heat olive oil in a Dutch oven or soup kettle. Add garlic, onion, carrot, parsley, basil and celery leaves. Toss vegetables lightly in oil until onion turns golden.
4. Add tomato, mushrooms, chopped frog meat and 6 cups (1.4 liters) water. Bring slowly to boiling; reduce heat and simmer until meat falls from bones.
5. Strain; season with salt and pepper to taste.
6. Add hind legs and simmer until tender.
7. To serve, pour soup into a heated tureen and sprinkle bread crumbs on top. Pass bread sticks.

Note: People in Uruguay and Argentina like frogs a lot and do not waste any of the meat. In the markets of Montevideo and Buenos Aires frogs are as much in demand as sirloins.

POT O' THE SEA

Makes 4 - 6 servings.

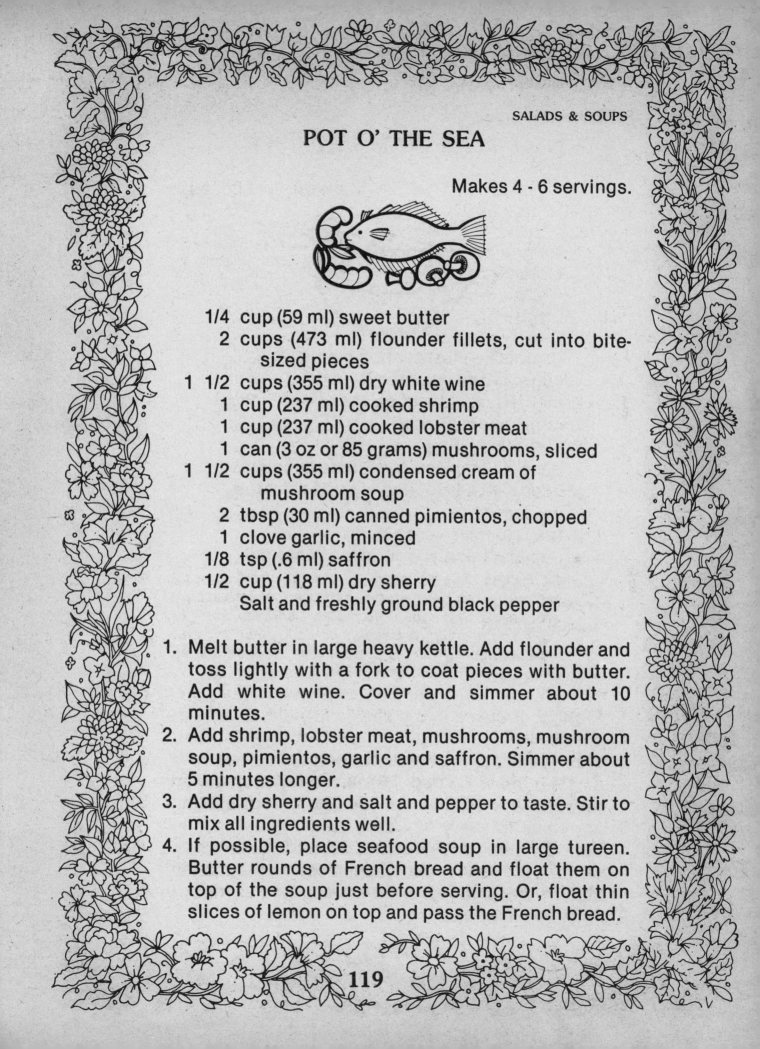

1/4 cup (59 ml) sweet butter
2 cups (473 ml) flounder fillets, cut into bite-sized pieces
1 1/2 cups (355 ml) dry white wine
1 cup (237 ml) cooked shrimp
1 cup (237 ml) cooked lobster meat
1 can (3 oz or 85 grams) mushrooms, sliced
1 1/2 cups (355 ml) condensed cream of mushroom soup
2 tbsp (30 ml) canned pimientos, chopped
1 clove garlic, minced
1/8 tsp (.6 ml) saffron
1/2 cup (118 ml) dry sherry
Salt and freshly ground black pepper

1. Melt butter in large heavy kettle. Add flounder and toss lightly with a fork to coat pieces with butter. Add white wine. Cover and simmer about 10 minutes.
2. Add shrimp, lobster meat, mushrooms, mushroom soup, pimientos, garlic and saffron. Simmer about 5 minutes longer.
3. Add dry sherry and salt and pepper to taste. Stir to mix all ingredients well.
4. If possible, place seafood soup in large tureen. Butter rounds of French bread and float them on top of the soup just before serving. Or, float thin slices of lemon on top and pass the French bread.

NEW YORK CLAM CHOWDER

Makes 6 - 8 servings.

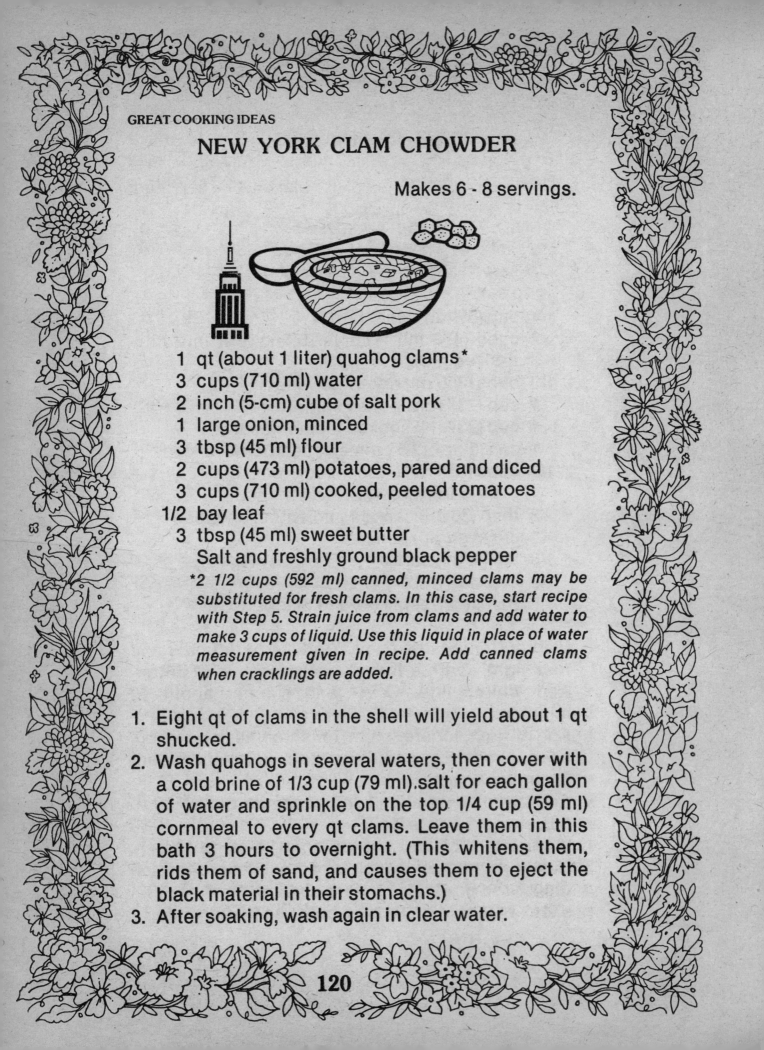

- 1 qt (about 1 liter) quahog clams*
- 3 cups (710 ml) water
- 2 inch (5-cm) cube of salt pork
- 1 large onion, minced
- 3 tbsp (45 ml) flour
- 2 cups (473 ml) potatoes, pared and diced
- 3 cups (710 ml) cooked, peeled tomatoes
- 1/2 bay leaf
- 3 tbsp (45 ml) sweet butter
  Salt and freshly ground black pepper

2 1/2 cups (592 ml) canned, minced clams may be substituted for fresh clams. In this case, start recipe with Step 5. Strain juice from clams and add water to make 3 cups of liquid. Use this liquid in place of water measurement given in recipe. Add canned clams when cracklings are added.

1. Eight qt of clams in the shell will yield about 1 qt shucked.
2. Wash quahogs in several waters, then cover with a cold brine of 1/3 cup (79 ml) salt for each gallon of water and sprinkle on the top 1/4 cup (59 ml) cornmeal to every qt clams. Leave them in this bath 3 hours to overnight. (This whitens them, rids them of sand, and causes them to eject the black material in their stomachs.)
3. After soaking, wash again in clear water.

4. The easiest way to open quahogs is to place them on a tray in a moderate oven until they open. After opening, cut through muscle holding shells together.
5. Wash quahogs in 3 cups water. Drain through cheesecloth. Reserve liquid. Cut hard part from soft part of clams and chop hard parts finely.
6. Chop salt pork finely. Mince onion.
7. Sauté salt pork very slowly in bottom of heavy kettle. Remove and reserve cracklings.
8. Add minced onions and hard part of clams to fat. Stir and cook slowly about 5 minutes.
9. Sift flour over onions and clams. Stir until blended.
10. Heat reserved clam water. Stir into onion-clam mixture.
11. Prepare and add potatoes, tomatoes and bay leaf.
12. Cover kettle and simmer until potatoes are done, but still firm.
13. Add cracklings, soft part of clams and butter. Simmer 3 minutes more. Place chowder in a hot tureen. Season with salt and pepper to taste.
14. Serve with Oyster crackers.

Variations: New England-Style Clam Chowder — Omit tomatoes and pour in 4 cups (946 ml) hot, *not* boiling milk after cracklings have been added. Do not let mixture boil. Serve with large chowder crackers.
Conch Chowder — Prepare recipe above and use conch meat to replace the clams. Cover 5 to 15 conch or large whelks with cold water and simmer 20 to 30 minutes. Remove from shell and beat white body meat in a canvas bag until it begins to disintegrate. Marinate 2 hours in 1/4 cup (59 ml) lime juice. After adding conch meat to chowder, simmer 3 to 5 minutes longer than for New York Clam Chowder.

JELLIED BOUILLON

Makes 6 servings.

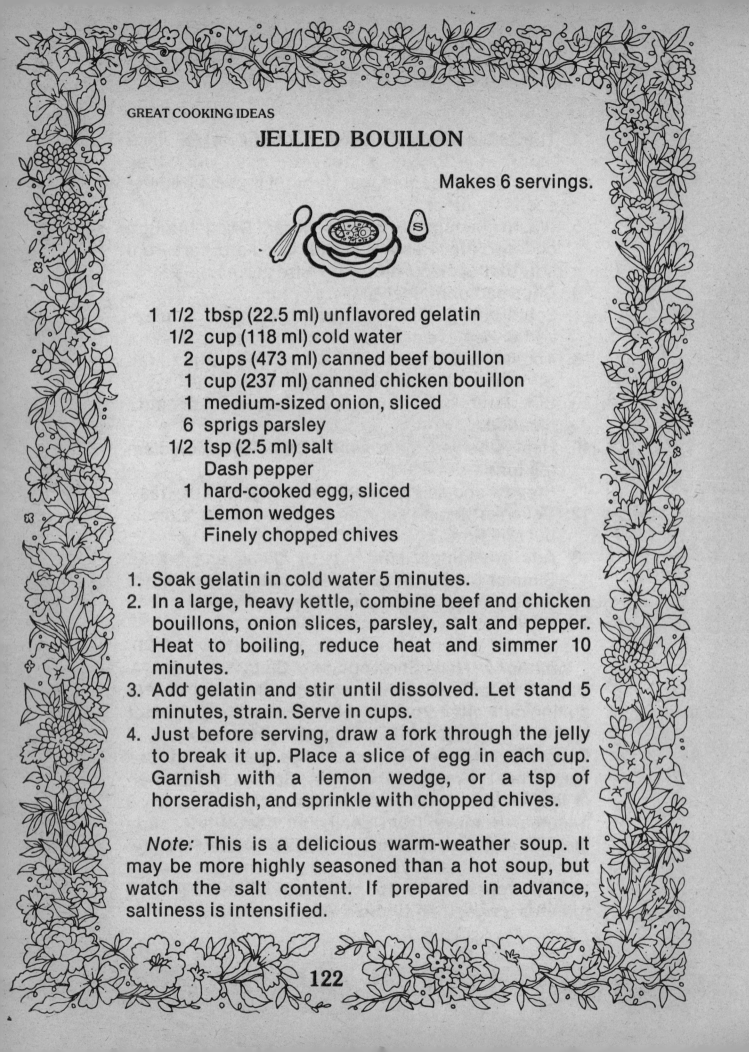

1 1/2 tbsp (22.5 ml) unflavored gelatin
1/2 cup (118 ml) cold water
2 cups (473 ml) canned beef bouillon
1 cup (237 ml) canned chicken bouillon
1 medium-sized onion, sliced
6 sprigs parsley
1/2 tsp (2.5 ml) salt
  Dash pepper
1 hard-cooked egg, sliced
  Lemon wedges
  Finely chopped chives

1. Soak gelatin in cold water 5 minutes.
2. In a large, heavy kettle, combine beef and chicken bouillons, onion slices, parsley, salt and pepper. Heat to boiling, reduce heat and simmer 10 minutes.
3. Add gelatin and stir until dissolved. Let stand 5 minutes, strain. Serve in cups.
4. Just before serving, draw a fork through the jelly to break it up. Place a slice of egg in each cup. Garnish with a lemon wedge, or a tsp of horseradish, and sprinkle with chopped chives.

Note: This is a delicious warm-weather soup. It may be more highly seasoned than a hot soup, but watch the salt content. If prepared in advance, saltiness is intensified.

JELLIED MADRILENE CONSOMMÉ

Makes 8 servings.

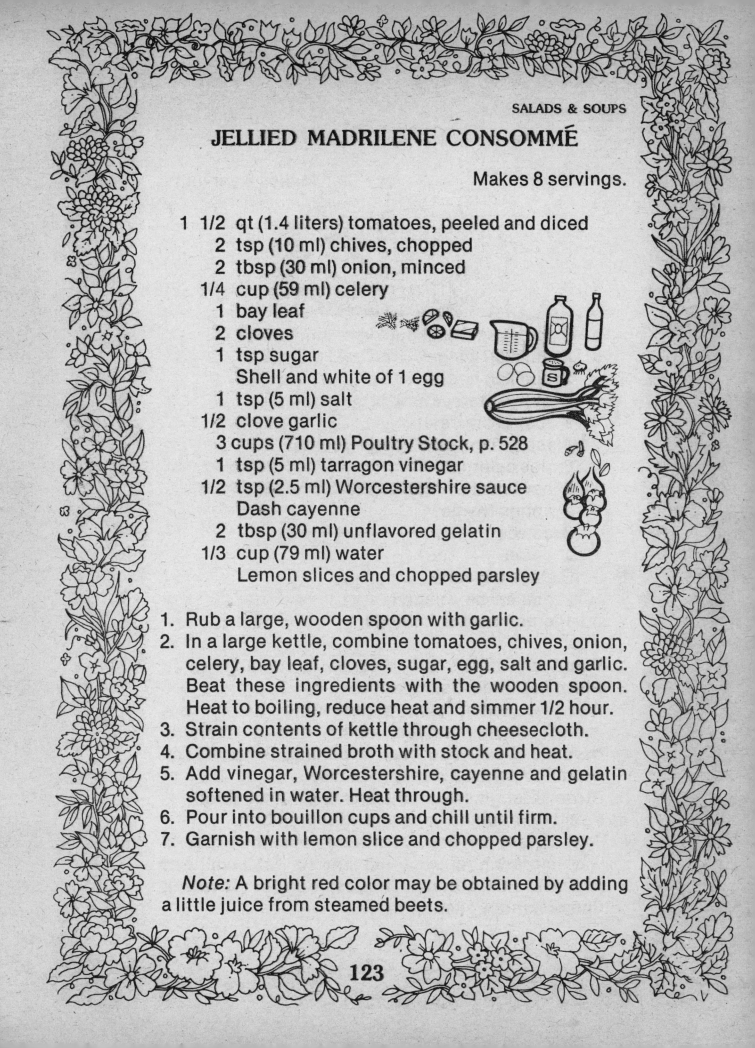

1 1/2 qt (1.4 liters) tomatoes, peeled and diced
    2 tsp (10 ml) chives, chopped
    2 tbsp (30 ml) onion, minced
  1/4 cup (59 ml) celery
    1 bay leaf
    2 cloves
    1 tsp sugar
       Shell and white of 1 egg
    1 tsp (5 ml) salt
  1/2 clove garlic
    3 cups (710 ml) Poultry Stock, p. 528
    1 tsp (5 ml) tarragon vinegar
  1/2 tsp (2.5 ml) Worcestershire sauce
       Dash cayenne
    2 tbsp (30 ml) unflavored gelatin
  1/3 cup (79 ml) water
       Lemon slices and chopped parsley

1. Rub a large, wooden spoon with garlic.
2. In a large kettle, combine tomatoes, chives, onion, celery, bay leaf, cloves, sugar, egg, salt and garlic. Beat these ingredients with the wooden spoon. Heat to boiling, reduce heat and simmer 1/2 hour.
3. Strain contents of kettle through cheesecloth.
4. Combine strained broth with stock and heat.
5. Add vinegar, Worcestershire, cayenne and gelatin softened in water. Heat through.
6. Pour into bouillon cups and chill until firm.
7. Garnish with lemon slice and chopped parsley.

Note: A bright red color may be obtained by adding a little juice from steamed beets.

JELLIED VEAL CONSOMMÉ

Makes 8 servings.

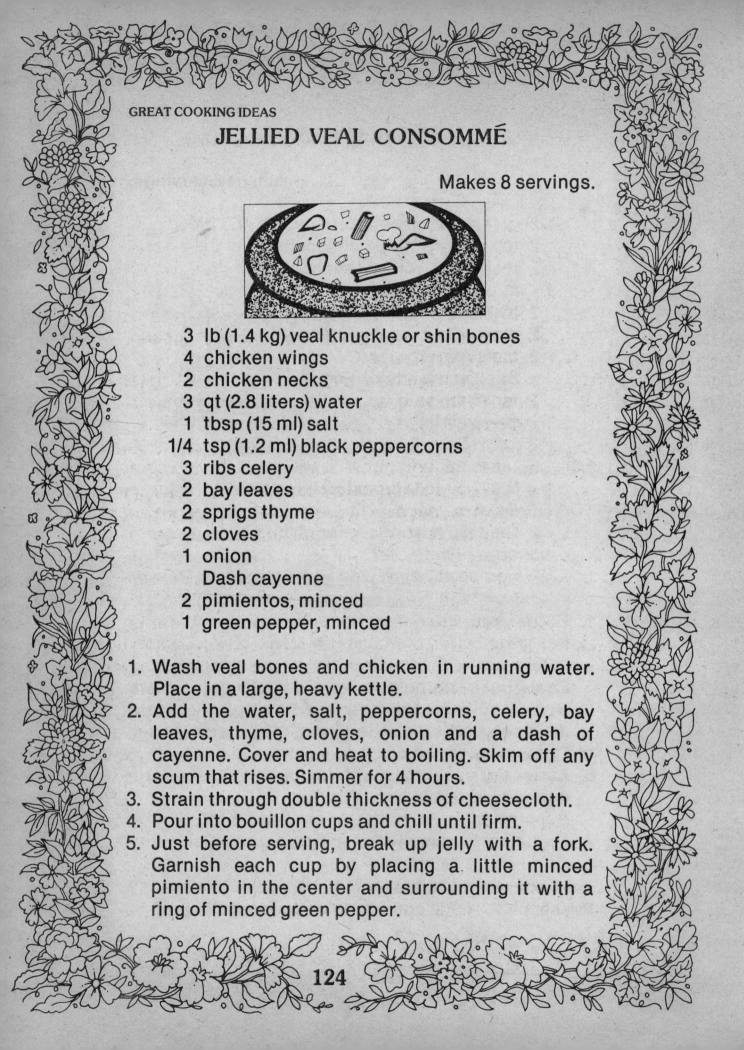

- 3 lb (1.4 kg) veal knuckle or shin bones
- 4 chicken wings
- 2 chicken necks
- 3 qt (2.8 liters) water
- 1 tbsp (15 ml) salt
- 1/4 tsp (1.2 ml) black peppercorns
- 3 ribs celery
- 2 bay leaves
- 2 sprigs thyme
- 2 cloves
- 1 onion
  Dash cayenne
- 2 pimientos, minced
- 1 green pepper, minced

1. Wash veal bones and chicken in running water. Place in a large, heavy kettle.
2. Add the water, salt, peppercorns, celery, bay leaves, thyme, cloves, onion and a dash of cayenne. Cover and heat to boiling. Skim off any scum that rises. Simmer for 4 hours.
3. Strain through double thickness of cheesecloth.
4. Pour into bouillon cups and chill until firm.
5. Just before serving, break up jelly with a fork. Garnish each cup by placing a little minced pimiento in the center and surrounding it with a ring of minced green pepper.

DUTCH CHERRY

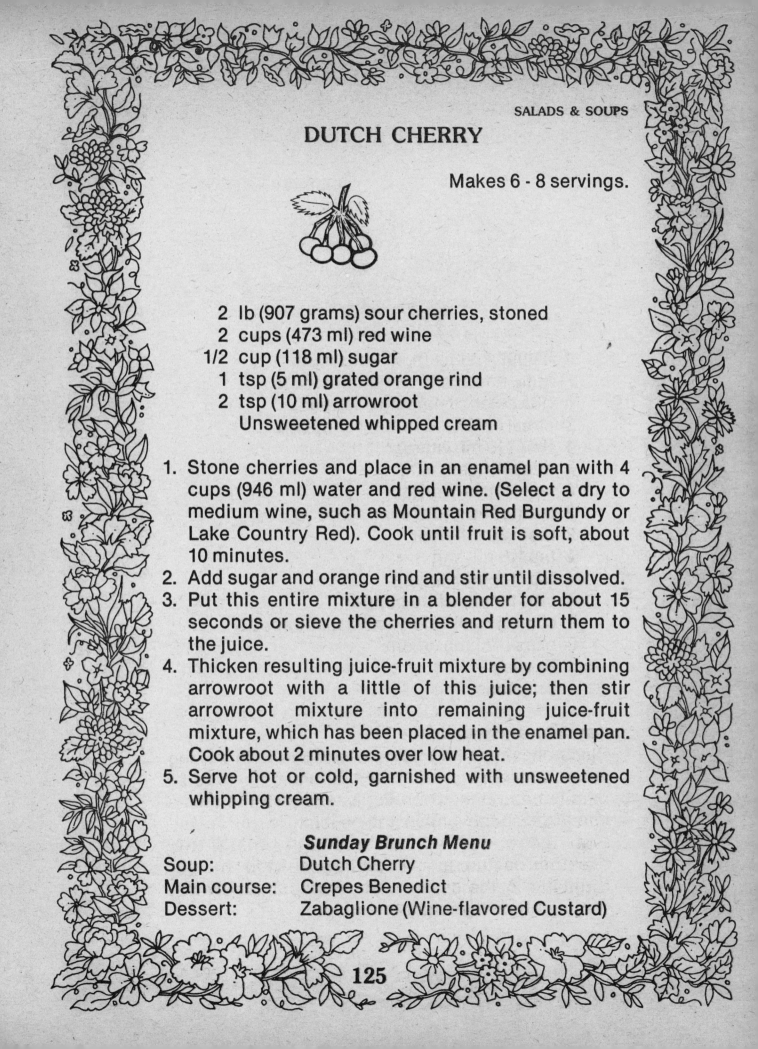

Makes 6 - 8 servings.

2 lb (907 grams) sour cherries, stoned
2 cups (473 ml) red wine
1/2 cup (118 ml) sugar
1 tsp (5 ml) grated orange rind
2 tsp (10 ml) arrowroot
Unsweetened whipped cream

1. Stone cherries and place in an enamel pan with 4 cups (946 ml) water and red wine. (Select a dry to medium wine, such as Mountain Red Burgundy or Lake Country Red). Cook until fruit is soft, about 10 minutes.
2. Add sugar and orange rind and stir until dissolved.
3. Put this entire mixture in a blender for about 15 seconds or sieve the cherries and return them to the juice.
4. Thicken resulting juice-fruit mixture by combining arrowroot with a little of this juice; then stir arrowroot mixture into remaining juice-fruit mixture, which has been placed in the enamel pan. Cook about 2 minutes over low heat.
5. Serve hot or cold, garnished with unsweetened whipping cream.

Sunday Brunch Menu

Soup: Dutch Cherry
Main course: Crepes Benedict
Dessert: Zabaglione (Wine-flavored Custard)

HEARTY CHESTNUT

Makes 6 - 8 servings.

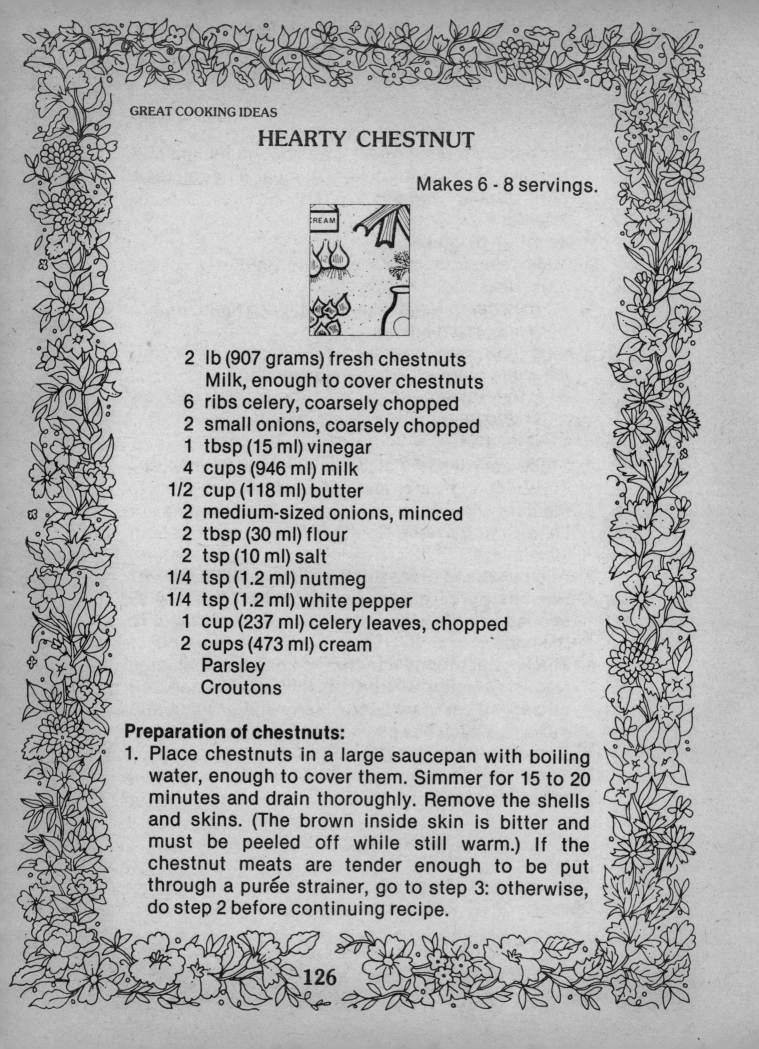

- 2 lb (907 grams) fresh chestnuts
  Milk, enough to cover chestnuts
- 6 ribs celery, coarsely chopped
- 2 small onions, coarsely chopped
- 1 tbsp (15 ml) vinegar
- 4 cups (946 ml) milk
- 1/2 cup (118 ml) butter
- 2 medium-sized onions, minced
- 2 tbsp (30 ml) flour
- 2 tsp (10 ml) salt
- 1/4 tsp (1.2 ml) nutmeg
- 1/4 tsp (1.2 ml) white pepper
- 1 cup (237 ml) celery leaves, chopped
- 2 cups (473 ml) cream
  Parsley
  Croutons

Preparation of chestnuts:

1. Place chestnuts in a large saucepan with boiling water, enough to cover them. Simmer for 15 to 20 minutes and drain thoroughly. Remove the shells and skins. (The brown inside skin is bitter and must be peeled off while still warm.) If the chestnut meats are tender enough to be put through a purée strainer, go to step 3: otherwise, do step 2 before continuing recipe.

2. Drop the chestnut meats into enough boiling milk to cover them. Add ribs of celery and onion. Cook until tender enough to put through a purée strainer.

Preparation of soup:

3. Mash chestnut meats and add gradually 4 cups milk. Beat until smooth.
4. Melt butter in large, heavy kettle and sauté onions until soft and golden.
5. Add flour, salt, nutmeg, white pepper and celery leaves to onions. Stir until combined.
6. Stir the chestnut-milk mixture slowly into the onion mixture. Simmer about 10 minutes.
7. Pour in cream and heat through, but do *not* boil.
8. Serve hot, garnished with chopped parsley and croutons.

Suggested Menu

Soup:	Hearty Chestnut
Main course:	Sliced Sirloin with Mushroom Sauce
Salad:	Fresh Mixed Greens with Garlic Dressing
Wine:	Cabernet Sauvignon; red Burgundy
Dessert:	COCONUT CREAM PIE, pp. 462, 463 Espresso or Regular Coffee

NOTES

FRESH FRUIT

Makes 6 servings.

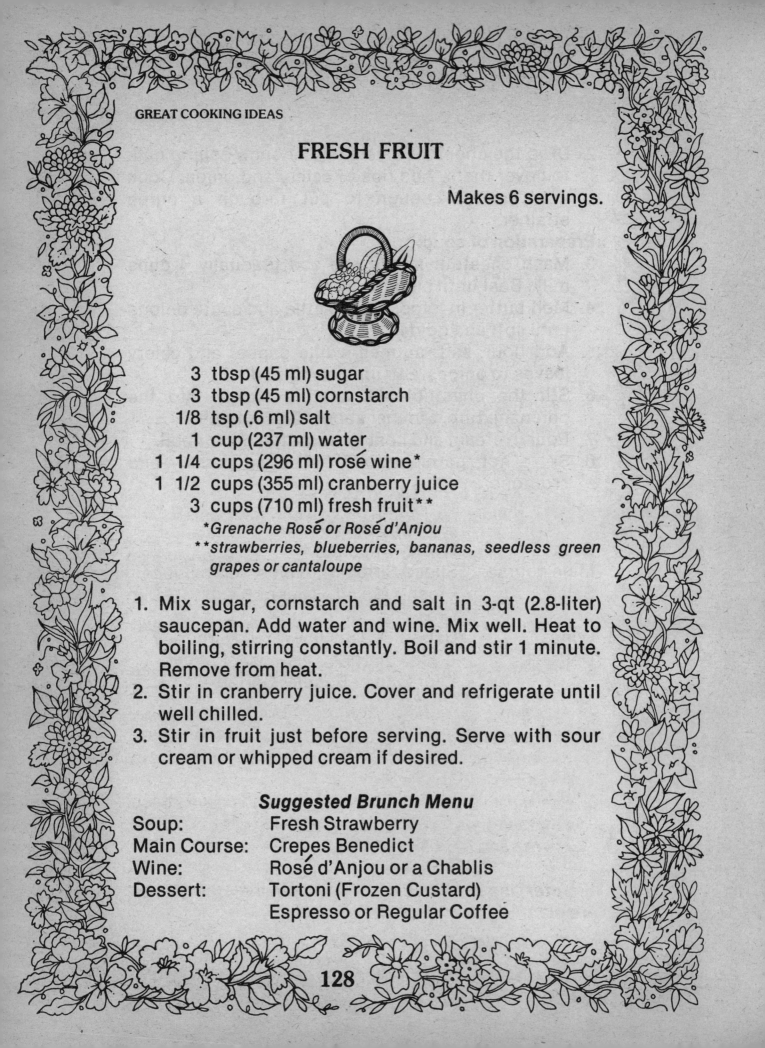

        3   tbsp (45 ml) sugar
        3   tbsp (45 ml) cornstarch
      1/8   tsp (.6 ml) salt
        1   cup (237 ml) water
    1 1/4   cups (296 ml) rosé wine*
    1 1/2   cups (355 ml) cranberry juice
        3   cups (710 ml) fresh fruit**

   *Grenache Rosé or Rosé d'Anjou
   **strawberries, blueberries, bananas, seedless green grapes or cantaloupe

1. Mix sugar, cornstarch and salt in 3-qt (2.8-liter) saucepan. Add water and wine. Mix well. Heat to boiling, stirring constantly. Boil and stir 1 minute. Remove from heat.
2. Stir in cranberry juice. Cover and refrigerate until well chilled.
3. Stir in fruit just before serving. Serve with sour cream or whipped cream if desired.

Suggested Brunch Menu

Soup: Fresh Strawberry
Main Course: Crepes Benedict
Wine: Rosé d'Anjou or a Chablis
Dessert: Tortoni (Frozen Custard)
                 Espresso or Regular Coffee

BEEF KIDNEY STEW

Makes 4 servings.

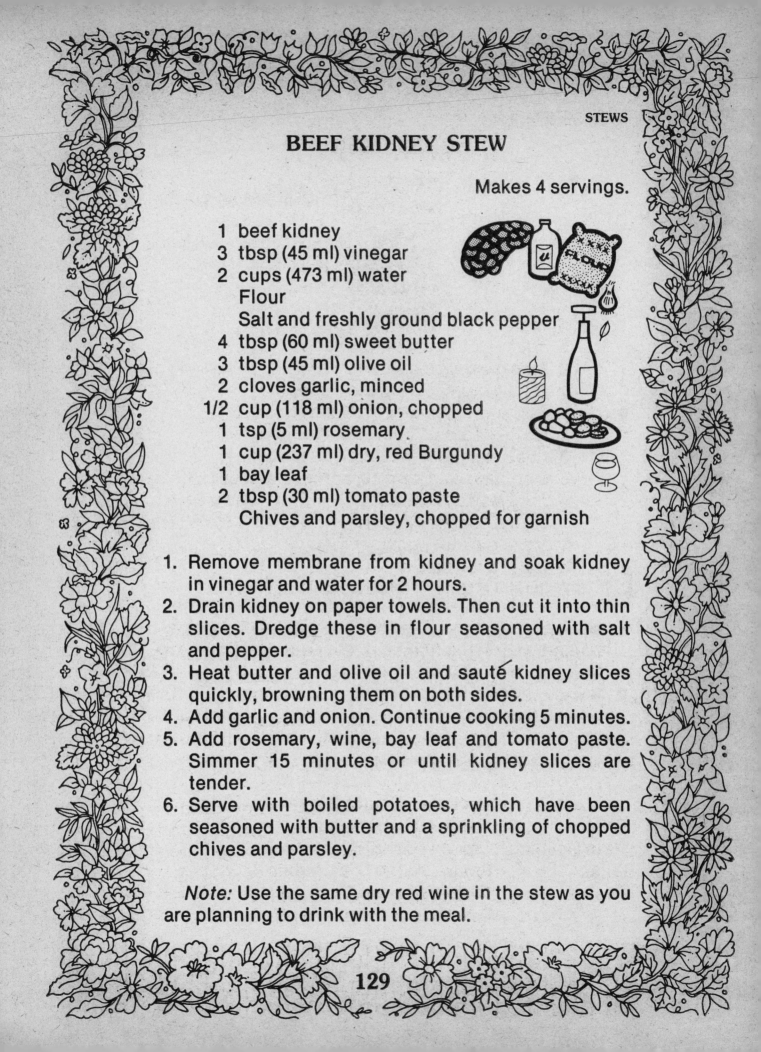

- 1 beef kidney
- 3 tbsp (45 ml) vinegar
- 2 cups (473 ml) water
- Flour
- Salt and freshly ground black pepper
- 4 tbsp (60 ml) sweet butter
- 3 tbsp (45 ml) olive oil
- 2 cloves garlic, minced
- 1/2 cup (118 ml) onion, chopped
- 1 tsp (5 ml) rosemary
- 1 cup (237 ml) dry, red Burgundy
- 1 bay leaf
- 2 tbsp (30 ml) tomato paste
- Chives and parsley, chopped for garnish

1. Remove membrane from kidney and soak kidney in vinegar and water for 2 hours.
2. Drain kidney on paper towels. Then cut it into thin slices. Dredge these in flour seasoned with salt and pepper.
3. Heat butter and olive oil and sauté kidney slices quickly, browning them on both sides.
4. Add garlic and onion. Continue cooking 5 minutes.
5. Add rosemary, wine, bay leaf and tomato paste. Simmer 15 minutes or until kidney slices are tender.
6. Serve with boiled potatoes, which have been seasoned with butter and a sprinkling of chopped chives and parsley.

Note: Use the same dry red wine in the stew as you are planning to drink with the meal.

BEEF STEW

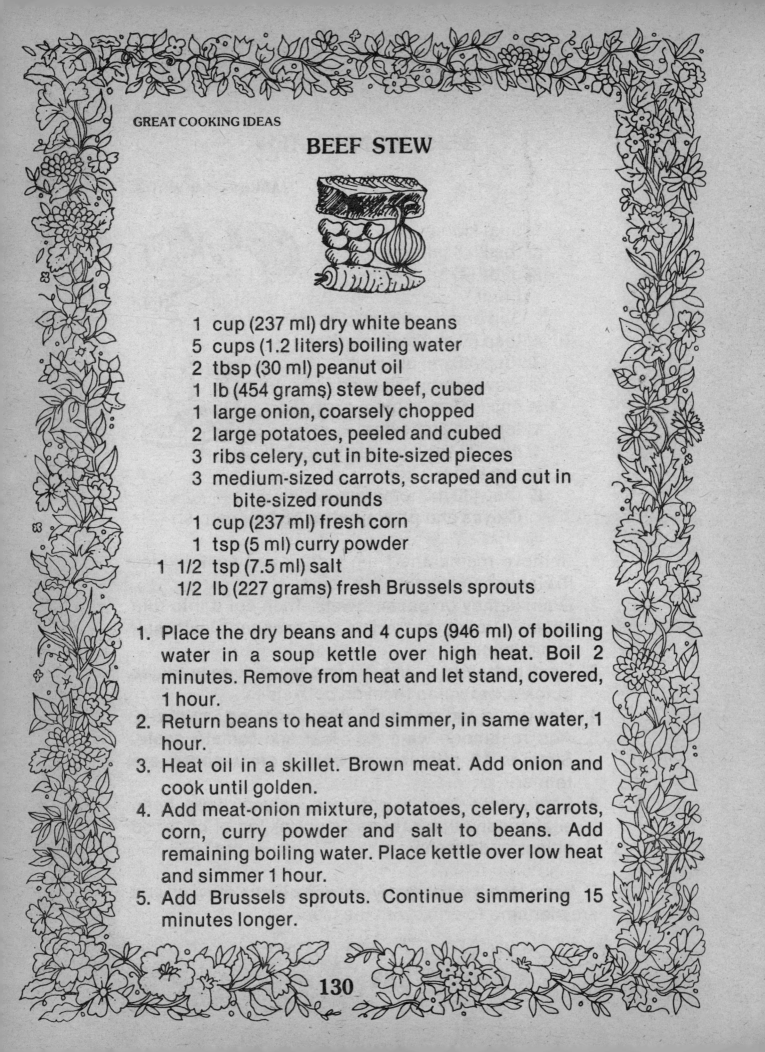

1 cup (237 ml) dry white beans
5 cups (1.2 liters) boiling water
2 tbsp (30 ml) peanut oil
1 lb (454 grams) stew beef, cubed
1 large onion, coarsely chopped
2 large potatoes, peeled and cubed
3 ribs celery, cut in bite-sized pieces
3 medium-sized carrots, scraped and cut in
    bite-sized rounds
1 cup (237 ml) fresh corn
1 tsp (5 ml) curry powder
1 1/2 tsp (7.5 ml) salt
1/2 lb (227 grams) fresh Brussels sprouts

1. Place the dry beans and 4 cups (946 ml) of boiling water in a soup kettle over high heat. Boil 2 minutes. Remove from heat and let stand, covered, 1 hour.
2. Return beans to heat and simmer, in same water, 1 hour.
3. Heat oil in a skillet. Brown meat. Add onion and cook until golden.
4. Add meat-onion mixture, potatoes, celery, carrots, corn, curry powder and salt to beans. Add remaining boiling water. Place kettle over low heat and simmer 1 hour.
5. Add Brussels sprouts. Continue simmering 15 minutes longer.

BELGIAN BEER BEEF

Makes 6 servings.

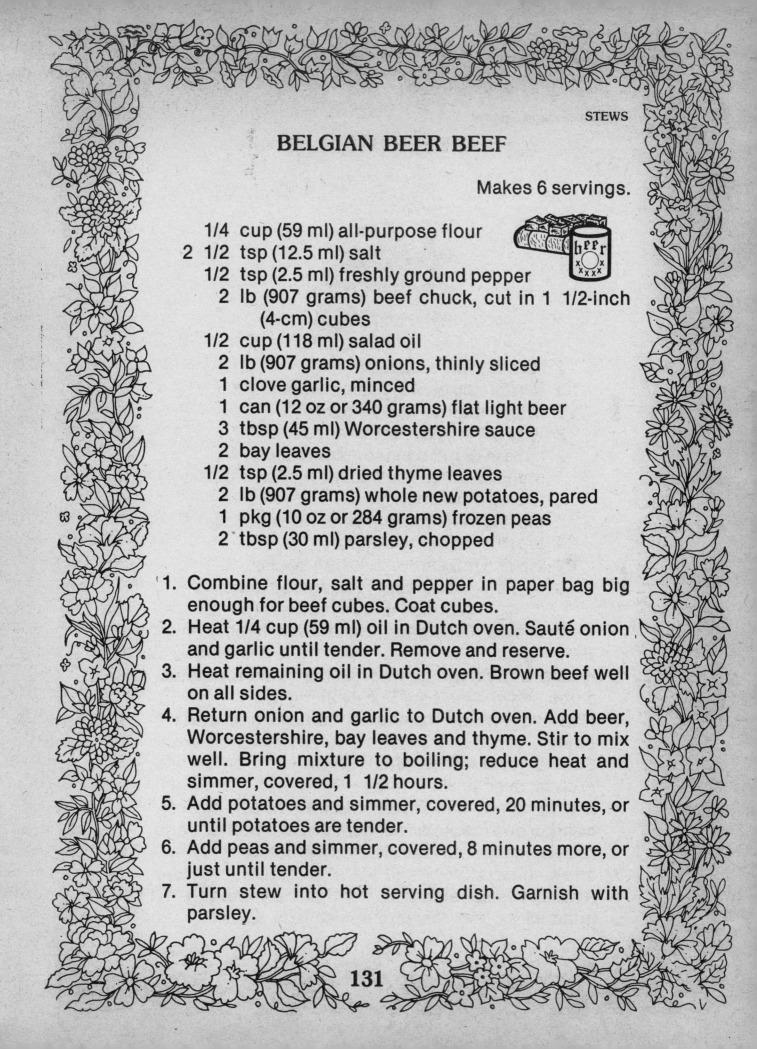

1/4 cup (59 ml) all-purpose flour
2 1/2 tsp (12.5 ml) salt
1/2 tsp (2.5 ml) freshly ground pepper
2 lb (907 grams) beef chuck, cut in 1 1/2-inch (4-cm) cubes
1/2 cup (118 ml) salad oil
2 lb (907 grams) onions, thinly sliced
1 clove garlic, minced
1 can (12 oz or 340 grams) flat light beer
3 tbsp (45 ml) Worcestershire sauce
2 bay leaves
1/2 tsp (2.5 ml) dried thyme leaves
2 lb (907 grams) whole new potatoes, pared
1 pkg (10 oz or 284 grams) frozen peas
2 tbsp (30 ml) parsley, chopped

1. Combine flour, salt and pepper in paper bag big enough for beef cubes. Coat cubes.
2. Heat 1/4 cup (59 ml) oil in Dutch oven. Sauté onion and garlic until tender. Remove and reserve.
3. Heat remaining oil in Dutch oven. Brown beef well on all sides.
4. Return onion and garlic to Dutch oven. Add beer, Worcestershire, bay leaves and thyme. Stir to mix well. Bring mixture to boiling; reduce heat and simmer, covered, 1 1/2 hours.
5. Add potatoes and simmer, covered, 20 minutes, or until potatoes are tender.
6. Add peas and simmer, covered, 8 minutes more, or just until tender.
7. Turn stew into hot serving dish. Garnish with parsley.

GROUND BEEF GOULASH

Makes 6 servings.

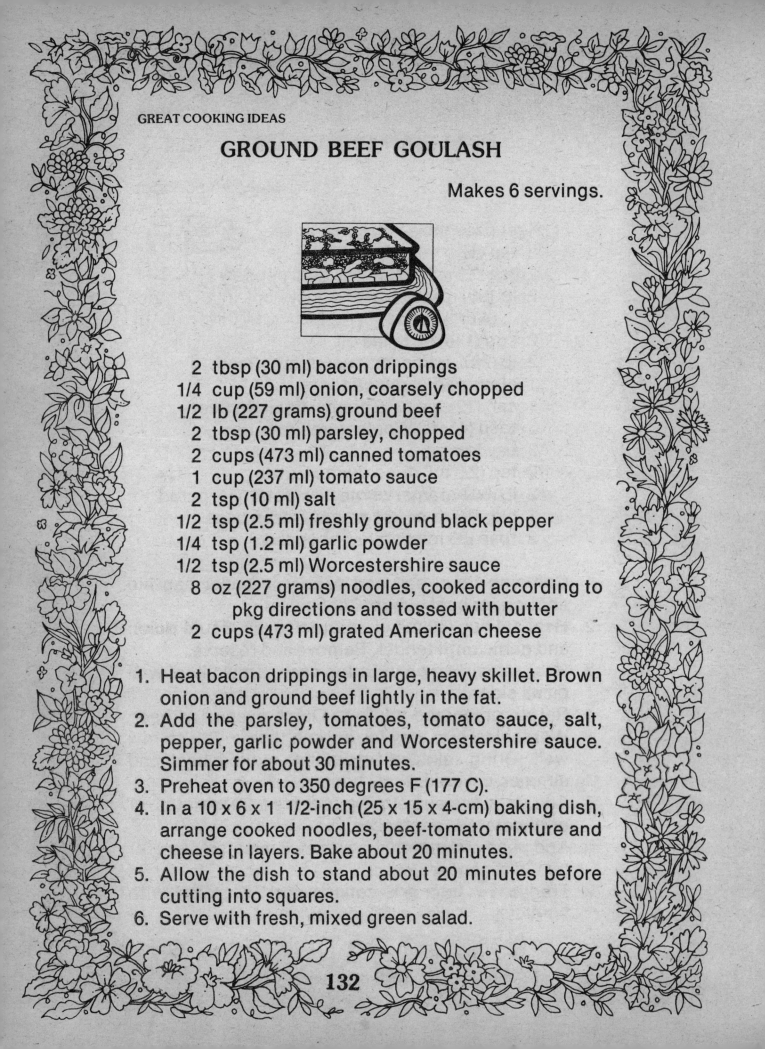

2 tbsp (30 ml) bacon drippings
1/4 cup (59 ml) onion, coarsely chopped
1/2 lb (227 grams) ground beef
2 tbsp (30 ml) parsley, chopped
2 cups (473 ml) canned tomatoes
1 cup (237 ml) tomato sauce
2 tsp (10 ml) salt
1/2 tsp (2.5 ml) freshly ground black pepper
1/4 tsp (1.2 ml) garlic powder
1/2 tsp (2.5 ml) Worcestershire sauce
8 oz (227 grams) noodles, cooked according to
   pkg directions and tossed with butter
2 cups (473 ml) grated American cheese

1. Heat bacon drippings in large, heavy skillet. Brown onion and ground beef lightly in the fat.
2. Add the parsley, tomatoes, tomato sauce, salt, pepper, garlic powder and Worcestershire sauce. Simmer for about 30 minutes.
3. Preheat oven to 350 degrees F (177 C).
4. In a 10 x 6 x 1 1/2-inch (25 x 15 x 4-cm) baking dish, arrange cooked noodles, beef-tomato mixture and cheese in layers. Bake about 20 minutes.
5. Allow the dish to stand about 20 minutes before cutting into squares.
6. Serve with fresh, mixed green salad.

HUNGARIAN GOULASH

Makes 4 - 6 servings.

3 lb (1.4 kg) top round, cut in 2-inch (5-cm) cubes
3 tbsp (45 ml) flour
1 tsp (5 ml) salt
1 tsp (5 ml) freshly ground black pepper
2 tsp (10 ml) paprika
4 tbsp (60 ml) butter
1 1/2 cups (355 ml) onions, chopped
1 green pepper, diced
1 cup (237 ml) tomato purée
1 cup (237 ml) Brown Stock, p. 526

1. Preheat oven to 350 degrees F (177 C).
2. Place flour, salt, pepper and paprika in a paper bag. Add meat cubes and shake thoroughly to coat cubes evenly with the flour mixture.
3. Heat butter in a large, heavy Dutch oven and brown meat cubes on all sides.
4. Add onions and green pepper. Sauté until onions are translucent.
5. Add tomato purée and stock. Cover and bake 2 or 3 hours or until meat is tender and flavorings are well blended.

Menu Suggestions

Main Course: Hungarian Goulash over buttered noodles or boiled new potatoes
Vegetables: Braised celery or cooked broccoli
Dessert: Apple Crisp with sweet sour cream; or Applesauce Cake
Beverages: Beer or Burgundy with the goulash Coffee with dessert

ITALIAN BEEF STEW

Makes 4 - 6 servings.

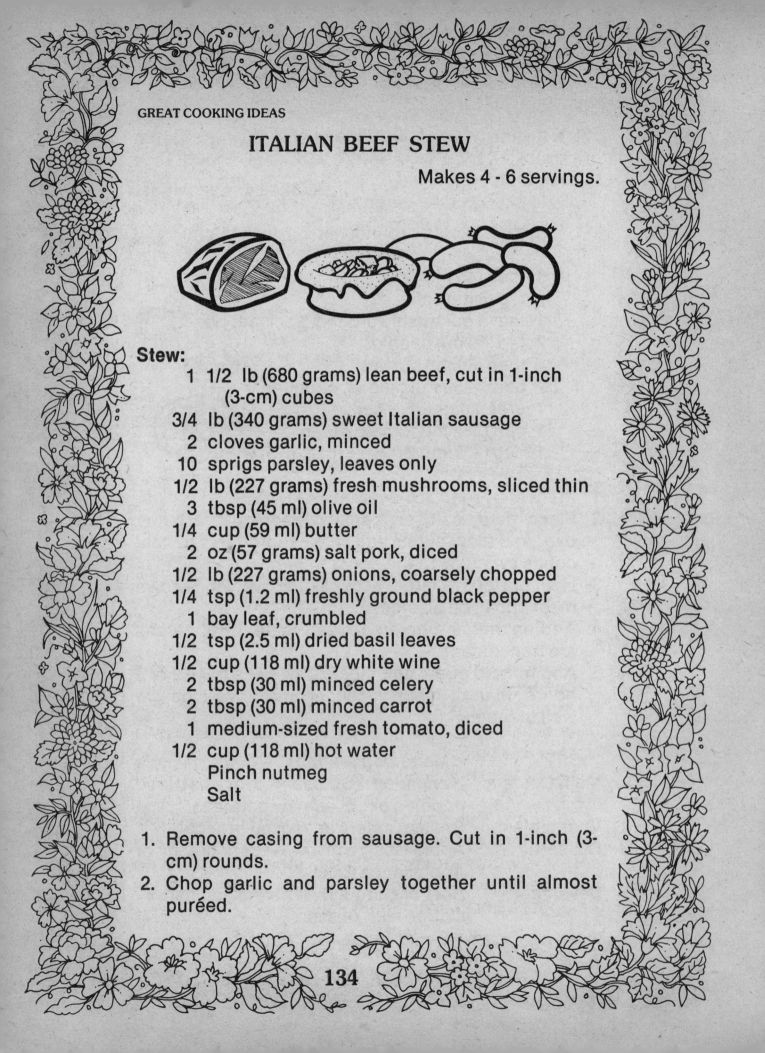

Stew:

- 1 1/2 lb (680 grams) lean beef, cut in 1-inch (3-cm) cubes
- 3/4 lb (340 grams) sweet Italian sausage
- 2 cloves garlic, minced
- 10 sprigs parsley, leaves only
- 1/2 lb (227 grams) fresh mushrooms, sliced thin
- 3 tbsp (45 ml) olive oil
- 1/4 cup (59 ml) butter
- 2 oz (57 grams) salt pork, diced
- 1/2 lb (227 grams) onions, coarsely chopped
- 1/4 tsp (1.2 ml) freshly ground black pepper
- 1 bay leaf, crumbled
- 1/2 tsp (2.5 ml) dried basil leaves
- 1/2 cup (118 ml) dry white wine
- 2 tbsp (30 ml) minced celery
- 2 tbsp (30 ml) minced carrot
- 1 medium-sized fresh tomato, diced
- 1/2 cup (118 ml) hot water
  Pinch nutmeg
  Salt

1. Remove casing from sausage. Cut in 1-inch (3-cm) rounds.
2. Chop garlic and parsley together until almost puréed.

3. Heat the olive oil, butter and salt pork in a Dutch oven. Add the onions and sauté slowly until they are lightly browned.
4. Add beef and sausage and cook for 10 minutes, stirring occasionally.
5. Add garlic and parsley, pepper and bay leaf. Stir and cook for 10 minutes.
6. Add wine. Stir. Simmer, covered, 10 minutes.
7. Add celery, carrot, tomatoes and mushrooms. Stir and cook for 10 minutes longer.
8. Add hot water, stir, cover and simmer for 40 minutes.
9. Sprinkle a little nutmeg over top of stew. Simmer, uncovered, an additional 10 minutes, or until meat is tender.
10. Taste for salt and add, if needed.

Polenta:

    1 cup (237 ml) yellow cornmeal
    1 cup (237 ml) cold water
    1 tsp (5 ml) salt
    2 tbsp (30 ml) butter
  3/4 cup (177 ml) melted butter
  3/4 cup (177 ml) grated Parmesan cheese

1. Bring 4 cups (946 ml) of water to boiling in a saucepan.
2. In a mixing bowl, combine cornmeal, cold water and salt. Stir into boiling water. Stir constantly over low heat for about 15 minutes.
3. Add 2 tbsp butter and stir.

To serve: Put Polenta in large, shallow individual serving bowls. Pour melted butter over Polenta and sprinkle with Parmesan. Spoon stew and gravy on top. Serve with a light, dry red wine, such as Valpolicella or Gamay Beaujolais.

JUST PLAIN STEW

Makes 4 - 6 servings.

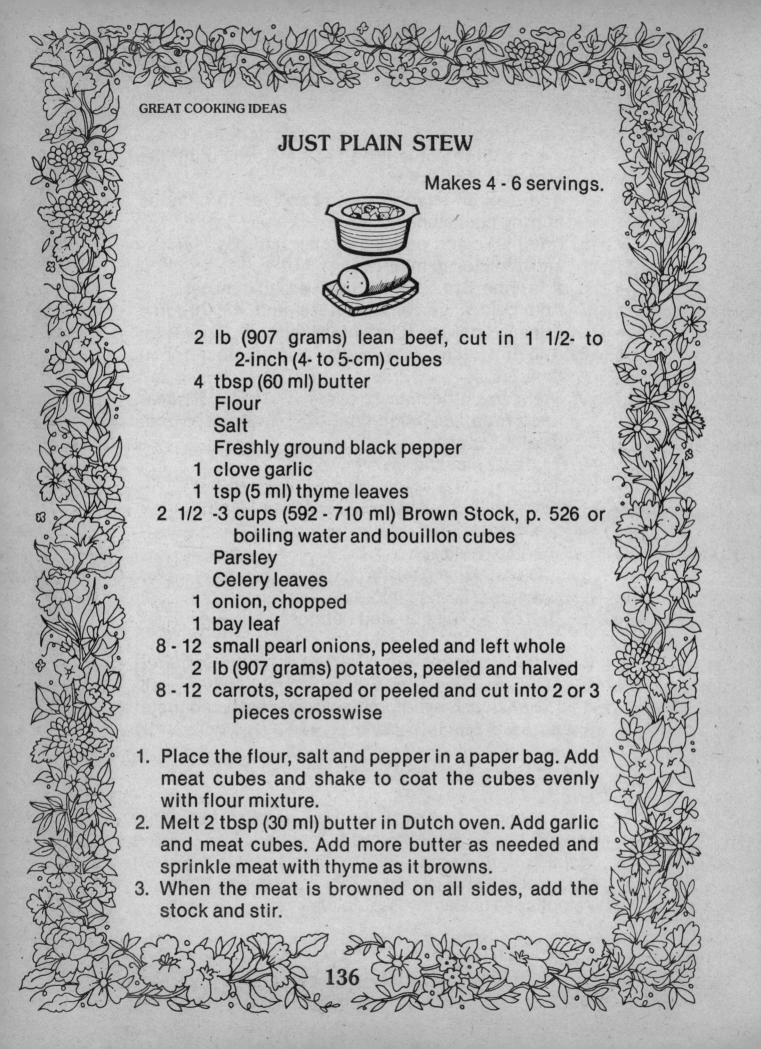

2 lb (907 grams) lean beef, cut in 1 1/2- to 2-inch (4- to 5-cm) cubes
4 tbsp (60 ml) butter
Flour
Salt
Freshly ground black pepper
1 clove garlic
1 tsp (5 ml) thyme leaves
2 1/2 -3 cups (592 - 710 ml) Brown Stock, p. 526 or boiling water and bouillon cubes
Parsley
Celery leaves
1 onion, chopped
1 bay leaf
8 - 12 small pearl onions, peeled and left whole
2 lb (907 grams) potatoes, peeled and halved
8 - 12 carrots, scraped or peeled and cut into 2 or 3 pieces crosswise

1. Place the flour, salt and pepper in a paper bag. Add meat cubes and shake to coat the cubes evenly with flour mixture.
2. Melt 2 tbsp (30 ml) butter in Dutch oven. Add garlic and meat cubes. Add more butter as needed and sprinkle meat with thyme as it browns.
3. When the meat is browned on all sides, add the stock and stir.

4. Add a few sprigs of parsley, a few celery leaves, onion and bay leaf. Stir to combine ingredients. Bring to boiling, cover tightly and reduce heat to simmer. Cook gently 1 1/2 to 2 hours, or until meat is tender.
5. When meat is about half done, add pearl onions, potatoes and carrots.
6. When stew is done, thicken sauce, if desired, with 2 tbsp (30 ml) cornstarch dissolved in 1/4 cup (59 ml) water.

Variations: 1) Omit pearl onions, potatoes and carrots. Serve plain beef stew over rice, noodles or mashed potatoes.

2) Almost any vegetables you like can be added to the basic recipe. Other suggestions include: stalks of celery cut in 3 or 4 pieces, green beans, or frozen green peas (add peas during last 15 minutes of cooking.)

3) Use ingredients on above as far as "stock", except substitute basil for thyme. Add 1 chopped green pepper and 2 chopped onions when browning meat (Step 2). Halfway through cooking, add 3 or 4 fresh tomatoes, peeled, seeded and chopped. Serve with rice, mixed with chopped pimiento and garnished with chopped parsley.

NOTES

KENTUCKY BURGOO

Makes 10 - 12 servings.

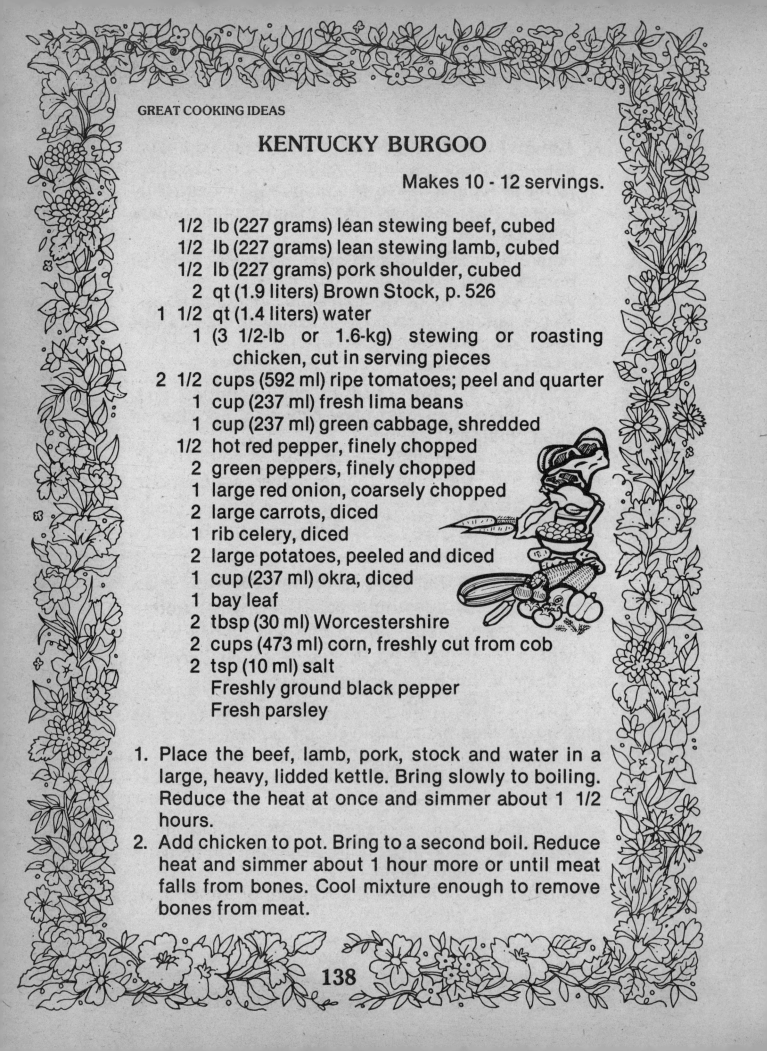

- 1/2 lb (227 grams) lean stewing beef, cubed
- 1/2 lb (227 grams) lean stewing lamb, cubed
- 1/2 lb (227 grams) pork shoulder, cubed
- 2 qt (1.9 liters) Brown Stock, p. 526
- 1 1/2 qt (1.4 liters) water
- 1 (3 1/2-lb or 1.6-kg) stewing or roasting chicken, cut in serving pieces
- 2 1/2 cups (592 ml) ripe tomatoes; peel and quarter
- 1 cup (237 ml) fresh lima beans
- 1 cup (237 ml) green cabbage, shredded
- 1/2 hot red pepper, finely chopped
- 2 green peppers, finely chopped
- 1 large red onion, coarsely chopped
- 2 large carrots, diced
- 1 rib celery, diced
- 2 large potatoes, peeled and diced
- 1 cup (237 ml) okra, diced
- 1 bay leaf
- 2 tbsp (30 ml) Worcestershire
- 2 cups (473 ml) corn, freshly cut from cob
- 2 tsp (10 ml) salt
  Freshly ground black pepper
  Fresh parsley

1. Place the beef, lamb, pork, stock and water in a large, heavy, lidded kettle. Bring slowly to boiling. Reduce the heat at once and simmer about 1 1/2 hours.
2. Add chicken to pot. Bring to a second boil. Reduce heat and simmer about 1 hour more or until meat falls from bones. Cool mixture enough to remove bones from meat.

3. Return meat to kettle. Add tomatoes, lima beans, cabbage, peppers, onion, carrots, celery, potatoes, okra, bay leaf and Worcestershire. Stir frequently as stew thickens. Simmer 45 minutes or more over very low heat.
4. Add fresh corn and simmer about 15 minutes longer, or until all vegetables are soft.
5. Add salt and freshly ground black pepper to taste.
6. Serve piping hot in deep bowls with squares of corn bread (see recipe below).

Corn Bread for Burgoo:

    3/4 cup (177 ml) all-purpose flour, sifted
    2 1/2 tsp (12.5 ml) baking powder
    1 tbsp (15 ml) sugar
    3/4 tsp (3.7 ml) salt
    1 1/4 cups (296 ml) yellow cornmeal
    1 egg
    2 1/2 tbsp (22.5 ml) bacon drippings
    1 cup (237 ml) milk

1. Preheat oven to 425 degrees F (218 C).
2. Sift flour, baking powder, sugar and salt together into a mixing bowl. Add cornmeal.
3. Beat egg is a separate bowl. Add bacon drippings and milk and beat thoroughly.
4. Add the egg mixture to flour mixture. Combine with a few rapid strokes. Place the batter in a 9 x 9 x 2-inch (23 x 23 x 5-cm) baking pan. Bake for 20 to 25 minutes.

Menu Suggestion

Main Course: Kentucky Burgoo with Corn Muffins
Dessert: Lemon Sponge Cake with Homemade Ice Cream
Beverages: Beer and Lemonade or other fruit drink

MEATBALL STEW

Makes 6 servings.

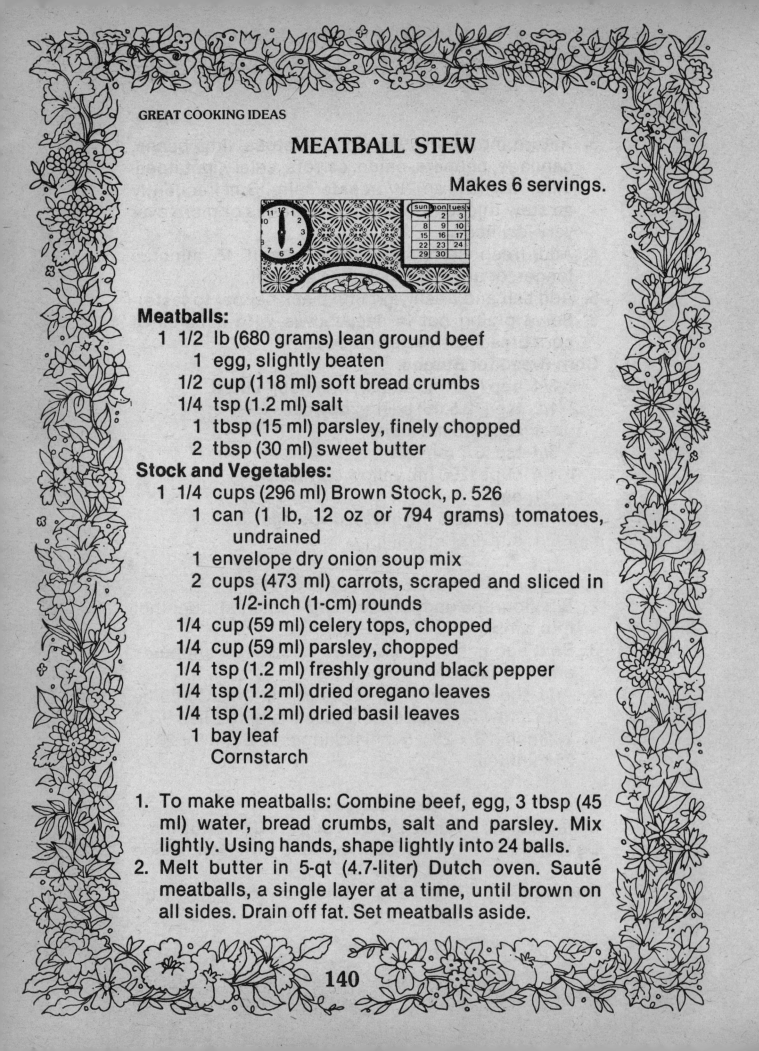

Meatballs:
- 1 1/2 lb (680 grams) lean ground beef
- 1 egg, slightly beaten
- 1/2 cup (118 ml) soft bread crumbs
- 1/4 tsp (1.2 ml) salt
- 1 tbsp (15 ml) parsley, finely chopped
- 2 tbsp (30 ml) sweet butter

Stock and Vegetables:
- 1 1/4 cups (296 ml) Brown Stock, p. 526
- 1 can (1 lb, 12 oz or 794 grams) tomatoes, undrained
- 1 envelope dry onion soup mix
- 2 cups (473 ml) carrots, scraped and sliced in 1/2-inch (1-cm) rounds
- 1/4 cup (59 ml) celery tops, chopped
- 1/4 cup (59 ml) parsley, chopped
- 1/4 tsp (1.2 ml) freshly ground black pepper
- 1/4 tsp (1.2 ml) dried oregano leaves
- 1/4 tsp (1.2 ml) dried basil leaves
- 1 bay leaf
- Cornstarch

1. To make meatballs: Combine beef, egg, 3 tbsp (45 ml) water, bread crumbs, salt and parsley. Mix lightly. Using hands, shape lightly into 24 balls.
2. Melt butter in 5-qt (4.7-liter) Dutch oven. Sauté meatballs, a single layer at a time, until brown on all sides. Drain off fat. Set meatballs aside.

3. In same Dutch oven, combine 2 cups (473 ml) water, stock, tomatoes, onion soup mix, carrots, celery tops, parsley, pepper, oregano, basil and bay leaf. Bring to boiling, then reduce heat to simmer. Cover. Stir occasionally to break up tomatoes. Cook 30 minutes.
4. Add meatballs and simmer 20 minutes longer.
5. To thicken: Mix 1 tbsp (15 ml) cornstarch with just enough cold water to make a thin liquid. Add this slowly to the contents of Dutch oven, stirring constantly. When sauce thickens, remove from heat.
6. Serve in tureen or individual bowls garnished with chopped parsley.

Serving Suggestions

Main Course: Meatball Stew over rice; or Stew with warm French bread
Salad: Fresh, mixed greens
Dessert: Fresh Fruit and Cheese
Beverages: Beer, coffee or tea

NOTES

MEAT BALL 'N' TOMATO STEW

Makes 8 servings.

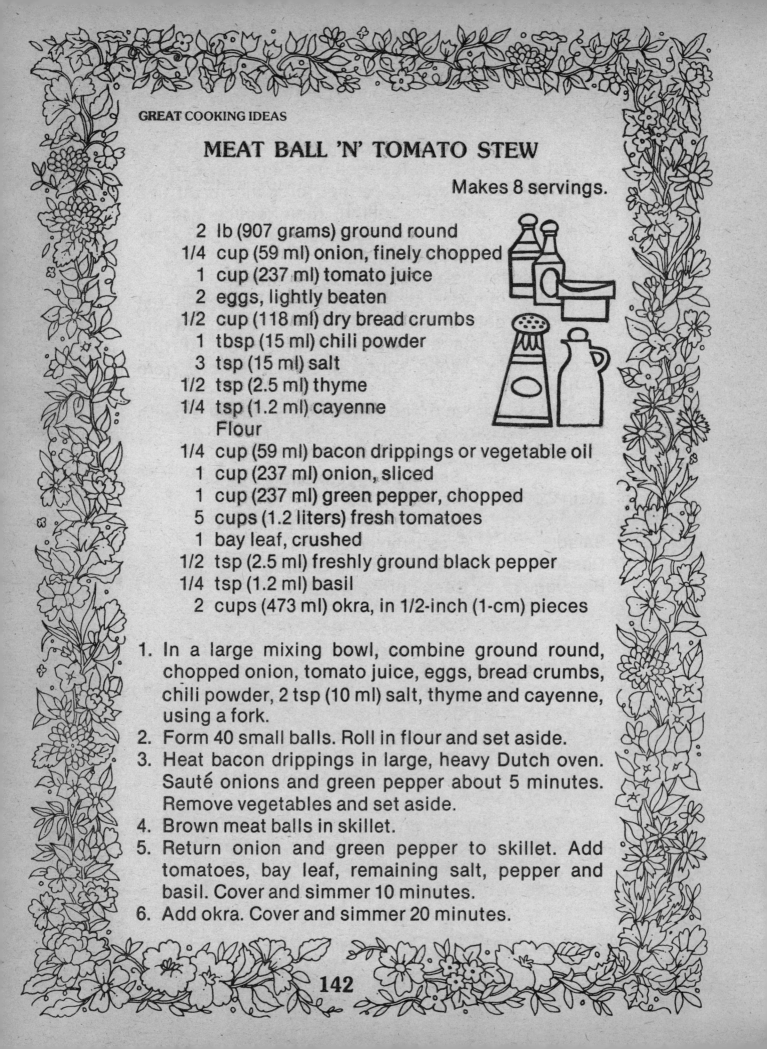

- 2 lb (907 grams) ground round
- 1/4 cup (59 ml) onion, finely chopped
- 1 cup (237 ml) tomato juice
- 2 eggs, lightly beaten
- 1/2 cup (118 ml) dry bread crumbs
- 1 tbsp (15 ml) chili powder
- 3 tsp (15 ml) salt
- 1/2 tsp (2.5 ml) thyme
- 1/4 tsp (1.2 ml) cayenne
- Flour
- 1/4 cup (59 ml) bacon drippings or vegetable oil
- 1 cup (237 ml) onion, sliced
- 1 cup (237 ml) green pepper, chopped
- 5 cups (1.2 liters) fresh tomatoes
- 1 bay leaf, crushed
- 1/2 tsp (2.5 ml) freshly ground black pepper
- 1/4 tsp (1.2 ml) basil
- 2 cups (473 ml) okra, in 1/2-inch (1-cm) pieces

1. In a large mixing bowl, combine ground round, chopped onion, tomato juice, eggs, bread crumbs, chili powder, 2 tsp (10 ml) salt, thyme and cayenne, using a fork.
2. Form 40 small balls. Roll in flour and set aside.
3. Heat bacon drippings in large, heavy Dutch oven. Sauté onions and green pepper about 5 minutes. Remove vegetables and set aside.
4. Brown meat balls in skillet.
5. Return onion and green pepper to skillet. Add tomatoes, bay leaf, remaining salt, pepper and basil. Cover and simmer 10 minutes.
6. Add okra. Cover and simmer 20 minutes.

MEATLOAF STEW

Makes 4 - 6 servings.

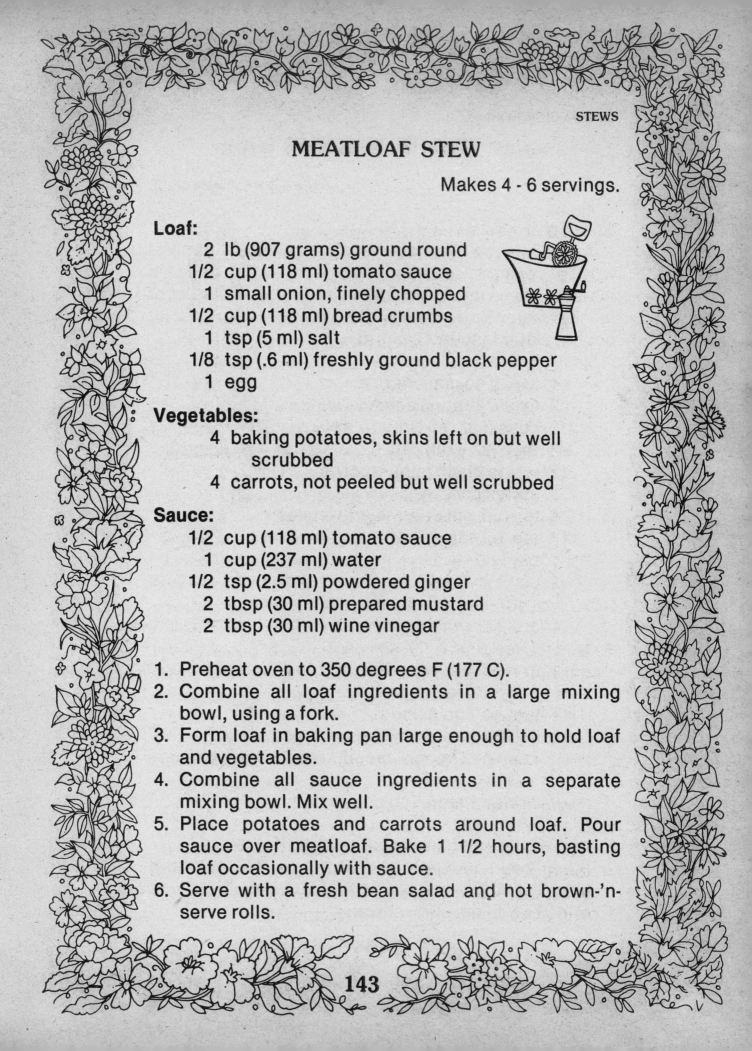

Loaf:

- 2 lb (907 grams) ground round
- 1/2 cup (118 ml) tomato sauce
- 1 small onion, finely chopped
- 1/2 cup (118 ml) bread crumbs
- 1 tsp (5 ml) salt
- 1/8 tsp (.6 ml) freshly ground black pepper
- 1 egg

Vegetables:

- 4 baking potatoes, skins left on but well scrubbed
- 4 carrots, not peeled but well scrubbed

Sauce:

- 1/2 cup (118 ml) tomato sauce
- 1 cup (237 ml) water
- 1/2 tsp (2.5 ml) powdered ginger
- 2 tbsp (30 ml) prepared mustard
- 2 tbsp (30 ml) wine vinegar

1. Preheat oven to 350 degrees F (177 C).
2. Combine all loaf ingredients in a large mixing bowl, using a fork.
3. Form loaf in baking pan large enough to hold loaf and vegetables.
4. Combine all sauce ingredients in a separate mixing bowl. Mix well.
5. Place potatoes and carrots around loaf. Pour sauce over meatloaf. Bake 1 1/2 hours, basting loaf occasionally with sauce.
6. Serve with a fresh bean salad and hot brown-'n-serve rolls.

PETITE MARMITE

Makes 8 - 10 servings.

About Marmites:

A marmite is a large earthenware or metal soup pot with a cover. It is taller than it is wide, and the material from which it is made adds a particular flavor to the soup. The pot should be "conditioned" by boiling water in it for 12 hours.

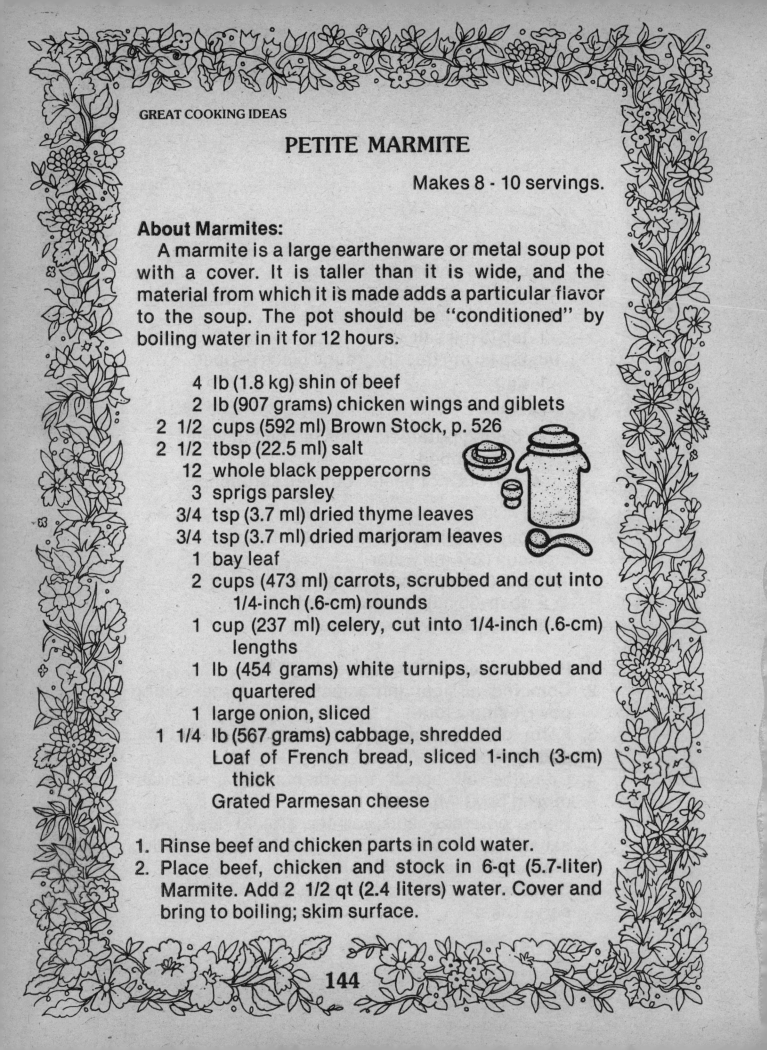

- 4 lb (1.8 kg) shin of beef
- 2 lb (907 grams) chicken wings and giblets
- 2 1/2 cups (592 ml) Brown Stock, p. 526
- 2 1/2 tbsp (22.5 ml) salt
- 12 whole black peppercorns
- 3 sprigs parsley
- 3/4 tsp (3.7 ml) dried thyme leaves
- 3/4 tsp (3.7 ml) dried marjoram leaves
- 1 bay leaf
- 2 cups (473 ml) carrots, scrubbed and cut into 1/4-inch (.6-cm) rounds
- 1 cup (237 ml) celery, cut into 1/4-inch (.6-cm) lengths
- 1 lb (454 grams) white turnips, scrubbed and quartered
- 1 large onion, sliced
- 1 1/4 lb (567 grams) cabbage, shredded
  Loaf of French bread, sliced 1-inch (3-cm) thick
  Grated Parmesan cheese

1. Rinse beef and chicken parts in cold water.
2. Place beef, chicken and stock in 6-qt (5.7-liter) Marmite. Add 2 1/2 qt (2.4 liters) water. Cover and bring to boiling; skim surface.

3. Add salt, peppercorns, parsley, thyme, marjoram and bay leaf. Cover kettle again, and simmer 2 1/2 hours, or just until meat is tender. Remove meat from soup; set aside.
4. Strain soup through coarse strainer. Pour back into Marmite. Discard chicken pieces and seasonings.
5. Add the carrot, leek, celery, turnips and onion. Simmer, covered, 1 1/2 hours.
6. Meanwhile, cut beef into large cubes; set aside.
7. Add cabbage. Cook, covered, 10 minutes, or just until cabbage is tender; skim off excess fat.
8. Sprinkle one side of each bread slice with cheese. Brown under broiler 1 minute, or until cheese is bubbly.

Serving Suggestion

Pour soup into individual hot bowls. Add a few pieces of meat to each one. Top with toasted bread slices. Serve hot. A glass of dry red Burgundy and a dessert of Brie (cheese) and fruit would compliment this dish.

NOTES

RED OXTAIL RAGOUT

Makes 8 servings.

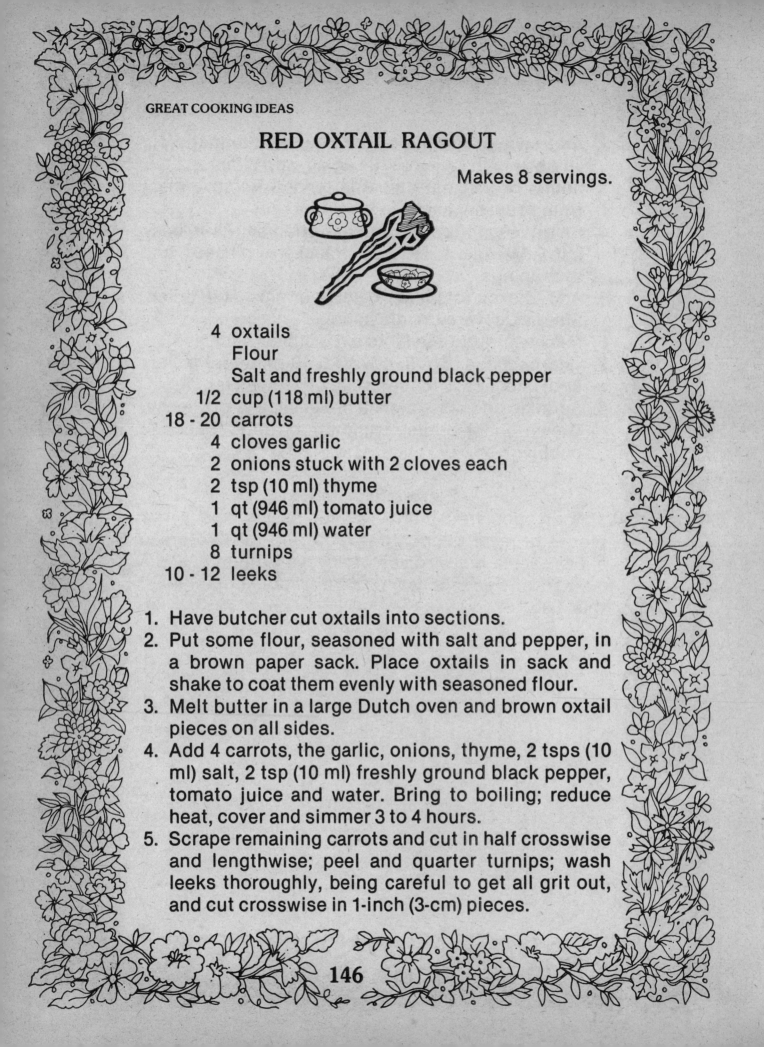

          4 oxtails
             Flour
             Salt and freshly ground black pepper
        1/2 cup (118 ml) butter
     18 - 20 carrots
          4 cloves garlic
          2 onions stuck with 2 cloves each
          2 tsp (10 ml) thyme
          1 qt (946 ml) tomato juice
          1 qt (946 ml) water
          8 turnips
     10 - 12 leeks

1. Have butcher cut oxtails into sections.
2. Put some flour, seasoned with salt and pepper, in a brown paper sack. Place oxtails in sack and shake to coat them evenly with seasoned flour.
3. Melt butter in a large Dutch oven and brown oxtail pieces on all sides.
4. Add 4 carrots, the garlic, onions, thyme, 2 tsps (10 ml) salt, 2 tsp (10 ml) freshly ground black pepper, tomato juice and water. Bring to boiling; reduce heat, cover and simmer 3 to 4 hours.
5. Scrape remaining carrots and cut in half crosswise and lengthwise; peel and quarter turnips; wash leeks thoroughly, being careful to get all grit out, and cut crosswise in 1-inch (3-cm) pieces.

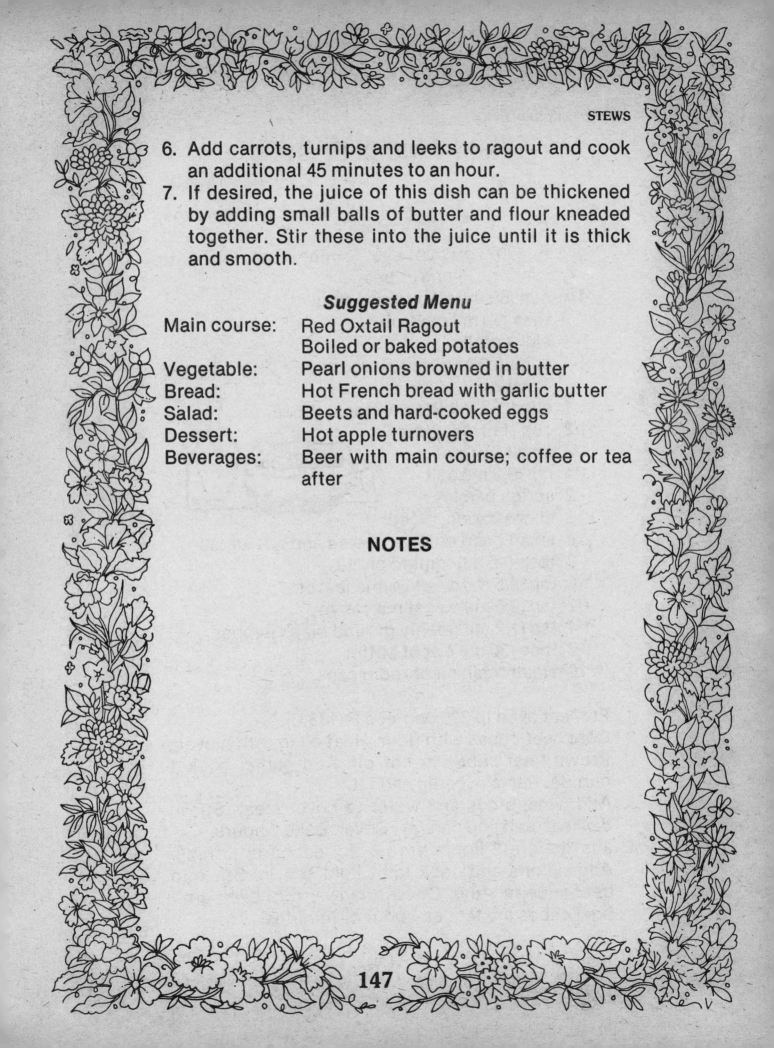

6. Add carrots, turnips and leeks to ragout and cook an additional 45 minutes to an hour.
7. If desired, the juice of this dish can be thickened by adding small balls of butter and flour kneaded together. Stir these into the juice until it is thick and smooth.

Suggested Menu

Main course: Red Oxtail Ragout
Boiled or baked potatoes
Vegetable: Pearl onions browned in butter
Bread: Hot French bread with garlic butter
Salad: Beets and hard-cooked eggs
Dessert: Hot apple turnovers
Beverages: Beer with main course; coffee or tea after

NOTES

RED WINE BEEF STEW

Makes 4 - 5 servings.

2 lb (907 grams) eye round roast, cut into 1-inch (3-cm) cubes
1/4 cup (59 ml) all-purpose flour
2 tbsp (30 ml) olive oil
1 clove garlic
1 1/4 cups (296 ml) red Burgundy or other dry red wine
1 cup (237 ml) Brown Stock, p. 526
1/2 cup (118 ml) water
1/2 small bay leaf
1 1/4 tsp (6.2 ml) salt
2 sprigs parsley
3 slices bacon, diced
18 small pearl onions, peeled and left whole
3 tbsp (45 ml) tomato paste
1/2 tsp (2.5 ml) dried thyme leaves
1/2 tsp (2.5 ml) sweet marjoram
1/4 tsp (1.2 ml) freshly ground black pepper
2 tbsp (30 ml) sweet butter
18 small fresh mushroom caps

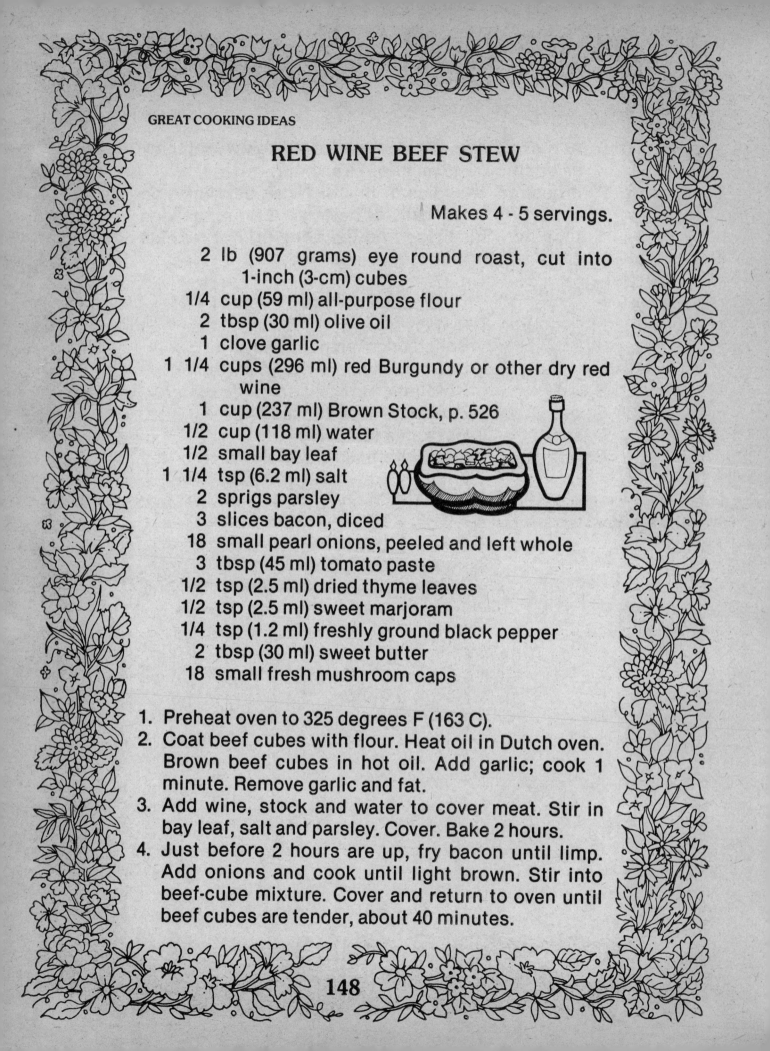

1. Preheat oven to 325 degrees F (163 C).
2. Coat beef cubes with flour. Heat oil in Dutch oven. Brown beef cubes in hot oil. Add garlic; cook 1 minute. Remove garlic and fat.
3. Add wine, stock and water to cover meat. Stir in bay leaf, salt and parsley. Cover. Bake 2 hours.
4. Just before 2 hours are up, fry bacon until limp. Add onions and cook until light brown. Stir into beef-cube mixture. Cover and return to oven until beef cubes are tender, about 40 minutes.

5. Stir in tomato paste, thyme and pepper. Re-cover and bake 10 minutes longer.
6. Melt butter in 6-inch skillet. Cook and stir mushrooms in butter until tender.
7. Arrange sautéed mushrooms on top of stew before serving.

Notes: 1) For added flavor, the beef may be marinated and refrigerated in the red wine. Drain and reserve wine for use in cooking the stew.

2) At the last minute before serving, flambé the stew with 1/4 cup (59 ml) brandy.

Serving Suggestions

For dinner: Over buttered egg noodles, or with French bread and a fresh green salad, which includes 2 kinds of lettuce, cucumber and radish slices, tossed with a light French garlic dressing

Wine: Côtes du Rhône Red; or Pinot Noir

Dessert: Camenbert or Brie and Fruit; or Cup Custard topped with fresh berries or caramel syrup, Coffee and Cognac

NOTES

OLD-FASHIONED GOULASH

Makes 6 servings.

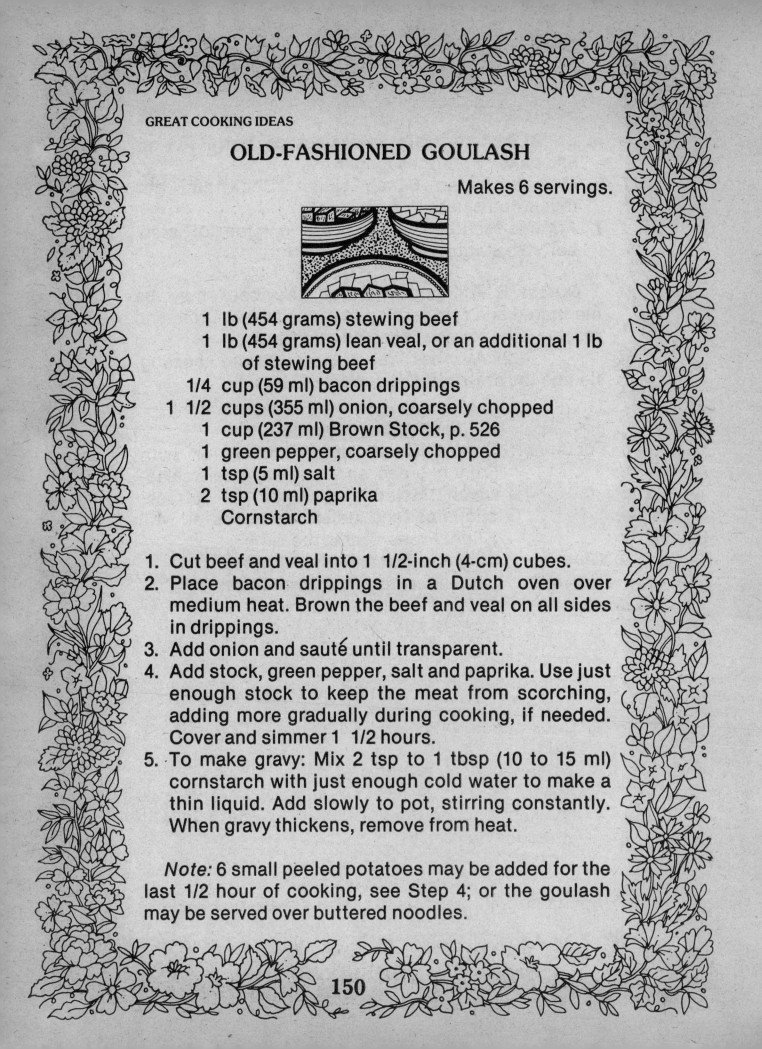

- 1 lb (454 grams) stewing beef
- 1 lb (454 grams) lean veal, or an additional 1 lb of stewing beef
- 1/4 cup (59 ml) bacon drippings
- 1 1/2 cups (355 ml) onion, coarsely chopped
- 1 cup (237 ml) Brown Stock, p. 526
- 1 green pepper, coarsely chopped
- 1 tsp (5 ml) salt
- 2 tsp (10 ml) paprika
- Cornstarch

1. Cut beef and veal into 1 1/2-inch (4-cm) cubes.
2. Place bacon drippings in a Dutch oven over medium heat. Brown the beef and veal on all sides in drippings.
3. Add onion and sauté until transparent.
4. Add stock, green pepper, salt and paprika. Use just enough stock to keep the meat from scorching, adding more gradually during cooking, if needed. Cover and simmer 1 1/2 hours.
5. To make gravy: Mix 2 tsp to 1 tbsp (10 to 15 ml) cornstarch with just enough cold water to make a thin liquid. Add slowly to pot, stirring constantly. When gravy thickens, remove from heat.

Note: 6 small peeled potatoes may be added for the last 1/2 hour of cooking, see Step 4; or the goulash may be served over buttered noodles.

CHICKEN 'N' NOODLE STEW

Makes 6 servings.

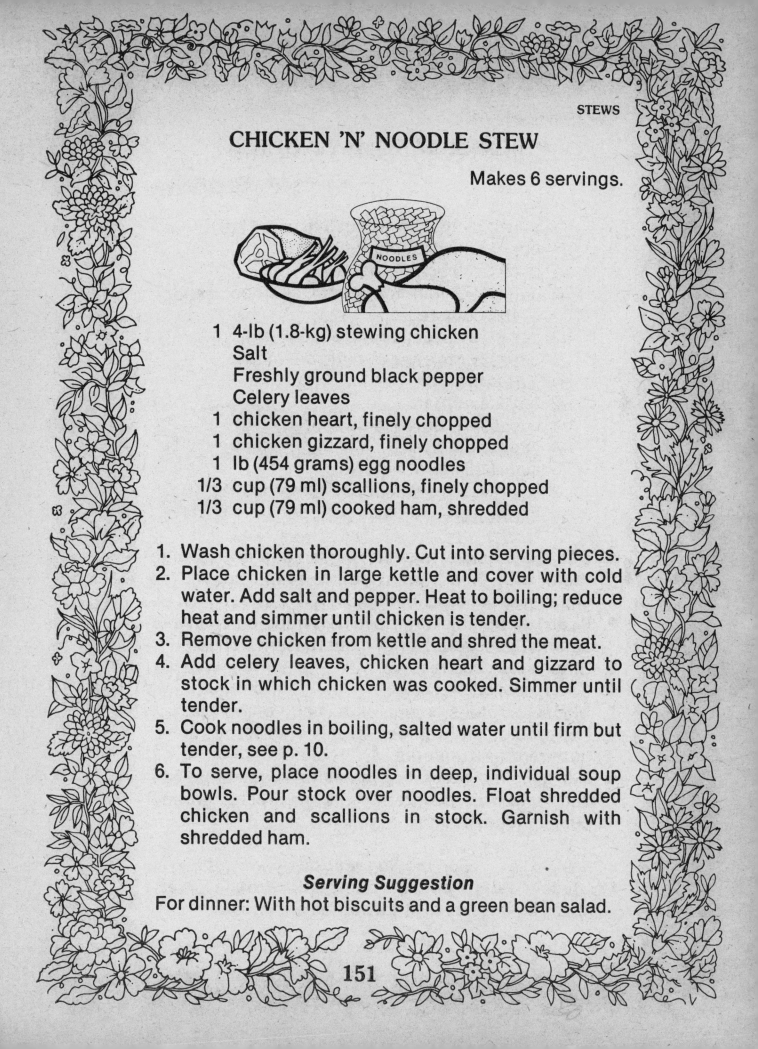

1   4-lb (1.8-kg) stewing chicken
Salt
Freshly ground black pepper
Celery leaves
1   chicken heart, finely chopped
1   chicken gizzard, finely chopped
1   lb (454 grams) egg noodles
1/3 cup (79 ml) scallions, finely chopped
1/3 cup (79 ml) cooked ham, shredded

1. Wash chicken thoroughly. Cut into serving pieces.
2. Place chicken in large kettle and cover with cold water. Add salt and pepper. Heat to boiling; reduce heat and simmer until chicken is tender.
3. Remove chicken from kettle and shred the meat.
4. Add celery leaves, chicken heart and gizzard to stock in which chicken was cooked. Simmer until tender.
5. Cook noodles in boiling, salted water until firm but tender, see p. 10.
6. To serve, place noodles in deep, individual soup bowls. Pour stock over noodles. Float shredded chicken and scallions in stock. Garnish with shredded ham.

Serving Suggestion
For dinner: With hot biscuits and a green bean salad.

CHICKEN 'N' TOMATO GUMBO

Makes 10 - 12 servings.

- 1 stewing chicken (about 3 lb or 1.4 kg)
- 1/4 cup (59 ml) bacon drippings
- 1 qt (946 ml) boiling water
- 2 cups (473 ml) tomatoes: skinned, seeded and chopped
- 1/2 cup (118 ml) corn cut from cob
- 1 cup (237 ml) okra, cut into 1/2-inch (1-cm) pieces
- 1/2 tsp (2.5 ml) salt
- 1/4 cup (59 ml) onion, diced
- 1/4 cup (59 ml) rice
- 5 cups (1.2 liters) water
- 2 tbsp (30 ml) quick-cooking tapioca
- Freshly ground black pepper

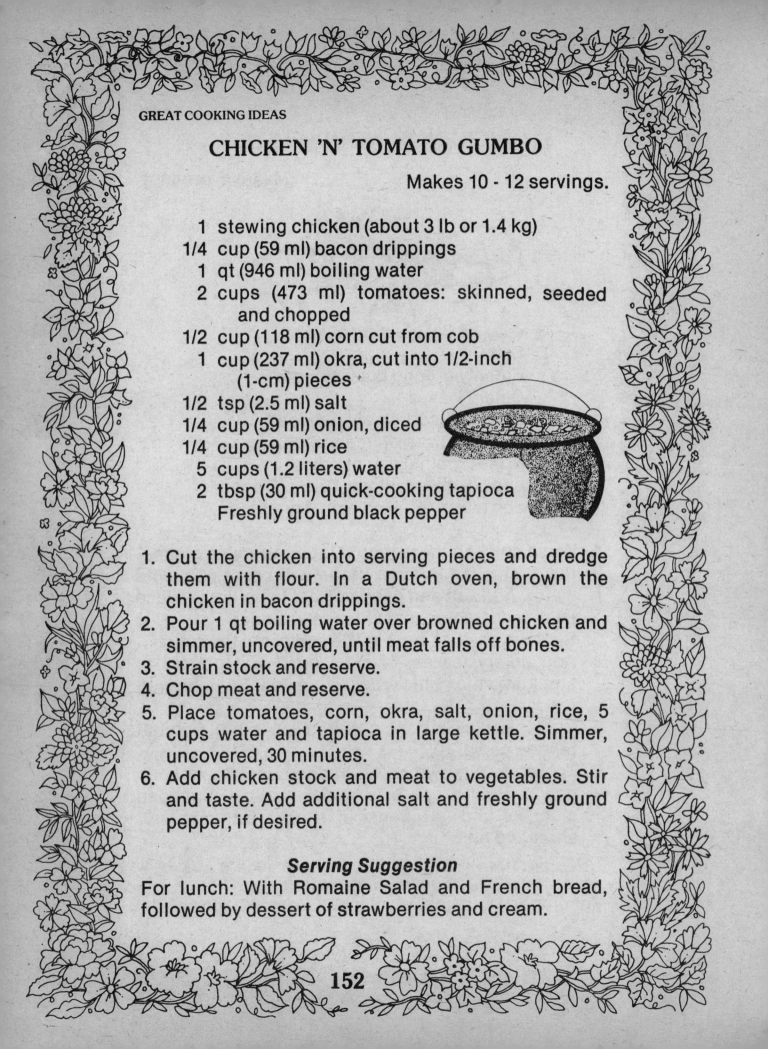

1. Cut the chicken into serving pieces and dredge them with flour. In a Dutch oven, brown the chicken in bacon drippings.
2. Pour 1 qt boiling water over browned chicken and simmer, uncovered, until meat falls off bones.
3. Strain stock and reserve.
4. Chop meat and reserve.
5. Place tomatoes, corn, okra, salt, onion, rice, 5 cups water and tapioca in large kettle. Simmer, uncovered, 30 minutes.
6. Add chicken stock and meat to vegetables. Stir and taste. Add additional salt and freshly ground pepper, if desired.

Serving Suggestion

For lunch: With Romaine Salad and French bread, followed by dessert of strawberries and cream.

CHICKEN CURRY

Makes 6 servings.

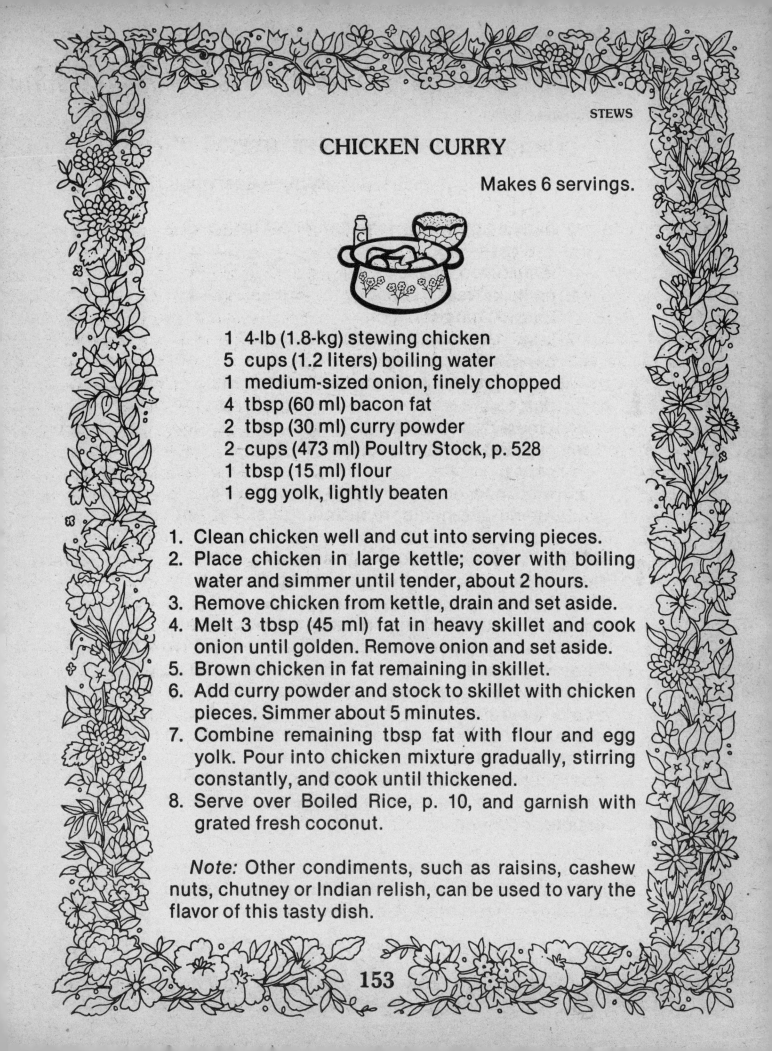

1 4-lb (1.8-kg) stewing chicken
5 cups (1.2 liters) boiling water
1 medium-sized onion, finely chopped
4 tbsp (60 ml) bacon fat
2 tbsp (30 ml) curry powder
2 cups (473 ml) Poultry Stock, p. 528
1 tbsp (15 ml) flour
1 egg yolk, lightly beaten

1. Clean chicken well and cut into serving pieces.
2. Place chicken in large kettle; cover with boiling water and simmer until tender, about 2 hours.
3. Remove chicken from kettle, drain and set aside.
4. Melt 3 tbsp (45 ml) fat in heavy skillet and cook onion until golden. Remove onion and set aside.
5. Brown chicken in fat remaining in skillet.
6. Add curry powder and stock to skillet with chicken pieces. Simmer about 5 minutes.
7. Combine remaining tbsp fat with flour and egg yolk. Pour into chicken mixture gradually, stirring constantly, and cook until thickened.
8. Serve over Boiled Rice, p. 10, and garnish with grated fresh coconut.

Note: Other condiments, such as raisins, cashew nuts, chutney or Indian relish, can be used to vary the flavor of this tasty dish.

CHICKEN-PEANUT BUTTER STEW

Makes 4 servings.

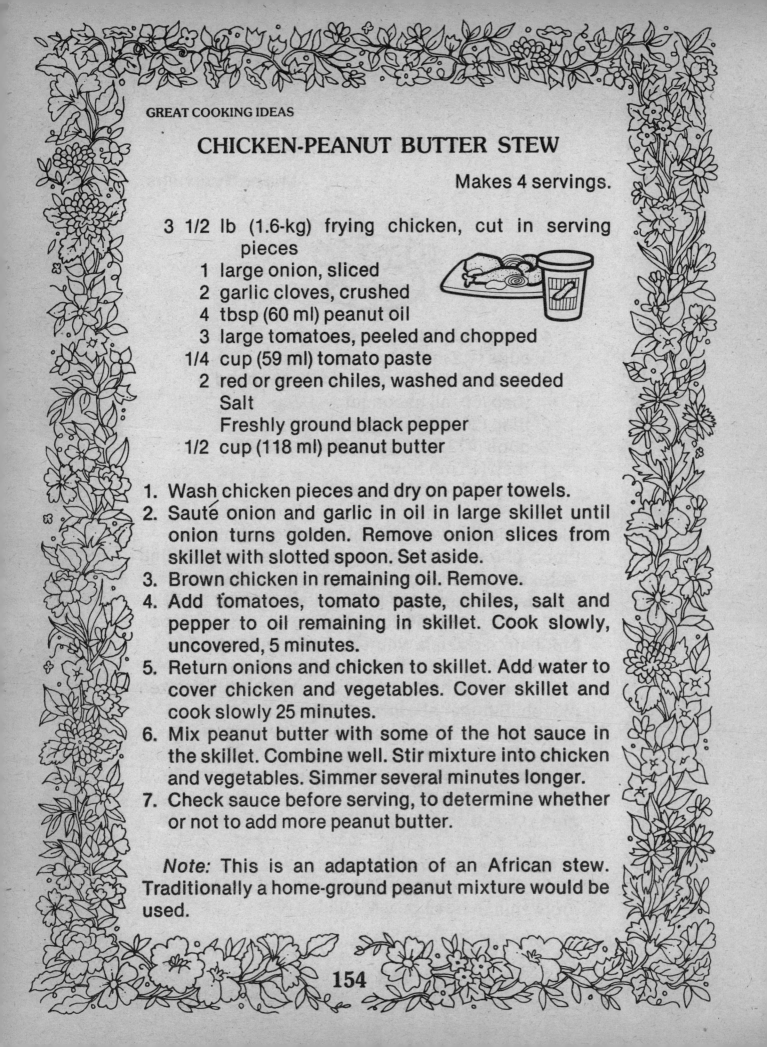

3 1/2 lb (1.6-kg) frying chicken, cut in serving pieces
1 large onion, sliced
2 garlic cloves, crushed
4 tbsp (60 ml) peanut oil
3 large tomatoes, peeled and chopped
1/4 cup (59 ml) tomato paste
2 red or green chiles, washed and seeded
 Salt
 Freshly ground black pepper
1/2 cup (118 ml) peanut butter

1. Wash chicken pieces and dry on paper towels.
2. Sauté onion and garlic in oil in large skillet until onion turns golden. Remove onion slices from skillet with slotted spoon. Set aside.
3. Brown chicken in remaining oil. Remove.
4. Add tomatoes, tomato paste, chiles, salt and pepper to oil remaining in skillet. Cook slowly, uncovered, 5 minutes.
5. Return onions and chicken to skillet. Add water to cover chicken and vegetables. Cover skillet and cook slowly 25 minutes.
6. Mix peanut butter with some of the hot sauce in the skillet. Combine well. Stir mixture into chicken and vegetables. Simmer several minutes longer.
7. Check sauce before serving, to determine whether or not to add more peanut butter.

Note: This is an adaptation of an African stew. Traditionally a home-ground peanut mixture would be used.

JIFFY CHICKEN STEW

Makes 6 servings.

2 slices raw bacon
1 cup (237 ml) onion, chopped
1 (3 lb or 1.4 kg) chicken, cut in serving pieces
1 1/4 cup (296 ml) Poultry Stock, p. 528
1 1/4 cup (296 ml) water
1/2 cup (118 ml) celery, diced
2 tsp (10 ml) salt
1 can (1 lb or 454 grams) stewed tomatoes
2 cups (473 ml) potatoes, peeled and diced
1 pkg (10 oz or 284 grams) frozen okra, thawed
1 pkg (10 oz or 284 grams) frozen lima beans, thawed
1 can (12 oz or 340 grams) whole-kernel corn, undrained
1 tbsp (15 ml) Worcestershire sauce
3 tbsp (45 ml) flour

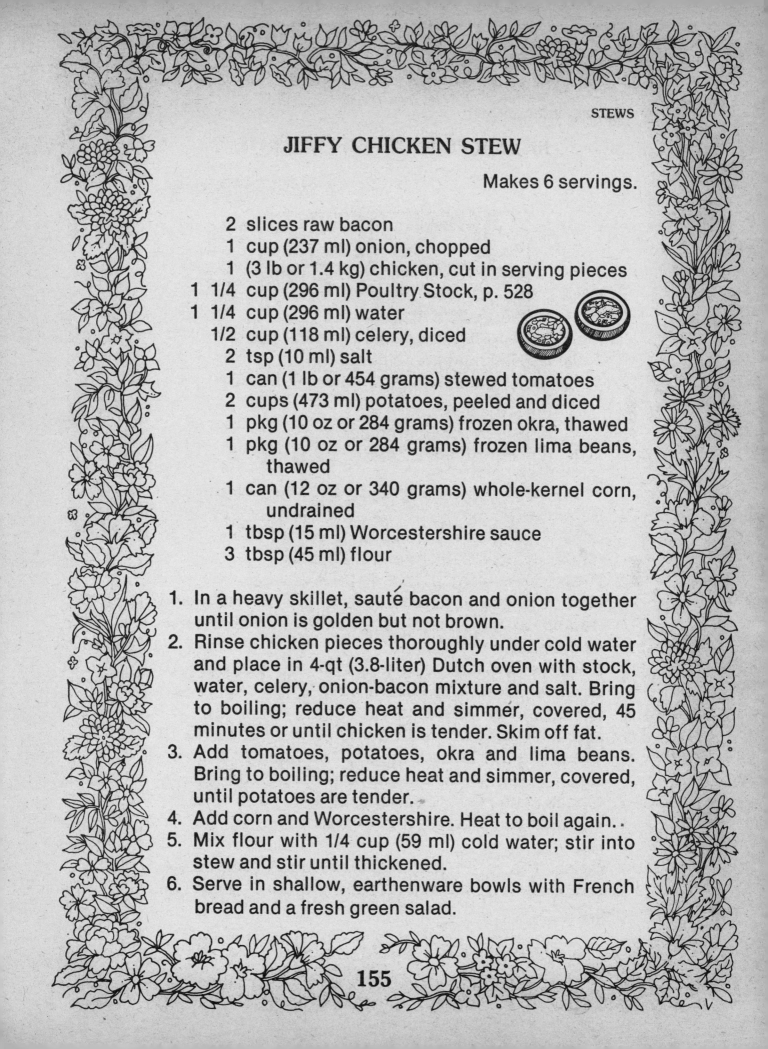

1. In a heavy skillet, sauté bacon and onion together until onion is golden but not brown.
2. Rinse chicken pieces thoroughly under cold water and place in 4-qt (3.8-liter) Dutch oven with stock, water, celery, onion-bacon mixture and salt. Bring to boiling; reduce heat and simmer, covered, 45 minutes or until chicken is tender. Skim off fat.
3. Add tomatoes, potatoes, okra and lima beans. Bring to boiling; reduce heat and simmer, covered, until potatoes are tender.
4. Add corn and Worcestershire. Heat to boil again..
5. Mix flour with 1/4 cup (59 ml) cold water; stir into stew and stir until thickened.
6. Serve in shallow, earthenware bowls with French bread and a fresh green salad.

MOROCCAN-STYLE CHICKEN

Makes 6 servings.

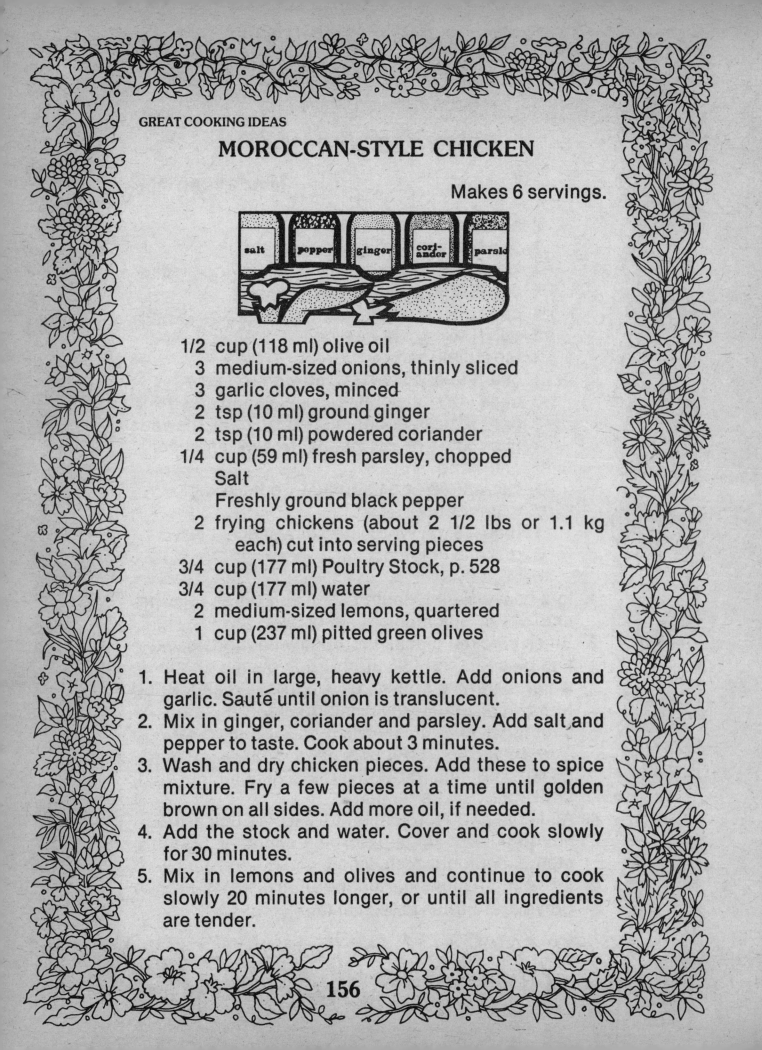

1/2	cup (118 ml) olive oil
3	medium-sized onions, thinly sliced
3	garlic cloves, minced
2	tsp (10 ml) ground ginger
2	tsp (10 ml) powdered coriander
1/4	cup (59 ml) fresh parsley, chopped
	Salt
	Freshly ground black pepper
2	frying chickens (about 2 1/2 lbs or 1.1 kg each) cut into serving pieces
3/4	cup (177 ml) Poultry Stock, p. 528
3/4	cup (177 ml) water
2	medium-sized lemons, quartered
1	cup (237 ml) pitted green olives

1. Heat oil in large, heavy kettle. Add onions and garlic. Sauté until onion is translucent.
2. Mix in ginger, coriander and parsley. Add salt and pepper to taste. Cook about 3 minutes.
3. Wash and dry chicken pieces. Add these to spice mixture. Fry a few pieces at a time until golden brown on all sides. Add more oil, if needed.
4. Add the stock and water. Cover and cook slowly for 30 minutes.
5. Mix in lemons and olives and continue to cook slowly 20 minutes longer, or until all ingredients are tender.

POLYNESIAN RAGOUT

Makes 8 servings.

8 chicken breasts, split in half
6 tbsp (90 ml) soybean or peanut oil
1/4 tsp (1.2 ml) salt
Freshly ground white pepper
2/3 cup (158 ml) pineapple juice, unsweetened
5 tbsp (75 ml) soy sauce
1 cup (237 ml) Poultry Stock, p. 528
1 cup (237 ml) wine vinegar
2/3 cup (158 ml) water chestnuts
2/3 cup (158 ml) sugar
6 tbsp (90 ml) fresh ginger, minced
3 cups (710 ml) crushed pineapple, drained
6 tbsp (90 ml) cornstarch
1/2 cup (118 ml) water
2 large green peppers, coarsely chopped

1. Remove skin from chicken breasts.
2. Heat oil in large Dutch oven. Sprinkle chicken with salt and pepper. Sauté on both sides until golden.
3. Add pineapple juice. Cover and cook slowly 5 minutes.
4. Remove Dutch oven from heat and cool chicken. Remove all meat and discard bones.
5. Cut meat into bite-sized pieces and return to Dutch oven. Add soy sauce, stock, vinegar, water chestnuts, sugar, ginger and pineapple. Cook slowly, covered, 30 minutes.
6. Dissolve cornstarch in water and stir into chicken mixture. Cook slowly, stirring frequently, for a few minutes until sauce is thickened.
7. Add peppers just before removing from heat.
8. Serve over buttered, Boiled Rice, p. 10.

WEST AFRICAN COUSCOUS

Makes 6 - 8 servings.

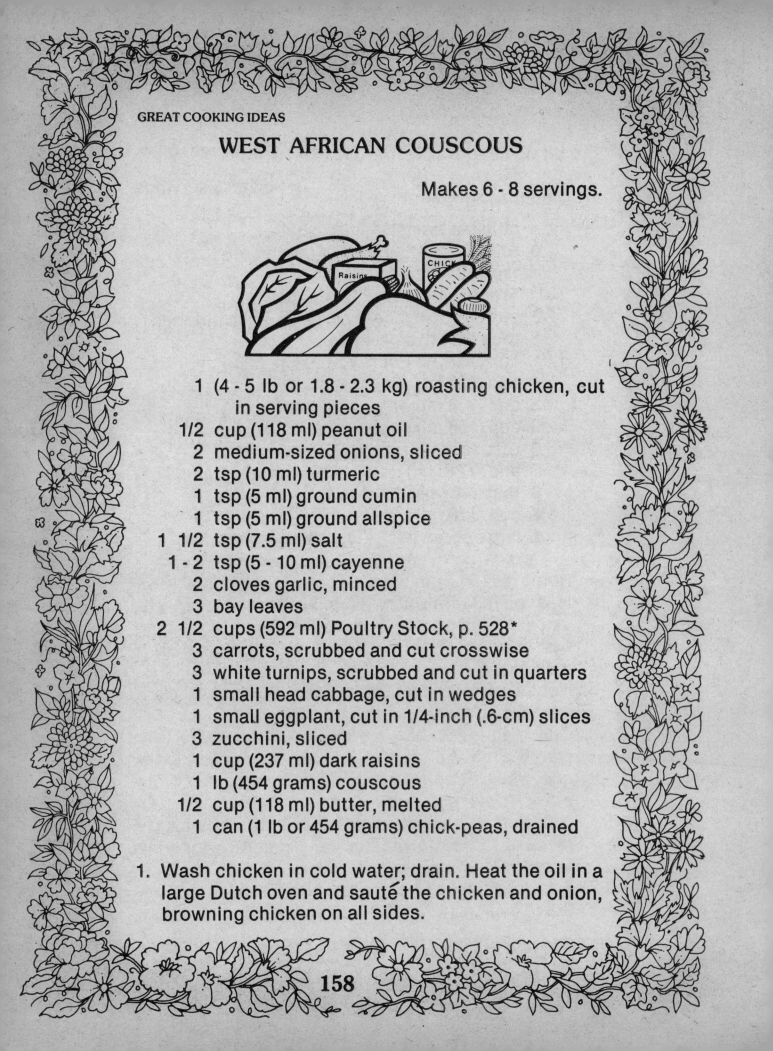

- 1 (4 - 5 lb or 1.8 - 2.3 kg) roasting chicken, cut in serving pieces
- 1/2 cup (118 ml) peanut oil
- 2 medium-sized onions, sliced
- 2 tsp (10 ml) turmeric
- 1 tsp (5 ml) ground cumin
- 1 tsp (5 ml) ground allspice
- 1 1/2 tsp (7.5 ml) salt
- 1 - 2 tsp (5 - 10 ml) cayenne
- 2 cloves garlic, minced
- 3 bay leaves
- 2 1/2 cups (592 ml) Poultry Stock, p. 528*
- 3 carrots, scrubbed and cut crosswise
- 3 white turnips, scrubbed and cut in quarters
- 1 small head cabbage, cut in wedges
- 1 small eggplant, cut in 1/4-inch (.6-cm) slices
- 3 zucchini, sliced
- 1 cup (237 ml) dark raisins
- 1 lb (454 grams) couscous
- 1/2 cup (118 ml) butter, melted
- 1 can (1 lb or 454 grams) chick-peas, drained

1. Wash chicken in cold water; drain. Heat the oil in a large Dutch oven and sauté the chicken and onion, browning chicken on all sides.

2. Add 1 1/2 tsp (7.5 ml) turmeric, cumin, allspice, salt, cayenne, garlic, bay leaves and stock. Combine ingredients well.
3. Add carrots, turnips and cabbage. Stir again to combine ingredients and cover. Cook 20 minutes.
4. Add eggplant and zucchini and cook 20 minutes more.
5. During last 20 minutes, place raisins in a small bowl and pour hot water to cover them. Let stand until needed.
6. Prepare couscous as package label directs. Toss with butter, drained raisins and the remaining turmeric. Then keep couscous hot by placing it in a colander lined with 2 towels, over hot water.
7. Add chick-peas to chicken and cook 5 minutes more.

Note: 2 cans (10 3/4 oz or 305 grams each) of undiluted, condensed, chicken broth may be substituted for Poultry Stock.

Serving Suggestion

For dinner: Place couscous on a large oval platter. Surround it with chicken pieces and vegetables. Pour sauce into separate bowl or gravy boat and serve with couscous.

SPANISH-STYLE CHICKEN STEW

Makes 8 - 10 servings.

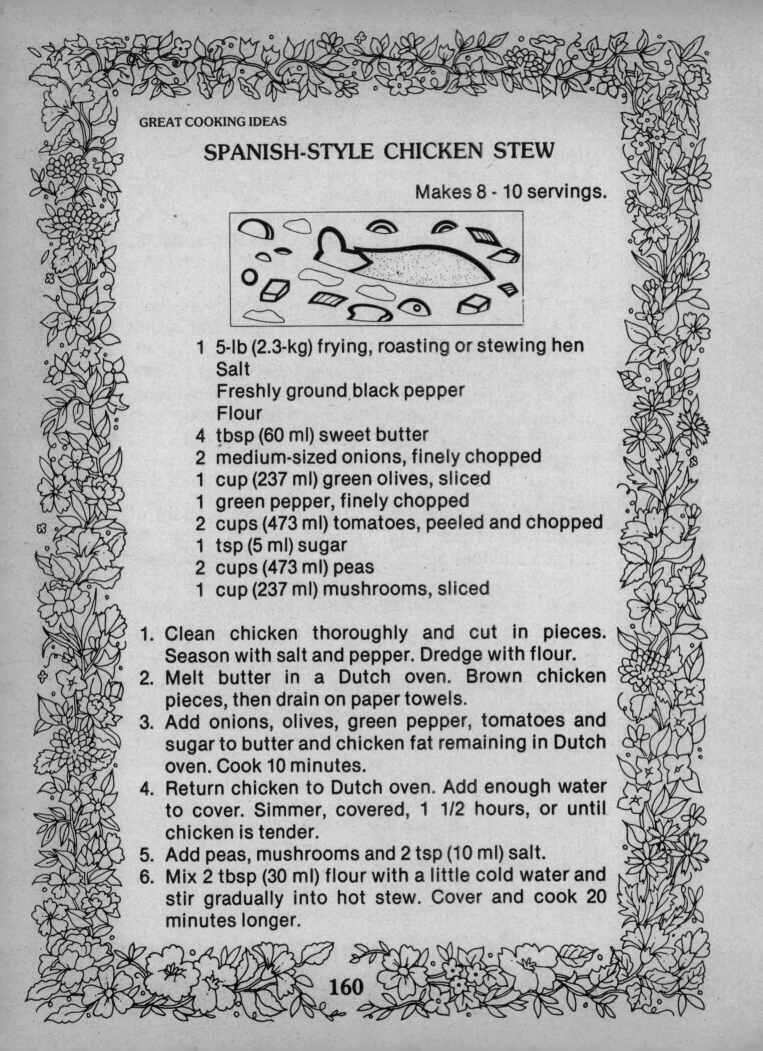

1 5-lb (2.3-kg) frying, roasting or stewing hen
   Salt
   Freshly ground black pepper
   Flour
4 tbsp (60 ml) sweet butter
2 medium-sized onions, finely chopped
1 cup (237 ml) green olives, sliced
1 green pepper, finely chopped
2 cups (473 ml) tomatoes, peeled and chopped
1 tsp (5 ml) sugar
2 cups (473 ml) peas
1 cup (237 ml) mushrooms, sliced

1. Clean chicken thoroughly and cut in pieces. Season with salt and pepper. Dredge with flour.
2. Melt butter in a Dutch oven. Brown chicken pieces, then drain on paper towels.
3. Add onions, olives, green pepper, tomatoes and sugar to butter and chicken fat remaining in Dutch oven. Cook 10 minutes.
4. Return chicken to Dutch oven. Add enough water to cover. Simmer, covered, 1 1/2 hours, or until chicken is tender.
5. Add peas, mushrooms and 2 tsp (10 ml) salt.
6. Mix 2 tbsp (30 ml) flour with a little cold water and stir gradually into hot stew. Cover and cook 20 minutes longer.

TURKEY CURRY

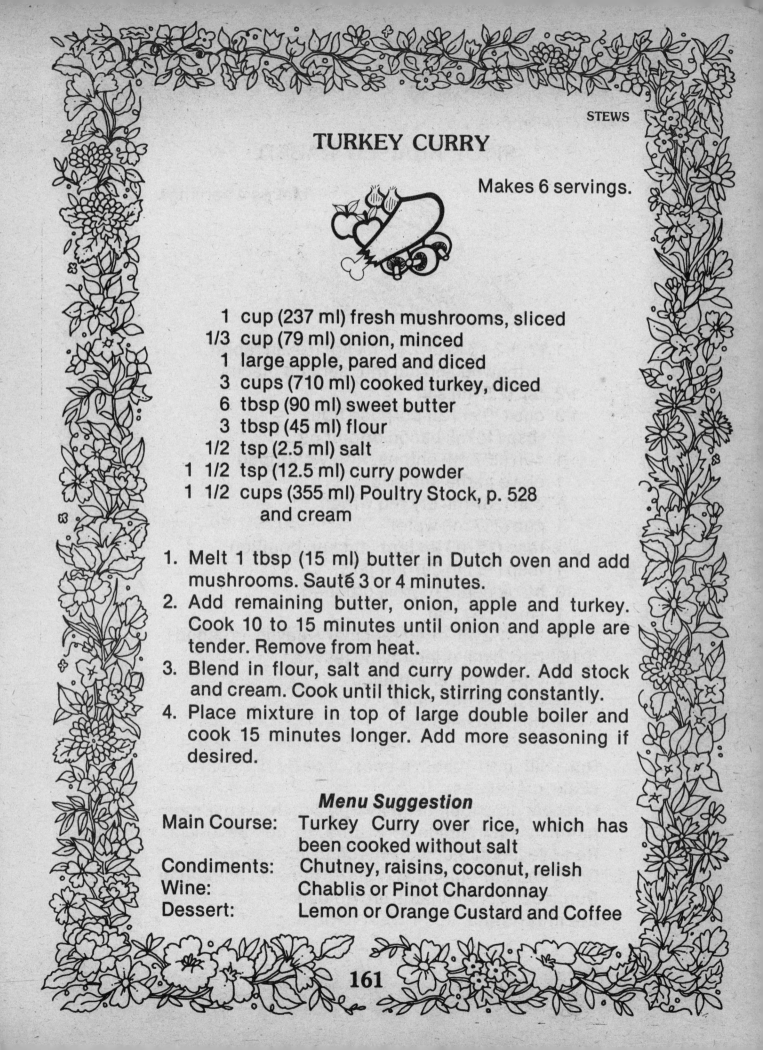

Makes 6 servings.

```
  1    cup (237 ml) fresh mushrooms, sliced
1/3    cup (79 ml) onion, minced
  1    large apple, pared and diced
  3    cups (710 ml) cooked turkey, diced
  6    tbsp (90 ml) sweet butter
  3    tbsp (45 ml) flour
1/2    tsp (2.5 ml) salt
1 1/2  tsp (12.5 ml) curry powder
1 1/2  cups (355 ml) Poultry Stock, p. 528
       and cream
```

1. Melt 1 tbsp (15 ml) butter in Dutch oven and add mushrooms. Sauté 3 or 4 minutes.
2. Add remaining butter, onion, apple and turkey. Cook 10 to 15 minutes until onion and apple are tender. Remove from heat.
3. Blend in flour, salt and curry powder. Add stock and cream. Cook until thick, stirring constantly.
4. Place mixture in top of large double boiler and cook 15 minutes longer. Add more seasoning if desired.

Menu Suggestion

Main Course: Turkey Curry over rice, which has been cooked without salt
Condiments: Chutney, raisins, coconut, relish
Wine: Chablis or Pinot Chardonnay
Dessert: Lemon or Orange Custard and Coffee

SPICY BRAISED RABBIT

Makes 4 servings.

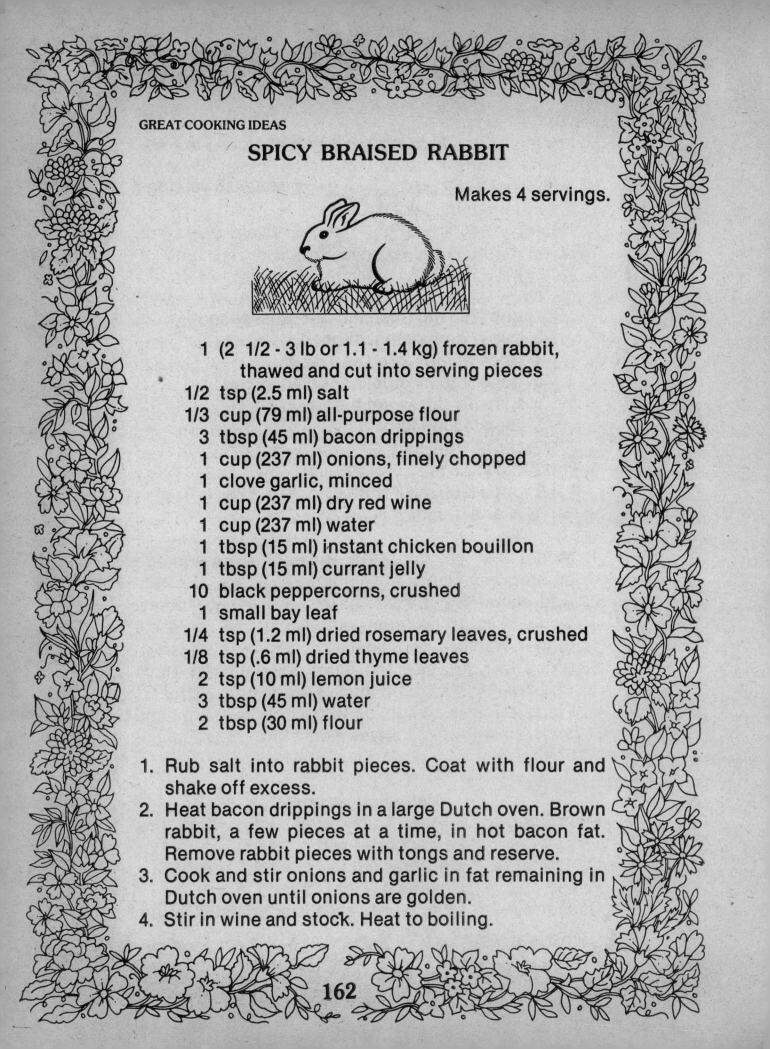

1 (2 1/2 - 3 lb or 1.1 - 1.4 kg) frozen rabbit, thawed and cut into serving pieces
1/2 tsp (2.5 ml) salt
1/3 cup (79 ml) all-purpose flour
3 tbsp (45 ml) bacon drippings
1 cup (237 ml) onions, finely chopped
1 clove garlic, minced
1 cup (237 ml) dry red wine
1 cup (237 ml) water
1 tbsp (15 ml) instant chicken bouillon
1 tbsp (15 ml) currant jelly
10 black peppercorns, crushed
1 small bay leaf
1/4 tsp (1.2 ml) dried rosemary leaves, crushed
1/8 tsp (.6 ml) dried thyme leaves
2 tsp (10 ml) lemon juice
3 tbsp (45 ml) water
2 tbsp (30 ml) flour

1. Rub salt into rabbit pieces. Coat with flour and shake off excess.
2. Heat bacon drippings in a large Dutch oven. Brown rabbit, a few pieces at a time, in hot bacon fat. Remove rabbit pieces with tongs and reserve.
3. Cook and stir onions and garlic in fat remaining in Dutch oven until onions are golden.
4. Stir in wine and stock. Heat to boiling.

5. Stir in jelly, peppercorns, bay leaf, rosemary and thyme. Return rabbit to Dutch oven. Heat to boiling, reduce heat, cover and simmer until rabbit is tender about 1 1/2 hours.
6. Remove bay leaf and discard. Place rabbit on warm platter; keep warm while preparing sauce.
7. Stir lemon juice into liquid in Dutch oven.
8. Combine water and flour in a cup and stir slowly into liquid in Dutch oven. Heat to boiling, stirring constantly. Boil and stir 1 minute. If sauce is too thick, stir in additional water until the desired consistency is reached.

Note: Rabbit or hare can be cooked by using any recipe calling for chicken. It is especially good in highly seasoned dishes, such as curries.

Menu Suggestion

Main course: Spicy Braised Rabbit with egg or green noodles, or a combination of wild and white or brown rice
Vegetable: Baked yellow (winter) squash
Wine: Claret or a dry rosé
Dessert: Apple Strudel or Custard Pie and Coffee

NOTES

GOULASH WITH SAUERKRAUT

Makes 4 servings.

- 2 tbsp (30 ml) sweet butter
- 6 tbsp (90 ml) onion, finely chopped
- 1/2 lb (227 grams) lean pork, cut in 1-inch (3-cm) cubes
- 1/2 lb (227 grams) veal, in 1-inch (3-cm) cubes
- 1 lb (454 grams) sauerkraut, drained
- 1 tsp (5 ml) caraway seed
- 1 cup (237 ml) sour cream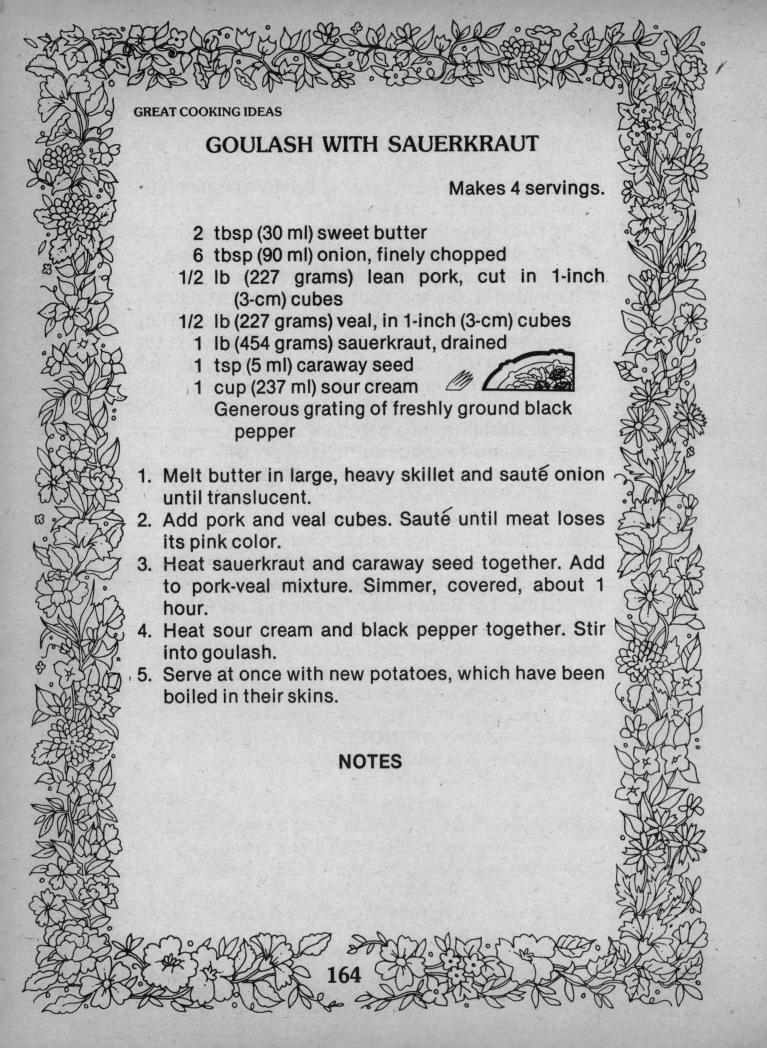
  Generous grating of freshly ground black pepper

1. Melt butter in large, heavy skillet and sauté onion until translucent.
2. Add pork and veal cubes. Sauté until meat loses its pink color.
3. Heat sauerkraut and caraway seed together. Add to pork-veal mixture. Simmer, covered, about 1 hour.
4. Heat sour cream and black pepper together. Stir into goulash.
5. Serve at once with new potatoes, which have been boiled in their skins.

NOTES

KIDNEY BEAN STEW

Makes 30 servings.

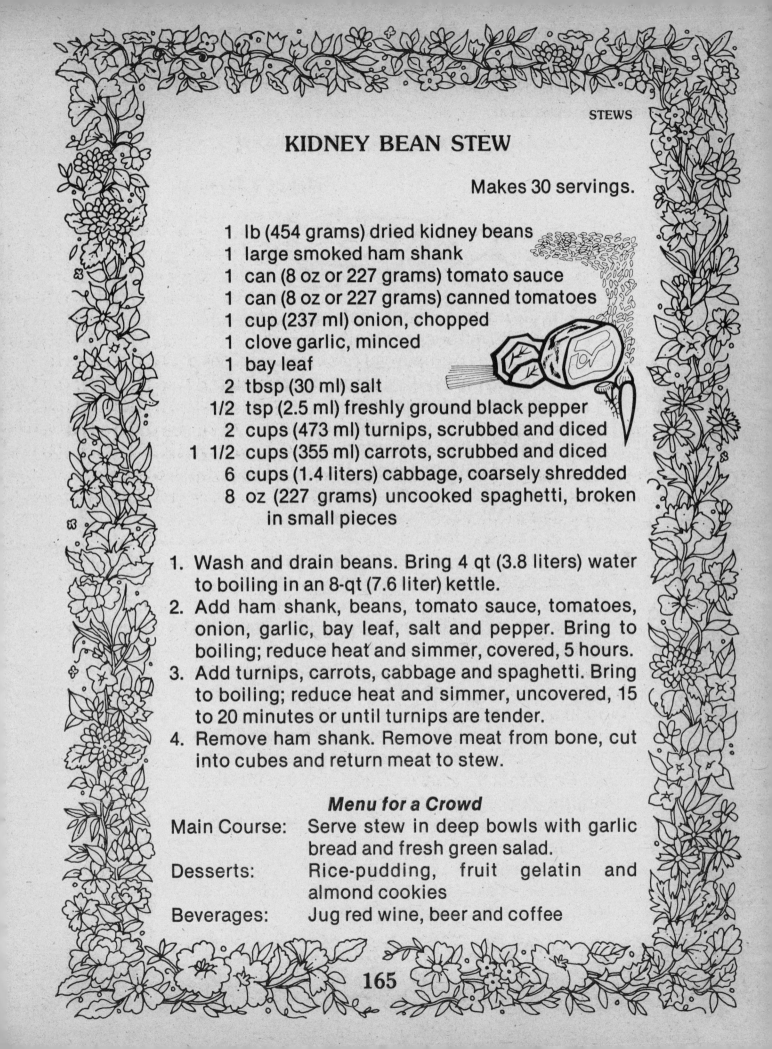

- 1 lb (454 grams) dried kidney beans
- 1 large smoked ham shank
- 1 can (8 oz or 227 grams) tomato sauce
- 1 can (8 oz or 227 grams) canned tomatoes
- 1 cup (237 ml) onion, chopped
- 1 clove garlic, minced
- 1 bay leaf
- 2 tbsp (30 ml) salt
- 1/2 tsp (2.5 ml) freshly ground black pepper
- 2 cups (473 ml) turnips, scrubbed and diced
- 1 1/2 cups (355 ml) carrots, scrubbed and diced
- 6 cups (1.4 liters) cabbage, coarsely shredded
- 8 oz (227 grams) uncooked spaghetti, broken in small pieces

1. Wash and drain beans. Bring 4 qt (3.8 liters) water to boiling in an 8-qt (7.6 liter) kettle.
2. Add ham shank, beans, tomato sauce, tomatoes, onion, garlic, bay leaf, salt and pepper. Bring to boiling; reduce heat and simmer, covered, 5 hours.
3. Add turnips, carrots, cabbage and spaghetti. Bring to boiling; reduce heat and simmer, uncovered, 15 to 20 minutes or until turnips are tender.
4. Remove ham shank. Remove meat from bone, cut into cubes and return meat to stew.

Menu for a Crowd

Main Course: Serve stew in deep bowls with garlic bread and fresh green salad.

Desserts: Rice-pudding, fruit gelatin and almond cookies

Beverages: Jug red wine, beer and coffee

PINEAPPLE PORK

Makes 6 servings.

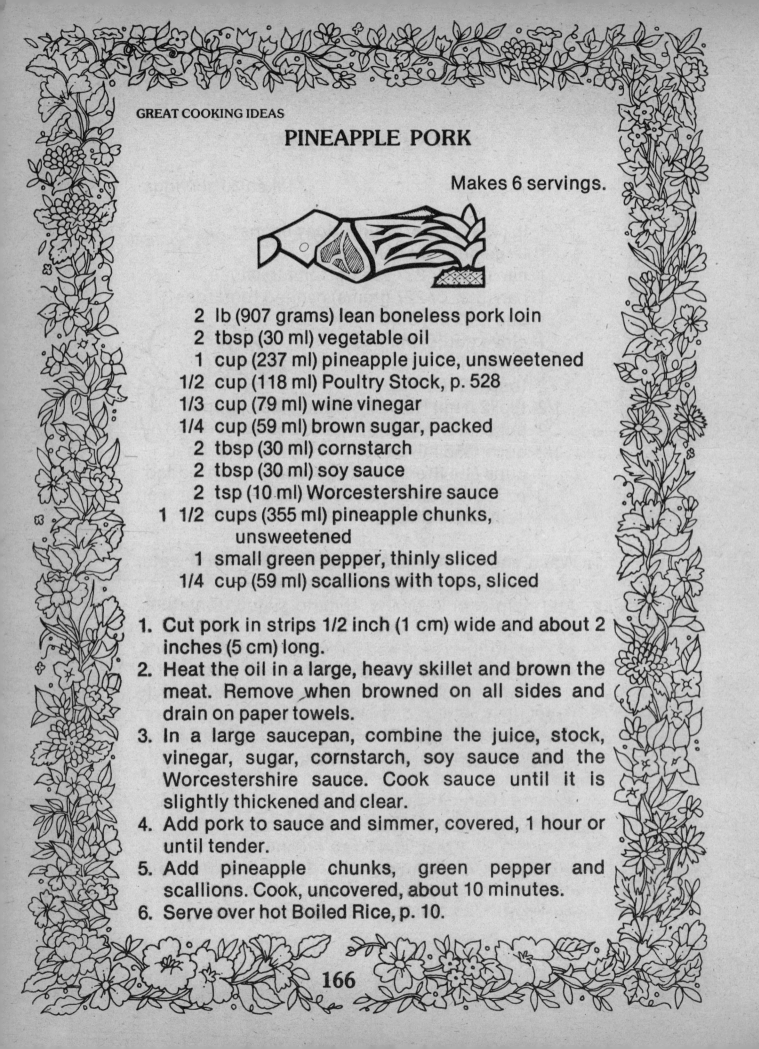

```
    2   lb (907 grams) lean boneless pork loin
    2   tbsp (30 ml) vegetable oil
    1   cup (237 ml) pineapple juice, unsweetened
  1/2   cup (118 ml) Poultry Stock, p. 528
  1/3   cup (79 ml) wine vinegar
  1/4   cup (59 ml) brown sugar, packed
    2   tbsp (30 ml) cornstarch
    2   tbsp (30 ml) soy sauce
    2   tsp (10 ml) Worcestershire sauce
1 1/2   cups (355 ml) pineapple chunks,
          unsweetened
    1   small green pepper, thinly sliced
  1/4   cup (59 ml) scallions with tops, sliced
```

1. Cut pork in strips 1/2 inch (1 cm) wide and about 2 inches (5 cm) long.
2. Heat the oil in a large, heavy skillet and brown the meat. Remove when browned on all sides and drain on paper towels.
3. In a large saucepan, combine the juice, stock, vinegar, sugar, cornstarch, soy sauce and the Worcestershire sauce. Cook sauce until it is slightly thickened and clear.
4. Add pork to sauce and simmer, covered, 1 hour or until tender.
5. Add pineapple chunks, green pepper and scallions. Cook, uncovered, about 10 minutes.
6. Serve over hot Boiled Rice, p. 10.

PORK GOULASH

Makes 6 servings.

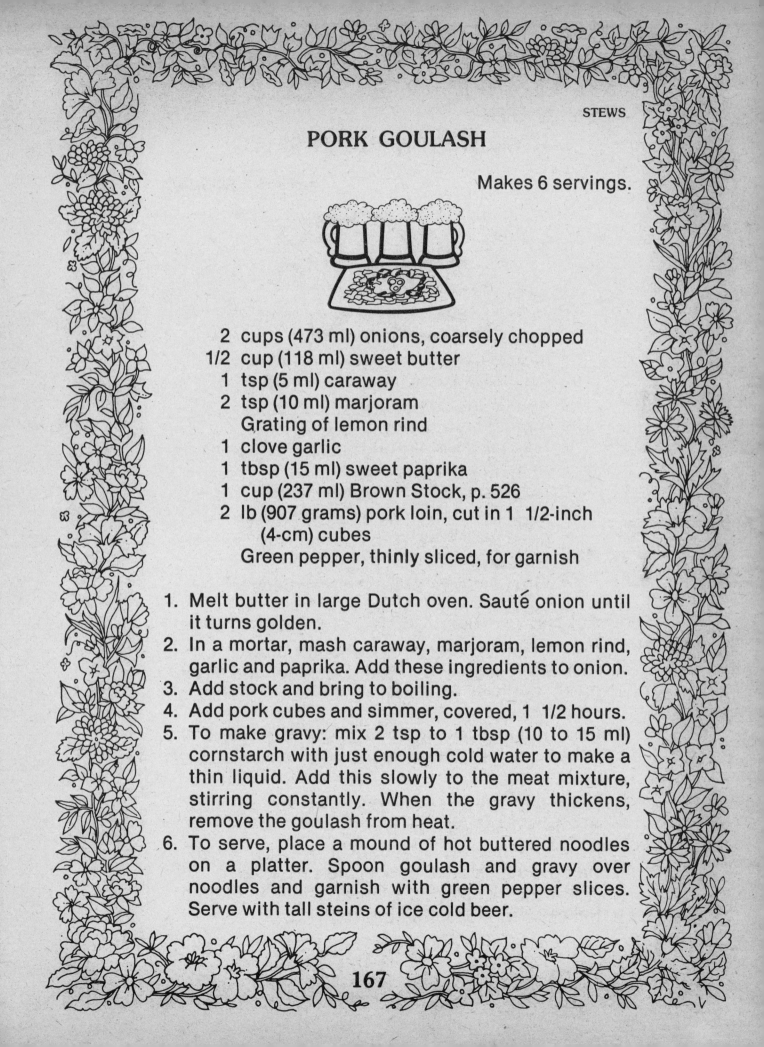

2 cups (473 ml) onions, coarsely chopped
1/2 cup (118 ml) sweet butter
1 tsp (5 ml) caraway
2 tsp (10 ml) marjoram
Grating of lemon rind
1 clove garlic
1 tbsp (15 ml) sweet paprika
1 cup (237 ml) Brown Stock, p. 526
2 lb (907 grams) pork loin, cut in 1 1/2-inch (4-cm) cubes
Green pepper, thinly sliced, for garnish

1. Melt butter in large Dutch oven. Sauté onion until it turns golden.
2. In a mortar, mash caraway, marjoram, lemon rind, garlic and paprika. Add these ingredients to onion.
3. Add stock and bring to boiling.
4. Add pork cubes and simmer, covered, 1 1/2 hours.
5. To make gravy: mix 2 tsp to 1 tbsp (10 to 15 ml) cornstarch with just enough cold water to make a thin liquid. Add this slowly to the meat mixture, stirring constantly. When the gravy thickens, remove the goulash from heat.
6. To serve, place a mound of hot buttered noodles on a platter. Spoon goulash and gravy over noodles and garnish with green pepper slices. Serve with tall steins of ice cold beer.

STEW WEST-AFRICAN STYLE

Makes 10 servings.

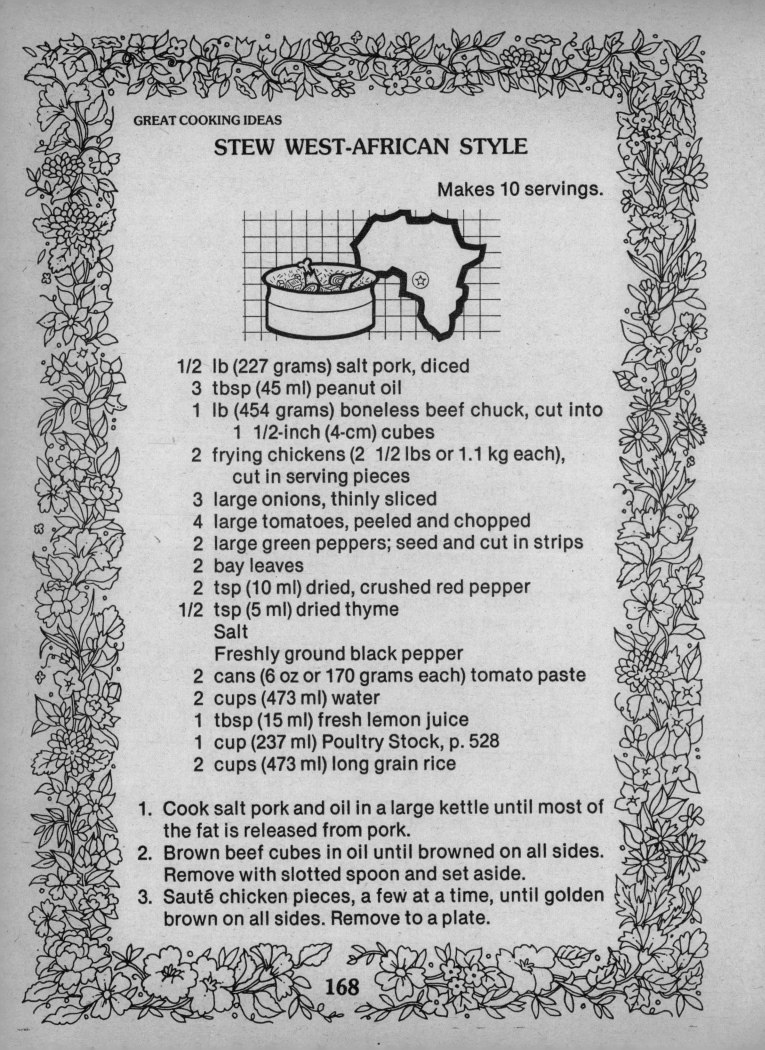

1/2 lb (227 grams) salt pork, diced
3 tbsp (45 ml) peanut oil
1 lb (454 grams) boneless beef chuck, cut into
   1 1/2-inch (4-cm) cubes
2 frying chickens (2 1/2 lbs or 1.1 kg each),
   cut in serving pieces
3 large onions, thinly sliced
4 large tomatoes, peeled and chopped
2 large green peppers; seed and cut in strips
2 bay leaves
2 tsp (10 ml) dried, crushed red pepper
1/2 tsp (5 ml) dried thyme
   Salt
   Freshly ground black pepper
2 cans (6 oz or 170 grams each) tomato paste
2 cups (473 ml) water
1 tbsp (15 ml) fresh lemon juice
1 cup (237 ml) Poultry Stock, p. 528
2 cups (473 ml) long grain rice

1. Cook salt pork and oil in a large kettle until most of
   the fat is released from pork.
2. Brown beef cubes in oil until browned on all sides.
   Remove with slotted spoon and set aside.
3. Sauté chicken pieces, a few at a time, until golden
   brown on all sides. Remove to a plate.

4. Sauté onions in oil until translucent. Stir in tomatoes and green peppers. Add more oil if needed and sauté 2 minutes longer.
5. Add bay leaves, crushed red pepper, thyme, salt and pepper to taste, tomato paste, 1 cup (237 ml) water and lemon juice. Mix well. Cook until hot through.
6. Return beef and chicken to kettle. Add remaining water and stock. Bring to a boil. Reduce heat, cover, and simmer 30 minutes.
7. Add rice and continue to simmer another 30 minutes, or until chicken is tender and nearly all liquid has been taken up by the rice.

Suggested Menu

Main Course:	Stew West-African Style
Salad:	Fresh Spinach
Bread:	Pumpernickel or other dark bread and sweet butter
Dessert:	Coconut Cream Pie, pp. 462, 463
Beverages:	Beer or Lemonade with main course Coffee or Tea with dessert

NOTES

BAKED LAMB STEW

Makes 4 servings.

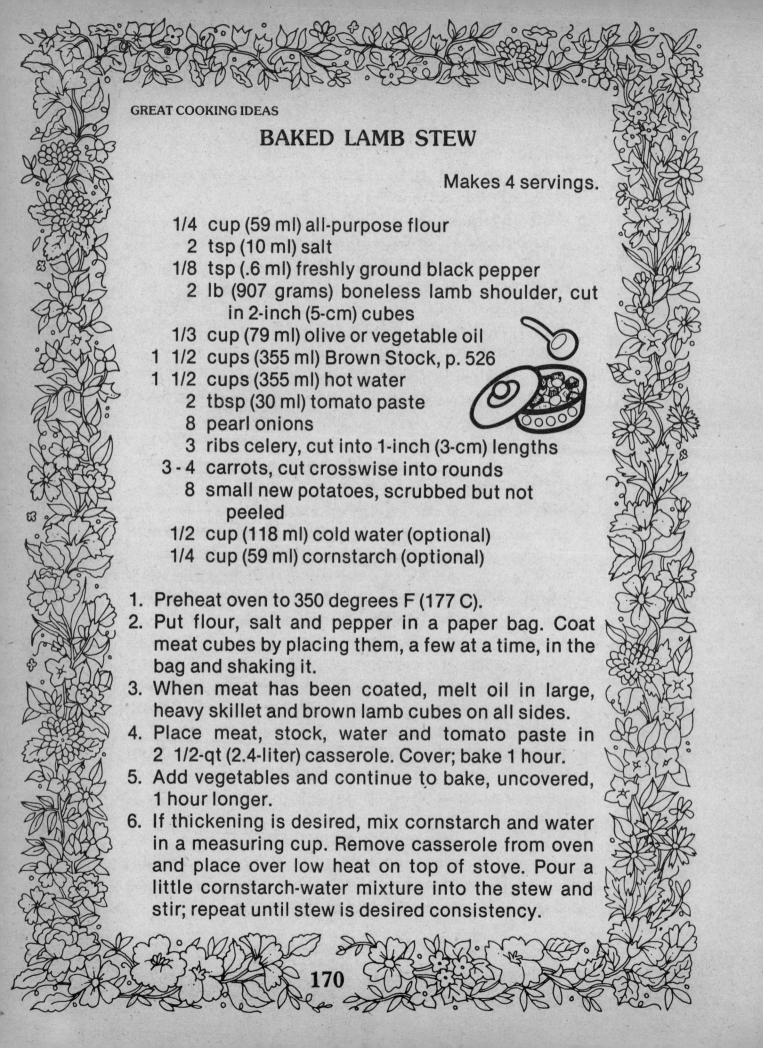

1/4 cup (59 ml) all-purpose flour
2 tsp (10 ml) salt
1/8 tsp (.6 ml) freshly ground black pepper
2 lb (907 grams) boneless lamb shoulder, cut
   in 2-inch (5-cm) cubes
1/3 cup (79 ml) olive or vegetable oil
1 1/2 cups (355 ml) Brown Stock, p. 526
1 1/2 cups (355 ml) hot water
2 tbsp (30 ml) tomato paste
8 pearl onions
3 ribs celery, cut into 1-inch (3-cm) lengths
3 - 4 carrots, cut crosswise into rounds
8 small new potatoes, scrubbed but not
   peeled
1/2 cup (118 ml) cold water (optional)
1/4 cup (59 ml) cornstarch (optional)

1. Preheat oven to 350 degrees F (177 C).
2. Put flour, salt and pepper in a paper bag. Coat meat cubes by placing them, a few at a time, in the bag and shaking it.
3. When meat has been coated, melt oil in large, heavy skillet and brown lamb cubes on all sides.
4. Place meat, stock, water and tomato paste in 2 1/2-qt (2.4-liter) casserole. Cover; bake 1 hour.
5. Add vegetables and continue to bake, uncovered, 1 hour longer.
6. If thickening is desired, mix cornstarch and water in a measuring cup. Remove casserole from oven and place over low heat on top of stove. Pour a little cornstarch-water mixture into the stew and stir; repeat until stew is desired consistency.

BLARNEY-STONE STEW

Makes 6 servings.

4 lb (1.8 kg) lean shoulder or breast of lamb
6 medium-sized potatoes, peeled and sliced to 1/8-inch (.3-cm) thickness
6 medium-sized onions, thinly sliced
  Salt
  Freshly ground black pepper
1 leek, washed and sliced in rounds
1 rib celery, cut in 3 or 4 pieces
3 sprigs parsley
1 bay leaf
1 tsp (5 ml) thyme
2 cups (473 ml) Brown Stock, p. 526

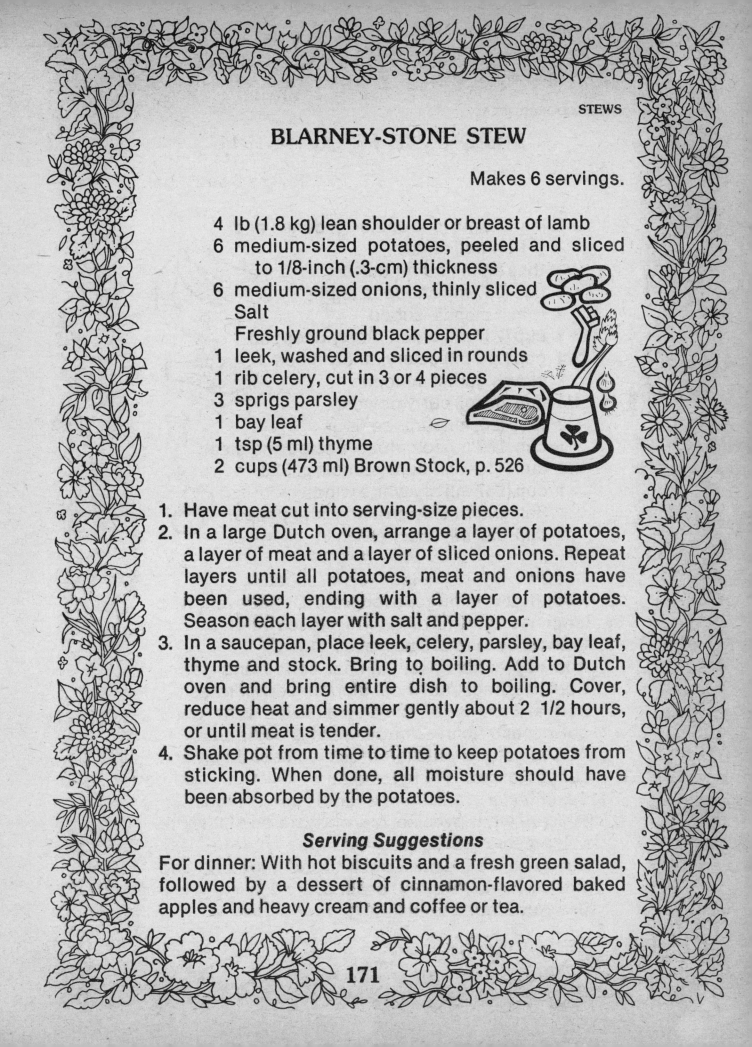

1. Have meat cut into serving-size pieces.
2. In a large Dutch oven, arrange a layer of potatoes, a layer of meat and a layer of sliced onions. Repeat layers until all potatoes, meat and onions have been used, ending with a layer of potatoes. Season each layer with salt and pepper.
3. In a saucepan, place leek, celery, parsley, bay leaf, thyme and stock. Bring to boiling. Add to Dutch oven and bring entire dish to boiling. Cover, reduce heat and simmer gently about 2 1/2 hours, or until meat is tender.
4. Shake pot from time to time to keep potatoes from sticking. When done, all moisture should have been absorbed by the potatoes.

Serving Suggestions

For dinner: With hot biscuits and a fresh green salad, followed by a dessert of cinnamon-flavored baked apples and heavy cream and coffee or tea.

CURRIED LAMB FRENCH-STYLE

Makes 8 servings.

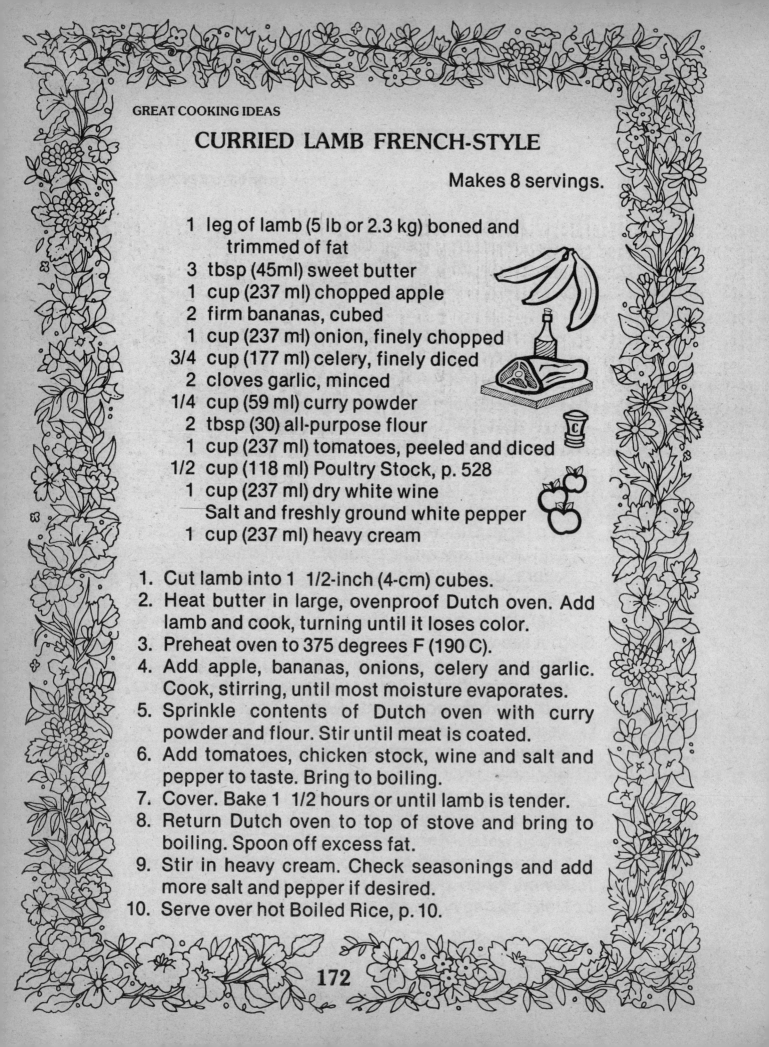

1 leg of lamb (5 lb or 2.3 kg) boned and
   trimmed of fat
3 tbsp (45ml) sweet butter
1 cup (237 ml) chopped apple
2 firm bananas, cubed
1 cup (237 ml) onion, finely chopped
3/4 cup (177 ml) celery, finely diced
2 cloves garlic, minced
1/4 cup (59 ml) curry powder
2 tbsp (30) all-purpose flour
1 cup (237 ml) tomatoes, peeled and diced
1/2 cup (118 ml) Poultry Stock, p. 528
1 cup (237 ml) dry white wine
   Salt and freshly ground white pepper
1 cup (237 ml) heavy cream

1. Cut lamb into 1 1/2-inch (4-cm) cubes.
2. Heat butter in large, ovenproof Dutch oven. Add lamb and cook, turning until it loses color.
3. Preheat oven to 375 degrees F (190 C).
4. Add apple, bananas, onions, celery and garlic. Cook, stirring, until most moisture evaporates.
5. Sprinkle contents of Dutch oven with curry powder and flour. Stir until meat is coated.
6. Add tomatoes, chicken stock, wine and salt and pepper to taste. Bring to boiling.
7. Cover. Bake 1 1/2 hours or until lamb is tender.
8. Return Dutch oven to top of stove and bring to boiling. Spoon off excess fat.
9. Stir in heavy cream. Check seasonings and add more salt and pepper if desired.
10. Serve over hot Boiled Rice, p. 10.

LAMB STEW WITH WHITE WINE

Makes 6 servings.

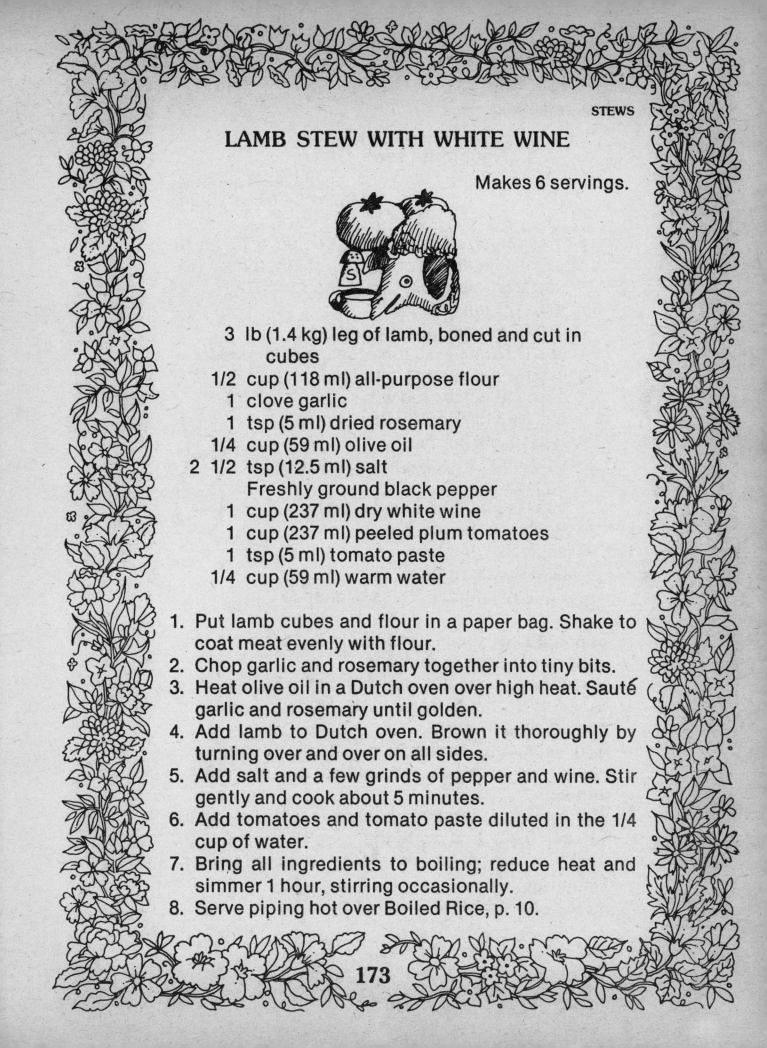

3 lb (1.4 kg) leg of lamb, boned and cut in cubes
1/2 cup (118 ml) all-purpose flour
1 clove garlic
1 tsp (5 ml) dried rosemary
1/4 cup (59 ml) olive oil
2 1/2 tsp (12.5 ml) salt
Freshly ground black pepper
1 cup (237 ml) dry white wine
1 cup (237 ml) peeled plum tomatoes
1 tsp (5 ml) tomato paste
1/4 cup (59 ml) warm water

1. Put lamb cubes and flour in a paper bag. Shake to coat meat evenly with flour.
2. Chop garlic and rosemary together into tiny bits.
3. Heat olive oil in a Dutch oven over high heat. Sauté garlic and rosemary until golden.
4. Add lamb to Dutch oven. Brown it thoroughly by turning over and over on all sides.
5. Add salt and a few grinds of pepper and wine. Stir gently and cook about 5 minutes.
6. Add tomatoes and tomato paste diluted in the 1/4 cup of water.
7. Bring all ingredients to boiling; reduce heat and simmer 1 hour, stirring occasionally.
8. Serve piping hot over Boiled Rice, p. 10.

MOUSSAKA
(Eggplant-Lamb Stew)

Makes 8 - 10 servings.

3 medium-sized eggplants, peeled and cut in long slices about 1/2 inch (1 cm) thick
1 cup (237 ml) onion, finely chopped
3/4 cup (177 ml) olive oil
2 lb (907 grams) lean ground lamb
1 cup (237 ml) fresh tomatoes, well-drained
1/3 cup (79 ml) parsley, chopped
1/2 cup (118 ml) dry red wine
1/2 cup (118 ml) Poultry Stock, p. 528
1/4 tsp (1.2 ml) nutmeg
Grating of freshly ground black pepper
3 egg whites
1/2 cup (118 ml) fine bread crumbs
Bechamel Sauce, below
3 egg yolks, beaten
Grating of nutmeg
Freshly grated Parmesan cheese

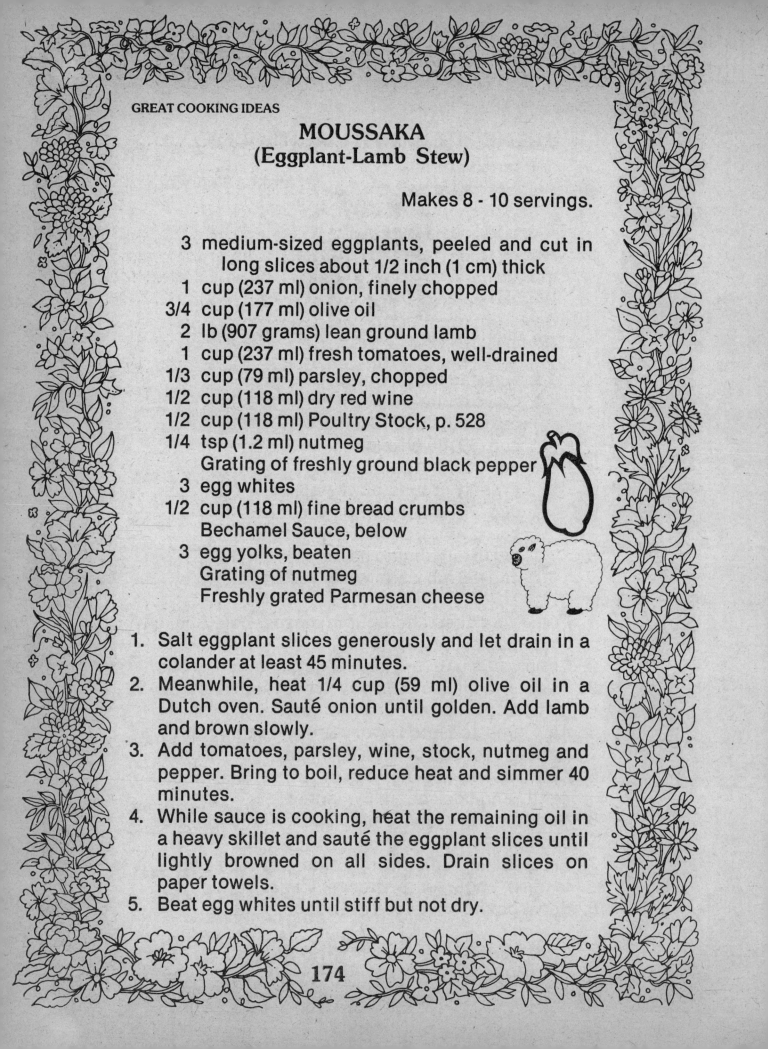

1. Salt eggplant slices generously and let drain in a colander at least 45 minutes.
2. Meanwhile, heat 1/4 cup (59 ml) olive oil in a Dutch oven. Sauté onion until golden. Add lamb and brown slowly.
3. Add tomatoes, parsley, wine, stock, nutmeg and pepper. Bring to boil, reduce heat and simmer 40 minutes.
4. While sauce is cooking, heat the remaining oil in a heavy skillet and sauté the eggplant slices until lightly browned on all sides. Drain slices on paper towels.
5. Beat egg whites until stiff but not dry.

6. When the sauce is done, fold in the egg whites and bread crumbs.
7. Prepare sauce, see below.
8. Preheat oven to 350 degrees F (177 C).
9. Assemble ingredients in a 9 x 13-inch (33 x 23-cm) baking dish: Layer of eggplant, layer of meat mixture and second eggplant layer. Cover with Bechamel Sauce. Sprinkle with Parmesan.
10. Bake until thoroughly heated, but do *not* boil.
11. Remove moussaka from oven. Allow to cool 30 minutes or longer. Cut into 8 to 10 squares. Serve sprinkled with Parmesan. However, it is preferable to refrigerate overnight before serving.
12. To heat: Preheat oven to 500 degrees F (260 C). Cut moussaka in 8 to 10 pieces. Pour thin layer of milk into bottom of one or more baking pans. Arrange squares in pan. Bake until hot, about 15 minutes. Transfer squares to individual dishes, sprinkle with Parmesan and serve.

Bechamel Sauce for Moussaka:

        1/4 lb (113 grams) sweet butter
          6 tbsp (90 ml) flour
        1/4 cup (59 ml) cornstarch
      3 1/2 cups (828 ml) hot milk
          2 small eggs, lightly beaten
        1/8 tsp (.6 ml) nutmeg

1. Heat butter in a 1 1/2-qt (1.5-liter) saucepan. When melted, add flour, stirring with wire whisk. Add cornstarch and stir to blend.
2. Add about 1/3 of milk, stirring rapidly with whisk. Quickly add another 1/3 milk, stirring rapidly and constantly. Do same with remaining milk.
3. When thickened and smooth, remove from heat. Beat the eggs and nutmeg. Add to sauce, stirring with whisk. Cook briefly, stirring constantly.

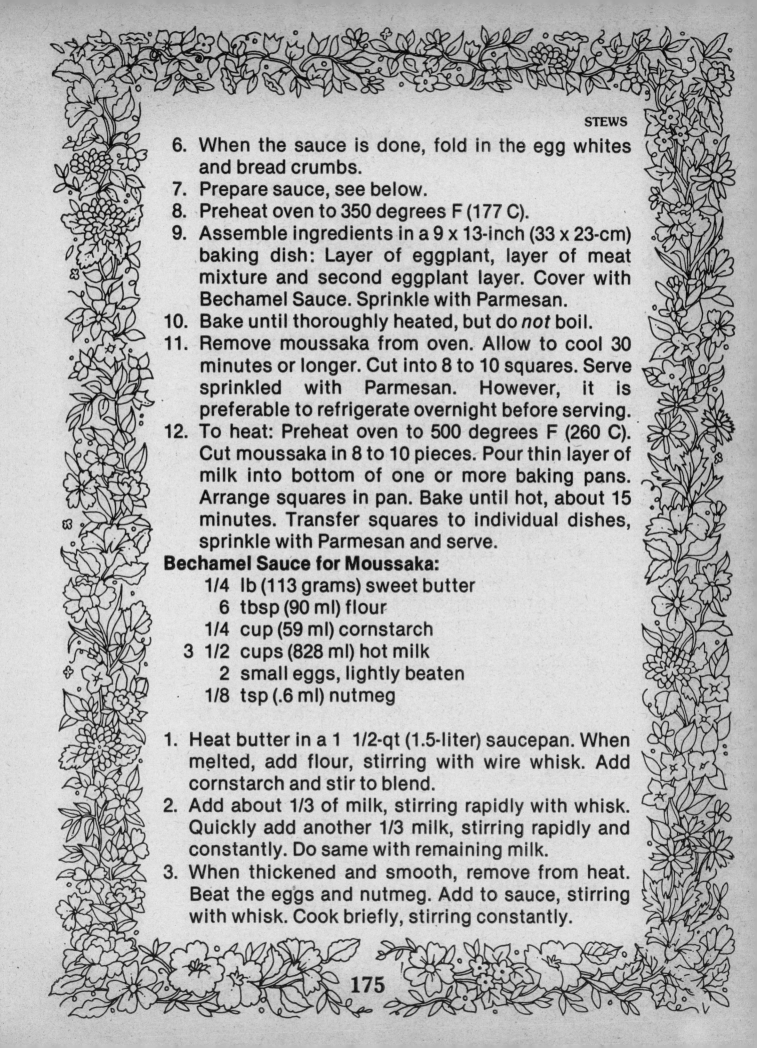

SPRING LAMB RAGOUT

Makes 6 servings.

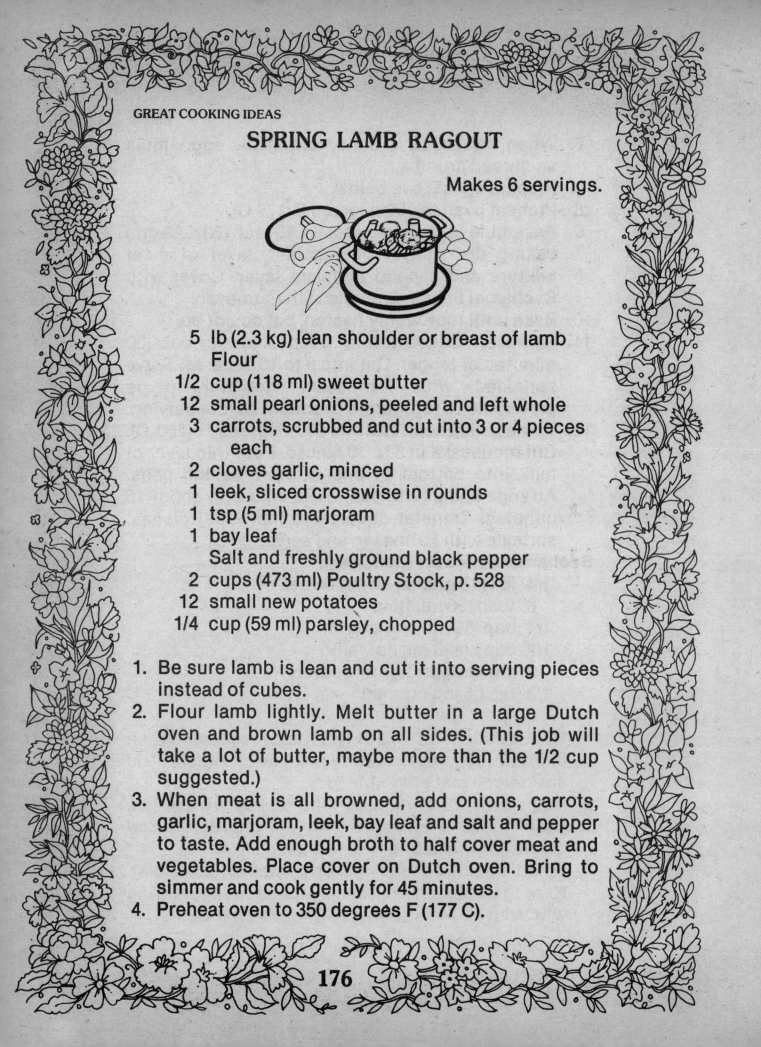

- 5 lb (2.3 kg) lean shoulder or breast of lamb
  Flour
- 1/2 cup (118 ml) sweet butter
- 12 small pearl onions, peeled and left whole
- 3 carrots, scrubbed and cut into 3 or 4 pieces each
- 2 cloves garlic, minced
- 1 leek, sliced crosswise in rounds
- 1 tsp (5 ml) marjoram
- 1 bay leaf
  Salt and freshly ground black pepper
- 2 cups (473 ml) Poultry Stock, p. 528
- 12 small new potatoes
- 1/4 cup (59 ml) parsley, chopped

1. Be sure lamb is lean and cut it into serving pieces instead of cubes.
2. Flour lamb lightly. Melt butter in a large Dutch oven and brown lamb on all sides. (This job will take a lot of butter, maybe more than the 1/2 cup suggested.)
3. When meat is all browned, add onions, carrots, garlic, marjoram, leek, bay leaf and salt and pepper to taste. Add enough broth to half cover meat and vegetables. Place cover on Dutch oven. Bring to simmer and cook gently for 45 minutes.
4. Preheat oven to 350 degrees F (177 C).

5. Remove lamb, onions and carrots and place them in a casserole. Add potatoes, which have been parboiled for 10 minutes in salted water.

6. Skim fat from liquid in which meat was cooked and strain sauce through a sieve lined with a piece of fine linen.

7. Pour strained sauce over the meat and vegetables in casserole. Sprinkle chopped parsley on top. Cover and bake for 45 minutes to an hour.

8. If desired, thicken sauce by adding small balls, about the size of a green pea, of butter and flour kneaded together. Stir these, a few at a time, into stew until liquid becomes thick and smooth.

9. Serve from the casserole.

Suggested Menu

Soup:	Consommé
Main Course:	Spring Lamb Ragout
Salad:	Fresh mixed greens, cucumbers and radishes tossed with a French dressing
Bread:	Toasted French
Wine:	Cabernet Sauvignon or Zinfandel
Dessert:	Pineapple Sponge Custard
	Coffee or Tea

NOTES

VEAL SAUTÉ WITH SPAETZLE

Makes 8 servings.

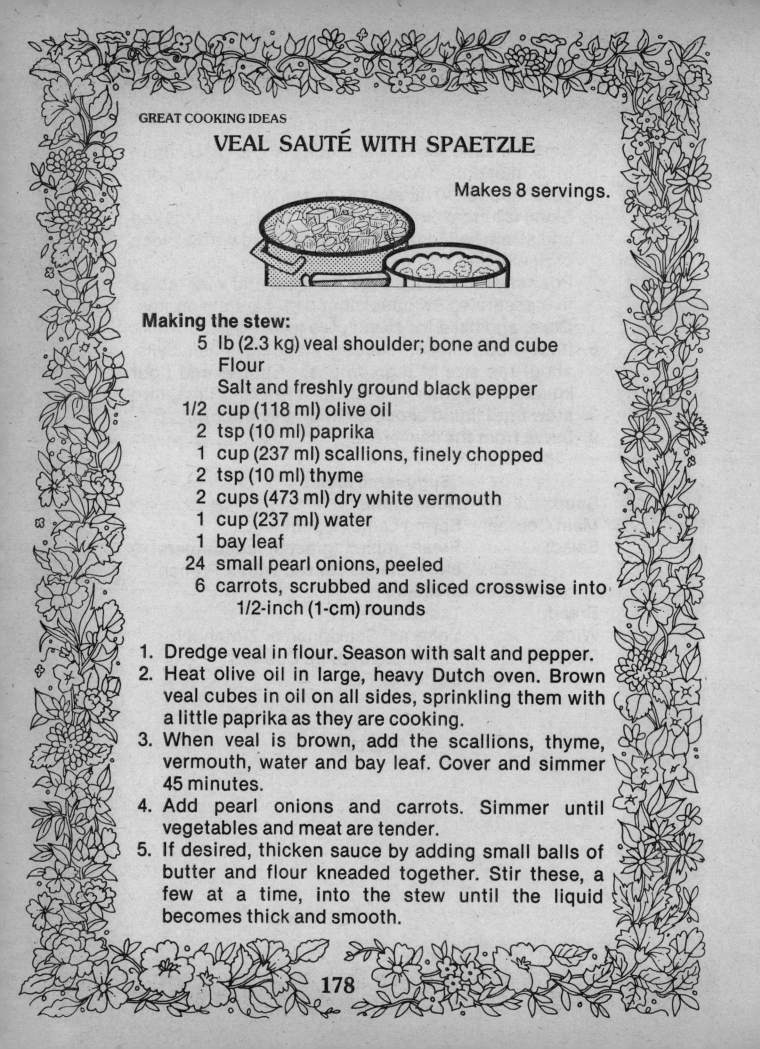

Making the stew:

   5 lb (2.3 kg) veal shoulder; bone and cube
      Flour
      Salt and freshly ground black pepper
 1/2 cup (118 ml) olive oil
   2 tsp (10 ml) paprika
   1 cup (237 ml) scallions, finely chopped
   2 tsp (10 ml) thyme
   2 cups (473 ml) dry white vermouth
   1 cup (237 ml) water
   1 bay leaf
  24 small pearl onions, peeled
   6 carrots, scrubbed and sliced crosswise into
      1/2-inch (1-cm) rounds

1. Dredge veal in flour. Season with salt and pepper.
2. Heat olive oil in large, heavy Dutch oven. Brown veal cubes in oil on all sides, sprinkling them with a little paprika as they are cooking.
3. When veal is brown, add the scallions, thyme, vermouth, water and bay leaf. Cover and simmer 45 minutes.
4. Add pearl onions and carrots. Simmer until vegetables and meat are tender.
5. If desired, thicken sauce by adding small balls of butter and flour kneaded together. Stir these, a few at a time, into the stew until the liquid becomes thick and smooth.

Making the spaetzle:

        6 eggs
        6 cups (1.4 liters) sifted flour
        1 tsp (5 ml) salt
        2 cups (473 ml) milk
           Boiling water
           Sweet butter

1. Place eggs in large mixing bowl. Beat lightly with a fork.
2. Add flour, which has been sifted, and salt. (An electric mixer can be used for this job).
3. When the eggs, flour and salt are well blended, gradually add the milk. Continue beating for about 4 minutes.
4. Drop tiny balls of this dough from end of a small spoon into briskly boiling water. The spaetzle are cooked when they rise to the surface.
5. Drain spaetzle on paper towels. Melt butter into large skillet and sauté spaetzle quickly.
6. Serve Veal Sauté over the Spaetzle.

NOTES

EXOTIC VEAL RAGOUT

Makes 6 servings.

3 lb (1.4 kg) veal shoulder, cut in 1 1/2-inch (4-cm) cubes
4 tbsp (60 ml) olive oil
1 large onion, coarsely chopped
2 tbsp (30 ml) flour
1 cup (237 ml) dry white wine*
3/4 cup (177 ml) Brown Stock, p. 526
1/2 cup (118 ml) tomato purée
2 cloves garlic, cut in half
  Bouquet garni (tie in a cheesecloth bag):
    2 large sprigs parsley, 1 bay leaf, 1/2 tsp (2.5 ml) dried thyme leaves
1 small strip orange peel (optional)
  Salt and freshly ground black pepper
1/2 lb (227 grams) fresh mushrooms, sliced thick
3 tbsp (45 ml) parsley, coarsely chopped

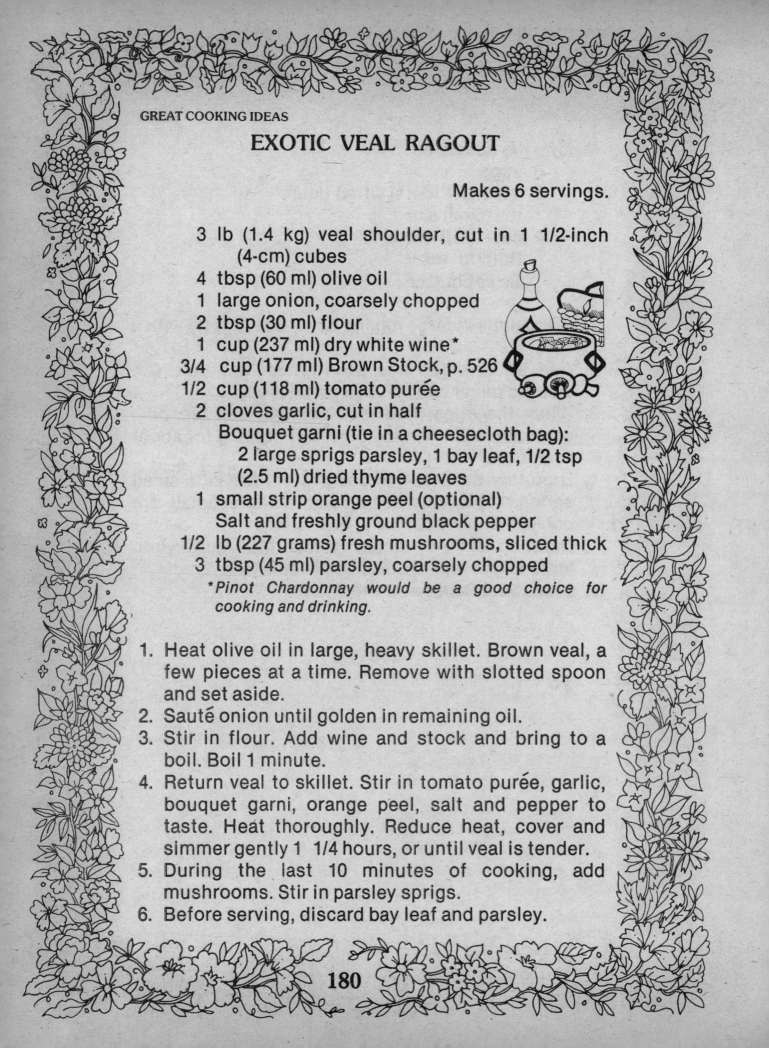

Pinot Chardonnay would be a good choice for cooking and drinking.

1. Heat olive oil in large, heavy skillet. Brown veal, a few pieces at a time. Remove with slotted spoon and set aside.
2. Sauté onion until golden in remaining oil.
3. Stir in flour. Add wine and stock and bring to a boil. Boil 1 minute.
4. Return veal to skillet. Stir in tomato purée, garlic, bouquet garni, orange peel, salt and pepper to taste. Heat thoroughly. Reduce heat, cover and simmer gently 1 1/4 hours, or until veal is tender.
5. During the last 10 minutes of cooking, add mushrooms. Stir in parsley sprigs.
6. Before serving, discard bay leaf and parsley.

VEAL STEW

Makes 6 servings.

2 tbsp (30 ml) sweet butter
1/2 cup (118 ml) onion, minced
2 lb (907 grams) boned veal shoulder, cut in 1 1/2-inch (4-cm) cubes
1 1/4 cups (296 ml) Veal Stock, p. 529
1 1/4 cups (296 ml) water
3/4 tsp (3.7 ml) salt
1/2 tsp (2.5 ml) marjoram
1 1/2 cups (355 ml) carrots, scraped and cut into 1-inch (3-cm) pieces
1 cup (237 ml) celery, diced
2 medium-sized yellow summer squash, diced
1 pkg (10 oz or 284 grams) frozen peas
1 tbsp (15 ml) flour

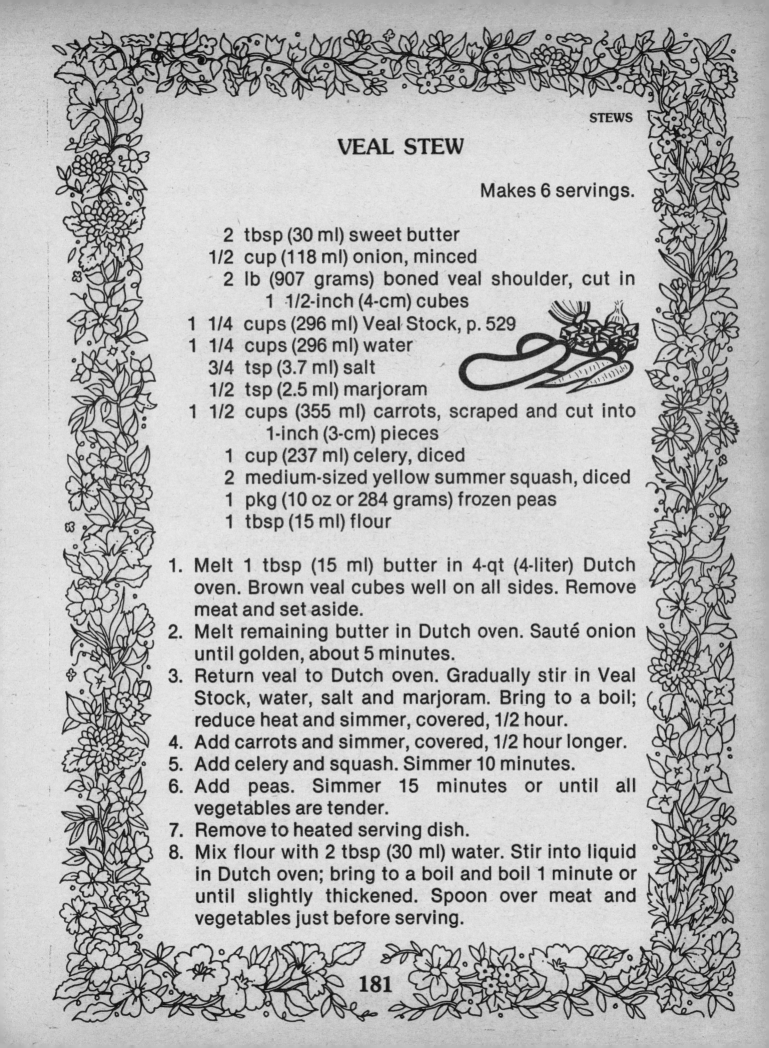

1. Melt 1 tbsp (15 ml) butter in 4-qt (4-liter) Dutch oven. Brown veal cubes well on all sides. Remove meat and set aside.
2. Melt remaining butter in Dutch oven. Sauté onion until golden, about 5 minutes.
3. Return veal to Dutch oven. Gradually stir in Veal Stock, water, salt and marjoram. Bring to a boil; reduce heat and simmer, covered, 1/2 hour.
4. Add carrots and simmer, covered, 1/2 hour longer.
5. Add celery and squash. Simmer 10 minutes.
6. Add peas. Simmer 15 minutes or until all vegetables are tender.
7. Remove to heated serving dish.
8. Mix flour with 2 tbsp (30 ml) water. Stir into liquid in Dutch oven; bring to a boil and boil 1 minute or until slightly thickened. Spoon over meat and vegetables just before serving.

BOUILLABAISE

Makes 4 servings.

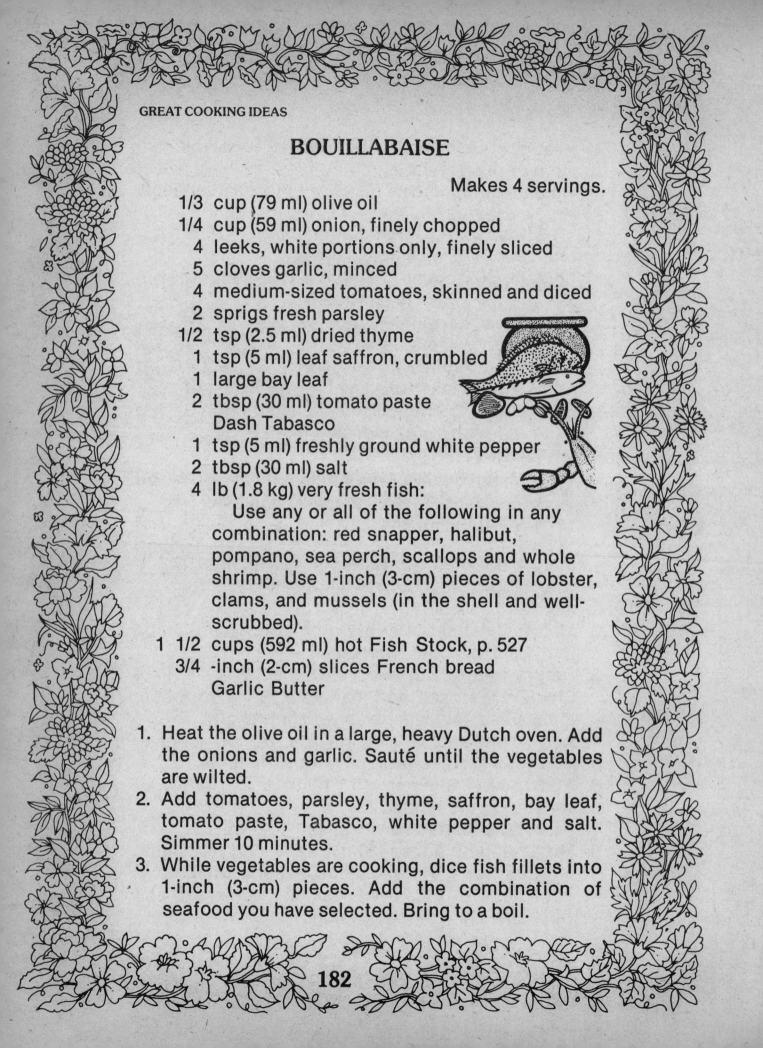

1/3 cup (79 ml) olive oil
1/4 cup (59 ml) onion, finely chopped
4 leeks, white portions only, finely sliced
5 cloves garlic, minced
4 medium-sized tomatoes, skinned and diced
2 sprigs fresh parsley
1/2 tsp (2.5 ml) dried thyme
1 tsp (5 ml) leaf saffron, crumbled
1 large bay leaf
2 tbsp (30 ml) tomato paste
Dash Tabasco
1 tsp (5 ml) freshly ground white pepper
2 tbsp (30 ml) salt
4 lb (1.8 kg) very fresh fish:
Use any or all of the following in any combination: red snapper, halibut, pompano, sea perch, scallops and whole shrimp. Use 1-inch (3-cm) pieces of lobster, clams, and mussels (in the shell and well-scrubbed).
1 1/2 cups (592 ml) hot Fish Stock, p. 527
3/4 -inch (2-cm) slices French bread
Garlic Butter

1. Heat the olive oil in a large, heavy Dutch oven. Add the onions and garlic. Sauté until the vegetables are wilted.
2. Add tomatoes, parsley, thyme, saffron, bay leaf, tomato paste, Tabasco, white pepper and salt. Simmer 10 minutes.
3. While vegetables are cooking, dice fish fillets into 1-inch (3-cm) pieces. Add the combination of seafood you have selected. Bring to a boil.

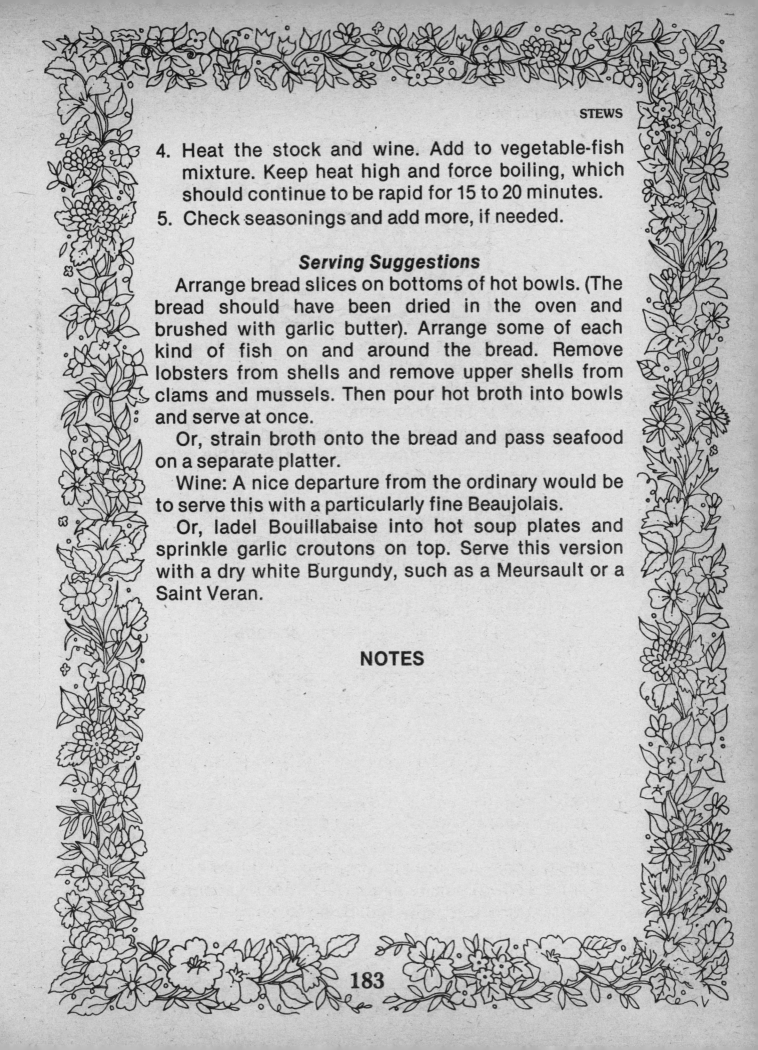

4. Heat the stock and wine. Add to vegetable-fish mixture. Keep heat high and force boiling, which should continue to be rapid for 15 to 20 minutes.
5. Check seasonings and add more, if needed.

Serving Suggestions

Arrange bread slices on bottoms of hot bowls. (The bread should have been dried in the oven and brushed with garlic butter). Arrange some of each kind of fish on and around the bread. Remove lobsters from shells and remove upper shells from clams and mussels. Then pour hot broth into bowls and serve at once.

Or, strain broth onto the bread and pass seafood on a separate platter.

Wine: A nice departure from the ordinary would be to serve this with a particularly fine Beaujolais.

Or, ladel Bouillabaise into hot soup plates and sprinkle garlic croutons on top. Serve this version with a dry white Burgundy, such as a Meursault or a Saint Veran.

NOTES

CAVEMAN STEW

Makes 4 - 6 servings.

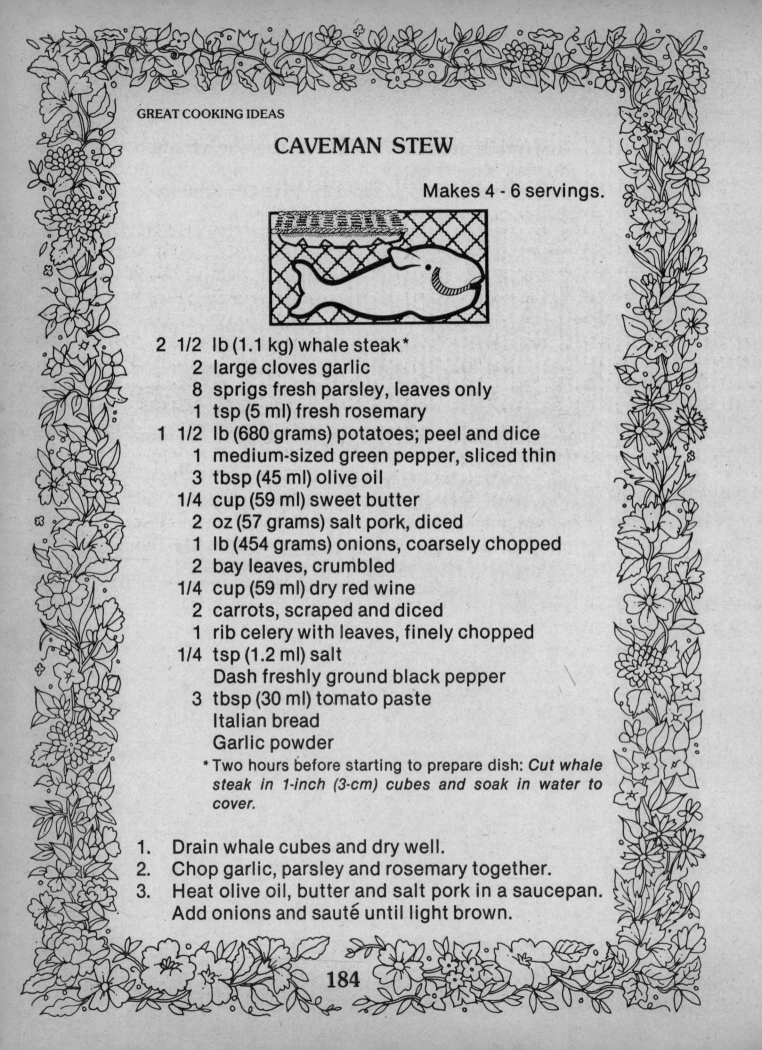

2 1/2 lb (1.1 kg) whale steak*
    2 large cloves garlic
    8 sprigs fresh parsley, leaves only
    1 tsp (5 ml) fresh rosemary
1 1/2 lb (680 grams) potatoes; peel and dice
    1 medium-sized green pepper, sliced thin
    3 tbsp (45 ml) olive oil
1/4 cup (59 ml) sweet butter
    2 oz (57 grams) salt pork, diced
    1 lb (454 grams) onions, coarsely chopped
    2 bay leaves, crumbled
1/4 cup (59 ml) dry red wine
    2 carrots, scraped and diced
    1 rib celery with leaves, finely chopped
1/4 tsp (1.2 ml) salt
    Dash freshly ground black pepper
    3 tbsp (30 ml) tomato paste
    Italian bread
    Garlic powder

* Two hours before starting to prepare dish: *Cut whale steak in 1-inch (3-cm) cubes and soak in water to cover.*

1. Drain whale cubes and dry well.
2. Chop garlic, parsley and rosemary together.
3. Heat olive oil, butter and salt pork in a saucepan. Add onions and sauté until light brown.

4. Add whale meat and brown slowly 10 minutes, stirring once or twice.
5. Add garlic, parsley, rosemary and bay leaves. Stir and cook 8 minutes.
6. Add wine, cover and cook 5 minutes.
7. Add carrots, celery, potatoes, green pepper, salt and pepper. Combine ingredients thoroughly.
8. Mix tomato paste with 1 cup (237 ml) warm water. Add to stew and stir well. Cook slowly about 1 1/2 hours, or until whale steak is tender.
9. To make garlic bread — Slice bread, but do not detach slices. Combine 1/8 tsp (.6 ml) garlic powder with 3 tbsp (45 ml) softened butter. Spread one side of each bread slice liberally with garlic butter. Wrap loaf in aluminum foil. Place in hot oven 5 minutes.
10. For each serving, place 2 slices of bread in an individual bowl and spoon a large portion of stew on top. Serve with a red Chianti or a dry red French or California Burgundy.

NOTES

185

BOSTON BAY STEW

Makes 4 servings.

3 cups (710 ml) oysters and liquid
4 tbsp (60 ml) butter
1 cup (237 ml) milk
2 cups (473 ml) cream
Celery salt
Worcestershire
Paprika

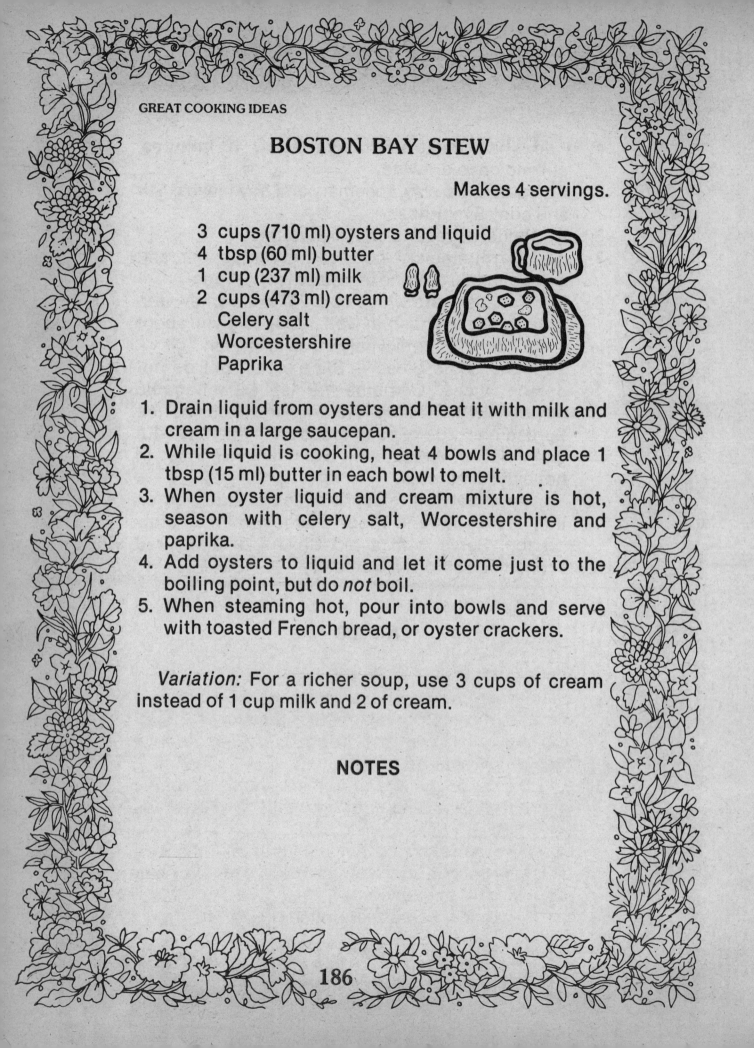

1. Drain liquid from oysters and heat it with milk and cream in a large saucepan.
2. While liquid is cooking, heat 4 bowls and place 1 tbsp (15 ml) butter in each bowl to melt.
3. When oyster liquid and cream mixture is hot, season with celery salt, Worcestershire and paprika.
4. Add oysters to liquid and let it come just to the boiling point, but do *not* boil.
5. When steaming hot, pour into bowls and serve with toasted French bread, or oyster crackers.

Variation: For a richer soup, use 3 cups of cream instead of 1 cup milk and 2 of cream.

NOTES

COUNTRY FISH-VEGETABLE STEW

Makes 4 servings.

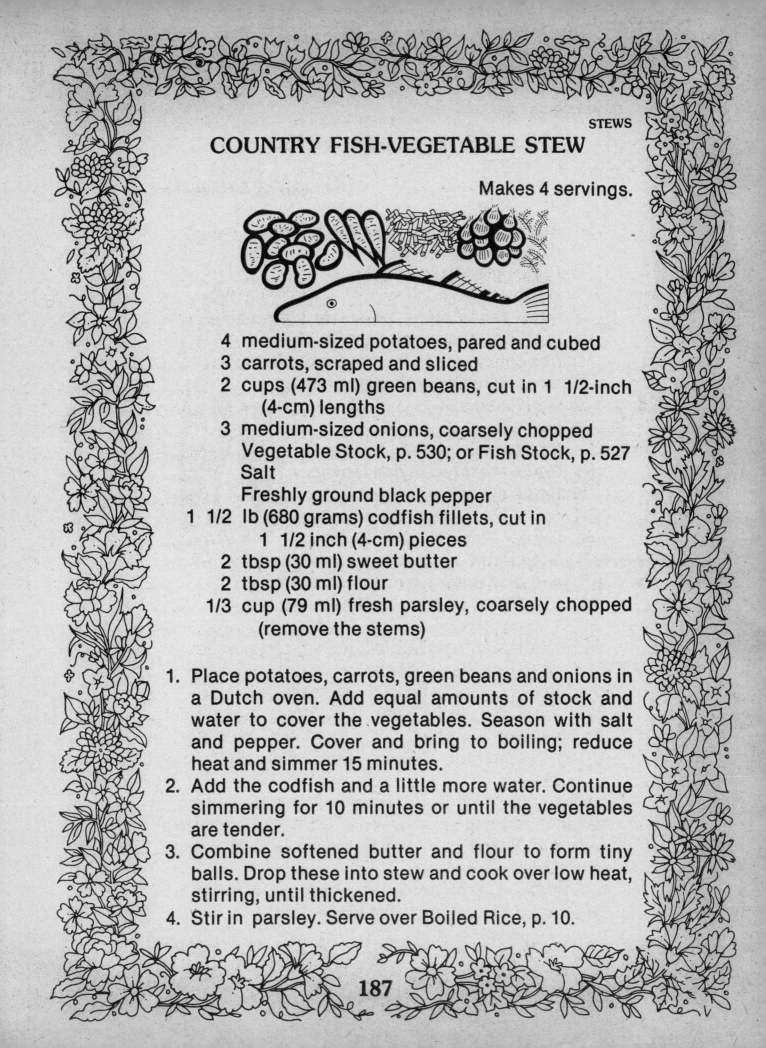

4 medium-sized potatoes, pared and cubed
3 carrots, scraped and sliced
2 cups (473 ml) green beans, cut in 1 1/2-inch
  (4-cm) lengths
3 medium-sized onions, coarsely chopped
  Vegetable Stock, p. 530; or Fish Stock, p. 527
  Salt
  Freshly ground black pepper
1 1/2 lb (680 grams) codfish fillets, cut in
      1 1/2 inch (4-cm) pieces
2 tbsp (30 ml) sweet butter
2 tbsp (30 ml) flour
1/3 cup (79 ml) fresh parsley, coarsely chopped
  (remove the stems)

1. Place potatoes, carrots, green beans and onions in a Dutch oven. Add equal amounts of stock and water to cover the vegetables. Season with salt and pepper. Cover and bring to boiling; reduce heat and simmer 15 minutes.
2. Add the codfish and a little more water. Continue simmering for 10 minutes or until the vegetables are tender.
3. Combine softened butter and flour to form tiny balls. Drop these into stew and cook over low heat, stirring, until thickened.
4. Stir in parsley. Serve over Boiled Rice, p. 10.

FISH IN WHITE WINE

Makes 6 - 8 servings.

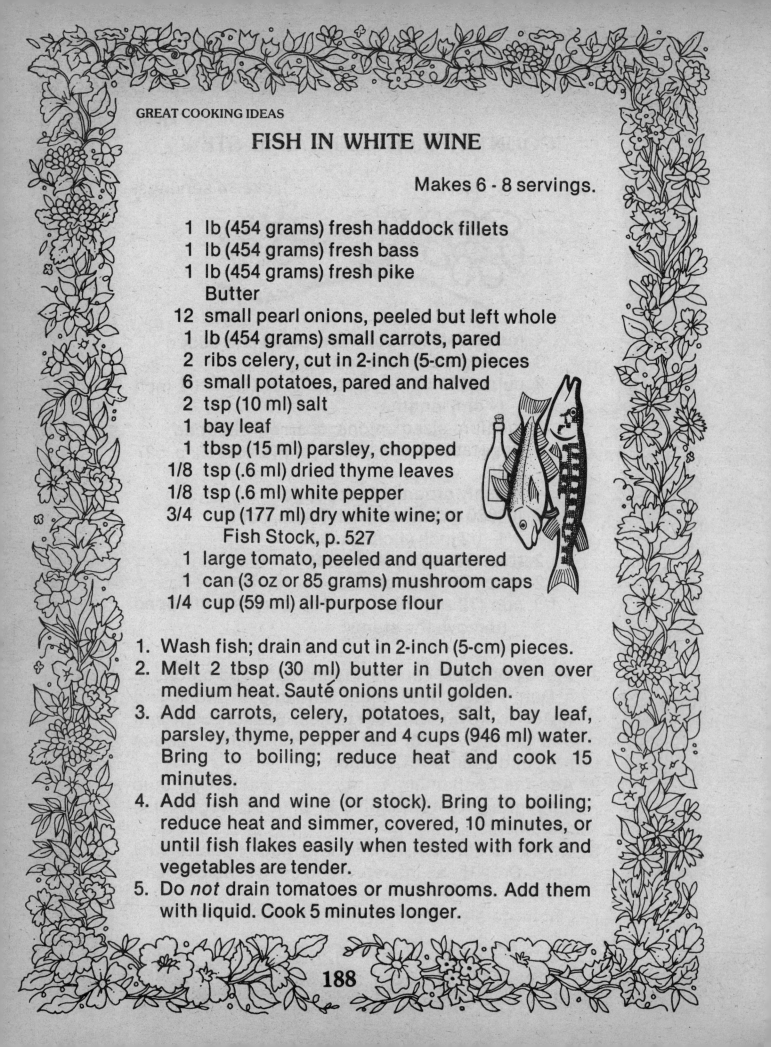

1   lb (454 grams) fresh haddock fillets
1   lb (454 grams) fresh bass
1   lb (454 grams) fresh pike
    Butter
12 small pearl onions, peeled but left whole
1   lb (454 grams) small carrots, pared
2   ribs celery, cut in 2-inch (5-cm) pieces
6   small potatoes, pared and halved
2   tsp (10 ml) salt
1   bay leaf
1   tbsp (15 ml) parsley, chopped
1/8 tsp (.6 ml) dried thyme leaves
1/8 tsp (.6 ml) white pepper
3/4 cup (177 ml) dry white wine; or
    Fish Stock, p. 527
1   large tomato, peeled and quartered
1   can (3 oz or 85 grams) mushroom caps
1/4 cup (59 ml) all-purpose flour

1. Wash fish; drain and cut in 2-inch (5-cm) pieces.
2. Melt 2 tbsp (30 ml) butter in Dutch oven over medium heat. Sauté onions until golden.
3. Add carrots, celery, potatoes, salt, bay leaf, parsley, thyme, pepper and 4 cups (946 ml) water. Bring to boiling; reduce heat and cook 15 minutes.
4. Add fish and wine (or stock). Bring to boiling; reduce heat and simmer, covered, 10 minutes, or until fish flakes easily when tested with fork and vegetables are tender.
5. Do *not* drain tomatoes or mushrooms. Add them with liquid. Cook 5 minutes longer.

6. Remove fish and vegetables to heated serving bowl with slotted spoon. Cover and keep warm.
7. Bring fish broth to boiling; boil until reduced to 2 cups.
8. Melt 4 tbsp (59 ml) of butter in a 1-qt (1-liter) saucepan. Blend in flour. Remove from heat.
9. Stir fish broth gradually into butter-flour mixture. Return to heat and bring to boiling, stirring constantly. Reduce heat and cook, still stirring, until sauce thickens, about 1 minute.
10. Pour sauce over fish and vegetables in serving bowl. Garnish with chopped parsley.

Menu Suggestion

Appetizer: 2 or 3 stuffed clams per person
Main Course: Fish in White Wine
Salad: Asparagus with Vinaigrette dressing
Wine: Chenin Blanc or Soave
Dessert: Caramel Custard
            Coffee or Tea

NOTES

NEW ENGLAND CLAM STEW

Makes 8 servings.

4 cans (8 oz or 227 grams each) minced clams
3/4 cup (177 ml) butter
1/2 tsp (2.5 ml) celery salt
Dash Worcestershire
Paprika
6 cups (1.4 liters) half milk and half cream
1 tsp (5 ml) lemon juice (optional)

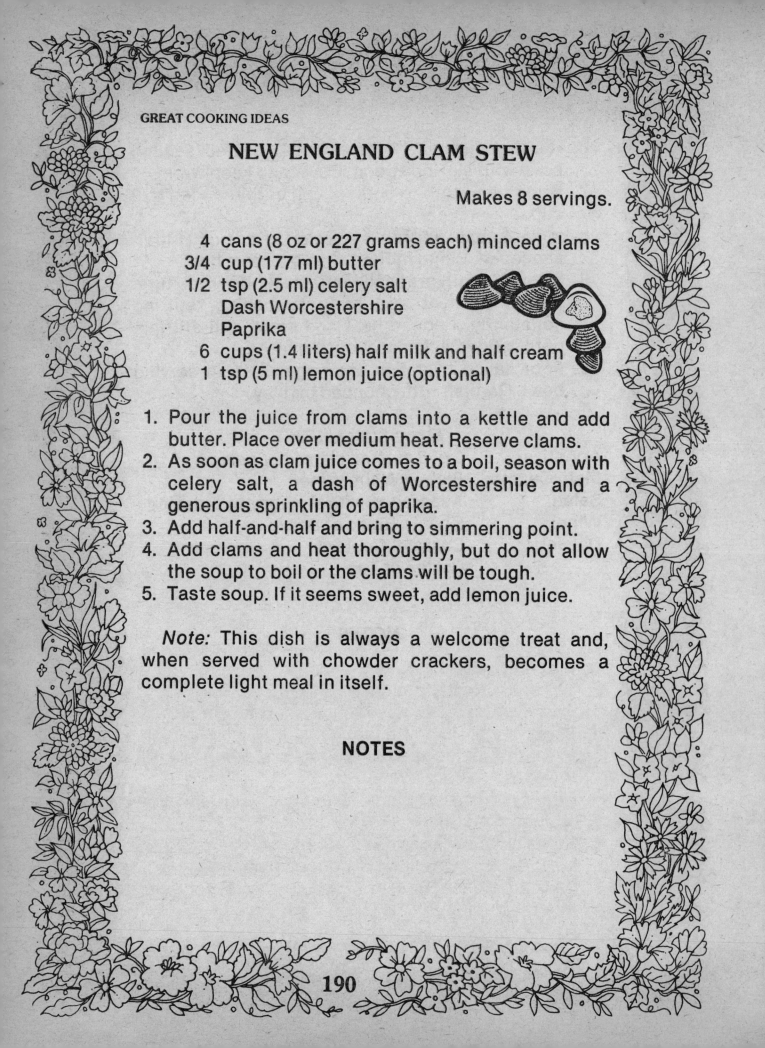

1. Pour the juice from clams into a kettle and add butter. Place over medium heat. Reserve clams.
2. As soon as clam juice comes to a boil, season with celery salt, a dash of Worcestershire and a generous sprinkling of paprika.
3. Add half-and-half and bring to simmering point.
4. Add clams and heat thoroughly, but do not allow the soup to boil or the clams will be tough.
5. Taste soup. If it seems sweet, add lemon juice.

Note: This dish is always a welcome treat and, when served with chowder crackers, becomes a complete light meal in itself.

NOTES

SEAFOOD GUMBO

Makes 6 servings.

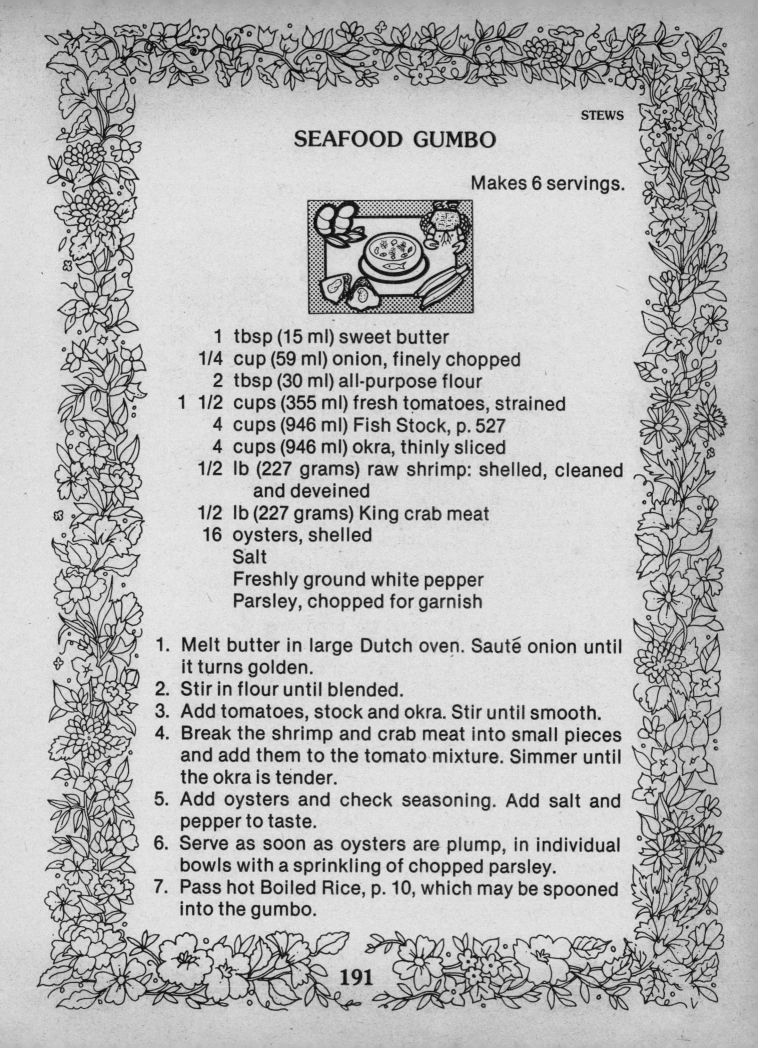

1 tbsp (15 ml) sweet butter
1/4 cup (59 ml) onion, finely chopped
2 tbsp (30 ml) all-purpose flour
1 1/2 cups (355 ml) fresh tomatoes, strained
4 cups (946 ml) Fish Stock, p. 527
4 cups (946 ml) okra, thinly sliced
1/2 lb (227 grams) raw shrimp: shelled, cleaned and deveined
1/2 lb (227 grams) King crab meat
16 oysters, shelled
Salt
Freshly ground white pepper
Parsley, chopped for garnish

1. Melt butter in large Dutch oven. Sauté onion until it turns golden.
2. Stir in flour until blended.
3. Add tomatoes, stock and okra. Stir until smooth.
4. Break the shrimp and crab meat into small pieces and add them to the tomato mixture. Simmer until the okra is tender.
5. Add oysters and check seasoning. Add salt and pepper to taste.
6. Serve as soon as oysters are plump, in individual bowls with a sprinkling of chopped parsley.
7. Pass hot Boiled Rice, p. 10, which may be spooned into the gumbo.

VEGETABLE STEW

Makes 6 - 8 servings.

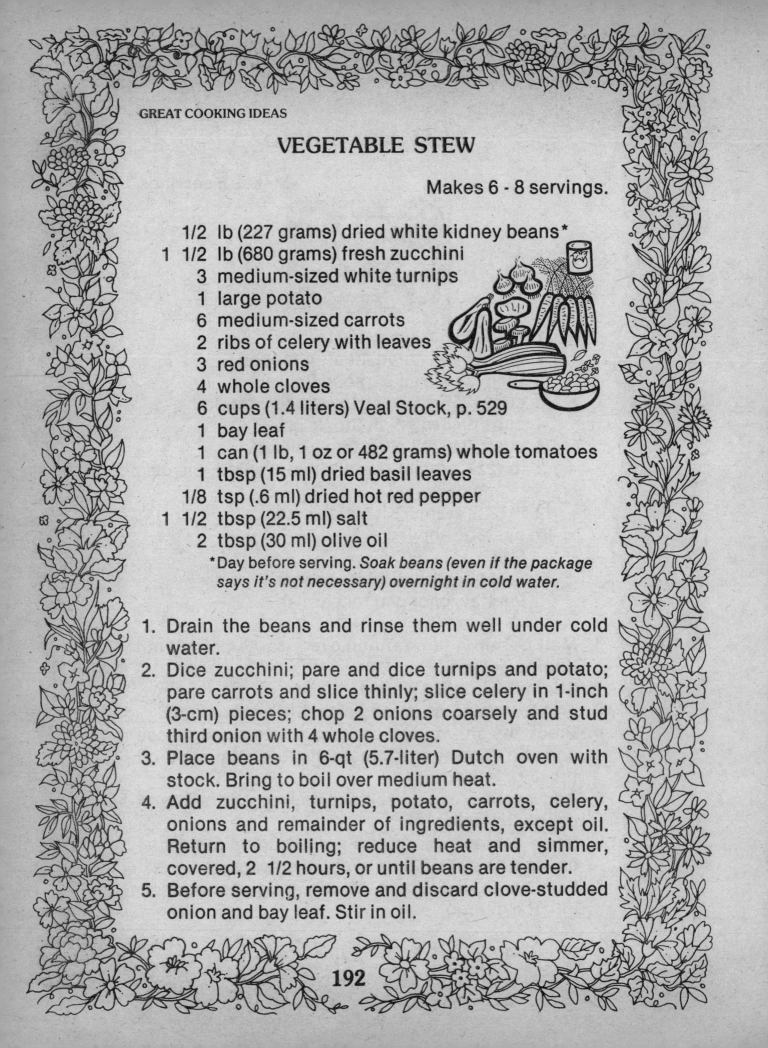

1/2 lb (227 grams) dried white kidney beans*
1 1/2 lb (680 grams) fresh zucchini
3 medium-sized white turnips
1 large potato
6 medium-sized carrots
2 ribs of celery with leaves
3 red onions
4 whole cloves
6 cups (1.4 liters) Veal Stock, p. 529
1 bay leaf
1 can (1 lb, 1 oz or 482 grams) whole tomatoes
1 tbsp (15 ml) dried basil leaves
1/8 tsp (.6 ml) dried hot red pepper
1 1/2 tbsp (22.5 ml) salt
2 tbsp (30 ml) olive oil

*Day before serving. *Soak beans (even if the package says it's not necessary) overnight in cold water.*

1. Drain the beans and rinse them well under cold water.
2. Dice zucchini; pare and dice turnips and potato; pare carrots and slice thinly; slice celery in 1-inch (3-cm) pieces; chop 2 onions coarsely and stud third onion with 4 whole cloves.
3. Place beans in 6-qt (5.7-liter) Dutch oven with stock. Bring to boil over medium heat.
4. Add zucchini, turnips, potato, carrots, celery, onions and remainder of ingredients, except oil. Return to boiling; reduce heat and simmer, covered, 2 1/2 hours, or until beans are tender.
5. Before serving, remove and discard clove-studded onion and bay leaf. Stir in oil.

BEEF BAKED WITH MUSHROOMS

Makes 6 servings.

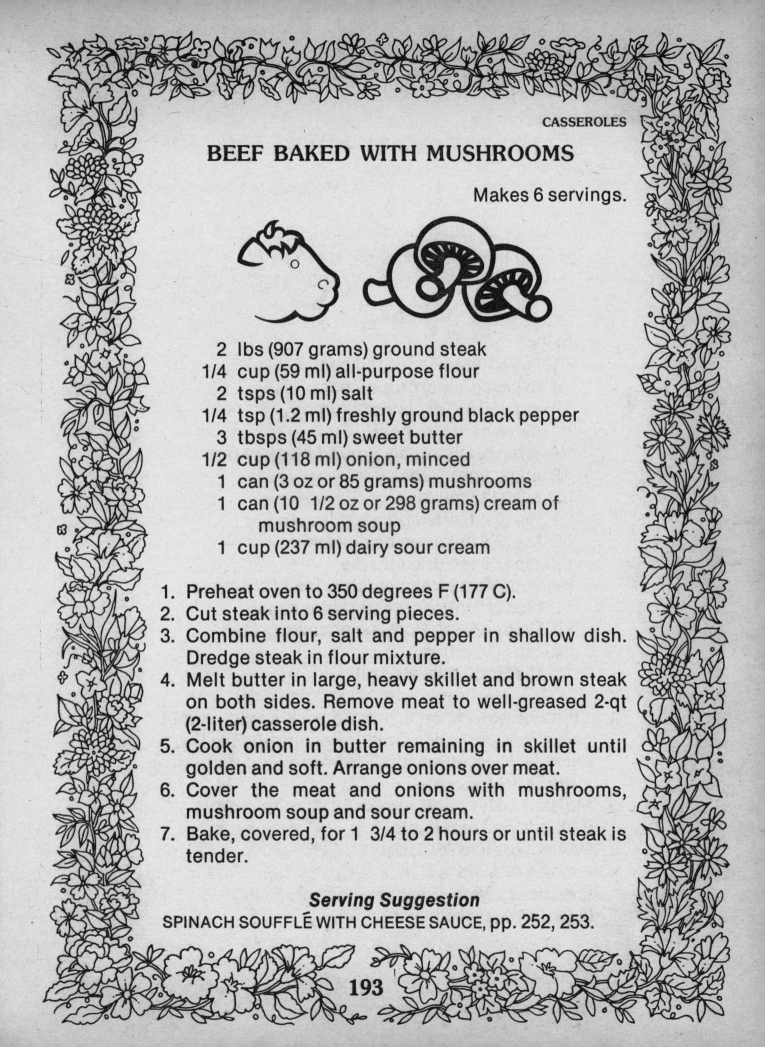

2 lbs (907 grams) ground steak
1/4 cup (59 ml) all-purpose flour
2 tsps (10 ml) salt
1/4 tsp (1.2 ml) freshly ground black pepper
3 tbsps (45 ml) sweet butter
1/2 cup (118 ml) onion, minced
1 can (3 oz or 85 grams) mushrooms
1 can (10 1/2 oz or 298 grams) cream of
   mushroom soup
1 cup (237 ml) dairy sour cream

1. Preheat oven to 350 degrees F (177 C).
2. Cut steak into 6 serving pieces.
3. Combine flour, salt and pepper in shallow dish. Dredge steak in flour mixture.
4. Melt butter in large, heavy skillet and brown steak on both sides. Remove meat to well-greased 2-qt (2-liter) casserole dish.
5. Cook onion in butter remaining in skillet until golden and soft. Arrange onions over meat.
6. Cover the meat and onions with mushrooms, mushroom soup and sour cream.
7. Bake, covered, for 1 3/4 to 2 hours or until steak is tender.

Serving Suggestion
SPINACH SOUFFLÉ WITH CHEESE SAUCE, pp. 252, 253.

BAKED CHILI 'N' MEATBALLS

Makes 6 to 8 servings.

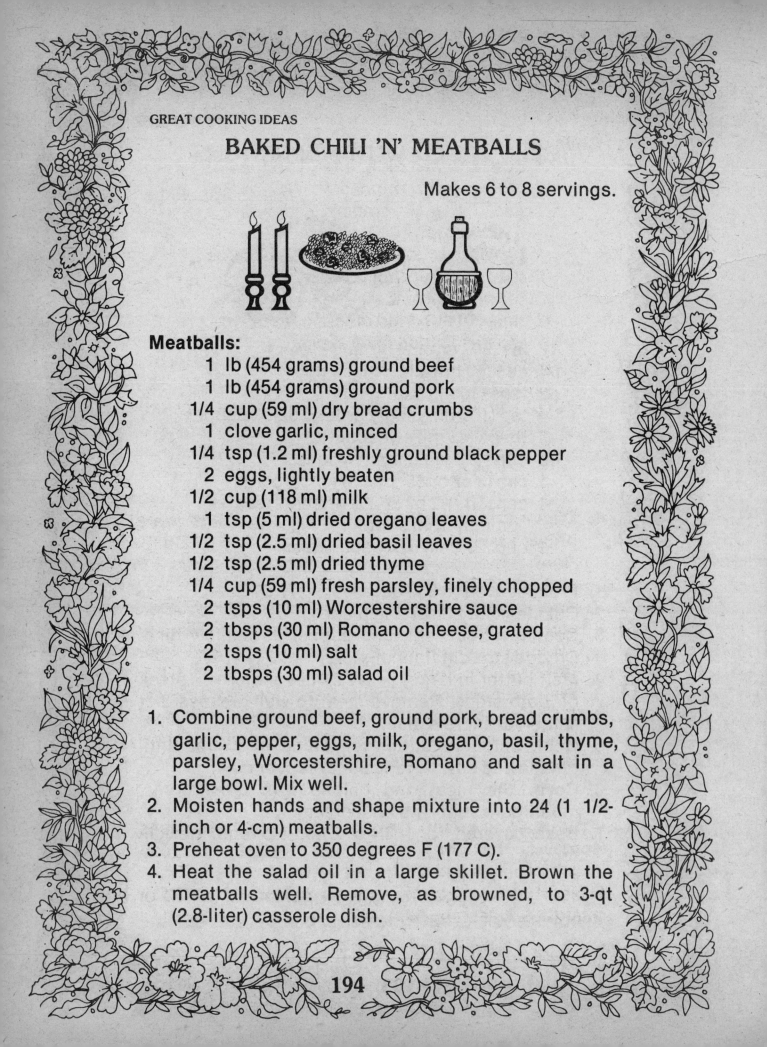

Meatballs:

- 1 lb (454 grams) ground beef
- 1 lb (454 grams) ground pork
- 1/4 cup (59 ml) dry bread crumbs
- 1 clove garlic, minced
- 1/4 tsp (1.2 ml) freshly ground black pepper
- 2 eggs, lightly beaten
- 1/2 cup (118 ml) milk
- 1 tsp (5 ml) dried oregano leaves
- 1/2 tsp (2.5 ml) dried basil leaves
- 1/2 tsp (2.5 ml) dried thyme
- 1/4 cup (59 ml) fresh parsley, finely chopped
- 2 tsps (10 ml) Worcestershire sauce
- 2 tbsps (30 ml) Romano cheese, grated
- 2 tsps (10 ml) salt
- 2 tbsps (30 ml) salad oil

1. Combine ground beef, ground pork, bread crumbs, garlic, pepper, eggs, milk, oregano, basil, thyme, parsley, Worcestershire, Romano and salt in a large bowl. Mix well.
2. Moisten hands and shape mixture into 24 (1 1/2-inch or 4-cm) meatballs.
3. Preheat oven to 350 degrees F (177 C).
4. Heat the salad oil in a large skillet. Brown the meatballs well. Remove, as browned, to 3-qt (2.8-liter) casserole dish.

Chili:

- 1 cup (237 ml) onion, finely chopped
- 2 cloves garlic, minced
- 1 can (1 lb or 454 grams) tomatoes, undrained
- 1 can (8 oz or 227 grams) tomato sauce
- 2 tbsps (30 ml) chili powder
- 2 tsps (10 ml) salt
- 2 tsps (10 ml) dried oregano leaves
- 1 tsp (5 ml) dried basil leaves
- 1 1/2 tbsps (22.5 ml) all-purpose flour
- 1 cup (237 ml) red wine or 2 beef-flavored bouillon cubes dissolved in 1 cup (237 ml) water
- 2 cans (15 1/2 oz or 439 grams each) kidney beans, drained

1. Discard from skillet (in which meatballs were browned) all drippings except for 2 tbsps (30 ml). Heat drippings and sauté onions and garlic for about 5 minutes.
2. Add the tomatoes, tomato sauce, chili powder, salt, oregano, basil and 1/4 cup (59 ml) red wine or 1/4 cup beef bouillon. Bring to boiling and simmer for about 5 minutes.
3. Pour sauce over meatballs. Bake, covered, 1 hour.
4. Combine flour with remaining wine, or beef bouillon, and stir into casserole along with beans.
5. Bake, covered, 30 minutes longer.

Serving Suggestions

With main course: Tossed salad which includes Romaine lettuce, watercress, radishes, fresh Zucchini slices and a little red onion.

Dessert: ORANGE CUSTARD WITH MERINGUE, p. 473 or ORANGE SOUFFLÉ, pp. 486, 487

BEEFY-CORN 'N' COTTAGE CHEESE BAKE

Makes about 8 servings.

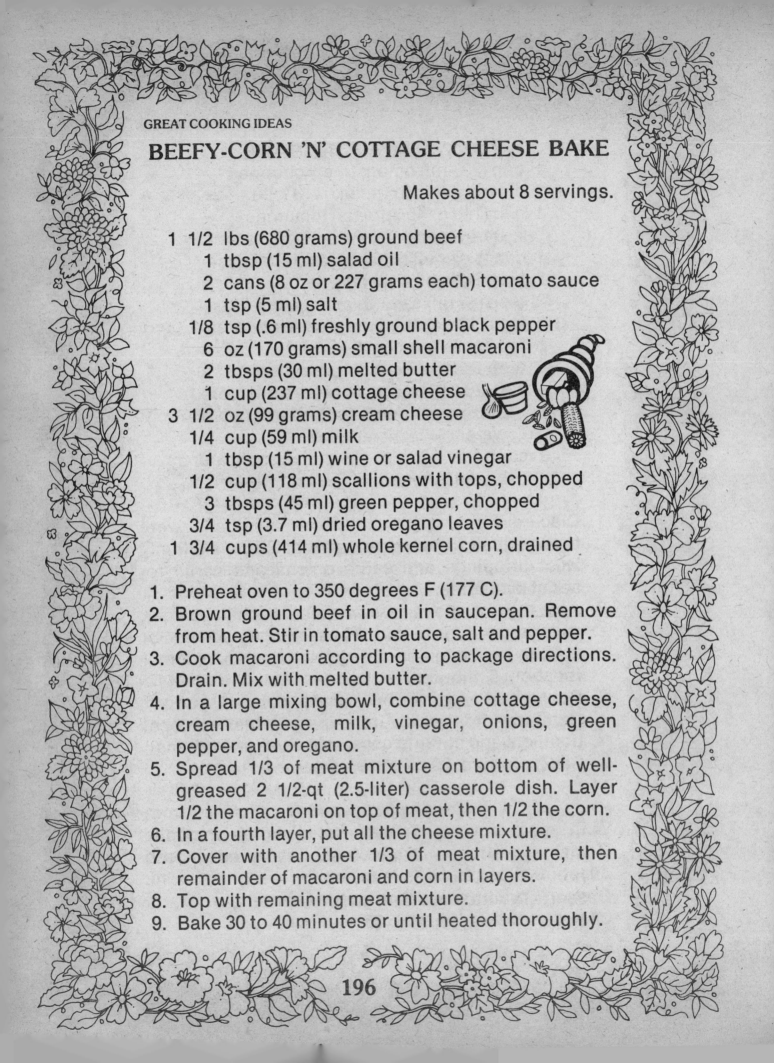

1 1/2	lbs (680 grams)	ground beef
1	tbsp (15 ml)	salad oil
2	cans (8 oz or 227 grams each)	tomato sauce
1	tsp (5 ml)	salt
1/8	tsp (.6 ml)	freshly ground black pepper
6	oz (170 grams)	small shell macaroni
2	tbsps (30 ml)	melted butter
1	cup (237 ml)	cottage cheese
3 1/2	oz (99 grams)	cream cheese
1/4	cup (59 ml)	milk
1	tbsp (15 ml)	wine or salad vinegar
1/2	cup (118 ml)	scallions with tops, chopped
3	tbsps (45 ml)	green pepper, chopped
3/4	tsp (3.7 ml)	dried oregano leaves
1 3/4	cups (414 ml)	whole kernel corn, drained

1. Preheat oven to 350 degrees F (177 C).
2. Brown ground beef in oil in saucepan. Remove from heat. Stir in tomato sauce, salt and pepper.
3. Cook macaroni according to package directions. Drain. Mix with melted butter.
4. In a large mixing bowl, combine cottage cheese, cream cheese, milk, vinegar, onions, green pepper, and oregano.
5. Spread 1/3 of meat mixture on bottom of well-greased 2 1/2-qt (2.5-liter) casserole dish. Layer 1/2 the macaroni on top of meat, then 1/2 the corn.
6. In a fourth layer, put all the cheese mixture.
7. Cover with another 1/3 of meat mixture, then remainder of macaroni and corn in layers.
8. Top with remaining meat mixture.
9. Bake 30 to 40 minutes or until heated thoroughly.

BEEFY MACARONI BAKE

Makes 4 servings.

1 pkg (7 oz or 198 grams) long macaroni
3/4 lb (340 grams) ground beef
1 small onion, chopped
1/2 can (4 oz or 113 grams) tomato sauce
1/2 cup (118 ml) dry white wine or canned beef broth
1 tsp (5 ml) salt (reduce amount to 1/2 tsp if broth is used)
6 oz (170 grams) Parmesan cheese, grated
1/8 tsp (.6 ml) ground nutmeg
1 1/4 cups (296 ml) milk
3 tbsps (45 ml) butter
2 eggs, beaten

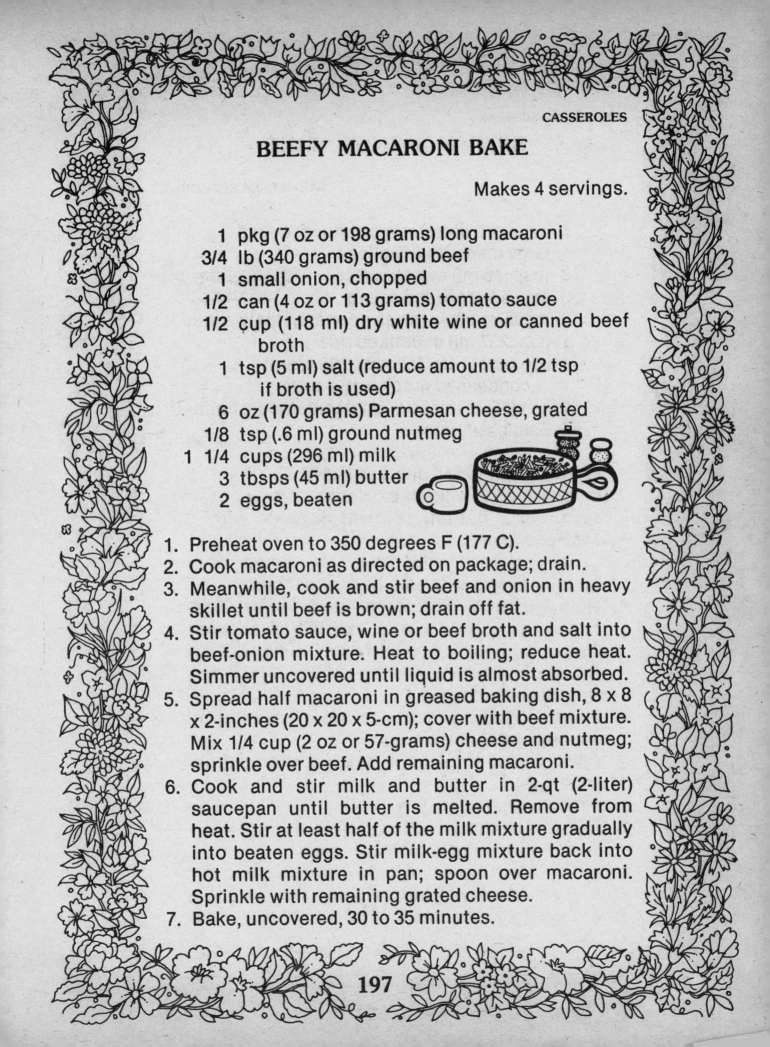

1. Preheat oven to 350 degrees F (177 C).
2. Cook macaroni as directed on package; drain.
3. Meanwhile, cook and stir beef and onion in heavy skillet until beef is brown; drain off fat.
4. Stir tomato sauce, wine or beef broth and salt into beef-onion mixture. Heat to boiling; reduce heat. Simmer uncovered until liquid is almost absorbed.
5. Spread half macaroni in greased baking dish, 8 x 8 x 2-inches (20 x 20 x 5-cm); cover with beef mixture. Mix 1/4 cup (2 oz or 57-grams) cheese and nutmeg; sprinkle over beef. Add remaining macaroni.
6. Cook and stir milk and butter in 2-qt (2-liter) saucepan until butter is melted. Remove from heat. Stir at least half of the milk mixture gradually into beaten eggs. Stir milk-egg mixture back into hot milk mixture in pan; spoon over macaroni. Sprinkle with remaining grated cheese.
7. Bake, uncovered, 30 to 35 minutes.

BRITISH BURGER BAKE

Makes 12 servings.

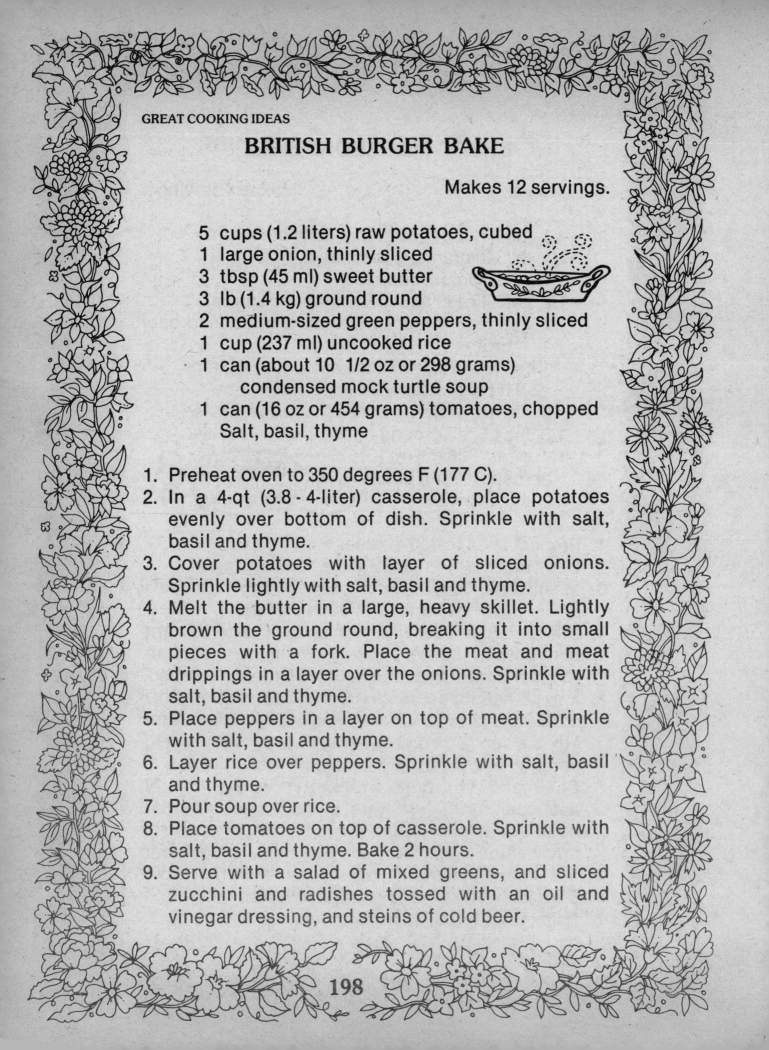

- 5 cups (1.2 liters) raw potatoes, cubed
- 1 large onion, thinly sliced
- 3 tbsp (45 ml) sweet butter
- 3 lb (1.4 kg) ground round
- 2 medium-sized green peppers, thinly sliced
- 1 cup (237 ml) uncooked rice
- 1 can (about 10 1/2 oz or 298 grams) condensed mock turtle soup
- 1 can (16 oz or 454 grams) tomatoes, chopped
  Salt, basil, thyme

1. Preheat oven to 350 degrees F (177 C).
2. In a 4-qt (3.8 - 4-liter) casserole, place potatoes evenly over bottom of dish. Sprinkle with salt, basil and thyme.
3. Cover potatoes with layer of sliced onions. Sprinkle lightly with salt, basil and thyme.
4. Melt the butter in a large, heavy skillet. Lightly brown the ground round, breaking it into small pieces with a fork. Place the meat and meat drippings in a layer over the onions. Sprinkle with salt, basil and thyme.
5. Place peppers in a layer on top of meat. Sprinkle with salt, basil and thyme.
6. Layer rice over peppers. Sprinkle with salt, basil and thyme.
7. Pour soup over rice.
8. Place tomatoes on top of casserole. Sprinkle with salt, basil and thyme. Bake 2 hours.
9. Serve with a salad of mixed greens, and sliced zucchini and radishes tossed with an oil and vinegar dressing, and steins of cold beer.

CORN BAKED WITH DRIED BEEF

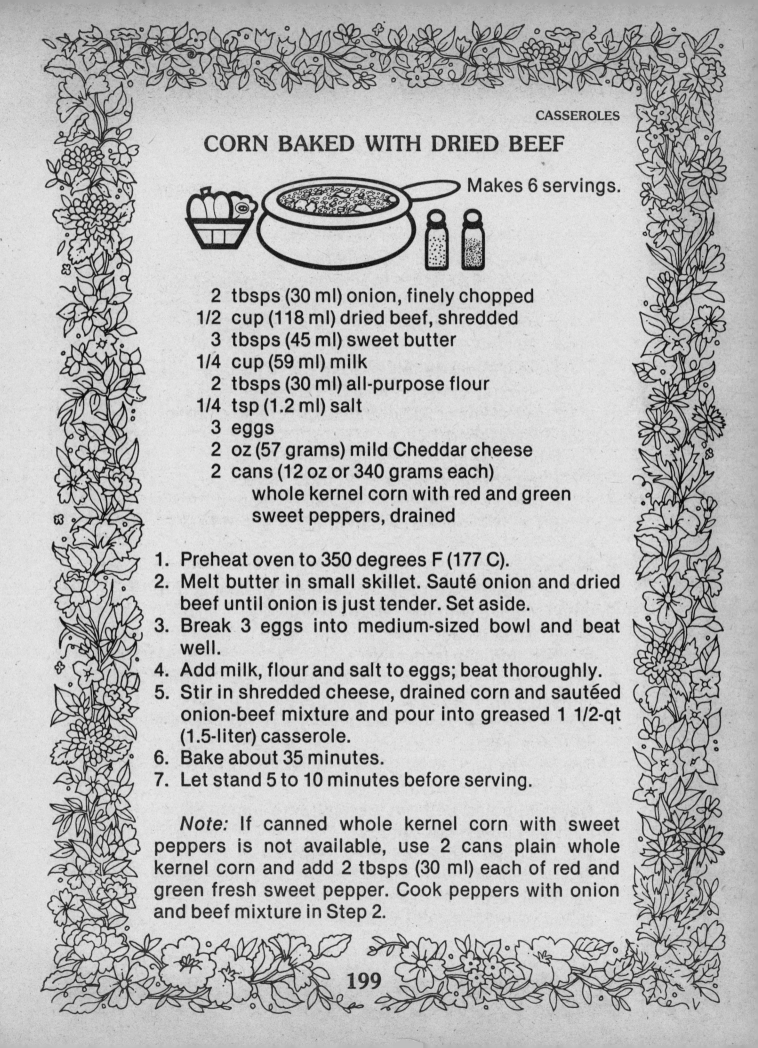

Makes 6 servings.

2 tbsps (30 ml) onion, finely chopped
1/2 cup (118 ml) dried beef, shredded
3 tbsps (45 ml) sweet butter
1/4 cup (59 ml) milk
2 tbsps (30 ml) all-purpose flour
1/4 tsp (1.2 ml) salt
3 eggs
2 oz (57 grams) mild Cheddar cheese
2 cans (12 oz or 340 grams each)
    whole kernel corn with red and green
    sweet peppers, drained

1. Preheat oven to 350 degrees F (177 C).
2. Melt butter in small skillet. Sauté onion and dried beef until onion is just tender. Set aside.
3. Break 3 eggs into medium-sized bowl and beat well.
4. Add milk, flour and salt to eggs; beat thoroughly.
5. Stir in shredded cheese, drained corn and sautéed onion-beef mixture and pour into greased 1 1/2-qt (1.5-liter) casserole.
6. Bake about 35 minutes.
7. Let stand 5 to 10 minutes before serving.

Note: If canned whole kernel corn with sweet peppers is not available, use 2 cans plain whole kernel corn and add 2 tbsps (30 ml) each of red and green fresh sweet pepper. Cook peppers with onion and beef mixture in Step 2.

HAMBURGER 'N' CHEESE CASSEROLE

Makes 18 servings.

16 oz (454 grams) medium noodles, uncooked
2 lbs (908 grams) ground beef
2 cans (15 oz or 425 grams each) tomato sauce
1 tbsp (15 ml) sugar
2 tsps (10 ml) salt
1/2 tsp (2.5 ml) garlic powder
1/2 tsp (2.5 ml) freshly ground black pepper
2 cups (473 ml) cream-style cottage cheese
2 pkgs (8 oz or 227 grams each) cream cheese, softened
1 cup (237 ml) dairy sour cream
2 bunches scallions, with tops, diced
1 medium-sized green pepper, chopped
1/2 cup (118 ml) Parmesan cheese, shredded

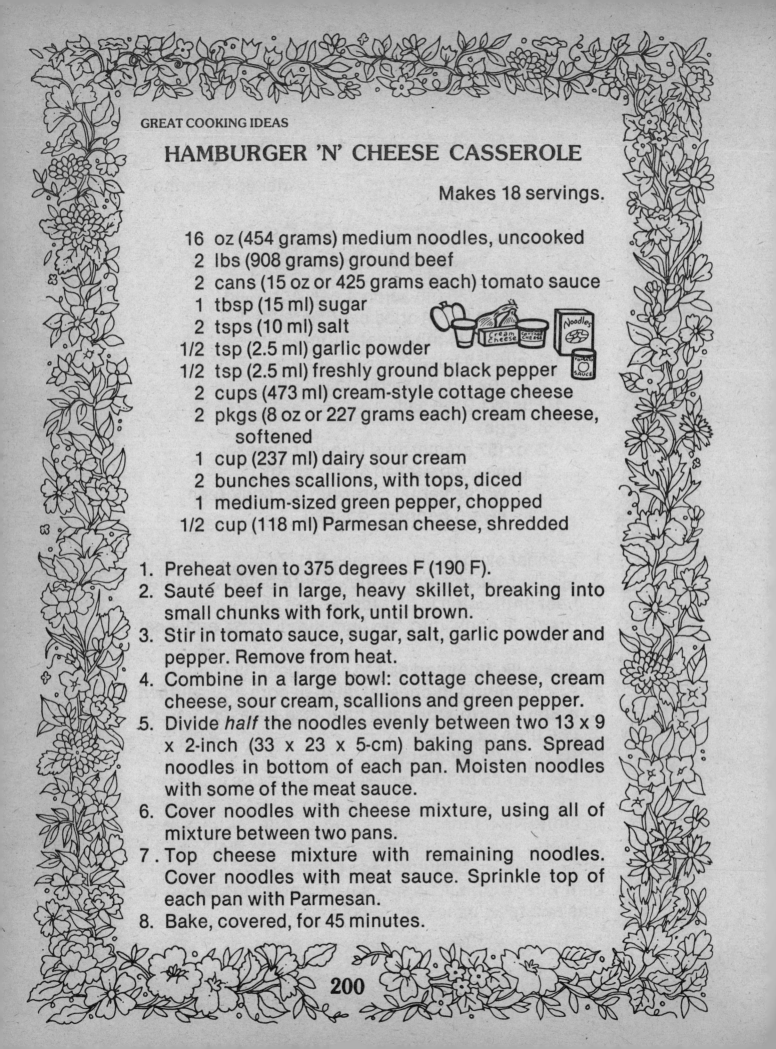

1. Preheat oven to 375 degrees F (190 F).
2. Sauté beef in large, heavy skillet, breaking into small chunks with fork, until brown.
3. Stir in tomato sauce, sugar, salt, garlic powder and pepper. Remove from heat.
4. Combine in a large bowl: cottage cheese, cream cheese, sour cream, scallions and green pepper.
5. Divide *half* the noodles evenly between two 13 x 9 x 2-inch (33 x 23 x 5-cm) baking pans. Spread noodles in bottom of each pan. Moisten noodles with some of the meat sauce.
6. Cover noodles with cheese mixture, using all of mixture between two pans.
7. Top cheese mixture with remaining noodles. Cover noodles with meat sauce. Sprinkle top of each pan with Parmesan.
8. Bake, covered, for 45 minutes.

HAMBURGER 'N' CORN BAKE

Makes 6 servings.

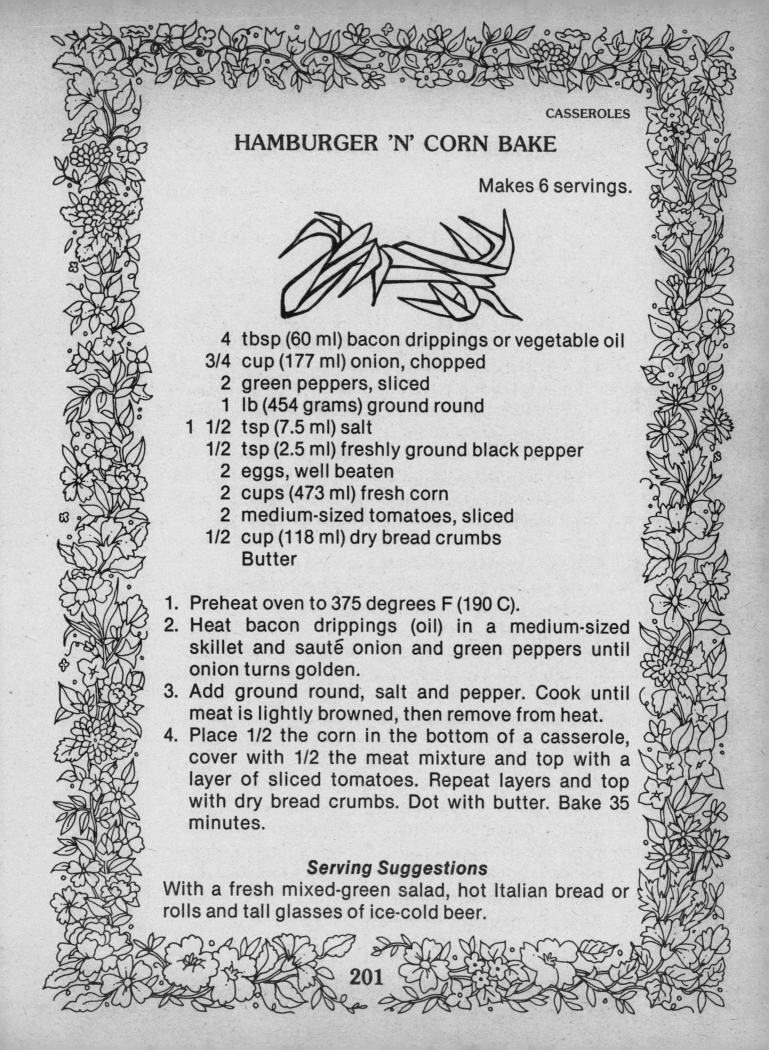

4 tbsp (60 ml) bacon drippings or vegetable oil
3/4 cup (177 ml) onion, chopped
2 green peppers, sliced
1 lb (454 grams) ground round
1 1/2 tsp (7.5 ml) salt
1/2 tsp (2.5 ml) freshly ground black pepper
2 eggs, well beaten
2 cups (473 ml) fresh corn
2 medium-sized tomatoes, sliced
1/2 cup (118 ml) dry bread crumbs
Butter

1. Preheat oven to 375 degrees F (190 C).
2. Heat bacon drippings (oil) in a medium-sized skillet and sauté onion and green peppers until onion turns golden.
3. Add ground round, salt and pepper. Cook until meat is lightly browned, then remove from heat.
4. Place 1/2 the corn in the bottom of a casserole, cover with 1/2 the meat mixture and top with a layer of sliced tomatoes. Repeat layers and top with dry bread crumbs. Dot with butter. Bake 35 minutes.

Serving Suggestions

With a fresh mixed-green salad, hot Italian bread or rolls and tall glasses of ice-cold beer.

MEAT BALLS 'N' GREEN NOODLE BAKE

Makes 6 servings.

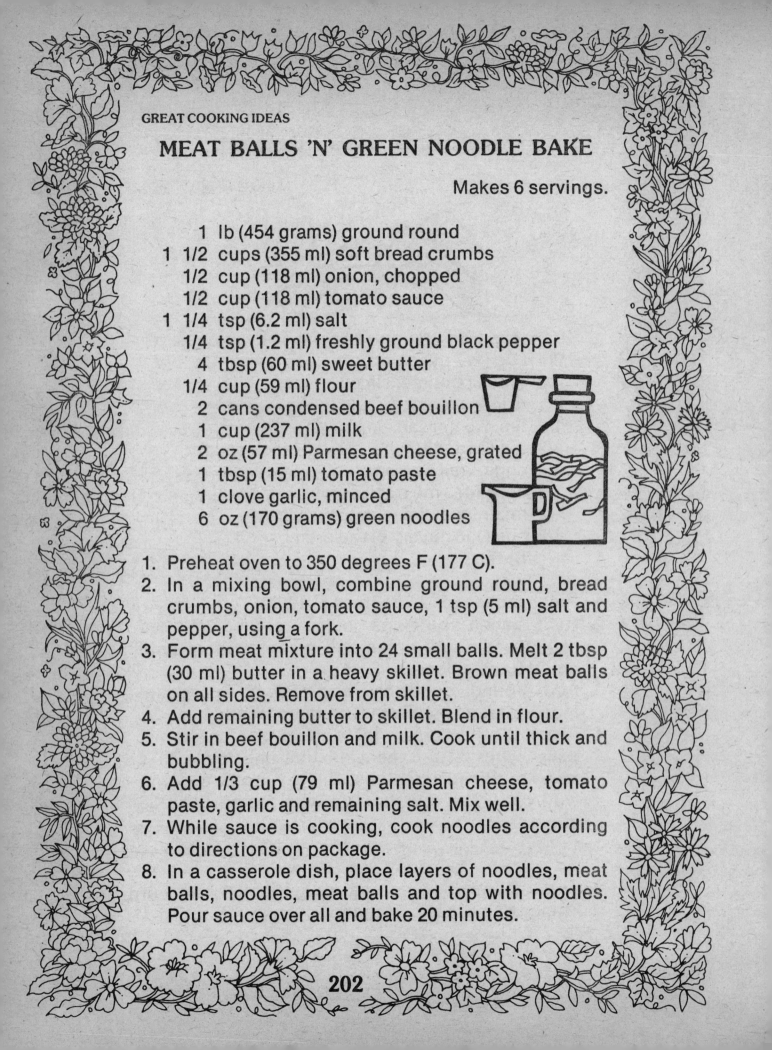

1	lb (454 grams)	ground round
1 1/2	cups (355 ml)	soft bread crumbs
1/2	cup (118 ml)	onion, chopped
1/2	cup (118 ml)	tomato sauce
1 1/4	tsp (6.2 ml)	salt
1/4	tsp (1.2 ml)	freshly ground black pepper
4	tbsp (60 ml)	sweet butter
1/4	cup (59 ml)	flour
2	cans	condensed beef bouillon
1	cup (237 ml)	milk
2	oz (57 ml)	Parmesan cheese, grated
1	tbsp (15 ml)	tomato paste
1	clove	garlic, minced
6	oz (170 grams)	green noodles

1. Preheat oven to 350 degrees F (177 C).
2. In a mixing bowl, combine ground round, bread crumbs, onion, tomato sauce, 1 tsp (5 ml) salt and pepper, using a fork.
3. Form meat mixture into 24 small balls. Melt 2 tbsp (30 ml) butter in a heavy skillet. Brown meat balls on all sides. Remove from skillet.
4. Add remaining butter to skillet. Blend in flour.
5. Stir in beef bouillon and milk. Cook until thick and bubbling.
6. Add 1/3 cup (79 ml) Parmesan cheese, tomato paste, garlic and remaining salt. Mix well.
7. While sauce is cooking, cook noodles according to directions on package.
8. In a casserole dish, place layers of noodles, meat balls, noodles, meat balls and top with noodles. Pour sauce over all and bake 20 minutes.

SPINACH-HAMBURGER BAKE

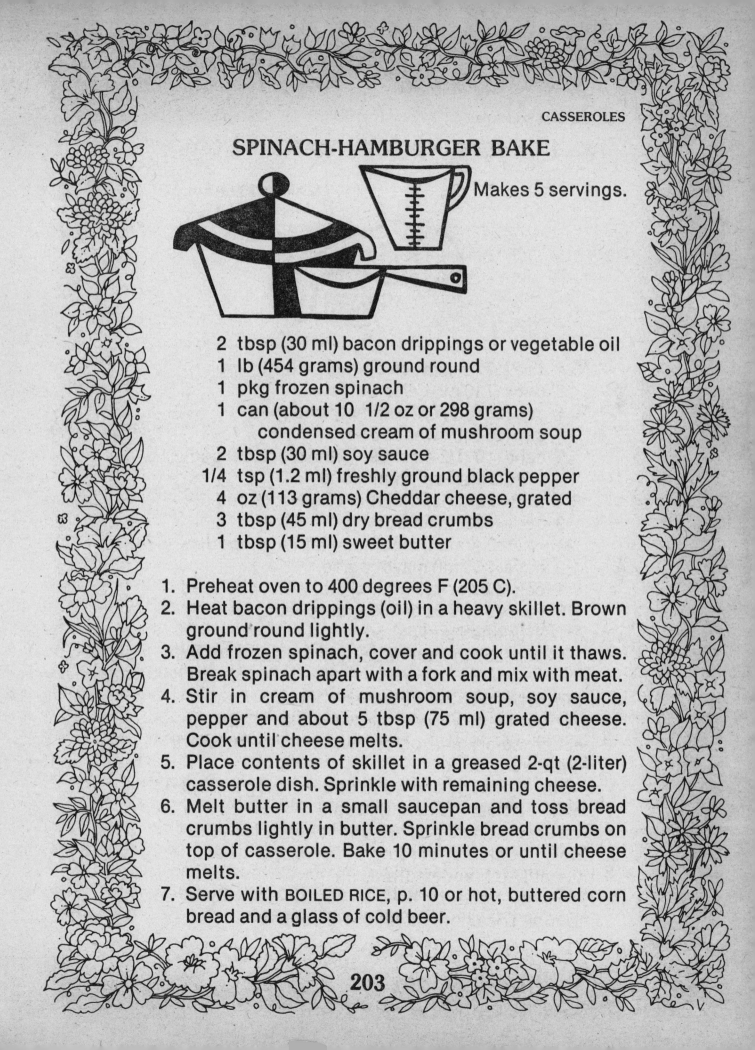

Makes 5 servings.

2 tbsp (30 ml) bacon drippings or vegetable oil
1 lb (454 grams) ground round
1 pkg frozen spinach
1 can (about 10 1/2 oz or 298 grams)
    condensed cream of mushroom soup
2 tbsp (30 ml) soy sauce
1/4 tsp (1.2 ml) freshly ground black pepper
4 oz (113 grams) Cheddar cheese, grated
3 tbsp (45 ml) dry bread crumbs
1 tbsp (15 ml) sweet butter

1. Preheat oven to 400 degrees F (205 C).
2. Heat bacon drippings (oil) in a heavy skillet. Brown ground round lightly.
3. Add frozen spinach, cover and cook until it thaws. Break spinach apart with a fork and mix with meat.
4. Stir in cream of mushroom soup, soy sauce, pepper and about 5 tbsp (75 ml) grated cheese. Cook until cheese melts.
5. Place contents of skillet in a greased 2-qt (2-liter) casserole dish. Sprinkle with remaining cheese.
6. Melt butter in a small saucepan and toss bread crumbs lightly in butter. Sprinkle bread crumbs on top of casserole. Bake 10 minutes or until cheese melts.
7. Serve with BOILED RICE, p. 10 or hot, buttered corn bread and a glass of cold beer.

ALMOND-TUNA BAKE

Makes 16 servings.

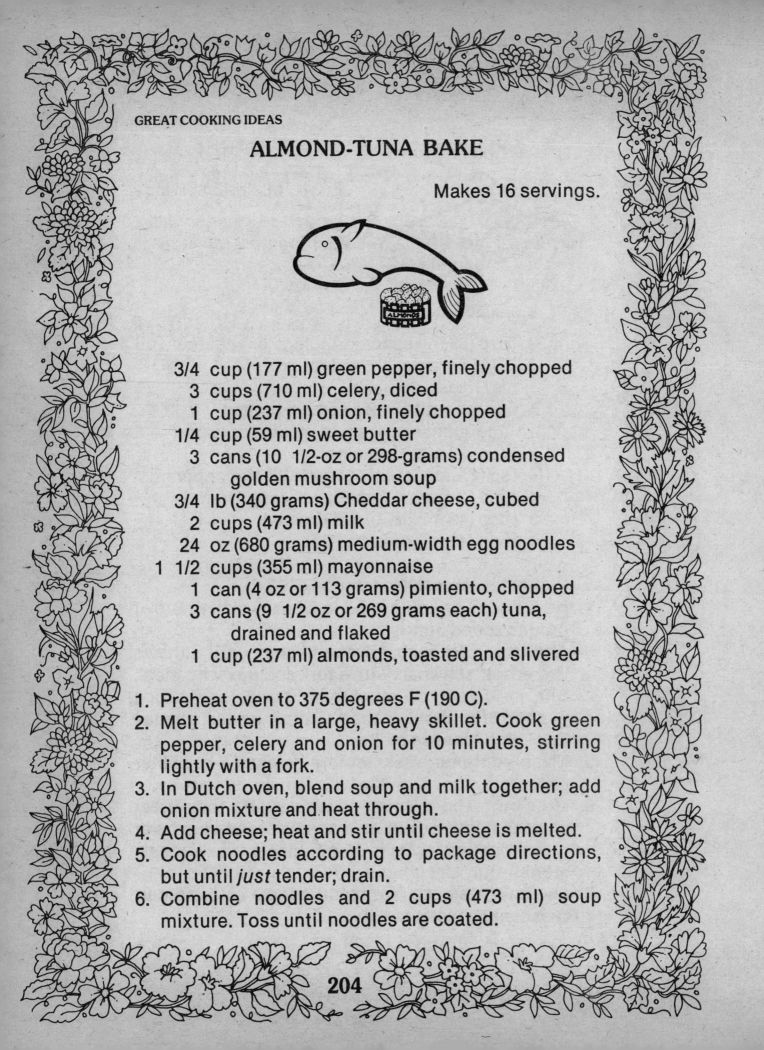

- 3/4 cup (177 ml) green pepper, finely chopped
- 3 cups (710 ml) celery, diced
- 1 cup (237 ml) onion, finely chopped
- 1/4 cup (59 ml) sweet butter
- 3 cans (10 1/2-oz or 298-grams) condensed golden mushroom soup
- 3/4 lb (340 grams) Cheddar cheese, cubed
- 2 cups (473 ml) milk
- 24 oz (680 grams) medium-width egg noodles
- 1 1/2 cups (355 ml) mayonnaise
- 1 can (4 oz or 113 grams) pimiento, chopped
- 3 cans (9 1/2 oz or 269 grams each) tuna, drained and flaked
- 1 cup (237 ml) almonds, toasted and slivered

1. Preheat oven to 375 degrees F (190 C).
2. Melt butter in a large, heavy skillet. Cook green pepper, celery and onion for 10 minutes, stirring lightly with a fork.
3. In Dutch oven, blend soup and milk together; add onion mixture and heat through.
4. Add cheese; heat and stir until cheese is melted.
5. Cook noodles according to package directions, but until *just* tender; drain.
6. Combine noodles and 2 cups (473 ml) soup mixture. Toss until noodles are coated.

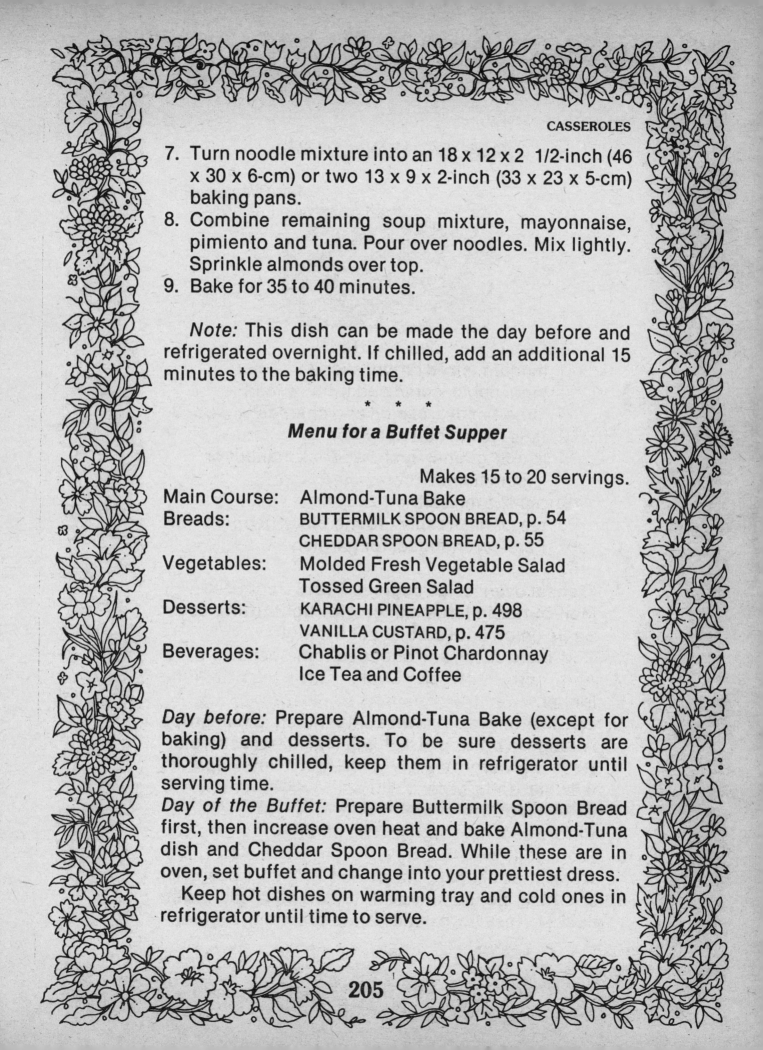

7. Turn noodle mixture into an 18 x 12 x 2 1/2-inch (46 x 30 x 6-cm) or two 13 x 9 x 2-inch (33 x 23 x 5-cm) baking pans.
8. Combine remaining soup mixture, mayonnaise, pimiento and tuna. Pour over noodles. Mix lightly. Sprinkle almonds over top.
9. Bake for 35 to 40 minutes.

Note: This dish can be made the day before and refrigerated overnight. If chilled, add an additional 15 minutes to the baking time.

* * *

Menu for a Buffet Supper

Makes 15 to 20 servings.

Main Course:	Almond-Tuna Bake
Breads:	BUTTERMILK SPOON BREAD, p. 54
	CHEDDAR SPOON BREAD, p. 55
Vegetables:	Molded Fresh Vegetable Salad
	Tossed Green Salad
Desserts:	KARACHI PINEAPPLE, p. 498
	VANILLA CUSTARD, p. 475
Beverages:	Chablis or Pinot Chardonnay
	Ice Tea and Coffee

Day before: Prepare Almond-Tuna Bake (except for baking) and desserts. To be sure desserts are thoroughly chilled, keep them in refrigerator until serving time.

Day of the Buffet: Prepare Buttermilk Spoon Bread first, then increase oven heat and bake Almond-Tuna dish and Cheddar Spoon Bread. While these are in oven, set buffet and change into your prettiest dress.

Keep hot dishes on warming tray and cold ones in refrigerator until time to serve.

BAKED CURRIED FISH

Makes 4 servings.

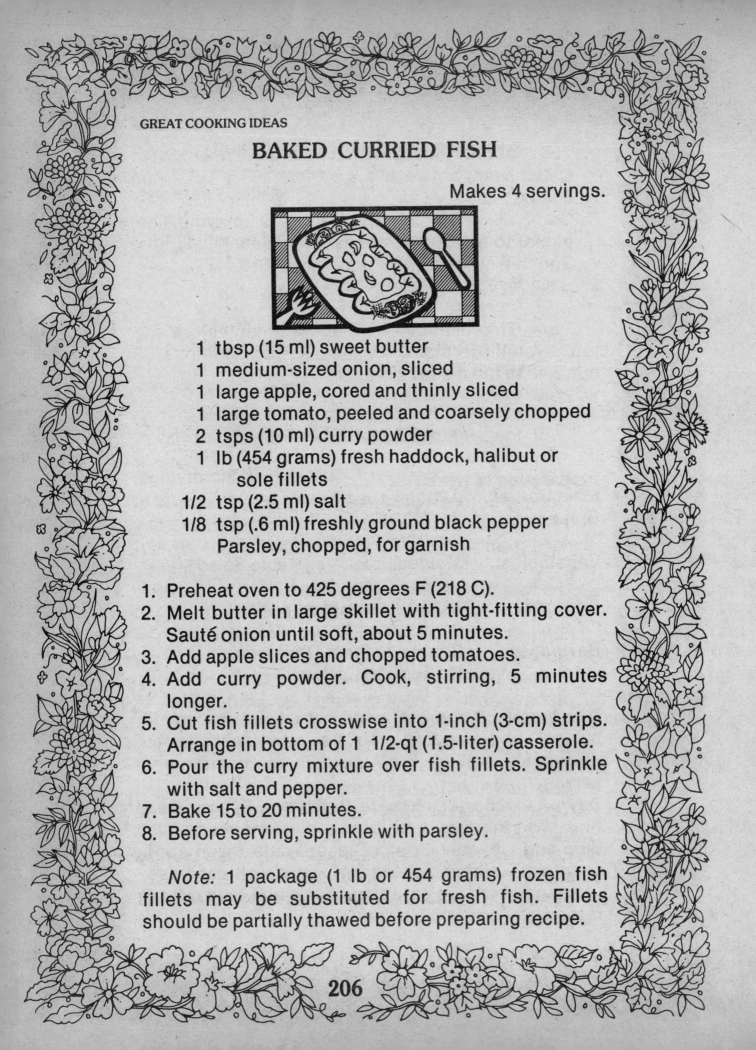

1 tbsp (15 ml) sweet butter
1 medium-sized onion, sliced
1 large apple, cored and thinly sliced
1 large tomato, peeled and coarsely chopped
2 tsps (10 ml) curry powder
1 lb (454 grams) fresh haddock, halibut or
    sole fillets
1/2 tsp (2.5 ml) salt
1/8 tsp (.6 ml) freshly ground black pepper
Parsley, chopped, for garnish

1. Preheat oven to 425 degrees F (218 C).
2. Melt butter in large skillet with tight-fitting cover. Sauté onion until soft, about 5 minutes.
3. Add apple slices and chopped tomatoes.
4. Add curry powder. Cook, stirring, 5 minutes longer.
5. Cut fish fillets crosswise into 1-inch (3-cm) strips. Arrange in bottom of 1 1/2-qt (1.5-liter) casserole.
6. Pour the curry mixture over fish fillets. Sprinkle with salt and pepper.
7. Bake 15 to 20 minutes.
8. Before serving, sprinkle with parsley.

Note: 1 package (1 lb or 454 grams) frozen fish fillets may be substituted for fresh fish. Fillets should be partially thawed before preparing recipe.

BLACK-EYED PEAS 'N' TUNA

Makes 6 servings.

2 cups (473 ml) dried black-eyed peas
1/2 cup (118 ml) onion, finely chopped
3 tbsps (45 ml) vegetable oil
1 large tomato, chopped
2 tsps (10 ml) crushed hot red peppers
2 cans (7 oz or 198 grams each) tuna, flaked
2 tbsps (30 ml) tomato paste
1/2 tsp (2.5 ml) salt
1/4 cup (59 ml) dry bread crumbs
2 tbsps (30 ml) butter

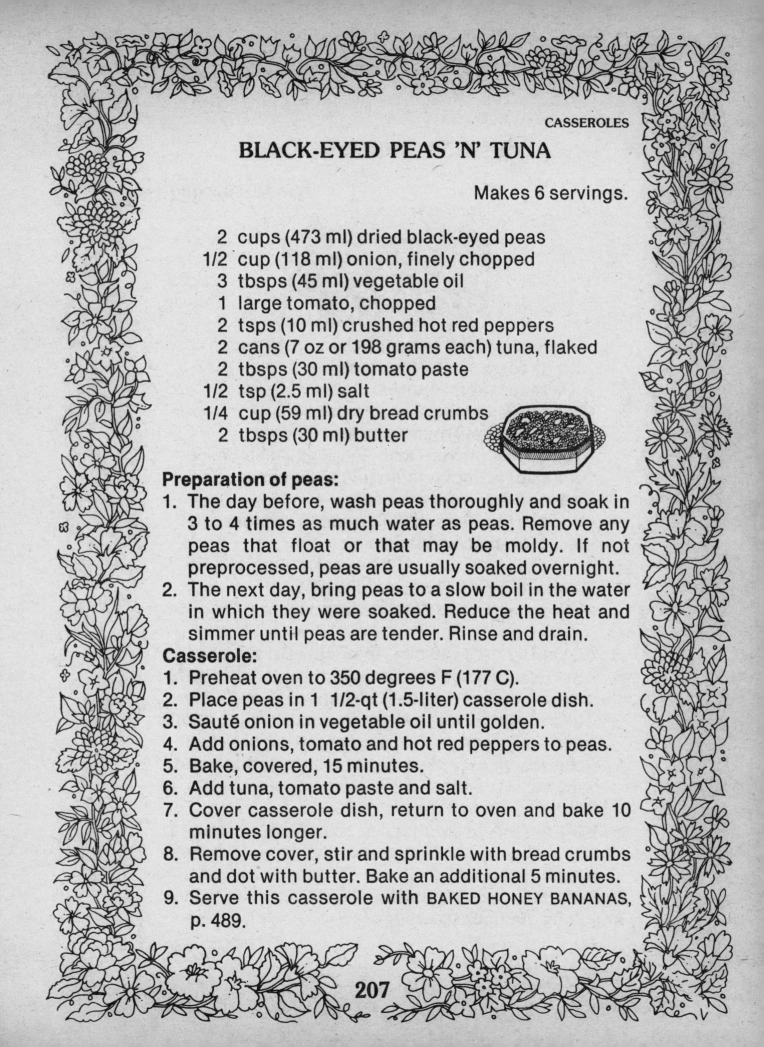

Preparation of peas:
1. The day before, wash peas thoroughly and soak in 3 to 4 times as much water as peas. Remove any peas that float or that may be moldy. If not preprocessed, peas are usually soaked overnight.
2. The next day, bring peas to a slow boil in the water in which they were soaked. Reduce the heat and simmer until peas are tender. Rinse and drain.

Casserole:
1. Preheat oven to 350 degrees F (177 C).
2. Place peas in 1 1/2-qt (1.5-liter) casserole dish.
3. Sauté onion in vegetable oil until golden.
4. Add onions, tomato and hot red peppers to peas.
5. Bake, covered, 15 minutes.
6. Add tuna, tomato paste and salt.
7. Cover casserole dish, return to oven and bake 10 minutes longer.
8. Remove cover, stir and sprinkle with bread crumbs and dot with butter. Bake an additional 5 minutes.
9. Serve this casserole with BAKED HONEY BANANAS, p. 489.

CRAB 'N' SHRIMP BAKE

Makes 6 to 8 servings.

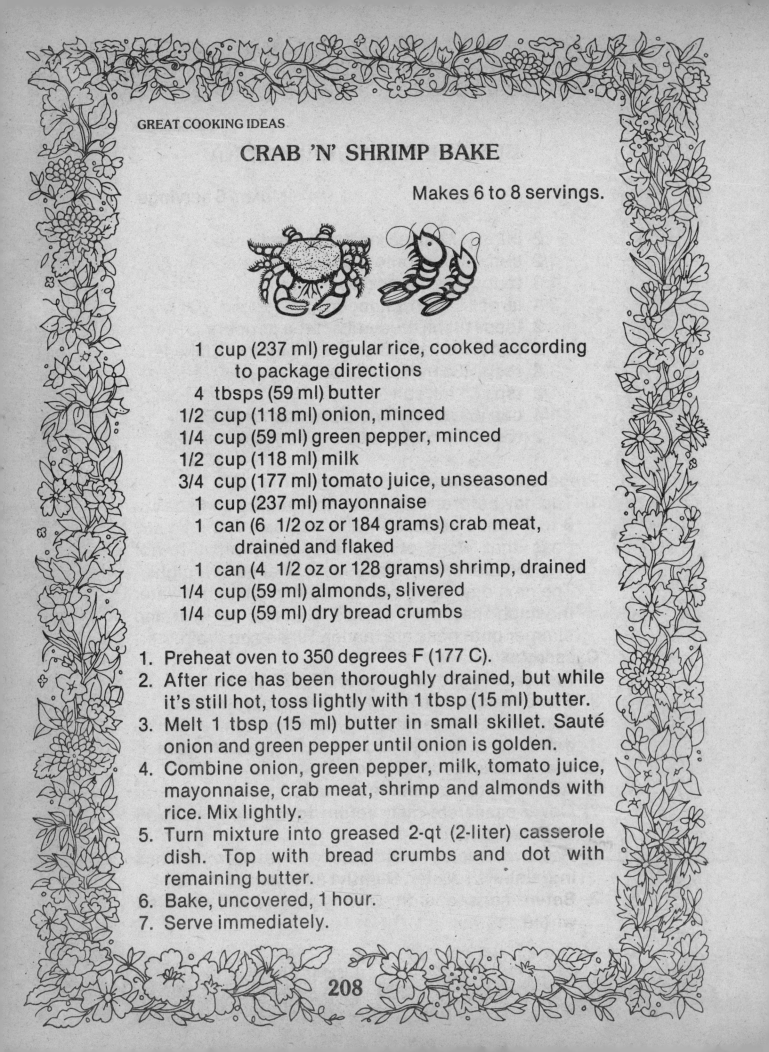

1 cup (237 ml) regular rice, cooked according
   to package directions
4 tbsps (59 ml) butter
1/2 cup (118 ml) onion, minced
1/4 cup (59 ml) green pepper, minced
1/2 cup (118 ml) milk
3/4 cup (177 ml) tomato juice, unseasoned
1 cup (237 ml) mayonnaise
1 can (6 1/2 oz or 184 grams) crab meat,
   drained and flaked
1 can (4 1/2 oz or 128 grams) shrimp, drained
1/4 cup (59 ml) almonds, slivered
1/4 cup (59 ml) dry bread crumbs

1. Preheat oven to 350 degrees F (177 C).
2. After rice has been thoroughly drained, but while it's still hot, toss lightly with 1 tbsp (15 ml) butter.
3. Melt 1 tbsp (15 ml) butter in small skillet. Sauté onion and green pepper until onion is golden.
4. Combine onion, green pepper, milk, tomato juice, mayonnaise, crab meat, shrimp and almonds with rice. Mix lightly.
5. Turn mixture into greased 2-qt (2-liter) casserole dish. Top with bread crumbs and dot with remaining butter.
6. Bake, uncovered, 1 hour.
7. Serve immediately.

CREAMED SHRIMP

Makes 8 to 10 servings.

3 lbs (1.4 kg) small fresh shrimp
2 tbsps (30 ml) lemon juice
1/4 cup (59 ml) salad oil
3/4 cup (177 ml) regular rice, uncooked
3 tbsps (45 ml) sweet butter
1/4 cup (59 ml) green pepper, diced
1/4 cup (59 ml) onion, diced
1 1/2 tsps (7.5 ml) salt
1/8 tsp (.6 ml) freshly ground black pepper
1 can (10 1/2 oz or 298 grams) condensed
    tomato soup
1 cup (237 ml) light cream
1/2 cup (118 ml) dry sherry or canned
    chicken broth
1/2 cup (118 ml) almonds, slivered
Parlsey for garnish

1. Clean and devein shrimp. Reserve 5 for garnish. Place remaining shrimp in a 2 1/2-qt (2.5-liter) casserole dish.
2. Pour lemon juice and salad oil over shrimp.
3. Cook rice according to package directions.
4. Melt butter in a medium-size saucepan. Add the green pepper and onion. Cook over low direct heat about 5 minutes.
5. Remove from heat and stir in salt, pepper, tomato soup, cream, sherry *or* chicken broth, almonds and cooked rice.
6. Pour mixture over the shrimp in casserole. Toss ingredients together lightly. Bake about 1 hour.
7. Before serving, garnish with parsley and reserved whole shrimp.

OYSTER-SPAGHETTI BAKE

Makes 4 servings.

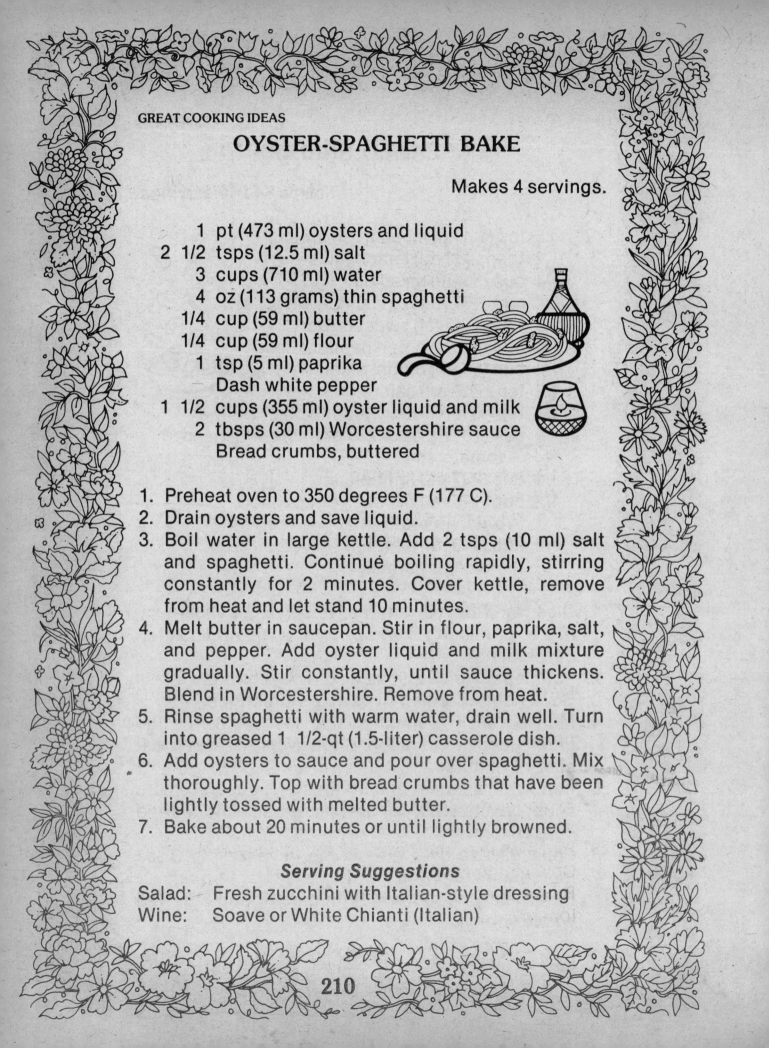

1 pt (473 ml) oysters and liquid
2 1/2 tsps (12.5 ml) salt
3 cups (710 ml) water
4 oz (113 grams) thin spaghetti
1/4 cup (59 ml) butter
1/4 cup (59 ml) flour
1 tsp (5 ml) paprika
Dash white pepper
1 1/2 cups (355 ml) oyster liquid and milk
2 tbsps (30 ml) Worcestershire sauce
Bread crumbs, buttered

1. Preheat oven to 350 degrees F (177 C).
2. Drain oysters and save liquid.
3. Boil water in large kettle. Add 2 tsps (10 ml) salt and spaghetti. Continue boiling rapidly, stirring constantly for 2 minutes. Cover kettle, remove from heat and let stand 10 minutes.
4. Melt butter in saucepan. Stir in flour, paprika, salt, and pepper. Add oyster liquid and milk mixture gradually. Stir constantly, until sauce thickens. Blend in Worcestershire. Remove from heat.
5. Rinse spaghetti with warm water, drain well. Turn into greased 1 1/2-qt (1.5-liter) casserole dish.
6. Add oysters to sauce and pour over spaghetti. Mix thoroughly. Top with bread crumbs that have been lightly tossed with melted butter.
7. Bake about 20 minutes or until lightly browned.

Serving Suggestions
Salad: Fresh zucchini with Italian-style dressing
Wine: Soave or White Chianti (Italian)

QUICK OYSTER CASSEROLE

Makes 3 or 4 servings.

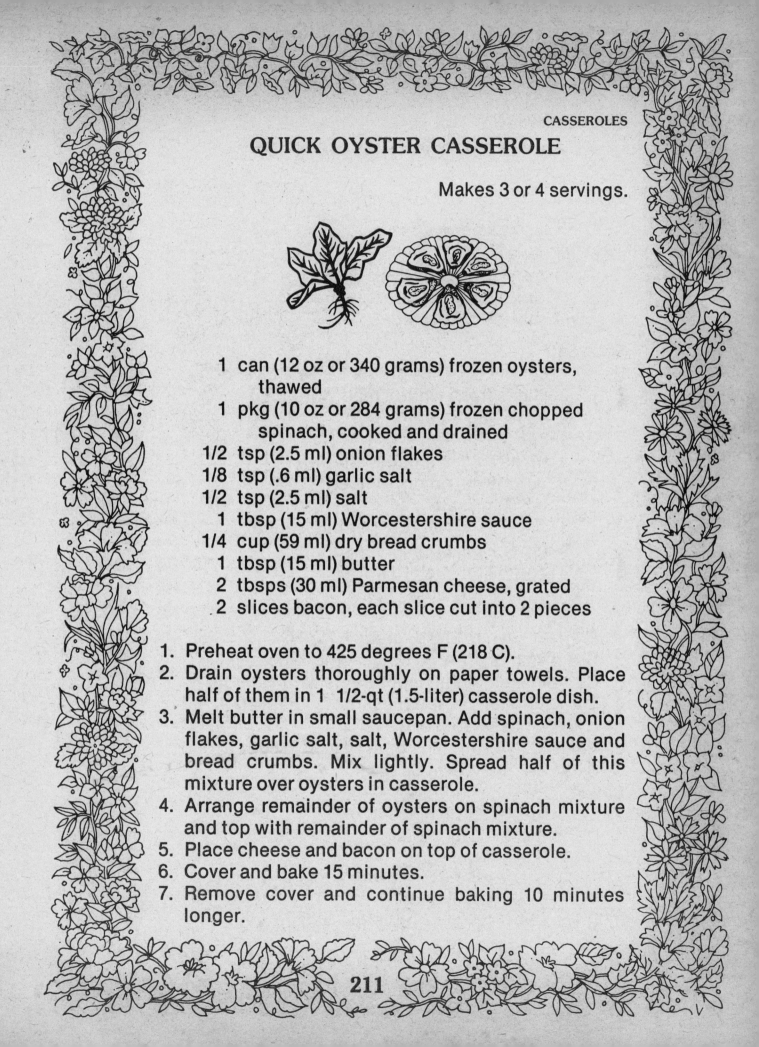

1 can (12 oz or 340 grams) frozen oysters,
  thawed
1 pkg (10 oz or 284 grams) frozen chopped
  spinach, cooked and drained
1/2 tsp (2.5 ml) onion flakes
1/8 tsp (.6 ml) garlic salt
1/2 tsp (2.5 ml) salt
1 tbsp (15 ml) Worcestershire sauce
1/4 cup (59 ml) dry bread crumbs
1 tbsp (15 ml) butter
2 tbsps (30 ml) Parmesan cheese, grated
2 slices bacon, each slice cut into 2 pieces

1. Preheat oven to 425 degrees F (218 C).
2. Drain oysters thoroughly on paper towels. Place half of them in 1 1/2-qt (1.5-liter) casserole dish.
3. Melt butter in small saucepan. Add spinach, onion flakes, garlic salt, salt, Worcestershire sauce and bread crumbs. Mix lightly. Spread half of this mixture over oysters in casserole.
4. Arrange remainder of oysters on spinach mixture and top with remainder of spinach mixture.
5. Place cheese and bacon on top of casserole.
6. Cover and bake 15 minutes.
7. Remove cover and continue baking 10 minutes longer.

GREAT COOKING IDEAS

SALMON WITH OLIVE SAUCE

Makes 8 servings.

Salmon:
- 2 cans (1 lb or 454 grams each) red salmon
- 6 slices fresh white bread, shredded
- 2 eggs, well-beaten
- 1 cup (237 ml) milk
- 2 tbsps (30 ml) snipped parsley
- 1/4 cup (59 ml) onion, minced
- 1 tsp (5 ml) salt
- 1 tbsp (15 ml) Worcestershire sauce
- 1/4 tsp (1.2 ml) poultry seasoning
- 1/4 cup (59 ml) melted butter
- 1/4 cup (59 ml) lemon juice

1. Preheat oven to 350 degrees F (177 C).
2. Flake salmon in large bowl; remove bones.
3. Combine remaining ingredients with salmon.
4. Turn the salmon mixture into a greased 1 1/2-qt (1.5-liter) casserole dish.
5. Bake 50 to 60 minutes or until firm in center.
6. Serve hot with Olive Sauce.

Sauce:
- 2 tbsps (30 ml) butter
- 2 tbsps (30 ml) flour
- 1/2 tsp (2. 5 ml) salt
- 1/8 tsp (.6 ml) freshly ground black pepper
- 1 cup (237 ml) milk
- 1/2 cup (118 ml) stuffed olives, sliced

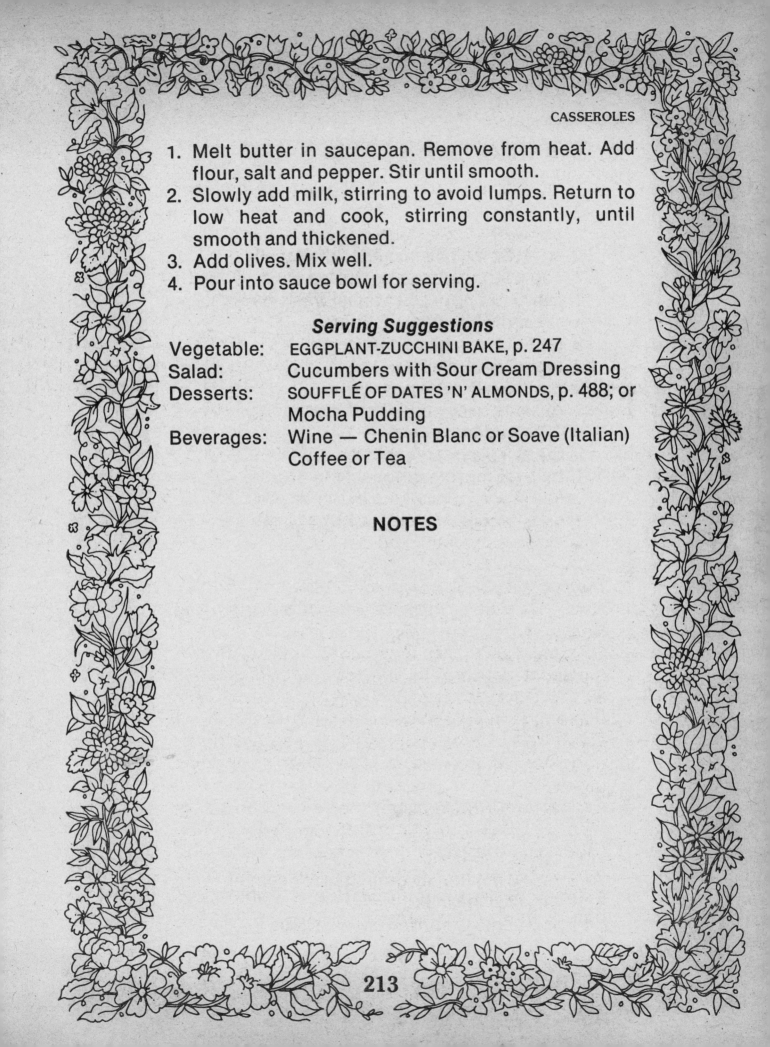

1. Melt butter in saucepan. Remove from heat. Add flour, salt and pepper. Stir until smooth.
2. Slowly add milk, stirring to avoid lumps. Return to low heat and cook, stirring constantly, until smooth and thickened.
3. Add olives. Mix well.
4. Pour into sauce bowl for serving.

Serving Suggestions

Vegetable: EGGPLANT-ZUCCHINI BAKE, p. 247
Salad: Cucumbers with Sour Cream Dressing
Desserts: SOUFFLÉ OF DATES 'N' ALMONDS, p. 488; or Mocha Pudding
Beverages: Wine — Chenin Blanc or Soave (Italian) Coffee or Tea

NOTES

TUNA-MACARONI-CHEESE BAKE

Makes 8 to 10 servings.

- 1 pkg (7 oz or 198 grams) elbow macaroni
- 1 cup (237 ml) celery, sliced diagonally
- 1/2 cup (118 ml) pimiento-stuffed olives, sliced
- 1 can (9 1/2 oz or 269 grams) water-packed, solid white tuna, drained
- 2 tbsps (30 ml) onion, minced
- 1 1/2 tsps (7.5 ml) salt
- 1/2 tsp (2.5 ml) white pepper
- 12 oz (340 grams) mild Cheddar cheese, shredded
- 3 tbsps (45 ml) sweet butter
- 1 tbsp (15 ml) all-purpose flour
- 1 cup (237 ml) dairy sour cream
- 1 cup (237 ml) dry white wine or canned chicken broth

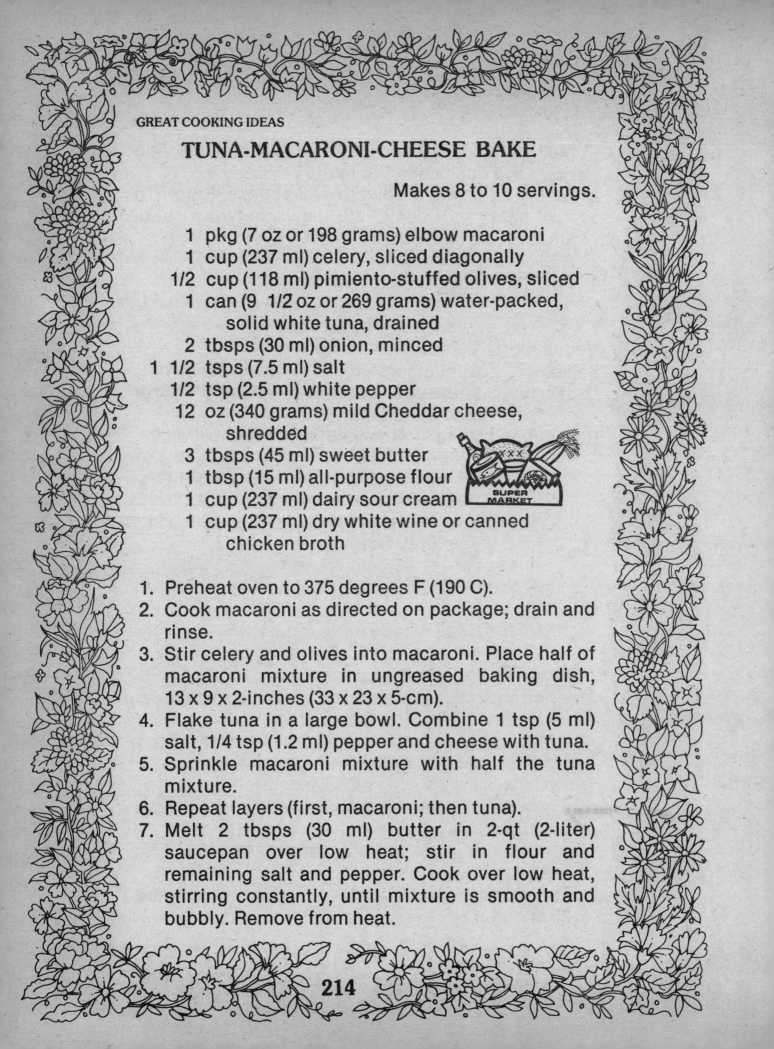

1. Preheat oven to 375 degrees F (190 C).
2. Cook macaroni as directed on package; drain and rinse.
3. Stir celery and olives into macaroni. Place half of macaroni mixture in ungreased baking dish, 13 x 9 x 2-inches (33 x 23 x 5-cm).
4. Flake tuna in a large bowl. Combine 1 tsp (5 ml) salt, 1/4 tsp (1.2 ml) pepper and cheese with tuna.
5. Sprinkle macaroni mixture with half the tuna mixture.
6. Repeat layers (first, macaroni; then tuna).
7. Melt 2 tbsps (30 ml) butter in 2-qt (2-liter) saucepan over low heat; stir in flour and remaining salt and pepper. Cook over low heat, stirring constantly, until mixture is smooth and bubbly. Remove from heat.

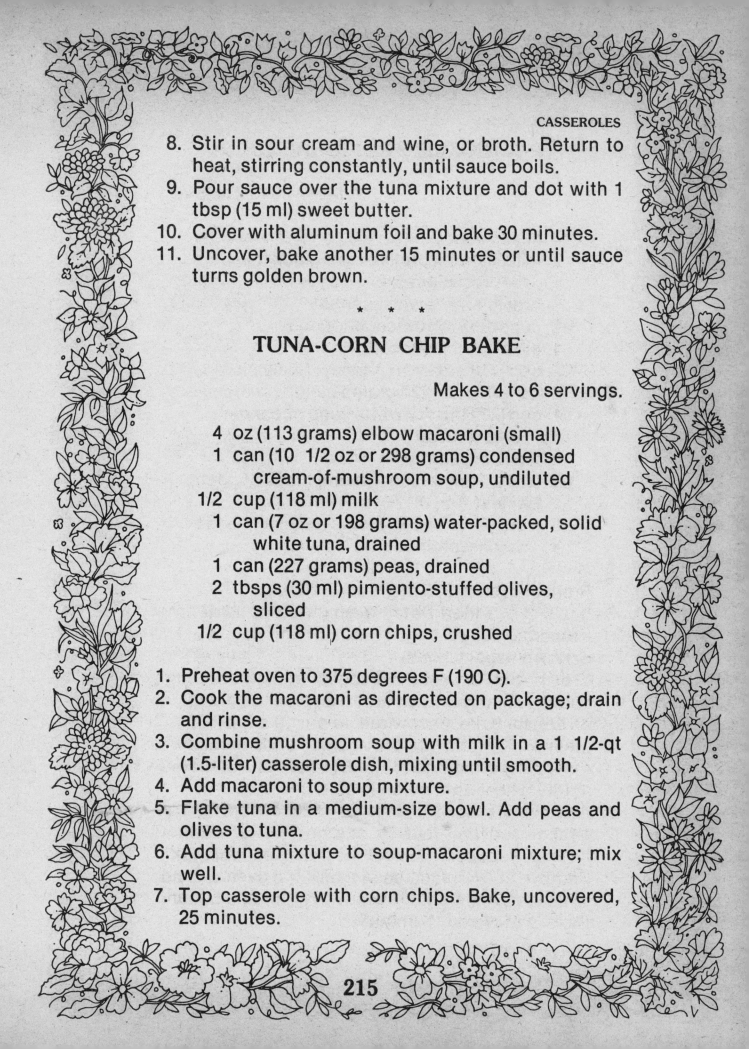

8. Stir in sour cream and wine, or broth. Return to heat, stirring constantly, until sauce boils.
9. Pour sauce over the tuna mixture and dot with 1 tbsp (15 ml) sweet butter.
10. Cover with aluminum foil and bake 30 minutes.
11. Uncover, bake another 15 minutes or until sauce turns golden brown.

* * *

TUNA-CORN CHIP BAKE

Makes 4 to 6 servings.

4 oz (113 grams) elbow macaroni (small)
1 can (10 1/2 oz or 298 grams) condensed cream-of-mushroom soup, undiluted
1/2 cup (118 ml) milk
1 can (7 oz or 198 grams) water-packed, solid white tuna, drained
1 can (227 grams) peas, drained
2 tbsps (30 ml) pimiento-stuffed olives, sliced
1/2 cup (118 ml) corn chips, crushed

1. Preheat oven to 375 degrees F (190 C).
2. Cook the macaroni as directed on package; drain and rinse.
3. Combine mushroom soup with milk in a 1 1/2-qt (1.5-liter) casserole dish, mixing until smooth.
4. Add macaroni to soup mixture.
5. Flake tuna in a medium-size bowl. Add peas and olives to tuna.
6. Add tuna mixture to soup-macaroni mixture; mix well.
7. Top casserole with corn chips. Bake, uncovered, 25 minutes.

CHICKEN 'N' SAUSAGES

Makes 6 to 8 servings.

- 4 slices bacon
- 2 lb (908 gram) broiler-fryer chicken, cut in serving pieces
- 6 brown-and-serve sausages
- 1 1/2 cups (355 ml) onion, chopped
- 1 clove garlic, minced
- 1/2 cup (118 ml) fresh parsley, finely chopped
- 2 cans (8 oz or 227 grams each) tomato sauce
- 1 cup (237 ml) dry white wine or canned chicken broth
- 1 tsp (5 ml) salt
- 1/2 tsp (2.5 ml) freshly ground black pepper
- 1 bay leaf
- 3 cans (20 oz or 567 grams each) white kidney beans, drained

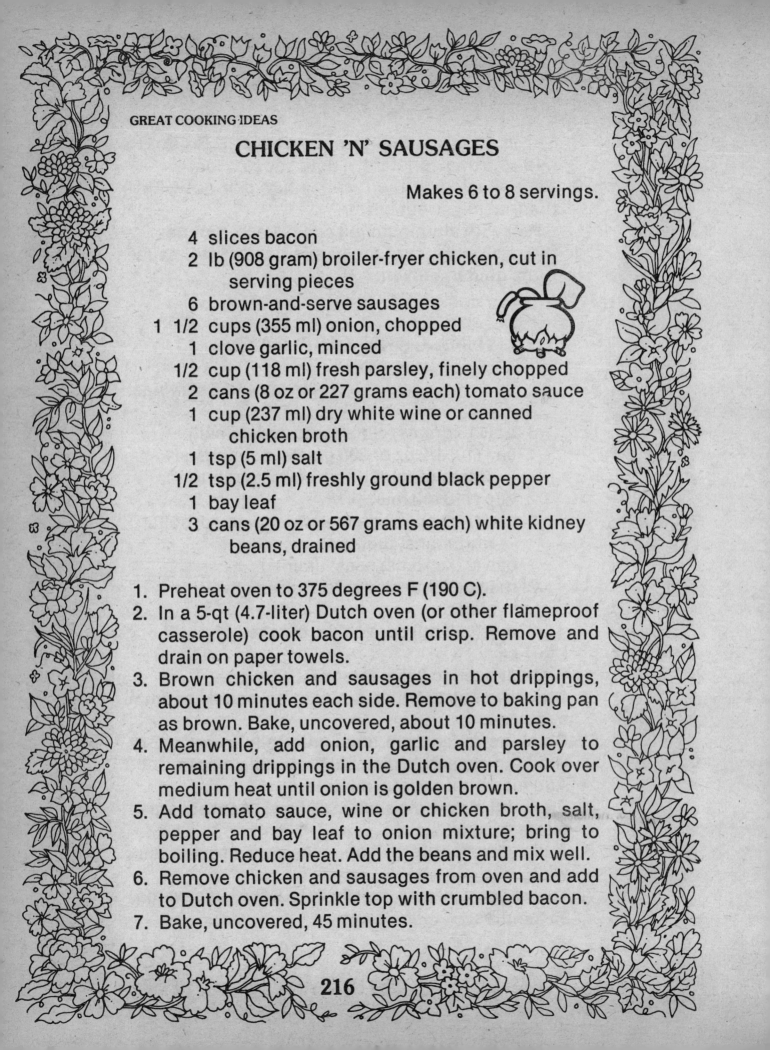

1. Preheat oven to 375 degrees F (190 C).
2. In a 5-qt (4.7-liter) Dutch oven (or other flameproof casserole) cook bacon until crisp. Remove and drain on paper towels.
3. Brown chicken and sausages in hot drippings, about 10 minutes each side. Remove to baking pan as brown. Bake, uncovered, about 10 minutes.
4. Meanwhile, add onion, garlic and parsley to remaining drippings in the Dutch oven. Cook over medium heat until onion is golden brown.
5. Add tomato sauce, wine or chicken broth, salt, pepper and bay leaf to onion mixture; bring to boiling. Reduce heat. Add the beans and mix well.
6. Remove chicken and sausages from oven and add to Dutch oven. Sprinkle top with crumbled bacon.
7. Bake, uncovered, 45 minutes.

CHICKEN-APPLE BAKE

Makes 5 servings.

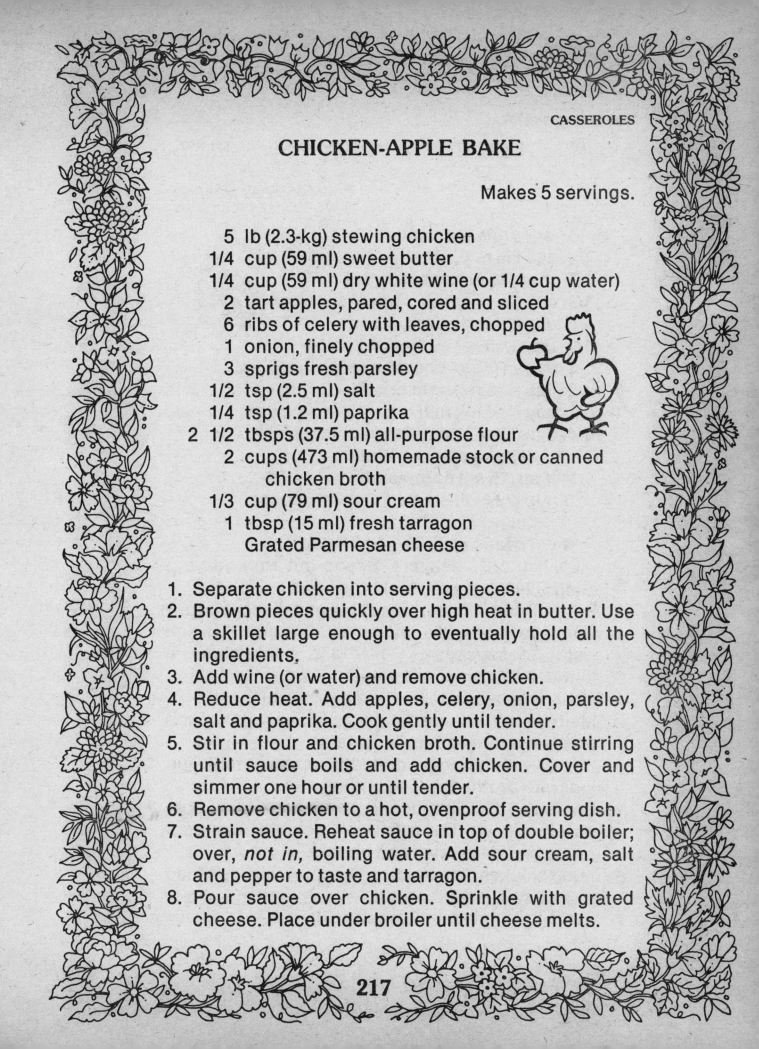

    5 lb (2.3-kg) stewing chicken
  1/4 cup (59 ml) sweet butter
  1/4 cup (59 ml) dry white wine (or 1/4 cup water)
    2 tart apples, pared, cored and sliced
    6 ribs of celery with leaves, chopped
    1 onion, finely chopped
    3 sprigs fresh parsley
  1/2 tsp (2.5 ml) salt
  1/4 tsp (1.2 ml) paprika
2 1/2 tbsps (37.5 ml) all-purpose flour
    2 cups (473 ml) homemade stock or canned
       chicken broth
  1/3 cup (79 ml) sour cream
    1 tbsp (15 ml) fresh tarragon
       Grated Parmesan cheese

1. Separate chicken into serving pieces.
2. Brown pieces quickly over high heat in butter. Use a skillet large enough to eventually hold all the ingredients.
3. Add wine (or water) and remove chicken.
4. Reduce heat. Add apples, celery, onion, parsley, salt and paprika. Cook gently until tender.
5. Stir in flour and chicken broth. Continue stirring until sauce boils and add chicken. Cover and simmer one hour or until tender.
6. Remove chicken to a hot, ovenproof serving dish.
7. Strain sauce. Reheat sauce in top of double boiler; over, *not in,* boiling water. Add sour cream, salt and pepper to taste and tarragon.
8. Pour sauce over chicken. Sprinkle with grated cheese. Place under broiler until cheese melts.

CHICKEN CURRY IN PINEAPPLE SHELLS

Makes 4 servings.

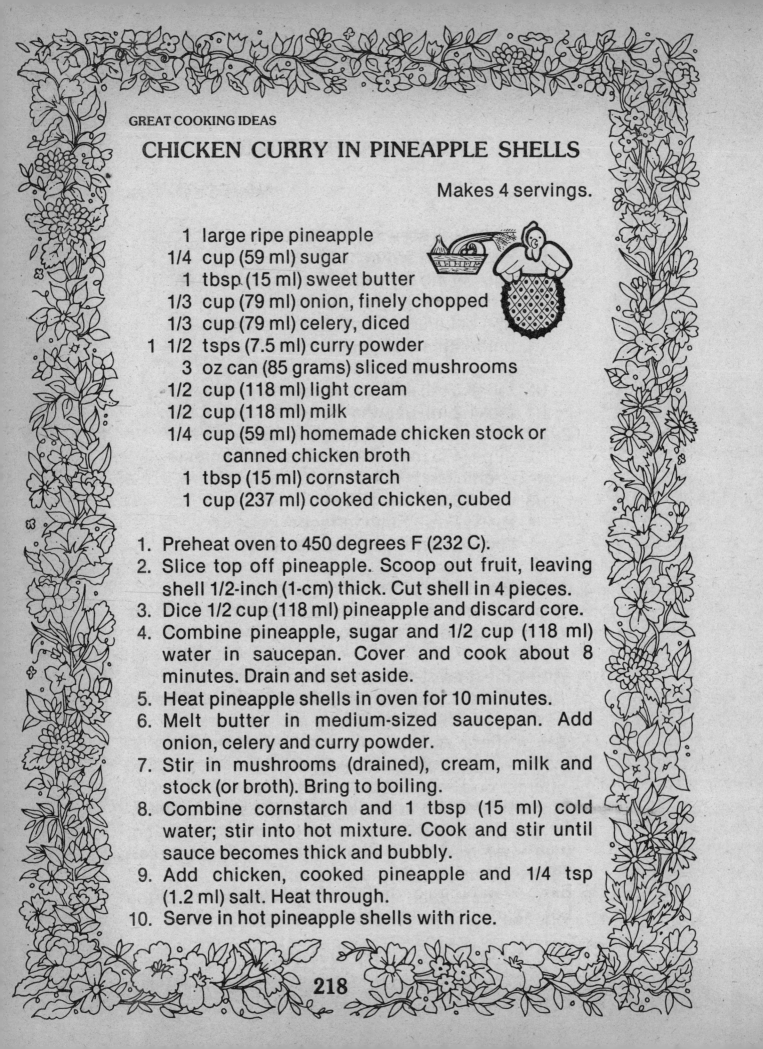

1 large ripe pineapple
1/4 cup (59 ml) sugar
1 tbsp (15 ml) sweet butter
1/3 cup (79 ml) onion, finely chopped
1/3 cup (79 ml) celery, diced
1 1/2 tsps (7.5 ml) curry powder
3 oz can (85 grams) sliced mushrooms
1/2 cup (118 ml) light cream
1/2 cup (118 ml) milk
1/4 cup (59 ml) homemade chicken stock or
   canned chicken broth
1 tbsp (15 ml) cornstarch
1 cup (237 ml) cooked chicken, cubed

1. Preheat oven to 450 degrees F (232 C).
2. Slice top off pineapple. Scoop out fruit, leaving shell 1/2-inch (1-cm) thick. Cut shell in 4 pieces.
3. Dice 1/2 cup (118 ml) pineapple and discard core.
4. Combine pineapple, sugar and 1/2 cup (118 ml) water in saucepan. Cover and cook about 8 minutes. Drain and set aside.
5. Heat pineapple shells in oven for 10 minutes.
6. Melt butter in medium-sized saucepan. Add onion, celery and curry powder.
7. Stir in mushrooms (drained), cream, milk and stock (or broth). Bring to boiling.
8. Combine cornstarch and 1 tbsp (15 ml) cold water; stir into hot mixture. Cook and stir until sauce becomes thick and bubbly.
9. Add chicken, cooked pineapple and 1/4 tsp (1.2 ml) salt. Heat through.
10. Serve in hot pineapple shells with rice.

CHICKEN-LASAGNA BAKE

Makes 8 servings.

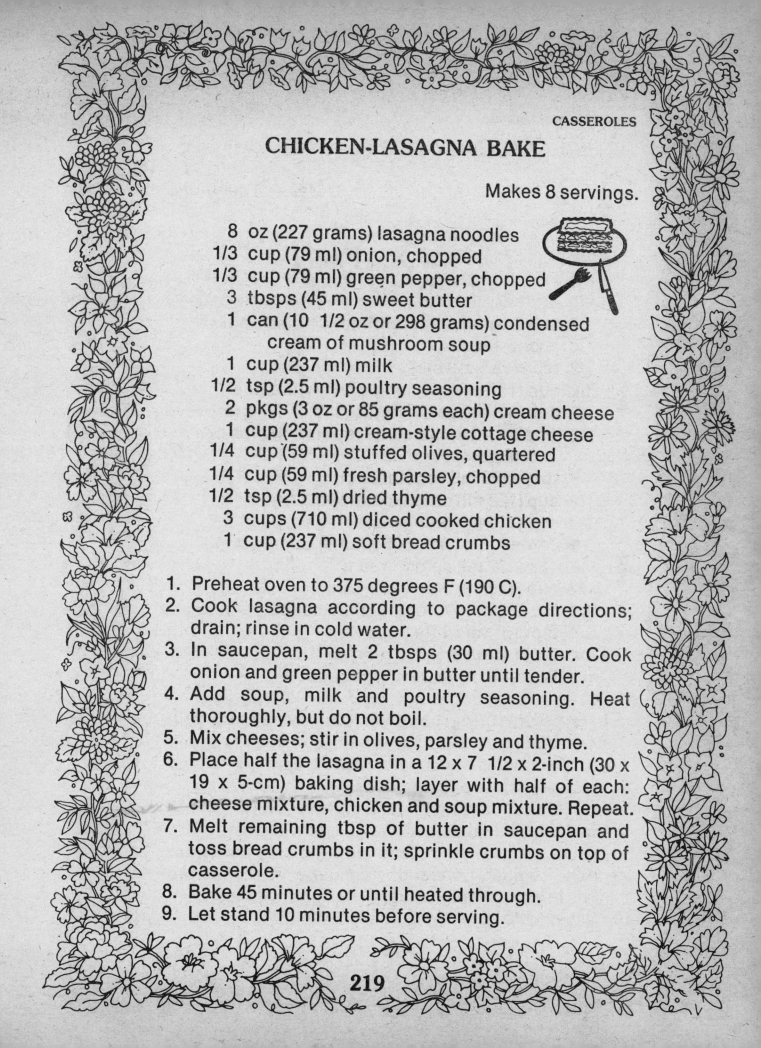

8 oz (227 grams) lasagna noodles
1/3 cup (79 ml) onion, chopped
1/3 cup (79 ml) green pepper, chopped
3 tbsps (45 ml) sweet butter
1 can (10 1/2 oz or 298 grams) condensed
   cream of mushroom soup
1 cup (237 ml) milk
1/2 tsp (2.5 ml) poultry seasoning
2 pkgs (3 oz or 85 grams each) cream cheese
1 cup (237 ml) cream-style cottage cheese
1/4 cup (59 ml) stuffed olives, quartered
1/4 cup (59 ml) fresh parsley, chopped
1/2 tsp (2.5 ml) dried thyme
3 cups (710 ml) diced cooked chicken
1 cup (237 ml) soft bread crumbs

1. Preheat oven to 375 degrees F (190 C).
2. Cook lasagna according to package directions; drain; rinse in cold water.
3. In saucepan, melt 2 tbsps (30 ml) butter. Cook onion and green pepper in butter until tender.
4. Add soup, milk and poultry seasoning. Heat thoroughly, but do not boil.
5. Mix cheeses; stir in olives, parsley and thyme.
6. Place half the lasagna in a 12 x 7 1/2 x 2-inch (30 x 19 x 5-cm) baking dish; layer with half of each: cheese mixture, chicken and soup mixture. Repeat.
7. Melt remaining tbsp of butter in saucepan and toss bread crumbs in it; sprinkle crumbs on top of casserole.
8. Bake 45 minutes or until heated through.
9. Let stand 10 minutes before serving.

CHICKEN-SHRIMP BAKE

Makes 6 servings.

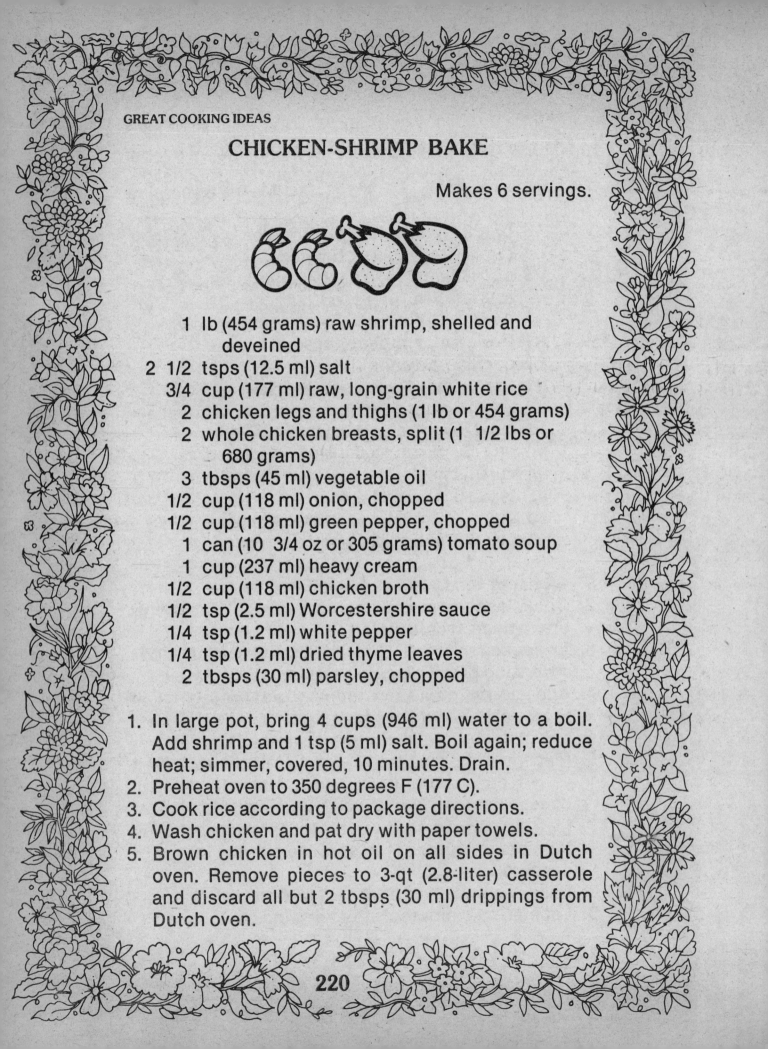

- 1 lb (454 grams) raw shrimp, shelled and deveined
- 2 1/2 tsps (12.5 ml) salt
- 3/4 cup (177 ml) raw, long-grain white rice
- 2 chicken legs and thighs (1 lb or 454 grams)
- 2 whole chicken breasts, split (1 1/2 lbs or 680 grams)
- 3 tbsps (45 ml) vegetable oil
- 1/2 cup (118 ml) onion, chopped
- 1/2 cup (118 ml) green pepper, chopped
- 1 can (10 3/4 oz or 305 grams) tomato soup
- 1 cup (237 ml) heavy cream
- 1/2 cup (118 ml) chicken broth
- 1/2 tsp (2.5 ml) Worcestershire sauce
- 1/4 tsp (1.2 ml) white pepper
- 1/4 tsp (1.2 ml) dried thyme leaves
- 2 tbsps (30 ml) parsley, chopped

1. In large pot, bring 4 cups (946 ml) water to a boil. Add shrimp and 1 tsp (5 ml) salt. Boil again; reduce heat; simmer, covered, 10 minutes. Drain.
2. Preheat oven to 350 degrees F (177 C).
3. Cook rice according to package directions.
4. Wash chicken and pat dry with paper towels.
5. Brown chicken in hot oil on all sides in Dutch oven. Remove pieces to 3-qt (2.8-liter) casserole and discard all but 2 tbsps (30 ml) drippings from Dutch oven.

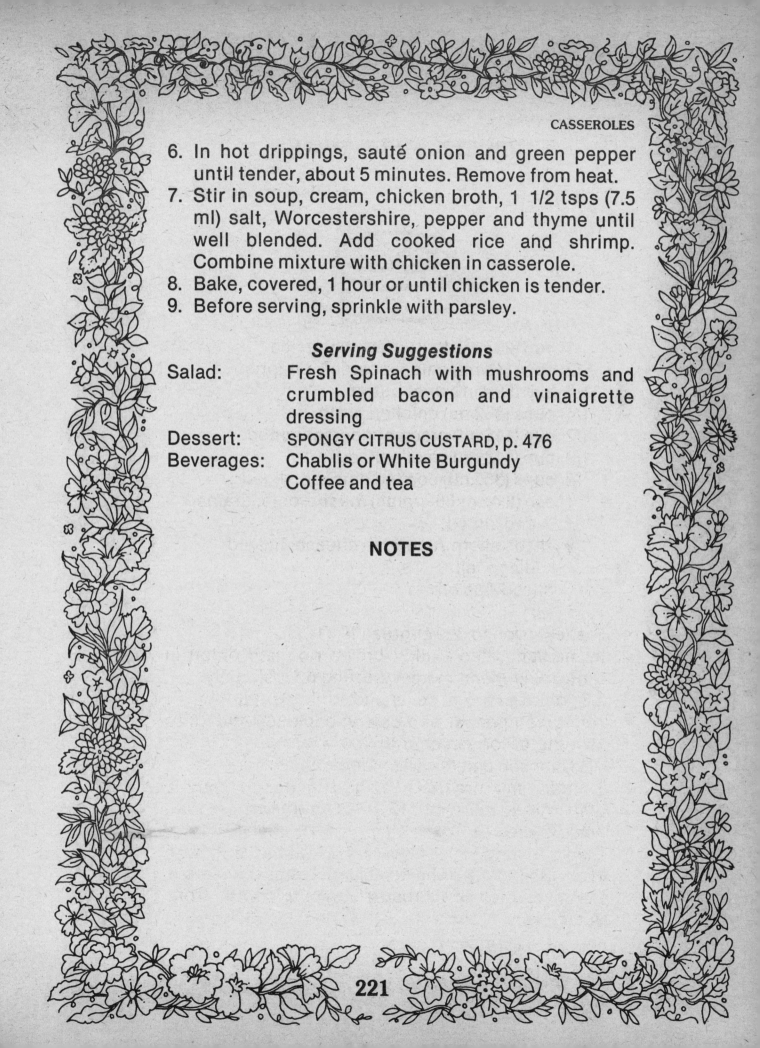

6. In hot drippings, sauté onion and green pepper until tender, about 5 minutes. Remove from heat.
7. Stir in soup, cream, chicken broth, 1 1/2 tsps (7.5 ml) salt, Worcestershire, pepper and thyme until well blended. Add cooked rice and shrimp. Combine mixture with chicken in casserole.
8. Bake, covered, 1 hour or until chicken is tender.
9. Before serving, sprinkle with parsley.

Serving Suggestions

Salad: Fresh Spinach with mushrooms and crumbled bacon and vinaigrette dressing
Dessert: SPONGY CITRUS CUSTARD, p. 476
Beverages: Chablis or White Burgundy
            Coffee and tea

NOTES

CHICKEN-RICE BAKE

Makes 5 or 6 servings.

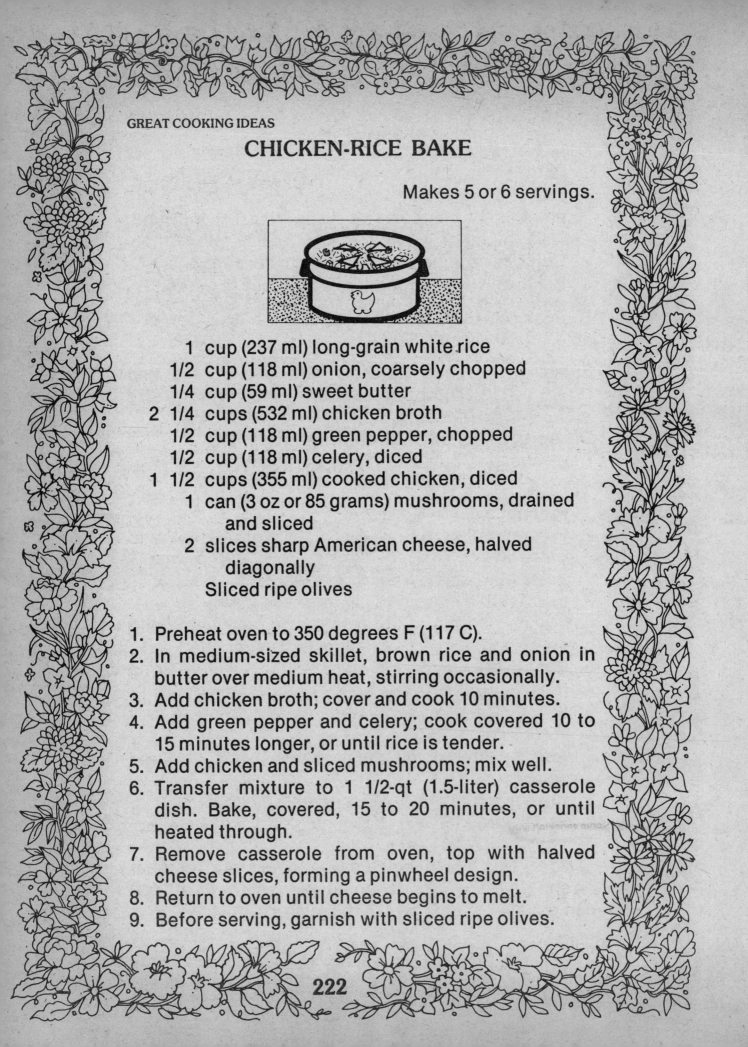

    1   cup (237 ml) long-grain white rice
  1/2   cup (118 ml) onion, coarsely chopped
  1/4   cup (59 ml) sweet butter
  2 1/4 cups (532 ml) chicken broth
  1/2   cup (118 ml) green pepper, chopped
  1/2   cup (118 ml) celery, diced
  1 1/2 cups (355 ml) cooked chicken, diced
    1   can (3 oz or 85 grams) mushrooms, drained
        and sliced
    2   slices sharp American cheese, halved
        diagonally
        Sliced ripe olives

1. Preheat oven to 350 degrees F (117 C).
2. In medium-sized skillet, brown rice and onion in butter over medium heat, stirring occasionally.
3. Add chicken broth; cover and cook 10 minutes.
4. Add green pepper and celery; cook covered 10 to 15 minutes longer, or until rice is tender.
5. Add chicken and sliced mushrooms; mix well.
6. Transfer mixture to 1 1/2-qt (1.5-liter) casserole dish. Bake, covered, 15 to 20 minutes, or until heated through.
7. Remove casserole from oven, top with halved cheese slices, forming a pinwheel design.
8. Return to oven until cheese begins to melt.
9. Before serving, garnish with sliced ripe olives.

JAMBALAYA

Makes 6 to 8 servings.

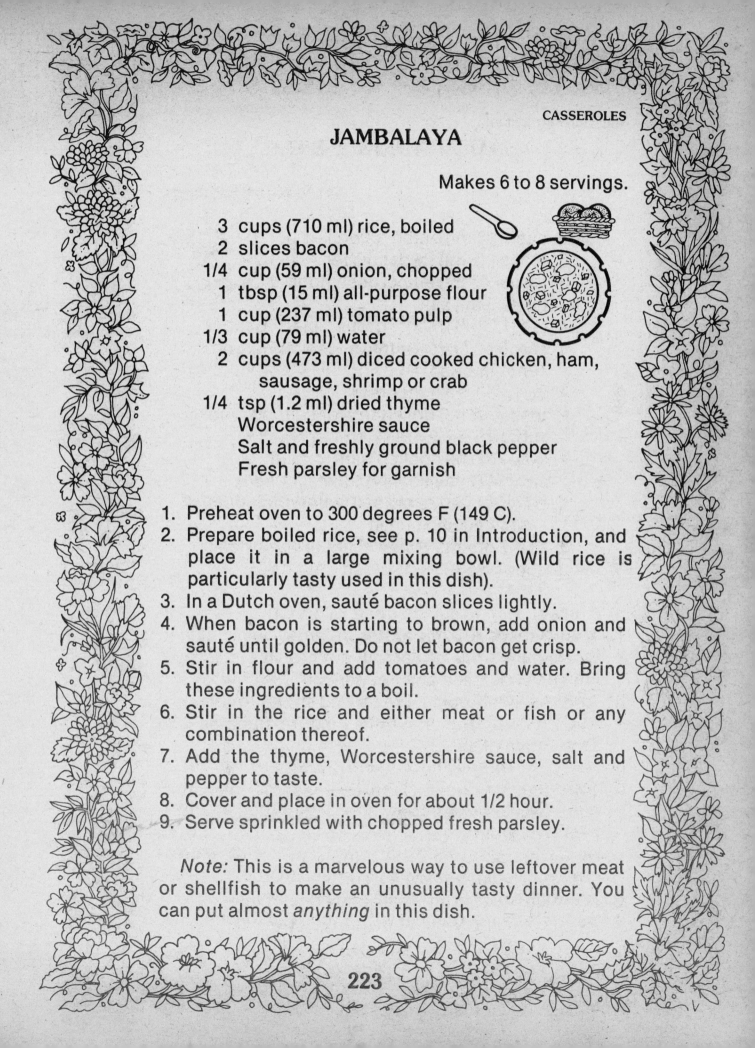

- 3 cups (710 ml) rice, boiled
- 2 slices bacon
- 1/4 cup (59 ml) onion, chopped
- 1 tbsp (15 ml) all-purpose flour
- 1 cup (237 ml) tomato pulp
- 1/3 cup (79 ml) water
- 2 cups (473 ml) diced cooked chicken, ham, sausage, shrimp or crab
- 1/4 tsp (1.2 ml) dried thyme
  Worcestershire sauce
  Salt and freshly ground black pepper
  Fresh parsley for garnish

1. Preheat oven to 300 degrees F (149 C).
2. Prepare boiled rice, see p. 10 in Introduction, and place it in a large mixing bowl. (Wild rice is particularly tasty used in this dish).
3. In a Dutch oven, sauté bacon slices lightly.
4. When bacon is starting to brown, add onion and sauté until golden. Do not let bacon get crisp.
5. Stir in flour and add tomatoes and water. Bring these ingredients to a boil.
6. Stir in the rice and either meat or fish or any combination thereof.
7. Add the thyme, Worcestershire sauce, salt and pepper to taste.
8. Cover and place in oven for about 1/2 hour.
9. Serve sprinkled with chopped fresh parsley.

Note: This is a marvelous way to use leftover meat or shellfish to make an unusually tasty dinner. You can put almost *anything* in this dish.

HAM 'N' TURKEY BAKE

Makes 6 servings.

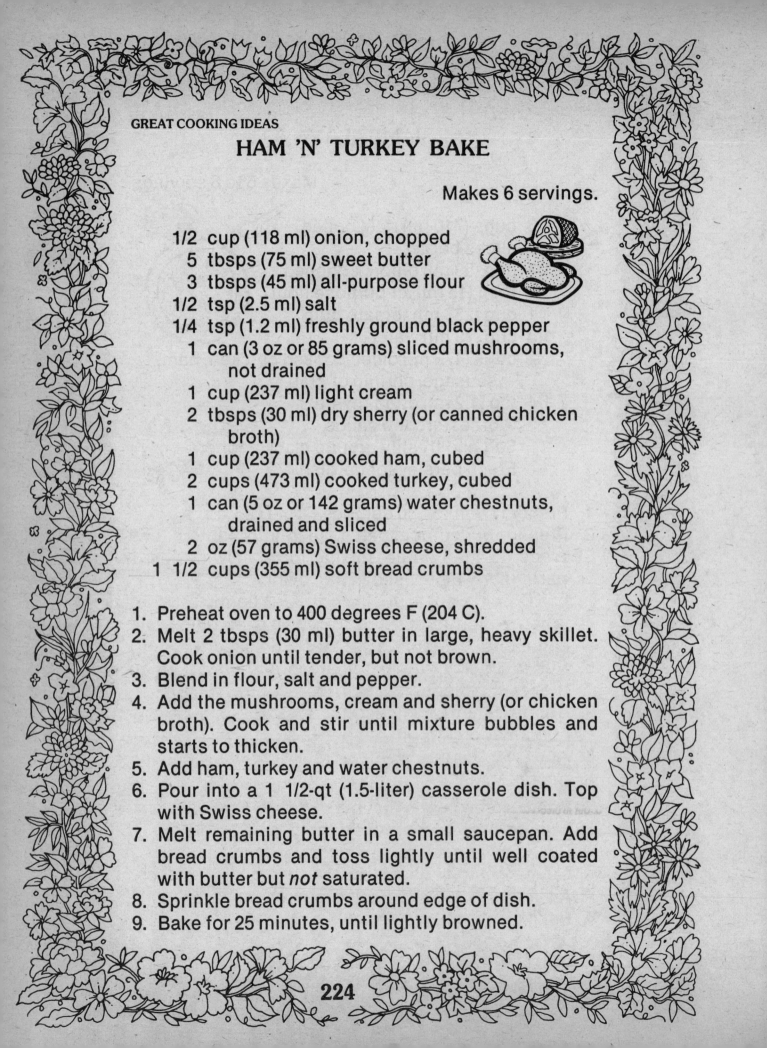

- 1/2 cup (118 ml) onion, chopped
- 5 tbsps (75 ml) sweet butter
- 3 tbsps (45 ml) all-purpose flour
- 1/2 tsp (2.5 ml) salt
- 1/4 tsp (1.2 ml) freshly ground black pepper
- 1 can (3 oz or 85 grams) sliced mushrooms, not drained
- 1 cup (237 ml) light cream
- 2 tbsps (30 ml) dry sherry (or canned chicken broth)
- 1 cup (237 ml) cooked ham, cubed
- 2 cups (473 ml) cooked turkey, cubed
- 1 can (5 oz or 142 grams) water chestnuts, drained and sliced
- 2 oz (57 grams) Swiss cheese, shredded
- 1 1/2 cups (355 ml) soft bread crumbs

1. Preheat oven to 400 degrees F (204 C).
2. Melt 2 tbsps (30 ml) butter in large, heavy skillet. Cook onion until tender, but not brown.
3. Blend in flour, salt and pepper.
4. Add the mushrooms, cream and sherry (or chicken broth). Cook and stir until mixture bubbles and starts to thicken.
5. Add ham, turkey and water chestnuts.
6. Pour into a 1 1/2-qt (1.5-liter) casserole dish. Top with Swiss cheese.
7. Melt remaining butter in a small saucepan. Add bread crumbs and toss lightly until well coated with butter but *not* saturated.
8. Sprinkle bread crumbs around edge of dish.
9. Bake for 25 minutes, until lightly browned.

HAM 'N' VEGETABLES

Makes 24 servings.

4 pkgs (9 oz or 255 grams each) frozen cut
    green beans
4 cans (1 lb or 454 grams each) whole kernel
    corn, drained
4 cans (1 lb or 454 grams each) cream-style
    corn
6 slices white bread, torn to make soft crumbs
4 eggs, well-beaten
1/4 cup (59 ml) onion, minced
4 tsps (20 ml) dry mustard
4 tsps (20 ml) dried basil, crushed
2 tsps (10 ml) salt
1/8 tsp (.6 ml) freshly ground black pepper
3 lbs (1.4 kg) boneless cooked ham, sliced
    1/2-inch (1-cm) thick
2 cans (6 oz or 170 grams each) sliced
    mushrooms, drained

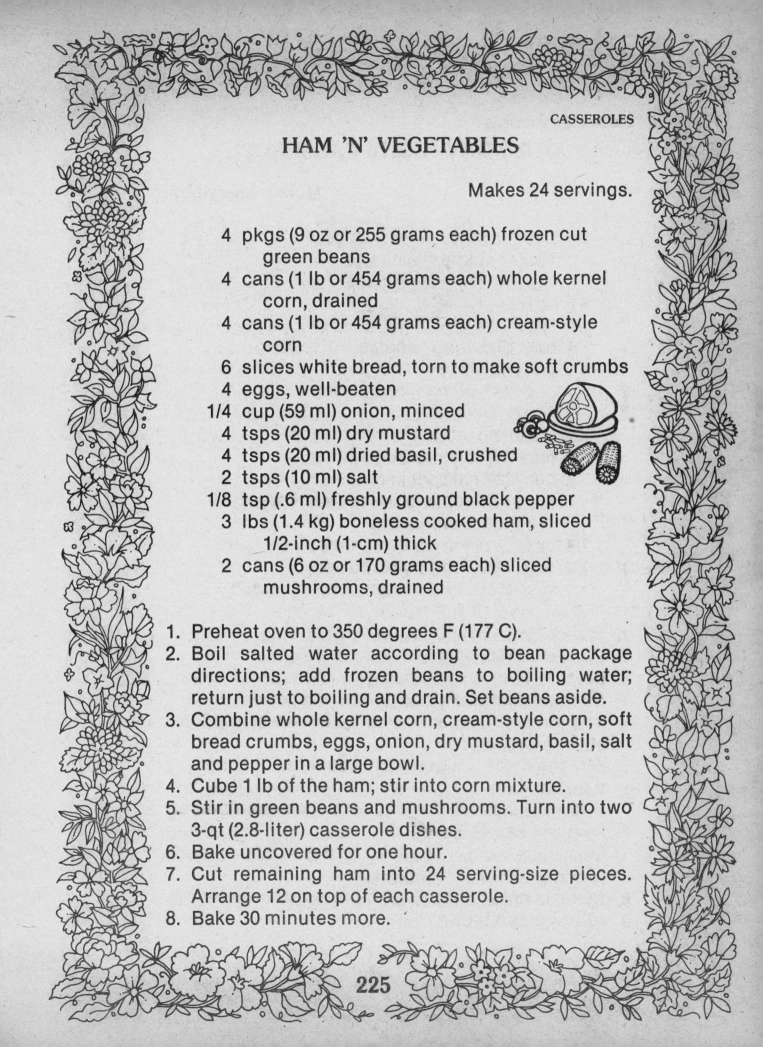

1. Preheat oven to 350 degrees F (177 C).
2. Boil salted water according to bean package
   directions; add frozen beans to boiling water;
   return just to boiling and drain. Set beans aside.
3. Combine whole kernel corn, cream-style corn, soft
   bread crumbs, eggs, onion, dry mustard, basil, salt
   and pepper in a large bowl.
4. Cube 1 lb of the ham; stir into corn mixture.
5. Stir in green beans and mushrooms. Turn into two
   3-qt (2.8-liter) casserole dishes.
6. Bake uncovered for one hour.
7. Cut remaining ham into 24 serving-size pieces.
   Arrange 12 on top of each casserole.
8. Bake 30 minutes more.

SATURDAY-NIGHT CASSEROLE

Makes 6 servings.

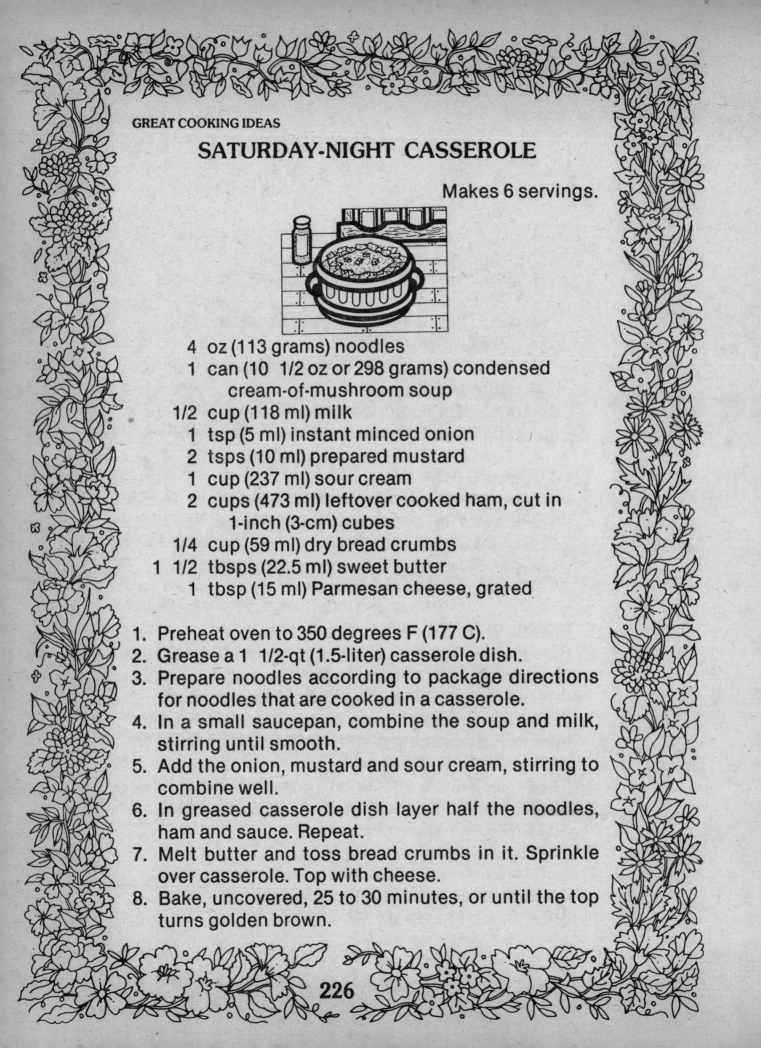

4 oz (113 grams) noodles
1 can (10 1/2 oz or 298 grams) condensed
   cream-of-mushroom soup
1/2 cup (118 ml) milk
1 tsp (5 ml) instant minced onion
2 tsps (10 ml) prepared mustard
1 cup (237 ml) sour cream
2 cups (473 ml) leftover cooked ham, cut in
   1-inch (3-cm) cubes
1/4 cup (59 ml) dry bread crumbs
1 1/2 tbsps (22.5 ml) sweet butter
1 tbsp (15 ml) Parmesan cheese, grated

1. Preheat oven to 350 degrees F (177 C).
2. Grease a 1 1/2-qt (1.5-liter) casserole dish.
3. Prepare noodles according to package directions for noodles that are cooked in a casserole.
4. In a small saucepan, combine the soup and milk, stirring until smooth.
5. Add the onion, mustard and sour cream, stirring to combine well.
6. In greased casserole dish layer half the noodles, ham and sauce. Repeat.
7. Melt butter and toss bread crumbs in it. Sprinkle over casserole. Top with cheese.
8. Bake, uncovered, 25 to 30 minutes, or until the top turns golden brown.

SAUSAGE BAKED WITH SWEET POTATOES 'N' APPLES

Makes 8 servings.

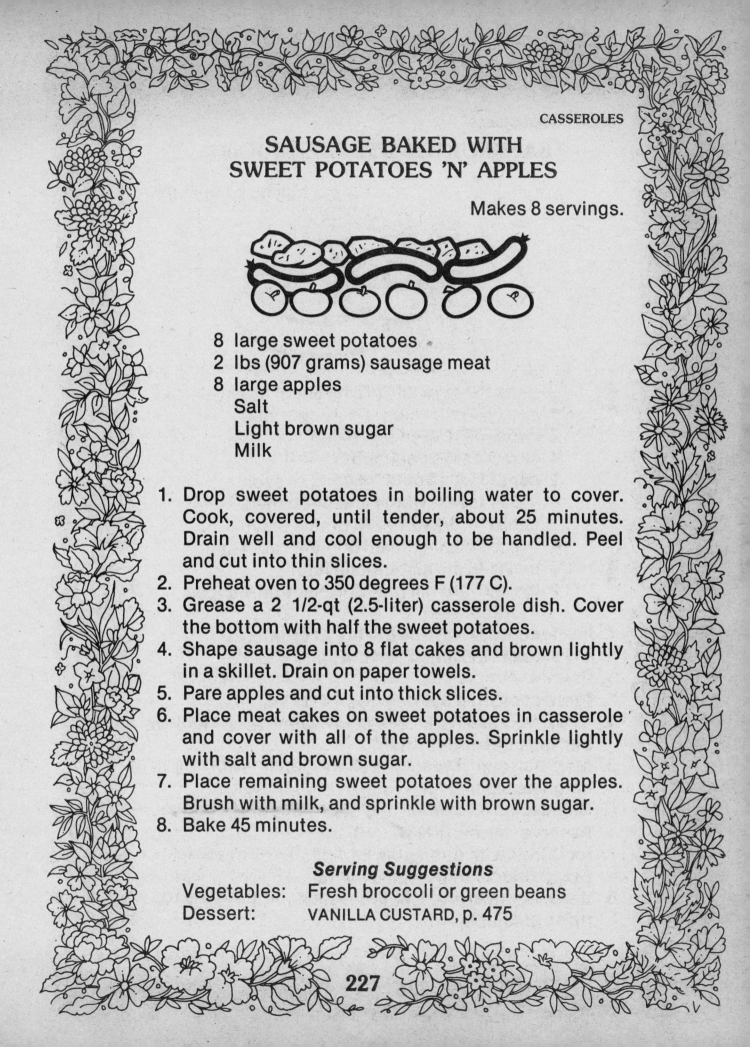

8 large sweet potatoes
2 lbs (907 grams) sausage meat
8 large apples
Salt
Light brown sugar
Milk

1. Drop sweet potatoes in boiling water to cover. Cook, covered, until tender, about 25 minutes. Drain well and cool enough to be handled. Peel and cut into thin slices.
2. Preheat oven to 350 degrees F (177 C).
3. Grease a 2 1/2-qt (2.5-liter) casserole dish. Cover the bottom with half the sweet potatoes.
4. Shape sausage into 8 flat cakes and brown lightly in a skillet. Drain on paper towels.
5. Pare apples and cut into thick slices.
6. Place meat cakes on sweet potatoes in casserole and cover with all of the apples. Sprinkle lightly with salt and brown sugar.
7. Place remaining sweet potatoes over the apples. Brush with milk, and sprinkle with brown sugar.
8. Bake 45 minutes.

Serving Suggestions

Vegetables: Fresh broccoli or green beans
Dessert: VANILLA CUSTARD, p. 475

FRANKFURTER-LIMA BEAN BAKE

Makes 16 to 18 servings.

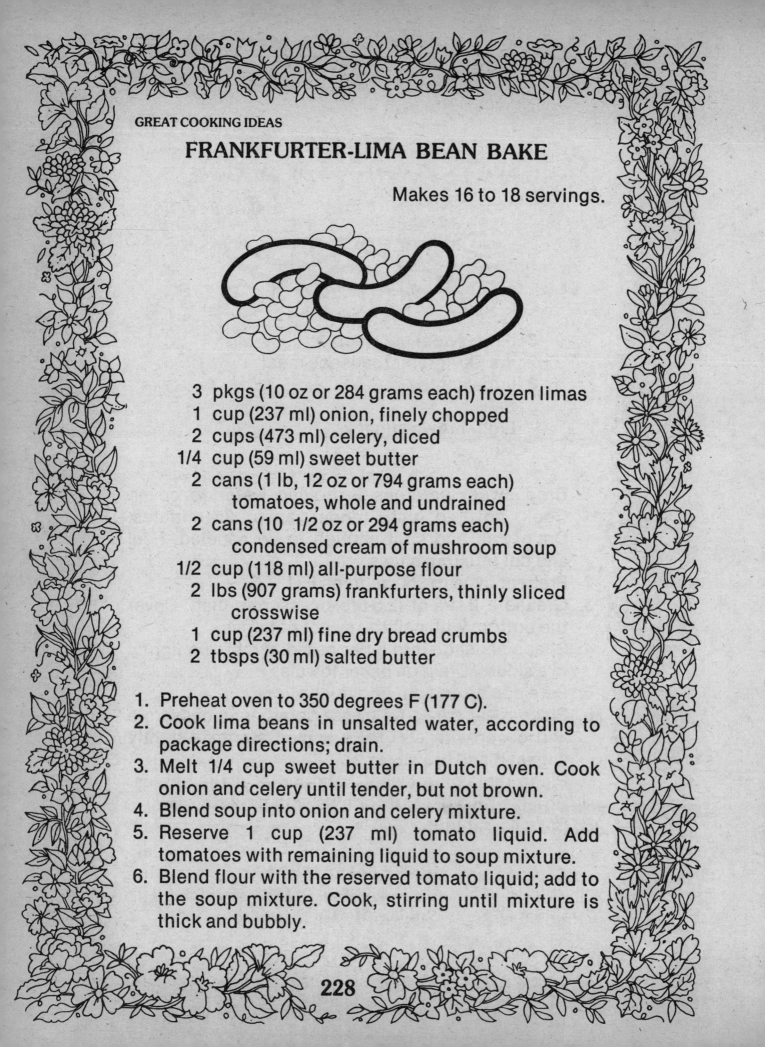

    3 pkgs (10 oz or 284 grams each) frozen limas
    1 cup (237 ml) onion, finely chopped
    2 cups (473 ml) celery, diced
  1/4 cup (59 ml) sweet butter
    2 cans (1 lb, 12 oz or 794 grams each)
          tomatoes, whole and undrained
    2 cans (10 1/2 oz or 294 grams each)
          condensed cream of mushroom soup
  1/2 cup (118 ml) all-purpose flour
    2 lbs (907 grams) frankfurters, thinly sliced
          crosswise
    1 cup (237 ml) fine dry bread crumbs
    2 tbsps (30 ml) salted butter

1. Preheat oven to 350 degrees F (177 C).
2. Cook lima beans in unsalted water, according to package directions; drain.
3. Melt 1/4 cup sweet butter in Dutch oven. Cook onion and celery until tender, but not brown.
4. Blend soup into onion and celery mixture.
5. Reserve 1 cup (237 ml) tomato liquid. Add tomatoes with remaining liquid to soup mixture.
6. Blend flour with the reserved tomato liquid; add to the soup mixture. Cook, stirring until mixture is thick and bubbly.

7. Divide lima beans and frankfurters evenly between two 13 x 9 x 2-inch (33 x 23 x 5-cm) baking pans. Pour half of tomato mixture in each. Mix lightly.
8. Melt 2 tbsps salted butter in saucepan. Add bread crumbs and toss lightly. Sprinkle crumbs evenly over both pans. Bake 30 minutes.
9. Let stand 10 minutes before serving.

* * *

Menu for a Buffet Supper

Makes 20 servings.

Main Course:	Frankfurter-Lima Bean Bake
Bread:	Hot Rolls or Italian Bread
Vegetables:	CHEESE SCALLOPED POTATOES, p. 447*
	FRESH YAMS BAKED WITH PECANS, p. 249
	ALMOND BROCCOLI, p. 437
Desserts:	Spice Cake
	RICE PUDDING, p. 472*
Beverages:	Hot Mulled Cider
	Beer
	Iced Tea and Coffee

*double recipe

Day before: Make desserts and chill Rice Pudding.
Day of buffet: Prepare Cheese Scalloped Potatoes first. While it's in oven, prepare Frankfurter-Lima Bean Bake, Yams with Pecans and Almond Broccoli. Bake main course, then put Yam dish in oven. When baked for 15 minutes, put Almond Broccoli in oven. Continue baking for another 20 minutes. While vegetables are baking, set buffet table with Halloween, or other seasonal, decorations. Keep dishes on warming tray until time to serve.

FRANKFURTERS WITH CORN BREAD TOPPING

Makes 6 to 8 servings.

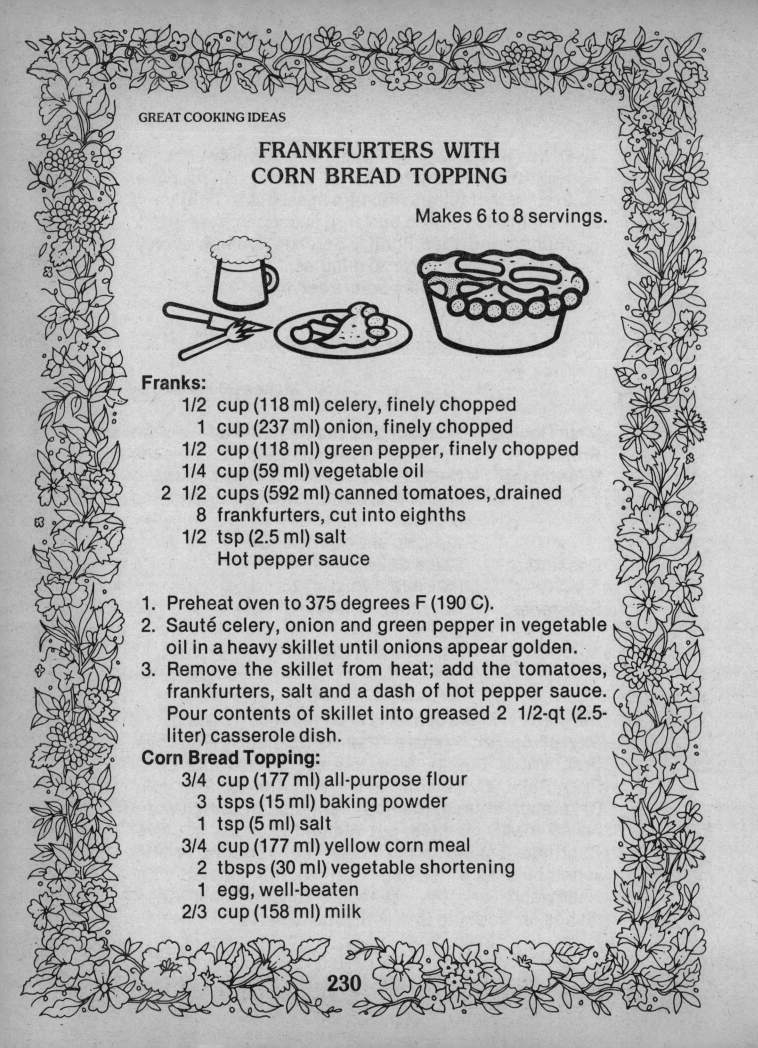

Franks:

    1/2 cup (118 ml) celery, finely chopped
      1 cup (237 ml) onion, finely chopped
    1/2 cup (118 ml) green pepper, finely chopped
    1/4 cup (59 ml) vegetable oil
  2 1/2 cups (592 ml) canned tomatoes, drained
      8 frankfurters, cut into eighths
    1/2 tsp (2.5 ml) salt
         Hot pepper sauce

1. Preheat oven to 375 degrees F (190 C).
2. Sauté celery, onion and green pepper in vegetable oil in a heavy skillet until onions appear golden.
3. Remove the skillet from heat; add the tomatoes, frankfurters, salt and a dash of hot pepper sauce. Pour contents of skillet into greased 2 1/2-qt (2.5-liter) casserole dish.

Corn Bread Topping:

    3/4 cup (177 ml) all-purpose flour
      3 tsps (15 ml) baking powder
      1 tsp (5 ml) salt
    3/4 cup (177 ml) yellow corn meal
      2 tbsps (30 ml) vegetable shortening
      1 egg, well-beaten
    2/3 cup (158 ml) milk

1. Sift flour, baking powder and salt together.
2. Stir in corn meal.
3. Cut shortening into flour mixture until well blended.
4. Add well-beaten egg and milk. Mix until dry ingredients are moistened.
5. Pour corn meal batter on top of tomato-frankfurter mixture in casserole.
6. Topping may be garnished with an additional frankfurter cut into thin rounds.
7. Bake uncovered about 35 minutes.

* * *

Variation: One package (11 3/4 oz or 333 grams) corn muffin mix may be substituted for homemade Corn Bread Topping. Simply prepare mix according to package directions and go to Step 5 of the Topping instructions.

Serving Suggestions

Vegetable: GREEN BEAN BAKE, p. 250
Dessert: Fresh peach cobbler or your favorite ice cream
Beverages: Red Chianti (Italian) or Beer
Coffee or Tea after dinner

NOTES

LAMB SHANK 'N' BEAN BAKE

Makes 8 servings.

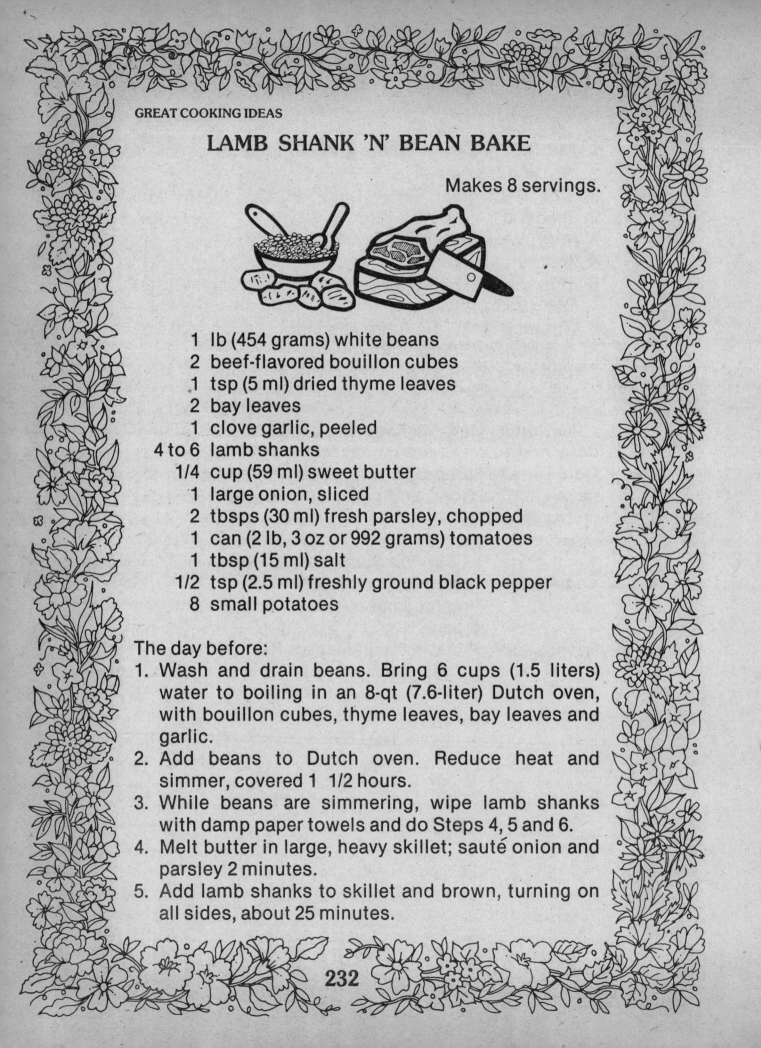

- 1 lb (454 grams) white beans
- 2 beef-flavored bouillon cubes
- 1 tsp (5 ml) dried thyme leaves
- 2 bay leaves
- 1 clove garlic, peeled
- 4 to 6 lamb shanks
- 1/4 cup (59 ml) sweet butter
- 1 large onion, sliced
- 2 tbsps (30 ml) fresh parsley, chopped
- 1 can (2 lb, 3 oz or 992 grams) tomatoes
- 1 tbsp (15 ml) salt
- 1/2 tsp (2.5 ml) freshly ground black pepper
- 8 small potatoes

The day before:

1. Wash and drain beans. Bring 6 cups (1.5 liters) water to boiling in an 8-qt (7.6-liter) Dutch oven, with bouillon cubes, thyme leaves, bay leaves and garlic.
2. Add beans to Dutch oven. Reduce heat and simmer, covered 1 1/2 hours.
3. While beans are simmering, wipe lamb shanks with damp paper towels and do Steps 4, 5 and 6.
4. Melt butter in large, heavy skillet; sauté onion and parsley 2 minutes.
5. Add lamb shanks to skillet and brown, turning on all sides, about 25 minutes.

6. Add undrained tomatoes to skillet and simmer, covered, 1 hour.
7. Add the lamb shanks and tomato mixture to beans; sprinkle with salt and pepper. Cover and refrigerate overnight.

Next day:
1. Preheat oven to 375 degrees F (190 C).
2. Pare the potatoes and slice them into 1/4-inch (.6-cm) slices.
3. Arrange potato slices over beans. Bake lamb shanks and beans, uncovered, 1 1/2 hours, or until potatoes are cooked and shanks tender.
4. Before serving: turn into large, shallow serving dish, sprinkle with chopped parsley.

Serving Suggestions

Vegetables:	ACORN SQUASH BAKE, p. 238; or
	BAKED BRUSSELS SPROUTS, p. 240
Salad:	Wilted Lettuce
Dessert:	ORANGE SOUFFLÉ, pp. 486, 487
Beverages:	White Burgundy, or
	Grey Riesling
	Coffee or Tea after dinner

NOTES

RUMANIAN CASSEROLE

Makes 6 servings.

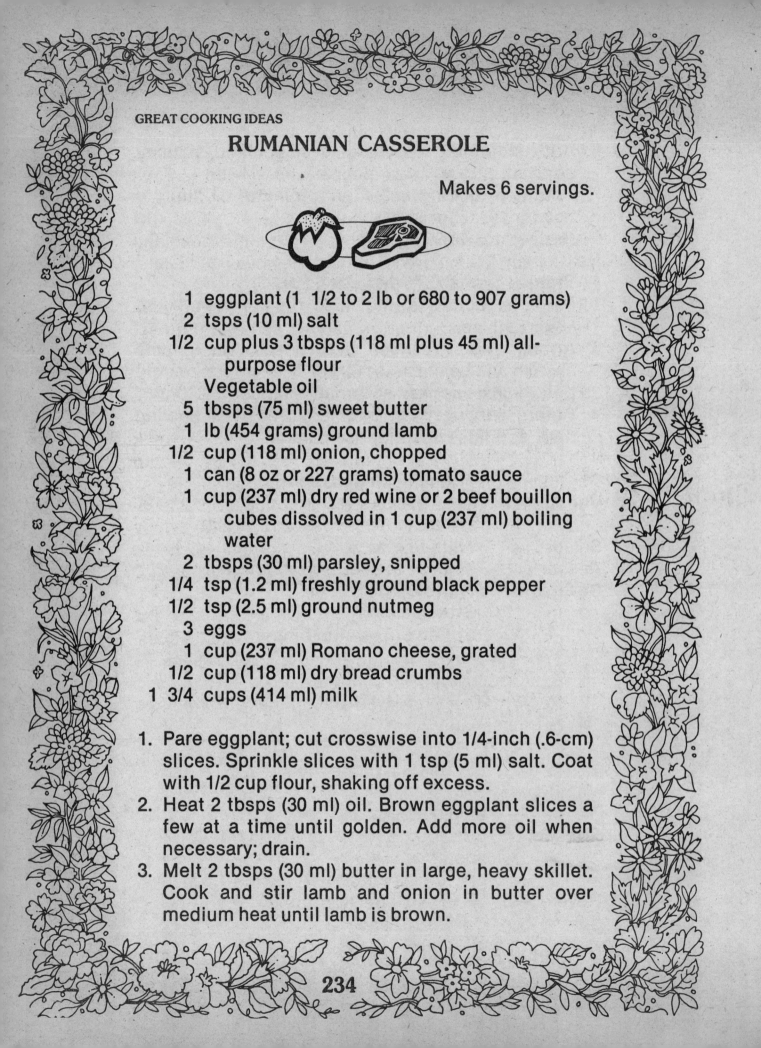

- 1 eggplant (1 1/2 to 2 lb or 680 to 907 grams)
- 2 tsps (10 ml) salt
- 1/2 cup plus 3 tbsps (118 ml plus 45 ml) all-purpose flour
  Vegetable oil
- 5 tbsps (75 ml) sweet butter
- 1 lb (454 grams) ground lamb
- 1/2 cup (118 ml) onion, chopped
- 1 can (8 oz or 227 grams) tomato sauce
- 1 cup (237 ml) dry red wine or 2 beef bouillon cubes dissolved in 1 cup (237 ml) boiling water
- 2 tbsps (30 ml) parsley, snipped
- 1/4 tsp (1.2 ml) freshly ground black pepper
- 1/2 tsp (2.5 ml) ground nutmeg
- 3 eggs
- 1 cup (237 ml) Romano cheese, grated
- 1/2 cup (118 ml) dry bread crumbs
- 1 3/4 cups (414 ml) milk

1. Pare eggplant; cut crosswise into 1/4-inch (.6-cm) slices. Sprinkle slices with 1 tsp (5 ml) salt. Coat with 1/2 cup flour, shaking off excess.
2. Heat 2 tbsps (30 ml) oil. Brown eggplant slices a few at a time until golden. Add more oil when necessary; drain.
3. Melt 2 tbsps (30 ml) butter in large, heavy skillet. Cook and stir lamb and onion in butter over medium heat until lamb is brown.

4. Stir in tomato sauce, wine or bouillon, parsley, 1/2 tsp (2.5 ml) salt, pepper and 1/4 tsp (1.2 ml) nutmeg. Cook, uncovered, until half of liquid is absorbed, about 20 minutes.
5. Stir in 1 beaten egg, 1/2 cup (118 ml) cheese and 1/4 cup (59 ml) bread crumbs. Remove from heat.
6. Preheat oven to 375 degrees F (190 C).
7. Melt remaining butter in 2-qt (2-liter) saucepan. Stir in 3 tbsps flour, remaining salt and nutmeg. Cook over low heat, stirring constantly, until mixture is smooth and bubbly.
8. Add milk, stirring constantly, until sauce boils. Beat remaining 2 eggs lightly. Stir small amount of hot milk mixture into eggs. Stir egg-milk mixture back into hot mixture in pan. Add 1/4 cup (59 ml) cheese and stir until it is melted.
9. Grease baking dish 9 x 9 x 2-inches (23 x 23 x 5-cm). Sprinkle 1/4 cup (59 ml) bread crumbs evenly in dish. Arrange half of the eggplant slices in dish; cover with lamb mixture. Sprinkle with 2 tbsps (30 ml) cheese.
10. Place remaining eggplant slices on top of cheese. Pour sauce over eggplant slices. Sprinkle with remaining 2 tbsps (30 ml) cheese.
11. Bake, uncovered, 45 minutes.
12. Remove dish from oven and let stand 20 minutes before serving.

Serving Suggestions

Vegetables: BAKED MUSHROOMS, p. 239; or
BAKED RICE, p. 240
Dessert: CHOCOLATE-PECAN UPSIDE DOWN
PUDDING, p. 469
or ORANGE MINCEMEAT PUDDING, p. 470
Beverages: Wine — Claret (California)
Coffee or Tea

VEAL MARENGO BAKE

Makes 12 servings.

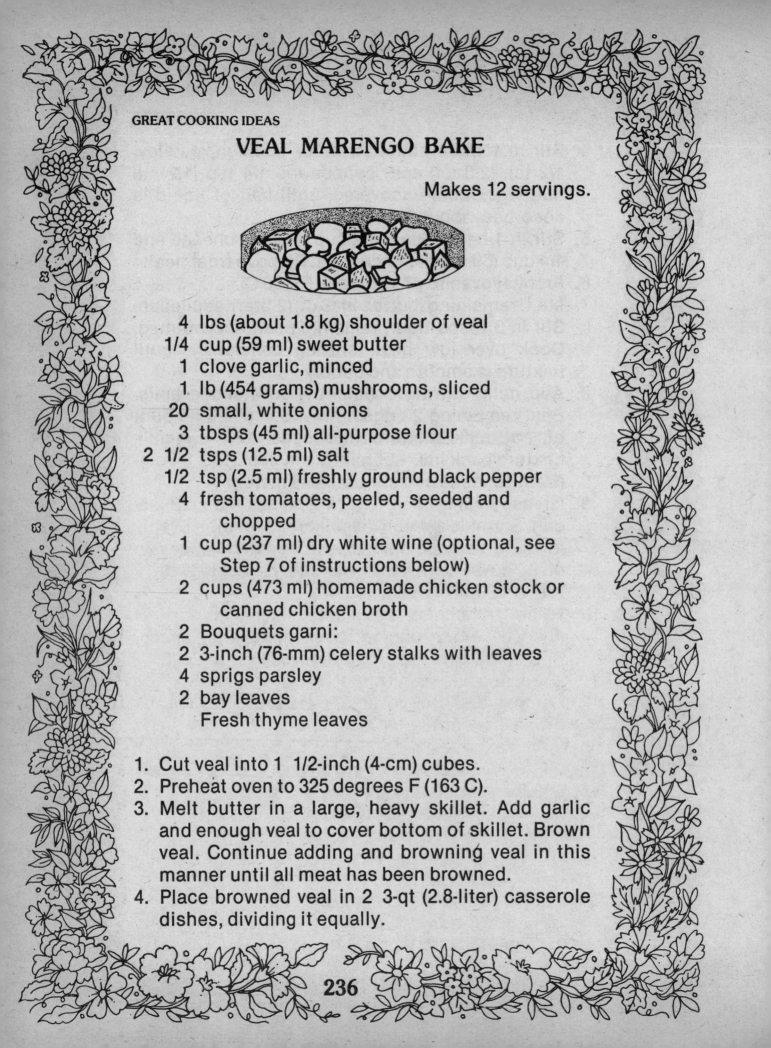

- 4 lbs (about 1.8 kg) shoulder of veal
- 1/4 cup (59 ml) sweet butter
- 1 clove garlic, minced
- 1 lb (454 grams) mushrooms, sliced
- 20 small, white onions
- 3 tbsps (45 ml) all-purpose flour
- 2 1/2 tsps (12.5 ml) salt
- 1/2 tsp (2.5 ml) freshly ground black pepper
- 4 fresh tomatoes, peeled, seeded and chopped
- 1 cup (237 ml) dry white wine (optional, see Step 7 of instructions below)
- 2 cups (473 ml) homemade chicken stock or canned chicken broth
- 2 Bouquets garni:
- 2 3-inch (76-mm) celery stalks with leaves
- 4 sprigs parsley
- 2 bay leaves
   Fresh thyme leaves

1. Cut veal into 1 1/2-inch (4-cm) cubes.
2. Preheat oven to 325 degrees F (163 C).
3. Melt butter in a large, heavy skillet. Add garlic and enough veal to cover bottom of skillet. Brown veal. Continue adding and browning veal in this manner until all meat has been browned.
4. Place browned veal in 2 3-qt (2.8-liter) casserole dishes, dividing it equally.

236

5. Add additional butter to skillet, if necessary; then brown mushrooms by tossing them lightly in skillet and sauté onions until golden.
6. Divide the mushrooms and onions evenly and arrange over meat.
7. Stir flour, salt and pepper into butter remaining in skillet. Add tomatoes, wine and broth. (If wine is not being used, substitute an additional cup, 237 ml, of chicken broth.) Pour over veal mixture.
8. Make a bouquet garni for each casserole dish by tying together a celery stalk, 2 sprigs parsley, a bay leaf and a pinch of fresh thyme into a small piece of cheesecloth with white string. Place a bouquet in each casserole.
9. Cover casseroles and bake for 1 1/4 hours.
10. Remove herb bouquets before serving.

Serving Suggestions

Salad:	Zucchini with Italian-style dressing
Dessert:	CHOCOLATE BREAD PUDDING, p. 468 or; RICE PUDDING, p. 472
Beverages:	Pinot St. George; or Lake Country Red (California) Espresso or regular coffee

NOTES

ACORN SQUASH BAKE

Makes 6 servings.

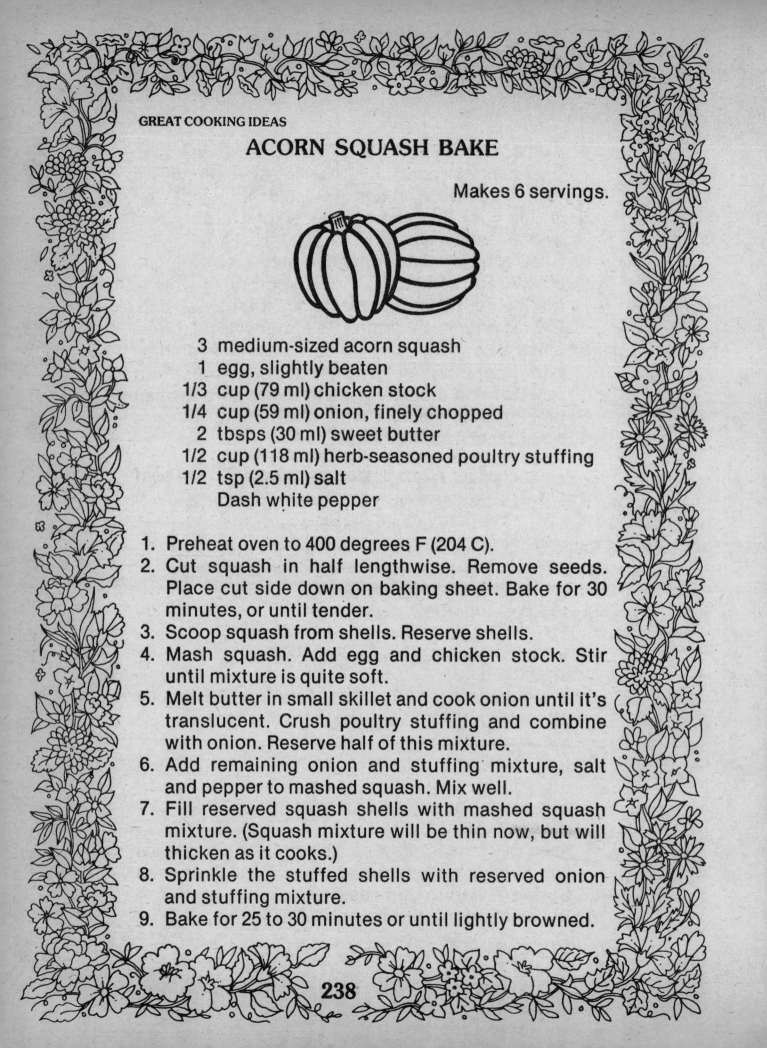

3 medium-sized acorn squash
1 egg, slightly beaten
1/3 cup (79 ml) chicken stock
1/4 cup (59 ml) onion, finely chopped
2 tbsps (30 ml) sweet butter
1/2 cup (118 ml) herb-seasoned poultry stuffing
1/2 tsp (2.5 ml) salt
    Dash white pepper

1. Preheat oven to 400 degrees F (204 C).
2. Cut squash in half lengthwise. Remove seeds. Place cut side down on baking sheet. Bake for 30 minutes, or until tender.
3. Scoop squash from shells. Reserve shells.
4. Mash squash. Add egg and chicken stock. Stir until mixture is quite soft.
5. Melt butter in small skillet and cook onion until it's translucent. Crush poultry stuffing and combine with onion. Reserve half of this mixture.
6. Add remaining onion and stuffing mixture, salt and pepper to mashed squash. Mix well.
7. Fill reserved squash shells with mashed squash mixture. (Squash mixture will be thin now, but will thicken as it cooks.)
8. Sprinkle the stuffed shells with reserved onion and stuffing mixture.
9. Bake for 25 to 30 minutes or until lightly browned.

BAKED MUSHROOMS

Makes 6 servings.

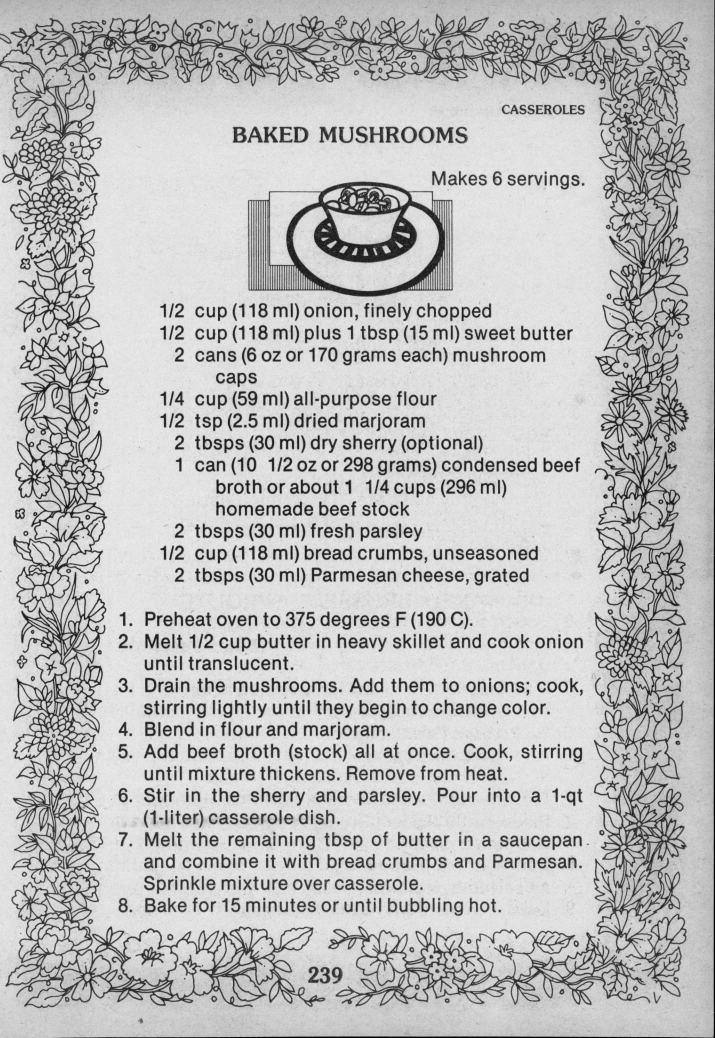

- 1/2 cup (118 ml) onion, finely chopped
- 1/2 cup (118 ml) plus 1 tbsp (15 ml) sweet butter
- 2 cans (6 oz or 170 grams each) mushroom caps
- 1/4 cup (59 ml) all-purpose flour
- 1/2 tsp (2.5 ml) dried marjoram
- 2 tbsps (30 ml) dry sherry (optional)
- 1 can (10 1/2 oz or 298 grams) condensed beef broth or about 1 1/4 cups (296 ml) homemade beef stock
- 2 tbsps (30 ml) fresh parsley
- 1/2 cup (118 ml) bread crumbs, unseasoned
- 2 tbsps (30 ml) Parmesan cheese, grated

1. Preheat oven to 375 degrees F (190 C).
2. Melt 1/2 cup butter in heavy skillet and cook onion until translucent.
3. Drain the mushrooms. Add them to onions; cook, stirring lightly until they begin to change color.
4. Blend in flour and marjoram.
5. Add beef broth (stock) all at once. Cook, stirring until mixture thickens. Remove from heat.
6. Stir in the sherry and parsley. Pour into a 1-qt (1-liter) casserole dish.
7. Melt the remaining tbsp of butter in a saucepan and combine it with bread crumbs and Parmesan. Sprinkle mixture over casserole.
8. Bake for 15 minutes or until bubbling hot.

COTTAGE CHEESE NOODLE BAKE

Makes 8 servings.

8 oz (227 grams) egg noddles
1/4 cup (59 ml) onion, finely chopped
1 clove garlic, minced
2 tbsps (30 ml) sweet butter
1 1/2 cups (355 ml) cream-style cottage cheese
1 cup (237 ml) dairy sour cream
1 tsp (5 ml) Worcestershire sauce
Dash hot red pepper sauce
2 tbsps (30 ml) dried parsley flakes
1 tsp (5 ml) dried basil, crushed
1/2 tsp (2.5 ml) salt
Dash white pepper

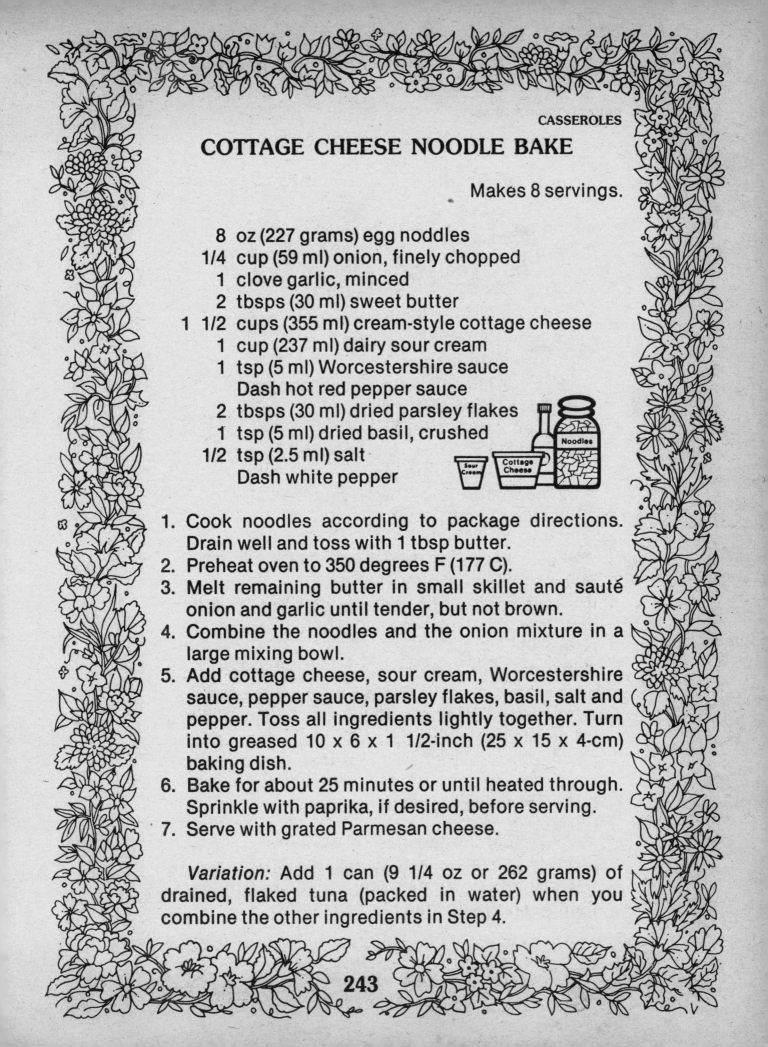

1. Cook noodles according to package directions. Drain well and toss with 1 tbsp butter.
2. Preheat oven to 350 degrees F (177 C).
3. Melt remaining butter in small skillet and sauté onion and garlic until tender, but not brown.
4. Combine the noodles and the onion mixture in a large mixing bowl.
5. Add cottage cheese, sour cream, Worcestershire sauce, pepper sauce, parsley flakes, basil, salt and pepper. Toss all ingredients lightly together. Turn into greased 10 x 6 x 1 1/2-inch (25 x 15 x 4-cm) baking dish.
6. Bake for about 25 minutes or until heated through. Sprinkle with paprika, if desired, before serving.
7. Serve with grated Parmesan cheese.

Variation: Add 1 can (9 1/4 oz or 262 grams) of drained, flaked tuna (packed in water) when you combine the other ingredients in Step 4.

CORN 'N' SWISS CHEESE BAKE

Makes 4 to 6 servings.

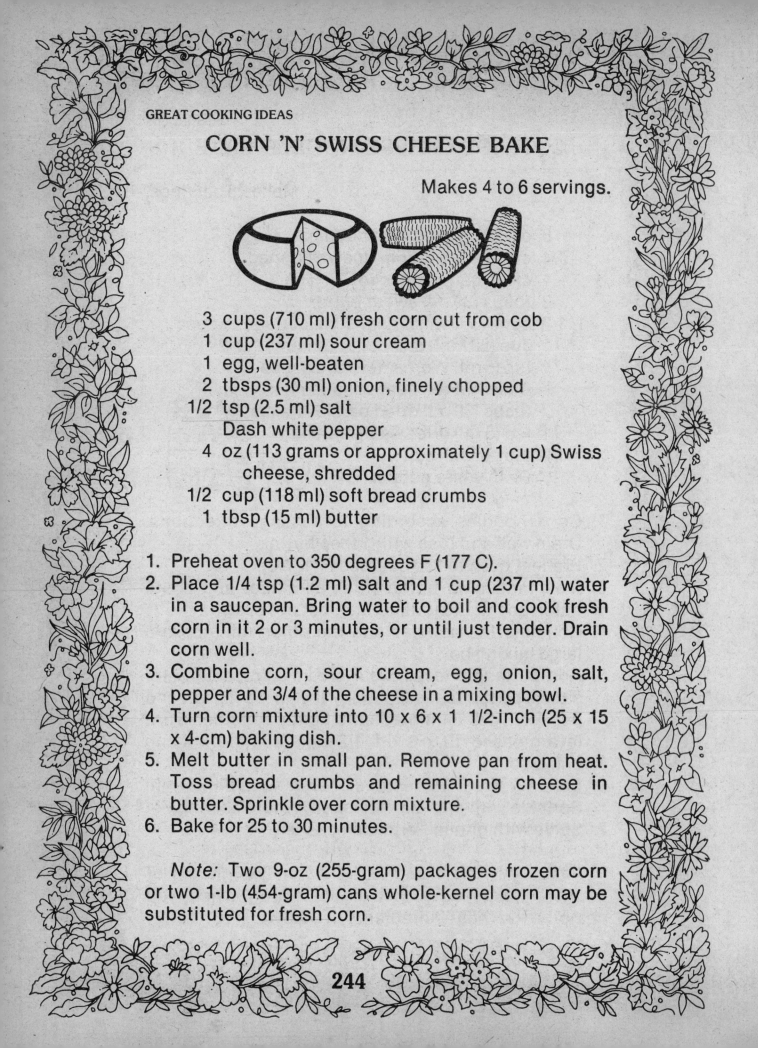

    3 cups (710 ml) fresh corn cut from cob
    1 cup (237 ml) sour cream
    1 egg, well-beaten
    2 tbsps (30 ml) onion, finely chopped
  1/2 tsp (2.5 ml) salt
       Dash white pepper
    4 oz (113 grams or approximately 1 cup) Swiss
       cheese, shredded
  1/2 cup (118 ml) soft bread crumbs
    1 tbsp (15 ml) butter

1. Preheat oven to 350 degrees F (177 C).
2. Place 1/4 tsp (1.2 ml) salt and 1 cup (237 ml) water in a saucepan. Bring water to boil and cook fresh corn in it 2 or 3 minutes, or until just tender. Drain corn well.
3. Combine corn, sour cream, egg, onion, salt, pepper and 3/4 of the cheese in a mixing bowl.
4. Turn corn mixture into 10 x 6 x 1 1/2-inch (25 x 15 x 4-cm) baking dish.
5. Melt butter in small pan. Remove pan from heat. Toss bread crumbs and remaining cheese in butter. Sprinkle over corn mixture.
6. Bake for 25 to 30 minutes.

Note: Two 9-oz (255-gram) packages frozen corn or two 1-lb (454-gram) cans whole-kernel corn may be substituted for fresh corn.

CORN PUDDING CASSEROLE

Makes 8 servings.

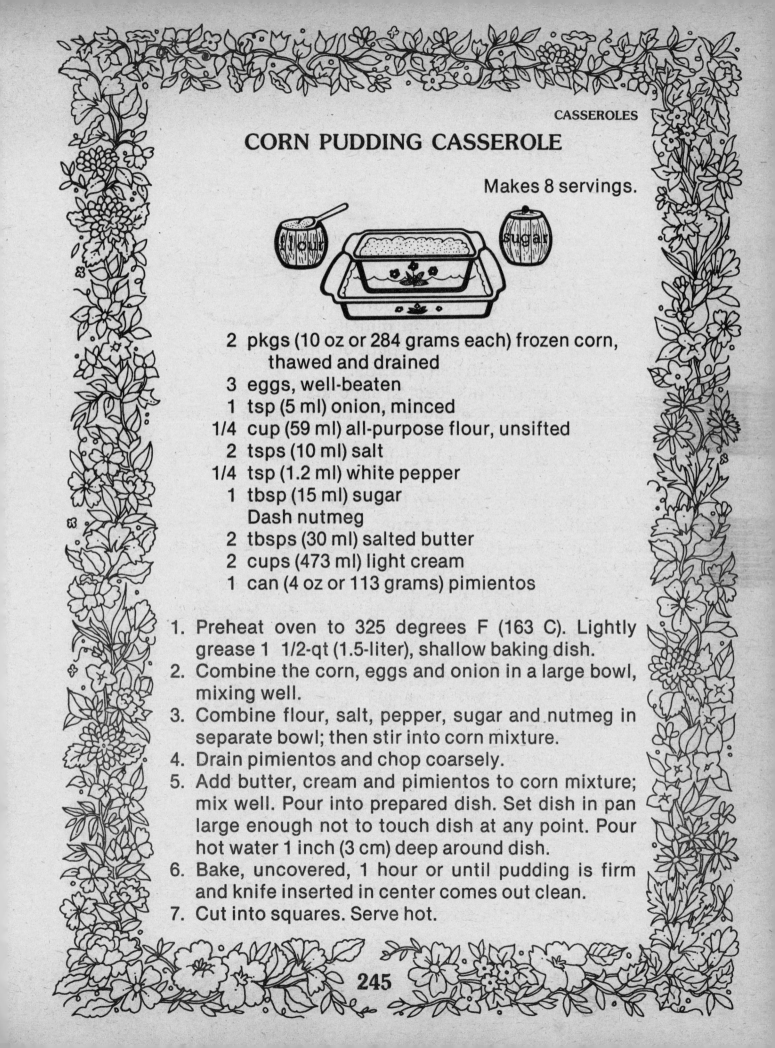

2 pkgs (10 oz or 284 grams each) frozen corn,
   thawed and drained
3 eggs, well-beaten
1 tsp (5 ml) onion, minced
1/4 cup (59 ml) all-purpose flour, unsifted
2 tsps (10 ml) salt
1/4 tsp (1.2 ml) white pepper
1 tbsp (15 ml) sugar
   Dash nutmeg
2 tbsps (30 ml) salted butter
2 cups (473 ml) light cream
1 can (4 oz or 113 grams) pimientos

1. Preheat oven to 325 degrees F (163 C). Lightly grease 1 1/2-qt (1.5-liter), shallow baking dish.
2. Combine the corn, eggs and onion in a large bowl, mixing well.
3. Combine flour, salt, pepper, sugar and nutmeg in separate bowl; then stir into corn mixture.
4. Drain pimientos and chop coarsely.
5. Add butter, cream and pimientos to corn mixture; mix well. Pour into prepared dish. Set dish in pan large enough not to touch dish at any point. Pour hot water 1 inch (3 cm) deep around dish.
6. Bake, uncovered, 1 hour or until pudding is firm and knife inserted in center comes out clean.
7. Cut into squares. Serve hot.

CURRIED FRUIT, NUTS AND RICE

Makes 10 servings.

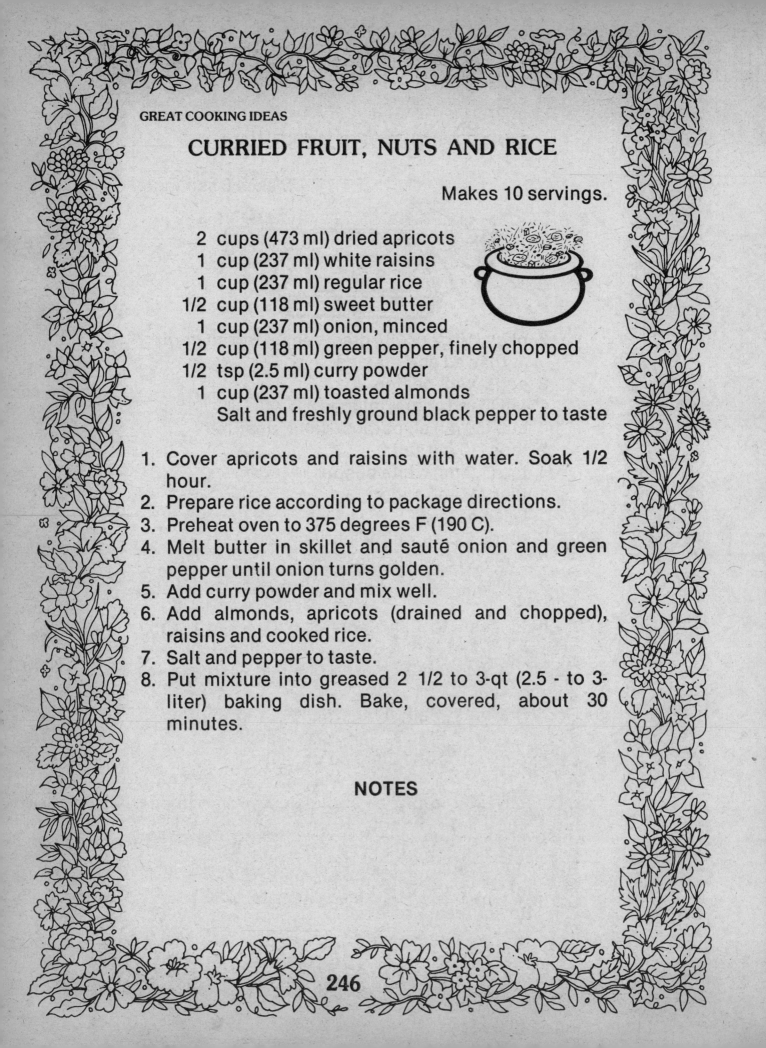

2 cups (473 ml) dried apricots
1 cup (237 ml) white raisins
1 cup (237 ml) regular rice
1/2 cup (118 ml) sweet butter
1 cup (237 ml) onion, minced
1/2 cup (118 ml) green pepper, finely chopped
1/2 tsp (2.5 ml) curry powder
1 cup (237 ml) toasted almonds
Salt and freshly ground black pepper to taste

1. Cover apricots and raisins with water. Soak 1/2 hour.
2. Prepare rice according to package directions.
3. Preheat oven to 375 degrees F (190 C).
4. Melt butter in skillet and sauté onion and green pepper until onion turns golden.
5. Add curry powder and mix well.
6. Add almonds, apricots (drained and chopped), raisins and cooked rice.
7. Salt and pepper to taste.
8. Put mixture into greased 2 1/2 to 3-qt (2.5 - to 3-liter) baking dish. Bake, covered, about 30 minutes.

NOTES

EGGPLANT-ZUCCHINI BAKE

Makes 8 servings.

2 1/2 cups (14 oz or about 397 grams) eggplant
1/3 cup (79 ml) olive oil
3/4 cup (177 ml) onions, thinly sliced
2 cloves garlic
1/2 cup (118 ml) whole pitted black olives
4 green peppers, seeds and membrane removed, cut in thin strips
3 cups (710 ml) zucchini, cut in 1/2-inch (1-cm) slices
2 cups (473 ml) tomatoes, peeled, seeded and quartered
1/2 tsp (2.5 ml) dried oregano
Salt
Freshly ground black pepper

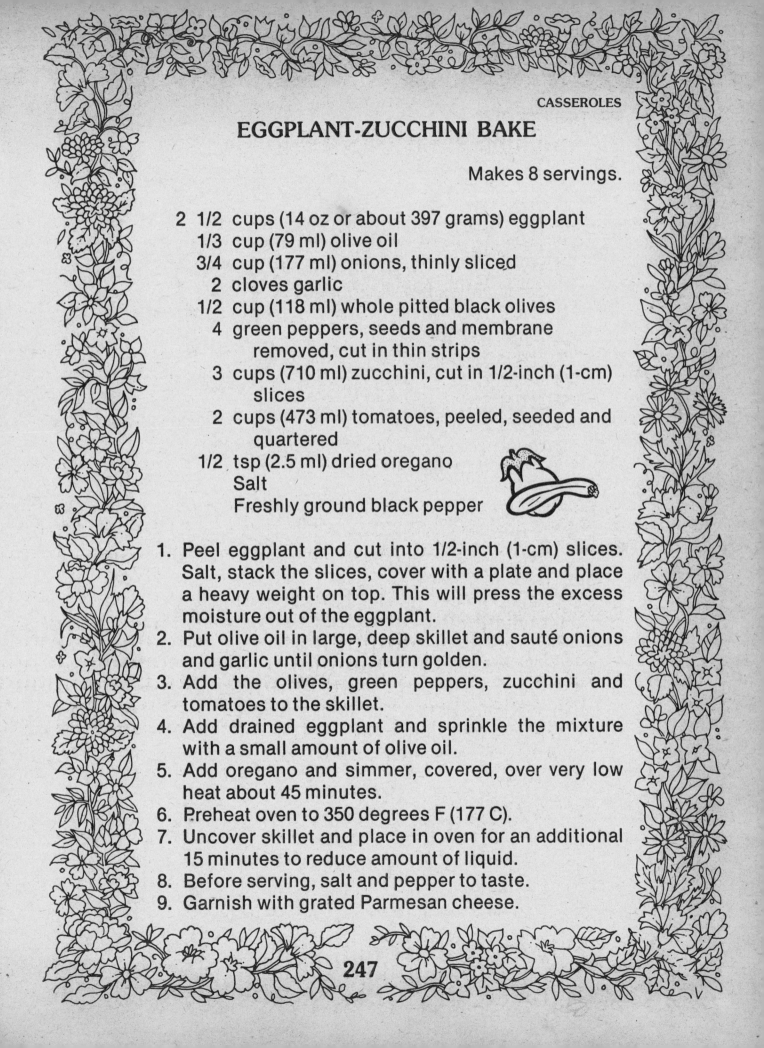

1. Peel eggplant and cut into 1/2-inch (1-cm) slices. Salt, stack the slices, cover with a plate and place a heavy weight on top. This will press the excess moisture out of the eggplant.
2. Put olive oil in large, deep skillet and sauté onions and garlic until onions turn golden.
3. Add the olives, green peppers, zucchini and tomatoes to the skillet.
4. Add drained eggplant and sprinkle the mixture with a small amount of olive oil.
5. Add oregano and simmer, covered, over very low heat about 45 minutes.
6. Preheat oven to 350 degrees F (177 C).
7. Uncover skillet and place in oven for an additional 15 minutes to reduce amount of liquid.
8. Before serving, salt and pepper to taste.
9. Garnish with grated Parmesan cheese.

EGGPLANT SCALLOP

Makes 4 servings.

1 1/2 to 2 lb (681 to 908 grams) eggplant
1/2 cup (118 ml) boiling water
2 tbsps (30 ml) parsley, chopped
1 small onion, finely chopped
1/2 cup (118 ml) milk
2 eggs, well beaten
4 tbsps (59 ml) butter
3/4 cup (177 ml) cracker crumbs
1/4 tsp (1.2 ml) salt
1/4 tsp (1.2 ml) paprika
2 oz (57 grams) Parmesan cheese, grated
Crisp, crumbled bacon for garnish

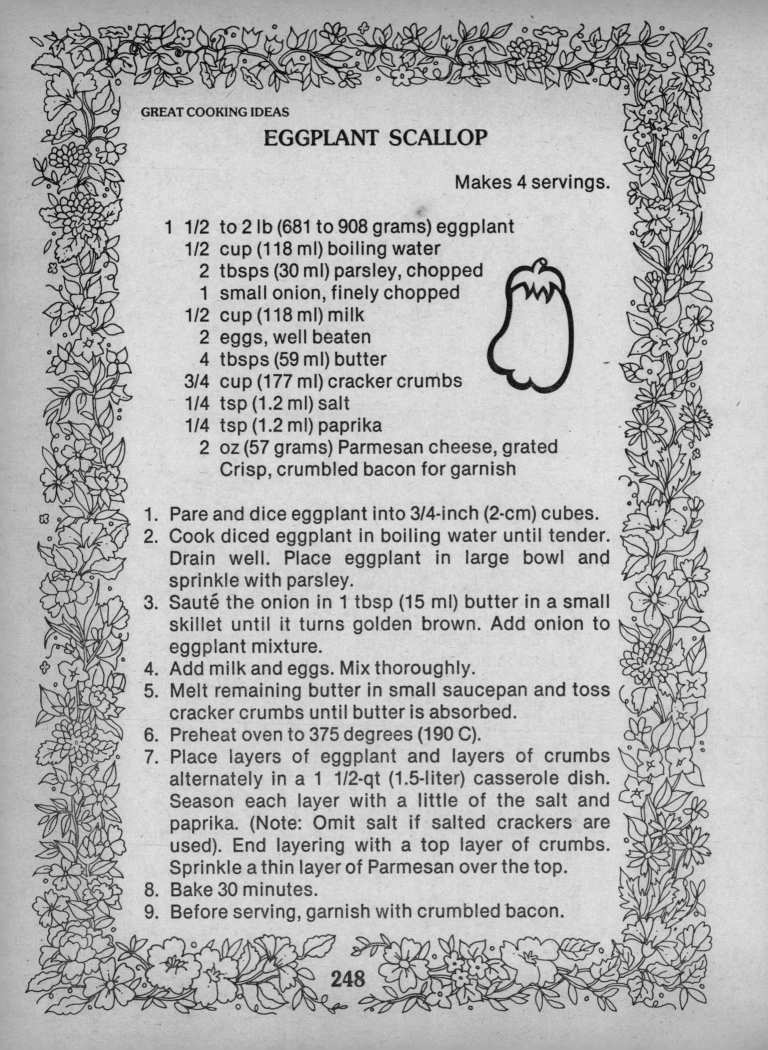

1. Pare and dice eggplant into 3/4-inch (2-cm) cubes.
2. Cook diced eggplant in boiling water until tender. Drain well. Place eggplant in large bowl and sprinkle with parsley.
3. Sauté the onion in 1 tbsp (15 ml) butter in a small skillet until it turns golden brown. Add onion to eggplant mixture.
4. Add milk and eggs. Mix thoroughly.
5. Melt remaining butter in small saucepan and toss cracker crumbs until butter is absorbed.
6. Preheat oven to 375 degrees (190 C).
7. Place layers of eggplant and layers of crumbs alternately in a 1 1/2-qt (1.5-liter) casserole dish. Season each layer with a little of the salt and paprika. (Note: Omit salt if salted crackers are used). End layering with a top layer of crumbs. Sprinkle a thin layer of Parmesan over the top.
8. Bake 30 minutes.
9. Before serving, garnish with crumbled bacon.

FRESH YAMS BAKED WITH PECANS

Makes 8 servings.

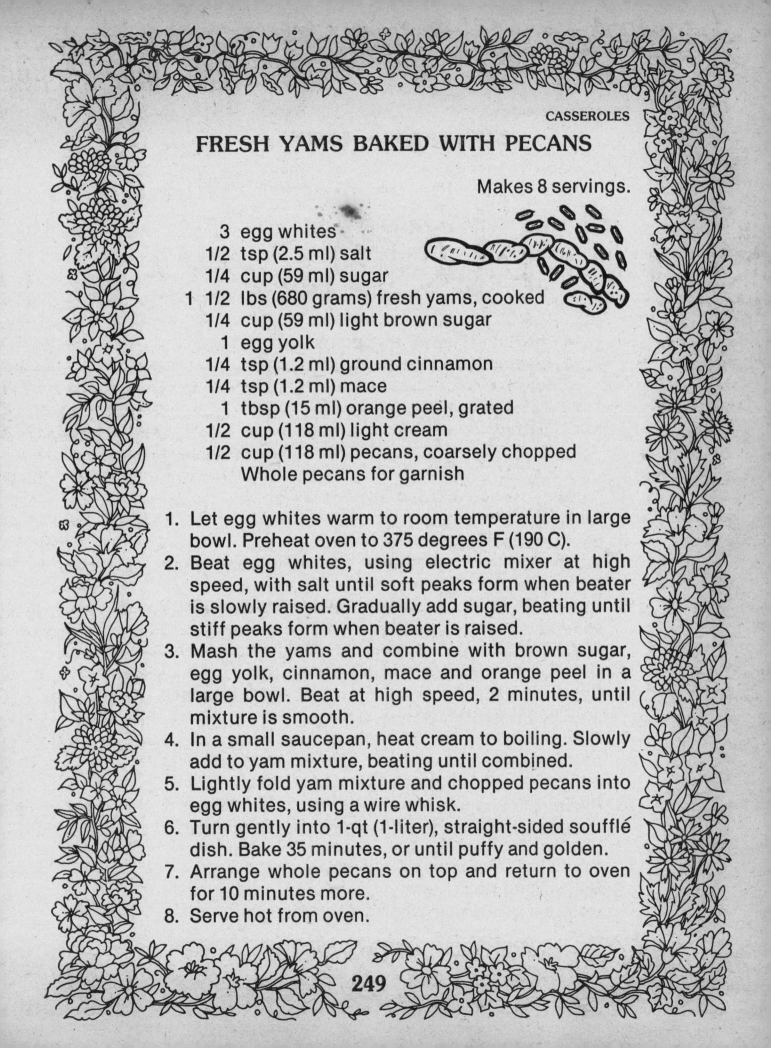

     3   egg whites
    1/2 tsp (2.5 ml) salt
    1/4 cup (59 ml) sugar
  1 1/2 lbs (680 grams) fresh yams, cooked
    1/4 cup (59 ml) light brown sugar
     1   egg yolk
    1/4 tsp (1.2 ml) ground cinnamon
    1/4 tsp (1.2 ml) mace
     1   tbsp (15 ml) orange peel, grated
    1/2 cup (118 ml) light cream
    1/2 cup (118 ml) pecans, coarsely chopped
         Whole pecans for garnish

1. Let egg whites warm to room temperature in large bowl. Preheat oven to 375 degrees F (190 C).
2. Beat egg whites, using electric mixer at high speed, with salt until soft peaks form when beater is slowly raised. Gradually add sugar, beating until stiff peaks form when beater is raised.
3. Mash the yams and combine with brown sugar, egg yolk, cinnamon, mace and orange peel in a large bowl. Beat at high speed, 2 minutes, until mixture is smooth.
4. In a small saucepan, heat cream to boiling. Slowly add to yam mixture, beating until combined.
5. Lightly fold yam mixture and chopped pecans into egg whites, using a wire whisk.
6. Turn gently into 1-qt (1-liter), straight-sided soufflé dish. Bake 35 minutes, or until puffy and golden.
7. Arrange whole pecans on top and return to oven for 10 minutes more.
8. Serve hot from oven.

GREEN BEAN BAKE

Makes 6 servings.

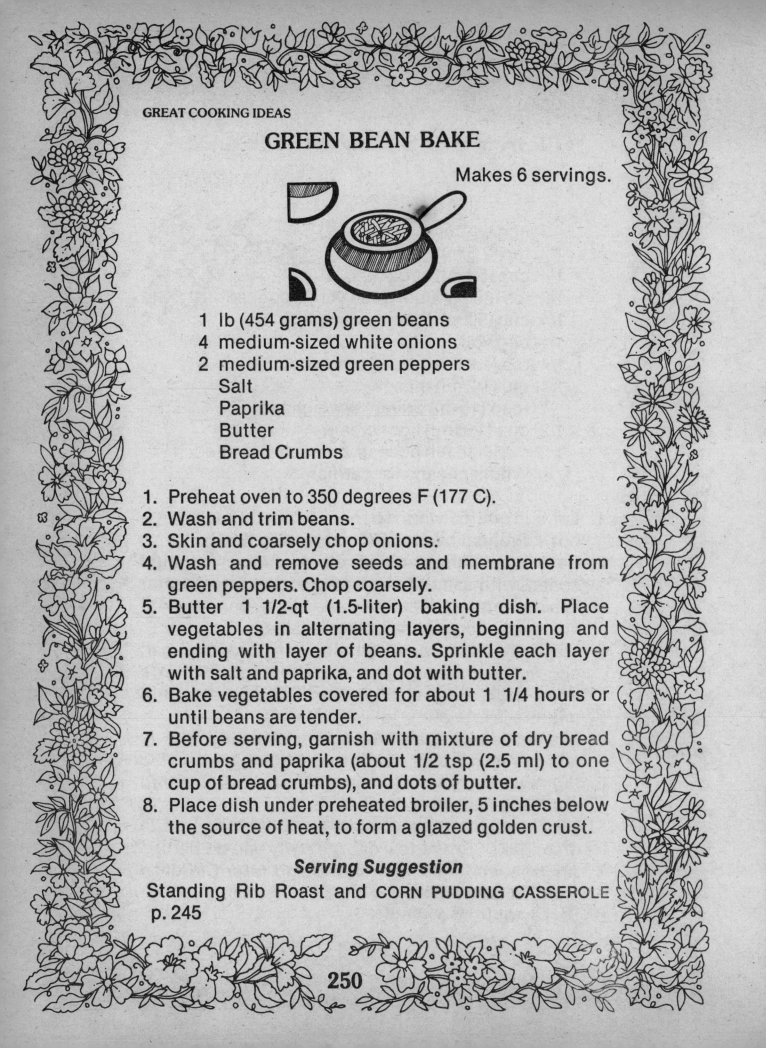

1 lb (454 grams) green beans
4 medium-sized white onions
2 medium-sized green peppers
Salt
Paprika
Butter
Bread Crumbs

1. Preheat oven to 350 degrees F (177 C).
2. Wash and trim beans.
3. Skin and coarsely chop onions.
4. Wash and remove seeds and membrane from green peppers. Chop coarsely.
5. Butter 1 1/2-qt (1.5-liter) baking dish. Place vegetables in alternating layers, beginning and ending with layer of beans. Sprinkle each layer with salt and paprika, and dot with butter.
6. Bake vegetables covered for about 1 1/4 hours or until beans are tender.
7. Before serving, garnish with mixture of dry bread crumbs and paprika (about 1/2 tsp (2.5 ml) to one cup of bread crumbs), and dots of butter.
8. Place dish under preheated broiler, 5 inches below the source of heat, to form a glazed golden crust.

Serving Suggestion

Standing Rib Roast and CORN PUDDING CASSEROLE p. 245

LEFTOVER NOODLE BAKE

Makes 6 servings.

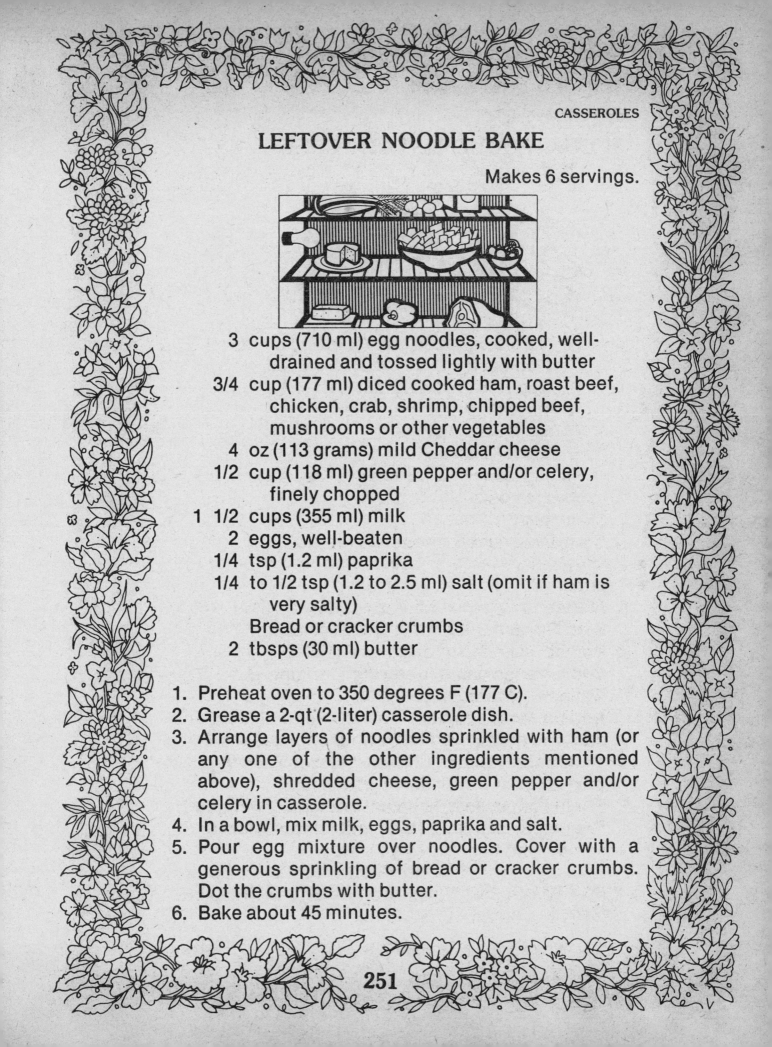

    3   cups (710 ml) egg noodles, cooked, well-
        drained and tossed lightly with butter
  3/4   cup (177 ml) diced cooked ham, roast beef,
        chicken, crab, shrimp, chipped beef,
        mushrooms or other vegetables
    4   oz (113 grams) mild Cheddar cheese
  1/2   cup (118 ml) green pepper and/or celery,
        finely chopped
1 1/2   cups (355 ml) milk
    2   eggs, well-beaten
  1/4   tsp (1.2 ml) paprika
  1/4   to 1/2 tsp (1.2 to 2.5 ml) salt (omit if ham is
        very salty)
        Bread or cracker crumbs
    2   tbsps (30 ml) butter

1. Preheat oven to 350 degrees F (177 C).
2. Grease a 2-qt (2-liter) casserole dish.
3. Arrange layers of noodles sprinkled with ham (or
   any one of the other ingredients mentioned
   above), shredded cheese, green pepper and/or
   celery in casserole.
4. In a bowl, mix milk, eggs, paprika and salt.
5. Pour egg mixture over noodles. Cover with a
   generous sprinkling of bread or cracker crumbs.
   Dot the crumbs with butter.
6. Bake about 45 minutes.

SPINACH SOUFFLÉ WITH CHEESE SAUCE

Makes 4 to 6 servings.

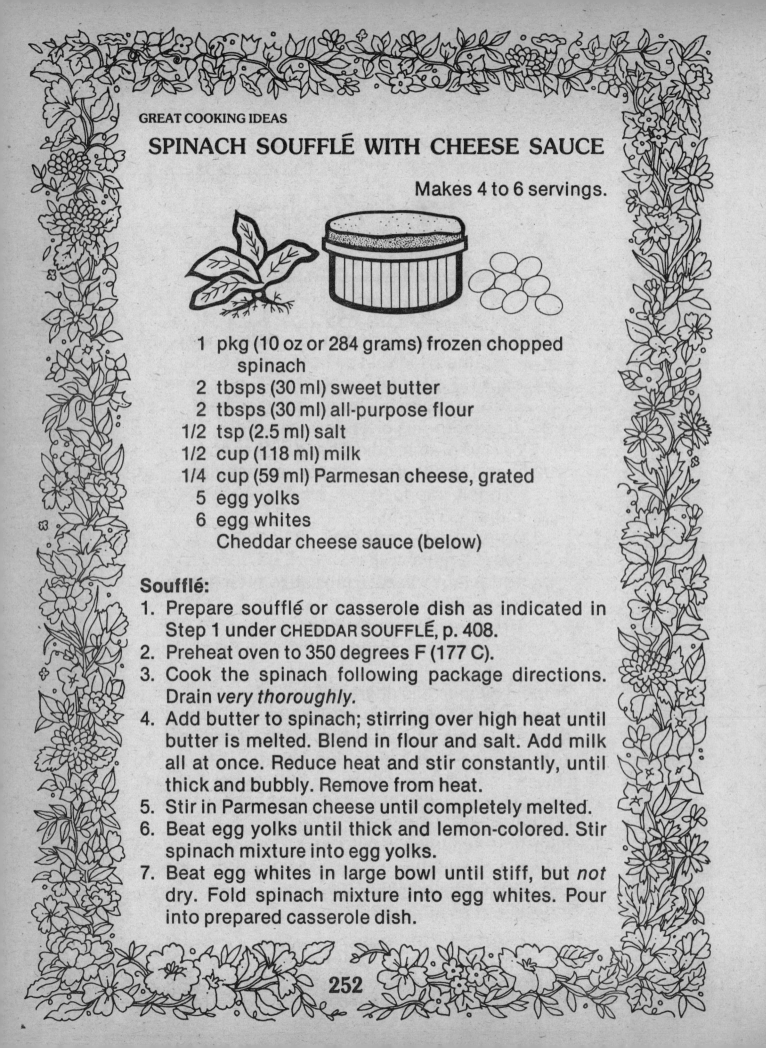

1 pkg (10 oz or 284 grams) frozen chopped spinach
2 tbsps (30 ml) sweet butter
2 tbsps (30 ml) all-purpose flour
1/2 tsp (2.5 ml) salt
1/2 cup (118 ml) milk
1/4 cup (59 ml) Parmesan cheese, grated
5 egg yolks
6 egg whites
   Cheddar cheese sauce (below)

Soufflé:

1. Prepare soufflé or casserole dish as indicated in Step 1 under CHEDDAR SOUFFLÉ, p. 408.
2. Preheat oven to 350 degrees F (177 C).
3. Cook the spinach following package directions. Drain *very thoroughly.*
4. Add butter to spinach; stirring over high heat until butter is melted. Blend in flour and salt. Add milk all at once. Reduce heat and stir constantly, until thick and bubbly. Remove from heat.
5. Stir in Parmesan cheese until completely melted.
6. Beat egg yolks until thick and lemon-colored. Stir spinach mixture into egg yolks.
7. Beat egg whites in large bowl until stiff, but *not* dry. Fold spinach mixture into egg whites. Pour into prepared casserole dish.

8. Bake for 30 to 35 minutes or until set.
9. Serve immediately with Cheddar Cheese Sauce.

Sauce:

    1 can (10 1/2 oz or 305 grams) condensed
        mushroom soup
1/3 cup (79 ml) milk
    4 oz (113 grams) sharp natural Cheddar
        cheese, shredded

1. Combine soup with milk and heat through, do *not* boil.
2. Add cheese and stir to melt.

* * *

GREEN BEAN-MUSHROOM BAKE

Makes 6 to 8 servings.

   2 pkgs (9 oz or 255 grams each) frozen cut
      green beans
   4 tbsps (59 ml) butter
1/2 tsp (2.5 ml) salt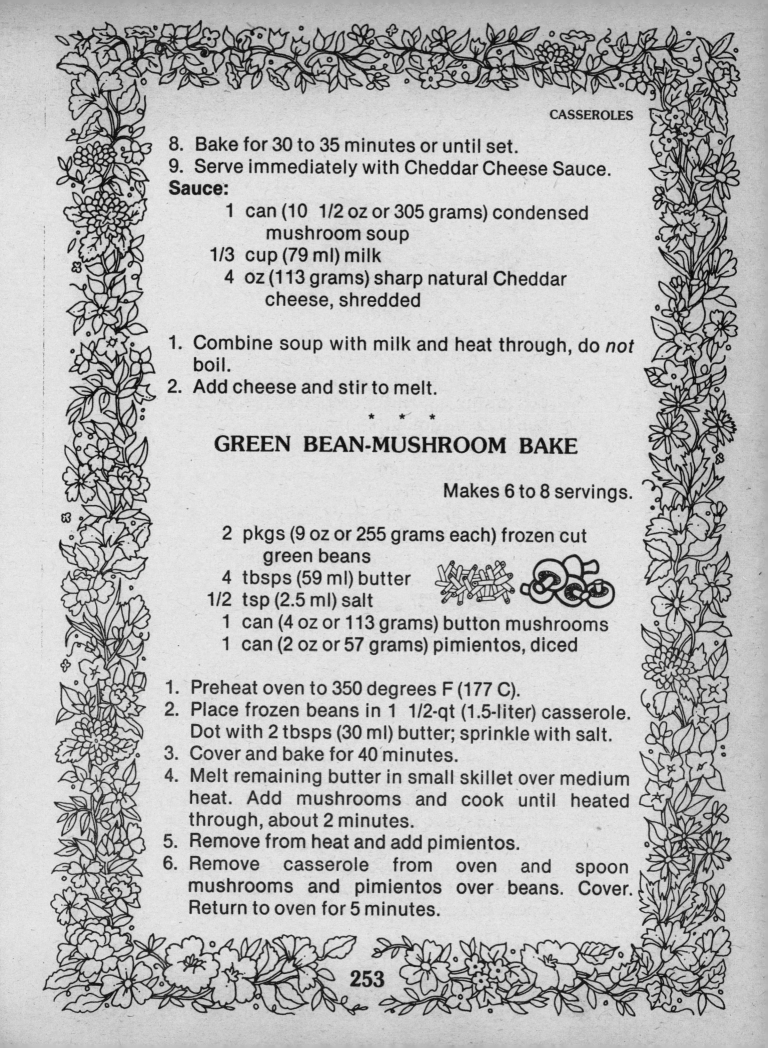
   1 can (4 oz or 113 grams) button mushrooms
   1 can (2 oz or 57 grams) pimientos, diced

1. Preheat oven to 350 degrees F (177 C).
2. Place frozen beans in 1 1/2-qt (1.5-liter) casserole. Dot with 2 tbsps (30 ml) butter; sprinkle with salt.
3. Cover and bake for 40 minutes.
4. Melt remaining butter in small skillet over medium heat. Add mushrooms and cook until heated through, about 2 minutes.
5. Remove from heat and add pimientos.
6. Remove casserole from oven and spoon mushrooms and pimientos over beans. Cover. Return to oven for 5 minutes.

STUFFED MACARONI SHELLS

Makes 6 servings.

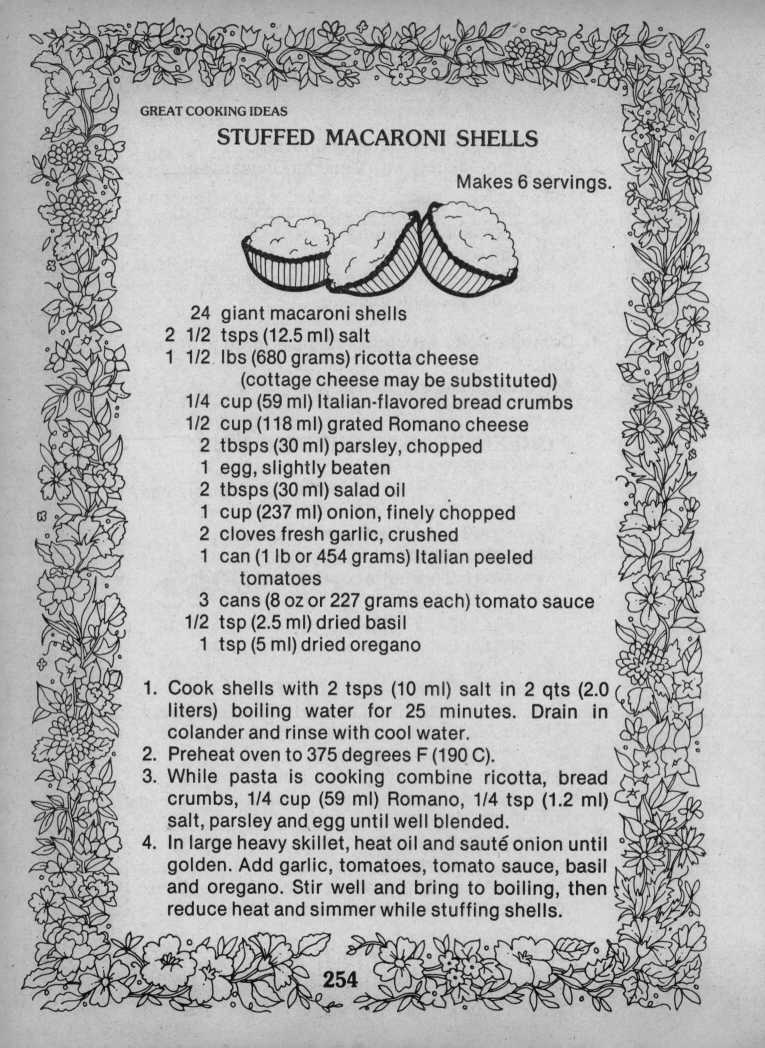

```
 24  giant macaroni shells
2 1/2  tsps (12.5 ml) salt
1 1/2  lbs (680 grams) ricotta cheese
         (cottage cheese may be substituted)
 1/4  cup (59 ml) Italian-flavored bread crumbs
 1/2  cup (118 ml) grated Romano cheese
   2  tbsps (30 ml) parsley, chopped
   1  egg, slightly beaten
   2  tbsps (30 ml) salad oil
   1  cup (237 ml) onion, finely chopped
   2  cloves fresh garlic, crushed
   1  can (1 lb or 454 grams) Italian peeled
         tomatoes
   3  cans (8 oz or 227 grams each) tomato sauce
 1/2  tsp (2.5 ml) dried basil
   1  tsp (5 ml) dried oregano
```

1. Cook shells with 2 tsps (10 ml) salt in 2 qts (2.0 liters) boiling water for 25 minutes. Drain in colander and rinse with cool water.
2. Preheat oven to 375 degrees F (190 C).
3. While pasta is cooking combine ricotta, bread crumbs, 1/4 cup (59 ml) Romano, 1/4 tsp (1.2 ml) salt, parsley and egg until well blended.
4. In large heavy skillet, heat oil and sauté onion until golden. Add garlic, tomatoes, tomato sauce, basil and oregano. Stir well and bring to boiling, then reduce heat and simmer while stuffing shells.

5. Spoon cheese mixture into shells. Arrange shells, cheese side up, in 9 x 13 x 2-inch (23 x 33 x 5-cm) baking dish. Pour sauce over top and around shells. Cover with foil. Bake 30 minutes. Remove from oven.
6. Sprinkle with remaining Romano cheese. Return to oven and bake, uncovered, 15 minutes longer, or until cheese is lightly browned.

Suggested Menu

Antipasto
Stuffed Macaroni Shells
Fresh green salad with sliced mushrooms, zucchini and red onion
Hot Italian Bread with Garlic Butter
Wine: Pinot Blanc or Soave (Italian)
Italian pastry, tortoni or SPONGY CITRUS CUSTARD, p. 476
Espresso or regular coffee

NOTES

MACARONI-CHEESE PUFF

Makes 6 servings.

3/4 cup (177 ml) small shell macaroni, uncooked
1 1/2 cups (355 ml) milk
6 oz (170 grams) sharp Cheddar cheese
4 tbsps butter
3 egg yolks
1 cup (237 ml) soft bread crumbs
1/4 cup (59 ml) canned pimiento, finely chopped
1 tbsp (15 ml) fresh parsley, minced
1 tbsp (15 ml) onion, minced
1/2 tsp (2.5 ml) dry mustard
1/8 tsp (.6 ml) white pepper
3 egg whites
1/4 tsp (1.2 ml) cream of tartar

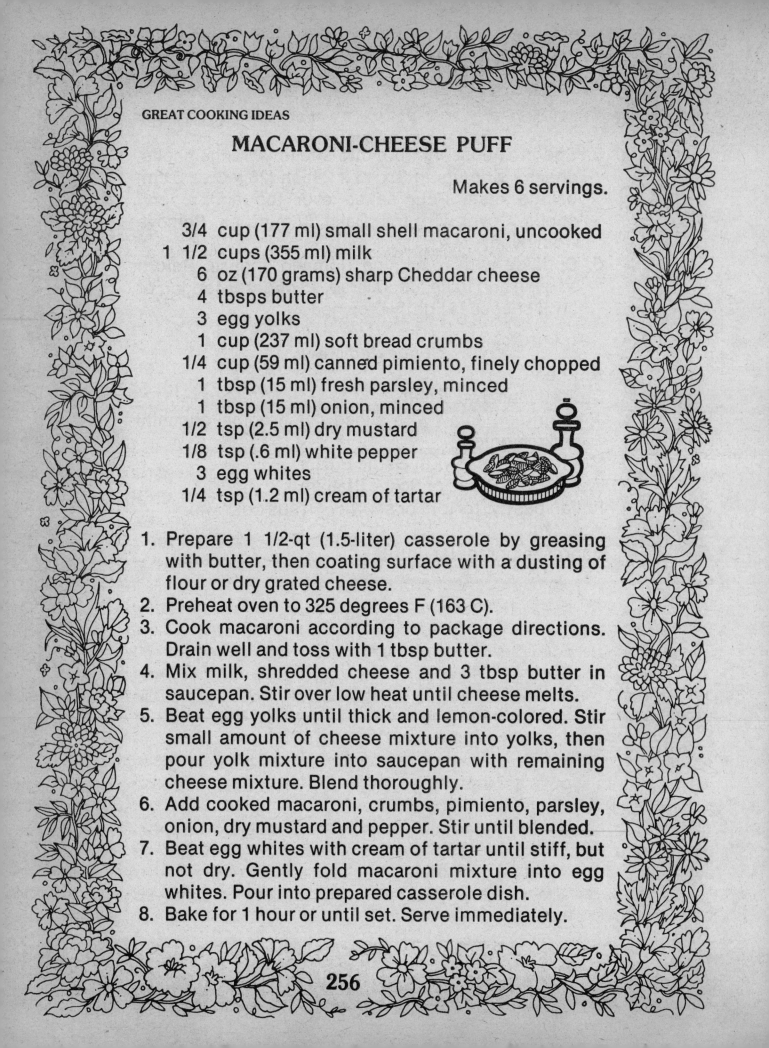

1. Prepare 1 1/2-qt (1.5-liter) casserole by greasing with butter, then coating surface with a dusting of flour or dry grated cheese.
2. Preheat oven to 325 degrees F (163 C).
3. Cook macaroni according to package directions. Drain well and toss with 1 tbsp butter.
4. Mix milk, shredded cheese and 3 tbsp butter in saucepan. Stir over low heat until cheese melts.
5. Beat egg yolks until thick and lemon-colored. Stir small amount of cheese mixture into yolks, then pour yolk mixture into saucepan with remaining cheese mixture. Blend thoroughly.
6. Add cooked macaroni, crumbs, pimiento, parsley, onion, dry mustard and pepper. Stir until blended.
7. Beat egg whites with cream of tartar until stiff, but not dry. Gently fold macaroni mixture into egg whites. Pour into prepared casserole dish.
8. Bake for 1 hour or until set. Serve immediately.

BEEF CURRY

Makes 4 - 6 servings.

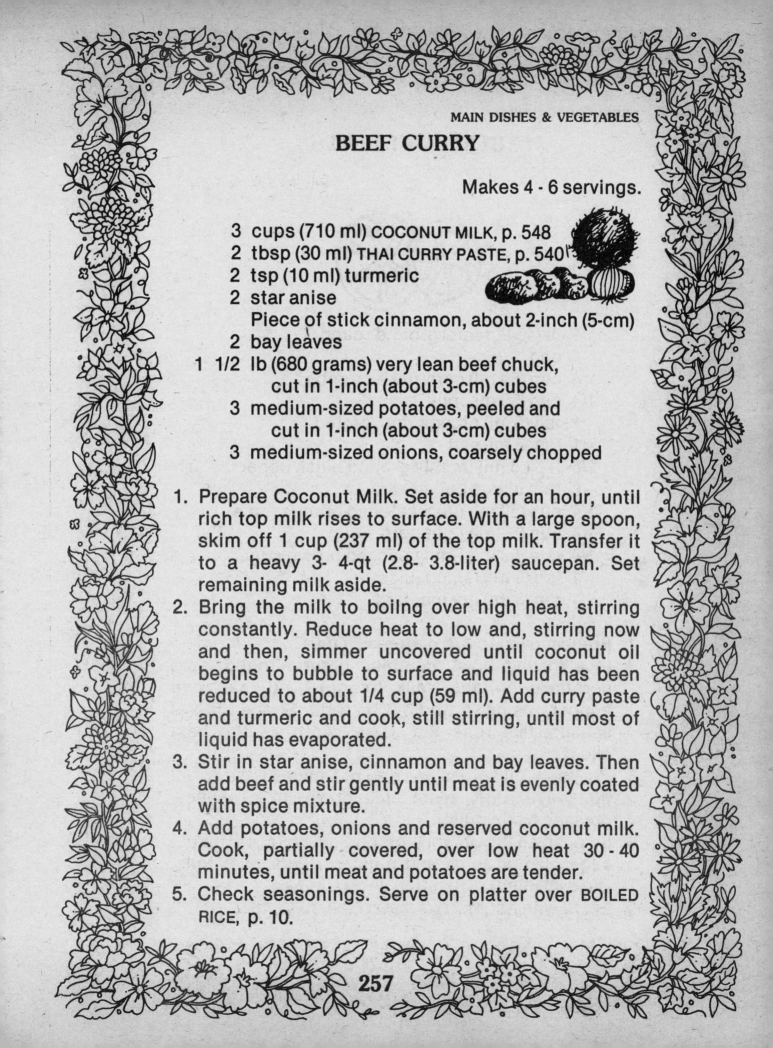

- 3 cups (710 ml) COCONUT MILK, p. 548
- 2 tbsp (30 ml) THAI CURRY PASTE, p. 540
- 2 tsp (10 ml) turmeric
- 2 star anise
- Piece of stick cinnamon, about 2-inch (5-cm)
- 2 bay leaves
- 1 1/2 lb (680 grams) very lean beef chuck, cut in 1-inch (about 3-cm) cubes
- 3 medium-sized potatoes, peeled and cut in 1-inch (about 3-cm) cubes
- 3 medium-sized onions, coarsely chopped

1. Prepare Coconut Milk. Set aside for an hour, until rich top milk rises to surface. With a large spoon, skim off 1 cup (237 ml) of the top milk. Transfer it to a heavy 3- 4-qt (2.8- 3.8-liter) saucepan. Set remaining milk aside.
2. Bring the milk to boilng over high heat, stirring constantly. Reduce heat to low and, stirring now and then, simmer uncovered until coconut oil begins to bubble to surface and liquid has been reduced to about 1/4 cup (59 ml). Add curry paste and turmeric and cook, still stirring, until most of liquid has evaporated.
3. Stir in star anise, cinnamon and bay leaves. Then add beef and stir gently until meat is evenly coated with spice mixture.
4. Add potatoes, onions and reserved coconut milk. Cook, partially covered, over low heat 30 - 40 minutes, until meat and potatoes are tender.
5. Check seasonings. Serve on platter over BOILED RICE, p. 10.

BEEF-HAM ROLLS

Makes 4 servings.

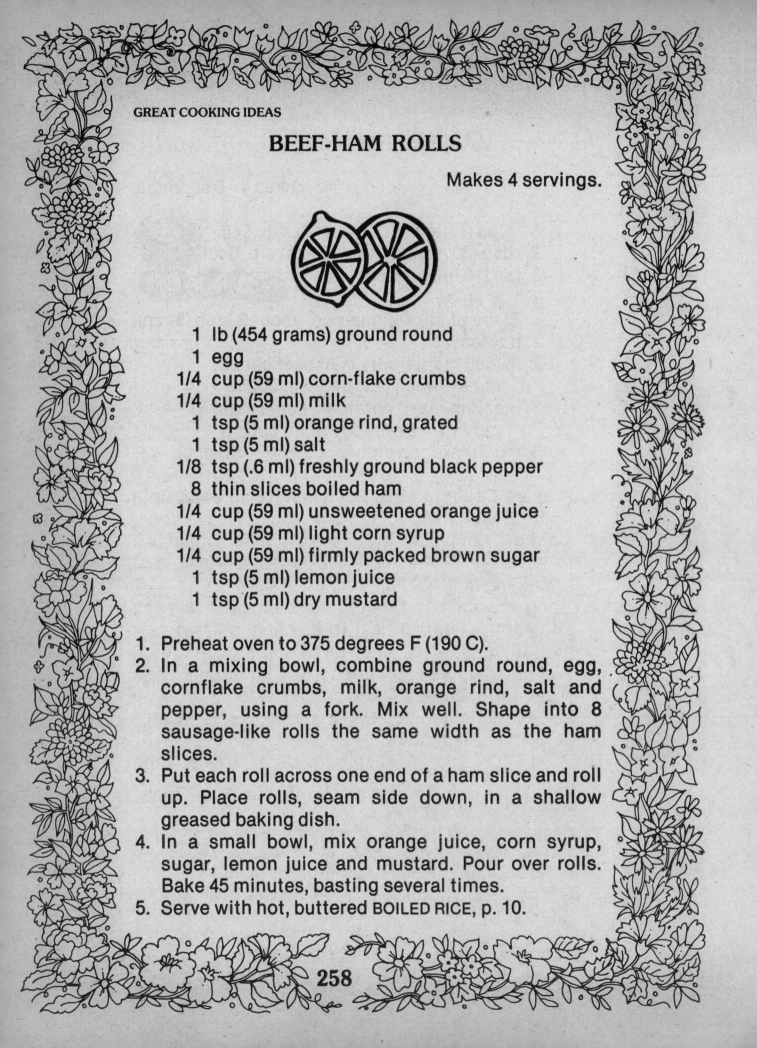

```
  1  lb (454 grams) ground round
  1  egg
1/4  cup (59 ml) corn-flake crumbs
1/4  cup (59 ml) milk
  1  tsp (5 ml) orange rind, grated
  1  tsp (5 ml) salt
1/8  tsp (.6 ml) freshly ground black pepper
  8  thin slices boiled ham
1/4  cup (59 ml) unsweetened orange juice
1/4  cup (59 ml) light corn syrup
1/4  cup (59 ml) firmly packed brown sugar
  1  tsp (5 ml) lemon juice
  1  tsp (5 ml) dry mustard
```

1. Preheat oven to 375 degrees F (190 C).
2. In a mixing bowl, combine ground round, egg, cornflake crumbs, milk, orange rind, salt and pepper, using a fork. Mix well. Shape into 8 sausage-like rolls the same width as the ham slices.
3. Put each roll across one end of a ham slice and roll up. Place rolls, seam side down, in a shallow greased baking dish.
4. In a small bowl, mix orange juice, corn syrup, sugar, lemon juice and mustard. Pour over rolls. Bake 45 minutes, basting several times.
5. Serve with hot, buttered BOILED RICE, p. 10.

BEEF STROGANOFF

Makes 4 servings.

1/2 cup (118 ml) Brown Stock p. 526; or 1 beef bouillon cube dissolved in 1/2 cup (118 ml) boiling water
1 lb (454 grams) sirloin steak, about 1/2-inch (1-cm) thick
2 tbsp (30 ml) sweet butter
8 oz (227 grams) fresh mushrooms, sliced
1 medium-sized onion, thinly sliced
1 clove garlic, minced
3/4 cup (177 ml) dry red wine
1/2 tsp (2.5 ml) Worcestershire sauce
1 tsp (5 ml) salt
3 tbsp (45 ml) flour
1 cup (237 ml) sour cream
1 pkg (8 oz or 227 grams) egg noodles, cooked and drained, then tossed with butter

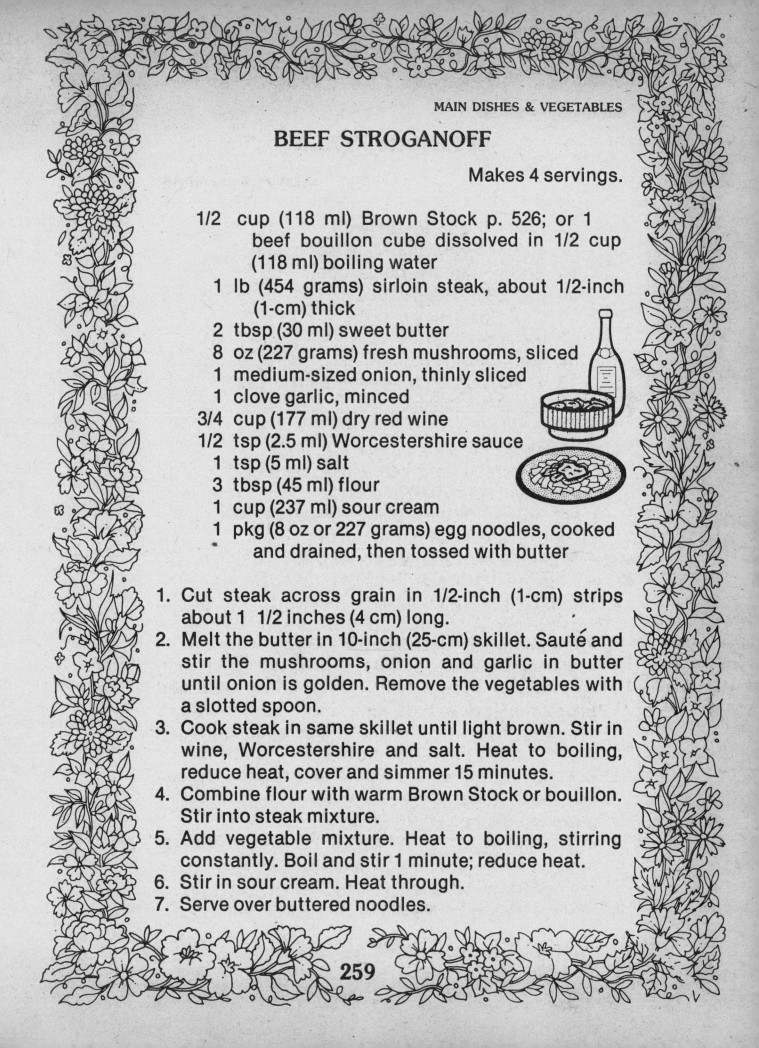

1. Cut steak across grain in 1/2-inch (1-cm) strips about 1 1/2 inches (4 cm) long.
2. Melt the butter in 10-inch (25-cm) skillet. Sauté and stir the mushrooms, onion and garlic in butter until onion is golden. Remove the vegetables with a slotted spoon.
3. Cook steak in same skillet until light brown. Stir in wine, Worcestershire and salt. Heat to boiling, reduce heat, cover and simmer 15 minutes.
4. Combine flour with warm Brown Stock or bouillon. Stir into steak mixture.
5. Add vegetable mixture. Heat to boiling, stirring constantly. Boil and stir 1 minute; reduce heat.
6. Stir in sour cream. Heat through.
7. Serve over buttered noodles.

BEEF TURNOVERS

Makes 6 servings.

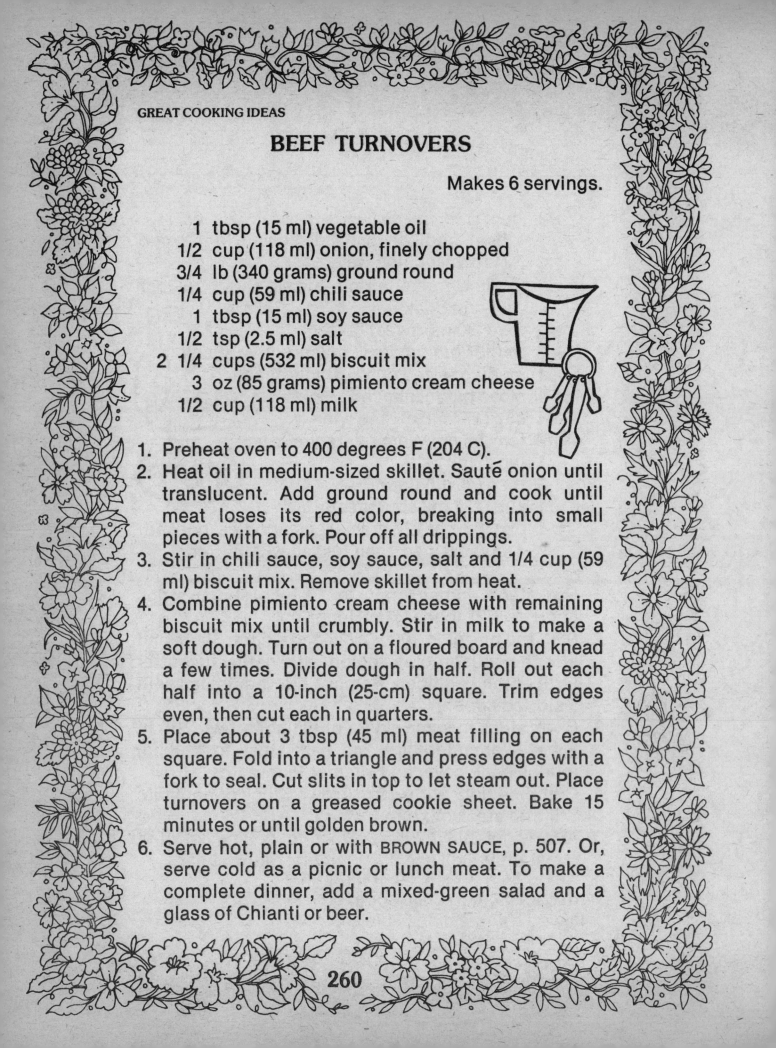

- 1 tbsp (15 ml) vegetable oil
- 1/2 cup (118 ml) onion, finely chopped
- 3/4 lb (340 grams) ground round
- 1/4 cup (59 ml) chili sauce
- 1 tbsp (15 ml) soy sauce
- 1/2 tsp (2.5 ml) salt
- 2 1/4 cups (532 ml) biscuit mix
- 3 oz (85 grams) pimiento cream cheese
- 1/2 cup (118 ml) milk

1. Preheat oven to 400 degrees F (204 C).
2. Heat oil in medium-sized skillet. Sauté onion until translucent. Add ground round and cook until meat loses its red color, breaking into small pieces with a fork. Pour off all drippings.
3. Stir in chili sauce, soy sauce, salt and 1/4 cup (59 ml) biscuit mix. Remove skillet from heat.
4. Combine pimiento cream cheese with remaining biscuit mix until crumbly. Stir in milk to make a soft dough. Turn out on a floured board and knead a few times. Divide dough in half. Roll out each half into a 10-inch (25-cm) square. Trim edges even, then cut each in quarters.
5. Place about 3 tbsp (45 ml) meat filling on each square. Fold into a triangle and press edges with a fork to seal. Cut slits in top to let steam out. Place turnovers on a greased cookie sheet. Bake 15 minutes or until golden brown.
6. Serve hot, plain or with BROWN SAUCE, p. 507. Or, serve cold as a picnic or lunch meat. To make a complete dinner, add a mixed-green salad and a glass of Chianti or beer.

BEEF WITH ALMONDS

Makes 6 servings.

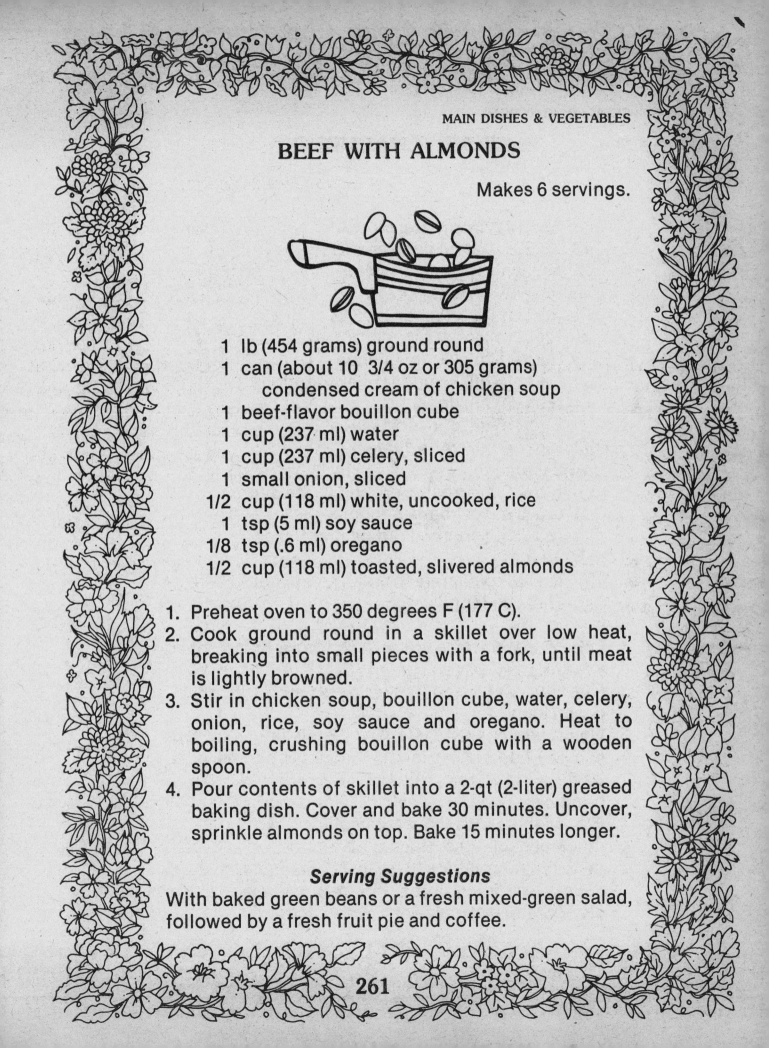

1 lb (454 grams) ground round
1 can (about 10 3/4 oz or 305 grams)
   condensed cream of chicken soup
1 beef-flavor bouillon cube
1 cup (237 ml) water
1 cup (237 ml) celery, sliced
1 small onion, sliced
1/2 cup (118 ml) white, uncooked, rice
1 tsp (5 ml) soy sauce
1/8 tsp (.6 ml) oregano
1/2 cup (118 ml) toasted, slivered almonds

1. Preheat oven to 350 degrees F (177 C).
2. Cook ground round in a skillet over low heat, breaking into small pieces with a fork, until meat is lightly browned.
3. Stir in chicken soup, bouillon cube, water, celery, onion, rice, soy sauce and oregano. Heat to boiling, crushing bouillon cube with a wooden spoon.
4. Pour contents of skillet into a 2-qt (2-liter) greased baking dish. Cover and bake 30 minutes. Uncover, sprinkle almonds on top. Bake 15 minutes longer.

Serving Suggestions

With baked green beans or a fresh mixed-green salad, followed by a fresh fruit pie and coffee.

BEEF WITH WATERCRESS

Makes 2 - 4 servings.*

2 tsp (10 ml) cornstarch
10 oz (284 grams) flank steak
1 egg white
1/2 tsp (2.5 ml) salt
1 tsp (5 ml) PEPPER OIL, p. 513
1 tsp (5 ml) fresh ginger root, minced
1 tbsp (15 ml) garlic, minced
1 tbsp (15 ml) scallion, finely chopped
4 tbsp (60 ml) dry sherry
1 tbsp (15 ml) dark soy sauce
1 1/2 tsp (7.5 ml) white vinegar
Sesame oil
1/4 tsp (1.2 ml) freshly ground white pepper
1 tsp (5 ml) cayenne pepper
1 tsp (5 ml) crushed red pepper flakes
Peanut oil
1/4 lb (113 grams) fresh watercress, cut in 3-inch (8-cm) lengths

1. Dissolve the cornstarch in 2 tbsp (30 ml) cold water.
2. Cut flank steak into thin strips about 3 1/2 inches (9 cm) long.
3. Combine egg white, 1/4 tsp (1.2 ml) salt, 1 1/2 tsp (7.5 ml) cornstarch mixture and pepper oil in a bowl. Place steak pieces in bowl and, using hands, mix well.
4. Place ginger, garlic and scallions within easy reach of cooking surface.
5. In a bowl, combine 3 tbsp (45 ml) sherry, soy sauce, remaining cornstarch paste, vinegar, 1 1/2 tsp (7.5 ml) sesame oil and white pepper.

6. In a tiny bowl, combine cayenne and crushed red pepper with enough sesame oil to drench.

7. Heat 2 tbsp (30 ml) of peanut oil until very hot, but not smoking, in a wok or heavy skillet. Add watercress. Quickly stir in remaining sherry and salt. Stir lightly 2 or 3 times with wooden spoons and remove to warm serving dish.

8. In a clean wok or skillet, heat 2 cups (473 ml) peanut oil until it begins to bubble. Add beef strips. Stir-fry until strips loose red color, about 15 seconds.

9. Add all prepared ingredients, except cayenne and crushed red pepper mixture. Stir all ingredients together very briefly. Add pepper mixture and continue stirring another 15 seconds. This should result in beef being barely browned outside and quite rare inside. If more well-done meat is desired, cook an additional 1/2 minute.

10. When meat is done, remove from wok with slotted spoon and place next to watercress on serving dish. Serve immediately.

If served with other dishes, this recipe is enough for 4; other-wise, it's dinner for 2.

NOTES

CANNELLONI
(Beef-Stuffed Pasta Rolls)

Makes 4 - 6 servings.

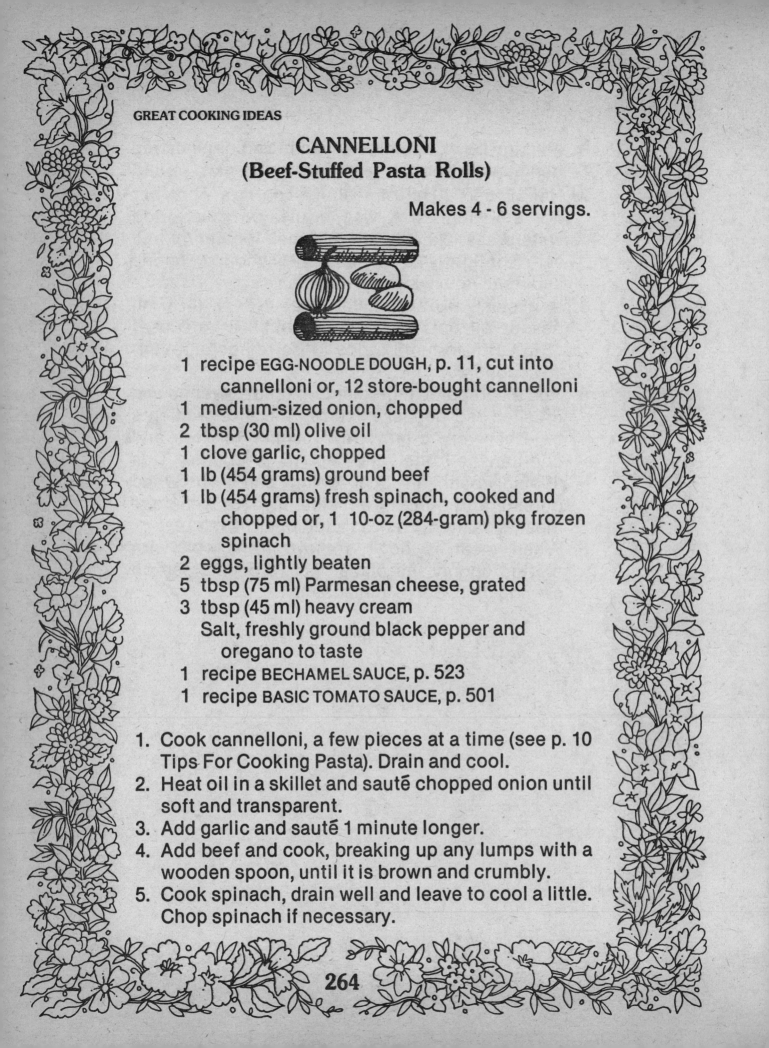

1 recipe EGG-NOODLE DOUGH, p. 11, cut into cannelloni or, 12 store-bought cannelloni
1 medium-sized onion, chopped
2 tbsp (30 ml) olive oil
1 clove garlic, chopped
1 lb (454 grams) ground beef
1 lb (454 grams) fresh spinach, cooked and chopped or, 1 10-oz (284-gram) pkg frozen spinach
2 eggs, lightly beaten
5 tbsp (75 ml) Parmesan cheese, grated
3 tbsp (45 ml) heavy cream
Salt, freshly ground black pepper and oregano to taste
1 recipe BECHAMEL SAUCE, p. 523
1 recipe BASIC TOMATO SAUCE, p. 501

1. Cook cannelloni, a few pieces at a time (see p. 10 Tips For Cooking Pasta). Drain and cool.
2. Heat oil in a skillet and sauté chopped onion until soft and transparent.
3. Add garlic and sauté 1 minute longer.
4. Add beef and cook, breaking up any lumps with a wooden spoon, until it is brown and crumbly.
5. Cook spinach, drain well and leave to cool a little. Chop spinach if necessary.

6. In a large mixing bowl, combine beef mixture, spinach, eggs, Parmesan, cream, salt, pepper and oregano. Mix well with a fork.

7. Spread a thin layer of Basic Tomato Sauce in a baking dish 13 x 9 x 2 inches (33 x 23 x 5 cm).

8. If homemade squares of pasta are used, place 1 heaping tsp filling onto each square, fold both sides toward middle and place each cannelloni, seam side down, into baking dish. If store-bought cannelloni are used, they can be filled with a tsp. Place cannelloni in single layer in baking dish.

9. Layer the Bechamel Sauce evenly over the cannelloni. Cover Bechamel layer with remaining Tomato Sauce. Sprinkle with Parmesan.*

10. Preheat oven to 375 degrees F (190 C).

11. Bake 20 minutes if dish is being baked right away; 40 minutes if it has been allowed to get cold.

*Up to this point this dish can be made several hours before the appointed dinner hour. Cover with foil until ready to bake.

Serving Suggestions

With crusty warm bread, SPINACH SALAD, p. 77 or, a mixed green salad and a glass of dry red wine.

NOTES

CHILI-CORNBREAD PIE

Makes 8 servings.

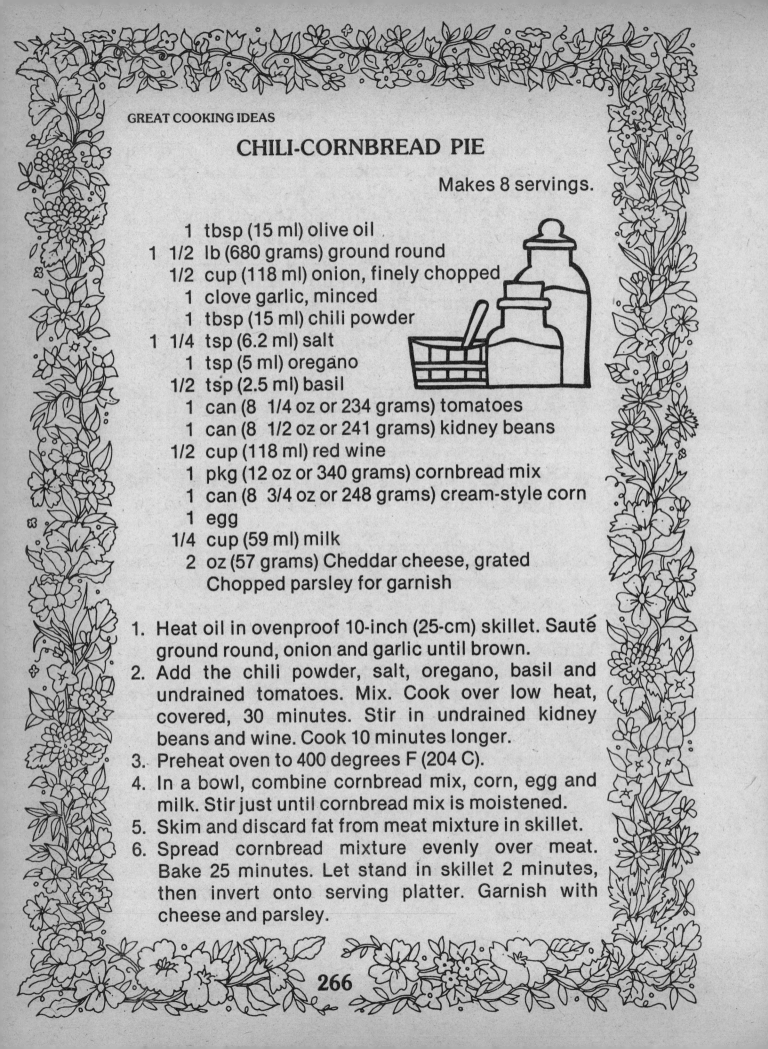

- 1 tbsp (15 ml) olive oil
- 1 1/2 lb (680 grams) ground round
- 1/2 cup (118 ml) onion, finely chopped
- 1 clove garlic, minced
- 1 tbsp (15 ml) chili powder
- 1 1/4 tsp (6.2 ml) salt
- 1 tsp (5 ml) oregano
- 1/2 tsp (2.5 ml) basil
- 1 can (8 1/4 oz or 234 grams) tomatoes
- 1 can (8 1/2 oz or 241 grams) kidney beans
- 1/2 cup (118 ml) red wine
- 1 pkg (12 oz or 340 grams) cornbread mix
- 1 can (8 3/4 oz or 248 grams) cream-style corn
- 1 egg
- 1/4 cup (59 ml) milk
- 2 oz (57 grams) Cheddar cheese, grated
- Chopped parsley for garnish

1. Heat oil in ovenproof 10-inch (25-cm) skillet. Sauté ground round, onion and garlic until brown.
2. Add the chili powder, salt, oregano, basil and undrained tomatoes. Mix. Cook over low heat, covered, 30 minutes. Stir in undrained kidney beans and wine. Cook 10 minutes longer.
3. Preheat oven to 400 degrees F (204 C).
4. In a bowl, combine cornbread mix, corn, egg and milk. Stir just until cornbread mix is moistened.
5. Skim and discard fat from meat mixture in skillet.
6. Spread cornbread mixture evenly over meat. Bake 25 minutes. Let stand in skillet 2 minutes, then invert onto serving platter. Garnish with cheese and parsley.

CHINESE MEAT BALLS

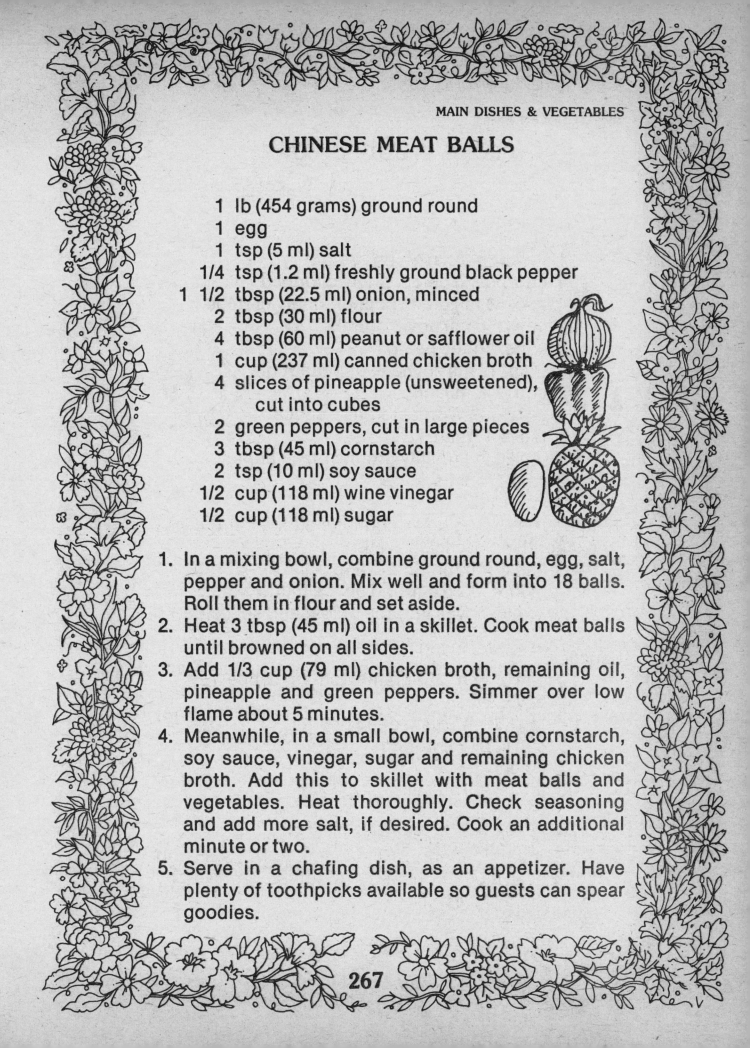

1 lb (454 grams) ground round
1 egg
1 tsp (5 ml) salt
1/4 tsp (1.2 ml) freshly ground black pepper
1 1/2 tbsp (22.5 ml) onion, minced
2 tbsp (30 ml) flour
4 tbsp (60 ml) peanut or safflower oil
1 cup (237 ml) canned chicken broth
4 slices of pineapple (unsweetened), cut into cubes
2 green peppers, cut in large pieces
3 tbsp (45 ml) cornstarch
2 tsp (10 ml) soy sauce
1/2 cup (118 ml) wine vinegar
1/2 cup (118 ml) sugar

1. In a mixing bowl, combine ground round, egg, salt, pepper and onion. Mix well and form into 18 balls. Roll them in flour and set aside.
2. Heat 3 tbsp (45 ml) oil in a skillet. Cook meat balls until browned on all sides.
3. Add 1/3 cup (79 ml) chicken broth, remaining oil, pineapple and green peppers. Simmer over low flame about 5 minutes.
4. Meanwhile, in a small bowl, combine cornstarch, soy sauce, vinegar, sugar and remaining chicken broth. Add this to skillet with meat balls and vegetables. Heat thoroughly. Check seasoning and add more salt, if desired. Cook an additional minute or two.
5. Serve in a chafing dish, as an appetizer. Have plenty of toothpicks available so guests can spear goodies.

CLOVE-STUDDED LOAF

Makes 4 servings.

Loaf:

- 1 lb (454 grams) ground round
- 1/4 cup (59 ml) onion, finely chopped
- 1/4 cup (59 ml) green pepper, finely chopped
- 1/2 cup (118 ml) bread crumbs
- 2 eggs, lightly beaten
- 1 tbsp (15 ml) soybean or peanut oil
- 1/2 cup (118 ml) milk
- 1 tsp (5 ml) Worcestershire sauce
- 1 tsp (5 ml) salt
- 1/8 tsp (.6 ml) freshly ground black pepper
- 12 whole cloves

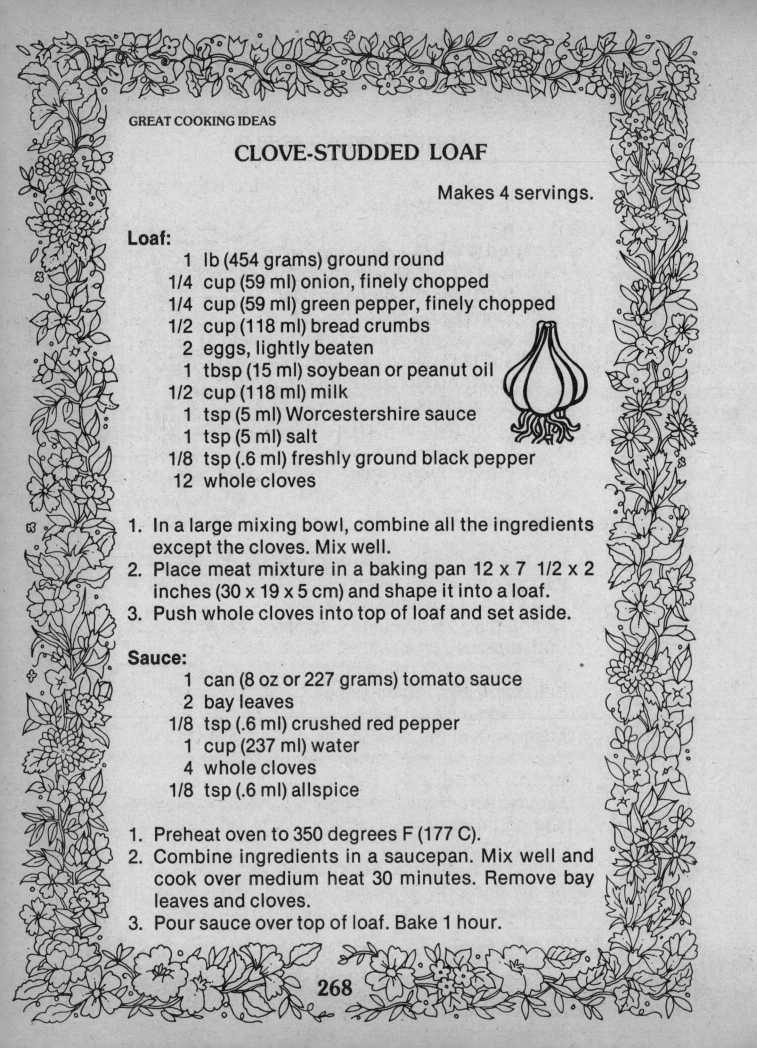

1. In a large mixing bowl, combine all the ingredients except the cloves. Mix well.
2. Place meat mixture in a baking pan 12 x 7 1/2 x 2 inches (30 x 19 x 5 cm) and shape it into a loaf.
3. Push whole cloves into top of loaf and set aside.

Sauce:

- 1 can (8 oz or 227 grams) tomato sauce
- 2 bay leaves
- 1/8 tsp (.6 ml) crushed red pepper
- 1 cup (237 ml) water
- 4 whole cloves
- 1/8 tsp (.6 ml) allspice

1. Preheat oven to 350 degrees F (177 C).
2. Combine ingredients in a saucepan. Mix well and cook over medium heat 30 minutes. Remove bay leaves and cloves.
3. Pour sauce over top of loaf. Bake 1 hour.

COUNTRY-STYLE BEEF PIE

Makes 6 servings.

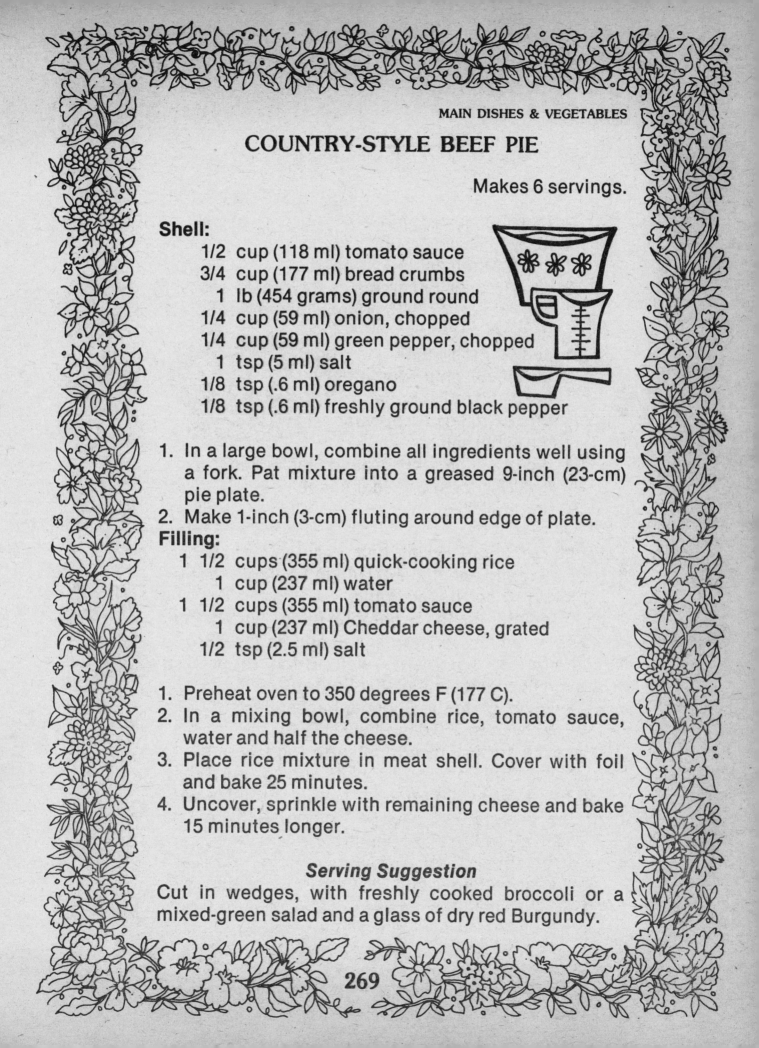

Shell:
- 1/2 cup (118 ml) tomato sauce
- 3/4 cup (177 ml) bread crumbs
- 1 lb (454 grams) ground round
- 1/4 cup (59 ml) onion, chopped
- 1/4 cup (59 ml) green pepper, chopped
- 1 tsp (5 ml) salt
- 1/8 tsp (.6 ml) oregano
- 1/8 tsp (.6 ml) freshly ground black pepper

1. In a large bowl, combine all ingredients well using a fork. Pat mixture into a greased 9-inch (23-cm) pie plate.
2. Make 1-inch (3-cm) fluting around edge of plate.

Filling:
- 1 1/2 cups (355 ml) quick-cooking rice
- 1 cup (237 ml) water
- 1 1/2 cups (355 ml) tomato sauce
- 1 cup (237 ml) Cheddar cheese, grated
- 1/2 tsp (2.5 ml) salt

1. Preheat oven to 350 degrees F (177 C).
2. In a mixing bowl, combine rice, tomato sauce, water and half the cheese.
3. Place rice mixture in meat shell. Cover with foil and bake 25 minutes.
4. Uncover, sprinkle with remaining cheese and bake 15 minutes longer.

Serving Suggestion

Cut in wedges, with freshly cooked broccoli or a mixed-green salad and a glass of dry red Burgundy.

ENCHILADAS

Makes 8 servings.

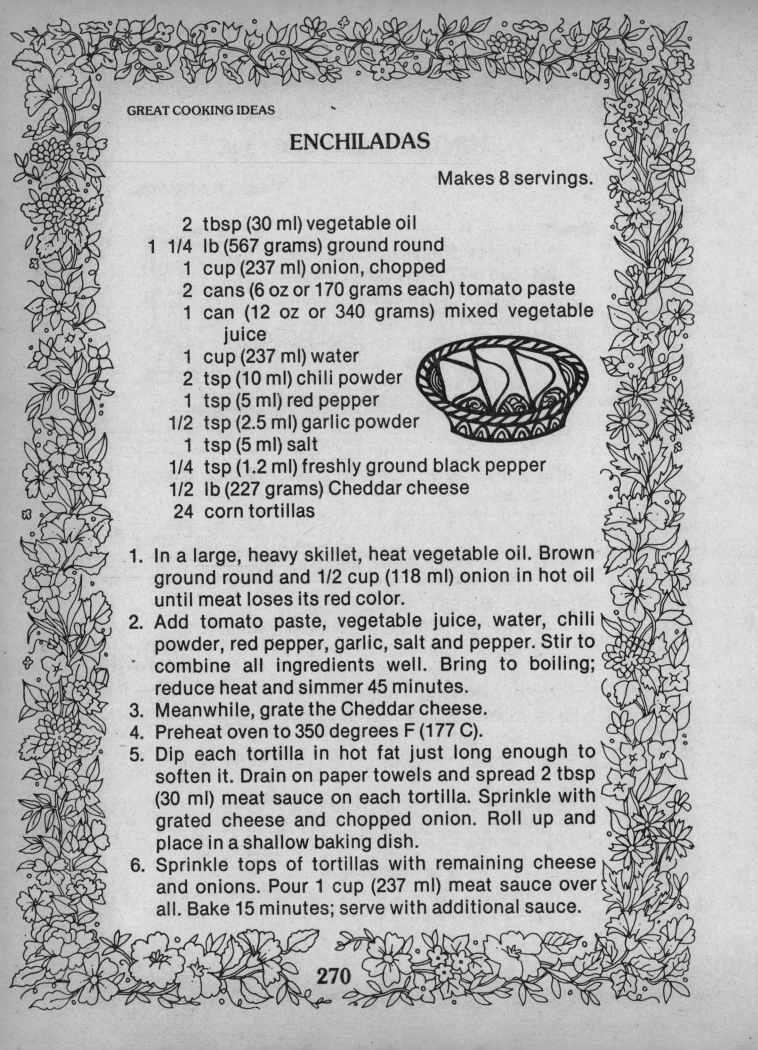

2 tbsp (30 ml) vegetable oil
1 1/4 lb (567 grams) ground round
1 cup (237 ml) onion, chopped
2 cans (6 oz or 170 grams each) tomato paste
1 can (12 oz or 340 grams) mixed vegetable juice
1 cup (237 ml) water
2 tsp (10 ml) chili powder
1 tsp (5 ml) red pepper
1/2 tsp (2.5 ml) garlic powder
1 tsp (5 ml) salt
1/4 tsp (1.2 ml) freshly ground black pepper
1/2 lb (227 grams) Cheddar cheese
24 corn tortillas

1. In a large, heavy skillet, heat vegetable oil. Brown ground round and 1/2 cup (118 ml) onion in hot oil until meat loses its red color.
2. Add tomato paste, vegetable juice, water, chili powder, red pepper, garlic, salt and pepper. Stir to combine all ingredients well. Bring to boiling; reduce heat and simmer 45 minutes.
3. Meanwhile, grate the Cheddar cheese.
4. Preheat oven to 350 degrees F (177 C).
5. Dip each tortilla in hot fat just long enough to soften it. Drain on paper towels and spread 2 tbsp (30 ml) meat sauce on each tortilla. Sprinkle with grated cheese and chopped onion. Roll up and place in a shallow baking dish.
6. Sprinkle tops of tortillas with remaining cheese and onions. Pour 1 cup (237 ml) meat sauce over all. Bake 15 minutes; serve with additional sauce.

GERMAN MEAT BALLS

Makes 4 servings.

Meat Balls:

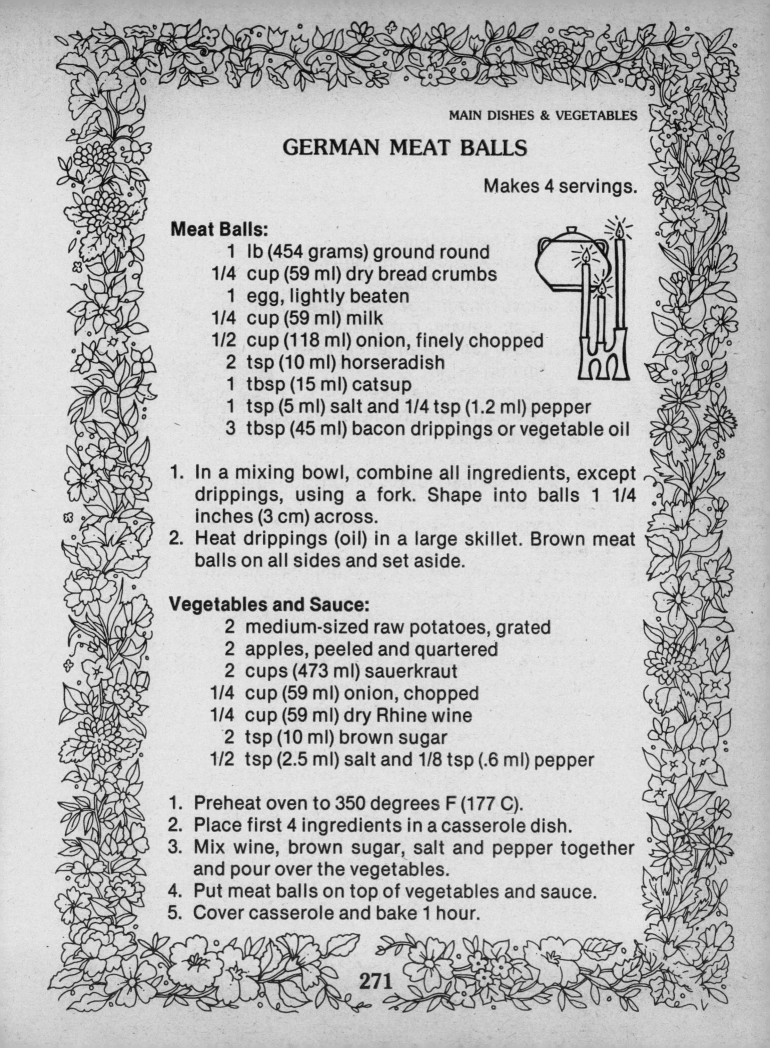

- 1 lb (454 grams) ground round
- 1/4 cup (59 ml) dry bread crumbs
- 1 egg, lightly beaten
- 1/4 cup (59 ml) milk
- 1/2 cup (118 ml) onion, finely chopped
- 2 tsp (10 ml) horseradish
- 1 tbsp (15 ml) catsup
- 1 tsp (5 ml) salt and 1/4 tsp (1.2 ml) pepper
- 3 tbsp (45 ml) bacon drippings or vegetable oil

1. In a mixing bowl, combine all ingredients, except drippings, using a fork. Shape into balls 1 1/4 inches (3 cm) across.
2. Heat drippings (oil) in a large skillet. Brown meat balls on all sides and set aside.

Vegetables and Sauce:

- 2 medium-sized raw potatoes, grated
- 2 apples, peeled and quartered
- 2 cups (473 ml) sauerkraut
- 1/4 cup (59 ml) onion, chopped
- 1/4 cup (59 ml) dry Rhine wine
- 2 tsp (10 ml) brown sugar
- 1/2 tsp (2.5 ml) salt and 1/8 tsp (.6 ml) pepper

1. Preheat oven to 350 degrees F (177 C).
2. Place first 4 ingredients in a casserole dish.
3. Mix wine, brown sugar, salt and pepper together and pour over the vegetables.
4. Put meat balls on top of vegetables and sauce.
5. Cover casserole and bake 1 hour.

GINGER BEEF

Makes 4 servings.

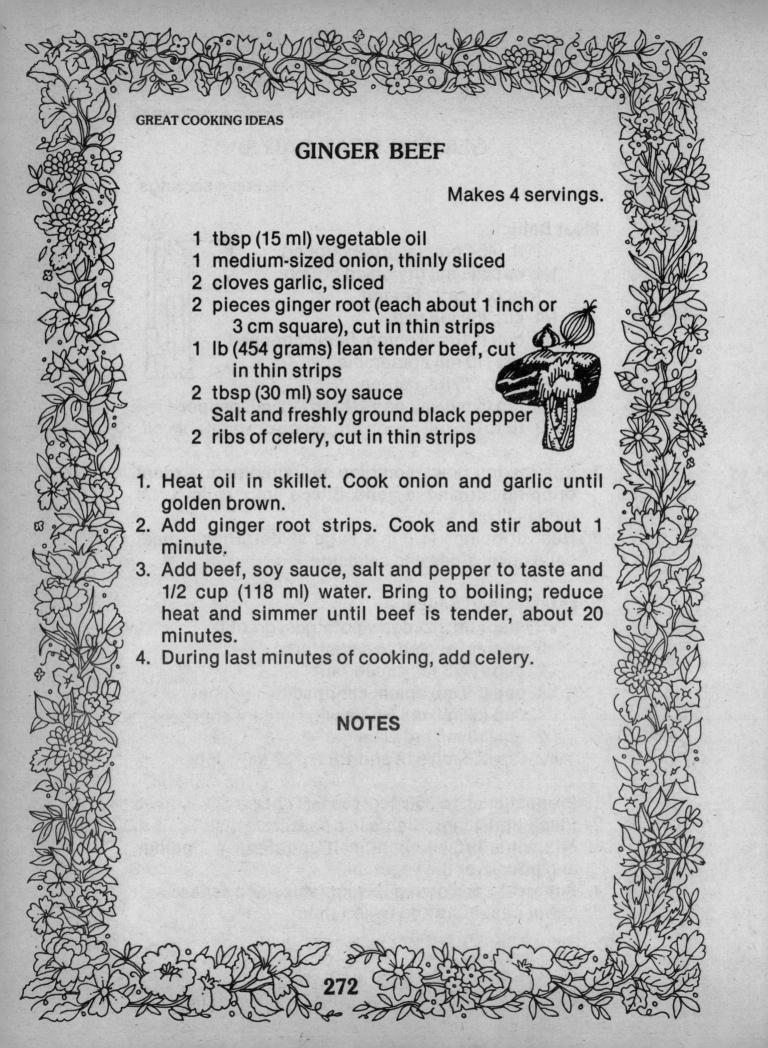

1 tbsp (15 ml) vegetable oil
1 medium-sized onion, thinly sliced
2 cloves garlic, sliced
2 pieces ginger root (each about 1 inch or
    3 cm square), cut in thin strips
1 lb (454 grams) lean tender beef, cut
    in thin strips
2 tbsp (30 ml) soy sauce
  Salt and freshly ground black pepper
2 ribs of celery, cut in thin strips

1. Heat oil in skillet. Cook onion and garlic until golden brown.
2. Add ginger root strips. Cook and stir about 1 minute.
3. Add beef, soy sauce, salt and pepper to taste and 1/2 cup (118 ml) water. Bring to boiling; reduce heat and simmer until beef is tender, about 20 minutes.
4. During last minutes of cooking, add celery.

NOTES

GROUND BEEF 'N' FRUIT ROLL

Makes 8 - 10 servings.

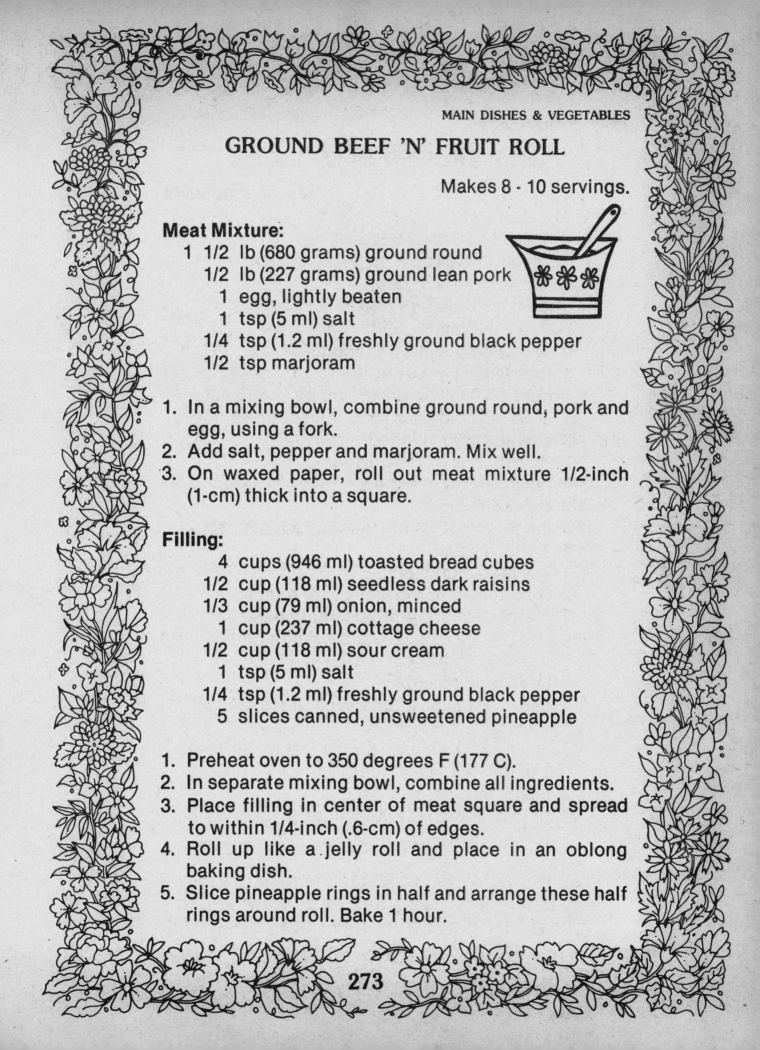

Meat Mixture:
- 1 1/2 lb (680 grams) ground round
- 1/2 lb (227 grams) ground lean pork
- 1 egg, lightly beaten
- 1 tsp (5 ml) salt
- 1/4 tsp (1.2 ml) freshly ground black pepper
- 1/2 tsp marjoram

1. In a mixing bowl, combine ground round, pork and egg, using a fork.
2. Add salt, pepper and marjoram. Mix well.
3. On waxed paper, roll out meat mixture 1/2-inch (1-cm) thick into a square.

Filling:
- 4 cups (946 ml) toasted bread cubes
- 1/2 cup (118 ml) seedless dark raisins
- 1/3 cup (79 ml) onion, minced
- 1 cup (237 ml) cottage cheese
- 1/2 cup (118 ml) sour cream
- 1 tsp (5 ml) salt
- 1/4 tsp (1.2 ml) freshly ground black pepper
- 5 slices canned, unsweetened pineapple

1. Preheat oven to 350 degrees F (177 C).
2. In separate mixing bowl, combine all ingredients.
3. Place filling in center of meat square and spread to within 1/4-inch (.6-cm) of edges.
4. Roll up like a jelly roll and place in an oblong baking dish.
5. Slice pineapple rings in half and arrange these half rings around roll. Bake 1 hour.

HOT GROUND BEEF TACOS

Makes 48.

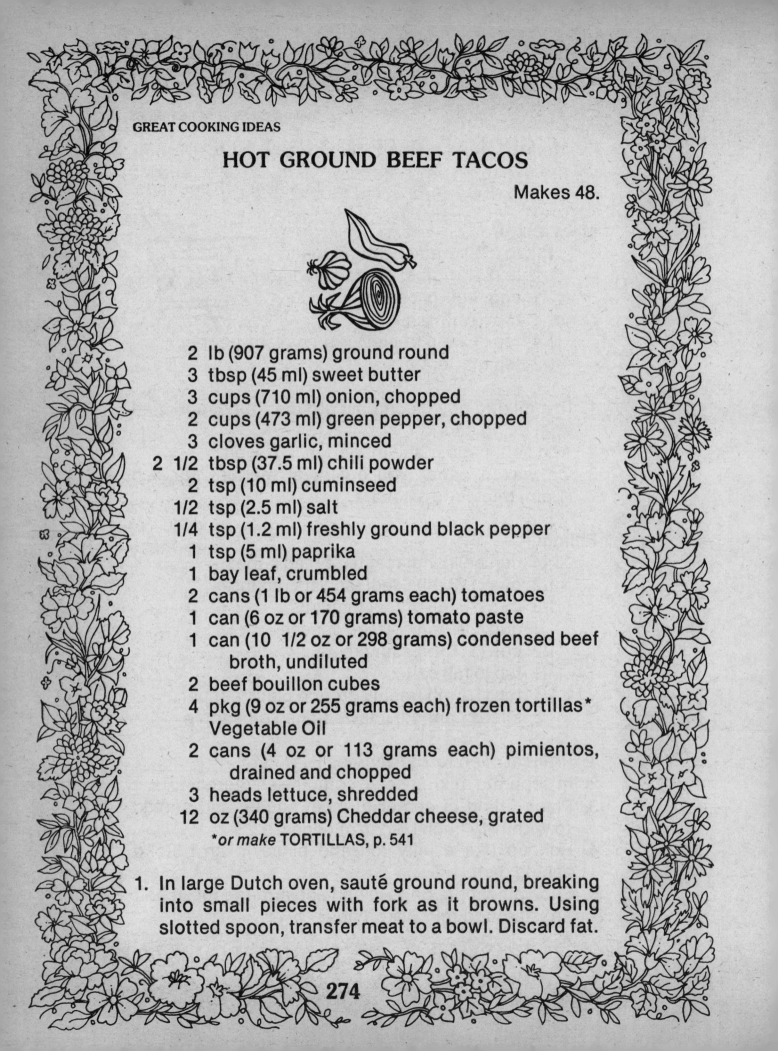

2 lb (907 grams) ground round
3 tbsp (45 ml) sweet butter
3 cups (710 ml) onion, chopped
2 cups (473 ml) green pepper, chopped
3 cloves garlic, minced
2 1/2 tbsp (37.5 ml) chili powder
2 tsp (10 ml) cuminseed
1/2 tsp (2.5 ml) salt
1/4 tsp (1.2 ml) freshly ground black pepper
1 tsp (5 ml) paprika
1 bay leaf, crumbled
2 cans (1 lb or 454 grams each) tomatoes
1 can (6 oz or 170 grams) tomato paste
1 can (10 1/2 oz or 298 grams) condensed beef
    broth, undiluted
2 beef bouillon cubes
4 pkg (9 oz or 255 grams each) frozen tortillas*
    Vegetable Oil
2 cans (4 oz or 113 grams each) pimientos,
    drained and chopped
3 heads lettuce, shredded
12 oz (340 grams) Cheddar cheese, grated
    *or make TORTILLAS, p. 541

1. In large Dutch oven, sauté ground round, breaking
   into small pieces with fork as it browns. Using
   slotted spoon, transfer meat to a bowl. Discard fat.

2. Melt butter in same Dutch oven, sauté onion, green pepper and garlic over medium heat, stirring occasionally, until onion turns golden.

3. Stir in chili powder, cumin, salt, pepper, paprika and bay leaf. Cook gently, stirring, about 5 minutes.

4. Add browned meat, tomatoes, tomato paste, beef broth and bouillon cubes. Stir, breaking up tomatoes with a wooden spoon. Bring to boiling; reduce heat and simmer, uncovered, stirring occasionally, 1/2 hour.

5. Meanwhile thaw tortillas as package directs. Pour 1/2 inch (1 cm) vegetable oil into a skillet, heat tortillas as package directs for tacos.

6. To serve: heat chili mixture to boiling. Stir in pimientos. Place about 1/4 cup (59 ml) shredded lettuce in bottom of each taco. Spoon 1/4 cup (59 ml) chili over lettuce. Sprinkle with 1 tbsp (15 ml) grated cheese. Serve at once with HOT GREEN SAUCE, p. 515.

Serving Suggestion

As a one-dish meal, with Sangria or cold beer, for a group of 8 to 12. Follow the main course with a gelatin and fruit dessert and coffee; or serve as one of the dishes at a buffet dinner.

NOTES

HOMINY PIE

Makes 8 servings.

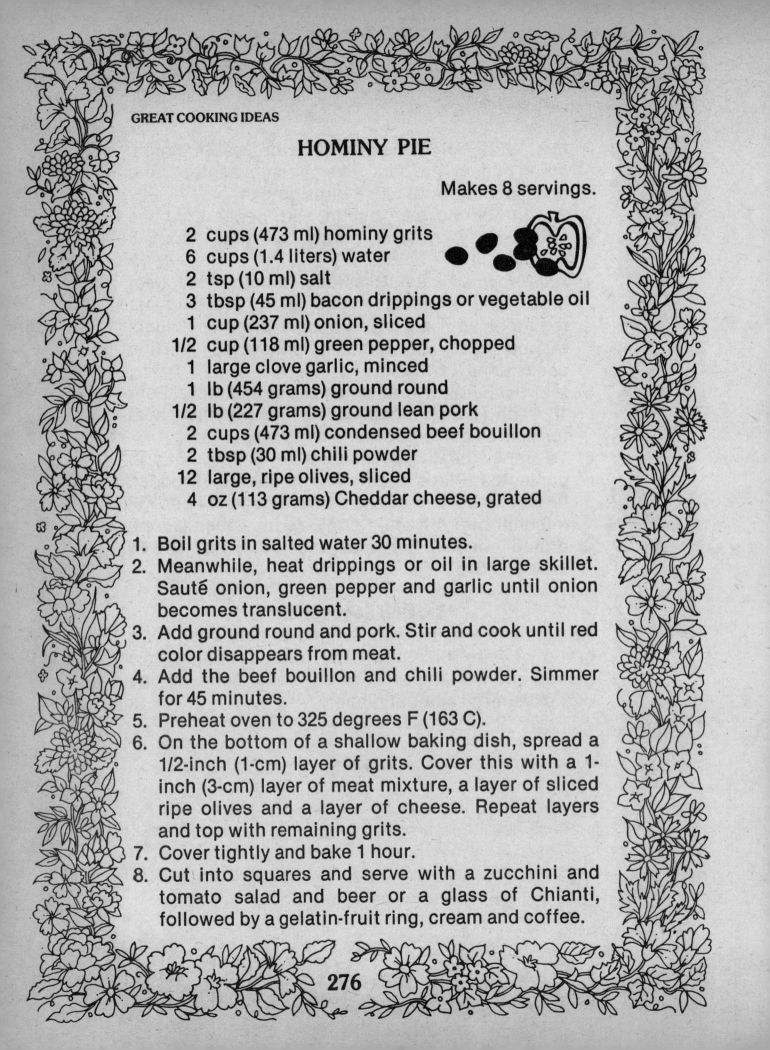

2 cups (473 ml) hominy grits
6 cups (1.4 liters) water
2 tsp (10 ml) salt
3 tbsp (45 ml) bacon drippings or vegetable oil
1 cup (237 ml) onion, sliced
1/2 cup (118 ml) green pepper, chopped
1 large clove garlic, minced
1 lb (454 grams) ground round
1/2 lb (227 grams) ground lean pork
2 cups (473 ml) condensed beef bouillon
2 tbsp (30 ml) chili powder
12 large, ripe olives, sliced
4 oz (113 grams) Cheddar cheese, grated

1. Boil grits in salted water 30 minutes.
2. Meanwhile, heat drippings or oil in large skillet. Sauté onion, green pepper and garlic until onion becomes translucent.
3. Add ground round and pork. Stir and cook until red color disappears from meat.
4. Add the beef bouillon and chili powder. Simmer for 45 minutes.
5. Preheat oven to 325 degrees F (163 C).
6. On the bottom of a shallow baking dish, spread a 1/2-inch (1-cm) layer of grits. Cover this with a 1-inch (3-cm) layer of meat mixture, a layer of sliced ripe olives and a layer of cheese. Repeat layers and top with remaining grits.
7. Cover tightly and bake 1 hour.
8. Cut into squares and serve with a zucchini and tomato salad and beer or a glass of Chianti, followed by a gelatin-fruit ring, cream and coffee.

ISLAND LOAF

Makes 8 servings.

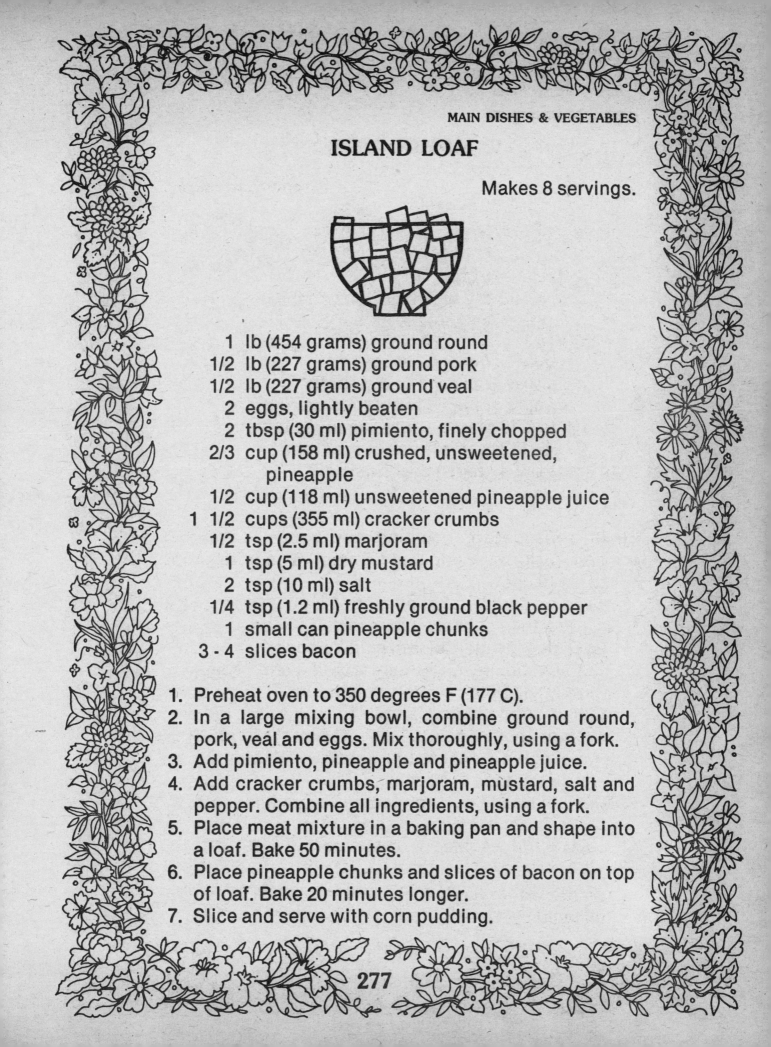

1	lb (454 grams)	ground round
1/2	lb (227 grams)	ground pork
1/2	lb (227 grams)	ground veal
2		eggs, lightly beaten
2	tbsp (30 ml)	pimiento, finely chopped
2/3	cup (158 ml)	crushed, unsweetened, pineapple
1/2	cup (118 ml)	unsweetened pineapple juice
1 1/2	cups (355 ml)	cracker crumbs
1/2	tsp (2.5 ml)	marjoram
1	tsp (5 ml)	dry mustard
2	tsp (10 ml)	salt
1/4	tsp (1.2 ml)	freshly ground black pepper
1		small can pineapple chunks
3 - 4		slices bacon

1. Preheat oven to 350 degrees F (177 C).
2. In a large mixing bowl, combine ground round, pork, veal and eggs. Mix thoroughly, using a fork.
3. Add pimiento, pineapple and pineapple juice.
4. Add cracker crumbs, marjoram, mustard, salt and pepper. Combine all ingredients, using a fork.
5. Place meat mixture in a baking pan and shape into a loaf. Bake 50 minutes.
6. Place pineapple chunks and slices of bacon on top of loaf. Bake 20 minutes longer.
7. Slice and serve with corn pudding.

JAPANESE BRISKET

Makes 4 servings.

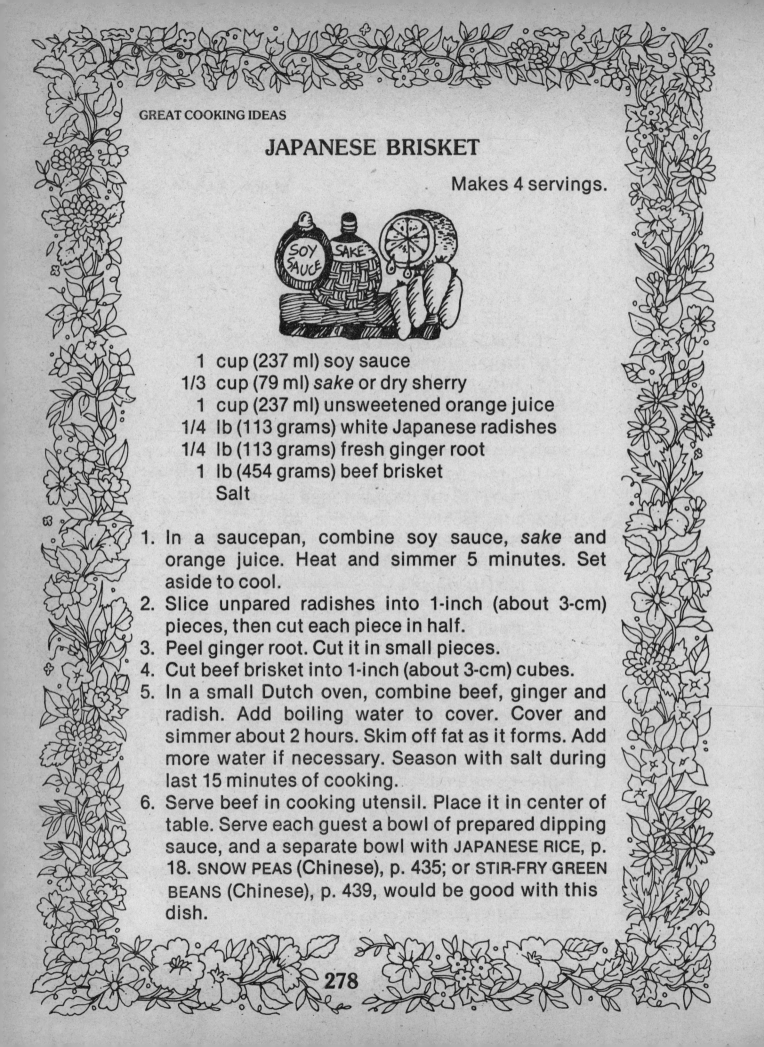

1 cup (237 ml) soy sauce
1/3 cup (79 ml) *sake* or dry sherry
1 cup (237 ml) unsweetened orange juice
1/4 lb (113 grams) white Japanese radishes
1/4 lb (113 grams) fresh ginger root
1 lb (454 grams) beef brisket
Salt

1. In a saucepan, combine soy sauce, *sake* and orange juice. Heat and simmer 5 minutes. Set aside to cool.
2. Slice unpared radishes into 1-inch (about 3-cm) pieces, then cut each piece in half.
3. Peel ginger root. Cut it in small pieces.
4. Cut beef brisket into 1-inch (about 3-cm) cubes.
5. In a small Dutch oven, combine beef, ginger and radish. Add boiling water to cover. Cover and simmer about 2 hours. Skim off fat as it forms. Add more water if necessary. Season with salt during last 15 minutes of cooking.
6. Serve beef in cooking utensil. Place it in center of table. Serve each guest a bowl of prepared dipping sauce, and a separate bowl with JAPANESE RICE, p. 18. SNOW PEAS (Chinese), p. 435; or STIR-FRY GREEN BEANS (Chinese), p. 439, would be good with this dish.

LEMONY BEEF PATTIES

Makes 6 servings.

Patties:

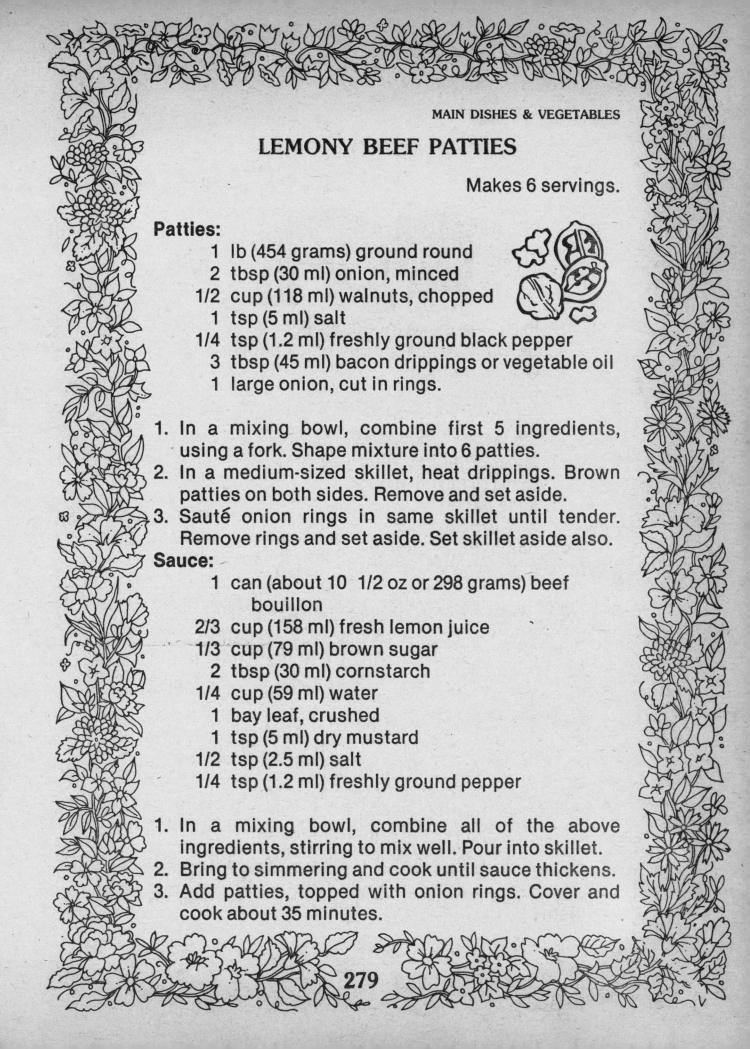

- 1 lb (454 grams) ground round
- 2 tbsp (30 ml) onion, minced
- 1/2 cup (118 ml) walnuts, chopped
- 1 tsp (5 ml) salt
- 1/4 tsp (1.2 ml) freshly ground black pepper
- 3 tbsp (45 ml) bacon drippings or vegetable oil
- 1 large onion, cut in rings.

1. In a mixing bowl, combine first 5 ingredients, using a fork. Shape mixture into 6 patties.
2. In a medium-sized skillet, heat drippings. Brown patties on both sides. Remove and set aside.
3. Sauté onion rings in same skillet until tender. Remove rings and set aside. Set skillet aside also.

Sauce:

- 1 can (about 10 1/2 oz or 298 grams) beef bouillon
- 2/3 cup (158 ml) fresh lemon juice
- 1/3 cup (79 ml) brown sugar
- 2 tbsp (30 ml) cornstarch
- 1/4 cup (59 ml) water
- 1 bay leaf, crushed
- 1 tsp (5 ml) dry mustard
- 1/2 tsp (2.5 ml) salt
- 1/4 tsp (1.2 ml) freshly ground pepper

1. In a mixing bowl, combine all of the above ingredients, stirring to mix well. Pour into skillet.
2. Bring to simmering and cook until sauce thickens.
3. Add patties, topped with onion rings. Cover and cook about 35 minutes.

MARINATED ROAST BEEF

Makes 4 - 6 servings.

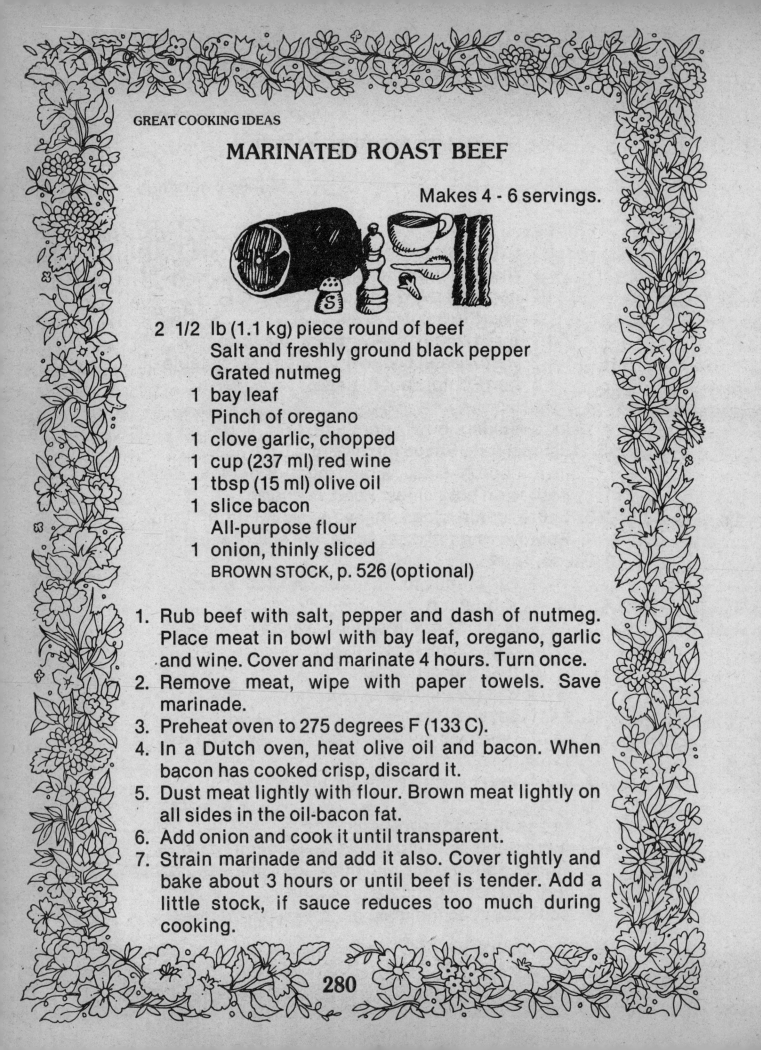

2 1/2 lb (1.1 kg) piece round of beef
Salt and freshly ground black pepper
Grated nutmeg
1 bay leaf
Pinch of oregano
1 clove garlic, chopped
1 cup (237 ml) red wine
1 tbsp (15 ml) olive oil
1 slice bacon
All-purpose flour
1 onion, thinly sliced
BROWN STOCK, p. 526 (optional)

1. Rub beef with salt, pepper and dash of nutmeg. Place meat in bowl with bay leaf, oregano, garlic and wine. Cover and marinate 4 hours. Turn once.
2. Remove meat, wipe with paper towels. Save marinade.
3. Preheat oven to 275 degrees F (133 C).
4. In a Dutch oven, heat olive oil and bacon. When bacon has cooked crisp, discard it.
5. Dust meat lightly with flour. Brown meat lightly on all sides in the oil-bacon fat.
6. Add onion and cook it until transparent.
7. Strain marinade and add it also. Cover tightly and bake about 3 hours or until beef is tender. Add a little stock, if sauce reduces too much during cooking.

MEAT BALLS IN ALMOND SAUCE

Makes 4 servings.

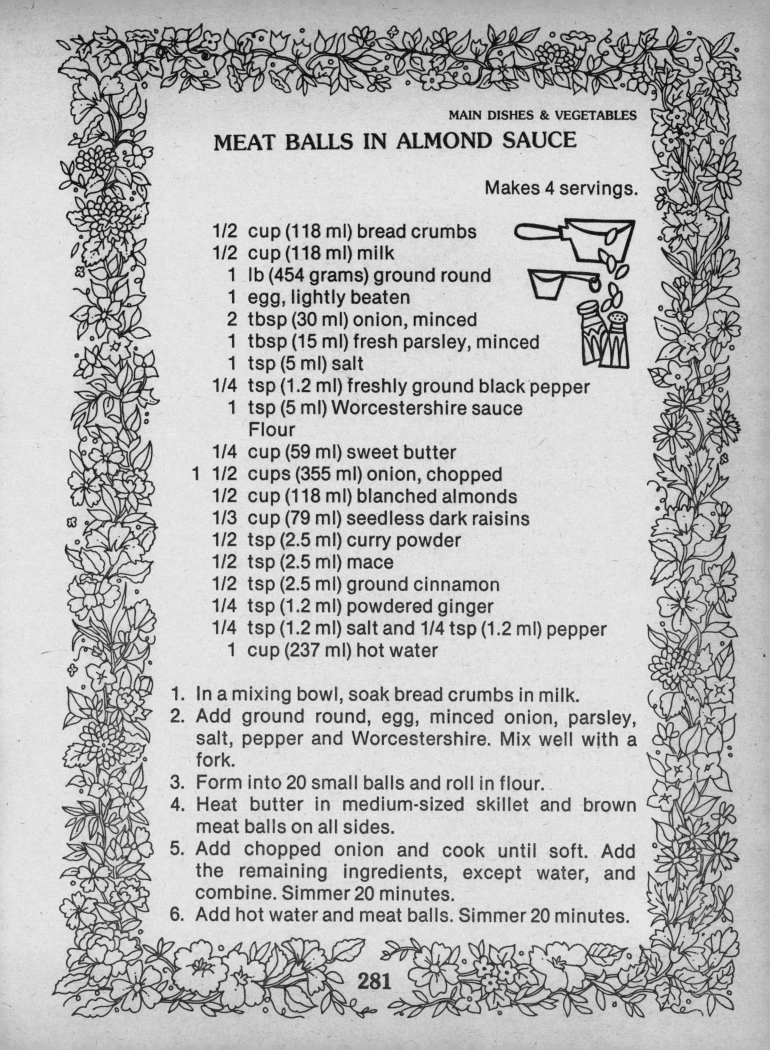

1/2 cup (118 ml) bread crumbs
1/2 cup (118 ml) milk
  1 lb (454 grams) ground round
  1 egg, lightly beaten
  2 tbsp (30 ml) onion, minced
  1 tbsp (15 ml) fresh parsley, minced
  1 tsp (5 ml) salt
1/4 tsp (1.2 ml) freshly ground black pepper
  1 tsp (5 ml) Worcestershire sauce
     Flour
1/4 cup (59 ml) sweet butter
1 1/2 cups (355 ml) onion, chopped
1/2 cup (118 ml) blanched almonds
1/3 cup (79 ml) seedless dark raisins
1/2 tsp (2.5 ml) curry powder
1/2 tsp (2.5 ml) mace
1/2 tsp (2.5 ml) ground cinnamon
1/4 tsp (1.2 ml) powdered ginger
1/4 tsp (1.2 ml) salt and 1/4 tsp (1.2 ml) pepper
  1 cup (237 ml) hot water

1. In a mixing bowl, soak bread crumbs in milk.
2. Add ground round, egg, minced onion, parsley, salt, pepper and Worcestershire. Mix well with a fork.
3. Form into 20 small balls and roll in flour.
4. Heat butter in medium-sized skillet and brown meat balls on all sides.
5. Add chopped onion and cook until soft. Add the remaining ingredients, except water, and combine. Simmer 20 minutes.
6. Add hot water and meat balls. Simmer 20 minutes.

MEAT LOAF SICILIAN-STYLE

Makes 4 - 6 servings.

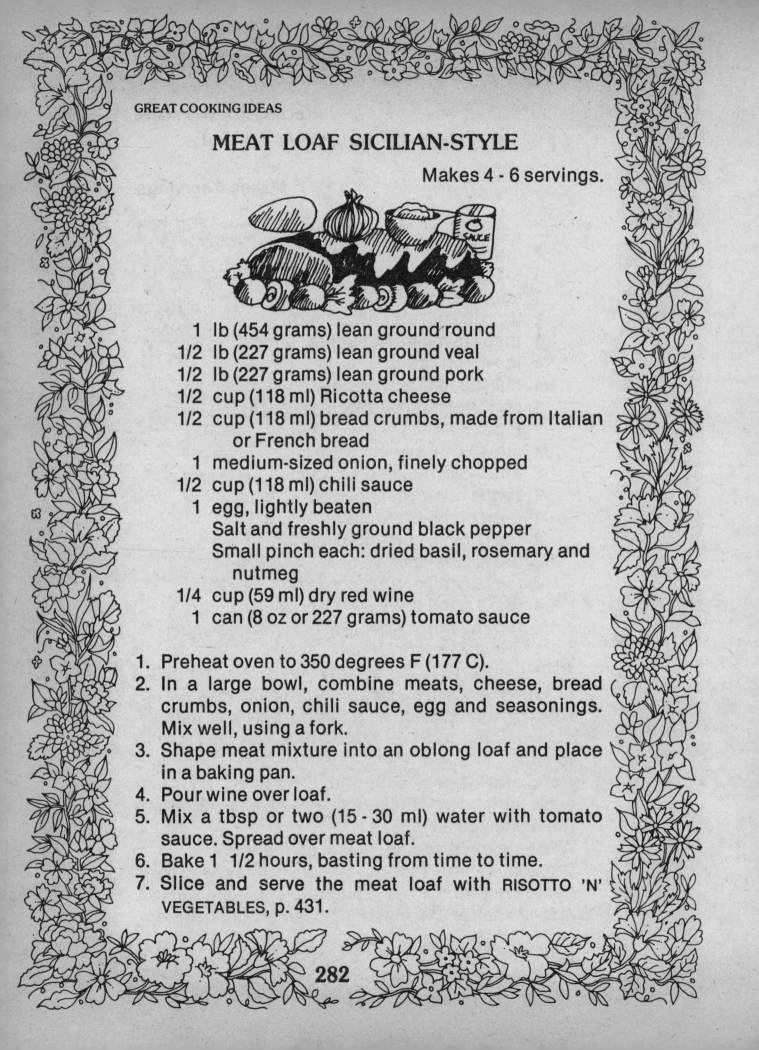

```
 1   lb (454 grams) lean ground round
1/2  lb (227 grams) lean ground veal
1/2  lb (227 grams) lean ground pork
1/2  cup (118 ml) Ricotta cheese
1/2  cup (118 ml) bread crumbs, made from Italian
       or French bread
 1   medium-sized onion, finely chopped
1/2  cup (118 ml) chili sauce
 1   egg, lightly beaten
     Salt and freshly ground black pepper
     Small pinch each: dried basil, rosemary and
       nutmeg
1/4  cup (59 ml) dry red wine
 1   can (8 oz or 227 grams) tomato sauce
```

1. Preheat oven to 350 degrees F (177 C).
2. In a large bowl, combine meats, cheese, bread crumbs, onion, chili sauce, egg and seasonings. Mix well, using a fork.
3. Shape meat mixture into an oblong loaf and place in a baking pan.
4. Pour wine over loaf.
5. Mix a tbsp or two (15 - 30 ml) water with tomato sauce. Spread over meat loaf.
6. Bake 1 1/2 hours, basting from time to time.
7. Slice and serve the meat loaf with RISOTTO 'N' VEGETABLES, p. 431.

MEXICAN CHILI

Makes 8 servings.

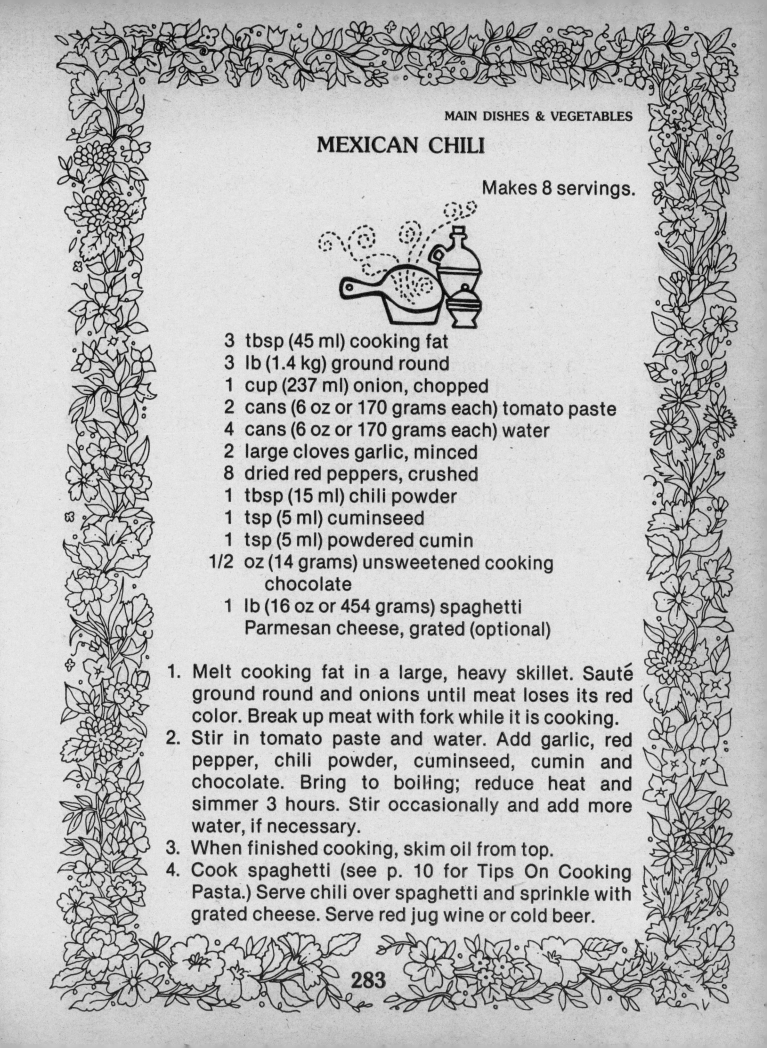

3 tbsp (45 ml) cooking fat
3 lb (1.4 kg) ground round
1 cup (237 ml) onion, chopped
2 cans (6 oz or 170 grams each) tomato paste
4 cans (6 oz or 170 grams each) water
2 large cloves garlic, minced
8 dried red peppers, crushed
1 tbsp (15 ml) chili powder
1 tsp (5 ml) cuminseed
1 tsp (5 ml) powdered cumin
1/2 oz (14 grams) unsweetened cooking chocolate
1 lb (16 oz or 454 grams) spaghetti
Parmesan cheese, grated (optional)

1. Melt cooking fat in a large, heavy skillet. Sauté ground round and onions until meat loses its red color. Break up meat with fork while it is cooking.
2. Stir in tomato paste and water. Add garlic, red pepper, chili powder, cuminseed, cumin and chocolate. Bring to boiling; reduce heat and simmer 3 hours. Stir occasionally and add more water, if necessary.
3. When finished cooking, skim oil from top.
4. Cook spaghetti (see p. 10 for Tips On Cooking Pasta.) Serve chili over spaghetti and sprinkle with grated cheese. Serve red jug wine or cold beer.

PEPPER POT

Makes 6 servings.

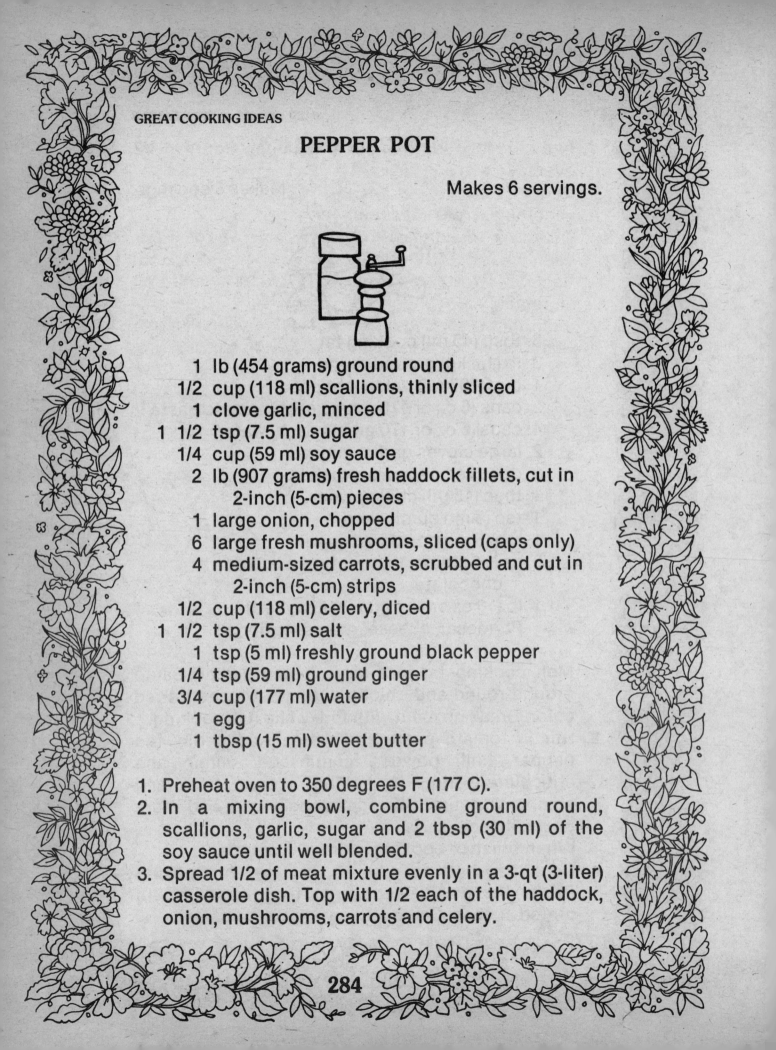

- 1 lb (454 grams) ground round
- 1/2 cup (118 ml) scallions, thinly sliced
- 1 clove garlic, minced
- 1 1/2 tsp (7.5 ml) sugar
- 1/4 cup (59 ml) soy sauce
- 2 lb (907 grams) fresh haddock fillets, cut in 2-inch (5-cm) pieces
- 1 large onion, chopped
- 6 large fresh mushrooms, sliced (caps only)
- 4 medium-sized carrots, scrubbed and cut in 2-inch (5-cm) strips
- 1/2 cup (118 ml) celery, diced
- 1 1/2 tsp (7.5 ml) salt
- 1 tsp (5 ml) freshly ground black pepper
- 1/4 tsp (59 ml) ground ginger
- 3/4 cup (177 ml) water
- 1 egg
- 1 tbsp (15 ml) sweet butter

1. Preheat oven to 350 degrees F (177 C).
2. In a mixing bowl, combine ground round, scallions, garlic, sugar and 2 tbsp (30 ml) of the soy sauce until well blended.
3. Spread 1/2 of meat mixture evenly in a 3-qt (3-liter) casserole dish. Top with 1/2 each of the haddock, onion, mushrooms, carrots and celery.

4. In a cup, mix salt, pepper and ginger. Sprinkle 1/2 over layers in casserole.

5. Repeat layers of meat mixture, haddock, vegetables, and seasoning mixture.

6. Combine remaining soy sauce with water. Pour over layers. Cover tightly. Bake 1 hour or until haddock flakes easily with a fork and all vegetables are tender.

7. Just before serving, beat egg well in a small bowl. Melt butter in a small skillet and cook egg, turning once, just until it's tender. Remove egg from skillet and place on cutting board. Slice in thin strips.

8. Use strips to make a petal-design garnish on top of dish.

9. Serve in shallow bowls with chopsticks or use spoons.

NOTES

ONION PIE

Makes 6 servings.

Pastry:

    1 1/2 cups (355 ml) prepared biscuit mix
      1/2 cup (118 ml) milk

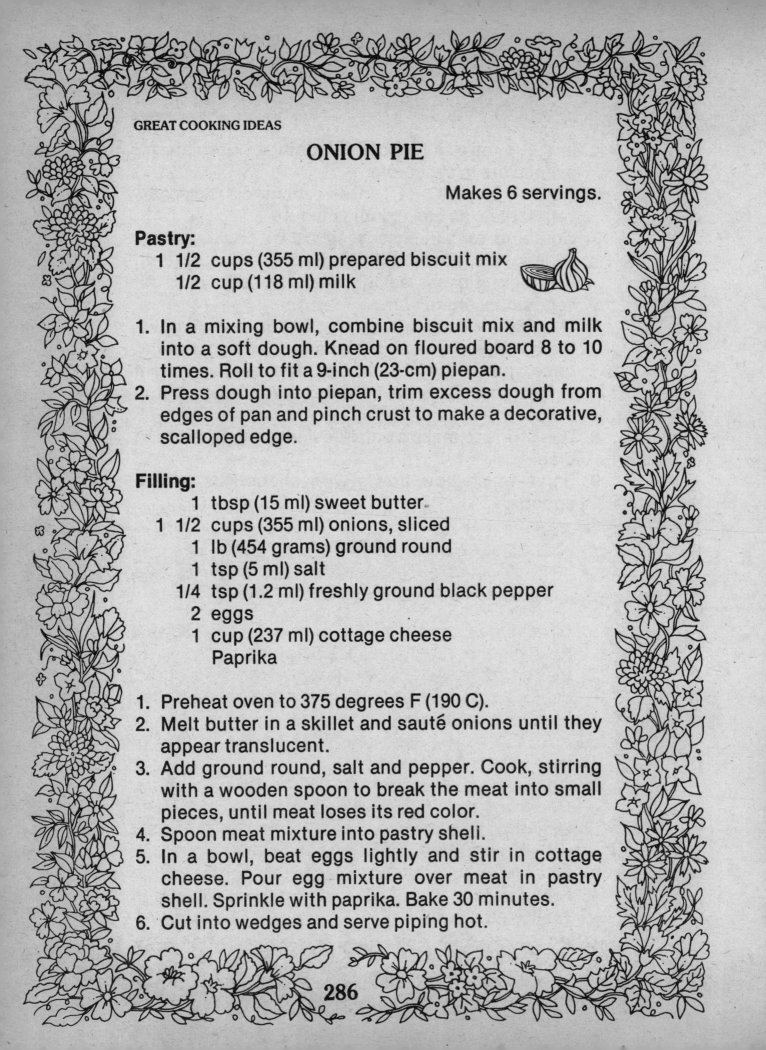

1. In a mixing bowl, combine biscuit mix and milk into a soft dough. Knead on floured board 8 to 10 times. Roll to fit a 9-inch (23-cm) piepan.
2. Press dough into piepan, trim excess dough from edges of pan and pinch crust to make a decorative, scalloped edge.

Filling:

      1 tbsp (15 ml) sweet butter
    1 1/2 cups (355 ml) onions, sliced
      1 lb (454 grams) ground round
      1 tsp (5 ml) salt
      1/4 tsp (1.2 ml) freshly ground black pepper
      2 eggs
      1 cup (237 ml) cottage cheese
         Paprika

1. Preheat oven to 375 degrees F (190 C).
2. Melt butter in a skillet and sauté onions until they appear translucent.
3. Add ground round, salt and pepper. Cook, stirring with a wooden spoon to break the meat into small pieces, until meat loses its red color.
4. Spoon meat mixture into pastry shell.
5. In a bowl, beat eggs lightly and stir in cottage cheese. Pour egg mixture over meat in pastry shell. Sprinkle with paprika. Bake 30 minutes.
6. Cut into wedges and serve piping hot.

PEPPER STEAK

Makes 4 servings.

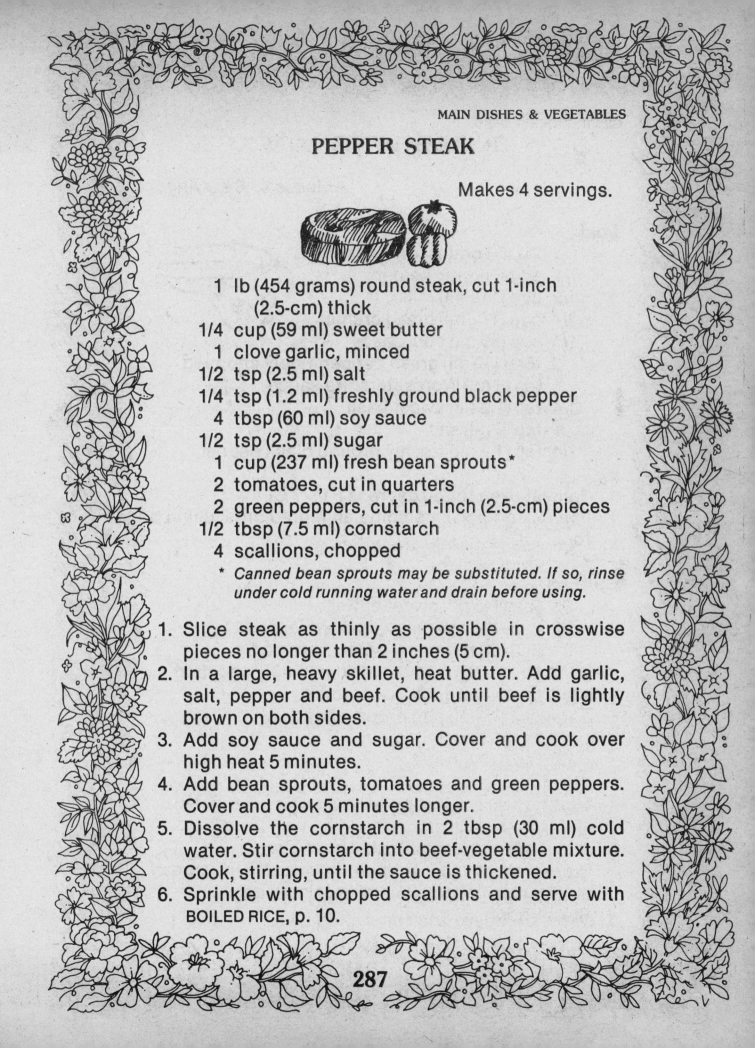

    1 lb (454 grams) round steak, cut 1-inch
       (2.5-cm) thick
  1/4 cup (59 ml) sweet butter
    1 clove garlic, minced
  1/2 tsp (2.5 ml) salt
  1/4 tsp (1.2 ml) freshly ground black pepper
    4 tbsp (60 ml) soy sauce
  1/2 tsp (2.5 ml) sugar
    1 cup (237 ml) fresh bean sprouts*
    2 tomatoes, cut in quarters
    2 green peppers, cut in 1-inch (2.5-cm) pieces
  1/2 tbsp (7.5 ml) cornstarch
    4 scallions, chopped

  * *Canned bean sprouts may be substituted. If so, rinse
    under cold running water and drain before using.*

1. Slice steak as thinly as possible in crosswise pieces no longer than 2 inches (5 cm).
2. In a large, heavy skillet, heat butter. Add garlic, salt, pepper and beef. Cook until beef is lightly brown on both sides.
3. Add soy sauce and sugar. Cover and cook over high heat 5 minutes.
4. Add bean sprouts, tomatoes and green peppers. Cover and cook 5 minutes longer.
5. Dissolve the cornstarch in 2 tbsp (30 ml) cold water. Stir cornstarch into beef-vegetable mixture. Cook, stirring, until the sauce is thickened.
6. Sprinkle with chopped scallions and serve with BOILED RICE, p. 10.

PICKLE-STUFFED LOAF

Makes 4 - 6 servings.

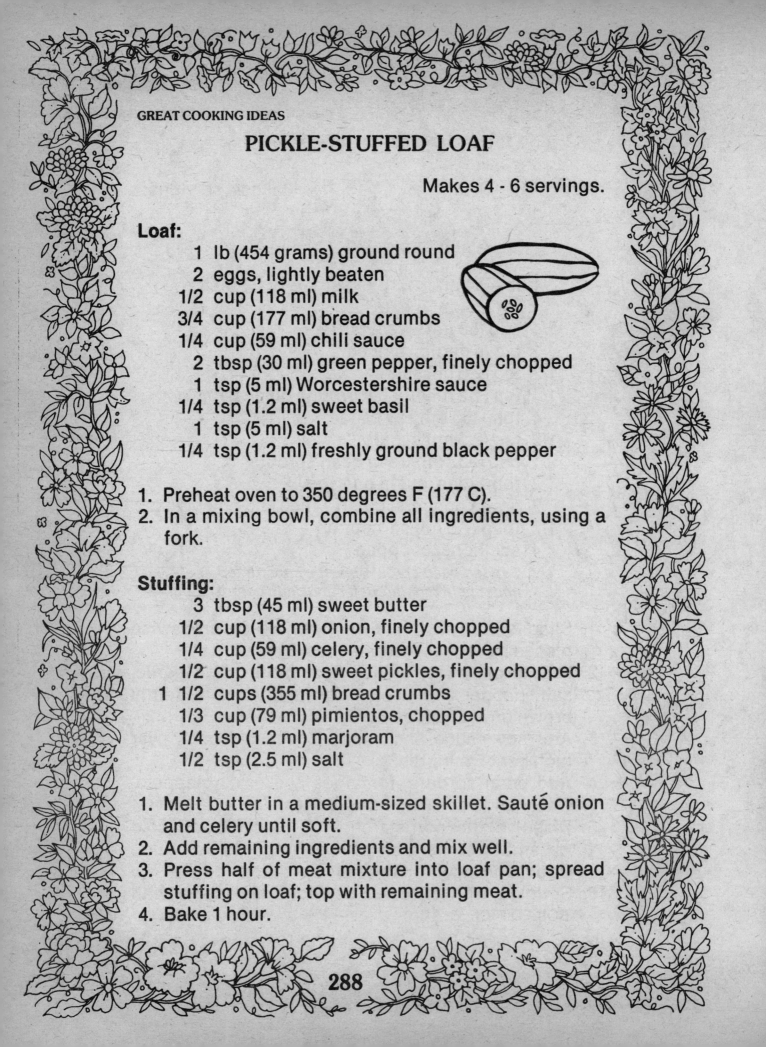

Loaf:

- 1 lb (454 grams) ground round
- 2 eggs, lightly beaten
- 1/2 cup (118 ml) milk
- 3/4 cup (177 ml) bread crumbs
- 1/4 cup (59 ml) chili sauce
- 2 tbsp (30 ml) green pepper, finely chopped
- 1 tsp (5 ml) Worcestershire sauce
- 1/4 tsp (1.2 ml) sweet basil
- 1 tsp (5 ml) salt
- 1/4 tsp (1.2 ml) freshly ground black pepper

1. Preheat oven to 350 degrees F (177 C).
2. In a mixing bowl, combine all ingredients, using a fork.

Stuffing:

- 3 tbsp (45 ml) sweet butter
- 1/2 cup (118 ml) onion, finely chopped
- 1/4 cup (59 ml) celery, finely chopped
- 1/2 cup (118 ml) sweet pickles, finely chopped
- 1 1/2 cups (355 ml) bread crumbs
- 1/3 cup (79 ml) pimientos, chopped
- 1/4 tsp (1.2 ml) marjoram
- 1/2 tsp (2.5 ml) salt

1. Melt butter in a medium-sized skillet. Sauté onion and celery until soft.
2. Add remaining ingredients and mix well.
3. Press half of meat mixture into loaf pan; spread stuffing on loaf; top with remaining meat.
4. Bake 1 hour.

PINEAPPLE MEAT BALLS

Makes 8 servings.

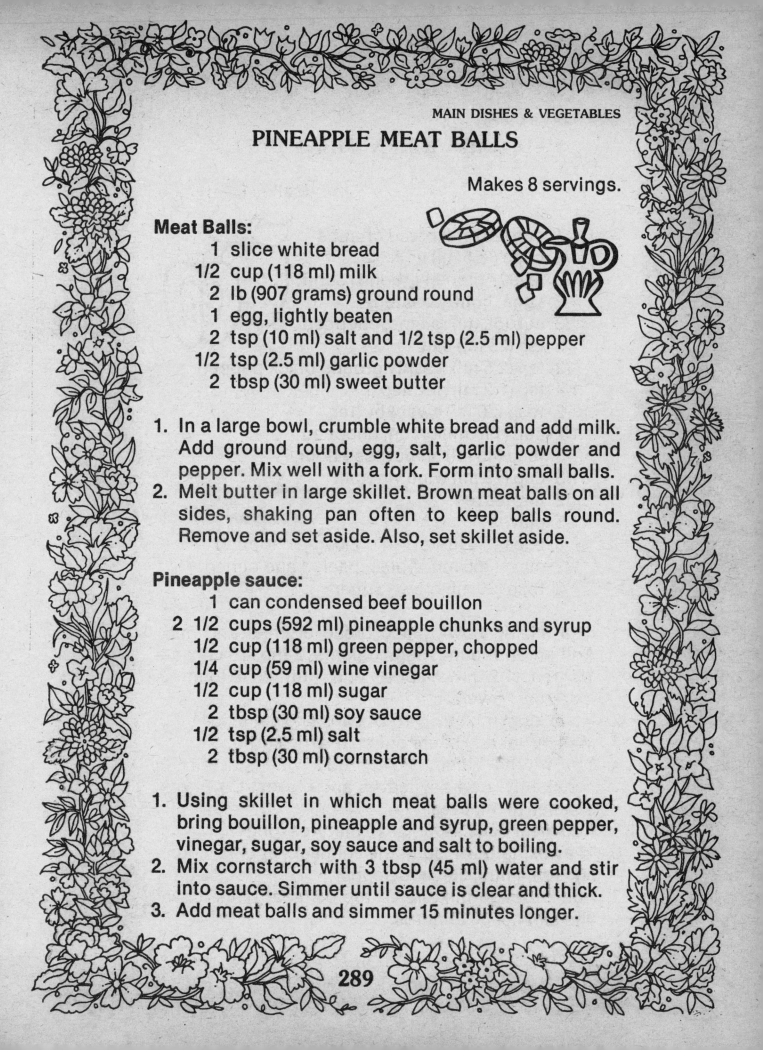

Meat Balls:
- 1 slice white bread
- 1/2 cup (118 ml) milk
- 2 lb (907 grams) ground round
- 1 egg, lightly beaten
- 2 tsp (10 ml) salt and 1/2 tsp (2.5 ml) pepper
- 1/2 tsp (2.5 ml) garlic powder
- 2 tbsp (30 ml) sweet butter

1. In a large bowl, crumble white bread and add milk. Add ground round, egg, salt, garlic powder and pepper. Mix well with a fork. Form into small balls.
2. Melt butter in large skillet. Brown meat balls on all sides, shaking pan often to keep balls round. Remove and set aside. Also, set skillet aside.

Pineapple sauce:
- 1 can condensed beef bouillon
- 2 1/2 cups (592 ml) pineapple chunks and syrup
- 1/2 cup (118 ml) green pepper, chopped
- 1/4 cup (59 ml) wine vinegar
- 1/2 cup (118 ml) sugar
- 2 tbsp (30 ml) soy sauce
- 1/2 tsp (2.5 ml) salt
- 2 tbsp (30 ml) cornstarch

1. Using skillet in which meat balls were cooked, bring bouillon, pineapple and syrup, green pepper, vinegar, sugar, soy sauce and salt to boiling.
2. Mix cornstarch with 3 tbsp (45 ml) water and stir into sauce. Simmer until sauce is clear and thick.
3. Add meat balls and simmer 15 minutes longer.

RED CABBAGE 'N' MEAT BALLS

Makes 6 servings.

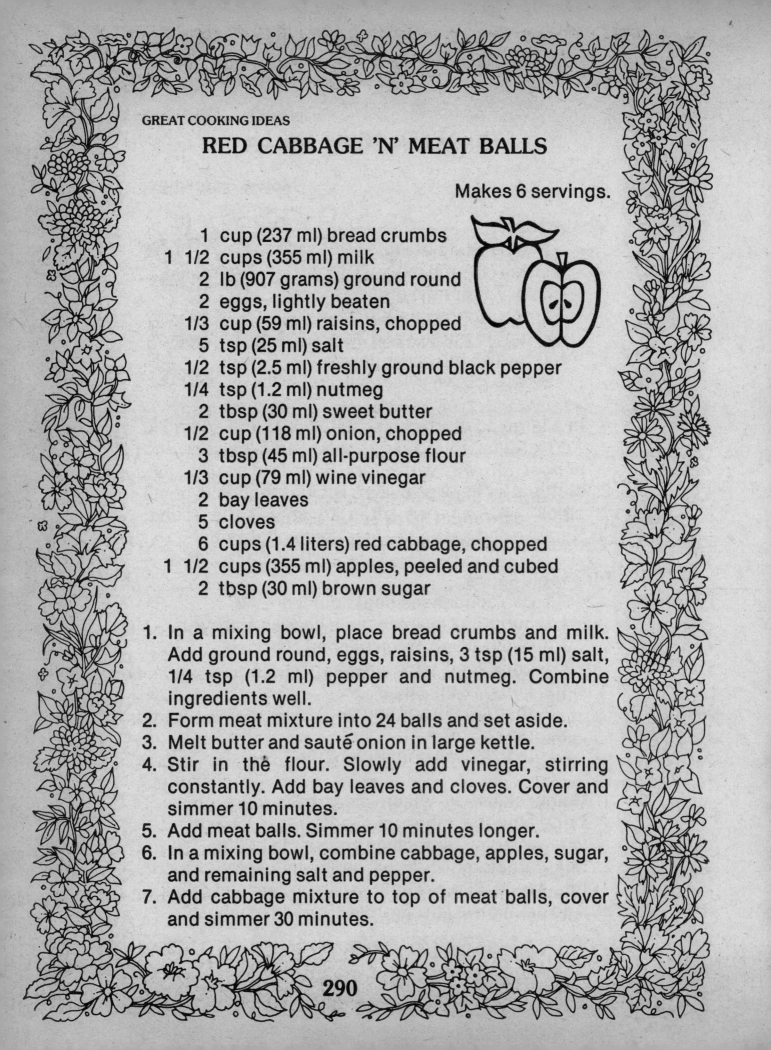

          1   cup (237 ml) bread crumbs
     1 1/2   cups (355 ml) milk
          2   lb (907 grams) ground round
          2   eggs, lightly beaten
        1/3   cup (59 ml) raisins, chopped
          5   tsp (25 ml) salt
        1/2   tsp (2.5 ml) freshly ground black pepper
        1/4   tsp (1.2 ml) nutmeg
          2   tbsp (30 ml) sweet butter
        1/2   cup (118 ml) onion, chopped
          3   tbsp (45 ml) all-purpose flour
        1/3   cup (79 ml) wine vinegar
          2   bay leaves
          5   cloves
          6   cups (1.4 liters) red cabbage, chopped
     1 1/2   cups (355 ml) apples, peeled and cubed
          2   tbsp (30 ml) brown sugar

1. In a mixing bowl, place bread crumbs and milk. Add ground round, eggs, raisins, 3 tsp (15 ml) salt, 1/4 tsp (1.2 ml) pepper and nutmeg. Combine ingredients well.
2. Form meat mixture into 24 balls and set aside.
3. Melt butter and sauté onion in large kettle.
4. Stir in the flour. Slowly add vinegar, stirring constantly. Add bay leaves and cloves. Cover and simmer 10 minutes.
5. Add meat balls. Simmer 10 minutes longer.
6. In a mixing bowl, combine cabbage, apples, sugar, and remaining salt and pepper.
7. Add cabbage mixture to top of meat balls, cover and simmer 30 minutes.

RUSSIAN MEAT BALLS

Makes 8 servings.

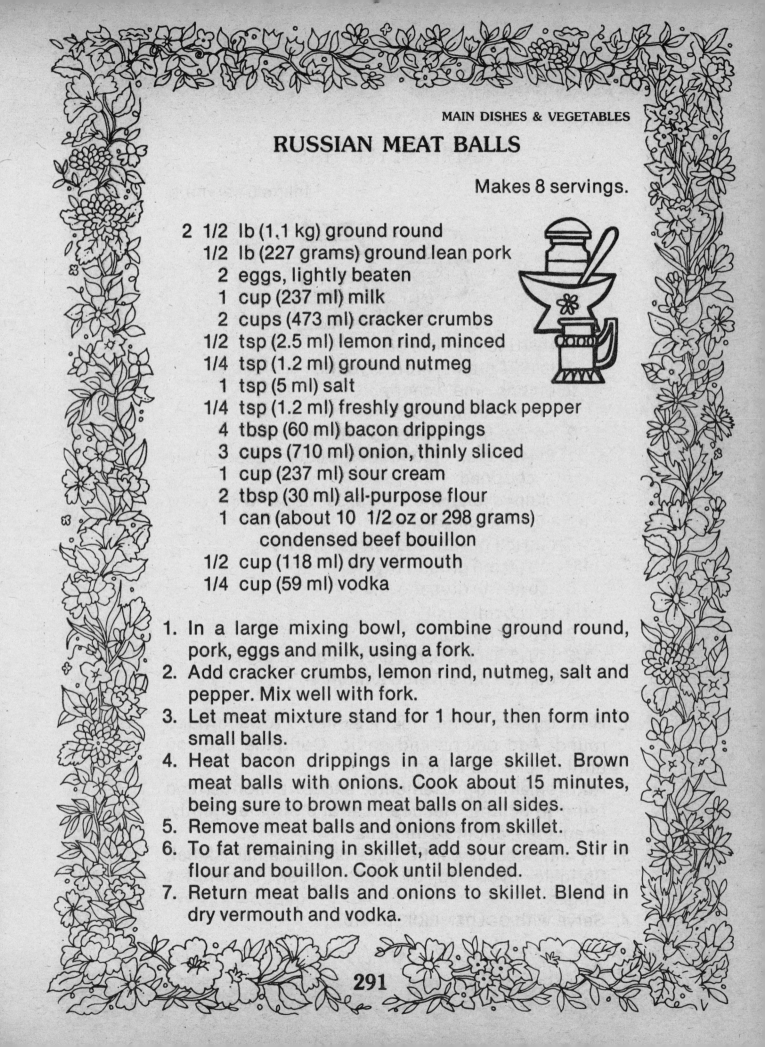

- 2 1/2 lb (1.1 kg) ground round
- 1/2 lb (227 grams) ground lean pork
- 2 eggs, lightly beaten
- 1 cup (237 ml) milk
- 2 cups (473 ml) cracker crumbs
- 1/2 tsp (2.5 ml) lemon rind, minced
- 1/4 tsp (1.2 ml) ground nutmeg
- 1 tsp (5 ml) salt
- 1/4 tsp (1.2 ml) freshly ground black pepper
- 4 tbsp (60 ml) bacon drippings
- 3 cups (710 ml) onion, thinly sliced
- 1 cup (237 ml) sour cream
- 2 tbsp (30 ml) all-purpose flour
- 1 can (about 10 1/2 oz or 298 grams) condensed beef bouillon
- 1/2 cup (118 ml) dry vermouth
- 1/4 cup (59 ml) vodka

1. In a large mixing bowl, combine ground round, pork, eggs and milk, using a fork.
2. Add cracker crumbs, lemon rind, nutmeg, salt and pepper. Mix well with fork.
3. Let meat mixture stand for 1 hour, then form into small balls.
4. Heat bacon drippings in a large skillet. Brown meat balls with onions. Cook about 15 minutes, being sure to brown meat balls on all sides.
5. Remove meat balls and onions from skillet.
6. To fat remaining in skillet, add sour cream. Stir in flour and bouillon. Cook until blended.
7. Return meat balls and onions to skillet. Blend in dry vermouth and vodka.

SPANISH-STYLE HASH

Makes 6 servings.

- 4 tbsp (60 ml) olive oil
- 2 lb (907 grams) ground round
- 2 onions, finely chopped
- 1 clove garlic, minced
- 2 apples, peeled, cored and chopped
- 1 lb (454 grams) tomatoes, peeled, seeded and chopped
- 3 canned *jalapeno* chiles, seeded and sliced
- 1/2 cup (118 ml) raisins
- 1/4 cup (59 ml) stuffed olives, halved
- 1/8 tsp (.6 ml) ground thyme
- 1/8 tsp (.6 ml) oregano
- 1/8 tsp (.6 ml) basil
- 2 tsp (10 ml) salt
- 1/2 tsp (2.5 ml) freshly ground black pepper
- 1/4 cup (59 ml) slivered almonds

1. Heat oil in a large, heavy skillet. Brown ground round. Add onions and garlic. Continue cooking until onions are wilted.
2. Add remaining ingredients, except almonds, and bring to boiling. Reduce heat and simmer gently, uncovered, about 20 minutes.
3. Fry almonds in a little olive oil in a small skillet. Sprinkle over top of Hash. Cook 2 minutes longer.
4. Serve with GOLDEN RICE, p. 418.

STEAK 'N' PIMIENTOS

Makes 4 servings.

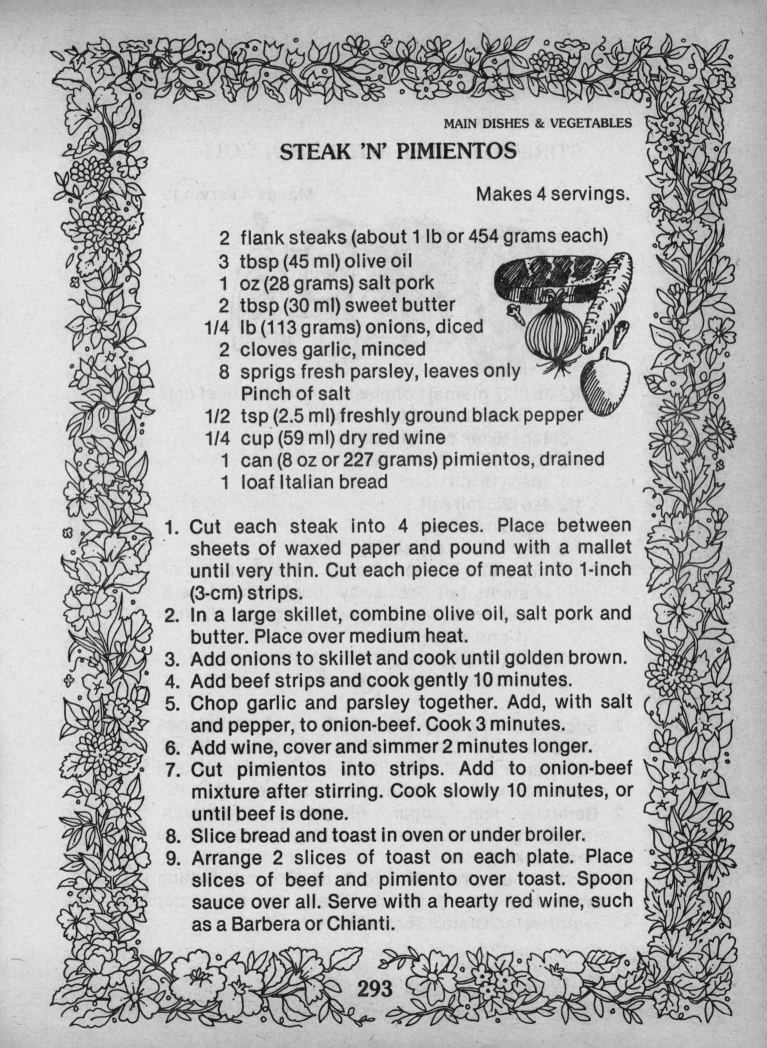

 2   flank steaks (about 1 lb or 454 grams each)
 3   tbsp (45 ml) olive oil
 1   oz (28 grams) salt pork
 2   tbsp (30 ml) sweet butter
1/4 lb (113 grams) onions, diced
 2   cloves garlic, minced
 8   sprigs fresh parsley, leaves only
     Pinch of salt
1/2 tsp (2.5 ml) freshly ground black pepper
1/4 cup (59 ml) dry red wine
 1   can (8 oz or 227 grams) pimientos, drained
 1   loaf Italian bread

1. Cut each steak into 4 pieces. Place between sheets of waxed paper and pound with a mallet until very thin. Cut each piece of meat into 1-inch (3-cm) strips.
2. In a large skillet, combine olive oil, salt pork and butter. Place over medium heat.
3. Add onions to skillet and cook until golden brown.
4. Add beef strips and cook gently 10 minutes.
5. Chop garlic and parsley together. Add, with salt and pepper, to onion-beef. Cook 3 minutes.
6. Add wine, cover and simmer 2 minutes longer.
7. Cut pimientos into strips. Add to onion-beef mixture after stirring. Cook slowly 10 minutes, or until beef is done.
8. Slice bread and toast in oven or under broiler.
9. Arrange 2 slices of toast on each plate. Place slices of beef and pimiento over toast. Spoon sauce over all. Serve with a hearty red wine, such as a Barbera or Chianti.

STIR-FRIED BEEF WITH BROCCOLI

Makes 4 servings.

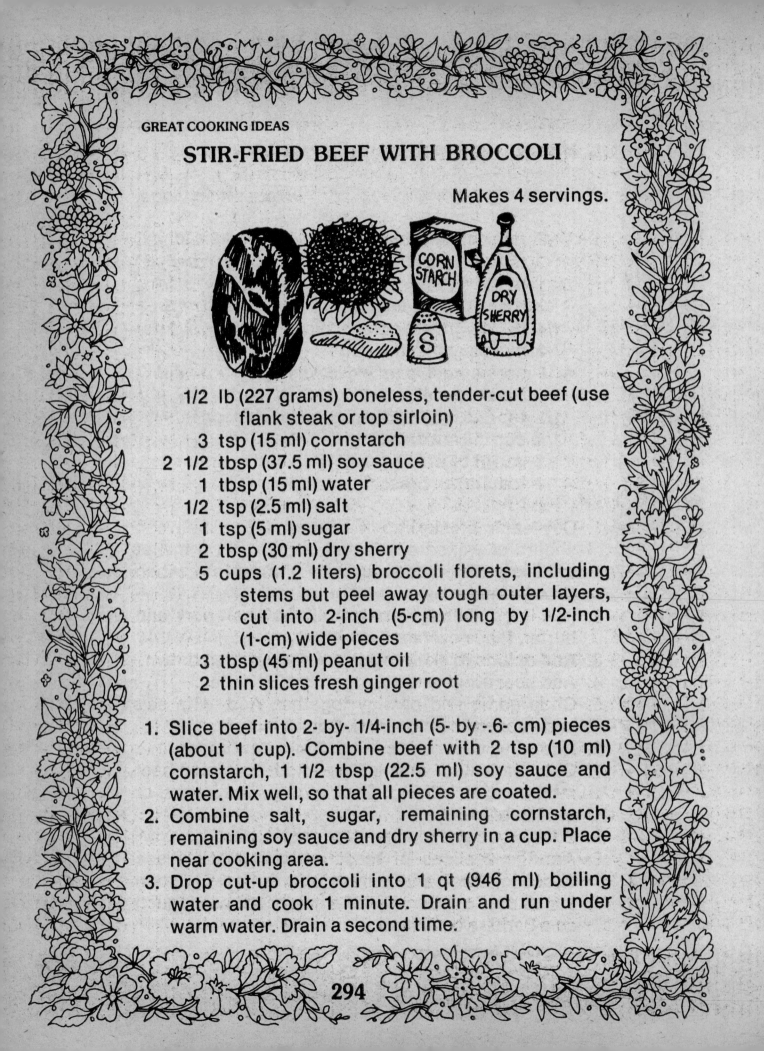

1/2 lb (227 grams) boneless, tender-cut beef (use flank steak or top sirloin)

3 tsp (15 ml) cornstarch

2 1/2 tbsp (37.5 ml) soy sauce

1 tbsp (15 ml) water

1/2 tsp (2.5 ml) salt

1 tsp (5 ml) sugar

2 tbsp (30 ml) dry sherry

5 cups (1.2 liters) broccoli florets, including stems but peel away tough outer layers, cut into 2-inch (5-cm) long by 1/2-inch (1-cm) wide pieces

3 tbsp (45 ml) peanut oil

2 thin slices fresh ginger root

1. Slice beef into 2- by- 1/4-inch (5- by -.6- cm) pieces (about 1 cup). Combine beef with 2 tsp (10 ml) cornstarch, 1 1/2 tbsp (22.5 ml) soy sauce and water. Mix well, so that all pieces are coated.
2. Combine salt, sugar, remaining cornstarch, remaining soy sauce and dry sherry in a cup. Place near cooking area.
3. Drop cut-up broccoli into 1 qt (946 ml) boiling water and cook 1 minute. Drain and run under warm water. Drain a second time.

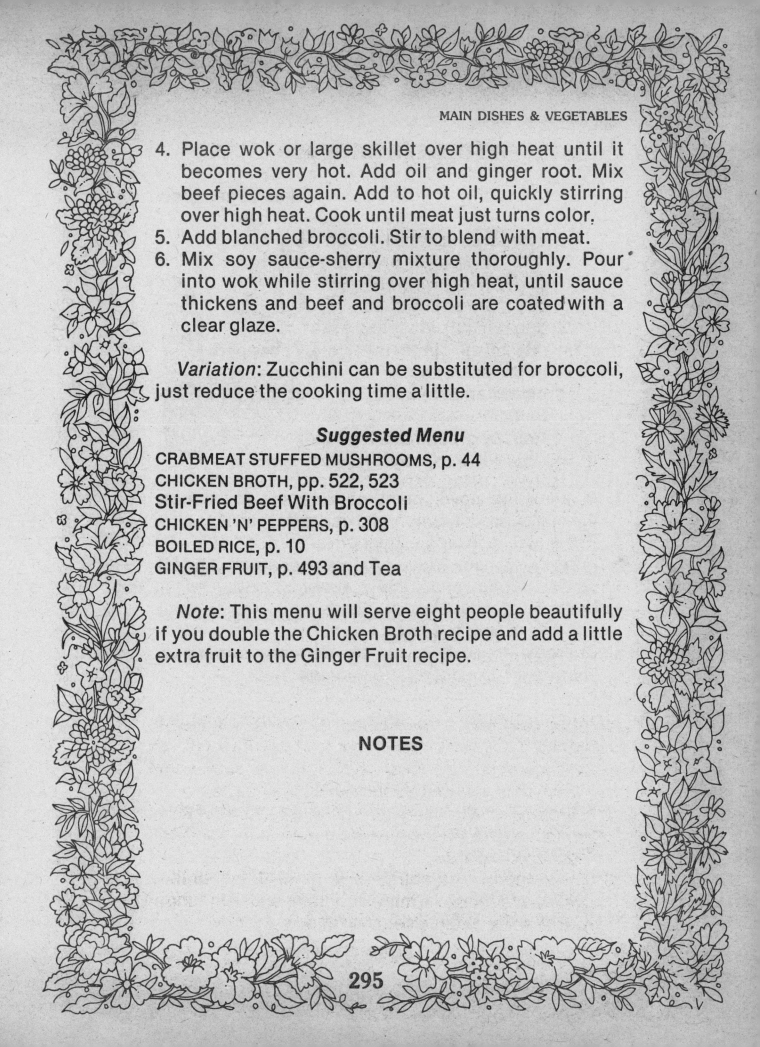

4. Place wok or large skillet over high heat until it becomes very hot. Add oil and ginger root. Mix beef pieces again. Add to hot oil, quickly stirring over high heat. Cook until meat just turns color.
5. Add blanched broccoli. Stir to blend with meat.
6. Mix soy sauce-sherry mixture thoroughly. Pour into wok while stirring over high heat, until sauce thickens and beef and broccoli are coated with a clear glaze.

Variation: Zucchini can be substituted for broccoli, just reduce the cooking time a little.

Suggested Menu

CRABMEAT STUFFED MUSHROOMS, p. 44
CHICKEN BROTH, pp. 522, 523
Stir-Fried Beef With Broccoli
CHICKEN 'N' PEPPERS, p. 308
BOILED RICE, p. 10
GINGER FRUIT, p. 493 and Tea

Note: This menu will serve eight people beautifully if you double the Chicken Broth recipe and add a little extra fruit to the Ginger Fruit recipe.

NOTES

STEAK HAWAIIAN

Makes 12 servings.

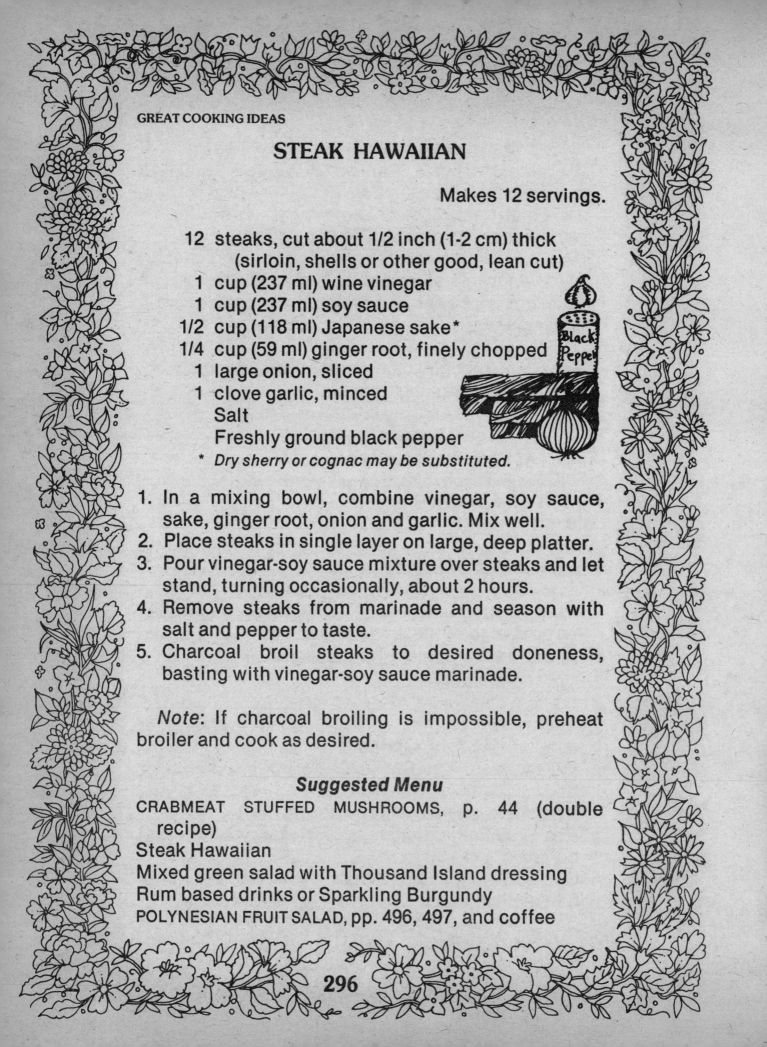

12 steaks, cut about 1/2 inch (1-2 cm) thick
  (sirloin, shells or other good, lean cut)
1 cup (237 ml) wine vinegar
1 cup (237 ml) soy sauce
1/2 cup (118 ml) Japanese sake*
1/4 cup (59 ml) ginger root, finely chopped
1 large onion, sliced
1 clove garlic, minced
  Salt
  Freshly ground black pepper

* *Dry sherry or cognac may be substituted.*

1. In a mixing bowl, combine vinegar, soy sauce, sake, ginger root, onion and garlic. Mix well.
2. Place steaks in single layer on large, deep platter.
3. Pour vinegar-soy sauce mixture over steaks and let stand, turning occasionally, about 2 hours.
4. Remove steaks from marinade and season with salt and pepper to taste.
5. Charcoal broil steaks to desired doneness, basting with vinegar-soy sauce marinade.

Note: If charcoal broiling is impossible, preheat broiler and cook as desired.

Suggested Menu

CRABMEAT STUFFED MUSHROOMS, p. 44 (double recipe)
Steak Hawaiian
Mixed green salad with Thousand Island dressing
Rum based drinks or Sparkling Burgundy
POLYNESIAN FRUIT SALAD, pp. 496, 497, and coffee

STUFFED EGGPLANT

Makes 4 servings.

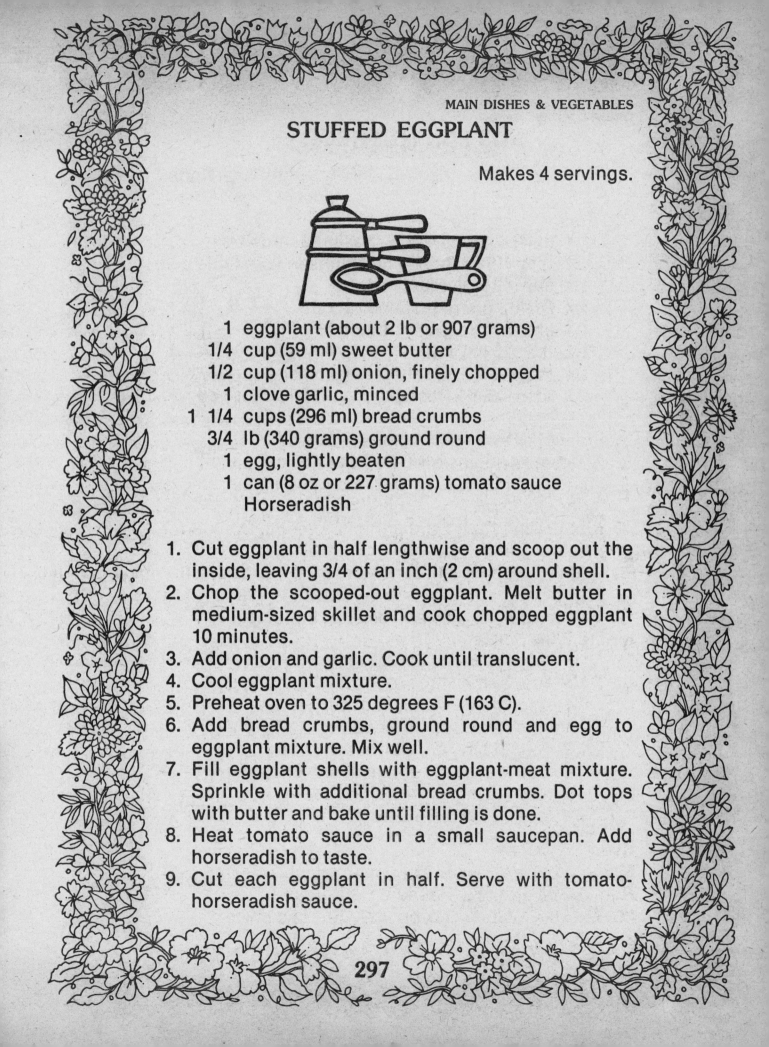

1   eggplant (about 2 lb or 907 grams)
1/4 cup (59 ml) sweet butter
1/2 cup (118 ml) onion, finely chopped
1   clove garlic, minced
1 1/4 cups (296 ml) bread crumbs
3/4 lb (340 grams) ground round
1   egg, lightly beaten
1   can (8 oz or 227 grams) tomato sauce
     Horseradish

1. Cut eggplant in half lengthwise and scoop out the inside, leaving 3/4 of an inch (2 cm) around shell.
2. Chop the scooped-out eggplant. Melt butter in medium-sized skillet and cook chopped eggplant 10 minutes.
3. Add onion and garlic. Cook until translucent.
4. Cool eggplant mixture.
5. Preheat oven to 325 degrees F (163 C).
6. Add bread crumbs, ground round and egg to eggplant mixture. Mix well.
7. Fill eggplant shells with eggplant-meat mixture. Sprinkle with additional bread crumbs. Dot tops with butter and bake until filling is done.
8. Heat tomato sauce in a small saucepan. Add horseradish to taste.
9. Cut each eggplant in half. Serve with tomato-horseradish sauce.

STUFFED MUSHROOMS

Makes 4 servings.

Stuffing:

    1 lb (454 grams) large, fresh mushrooms
    1 tbsp (15 ml) bacon drippings or vegetable oil
  1/4 cup (59 ml) onion, minced
  1/4 lb (113 grams) ground round
    1 small clove garlic, minced
  1/2 tsp (2.5 ml) salt
  1/4 tsp (1.2 ml) freshly ground black pepper
    1 tbsp (15 ml) fresh parsley, finely chopped

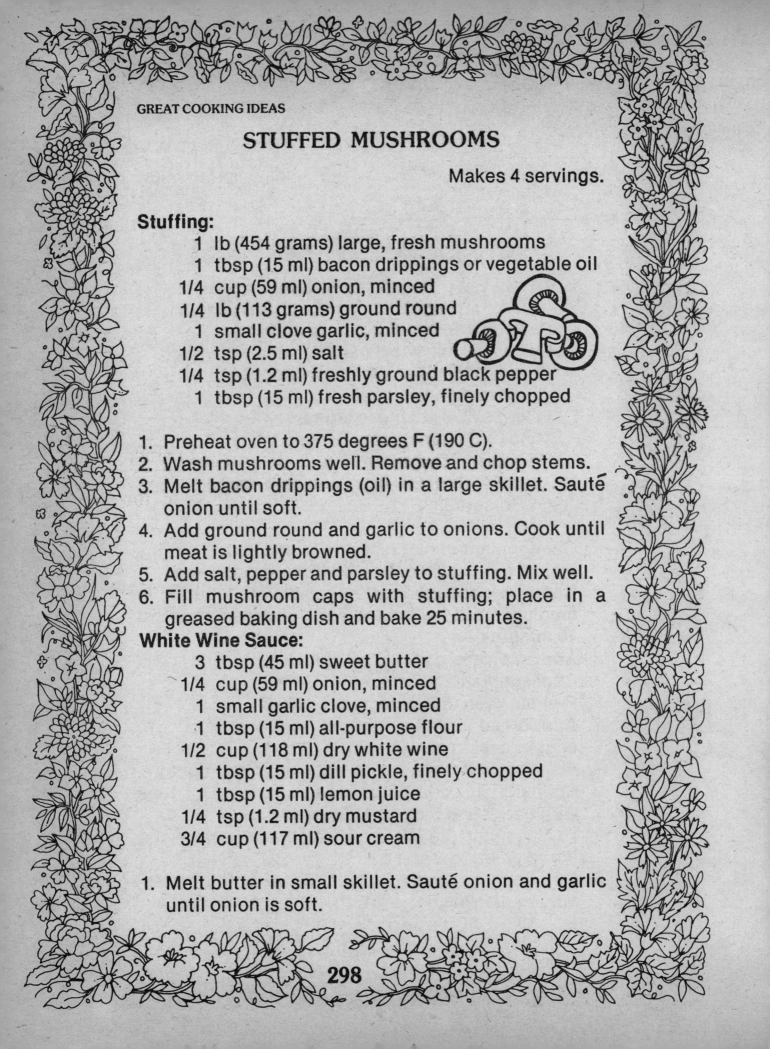

1. Preheat oven to 375 degrees F (190 C).
2. Wash mushrooms well. Remove and chop stems.
3. Melt bacon drippings (oil) in a large skillet. Sauté onion until soft.
4. Add ground round and garlic to onions. Cook until meat is lightly browned.
5. Add salt, pepper and parsley to stuffing. Mix well.
6. Fill mushroom caps with stuffing; place in a greased baking dish and bake 25 minutes.

White Wine Sauce:

    3 tbsp (45 ml) sweet butter
  1/4 cup (59 ml) onion, minced
    1 small garlic clove, minced
    1 tbsp (15 ml) all-purpose flour
  1/2 cup (118 ml) dry white wine
    1 tbsp (15 ml) dill pickle, finely chopped
    1 tbsp (15 ml) lemon juice
  1/4 tsp (1.2 ml) dry mustard
  3/4 cup (117 ml) sour cream

1. Melt butter in small skillet. Sauté onion and garlic until onion is soft.

2. Stir in flour. Add wine, pickle, lemon juice and dry mustard. Mix well.
3. Just before serving, stir sour cream into sauce and pour over mushrooms.

Variation: Substitute the following Rosemary Wine Sauce for White Wine Sauce.

Rosemary Wine Sauce:
- 1/2 cup (118 ml) dry sherry
- 1 tsp (5 ml) mixed dried marjoram, rosemary, sage, thyme and basil
- 1 cup (237 ml) BROWN SAUCE, p. 507

1. Heat sherry to boiling in a small saucepan.
2. Add mixed herbs and remove from heat. Let stand 5 to 10 minutes.
3. Strain off herb-flavored wine and add it to the Brown Sauce, which has been heated.

Serving Suggestions
With a salad Nicoise or cucumber salad, warm French bread and a Muscadet or Gamay Beaujolais.

NOTES

SWEDISH MEAT BALLS
(With Cream Gravy)

Makes 25 servings.

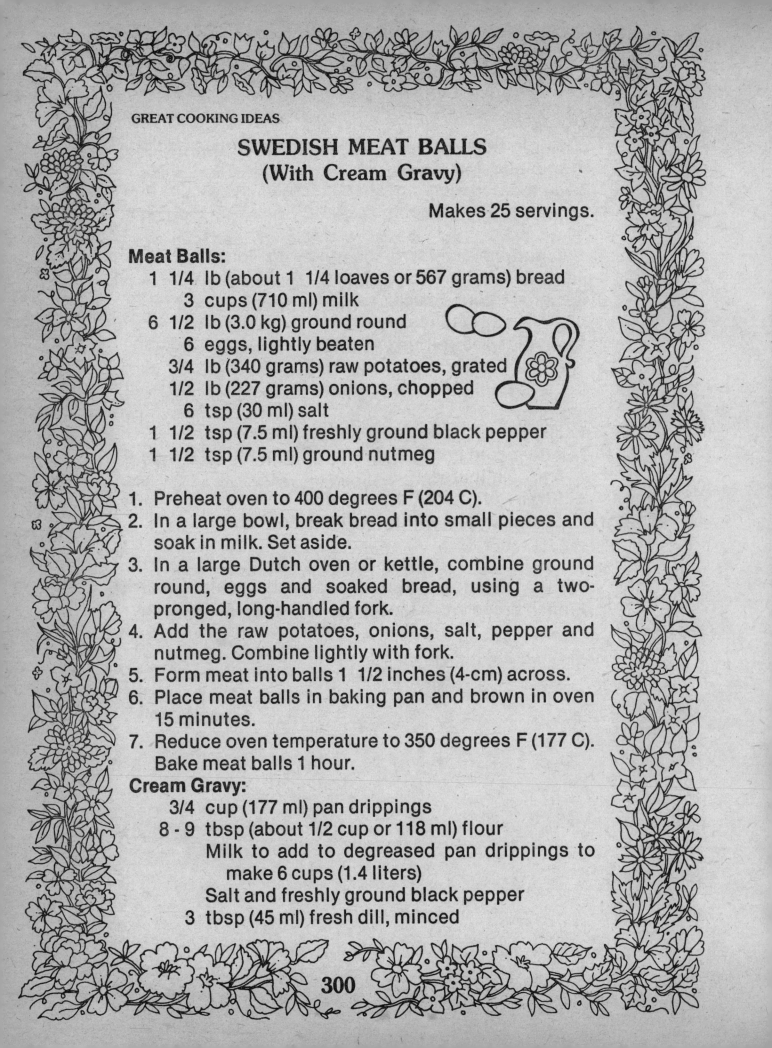

Meat Balls:
- 1 1/4 lb (about 1 1/4 loaves or 567 grams) bread
- 3 cups (710 ml) milk
- 6 1/2 lb (3.0 kg) ground round
- 6 eggs, lightly beaten
- 3/4 lb (340 grams) raw potatoes, grated
- 1/2 lb (227 grams) onions, chopped
- 6 tsp (30 ml) salt
- 1 1/2 tsp (7.5 ml) freshly ground black pepper
- 1 1/2 tsp (7.5 ml) ground nutmeg

1. Preheat oven to 400 degrees F (204 C).
2. In a large bowl, break bread into small pieces and soak in milk. Set aside.
3. In a large Dutch oven or kettle, combine ground round, eggs and soaked bread, using a two-pronged, long-handled fork.
4. Add the raw potatoes, onions, salt, pepper and nutmeg. Combine lightly with fork.
5. Form meat into balls 1 1/2 inches (4-cm) across.
6. Place meat balls in baking pan and brown in oven 15 minutes.
7. Reduce oven temperature to 350 degrees F (177 C). Bake meat balls 1 hour.

Cream Gravy:
- 3/4 cup (177 ml) pan drippings
- 8 - 9 tbsp (about 1/2 cup or 118 ml) flour
- Milk to add to degreased pan drippings to make 6 cups (1.4 liters)
- Salt and freshly ground black pepper
- 3 tbsp (45 ml) fresh dill, minced

1. Measure 3/4 cup pan drippings into a cup. Pour the remaining drippings into a heatproof glass container.
2. Clarify drippings by submerging the container in cold water. The fat will rise at once and can be spooned off.
3. Put 3/4 cup drippings in a large skillet over low heat and stir in flour with a wire whisk until the mixture is smooth and bubbly.
4. Measure degreased pan drippings and add enough milk to make 6 cups. Add this mixture slowly to flour mixture, stirring, until gravy begins to thicken.
5. Season gravy with salt and pepper to taste.
6. To serve, pour Cream Gravy over meat balls and sprinkle lightly with chopped chives.

Suggested Buffet Menu

Serve Swedish Meat Balls and Gravy
Side Dishes: Small potato dumplings and a tray of sliced fresh carrots and zucchini
Desserts: Chilled lemon meringue and coconut cream pies, vanilla custard and fresh fruit bowl
Beverages: Chilled dry white wine, beer and coffee

NOTES

STUFFED MEAT LOAF

Makes 10 servings.

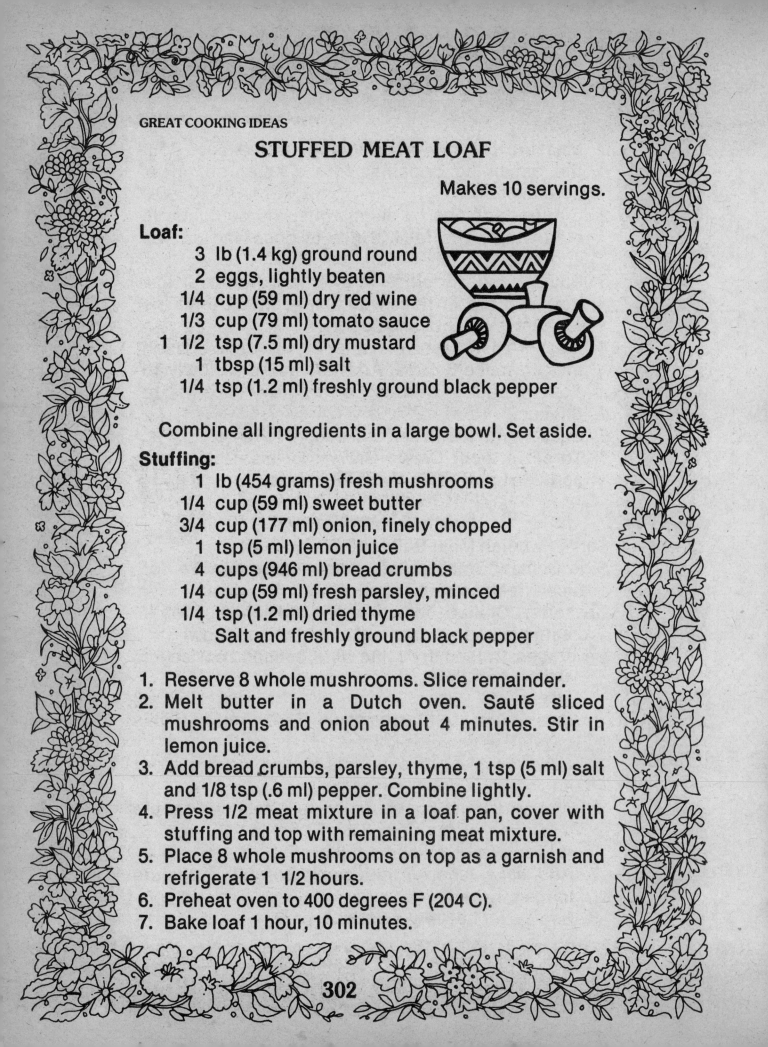

Loaf:

- 3 lb (1.4 kg) ground round
- 2 eggs, lightly beaten
- 1/4 cup (59 ml) dry red wine
- 1/3 cup (79 ml) tomato sauce
- 1 1/2 tsp (7.5 ml) dry mustard
- 1 tbsp (15 ml) salt
- 1/4 tsp (1.2 ml) freshly ground black pepper

Combine all ingredients in a large bowl. Set aside.

Stuffing:

- 1 lb (454 grams) fresh mushrooms
- 1/4 cup (59 ml) sweet butter
- 3/4 cup (177 ml) onion, finely chopped
- 1 tsp (5 ml) lemon juice
- 4 cups (946 ml) bread crumbs
- 1/4 cup (59 ml) fresh parsley, minced
- 1/4 tsp (1.2 ml) dried thyme
- Salt and freshly ground black pepper

1. Reserve 8 whole mushrooms. Slice remainder.
2. Melt butter in a Dutch oven. Sauté sliced mushrooms and onion about 4 minutes. Stir in lemon juice.
3. Add bread crumbs, parsley, thyme, 1 tsp (5 ml) salt and 1/8 tsp (.6 ml) pepper. Combine lightly.
4. Press 1/2 meat mixture in a loaf pan, cover with stuffing and top with remaining meat mixture.
5. Place 8 whole mushrooms on top as a garnish and refrigerate 1 1/2 hours.
6. Preheat oven to 400 degrees F (204 C).
7. Bake loaf 1 hour, 10 minutes.

SUKIYAKI*

Makes 8 servings.

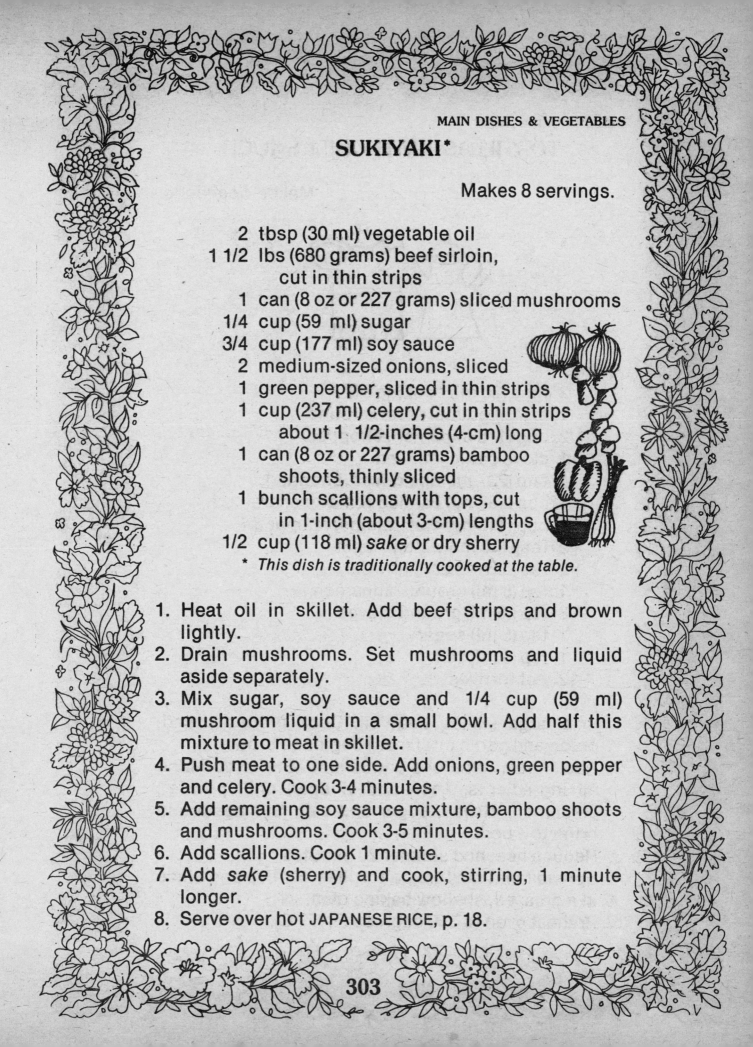

2 tbsp (30 ml) vegetable oil
1 1/2 lbs (680 grams) beef sirloin,
  cut in thin strips
1 can (8 oz or 227 grams) sliced mushrooms
1/4 cup (59 ml) sugar
3/4 cup (177 ml) soy sauce
2 medium-sized onions, sliced
1 green pepper, sliced in thin strips
1 cup (237 ml) celery, cut in thin strips
  about 1 1/2-inches (4-cm) long
1 can (8 oz or 227 grams) bamboo
  shoots, thinly sliced
1 bunch scallions with tops, cut
  in 1-inch (about 3-cm) lengths
1/2 cup (118 ml) *sake* or dry sherry

* *This dish is traditionally cooked at the table.*

1. Heat oil in skillet. Add beef strips and brown lightly.
2. Drain mushrooms. Set mushrooms and liquid aside separately.
3. Mix sugar, soy sauce and 1/4 cup (59 ml) mushroom liquid in a small bowl. Add half this mixture to meat in skillet.
4. Push meat to one side. Add onions, green pepper and celery. Cook 3-4 minutes.
5. Add remaining soy sauce mixture, bamboo shoots and mushrooms. Cook 3-5 minutes.
6. Add scallions. Cook 1 minute.
7. Add *sake* (sherry) and cook, stirring, 1 minute longer.
8. Serve over hot JAPANESE RICE, p. 18.

TORTILLAS WITH CHILI SAUCE

Makes 4 servings.

Filling:

2 tbsp (30 ml) cooking oil
1 lb (454 grams) ground round
1/2 cup (118 ml) onion, chopped
1 clove garlic, minced
1 cup (237 ml) ripe olives, chopped
1 cup (237 ml) canned tomatoes, drained
1/2 cup (118 ml) dark raisins, chopped
2 tbsp (30 ml) wine vinegar
1/2 tsp (2.5 ml) chili powder
1 tsp (5 ml) ground cinnamon
1/8 tsp (.6 ml) ground cloves
1 tsp (5 ml) sugar
1 tsp (5 ml) salt
12 hot tortillas

1. In a large skillet, heat oil. Cook ground round, onion and garlic until meat begins to brown.
2. Add olives, tomatoes and raisins. Stir to combine all ingredients. Then add vinegar, chili powder, cinnamon, cloves, sugar and salt. Stir again and bring to a boil.
3. Reduce heat and simmer 20 minutes.
4. Spread meat mixture on tortillas. Roll up and place in a greased, shallow baking dish.
5. Preheat oven to 350 degrees F (177 C)

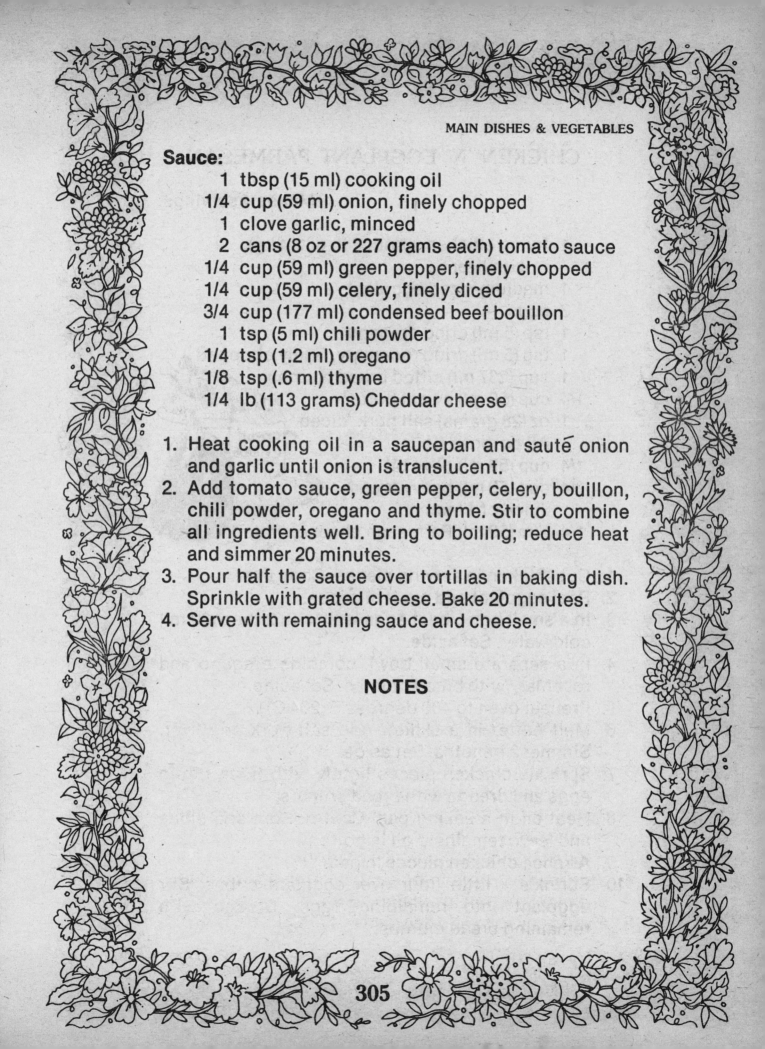

Sauce:

1	tbsp (15 ml) cooking oil
1/4	cup (59 ml) onion, finely chopped
1	clove garlic, minced
2	cans (8 oz or 227 grams each) tomato sauce
1/4	cup (59 ml) green pepper, finely chopped
1/4	cup (59 ml) celery, finely diced
3/4	cup (177 ml) condensed beef bouillon
1	tsp (5 ml) chili powder
1/4	tsp (1.2 ml) oregano
1/8	tsp (.6 ml) thyme
1/4	lb (113 grams) Cheddar cheese

1. Heat cooking oil in a saucepan and sauté onion and garlic until onion is translucent.
2. Add tomato sauce, green pepper, celery, bouillon, chili powder, oregano and thyme. Stir to combine all ingredients well. Bring to boiling; reduce heat and simmer 20 minutes.
3. Pour half the sauce over tortillas in baking dish. Sprinkle with grated cheese. Bake 20 minutes.
4. Serve with remaining sauce and cheese.

NOTES

CHICKEN 'N' EGGPLANT PARMESAN

Makes 4 servings.

1 frying chicken (about 3 lb or 1.4 kg), with liver
1 medium-sized eggplant
3 eggs
1 tsp (5 ml) dried oregano
1 tsp (5 ml) dried rosemary, finely chopped
1 cup (237 ml) sifted bread crumbs
1/4 cup (59 ml) sweet butter
1 oz (28 grams) salt pork, diced
   All-purpose flour
1/4 cup (59 ml) olive oil
1/4 cup (59 ml) heavy cream
   Juice of 1 lemon
1/4 cup (59 ml) Parmesan cheese, grated

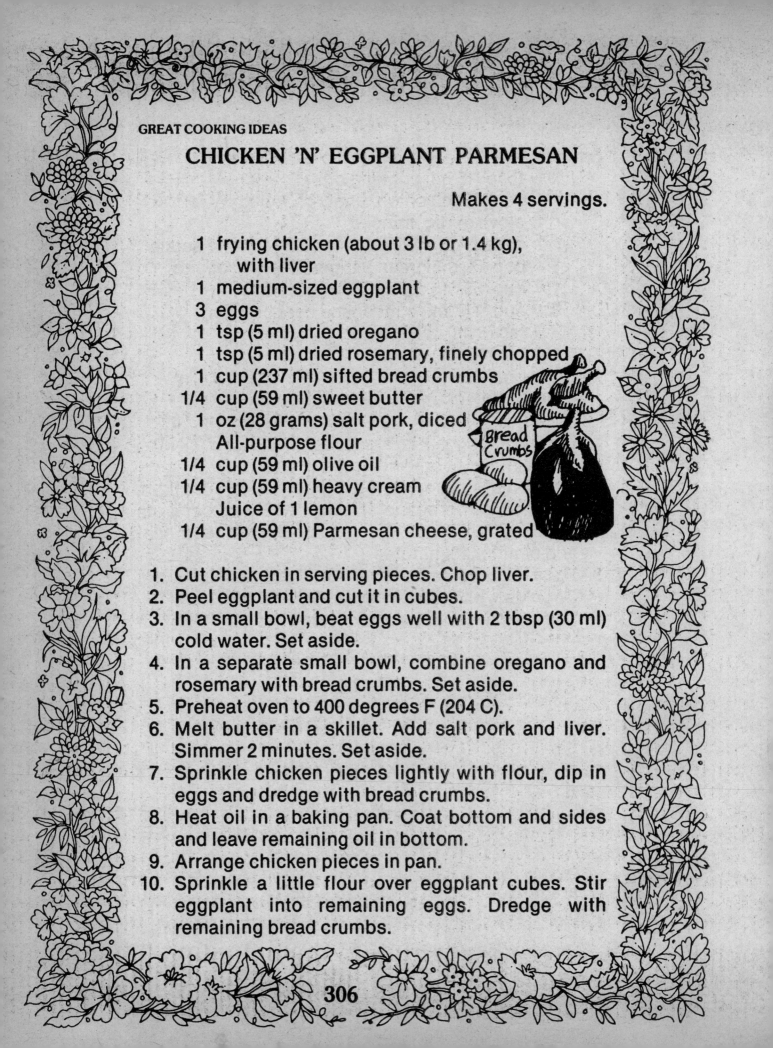

1. Cut chicken in serving pieces. Chop liver.
2. Peel eggplant and cut it in cubes.
3. In a small bowl, beat eggs well with 2 tbsp (30 ml) cold water. Set aside.
4. In a separate small bowl, combine oregano and rosemary with bread crumbs. Set aside.
5. Preheat oven to 400 degrees F (204 C).
6. Melt butter in a skillet. Add salt pork and liver. Simmer 2 minutes. Set aside.
7. Sprinkle chicken pieces lightly with flour, dip in eggs and dredge with bread crumbs.
8. Heat oil in a baking pan. Coat bottom and sides and leave remaining oil in bottom.
9. Arrange chicken pieces in pan.
10. Sprinkle a little flour over eggplant cubes. Stir eggplant into remaining eggs. Dredge with remaining bread crumbs.

11. Fill in empty spaces around and over chicken with eggplant.
12. Add cream to butter-liver mixture. Spoon over chicken and eggplant.
13. Sprinkle lemon juice and cheese over top. Place in oven 30 minutes. Reduce oven heat to 350 degrees F (177 C). Bake 30 minutes longer, or until tender.

* * *

LEMON-FLAVORED CHICKEN

Makes 4 servings.

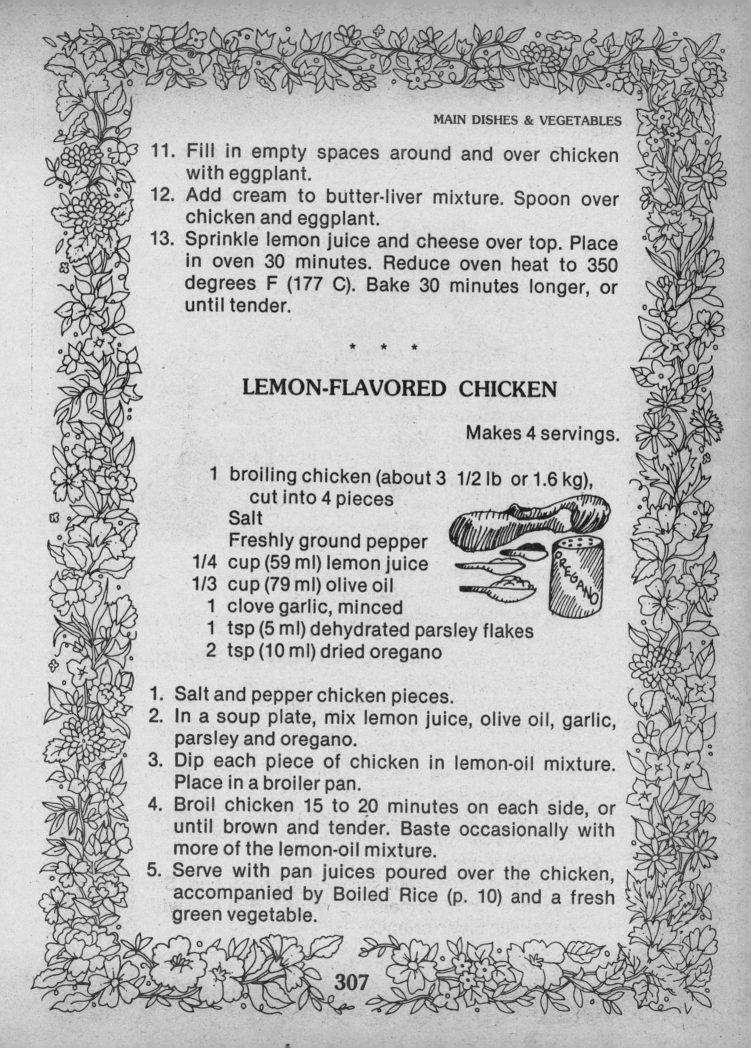

1 broiling chicken (about 3 1/2 lb or 1.6 kg), cut into 4 pieces
  Salt
  Freshly ground pepper
1/4 cup (59 ml) lemon juice
1/3 cup (79 ml) olive oil
1 clove garlic, minced
1 tsp (5 ml) dehydrated parsley flakes
2 tsp (10 ml) dried oregano

1. Salt and pepper chicken pieces.
2. In a soup plate, mix lemon juice, olive oil, garlic, parsley and oregano.
3. Dip each piece of chicken in lemon-oil mixture. Place in a broiler pan.
4. Broil chicken 15 to 20 minutes on each side, or until brown and tender. Baste occasionally with more of the lemon-oil mixture.
5. Serve with pan juices poured over the chicken, accompanied by Boiled Rice (p. 10) and a fresh green vegetable.

CHICKEN 'N' PEPPERS

Makes 6 servings.

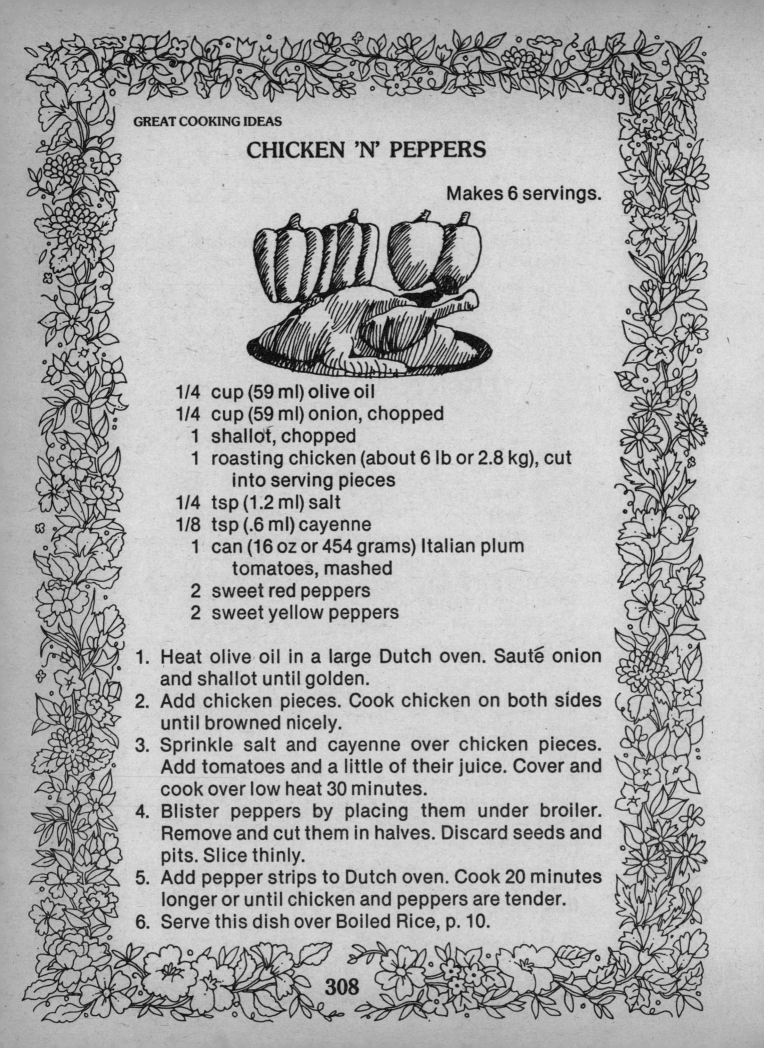

1/4 cup (59 ml) olive oil
1/4 cup (59 ml) onion, chopped
1 shallot, chopped
1 roasting chicken (about 6 lb or 2.8 kg), cut into serving pieces
1/4 tsp (1.2 ml) salt
1/8 tsp (.6 ml) cayenne
1 can (16 oz or 454 grams) Italian plum tomatoes, mashed
2 sweet red peppers
2 sweet yellow peppers

1. Heat olive oil in a large Dutch oven. Sauté onion and shallot until golden.
2. Add chicken pieces. Cook chicken on both sides until browned nicely.
3. Sprinkle salt and cayenne over chicken pieces. Add tomatoes and a little of their juice. Cover and cook over low heat 30 minutes.
4. Blister peppers by placing them under broiler. Remove and cut them in halves. Discard seeds and pits. Slice thinly.
5. Add pepper strips to Dutch oven. Cook 20 minutes longer or until chicken and peppers are tender.
6. Serve this dish over Boiled Rice, p. 10.

CHICKEN 'N' SNOW PEAS

Makes 6 servings.

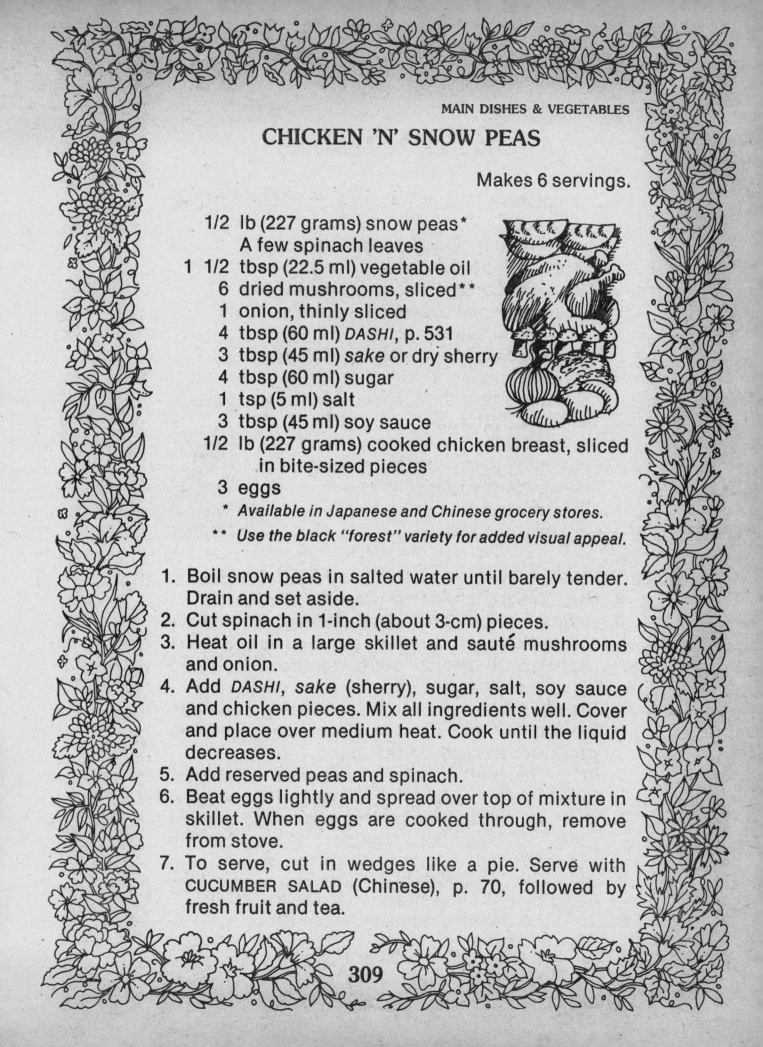

1/2 lb (227 grams) snow peas*
     A few spinach leaves
1 1/2 tbsp (22.5 ml) vegetable oil
   6 dried mushrooms, sliced**
   1 onion, thinly sliced
   4 tbsp (60 ml) *DASHI*, p. 531
   3 tbsp (45 ml) *sake* or dry sherry
   4 tbsp (60 ml) sugar
   1 tsp (5 ml) salt
   3 tbsp (45 ml) soy sauce
1/2 lb (227 grams) cooked chicken breast, sliced
     in bite-sized pieces
   3 eggs

  * *Available in Japanese and Chinese grocery stores.*

 ** *Use the black "forest" variety for added visual appeal.*

1. Boil snow peas in salted water until barely tender. Drain and set aside.
2. Cut spinach in 1-inch (about 3-cm) pieces.
3. Heat oil in a large skillet and sauté mushrooms and onion.
4. Add *DASHI*, *sake* (sherry), sugar, salt, soy sauce and chicken pieces. Mix all ingredients well. Cover and place over medium heat. Cook until the liquid decreases.
5. Add reserved peas and spinach.
6. Beat eggs lightly and spread over top of mixture in skillet. When eggs are cooked through, remove from stove.
7. To serve, cut in wedges like a pie. Serve with CUCUMBER SALAD (Chinese), p. 70, followed by fresh fruit and tea.

CHICKEN 'N' RICE

3 chickens (3 lb or 1.4 kg each), cut in 6 pieces
    each
    Salt and freshly ground black pepper
3 cups (710 ml) olive oil
2 cloves garlic; 1 whole, 1 minced
2 green peppers, seeded and cut in 1-inch
    (3-cm) strips
1 large can (2 lb or 907 grams) Italian plum
    tomatoes
2 cans (8 oz or 227 grams each) tomato sauce
1/2 tsp (2.5 ml) sugar
3 cups (710 ml) uncooked rice
3 cups (710 ml) POULTRY STOCK, p. 528
1/8 tsp (.6 ml) saffron
1 can (1 lb or 454 grams) tiny peas
1 small can pimientos

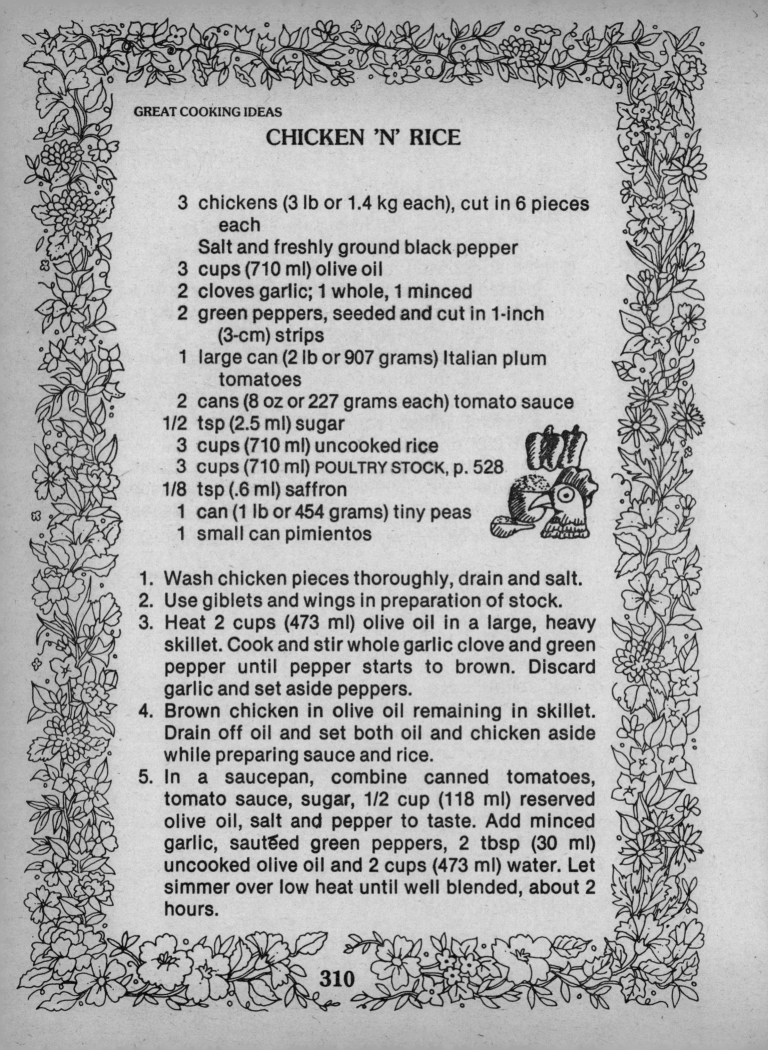

1. Wash chicken pieces thoroughly, drain and salt.
2. Use giblets and wings in preparation of stock.
3. Heat 2 cups (473 ml) olive oil in a large, heavy skillet. Cook and stir whole garlic clove and green pepper until pepper starts to brown. Discard garlic and set aside peppers.
4. Brown chicken in olive oil remaining in skillet. Drain off oil and set both oil and chicken aside while preparing sauce and rice.
5. In a saucepan, combine canned tomatoes, tomato sauce, sugar, 1/2 cup (118 ml) reserved olive oil, salt and pepper to taste. Add minced garlic, sautéed green peppers, 2 tbsp (30 ml) uncooked olive oil and 2 cups (473 ml) water. Let simmer over low heat until well blended, about 2 hours.

6. Wash rice in a bowl of cold, salted water. Rinse in tepid water.
7. Bring stock to boiling in a large saucepan.
8. Heat remaining olive oil until it is hot enough to brown a cube of bread.
9. Add hot oil, 1 tsp (5 ml) salt and saffron to stock. Mix well. Add rice and allow mixture to come to boiling, uncovered. After 5 minutes, cover, reduce heat and cook 25 minutes longer.
10. When liquid has been absorbed, remove lid and stir rice gently from sides and bottom of pan.
11. Add chicken to sauce (Step 5) and let simmer until nearly tender, about 30 minutes.
12. Preheat oven to 375 degrees F (190 C).
13. In a 12-inch (30-cm) glass or pottery baking dish, arrange a layer of cooked rice 1 inch (3 cm) deep. Place a layer of chicken on top of rice. Repeat layers. Cover with a layer of rice, topped with a layer of peas. Bake, uncovered 30 minutes.
14. A few minutes before serving, garnish with strips of pimiento.

NOTES

CHICKEN FRENCH COUNTRY-STYLE

Makes 4 or 5 servings.

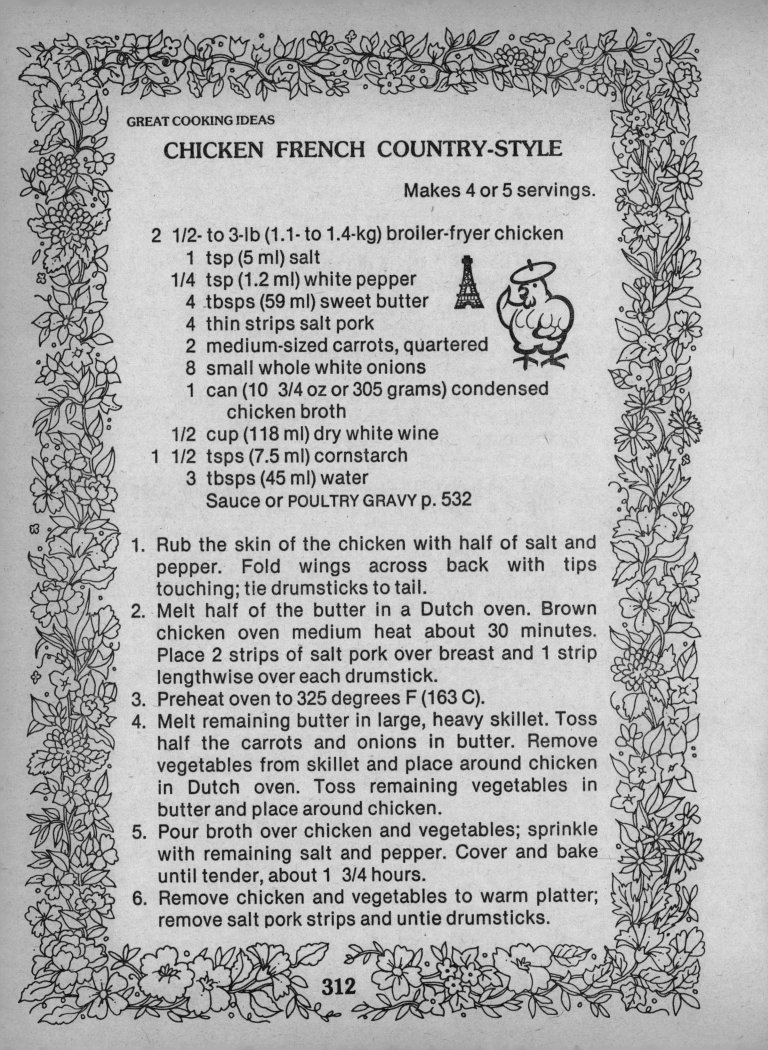

2 1/2- to 3-lb (1.1- to 1.4-kg) broiler-fryer chicken
1 tsp (5 ml) salt
1/4 tsp (1.2 ml) white pepper
4 tbsps (59 ml) sweet butter
4 thin strips salt pork
2 medium-sized carrots, quartered
8 small whole white onions
1 can (10 3/4 oz or 305 grams) condensed
  chicken broth
1/2 cup (118 ml) dry white wine
1 1/2 tsps (7.5 ml) cornstarch
3 tbsps (45 ml) water
Sauce or POULTRY GRAVY p. 532

1. Rub the skin of the chicken with half of salt and pepper. Fold wings across back with tips touching; tie drumsticks to tail.
2. Melt half of the butter in a Dutch oven. Brown chicken oven medium heat about 30 minutes. Place 2 strips of salt pork over breast and 1 strip lengthwise over each drumstick.
3. Preheat oven to 325 degrees F (163 C).
4. Melt remaining butter in large, heavy skillet. Toss half the carrots and onions in butter. Remove vegetables from skillet and place around chicken in Dutch oven. Toss remaining vegetables in butter and place around chicken.
5. Pour broth over chicken and vegetables; sprinkle with remaining salt and pepper. Cover and bake until tender, about 1 3/4 hours.
6. Remove chicken and vegetables to warm platter; remove salt pork strips and untie drumsticks.

Sauce:

1. Stir white wine into chicken broth remaining in Dutch oven. Heat to boiling, stirring constantly. Boil and stir 3 minutes. Mix cornstarch and water; stir into wine broth. Heat again to boiling, stirring constantly. Boil and stir 3 more minutes; skim off fat. Serve sauce with chicken and vegetables.

* * *

BAMBOO CHICKEN

Makes 6 servings.

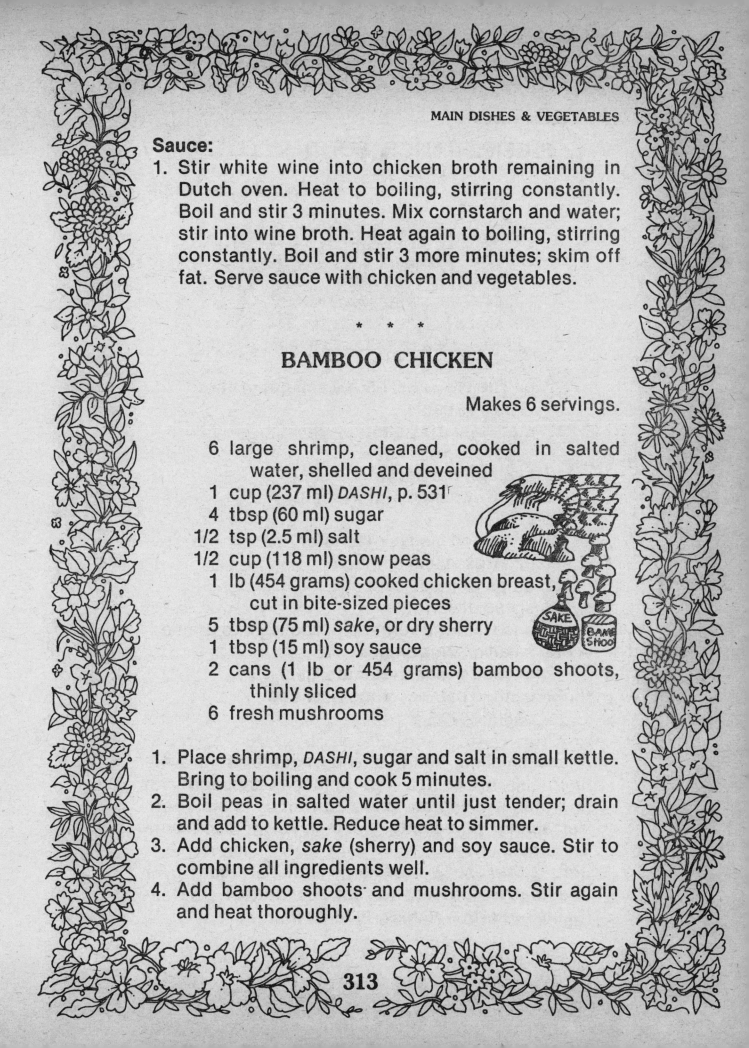

6 large shrimp, cleaned, cooked in salted water, shelled and deveined
1 cup (237 ml) *DASHI*, p. 531
4 tbsp (60 ml) sugar
1/2 tsp (2.5 ml) salt
1/2 cup (118 ml) snow peas
1 lb (454 grams) cooked chicken breast, cut in bite-sized pieces
5 tbsp (75 ml) *sake*, or dry sherry
1 tbsp (15 ml) soy sauce
2 cans (1 lb or 454 grams) bamboo shoots, thinly sliced
6 fresh mushrooms

1. Place shrimp, *DASHI*, sugar and salt in small kettle. Bring to boiling and cook 5 minutes.
2. Boil peas in salted water until just tender; drain and add to kettle. Reduce heat to simmer.
3. Add chicken, *sake* (sherry) and soy sauce. Stir to combine all ingredients well.
4. Add bamboo shoots and mushrooms. Stir again and heat thoroughly.

CHICKEN 'N' SEAFOOD SKILLET

Makes 6 servings.

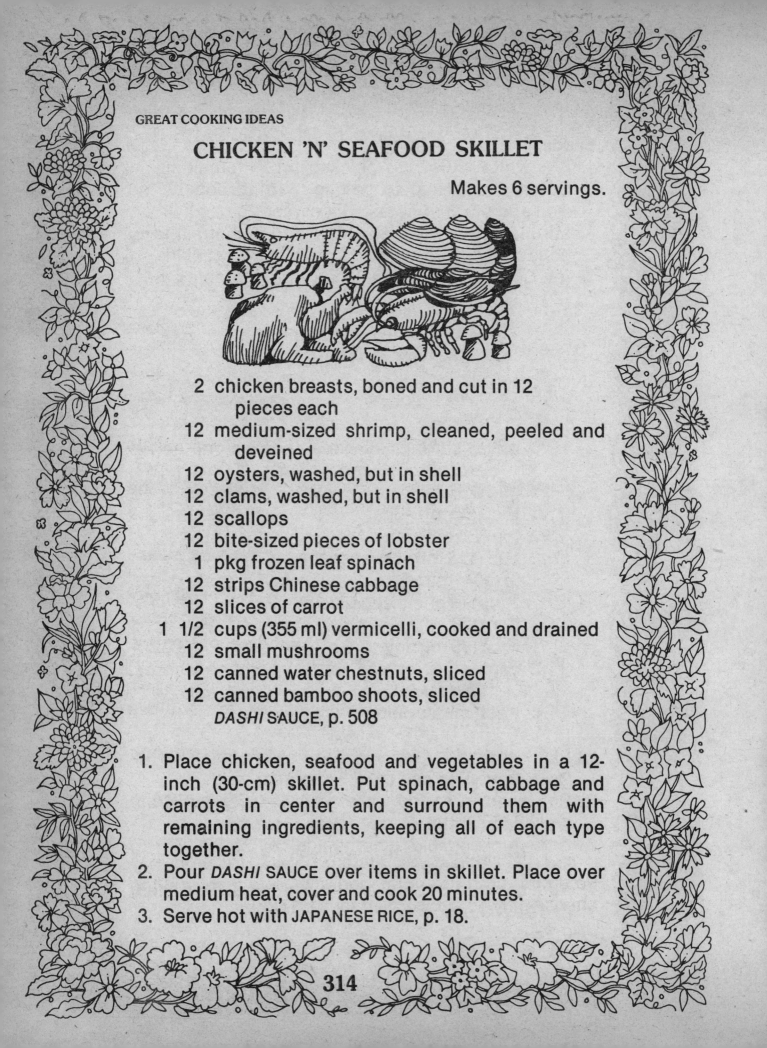

2	chicken breasts, boned and cut in 12 pieces each
12	medium-sized shrimp, cleaned, peeled and deveined
12	oysters, washed, but in shell
12	clams, washed, but in shell
12	scallops
12	bite-sized pieces of lobster
1	pkg frozen leaf spinach
12	strips Chinese cabbage
12	slices of carrot
1 1/2	cups (355 ml) vermicelli, cooked and drained
12	small mushrooms
12	canned water chestnuts, sliced
12	canned bamboo shoots, sliced
	DASHI SAUCE, p. 508

1. Place chicken, seafood and vegetables in a 12-inch (30-cm) skillet. Put spinach, cabbage and carrots in center and surround them with remaining ingredients, keeping all of each type together.
2. Pour DASHI SAUCE over items in skillet. Place over medium heat, cover and cook 20 minutes.
3. Serve hot with JAPANESE RICE, p. 18.

CHICKEN BREASTS 'N' TRUFFLES

Makes 4 servings.

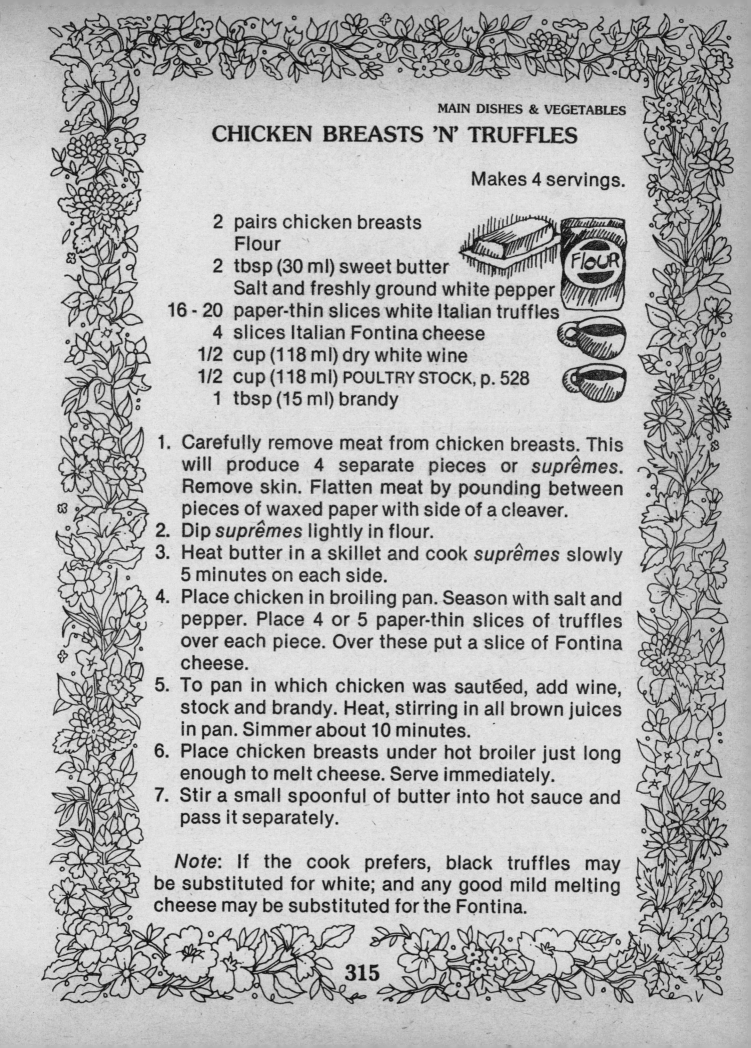

- 2 pairs chicken breasts
  Flour
- 2 tbsp (30 ml) sweet butter
  Salt and freshly ground white pepper
- 16 - 20 paper-thin slices white Italian truffles
- 4 slices Italian Fontina cheese
- 1/2 cup (118 ml) dry white wine
- 1/2 cup (118 ml) POULTRY STOCK, p. 528
- 1 tbsp (15 ml) brandy

1. Carefully remove meat from chicken breasts. This will produce 4 separate pieces or *suprêmes*. Remove skin. Flatten meat by pounding between pieces of waxed paper with side of a cleaver.
2. Dip *suprêmes* lightly in flour.
3. Heat butter in a skillet and cook *suprêmes* slowly 5 minutes on each side.
4. Place chicken in broiling pan. Season with salt and pepper. Place 4 or 5 paper-thin slices of truffles over each piece. Over these put a slice of Fontina cheese.
5. To pan in which chicken was sautéed, add wine, stock and brandy. Heat, stirring in all brown juices in pan. Simmer about 10 minutes.
6. Place chicken breasts under hot broiler just long enough to melt cheese. Serve immediately.
7. Stir a small spoonful of butter into hot sauce and pass it separately.

Note: If the cook prefers, black truffles may be substituted for white; and any good mild melting cheese may be substituted for the Fontina.

CHICKEN BREASTS BAKED WITH BACON AND CHEESE

Makes 4 - 6 servings.

- 2 pairs chicken breasts
  Salt and freshly ground black pepper
  Flour
- 1 egg, beaten lightly with a few drops water
  Fine bread crumbs
- 6 tbsp (90 ml) sweet butter
- 4 tbsp (60 ml) olive oil
- 16 slices Canadian bacon
- 8 thin slices Fontina cheese

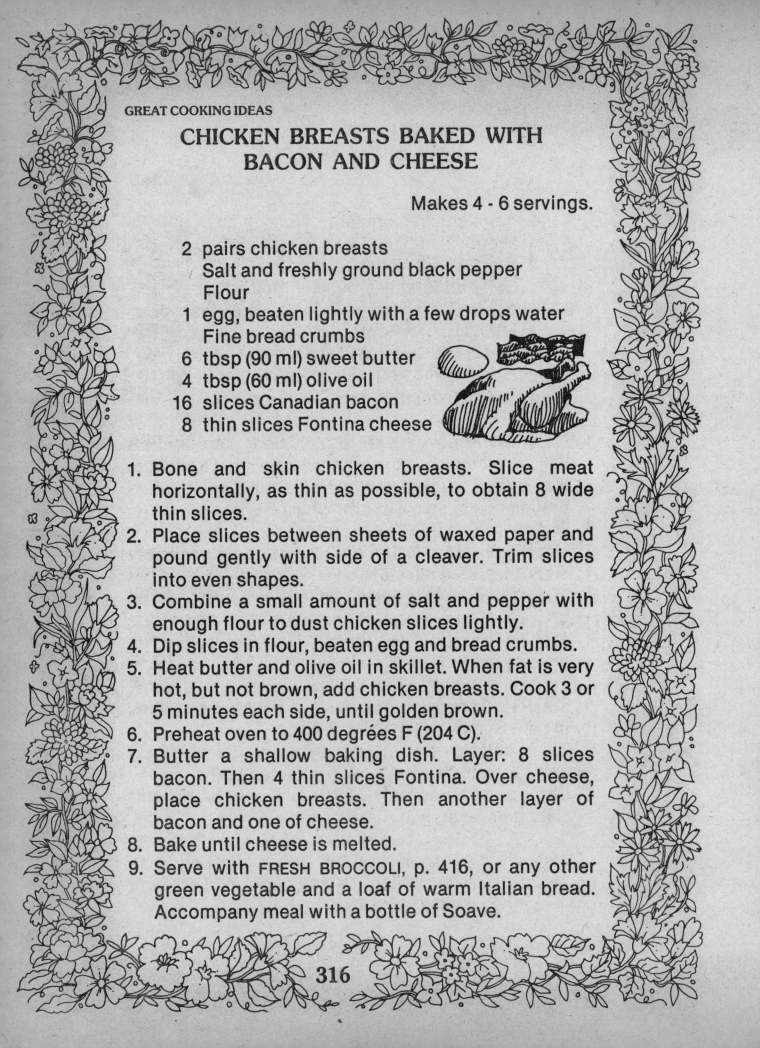

1. Bone and skin chicken breasts. Slice meat horizontally, as thin as possible, to obtain 8 wide thin slices.
2. Place slices between sheets of waxed paper and pound gently with side of a cleaver. Trim slices into even shapes.
3. Combine a small amount of salt and pepper with enough flour to dust chicken slices lightly.
4. Dip slices in flour, beaten egg and bread crumbs.
5. Heat butter and olive oil in skillet. When fat is very hot, but not brown, add chicken breasts. Cook 3 or 5 minutes each side, until golden brown.
6. Preheat oven to 400 degrées F (204 C).
7. Butter a shallow baking dish. Layer: 8 slices bacon. Then 4 thin slices Fontina. Over cheese, place chicken breasts. Then another layer of bacon and one of cheese.
8. Bake until cheese is melted.
9. Serve with FRESH BROCCOLI, p. 416, or any other green vegetable and a loaf of warm Italian bread. Accompany meal with a bottle of Soave.

CHICKEN CUSTARD

Makes 6 servings.

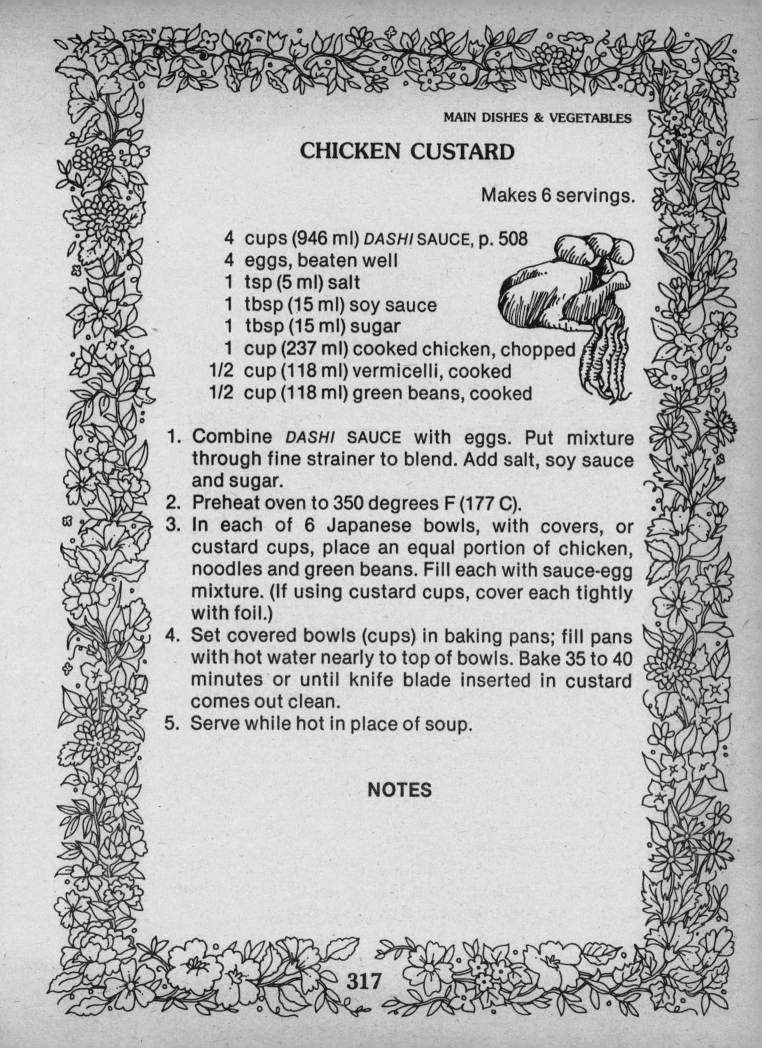

4 cups (946 ml) *DASHI* SAUCE, p. 508
4 eggs, beaten well
1 tsp (5 ml) salt
1 tbsp (15 ml) soy sauce
1 tbsp (15 ml) sugar
1 cup (237 ml) cooked chicken, chopped
1/2 cup (118 ml) vermicelli, cooked
1/2 cup (118 ml) green beans, cooked

1. Combine *DASHI* SAUCE with eggs. Put mixture through fine strainer to blend. Add salt, soy sauce and sugar.
2. Preheat oven to 350 degrees F (177 C).
3. In each of 6 Japanese bowls, with covers, or custard cups, place an equal portion of chicken, noodles and green beans. Fill each with sauce-egg mixture. (If using custard cups, cover each tightly with foil.)
4. Set covered bowls (cups) in baking pans; fill pans with hot water nearly to top of bowls. Bake 35 to 40 minutes or until knife blade inserted in custard comes out clean.
5. Serve while hot in place of soup.

NOTES

CHICKEN FLORENTINE

Makes 6 - 8 servings.

- 1/2 cup (118 ml) flour
- 1/4 tsp (1.2 ml) salt
- 1/4 tsp (1.2 ml) freshly ground black pepper
- 1 egg
- 1 tbsp (15 ml) red wine
- 4 chicken breasts, boned, skinned and cut in halves
- 2 oz (57 grams) Parmesan cheese, grated
- 1/2 cup (118 ml) bread crumbs
- 3/4 cup (177 ml) sweet butter
- Juice of 1/2 lemon
- 1 pkg frozen spinach, cooked, drained and chopped
- 1 lb (454 grams) fresh mushrooms

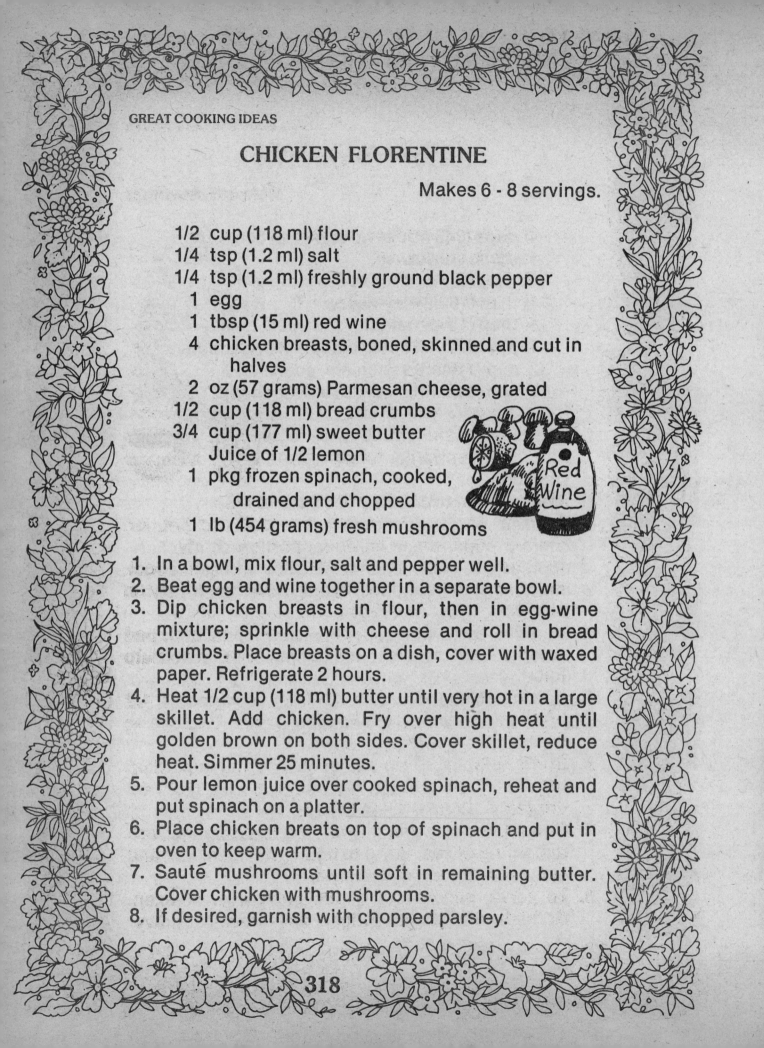

1. In a bowl, mix flour, salt and pepper well.
2. Beat egg and wine together in a separate bowl.
3. Dip chicken breasts in flour, then in egg-wine mixture; sprinkle with cheese and roll in bread crumbs. Place breasts on a dish, cover with waxed paper. Refrigerate 2 hours.
4. Heat 1/2 cup (118 ml) butter until very hot in a large skillet. Add chicken. Fry over high heat until golden brown on both sides. Cover skillet, reduce heat. Simmer 25 minutes.
5. Pour lemon juice over cooked spinach, reheat and put spinach on a platter.
6. Place chicken breats on top of spinach and put in oven to keep warm.
7. Sauté mushrooms until soft in remaining butter. Cover chicken with mushrooms.
8. If desired, garnish with chopped parsley.

CHICKEN WITH OLIVES

Makes 6 servings.

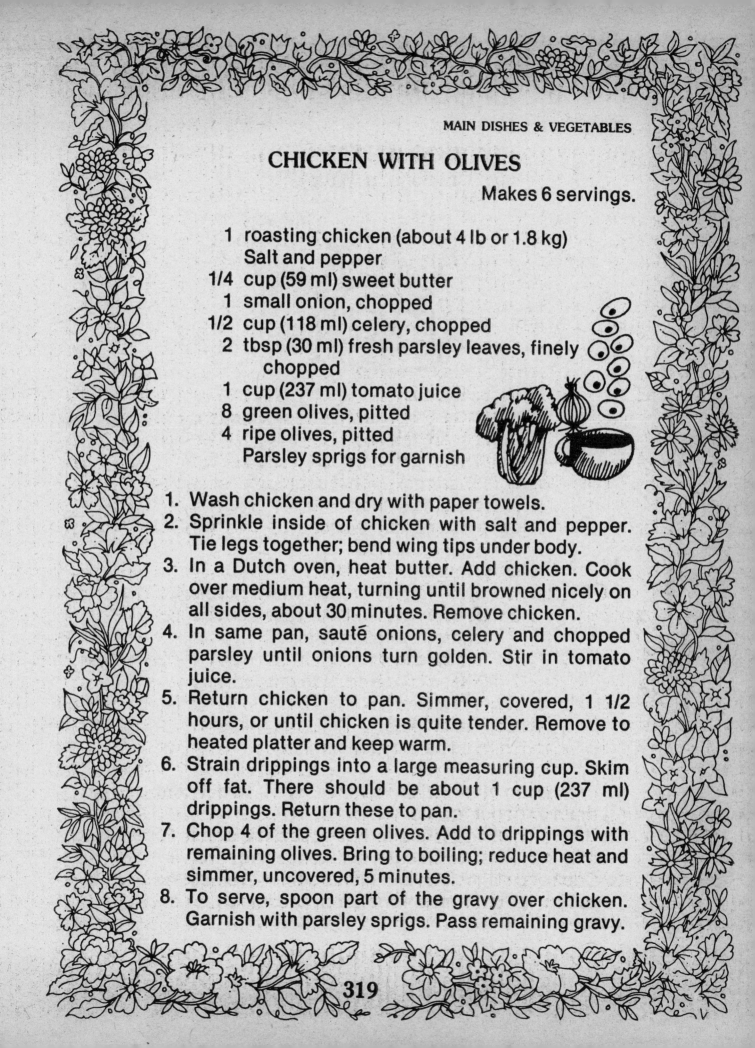

- 1 roasting chicken (about 4 lb or 1.8 kg)
  Salt and pepper
- 1/4 cup (59 ml) sweet butter
- 1 small onion, chopped
- 1/2 cup (118 ml) celery, chopped
- 2 tbsp (30 ml) fresh parsley leaves, finely chopped
- 1 cup (237 ml) tomato juice
- 8 green olives, pitted
- 4 ripe olives, pitted
  Parsley sprigs for garnish

1. Wash chicken and dry with paper towels.
2. Sprinkle inside of chicken with salt and pepper. Tie legs together; bend wing tips under body.
3. In a Dutch oven, heat butter. Add chicken. Cook over medium heat, turning until browned nicely on all sides, about 30 minutes. Remove chicken.
4. In same pan, sauté onions, celery and chopped parsley until onions turn golden. Stir in tomato juice.
5. Return chicken to pan. Simmer, covered, 1 1/2 hours, or until chicken is quite tender. Remove to heated platter and keep warm.
6. Strain drippings into a large measuring cup. Skim off fat. There should be about 1 cup (237 ml) drippings. Return these to pan.
7. Chop 4 of the green olives. Add to drippings with remaining olives. Bring to boiling; reduce heat and simmer, uncovered, 5 minutes.
8. To serve, spoon part of the gravy over chicken. Garnish with parsley sprigs. Pass remaining gravy.

COQ AU VIN
(Chicken In Wine)

Makes 4 servings.

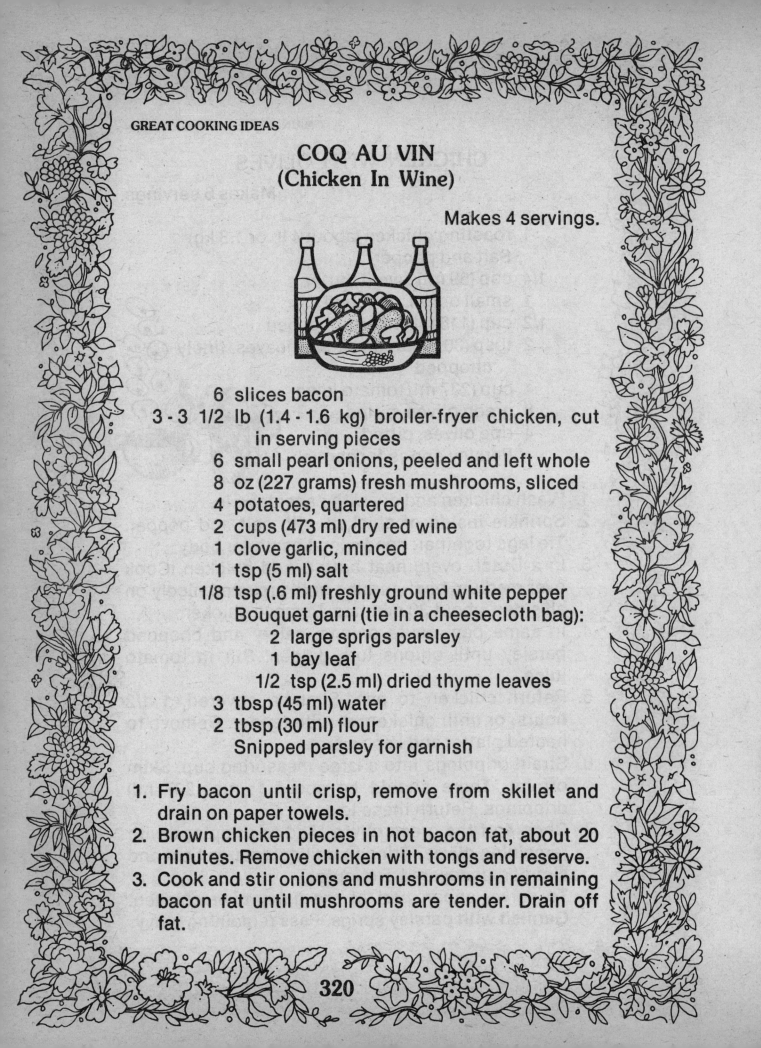

6 slices bacon

3 - 3 1/2 lb (1.4 - 1.6 kg) broiler-fryer chicken, cut in serving pieces

6 small pearl onions, peeled and left whole

8 oz (227 grams) fresh mushrooms, sliced

4 potatoes, quartered

2 cups (473 ml) dry red wine

1 clove garlic, minced

1 tsp (5 ml) salt

1/8 tsp (.6 ml) freshly ground white pepper

Bouquet garni (tie in a cheesecloth bag):
    2 large sprigs parsley
    1 bay leaf
    1/2 tsp (2.5 ml) dried thyme leaves

3 tbsp (45 ml) water

2 tbsp (30 ml) flour

Snipped parsley for garnish

1. Fry bacon until crisp, remove from skillet and drain on paper towels.

2. Brown chicken pieces in hot bacon fat, about 20 minutes. Remove chicken with tongs and reserve.

3. Cook and stir onions and mushrooms in remaining bacon fat until mushrooms are tender. Drain off fat.

4. Return chicken pieces to skillet.
5. Crumble bacon into skillet. Stir in potatoes, wine, garlic, salt and pepper and the bouquet garni. Heat to boiling, reduce heat, cover and simmer about 1 hour, until chicken is tender.
6. Remove bouquet garni and discard.
7. Remove chicken and vegetables to warm serving dish and keep warm while preparing sauce.
8. Skim excess fat off liquid. Mix 3 tbsp water and flour in a cup. Stir flour mixture slowly into liquid. Heat to boiling, stirring constantly. Boil and stir 1 minute.
9. Pour sauce over chicken and sprinkle with parsley.

Suggested Menu

Soup: Consommé
Main Course: Coq au Vin with buttered noodles or warm French bread
Salad: Sliced tomatoes and cucumbers with a light French dressing
Wine: Grey Riesling or Pinot Chardonnay
Dessert: Bavarian cream or fruit salad with cream
Coffee and Cognac

NOTES

CHICKEN WITH WATER CHESTNUTS

Makes 6 - 8 servings.

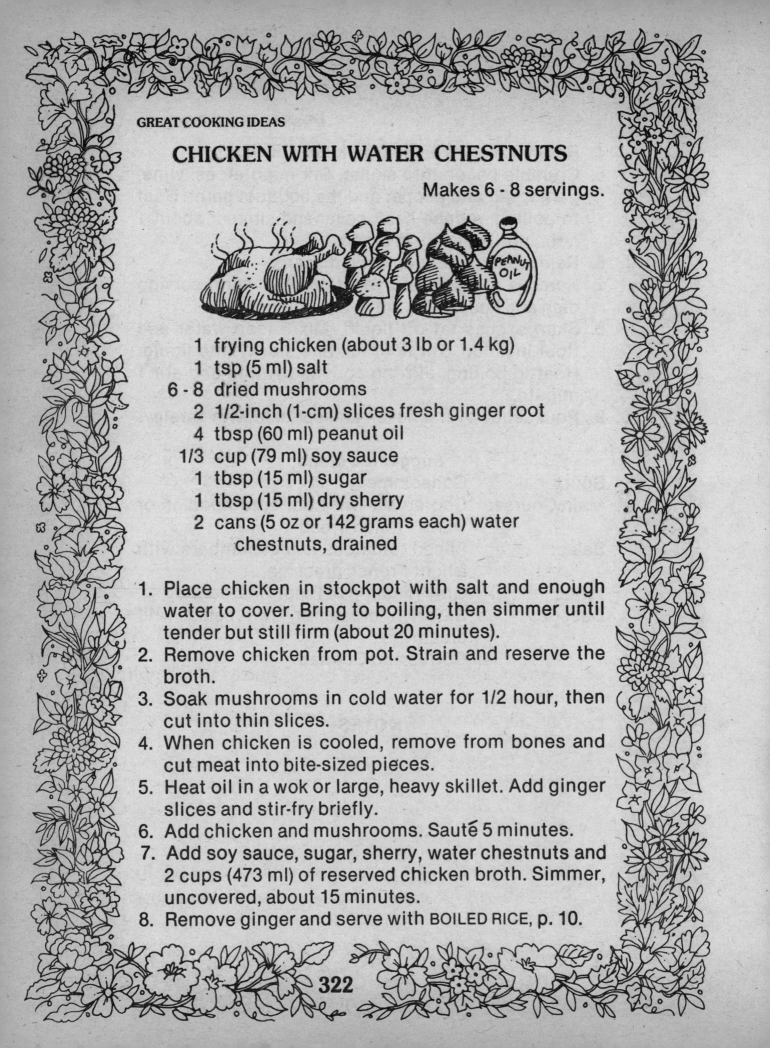

- 1 frying chicken (about 3 lb or 1.4 kg)
- 1 tsp (5 ml) salt
- 6 - 8 dried mushrooms
- 2 1/2-inch (1-cm) slices fresh ginger root
- 4 tbsp (60 ml) peanut oil
- 1/3 cup (79 ml) soy sauce
- 1 tbsp (15 ml) sugar
- 1 tbsp (15 ml) dry sherry
- 2 cans (5 oz or 142 grams each) water chestnuts, drained

1. Place chicken in stockpot with salt and enough water to cover. Bring to boiling, then simmer until tender but still firm (about 20 minutes).
2. Remove chicken from pot. Strain and reserve the broth.
3. Soak mushrooms in cold water for 1/2 hour, then cut into thin slices.
4. When chicken is cooled, remove from bones and cut meat into bite-sized pieces.
5. Heat oil in a wok or large, heavy skillet. Add ginger slices and stir-fry briefly.
6. Add chicken and mushrooms. Sauté 5 minutes.
7. Add soy sauce, sugar, sherry, water chestnuts and 2 cups (473 ml) of reserved chicken broth. Simmer, uncovered, about 15 minutes.
8. Remove ginger and serve with BOILED RICE, p. 10.

MALAYAN CHICKEN

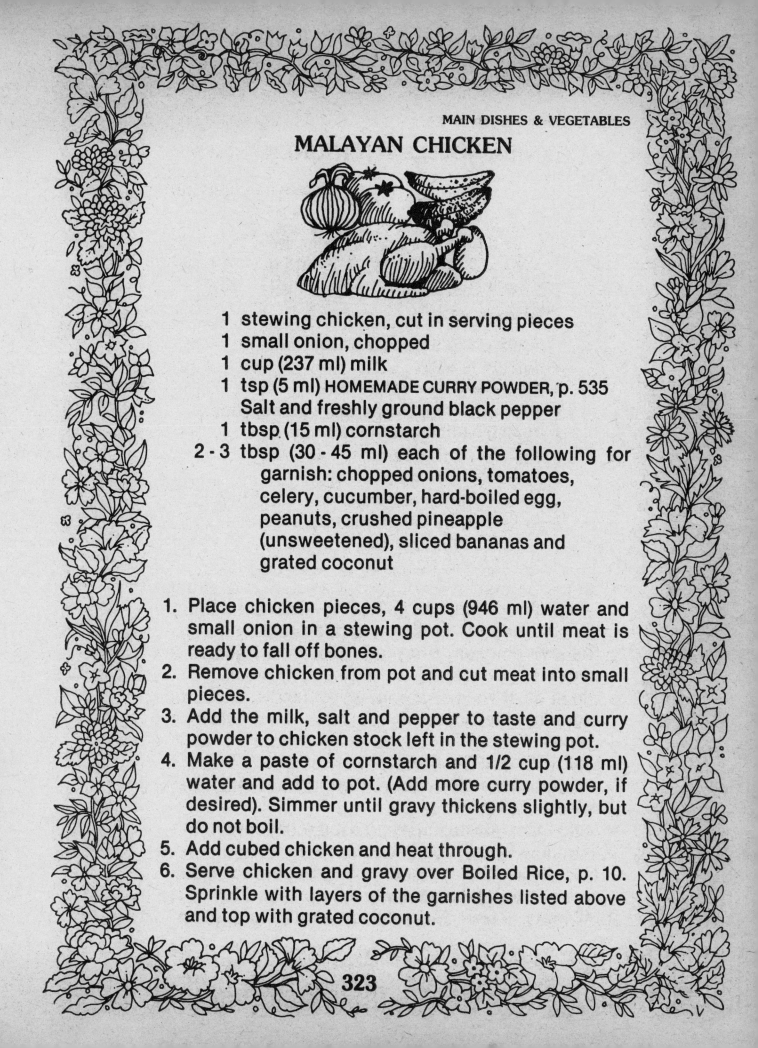

1 stewing chicken, cut in serving pieces
1 small onion, chopped
1 cup (237 ml) milk
1 tsp (5 ml) HOMEMADE CURRY POWDER, p. 535
Salt and freshly ground black pepper
1 tbsp (15 ml) cornstarch
2 - 3 tbsp (30 - 45 ml) each of the following for garnish: chopped onions, tomatoes, celery, cucumber, hard-boiled egg, peanuts, crushed pineapple (unsweetened), sliced bananas and grated coconut

1. Place chicken pieces, 4 cups (946 ml) water and small onion in a stewing pot. Cook until meat is ready to fall off bones.
2. Remove chicken from pot and cut meat into small pieces.
3. Add the milk, salt and pepper to taste and curry powder to chicken stock left in the stewing pot.
4. Make a paste of cornstarch and 1/2 cup (118 ml) water and add to pot. (Add more curry powder, if desired). Simmer until gravy thickens slightly, but do not boil.
5. Add cubed chicken and heat through.
6. Serve chicken and gravy over Boiled Rice, p. 10. Sprinkle with layers of the garnishes listed above and top with grated coconut.

VERMICELLI 'N' CHICKEN

Makes 4 servings.

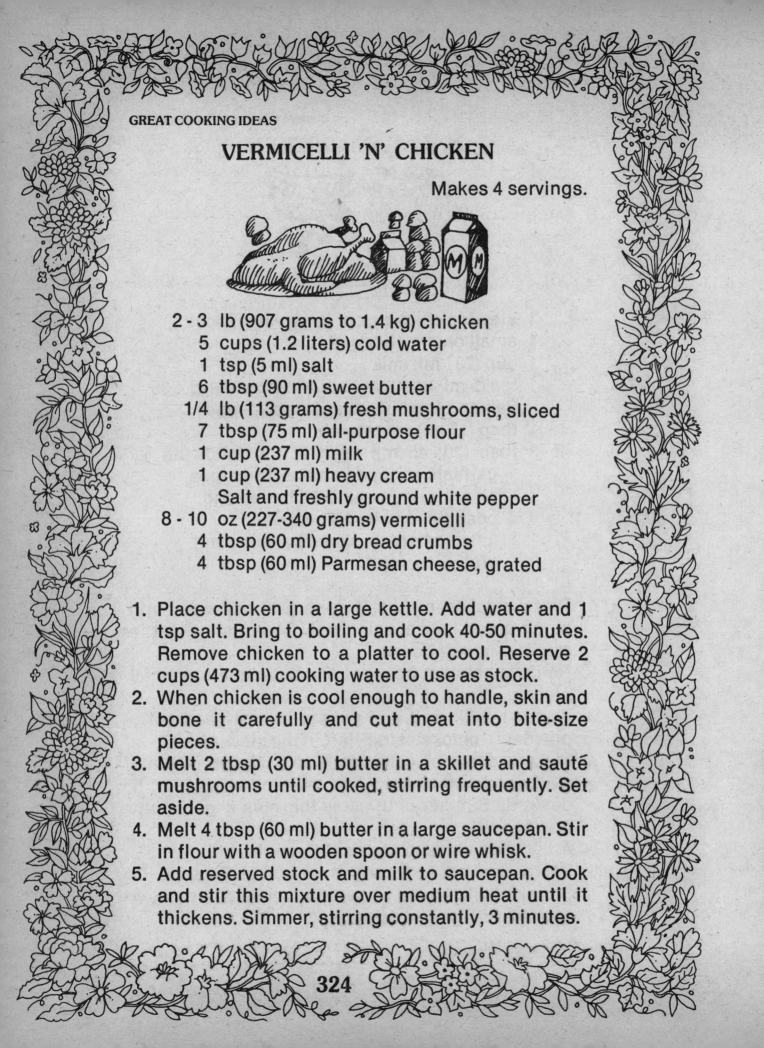

2 - 3 lb (907 grams to 1.4 kg) chicken
5 cups (1.2 liters) cold water
1 tsp (5 ml) salt
6 tbsp (90 ml) sweet butter
1/4 lb (113 grams) fresh mushrooms, sliced
7 tbsp (75 ml) all-purpose flour
1 cup (237 ml) milk
1 cup (237 ml) heavy cream
Salt and freshly ground white pepper
8 - 10 oz (227-340 grams) vermicelli
4 tbsp (60 ml) dry bread crumbs
4 tbsp (60 ml) Parmesan cheese, grated

1. Place chicken in a large kettle. Add water and 1 tsp salt. Bring to boiling and cook 40-50 minutes. Remove chicken to a platter to cool. Reserve 2 cups (473 ml) cooking water to use as stock.
2. When chicken is cool enough to handle, skin and bone it carefully and cut meat into bite-size pieces.
3. Melt 2 tbsp (30 ml) butter in a skillet and sauté mushrooms until cooked, stirring frequently. Set aside.
4. Melt 4 tbsp (60 ml) butter in a large saucepan. Stir in flour with a wooden spoon or wire whisk.
5. Add reserved stock and milk to saucepan. Cook and stir this mixture over medium heat until it thickens. Simmer, stirring constantly, 3 minutes.

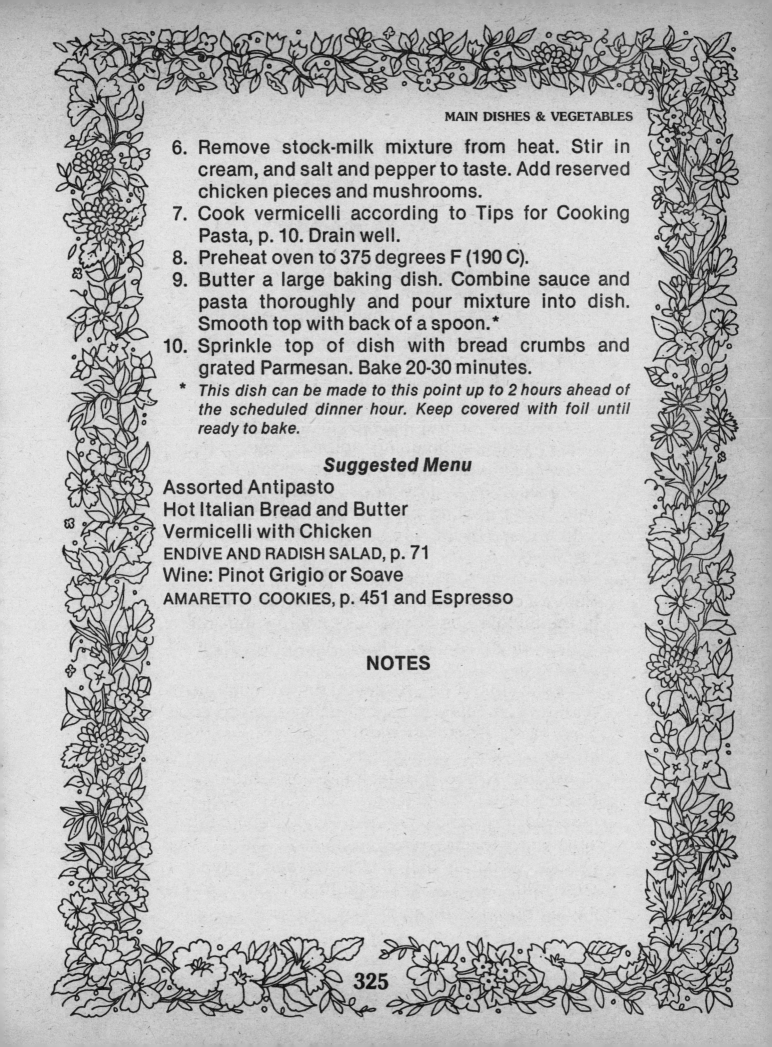

6. Remove stock-milk mixture from heat. Stir in cream, and salt and pepper to taste. Add reserved chicken pieces and mushrooms.

7. Cook vermicelli according to Tips for Cooking Pasta, p. 10. Drain well.

8. Preheat oven to 375 degrees F (190 C).

9. Butter a large baking dish. Combine sauce and pasta thoroughly and pour mixture into dish. Smooth top with back of a spoon.*

10. Sprinkle top of dish with bread crumbs and grated Parmesan. Bake 20-30 minutes.

   * *This dish can be made to this point up to 2 hours ahead of the scheduled dinner hour. Keep covered with foil until ready to bake.*

Suggested Menu

Assorted Antipasto
Hot Italian Bread and Butter
Vermicelli with Chicken
ENDIVE AND RADISH SALAD, p. 71
Wine: Pinot Grigio or Soave
AMARETTO COOKIES, p. 451 and Espresso

NOTES

SHANGHAI DUCK

Makes 6 - 10 servings.

1 fresh or frozen duck (about 5 lb or 2.3 kg)
1 tsp (5 ml) salt
6 tbsp (90 ml) dark soy sauce
1 whole star anise
2 scallions, cut in 2-inch (5-cm) pieces
1 1/2 tbsp (22.5 ml) sugar
1/4 cup (59 ml) dry sherry
2 tsp (10 ml) sesame oil

1. Trim extra skin and excess fat from duck. Skin neck. Rinse, including giblets and neck, thoroughly. Drain and dry with paper towels.
2. Place duck in a large pot. Sprinkle inside with salt. Using basting brush, coat outside of duck with 1 tbsp (15 ml) soy sauce. Let stand 1 hour, turning once.
3. Preheat oven to 400 degrees F (204 C).
4. Remove oven racks. Oil one and return it to oven in the middle position. Pour 1 inch water into a large, flat broiler pan. Place this on lowest level of oven.
5. Take duck out of pot, reserving pot with marinade for later use. Place duck, breast side up, on oiled oven rack. Roast 30 minutes or until skin is brown.
6. Allow duck to cool 10 min. for easier handling.
7. Place an asbestos pad on burner. On it place the reserved pot and marinade. Add star anise, scallions, sugar, remaining soy sauce and enough water to half cover the duck, about 4 cups (946 ml). Bring sauce to boiling, stirring constantly.

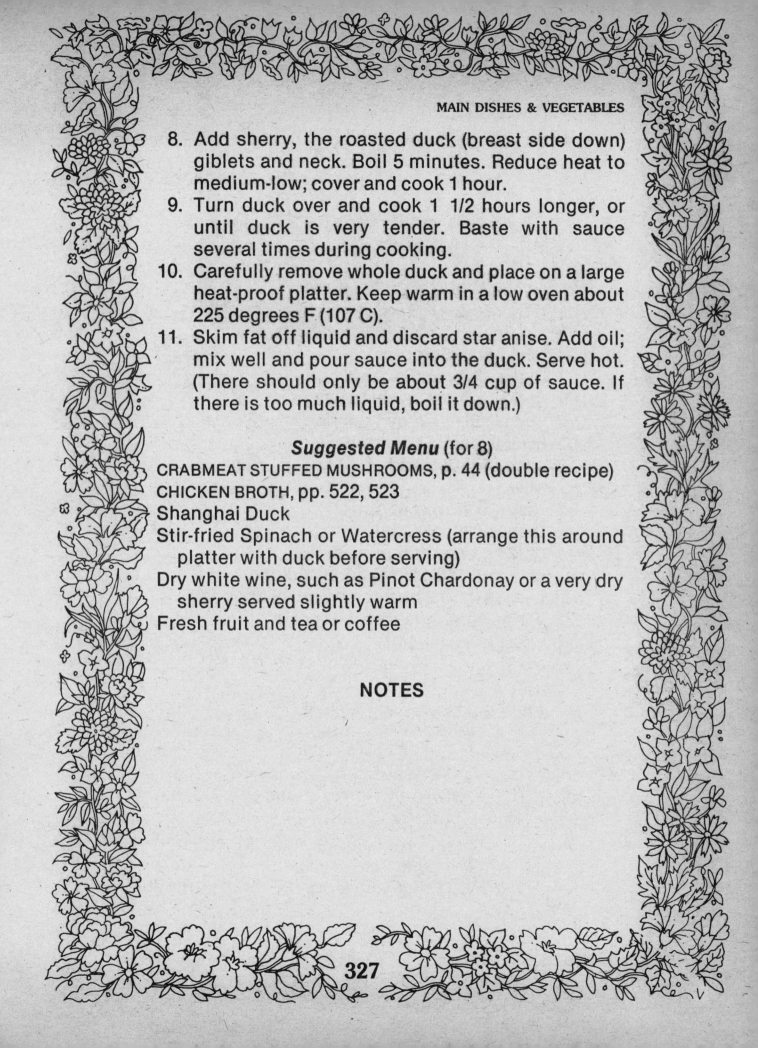

8. Add sherry, the roasted duck (breast side down) giblets and neck. Boil 5 minutes. Reduce heat to medium-low; cover and cook 1 hour.

9. Turn duck over and cook 1 1/2 hours longer, or until duck is very tender. Baste with sauce several times during cooking.

10. Carefully remove whole duck and place on a large heat-proof platter. Keep warm in a low oven about 225 degrees F (107 C).

11. Skim fat off liquid and discard star anise. Add oil; mix well and pour sauce into the duck. Serve hot. (There should only be about 3/4 cup of sauce. If there is too much liquid, boil it down.)

Suggested Menu (for 8)

CRABMEAT STUFFED MUSHROOMS, p. 44 (double recipe)
CHICKEN BROTH, pp. 522, 523
Shanghai Duck
Stir-fried Spinach or Watercress (arrange this around platter with duck before serving)
Dry white wine, such as Pinot Chardonay or a very dry sherry served slightly warm
Fresh fruit and tea or coffee

NOTES

TURKEY 'N' CHESTNUT DRESSING

Makes 10 - 12 servings.

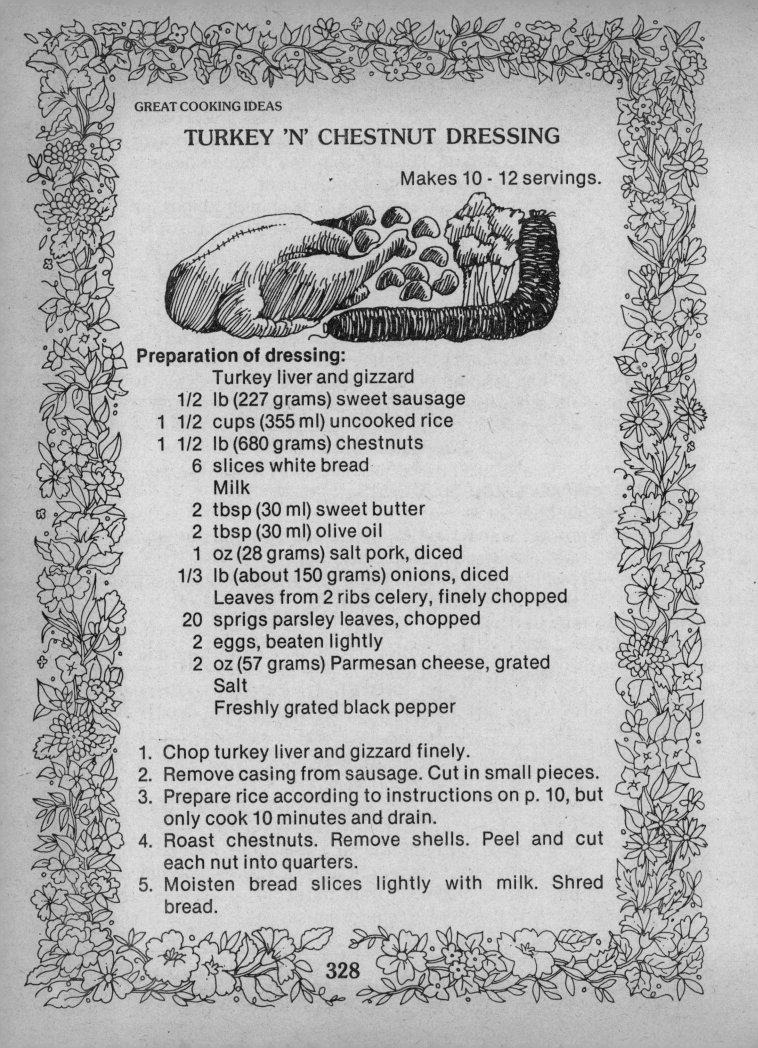

Preparation of dressing:

	Turkey liver and gizzard
1/2	lb (227 grams) sweet sausage
1 1/2	cups (355 ml) uncooked rice
1 1/2	lb (680 grams) chestnuts
6	slices white bread
	Milk
2	tbsp (30 ml) sweet butter
2	tbsp (30 ml) olive oil
1	oz (28 grams) salt pork, diced
1/3	lb (about 150 grams) onions, diced
	Leaves from 2 ribs celery, finely chopped
20	sprigs parsley leaves, chopped
2	eggs, beaten lightly
2	oz (57 grams) Parmesan cheese, grated
	Salt
	Freshly grated black pepper

1. Chop turkey liver and gizzard finely.
2. Remove casing from sausage. Cut in small pieces.
3. Prepare rice according to instructions on p. 10, but only cook 10 minutes and drain.
4. Roast chestnuts. Remove shells. Peel and cut each nut into quarters.
5. Moisten bread slices lightly with milk. Shred bread.

6. In a skillet, combine butter, oil and salt pork. Add onions and cook to golden brown.
7. Add chopped liver and gizzard, sausage pieces and celery leaves to onions in skillet. Cook slowly 15 minutes. Remove from heat.
8. Add drained rice, chestnuts, bread, parsley, eggs and cheese. Season with salt and pepper to taste. Mix well.

Preparation of bird:

6 tbsp (90 ml) sweet butter
2 tbsp (30 ml) olive oil
1 turkey (16-18 lb or 7-8 kg)
Chestnut Stuffing
5 thin slices salt pork
1 tbsp (15 ml) fresh rosemary
Salt
Freshly ground black pepper

1. Combine 2 tbsp (30 ml) butter with olive oil. Rub turkey inside and out with mixture.
2. Preheat oven to 400 degrees F (204 C).
3. Stuff the bird and sew both openings closed.
4. Oil a roasting pan with olive oil. Place turkey in it, breast side down. Brown 5 minutes. Turn over and brown 5 minutes longer.
5. Lay slices of pork on top of breast and legs.
6. Sprinkle rosemary, salt and pepper over turkey.
7. Reduce heat to 350 degrees F (177 C). Bake turkey 25 minutes per lb. Baste frequently. When bird is cooked, remove from pan and keep warm.
8. Make gravy: Pour off grease from roasting pan. Place pan on top of stove. Add remaining butter and 2 cups (473 ml) boiling water. Bring to a boil. Simmer 7-8 minutes, until gravy thickens. (Do not use flour to thicken.) Strain and serve.
9. Serve with whole cranberry sauce.

PHEASANT 'N' WILD RICE DRESSING

Makes 6 servings.

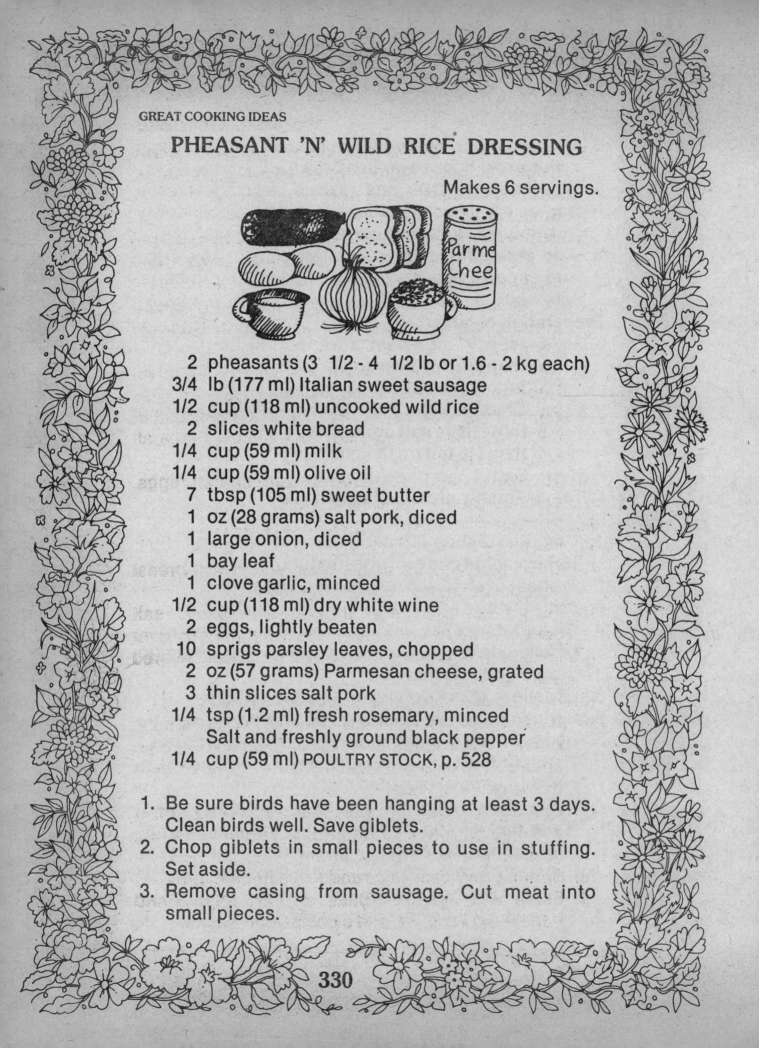

2	pheasants (3 1/2 - 4 1/2 lb or 1.6 - 2 kg each)
3/4	lb (177 ml) Italian sweet sausage
1/2	cup (118 ml) uncooked wild rice
2	slices white bread
1/4	cup (59 ml) milk
1/4	cup (59 ml) olive oil
7	tbsp (105 ml) sweet butter
1	oz (28 grams) salt pork, diced
1	large onion, diced
1	bay leaf
1	clove garlic, minced
1/2	cup (118 ml) dry white wine
2	eggs, lightly beaten
10	sprigs parsley leaves, chopped
2	oz (57 grams) Parmesan cheese, grated
3	thin slices salt pork
1/4	tsp (1.2 ml) fresh rosemary, minced
	Salt and freshly ground black pepper
1/4	cup (59 ml) POULTRY STOCK, p. 528

1. Be sure birds have been hanging at least 3 days. Clean birds well. Save giblets.
2. Chop giblets in small pieces to use in stuffing. Set aside.
3. Remove casing from sausage. Cut meat into small pieces.

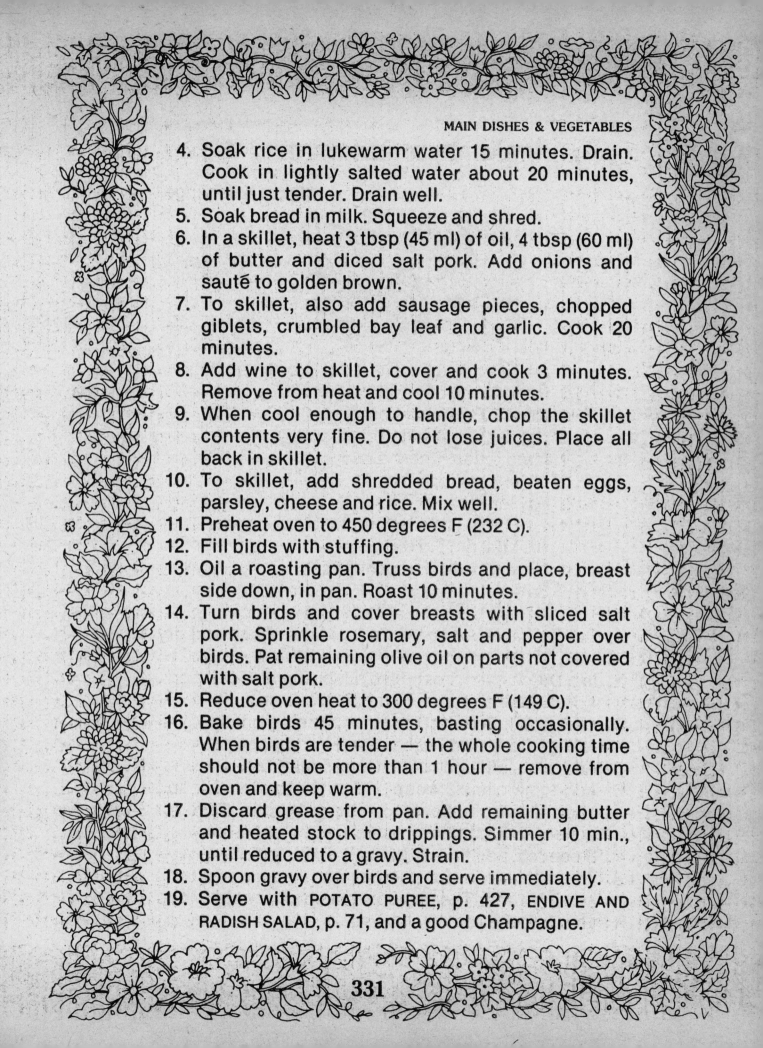

4. Soak rice in lukewarm water 15 minutes. Drain. Cook in lightly salted water about 20 minutes, until just tender. Drain well.
5. Soak bread in milk. Squeeze and shred.
6. In a skillet, heat 3 tbsp (45 ml) of oil, 4 tbsp (60 ml) of butter and diced salt pork. Add onions and sauté to golden brown.
7. To skillet, also add sausage pieces, chopped giblets, crumbled bay leaf and garlic. Cook 20 minutes.
8. Add wine to skillet, cover and cook 3 minutes. Remove from heat and cool 10 minutes.
9. When cool enough to handle, chop the skillet contents very fine. Do not lose juices. Place all back in skillet.
10. To skillet, add shredded bread, beaten eggs, parsley, cheese and rice. Mix well.
11. Preheat oven to 450 degrees F (232 C).
12. Fill birds with stuffing.
13. Oil a roasting pan. Truss birds and place, breast side down, in pan. Roast 10 minutes.
14. Turn birds and cover breasts with sliced salt pork. Sprinkle rosemary, salt and pepper over birds. Pat remaining olive oil on parts not covered with salt pork.
15. Reduce oven heat to 300 degrees F (149 C).
16. Bake birds 45 minutes, basting occasionally. When birds are tender — the whole cooking time should not be more than 1 hour — remove from oven and keep warm.
17. Discard grease from pan. Add remaining butter and heated stock to drippings. Simmer 10 min., until reduced to a gravy. Strain.
18. Spoon gravy over birds and serve immediately.
19. Serve with POTATO PUREE, p. 427, ENDIVE AND RADISH SALAD, p. 71, and a good Champagne.

RABBIT IN RED WINE

Makes 4 servings.

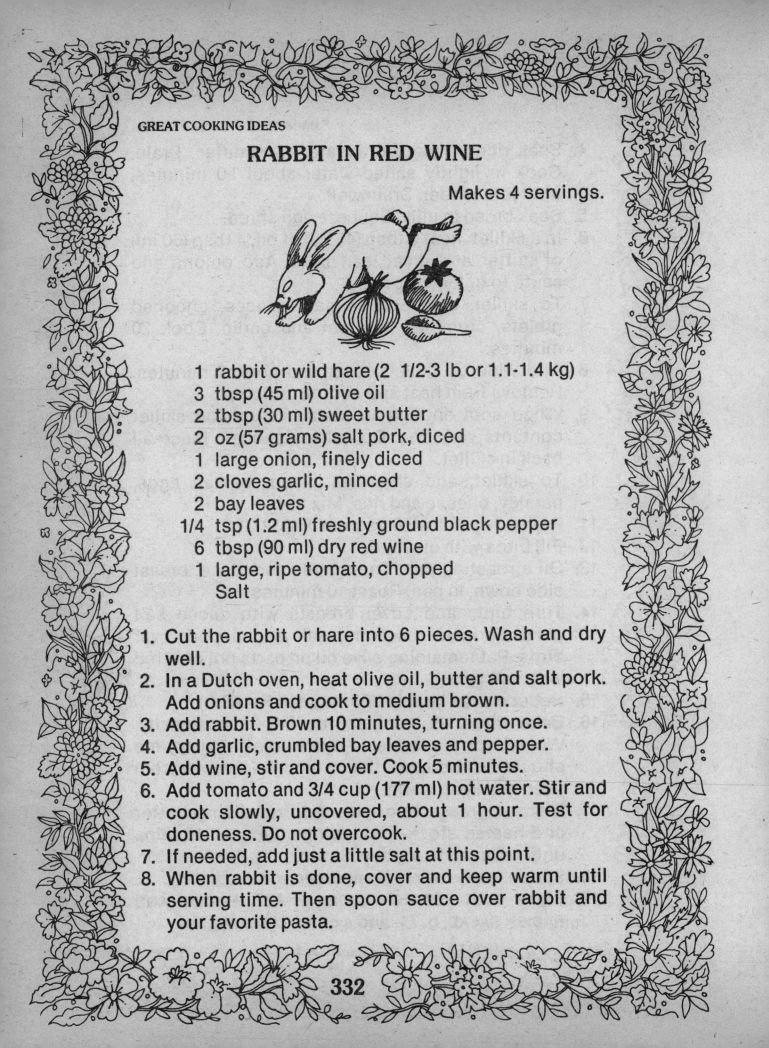

- 1 rabbit or wild hare (2 1/2-3 lb or 1.1-1.4 kg)
- 3 tbsp (45 ml) olive oil
- 2 tbsp (30 ml) sweet butter
- 2 oz (57 grams) salt pork, diced
- 1 large onion, finely diced
- 2 cloves garlic, minced
- 2 bay leaves
- 1/4 tsp (1.2 ml) freshly ground black pepper
- 6 tbsp (90 ml) dry red wine
- 1 large, ripe tomato, chopped
- Salt

1. Cut the rabbit or hare into 6 pieces. Wash and dry well.
2. In a Dutch oven, heat olive oil, butter and salt pork. Add onions and cook to medium brown.
3. Add rabbit. Brown 10 minutes, turning once.
4. Add garlic, crumbled bay leaves and pepper.
5. Add wine, stir and cover. Cook 5 minutes.
6. Add tomato and 3/4 cup (177 ml) hot water. Stir and cook slowly, uncovered, about 1 hour. Test for doneness. Do not overcook.
7. If needed, add just a little salt at this point.
8. When rabbit is done, cover and keep warm until serving time. Then spoon sauce over rabbit and your favorite pasta.

CHOP SUEY

Makes 4 servings.

1 cup (237 ml) cooked meat*, diced
Salt and freshly ground black pepper
2 tbsp (30 ml) vinegar
1 cup (237 ml) fresh mushrooms, chopped
2 medium-sized onions
Sweet butter
1 cup (237 ml) fresh bean sprouts, or 1 can
   (5 oz or 142 grams) bamboo shoots
Soy sauce
1 tsp (5 ml) sugar
Pinch of allspice
1/2 lb (227 grams) fresh shrimp, cooked, cleaned
   and deveined

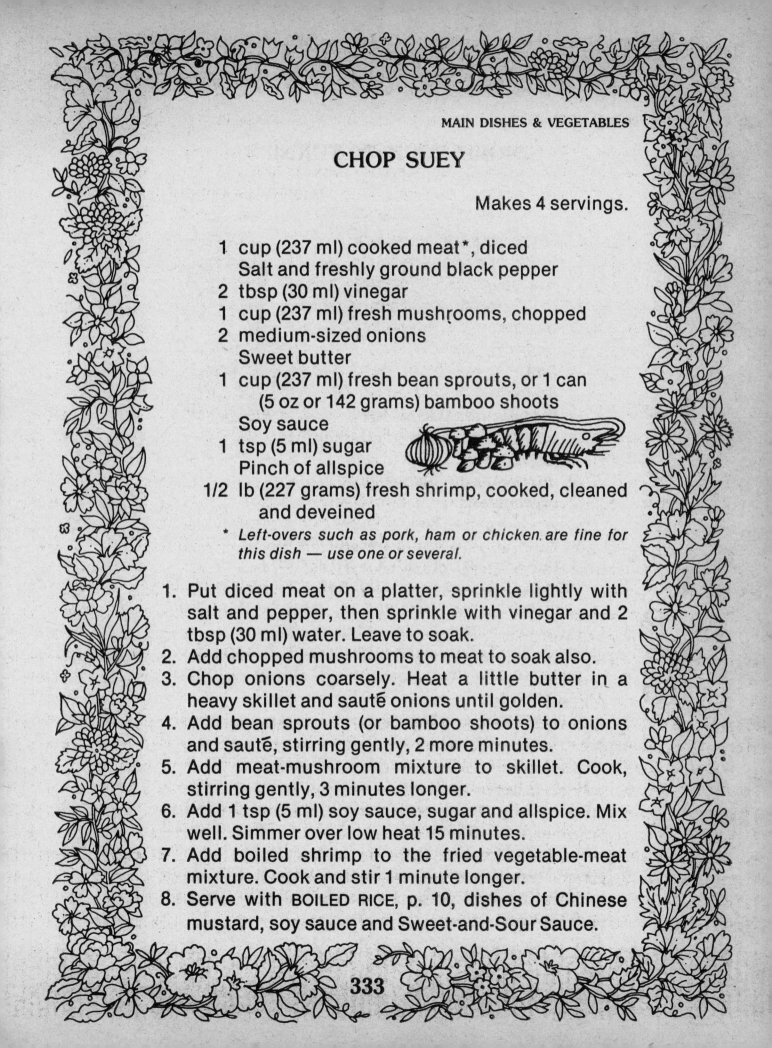

  * *Left-overs such as pork, ham or chicken are fine for this dish — use one or several.*

1. Put diced meat on a platter, sprinkle lightly with salt and pepper, then sprinkle with vinegar and 2 tbsp (30 ml) water. Leave to soak.
2. Add chopped mushrooms to meat to soak also.
3. Chop onions coarsely. Heat a little butter in a heavy skillet and sauté onions until golden.
4. Add bean sprouts (or bamboo shoots) to onions and sauté, stirring gently, 2 more minutes.
5. Add meat-mushroom mixture to skillet. Cook, stirring gently, 3 minutes longer.
6. Add 1 tsp (5 ml) soy sauce, sugar and allspice. Mix well. Simmer over low heat 15 minutes.
7. Add boiled shrimp to the fried vegetable-meat mixture. Cook and stir 1 minute longer.
8. Serve with BOILED RICE, p. 10, dishes of Chinese mustard, soy sauce and Sweet-and-Sour Sauce.

GINGKO PORK 'N' TURNIPS

Makes 4 servings.

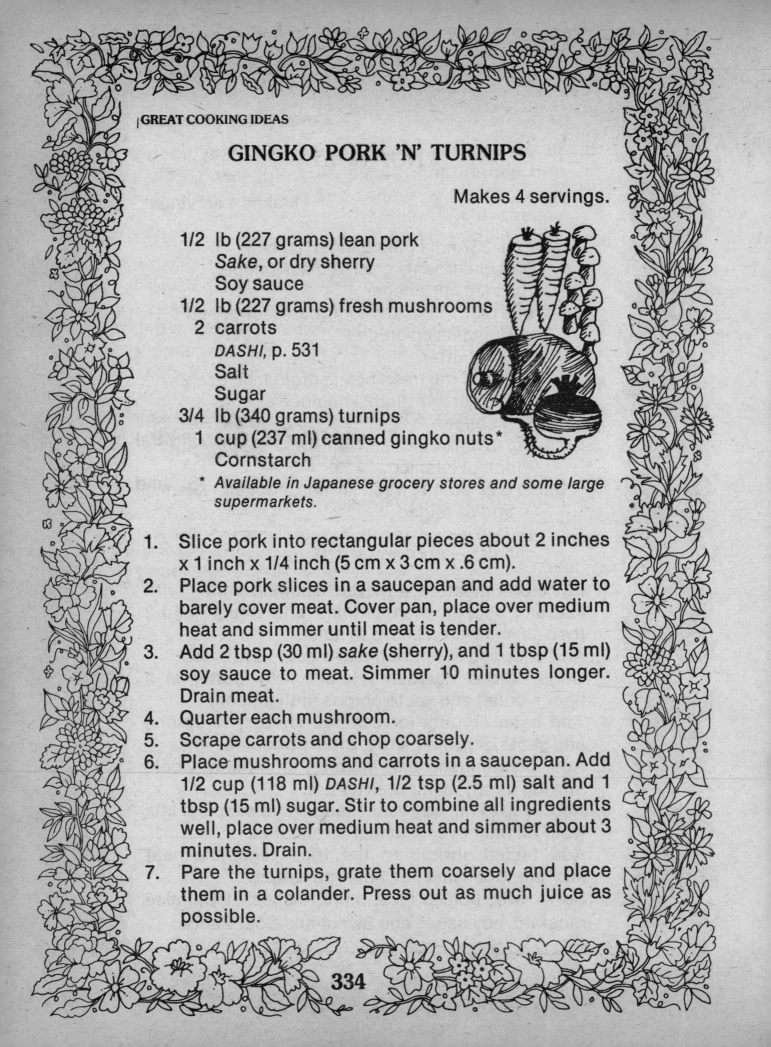

1/2 lb (227 grams) lean pork
Sake, or dry sherry
Soy sauce
1/2 lb (227 grams) fresh mushrooms
2 carrots
DASHI, p. 531
Salt
Sugar
3/4 lb (340 grams) turnips
1 cup (237 ml) canned gingko nuts*
Cornstarch

* *Available in Japanese grocery stores and some large supermarkets.*

1. Slice pork into rectangular pieces about 2 inches x 1 inch x 1/4 inch (5 cm x 3 cm x .6 cm).
2. Place pork slices in a saucepan and add water to barely cover meat. Cover pan, place over medium heat and simmer until meat is tender.
3. Add 2 tbsp (30 ml) *sake* (sherry), and 1 tbsp (15 ml) soy sauce to meat. Simmer 10 minutes longer. Drain meat.
4. Quarter each mushroom.
5. Scrape carrots and chop coarsely.
6. Place mushrooms and carrots in a saucepan. Add 1/2 cup (118 ml) *DASHI*, 1/2 tsp (2.5 ml) salt and 1 tbsp (15 ml) sugar. Stir to combine all ingredients well, place over medium heat and simmer about 3 minutes. Drain.
7. Pare the turnips, grate them coarsely and place them in a colander. Press out as much juice as possible.

8. In deep bowls, arrange pork slices, mushrooms and carrots and gingko nuts. Top each with a large mound of grated turnip. Place bowls in a steamer for 20 minutes.
9. Meanwhile, in a saucepan, combine 1 cup (237 ml) DASHI, 1 tbsp (15 ml) *sake* (sherry), 1 tsp (5 ml) sugar, 2 tsp (10 ml) soy sauce and 1/2 tsp (2.5 ml) salt. Place over medium heat. Simmer 5 minutes.
10. In a cup, combine 2 tsp (10 ml) cornstarch with 2 tsp (10 ml) water and mix well. Stir this mixture into sauce and cook until it thickens slightly. Remove from stove.
11. Remove bowls from steamer and spoon off any excess juice which has formed. Pour several spoonfuls of sauce over each bowl.
12. Serve hot with JAPANESE RICE, p. 18, and CUCUMBER SALAD (Chinese), p. 70.

Note: A steamer can be created by placing a rack in a deep roasting pan, filling roaster with water nearly up to rack and setting bowls on rack.

NOTES

FETTUCCINE ROMAN-STYLE

Makes 4 servings.

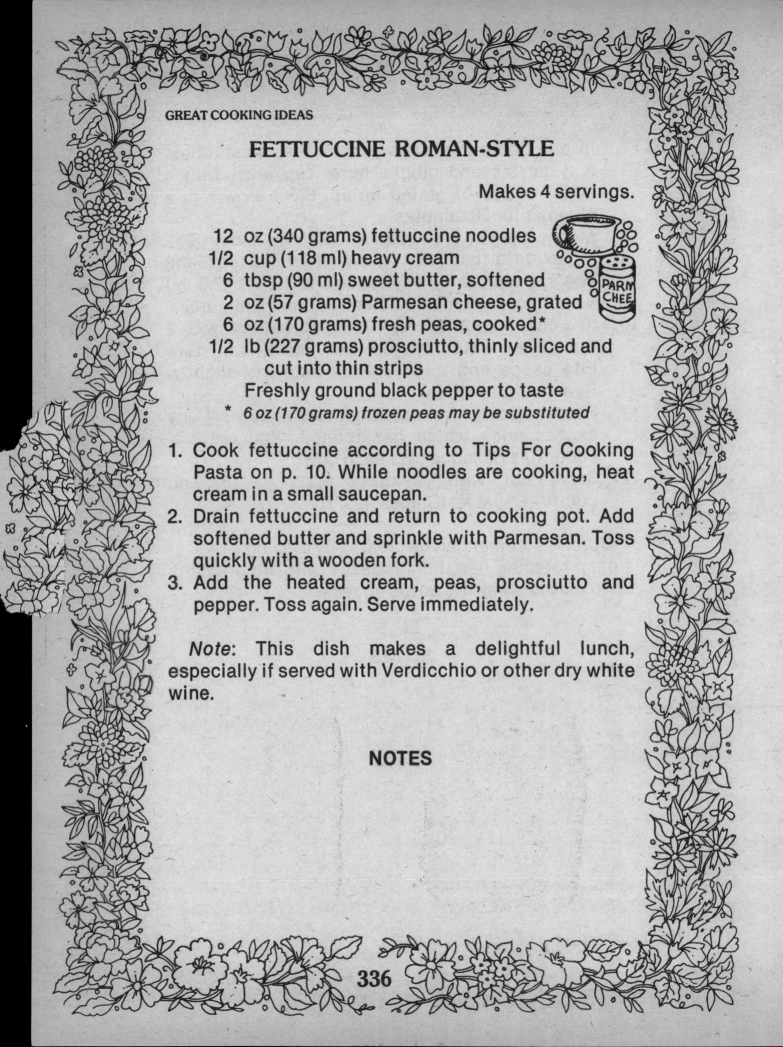

- 12 oz (340 grams) fettuccine noodles
- 1/2 cup (118 ml) heavy cream
- 6 tbsp (90 ml) sweet butter, softened
- 2 oz (57 grams) Parmesan cheese, grated
- 6 oz (170 grams) fresh peas, cooked*
- 1/2 lb (227 grams) prosciutto, thinly sliced and cut into thin strips
- Freshly ground black pepper to taste

* *6 oz (170 grams) frozen peas may be substituted*

1. Cook fettuccine according to Tips For Cooking Pasta on p. 10. While noodles are cooking, heat cream in a small saucepan.
2. Drain fettuccine and return to cooking pot. Add softened butter and sprinkle with Parmesan. Toss quickly with a wooden fork.
3. Add the heated cream, peas, prosciutto and pepper. Toss again. Serve immediately.

Note: This dish makes a delightful lunch, especially if served with Verdicchio or other dry white wine.

NOTES

MARINATED PORK ROAST

Makes 6 servings.

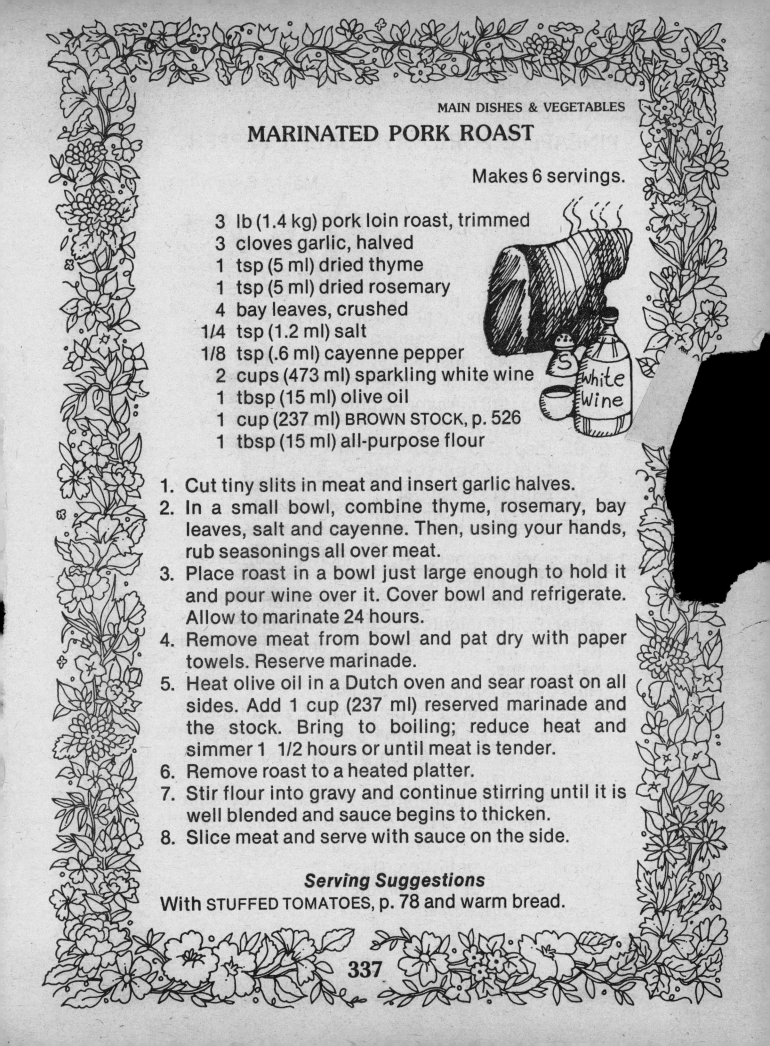

3 lb (1.4 kg) pork loin roast, trimmed
3 cloves garlic, halved
1 tsp (5 ml) dried thyme
1 tsp (5 ml) dried rosemary
4 bay leaves, crushed
1/4 tsp (1.2 ml) salt
1/8 tsp (.6 ml) cayenne pepper
2 cups (473 ml) sparkling white wine
1 tbsp (15 ml) olive oil
1 cup (237 ml) BROWN STOCK, p. 526
1 tbsp (15 ml) all-purpose flour

1. Cut tiny slits in meat and insert garlic halves.
2. In a small bowl, combine thyme, rosemary, bay leaves, salt and cayenne. Then, using your hands, rub seasonings all over meat.
3. Place roast in a bowl just large enough to hold it and pour wine over it. Cover bowl and refrigerate. Allow to marinate 24 hours.
4. Remove meat from bowl and pat dry with paper towels. Reserve marinade.
5. Heat olive oil in a Dutch oven and sear roast on all sides. Add 1 cup (237 ml) reserved marinade and the stock. Bring to boiling; reduce heat and simmer 1 1/2 hours or until meat is tender.
6. Remove roast to a heated platter.
7. Stir flour into gravy and continue stirring until it is well blended and sauce begins to thicken.
8. Slice meat and serve with sauce on the side.

Serving Suggestions

With STUFFED TOMATOES, p. 78 and warm bread.

PINEAPPLE PORK WITH GREEN PEPPERS

Makes 6 servings.

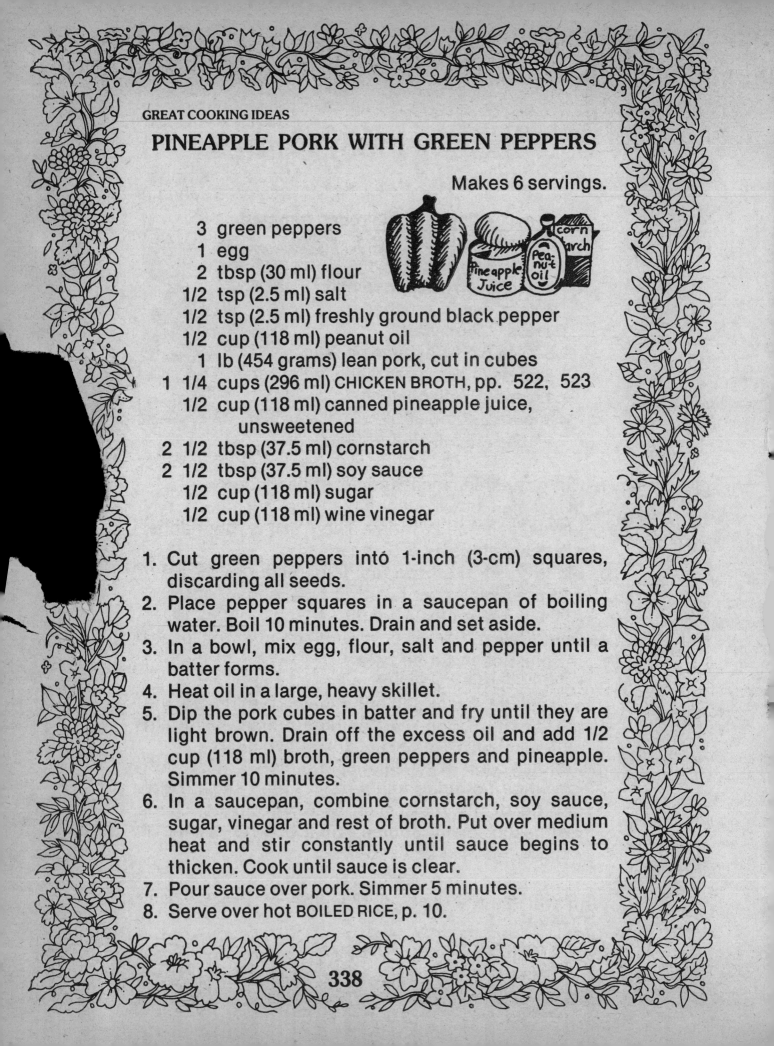

- 3 green peppers
- 1 egg
- 2 tbsp (30 ml) flour
- 1/2 tsp (2.5 ml) salt
- 1/2 tsp (2.5 ml) freshly ground black pepper
- 1/2 cup (118 ml) peanut oil
- 1 lb (454 grams) lean pork, cut in cubes
- 1 1/4 cups (296 ml) CHICKEN BROTH, pp. 522, 523
- 1/2 cup (118 ml) canned pineapple juice, unsweetened
- 2 1/2 tbsp (37.5 ml) cornstarch
- 2 1/2 tbsp (37.5 ml) soy sauce
- 1/2 cup (118 ml) sugar
- 1/2 cup (118 ml) wine vinegar

1. Cut green peppers into 1-inch (3-cm) squares, discarding all seeds.
2. Place pepper squares in a saucepan of boiling water. Boil 10 minutes. Drain and set aside.
3. In a bowl, mix egg, flour, salt and pepper until a batter forms.
4. Heat oil in a large, heavy skillet.
5. Dip the pork cubes in batter and fry until they are light brown. Drain off the excess oil and add 1/2 cup (118 ml) broth, green peppers and pineapple. Simmer 10 minutes.
6. In a saucepan, combine cornstarch, soy sauce, sugar, vinegar and rest of broth. Put over medium heat and stir constantly until sauce begins to thicken. Cook until sauce is clear.
7. Pour sauce over pork. Simmer 5 minutes.
8. Serve over hot BOILED RICE, p. 10.

PORK CHOPS WITH ANCHOVIES

Makes 6 servings.

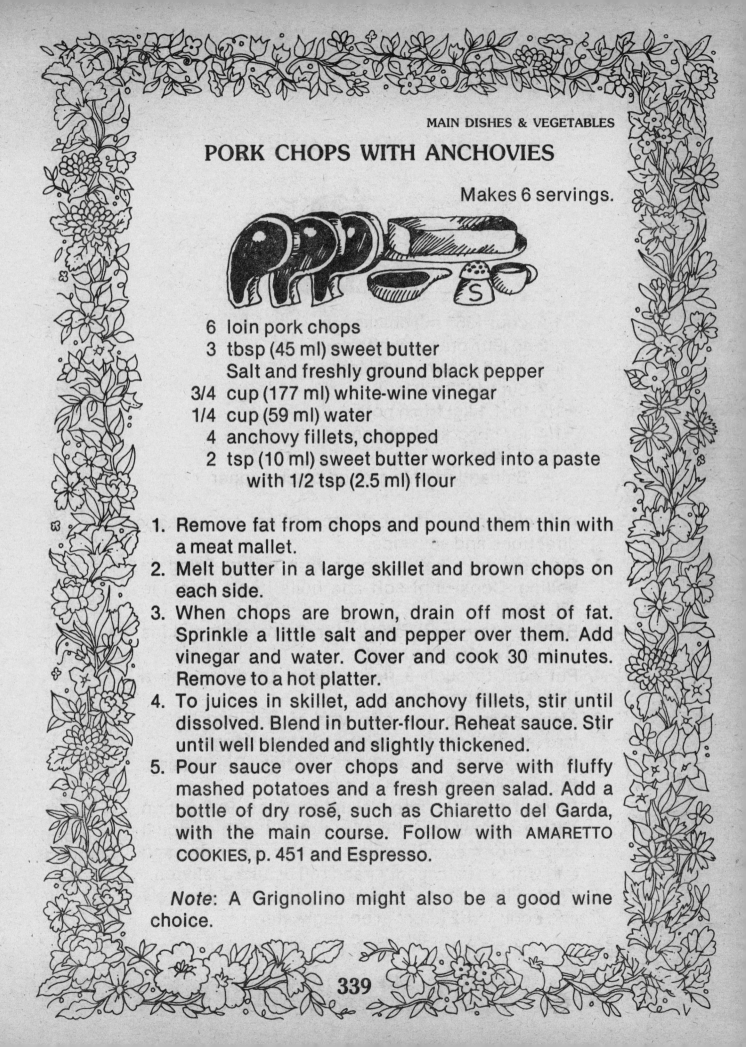

6 loin pork chops
3 tbsp (45 ml) sweet butter
Salt and freshly ground black pepper
3/4 cup (177 ml) white-wine vinegar
1/4 cup (59 ml) water
4 anchovy fillets, chopped
2 tsp (10 ml) sweet butter worked into a paste
  with 1/2 tsp (2.5 ml) flour

1. Remove fat from chops and pound them thin with a meat mallet.
2. Melt butter in a large skillet and brown chops on each side.
3. When chops are brown, drain off most of fat. Sprinkle a little salt and pepper over them. Add vinegar and water. Cover and cook 30 minutes. Remove to a hot platter.
4. To juices in skillet, add anchovy fillets, stir until dissolved. Blend in butter-flour. Reheat sauce. Stir until well blended and slightly thickened.
5. Pour sauce over chops and serve with fluffy mashed potatoes and a fresh green salad. Add a bottle of dry rosé, such as Chiaretto del Garda, with the main course. Follow with AMARETTO COOKIES, p. 451 and Espresso.

Note: A Grignolino might also be a good wine choice.

PORK NACTAMALES

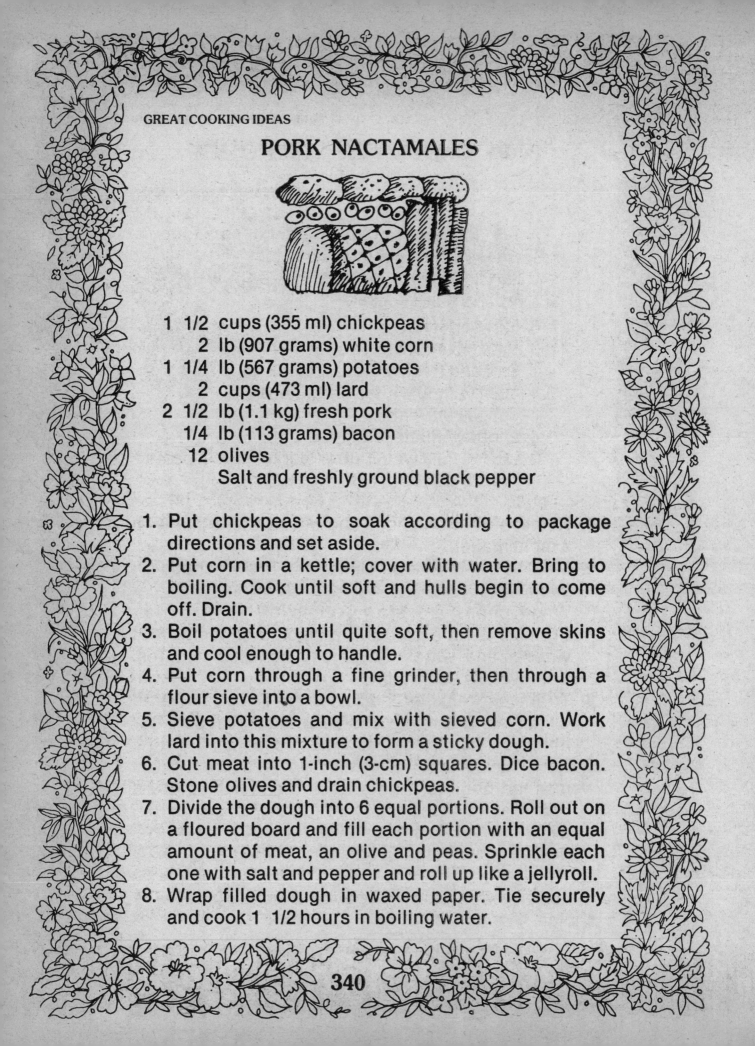

1 1/2 cups (355 ml) chickpeas
2 lb (907 grams) white corn
1 1/4 lb (567 grams) potatoes
2 cups (473 ml) lard
2 1/2 lb (1.1 kg) fresh pork
1/4 lb (113 grams) bacon
12 olives
Salt and freshly ground black pepper

1. Put chickpeas to soak according to package directions and set aside.
2. Put corn in a kettle; cover with water. Bring to boiling. Cook until soft and hulls begin to come off. Drain.
3. Boil potatoes until quite soft, then remove skins and cool enough to handle.
4. Put corn through a fine grinder, then through a flour sieve into a bowl.
5. Sieve potatoes and mix with sieved corn. Work lard into this mixture to form a sticky dough.
6. Cut meat into 1-inch (3-cm) squares. Dice bacon. Stone olives and drain chickpeas.
7. Divide the dough into 6 equal portions. Roll out on a floured board and fill each portion with an equal amount of meat, an olive and peas. Sprinkle each one with salt and pepper and roll up like a jellyroll.
8. Wrap filled dough in waxed paper. Tie securely and cook 1 1/2 hours in boiling water.

PORK ROAST WITH CHESTNUTS

Makes 8 servings.

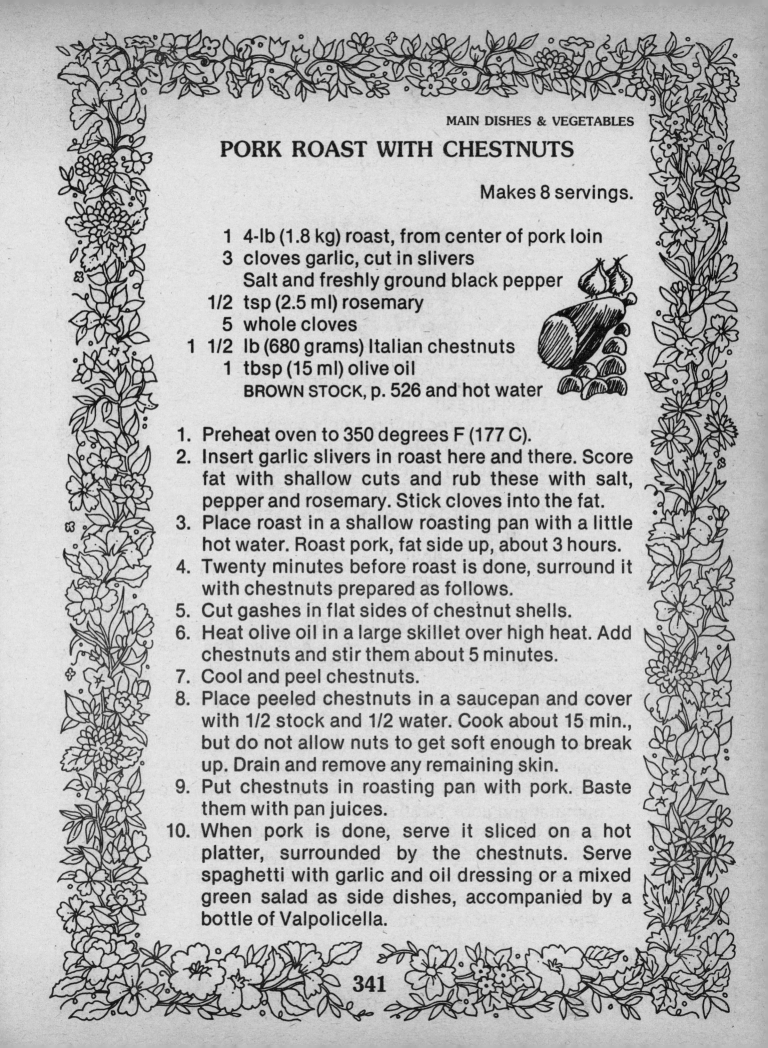

- 1   4-lb (1.8 kg) roast, from center of pork loin
- 3   cloves garlic, cut in slivers
  Salt and freshly ground black pepper
- 1/2   tsp (2.5 ml) rosemary
- 5   whole cloves
- 1 1/2   lb (680 grams) Italian chestnuts
- 1   tbsp (15 ml) olive oil
  BROWN STOCK, p. 526 and hot water

1. Preheat oven to 350 degrees F (177 C).
2. Insert garlic slivers in roast here and there. Score fat with shallow cuts and rub these with salt, pepper and rosemary. Stick cloves into the fat.
3. Place roast in a shallow roasting pan with a little hot water. Roast pork, fat side up, about 3 hours.
4. Twenty minutes before roast is done, surround it with chestnuts prepared as follows.
5. Cut gashes in flat sides of chestnut shells.
6. Heat olive oil in a large skillet over high heat. Add chestnuts and stir them about 5 minutes.
7. Cool and peel chestnuts.
8. Place peeled chestnuts in a saucepan and cover with 1/2 stock and 1/2 water. Cook about 15 min., but do not allow nuts to get soft enough to break up. Drain and remove any remaining skin.
9. Put chestnuts in roasting pan with pork. Baste them with pan juices.
10. When pork is done, serve it sliced on a hot platter, surrounded by the chestnuts. Serve spaghetti with garlic and oil dressing or a mixed green salad as side dishes, accompanied by a bottle of Valpolicella.

PORK SKILLET

Makes 6 servings.

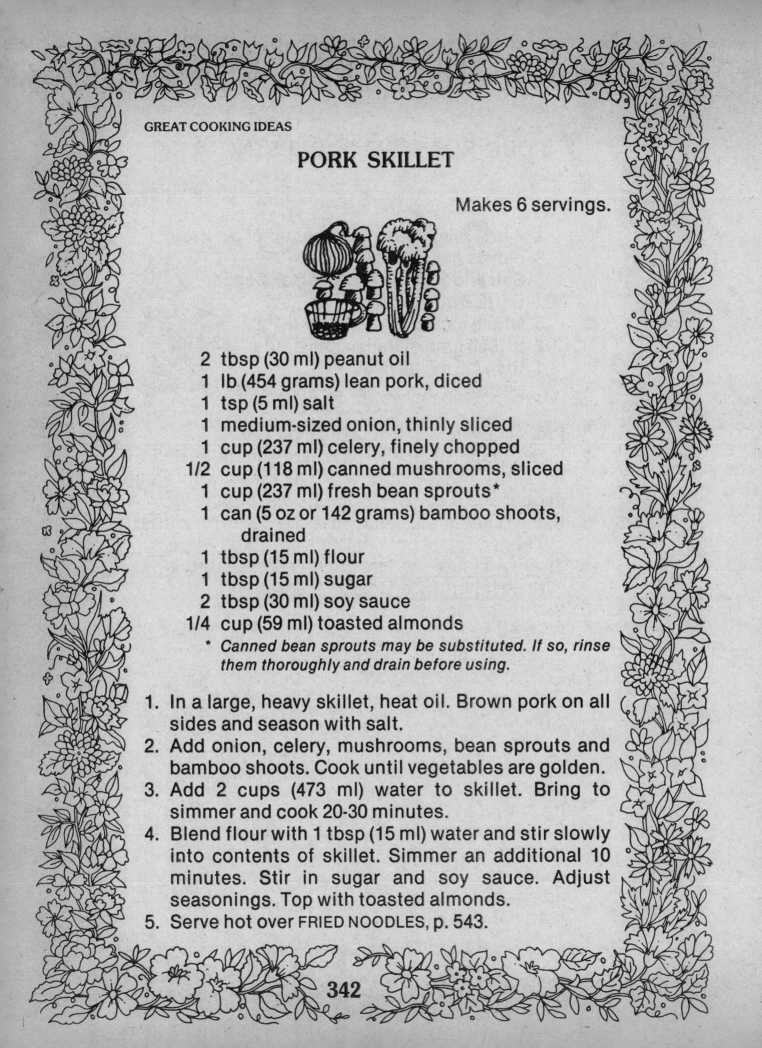

2 tbsp (30 ml) peanut oil
1 lb (454 grams) lean pork, diced
1 tsp (5 ml) salt
1 medium-sized onion, thinly sliced
1 cup (237 ml) celery, finely chopped
1/2 cup (118 ml) canned mushrooms, sliced
1 cup (237 ml) fresh bean sprouts*
1 can (5 oz or 142 grams) bamboo shoots, drained
1 tbsp (15 ml) flour
1 tbsp (15 ml) sugar
2 tbsp (30 ml) soy sauce
1/4 cup (59 ml) toasted almonds

Canned bean sprouts may be substituted. If so, rinse them thoroughly and drain before using.

1. In a large, heavy skillet, heat oil. Brown pork on all sides and season with salt.
2. Add onion, celery, mushrooms, bean sprouts and bamboo shoots. Cook until vegetables are golden.
3. Add 2 cups (473 ml) water to skillet. Bring to simmer and cook 20-30 minutes.
4. Blend flour with 1 tbsp (15 ml) water and stir slowly into contents of skillet. Simmer an additional 10 minutes. Stir in sugar and soy sauce. Adjust seasonings. Top with toasted almonds.
5. Serve hot over FRIED NOODLES, p. 543.

SAUSAGES 'N' LENTILS IN WHITE WINE

Makes 6 servings.

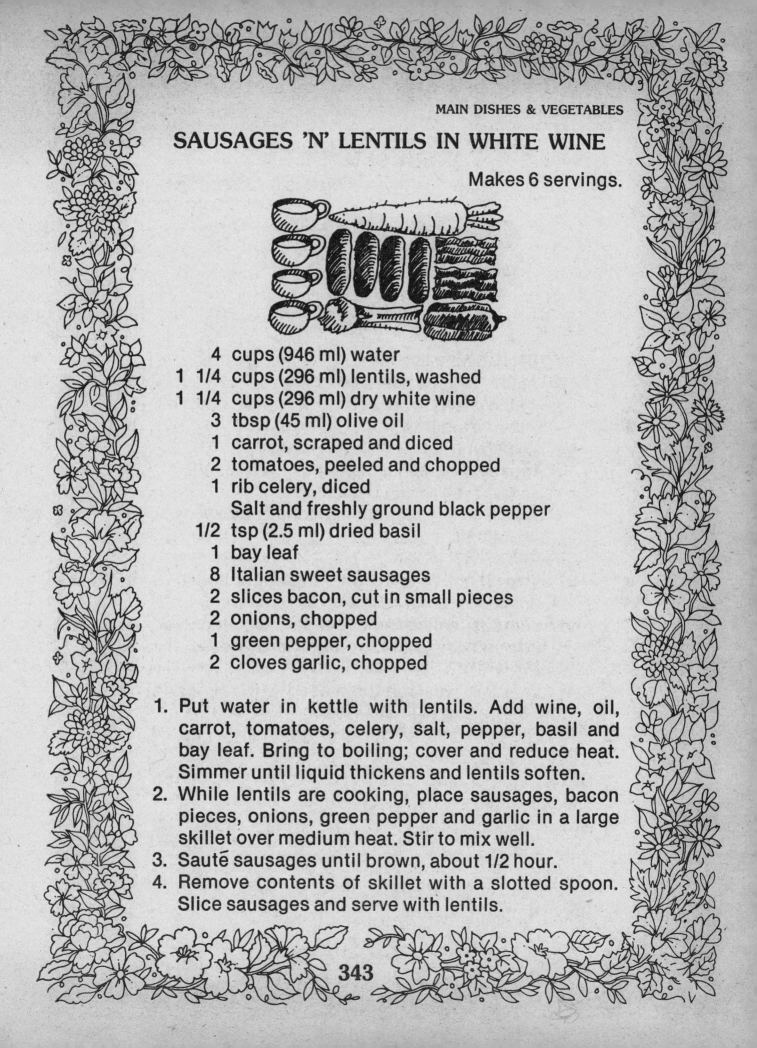

```
 4     cups (946 ml) water
 1 1/4 cups (296 ml) lentils, washed
 1 1/4 cups (296 ml) dry white wine
 3     tbsp (45 ml) olive oil
 1     carrot, scraped and diced
 2     tomatoes, peeled and chopped
 1     rib celery, diced
       Salt and freshly ground black pepper
 1/2   tsp (2.5 ml) dried basil
 1     bay leaf
 8     Italian sweet sausages
 2     slices bacon, cut in small pieces
 2     onions, chopped
 1     green pepper, chopped
 2     cloves garlic, chopped
```

1. Put water in kettle with lentils. Add wine, oil, carrot, tomatoes, celery, salt, pepper, basil and bay leaf. Bring to boiling; cover and reduce heat. Simmer until liquid thickens and lentils soften.
2. While lentils are cooking, place sausages, bacon pieces, onions, green pepper and garlic in a large skillet over medium heat. Stir to mix well.
3. Sauté sausages until brown, about 1/2 hour.
4. Remove contents of skillet with a slotted spoon. Slice sausages and serve with lentils.

SPARERIBS 'N' SAUSAGES

Makes 6 - 8 servings.

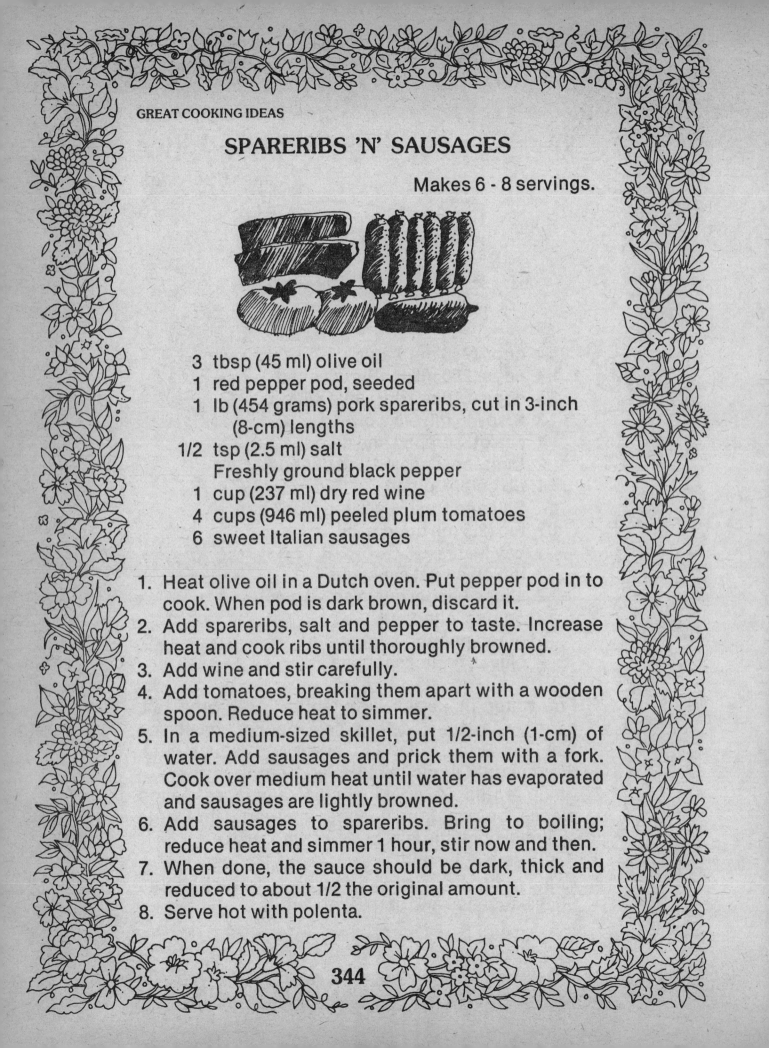

3 tbsp (45 ml) olive oil
1 red pepper pod, seeded
1 lb (454 grams) pork spareribs, cut in 3-inch (8-cm) lengths
1/2 tsp (2.5 ml) salt
  Freshly ground black pepper
1 cup (237 ml) dry red wine
4 cups (946 ml) peeled plum tomatoes
6 sweet Italian sausages

1. Heat olive oil in a Dutch oven. Put pepper pod in to cook. When pod is dark brown, discard it.
2. Add spareribs, salt and pepper to taste. Increase heat and cook ribs until thoroughly browned.
3. Add wine and stir carefully.
4. Add tomatoes, breaking them apart with a wooden spoon. Reduce heat to simmer.
5. In a medium-sized skillet, put 1/2-inch (1-cm) of water. Add sausages and prick them with a fork. Cook over medium heat until water has evaporated and sausages are lightly browned.
6. Add sausages to spareribs. Bring to boiling; reduce heat and simmer 1 hour, stir now and then.
7. When done, the sauce should be dark, thick and reduced to about 1/2 the original amount.
8. Serve hot with polenta.

SPARERIBS WITH SWEET 'N' SOUR SAUCE

Makes 4 servings.*

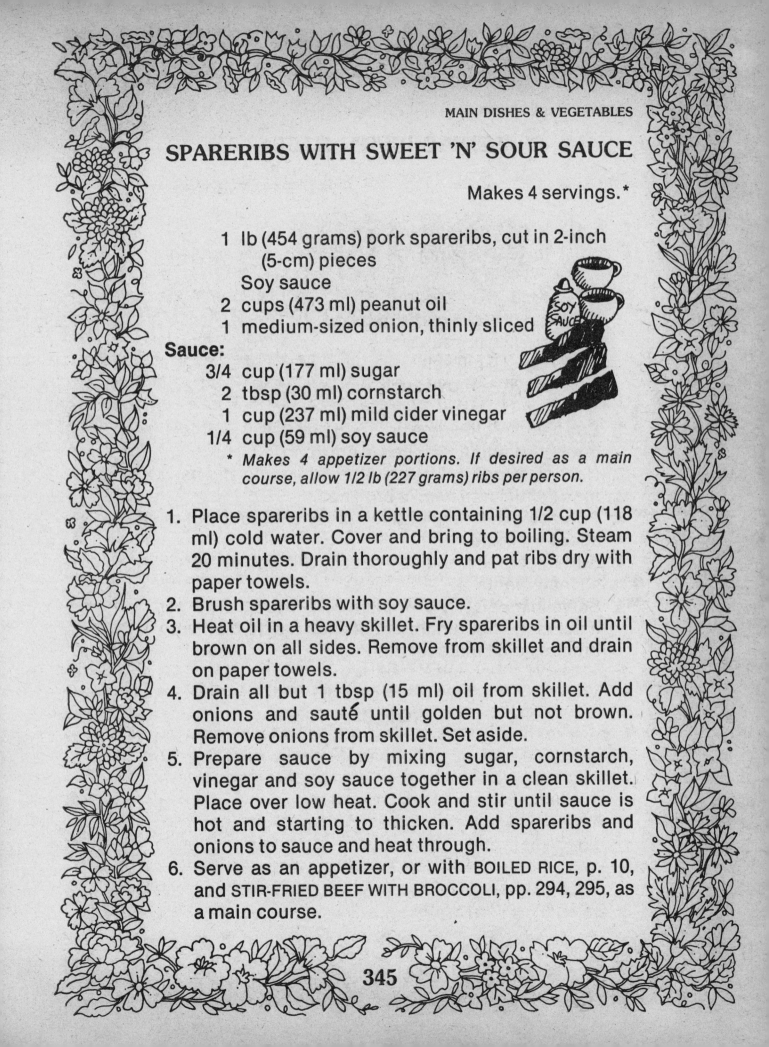

1 lb (454 grams) pork spareribs, cut in 2-inch (5-cm) pieces
  Soy sauce
2 cups (473 ml) peanut oil
1 medium-sized onion, thinly sliced

Sauce:

3/4 cup (177 ml) sugar
2 tbsp (30 ml) cornstarch
1 cup (237 ml) mild cider vinegar
1/4 cup (59 ml) soy sauce

* Makes 4 appetizer portions. If desired as a main course, allow 1/2 lb (227 grams) ribs per person.

1. Place spareribs in a kettle containing 1/2 cup (118 ml) cold water. Cover and bring to boiling. Steam 20 minutes. Drain thoroughly and pat ribs dry with paper towels.
2. Brush spareribs with soy sauce.
3. Heat oil in a heavy skillet. Fry spareribs in oil until brown on all sides. Remove from skillet and drain on paper towels.
4. Drain all but 1 tbsp (15 ml) oil from skillet. Add onions and sauté until golden but not brown. Remove onions from skillet. Set aside.
5. Prepare sauce by mixing sugar, cornstarch, vinegar and soy sauce together in a clean skillet. Place over low heat. Cook and stir until sauce is hot and starting to thicken. Add spareribs and onions to sauce and heat through.
6. Serve as an appetizer, or with BOILED RICE, p. 10, and STIR-FRIED BEEF WITH BROCCOLI, pp. 294, 295, as a main course.

SPINACH WITH HAM

Makes 4 servings.

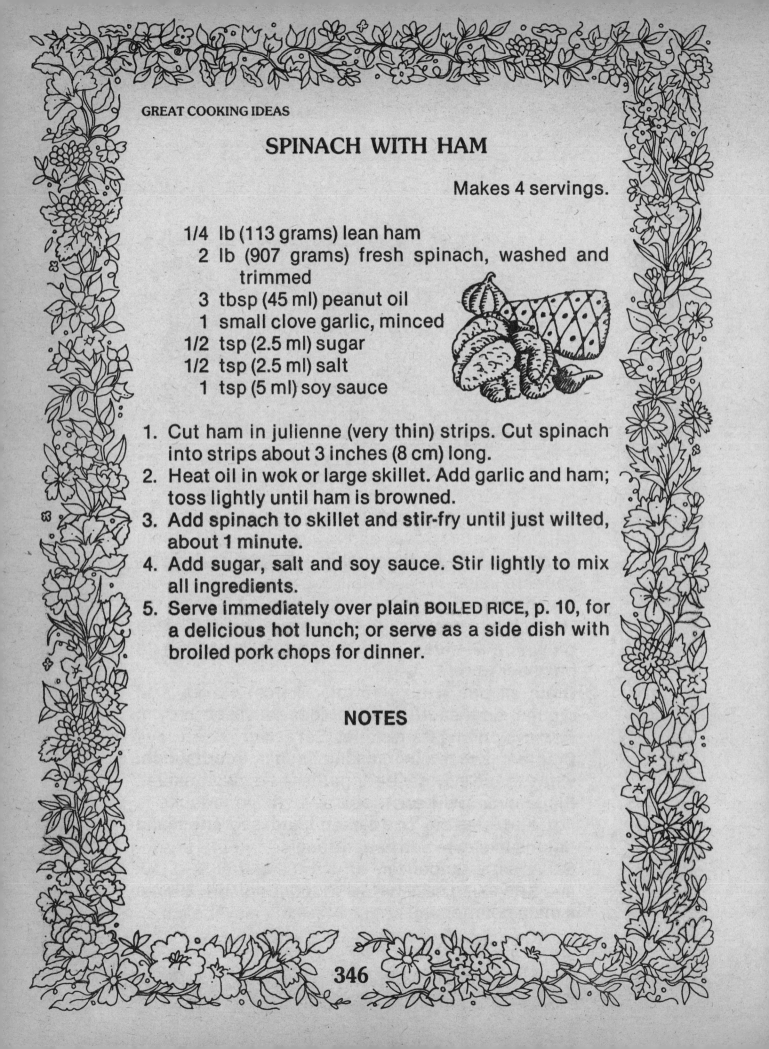

1/4 lb (113 grams) lean ham
2 lb (907 grams) fresh spinach, washed and trimmed
3 tbsp (45 ml) peanut oil
1 small clove garlic, minced
1/2 tsp (2.5 ml) sugar
1/2 tsp (2.5 ml) salt
1 tsp (5 ml) soy sauce

1. Cut ham in julienne (very thin) strips. Cut spinach into strips about 3 inches (8 cm) long.
2. Heat oil in wok or large skillet. Add garlic and ham; toss lightly until ham is browned.
3. Add spinach to skillet and stir-fry until just wilted, about 1 minute.
4. Add sugar, salt and soy sauce. Stir lightly to mix all ingredients.
5. Serve immediately over plain BOILED RICE, p. 10, for a delicious hot lunch; or serve as a side dish with broiled pork chops for dinner.

NOTES

STUFFED CUCUMBERS

Makes 6 servings.

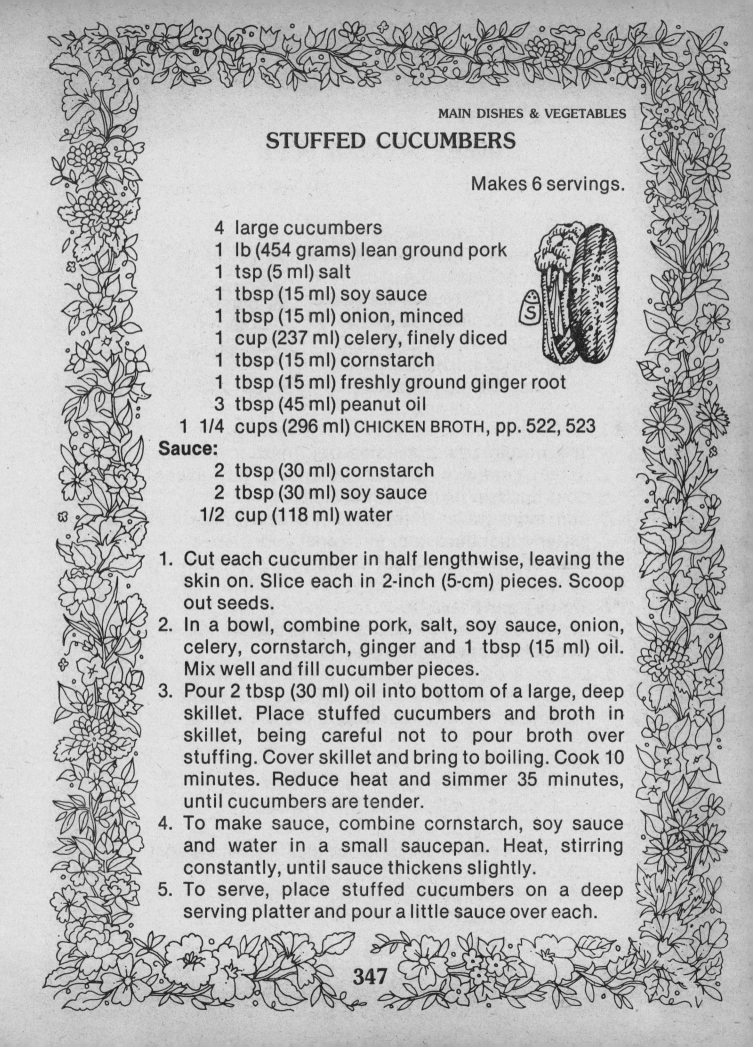

4 large cucumbers
1 lb (454 grams) lean ground pork
1 tsp (5 ml) salt
1 tbsp (15 ml) soy sauce
1 tbsp (15 ml) onion, minced
1 cup (237 ml) celery, finely diced
1 tbsp (15 ml) cornstarch
1 tbsp (15 ml) freshly ground ginger root
3 tbsp (45 ml) peanut oil
1 1/4 cups (296 ml) CHICKEN BROTH, pp. 522, 523

Sauce:

2 tbsp (30 ml) cornstarch
2 tbsp (30 ml) soy sauce
1/2 cup (118 ml) water

1. Cut each cucumber in half lengthwise, leaving the skin on. Slice each in 2-inch (5-cm) pieces. Scoop out seeds.
2. In a bowl, combine pork, salt, soy sauce, onion, celery, cornstarch, ginger and 1 tbsp (15 ml) oil. Mix well and fill cucumber pieces.
3. Pour 2 tbsp (30 ml) oil into bottom of a large, deep skillet. Place stuffed cucumbers and broth in skillet, being careful not to pour broth over stuffing. Cover skillet and bring to boiling. Cook 10 minutes. Reduce heat and simmer 35 minutes, until cucumbers are tender.
4. To make sauce, combine cornstarch, soy sauce and water in a small saucepan. Heat, stirring constantly, until sauce thickens slightly.
5. To serve, place stuffed cucumbers on a deep serving platter and pour a little sauce over each.

SWEET 'N' SOUR PORK

Makes 4 - 6 servings.

Pork:

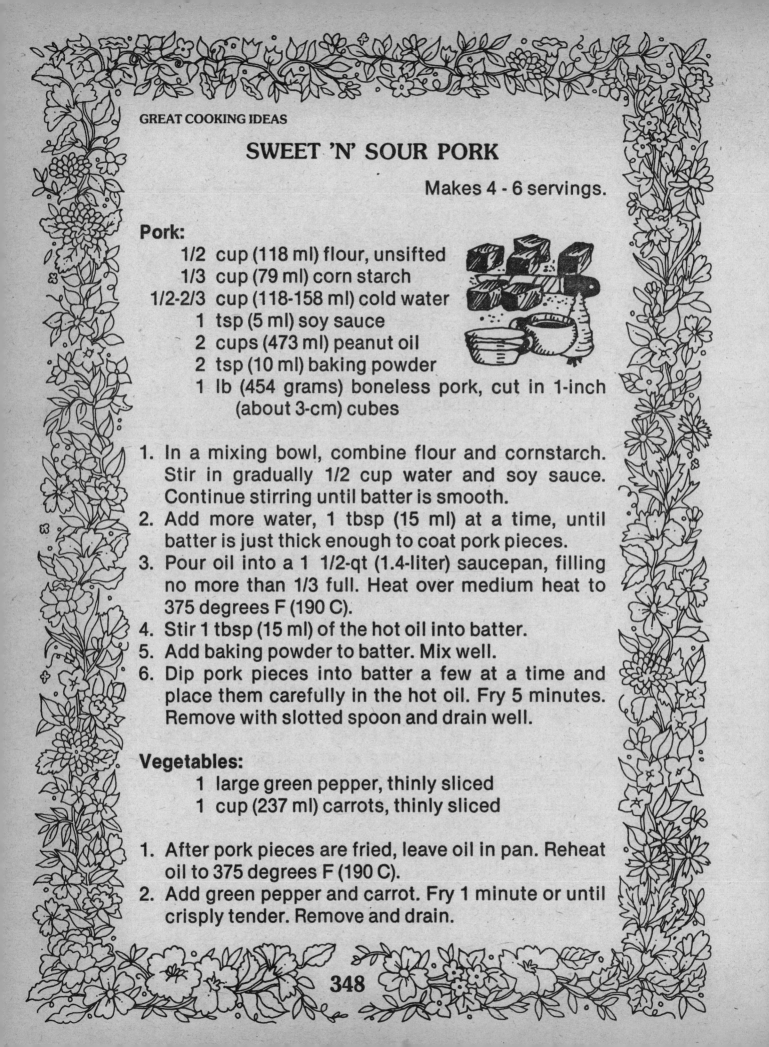

- 1/2 cup (118 ml) flour, unsifted
- 1/3 cup (79 ml) corn starch
- 1/2-2/3 cup (118-158 ml) cold water
- 1 tsp (5 ml) soy sauce
- 2 cups (473 ml) peanut oil
- 2 tsp (10 ml) baking powder
- 1 lb (454 grams) boneless pork, cut in 1-inch (about 3-cm) cubes

1. In a mixing bowl, combine flour and cornstarch. Stir in gradually 1/2 cup water and soy sauce. Continue stirring until batter is smooth.
2. Add more water, 1 tbsp (15 ml) at a time, until batter is just thick enough to coat pork pieces.
3. Pour oil into a 1 1/2-qt (1.4-liter) saucepan, filling no more than 1/3 full. Heat over medium heat to 375 degrees F (190 C).
4. Stir 1 tbsp (15 ml) of the hot oil into batter.
5. Add baking powder to batter. Mix well.
6. Dip pork pieces into batter a few at a time and place them carefully in the hot oil. Fry 5 minutes. Remove with slotted spoon and drain well.

Vegetables:

- 1 large green pepper, thinly sliced
- 1 cup (237 ml) carrots, thinly sliced

1. After pork pieces are fried, leave oil in pan. Reheat oil to 375 degrees F (190 C).
2. Add green pepper and carrot. Fry 1 minute or until crisply tender. Remove and drain.

348

Sauce:

    1   can (8 oz or 227 grams) pineapple chunks,
          unsweetened
    1/3 cup (79 ml) wine vinegar
    1   tbsp (15 ml) cornstarch
    1/3 cup (79 ml) dark corn syrup
    1   tbsp (15 ml) sugar
    2   tbsp (30 ml) dry sherry
    1/2 tsp (2.5 ml) salt

1. Drain pineapple, reserving 1/4 cup (59 ml) of the juice.
2. In a large, heavy skillet, combine the vinegar and cornstarch until it forms a smooth paste. Add corn syrup, sugar, sherry, salt and reserved pineapple juice. Bring to boiling, stirring constantly, over medium heat.
3. Add pork pieces, vegetables and pineapple chunks. Bring to a second boil while stirring constantly. Boil about 1 minute. Serve hot.

Suggested Menu
(for 6)

SHRIMP TOAST, p. 46
CHICKEN BROTH, pp. 522, 523
POACHED HADDOCK, p. 378
Sweet and Sour Pork
BOILED RICE, p. 10
Dry white wine, such as Chablis or Pinot Blanc*
GINGER FRUIT, p. 493, and Tea

*For those who would like to make this a completely Chinese dinner, obtain some Shaohsing wine. It should be served with the food, warm (or hot), from a porcelain or pewter wine pot. Use small special wine cups instead of glasses.

TOAST SQUARES WITH SPICY PORK

Makes 4 - 6 servings.

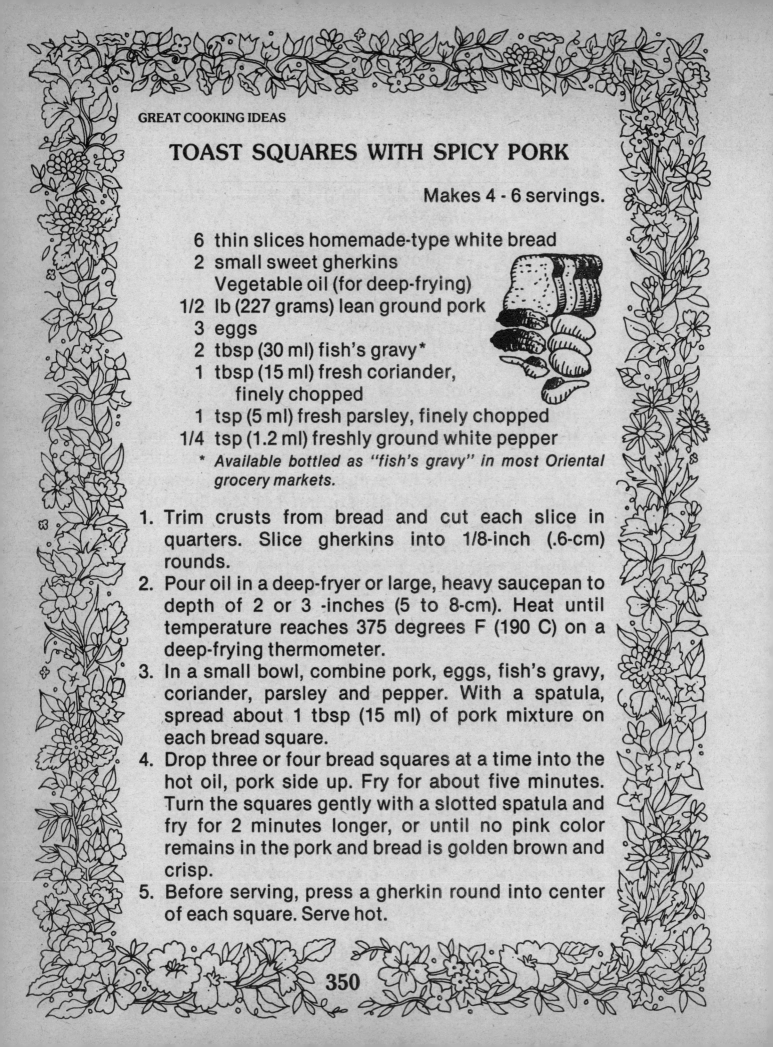

- 6 thin slices homemade-type white bread
- 2 small sweet gherkins
  Vegetable oil (for deep-frying)
- 1/2 lb (227 grams) lean ground pork
- 3 eggs
- 2 tbsp (30 ml) fish's gravy*
- 1 tbsp (15 ml) fresh coriander,
  finely chopped
- 1 tsp (5 ml) fresh parsley, finely chopped
- 1/4 tsp (1.2 ml) freshly ground white pepper

  * *Available bottled as "fish's gravy" in most Oriental
  grocery markets.*

1. Trim crusts from bread and cut each slice in quarters. Slice gherkins into 1/8-inch (.6-cm) rounds.
2. Pour oil in a deep-fryer or large, heavy saucepan to depth of 2 or 3 -inches (5 to 8-cm). Heat until temperature reaches 375 degrees F (190 C) on a deep-frying thermometer.
3. In a small bowl, combine pork, eggs, fish's gravy, coriander, parsley and pepper. With a spatula, spread about 1 tbsp (15 ml) of pork mixture on each bread square.
4. Drop three or four bread squares at a time into the hot oil, pork side up. Fry for about five minutes. Turn the squares gently with a slotted spatula and fry for 2 minutes longer, or until no pink color remains in the pork and bread is golden brown and crisp.
5. Before serving, press a gherkin round into center of each square. Serve hot.

VEGETABLE-RICE

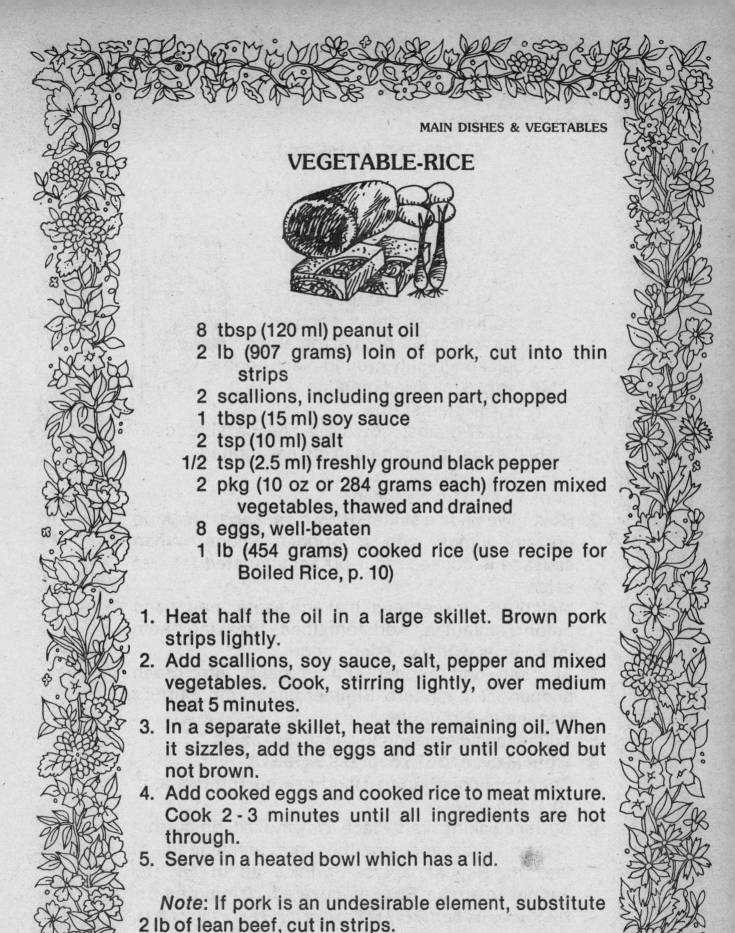

8 tbsp (120 ml) peanut oil
2 lb (907 grams) loin of pork, cut into thin strips
2 scallions, including green part, chopped
1 tbsp (15 ml) soy sauce
2 tsp (10 ml) salt
1/2 tsp (2.5 ml) freshly ground black pepper
2 pkg (10 oz or 284 grams each) frozen mixed vegetables, thawed and drained
8 eggs, well-beaten
1 lb (454 grams) cooked rice (use recipe for Boiled Rice, p. 10)

1. Heat half the oil in a large skillet. Brown pork strips lightly.
2. Add scallions, soy sauce, salt, pepper and mixed vegetables. Cook, stirring lightly, over medium heat 5 minutes.
3. In a separate skillet, heat the remaining oil. When it sizzles, add the eggs and stir until cooked but not brown.
4. Add cooked eggs and cooked rice to meat mixture. Cook 2 - 3 minutes until all ingredients are hot through.
5. Serve in a heated bowl which has a lid.

Note: If pork is an undesirable element, substitute 2 lb of lean beef, cut in strips.

ZITI 'N' SAUSAGE

Makes 4 servings.

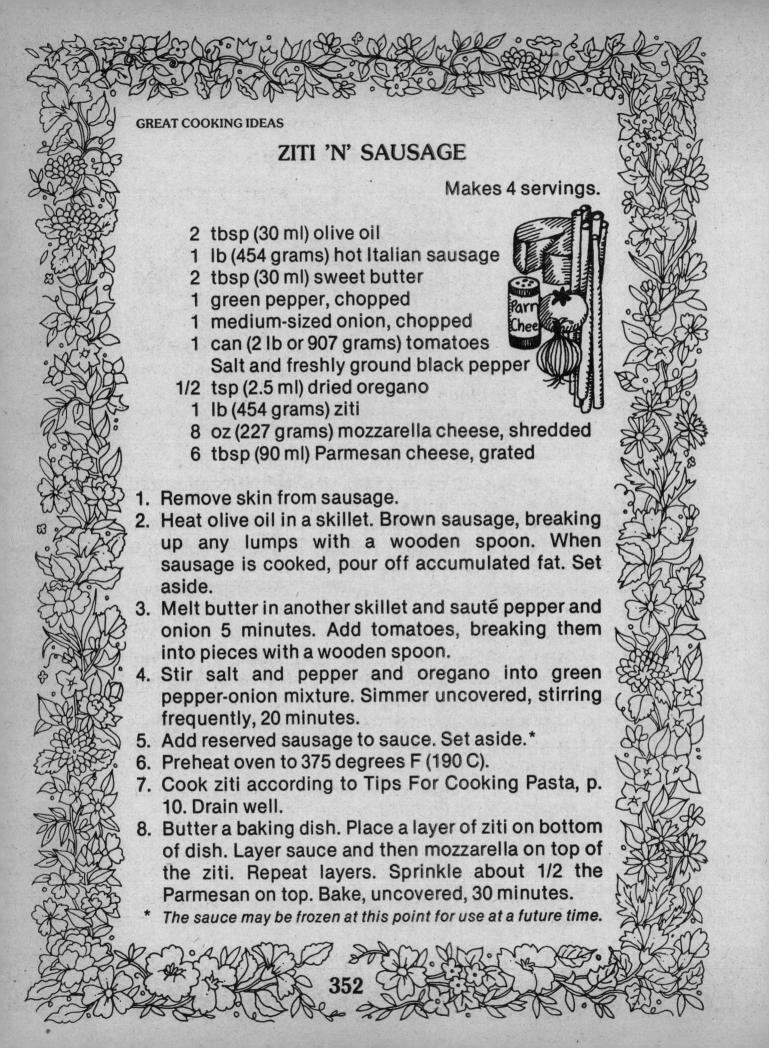

- 2 tbsp (30 ml) olive oil
- 1 lb (454 grams) hot Italian sausage
- 2 tbsp (30 ml) sweet butter
- 1 green pepper, chopped
- 1 medium-sized onion, chopped
- 1 can (2 lb or 907 grams) tomatoes
  Salt and freshly ground black pepper
- 1/2 tsp (2.5 ml) dried oregano
- 1 lb (454 grams) ziti
- 8 oz (227 grams) mozzarella cheese, shredded
- 6 tbsp (90 ml) Parmesan cheese, grated

1. Remove skin from sausage.
2. Heat olive oil in a skillet. Brown sausage, breaking up any lumps with a wooden spoon. When sausage is cooked, pour off accumulated fat. Set aside.
3. Melt butter in another skillet and sauté pepper and onion 5 minutes. Add tomatoes, breaking them into pieces with a wooden spoon.
4. Stir salt and pepper and oregano into green pepper-onion mixture. Simmer uncovered, stirring frequently, 20 minutes.
5. Add reserved sausage to sauce. Set aside.*
6. Preheat oven to 375 degrees F (190 C).
7. Cook ziti according to Tips For Cooking Pasta, p. 10. Drain well.
8. Butter a baking dish. Place a layer of ziti on bottom of dish. Layer sauce and then mozzarella on top of the ziti. Repeat layers. Sprinkle about 1/2 the Parmesan on top. Bake, uncovered, 30 minutes.

* *The sauce may be frozen at this point for use at a future time.*

CAVATELLI 'N' LAMB

Makes 4 servings.

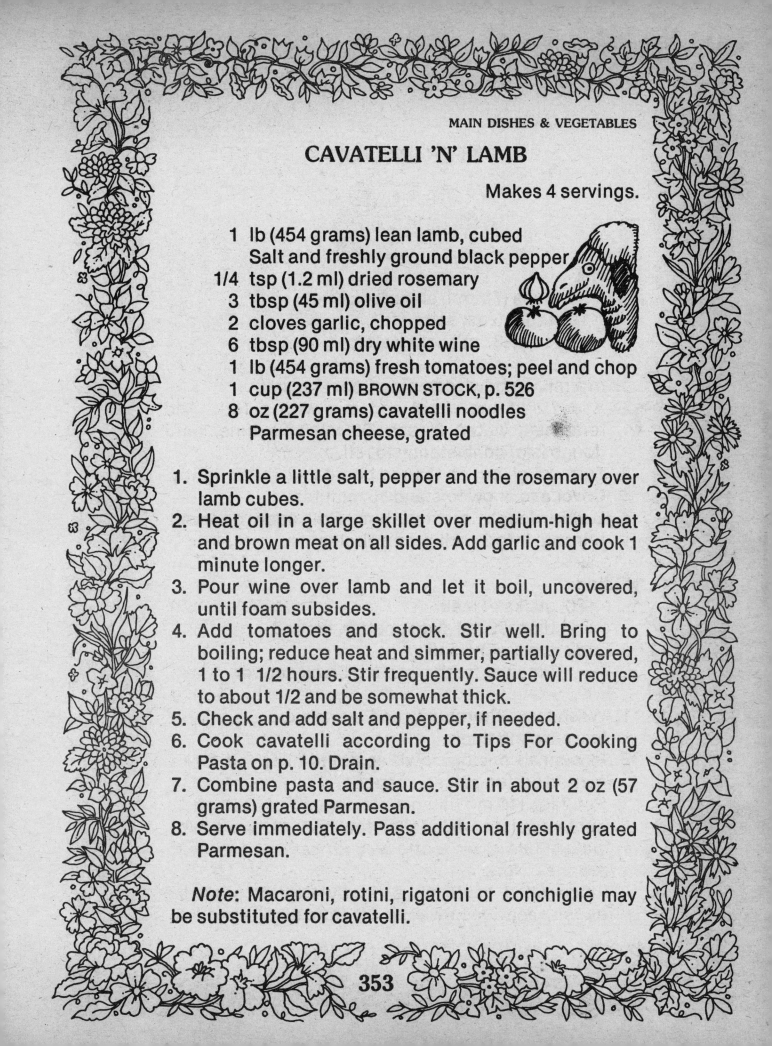

- 1 lb (454 grams) lean lamb, cubed
   Salt and freshly ground black pepper
- 1/4 tsp (1.2 ml) dried rosemary
- 3 tbsp (45 ml) olive oil
- 2 cloves garlic, chopped
- 6 tbsp (90 ml) dry white wine
- 1 lb (454 grams) fresh tomatoes; peel and chop
- 1 cup (237 ml) BROWN STOCK, p. 526
- 8 oz (227 grams) cavatelli noodles
   Parmesan cheese, grated

1. Sprinkle a little salt, pepper and the rosemary over lamb cubes.
2. Heat oil in a large skillet over medium-high heat and brown meat on all sides. Add garlic and cook 1 minute longer.
3. Pour wine over lamb and let it boil, uncovered, until foam subsides.
4. Add tomatoes and stock. Stir well. Bring to boiling; reduce heat and simmer, partially covered, 1 to 1 1/2 hours. Stir frequently. Sauce will reduce to about 1/2 and be somewhat thick.
5. Check and add salt and pepper, if needed.
6. Cook cavatelli according to Tips For Cooking Pasta on p. 10. Drain.
7. Combine pasta and sauce. Stir in about 2 oz (57 grams) grated Parmesan.
8. Serve immediately. Pass additional freshly grated Parmesan.

Note: Macaroni, rotini, rigatoni or conchiglie may be substituted for cavatelli.

LEEK RAVIOLI

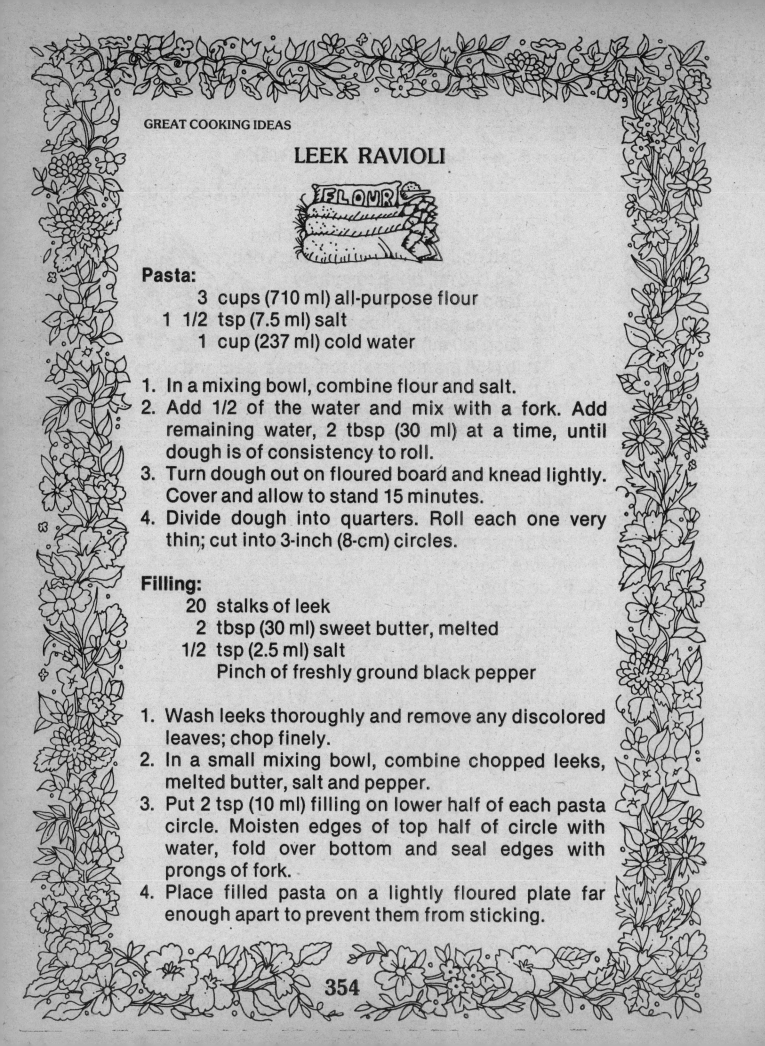

Pasta:

      3 cups (710 ml) all-purpose flour
  1 1/2 tsp (7.5 ml) salt
      1 cup (237 ml) cold water

1. In a mixing bowl, combine flour and salt.
2. Add 1/2 of the water and mix with a fork. Add remaining water, 2 tbsp (30 ml) at a time, until dough is of consistency to roll.
3. Turn dough out on floured board and knead lightly. Cover and allow to stand 15 minutes.
4. Divide dough into quarters. Roll each one very thin; cut into 3-inch (8-cm) circles.

Filling:

     20 stalks of leek
      2 tbsp (30 ml) sweet butter, melted
    1/2 tsp (2.5 ml) salt
         Pinch of freshly ground black pepper

1. Wash leeks thoroughly and remove any discolored leaves; chop finely.
2. In a small mixing bowl, combine chopped leeks, melted butter, salt and pepper.
3. Put 2 tsp (10 ml) filling on lower half of each pasta circle. Moisten edges of top half of circle with water, fold over bottom and seal edges with prongs of fork.
4. Place filled pasta on a lightly floured plate far enough apart to prevent them from sticking.

5. Fill a large kettle 3/4 full with water. Bring to a rolling boil.
6. Drop filled pasta into boiling water. Allow water to return to boiling. Cook 5 minutes. Remove with slotted spoon.

Sour Cream Mixture:

    1 pt (473 ml) sour cream
1/2 tsp (2.5 ml) garlic powder
1/2 tsp (2.5 ml) salt

1. In a small bowl, combine sour cream, garlic powder and salt. Mix thoroughly.
2. Spread a thin layer of sour cream over a platter. Place the drained pasta semi-circles on the platter and cover with the remaining sour cream mixture.

Meat Sauce:

1/2 cup (118 ml) sweet butter
  2 cups (473 ml) onions, chopped
  1 lb (454 grams) lean ground lamb
  1 tsp (5 ml) salt
1/2 tsp (2.5 ml) freshly ground black pepper
  2 tbsp (30 ml) tomato sauce
  2 tbsp (30 ml) mint leaves, chopped

1. Melt butter in a skillet and sauté onions until lightly browned.
2. Add lamb, salt, pepper and tomato sauce. Stir and cook over low heat until meat loses its pinkish color.
3. Add 1 cup (237 ml) water. Cook slowly until water evaporates.
4. Spoon lamb sauce over top of pasta and sour cream mixture. Sprinkle with chopped mint before serving.

MARINATED LAMB CURRY

Makes 4 - 6 servings.

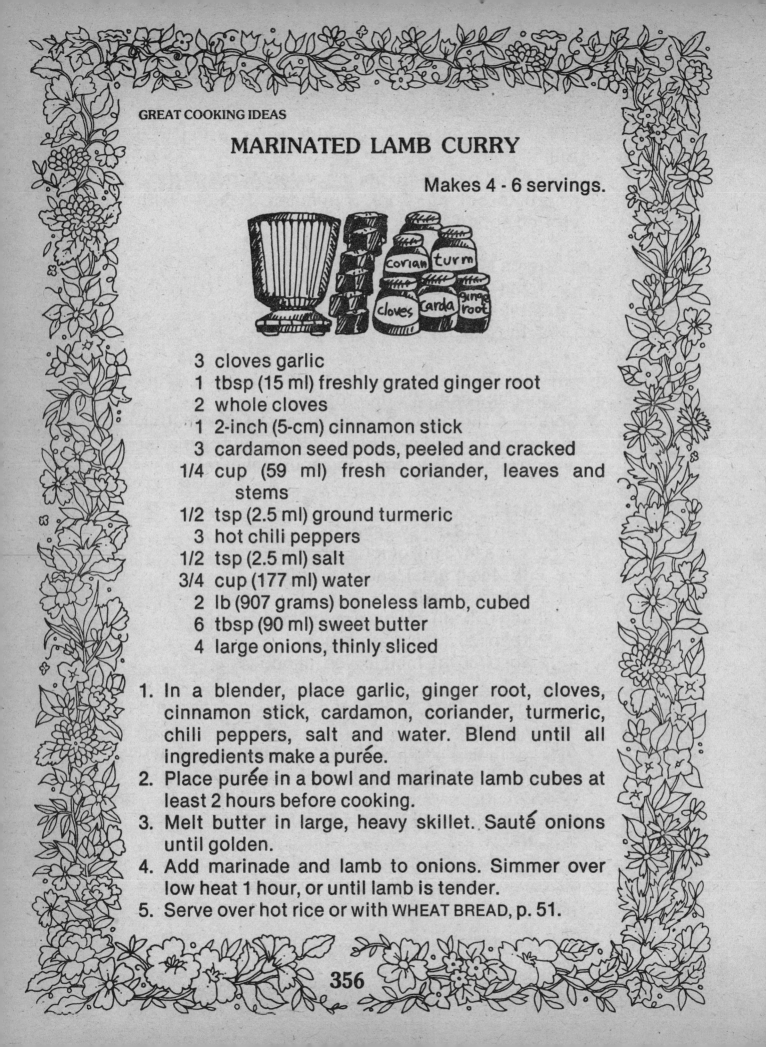

3 cloves garlic
1 tbsp (15 ml) freshly grated ginger root
2 whole cloves
1 2-inch (5-cm) cinnamon stick
3 cardamon seed pods, peeled and cracked
1/4 cup (59 ml) fresh coriander, leaves and stems
1/2 tsp (2.5 ml) ground turmeric
3 hot chili peppers
1/2 tsp (2.5 ml) salt
3/4 cup (177 ml) water
2 lb (907 grams) boneless lamb, cubed
6 tbsp (90 ml) sweet butter
4 large onions, thinly sliced

1. In a blender, place garlic, ginger root, cloves, cinnamon stick, cardamon, coriander, turmeric, chili peppers, salt and water. Blend until all ingredients make a purée.
2. Place purée in a bowl and marinate lamb cubes at least 2 hours before cooking.
3. Melt butter in large, heavy skillet. Sauté onions until golden.
4. Add marinade and lamb to onions. Simmer over low heat 1 hour, or until lamb is tender.
5. Serve over hot rice or with WHEAT BREAD, p. 51.

INDIAN VEAL CURRY

Makes 6 servings.

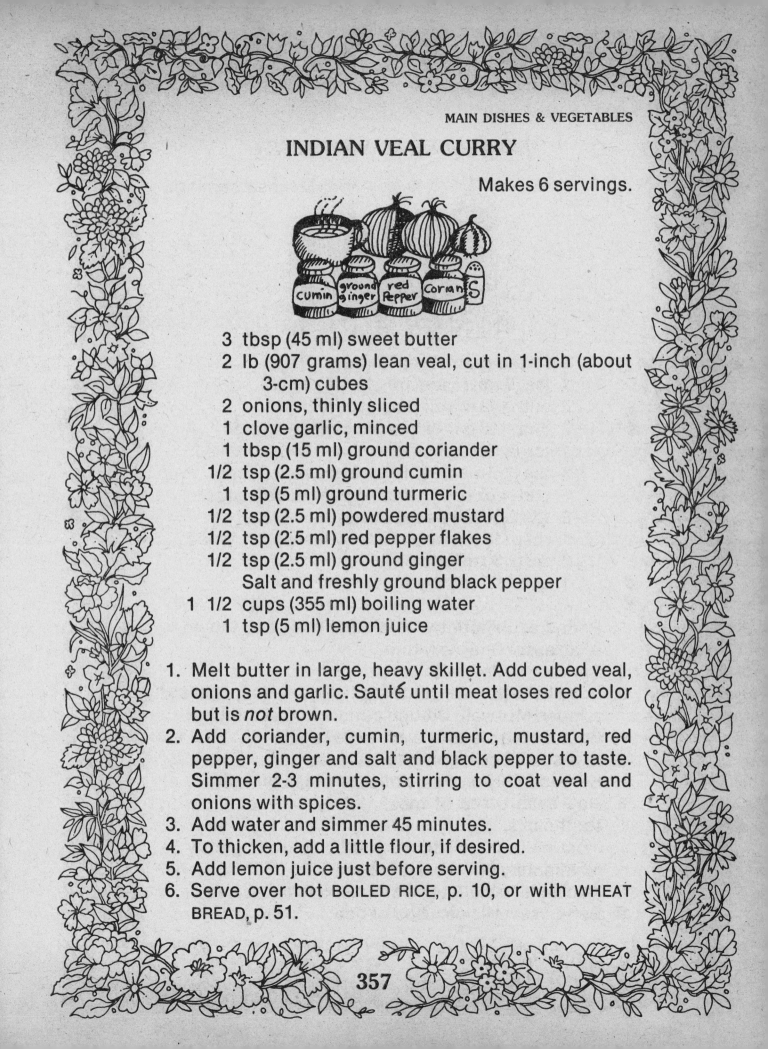

3 tbsp (45 ml) sweet butter
2 lb (907 grams) lean veal, cut in 1-inch (about 3-cm) cubes
2 onions, thinly sliced
1 clove garlic, minced
1 tbsp (15 ml) ground coriander
1/2 tsp (2.5 ml) ground cumin
1 tsp (5 ml) ground turmeric
1/2 tsp (2.5 ml) powdered mustard
1/2 tsp (2.5 ml) red pepper flakes
1/2 tsp (2.5 ml) ground ginger
Salt and freshly ground black pepper
1 1/2 cups (355 ml) boiling water
1 tsp (5 ml) lemon juice

1. Melt butter in large, heavy skillet. Add cubed veal, onions and garlic. Sauté until meat loses red color but is *not* brown.
2. Add coriander, cumin, turmeric, mustard, red pepper, ginger and salt and black pepper to taste. Simmer 2-3 minutes, stirring to coat veal and onions with spices.
3. Add water and simmer 45 minutes.
4. To thicken, add a little flour, if desired.
5. Add lemon juice just before serving.
6. Serve over hot BOILED RICE, p. 10, or with WHEAT BREAD, p. 51.

ROLLED VEAL WITH PÂTÉ

Makes 6 servings.

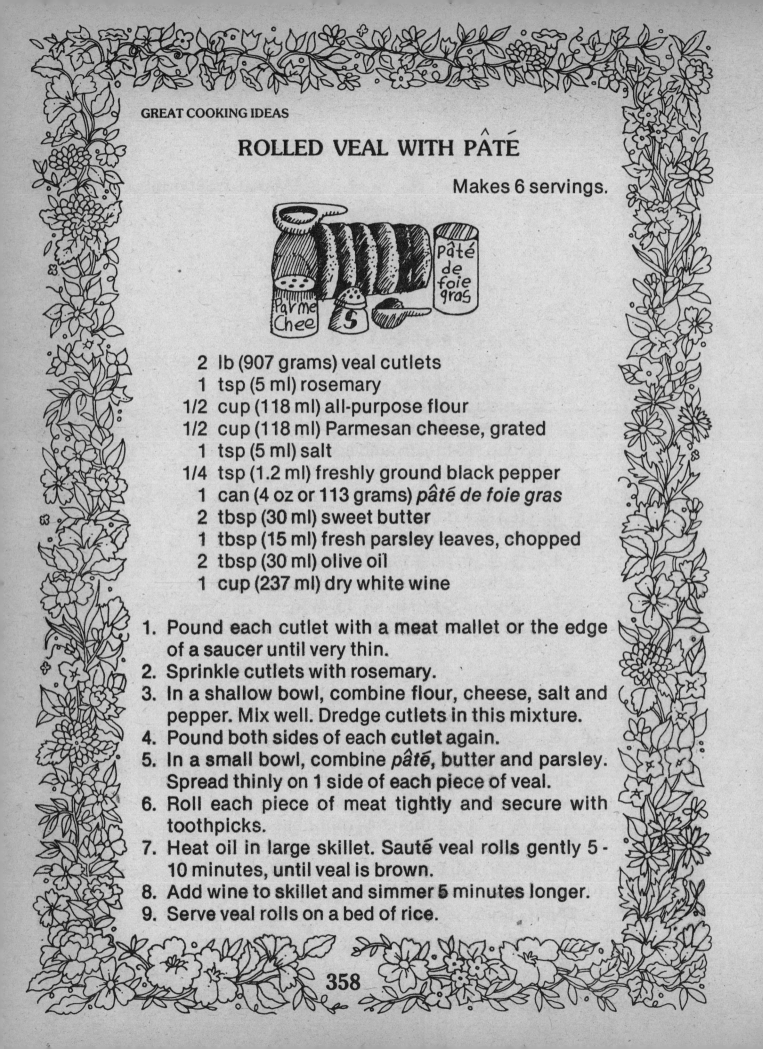

2	lb (907 grams) veal cutlets
1	tsp (5 ml) rosemary
1/2	cup (118 ml) all-purpose flour
1/2	cup (118 ml) Parmesan cheese, grated
1	tsp (5 ml) salt
1/4	tsp (1.2 ml) freshly ground black pepper
1	can (4 oz or 113 grams) *pâté de foie gras*
2	tbsp (30 ml) sweet butter
1	tbsp (15 ml) fresh parsley leaves, chopped
2	tbsp (30 ml) olive oil
1	cup (237 ml) dry white wine

1. Pound each cutlet with a meat mallet or the edge of a saucer until very thin.
2. Sprinkle cutlets with rosemary.
3. In a shallow bowl, combine flour, cheese, salt and pepper. Mix well. Dredge cutlets in this mixture.
4. Pound both sides of each cutlet again.
5. In a small bowl, combine *pâté*, butter and parsley. Spread thinly on 1 side of each piece of veal.
6. Roll each piece of meat tightly and secure with toothpicks.
7. Heat oil in large skillet. Sauté veal rolls gently 5 - 10 minutes, until veal is brown.
8. Add wine to skillet and simmer 5 minutes longer.
9. Serve veal rolls on a bed of rice.

VEAL CUTLETS PARMESAN

Makes 6 servings.

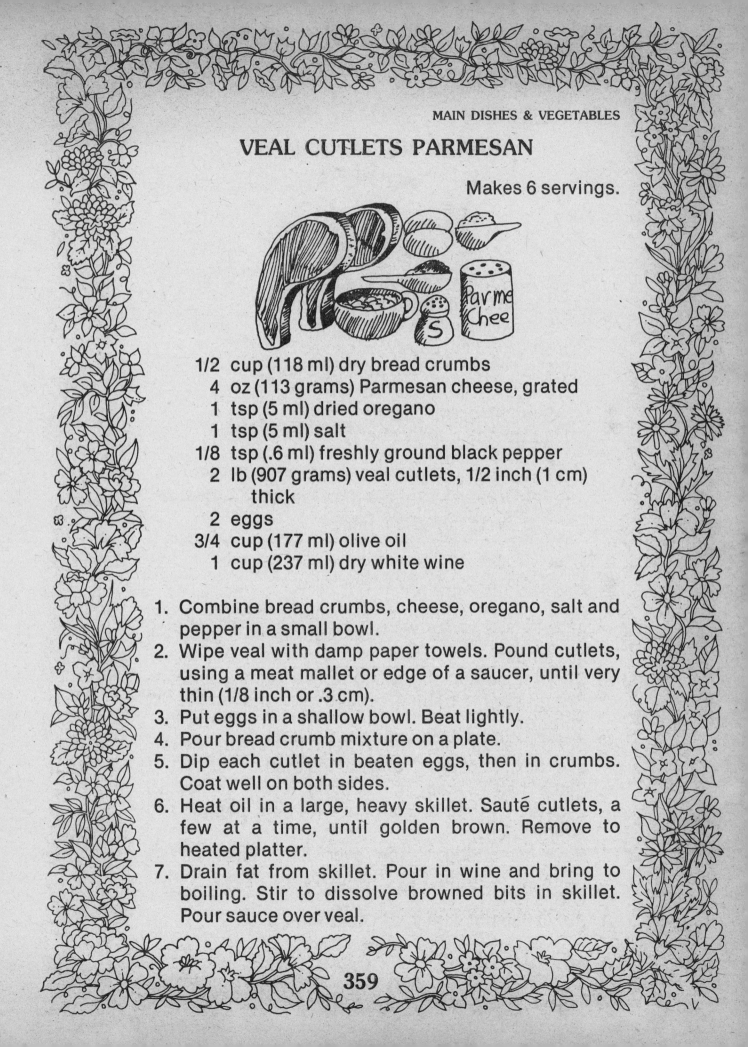

1/2 cup (118 ml) dry bread crumbs
4 oz (113 grams) Parmesan cheese, grated
1 tsp (5 ml) dried oregano
1 tsp (5 ml) salt
1/8 tsp (.6 ml) freshly ground black pepper
2 lb (907 grams) veal cutlets, 1/2 inch (1 cm) thick
2 eggs
3/4 cup (177 ml) olive oil
1 cup (237 ml) dry white wine

1. Combine bread crumbs, cheese, oregano, salt and pepper in a small bowl.
2. Wipe veal with damp paper towels. Pound cutlets, using a meat mallet or edge of a saucer, until very thin (1/8 inch or .3 cm).
3. Put eggs in a shallow bowl. Beat lightly.
4. Pour bread crumb mixture on a plate.
5. Dip each cutlet in beaten eggs, then in crumbs. Coat well on both sides.
6. Heat oil in a large, heavy skillet. Sauté cutlets, a few at a time, until golden brown. Remove to heated platter.
7. Drain fat from skillet. Pour in wine and bring to boiling. Stir to dissolve browned bits in skillet. Pour sauce over veal.

BAKED RED SNAPPER

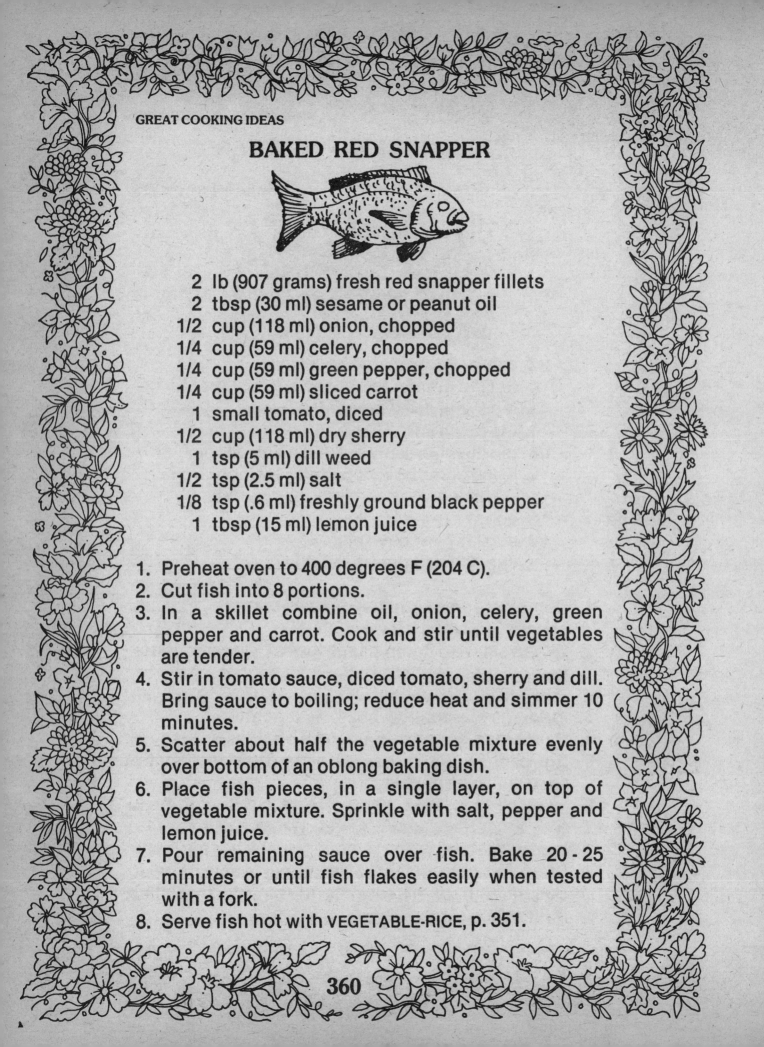

```
  2   lb (907 grams) fresh red snapper fillets
  2   tbsp (30 ml) sesame or peanut oil
1/2   cup (118 ml) onion, chopped
1/4   cup (59 ml) celery, chopped
1/4   cup (59 ml) green pepper, chopped
1/4   cup (59 ml) sliced carrot
  1   small tomato, diced
1/2   cup (118 ml) dry sherry
  1   tsp (5 ml) dill weed
1/2   tsp (2.5 ml) salt
1/8   tsp (.6 ml) freshly ground black pepper
  1   tbsp (15 ml) lemon juice
```

1. Preheat oven to 400 degrees F (204 C).
2. Cut fish into 8 portions.
3. In a skillet combine oil, onion, celery, green pepper and carrot. Cook and stir until vegetables are tender.
4. Stir in tomato sauce, diced tomato, sherry and dill. Bring sauce to boiling; reduce heat and simmer 10 minutes.
5. Scatter about half the vegetable mixture evenly over bottom of an oblong baking dish.
6. Place fish pieces, in a single layer, on top of vegetable mixture. Sprinkle with salt, pepper and lemon juice.
7. Pour remaining sauce over fish. Bake 20 - 25 minutes or until fish flakes easily when tested with a fork.
8. Serve fish hot with VEGETABLE-RICE, p. 351.

BAKED SHRIMP 'N' CHEESE

Makes 4 servings.

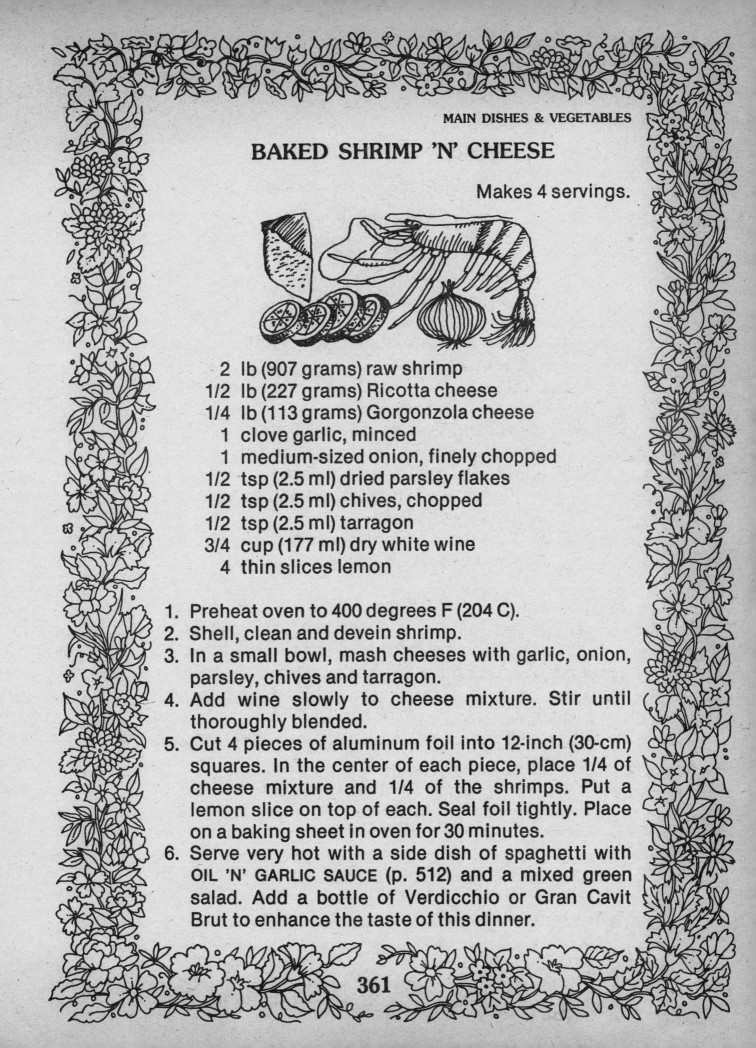

2	lb (907 grams) raw shrimp
1/2	lb (227 grams) Ricotta cheese
1/4	lb (113 grams) Gorgonzola cheese
1	clove garlic, minced
1	medium-sized onion, finely chopped
1/2	tsp (2.5 ml) dried parsley flakes
1/2	tsp (2.5 ml) chives, chopped
1/2	tsp (2.5 ml) tarragon
3/4	cup (177 ml) dry white wine
4	thin slices lemon

1. Preheat oven to 400 degrees F (204 C).
2. Shell, clean and devein shrimp.
3. In a small bowl, mash cheeses with garlic, onion, parsley, chives and tarragon.
4. Add wine slowly to cheese mixture. Stir until thoroughly blended.
5. Cut 4 pieces of aluminum foil into 12-inch (30-cm) squares. In the center of each piece, place 1/4 of cheese mixture and 1/4 of the shrimps. Put a lemon slice on top of each. Seal foil tightly. Place on a baking sheet in oven for 30 minutes.
6. Serve very hot with a side dish of spaghetti with OIL 'N' GARLIC SAUCE (p. 512) and a mixed green salad. Add a bottle of Verdicchio or Gran Cavit Brut to enhance the taste of this dinner.

BAKED SWORDFISH

Makes 6 servings.

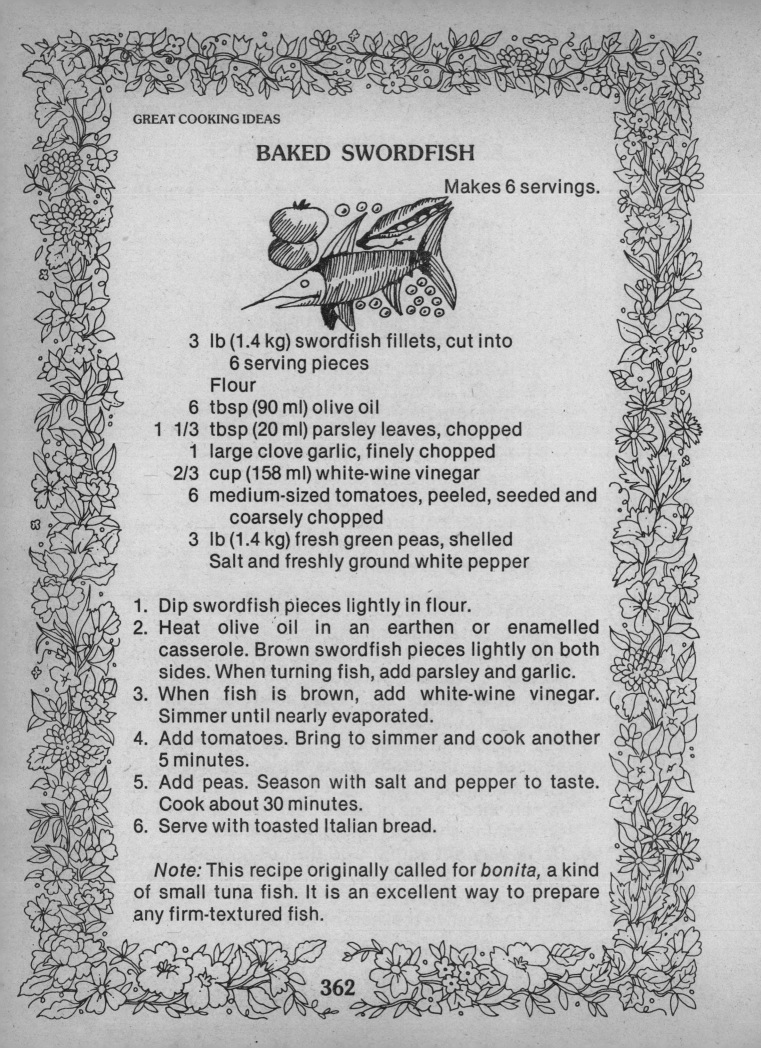

3 lb (1.4 kg) swordfish fillets, cut into
    6 serving pieces
Flour
6 tbsp (90 ml) olive oil
1 1/3 tbsp (20 ml) parsley leaves, chopped
1 large clove garlic, finely chopped
2/3 cup (158 ml) white-wine vinegar
6 medium-sized tomatoes, peeled, seeded and
    coarsely chopped
3 lb (1.4 kg) fresh green peas, shelled
Salt and freshly ground white pepper

1. Dip swordfish pieces lightly in flour.
2. Heat olive oil in an earthen or enamelled casserole. Brown swordfish pieces lightly on both sides. When turning fish, add parsley and garlic.
3. When fish is brown, add white-wine vinegar. Simmer until nearly evaporated.
4. Add tomatoes. Bring to simmer and cook another 5 minutes.
5. Add peas. Season with salt and pepper to taste. Cook about 30 minutes.
6. Serve with toasted Italian bread.

Note: This recipe originally called for *bonita,* a kind of small tuna fish. It is an excellent way to prepare any firm-textured fish.

BARBECUED PRAWNS

Makes 4 servings.

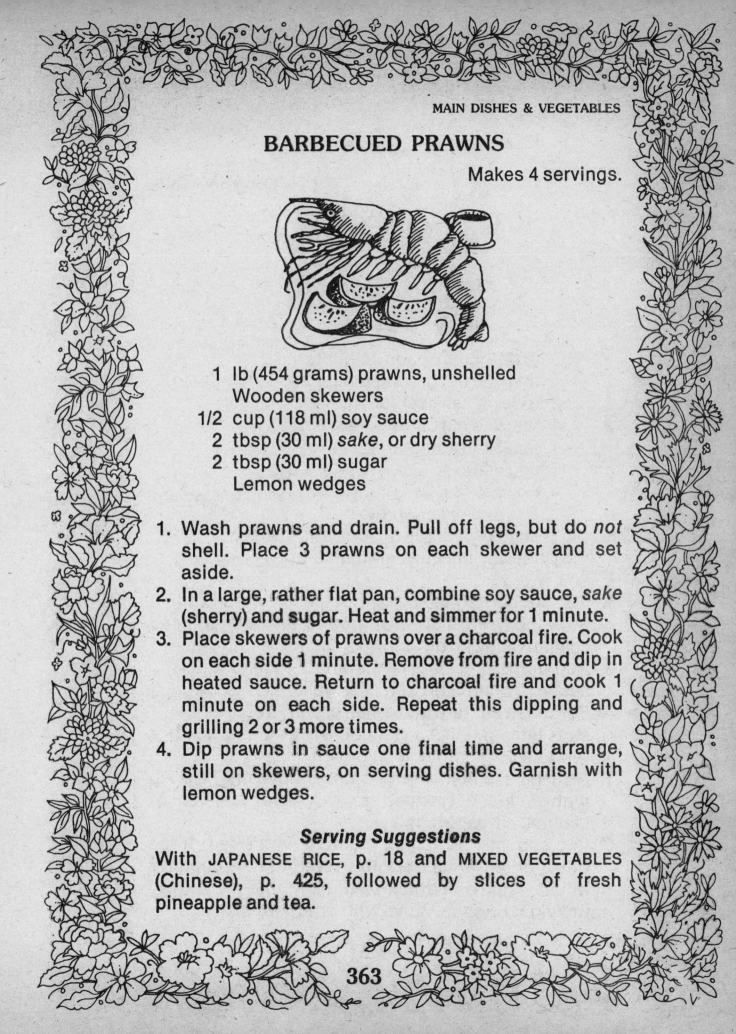

     1 lb (454 grams) prawns, unshelled
        Wooden skewers
   1/2 cup (118 ml) soy sauce
     2 tbsp (30 ml) *sake*, or dry sherry
     2 tbsp (30 ml) sugar
        Lemon wedges

1. Wash prawns and drain. Pull off legs, but do *not* shell. Place 3 prawns on each skewer and set aside.
2. In a large, rather flat pan, combine soy sauce, *sake* (sherry) and sugar. Heat and simmer for 1 minute.
3. Place skewers of prawns over a charcoal fire. Cook on each side 1 minute. Remove from fire and dip in heated sauce. Return to charcoal fire and cook 1 minute on each side. Repeat this dipping and grilling 2 or 3 more times.
4. Dip prawns in sauce one final time and arrange, still on skewers, on serving dishes. Garnish with lemon wedges.

Serving Suggestions

With JAPANESE RICE, p. 18 and MIXED VEGETABLES (Chinese), p. 425, followed by slices of fresh pineapple and tea.

BONITO CROQUETTES

Makes 4 servings.

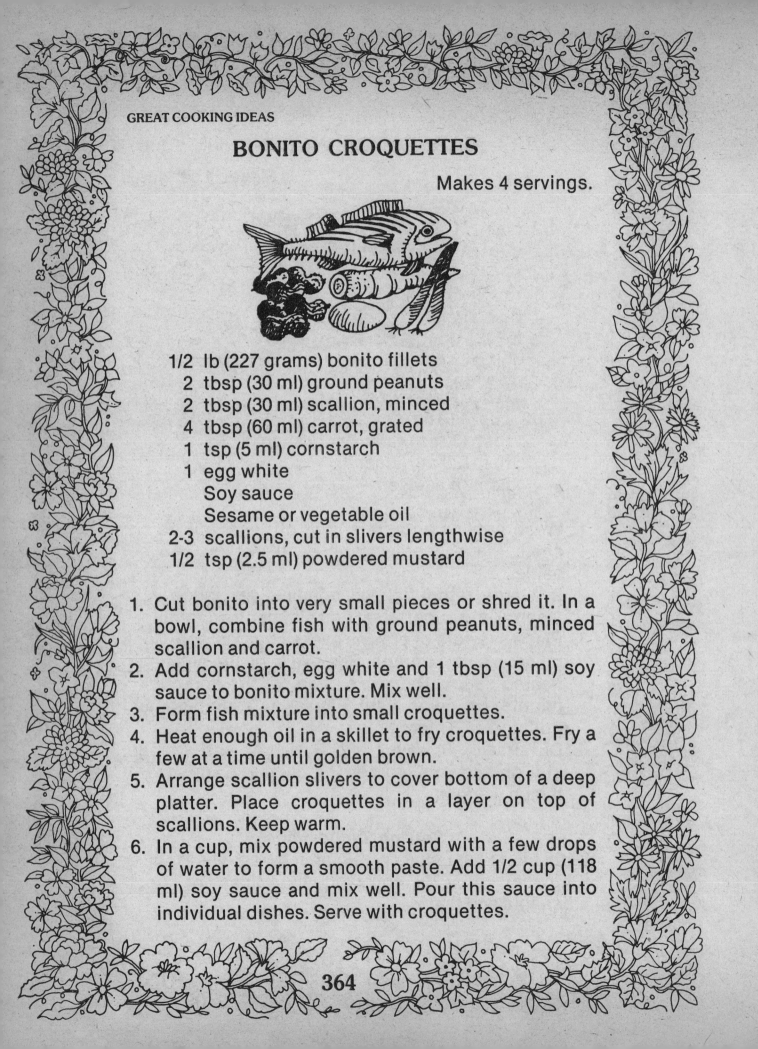

1/2 lb (227 grams) bonito fillets
2 tbsp (30 ml) ground peanuts
2 tbsp (30 ml) scallion, minced
4 tbsp (60 ml) carrot, grated
1 tsp (5 ml) cornstarch
1 egg white
Soy sauce
Sesame or vegetable oil
2-3 scallions, cut in slivers lengthwise
1/2 tsp (2.5 ml) powdered mustard

1. Cut bonito into very small pieces or shred it. In a bowl, combine fish with ground peanuts, minced scallion and carrot.
2. Add cornstarch, egg white and 1 tbsp (15 ml) soy sauce to bonito mixture. Mix well.
3. Form fish mixture into small croquettes.
4. Heat enough oil in a skillet to fry croquettes. Fry a few at a time until golden brown.
5. Arrange scallion slivers to cover bottom of a deep platter. Place croquettes in a layer on top of scallions. Keep warm.
6. In a cup, mix powdered mustard with a few drops of water to form a smooth paste. Add 1/2 cup (118 ml) soy sauce and mix well. Pour this sauce into individual dishes. Serve with croquettes.

BROILED GREY SOLE

Makes 4 servings.

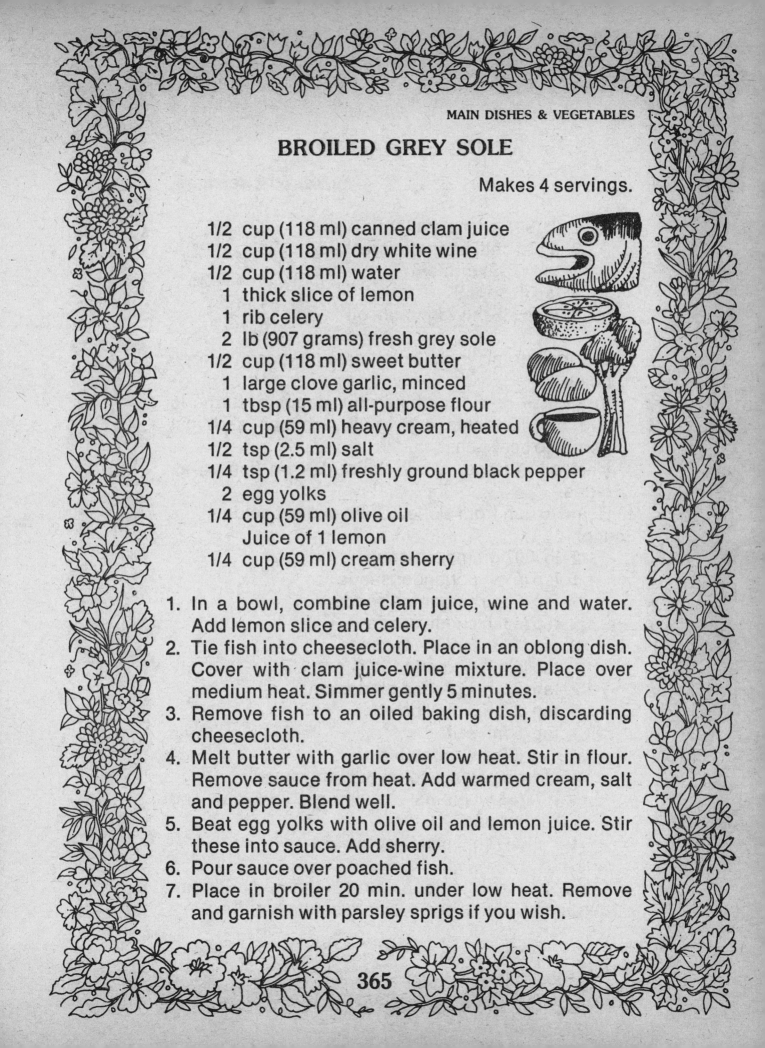

1/2 cup (118 ml) canned clam juice
1/2 cup (118 ml) dry white wine
1/2 cup (118 ml) water
  1 thick slice of lemon
  1 rib celery
  2 lb (907 grams) fresh grey sole
1/2 cup (118 ml) sweet butter
  1 large clove garlic, minced
  1 tbsp (15 ml) all-purpose flour
1/4 cup (59 ml) heavy cream, heated
1/2 tsp (2.5 ml) salt
1/4 tsp (1.2 ml) freshly ground black pepper
  2 egg yolks
1/4 cup (59 ml) olive oil
     Juice of 1 lemon
1/4 cup (59 ml) cream sherry

1. In a bowl, combine clam juice, wine and water. Add lemon slice and celery.
2. Tie fish into cheesecloth. Place in an oblong dish. Cover with clam juice-wine mixture. Place over medium heat. Simmer gently 5 minutes.
3. Remove fish to an oiled baking dish, discarding cheesecloth.
4. Melt butter with garlic over low heat. Stir in flour. Remove sauce from heat. Add warmed cream, salt and pepper. Blend well.
5. Beat egg yolks with olive oil and lemon juice. Stir these into sauce. Add sherry.
6. Pour sauce over poached fish.
7. Place in broiler 20 min. under low heat. Remove and garnish with parsley sprigs if you wish.

CURRIED HALIBUT

Makes 6 - 8 servings.

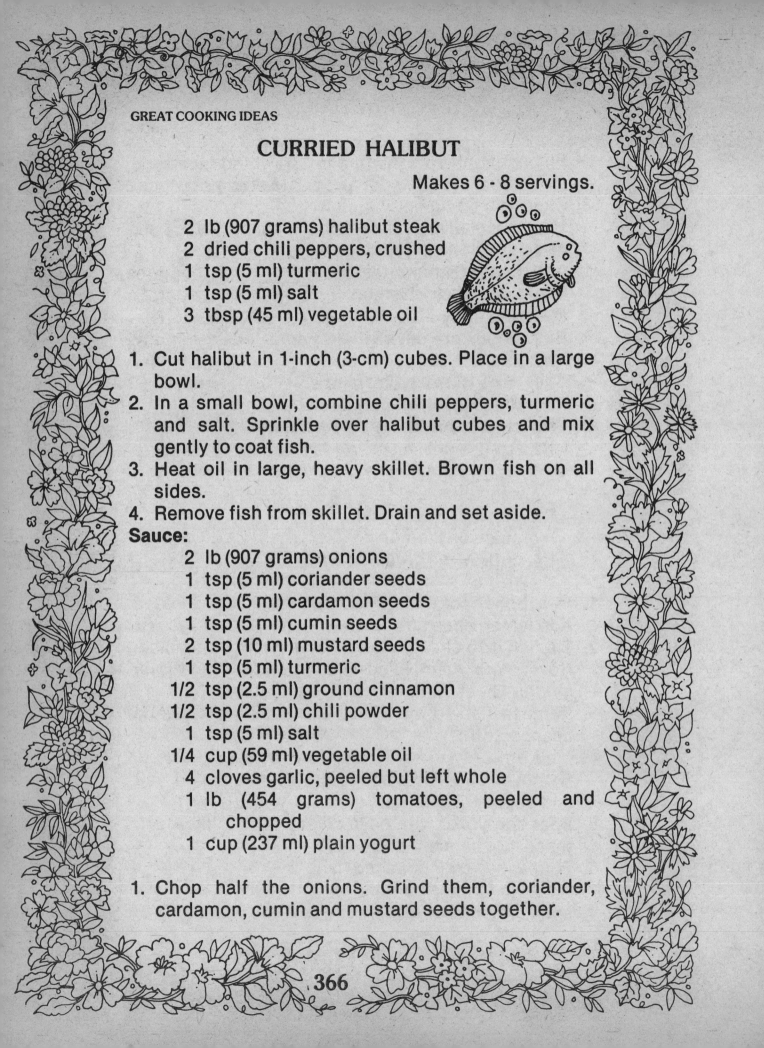

2 lb (907 grams) halibut steak
2 dried chili peppers, crushed
1 tsp (5 ml) turmeric
1 tsp (5 ml) salt
3 tbsp (45 ml) vegetable oil

1. Cut halibut in 1-inch (3-cm) cubes. Place in a large bowl.
2. In a small bowl, combine chili peppers, turmeric and salt. Sprinkle over halibut cubes and mix gently to coat fish.
3. Heat oil in large, heavy skillet. Brown fish on all sides.
4. Remove fish from skillet. Drain and set aside.

Sauce:

2 lb (907 grams) onions
1 tsp (5 ml) coriander seeds
1 tsp (5 ml) cardamon seeds
1 tsp (5 ml) cumin seeds
2 tsp (10 ml) mustard seeds
1 tsp (5 ml) turmeric
1/2 tsp (2.5 ml) ground cinnamon
1/2 tsp (2.5 ml) chili powder
1 tsp (5 ml) salt
1/4 cup (59 ml) vegetable oil
4 cloves garlic, peeled but left whole
1 lb (454 grams) tomatoes, peeled and chopped
1 cup (237 ml) plain yogurt

1. Chop half the onions. Grind them, coriander, cardamon, cumin and mustard seeds together.

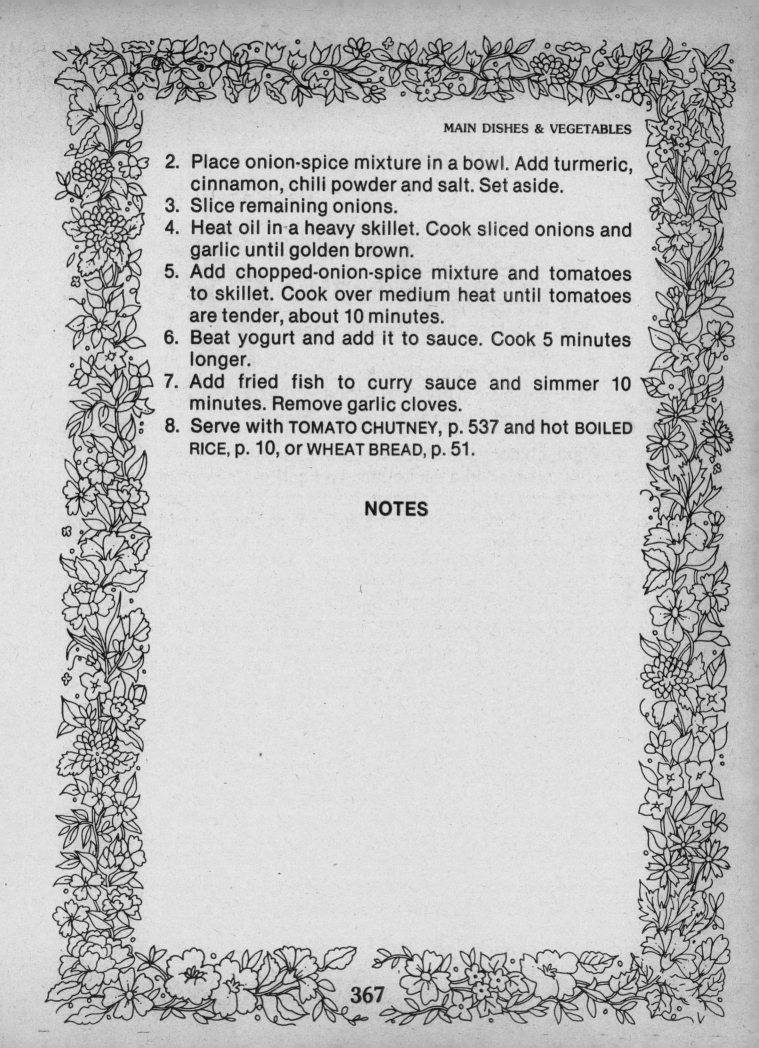

2. Place onion-spice mixture in a bowl. Add turmeric, cinnamon, chili powder and salt. Set aside.
3. Slice remaining onions.
4. Heat oil in a heavy skillet. Cook sliced onions and garlic until golden brown.
5. Add chopped-onion-spice mixture and tomatoes to skillet. Cook over medium heat until tomatoes are tender, about 10 minutes.
6. Beat yogurt and add it to sauce. Cook 5 minutes longer.
7. Add fried fish to curry sauce and simmer 10 minutes. Remove garlic cloves.
8. Serve with TOMATO CHUTNEY, p. 537 and hot BOILED RICE, p. 10, or WHEAT BREAD, p. 51.

NOTES

CHICORY WITH ANCHOVIES 'N' TOMATOES

Makes 4 servings.

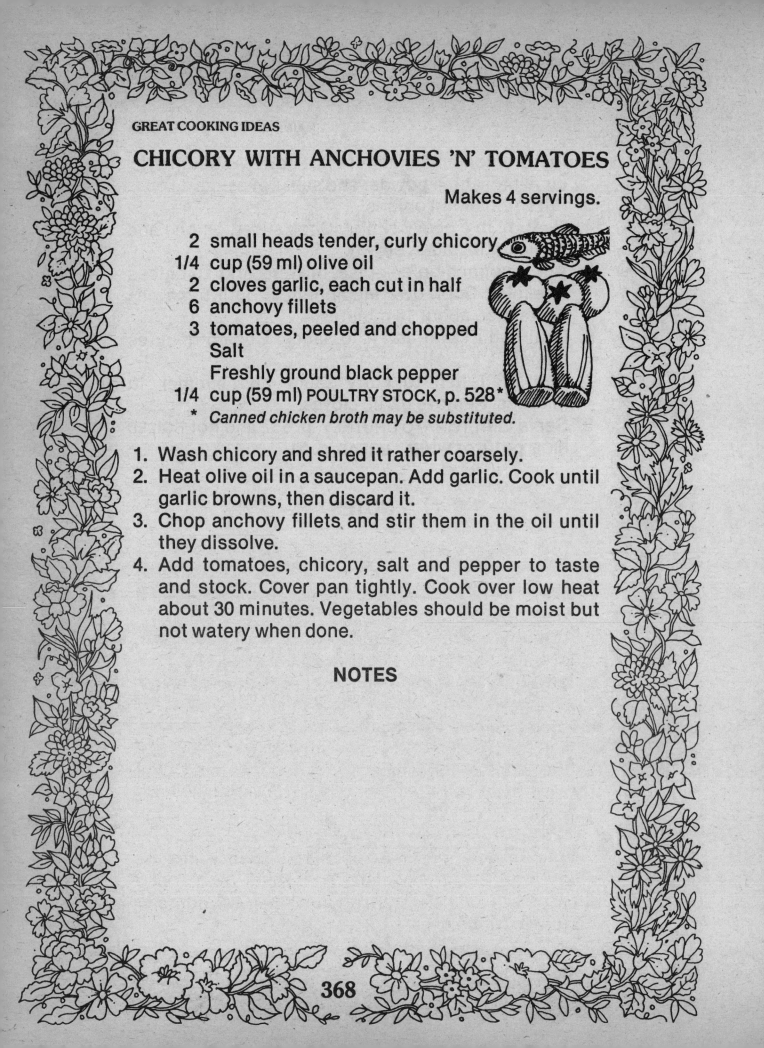

2 small heads tender, curly chicory
1/4 cup (59 ml) olive oil
2 cloves garlic, each cut in half
6 anchovy fillets
3 tomatoes, peeled and chopped
Salt
Freshly ground black pepper
1/4 cup (59 ml) POULTRY STOCK, p. 528*
* *Canned chicken broth may be substituted.*

1. Wash chicory and shred it rather coarsely.
2. Heat olive oil in a saucepan. Add garlic. Cook until garlic browns, then discard it.
3. Chop anchovy fillets and stir them in the oil until they dissolve.
4. Add tomatoes, chicory, salt and pepper to taste and stock. Cover pan tightly. Cook over low heat about 30 minutes. Vegetables should be moist but not watery when done.

NOTES

DEVILED FISH

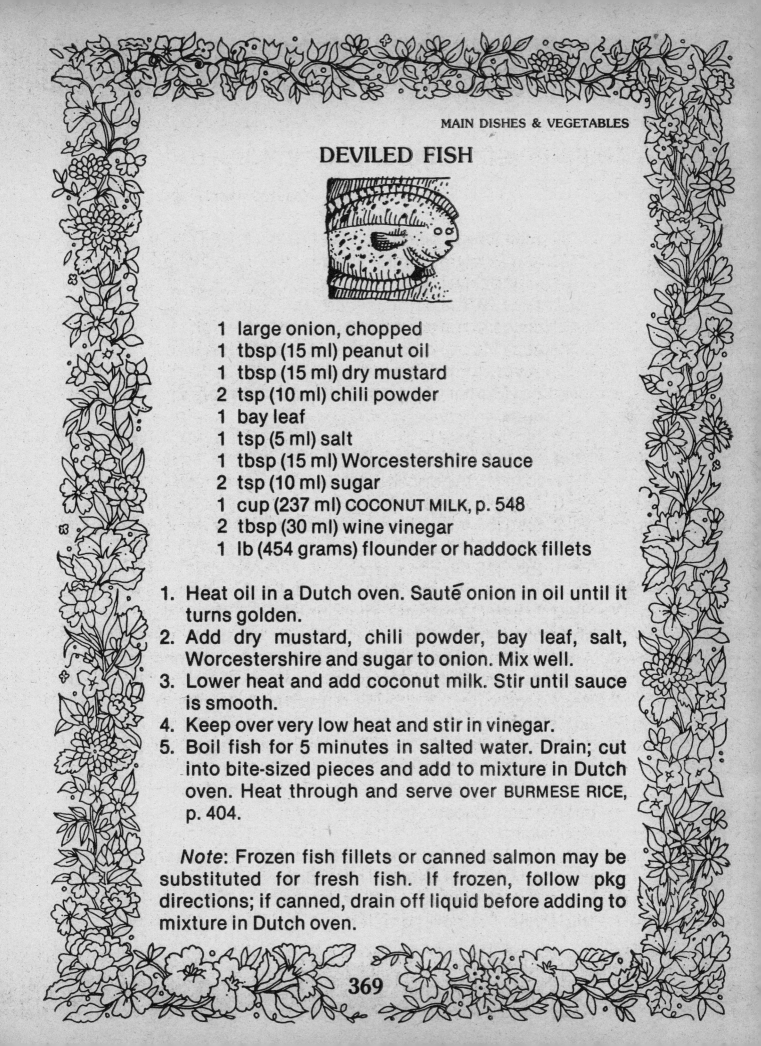

1 large onion, chopped
1 tbsp (15 ml) peanut oil
1 tbsp (15 ml) dry mustard
2 tsp (10 ml) chili powder
1 bay leaf
1 tsp (5 ml) salt
1 tbsp (15 ml) Worcestershire sauce
2 tsp (10 ml) sugar
1 cup (237 ml) COCONUT MILK, p. 548
2 tbsp (30 ml) wine vinegar
1 lb (454 grams) flounder or haddock fillets

1. Heat oil in a Dutch oven. Sauté onion in oil until it turns golden.
2. Add dry mustard, chili powder, bay leaf, salt, Worcestershire and sugar to onion. Mix well.
3. Lower heat and add coconut milk. Stir until sauce is smooth.
4. Keep over very low heat and stir in vinegar.
5. Boil fish for 5 minutes in salted water. Drain; cut into bite-sized pieces and add to mixture in Dutch oven. Heat through and serve over BURMESE RICE, p. 404.

Note: Frozen fish fillets or canned salmon may be substituted for fresh fish. If frozen, follow pkg directions; if canned, drain off liquid before adding to mixture in Dutch oven.

EGG-SHRIMP OMELET

Makes 4 servings.

- 4 tbsp (60 ml) peanut oil
- 1/2 lb (227 grams) small shrimp, cleaned, shelled and deveined
- 1/2 cup (118 ml) onion, sliced lengthwise
- 1/2 cup (118 ml) carrot, cut in very thin strips
- 1/2 cup (118 ml) cucumber, seeded and cut into very thin strips
- 1 can (4 oz or 113 grams) sliced mushrooms
- 6 eggs
- 1 tsp (5 ml) salt
- 1/4 tsp (1.2 ml) ground ginger
- 1 tbsp (15 ml) dry sherry
- 3 tbsp (45 ml) tomato purée
- 2 tbsp (30 ml) white-wine vinegar
- 2 tbsp (30 ml) sugar
- 1 tbsp (15 ml) cornstarch

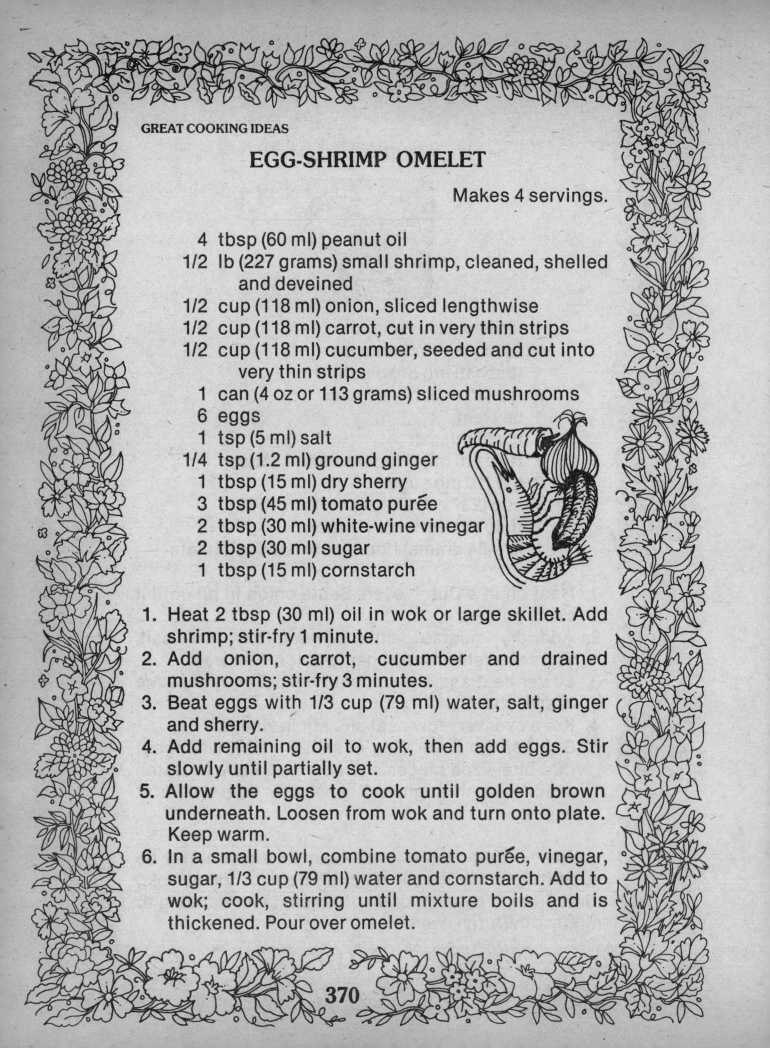

1. Heat 2 tbsp (30 ml) oil in wok or large skillet. Add shrimp; stir-fry 1 minute.
2. Add onion, carrot, cucumber and drained mushrooms; stir-fry 3 minutes.
3. Beat eggs with 1/3 cup (79 ml) water, salt, ginger and sherry.
4. Add remaining oil to wok, then add eggs. Stir slowly until partially set.
5. Allow the eggs to cook until golden brown underneath. Loosen from wok and turn onto plate. Keep warm.
6. In a small bowl, combine tomato purée, vinegar, sugar, 1/3 cup (79 ml) water and cornstarch. Add to wok; cook, stirring until mixture boils and is thickened. Pour over omelet.

LINGUINE 'N' WHITE CLAM SAUCE

Makes 4 - 6 servings.

18 - 24 cherrystone clams*
     7   tbsp (105 ml) olive oil
     3   cloves garlic, quartered
     3   tbsp (45 ml) fresh parsley leaves, chopped
   1/4   tsp (1.2 ml) dried red pepper flakes
   1/4   tsp (1.2 ml) dried basil
     2   shallots, finely chopped
     1   cup (237 ml) dry white wine
     1   lb (454 grams) linguine

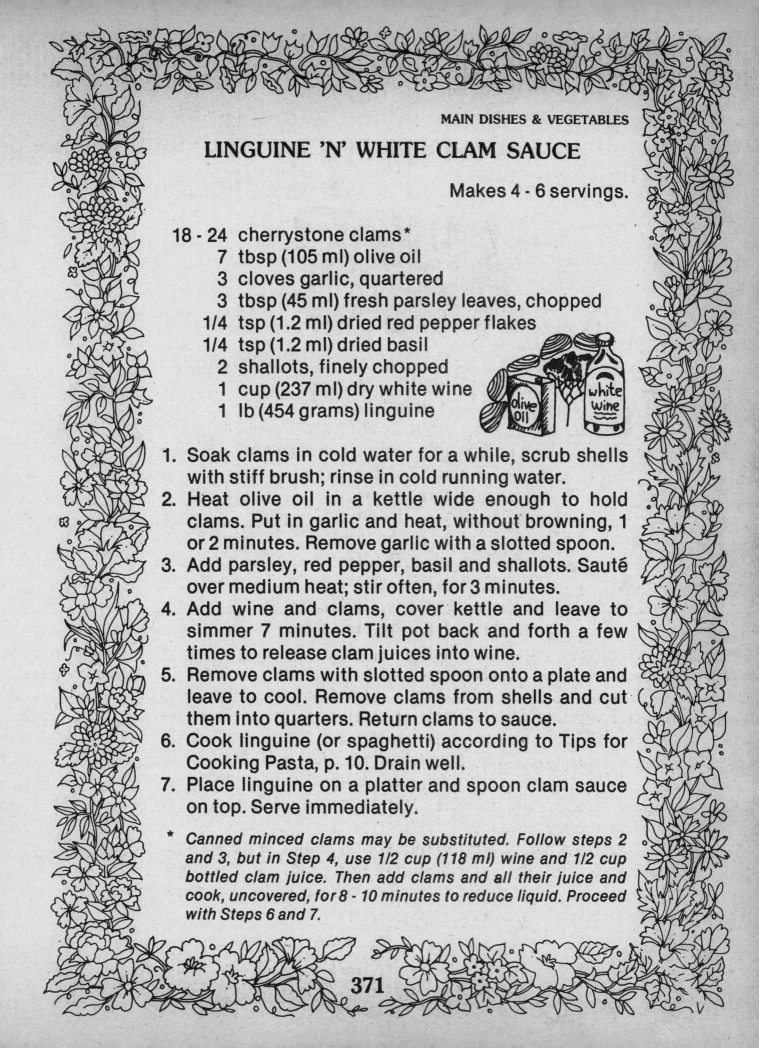

1. Soak clams in cold water for a while, scrub shells with stiff brush; rinse in cold running water.
2. Heat olive oil in a kettle wide enough to hold clams. Put in garlic and heat, without browning, 1 or 2 minutes. Remove garlic with a slotted spoon.
3. Add parsley, red pepper, basil and shallots. Sauté over medium heat; stir often, for 3 minutes.
4. Add wine and clams, cover kettle and leave to simmer 7 minutes. Tilt pot back and forth a few times to release clam juices into wine.
5. Remove clams with slotted spoon onto a plate and leave to cool. Remove clams from shells and cut them into quarters. Return clams to sauce.
6. Cook linguine (or spaghetti) according to Tips for Cooking Pasta, p. 10. Drain well.
7. Place linguine on a platter and spoon clam sauce on top. Serve immediately.

* *Canned minced clams may be substituted. Follow steps 2 and 3, but in Step 4, use 1/2 cup (118 ml) wine and 1/2 cup bottled clam juice. Then add clams and all their juice and cook, uncovered, for 8 - 10 minutes to reduce liquid. Proceed with Steps 6 and 7.*

MADRAS SHRIMP CURRY

Makes 4 - 6 servings.

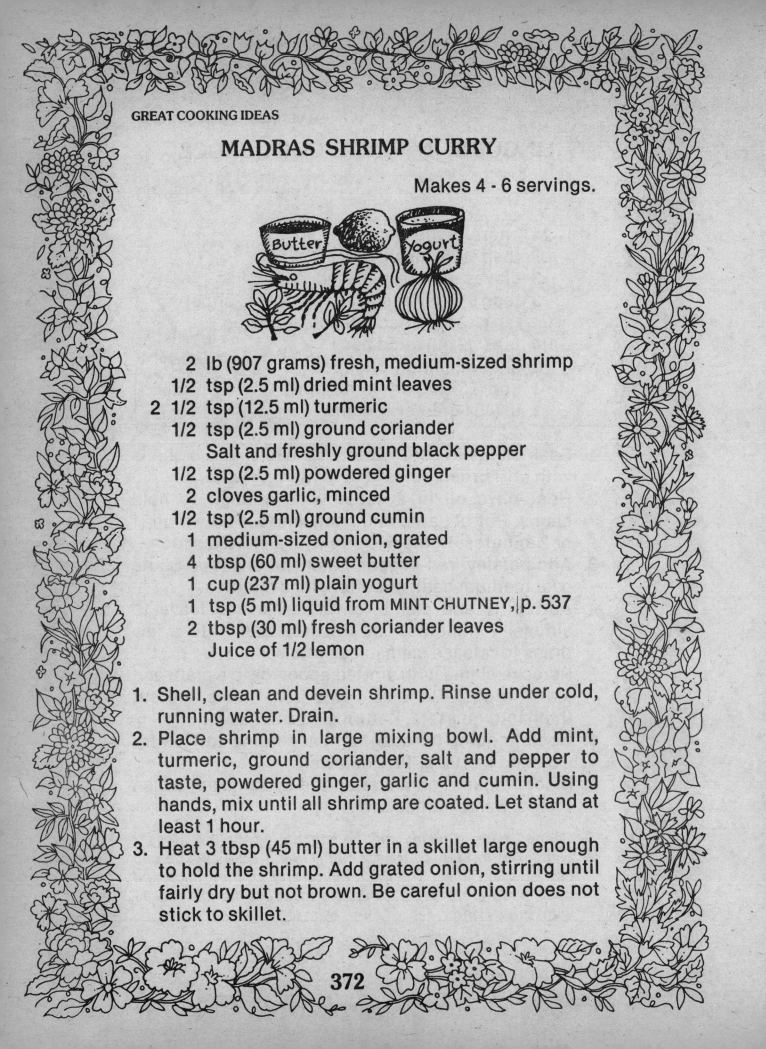

2 lb (907 grams) fresh, medium-sized shrimp
1/2 tsp (2.5 ml) dried mint leaves
2 1/2 tsp (12.5 ml) turmeric
1/2 tsp (2.5 ml) ground coriander
Salt and freshly ground black pepper
1/2 tsp (2.5 ml) powdered ginger
2 cloves garlic, minced
1/2 tsp (2.5 ml) ground cumin
1 medium-sized onion, grated
4 tbsp (60 ml) sweet butter
1 cup (237 ml) plain yogurt
1 tsp (5 ml) liquid from MINT CHUTNEY, p. 537
2 tbsp (30 ml) fresh coriander leaves
Juice of 1/2 lemon

1. Shell, clean and devein shrimp. Rinse under cold, running water. Drain.
2. Place shrimp in large mixing bowl. Add mint, turmeric, ground coriander, salt and pepper to taste, powdered ginger, garlic and cumin. Using hands, mix until all shrimp are coated. Let stand at least 1 hour.
3. Heat 3 tbsp (45 ml) butter in a skillet large enough to hold the shrimp. Add grated onion, stirring until fairly dry but not brown. Be careful onion does not stick to skillet.

4. Add remaining butter and marinated shrimp to skillet. Cook, stirring gently, until shrimp turn bright pink.
5. Add yogurt and chutney liquid. Simmer 10 minutes, covered. Remove cover and cook over medium heat 10 minutes longer.
6. Add fresh coriander leaves and lemon juice. Taste and add more salt and pepper, if desired.
7. Serve with BOILED RICE, p. 10 and the following condiments: MINT CHUTNEY, peanuts, India relish and grated coconut.

Note: If fresh coriander leaves are not available, substitute 2 tbsp (30 ml) chopped fresh parsley.

NOTES

MANILA CRAB

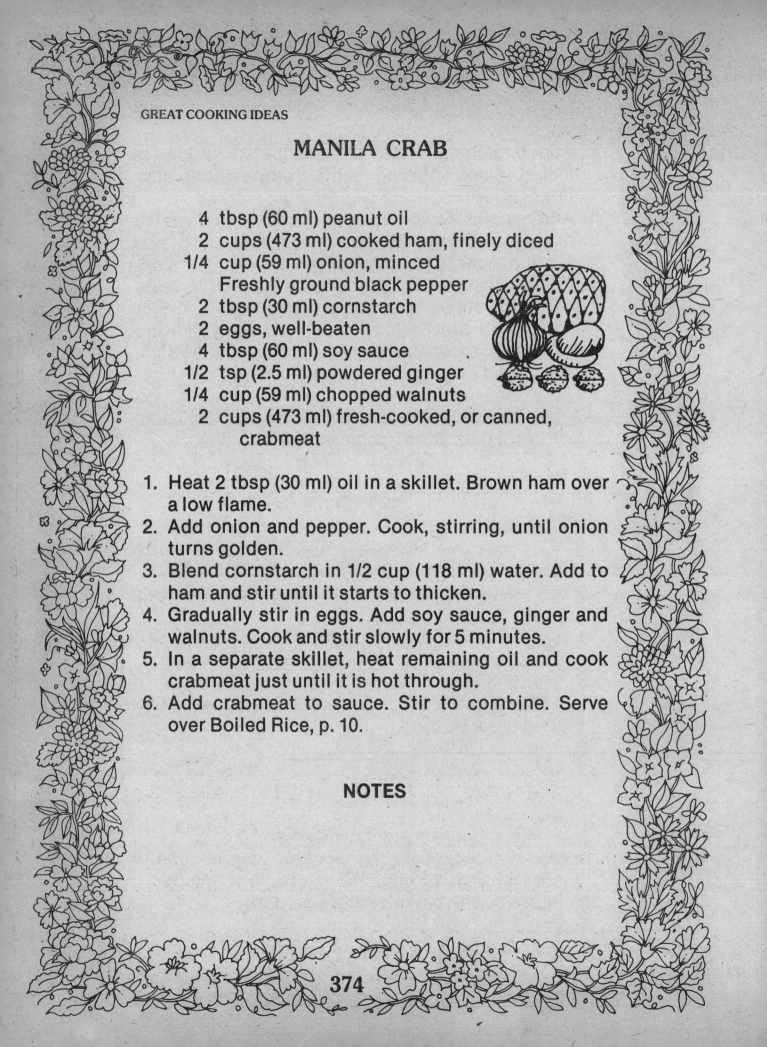

4 tbsp (60 ml) peanut oil
2 cups (473 ml) cooked ham, finely diced
1/4 cup (59 ml) onion, minced
Freshly ground black pepper
2 tbsp (30 ml) cornstarch
2 eggs, well-beaten
4 tbsp (60 ml) soy sauce
1/2 tsp (2.5 ml) powdered ginger
1/4 cup (59 ml) chopped walnuts
2 cups (473 ml) fresh-cooked, or canned, crabmeat

1. Heat 2 tbsp (30 ml) oil in a skillet. Brown ham over a low flame.
2. Add onion and pepper. Cook, stirring, until onion turns golden.
3. Blend cornstarch in 1/2 cup (118 ml) water. Add to ham and stir until it starts to thicken.
4. Gradually stir in eggs. Add soy sauce, ginger and walnuts. Cook and stir slowly for 5 minutes.
5. In a separate skillet, heat remaining oil and cook crabmeat just until it is hot through.
6. Add crabmeat to sauce. Stir to combine. Serve over Boiled Rice, p. 10.

NOTES

374

MUSSELS IN WINE

Makes 6 servings.

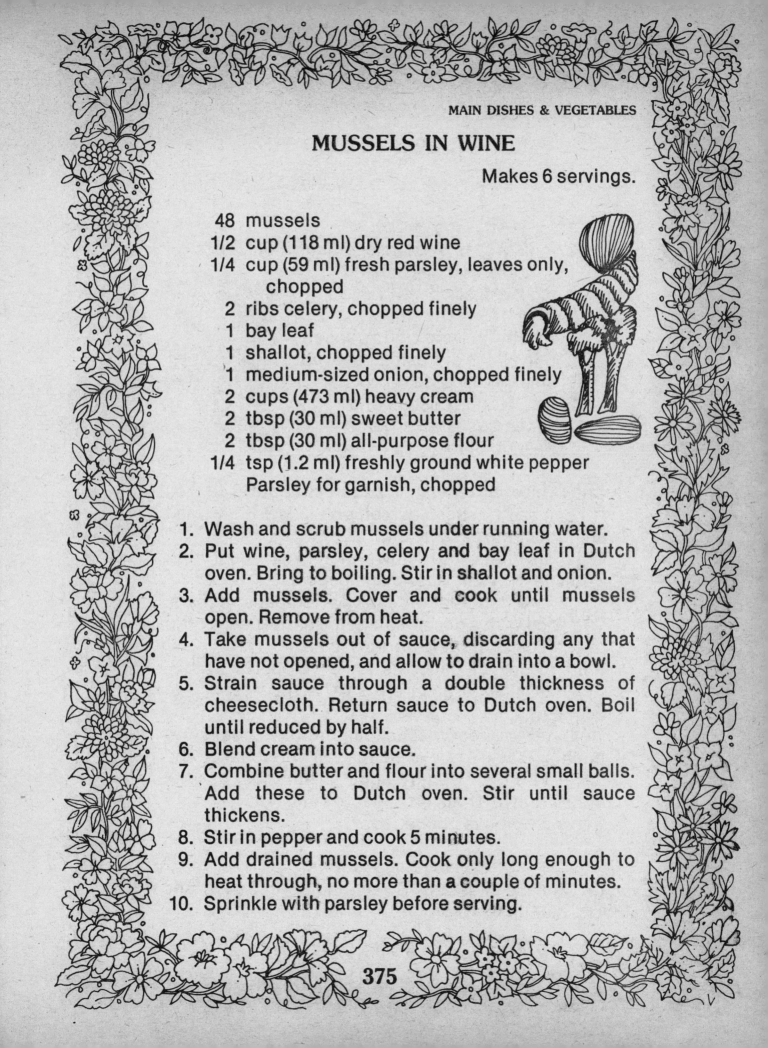

48 mussels
1/2 cup (118 ml) dry red wine
1/4 cup (59 ml) fresh parsley, leaves only, chopped
2 ribs celery, chopped finely
1 bay leaf
1 shallot, chopped finely
1 medium-sized onion, chopped finely
2 cups (473 ml) heavy cream
2 tbsp (30 ml) sweet butter
2 tbsp (30 ml) all-purpose flour
1/4 tsp (1.2 ml) freshly ground white pepper
Parsley for garnish, chopped

1. Wash and scrub mussels under running water.
2. Put wine, parsley, celery and bay leaf in Dutch oven. Bring to boiling. Stir in shallot and onion.
3. Add mussels. Cover and cook until mussels open. Remove from heat.
4. Take mussels out of sauce, discarding any that have not opened, and allow to drain into a bowl.
5. Strain sauce through a double thickness of cheesecloth. Return sauce to Dutch oven. Boil until reduced by half.
6. Blend cream into sauce.
7. Combine butter and flour into several small balls. Add these to Dutch oven. Stir until sauce thickens.
8. Stir in pepper and cook 5 minutes.
9. Add drained mussels. Cook only long enough to heat through, no more than a couple of minutes.
10. Sprinkle with parsley before serving.

PAPER-WRAPPED FRIED FISH

Makes 4 - 6 servings.

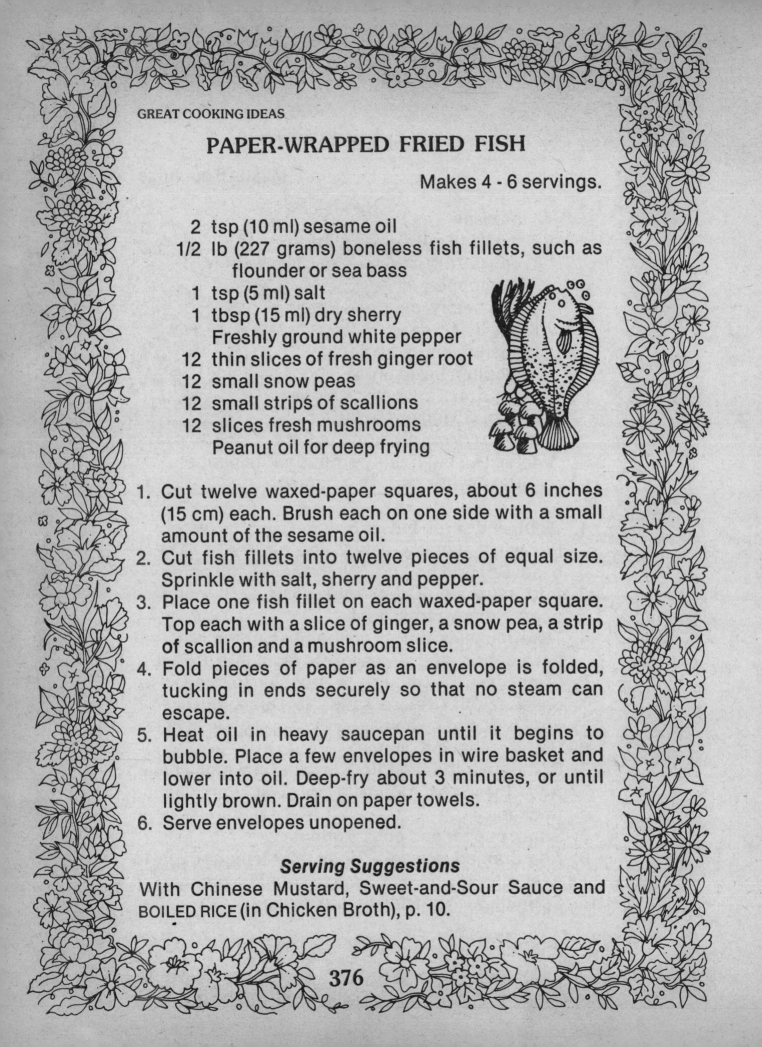

  2 tsp (10 ml) sesame oil
1/2 lb (227 grams) boneless fish fillets, such as flounder or sea bass
  1 tsp (5 ml) salt
  1 tbsp (15 ml) dry sherry
     Freshly ground white pepper
12 thin slices of fresh ginger root
12 small snow peas
12 small strips of scallions
12 slices fresh mushrooms
     Peanut oil for deep frying

1. Cut twelve waxed-paper squares, about 6 inches (15 cm) each. Brush each on one side with a small amount of the sesame oil.
2. Cut fish fillets into twelve pieces of equal size. Sprinkle with salt, sherry and pepper.
3. Place one fish fillet on each waxed-paper square. Top each with a slice of ginger, a snow pea, a strip of scallion and a mushroom slice.
4. Fold pieces of paper as an envelope is folded, tucking in ends securely so that no steam can escape.
5. Heat oil in heavy saucepan until it begins to bubble. Place a few envelopes in wire basket and lower into oil. Deep-fry about 3 minutes, or until lightly brown. Drain on paper towels.
6. Serve envelopes unopened.

Serving Suggestions

With Chinese Mustard, Sweet-and-Sour Sauce and BOILED RICE (in Chicken Broth), p. 10.

PEPPERY HOT LOBSTER

Makes 4 servings.

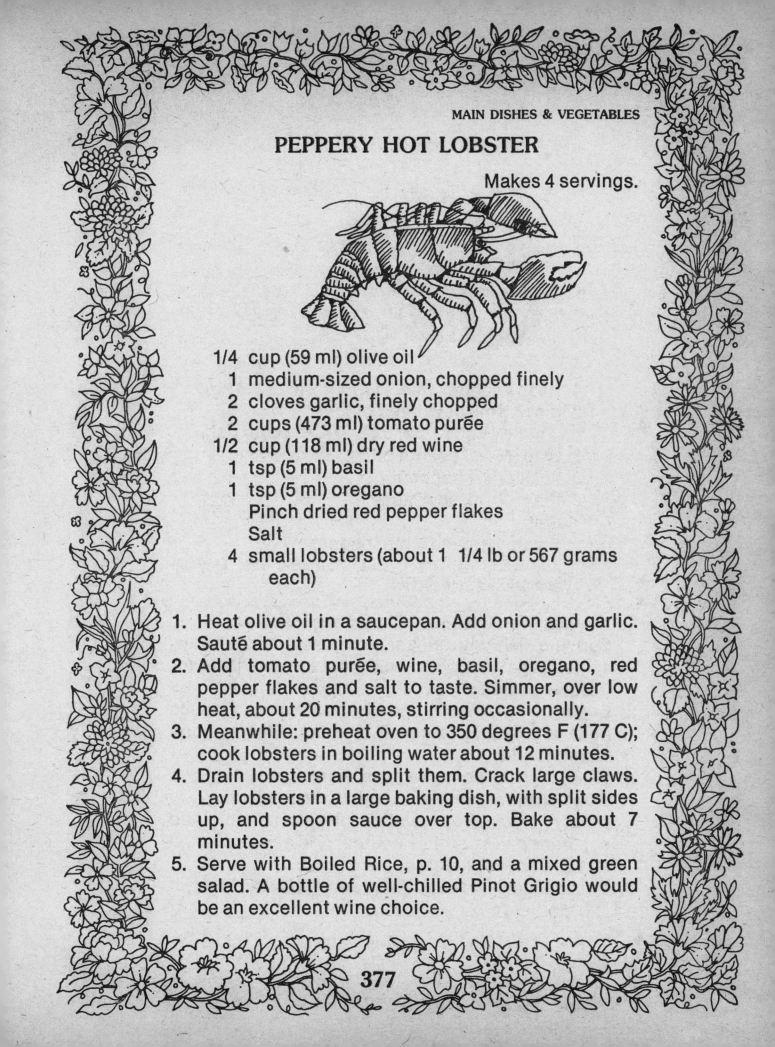

1/4 cup (59 ml) olive oil
  1 medium-sized onion, chopped finely
  2 cloves garlic, finely chopped
  2 cups (473 ml) tomato purée
1/2 cup (118 ml) dry red wine
  1 tsp (5 ml) basil
  1 tsp (5 ml) oregano
    Pinch dried red pepper flakes
    Salt
  4 small lobsters (about 1 1/4 lb or 567 grams each)

1. Heat olive oil in a saucepan. Add onion and garlic. Sauté about 1 minute.
2. Add tomato purée, wine, basil, oregano, red pepper flakes and salt to taste. Simmer, over low heat, about 20 minutes, stirring occasionally.
3. Meanwhile: preheat oven to 350 degrees F (177 C); cook lobsters in boiling water about 12 minutes.
4. Drain lobsters and split them. Crack large claws. Lay lobsters in a large baking dish, with split sides up, and spoon sauce over top. Bake about 7 minutes.
5. Serve with Boiled Rice, p. 10, and a mixed green salad. A bottle of well-chilled Pinot Grigio would be an excellent wine choice.

POACHED HADDOCK

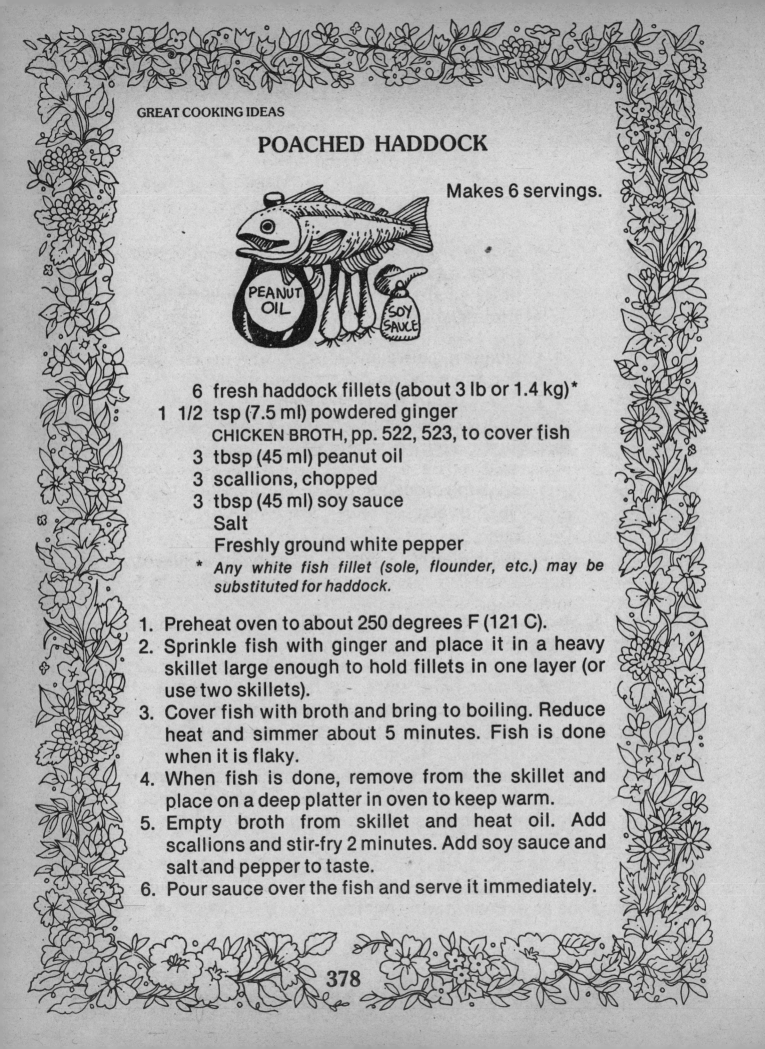

Makes 6 servings.

6	fresh haddock fillets (about 3 lb or 1.4 kg)*
1 1/2	tsp (7.5 ml) powdered ginger
	CHICKEN BROTH, pp. 522, 523, to cover fish
3	tbsp (45 ml) peanut oil
3	scallions, chopped
3	tbsp (45 ml) soy sauce
	Salt
	Freshly ground white pepper

* *Any white fish fillet (sole, flounder, etc.) may be substituted for haddock.*

1. Preheat oven to about 250 degrees F (121 C).
2. Sprinkle fish with ginger and place it in a heavy skillet large enough to hold fillets in one layer (or use two skillets).
3. Cover fish with broth and bring to boiling. Reduce heat and simmer about 5 minutes. Fish is done when it is flaky.
4. When fish is done, remove from the skillet and place on a deep platter in oven to keep warm.
5. Empty broth from skillet and heat oil. Add scallions and stir-fry 2 minutes. Add soy sauce and salt and pepper to taste.
6. Pour sauce over the fish and serve it immediately.

SALMON TERIYAKI

Makes 6 servings.

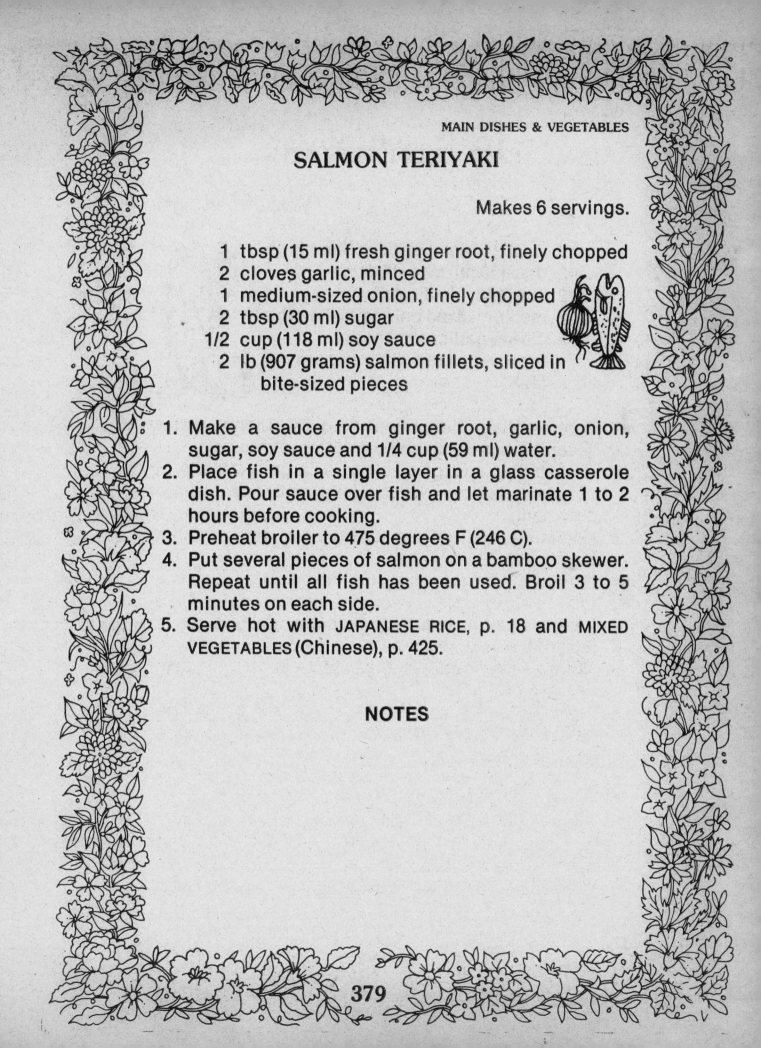

1 tbsp (15 ml) fresh ginger root, finely chopped
2 cloves garlic, minced
1 medium-sized onion, finely chopped
2 tbsp (30 ml) sugar
1/2 cup (118 ml) soy sauce
2 lb (907 grams) salmon fillets, sliced in
   bite-sized pieces

1. Make a sauce from ginger root, garlic, onion, sugar, soy sauce and 1/4 cup (59 ml) water.
2. Place fish in a single layer in a glass casserole dish. Pour sauce over fish and let marinate 1 to 2 hours before cooking.
3. Preheat broiler to 475 degrees F (246 C).
4. Put several pieces of salmon on a bamboo skewer. Repeat until all fish has been used. Broil 3 to 5 minutes on each side.
5. Serve hot with JAPANESE RICE, p. 18 and MIXED VEGETABLES (Chinese), p. 425.

NOTES

SALT CODFISH IN MILK

Makes 6 servings.

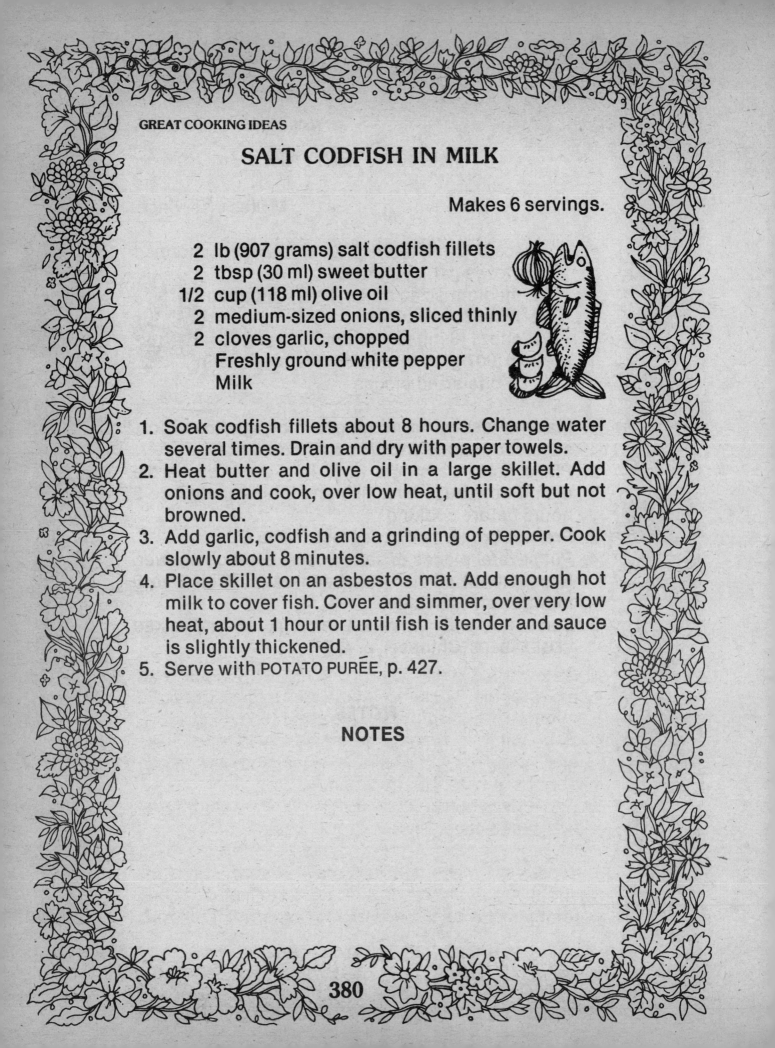

2 lb (907 grams) salt codfish fillets
2 tbsp (30 ml) sweet butter
1/2 cup (118 ml) olive oil
2 medium-sized onions, sliced thinly
2 cloves garlic, chopped
Freshly ground white pepper
Milk

1. Soak codfish fillets about 8 hours. Change water several times. Drain and dry with paper towels.
2. Heat butter and olive oil in a large skillet. Add onions and cook, over low heat, until soft but not browned.
3. Add garlic, codfish and a grinding of pepper. Cook slowly about 8 minutes.
4. Place skillet on an asbestos mat. Add enough hot milk to cover fish. Cover and simmer, over very low heat, about 1 hour or until fish is tender and sauce is slightly thickened.
5. Serve with POTATO PURÉE, p. 427.

NOTES

SCALLOP SKILLET

Makes 4 - 6 servings.

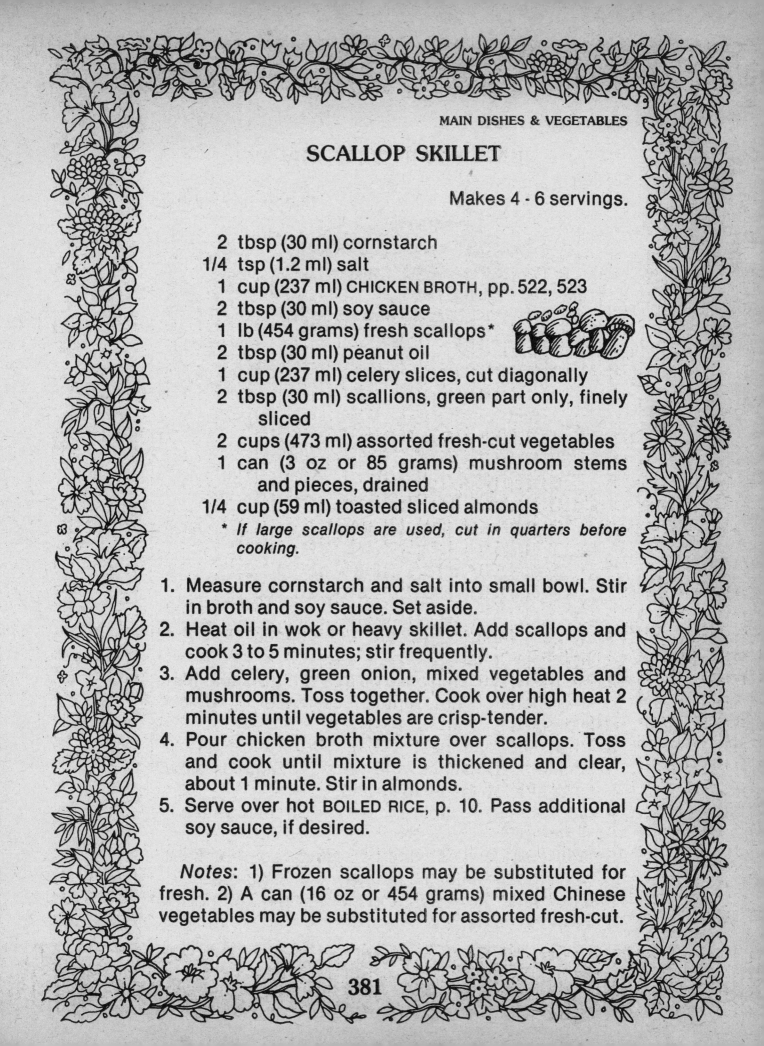

- 2 tbsp (30 ml) cornstarch
- 1/4 tsp (1.2 ml) salt
- 1 cup (237 ml) CHICKEN BROTH, pp. 522, 523
- 2 tbsp (30 ml) soy sauce
- 1 lb (454 grams) fresh scallops*
- 2 tbsp (30 ml) peanut oil
- 1 cup (237 ml) celery slices, cut diagonally
- 2 tbsp (30 ml) scallions, green part only, finely sliced
- 2 cups (473 ml) assorted fresh-cut vegetables
- 1 can (3 oz or 85 grams) mushroom stems and pieces, drained
- 1/4 cup (59 ml) toasted sliced almonds

If large scallops are used, cut in quarters before cooking.

1. Measure cornstarch and salt into small bowl. Stir in broth and soy sauce. Set aside.
2. Heat oil in wok or heavy skillet. Add scallops and cook 3 to 5 minutes; stir frequently.
3. Add celery, green onion, mixed vegetables and mushrooms. Toss together. Cook over high heat 2 minutes until vegetables are crisp-tender.
4. Pour chicken broth mixture over scallops. Toss and cook until mixture is thickened and clear, about 1 minute. Stir in almonds.
5. Serve over hot BOILED RICE, p. 10. Pass additional soy sauce, if desired.

Notes: 1) Frozen scallops may be substituted for fresh. 2) A can (16 oz or 454 grams) mixed Chinese vegetables may be substituted for assorted fresh-cut.

SEA BASS IN WINE SAUCE

Makes 4 servings.

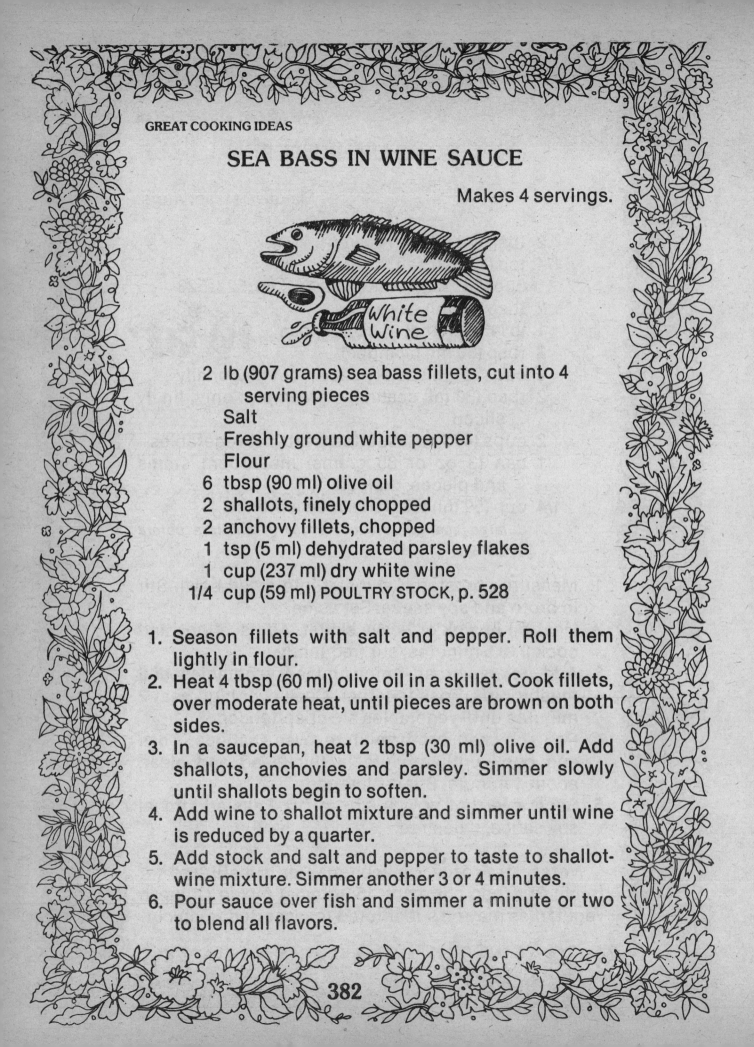

2 lb (907 grams) sea bass fillets, cut into 4
    serving pieces
Salt
Freshly ground white pepper
Flour
6 tbsp (90 ml) olive oil
2 shallots, finely chopped
2 anchovy fillets, chopped
1 tsp (5 ml) dehydrated parsley flakes
1 cup (237 ml) dry white wine
1/4 cup (59 ml) POULTRY STOCK, p. 528

1. Season fillets with salt and pepper. Roll them lightly in flour.
2. Heat 4 tbsp (60 ml) olive oil in a skillet. Cook fillets, over moderate heat, until pieces are brown on both sides.
3. In a saucepan, heat 2 tbsp (30 ml) olive oil. Add shallots, anchovies and parsley. Simmer slowly until shallots begin to soften.
4. Add wine to shallot mixture and simmer until wine is reduced by a quarter.
5. Add stock and salt and pepper to taste to shallot-wine mixture. Simmer another 3 or 4 minutes.
6. Pour sauce over fish and simmer a minute or two to blend all flavors.

SHRIMP IN COCONUT MILK

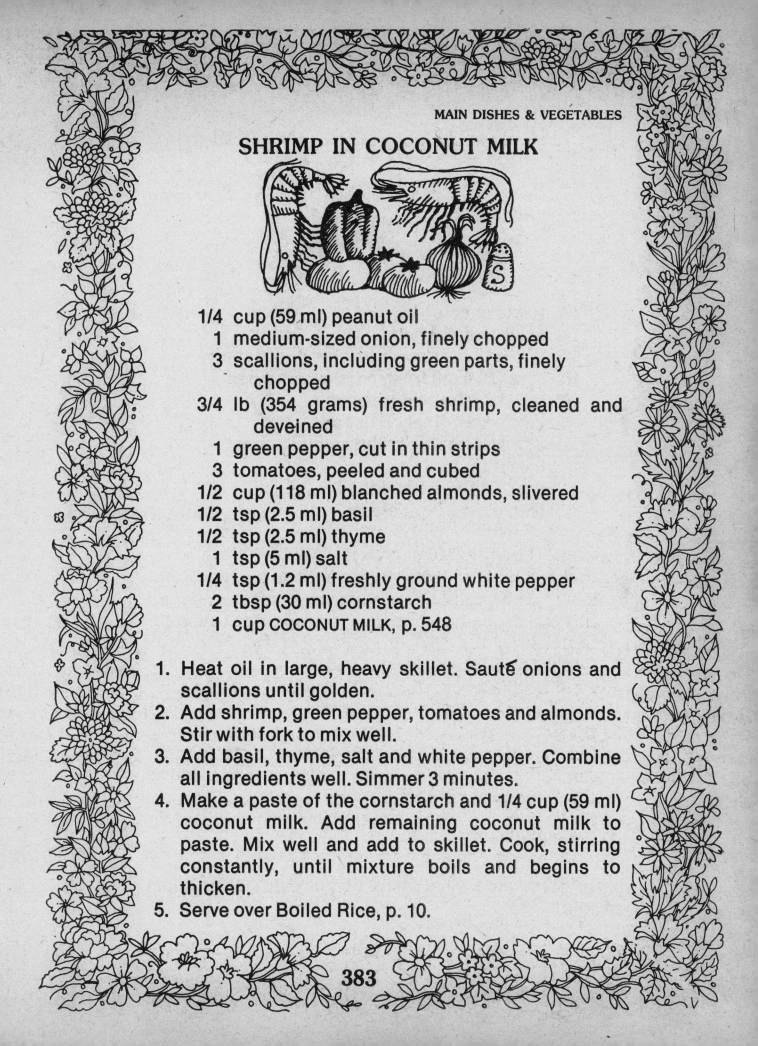

1/4 cup (59 ml) peanut oil
1 medium-sized onion, finely chopped
3 scallions, including green parts, finely chopped
3/4 lb (354 grams) fresh shrimp, cleaned and deveined
1 green pepper, cut in thin strips
3 tomatoes, peeled and cubed
1/2 cup (118 ml) blanched almonds, slivered
1/2 tsp (2.5 ml) basil
1/2 tsp (2.5 ml) thyme
1 tsp (5 ml) salt
1/4 tsp (1.2 ml) freshly ground white pepper
2 tbsp (30 ml) cornstarch
1 cup COCONUT MILK, p. 548

1. Heat oil in large, heavy skillet. Sauté onions and scallions until golden.
2. Add shrimp, green pepper, tomatoes and almonds. Stir with fork to mix well.
3. Add basil, thyme, salt and white pepper. Combine all ingredients well. Simmer 3 minutes.
4. Make a paste of the cornstarch and 1/4 cup (59 ml) coconut milk. Add remaining coconut milk to paste. Mix well and add to skillet. Cook, stirring constantly, until mixture boils and begins to thicken.
5. Serve over Boiled Rice, p. 10.

SOLE FILLETS BAKED IN WINE

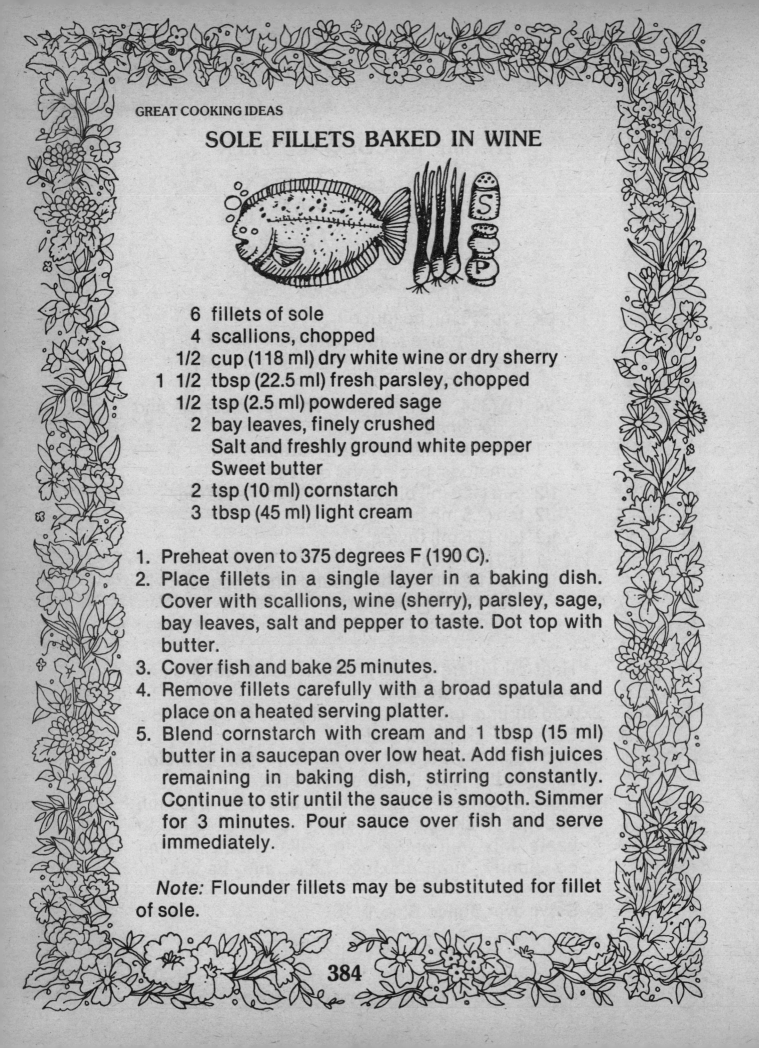

    6 fillets of sole
    4 scallions, chopped
  1/2 cup (118 ml) dry white wine or dry sherry
1 1/2 tbsp (22.5 ml) fresh parsley, chopped
  1/2 tsp (2.5 ml) powdered sage
    2 bay leaves, finely crushed
       Salt and freshly ground white pepper
       Sweet butter
    2 tsp (10 ml) cornstarch
    3 tbsp (45 ml) light cream

1. Preheat oven to 375 degrees F (190 C).
2. Place fillets in a single layer in a baking dish. Cover with scallions, wine (sherry), parsley, sage, bay leaves, salt and pepper to taste. Dot top with butter.
3. Cover fish and bake 25 minutes.
4. Remove fillets carefully with a broad spatula and place on a heated serving platter.
5. Blend cornstarch with cream and 1 tbsp (15 ml) butter in a saucepan over low heat. Add fish juices remaining in baking dish, stirring constantly. Continue to stir until the sauce is smooth. Simmer for 3 minutes. Pour sauce over fish and serve immediately.

Note: Flounder fillets may be substituted for fillet of sole.

SPICY SHRIMP

Makes 8 servings.

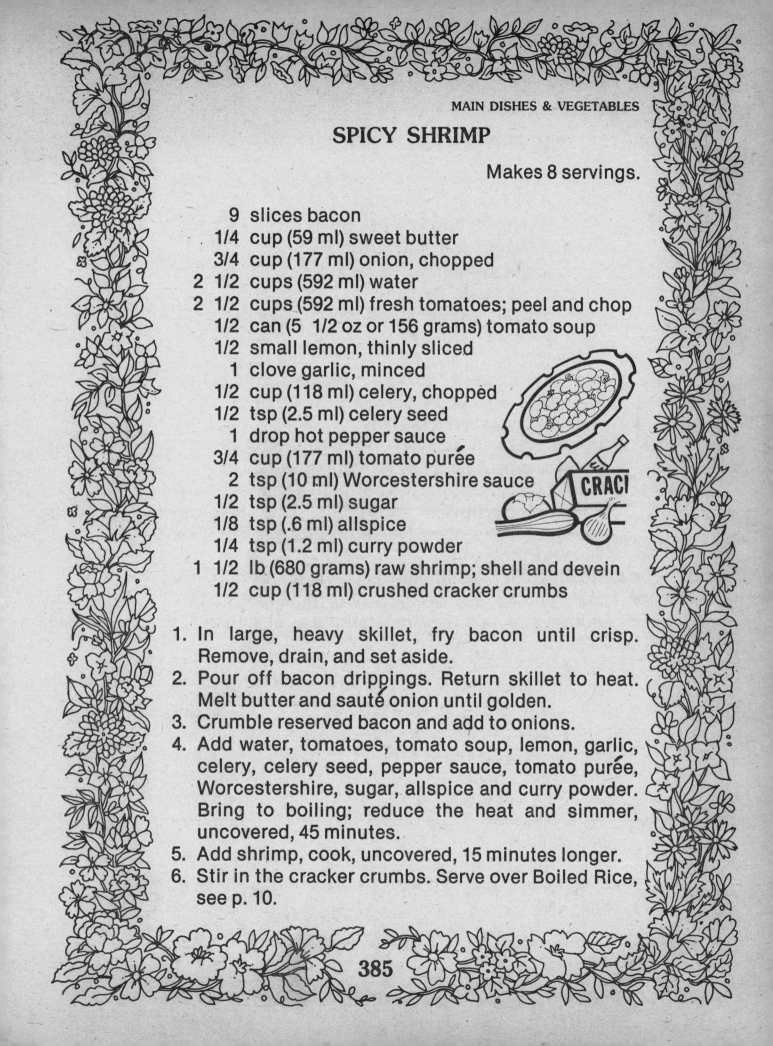

9	slices bacon
1/4	cup (59 ml) sweet butter
3/4	cup (177 ml) onion, chopped
2 1/2	cups (592 ml) water
2 1/2	cups (592 ml) fresh tomatoes; peel and chop
1/2	can (5 1/2 oz or 156 grams) tomato soup
1/2	small lemon, thinly sliced
1	clove garlic, minced
1/2	cup (118 ml) celery, chopped
1/2	tsp (2.5 ml) celery seed
1	drop hot pepper sauce
3/4	cup (177 ml) tomato purée
2	tsp (10 ml) Worcestershire sauce
1/2	tsp (2.5 ml) sugar
1/8	tsp (.6 ml) allspice
1/4	tsp (1.2 ml) curry powder
1 1/2	lb (680 grams) raw shrimp; shell and devein
1/2	cup (118 ml) crushed cracker crumbs

1. In large, heavy skillet, fry bacon until crisp. Remove, drain, and set aside.
2. Pour off bacon drippings. Return skillet to heat. Melt butter and sauté onion until golden.
3. Crumble reserved bacon and add to onions.
4. Add water, tomatoes, tomato soup, lemon, garlic, celery, celery seed, pepper sauce, tomato purée, Worcestershire, sugar, allspice and curry powder. Bring to boiling; reduce the heat and simmer, uncovered, 45 minutes.
5. Add shrimp, cook, uncovered, 15 minutes longer.
6. Stir in the cracker crumbs. Serve over Boiled Rice, see p. 10.

SPINACH WITH ANCHOVIES

Makes 4 servings.

1 lb (454 grams) fresh spinach
3 tbsp (45 ml) sweet butter
4 anchovy fillets, chopped
1 clove garlic, halved
Freshly ground black pepper
Dash of nutmeg

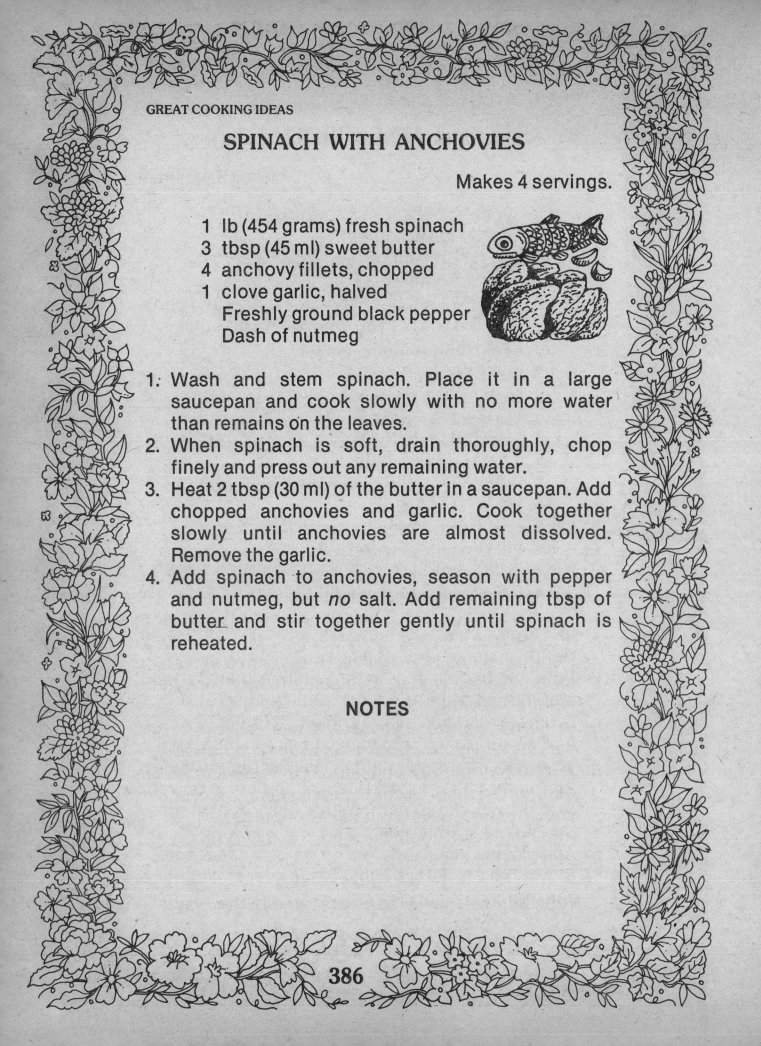

1. Wash and stem spinach. Place it in a large saucepan and cook slowly with no more water than remains on the leaves.
2. When spinach is soft, drain thoroughly, chop finely and press out any remaining water.
3. Heat 2 tbsp (30 ml) of the butter in a saucepan. Add chopped anchovies and garlic. Cook together slowly until anchovies are almost dissolved. Remove the garlic.
4. Add spinach to anchovies, season with pepper and nutmeg, but *no* salt. Add remaining tbsp of butter and stir together gently until spinach is reheated.

NOTES

STEAMED CLAMS 'N' TOMATOES

Makes 4 servings.

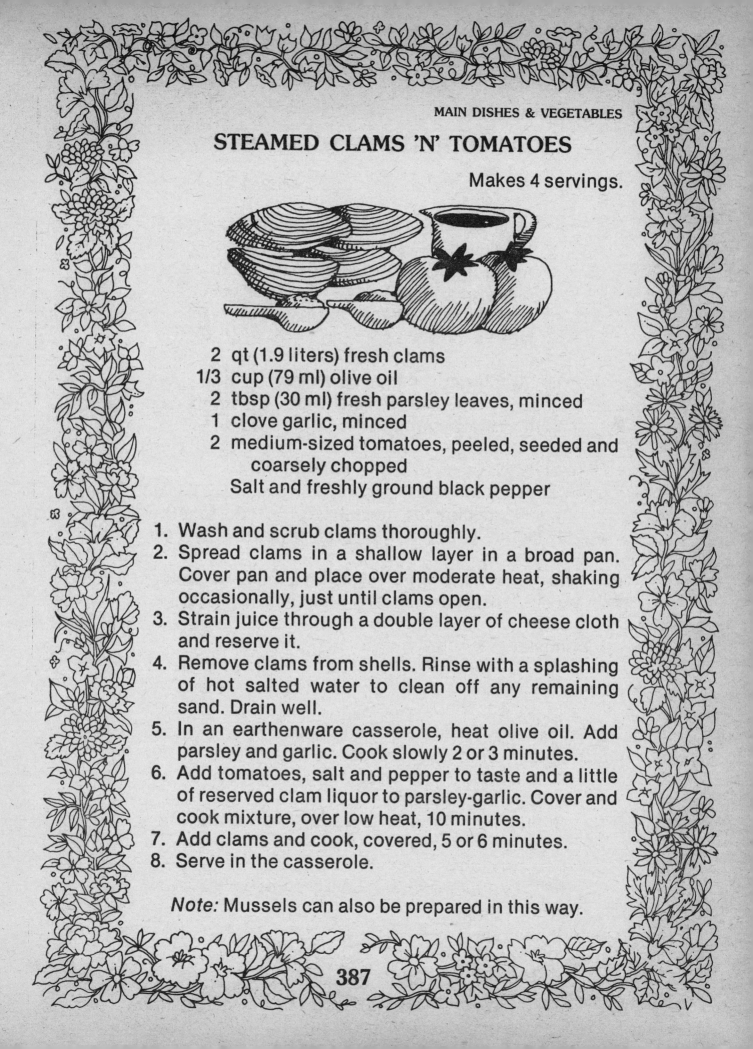

2 qt (1.9 liters) fresh clams
1/3 cup (79 ml) olive oil
2 tbsp (30 ml) fresh parsley leaves, minced
1 clove garlic, minced
2 medium-sized tomatoes, peeled, seeded and coarsely chopped
Salt and freshly ground black pepper

1. Wash and scrub clams thoroughly.
2. Spread clams in a shallow layer in a broad pan. Cover pan and place over moderate heat, shaking occasionally, just until clams open.
3. Strain juice through a double layer of cheese cloth and reserve it.
4. Remove clams from shells. Rinse with a splashing of hot salted water to clean off any remaining sand. Drain well.
5. In an earthenware casserole, heat olive oil. Add parsley and garlic. Cook slowly 2 or 3 minutes.
6. Add tomatoes, salt and pepper to taste and a little of reserved clam liquor to parsley-garlic. Cover and cook mixture, over low heat, 10 minutes.
7. Add clams and cook, covered, 5 or 6 minutes.
8. Serve in the casserole.

Note: Mussels can also be prepared in this way.

STEAMED EGGS WITH CRABMEAT

Makes 4 servings.

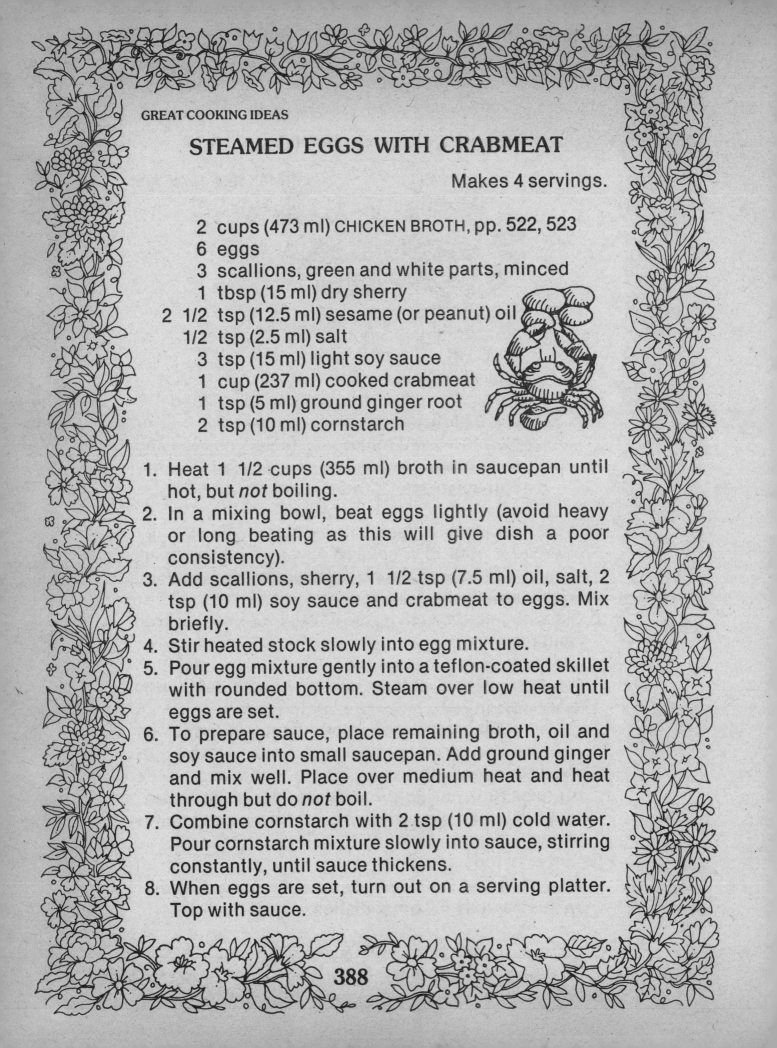

2 cups (473 ml) CHICKEN BROTH, pp. 522, 523
6 eggs
3 scallions, green and white parts, minced
1 tbsp (15 ml) dry sherry
2 1/2 tsp (12.5 ml) sesame (or peanut) oil
1/2 tsp (2.5 ml) salt
3 tsp (15 ml) light soy sauce
1 cup (237 ml) cooked crabmeat
1 tsp (5 ml) ground ginger root
2 tsp (10 ml) cornstarch

1. Heat 1 1/2 cups (355 ml) broth in saucepan until hot, but *not* boiling.
2. In a mixing bowl, beat eggs lightly (avoid heavy or long beating as this will give dish a poor consistency).
3. Add scallions, sherry, 1 1/2 tsp (7.5 ml) oil, salt, 2 tsp (10 ml) soy sauce and crabmeat to eggs. Mix briefly.
4. Stir heated stock slowly into egg mixture.
5. Pour egg mixture gently into a teflon-coated skillet with rounded bottom. Steam over low heat until eggs are set.
6. To prepare sauce, place remaining broth, oil and soy sauce into small saucepan. Add ground ginger and mix well. Place over medium heat and heat through but do *not* boil.
7. Combine cornstarch with 2 tsp (10 ml) cold water. Pour cornstarch mixture slowly into sauce, stirring constantly, until sauce thickens.
8. When eggs are set, turn out on a serving platter. Top with sauce.

STEAMED FLOUNDER

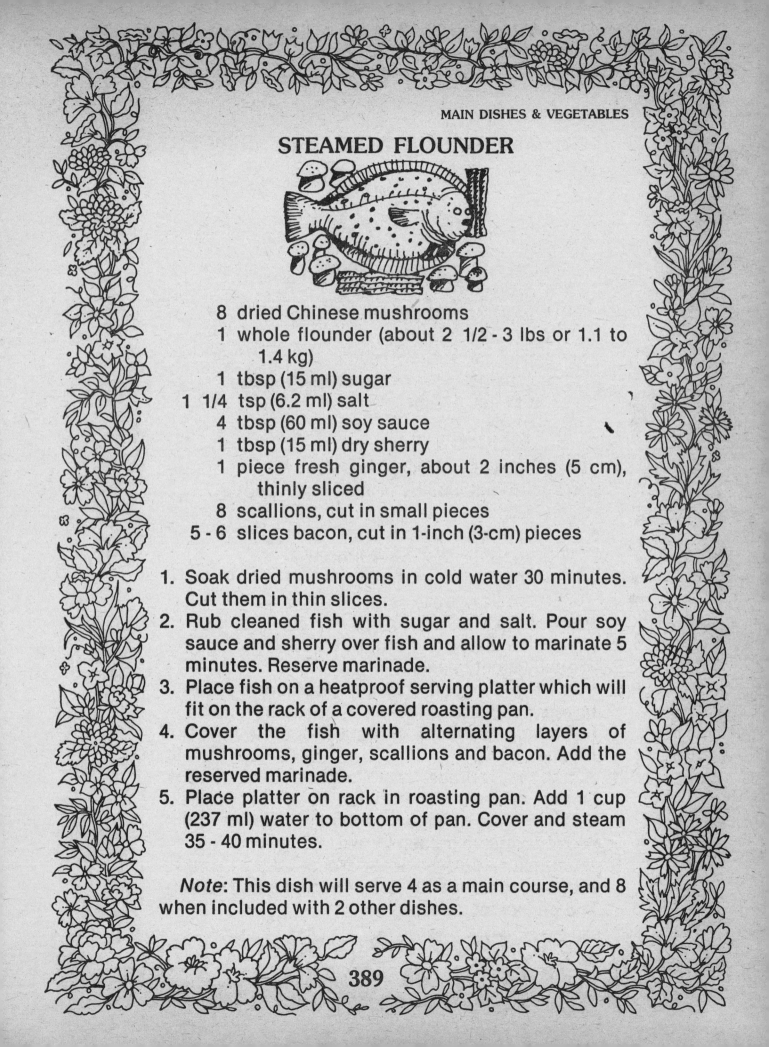

        8 dried Chinese mushrooms
        1 whole flounder (about 2 1/2 - 3 lbs or 1.1 to
             1.4 kg)
        1 tbsp (15 ml) sugar
    1 1/4 tsp (6.2 ml) salt
        4 tbsp (60 ml) soy sauce
        1 tbsp (15 ml) dry sherry
        1 piece fresh ginger, about 2 inches (5 cm),
             thinly sliced
        8 scallions, cut in small pieces
     5 - 6 slices bacon, cut in 1-inch (3-cm) pieces

1. Soak dried mushrooms in cold water 30 minutes.
   Cut them in thin slices.
2. Rub cleaned fish with sugar and salt. Pour soy
   sauce and sherry over fish and allow to marinate 5
   minutes. Reserve marinade.
3. Place fish on a heatproof serving platter which will
   fit on the rack of a covered roasting pan.
4. Cover the fish with alternating layers of
   mushrooms, ginger, scallions and bacon. Add the
   reserved marinade.
5. Place platter on rack in roasting pan. Add 1 cup
   (237 ml) water to bottom of pan. Cover and steam
   35 - 40 minutes.

Note: This dish will serve 4 as a main course, and 8
when included with 2 other dishes.

STUFFED BLUEFISH

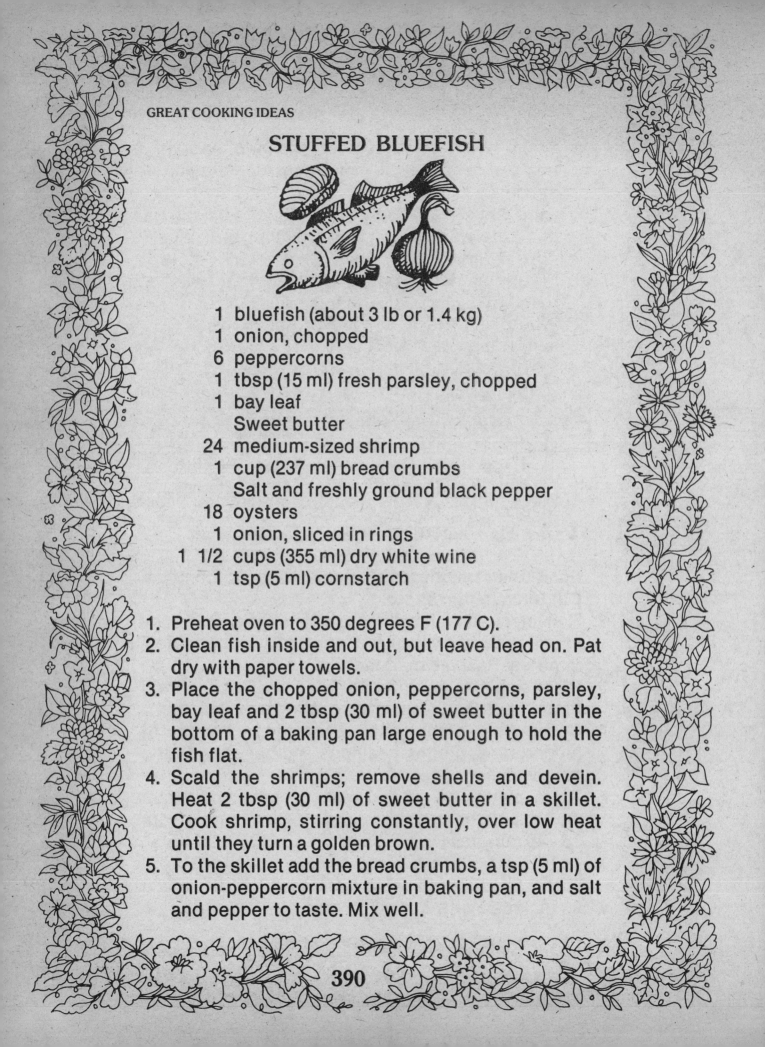

- 1 bluefish (about 3 lb or 1.4 kg)
- 1 onion, chopped
- 6 peppercorns
- 1 tbsp (15 ml) fresh parsley, chopped
- 1 bay leaf
  Sweet butter
- 24 medium-sized shrimp
- 1 cup (237 ml) bread crumbs
  Salt and freshly ground black pepper
- 18 oysters
- 1 onion, sliced in rings
- 1 1/2 cups (355 ml) dry white wine
- 1 tsp (5 ml) cornstarch

1. Preheat oven to 350 degrees F (177 C).
2. Clean fish inside and out, but leave head on. Pat dry with paper towels.
3. Place the chopped onion, peppercorns, parsley, bay leaf and 2 tbsp (30 ml) of sweet butter in the bottom of a baking pan large enough to hold the fish flat.
4. Scald the shrimps; remove shells and devein. Heat 2 tbsp (30 ml) of sweet butter in a skillet. Cook shrimp, stirring constantly, over low heat until they turn a golden brown.
5. To the skillet add the bread crumbs, a tsp (5 ml) of onion-peppercorn mixture in baking pan, and salt and pepper to taste. Mix well.

6. Drain liquid from oysters and add enough to mixture in skillet to make right consistency for stuffing.
7. Stuff the fish and sew it up. Place in baking pan, decorate with onion rings and pour in 1 cup (237 ml) of wine. Place in oven.
8. When fish is hot, begin to baste. As it dries, add remaining wine a little at a time.
9. When fish starts to brown, place oysters in a saucepan, cover and place over a slow fire. When they have curled, turn oysters into baking pan.
10. Combine cornstarch with a tbsp (15 ml) water and pour into liquid remaining in baking pan. Cook a few minutes longer, until sauce thickens slightly. (If there is not enough liquid left in the pan, add a little more wine to make sauce.)
11. Place fish on platter and cover with oyster sauce. Serve with Boiled Rice, p. 10.

NOTES

SZECHUAN SHRIMP

Makes 2 servings.*

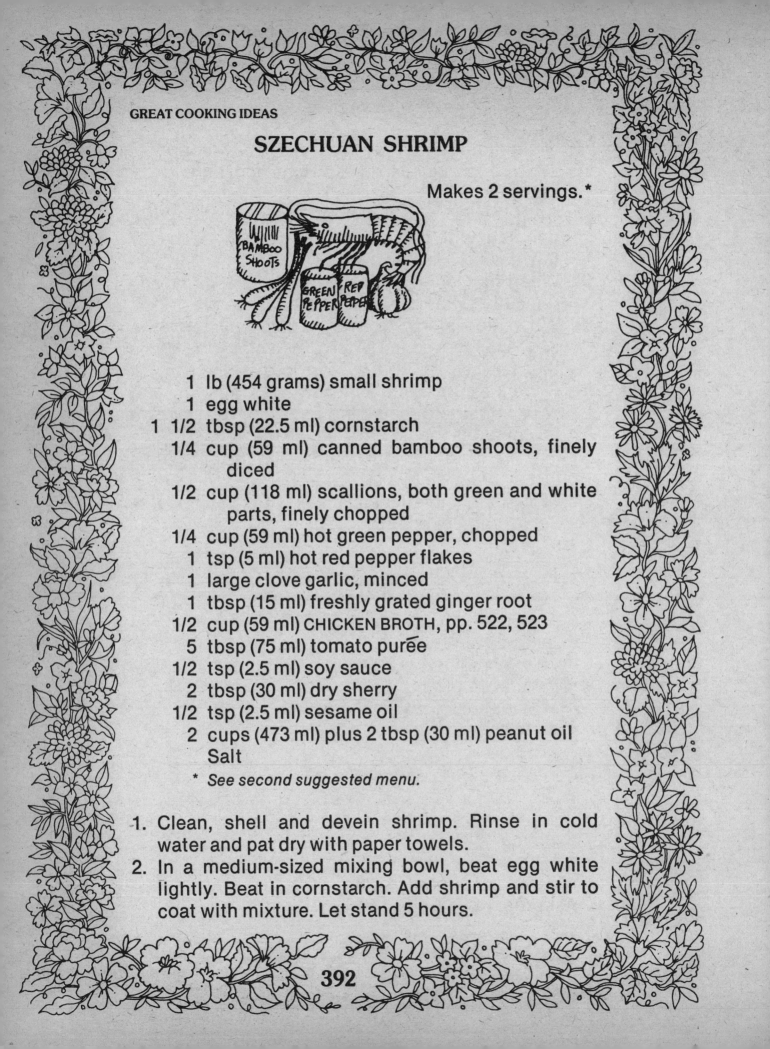

- 1 lb (454 grams) small shrimp
- 1 egg white
- 1 1/2 tbsp (22.5 ml) cornstarch
- 1/4 cup (59 ml) canned bamboo shoots, finely diced
- 1/2 cup (118 ml) scallions, both green and white parts, finely chopped
- 1/4 cup (59 ml) hot green pepper, chopped
- 1 tsp (5 ml) hot red pepper flakes
- 1 large clove garlic, minced
- 1 tbsp (15 ml) freshly grated ginger root
- 1/2 cup (59 ml) CHICKEN BROTH, pp. 522, 523
- 5 tbsp (75 ml) tomato purée
- 1/2 tsp (2.5 ml) soy sauce
- 2 tbsp (30 ml) dry sherry
- 1/2 tsp (2.5 ml) sesame oil
- 2 cups (473 ml) plus 2 tbsp (30 ml) peanut oil
- Salt

* See second suggested menu.

1. Clean, shell and devein shrimp. Rinse in cold water and pat dry with paper towels.
2. In a medium-sized mixing bowl, beat egg white lightly. Beat in cornstarch. Add shrimp and stir to coat with mixture. Let stand 5 hours.

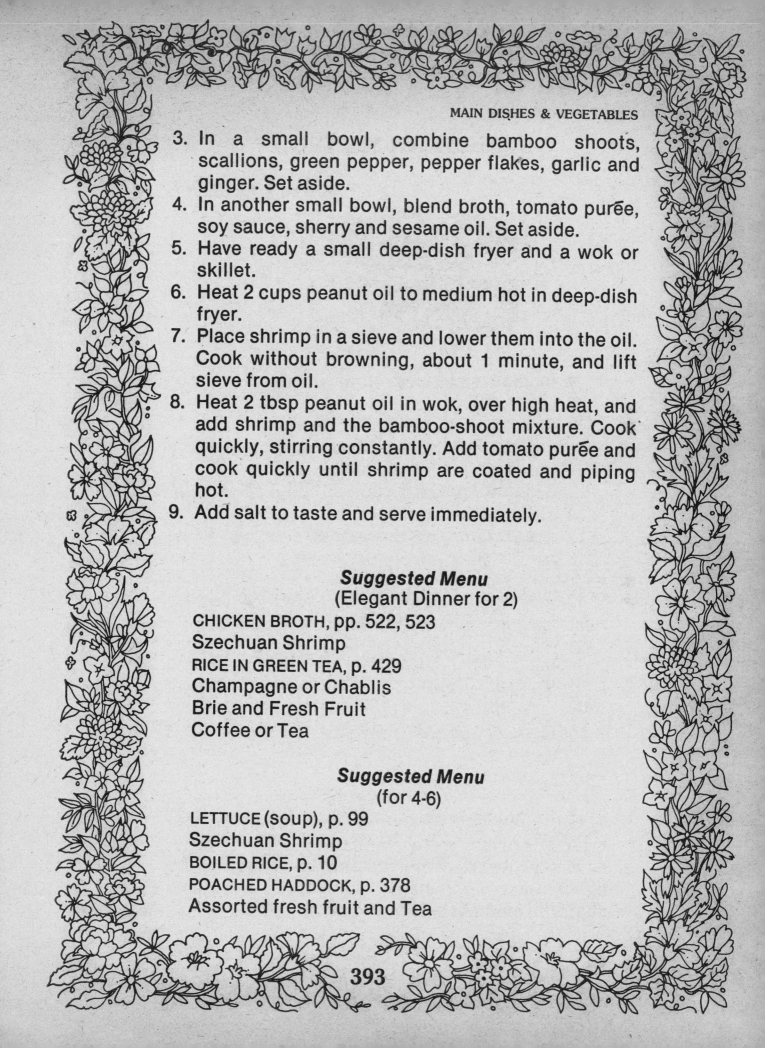

3. In a small bowl, combine bamboo shoots, scallions, green pepper, pepper flakes, garlic and ginger. Set aside.
4. In another small bowl, blend broth, tomato purée, soy sauce, sherry and sesame oil. Set aside.
5. Have ready a small deep-dish fryer and a wok or skillet.
6. Heat 2 cups peanut oil to medium hot in deep-dish fryer.
7. Place shrimp in a sieve and lower them into the oil. Cook without browning, about 1 minute, and lift sieve from oil.
8. Heat 2 tbsp peanut oil in wok, over high heat, and add shrimp and the bamboo-shoot mixture. Cook quickly, stirring constantly. Add tomato purée and cook quickly until shrimp are coated and piping hot.
9. Add salt to taste and serve immediately.

Suggested Menu
(Elegant Dinner for 2)
CHICKEN BROTH, pp. 522, 523
Szechuan Shrimp
RICE IN GREEN TEA, p. 429
Champagne or Chablis
Brie and Fresh Fruit
Coffee or Tea

Suggested Menu
(for 4-6)
LETTUCE (soup), p. 99
Szechuan Shrimp
BOILED RICE, p. 10
POACHED HADDOCK, p. 378
Assorted fresh fruit and Tea

STUFFED WHOLE TROUT

Makes 4 servings.

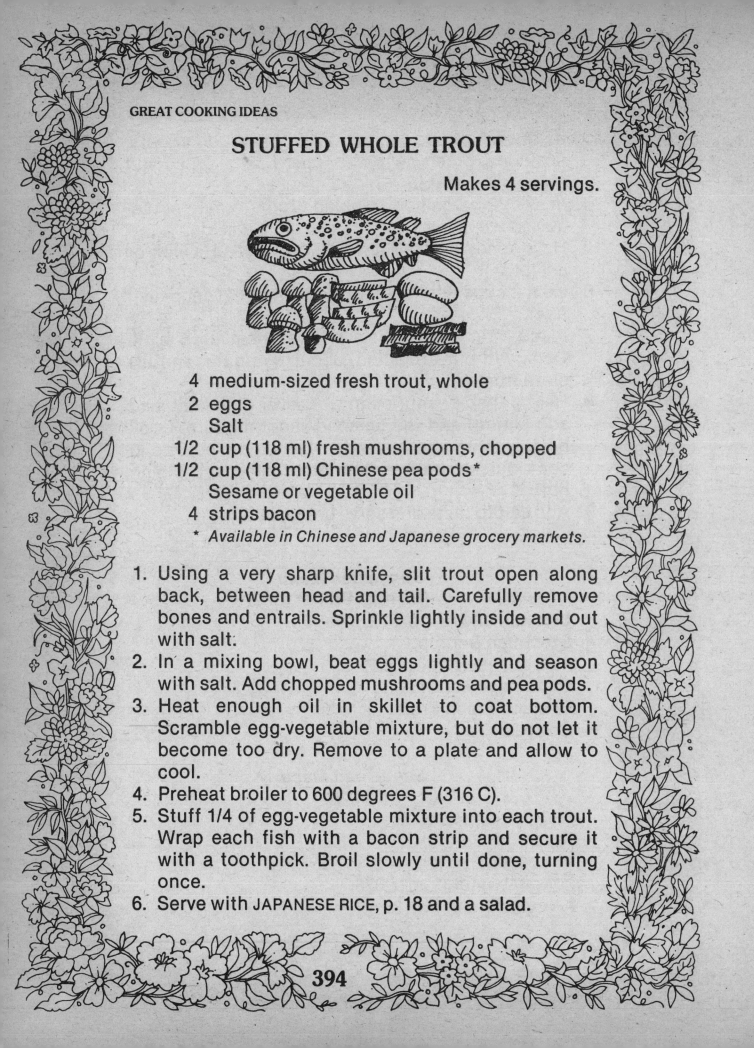

4   medium-sized fresh trout, whole
2   eggs
    Salt
1/2 cup (118 ml) fresh mushrooms, chopped
1/2 cup (118 ml) Chinese pea pods*
    Sesame or vegetable oil
4   strips bacon

* *Available in Chinese and Japanese grocery markets.*

1. Using a very sharp knife, slit trout open along back, between head and tail. Carefully remove bones and entrails. Sprinkle lightly inside and out with salt.
2. In a mixing bowl, beat eggs lightly and season with salt. Add chopped mushrooms and pea pods.
3. Heat enough oil in skillet to coat bottom. Scramble egg-vegetable mixture, but do not let it become too dry. Remove to a plate and allow to cool.
4. Preheat broiler to 600 degrees F (316 C).
5. Stuff 1/4 of egg-vegetable mixture into each trout. Wrap each fish with a bacon strip and secure it with a toothpick. Broil slowly until done, turning once.
6. Serve with JAPANESE RICE, p. 18 and a salad.

TAGLIATELLE 'N' FISH

Makes 6 servings.

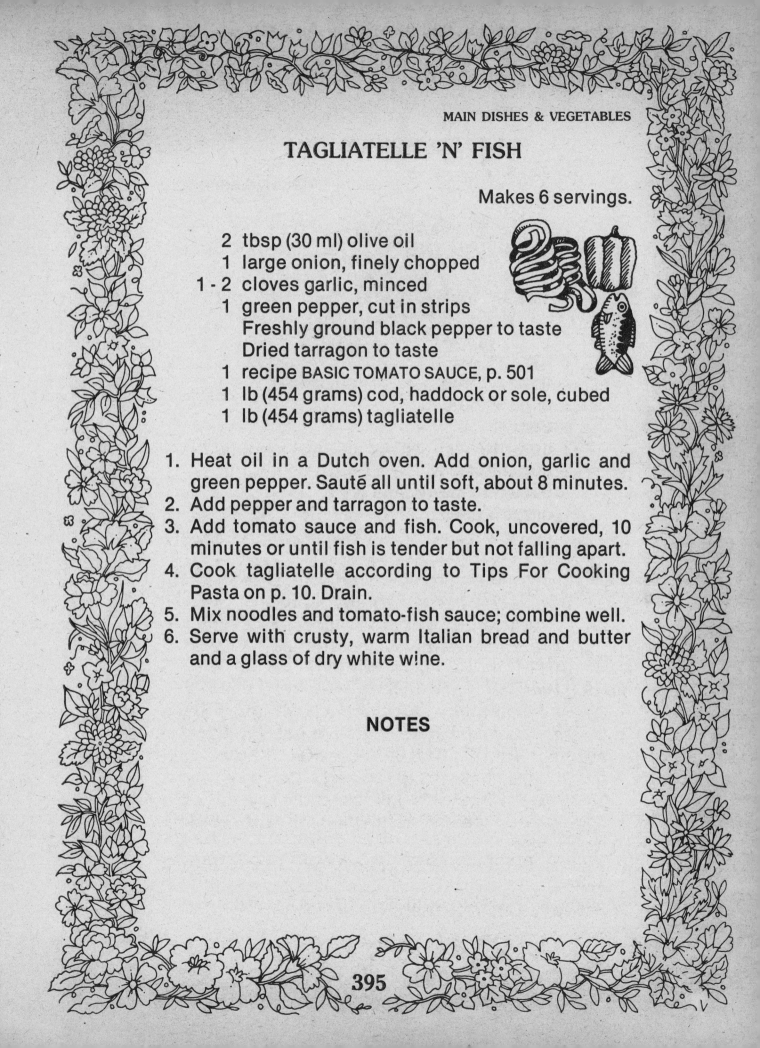

    2 tbsp (30 ml) olive oil
    1 large onion, finely chopped
1 - 2 cloves garlic, minced
    1 green pepper, cut in strips
       Freshly ground black pepper to taste
       Dried tarragon to taste
    1 recipe BASIC TOMATO SAUCE, p. 501
    1 lb (454 grams) cod, haddock or sole, cubed
    1 lb (454 grams) tagliatelle

1. Heat oil in a Dutch oven. Add onion, garlic and green pepper. Sauté all until soft, about 8 minutes.
2. Add pepper and tarragon to taste.
3. Add tomato sauce and fish. Cook, uncovered, 10 minutes or until fish is tender but not falling apart.
4. Cook tagliatelle according to Tips For Cooking Pasta on p. 10. Drain.
5. Mix noodles and tomato-fish sauce; combine well.
6. Serve with crusty, warm Italian bread and butter and a glass of dry white wine.

NOTES

TEMPURA

Makes 6 servings.

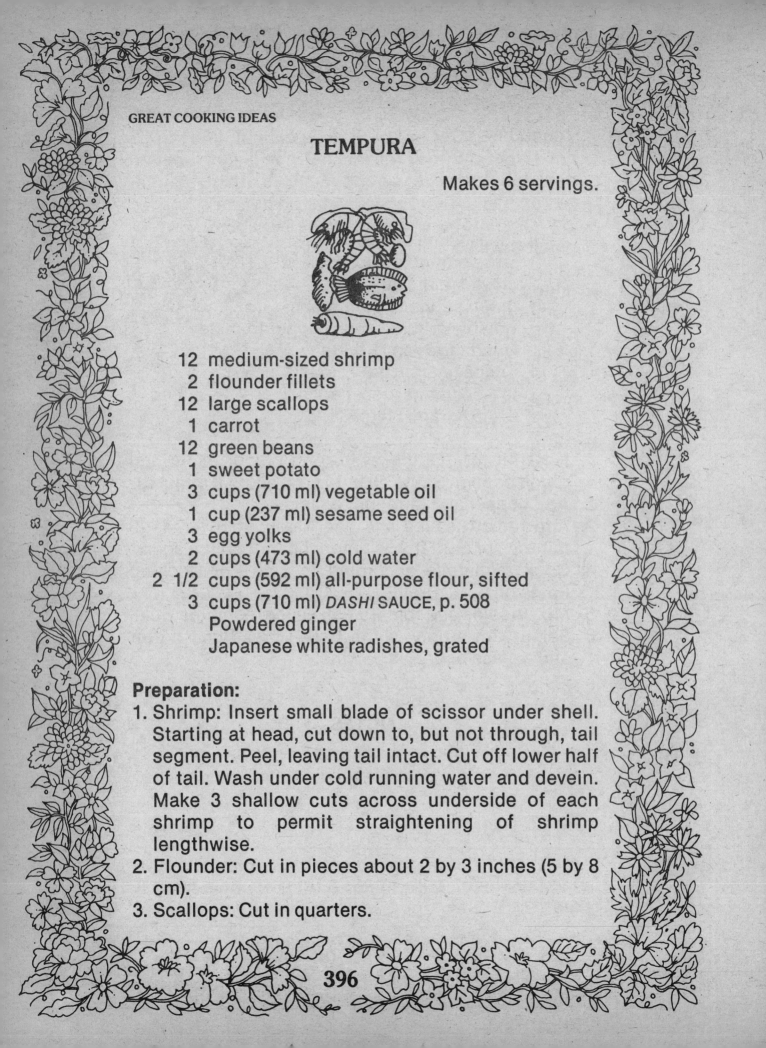

12 medium-sized shrimp
 2 flounder fillets
12 large scallops
 1 carrot
12 green beans
 1 sweet potato
 3 cups (710 ml) vegetable oil
 1 cup (237 ml) sesame seed oil
 3 egg yolks
 2 cups (473 ml) cold water
2 1/2 cups (592 ml) all-purpose flour, sifted
 3 cups (710 ml) *DASHI* SAUCE, p. 508
    Powdered ginger
    Japanese white radishes, grated

Preparation:

1. Shrimp: Insert small blade of scissor under shell. Starting at head, cut down to, but not through, tail segment. Peel, leaving tail intact. Cut off lower half of tail. Wash under cold running water and devein. Make 3 shallow cuts across underside of each shrimp to permit straightening of shrimp lengthwise.

2. Flounder: Cut in pieces about 2 by 3 inches (5 by 8 cm).

3. Scallops: Cut in quarters.

4. Vegetables: Cut carrot in slices about 1/8 inch (.3 cm) thick; cut green beans in 2-inch (5-cm) lengths; peel and cut sweet potato in slices about 1/8 inch (.3 cm) thick, then cut each slice in quarters.
5. Dry all seafood and vegetables between layers of paper towels.

Making batter:
1. Combine egg yolks with water in a large bowl and mix well.
2. Stir in flour gradually, stirring from bottom of bowl. Do not overbeat; some flour should remain floating on top of batter.

Cooking:
1. Heat oil in a deep-fat fryer. A deep-fat thermometer is necessary as 330 degrees F (164 C) must be maintained in order to obtain good results.
2. Hold shrimp by tail, dip in batter and drop gently, one at a time, into hot fat. Fry until golden brown, about 1 minute.
3. Dip each piece of remaining fish, shellfish and vegetables in batter, following same procedure. Fry until golden brown. (*Caution*: Fry only a few pieces at a time).
4. Remove fried morsels to paper towels to drain briefly.
5. To serve, give each person an individual bowl of *DASHI* SAUCE with ginger and grated radish added to sauce, a separate bowl with some of each type of fried food and a third bowl with JAPANESE RICE, p. 18.

Note: This dish should be eaten with chopsticks to obtain maximum enjoyment. A little practice is all it takes.

VERONA TROUT

Makes 4 servings.

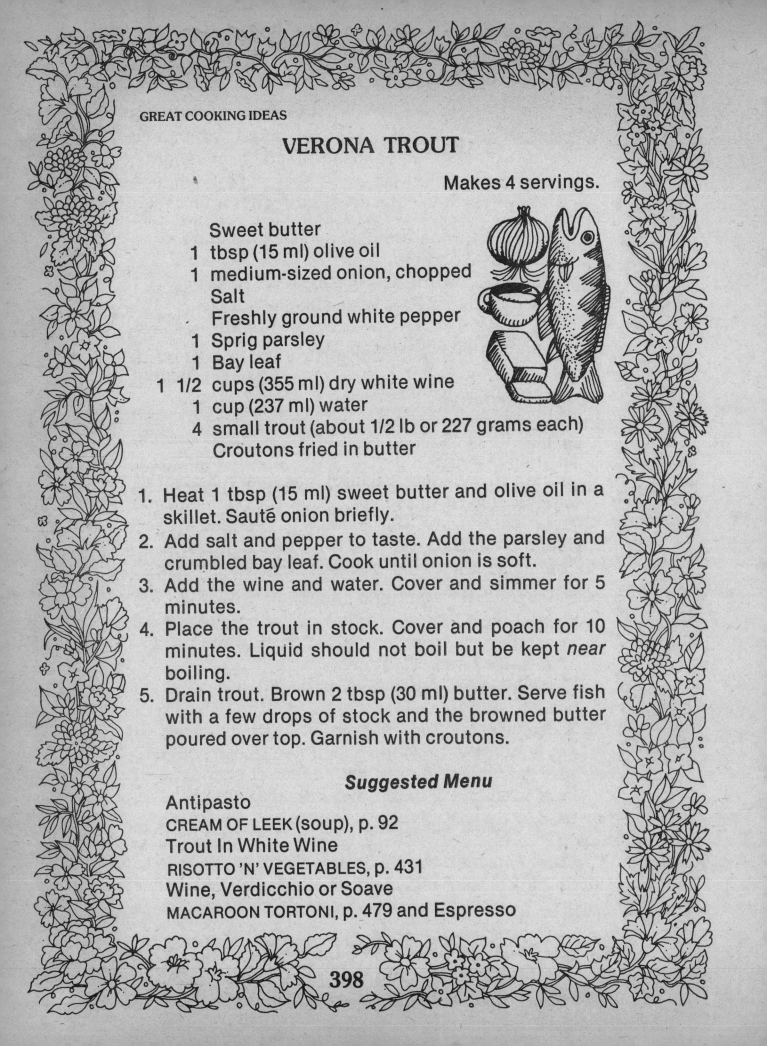

Sweet butter
1 tbsp (15 ml) olive oil
1 medium-sized onion, chopped
Salt
Freshly ground white pepper
1 Sprig parsley
1 Bay leaf
1 1/2 cups (355 ml) dry white wine
1 cup (237 ml) water
4 small trout (about 1/2 lb or 227 grams each)
Croutons fried in butter

1. Heat 1 tbsp (15 ml) sweet butter and olive oil in a skillet. Sauté onion briefly.
2. Add salt and pepper to taste. Add the parsley and crumbled bay leaf. Cook until onion is soft.
3. Add the wine and water. Cover and simmer for 5 minutes.
4. Place the trout in stock. Cover and poach for 10 minutes. Liquid should not boil but be kept *near* boiling.
5. Drain trout. Brown 2 tbsp (30 ml) butter. Serve fish with a few drops of stock and the browned butter poured over top. Garnish with croutons.

Suggested Menu

Antipasto
CREAM OF LEEK (soup), p. 92
Trout In White Wine
RISOTTO 'N' VEGETABLES, p. 431
Wine, Verdicchio or Soave
MACAROON TORTONI, p. 479 and Espresso

BAKED CAULIFLOWER

Makes 4 - 6 servings.

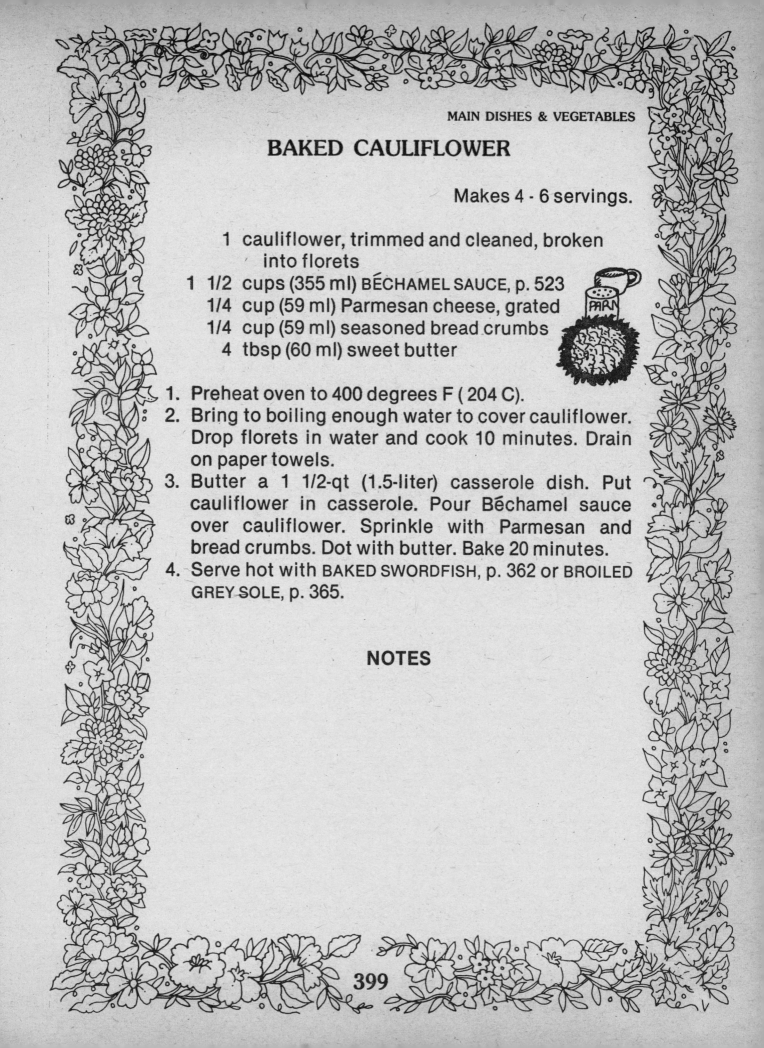

1 cauliflower, trimmed and cleaned, broken
  into florets
1 1/2 cups (355 ml) BÉCHAMEL SAUCE, p. 523
1/4 cup (59 ml) Parmesan cheese, grated
1/4 cup (59 ml) seasoned bread crumbs
4 tbsp (60 ml) sweet butter

1. Preheat oven to 400 degrees F (204 C).
2. Bring to boiling enough water to cover cauliflower. Drop florets in water and cook 10 minutes. Drain on paper towels.
3. Butter a 1 1/2-qt (1.5-liter) casserole dish. Put cauliflower in casserole. Pour Béchamel sauce over cauliflower. Sprinkle with Parmesan and bread crumbs. Dot with butter. Bake 20 minutes.
4. Serve hot with BAKED SWORDFISH, p. 362 or BROILED GREY SOLE, p. 365.

NOTES

BAMBOO SHOOTS 'N' GREEN BEANS

Makes 4 servings.

1/2 lb (227 grams) fresh green beans
1 tbsp (15 ml) vegetable oil
1/2 medium-sized onion, thinly sliced
1 tbsp (15 ml) dried shrimp*
Salt
1 cup (237 ml) canned bamboo shoots, sliced**

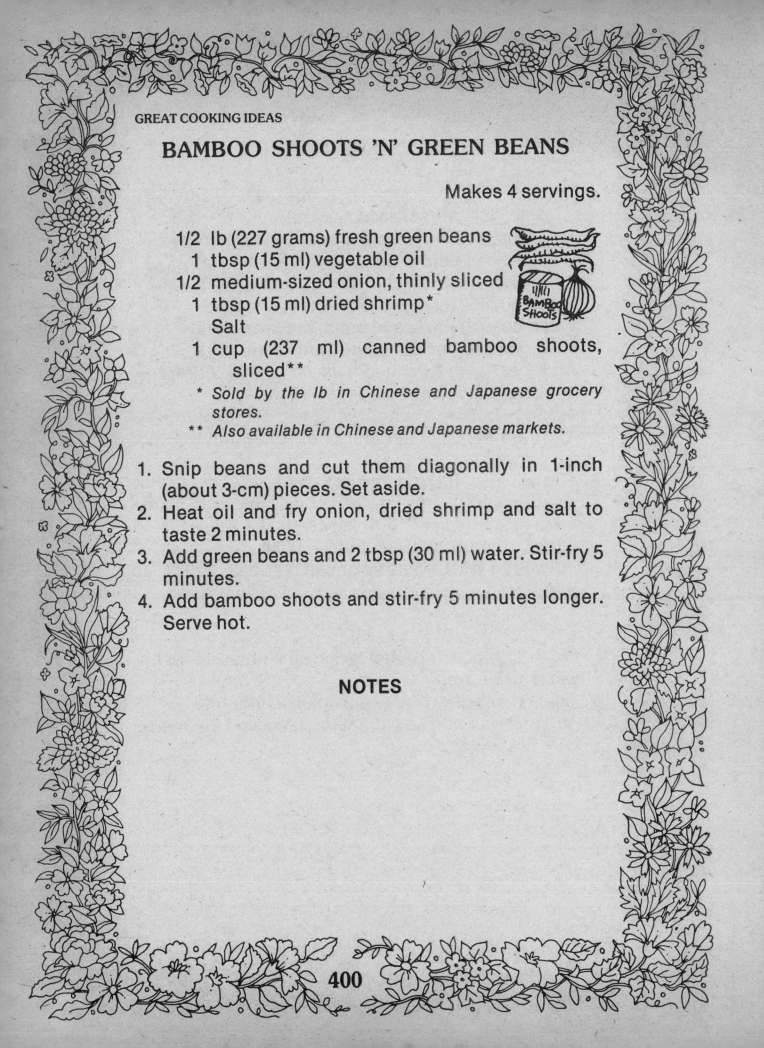

* Sold by the lb in Chinese and Japanese grocery stores.
** Also available in Chinese and Japanese markets.

1. Snip beans and cut them diagonally in 1-inch (about 3-cm) pieces. Set aside.
2. Heat oil and fry onion, dried shrimp and salt to taste 2 minutes.
3. Add green beans and 2 tbsp (30 ml) water. Stir-fry 5 minutes.
4. Add bamboo shoots and stir-fry 5 minutes longer. Serve hot.

NOTES

BEAN SPROUTS

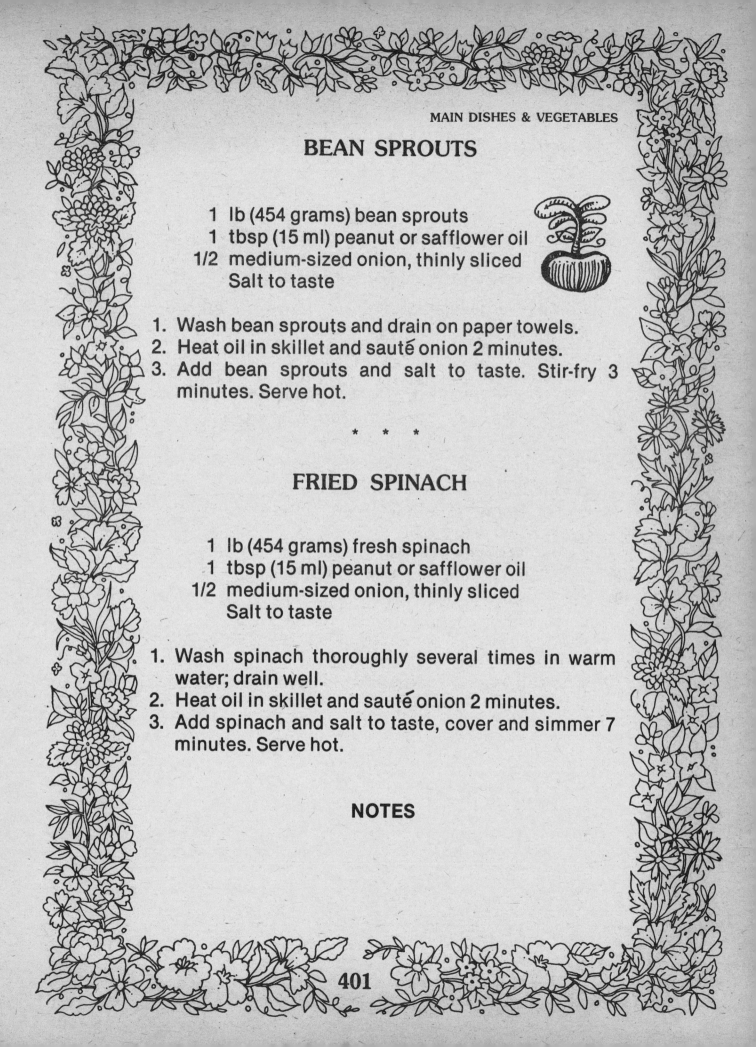

1 lb (454 grams) bean sprouts
1 tbsp (15 ml) peanut or safflower oil
1/2 medium-sized onion, thinly sliced
Salt to taste

1. Wash bean sprouts and drain on paper towels.
2. Heat oil in skillet and sauté onion 2 minutes.
3. Add bean sprouts and salt to taste. Stir-fry 3 minutes. Serve hot.

* * *

FRIED SPINACH

1 lb (454 grams) fresh spinach
1 tbsp (15 ml) peanut or safflower oil
1/2 medium-sized onion, thinly sliced
Salt to taste

1. Wash spinach thoroughly several times in warm water; drain well.
2. Heat oil in skillet and sauté onion 2 minutes.
3. Add spinach and salt to taste, cover and simmer 7 minutes. Serve hot.

NOTES

BROCCOLI WITH CHEESE SAUCE

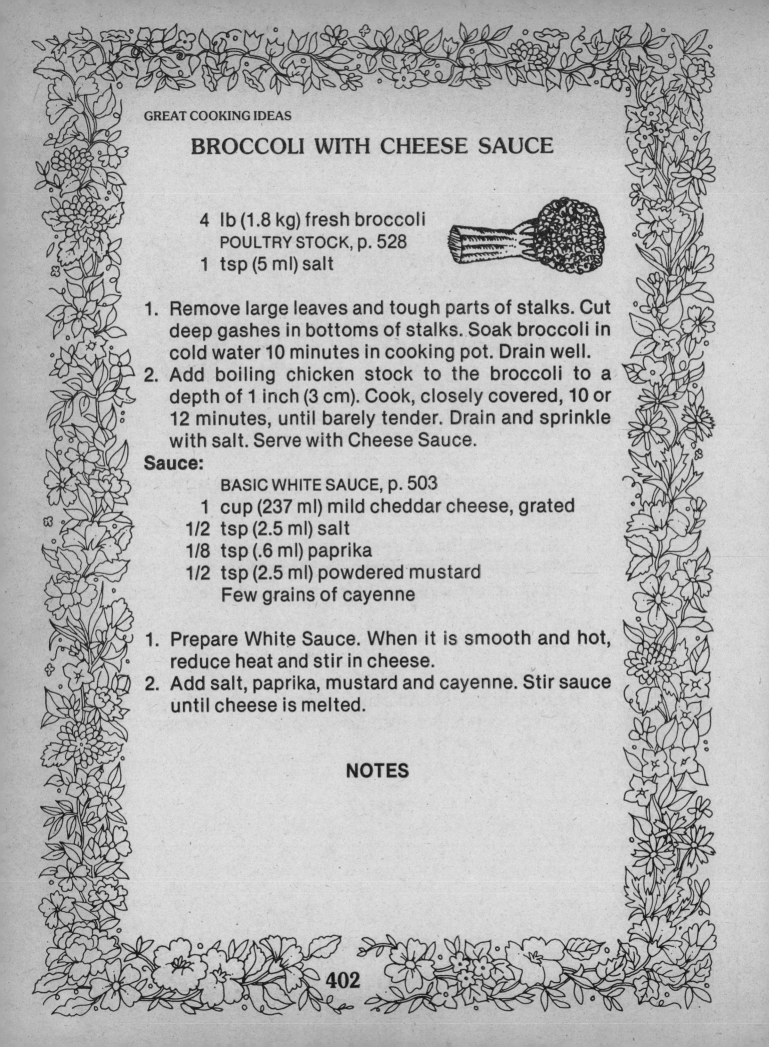

4 lb (1.8 kg) fresh broccoli
POULTRY STOCK, p. 528
1 tsp (5 ml) salt

1. Remove large leaves and tough parts of stalks. Cut deep gashes in bottoms of stalks. Soak broccoli in cold water 10 minutes in cooking pot. Drain well.
2. Add boiling chicken stock to the broccoli to a depth of 1 inch (3 cm). Cook, closely covered, 10 or 12 minutes, until barely tender. Drain and sprinkle with salt. Serve with Cheese Sauce.

Sauce:

BASIC WHITE SAUCE, p. 503
1 cup (237 ml) mild cheddar cheese, grated
1/2 tsp (2.5 ml) salt
1/8 tsp (.6 ml) paprika
1/2 tsp (2.5 ml) powdered mustard
Few grains of cayenne

1. Prepare White Sauce. When it is smooth and hot, reduce heat and stir in cheese.
2. Add salt, paprika, mustard and cayenne. Stir sauce until cheese is melted.

NOTES

BRUSSELS SPROUTS

Makes 4 servings.

1 lb (454 grams) fresh Brussels sprouts
  Wine vinegar
  Juice of 1/2 lemon
  Salt
2 tbsp (30 ml) sweet butter, melted
1 tbsp (15 ml) fresh parsley leaves,
  chopped finely

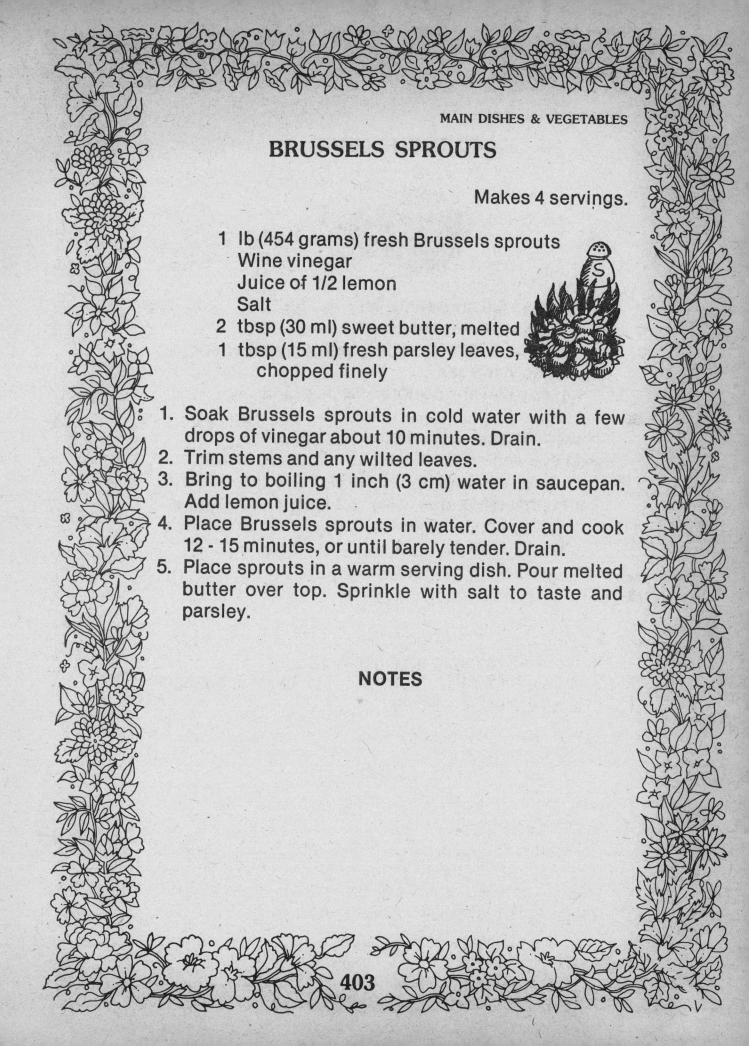

1. Soak Brussels sprouts in cold water with a few drops of vinegar about 10 minutes. Drain.
2. Trim stems and any wilted leaves.
3. Bring to boiling 1 inch (3 cm) water in saucepan. Add lemon juice.
4. Place Brussels sprouts in water. Cover and cook 12 - 15 minutes, or until barely tender. Drain.
5. Place sprouts in a warm serving dish. Pour melted butter over top. Sprinkle with salt to taste and parsley.

NOTES

BURMESE RICE

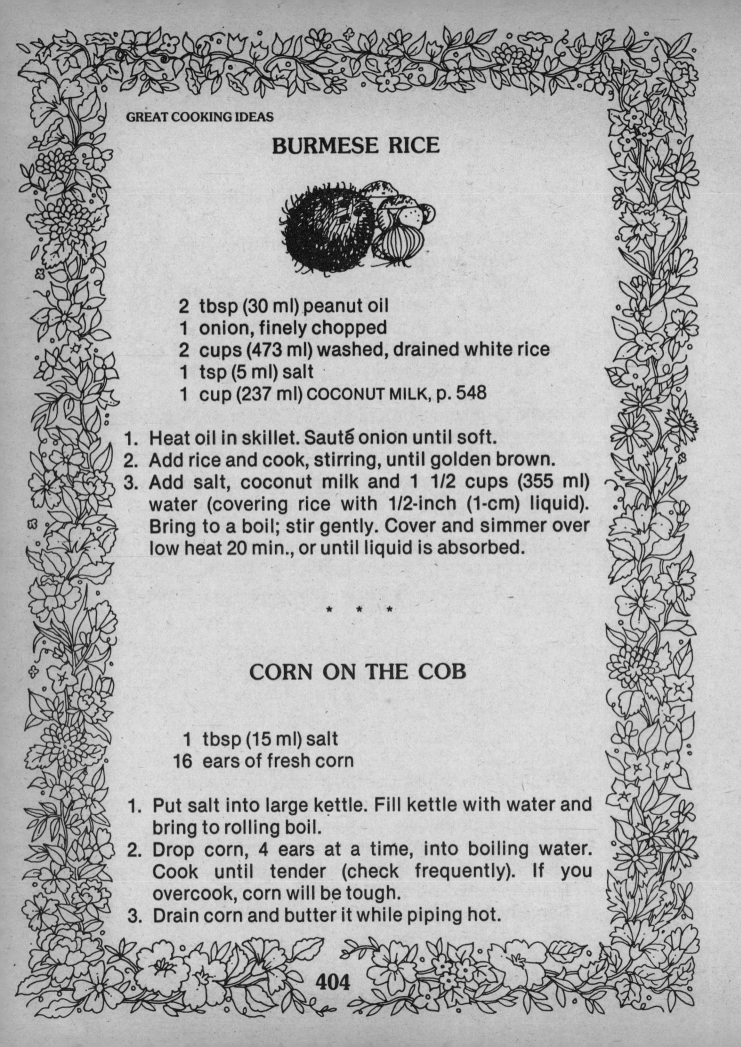

2 tbsp (30 ml) peanut oil
1 onion, finely chopped
2 cups (473 ml) washed, drained white rice
1 tsp (5 ml) salt
1 cup (237 ml) COCONUT MILK, p. 548

1. Heat oil in skillet. Sauté onion until soft.
2. Add rice and cook, stirring, until golden brown.
3. Add salt, coconut milk and 1 1/2 cups (355 ml) water (covering rice with 1/2-inch (1-cm) liquid). Bring to a boil; stir gently. Cover and simmer over low heat 20 min., or until liquid is absorbed.

* * *

CORN ON THE COB

1 tbsp (15 ml) salt
16 ears of fresh corn

1. Put salt into large kettle. Fill kettle with water and bring to rolling boil.
2. Drop corn, 4 ears at a time, into boiling water. Cook until tender (check frequently). If you overcook, corn will be tough.
3. Drain corn and butter it while piping hot.

BUTTERY ASPARAGUS

Makes 4 servings.

2 lb (907 grams) fresh asparagus
2 - 3 tbsp (30-45 ml) sweet butter, melted
Salt
Parmesan cheese, grated

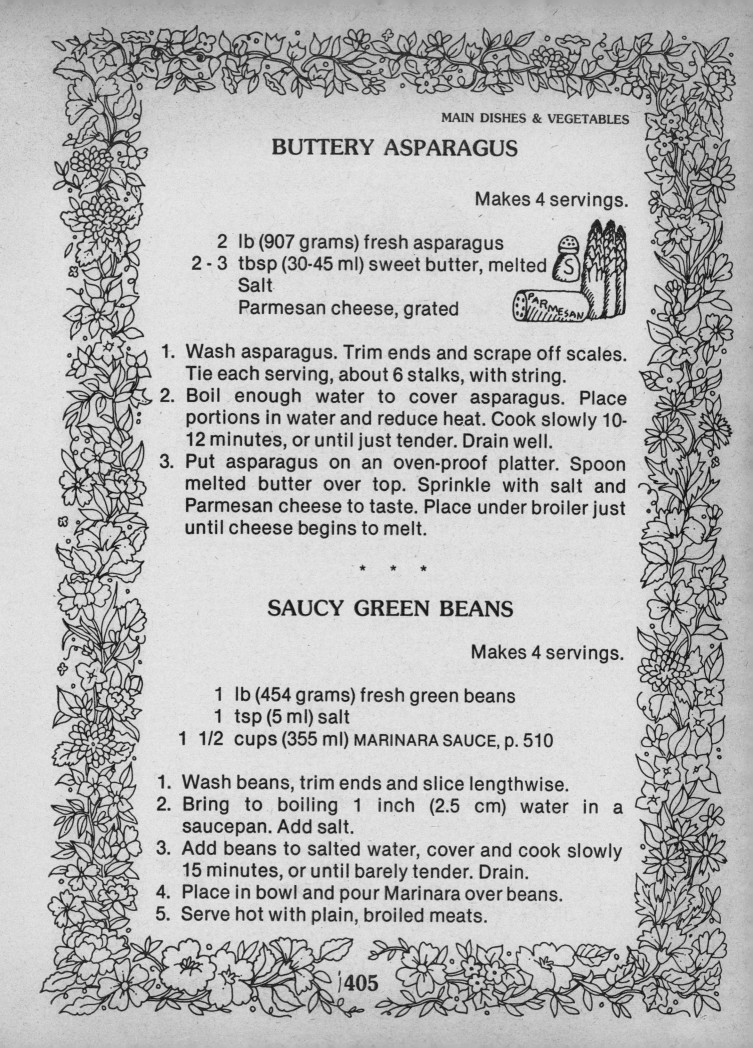

1. Wash asparagus. Trim ends and scrape off scales. Tie each serving, about 6 stalks, with string.
2. Boil enough water to cover asparagus. Place portions in water and reduce heat. Cook slowly 10-12 minutes, or until just tender. Drain well.
3. Put asparagus on an oven-proof platter. Spoon melted butter over top. Sprinkle with salt and Parmesan cheese to taste. Place under broiler just until cheese begins to melt.

* * *

SAUCY GREEN BEANS

Makes 4 servings.

1 lb (454 grams) fresh green beans
1 tsp (5 ml) salt
1 1/2 cups (355 ml) MARINARA SAUCE, p. 510

1. Wash beans, trim ends and slice lengthwise.
2. Bring to boiling 1 inch (2.5 cm) water in a saucepan. Add salt.
3. Add beans to salted water, cover and cook slowly 15 minutes, or until barely tender. Drain.
4. Place in bowl and pour Marinara over beans.
5. Serve hot with plain, broiled meats.

BUTTERY CARROTS

Makes 8 servings.

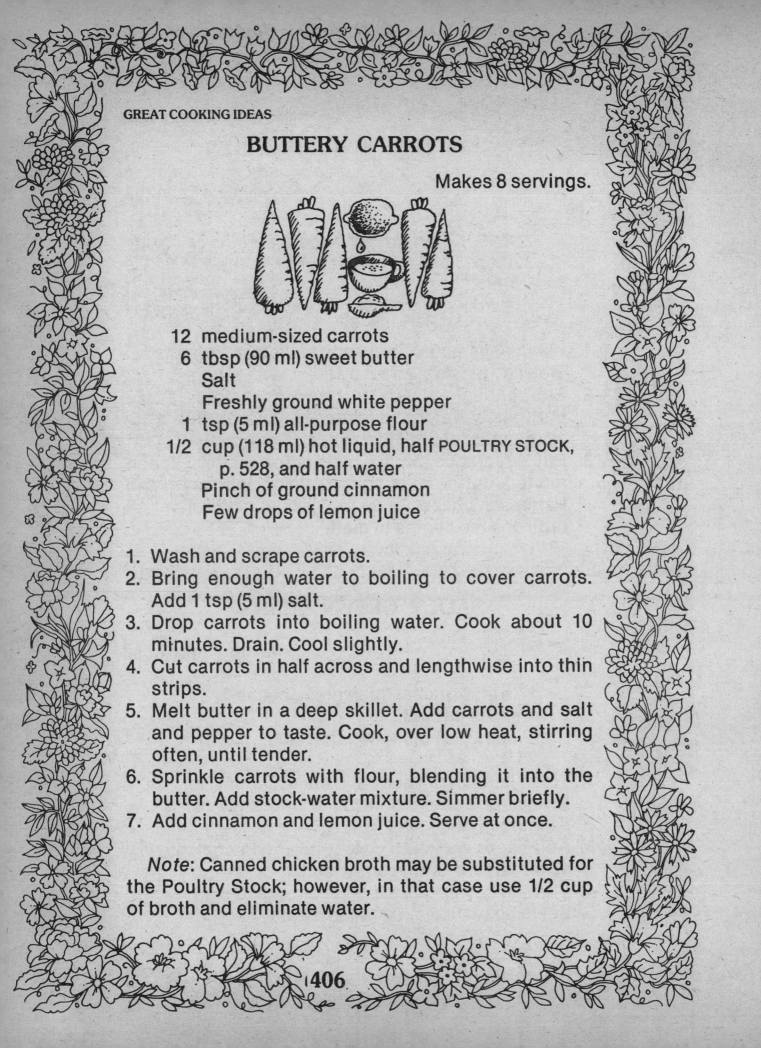

```
12  medium-sized carrots
 6  tbsp (90 ml) sweet butter
    Salt
    Freshly ground white pepper
 1  tsp (5 ml) all-purpose flour
1/2 cup (118 ml) hot liquid, half POULTRY STOCK,
       p. 528, and half water
    Pinch of ground cinnamon
    Few drops of lemon juice
```

1. Wash and scrape carrots.
2. Bring enough water to boiling to cover carrots. Add 1 tsp (5 ml) salt.
3. Drop carrots into boiling water. Cook about 10 minutes. Drain. Cool slightly.
4. Cut carrots in half across and lengthwise into thin strips.
5. Melt butter in a deep skillet. Add carrots and salt and pepper to taste. Cook, over low heat, stirring often, until tender.
6. Sprinkle carrots with flour, blending it into the butter. Add stock-water mixture. Simmer briefly.
7. Add cinnamon and lemon juice. Serve at once.

Note: Canned chicken broth may be substituted for the Poultry Stock; however, in that case use 1/2 cup of broth and eliminate water.

CABBAGE 'N' BEAN CAKES

Makes 4 servings.

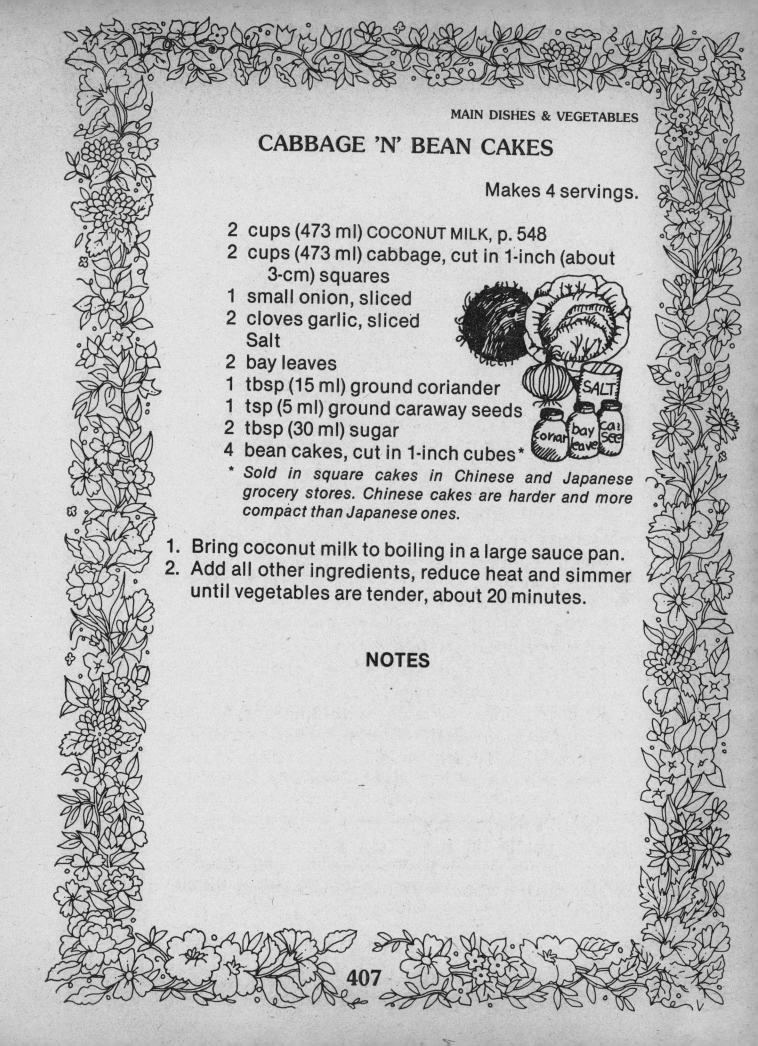

- 2 cups (473 ml) COCONUT MILK, p. 548
- 2 cups (473 ml) cabbage, cut in 1-inch (about 3-cm) squares
- 1 small onion, sliced
- 2 cloves garlic, sliced
- Salt
- 2 bay leaves
- 1 tbsp (15 ml) ground coriander
- 1 tsp (5 ml) ground caraway seeds
- 2 tbsp (30 ml) sugar
- 4 bean cakes, cut in 1-inch cubes*

* *Sold in square cakes in Chinese and Japanese grocery stores. Chinese cakes are harder and more compact than Japanese ones.*

1. Bring coconut milk to boiling in a large sauce pan.
2. Add all other ingredients, reduce heat and simmer until vegetables are tender, about 20 minutes.

NOTES

CHEDDAR SOUFFLÉ

Makes 6 to 8 servings.

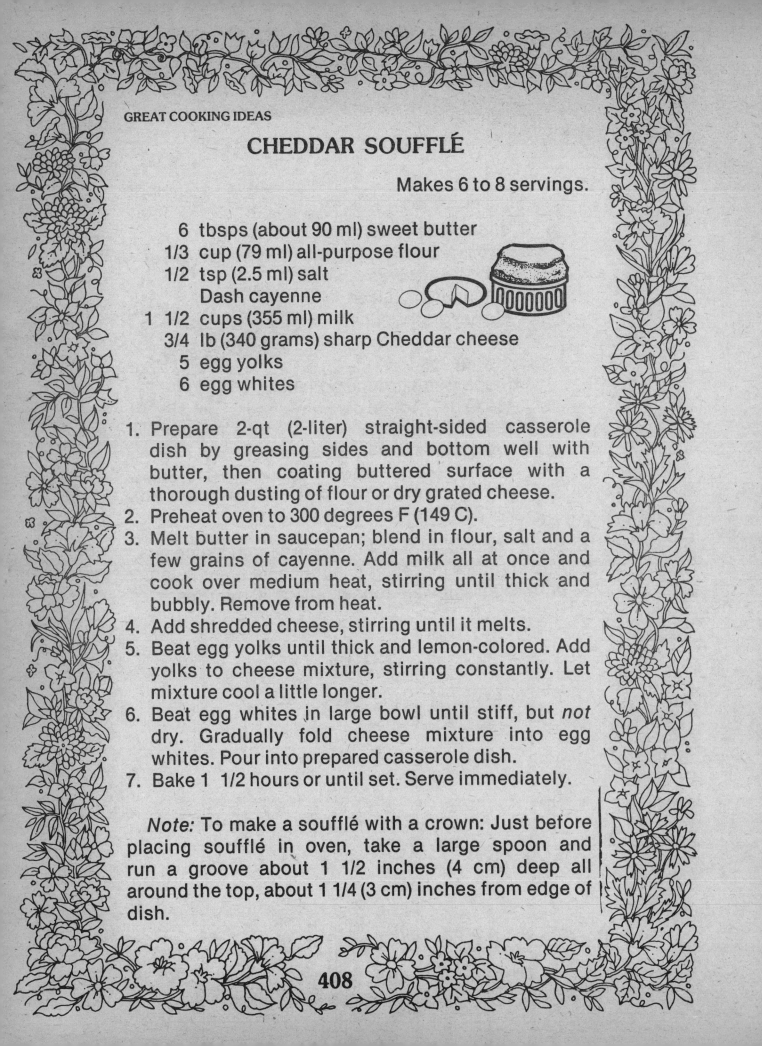

6	tbsps (about 90 ml) sweet butter
1/3	cup (79 ml) all-purpose flour
1/2	tsp (2.5 ml) salt
	Dash cayenne
1 1/2	cups (355 ml) milk
3/4	lb (340 grams) sharp Cheddar cheese
5	egg yolks
6	egg whites

1. Prepare 2-qt (2-liter) straight-sided casserole dish by greasing sides and bottom well with butter, then coating buttered surface with a thorough dusting of flour or dry grated cheese.
2. Preheat oven to 300 degrees F (149 C).
3. Melt butter in saucepan; blend in flour, salt and a few grains of cayenne. Add milk all at once and cook over medium heat, stirring until thick and bubbly. Remove from heat.
4. Add shredded cheese, stirring until it melts.
5. Beat egg yolks until thick and lemon-colored. Add yolks to cheese mixture, stirring constantly. Let mixture cool a little longer.
6. Beat egg whites in large bowl until stiff, but *not* dry. Gradually fold cheese mixture into egg whites. Pour into prepared casserole dish.
7. Bake 1 1/2 hours or until set. Serve immediately.

Note: To make a soufflé with a crown: Just before placing soufflé in oven, take a large spoon and run a groove about 1 1/2 inches (4 cm) deep all around the top, about 1 1/4 (3 cm) inches from edge of dish.

CHEESE FONDUE

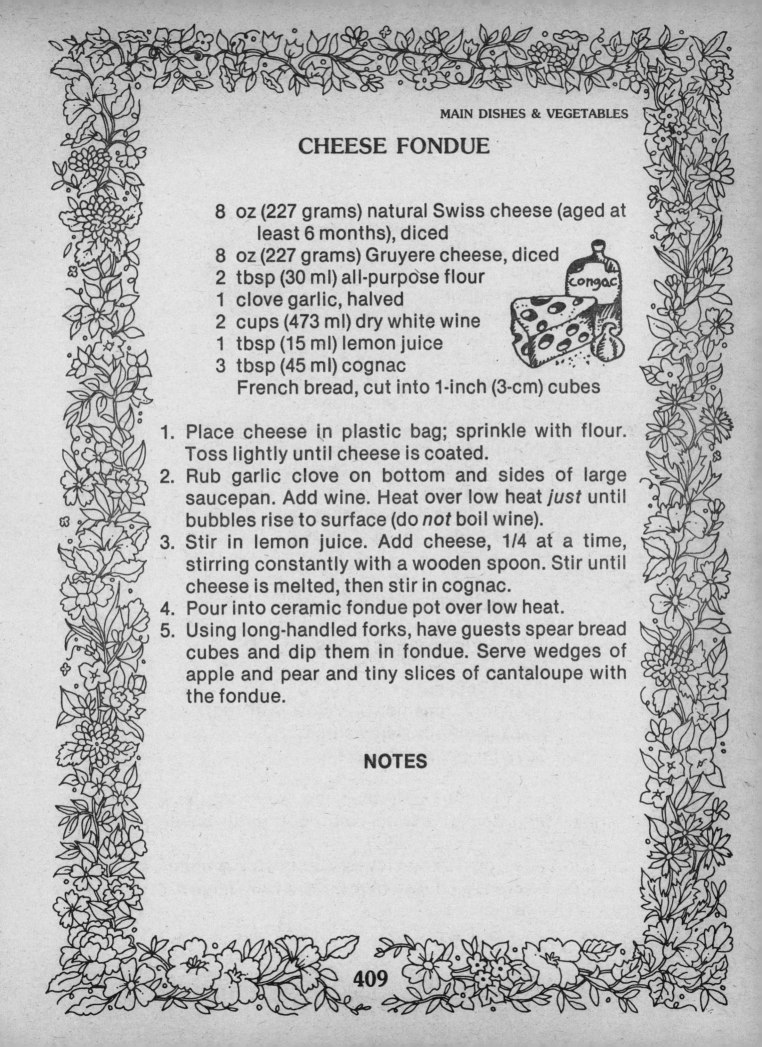

8 oz (227 grams) natural Swiss cheese (aged at least 6 months), diced
8 oz (227 grams) Gruyere cheese, diced
2 tbsp (30 ml) all-purpose flour
1 clove garlic, halved
2 cups (473 ml) dry white wine
1 tbsp (15 ml) lemon juice
3 tbsp (45 ml) cognac
French bread, cut into 1-inch (3-cm) cubes

1. Place cheese in plastic bag; sprinkle with flour. Toss lightly until cheese is coated.
2. Rub garlic clove on bottom and sides of large saucepan. Add wine. Heat over low heat *just* until bubbles rise to surface (do *not* boil wine).
3. Stir in lemon juice. Add cheese, 1/4 at a time, stirring constantly with a wooden spoon. Stir until cheese is melted, then stir in cognac.
4. Pour into ceramic fondue pot over low heat.
5. Using long-handled forks, have guests spear bread cubes and dip them in fondue. Serve wedges of apple and pear and tiny slices of cantaloupe with the fondue.

NOTES

CHEESY AVOCADOS

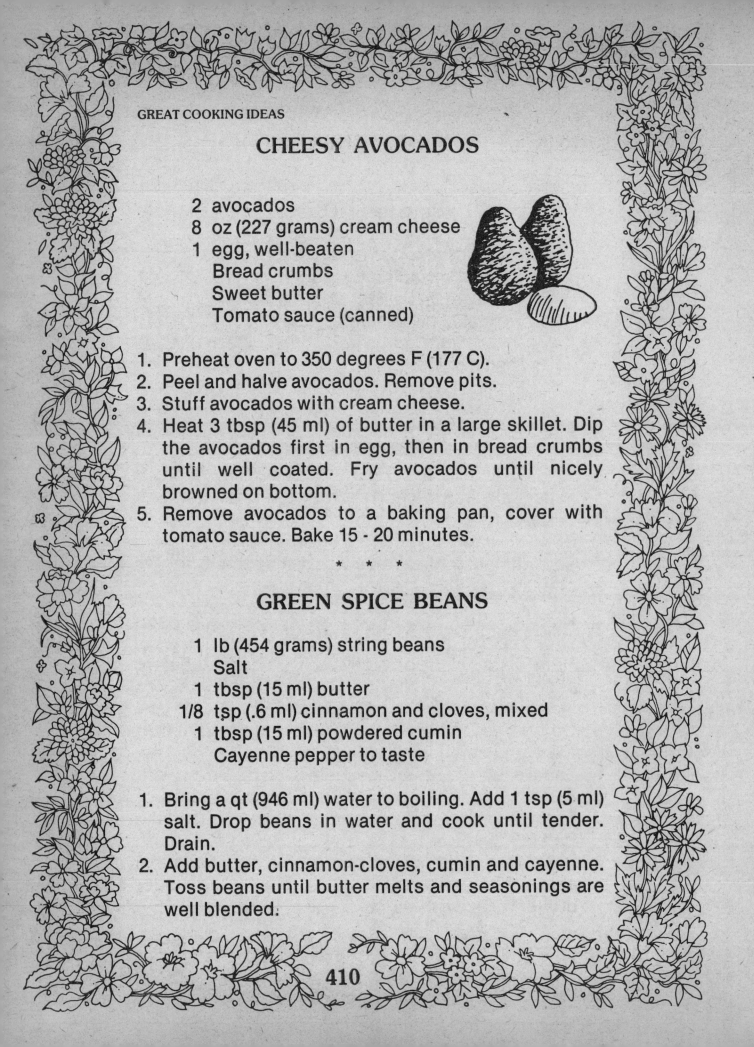

2 avocados
8 oz (227 grams) cream cheese
1 egg, well-beaten
Bread crumbs
Sweet butter
Tomato sauce (canned)

1. Preheat oven to 350 degrees F (177 C).
2. Peel and halve avocados. Remove pits.
3. Stuff avocados with cream cheese.
4. Heat 3 tbsp (45 ml) of butter in a large skillet. Dip the avocados first in egg, then in bread crumbs until well coated. Fry avocados until nicely browned on bottom.
5. Remove avocados to a baking pan, cover with tomato sauce. Bake 15 - 20 minutes.

* * *

GREEN SPICE BEANS

1 lb (454 grams) string beans
Salt
1 tbsp (15 ml) butter
1/8 tsp (.6 ml) cinnamon and cloves, mixed
1 tbsp (15 ml) powdered cumin
Cayenne pepper to taste

1. Bring a qt (946 ml) water to boiling. Add 1 tsp (5 ml) salt. Drop beans in water and cook until tender. Drain.
2. Add butter, cinnamon-cloves, cumin and cayenne. Toss beans until butter melts and seasonings are well blended.

CHEESY EGGPLANT

Makes 4 - 6 servings.

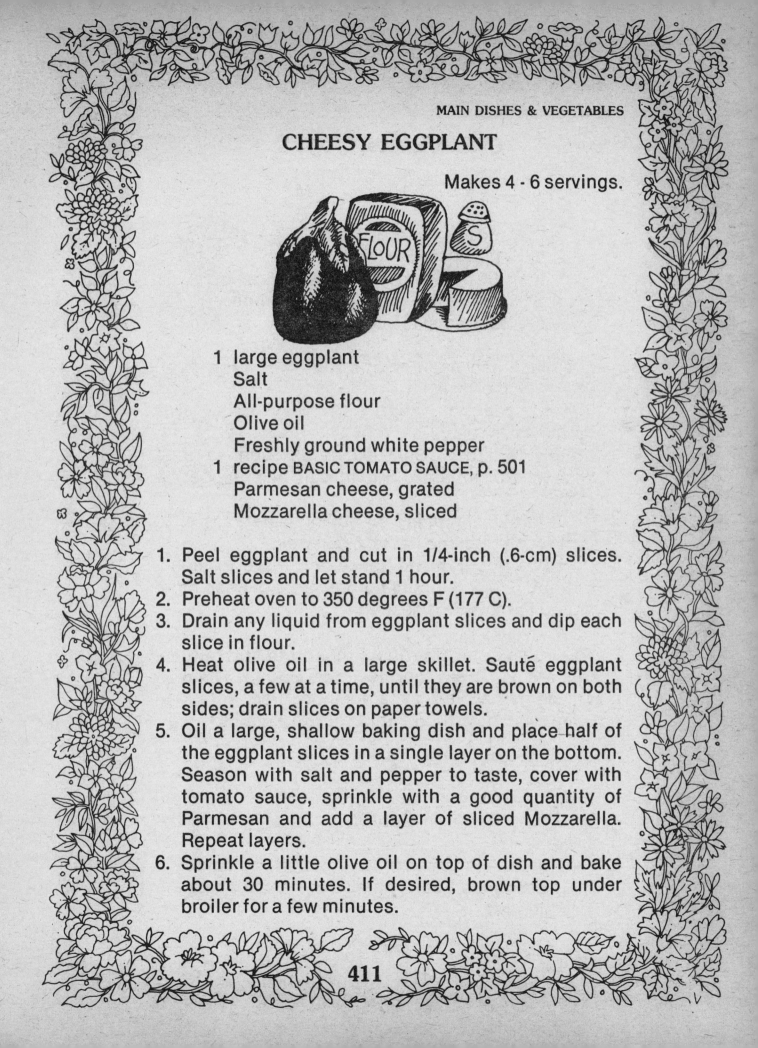

1 large eggplant
 Salt
 All-purpose flour
 Olive oil
 Freshly ground white pepper
1 recipe BASIC TOMATO SAUCE, p. 501
 Parmesan cheese, grated
 Mozzarella cheese, sliced

1. Peel eggplant and cut in 1/4-inch (.6-cm) slices. Salt slices and let stand 1 hour.
2. Preheat oven to 350 degrees F (177 C).
3. Drain any liquid from eggplant slices and dip each slice in flour.
4. Heat olive oil in a large skillet. Sauté eggplant slices, a few at a time, until they are brown on both sides; drain slices on paper towels.
5. Oil a large, shallow baking dish and place half of the eggplant slices in a single layer on the bottom. Season with salt and pepper to taste, cover with tomato sauce, sprinkle with a good quantity of Parmesan and add a layer of sliced Mozzarella. Repeat layers.
6. Sprinkle a little olive oil on top of dish and bake about 30 minutes. If desired, brown top under broiler for a few minutes.

CREAMED FETTUCCE

Makes 4 servings.

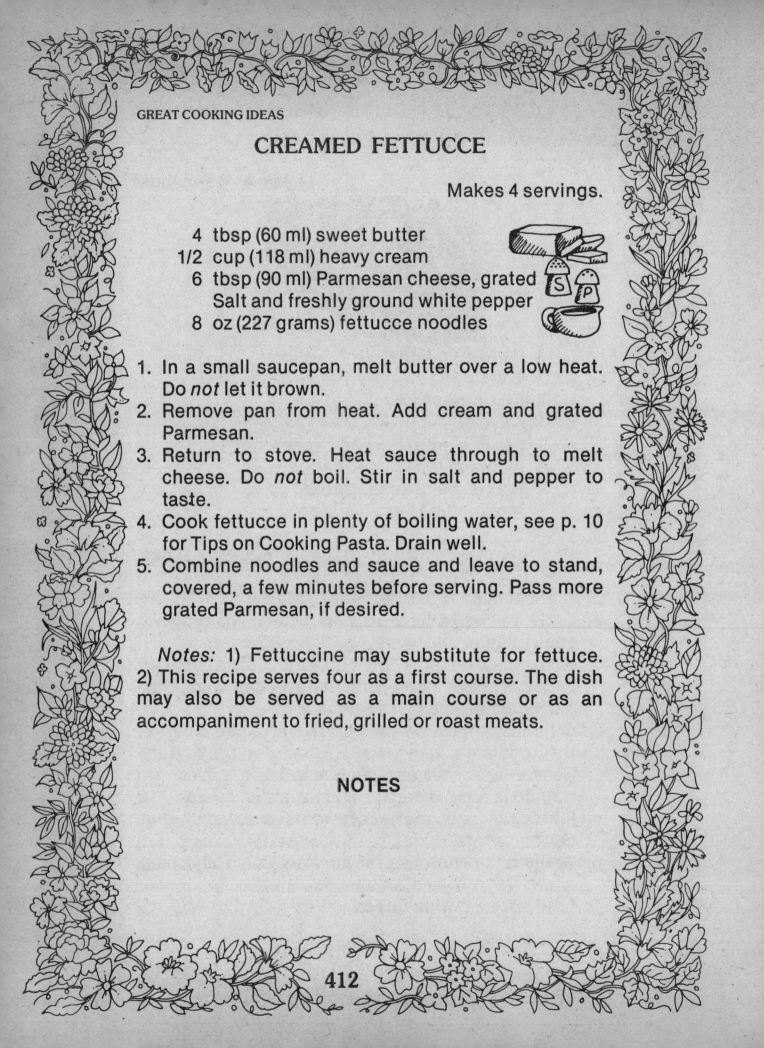

4 tbsp (60 ml) sweet butter
1/2 cup (118 ml) heavy cream
6 tbsp (90 ml) Parmesan cheese, grated
Salt and freshly ground white pepper
8 oz (227 grams) fettucce noodles

1. In a small saucepan, melt butter over a low heat. Do *not* let it brown.
2. Remove pan from heat. Add cream and grated Parmesan.
3. Return to stove. Heat sauce through to melt cheese. Do *not* boil. Stir in salt and pepper to taste.
4. Cook fettucce in plenty of boiling water, see p. 10 for Tips on Cooking Pasta. Drain well.
5. Combine noodles and sauce and leave to stand, covered, a few minutes before serving. Pass more grated Parmesan, if desired.

Notes: 1) Fettuccine may substitute for fettuce. 2) This recipe serves four as a first course. The dish may also be served as a main course or as an accompaniment to fried, grilled or roast meats.

NOTES

CURRIED BAKED RICE

Makes 6 servings.

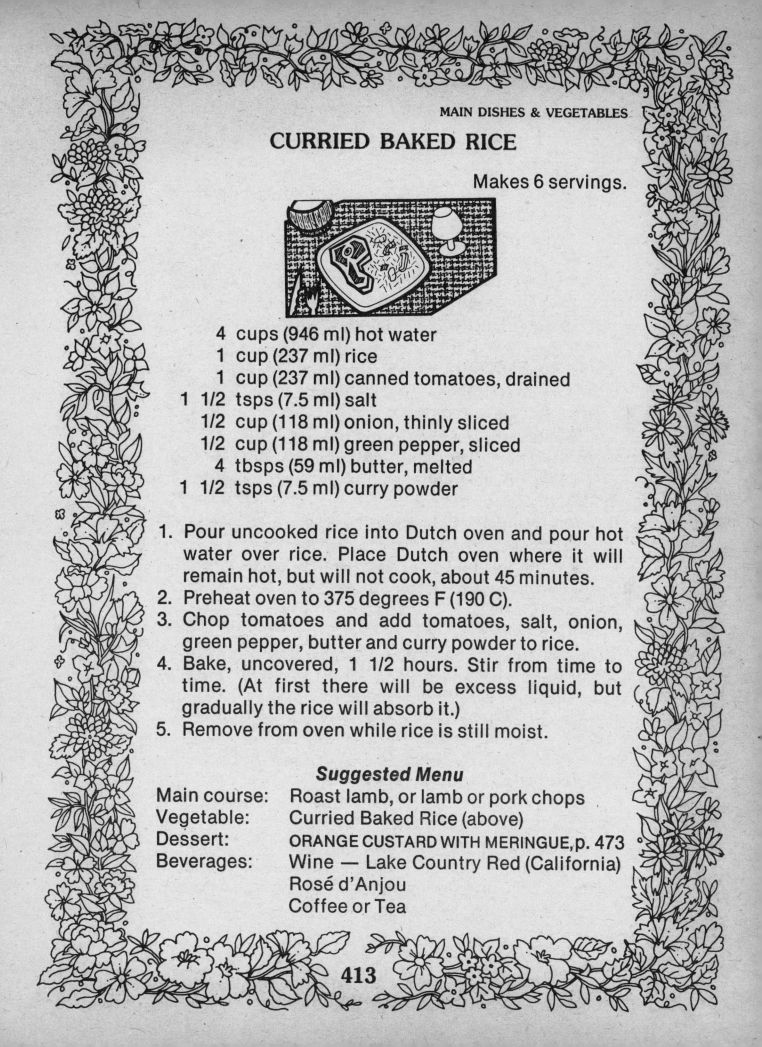

    4   cups (946 ml) hot water
    1   cup (237 ml) rice
    1   cup (237 ml) canned tomatoes, drained
1 1/2   tsps (7.5 ml) salt
  1/2   cup (118 ml) onion, thinly sliced
  1/2   cup (118 ml) green pepper, sliced
    4   tbsps (59 ml) butter, melted
1 1/2   tsps (7.5 ml) curry powder

1. Pour uncooked rice into Dutch oven and pour hot water over rice. Place Dutch oven where it will remain hot, but will not cook, about 45 minutes.
2. Preheat oven to 375 degrees F (190 C).
3. Chop tomatoes and add tomatoes, salt, onion, green pepper, butter and curry powder to rice.
4. Bake, uncovered, 1 1/2 hours. Stir from time to time. (At first there will be excess liquid, but gradually the rice will absorb it.)
5. Remove from oven while rice is still moist.

Suggested Menu

Main course: Roast lamb, or lamb or pork chops
Vegetable: Curried Baked Rice (above)
Dessert: ORANGE CUSTARD WITH MERINGUE, p. 473
Beverages: Wine — Lake Country Red (California)
Rosé d'Anjou
Coffee or Tea

FRUITY RICE CURRY

Makes 4 servings.

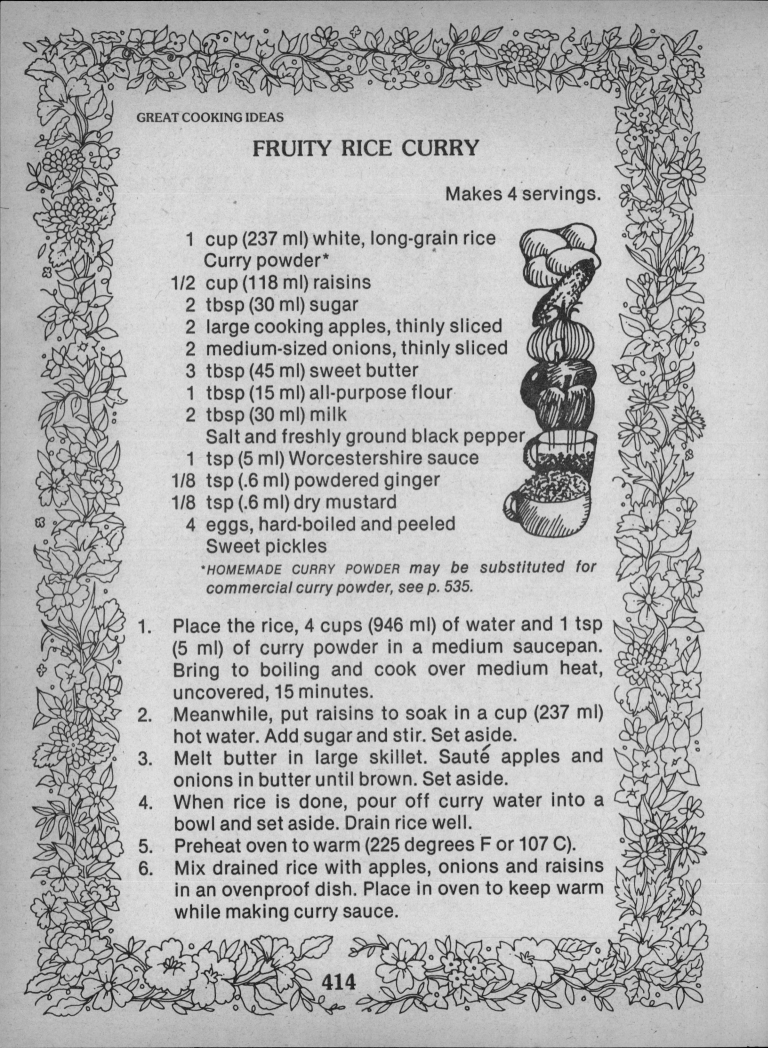

1 cup (237 ml) white, long-grain rice
Curry powder*
1/2 cup (118 ml) raisins
2 tbsp (30 ml) sugar
2 large cooking apples, thinly sliced
2 medium-sized onions, thinly sliced
3 tbsp (45 ml) sweet butter
1 tbsp (15 ml) all-purpose flour
2 tbsp (30 ml) milk
Salt and freshly ground black pepper
1 tsp (5 ml) Worcestershire sauce
1/8 tsp (.6 ml) powdered ginger
1/8 tsp (.6 ml) dry mustard
4 eggs, hard-boiled and peeled
Sweet pickles

*HOMEMADE CURRY POWDER may be substituted for commercial curry powder, see p. 535.

1. Place the rice, 4 cups (946 ml) of water and 1 tsp (5 ml) of curry powder in a medium saucepan. Bring to boiling and cook over medium heat, uncovered, 15 minutes.
2. Meanwhile, put raisins to soak in a cup (237 ml) hot water. Add sugar and stir. Set aside.
3. Melt butter in large skillet. Sauté apples and onions in butter until brown. Set aside.
4. When rice is done, pour off curry water into a bowl and set aside. Drain rice well.
5. Preheat oven to warm (225 degrees F or 107 C).
6. Mix drained rice with apples, onions and raisins in an ovenproof dish. Place in oven to keep warm while making curry sauce.

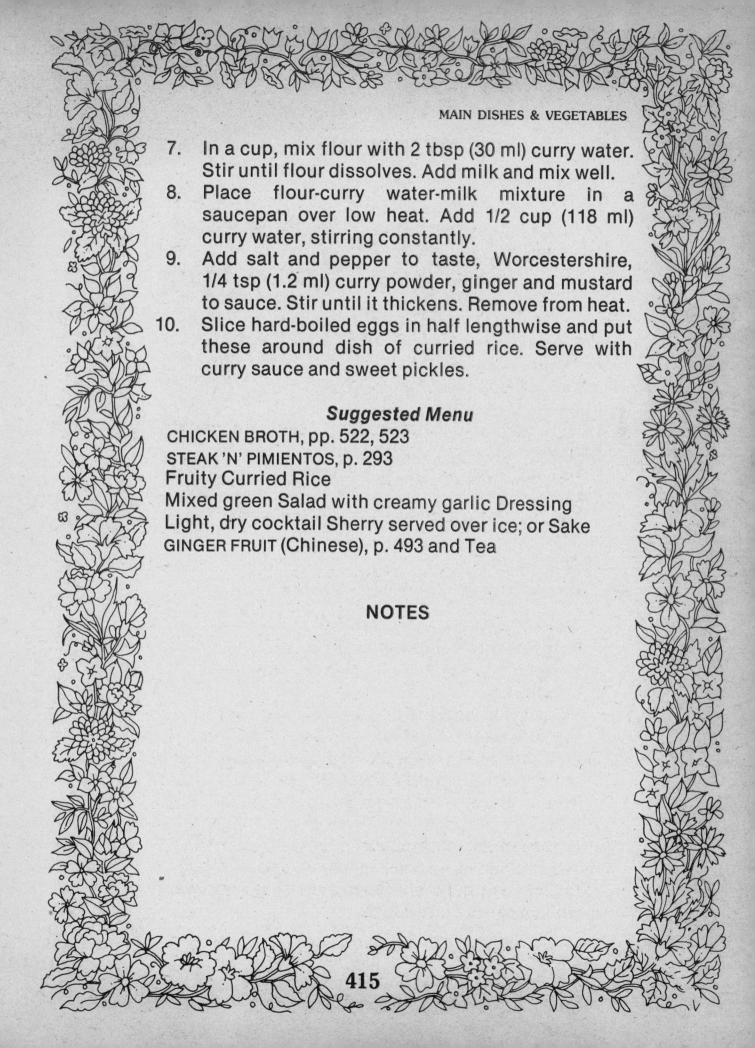

7. In a cup, mix flour with 2 tbsp (30 ml) curry water. Stir until flour dissolves. Add milk and mix well.
8. Place flour-curry water-milk mixture in a saucepan over low heat. Add 1/2 cup (118 ml) curry water, stirring constantly.
9. Add salt and pepper to taste, Worcestershire, 1/4 tsp (1.2 ml) curry powder, ginger and mustard to sauce. Stir until it thickens. Remove from heat.
10. Slice hard-boiled eggs in half lengthwise and put these around dish of curried rice. Serve with curry sauce and sweet pickles.

Suggested Menu

CHICKEN BROTH, pp. 522, 523
STEAK 'N' PIMIENTOS, p. 293
Fruity Curried Rice
Mixed green Salad with creamy garlic Dressing
Light, dry cocktail Sherry served over ice; or Sake
GINGER FRUIT (Chinese), p. 493 and Tea

NOTES

FAVA BEANS

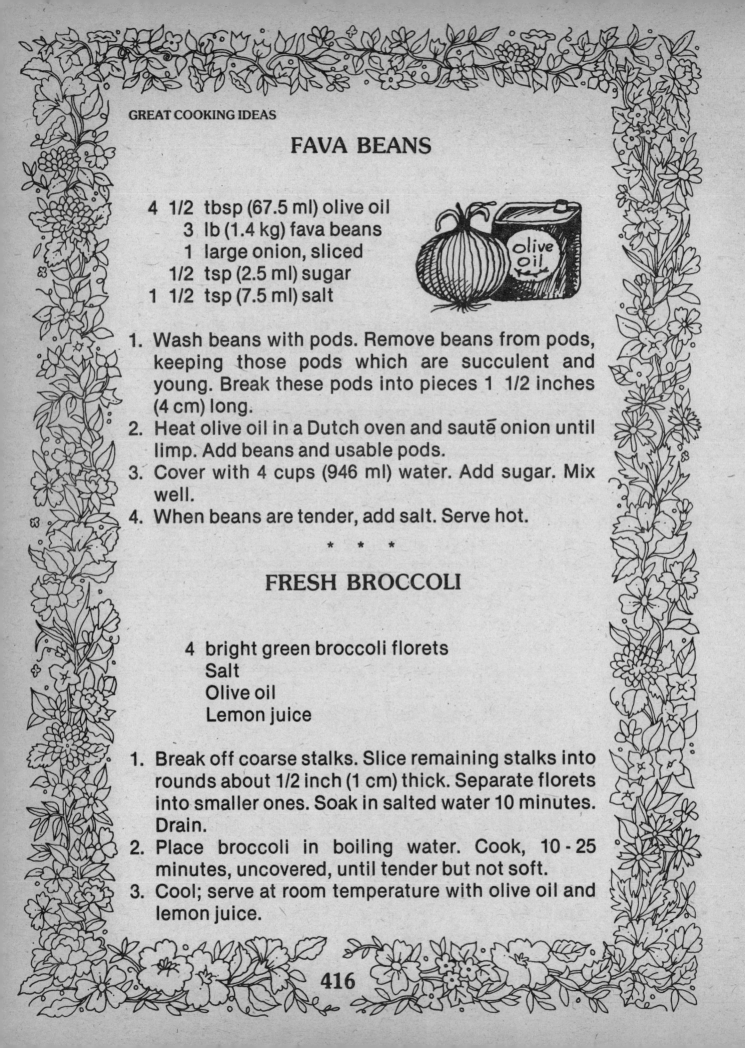

4 1/2 tbsp (67.5 ml) olive oil
3 lb (1.4 kg) fava beans
1 large onion, sliced
1/2 tsp (2.5 ml) sugar
1 1/2 tsp (7.5 ml) salt

1. Wash beans with pods. Remove beans from pods, keeping those pods which are succulent and young. Break these pods into pieces 1 1/2 inches (4 cm) long.
2. Heat olive oil in a Dutch oven and sauté onion until limp. Add beans and usable pods.
3. Cover with 4 cups (946 ml) water. Add sugar. Mix well.
4. When beans are tender, add salt. Serve hot.

* * *

FRESH BROCCOLI

4 bright green broccoli florets
Salt
Olive oil
Lemon juice

1. Break off coarse stalks. Slice remaining stalks into rounds about 1/2 inch (1 cm) thick. Separate florets into smaller ones. Soak in salted water 10 minutes. Drain.
2. Place broccoli in boiling water. Cook, 10 - 25 minutes, uncovered, until tender but not soft.
3. Cool; serve at room temperature with olive oil and lemon juice.

GLAZED CARROTS

8 cups (1.9 liters) carrots, thinly sliced
6 tbsp (90 ml) sweet butter
4 tbsp (60 ml) sugar
Salt
Chopped chives for garnish

1. In saucepan, combine carrots, butter and sugar. Season lightly with salt. Add 1 cup (237 ml) water and bring to a boil. Cover and cook 10 minutes, or until carrots are just tender.
2. Uncover at end of cooking time to evaporate water. Shake pan to glaze with butter and sugar.
3. Before serving, sprinkle with chives.

* * *

LYONNAISE POTATOES

1/2 cup (118 ml) sweet butter
9 medium-sized potatoes, pared and thinly sliced
2 medium-sized onions, sliced
3/4 tsp (3.7 ml) salt
Dash of freshly ground white pepper
3 tbsp (45 ml) parsley leaves, chopped

1. Heat butter in a large, heavy skillet. Sauté potato and onion slices, turning often, 15 - 20 minutes until golden brown and tender.
2. Before serving, sprinkle with salt, pepper and parsley.

GOLDEN RICE

Makes 6 servings.

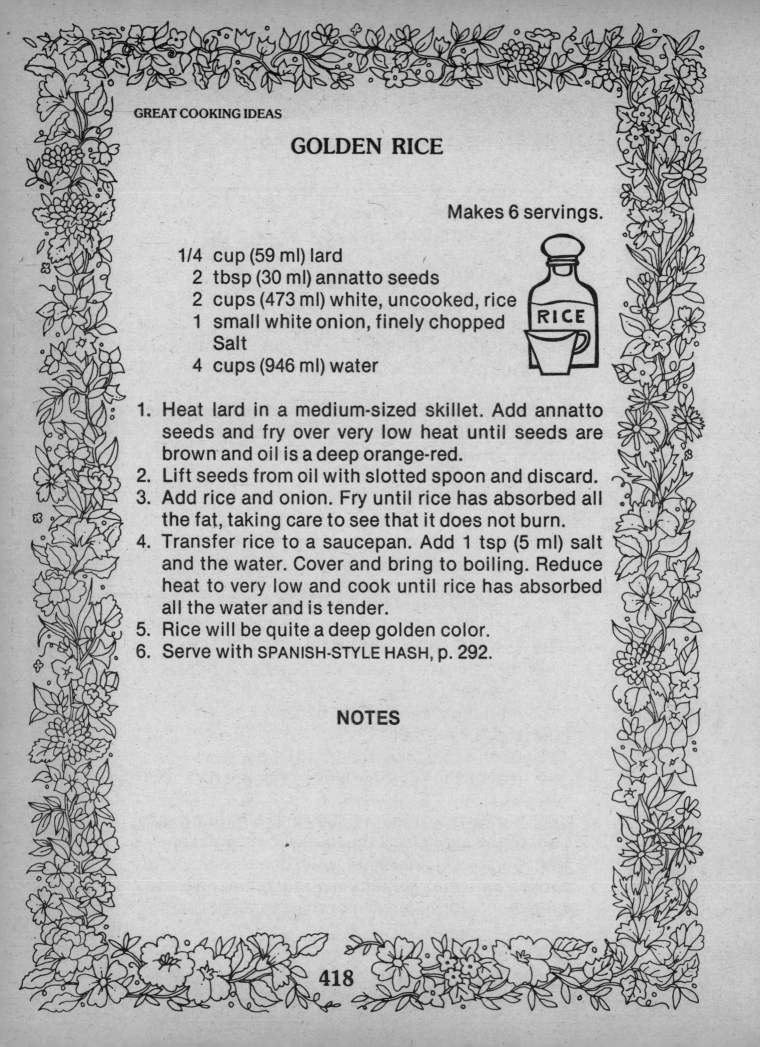

1/4 cup (59 ml) lard
2 tbsp (30 ml) annatto seeds
2 cups (473 ml) white, uncooked, rice
1 small white onion, finely chopped
Salt
4 cups (946 ml) water

1. Heat lard in a medium-sized skillet. Add annatto seeds and fry over very low heat until seeds are brown and oil is a deep orange-red.
2. Lift seeds from oil with slotted spoon and discard.
3. Add rice and onion. Fry until rice has absorbed all the fat, taking care to see that it does not burn.
4. Transfer rice to a saucepan. Add 1 tsp (5 ml) salt and the water. Cover and bring to boiling. Reduce heat to very low and cook until rice has absorbed all the water and is tender.
5. Rice will be quite a deep golden color.
6. Serve with SPANISH-STYLE HASH, p. 292.

NOTES

GREEN BEANS 'N' WATER CHESTNUTS

Makes 6 - 8 servings.

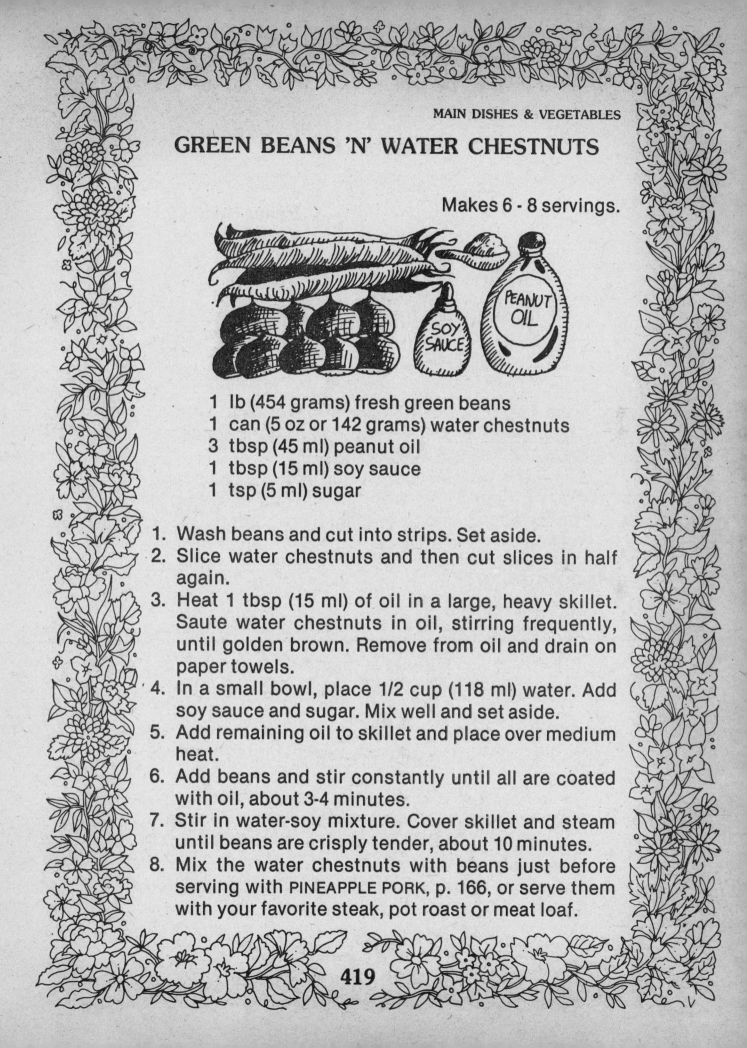

1 lb (454 grams) fresh green beans
1 can (5 oz or 142 grams) water chestnuts
3 tbsp (45 ml) peanut oil
1 tbsp (15 ml) soy sauce
1 tsp (5 ml) sugar

1. Wash beans and cut into strips. Set aside.
2. Slice water chestnuts and then cut slices in half again.
3. Heat 1 tbsp (15 ml) of oil in a large, heavy skillet. Saute water chestnuts in oil, stirring frequently, until golden brown. Remove from oil and drain on paper towels.
4. In a small bowl, place 1/2 cup (118 ml) water. Add soy sauce and sugar. Mix well and set aside.
5. Add remaining oil to skillet and place over medium heat.
6. Add beans and stir constantly until all are coated with oil, about 3-4 minutes.
7. Stir in water-soy mixture. Cover skillet and steam until beans are crisply tender, about 10 minutes.
8. Mix the water chestnuts with beans just before serving with PINEAPPLE PORK, p. 166, or serve them with your favorite steak, pot roast or meat loaf.

GREEN BEANS VINAIGRETTE

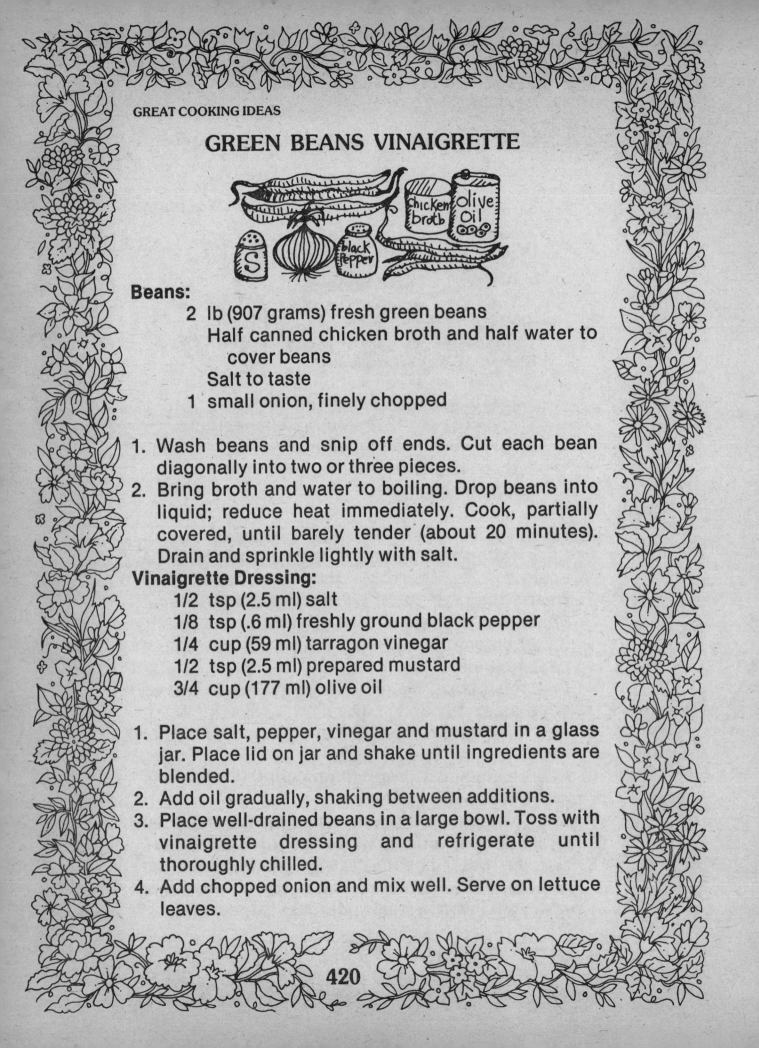

Beans:

2 lb (907 grams) fresh green beans

Half canned chicken broth and half water to cover beans

Salt to taste

1 small onion, finely chopped

1. Wash beans and snip off ends. Cut each bean diagonally into two or three pieces.
2. Bring broth and water to boiling. Drop beans into liquid; reduce heat immediately. Cook, partially covered, until barely tender (about 20 minutes). Drain and sprinkle lightly with salt.

Vinaigrette Dressing:

1/2 tsp (2.5 ml) salt

1/8 tsp (.6 ml) freshly ground black pepper

1/4 cup (59 ml) tarragon vinegar

1/2 tsp (2.5 ml) prepared mustard

3/4 cup (177 ml) olive oil

1. Place salt, pepper, vinegar and mustard in a glass jar. Place lid on jar and shake until ingredients are blended.
2. Add oil gradually, shaking between additions.
3. Place well-drained beans in a large bowl. Toss with vinaigrette dressing and refrigerate until thoroughly chilled.
4. Add chopped onion and mix well. Serve on lettuce leaves.

GREEN DUMPLINGS

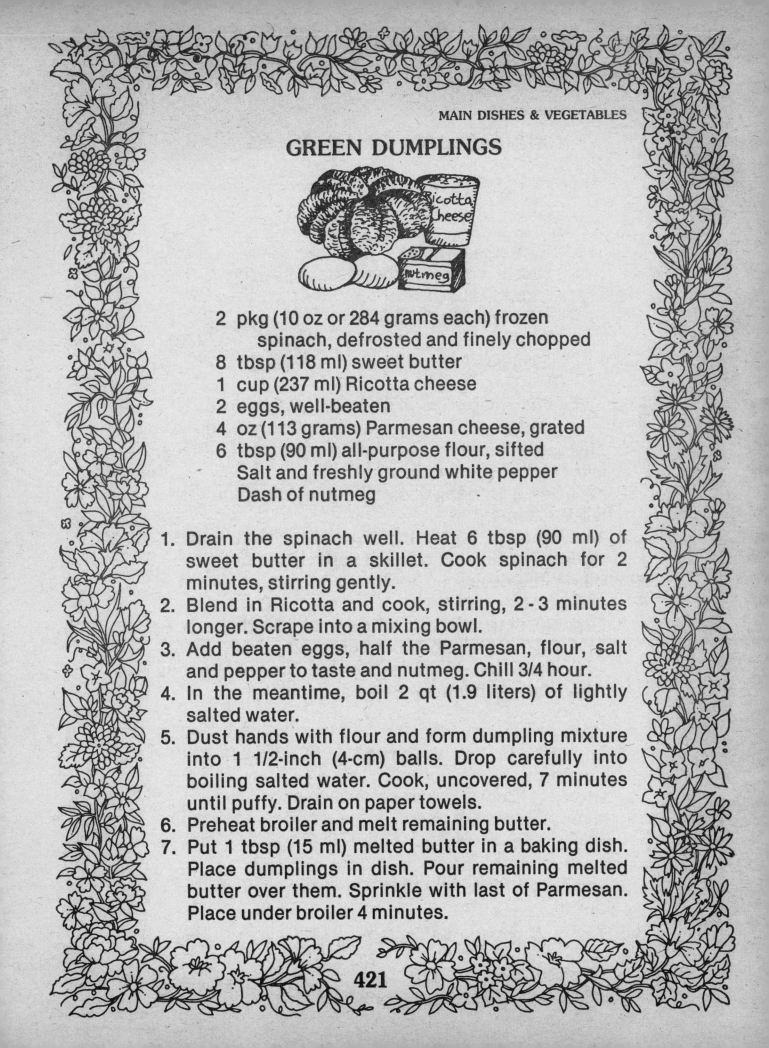

2 pkg (10 oz or 284 grams each) frozen
   spinach, defrosted and finely chopped
8 tbsp (118 ml) sweet butter
1 cup (237 ml) Ricotta cheese
2 eggs, well-beaten
4 oz (113 grams) Parmesan cheese, grated
6 tbsp (90 ml) all-purpose flour, sifted
   Salt and freshly ground white pepper
   Dash of nutmeg

1. Drain the spinach well. Heat 6 tbsp (90 ml) of sweet butter in a skillet. Cook spinach for 2 minutes, stirring gently.
2. Blend in Ricotta and cook, stirring, 2 - 3 minutes longer. Scrape into a mixing bowl.
3. Add beaten eggs, half the Parmesan, flour, salt and pepper to taste and nutmeg. Chill 3/4 hour.
4. In the meantime, boil 2 qt (1.9 liters) of lightly salted water.
5. Dust hands with flour and form dumpling mixture into 1 1/2-inch (4-cm) balls. Drop carefully into boiling salted water. Cook, uncovered, 7 minutes until puffy. Drain on paper towels.
6. Preheat broiler and melt remaining butter.
7. Put 1 tbsp (15 ml) melted butter in a baking dish. Place dumplings in dish. Pour remaining melted butter over them. Sprinkle with last of Parmesan. Place under broiler 4 minutes.

ITALIAN BAKED TOMATOES

Allow 1 large tomato
for each person.

Firm ripe tomatoes
Salt and freshly ground black pepper
Chopped basil
Small pinch of oregano
Butter
Split clove of garlic

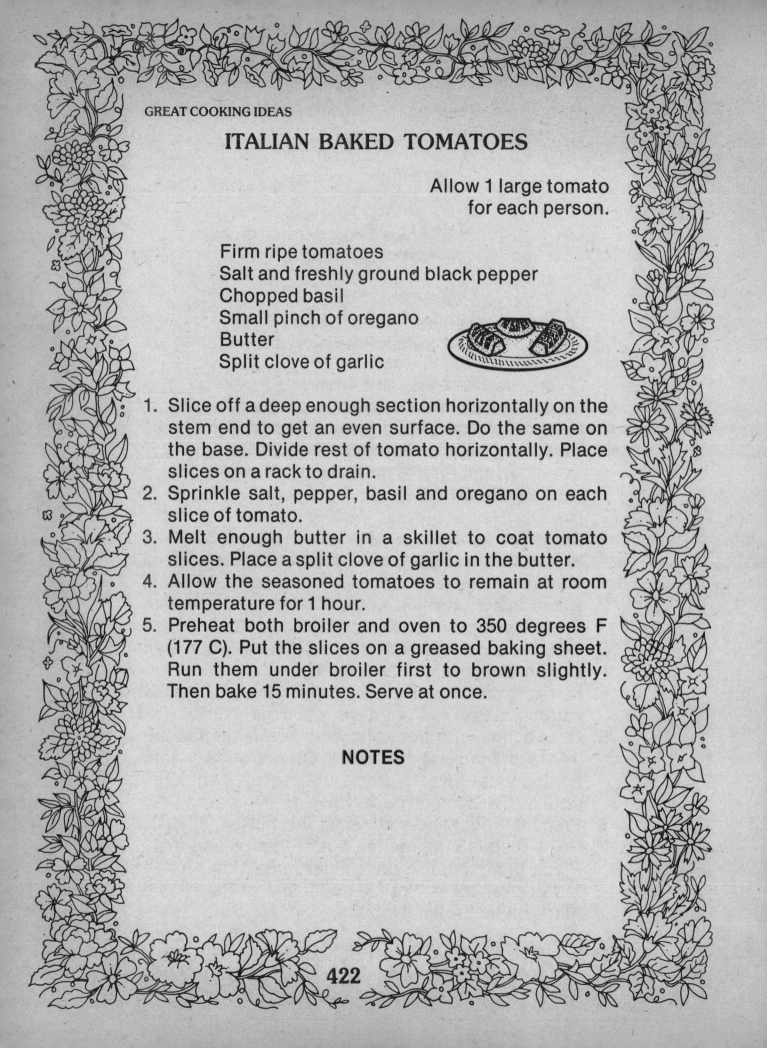

1. Slice off a deep enough section horizontally on the stem end to get an even surface. Do the same on the base. Divide rest of tomato horizontally. Place slices on a rack to drain.
2. Sprinkle salt, pepper, basil and oregano on each slice of tomato.
3. Melt enough butter in a skillet to coat tomato slices. Place a split clove of garlic in the butter.
4. Allow the seasoned tomatoes to remain at room temperature for 1 hour.
5. Preheat both broiler and oven to 350 degrees F (177 C). Put the slices on a greased baking sheet. Run them under broiler first to brown slightly. Then bake 15 minutes. Serve at once.

NOTES

LASAGNA

Makes 8 servings.

1/2 lb (227 grams) store-bought lasagna or 1/2
       recipe EGG-NOODLE DOUGH, p. 11
  1 tsp salt
  1 recipe BOLOGNESE SAUCE, p. 505
  1 recipe BECHAMEL SAUCE, p. 523
  5 tbsp (75 ml) Parmesan cheese, grated

1. Cook lasagna a few at a time in about 4 qts (3.8 liters) boiling water. Add salt when water is boiling. Cook noodles until *al dente* (see p. 10.) Drain in a colander and leave to cool slightly.
2. Butter a large baking dish, about 13 x 9 x 2 inches (33 x 23 x 5 cm).
3. Preheat oven to 350 degrees F (177 C).
4. Spread a thin layer of Bolognese Sauce over the bottom of the baking dish, followed by a layer of 1/3 the Bechamel Sauce, followed by a layer of 1/3 the lasagna noodles, slightly overlapping. Repeat these layers until all sauces have been used; finish with a layer of Bechamel. Sprinkle Parmesan cheese on top.*
5. Bake 25 minutes if cooking right away, about 40 minutes if dish has been allowed to get cold.

 * *Up to this point, lasagna can be made 2-3 hours in advance. Cover baking dish with foil until ready to bake.*

Variation: Substitute ricotta cheese and sliced mozzarella cheese for the Bechamel Sauce. About 1 lb (454 grams) of ricotta and 6-8 oz (170 to 227 grams) of mozzarella. Layer Bolognese Sauce, ricotta, mozzarella, and lasagna noodles. Repeat layers twice, ending with mozzarella.

MEXICAN RICE

Makes 4 servings.

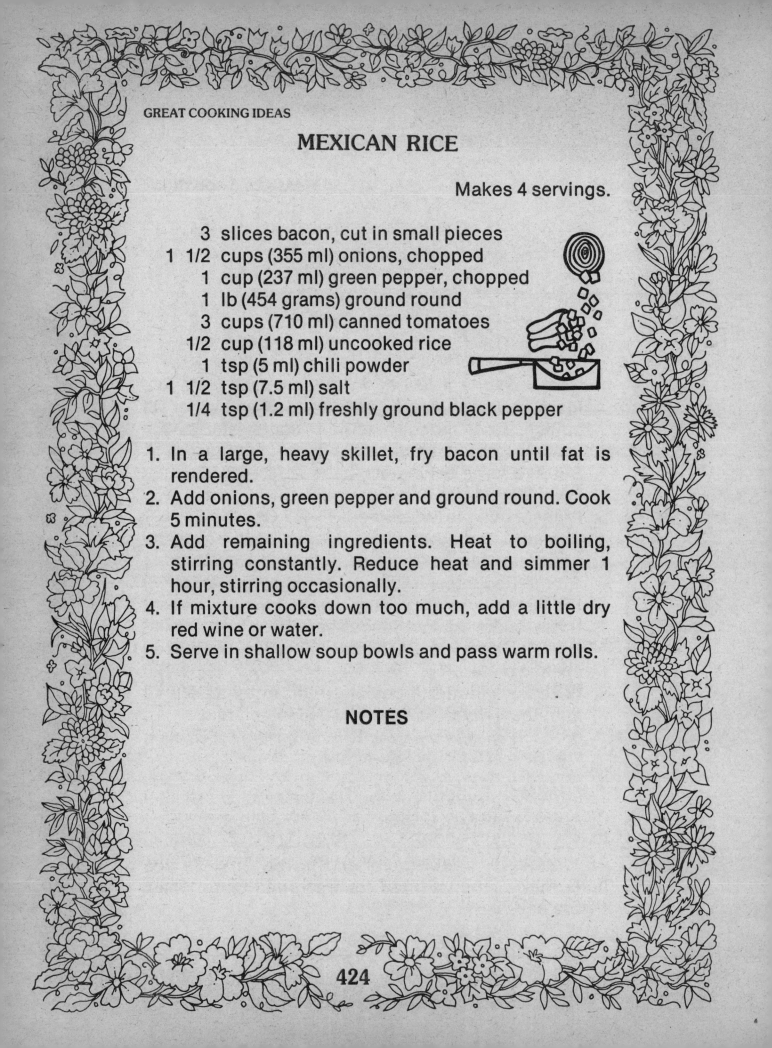

        3 slices bacon, cut in small pieces
1 1/2 cups (355 ml) onions, chopped
        1 cup (237 ml) green pepper, chopped
        1 lb (454 grams) ground round
        3 cups (710 ml) canned tomatoes
    1/2 cup (118 ml) uncooked rice
        1 tsp (5 ml) chili powder
1 1/2 tsp (7.5 ml) salt
    1/4 tsp (1.2 ml) freshly ground black pepper

1. In a large, heavy skillet, fry bacon until fat is rendered.
2. Add onions, green pepper and ground round. Cook 5 minutes.
3. Add remaining ingredients. Heat to boiling, stirring constantly. Reduce heat and simmer 1 hour, stirring occasionally.
4. If mixture cooks down too much, add a little dry red wine or water.
5. Serve in shallow soup bowls and pass warm rolls.

NOTES

MIXED VEGETABLES

Makes 4 - 6 servings.

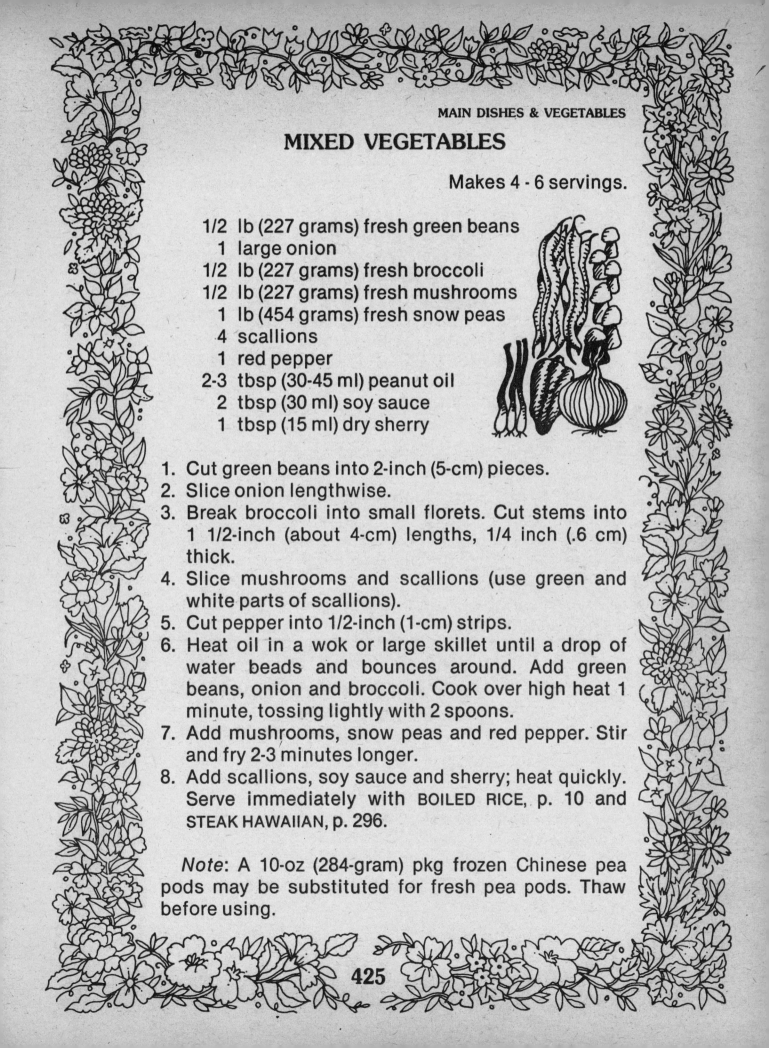

1/2	lb (227 grams) fresh green beans
1	large onion
1/2	lb (227 grams) fresh broccoli
1/2	lb (227 grams) fresh mushrooms
1	lb (454 grams) fresh snow peas
4	scallions
1	red pepper
2-3	tbsp (30-45 ml) peanut oil
2	tbsp (30 ml) soy sauce
1	tbsp (15 ml) dry sherry

1. Cut green beans into 2-inch (5-cm) pieces.
2. Slice onion lengthwise.
3. Break broccoli into small florets. Cut stems into 1 1/2-inch (about 4-cm) lengths, 1/4 inch (.6 cm) thick.
4. Slice mushrooms and scallions (use green and white parts of scallions).
5. Cut pepper into 1/2-inch (1-cm) strips.
6. Heat oil in a wok or large skillet until a drop of water beads and bounces around. Add green beans, onion and broccoli. Cook over high heat 1 minute, tossing lightly with 2 spoons.
7. Add mushrooms, snow peas and red pepper. Stir and fry 2-3 minutes longer.
8. Add scallions, soy sauce and sherry; heat quickly. Serve immediately with BOILED RICE, p. 10 and STEAK HAWAIIAN, p. 296.

Note: A 10-oz (284-gram) pkg frozen Chinese pea pods may be substituted for fresh pea pods. Thaw before using.

PORK FRIED RICE

Makes 6 servings.

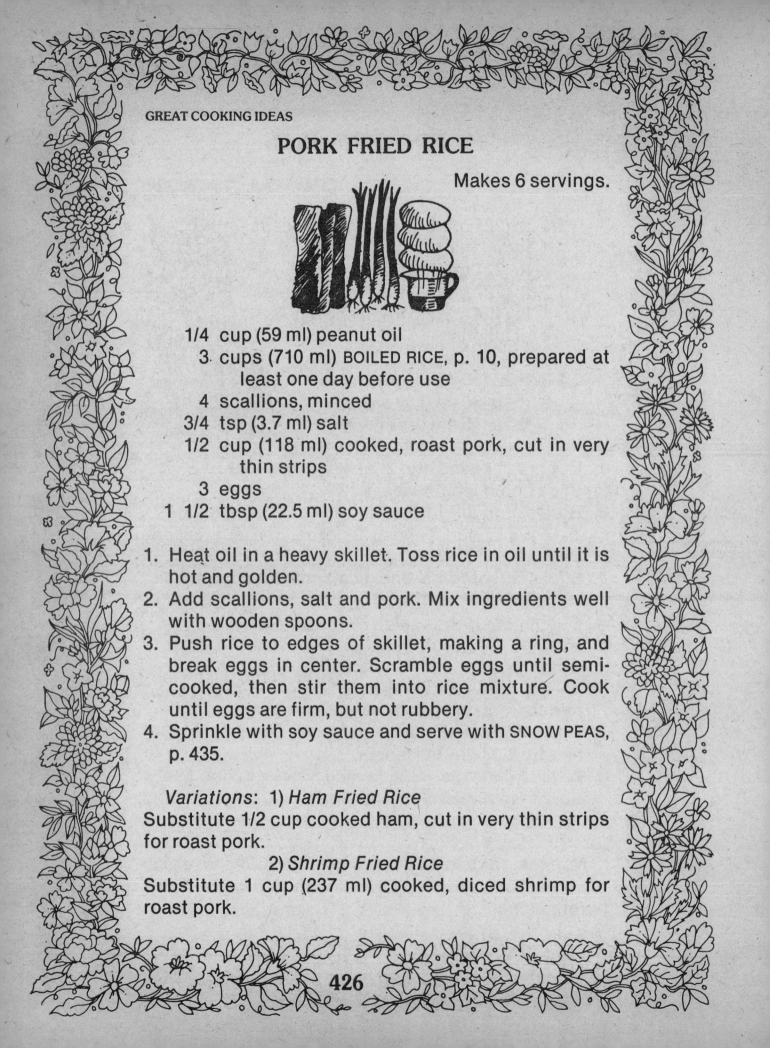

1/4 cup (59 ml) peanut oil
3 cups (710 ml) BOILED RICE, p. 10, prepared at least one day before use
4 scallions, minced
3/4 tsp (3.7 ml) salt
1/2 cup (118 ml) cooked, roast pork, cut in very thin strips
3 eggs
1 1/2 tbsp (22.5 ml) soy sauce

1. Heat oil in a heavy skillet. Toss rice in oil until it is hot and golden.
2. Add scallions, salt and pork. Mix ingredients well with wooden spoons.
3. Push rice to edges of skillet, making a ring, and break eggs in center. Scramble eggs until semi-cooked, then stir them into rice mixture. Cook until eggs are firm, but not rubbery.
4. Sprinkle with soy sauce and serve with SNOW PEAS, p. 435.

Variations: 1) *Ham Fried Rice*
Substitute 1/2 cup cooked ham, cut in very thin strips for roast pork.

2) *Shrimp Fried Rice*
Substitute 1 cup (237 ml) cooked, diced shrimp for roast pork.

POTATO PURÉE

Makes 6 servings.

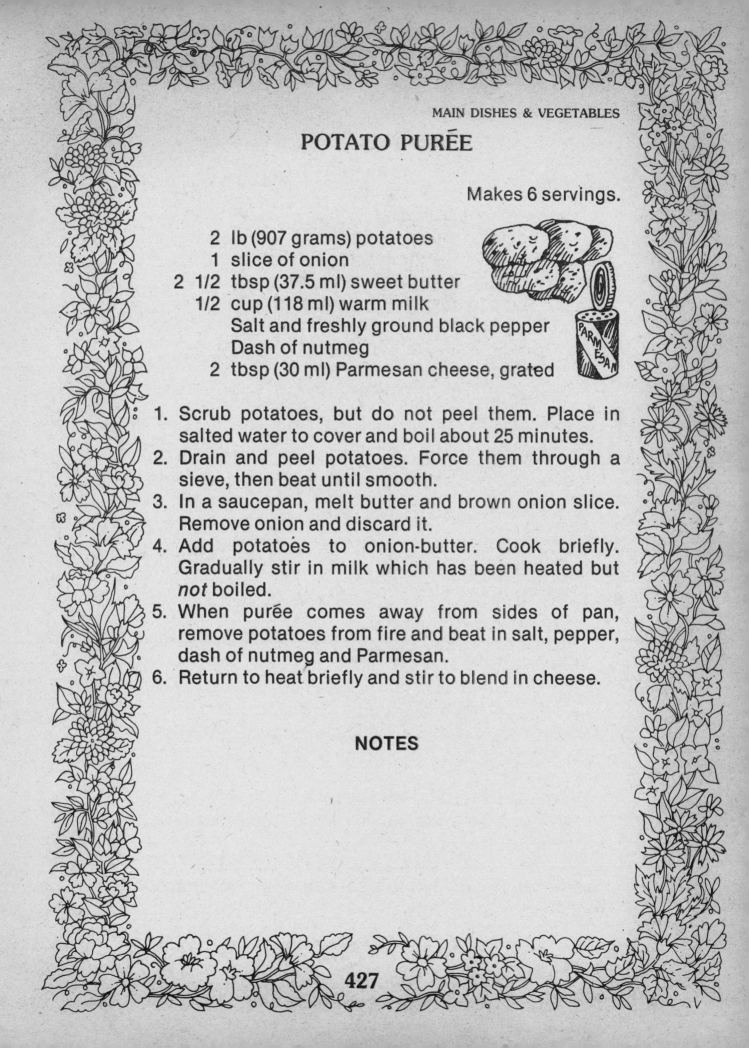

2 lb (907 grams) potatoes
1 slice of onion
2 1/2 tbsp (37.5 ml) sweet butter
1/2 cup (118 ml) warm milk
Salt and freshly ground black pepper
Dash of nutmeg
2 tbsp (30 ml) Parmesan cheese, grated

1. Scrub potatoes, but do not peel them. Place in salted water to cover and boil about 25 minutes.
2. Drain and peel potatoes. Force them through a sieve, then beat until smooth.
3. In a saucepan, melt butter and brown onion slice. Remove onion and discard it.
4. Add potatoes to onion-butter. Cook briefly. Gradually stir in milk which has been heated but *not* boiled.
5. When purée comes away from sides of pan, remove potatoes from fire and beat in salt, pepper, dash of nutmeg and Parmesan.
6. Return to heat briefly and stir to blend in cheese.

NOTES

427

RED PEPPER OMELET

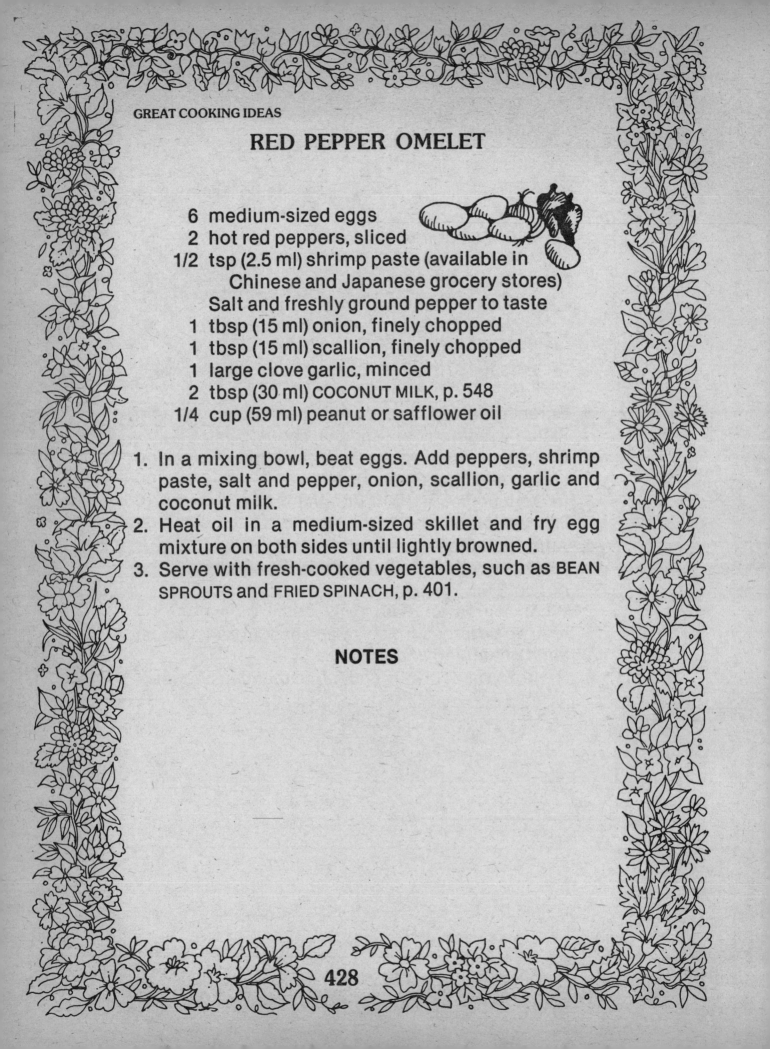

6 medium-sized eggs
2 hot red peppers, sliced
1/2 tsp (2.5 ml) shrimp paste (available in
  Chinese and Japanese grocery stores)
  Salt and freshly ground pepper to taste
1 tbsp (15 ml) onion, finely chopped
1 tbsp (15 ml) scallion, finely chopped
1 large clove garlic, minced
2 tbsp (30 ml) COCONUT MILK, p. 548
1/4 cup (59 ml) peanut or safflower oil

1. In a mixing bowl, beat eggs. Add peppers, shrimp paste, salt and pepper, onion, scallion, garlic and coconut milk.
2. Heat oil in a medium-sized skillet and fry egg mixture on both sides until lightly browned.
3. Serve with fresh-cooked vegetables, such as BEAN SPROUTS and FRIED SPINACH, p. 401.

NOTES

RICE IN GREEN TEA

Makes 4 - 6 servings.

2 tbsp (30 ml) green Japanese tea leaves
2 tbsp (30 ml) *sake* or dry sherry
1/2 tsp (2.5 ml) salt
2 cups (473 ml) white rice

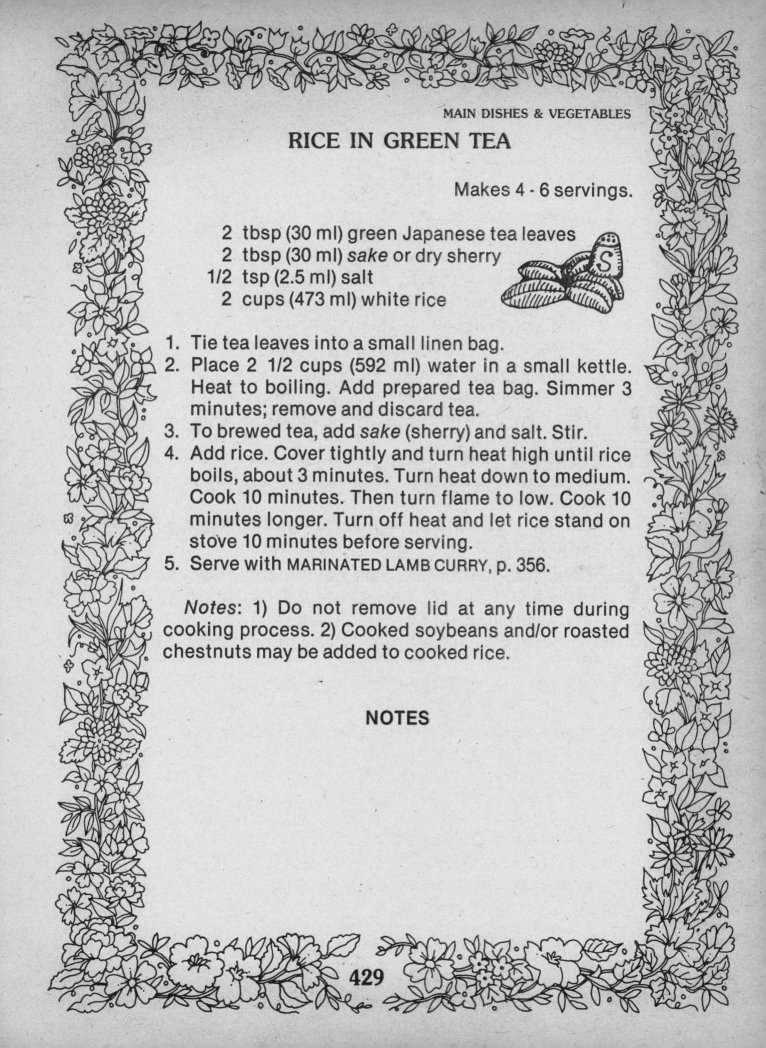

1. Tie tea leaves into a small linen bag.
2. Place 2 1/2 cups (592 ml) water in a small kettle. Heat to boiling. Add prepared tea bag. Simmer 3 minutes; remove and discard tea.
3. To brewed tea, add *sake* (sherry) and salt. Stir.
4. Add rice. Cover tightly and turn heat high until rice boils, about 3 minutes. Turn heat down to medium. Cook 10 minutes. Then turn flame to low. Cook 10 minutes longer. Turn off heat and let rice stand on stove 10 minutes before serving.
5. Serve with MARINATED LAMB CURRY, p. 356.

Notes: 1) Do not remove lid at any time during cooking process. 2) Cooked soybeans and/or roasted chestnuts may be added to cooked rice.

NOTES

RISOTTO

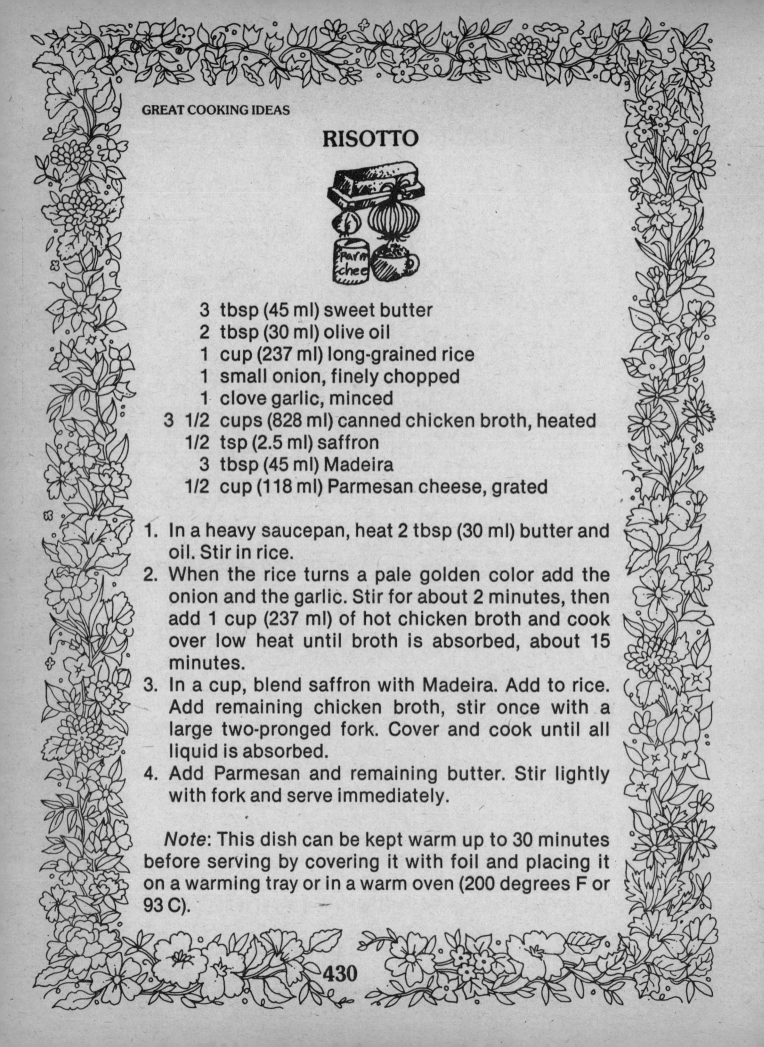

3 tbsp (45 ml) sweet butter
2 tbsp (30 ml) olive oil
1 cup (237 ml) long-grained rice
1 small onion, finely chopped
1 clove garlic, minced
3 1/2 cups (828 ml) canned chicken broth, heated
1/2 tsp (2.5 ml) saffron
3 tbsp (45 ml) Madeira
1/2 cup (118 ml) Parmesan cheese, grated

1. In a heavy saucepan, heat 2 tbsp (30 ml) butter and oil. Stir in rice.
2. When the rice turns a pale golden color add the onion and the garlic. Stir for about 2 minutes, then add 1 cup (237 ml) of hot chicken broth and cook over low heat until broth is absorbed, about 15 minutes.
3. In a cup, blend saffron with Madeira. Add to rice. Add remaining chicken broth, stir once with a large two-pronged fork. Cover and cook until all liquid is absorbed.
4. Add Parmesan and remaining butter. Stir lightly with fork and serve immediately.

Note: This dish can be kept warm up to 30 minutes before serving by covering it with foil and placing it on a warming tray or in a warm oven (200 degrees F or 93 C).

RISOTTO 'N' VEGETABLES

Makes 6 servings.

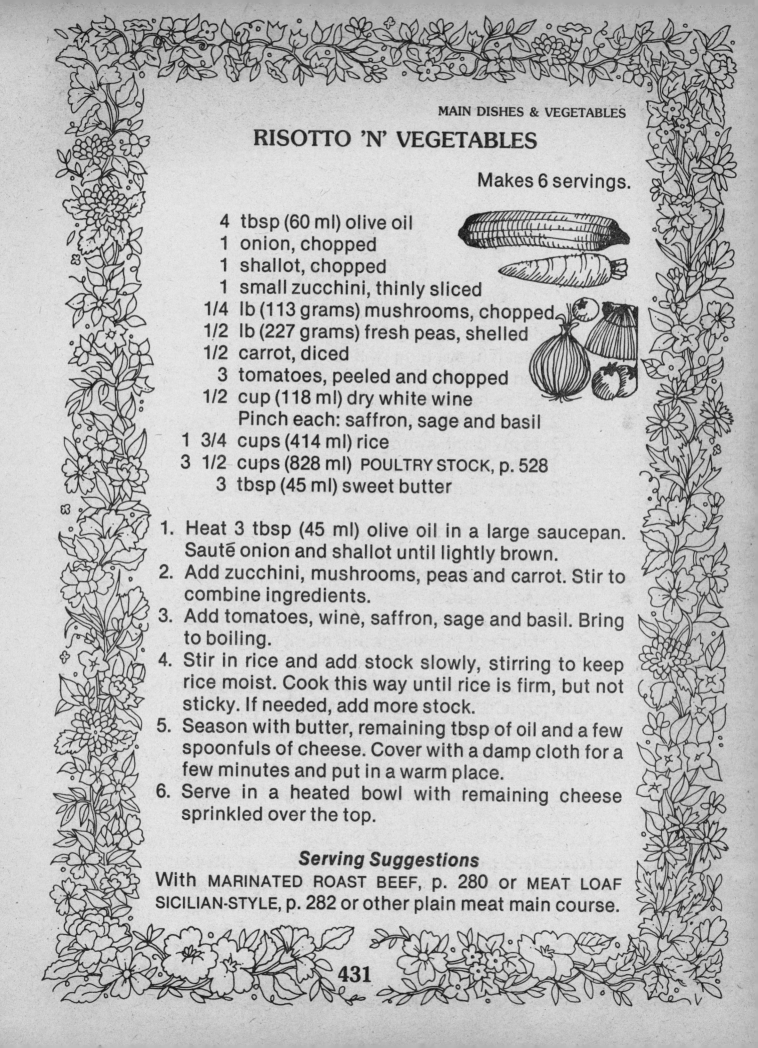

- 4 tbsp (60 ml) olive oil
- 1 onion, chopped
- 1 shallot, chopped
- 1 small zucchini, thinly sliced
- 1/4 lb (113 grams) mushrooms, chopped
- 1/2 lb (227 grams) fresh peas, shelled
- 1/2 carrot, diced
- 3 tomatoes, peeled and chopped
- 1/2 cup (118 ml) dry white wine
- Pinch each: saffron, sage and basil
- 1 3/4 cups (414 ml) rice
- 3 1/2 cups (828 ml) POULTRY STOCK, p. 528
- 3 tbsp (45 ml) sweet butter

1. Heat 3 tbsp (45 ml) olive oil in a large saucepan. Sauté onion and shallot until lightly brown.
2. Add zucchini, mushrooms, peas and carrot. Stir to combine ingredients.
3. Add tomatoes, wine, saffron, sage and basil. Bring to boiling.
4. Stir in rice and add stock slowly, stirring to keep rice moist. Cook this way until rice is firm, but not sticky. If needed, add more stock.
5. Season with butter, remaining tbsp of oil and a few spoonfuls of cheese. Cover with a damp cloth for a few minutes and put in a warm place.
6. Serve in a heated bowl with remaining cheese sprinkled over the top.

Serving Suggestions

With MARINATED ROAST BEEF, p. 280 or MEAT LOAF SICILIAN-STYLE, p. 282 or other plain meat main course.

ROMAN-STYLE PEPPERS

Makes 6 servings.

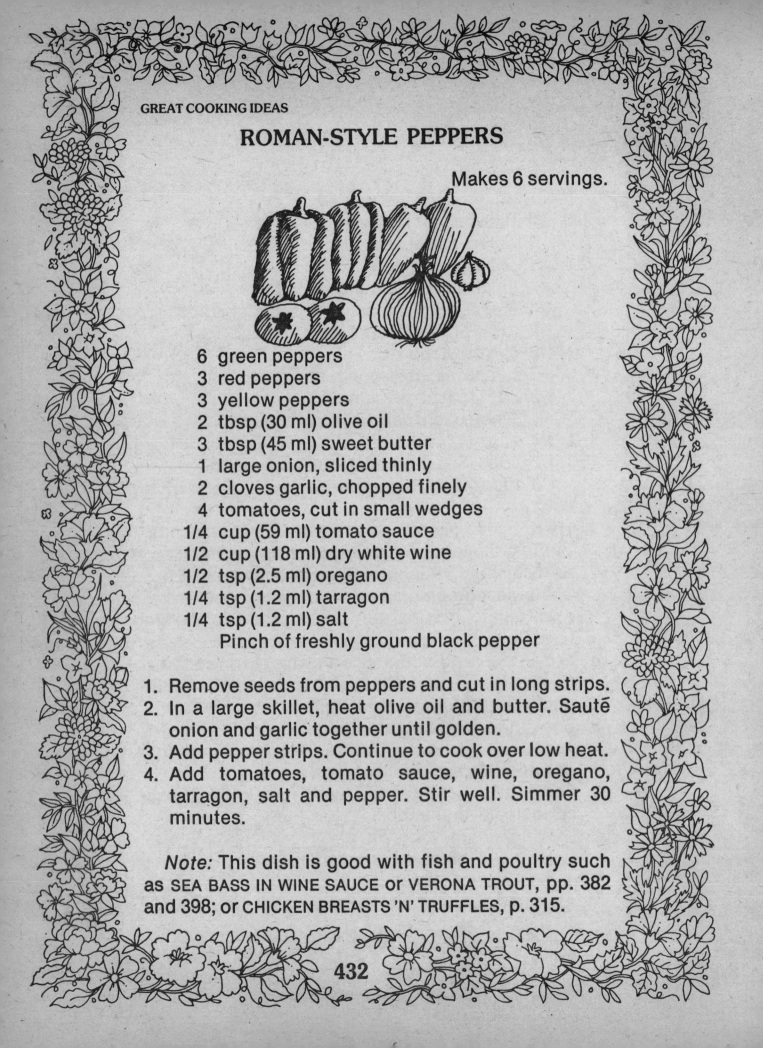

6 green peppers
3 red peppers
3 yellow peppers
2 tbsp (30 ml) olive oil
3 tbsp (45 ml) sweet butter
1 large onion, sliced thinly
2 cloves garlic, chopped finely
4 tomatoes, cut in small wedges
1/4 cup (59 ml) tomato sauce
1/2 cup (118 ml) dry white wine
1/2 tsp (2.5 ml) oregano
1/4 tsp (1.2 ml) tarragon
1/4 tsp (1.2 ml) salt
Pinch of freshly ground black pepper

1. Remove seeds from peppers and cut in long strips.
2. In a large skillet, heat olive oil and butter. Sauté onion and garlic together until golden.
3. Add pepper strips. Continue to cook over low heat.
4. Add tomatoes, tomato sauce, wine, oregano, tarragon, salt and pepper. Stir well. Simmer 30 minutes.

Note: This dish is good with fish and poultry such as SEA BASS IN WINE SAUCE or VERONA TROUT, pp. 382 and 398; or CHICKEN BREASTS 'N' TRUFFLES, p. 315.

SCALLOPED CORN

Makes 4 servings.

1 pkg (10 oz or 284 grams) frozen whole kernel corn, cooked and drained
3 tbsps (45 ml) sweet butter
1/4 cup (59 ml) onion, finely chopped
1/4 cup (59 ml) green pepper, finely chopped
2 tbsps (30 ml) flour
1 tsp (5 ml) salt
1/2 tsp (2.5 ml) paprika
1/4 tsp (1.2 ml) dry mustard
Dash white pepper
3/4 cup (177 ml) milk
1/2 cup (118 ml) natural Cheddar cheese, shredded
1 egg, lightly beaten
1/3 cup (79 ml) cracker crumbs

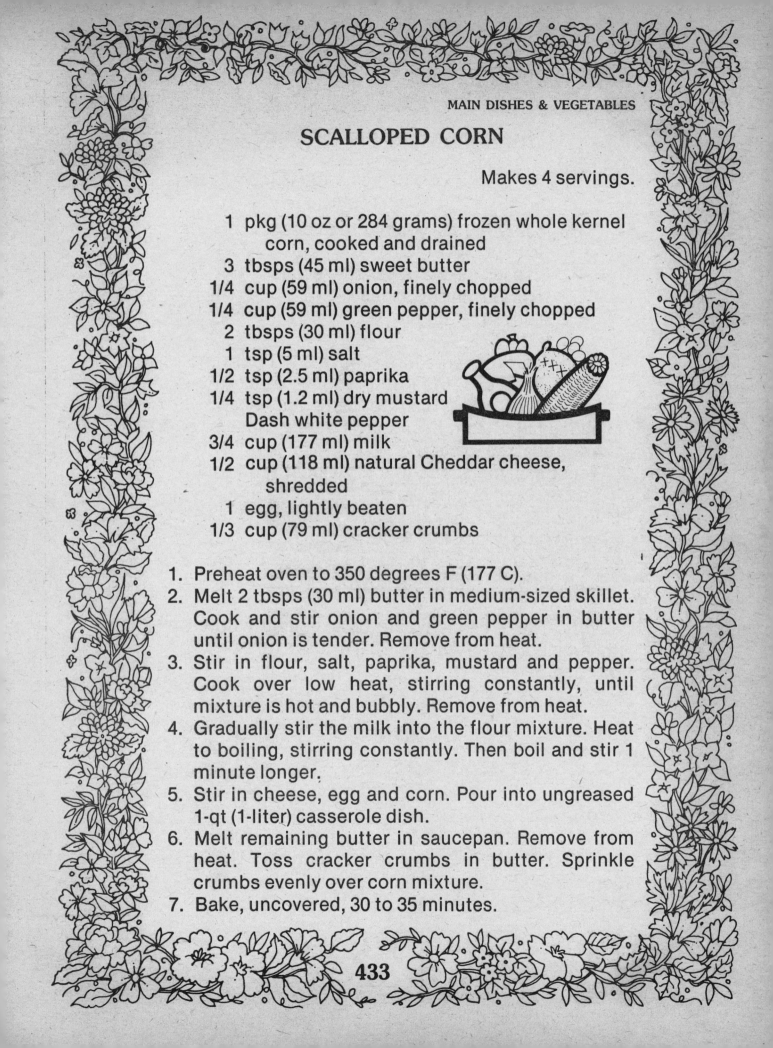

1. Preheat oven to 350 degrees F (177 C).
2. Melt 2 tbsps (30 ml) butter in medium-sized skillet. Cook and stir onion and green pepper in butter until onion is tender. Remove from heat.
3. Stir in flour, salt, paprika, mustard and pepper. Cook over low heat, stirring constantly, until mixture is hot and bubbly. Remove from heat.
4. Gradually stir the milk into the flour mixture. Heat to boiling, stirring constantly. Then boil and stir 1 minute longer.
5. Stir in cheese, egg and corn. Pour into ungreased 1-qt (1-liter) casserole dish.
6. Melt remaining butter in saucepan. Remove from heat. Toss cracker crumbs in butter. Sprinkle crumbs evenly over corn mixture.
7. Bake, uncovered, 30 to 35 minutes.

SESAME GREEN BEANS

Makes 4 servings.

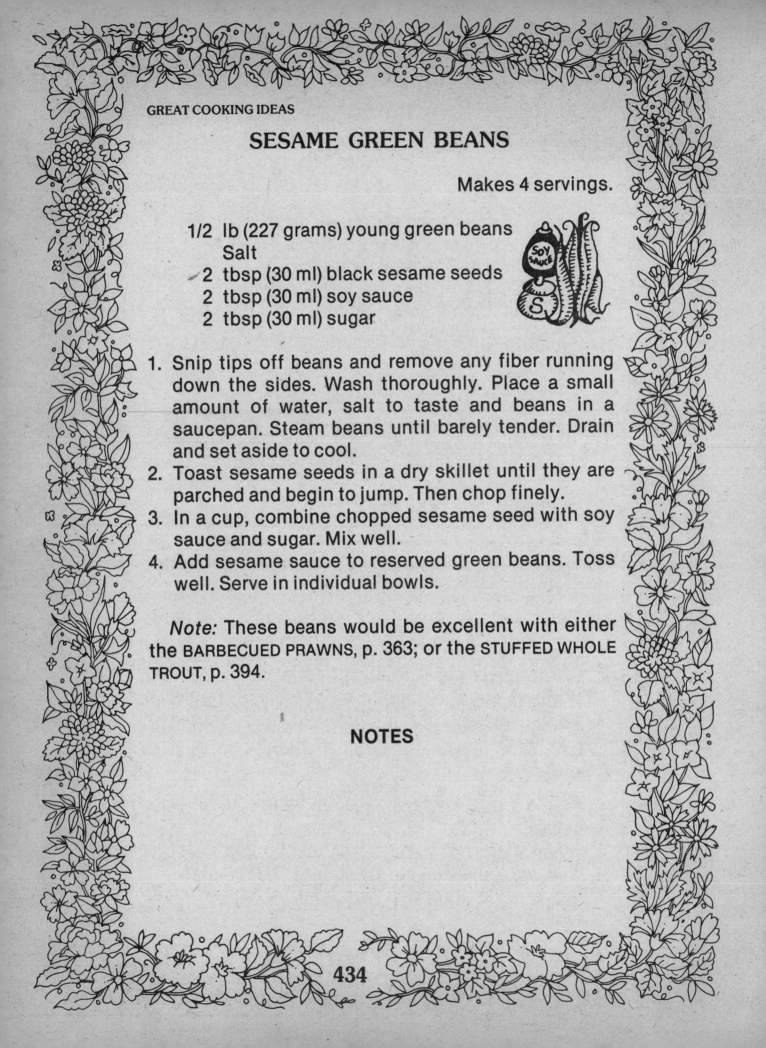

1/2 lb (227 grams) young green beans
    Salt
  2 tbsp (30 ml) black sesame seeds
  2 tbsp (30 ml) soy sauce
  2 tbsp (30 ml) sugar

1. Snip tips off beans and remove any fiber running down the sides. Wash thoroughly. Place a small amount of water, salt to taste and beans in a saucepan. Steam beans until barely tender. Drain and set aside to cool.
2. Toast sesame seeds in a dry skillet until they are parched and begin to jump. Then chop finely.
3. In a cup, combine chopped sesame seed with soy sauce and sugar. Mix well.
4. Add sesame sauce to reserved green beans. Toss well. Serve in individual bowls.

Note: These beans would be excellent with either the BARBECUED PRAWNS, p. 363; or the STUFFED WHOLE TROUT, p. 394.

NOTES

SNOW PEAS

Makes 4 servings.

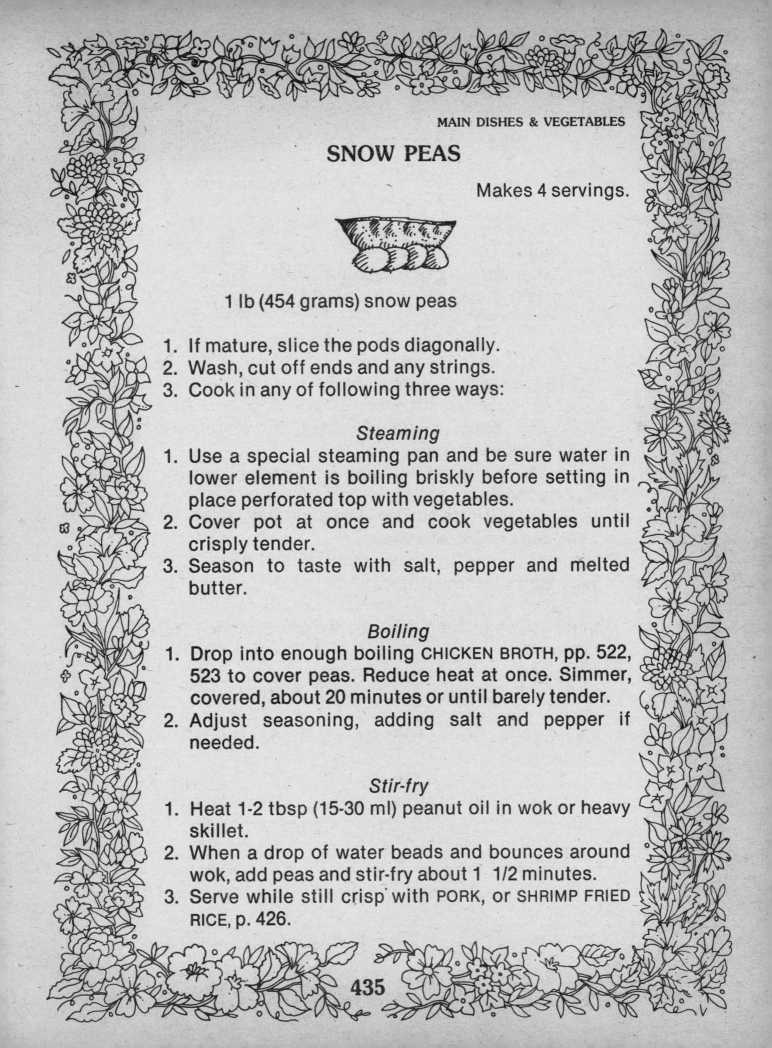

1 lb (454 grams) snow peas

1. If mature, slice the pods diagonally.
2. Wash, cut off ends and any strings.
3. Cook in any of following three ways:

Steaming

1. Use a special steaming pan and be sure water in lower element is boiling briskly before setting in place perforated top with vegetables.
2. Cover pot at once and cook vegetables until crisply tender.
3. Season to taste with salt, pepper and melted butter.

Boiling

1. Drop into enough boiling CHICKEN BROTH, pp. 522, 523 to cover peas. Reduce heat at once. Simmer, covered, about 20 minutes or until barely tender.
2. Adjust seasoning, adding salt and pepper if needed.

Stir-fry

1. Heat 1-2 tbsp (15-30 ml) peanut oil in wok or heavy skillet.
2. When a drop of water beads and bounces around wok, add peas and stir-fry about 1 1/2 minutes.
3. Serve while still crisp with PORK, or SHRIMP FRIED RICE, p. 426.

SNOW PEAS WITH WATER CHESTNUTS

Makes 4 - 6 servings.

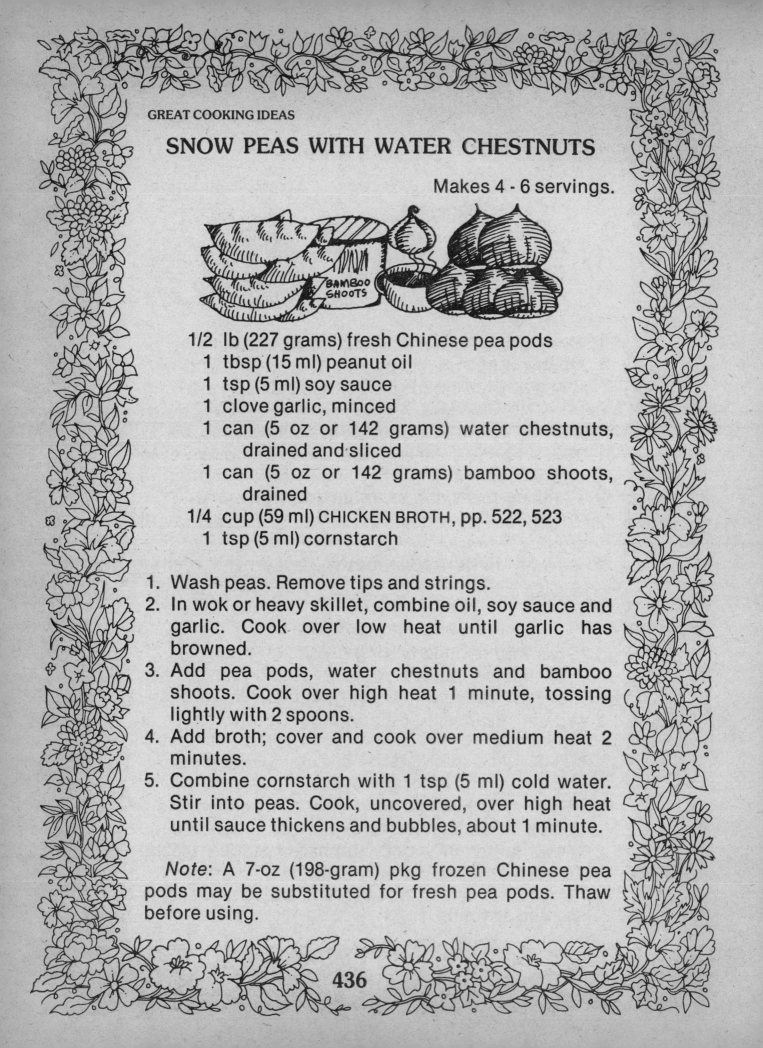

1/2 lb (227 grams) fresh Chinese pea pods
  1 tbsp (15 ml) peanut oil
  1 tsp (5 ml) soy sauce
  1 clove garlic, minced
  1 can (5 oz or 142 grams) water chestnuts, drained and sliced
  1 can (5 oz or 142 grams) bamboo shoots, drained
1/4 cup (59 ml) CHICKEN BROTH, pp. 522, 523
  1 tsp (5 ml) cornstarch

1. Wash peas. Remove tips and strings.
2. In wok or heavy skillet, combine oil, soy sauce and garlic. Cook over low heat until garlic has browned.
3. Add pea pods, water chestnuts and bamboo shoots. Cook over high heat 1 minute, tossing lightly with 2 spoons.
4. Add broth; cover and cook over medium heat 2 minutes.
5. Combine cornstarch with 1 tsp (5 ml) cold water. Stir into peas. Cook, uncovered, over high heat until sauce thickens and bubbles, about 1 minute.

Note: A 7-oz (198-gram) pkg frozen Chinese pea pods may be substituted for fresh pea pods. Thaw before using.

SOUR CREAM EGGPLANT

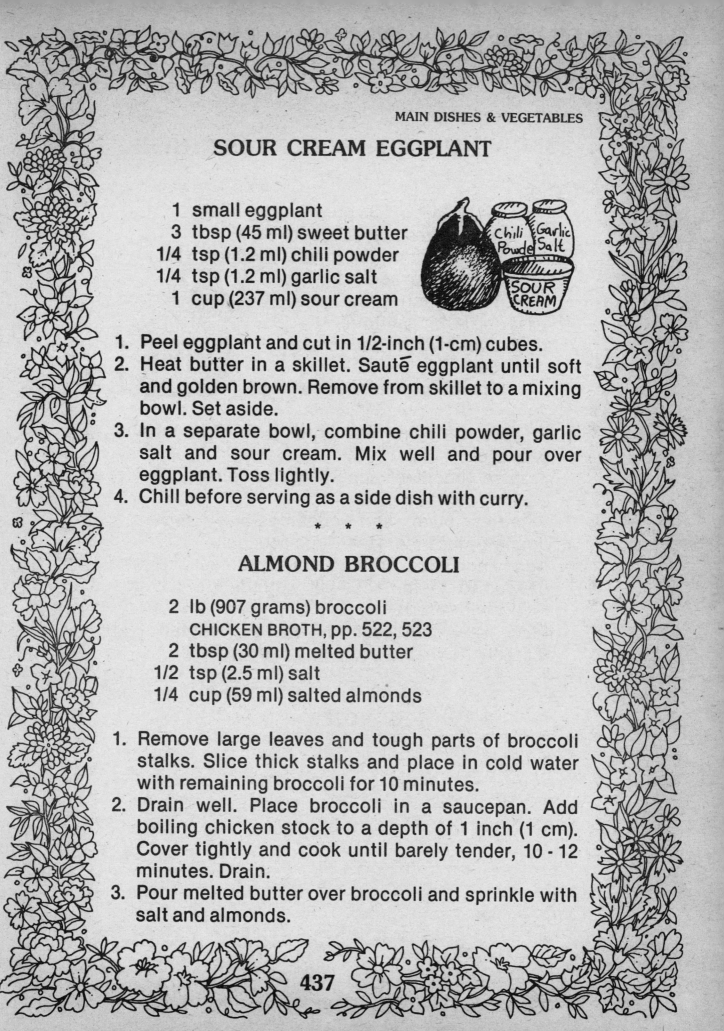

    1 small eggplant
    3 tbsp (45 ml) sweet butter
  1/4 tsp (1.2 ml) chili powder
  1/4 tsp (1.2 ml) garlic salt
    1 cup (237 ml) sour cream

1. Peel eggplant and cut in 1/2-inch (1-cm) cubes.
2. Heat butter in a skillet. Sauté eggplant until soft and golden brown. Remove from skillet to a mixing bowl. Set aside.
3. In a separate bowl, combine chili powder, garlic salt and sour cream. Mix well and pour over eggplant. Toss lightly.
4. Chill before serving as a side dish with curry.

* * *

ALMOND BROCCOLI

    2 lb (907 grams) broccoli
       CHICKEN BROTH, pp. 522, 523
    2 tbsp (30 ml) melted butter
  1/2 tsp (2.5 ml) salt
  1/4 cup (59 ml) salted almonds

1. Remove large leaves and tough parts of broccoli stalks. Slice thick stalks and place in cold water with remaining broccoli for 10 minutes.
2. Drain well. Place broccoli in a saucepan. Add boiling chicken stock to a depth of 1 inch (1 cm). Cover tightly and cook until barely tender, 10 - 12 minutes. Drain.
3. Pour melted butter over broccoli and sprinkle with salt and almonds.

SPINACH-NOODLE TOSS

2 pkg (10 oz or 284 grams each) frozen,
   chopped spinach, cooked
1 pkg (16 oz or 454 grams) medium-width egg
   noodles, cooked
1 tbsp (15 ml) lemon juice
1/4 tsp (1.2 ml) nutmeg
2 cups (473 ml) sour cream
   Salt
   Freshly ground black pepper

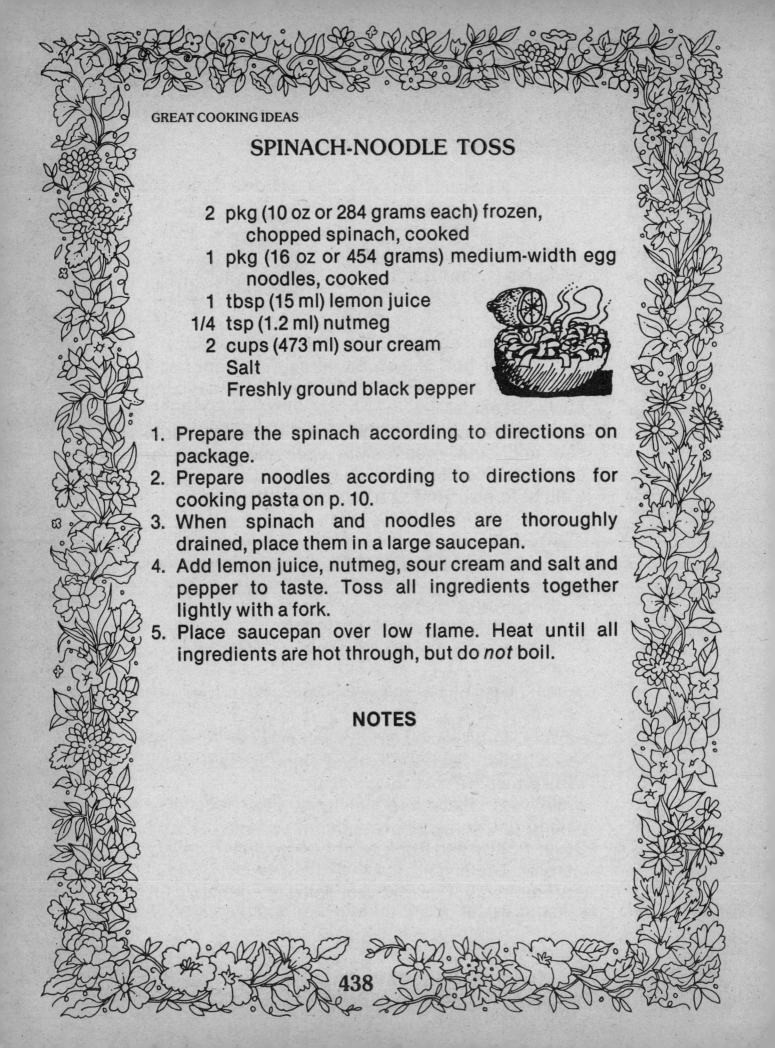

1. Prepare the spinach according to directions on package.
2. Prepare noodles according to directions for cooking pasta on p. 10.
3. When spinach and noodles are thoroughly drained, place them in a large saucepan.
4. Add lemon juice, nutmeg, sour cream and salt and pepper to taste. Toss all ingredients together lightly with a fork.
5. Place saucepan over low flame. Heat until all ingredients are hot through, but do *not* boil.

NOTES

STIR-FRY GREEN BEANS

Makes 4 servings.

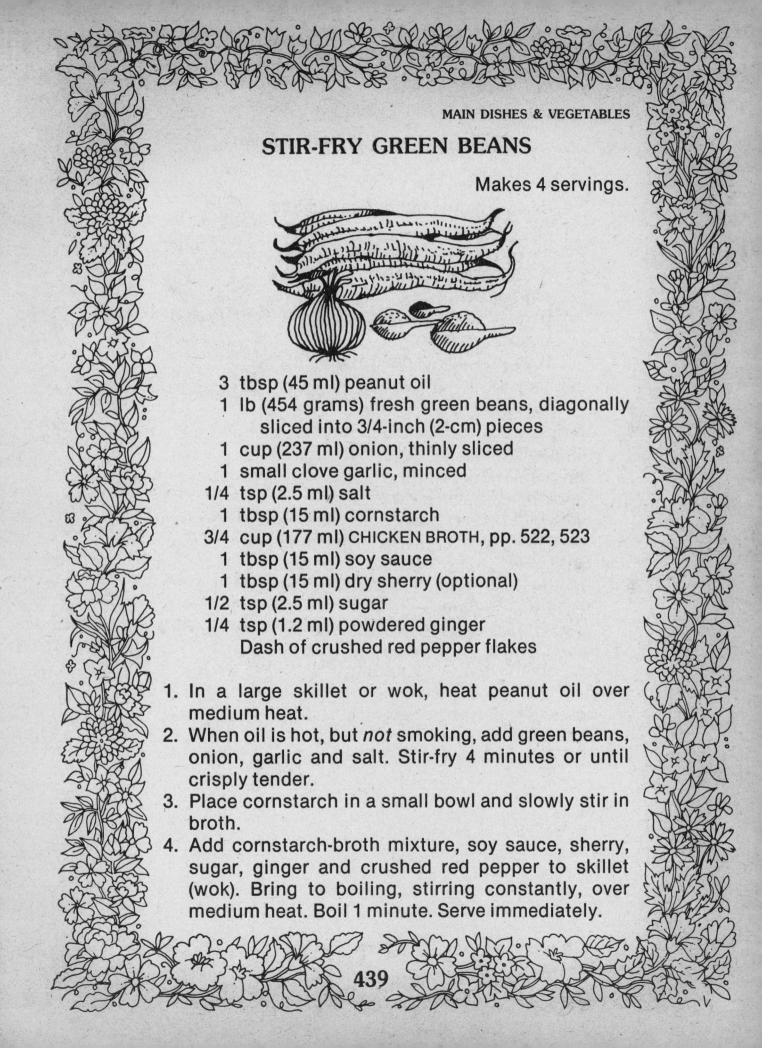

3 tbsp (45 ml) peanut oil
1 lb (454 grams) fresh green beans, diagonally
    sliced into 3/4-inch (2-cm) pieces
1 cup (237 ml) onion, thinly sliced
1 small clove garlic, minced
1/4 tsp (2.5 ml) salt
1 tbsp (15 ml) cornstarch
3/4 cup (177 ml) CHICKEN BROTH, pp. 522, 523
1 tbsp (15 ml) soy sauce
1 tbsp (15 ml) dry sherry (optional)
1/2 tsp (2.5 ml) sugar
1/4 tsp (1.2 ml) powdered ginger
    Dash of crushed red pepper flakes

1. In a large skillet or wok, heat peanut oil over medium heat.
2. When oil is hot, but *not* smoking, add green beans, onion, garlic and salt. Stir-fry 4 minutes or until crisply tender.
3. Place cornstarch in a small bowl and slowly stir in broth.
4. Add cornstarch-broth mixture, soy sauce, sherry, sugar, ginger and crushed red pepper to skillet (wok). Bring to boiling, stirring constantly, over medium heat. Boil 1 minute. Serve immediately.

STIR-FRY VEGETABLES

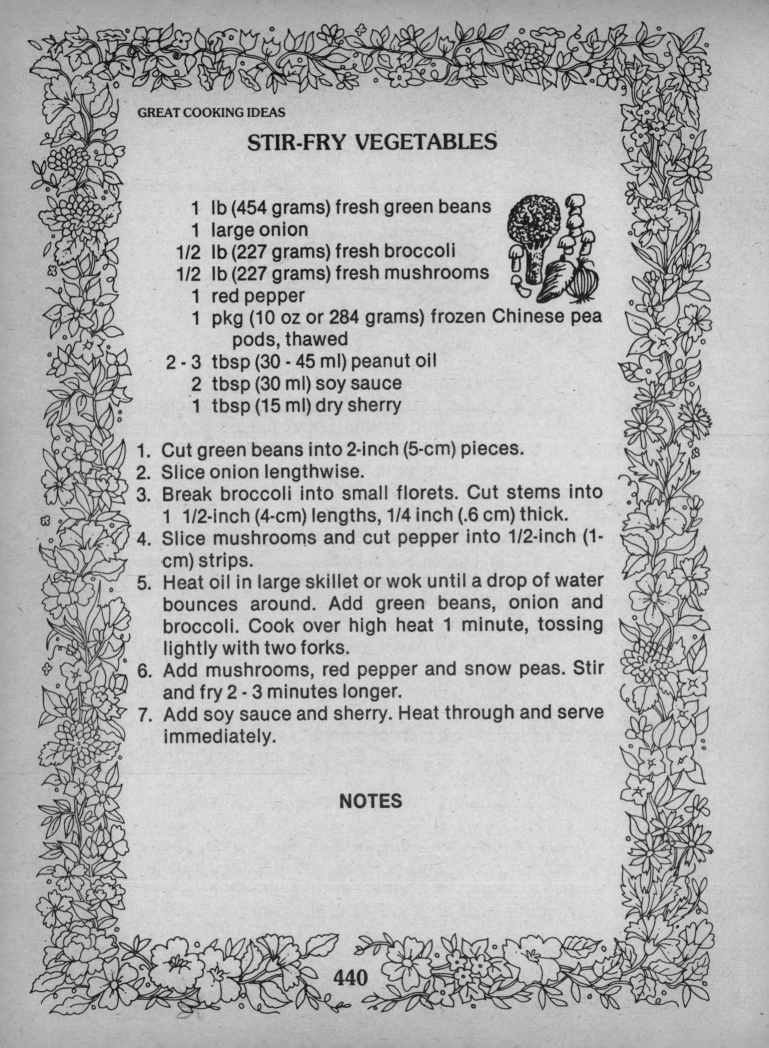

1 lb (454 grams) fresh green beans
1 large onion
1/2 lb (227 grams) fresh broccoli
1/2 lb (227 grams) fresh mushrooms
1 red pepper
1 pkg (10 oz or 284 grams) frozen Chinese pea pods, thawed
2 - 3 tbsp (30 - 45 ml) peanut oil
2 tbsp (30 ml) soy sauce
1 tbsp (15 ml) dry sherry

1. Cut green beans into 2-inch (5-cm) pieces.
2. Slice onion lengthwise.
3. Break broccoli into small florets. Cut stems into 1 1/2-inch (4-cm) lengths, 1/4 inch (.6 cm) thick.
4. Slice mushrooms and cut pepper into 1/2-inch (1-cm) strips.
5. Heat oil in large skillet or wok until a drop of water bounces around. Add green beans, onion and broccoli. Cook over high heat 1 minute, tossing lightly with two forks.
6. Add mushrooms, red pepper and snow peas. Stir and fry 2 - 3 minutes longer.
7. Add soy sauce and sherry. Heat through and serve immediately.

NOTES

STUFFED ARTICHOKES

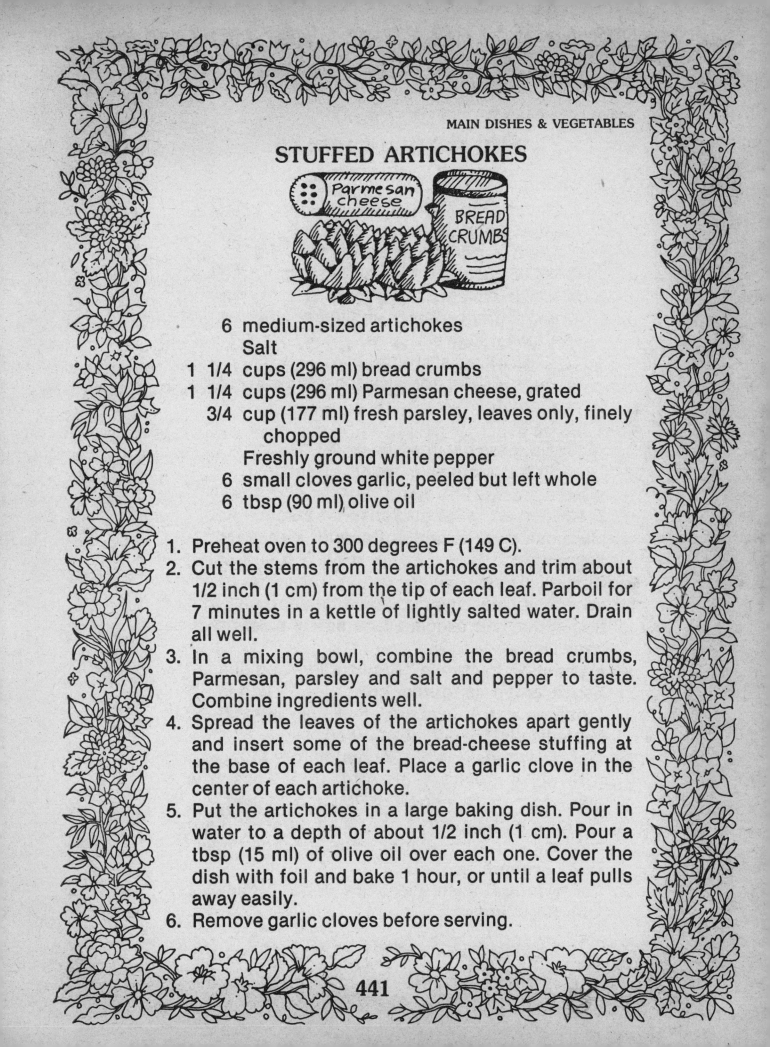

       6 medium-sized artichokes
          Salt
   1 1/4 cups (296 ml) bread crumbs
   1 1/4 cups (296 ml) Parmesan cheese, grated
     3/4 cup (177 ml) fresh parsley, leaves only, finely
          chopped
          Freshly ground white pepper
       6 small cloves garlic, peeled but left whole
       6 tbsp (90 ml) olive oil

1. Preheat oven to 300 degrees F (149 C).
2. Cut the stems from the artichokes and trim about 1/2 inch (1 cm) from the tip of each leaf. Parboil for 7 minutes in a kettle of lightly salted water. Drain all well.
3. In a mixing bowl, combine the bread crumbs, Parmesan, parsley and salt and pepper to taste. Combine ingredients well.
4. Spread the leaves of the artichokes apart gently and insert some of the bread-cheese stuffing at the base of each leaf. Place a garlic clove in the center of each artichoke.
5. Put the artichokes in a large baking dish. Pour in water to a depth of about 1/2 inch (1 cm). Pour a tbsp (15 ml) of olive oil over each one. Cover the dish with foil and bake 1 hour, or until a leaf pulls away easily.
6. Remove garlic cloves before serving.

STUFFED ZUCCHINI

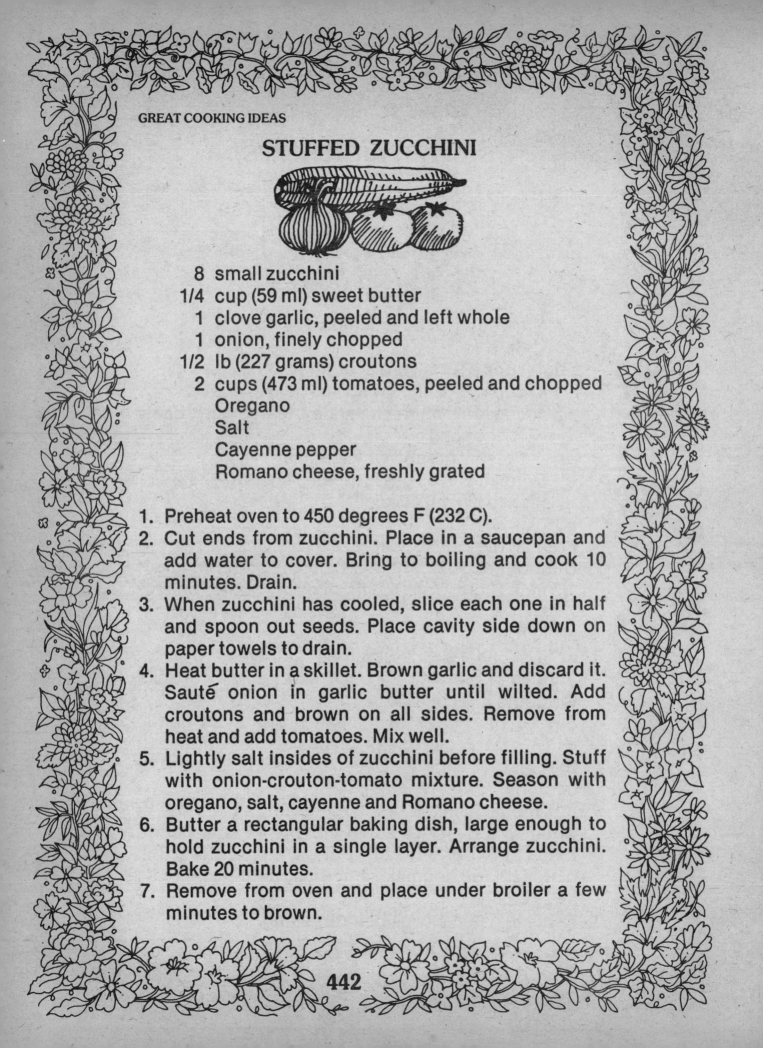

         8 small zucchini
       1/4 cup (59 ml) sweet butter
         1 clove garlic, peeled and left whole
         1 onion, finely chopped
       1/2 lb (227 grams) croutons
         2 cups (473 ml) tomatoes, peeled and chopped
            Oregano
            Salt
            Cayenne pepper
            Romano cheese, freshly grated

1. Preheat oven to 450 degrees F (232 C).
2. Cut ends from zucchini. Place in a saucepan and add water to cover. Bring to boiling and cook 10 minutes. Drain.
3. When zucchini has cooled, slice each one in half and spoon out seeds. Place cavity side down on paper towels to drain.
4. Heat butter in a skillet. Brown garlic and discard it. Sauté onion in garlic butter until wilted. Add croutons and brown on all sides. Remove from heat and add tomatoes. Mix well.
5. Lightly salt insides of zucchini before filling. Stuff with onion-crouton-tomato mixture. Season with oregano, salt, cayenne and Romano cheese.
6. Butter a rectangular baking dish, large enough to hold zucchini in a single layer. Arrange zucchini. Bake 20 minutes.
7. Remove from oven and place under broiler a few minutes to brown.

STUFFY TOMATOES

Makes 6 servings.

6 medium-sized tomatoes
1 1/2 cups (about 1/4 lb or 113 grams) fresh
mushrooms, chopped
3 tbsps (45 ml) sweet butter
1/2 cup (118 ml) sour cream
2 egg yolks, beaten
1/2 cup (118 ml) fine bread crumbs
1 tsp (5 ml) salt
1/8 tsp (.6 ml) dried thyme
Dash pepper
Dash garlic powder

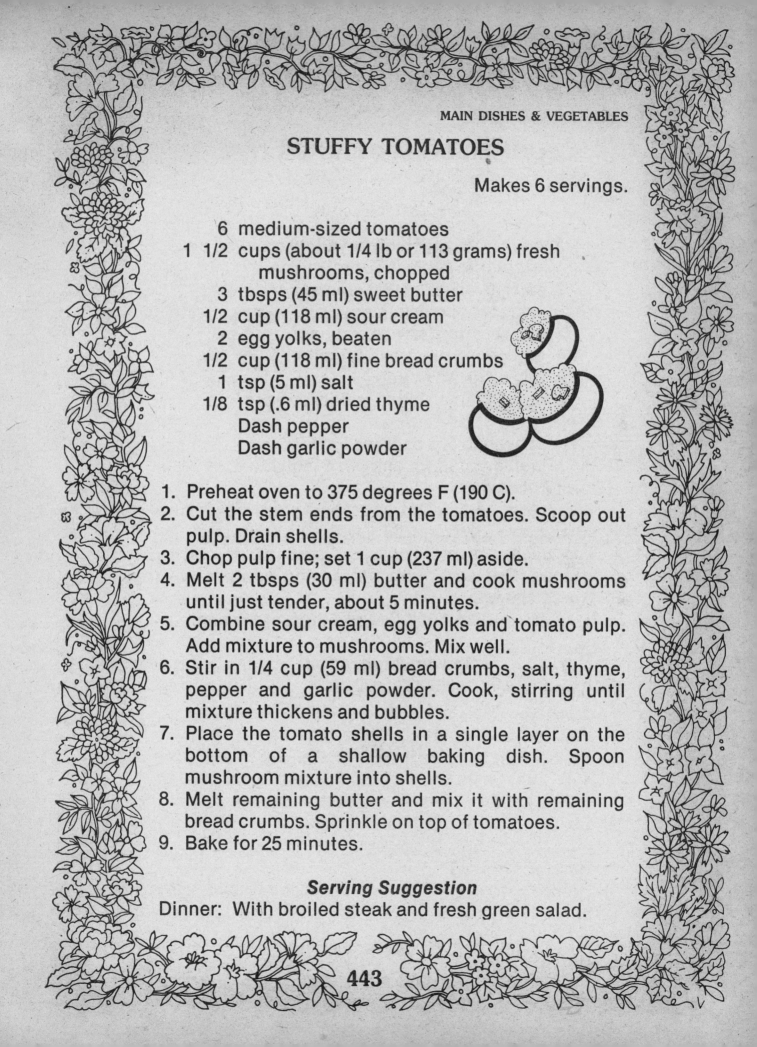

1. Preheat oven to 375 degrees F (190 C).
2. Cut the stem ends from the tomatoes. Scoop out pulp. Drain shells.
3. Chop pulp fine; set 1 cup (237 ml) aside.
4. Melt 2 tbsps (30 ml) butter and cook mushrooms until just tender, about 5 minutes.
5. Combine sour cream, egg yolks and tomato pulp. Add mixture to mushrooms. Mix well.
6. Stir in 1/4 cup (59 ml) bread crumbs, salt, thyme, pepper and garlic powder. Cook, stirring until mixture thickens and bubbles.
7. Place the tomato shells in a single layer on the bottom of a shallow baking dish. Spoon mushroom mixture into shells.
8. Melt remaining butter and mix it with remaining bread crumbs. Sprinkle on top of tomatoes.
9. Bake for 25 minutes.

Serving Suggestion
Dinner: With broiled steak and fresh green salad.

SUMMER SQUASH AU GRATIN

Makes 4 servings.

2 cups (473) zucchini, or yellow crooked neck
cut into 3/4-inch (2-cm) slices
1 can (10 1/2-oz or 298 grams) condensed
cream of chicken soup
1/2 cup (118 ml) dairy sour cream
1/4 cup (59 ml) dry bread crumbs
2 tbsps (30 ml) butter
2 oz (57 grams) mild Cheddar cheese, grated

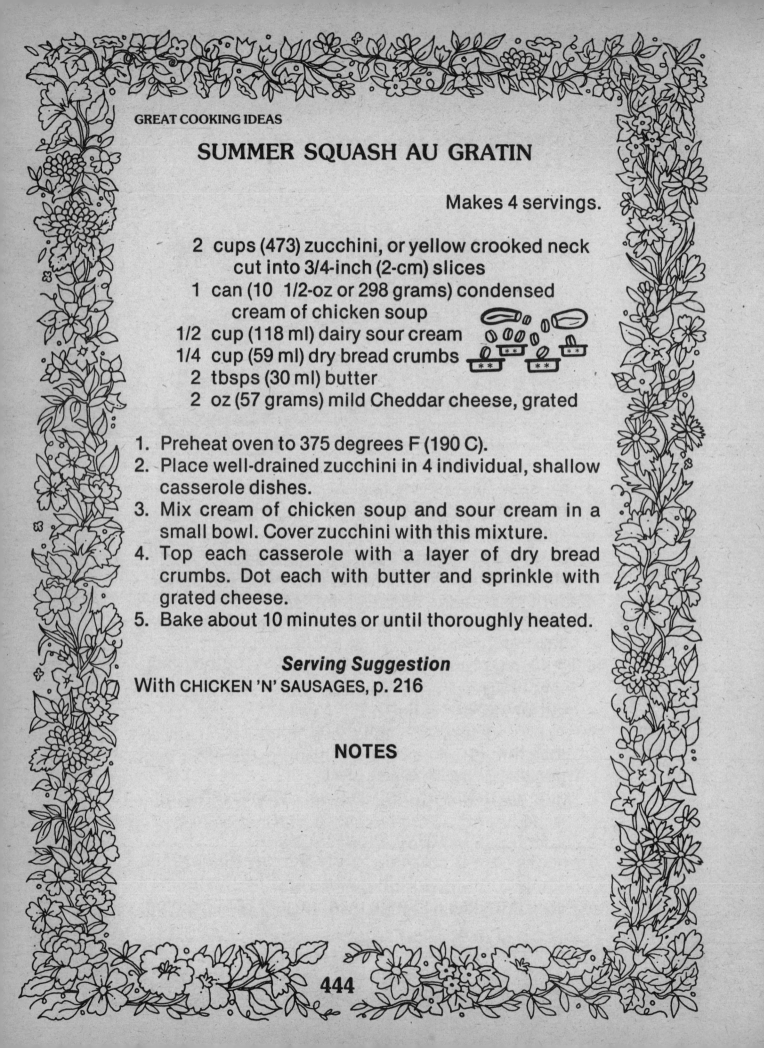

1. Preheat oven to 375 degrees F (190 C).
2. Place well-drained zucchini in 4 individual, shallow casserole dishes.
3. Mix cream of chicken soup and sour cream in a small bowl. Cover zucchini with this mixture.
4. Top each casserole with a layer of dry bread crumbs. Dot each with butter and sprinkle with grated cheese.
5. Bake about 10 minutes or until thoroughly heated.

Serving Suggestion
With CHICKEN 'N' SAUSAGES, p. 216

NOTES

SWEET POTATO AND APPLESAUCE SOUFFLÉ

Makes 6 servings.

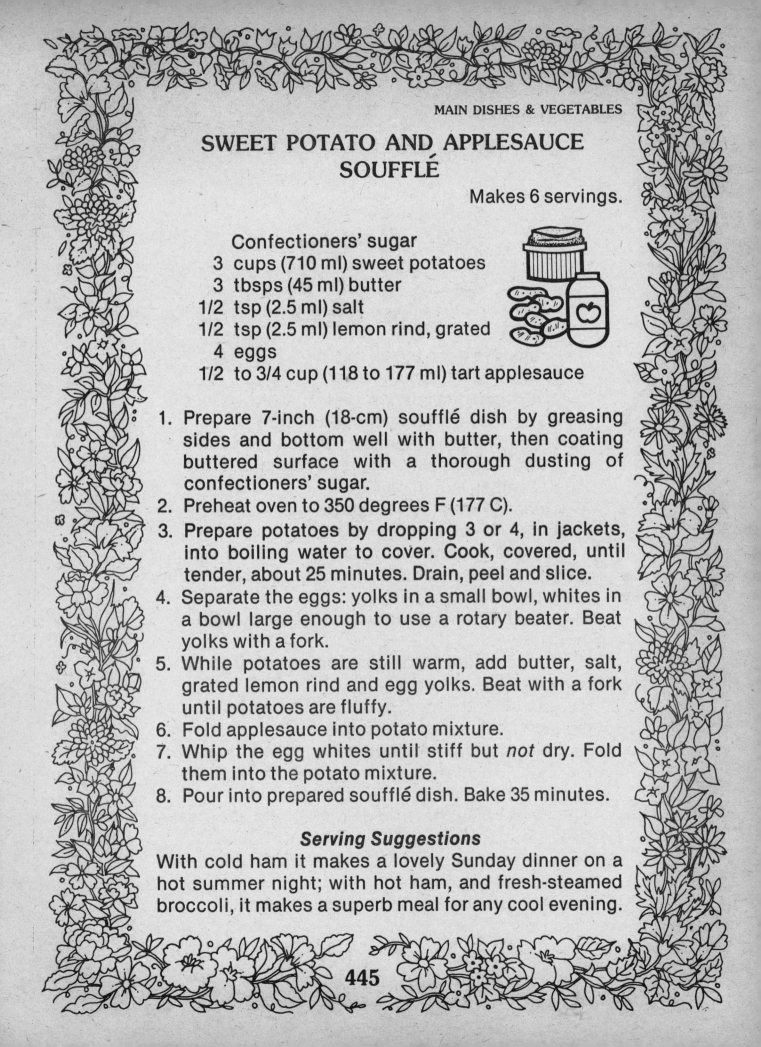

Confectioners' sugar
- 3 cups (710 ml) sweet potatoes
- 3 tbsps (45 ml) butter
- 1/2 tsp (2.5 ml) salt
- 1/2 tsp (2.5 ml) lemon rind, grated
- 4 eggs
- 1/2 to 3/4 cup (118 to 177 ml) tart applesauce

1. Prepare 7-inch (18-cm) soufflé dish by greasing sides and bottom well with butter, then coating buttered surface with a thorough dusting of confectioners' sugar.
2. Preheat oven to 350 degrees F (177 C).
3. Prepare potatoes by dropping 3 or 4, in jackets, into boiling water to cover. Cook, covered, until tender, about 25 minutes. Drain, peel and slice.
4. Separate the eggs: yolks in a small bowl, whites in a bowl large enough to use a rotary beater. Beat yolks with a fork.
5. While potatoes are still warm, add butter, salt, grated lemon rind and egg yolks. Beat with a fork until potatoes are fluffy.
6. Fold applesauce into potato mixture.
7. Whip the egg whites until stiff but *not* dry. Fold them into the potato mixture.
8. Pour into prepared soufflé dish. Bake 35 minutes.

Serving Suggestions

With cold ham it makes a lovely Sunday dinner on a hot summer night; with hot ham, and fresh-steamed broccoli, it makes a superb meal for any cool evening.

TASTY GREEN BEANS

Makes 6 servings.

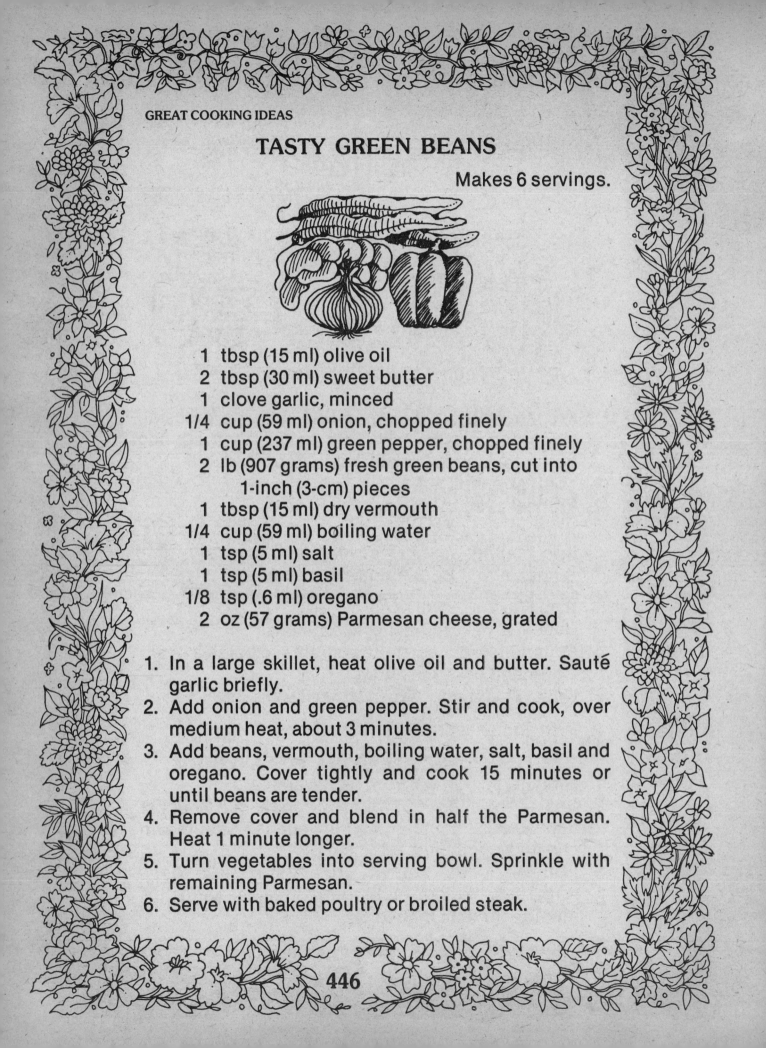

1 tbsp (15 ml) olive oil
2 tbsp (30 ml) sweet butter
1 clove garlic, minced
1/4 cup (59 ml) onion, chopped finely
1 cup (237 ml) green pepper, chopped finely
2 lb (907 grams) fresh green beans, cut into
   1-inch (3-cm) pieces
1 tbsp (15 ml) dry vermouth
1/4 cup (59 ml) boiling water
1 tsp (5 ml) salt
1 tsp (5 ml) basil
1/8 tsp (.6 ml) oregano
2 oz (57 grams) Parmesan cheese, grated

1. In a large skillet, heat olive oil and butter. Sauté garlic briefly.
2. Add onion and green pepper. Stir and cook, over medium heat, about 3 minutes.
3. Add beans, vermouth, boiling water, salt, basil and oregano. Cover tightly and cook 15 minutes or until beans are tender.
4. Remove cover and blend in half the Parmesan. Heat 1 minute longer.
5. Turn vegetables into serving bowl. Sprinkle with remaining Parmesan.
6. Serve with baked poultry or broiled steak.

ZESTY SCALLOPED POTATOES

Makes 6 servings.

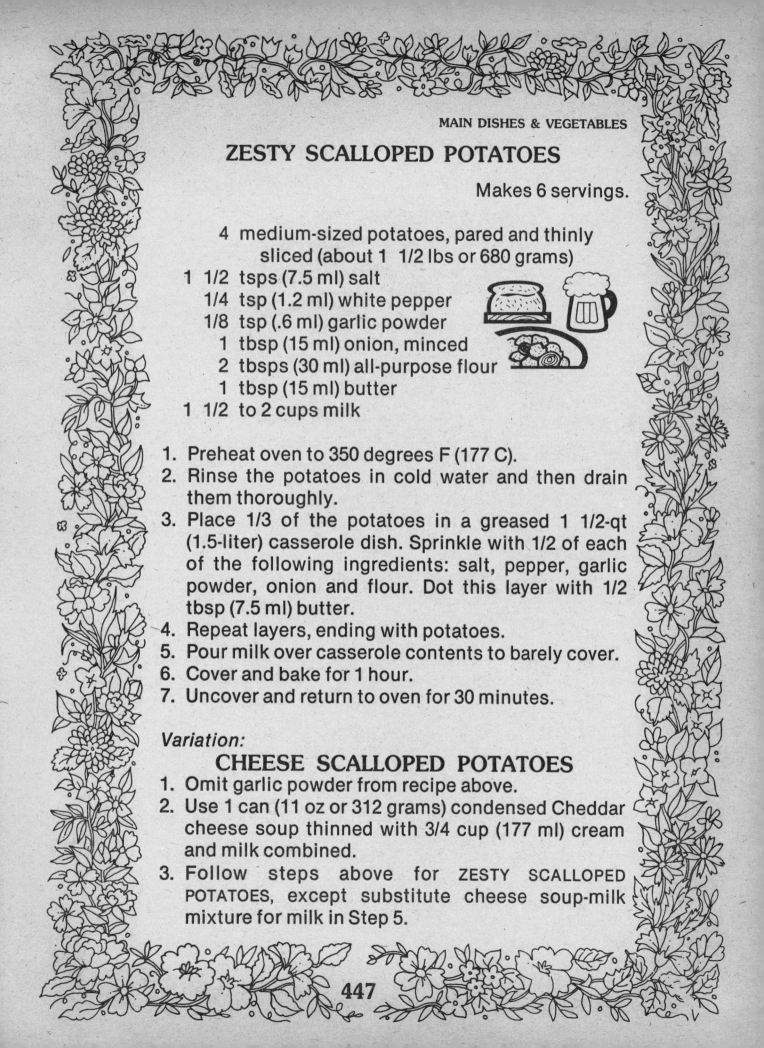

4 medium-sized potatoes, pared and thinly
    sliced (about 1 1/2 lbs or 680 grams)
1 1/2 tsps (7.5 ml) salt
1/4 tsp (1.2 ml) white pepper
1/8 tsp (.6 ml) garlic powder
1 tbsp (15 ml) onion, minced
2 tbsps (30 ml) all-purpose flour
1 tbsp (15 ml) butter
1 1/2 to 2 cups milk

1. Preheat oven to 350 degrees F (177 C).
2. Rinse the potatoes in cold water and then drain them thoroughly.
3. Place 1/3 of the potatoes in a greased 1 1/2-qt (1.5-liter) casserole dish. Sprinkle with 1/2 of each of the following ingredients: salt, pepper, garlic powder, onion and flour. Dot this layer with 1/2 tbsp (7.5 ml) butter.
4. Repeat layers, ending with potatoes.
5. Pour milk over casserole contents to barely cover.
6. Cover and bake for 1 hour.
7. Uncover and return to oven for 30 minutes.

Variation:
CHEESE SCALLOPED POTATOES
1. Omit garlic powder from recipe above.
2. Use 1 can (11 oz or 312 grams) condensed Cheddar cheese soup thinned with 3/4 cup (177 ml) cream and milk combined.
3. Follow steps above for ZESTY SCALLOPED POTATOES, except substitute cheese soup-milk mixture for milk in Step 5.

ZUCCHINI-CHEESE BAKE

Makes 6 servings.

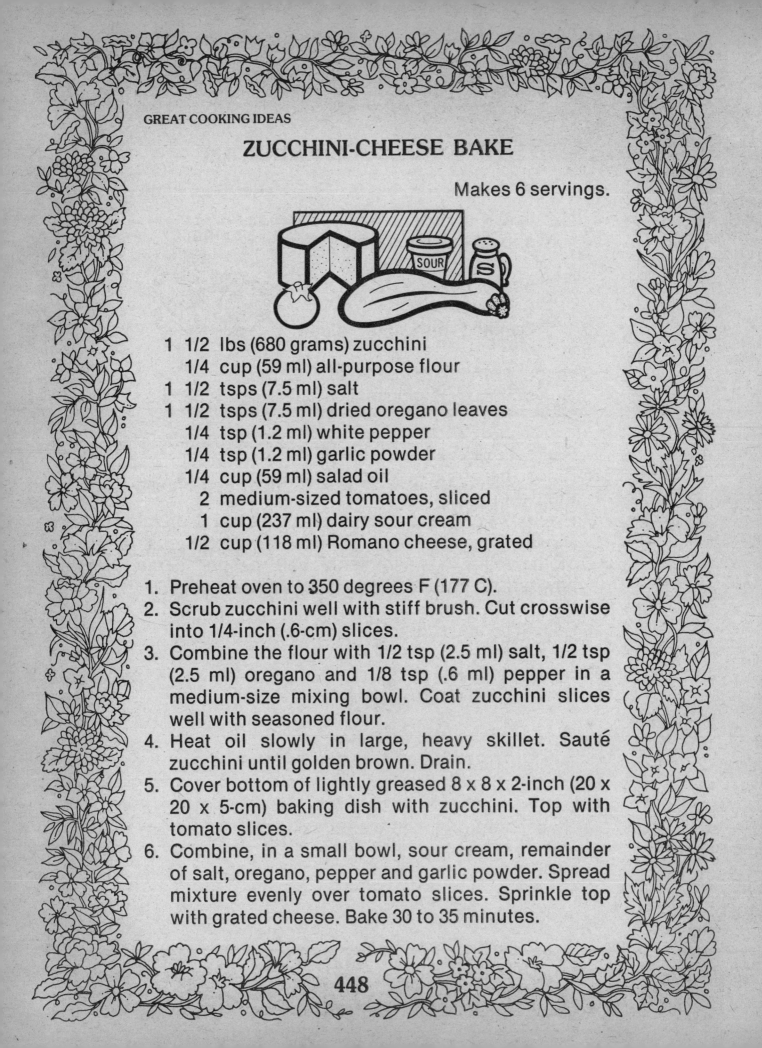

1 1/2	lbs (680 grams)	zucchini
1/4	cup (59 ml)	all-purpose flour
1 1/2	tsps (7.5 ml)	salt
1 1/2	tsps (7.5 ml)	dried oregano leaves
1/4	tsp (1.2 ml)	white pepper
1/4	tsp (1.2 ml)	garlic powder
1/4	cup (59 ml)	salad oil
2		medium-sized tomatoes, sliced
1	cup (237 ml)	dairy sour cream
1/2	cup (118 ml)	Romano cheese, grated

1. Preheat oven to 350 degrees F (177 C).
2. Scrub zucchini well with stiff brush. Cut crosswise into 1/4-inch (.6-cm) slices.
3. Combine the flour with 1/2 tsp (2.5 ml) salt, 1/2 tsp (2.5 ml) oregano and 1/8 tsp (.6 ml) pepper in a medium-size mixing bowl. Coat zucchini slices well with seasoned flour.
4. Heat oil slowly in large, heavy skillet. Sauté zucchini until golden brown. Drain.
5. Cover bottom of lightly greased 8 x 8 x 2-inch (20 x 20 x 5-cm) baking dish with zucchini. Top with tomato slices.
6. Combine, in a small bowl, sour cream, remainder of salt, oregano, pepper and garlic powder. Spread mixture evenly over tomato slices. Sprinkle top with grated cheese. Bake 30 to 35 minutes.

ALMOND MACAROONS

1/2 lb (227 grams) commercial almond paste
1 cup (237 ml) plus 2 tbsp (30 ml) fine
    granulated sugar
2 egg whites
  Safflower oil
  Candied fruits, finely diced

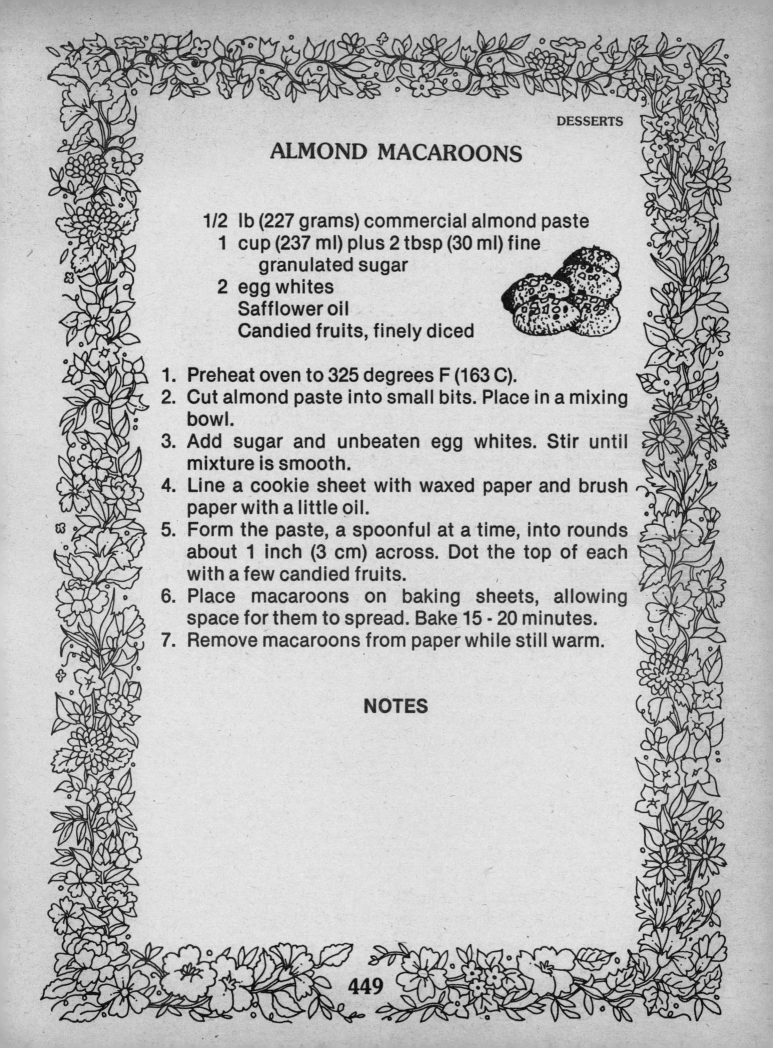

1. Preheat oven to 325 degrees F (163 C).
2. Cut almond paste into small bits. Place in a mixing bowl.
3. Add sugar and unbeaten egg whites. Stir until mixture is smooth.
4. Line a cookie sheet with waxed paper and brush paper with a little oil.
5. Form the paste, a spoonful at a time, into rounds about 1 inch (3 cm) across. Dot the top of each with a few candied fruits.
6. Place macaroons on baking sheets, allowing space for them to spread. Bake 15 - 20 minutes.
7. Remove macaroons from paper while still warm.

NOTES

ALMOND COOKIES

Makes about 4 doz. cookies.

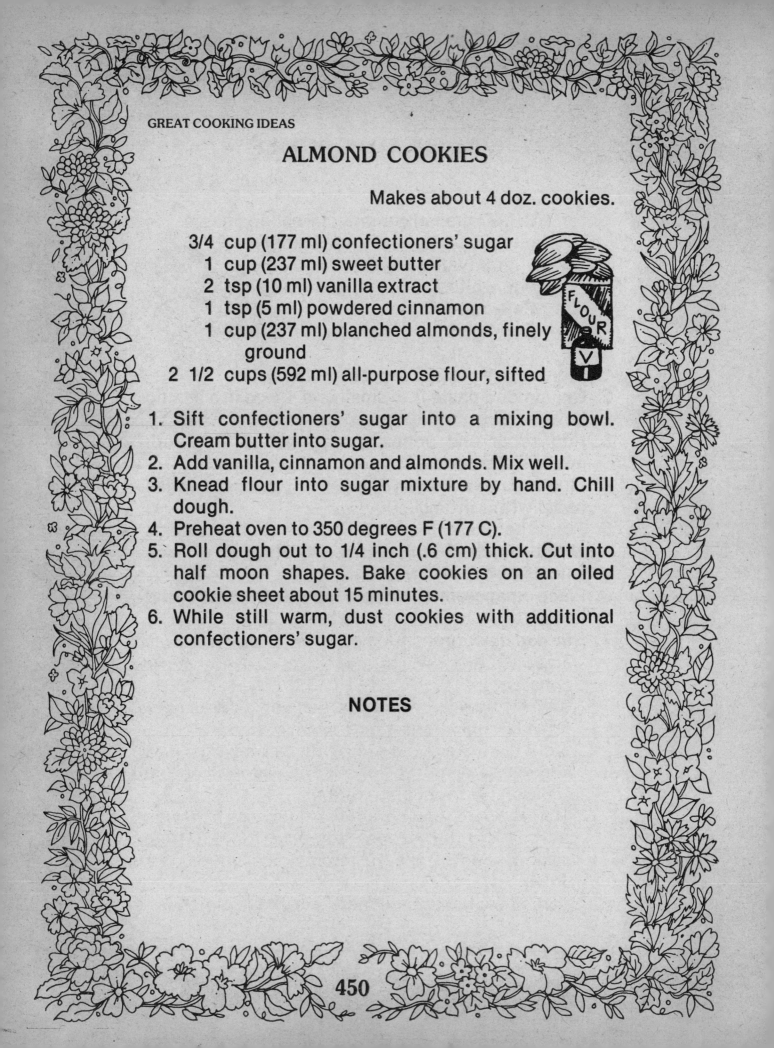

3/4 cup (177 ml) confectioners' sugar
1 cup (237 ml) sweet butter
2 tsp (10 ml) vanilla extract
1 tsp (5 ml) powdered cinnamon
1 cup (237 ml) blanched almonds, finely ground
2 1/2 cups (592 ml) all-purpose flour, sifted

1. Sift confectioners' sugar into a mixing bowl. Cream butter into sugar.
2. Add vanilla, cinnamon and almonds. Mix well.
3. Knead flour into sugar mixture by hand. Chill dough.
4. Preheat oven to 350 degrees F (177 C).
5. Roll dough out to 1/4 inch (.6 cm) thick. Cut into half moon shapes. Bake cookies on an oiled cookie sheet about 15 minutes.
6. While still warm, dust cookies with additional confectioners' sugar.

NOTES

AMARETTO COOKIES

Makes about 36 cookies.

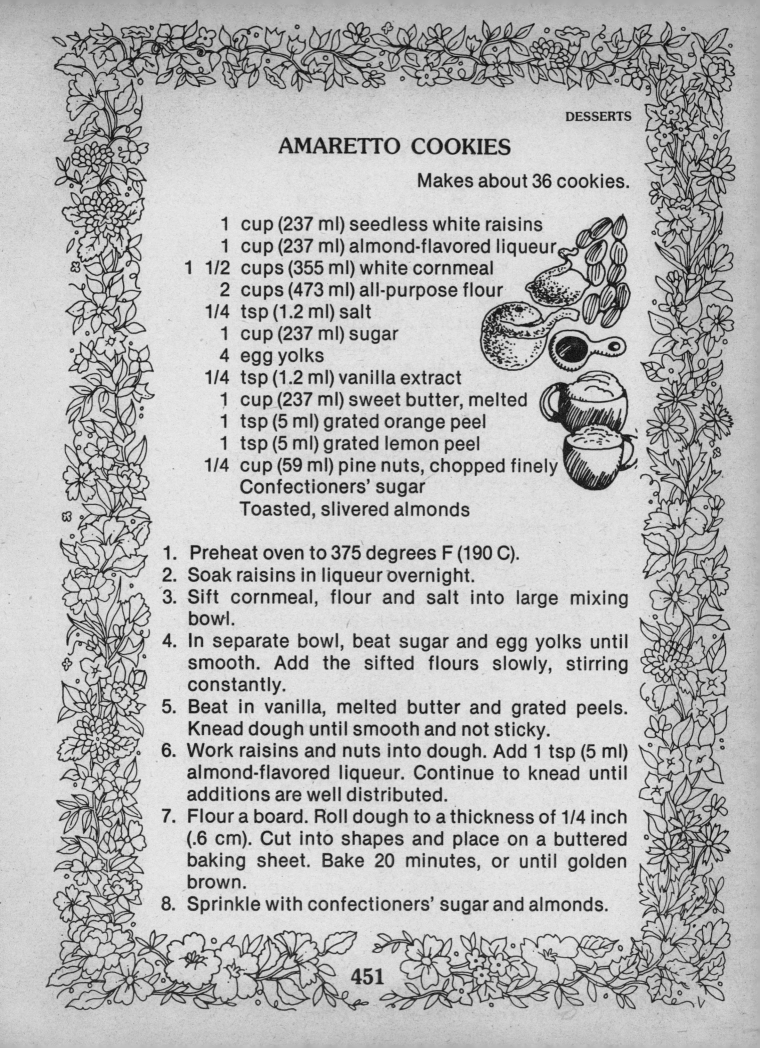

1 cup (237 ml) seedless white raisins
1 cup (237 ml) almond-flavored liqueur
1 1/2 cups (355 ml) white cornmeal
2 cups (473 ml) all-purpose flour
1/4 tsp (1.2 ml) salt
1 cup (237 ml) sugar
4 egg yolks
1/4 tsp (1.2 ml) vanilla extract
1 cup (237 ml) sweet butter, melted
1 tsp (5 ml) grated orange peel
1 tsp (5 ml) grated lemon peel
1/4 cup (59 ml) pine nuts, chopped finely
Confectioners' sugar
Toasted, slivered almonds

1. Preheat oven to 375 degrees F (190 C).
2. Soak raisins in liqueur overnight.
3. Sift cornmeal, flour and salt into large mixing bowl.
4. In separate bowl, beat sugar and egg yolks until smooth. Add the sifted flours slowly, stirring constantly.
5. Beat in vanilla, melted butter and grated peels. Knead dough until smooth and not sticky.
6. Work raisins and nuts into dough. Add 1 tsp (5 ml) almond-flavored liqueur. Continue to knead until additions are well distributed.
7. Flour a board. Roll dough to a thickness of 1/4 inch (.6 cm). Cut into shapes and place on a buttered baking sheet. Bake 20 minutes, or until golden brown.
8. Sprinkle with confectioners' sugar and almonds.

CINNAMON COOKIES*

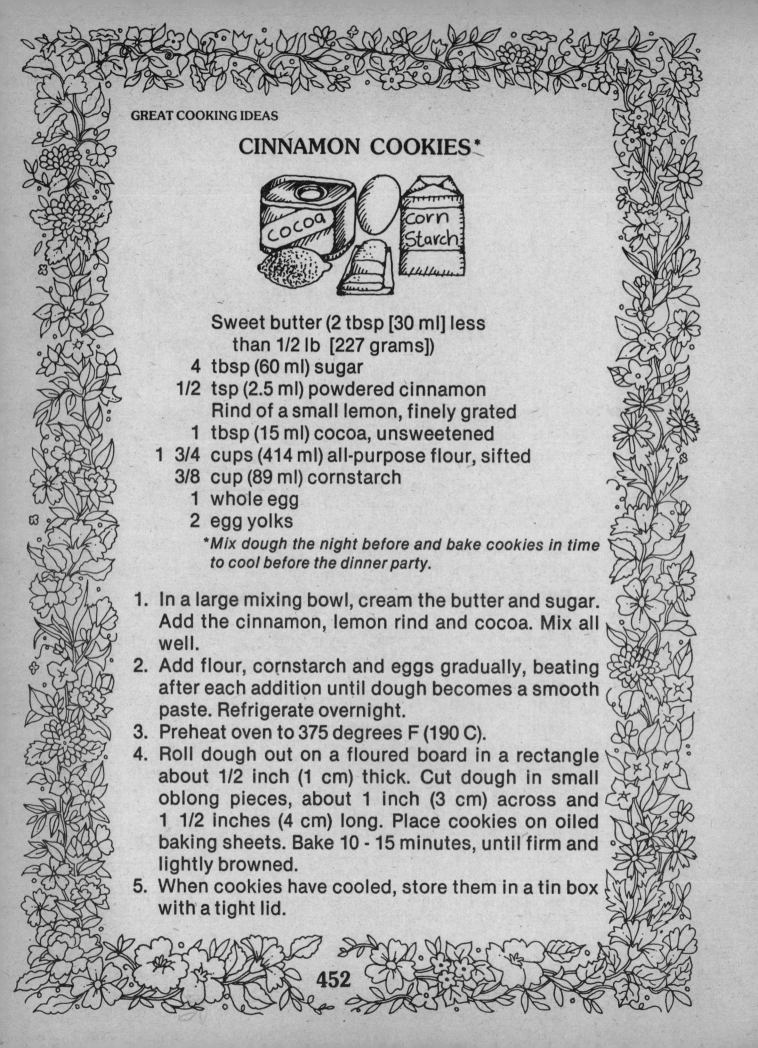

Sweet butter (2 tbsp [30 ml] less
   than 1/2 lb [227 grams])
4 tbsp (60 ml) sugar
1/2 tsp (2.5 ml) powdered cinnamon
   Rind of a small lemon, finely grated
1 tbsp (15 ml) cocoa, unsweetened
1 3/4 cups (414 ml) all-purpose flour, sifted
3/8 cup (89 ml) cornstarch
1 whole egg
2 egg yolks

*Mix dough the night before and bake cookies in time
to cool before the dinner party.*

1. In a large mixing bowl, cream the butter and sugar. Add the cinnamon, lemon rind and cocoa. Mix all well.
2. Add flour, cornstarch and eggs gradually, beating after each addition until dough becomes a smooth paste. Refrigerate overnight.
3. Preheat oven to 375 degrees F (190 C).
4. Roll dough out on a floured board in a rectangle about 1/2 inch (1 cm) thick. Cut dough in small oblong pieces, about 1 inch (3 cm) across and 1 1/2 inches (4 cm) long. Place cookies on oiled baking sheets. Bake 10 - 15 minutes, until firm and lightly browned.
5. When cookies have cooled, store them in a tin box with a tight lid.

PISTACHIO COOKIES

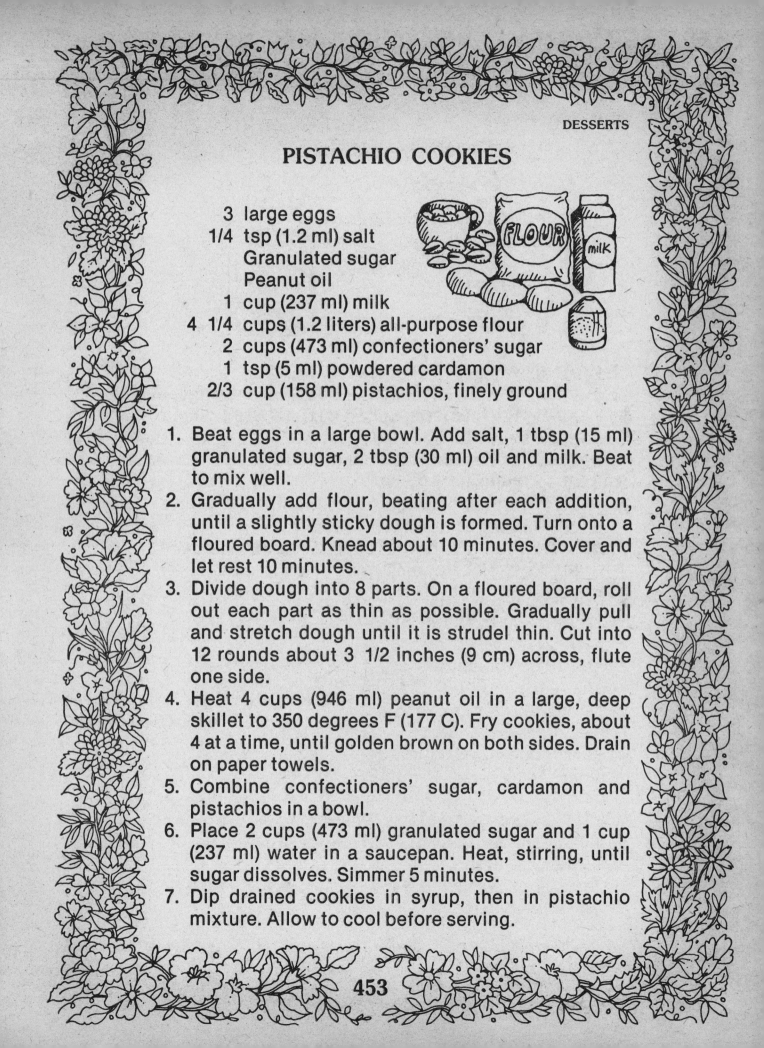

3 large eggs
1/4 tsp (1.2 ml) salt
Granulated sugar
Peanut oil
1 cup (237 ml) milk
4 1/4 cups (1.2 liters) all-purpose flour
2 cups (473 ml) confectioners' sugar
1 tsp (5 ml) powdered cardamon
2/3 cup (158 ml) pistachios, finely ground

1. Beat eggs in a large bowl. Add salt, 1 tbsp (15 ml) granulated sugar, 2 tbsp (30 ml) oil and milk. Beat to mix well.
2. Gradually add flour, beating after each addition, until a slightly sticky dough is formed. Turn onto a floured board. Knead about 10 minutes. Cover and let rest 10 minutes.
3. Divide dough into 8 parts. On a floured board, roll out each part as thin as possible. Gradually pull and stretch dough until it is strudel thin. Cut into 12 rounds about 3 1/2 inches (9 cm) across, flute one side.
4. Heat 4 cups (946 ml) peanut oil in a large, deep skillet to 350 degrees F (177 C). Fry cookies, about 4 at a time, until golden brown on both sides. Drain on paper towels.
5. Combine confectioners' sugar, cardamon and pistachios in a bowl.
6. Place 2 cups (473 ml) granulated sugar and 1 cup (237 ml) water in a saucepan. Heat, stirring, until sugar dissolves. Simmer 5 minutes.
7. Dip drained cookies in syrup, then in pistachio mixture. Allow to cool before serving.

CHEESECAKES

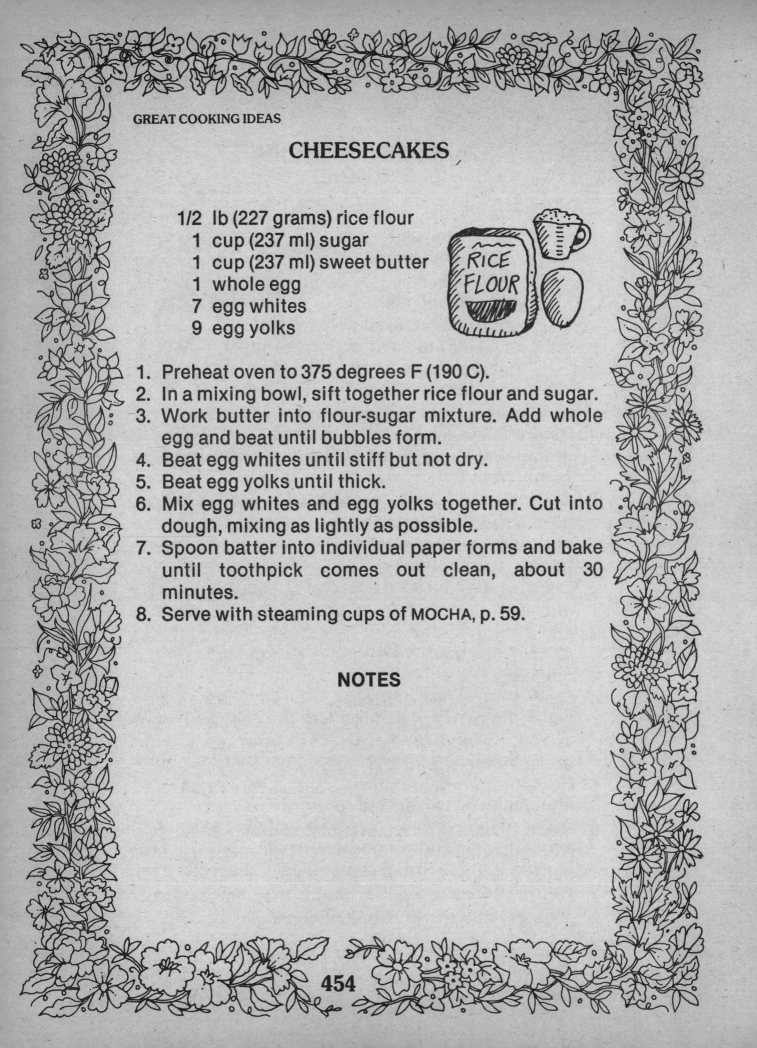

1/2 lb (227 grams) rice flour
1 cup (237 ml) sugar
1 cup (237 ml) sweet butter
1 whole egg
7 egg whites
9 egg yolks

1. Preheat oven to 375 degrees F (190 C).
2. In a mixing bowl, sift together rice flour and sugar.
3. Work butter into flour-sugar mixture. Add whole egg and beat until bubbles form.
4. Beat egg whites until stiff but not dry.
5. Beat egg yolks until thick.
6. Mix egg whites and egg yolks together. Cut into dough, mixing as lightly as possible.
7. Spoon batter into individual paper forms and bake until toothpick comes out clean, about 30 minutes.
8. Serve with steaming cups of MOCHA, p. 59.

NOTES

CREAM CHEESE CAKES
(Pakistani)

Makes 4 servings.

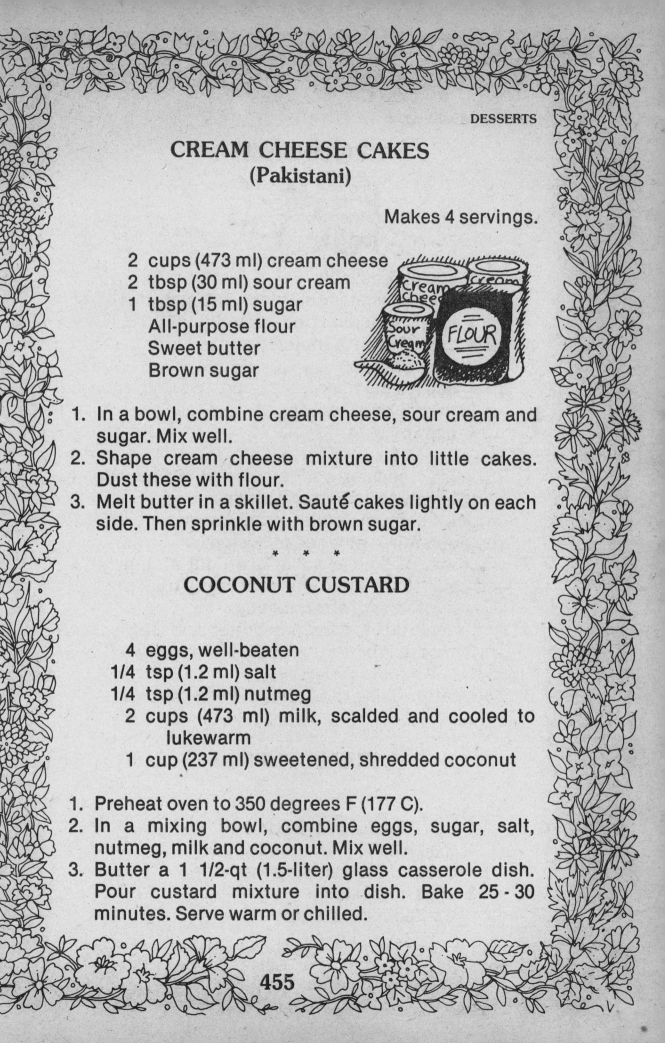

2 cups (473 ml) cream cheese
2 tbsp (30 ml) sour cream
1 tbsp (15 ml) sugar
All-purpose flour
Sweet butter
Brown sugar

1. In a bowl, combine cream cheese, sour cream and sugar. Mix well.
2. Shape cream cheese mixture into little cakes. Dust these with flour.
3. Melt butter in a skillet. Sauté cakes lightly on each side. Then sprinkle with brown sugar.

* * *

COCONUT CUSTARD

4 eggs, well-beaten
1/4 tsp (1.2 ml) salt
1/4 tsp (1.2 ml) nutmeg
2 cups (473 ml) milk, scalded and cooled to lukewarm
1 cup (237 ml) sweetened, shredded coconut

1. Preheat oven to 350 degrees F (177 C).
2. In a mixing bowl, combine eggs, sugar, salt, nutmeg, milk and coconut. Mix well.
3. Butter a 1 1/2-qt (1.5-liter) glass casserole dish. Pour custard mixture into dish. Bake 25 - 30 minutes. Serve warm or chilled.

CREAM FILLING

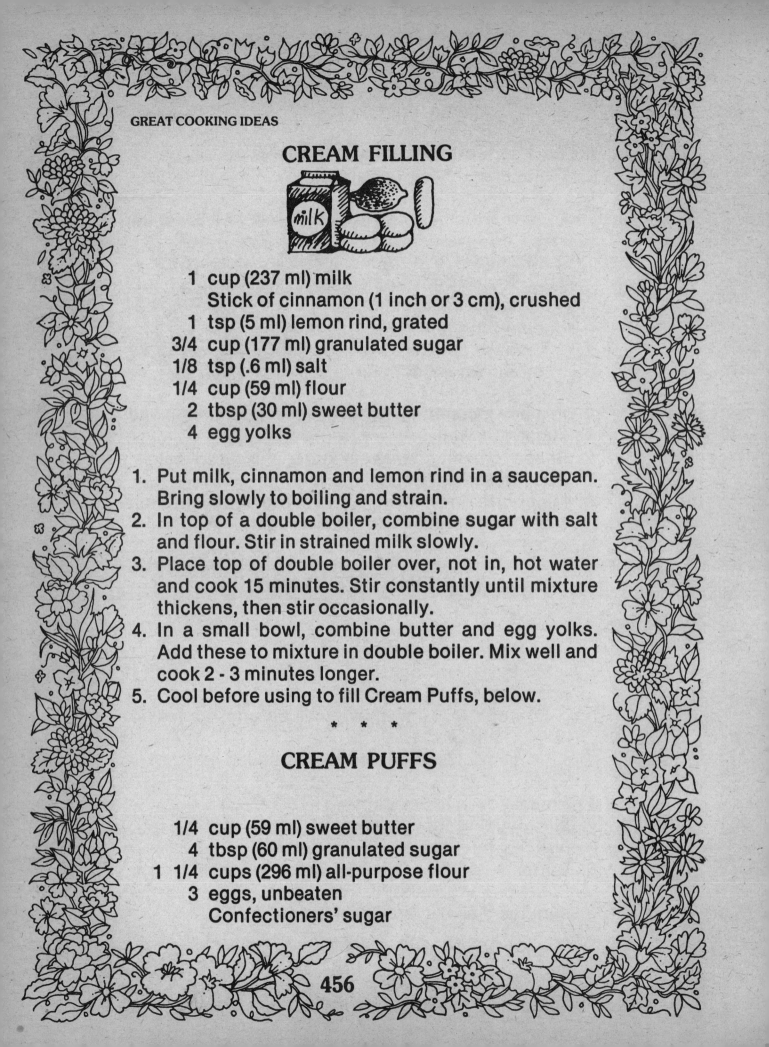

    1 cup (237 ml) milk
       Stick of cinnamon (1 inch or 3 cm), crushed
    1 tsp (5 ml) lemon rind, grated
  3/4 cup (177 ml) granulated sugar
  1/8 tsp (.6 ml) salt
  1/4 cup (59 ml) flour
    2 tbsp (30 ml) sweet butter
    4 egg yolks

1. Put milk, cinnamon and lemon rind in a saucepan. Bring slowly to boiling and strain.
2. In top of a double boiler, combine sugar with salt and flour. Stir in strained milk slowly.
3. Place top of double boiler over, not in, hot water and cook 15 minutes. Stir constantly until mixture thickens, then stir occasionally.
4. In a small bowl, combine butter and egg yolks. Add these to mixture in double boiler. Mix well and cook 2 - 3 minutes longer.
5. Cool before using to fill Cream Puffs, below.

* * *

CREAM PUFFS

  1/4 cup (59 ml) sweet butter
    4 tbsp (60 ml) granulated sugar
1 1/4 cups (296 ml) all-purpose flour
    3 eggs, unbeaten
       Confectioners' sugar

1. Put 1 cup (237 ml) of water, the butter and sugar in a saucepan. Bring to boiling. Stir flour in briskly until a smooth paste forms.
2. Remove from heat and stir a little more until dough forms a ball and does not stick to pan. Let stand 2 or 3 minutes.
3. Using a wooden spoon, stir in eggs one at a time. Let dough stand 30 minutes.
4. Preheat oven to 375 degrees F (190 C).
5. Stir dough a little and drop by tablespoons on buttered baking sheets, about 2 inches (5 cm) apart. Bake 15 - 20 minutes.
6. Open one side of each cream puff by inserting the nozzle of a pastry filler or knife carefully to make a small hole. Fill puffs with Cream Filling, above, and brush the outsides lightly with Confectioners' sugar.

NOTES

DELIGHTFUL TRIFLE

Makes 8 - 10 servings.

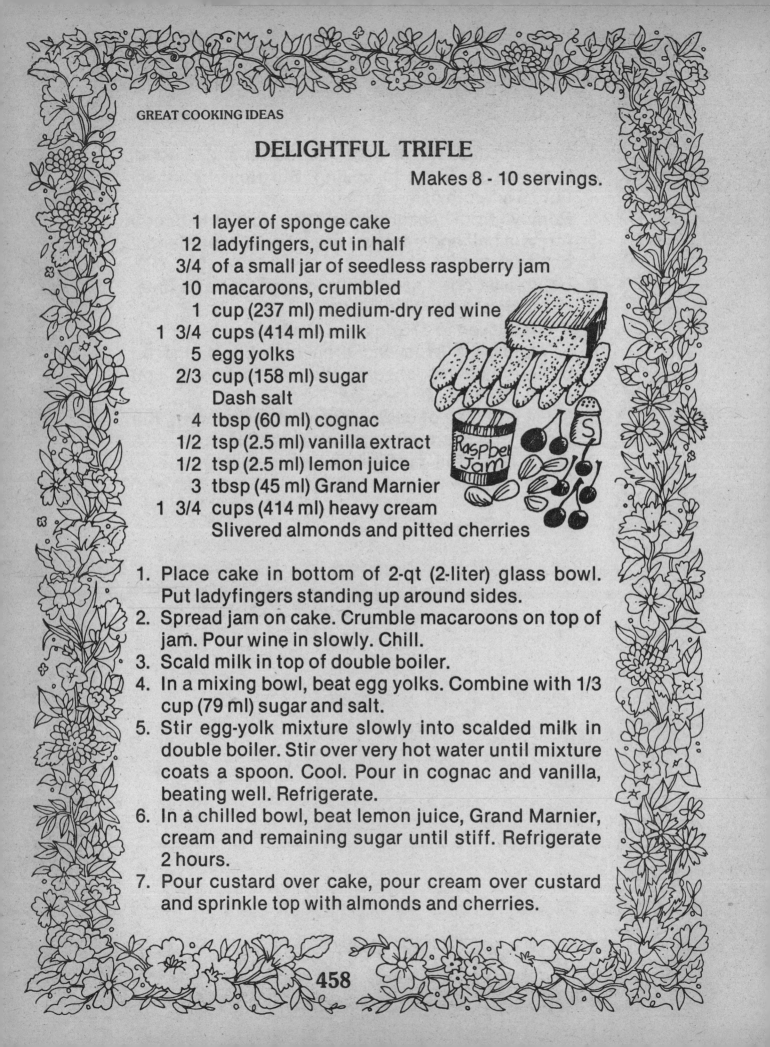

1	layer of sponge cake
12	ladyfingers, cut in half
3/4	of a small jar of seedless raspberry jam
10	macaroons, crumbled
1	cup (237 ml) medium-dry red wine
1 3/4	cups (414 ml) milk
5	egg yolks
2/3	cup (158 ml) sugar
	Dash salt
4	tbsp (60 ml) cognac
1/2	tsp (2.5 ml) vanilla extract
1/2	tsp (2.5 ml) lemon juice
3	tbsp (45 ml) Grand Marnier
1 3/4	cups (414 ml) heavy cream
	Slivered almonds and pitted cherries

1. Place cake in bottom of 2-qt (2-liter) glass bowl. Put ladyfingers standing up around sides.
2. Spread jam on cake. Crumble macaroons on top of jam. Pour wine in slowly. Chill.
3. Scald milk in top of double boiler.
4. In a mixing bowl, beat egg yolks. Combine with 1/3 cup (79 ml) sugar and salt.
5. Stir egg-yolk mixture slowly into scalded milk in double boiler. Stir over very hot water until mixture coats a spoon. Cool. Pour in cognac and vanilla, beating well. Refrigerate.
6. In a chilled bowl, beat lemon juice, Grand Marnier, cream and remaining sugar until stiff. Refrigerate 2 hours.
7. Pour custard over cake, pour cream over custard and sprinkle top with almonds and cherries.

NUTTY CARROT CAKE

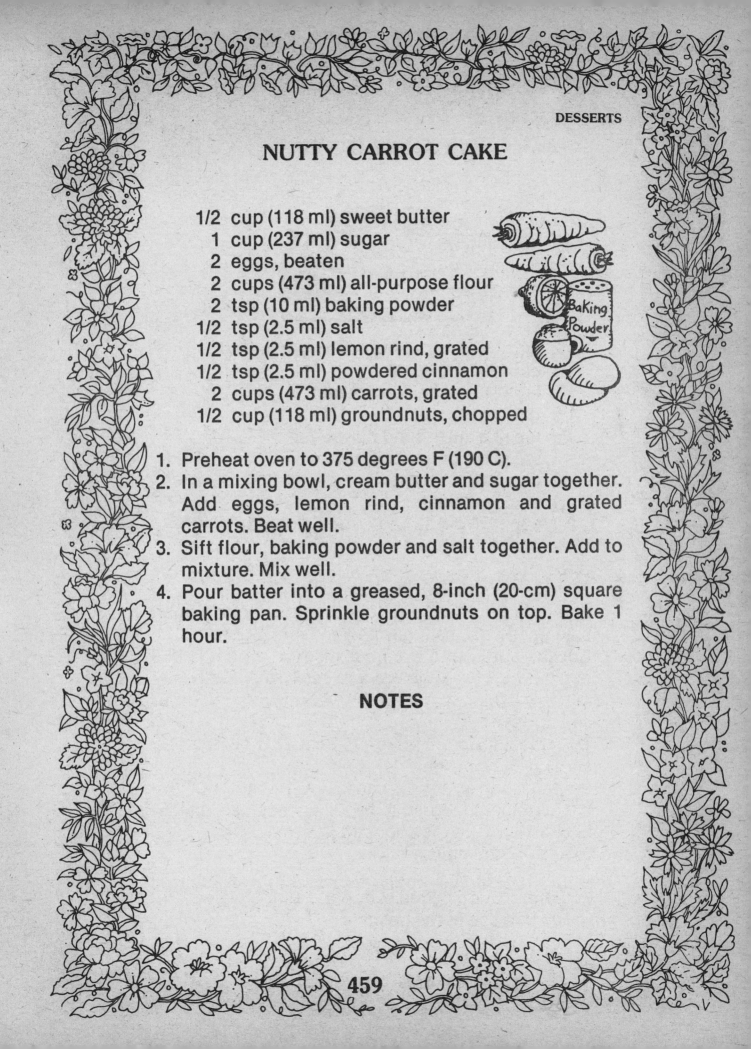

1/2 cup (118 ml) sweet butter
1 cup (237 ml) sugar
2 eggs, beaten
2 cups (473 ml) all-purpose flour
2 tsp (10 ml) baking powder
1/2 tsp (2.5 ml) salt
1/2 tsp (2.5 ml) lemon rind, grated
1/2 tsp (2.5 ml) powdered cinnamon
2 cups (473 ml) carrots, grated
1/2 cup (118 ml) groundnuts, chopped

1. Preheat oven to 375 degrees F (190 C).
2. In a mixing bowl, cream butter and sugar together. Add eggs, lemon rind, cinnamon and grated carrots. Beat well.
3. Sift flour, baking powder and salt together. Add to mixture. Mix well.
4. Pour batter into a greased, 8-inch (20-cm) square baking pan. Sprinkle groundnuts on top. Bake 1 hour.

NOTES

PECAN DELIGHT

Makes 9 servings.

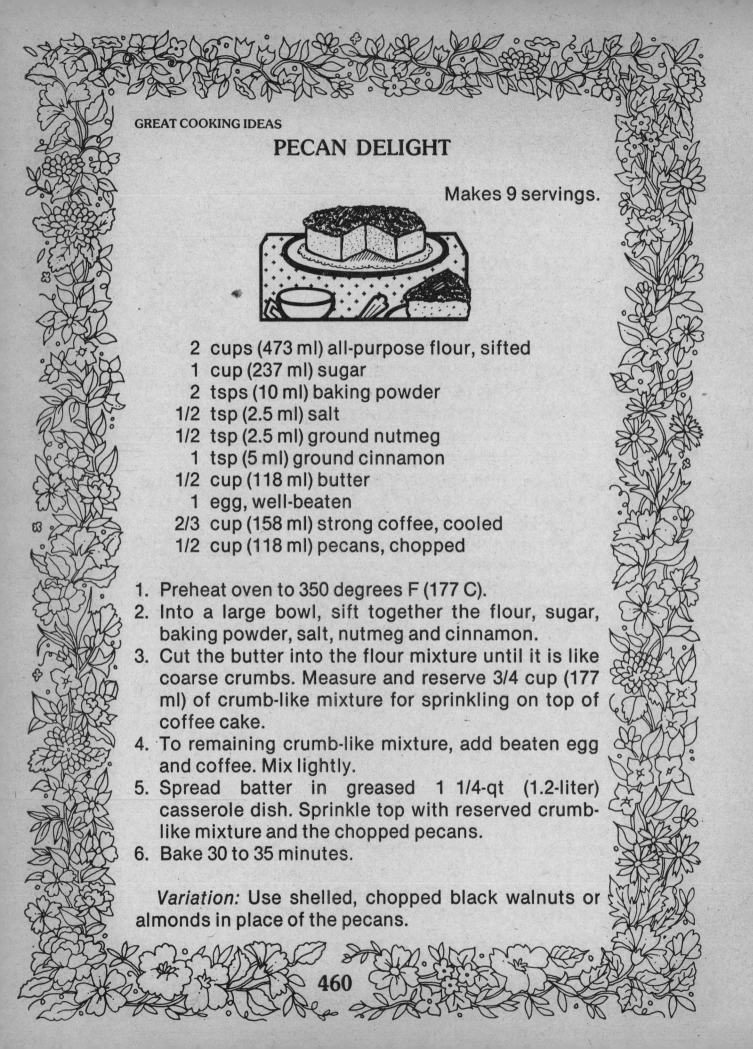

2	cups (473 ml) all-purpose flour, sifted
1	cup (237 ml) sugar
2	tsps (10 ml) baking powder
1/2	tsp (2.5 ml) salt
1/2	tsp (2.5 ml) ground nutmeg
1	tsp (5 ml) ground cinnamon
1/2	cup (118 ml) butter
1	egg, well-beaten
2/3	cup (158 ml) strong coffee, cooled
1/2	cup (118 ml) pecans, chopped

1. Preheat oven to 350 degrees F (177 C).
2. Into a large bowl, sift together the flour, sugar, baking powder, salt, nutmeg and cinnamon.
3. Cut the butter into the flour mixture until it is like coarse crumbs. Measure and reserve 3/4 cup (177 ml) of crumb-like mixture for sprinkling on top of coffee cake.
4. To remaining crumb-like mixture, add beaten egg and coffee. Mix lightly.
5. Spread batter in greased 1 1/4-qt (1.2-liter) casserole dish. Sprinkle top with reserved crumb-like mixture and the chopped pecans.
6. Bake 30 to 35 minutes.

Variation: Use shelled, chopped black walnuts or almonds in place of the pecans.

ROYAL STRAWBERRY SHORTCAKE

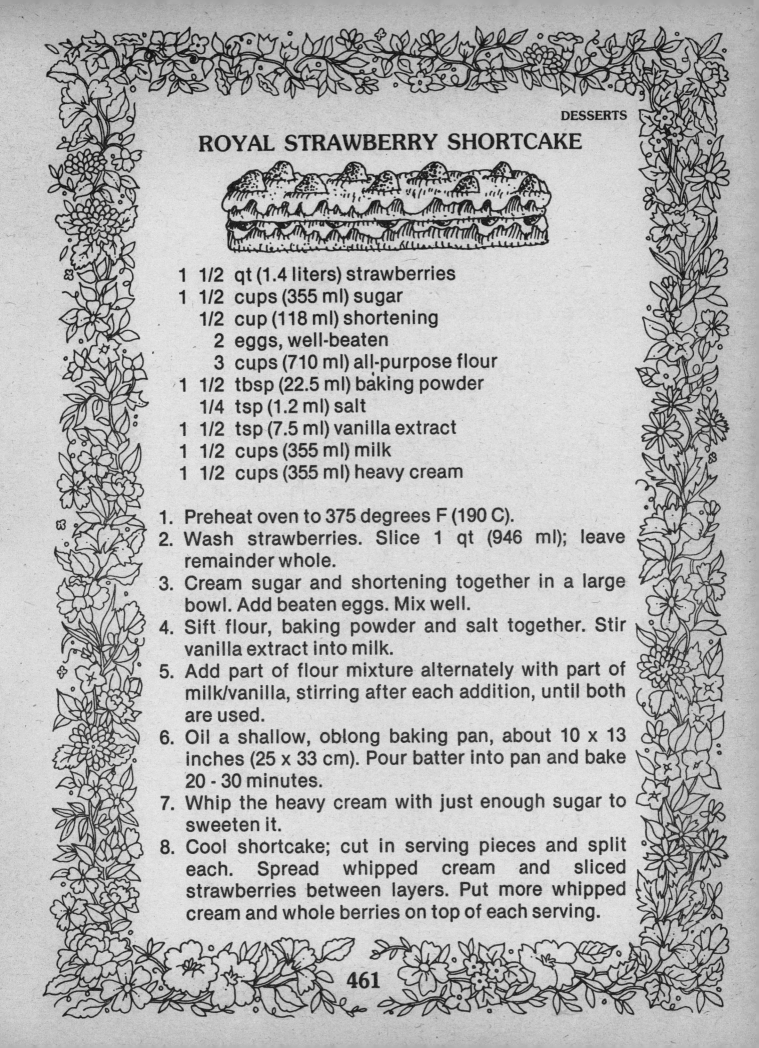

1 1/2 qt (1.4 liters) strawberries
1 1/2 cups (355 ml) sugar
   1/2 cup (118 ml) shortening
    2 eggs, well-beaten
    3 cups (710 ml) all-purpose flour
1 1/2 tbsp (22.5 ml) baking powder
   1/4 tsp (1.2 ml) salt
1 1/2 tsp (7.5 ml) vanilla extract
1 1/2 cups (355 ml) milk
1 1/2 cups (355 ml) heavy cream

1. Preheat oven to 375 degrees F (190 C).
2. Wash strawberries. Slice 1 qt (946 ml); leave remainder whole.
3. Cream sugar and shortening together in a large bowl. Add beaten eggs. Mix well.
4. Sift flour, baking powder and salt together. Stir vanilla extract into milk.
5. Add part of flour mixture alternately with part of milk/vanilla, stirring after each addition, until both are used.
6. Oil a shallow, oblong baking pan, about 10 x 13 inches (25 x 33 cm). Pour batter into pan and bake 20 - 30 minutes.
7. Whip the heavy cream with just enough sugar to sweeten it.
8. Cool shortcake; cut in serving pieces and split each. Spread whipped cream and sliced strawberries between layers. Put more whipped cream and whole berries on top of each serving.

COCONUT CREAM PIE

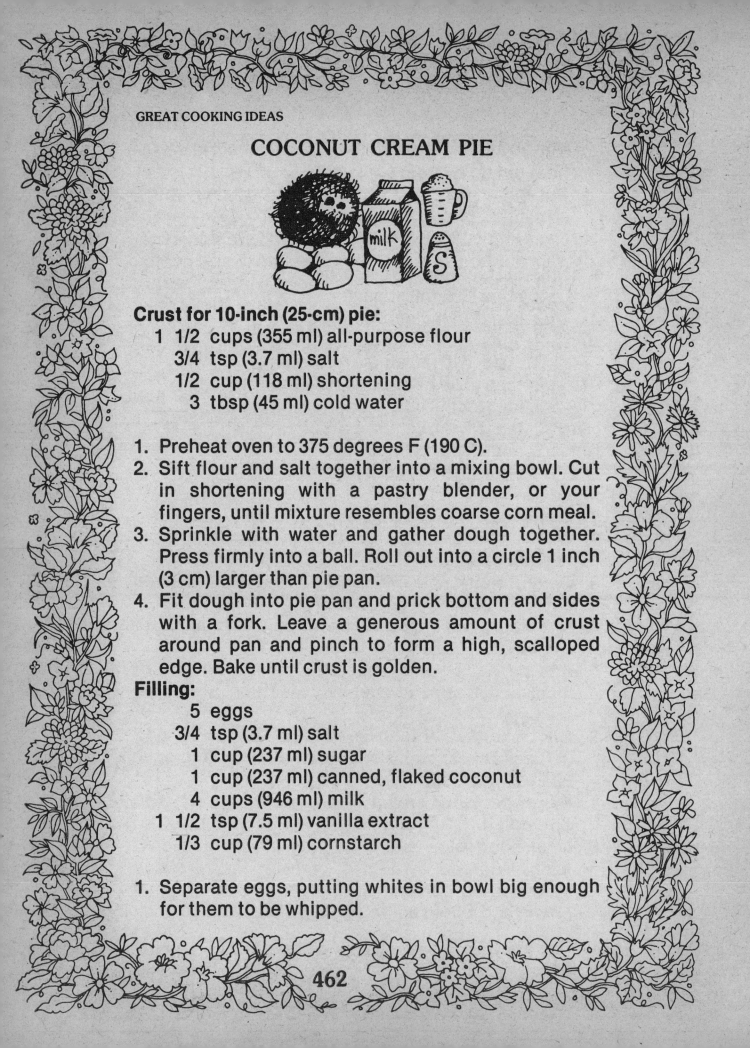

Crust for 10-inch (25-cm) pie:
   1 1/2 cups (355 ml) all-purpose flour
      3/4 tsp (3.7 ml) salt
      1/2 cup (118 ml) shortening
         3 tbsp (45 ml) cold water

1. Preheat oven to 375 degrees F (190 C).
2. Sift flour and salt together into a mixing bowl. Cut in shortening with a pastry blender, or your fingers, until mixture resembles coarse corn meal.
3. Sprinkle with water and gather dough together. Press firmly into a ball. Roll out into a circle 1 inch (3 cm) larger than pie pan.
4. Fit dough into pie pan and prick bottom and sides with a fork. Leave a generous amount of crust around pan and pinch to form a high, scalloped edge. Bake until crust is golden.

Filling:
         5 eggs
      3/4 tsp (3.7 ml) salt
         1 cup (237 ml) sugar
         1 cup (237 ml) canned, flaked coconut
         4 cups (946 ml) milk
   1 1/2 tsp (7.5 ml) vanilla extract
      1/3 cup (79 ml) cornstarch

1. Separate eggs, putting whites in bowl big enough for them to be whipped.

2. Put 3 cups (710 ml) milk in a saucepan over low heat but do *not* allow it to boil.
3. Put sugar, salt and cornstarch in a bowl. Stir in remaining milk, 1/4 at a time.
4. Beat egg yolks with fork and stir them into sugar-milk mixture. Pour this mixture slowly into heating milk. Raise flame to medium and cook, stirring constantly, until thick.
5. Add vanilla and coconut and mix well.
6. Whip egg whites with 2 tbsp (30 ml) sugar until stiff but not dry.
7. Pour filling into baked pie shell. Spread meringue over filling. Bake until meringue turns golden.

NOTES

CREAMY CHOCOLATE PIE

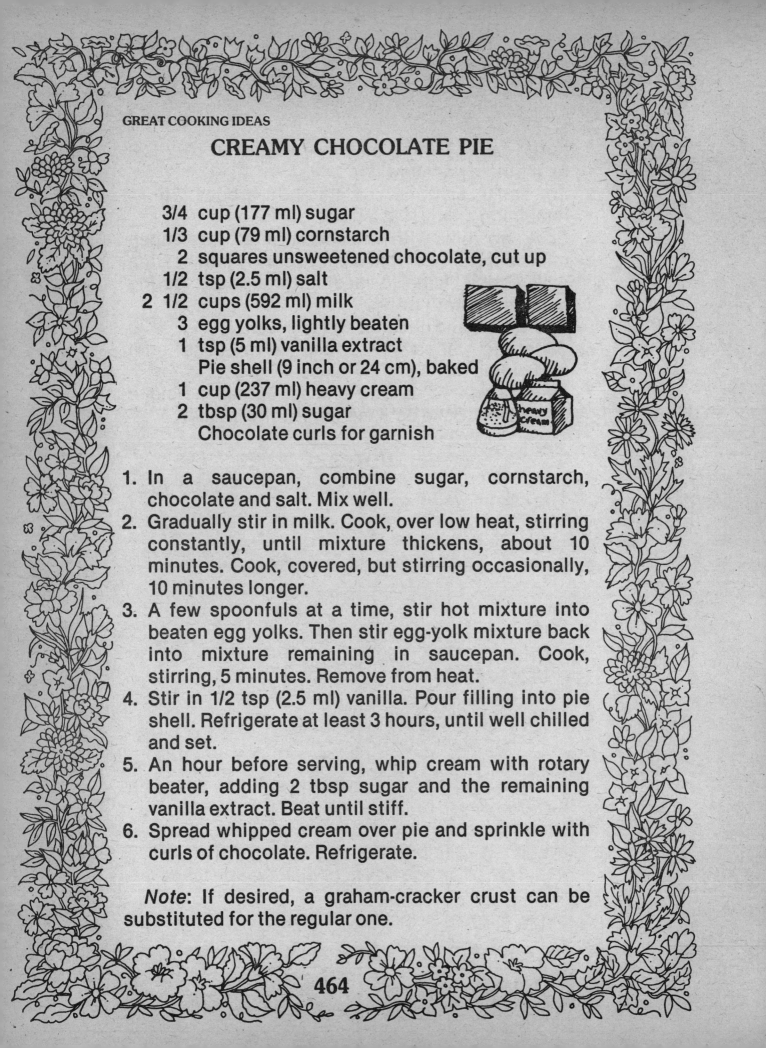

3/4 cup (177 ml) sugar
1/3 cup (79 ml) cornstarch
  2 squares unsweetened chocolate, cut up
1/2 tsp (2.5 ml) salt
2 1/2 cups (592 ml) milk
  3 egg yolks, lightly beaten
  1 tsp (5 ml) vanilla extract
    Pie shell (9 inch or 24 cm), baked
  1 cup (237 ml) heavy cream
  2 tbsp (30 ml) sugar
    Chocolate curls for garnish

1. In a saucepan, combine sugar, cornstarch, chocolate and salt. Mix well.
2. Gradually stir in milk. Cook, over low heat, stirring constantly, until mixture thickens, about 10 minutes. Cook, covered, but stirring occasionally, 10 minutes longer.
3. A few spoonfuls at a time, stir hot mixture into beaten egg yolks. Then stir egg-yolk mixture back into mixture remaining in saucepan. Cook, stirring, 5 minutes. Remove from heat.
4. Stir in 1/2 tsp (2.5 ml) vanilla. Pour filling into pie shell. Refrigerate at least 3 hours, until well chilled and set.
5. An hour before serving, whip cream with rotary beater, adding 2 tbsp sugar and the remaining vanilla extract. Beat until stiff.
6. Spread whipped cream over pie and sprinkle with curls of chocolate. Refrigerate.

Note: If desired, a graham-cracker crust can be substituted for the regular one.

PEACH COBBLER

Filling:
- 3 lb (1.4 kg) fresh peaches, peeled and sliced
- 1/2 cup (118 ml) sugar
- 2 tbsp (30 ml) all-purpose flour
- 1 tbsp (15 ml) lemon juice
- 3/4 tsp (3.7 ml) vanilla extract
- 1/2 tsp (2.5 ml) powdered cinnamon
- 1/4 tsp (1.2 ml) salt
- 2 tbsp (30 ml) sweet butter

1. In a mixing bowl, combine peaches, sugar, flour, lemon juice, vanilla extract, cinnamon, salt and 1/4 cup (59 ml) water. Mix well.
2. Turn filling into an 8 x 8 x 2-inch (20 x 20 x 5-cm) baking pan. Dot with butter.
3. Preheat oven to 375 degrees F (190 C).

Batter:
- 1/2 cup (118 ml) all-purpose flour
- 1/2 cup (118 ml) sugar
- 1/2 tsp (2.5 ml) baking powder
- 1/4 tsp (1.2 ml) salt
- 2 tbsp (30 ml) margarine, softened
- 1 egg, lightly beaten

1. In a bowl, combine all batter ingredients. Beat with wooden spoon until smooth.
2. Drop batter in 9 portions over filling, spacing evenly. (It will spread during baking.) Bake 35 - 40 minutes, or until crust is golden and peaches are tender.
3. Serve warm with vanilla ice cream.

CHERRY-MARSHMALLOW PUDDING

Makes 6 servings.

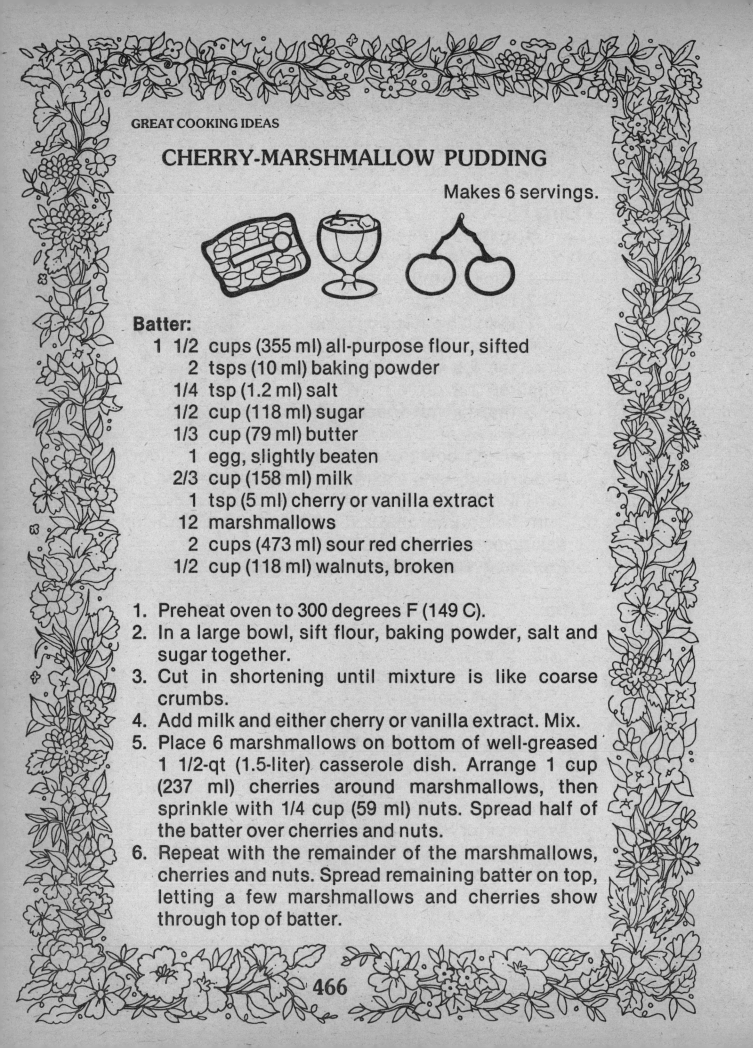

Batter:
- 1 1/2 cups (355 ml) all-purpose flour, sifted
- 2 tsps (10 ml) baking powder
- 1/4 tsp (1.2 ml) salt
- 1/2 cup (118 ml) sugar
- 1/3 cup (79 ml) butter
- 1 egg, slightly beaten
- 2/3 cup (158 ml) milk
- 1 tsp (5 ml) cherry or vanilla extract
- 12 marshmallows
- 2 cups (473 ml) sour red cherries
- 1/2 cup (118 ml) walnuts, broken

1. Preheat oven to 300 degrees F (149 C).
2. In a large bowl, sift flour, baking powder, salt and sugar together.
3. Cut in shortening until mixture is like coarse crumbs.
4. Add milk and either cherry or vanilla extract. Mix.
5. Place 6 marshmallows on bottom of well-greased 1 1/2-qt (1.5-liter) casserole dish. Arrange 1 cup (237 ml) cherries around marshmallows, then sprinkle with 1/4 cup (59 ml) nuts. Spread half of the batter over cherries and nuts.
6. Repeat with the remainder of the marshmallows, cherries and nuts. Spread remaining batter on top, letting a few marshmallows and cherries show through top of batter.

7. Bake about 1 hour and 20 minutes.
8. Serve with Cherry Sauce.

Cherry Sauce:

    1/4 cup (59 ml) sugar
      1 tbsp (15 ml) cornstarch
      1 cup (237 ml) cherry juice
    1/2 cup (118 ml) water
      2 marshmallows, cut into small pieces

1. In a small saucepan, mix the sugar and cornstarch together.
2. Add cherry juice and water gradually.
3. Cook over low heat, stirring constantly, until sauce is smooth and slightly thickened.
4. Add pieces of marshmallow just before serving.

NOTES

CHOCOLATE BREAD PUDDING

Makes 6 servings.

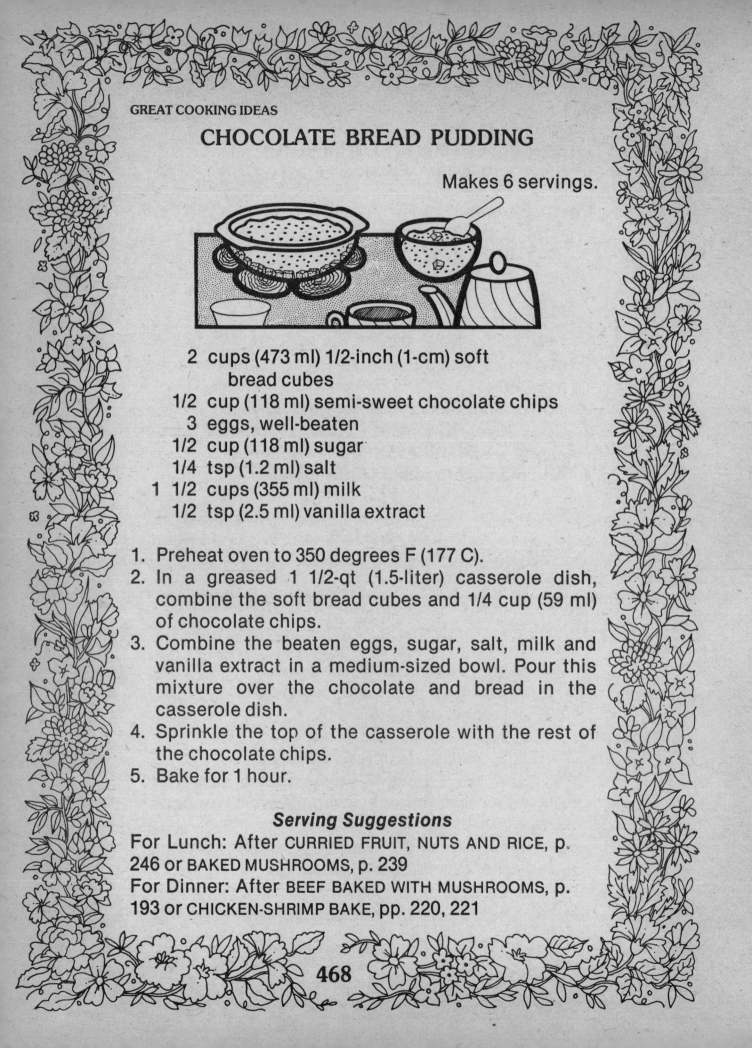

2 cups (473 ml) 1/2-inch (1-cm) soft
  bread cubes
1/2 cup (118 ml) semi-sweet chocolate chips
3 eggs, well-beaten
1/2 cup (118 ml) sugar
1/4 tsp (1.2 ml) salt
1 1/2 cups (355 ml) milk
1/2 tsp (2.5 ml) vanilla extract

1. Preheat oven to 350 degrees F (177 C).
2. In a greased 1 1/2-qt (1.5-liter) casserole dish, combine the soft bread cubes and 1/4 cup (59 ml) of chocolate chips.
3. Combine the beaten eggs, sugar, salt, milk and vanilla extract in a medium-sized bowl. Pour this mixture over the chocolate and bread in the casserole dish.
4. Sprinkle the top of the casserole with the rest of the chocolate chips.
5. Bake for 1 hour.

Serving Suggestions

For Lunch: After CURRIED FRUIT, NUTS AND RICE, p. 246 or BAKED MUSHROOMS, p. 239
For Dinner: After BEEF BAKED WITH MUSHROOMS, p. 193 or CHICKEN-SHRIMP BAKE, pp. 220, 221

CHOCOLATE-PECAN UPSIDE DOWN PUDDING

Makes 10 to 12 servings.

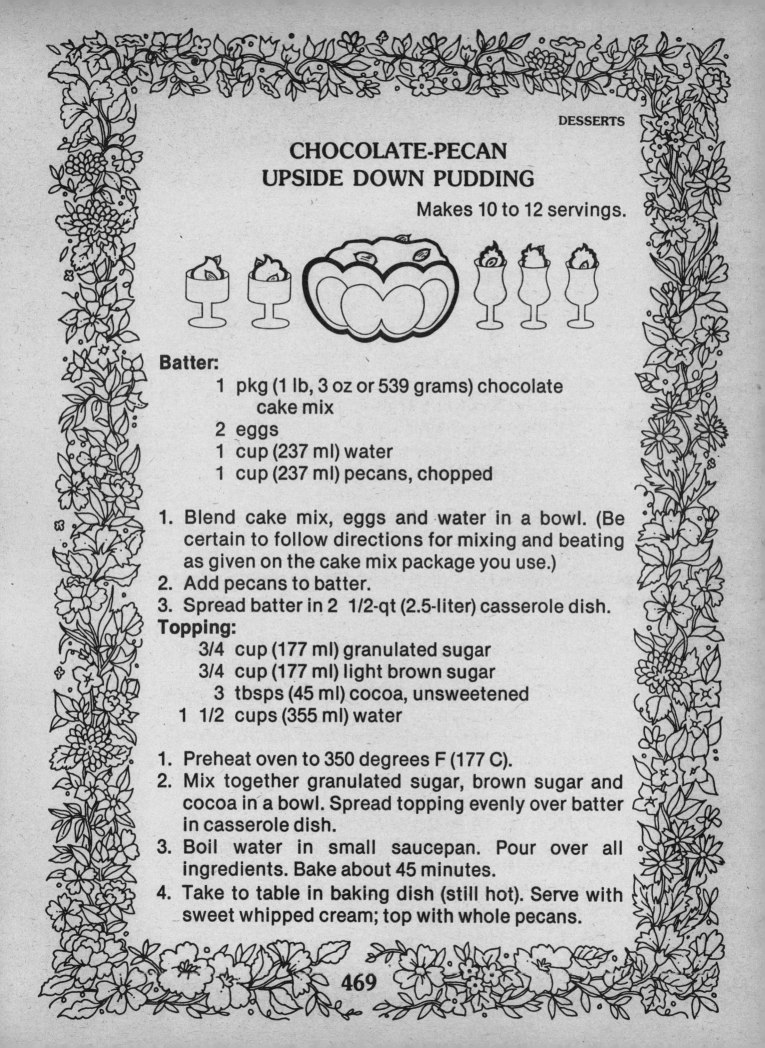

Batter:

- 1 pkg (1 lb, 3 oz or 539 grams) chocolate cake mix
- 2 eggs
- 1 cup (237 ml) water
- 1 cup (237 ml) pecans, chopped

1. Blend cake mix, eggs and water in a bowl. (Be certain to follow directions for mixing and beating as given on the cake mix package you use.)
2. Add pecans to batter.
3. Spread batter in 2 1/2-qt (2.5-liter) casserole dish.

Topping:

- 3/4 cup (177 ml) granulated sugar
- 3/4 cup (177 ml) light brown sugar
- 3 tbsps (45 ml) cocoa, unsweetened
- 1 1/2 cups (355 ml) water

1. Preheat oven to 350 degrees F (177 C).
2. Mix together granulated sugar, brown sugar and cocoa in a bowl. Spread topping evenly over batter in casserole dish.
3. Boil water in small saucepan. Pour over all ingredients. Bake about 45 minutes.
4. Take to table in baking dish (still hot). Serve with sweet whipped cream; top with whole pecans.

ORANGE MINCEMEAT PUDDING

Makes 6 servings.

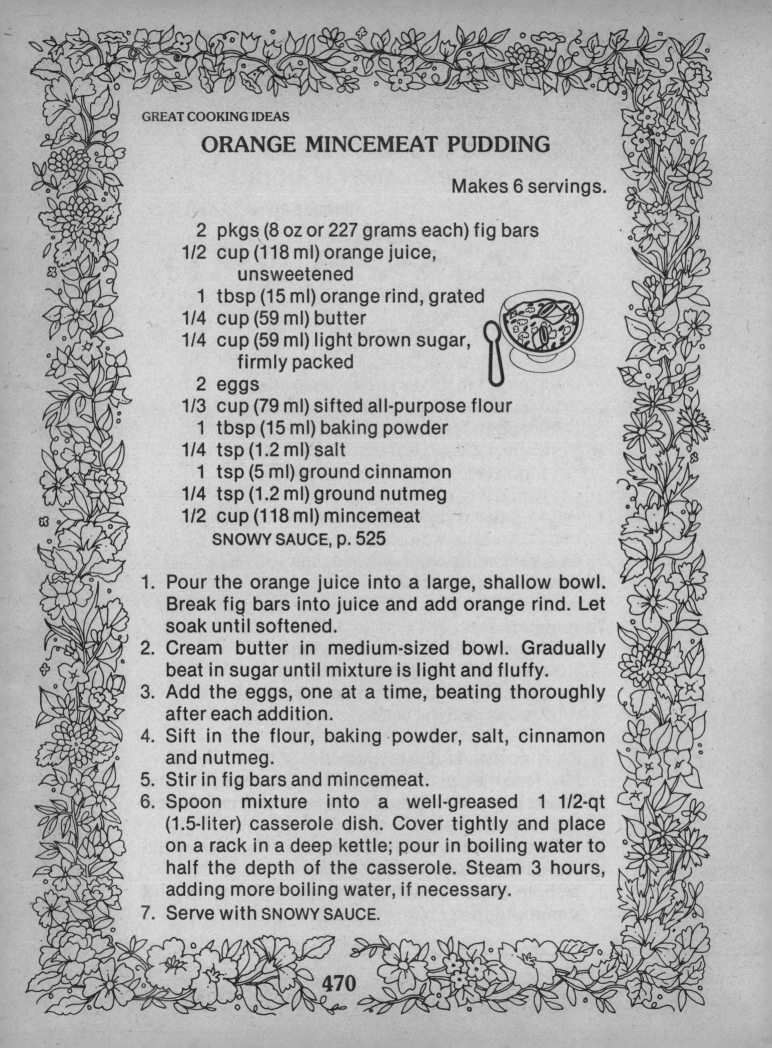

- 2 pkgs (8 oz or 227 grams each) fig bars
- 1/2 cup (118 ml) orange juice, unsweetened
- 1 tbsp (15 ml) orange rind, grated
- 1/4 cup (59 ml) butter
- 1/4 cup (59 ml) light brown sugar, firmly packed
- 2 eggs
- 1/3 cup (79 ml) sifted all-purpose flour
- 1 tbsp (15 ml) baking powder
- 1/4 tsp (1.2 ml) salt
- 1 tsp (5 ml) ground cinnamon
- 1/4 tsp (1.2 ml) ground nutmeg
- 1/2 cup (118 ml) mincemeat
- SNOWY SAUCE, p. 525

1. Pour the orange juice into a large, shallow bowl. Break fig bars into juice and add orange rind. Let soak until softened.
2. Cream butter in medium-sized bowl. Gradually beat in sugar until mixture is light and fluffy.
3. Add the eggs, one at a time, beating thoroughly after each addition.
4. Sift in the flour, baking powder, salt, cinnamon and nutmeg.
5. Stir in fig bars and mincemeat.
6. Spoon mixture into a well-greased 1 1/2-qt (1.5-liter) casserole dish. Cover tightly and place on a rack in a deep kettle; pour in boiling water to half the depth of the casserole. Steam 3 hours, adding more boiling water, if necessary.
7. Serve with SNOWY SAUCE.

PUMPKIN PUDDING

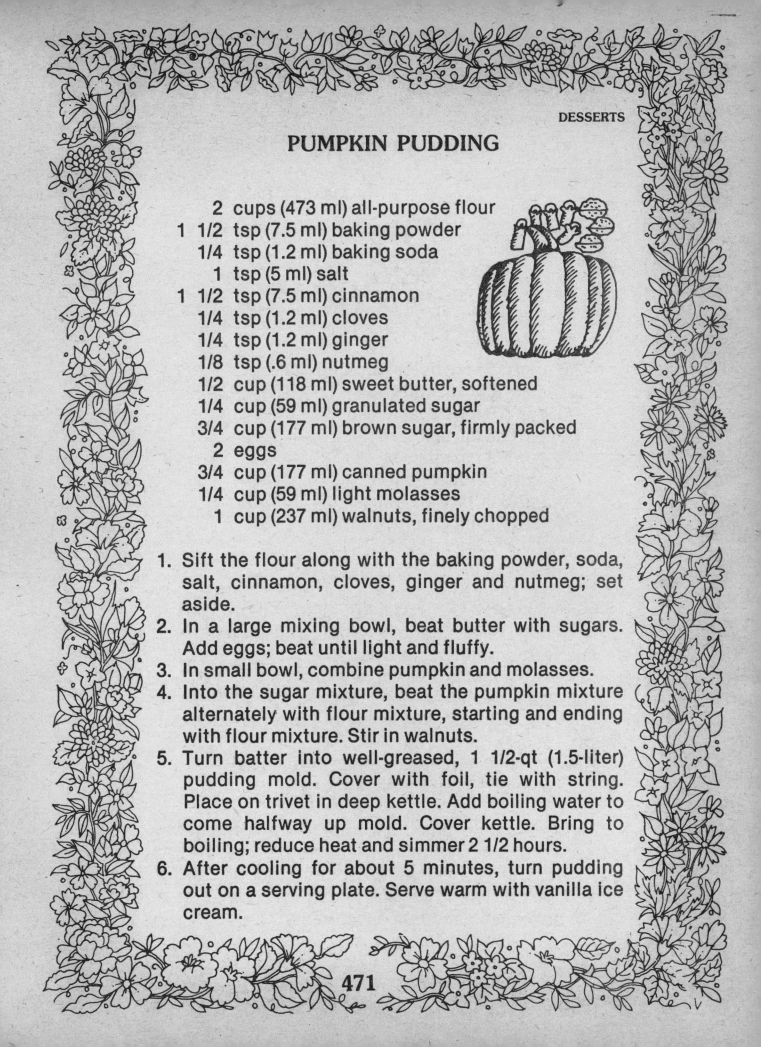

2 cups (473 ml) all-purpose flour
1 1/2 tsp (7.5 ml) baking powder
1/4 tsp (1.2 ml) baking soda
1 tsp (5 ml) salt
1 1/2 tsp (7.5 ml) cinnamon
1/4 tsp (1.2 ml) cloves
1/4 tsp (1.2 ml) ginger
1/8 tsp (.6 ml) nutmeg
1/2 cup (118 ml) sweet butter, softened
1/4 cup (59 ml) granulated sugar
3/4 cup (177 ml) brown sugar, firmly packed
2 eggs
3/4 cup (177 ml) canned pumpkin
1/4 cup (59 ml) light molasses
1 cup (237 ml) walnuts, finely chopped

1. Sift the flour along with the baking powder, soda, salt, cinnamon, cloves, ginger and nutmeg; set aside.
2. In a large mixing bowl, beat butter with sugars. Add eggs; beat until light and fluffy.
3. In small bowl, combine pumpkin and molasses.
4. Into the sugar mixture, beat the pumpkin mixture alternately with flour mixture, starting and ending with flour mixture. Stir in walnuts.
5. Turn batter into well-greased, 1 1/2-qt (1.5-liter) pudding mold. Cover with foil, tie with string. Place on trivet in deep kettle. Add boiling water to come halfway up mold. Cover kettle. Bring to boiling; reduce heat and simmer 2 1/2 hours.
6. After cooling for about 5 minutes, turn pudding out on a serving plate. Serve warm with vanilla ice cream.

RICE PUDDING

Makes 6 to 8 servings.

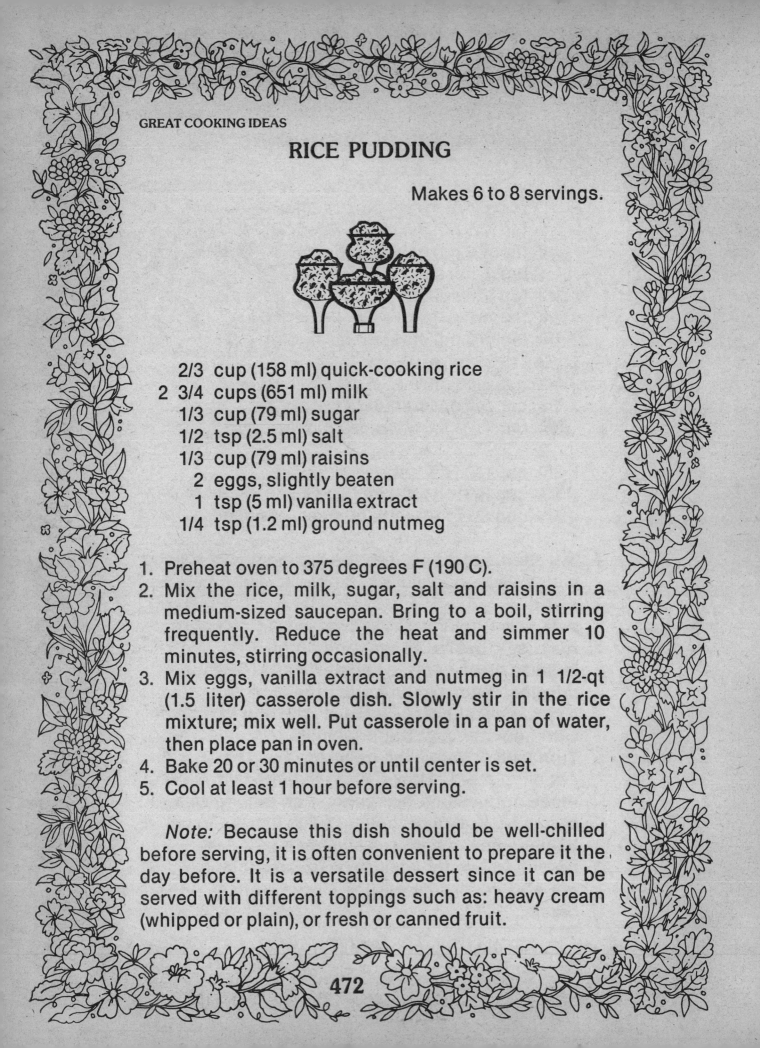

    2/3 cup (158 ml) quick-cooking rice
2 3/4 cups (651 ml) milk
    1/3 cup (79 ml) sugar
    1/2 tsp (2.5 ml) salt
    1/3 cup (79 ml) raisins
      2 eggs, slightly beaten
      1 tsp (5 ml) vanilla extract
    1/4 tsp (1.2 ml) ground nutmeg

1. Preheat oven to 375 degrees F (190 C).
2. Mix the rice, milk, sugar, salt and raisins in a medium-sized saucepan. Bring to a boil, stirring frequently. Reduce the heat and simmer 10 minutes, stirring occasionally.
3. Mix eggs, vanilla extract and nutmeg in 1 1/2-qt (1.5 liter) casserole dish. Slowly stir in the rice mixture; mix well. Put casserole in a pan of water, then place pan in oven.
4. Bake 20 or 30 minutes or until center is set.
5. Cool at least 1 hour before serving.

Note: Because this dish should be well-chilled before serving, it is often convenient to prepare it the day before. It is a versatile dessert since it can be served with different toppings such as: heavy cream (whipped or plain), or fresh or canned fruit.

ORANGE CUSTARD WITH MERINGUE

Makes 6 servings.

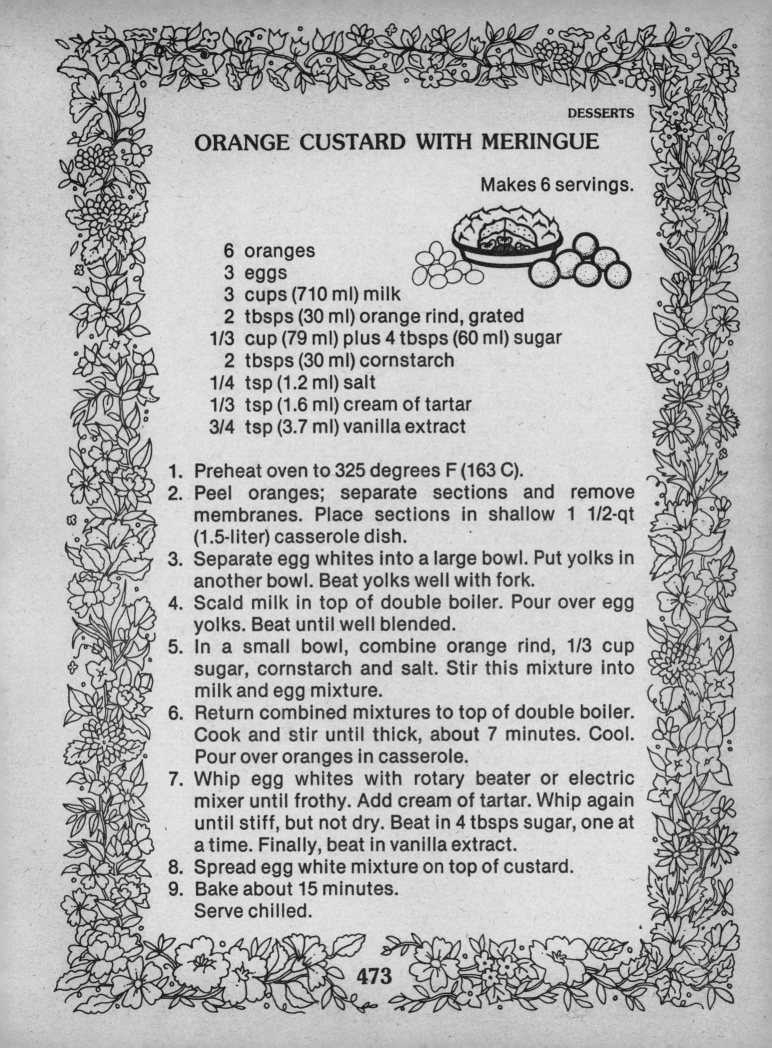

  6 oranges
  3 eggs
  3 cups (710 ml) milk
  2 tbsps (30 ml) orange rind, grated
1/3 cup (79 ml) plus 4 tbsps (60 ml) sugar
  2 tbsps (30 ml) cornstarch
1/4 tsp (1.2 ml) salt
1/3 tsp (1.6 ml) cream of tartar
3/4 tsp (3.7 ml) vanilla extract

1. Preheat oven to 325 degrees F (163 C).
2. Peel oranges; separate sections and remove membranes. Place sections in shallow 1 1/2-qt (1.5-liter) casserole dish.
3. Separate egg whites into a large bowl. Put yolks in another bowl. Beat yolks well with fork.
4. Scald milk in top of double boiler. Pour over egg yolks. Beat until well blended.
5. In a small bowl, combine orange rind, 1/3 cup sugar, cornstarch and salt. Stir this mixture into milk and egg mixture.
6. Return combined mixtures to top of double boiler. Cook and stir until thick, about 7 minutes. Cool. Pour over oranges in casserole.
7. Whip egg whites with rotary beater or electric mixer until frothy. Add cream of tartar. Whip again until stiff, but not dry. Beat in 4 tbsps sugar, one at a time. Finally, beat in vanilla extract.
8. Spread egg white mixture on top of custard.
9. Bake about 15 minutes.
Serve chilled.

CHOCOLATE MOUSSE

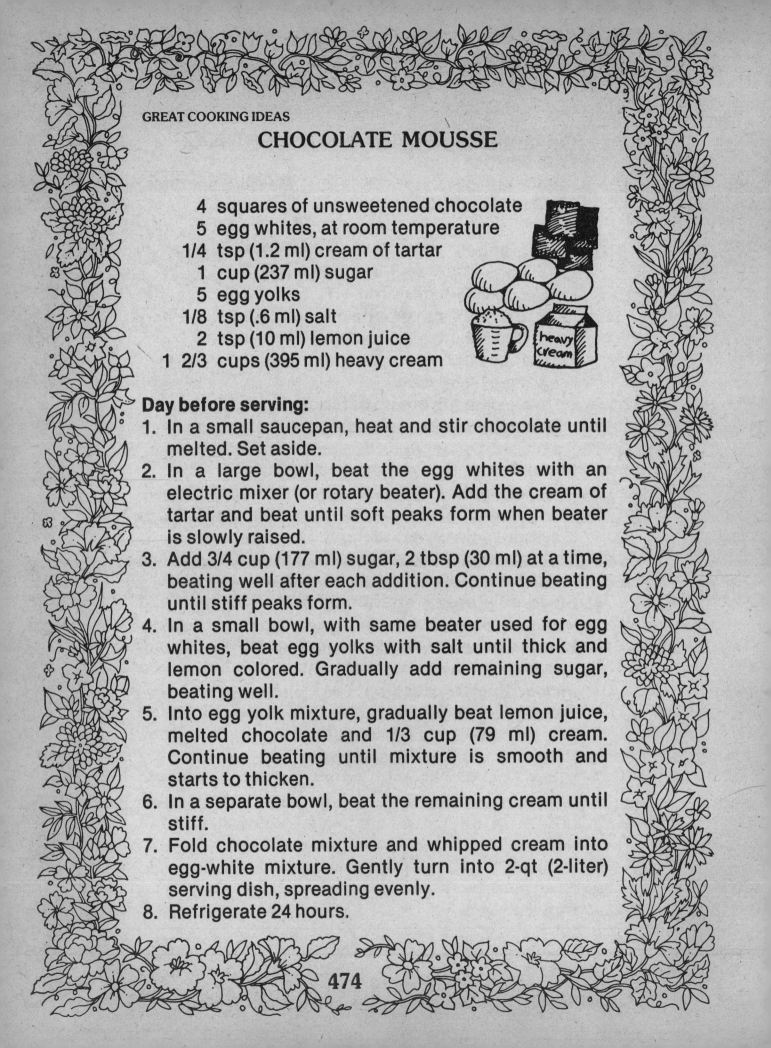

    4   squares of unsweetened chocolate
    5   egg whites, at room temperature
  1/4   tsp (1.2 ml) cream of tartar
    1   cup (237 ml) sugar
    5   egg yolks
  1/8   tsp (.6 ml) salt
    2   tsp (10 ml) lemon juice
  1 2/3 cups (395 ml) heavy cream

Day before serving:

1. In a small saucepan, heat and stir chocolate until melted. Set aside.
2. In a large bowl, beat the egg whites with an electric mixer (or rotary beater). Add the cream of tartar and beat until soft peaks form when beater is slowly raised.
3. Add 3/4 cup (177 ml) sugar, 2 tbsp (30 ml) at a time, beating well after each addition. Continue beating until stiff peaks form.
4. In a small bowl, with same beater used for egg whites, beat egg yolks with salt until thick and lemon colored. Gradually add remaining sugar, beating well.
5. Into egg yolk mixture, gradually beat lemon juice, melted chocolate and 1/3 cup (79 ml) cream. Continue beating until mixture is smooth and starts to thicken.
6. In a separate bowl, beat the remaining cream until stiff.
7. Fold chocolate mixture and whipped cream into egg-white mixture. Gently turn into 2-qt (2-liter) serving dish, spreading evenly.
8. Refrigerate 24 hours.

Day of serving:
9. Decorate top of Mousse with additional whipped cream and curls of semisweet chocolate.

* * *

VANILLA CUSTARD

Makes 8 to 10 servings.

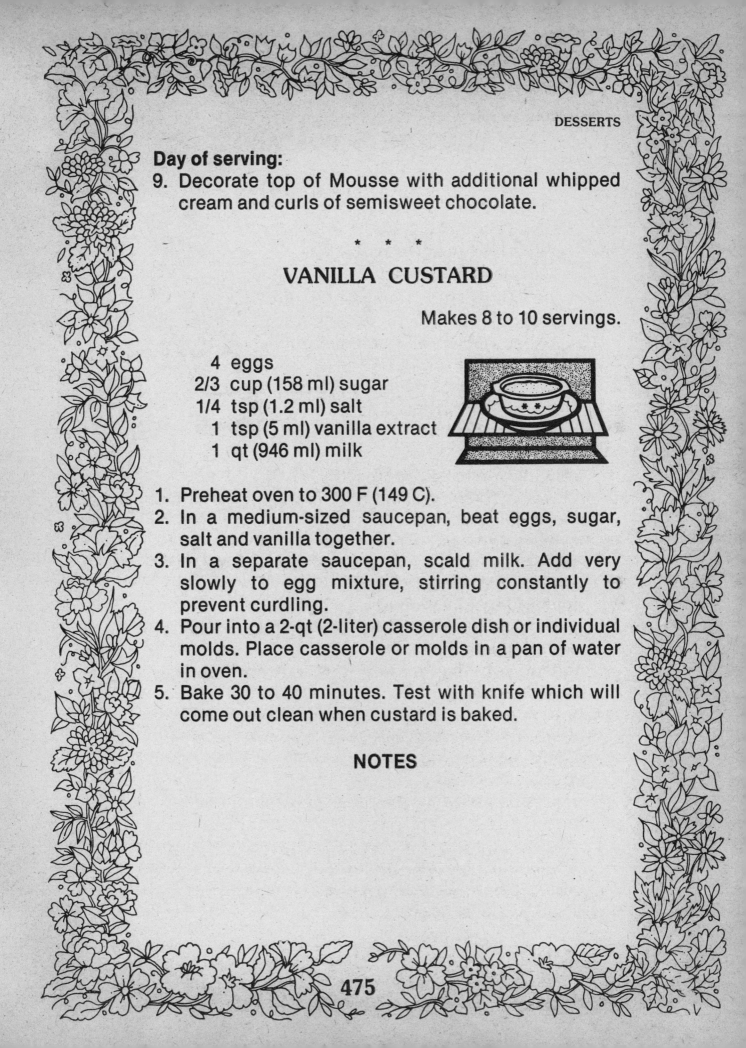

  4 eggs
2/3 cup (158 ml) sugar
1/4 tsp (1.2 ml) salt
  1 tsp (5 ml) vanilla extract
  1 qt (946 ml) milk

1. Preheat oven to 300 F (149 C).
2. In a medium-sized saucepan, beat eggs, sugar, salt and vanilla together.
3. In a separate saucepan, scald milk. Add very slowly to egg mixture, stirring constantly to prevent curdling.
4. Pour into a 2-qt (2-liter) casserole dish or individual molds. Place casserole or molds in a pan of water in oven.
5. Bake 30 to 40 minutes. Test with knife which will come out clean when custard is baked.

NOTES

SPONGY CITRUS CUSTARD

Makes 4 to 6 servings.

3/4 cup (177 ml) sugar
1 1/2 tbsps (22.5 ml) butter
1 tbsp (15 ml) orange rind, grated *or*
   2 tsps (10 ml) lemon rind, grated
3 eggs
3 tbsps (45 ml) all-purpose flour
1/3 cup (79 ml) orange juice *or*
   1/4 cup (59 ml) lemon juice
1 cup (237 ml) milk
Heavy cream

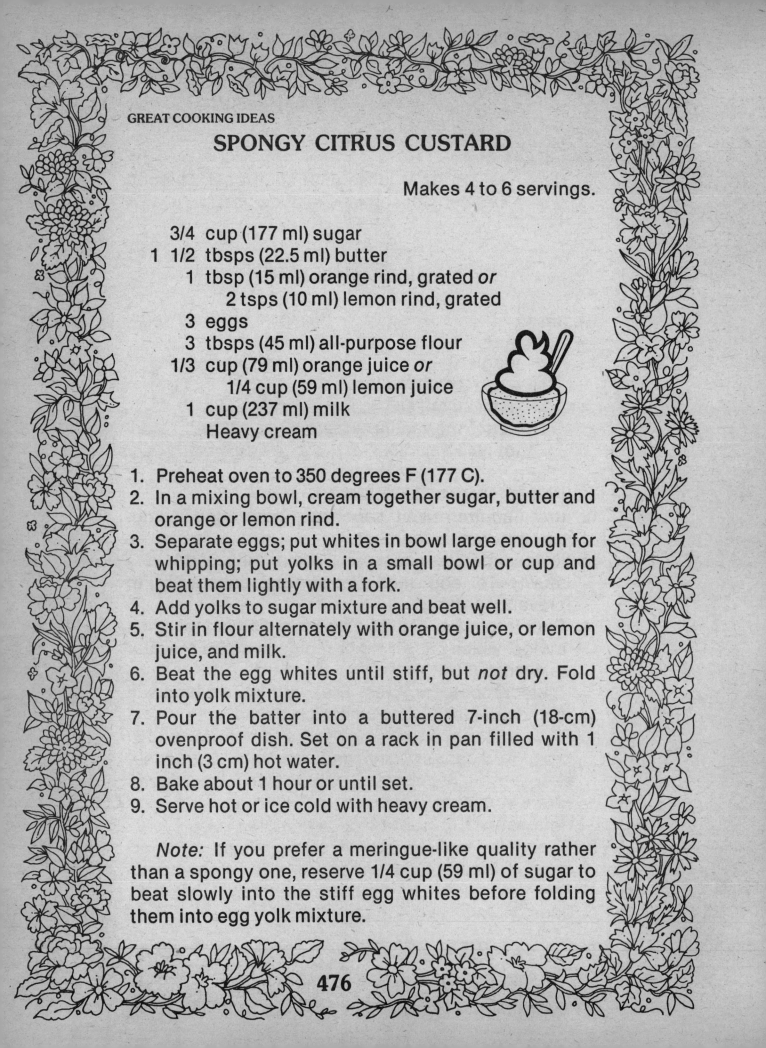

1. Preheat oven to 350 degrees F (177 C).
2. In a mixing bowl, cream together sugar, butter and orange or lemon rind.
3. Separate eggs; put whites in bowl large enough for whipping; put yolks in a small bowl or cup and beat them lightly with a fork.
4. Add yolks to sugar mixture and beat well.
5. Stir in flour alternately with orange juice, or lemon juice, and milk.
6. Beat the egg whites until stiff, but *not* dry. Fold into yolk mixture.
7. Pour the batter into a buttered 7-inch (18-cm) ovenproof dish. Set on a rack in pan filled with 1 inch (3 cm) hot water.
8. Bake about 1 hour or until set.
9. Serve hot or ice cold with heavy cream.

Note: If you prefer a meringue-like quality rather than a spongy one, reserve 1/4 cup (59 ml) of sugar to beat slowly into the stiff egg whites before folding them into egg yolk mixture.

FLAN

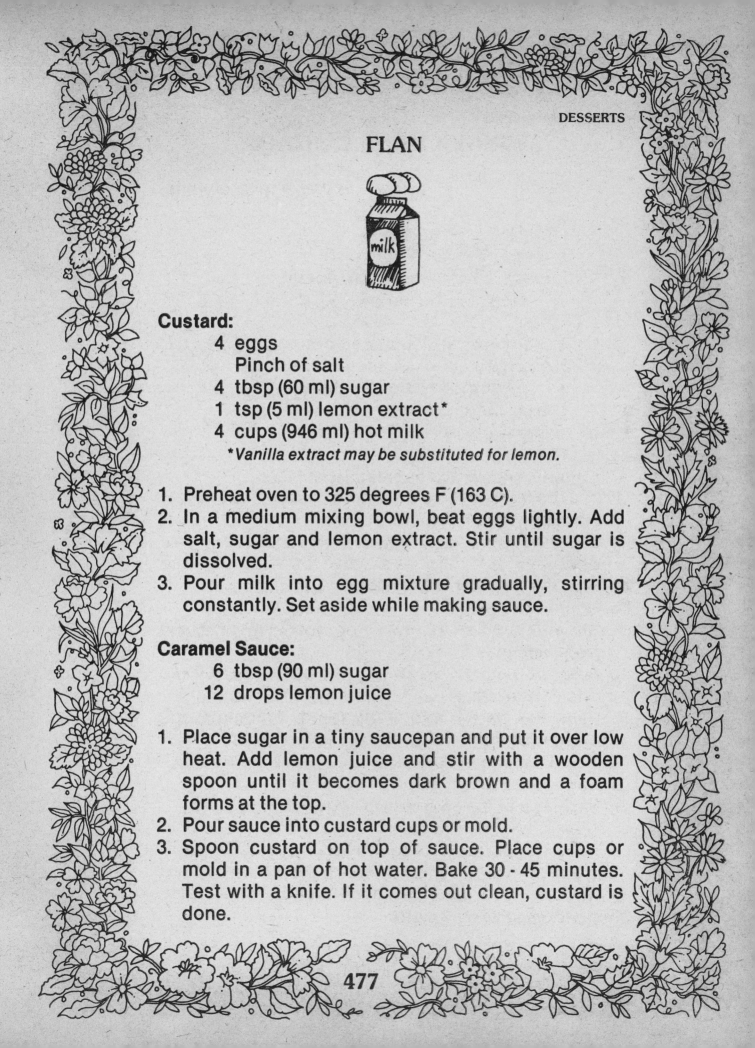

Custard:

    4 eggs
      Pinch of salt
    4 tbsp (60 ml) sugar
    1 tsp (5 ml) lemon extract*
    4 cups (946 ml) hot milk

   *Vanilla extract may be substituted for lemon.

1. Preheat oven to 325 degrees F (163 C).
2. In a medium mixing bowl, beat eggs lightly. Add salt, sugar and lemon extract. Stir until sugar is dissolved.
3. Pour milk into egg mixture gradually, stirring constantly. Set aside while making sauce.

Caramel Sauce:

    6 tbsp (90 ml) sugar
  12 drops lemon juice

1. Place sugar in a tiny saucepan and put it over low heat. Add lemon juice and stir with a wooden spoon until it becomes dark brown and a foam forms at the top.
2. Pour sauce into custard cups or mold.
3. Spoon custard on top of sauce. Place cups or mold in a pan of hot water. Bake 30 - 45 minutes. Test with a knife. If it comes out clean, custard is done.

FROZEN COFFEE CREAM

Makes 4 - 6 servings.

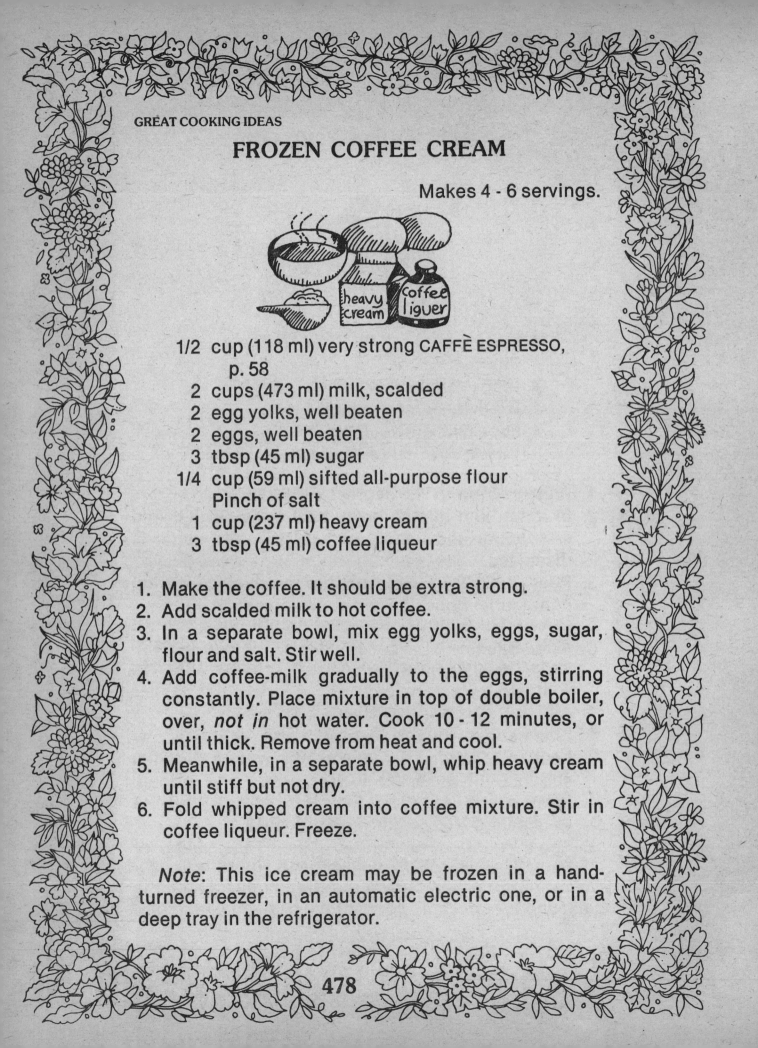

1/2 cup (118 ml) very strong CAFFÈ ESPRESSO,
      p. 58
  2 cups (473 ml) milk, scalded
  2 egg yolks, well beaten
  2 eggs, well beaten
  3 tbsp (45 ml) sugar
1/4 cup (59 ml) sifted all-purpose flour
     Pinch of salt
  1 cup (237 ml) heavy cream
  3 tbsp (45 ml) coffee liqueur

1. Make the coffee. It should be extra strong.
2. Add scalded milk to hot coffee.
3. In a separate bowl, mix egg yolks, eggs, sugar, flour and salt. Stir well.
4. Add coffee-milk gradually to the eggs, stirring constantly. Place mixture in top of double boiler, over, *not in* hot water. Cook 10 - 12 minutes, or until thick. Remove from heat and cool.
5. Meanwhile, in a separate bowl, whip heavy cream until stiff but not dry.
6. Fold whipped cream into coffee mixture. Stir in coffee liqueur. Freeze.

Note: This ice cream may be frozen in a hand-turned freezer, in an automatic electric one, or in a deep tray in the refrigerator.

478

MACAROON TORTONI

Makes 4 servings.

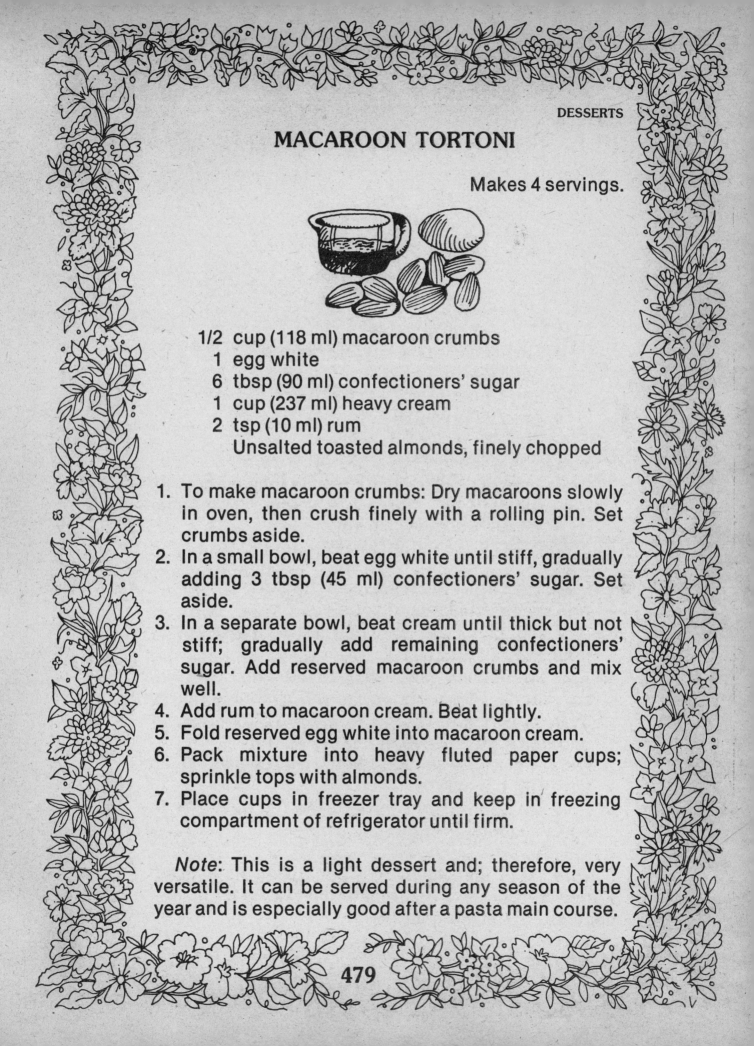

1/2 cup (118 ml) macaroon crumbs
1 egg white
6 tbsp (90 ml) confectioners' sugar
1 cup (237 ml) heavy cream
2 tsp (10 ml) rum
Unsalted toasted almonds, finely chopped

1. To make macaroon crumbs: Dry macaroons slowly in oven, then crush finely with a rolling pin. Set crumbs aside.
2. In a small bowl, beat egg white until stiff, gradually adding 3 tbsp (45 ml) confectioners' sugar. Set aside.
3. In a separate bowl, beat cream until thick but not stiff; gradually add remaining confectioners' sugar. Add reserved macaroon crumbs and mix well.
4. Add rum to macaroon cream. Beat lightly.
5. Fold reserved egg white into macaroon cream.
6. Pack mixture into heavy fluted paper cups; sprinkle tops with almonds.
7. Place cups in freezer tray and keep in freezing compartment of refrigerator until firm.

Note: This is a light dessert and; therefore, very versatile. It can be served during any season of the year and is especially good after a pasta main course.

MANDARIN ORANGE DELIGHT

Makes 8 servings.

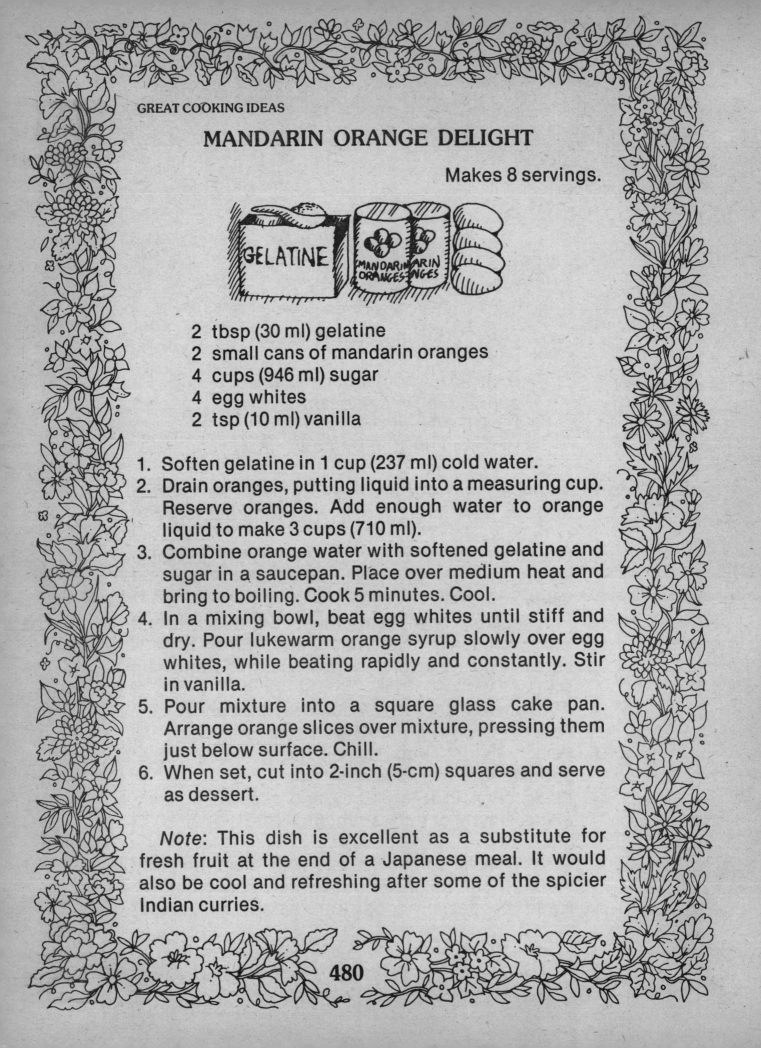

2 tbsp (30 ml) gelatine
2 small cans of mandarin oranges
4 cups (946 ml) sugar
4 egg whites
2 tsp (10 ml) vanilla

1. Soften gelatine in 1 cup (237 ml) cold water.
2. Drain oranges, putting liquid into a measuring cup. Reserve oranges. Add enough water to orange liquid to make 3 cups (710 ml).
3. Combine orange water with softened gelatine and sugar in a saucepan. Place over medium heat and bring to boiling. Cook 5 minutes. Cool.
4. In a mixing bowl, beat egg whites until stiff and dry. Pour lukewarm orange syrup slowly over egg whites, while beating rapidly and constantly. Stir in vanilla.
5. Pour mixture into a square glass cake pan. Arrange orange slices over mixture, pressing them just below surface. Chill.
6. When set, cut into 2-inch (5-cm) squares and serve as dessert.

Note: This dish is excellent as a substitute for fresh fruit at the end of a Japanese meal. It would also be cool and refreshing after some of the spicier Indian curries.

NUTTY APPLE CREAM

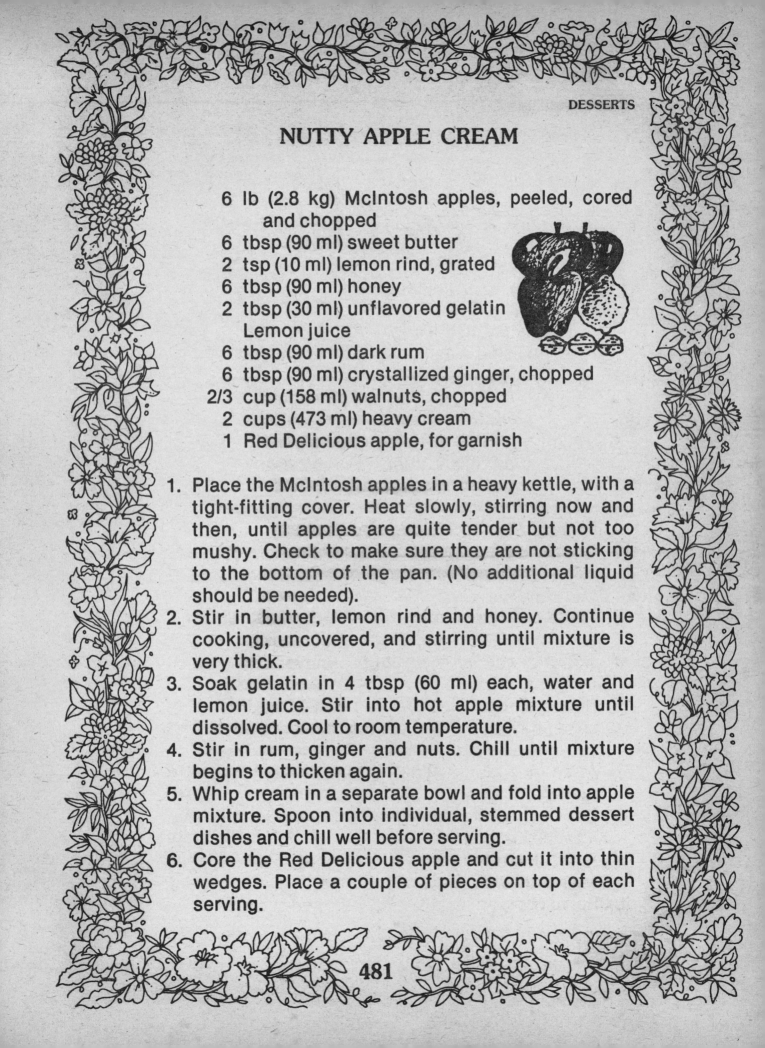

- 6 lb (2.8 kg) McIntosh apples, peeled, cored and chopped
- 6 tbsp (90 ml) sweet butter
- 2 tsp (10 ml) lemon rind, grated
- 6 tbsp (90 ml) honey
- 2 tbsp (30 ml) unflavored gelatin
  Lemon juice
- 6 tbsp (90 ml) dark rum
- 6 tbsp (90 ml) crystallized ginger, chopped
- 2/3 cup (158 ml) walnuts, chopped
- 2 cups (473 ml) heavy cream
- 1 Red Delicious apple, for garnish

1. Place the McIntosh apples in a heavy kettle, with a tight-fitting cover. Heat slowly, stirring now and then, until apples are quite tender but not too mushy. Check to make sure they are not sticking to the bottom of the pan. (No additional liquid should be needed).
2. Stir in butter, lemon rind and honey. Continue cooking, uncovered, and stirring until mixture is very thick.
3. Soak gelatin in 4 tbsp (60 ml) each, water and lemon juice. Stir into hot apple mixture until dissolved. Cool to room temperature.
4. Stir in rum, ginger and nuts. Chill until mixture begins to thicken again.
5. Whip cream in a separate bowl and fold into apple mixture. Spoon into individual, stemmed dessert dishes and chill well before serving.
6. Core the Red Delicious apple and cut it into thin wedges. Place a couple of pieces on top of each serving.

SINGAPORE TAPIOCA

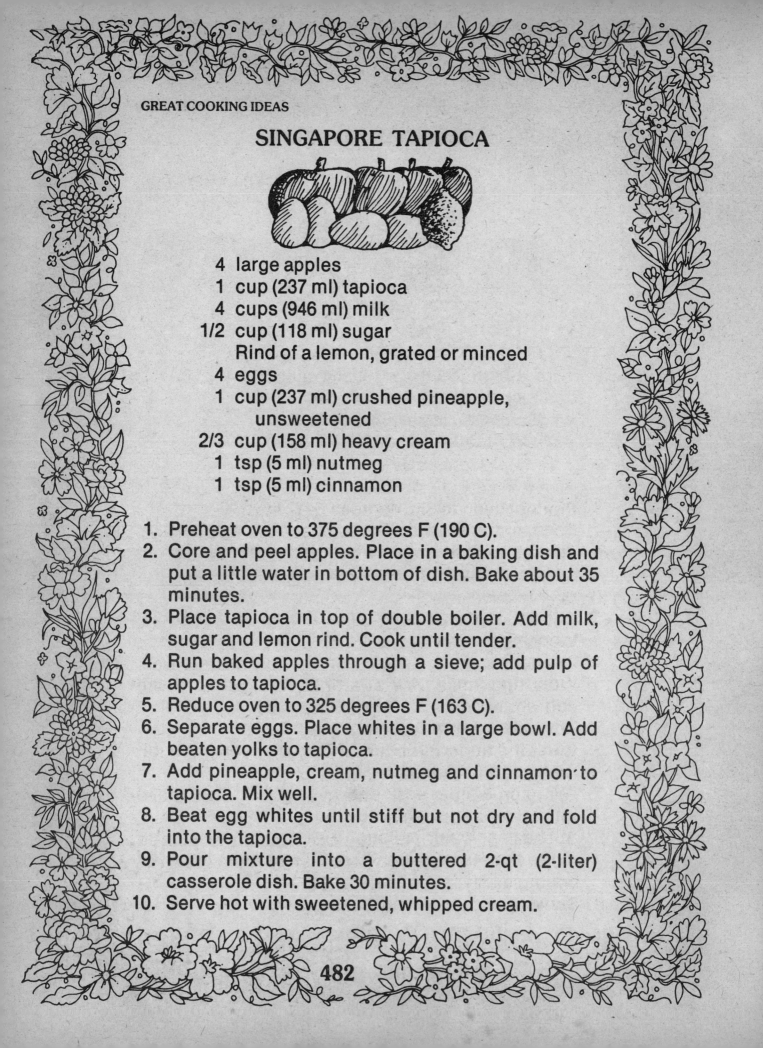

4 large apples
1 cup (237 ml) tapioca
4 cups (946 ml) milk
1/2 cup (118 ml) sugar
    Rind of a lemon, grated or minced
4 eggs
1 cup (237 ml) crushed pineapple,
    unsweetened
2/3 cup (158 ml) heavy cream
1 tsp (5 ml) nutmeg
1 tsp (5 ml) cinnamon

1. Preheat oven to 375 degrees F (190 C).
2. Core and peel apples. Place in a baking dish and put a little water in bottom of dish. Bake about 35 minutes.
3. Place tapioca in top of double boiler. Add milk, sugar and lemon rind. Cook until tender.
4. Run baked apples through a sieve; add pulp of apples to tapioca.
5. Reduce oven to 325 degrees F (163 C).
6. Separate eggs. Place whites in a large bowl. Add beaten yolks to tapioca.
7. Add pineapple, cream, nutmeg and cinnamon to tapioca. Mix well.
8. Beat egg whites until stiff but not dry and fold into the tapioca.
9. Pour mixture into a buttered 2-qt (2-liter) casserole dish. Bake 30 minutes.
10. Serve hot with sweetened, whipped cream.

APRICOT SOUFFLÉ

Makes 4 servings.

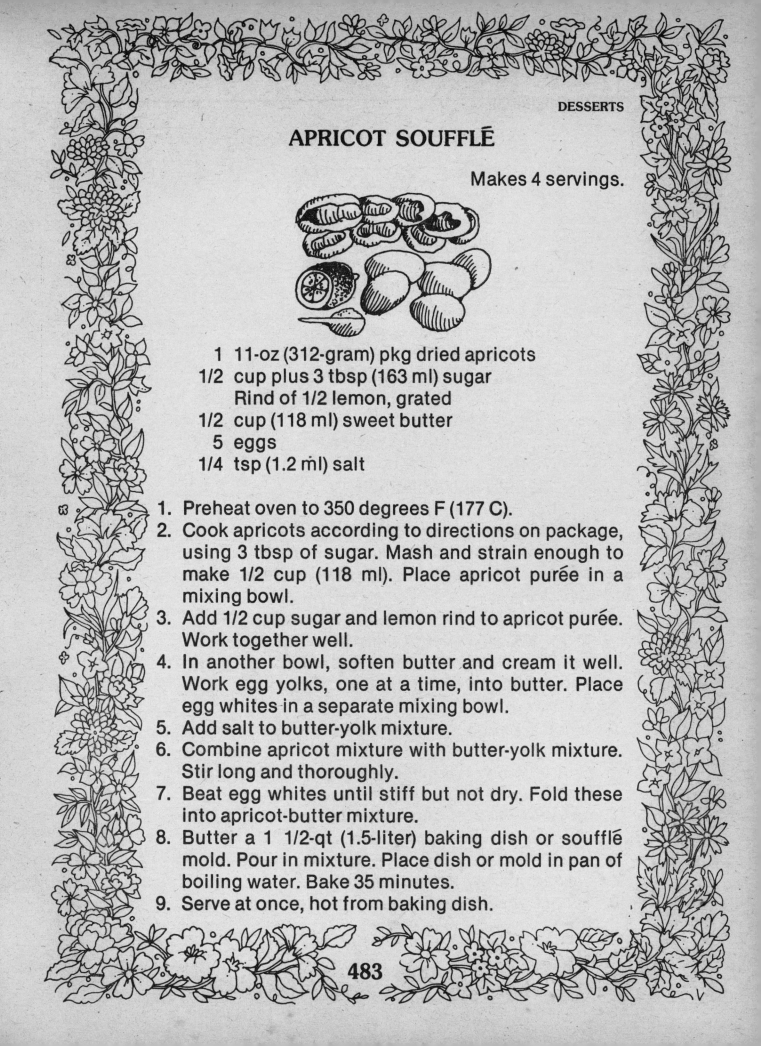

    1   11-oz (312-gram) pkg dried apricots
    1/2 cup plus 3 tbsp (163 ml) sugar
        Rind of 1/2 lemon, grated
    1/2 cup (118 ml) sweet butter
      5 eggs
    1/4 tsp (1.2 ml) salt

1. Preheat oven to 350 degrees F (177 C).
2. Cook apricots according to directions on package, using 3 tbsp of sugar. Mash and strain enough to make 1/2 cup (118 ml). Place apricot purée in a mixing bowl.
3. Add 1/2 cup sugar and lemon rind to apricot purée. Work together well.
4. In another bowl, soften butter and cream it well. Work egg yolks, one at a time, into butter. Place egg whites in a separate mixing bowl.
5. Add salt to butter-yolk mixture.
6. Combine apricot mixture with butter-yolk mixture. Stir long and thoroughly.
7. Beat egg whites until stiff but not dry. Fold these into apricot-butter mixture.
8. Butter a 1 1/2-qt (1.5-liter) baking dish or soufflé mold. Pour in mixture. Place dish or mold in pan of boiling water. Bake 35 minutes.
9. Serve at once, hot from baking dish.

CHOCOLATE-COFFEE SOUFFLÉ

Makes 6 servings.

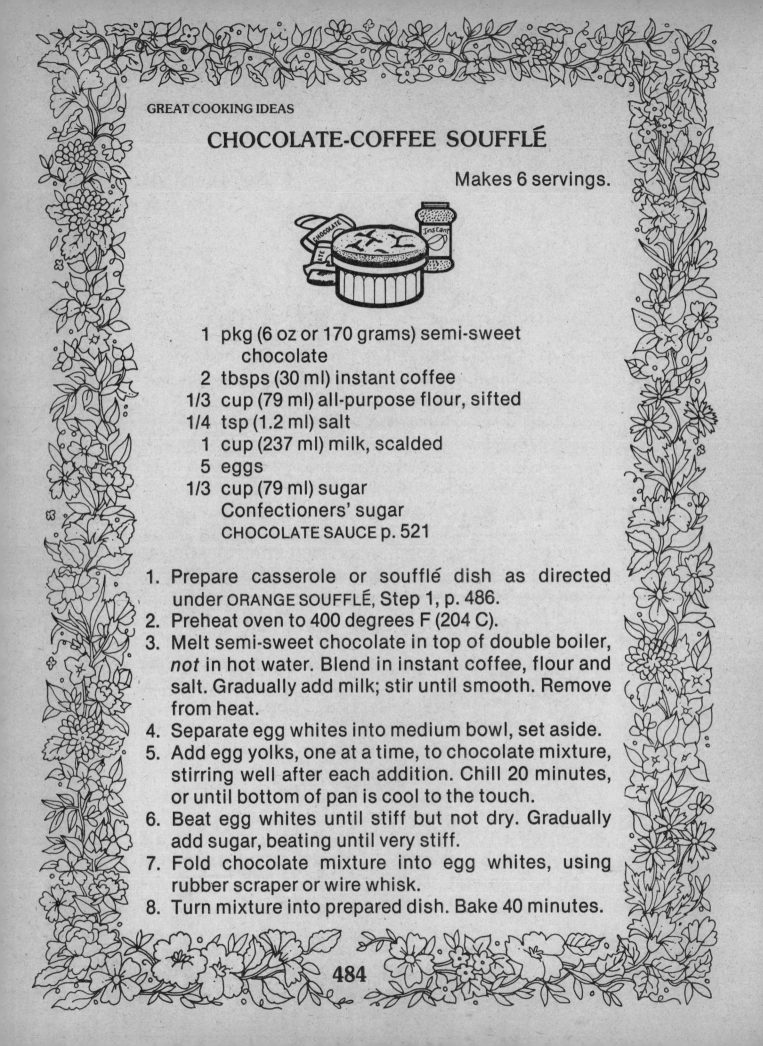

 1 pkg (6 oz or 170 grams) semi-sweet
    chocolate
 2 tbsps (30 ml) instant coffee
1/3 cup (79 ml) all-purpose flour, sifted
1/4 tsp (1.2 ml) salt
 1 cup (237 ml) milk, scalded
 5 eggs
1/3 cup (79 ml) sugar
    Confectioners' sugar
    CHOCOLATE SAUCE p. 521

1. Prepare casserole or soufflé dish as directed
   under ORANGE SOUFFLÉ, Step 1, p. 486.
2. Preheat oven to 400 degrees F (204 C).
3. Melt semi-sweet chocolate in top of double boiler,
   not in hot water. Blend in instant coffee, flour and
   salt. Gradually add milk; stir until smooth. Remove
   from heat.
4. Separate egg whites into medium bowl, set aside.
5. Add egg yolks, one at a time, to chocolate mixture,
   stirring well after each addition. Chill 20 minutes,
   or until bottom of pan is cool to the touch.
6. Beat egg whites until stiff but not dry. Gradually
   add sugar, beating until very stiff.
7. Fold chocolate mixture into egg whites, using
   rubber scraper or wire whisk.
8. Turn mixture into prepared dish. Bake 40 minutes.

9. Sprinkle top with confectioners' sugar. Serve immediately with CHOCOLATE SAUCE.

* * *

MARSALA CUSTARD

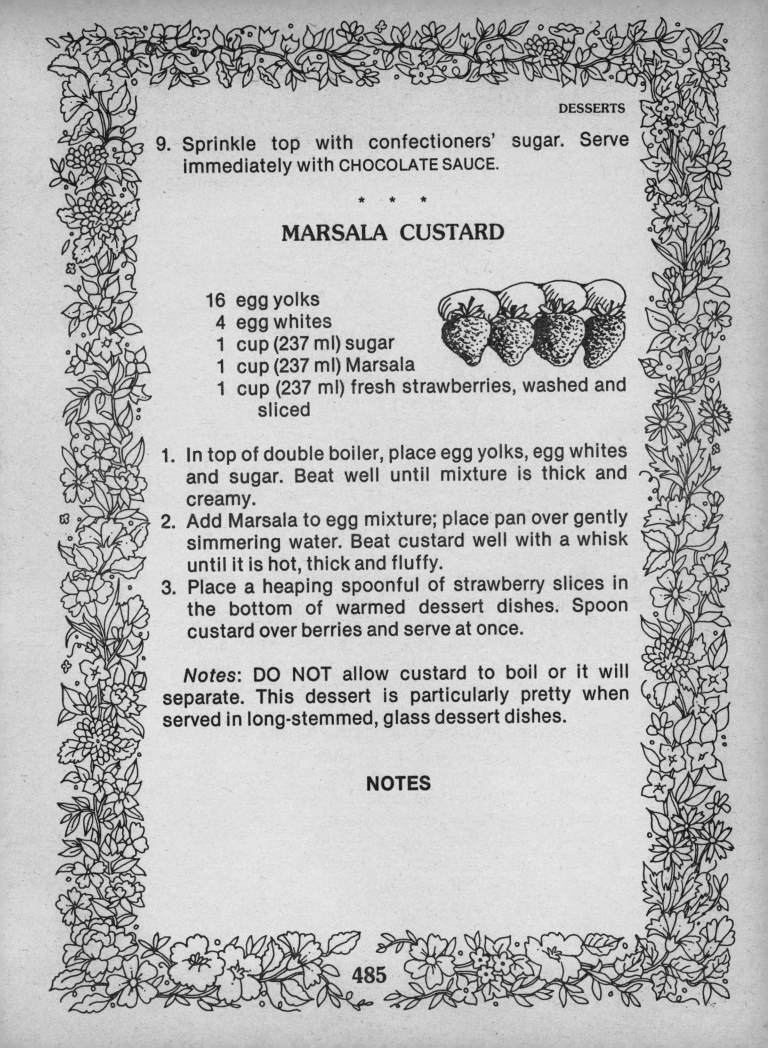

16 egg yolks
 4 egg whites
 1 cup (237 ml) sugar
 1 cup (237 ml) Marsala
 1 cup (237 ml) fresh strawberries, washed and sliced

1. In top of double boiler, place egg yolks, egg whites and sugar. Beat well until mixture is thick and creamy.
2. Add Marsala to egg mixture; place pan over gently simmering water. Beat custard well with a whisk until it is hot, thick and fluffy.
3. Place a heaping spoonful of strawberry slices in the bottom of warmed dessert dishes. Spoon custard over berries and serve at once.

Notes: DO NOT allow custard to boil or it will separate. This dessert is particularly pretty when served in long-stemmed, glass dessert dishes.

NOTES

ORANGE SOUFFLÉ

Makes 6 to 8 servings.

Confectioners' sugar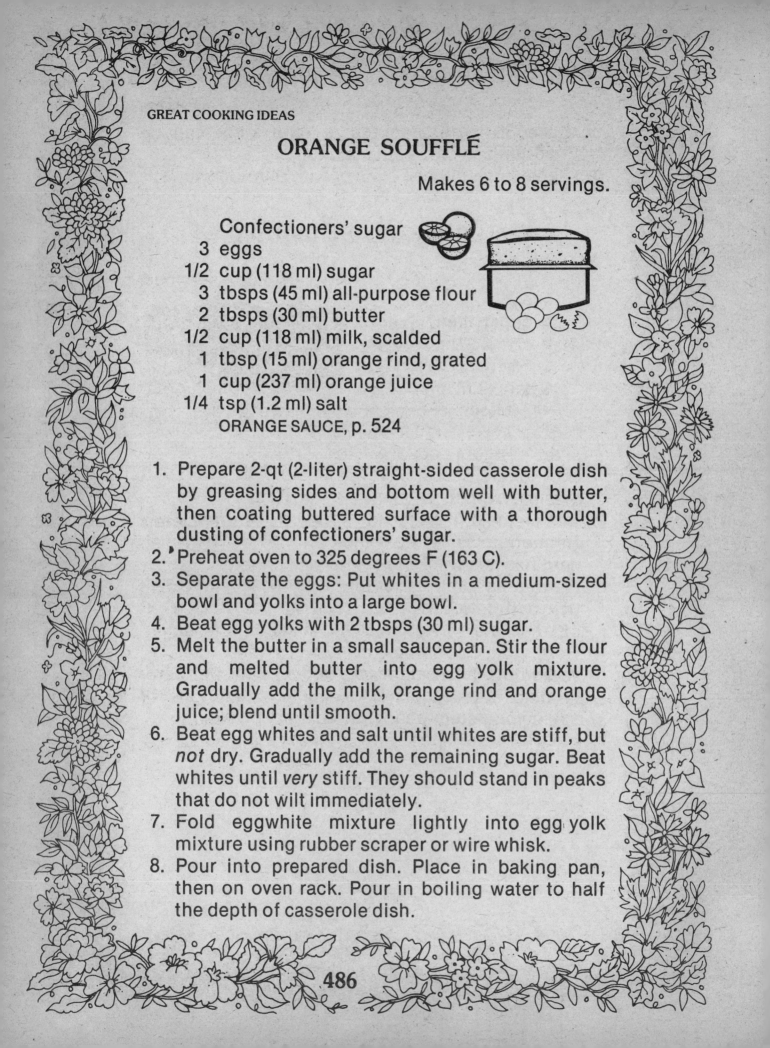
3 eggs
1/2 cup (118 ml) sugar
3 tbsps (45 ml) all-purpose flour
2 tbsps (30 ml) butter
1/2 cup (118 ml) milk, scalded
1 tbsp (15 ml) orange rind, grated
1 cup (237 ml) orange juice
1/4 tsp (1.2 ml) salt
ORANGE SAUCE, p. 524

1. Prepare 2-qt (2-liter) straight-sided casserole dish by greasing sides and bottom well with butter, then coating buttered surface with a thorough dusting of confectioners' sugar.
2. Preheat oven to 325 degrees F (163 C).
3. Separate the eggs: Put whites in a medium-sized bowl and yolks into a large bowl.
4. Beat egg yolks with 2 tbsps (30 ml) sugar.
5. Melt the butter in a small saucepan. Stir the flour and melted butter into egg yolk mixture. Gradually add the milk, orange rind and orange juice; blend until smooth.
6. Beat egg whites and salt until whites are stiff, but *not* dry. Gradually add the remaining sugar. Beat whites until *very* stiff. They should stand in peaks that do not wilt immediately.
7. Fold eggwhite mixture lightly into egg yolk mixture using rubber scraper or wire whisk.
8. Pour into prepared dish. Place in baking pan, then on oven rack. Pour in boiling water to half the depth of casserole dish.

9. Bake 35 to 40 minutes or until knife can be inserted and come out clean.
10. Serve immediately, plain or with ORANGE SAUCE.

* * *

APPLES BAKED IN RED WINE

Makes 4 servings.

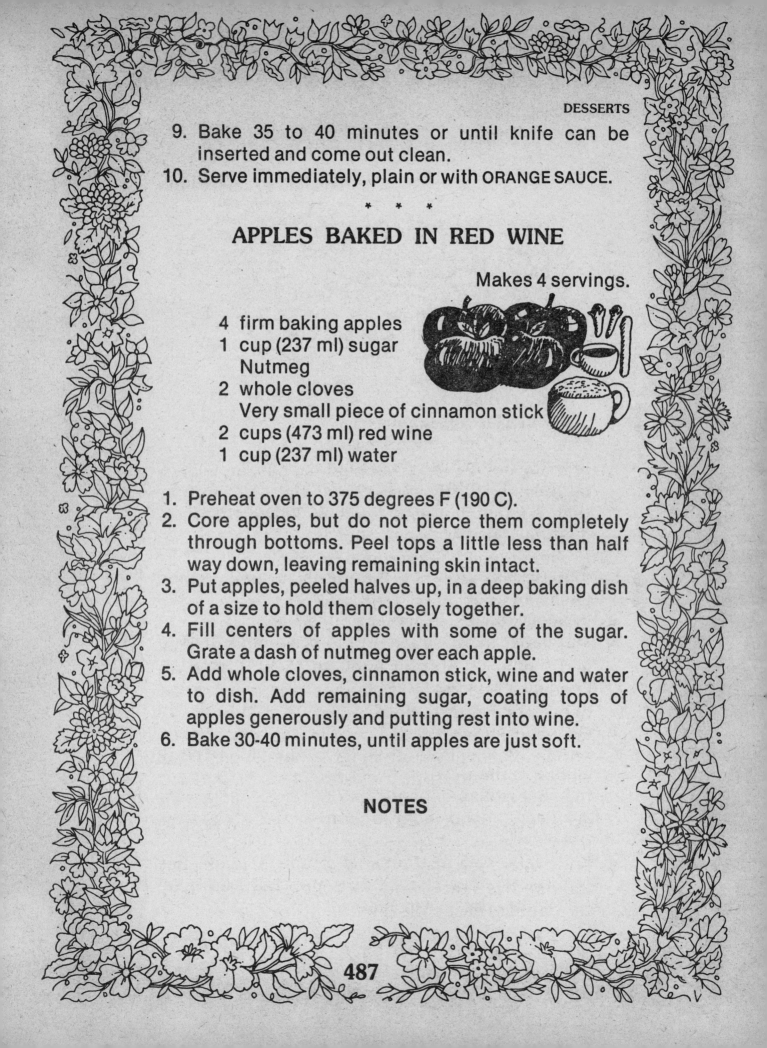

4 firm baking apples
1 cup (237 ml) sugar
   Nutmeg
2 whole cloves
   Very small piece of cinnamon stick
2 cups (473 ml) red wine
1 cup (237 ml) water

1. Preheat oven to 375 degrees F (190 C).
2. Core apples, but do not pierce them completely through bottoms. Peel tops a little less than half way down, leaving remaining skin intact.
3. Put apples, peeled halves up, in a deep baking dish of a size to hold them closely together.
4. Fill centers of apples with some of the sugar. Grate a dash of nutmeg over each apple.
5. Add whole cloves, cinnamon stick, wine and water to dish. Add remaining sugar, coating tops of apples generously and putting rest into wine.
6. Bake 30-40 minutes, until apples are just soft.

NOTES

SOUFFLÉ OF DATES 'N' ALMONDS

Makes 6 servings.

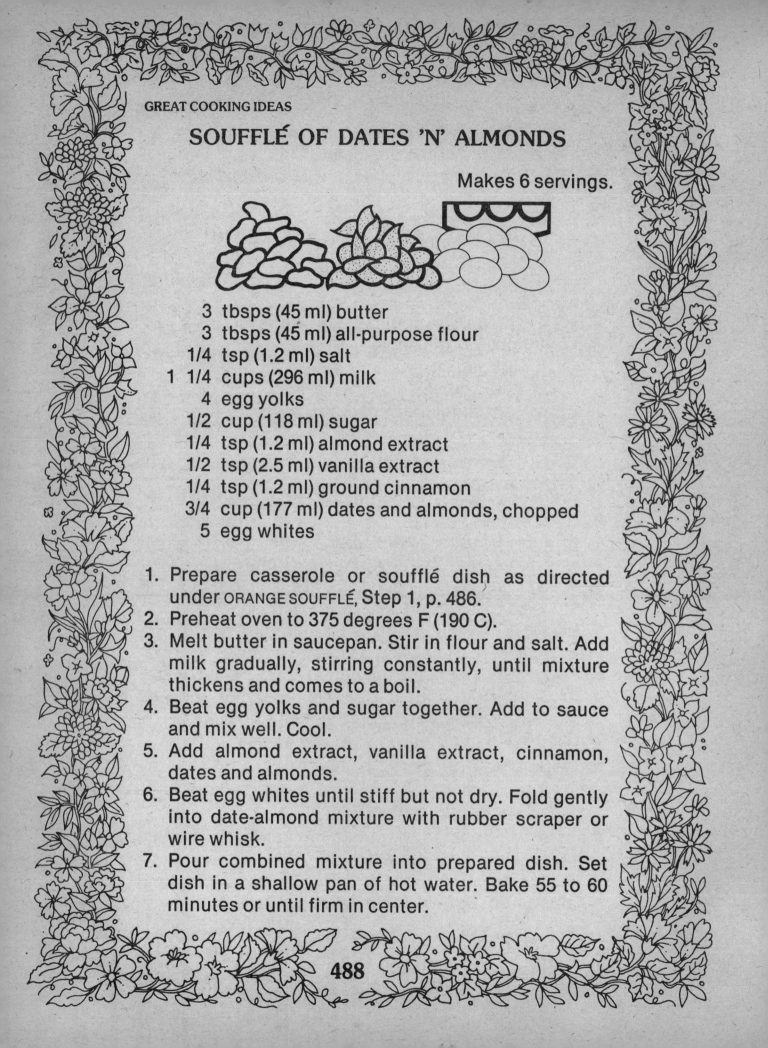

3 tbsps (45 ml) butter
3 tbsps (45 ml) all-purpose flour
1/4 tsp (1.2 ml) salt
1 1/4 cups (296 ml) milk
4 egg yolks
1/2 cup (118 ml) sugar
1/4 tsp (1.2 ml) almond extract
1/2 tsp (2.5 ml) vanilla extract
1/4 tsp (1.2 ml) ground cinnamon
3/4 cup (177 ml) dates and almonds, chopped
5 egg whites

1. Prepare casserole or soufflé dish as directed under ORANGE SOUFFLÉ, Step 1, p. 486.
2. Preheat oven to 375 degrees F (190 C).
3. Melt butter in saucepan. Stir in flour and salt. Add milk gradually, stirring constantly, until mixture thickens and comes to a boil.
4. Beat egg yolks and sugar together. Add to sauce and mix well. Cool.
5. Add almond extract, vanilla extract, cinnamon, dates and almonds.
6. Beat egg whites until stiff but not dry. Fold gently into date-almond mixture with rubber scraper or wire whisk.
7. Pour combined mixture into prepared dish. Set dish in a shallow pan of hot water. Bake 55 to 60 minutes or until firm in center.

BAKED HONEY BANANAS

Makes 6 servings.

3 bananas, ripe but firm
1 tbsp (15 ml) sweet butter, melted
1 tbsp (15 ml) lemon juice
2 tbsp (30 ml) honey

1. Preheat oven to 325 degrees F (163 C).
2. Peel bananas. Cut each one in half and place in a shallow baking dish.
3. In a tiny bowl, mix melted butter, lemon juice and honey. Brush this mixture on bananas. Bake 15 minutes.
4. Serve plain with MARINATED PORK ROAST, p. 337, or with heavy cream as a dessert.

* * *

BANANA DELIGHT

8 bananas
1 1/2 cups (355 ml) unsweetened orange juice
1 1/2 cups (355 ml) brown sugar
3/4 cup (177 ml) grated coconut
3/4 cup (177 ml) dry bread crumbs
1/2 tsp (2.5 ml) nutmeg
1/2 tsp (2.5 ml) cinnamon

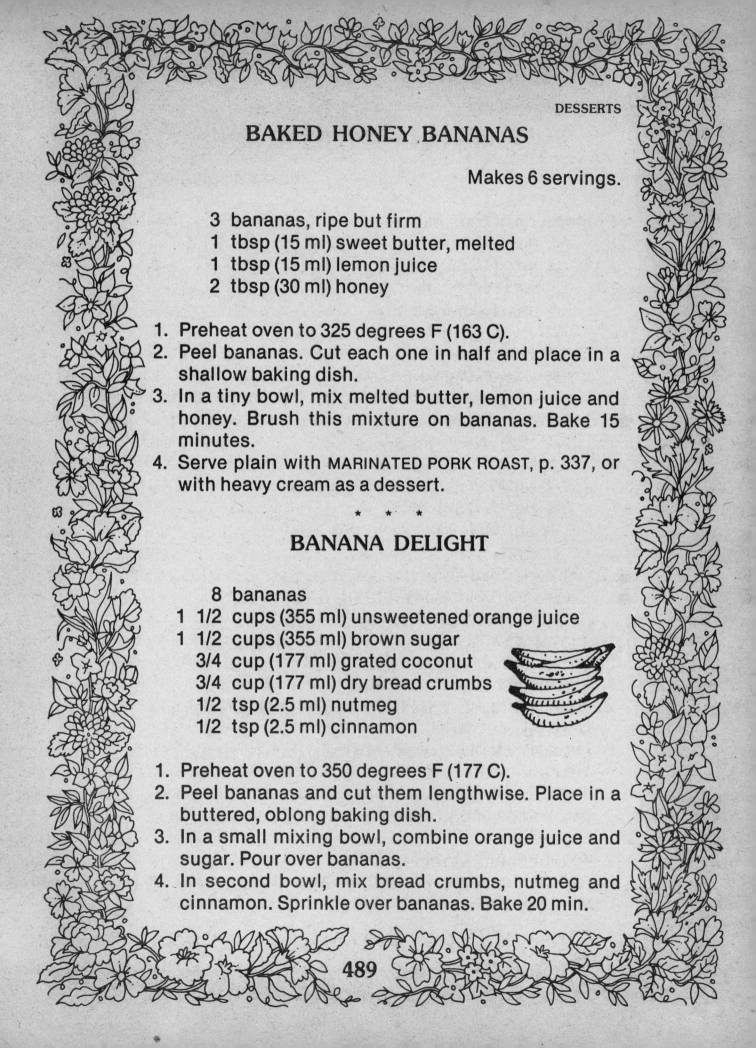

1. Preheat oven to 350 degrees F (177 C).
2. Peel bananas and cut them lengthwise. Place in a buttered, oblong baking dish.
3. In a small mixing bowl, combine orange juice and sugar. Pour over bananas.
4. In second bowl, mix bread crumbs, nutmeg and cinnamon. Sprinkle over bananas. Bake 20 min.

BANANA FRITTERS

Makes 4 servings.

Preparation of Bananas:

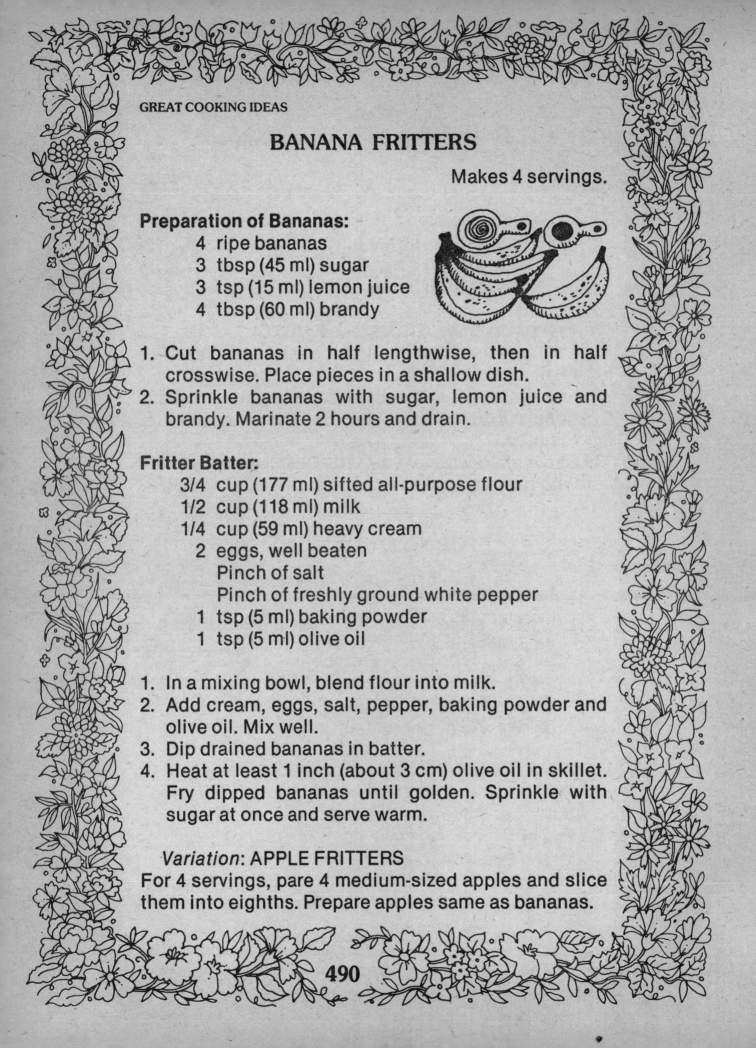

        4 ripe bananas
        3 tbsp (45 ml) sugar
        3 tsp (15 ml) lemon juice
        4 tbsp (60 ml) brandy

1. Cut bananas in half lengthwise, then in half crosswise. Place pieces in a shallow dish.
2. Sprinkle bananas with sugar, lemon juice and brandy. Marinate 2 hours and drain.

Fritter Batter:

        3/4 cup (177 ml) sifted all-purpose flour
        1/2 cup (118 ml) milk
        1/4 cup (59 ml) heavy cream
        2 eggs, well beaten
           Pinch of salt
           Pinch of freshly ground white pepper
        1 tsp (5 ml) baking powder
        1 tsp (5 ml) olive oil

1. In a mixing bowl, blend flour into milk.
2. Add cream, eggs, salt, pepper, baking powder and olive oil. Mix well.
3. Dip drained bananas in batter.
4. Heat at least 1 inch (about 3 cm) olive oil in skillet. Fry dipped bananas until golden. Sprinkle with sugar at once and serve warm.

Variation: APPLE FRITTERS

For 4 servings, pare 4 medium-sized apples and slice them into eighths. Prepare apples same as bananas.

COCO-NUTTY BANANAS

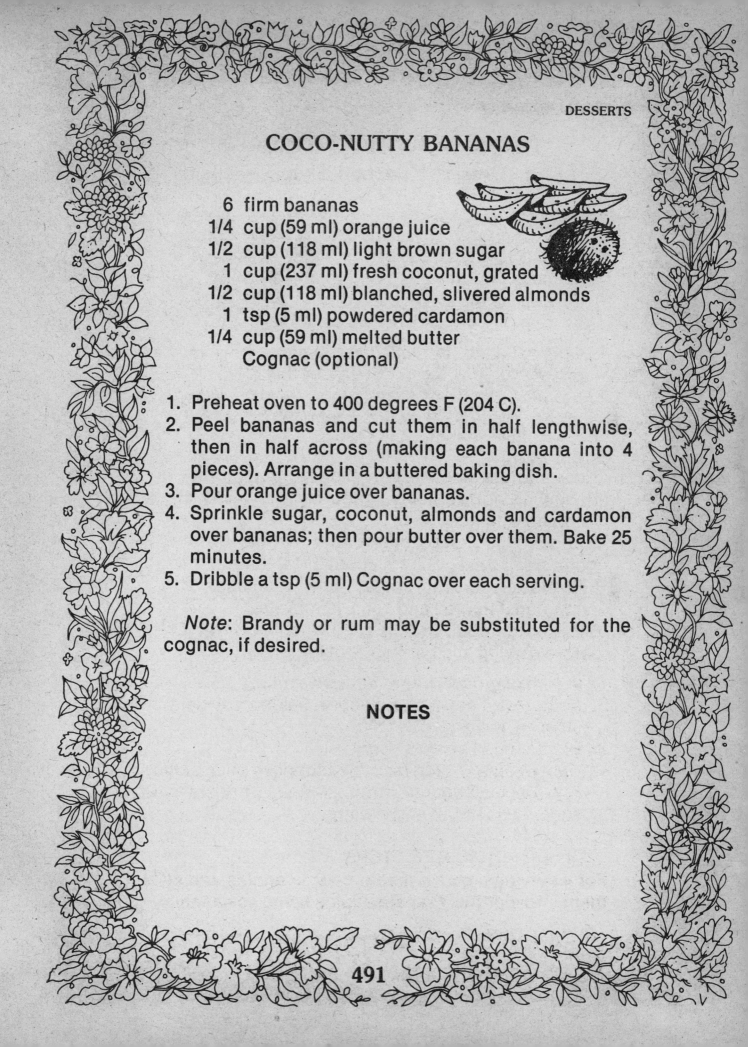

```
  6  firm bananas
1/4  cup (59 ml) orange juice
1/2  cup (118 ml) light brown sugar
  1  cup (237 ml) fresh coconut, grated
1/2  cup (118 ml) blanched, slivered almonds
  1  tsp (5 ml) powdered cardamon
1/4  cup (59 ml) melted butter
     Cognac (optional)
```

1. Preheat oven to 400 degrees F (204 C).
2. Peel bananas and cut them in half lengthwise, then in half across (making each banana into 4 pieces). Arrange in a buttered baking dish.
3. Pour orange juice over bananas.
4. Sprinkle sugar, coconut, almonds and cardamon over bananas; then pour butter over them. Bake 25 minutes.
5. Dribble a tsp (5 ml) Cognac over each serving.

Note: Brandy or rum may be substituted for the cognac, if desired.

NOTES

CARROTS WITH ALMONDS
(Dessert Pakistani-Style)

Makes 6 - 8 servings.

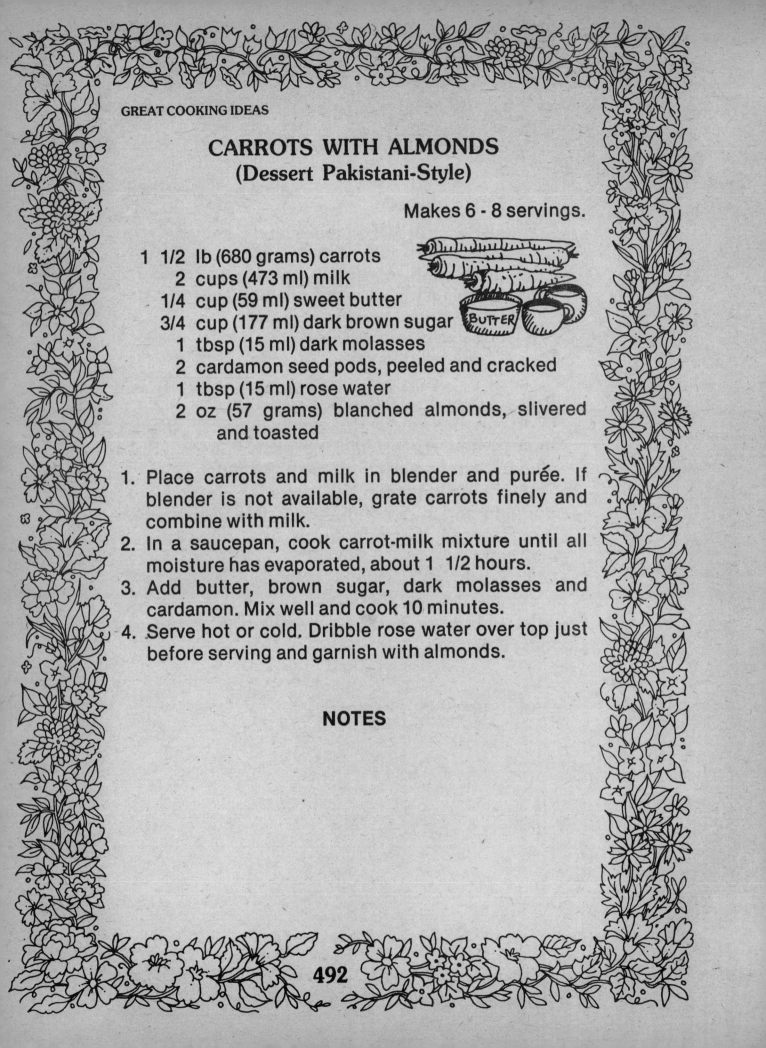

1 1/2 lb (680 grams) carrots
2 cups (473 ml) milk
1/4 cup (59 ml) sweet butter
3/4 cup (177 ml) dark brown sugar
1 tbsp (15 ml) dark molasses
2 cardamon seed pods, peeled and cracked
1 tbsp (15 ml) rose water
2 oz (57 grams) blanched almonds, slivered and toasted

1. Place carrots and milk in blender and purée. If blender is not available, grate carrots finely and combine with milk.
2. In a saucepan, cook carrot-milk mixture until all moisture has evaporated, about 1 1/2 hours.
3. Add butter, brown sugar, dark molasses and cardamon. Mix well and cook 10 minutes.
4. Serve hot or cold. Dribble rose water over top just before serving and garnish with almonds.

NOTES

GINGER FRUIT

Makes 4 - 6 servings.

1 can (16 oz or 454 grams) sliced peaches, drained
1 cup (237 ml) orange juice (unsweetened)
2 tsp (10 ml) fresh ginger, finely chopped
2 bananas
Kumquats*
Mint leaves

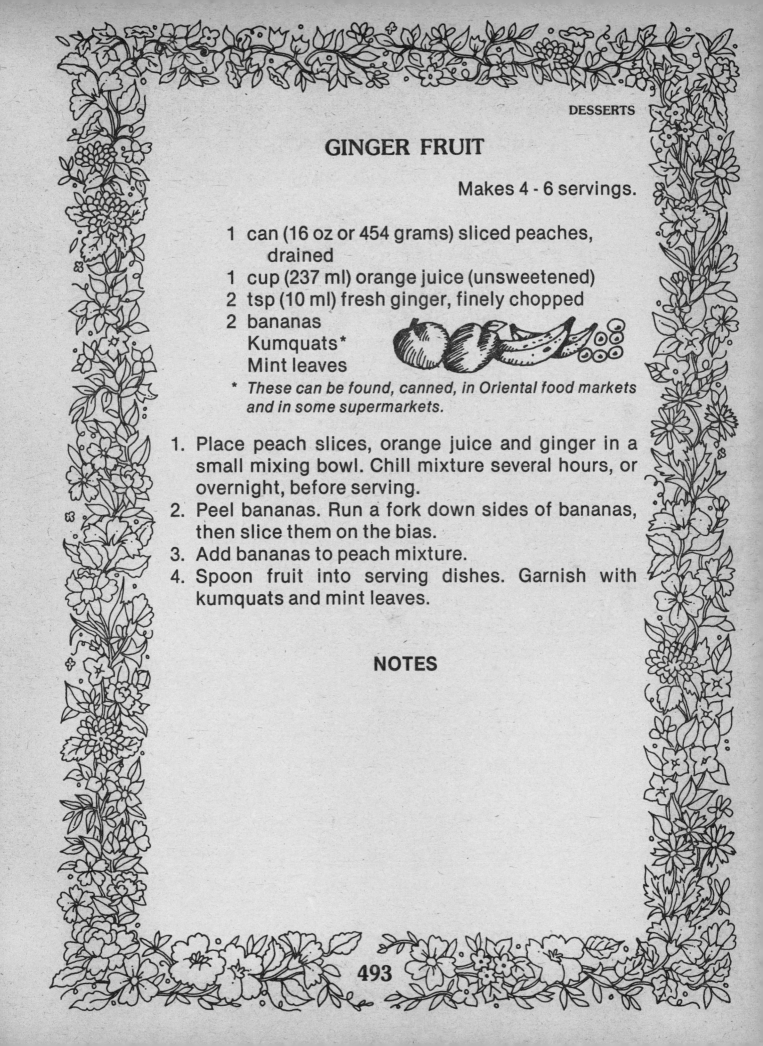

These can be found, canned, in Oriental food markets and in some supermarkets.

1. Place peach slices, orange juice and ginger in a small mixing bowl. Chill mixture several hours, or overnight, before serving.
2. Peel bananas. Run a fork down sides of bananas, then slice them on the bias.
3. Add bananas to peach mixture.
4. Spoon fruit into serving dishes. Garnish with kumquats and mint leaves.

NOTES

GRAPE JAM TURNOVERS

Makes 6 servings.

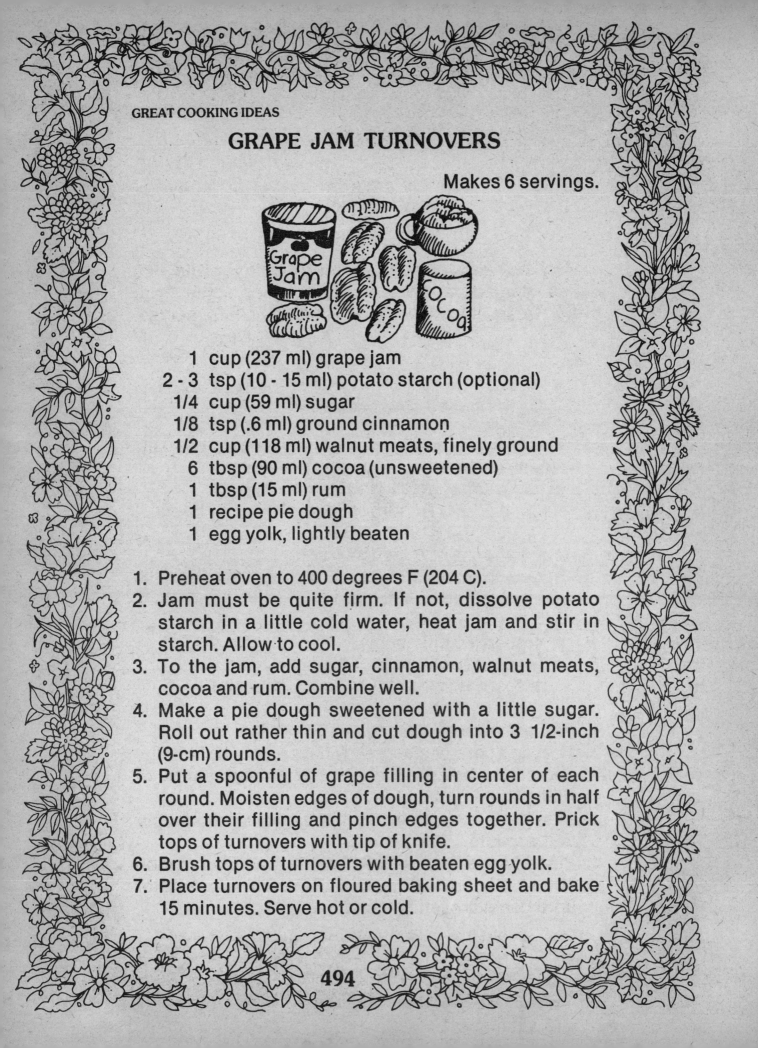

    1   cup (237 ml) grape jam
2 - 3   tsp (10 - 15 ml) potato starch (optional)
  1/4   cup (59 ml) sugar
  1/8   tsp (.6 ml) ground cinnamon
  1/2   cup (118 ml) walnut meats, finely ground
    6   tbsp (90 ml) cocoa (unsweetened)
    1   tbsp (15 ml) rum
    1   recipe pie dough
    1   egg yolk, lightly beaten

1. Preheat oven to 400 degrees F (204 C).
2. Jam must be quite firm. If not, dissolve potato starch in a little cold water, heat jam and stir in starch. Allow to cool.
3. To the jam, add sugar, cinnamon, walnut meats, cocoa and rum. Combine well.
4. Make a pie dough sweetened with a little sugar. Roll out rather thin and cut dough into 3 1/2-inch (9-cm) rounds.
5. Put a spoonful of grape filling in center of each round. Moisten edges of dough, turn rounds in half over their filling and pinch edges together. Prick tops of turnovers with tip of knife.
6. Brush tops of turnovers with beaten egg yolk.
7. Place turnovers on floured baking sheet and bake 15 minutes. Serve hot or cold.

DESSERTS

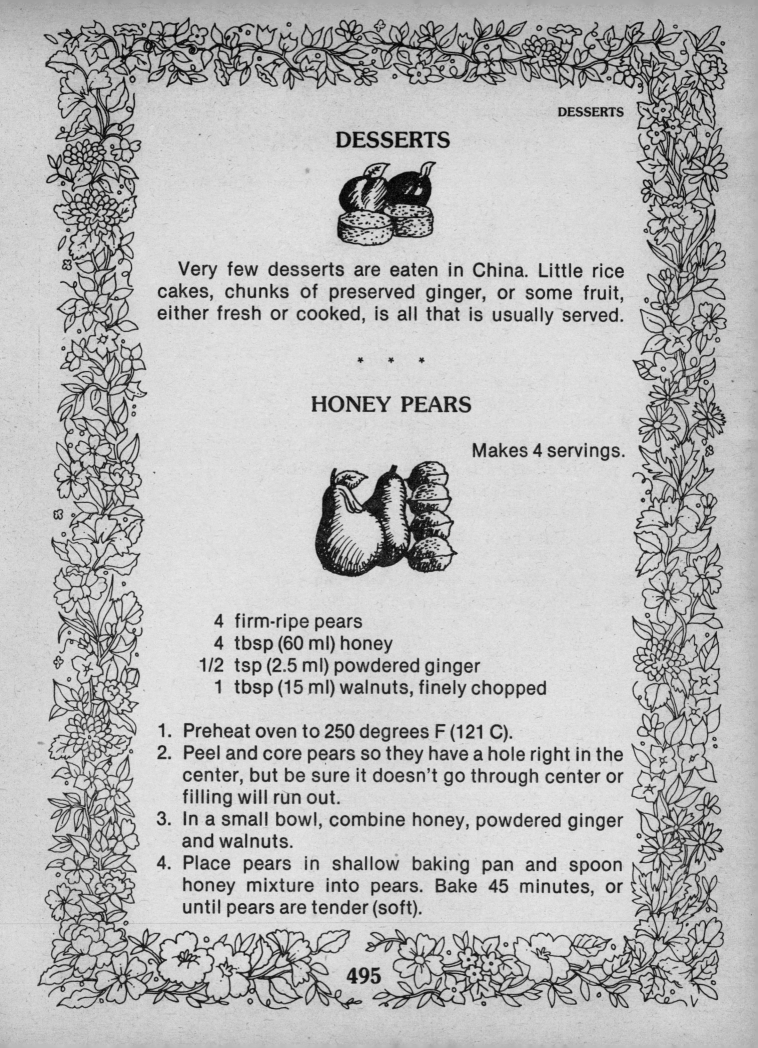

Very few desserts are eaten in China. Little rice cakes, chunks of preserved ginger, or some fruit, either fresh or cooked, is all that is usually served.

* * *

HONEY PEARS

Makes 4 servings.

4 firm-ripe pears
4 tbsp (60 ml) honey
1/2 tsp (2.5 ml) powdered ginger
1 tbsp (15 ml) walnuts, finely chopped

1. Preheat oven to 250 degrees F (121 C).
2. Peel and core pears so they have a hole right in the center, but be sure it doesn't go through center or filling will run out.
3. In a small bowl, combine honey, powdered ginger and walnuts.
4. Place pears in shallow baking pan and spoon honey mixture into pears. Bake 45 minutes, or until pears are tender (soft).

POLYNESIAN FRUIT SALAD

Makes 6 servings.

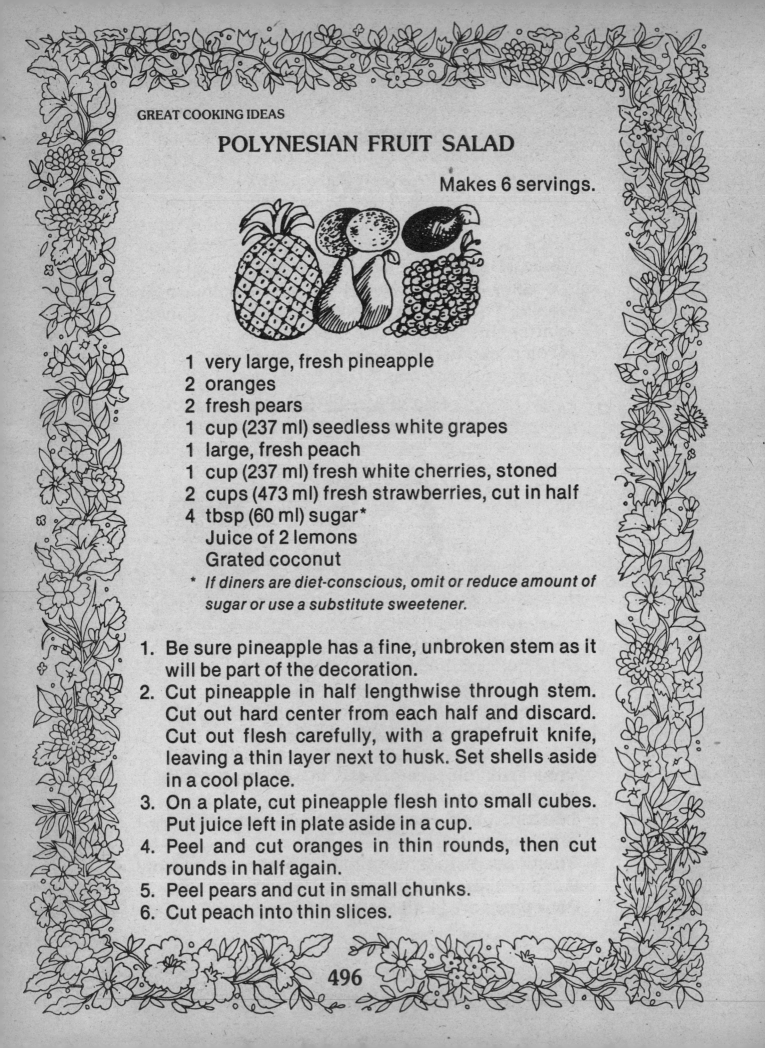

1 very large, fresh pineapple
2 oranges
2 fresh pears
1 cup (237 ml) seedless white grapes
1 large, fresh peach
1 cup (237 ml) fresh white cherries, stoned
2 cups (473 ml) fresh strawberries, cut in half
4 tbsp (60 ml) sugar*
Juice of 2 lemons
Grated coconut

* *If diners are diet-conscious, omit or reduce amount of sugar or use a substitute sweetener.*

1. Be sure pineapple has a fine, unbroken stem as it will be part of the decoration.
2. Cut pineapple in half lengthwise through stem. Cut out hard center from each half and discard. Cut out flesh carefully, with a grapefruit knife, leaving a thin layer next to husk. Set shells aside in a cool place.
3. On a plate, cut pineapple flesh into small cubes. Put juice left in plate aside in a cup.
4. Peel and cut oranges in thin rounds, then cut rounds in half again.
5. Peel pears and cut in small chunks.
6. Cut peach into thin slices.

7. In a large bowl, combine the pineapple cubes, orange slices, pear chunks, grapes, peach slices, cherries and strawberry halves. Mix all together so as not to break fruit, adding sugar, if desired.
8. Pour lemon juice and some of reserved pineapple juice over fruit in bowl. Mix lightly. Refrigerate salad at least 3 hours before serving.
9. To serve, spoon fruit salad into empty pineapple shells, which have been arranged on a large platter side by side, with leaves of one at one end of dish, and leaves of other at opposite end.
10. Sprinkle grated coconut over top.

* * *

STEWED FRUIT

Syrup:
    2 cups (473 ml) sugar
    4 cups (946 ml) water
   1/4 tsp (1.2 ml) salt

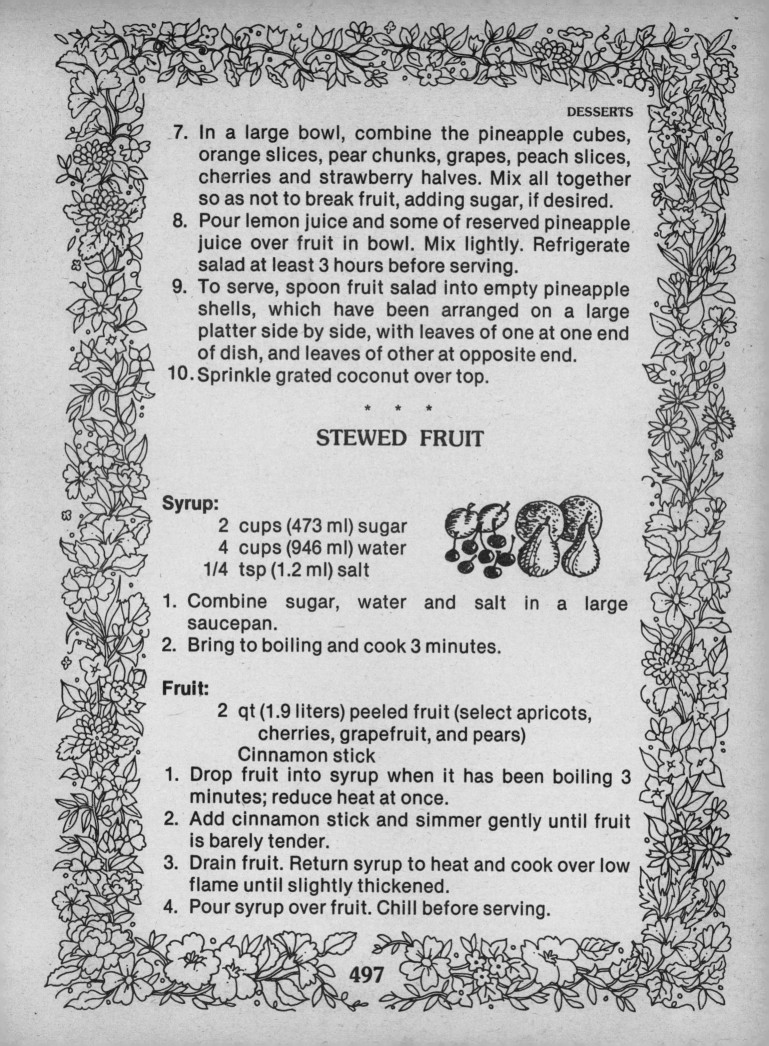

1. Combine sugar, water and salt in a large saucepan.
2. Bring to boiling and cook 3 minutes.

Fruit:
    2 qt (1.9 liters) peeled fruit (select apricots, cherries, grapefruit, and pears)
    Cinnamon stick

1. Drop fruit into syrup when it has been boiling 3 minutes; reduce heat at once.
2. Add cinnamon stick and simmer gently until fruit is barely tender.
3. Drain fruit. Return syrup to heat and cook over low flame until slightly thickened.
4. Pour syrup over fruit. Chill before serving.

KARACHI PINEAPPLE

Makes 4 servings.

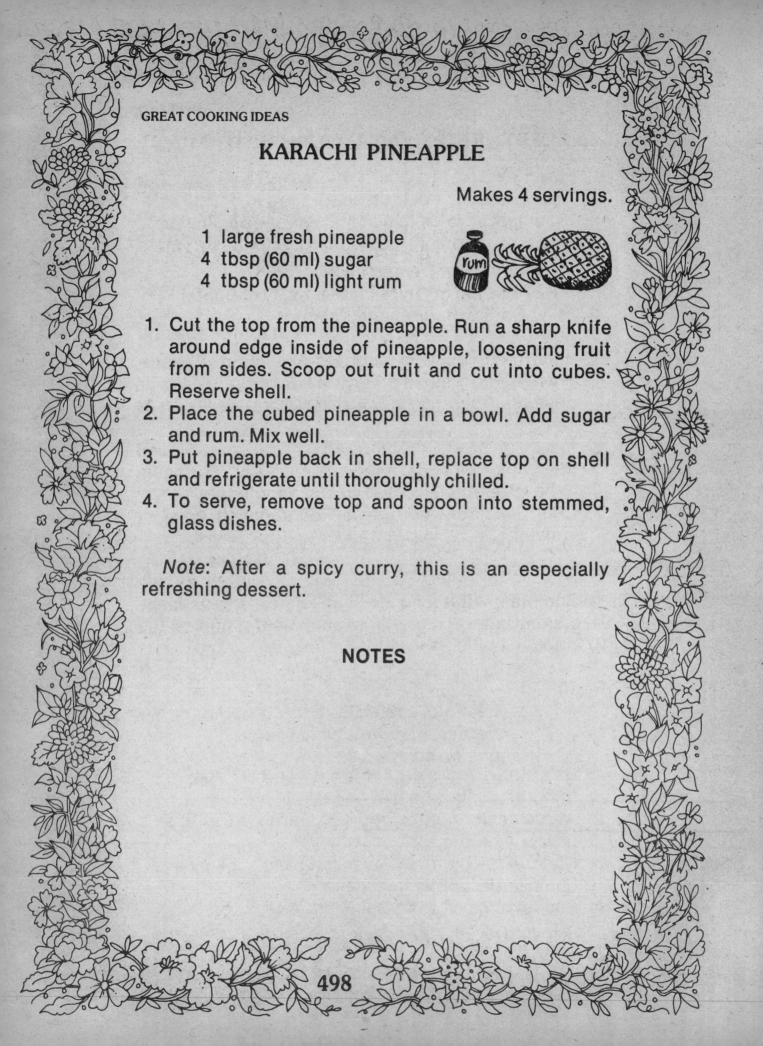

1 large fresh pineapple
4 tbsp (60 ml) sugar
4 tbsp (60 ml) light rum

1. Cut the top from the pineapple. Run a sharp knife around edge inside of pineapple, loosening fruit from sides. Scoop out fruit and cut into cubes. Reserve shell.
2. Place the cubed pineapple in a bowl. Add sugar and rum. Mix well.
3. Put pineapple back in shell, replace top on shell and refrigerate until thoroughly chilled.
4. To serve, remove top and spoon into stemmed, glass dishes.

Note: After a spicy curry, this is an especially refreshing dessert.

NOTES

SCULPTURED CANTALOUPE WITH MINT

Makes 6 - 8 servings.

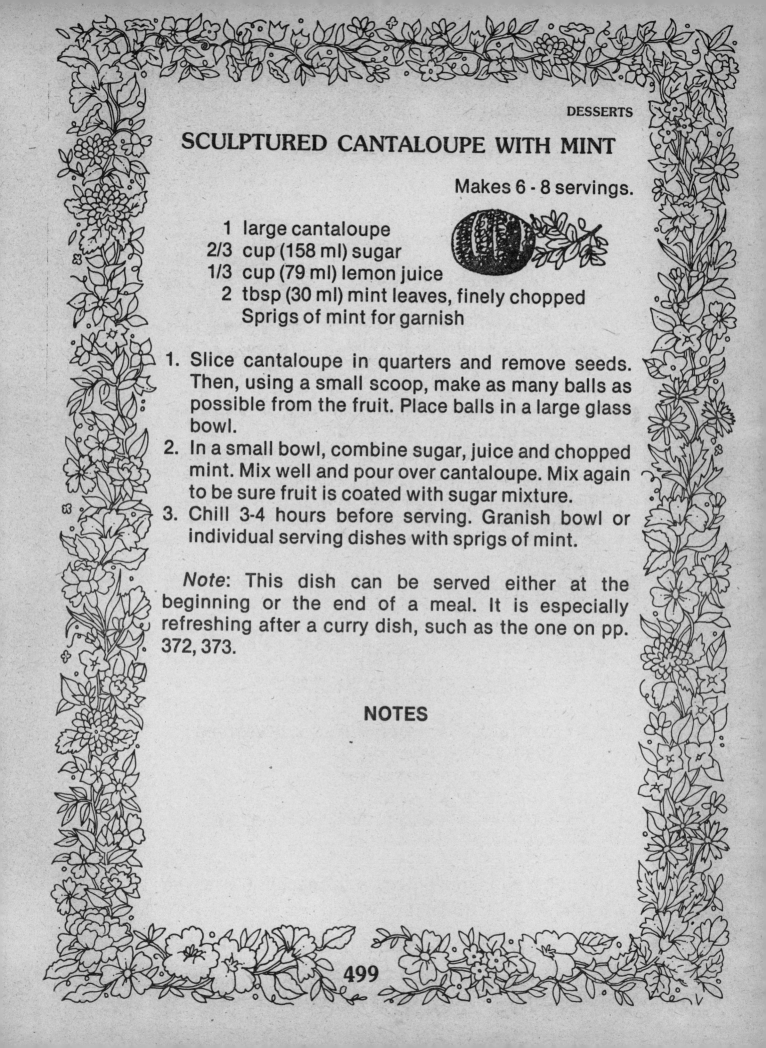

1 large cantaloupe
2/3 cup (158 ml) sugar
1/3 cup (79 ml) lemon juice
2 tbsp (30 ml) mint leaves, finely chopped
Sprigs of mint for garnish

1. Slice cantaloupe in quarters and remove seeds. Then, using a small scoop, make as many balls as possible from the fruit. Place balls in a large glass bowl.
2. In a small bowl, combine sugar, juice and chopped mint. Mix well and pour over cantaloupe. Mix again to be sure fruit is coated with sugar mixture.
3. Chill 3-4 hours before serving. Granish bowl or individual serving dishes with sprigs of mint.

Note: This dish can be served either at the beginning or the end of a meal. It is especially refreshing after a curry dish, such as the one on pp. 372, 373.

NOTES

BARBECUE SAUCE

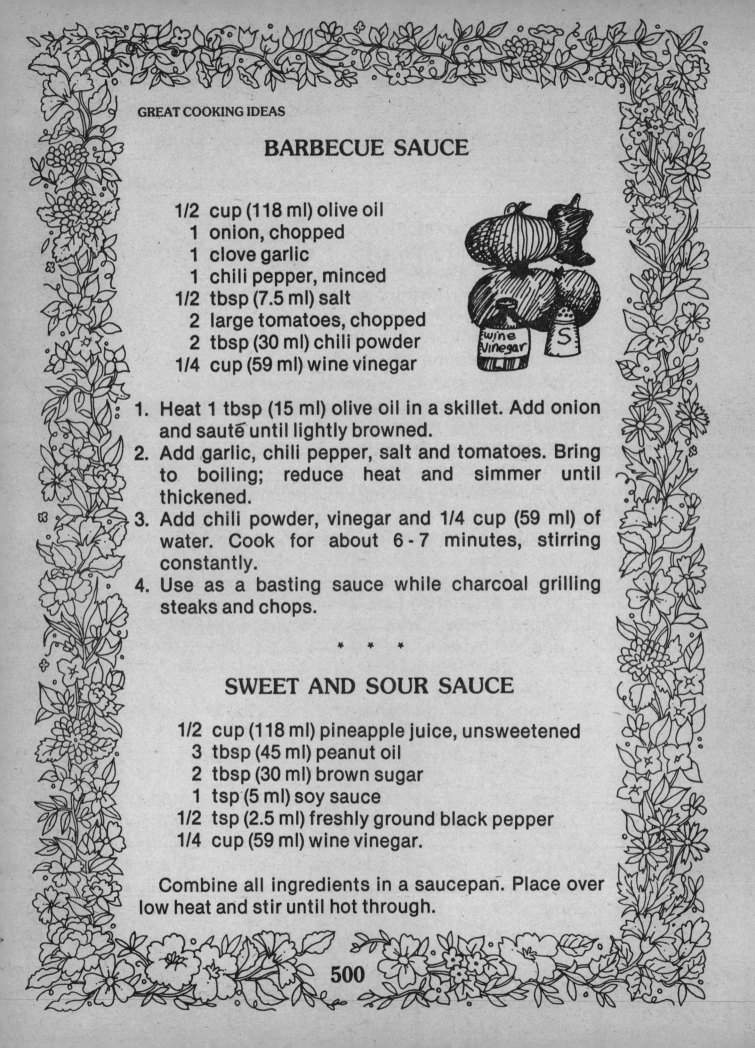

1/2 cup (118 ml) olive oil
1 onion, chopped
1 clove garlic
1 chili pepper, minced
1/2 tbsp (7.5 ml) salt
2 large tomatoes, chopped
2 tbsp (30 ml) chili powder
1/4 cup (59 ml) wine vinegar

1. Heat 1 tbsp (15 ml) olive oil in a skillet. Add onion and sauté until lightly browned.
2. Add garlic, chili pepper, salt and tomatoes. Bring to boiling; reduce heat and simmer until thickened.
3. Add chili powder, vinegar and 1/4 cup (59 ml) of water. Cook for about 6 - 7 minutes, stirring constantly.
4. Use as a basting sauce while charcoal grilling steaks and chops.

* * *

SWEET AND SOUR SAUCE

1/2 cup (118 ml) pineapple juice, unsweetened
3 tbsp (45 ml) peanut oil
2 tbsp (30 ml) brown sugar
1 tsp (5 ml) soy sauce
1/2 tsp (2.5 ml) freshly ground black pepper
1/4 cup (59 ml) wine vinegar.

Combine all ingredients in a saucepan. Place over low heat and stir until hot through.

BASIC TOMATO SAUCE

Makes about 2 cups.

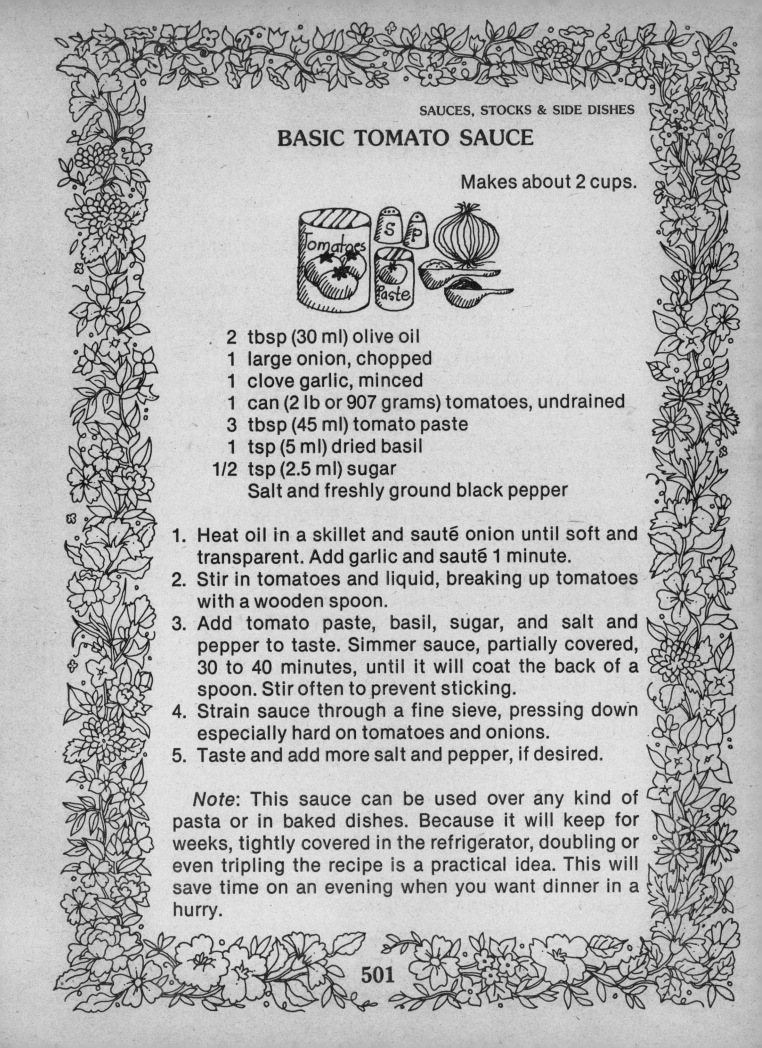

2 tbsp (30 ml) olive oil
1 large onion, chopped
1 clove garlic, minced
1 can (2 lb or 907 grams) tomatoes, undrained
3 tbsp (45 ml) tomato paste
1 tsp (5 ml) dried basil
1/2 tsp (2.5 ml) sugar
Salt and freshly ground black pepper

1. Heat oil in a skillet and sauté onion until soft and transparent. Add garlic and sauté 1 minute.
2. Stir in tomatoes and liquid, breaking up tomatoes with a wooden spoon.
3. Add tomato paste, basil, sugar, and salt and pepper to taste. Simmer sauce, partially covered, 30 to 40 minutes, until it will coat the back of a spoon. Stir often to prevent sticking.
4. Strain sauce through a fine sieve, pressing down especially hard on tomatoes and onions.
5. Taste and add more salt and pepper, if desired.

Note: This sauce can be used over any kind of pasta or in baked dishes. Because it will keep for weeks, tightly covered in the refrigerator, doubling or even tripling the recipe is a practical idea. This will save time on an evening when you want dinner in a hurry.

HOT TOMATO SAUCE

Makes 1 cup.

1 can (16 oz or 454 grams) tomatoes, drained and finely chopped
1 can (4 oz or 113 grams) green chili peppers, rinsed, seeded and chopped
1 small onion, finely chopped
1 tbsp (15 ml) wine vinegar
1 tsp (5 ml) sugar
1/8 tsp (.6 ml) salt

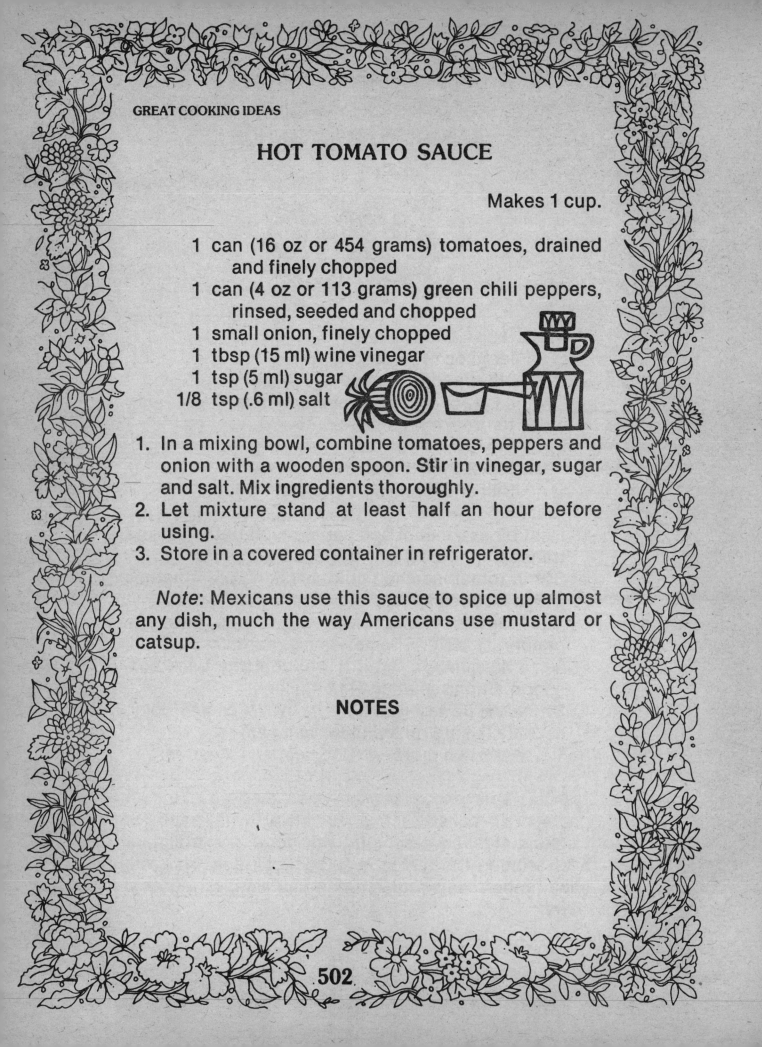

1. In a mixing bowl, combine tomatoes, peppers and onion with a wooden spoon. Stir in vinegar, sugar and salt. Mix ingredients thoroughly.
2. Let mixture stand at least half an hour before using.
3. Store in a covered container in refrigerator.

Note: Mexicans use this sauce to spice up almost any dish, much the way Americans use mustard or catsup.

NOTES

BASIC WHITE SAUCE

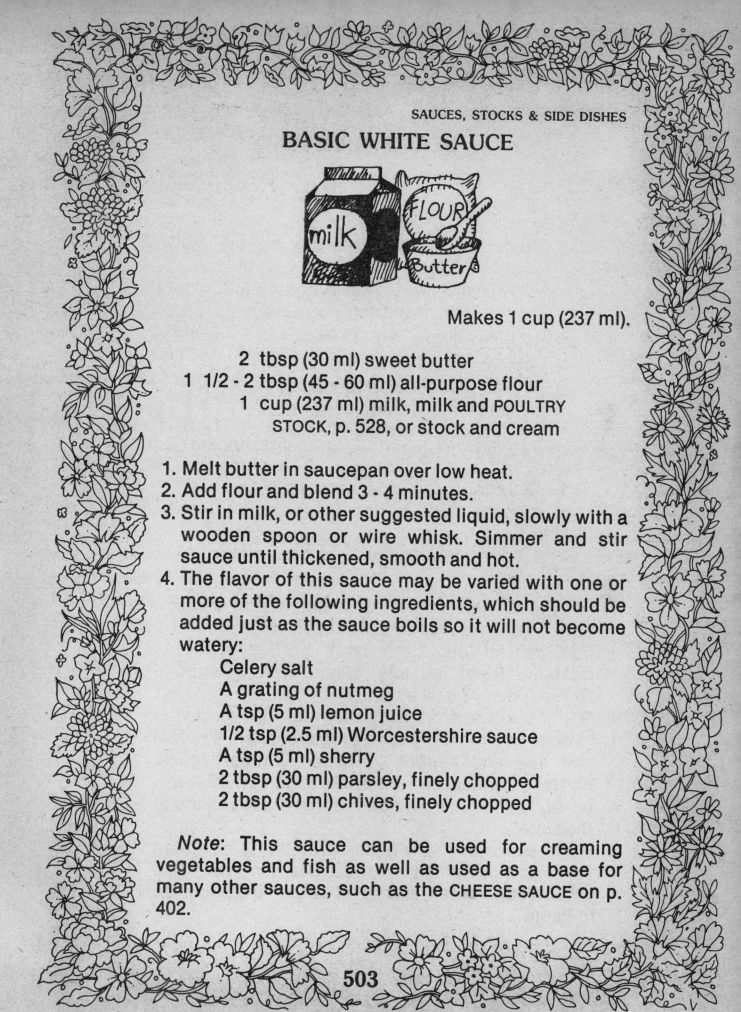

Makes 1 cup (237 ml).

2 tbsp (30 ml) sweet butter
1 1/2 - 2 tbsp (45 - 60 ml) all-purpose flour
1 cup (237 ml) milk, milk and POULTRY
STOCK, p. 528, or stock and cream

1. Melt butter in saucepan over low heat.
2. Add flour and blend 3 - 4 minutes.
3. Stir in milk, or other suggested liquid, slowly with a wooden spoon or wire whisk. Simmer and stir sauce until thickened, smooth and hot.
4. The flavor of this sauce may be varied with one or more of the following ingredients, which should be added just as the sauce boils so it will not become watery:
    Celery salt
    A grating of nutmeg
    A tsp (5 ml) lemon juice
    1/2 tsp (2.5 ml) Worcestershire sauce
    A tsp (5 ml) sherry
    2 tbsp (30 ml) parsley, finely chopped
    2 tbsp (30 ml) chives, finely chopped

Note: This sauce can be used for creaming vegetables and fish as well as used as a base for many other sauces, such as the CHEESE SAUCE on p. 402.

BEEF SAUCE

Makes 4 - 6 servings.

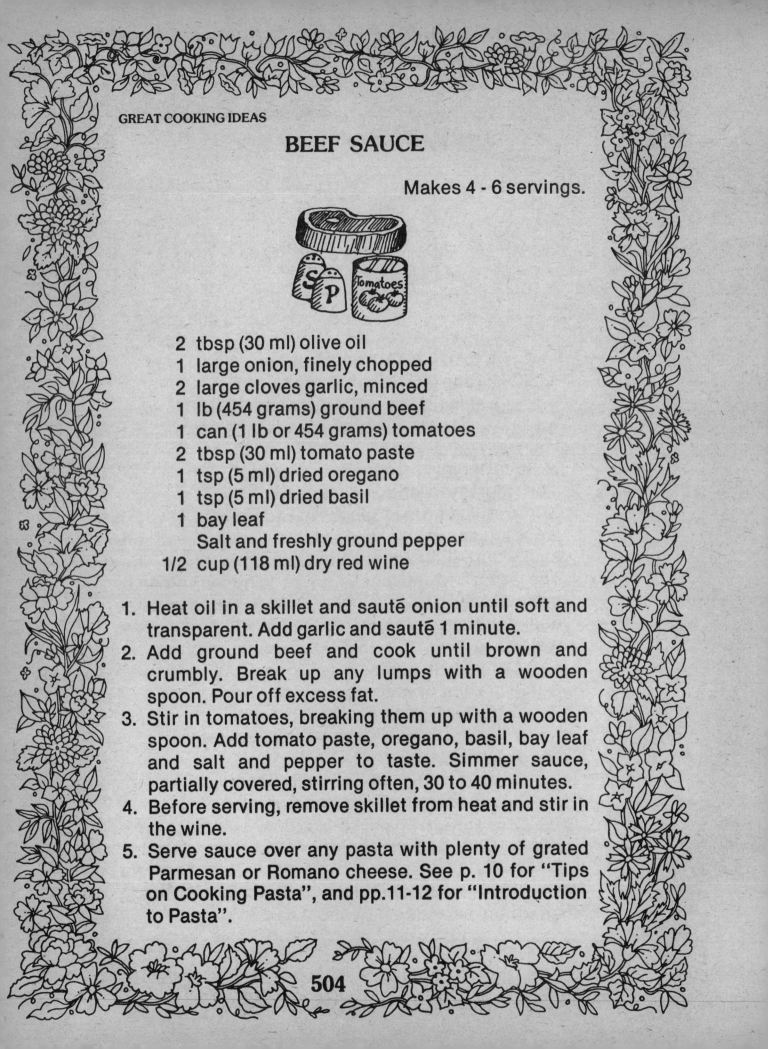

2 tbsp (30 ml) olive oil
1 large onion, finely chopped
2 large cloves garlic, minced
1 lb (454 grams) ground beef
1 can (1 lb or 454 grams) tomatoes
2 tbsp (30 ml) tomato paste
1 tsp (5 ml) dried oregano
1 tsp (5 ml) dried basil
1 bay leaf
Salt and freshly ground pepper
1/2 cup (118 ml) dry red wine

1. Heat oil in a skillet and sauté onion until soft and transparent. Add garlic and sauté 1 minute.
2. Add ground beef and cook until brown and crumbly. Break up any lumps with a wooden spoon. Pour off excess fat.
3. Stir in tomatoes, breaking them up with a wooden spoon. Add tomato paste, oregano, basil, bay leaf and salt and pepper to taste. Simmer sauce, partially covered, stirring often, 30 to 40 minutes.
4. Before serving, remove skillet from heat and stir in the wine.
5. Serve sauce over any pasta with plenty of grated Parmesan or Romano cheese. See p. 10 for "Tips on Cooking Pasta", and pp.11-12 for "Introduction to Pasta".

BOLOGNESE SAUCE

Makes 4 - 6 servings.

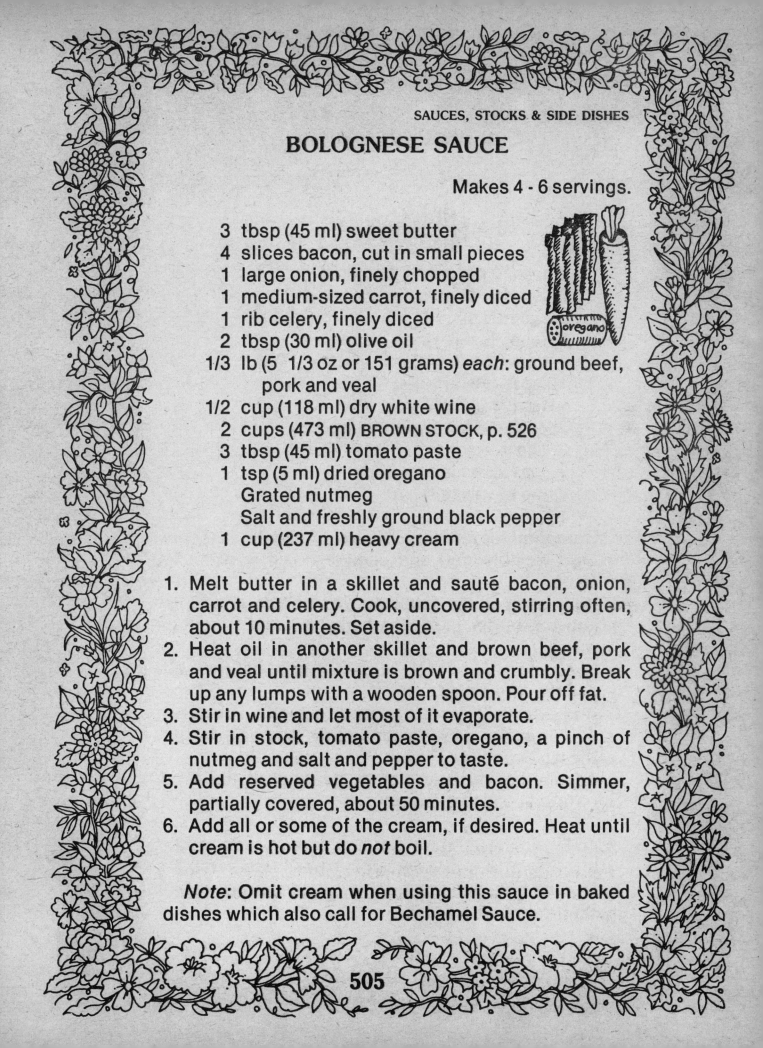

3 tbsp (45 ml) sweet butter
4 slices bacon, cut in small pieces
1 large onion, finely chopped
1 medium-sized carrot, finely diced
1 rib celery, finely diced
2 tbsp (30 ml) olive oil
1/3 lb (5 1/3 oz or 151 grams) *each*: ground beef,
     pork and veal
1/2 cup (118 ml) dry white wine
2 cups (473 ml) BROWN STOCK, p. 526
3 tbsp (45 ml) tomato paste
1 tsp (5 ml) dried oregano
   Grated nutmeg
   Salt and freshly ground black pepper
1 cup (237 ml) heavy cream

1. Melt butter in a skillet and sauté bacon, onion, carrot and celery. Cook, uncovered, stirring often, about 10 minutes. Set aside.
2. Heat oil in another skillet and brown beef, pork and veal until mixture is brown and crumbly. Break up any lumps with a wooden spoon. Pour off fat.
3. Stir in wine and let most of it evaporate.
4. Stir in stock, tomato paste, oregano, a pinch of nutmeg and salt and pepper to taste.
5. Add reserved vegetables and bacon. Simmer, partially covered, about 50 minutes.
6. Add all or some of the cream, if desired. Heat until cream is hot but do *not* boil.

Note: Omit cream when using this sauce in baked dishes which also call for Bechamel Sauce.

BEARNAISE SAUCE

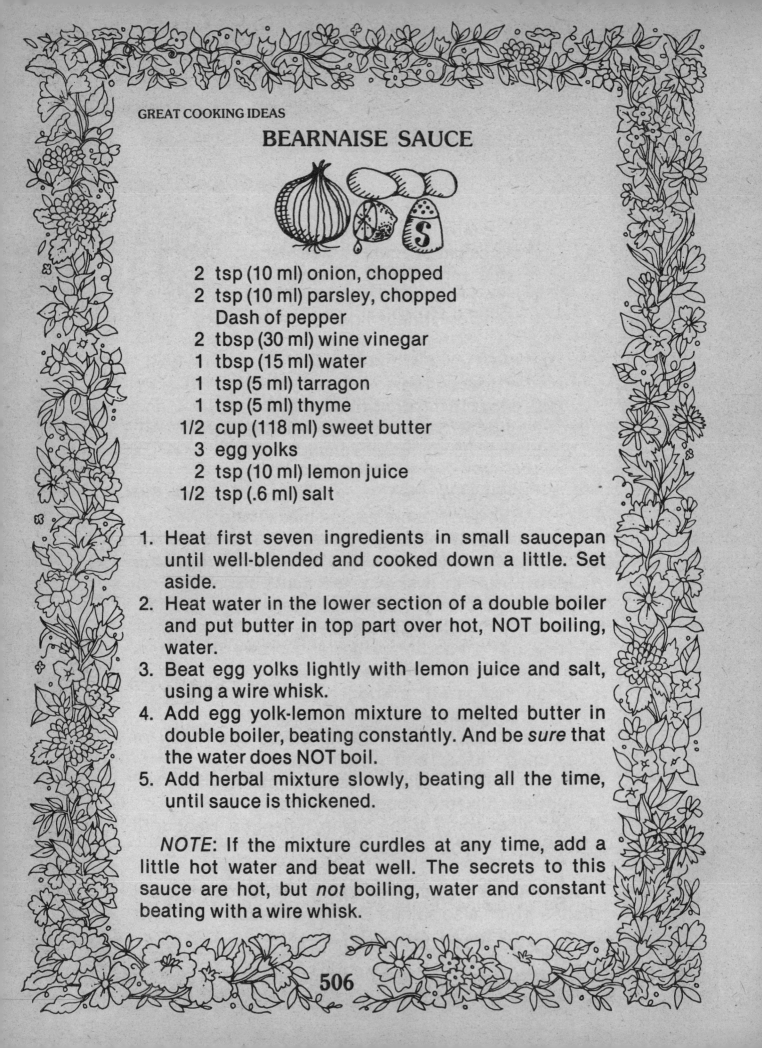

      2 tsp (10 ml) onion, chopped
      2 tsp (10 ml) parsley, chopped
         Dash of pepper
      2 tbsp (30 ml) wine vinegar
      1 tbsp (15 ml) water
      1 tsp (5 ml) tarragon
      1 tsp (5 ml) thyme
    1/2 cup (118 ml) sweet butter
      3 egg yolks
      2 tsp (10 ml) lemon juice
    1/2 tsp (.6 ml) salt

1. Heat first seven ingredients in small saucepan until well-blended and cooked down a little. Set aside.
2. Heat water in the lower section of a double boiler and put butter in top part over hot, NOT boiling, water.
3. Beat egg yolks lightly with lemon juice and salt, using a wire whisk.
4. Add egg yolk-lemon mixture to melted butter in double boiler, beating constantly. And be *sure* that the water does NOT boil.
5. Add herbal mixture slowly, beating all the time, until sauce is thickened.

NOTE: If the mixture curdles at any time, add a little hot water and beat well. The secrets to this sauce are hot, but *not* boiling, water and constant beating with a wire whisk.

506

BROWN SAUCE

Makes about 1 cup.

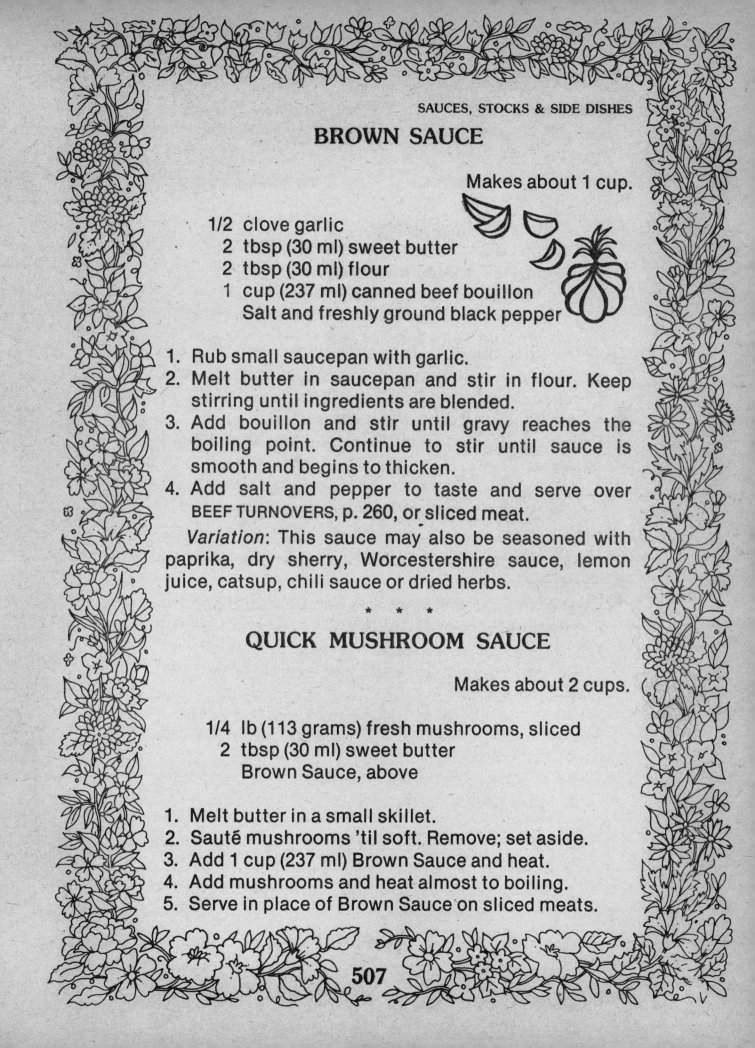

1/2 clove garlic
2 tbsp (30 ml) sweet butter
2 tbsp (30 ml) flour
1 cup (237 ml) canned beef bouillon
Salt and freshly ground black pepper

1. Rub small saucepan with garlic.
2. Melt butter in saucepan and stir in flour. Keep stirring until ingredients are blended.
3. Add bouillon and stir until gravy reaches the boiling point. Continue to stir until sauce is smooth and begins to thicken.
4. Add salt and pepper to taste and serve over BEEF TURNOVERS, p. 260, or sliced meat.

Variation: This sauce may also be seasoned with paprika, dry sherry, Worcestershire sauce, lemon juice, catsup, chili sauce or dried herbs.

* * *

QUICK MUSHROOM SAUCE

Makes about 2 cups.

1/4 lb (113 grams) fresh mushrooms, sliced
2 tbsp (30 ml) sweet butter
Brown Sauce, above

1. Melt butter in a small skillet.
2. Sauté mushrooms 'til soft. Remove; set aside.
3. Add 1 cup (237 ml) Brown Sauce and heat.
4. Add mushrooms and heat almost to boiling.
5. Serve in place of Brown Sauce on sliced meats.

DASHI SAUCE

Makes 6 servings.

7 cups (1.7 liters) water
3/4 cup (177 ml) dried bonito shavings*
3/4 cup (177 ml) Japanese soy sauce
3/4 cup (117 ml) *sake* or dry sherry
   * *Dried bonito fish is available in Japanese markets.*

1. Warm dried bonito before shaving.
2. Bring water to boiling in a large saucepan. Add bonito shavings and boil 3 minutes.
3. Strain liquid and discard shavings.
4. Combine strained liquid with soy sauce and *sake* (sherry).

* * *

CRISP FRIED ONION FLAKES

1. Cut 2 medium-sized onions in quarters, then in paper-thin slices.
2. Heat 2 tbsp (30 ml) vegetable oil in a skillet and fry onions until crisp and golden.
3. Drain on paper towels and store in tightly-covered glass jar. They can be kept for several weeks this way.

NOTES

HOT SHRIMP SAUCE

Makes about 2 cups.

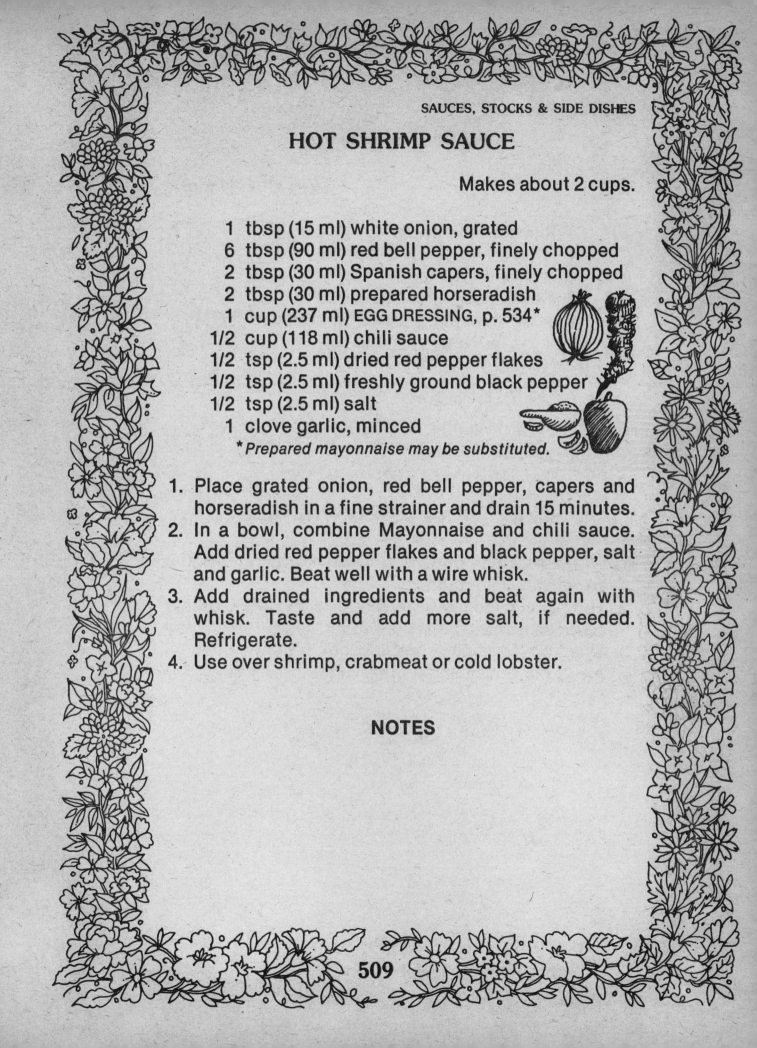

- 1 tbsp (15 ml) white onion, grated
- 6 tbsp (90 ml) red bell pepper, finely chopped
- 2 tbsp (30 ml) Spanish capers, finely chopped
- 2 tbsp (30 ml) prepared horseradish
- 1 cup (237 ml) EGG DRESSING, p. 534*
- 1/2 cup (118 ml) chili sauce
- 1/2 tsp (2.5 ml) dried red pepper flakes
- 1/2 tsp (2.5 ml) freshly ground black pepper
- 1/2 tsp (2.5 ml) salt
- 1 clove garlic, minced

Prepared mayonnaise may be substituted.

1. Place grated onion, red bell pepper, capers and horseradish in a fine strainer and drain 15 minutes.
2. In a bowl, combine Mayonnaise and chili sauce. Add dried red pepper flakes and black pepper, salt and garlic. Beat well with a wire whisk.
3. Add drained ingredients and beat again with whisk. Taste and add more salt, if needed. Refrigerate.
4. Use over shrimp, crabmeat or cold lobster.

NOTES

MARINARA SAUCE

Makes about 2 cups.

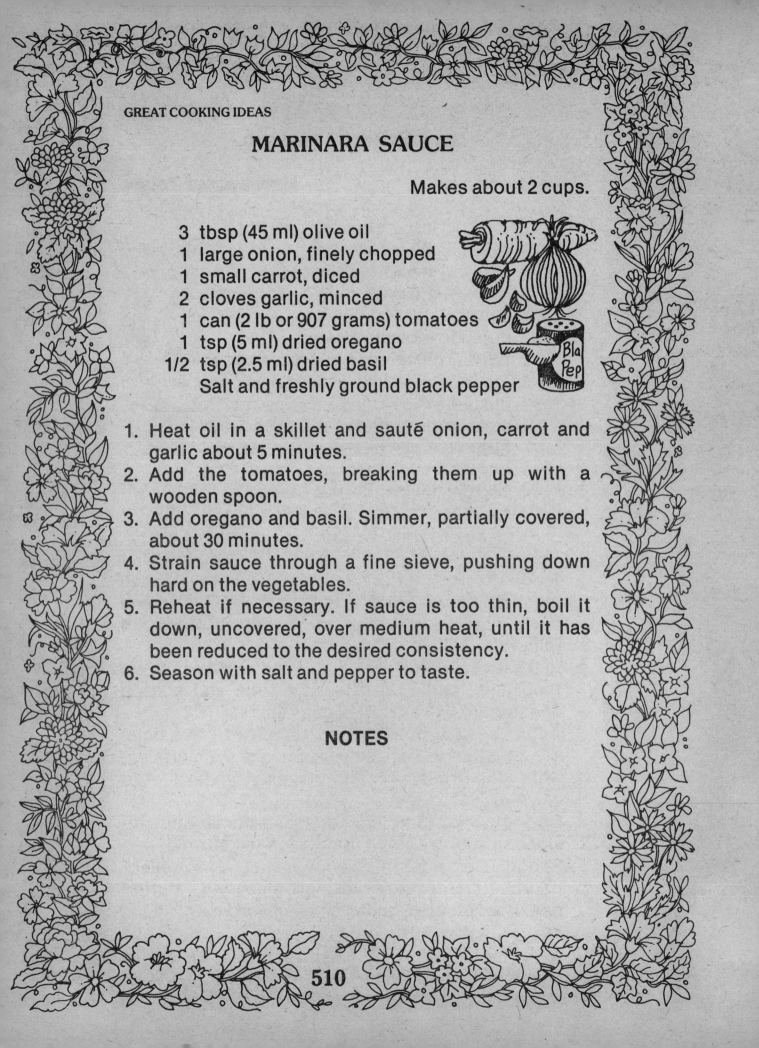

3 tbsp (45 ml) olive oil
1 large onion, finely chopped
1 small carrot, diced
2 cloves garlic, minced
1 can (2 lb or 907 grams) tomatoes
1 tsp (5 ml) dried oregano
1/2 tsp (2.5 ml) dried basil
Salt and freshly ground black pepper

1. Heat oil in a skillet and sauté onion, carrot and garlic about 5 minutes.
2. Add the tomatoes, breaking them up with a wooden spoon.
3. Add oregano and basil. Simmer, partially covered, about 30 minutes.
4. Strain sauce through a fine sieve, pushing down hard on the vegetables.
5. Reheat if necessary. If sauce is too thin, boil it down, uncovered, over medium heat, until it has been reduced to the desired consistency.
6. Season with salt and pepper to taste.

NOTES

MUSHROOM SAUCE

Makes about 3 cups.

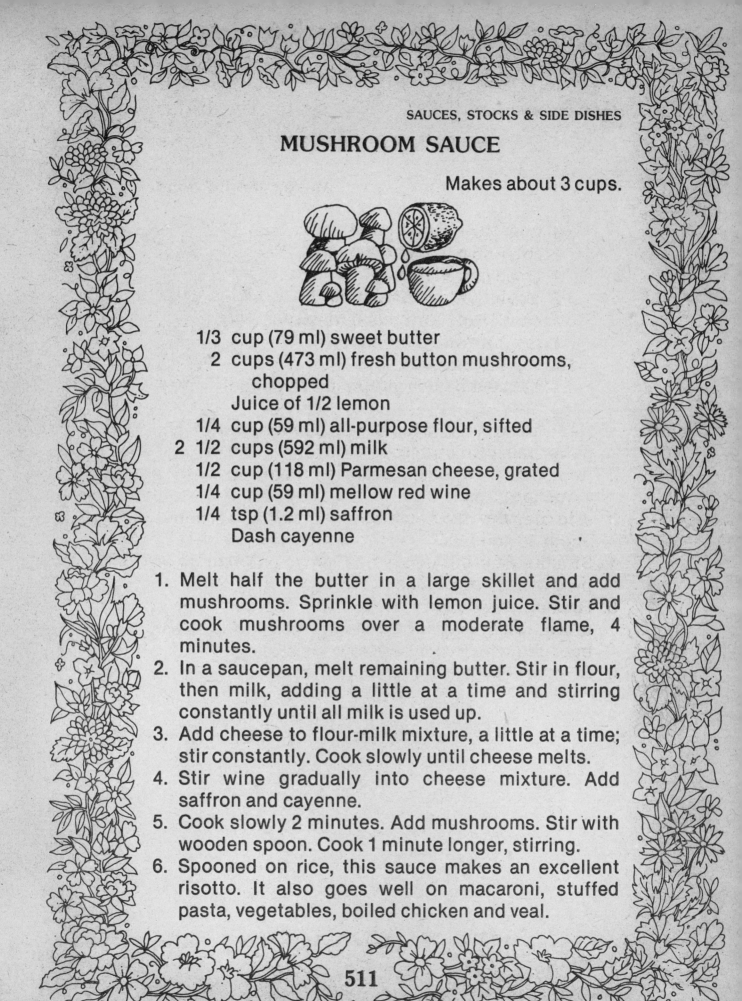

1/3 cup (79 ml) sweet butter
2 cups (473 ml) fresh button mushrooms, chopped
Juice of 1/2 lemon
1/4 cup (59 ml) all-purpose flour, sifted
2 1/2 cups (592 ml) milk
1/2 cup (118 ml) Parmesan cheese, grated
1/4 cup (59 ml) mellow red wine
1/4 tsp (1.2 ml) saffron
Dash cayenne

1. Melt half the butter in a large skillet and add mushrooms. Sprinkle with lemon juice. Stir and cook mushrooms over a moderate flame, 4 minutes.
2. In a saucepan, melt remaining butter. Stir in flour, then milk, adding a little at a time and stirring constantly until all milk is used up.
3. Add cheese to flour-milk mixture, a little at a time; stir constantly. Cook slowly until cheese melts.
4. Stir wine gradually into cheese mixture. Add saffron and cayenne.
5. Cook slowly 2 minutes. Add mushrooms. Stir with wooden spoon. Cook 1 minute longer, stirring.
6. Spooned on rice, this sauce makes an excellent risotto. It also goes well on macaroni, stuffed pasta, vegetables, boiled chicken and veal.

OIL 'N' GARLIC SAUCE

Makes 4 servings.

3/4 cup (177 ml) sweet butter
6 tbsp (90 ml) olive oil
4 cloves garlic, finely chopped
1/2 cup (118 ml) fresh parsley leaves, chopped
1/4 cup (59 ml) fresh leek, white part only, chopped
1/4 tsp (1.2 ml) salt
1/8 tsp (.6 ml) freshly ground white pepper
Dash oregano
Dash marjoram
1/4 cup (59 ml) dry red wine

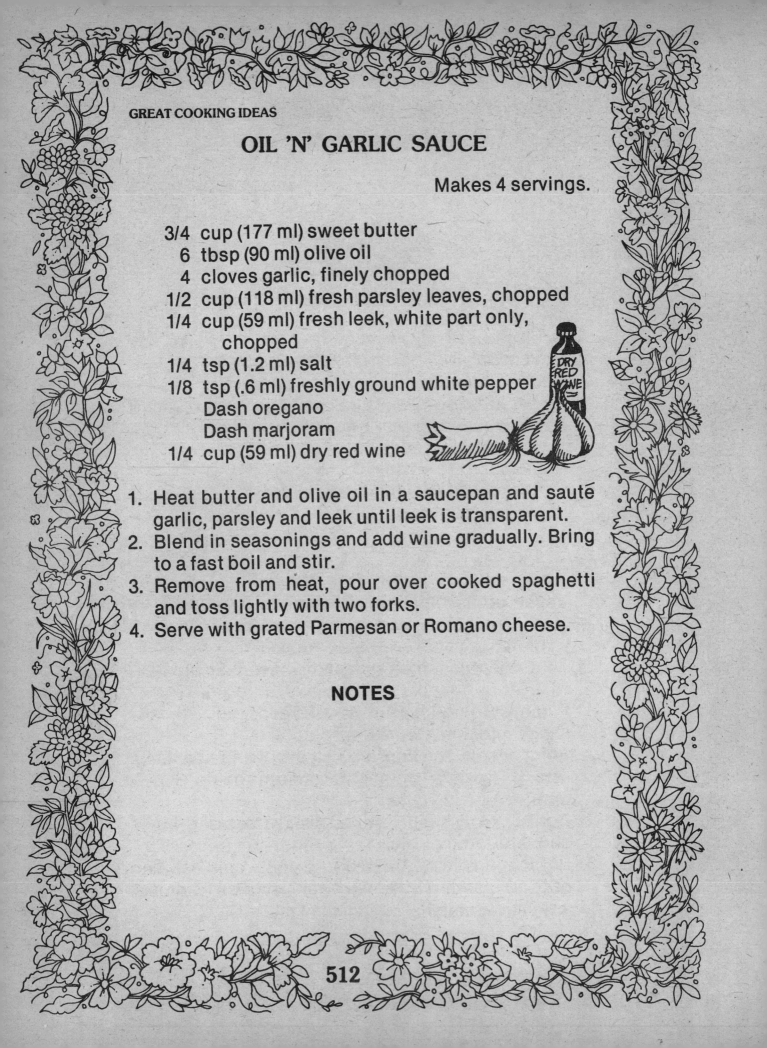

1. Heat butter and olive oil in a saucepan and sauté garlic, parsley and leek until leek is transparent.
2. Blend in seasonings and add wine gradually. Bring to a fast boil and stir.
3. Remove from heat, pour over cooked spaghetti and toss lightly with two forks.
4. Serve with grated Parmesan or Romano cheese.

NOTES

PEPPER OIL

Makes about 1 cup.

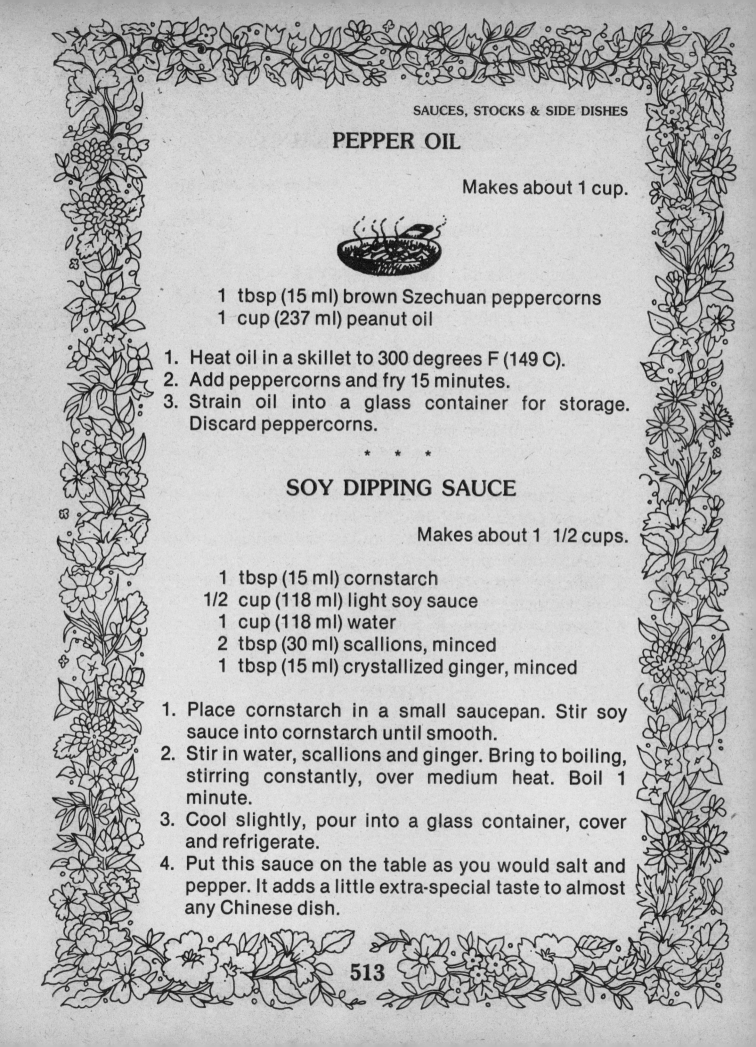

1 tbsp (15 ml) brown Szechuan peppercorns
1 cup (237 ml) peanut oil

1. Heat oil in a skillet to 300 degrees F (149 C).
2. Add peppercorns and fry 15 minutes.
3. Strain oil into a glass container for storage. Discard peppercorns.

* * *

SOY DIPPING SAUCE

Makes about 1 1/2 cups.

1 tbsp (15 ml) cornstarch
1/2 cup (118 ml) light soy sauce
1 cup (118 ml) water
2 tbsp (30 ml) scallions, minced
1 tbsp (15 ml) crystallized ginger, minced

1. Place cornstarch in a small saucepan. Stir soy sauce into cornstarch until smooth.
2. Stir in water, scallions and ginger. Bring to boiling, stirring constantly, over medium heat. Boil 1 minute.
3. Cool slightly, pour into a glass container, cover and refrigerate.
4. Put this sauce on the table as you would salt and pepper. It adds a little extra-special taste to almost any Chinese dish.

GREAT COOKING IDEAS

QUICK SEAFOOD SAUCE

Makes about 4 cups.

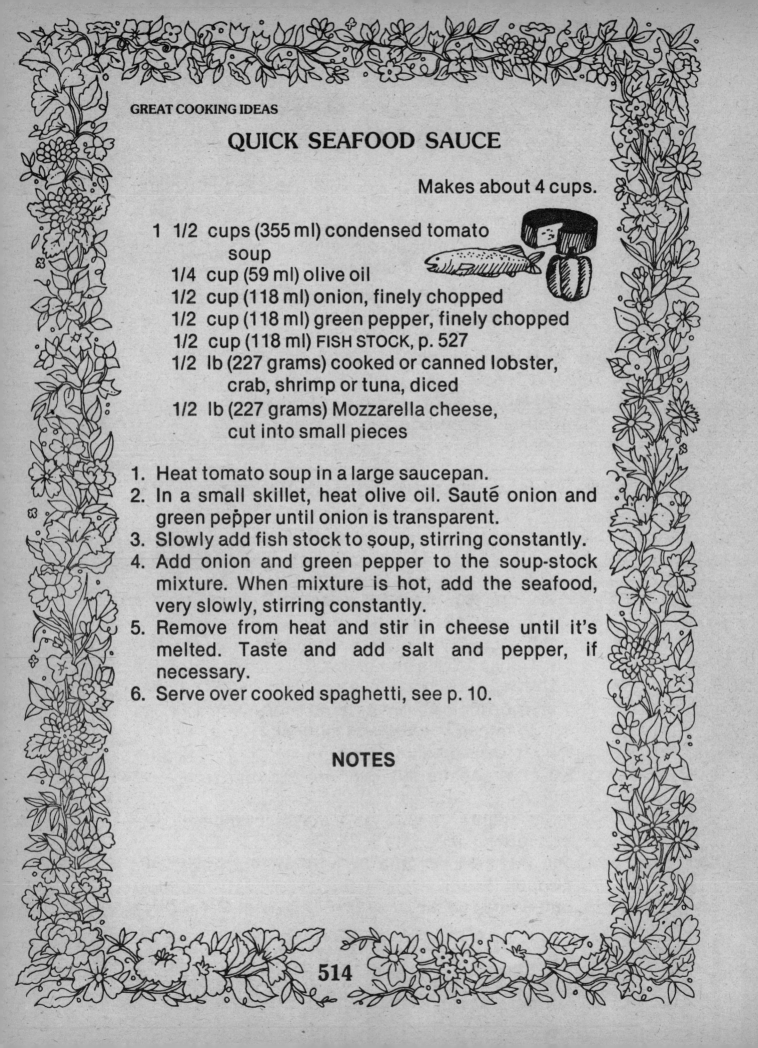

1 1/2 cups (355 ml) condensed tomato
           soup
      1/4 cup (59 ml) olive oil
      1/2 cup (118 ml) onion, finely chopped
      1/2 cup (118 ml) green pepper, finely chopped
      1/2 cup (118 ml) FISH STOCK, p. 527
      1/2 lb (227 grams) cooked or canned lobster,
           crab, shrimp or tuna, diced
      1/2 lb (227 grams) Mozzarella cheese,
           cut into small pieces

1. Heat tomato soup in a large saucepan.
2. In a small skillet, heat olive oil. Sauté onion and green pepper until onion is transparent.
3. Slowly add fish stock to soup, stirring constantly.
4. Add onion and green pepper to the soup-stock mixture. When mixture is hot, add the seafood, very slowly, stirring constantly.
5. Remove from heat and stir in cheese until it's melted. Taste and add salt and pepper, if necessary.
6. Serve over cooked spaghetti, see p. 10.

NOTES

RED HOT SAUCE

Makes 3 cups.

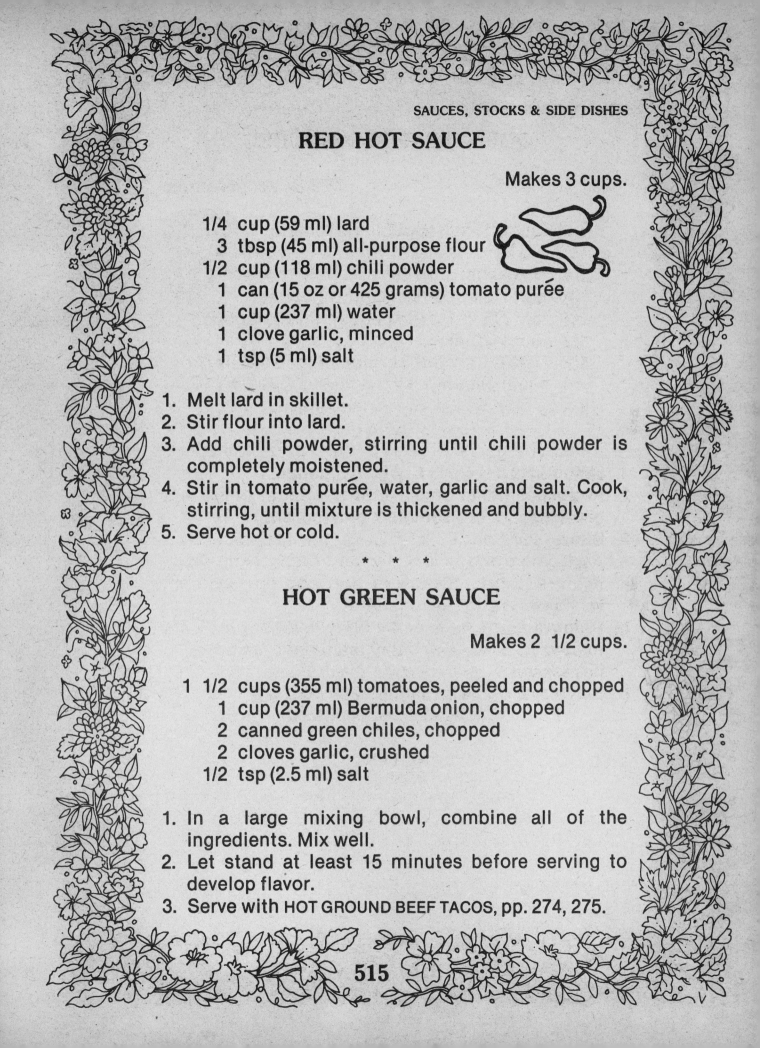

1/4 cup (59 ml) lard
  3 tbsp (45 ml) all-purpose flour
1/2 cup (118 ml) chili powder
  1 can (15 oz or 425 grams) tomato purée
  1 cup (237 ml) water
  1 clove garlic, minced
  1 tsp (5 ml) salt

1. Melt lard in skillet.
2. Stir flour into lard.
3. Add chili powder, stirring until chili powder is completely moistened.
4. Stir in tomato purée, water, garlic and salt. Cook, stirring, until mixture is thickened and bubbly.
5. Serve hot or cold.

* * *

HOT GREEN SAUCE

Makes 2 1/2 cups.

1 1/2 cups (355 ml) tomatoes, peeled and chopped
  1 cup (237 ml) Bermuda onion, chopped
  2 canned green chiles, chopped
  2 cloves garlic, crushed
1/2 tsp (2.5 ml) salt

1. In a large mixing bowl, combine all of the ingredients. Mix well.
2. Let stand at least 15 minutes before serving to develop flavor.
3. Serve with HOT GROUND BEEF TACOS, pp. 274, 275.

WHITE WINE SAUCE

Makes 1 3/4 cups.

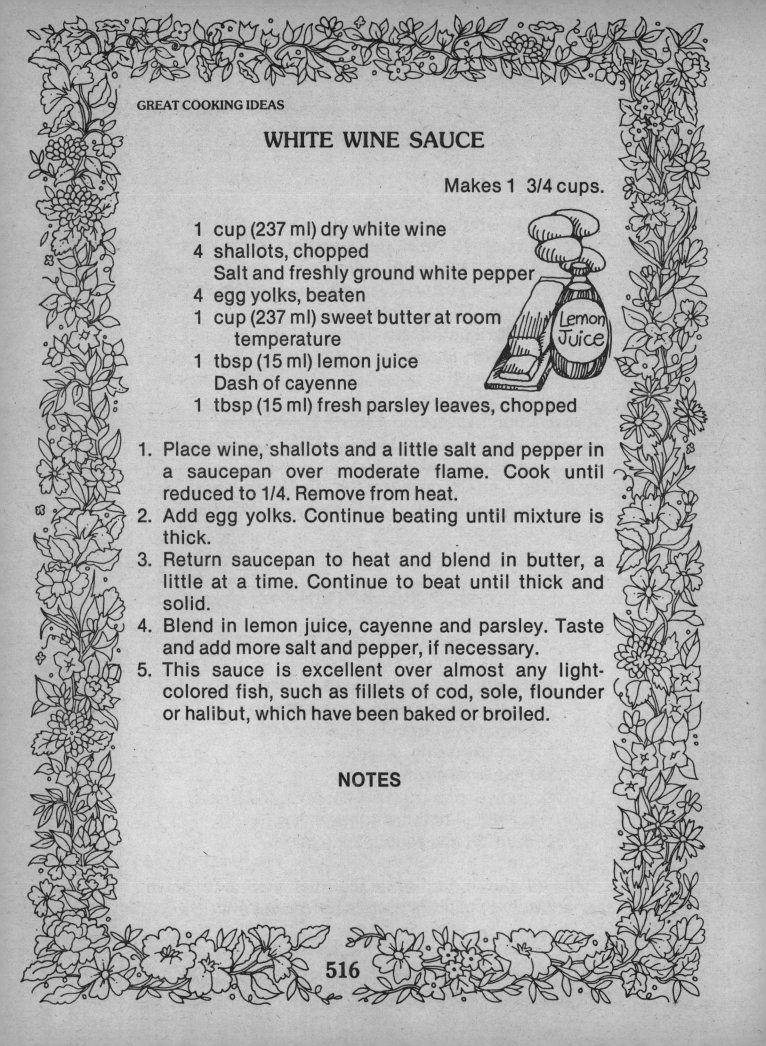

- 1 cup (237 ml) dry white wine
- 4 shallots, chopped
- Salt and freshly ground white pepper
- 4 egg yolks, beaten
- 1 cup (237 ml) sweet butter at room temperature
- 1 tbsp (15 ml) lemon juice
- Dash of cayenne
- 1 tbsp (15 ml) fresh parsley leaves, chopped

1. Place wine, shallots and a little salt and pepper in a saucepan over moderate flame. Cook until reduced to 1/4. Remove from heat.
2. Add egg yolks. Continue beating until mixture is thick.
3. Return saucepan to heat and blend in butter, a little at a time. Continue to beat until thick and solid.
4. Blend in lemon juice, cayenne and parsley. Taste and add more salt and pepper, if necessary.
5. This sauce is excellent over almost any light-colored fish, such as fillets of cod, sole, flounder or halibut, which have been baked or broiled.

NOTES

FISH BUTTER

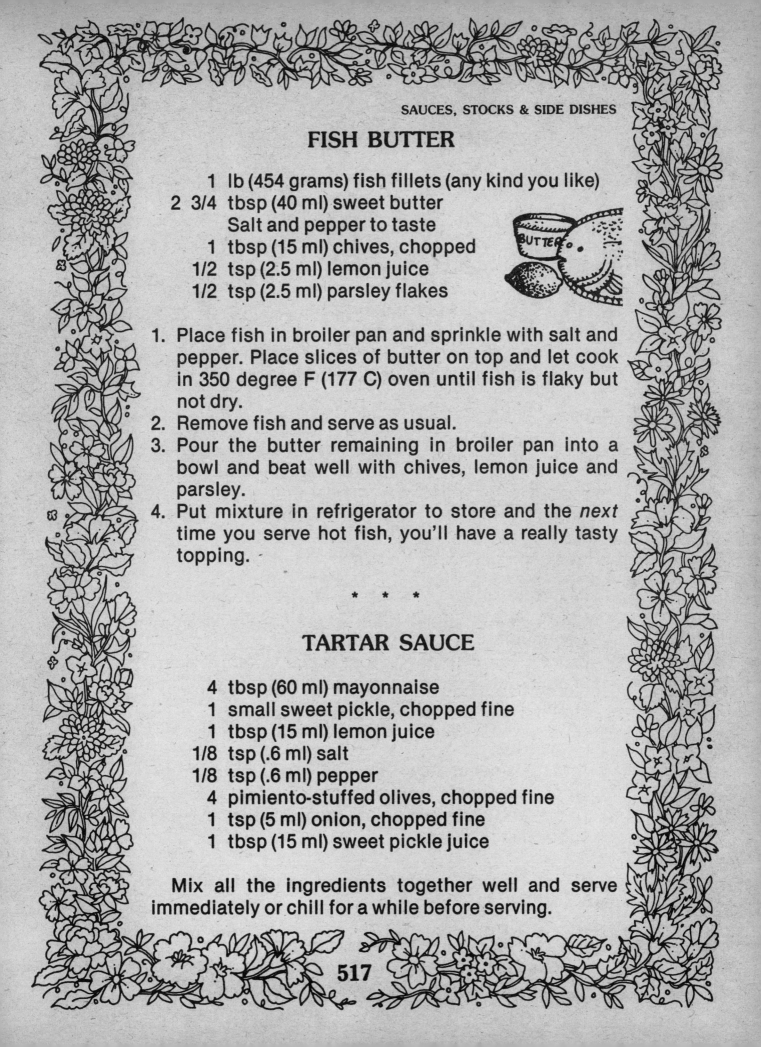

        1   lb (454 grams) fish fillets (any kind you like)
    2 3/4   tbsp (40 ml) sweet butter
            Salt and pepper to taste
        1   tbsp (15 ml) chives, chopped
      1/2   tsp (2.5 ml) lemon juice
      1/2   tsp (2.5 ml) parsley flakes

1. Place fish in broiler pan and sprinkle with salt and pepper. Place slices of butter on top and let cook in 350 degree F (177 C) oven until fish is flaky but not dry.
2. Remove fish and serve as usual.
3. Pour the butter remaining in broiler pan into a bowl and beat well with chives, lemon juice and parsley.
4. Put mixture in refrigerator to store and the *next* time you serve hot fish, you'll have a really tasty topping.

* * *

TARTAR SAUCE

        4   tbsp (60 ml) mayonnaise
        1   small sweet pickle, chopped fine
        1   tbsp (15 ml) lemon juice
      1/8   tsp (.6 ml) salt
      1/8   tsp (.6 ml) pepper
        4   pimiento-stuffed olives, chopped fine
        1   tsp (5 ml) onion, chopped fine
        1   tbsp (15 ml) sweet pickle juice

Mix all the ingredients together well and serve immediately or chill for a while before serving.

FRUIT DIPPING SAUCE

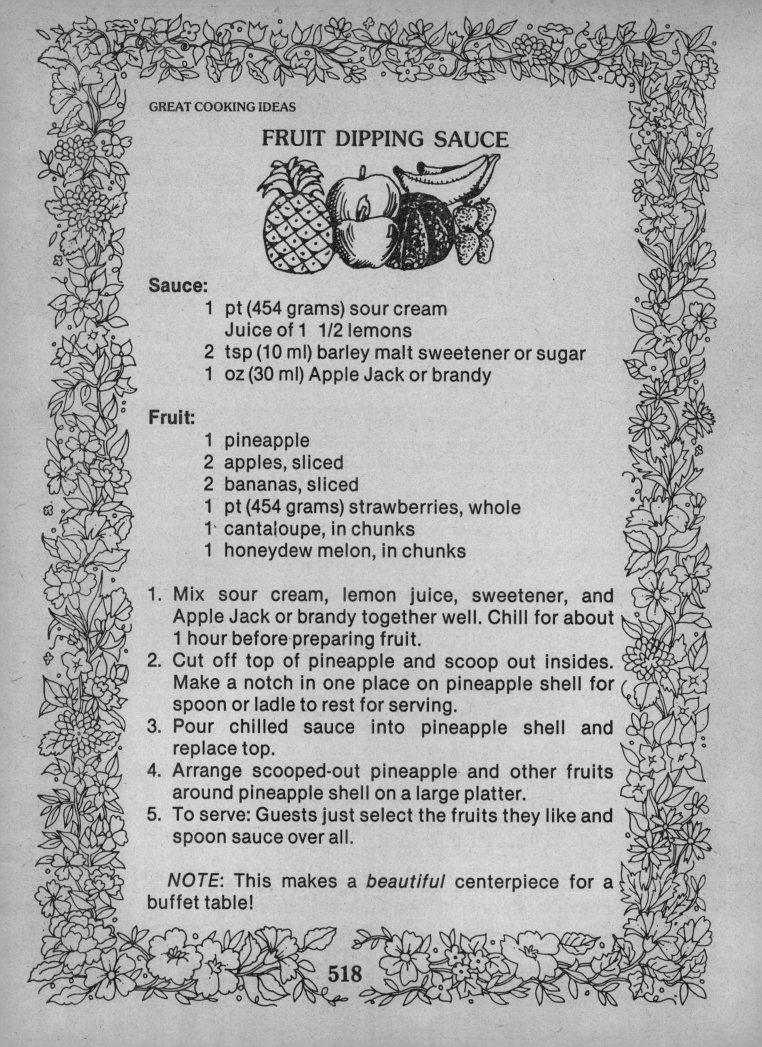

Sauce:

    1 pt (454 grams) sour cream
      Juice of 1 1/2 lemons
    2 tsp (10 ml) barley malt sweetener or sugar
    1 oz (30 ml) Apple Jack or brandy

Fruit:

    1 pineapple
    2 apples, sliced
    2 bananas, sliced
    1 pt (454 grams) strawberries, whole
    1 cantaloupe, in chunks
    1 honeydew melon, in chunks

1. Mix sour cream, lemon juice, sweetener, and Apple Jack or brandy together well. Chill for about 1 hour before preparing fruit.
2. Cut off top of pineapple and scoop out insides. Make a notch in one place on pineapple shell for spoon or ladle to rest for serving.
3. Pour chilled sauce into pineapple shell and replace top.
4. Arrange scooped-out pineapple and other fruits around pineapple shell on a large platter.
5. To serve: Guests just select the fruits they like and spoon sauce over all.

NOTE: This makes a *beautiful* centerpiece for a buffet table!

SESAME SAUCE

6 oz (170 grams) sesame seeds
1/2 cup (118 ml) soy sauce
1/2 cup (118 ml) sesame oil
2 tbsp (30 ml) white vinegar
1/4 cup (59 ml) water
2 medium-sized cloves garlic, crushed
1 tbsp (15 ml) red or black pepper
2 tbsp (30 ml) onion, chopped

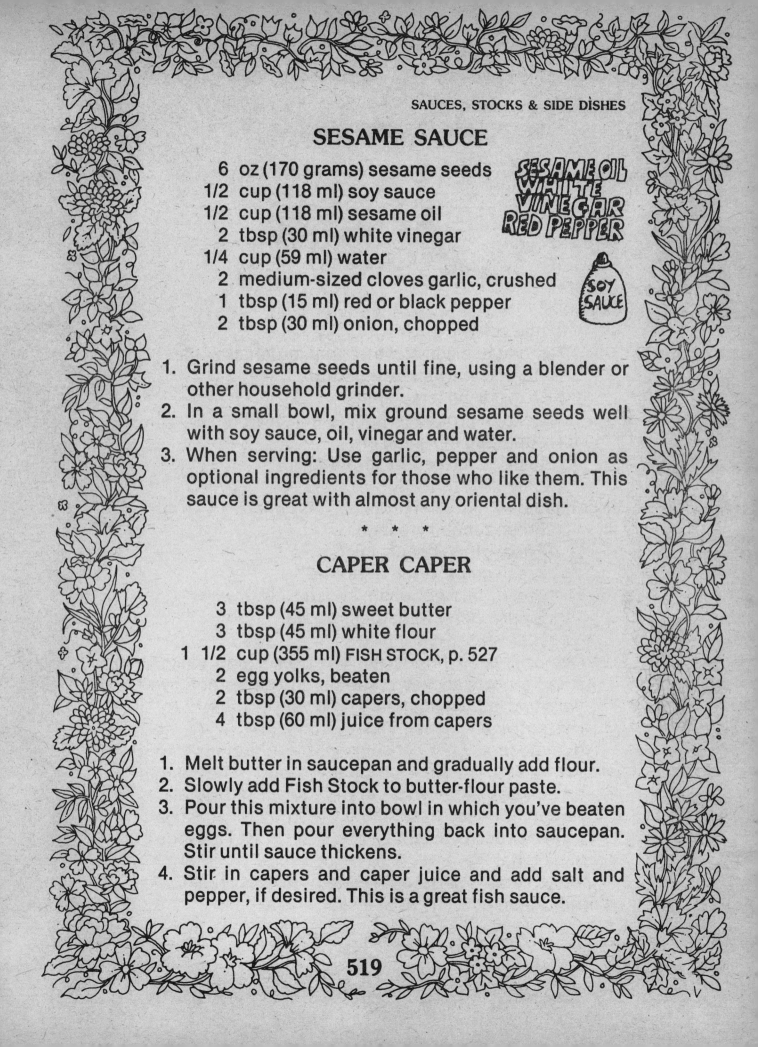

1. Grind sesame seeds until fine, using a blender or other household grinder.
2. In a small bowl, mix ground sesame seeds well with soy sauce, oil, vinegar and water.
3. When serving: Use garlic, pepper and onion as optional ingredients for those who like them. This sauce is great with almost any oriental dish.

* * *

CAPER CAPER

3 tbsp (45 ml) sweet butter
3 tbsp (45 ml) white flour
1 1/2 cup (355 ml) FISH STOCK, p. 527
2 egg yolks, beaten
2 tbsp (30 ml) capers, chopped
4 tbsp (60 ml) juice from capers

1. Melt butter in saucepan and gradually add flour.
2. Slowly add Fish Stock to butter-flour paste.
3. Pour this mixture into bowl in which you've beaten eggs. Then pour everything back into saucepan. Stir until sauce thickens.
4. Stir in capers and caper juice and add salt and pepper, if desired. This is a great fish sauce.

VEGETABLE DIPPING SAUCE

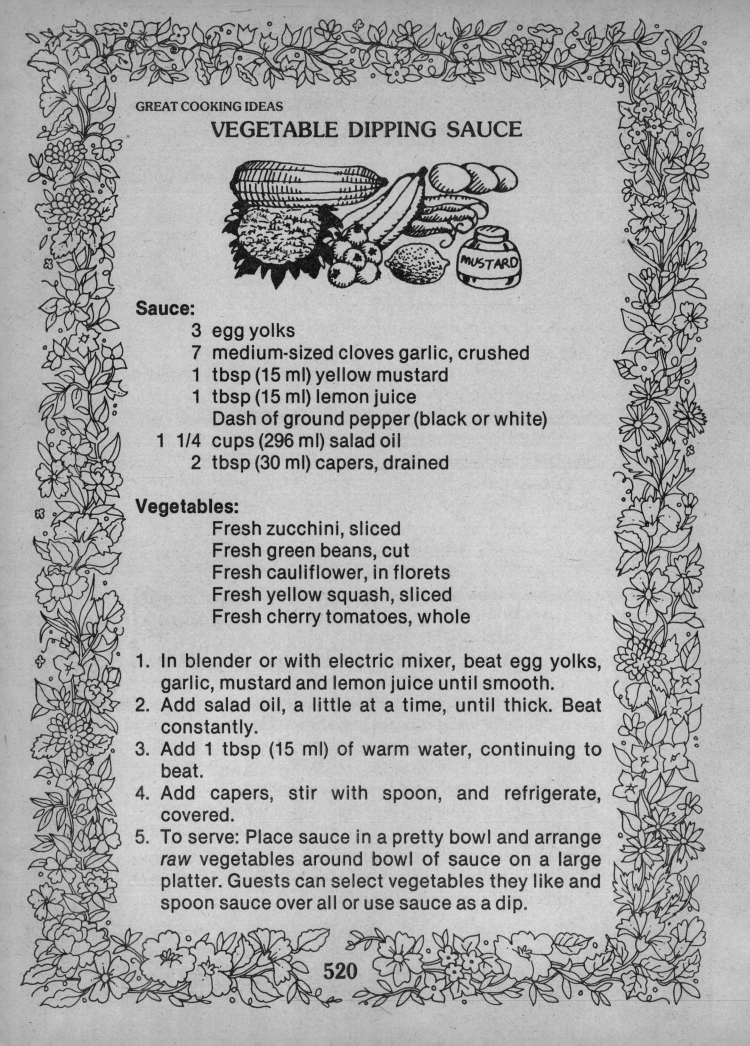

Sauce:

    3   egg yolks
    7   medium-sized cloves garlic, crushed
    1   tbsp (15 ml) yellow mustard
    1   tbsp (15 ml) lemon juice
        Dash of ground pepper (black or white)
1 1/4   cups (296 ml) salad oil
    2   tbsp (30 ml) capers, drained

Vegetables:

    Fresh zucchini, sliced
    Fresh green beans, cut
    Fresh cauliflower, in florets
    Fresh yellow squash, sliced
    Fresh cherry tomatoes, whole

1. In blender or with electric mixer, beat egg yolks, garlic, mustard and lemon juice until smooth.
2. Add salad oil, a little at a time, until thick. Beat constantly.
3. Add 1 tbsp (15 ml) of warm water, continuing to beat.
4. Add capers, stir with spoon, and refrigerate, covered.
5. To serve: Place sauce in a pretty bowl and arrange *raw* vegetables around bowl of sauce on a large platter. Guests can select vegetables they like and spoon sauce over all or use sauce as a dip.

CHOCOLATE SAUCE

Makes 1 3/4 cups

1 pkg (6 oz or 170 grams) semi-sweet
    chocolate
2/3 cup (158 ml) milk, scalded
2 tbsps (30 ml) butter
1/8 tsp (.6 ml) salt
1 tsp (5 ml) vanilla extract

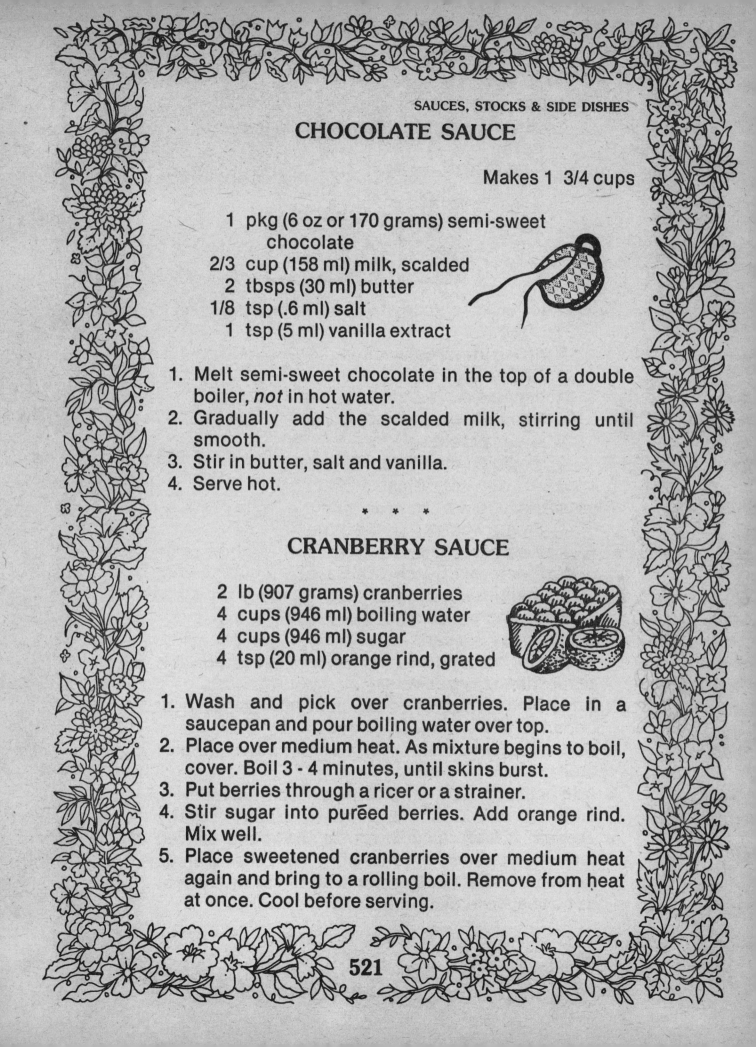

1. Melt semi-sweet chocolate in the top of a double boiler, *not* in hot water.
2. Gradually add the scalded milk, stirring until smooth.
3. Stir in butter, salt and vanilla.
4. Serve hot.

* * *

CRANBERRY SAUCE

2 lb (907 grams) cranberries
4 cups (946 ml) boiling water
4 cups (946 ml) sugar
4 tsp (20 ml) orange rind, grated

1. Wash and pick over cranberries. Place in a saucepan and pour boiling water over top.
2. Place over medium heat. As mixture begins to boil, cover. Boil 3 - 4 minutes, until skins burst.
3. Put berries through a ricer or a strainer.
4. Stir sugar into puréed berries. Add orange rind. Mix well.
5. Place sweetened cranberries over medium heat again and bring to a rolling boil. Remove from heat at once. Cool before serving.

CHICKEN BROTH

Makes about 2 qt.

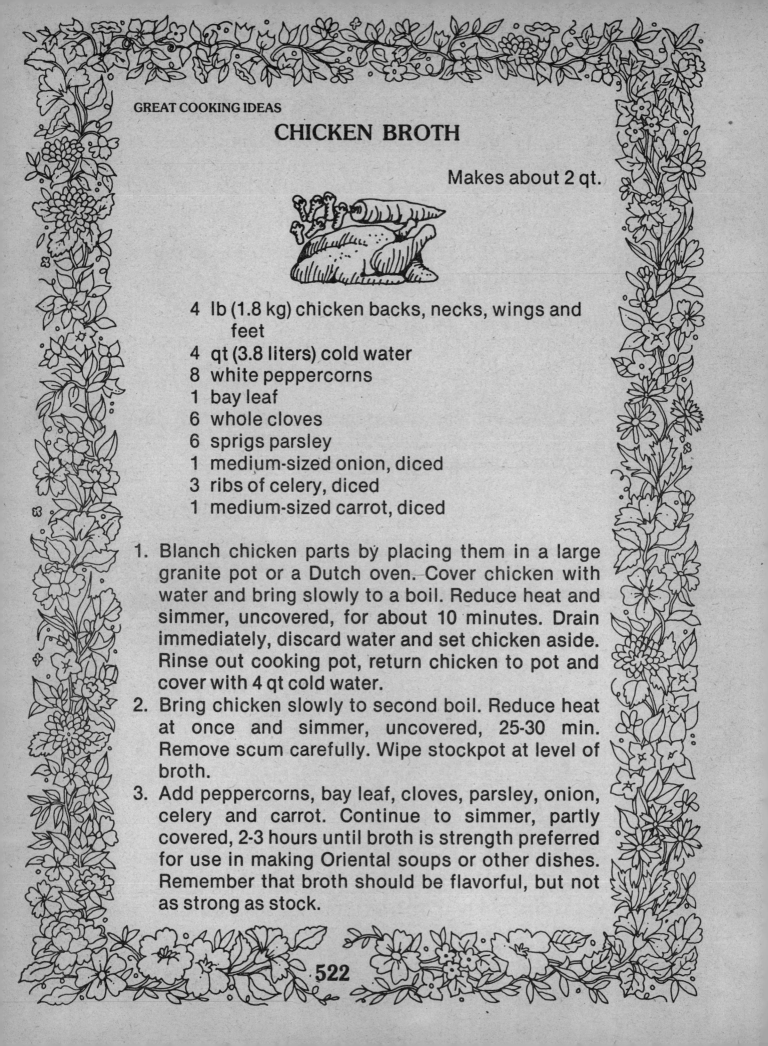

    4 lb (1.8 kg) chicken backs, necks, wings and
       feet
    4 qt (3.8 liters) cold water
    8 white peppercorns
    1 bay leaf
    6 whole cloves
    6 sprigs parsley
    1 medium-sized onion, diced
    3 ribs of celery, diced
    1 medium-sized carrot, diced

1. Blanch chicken parts by placing them in a large granite pot or a Dutch oven. Cover chicken with water and bring slowly to a boil. Reduce heat and simmer, uncovered, for about 10 minutes. Drain immediately, discard water and set chicken aside. Rinse out cooking pot, return chicken to pot and cover with 4 qt cold water.

2. Bring chicken slowly to second boil. Reduce heat at once and simmer, uncovered, 25-30 min. Remove scum carefully. Wipe stockpot at level of broth.

3. Add peppercorns, bay leaf, cloves, parsley, onion, celery and carrot. Continue to simmer, partly covered, 2-3 hours until broth is strength preferred for use in making Oriental soups or other dishes. Remember that broth should be flavorful, but not as strong as stock.

4. Strain the broth by ladling it through 2 layers of cheesecloth that have been wrung out in water. Cool it, uncovered. Store tightly covered and refrigerated. The grease will rise in a solid mass which serves as a protective coating. Do not remove this grease until you are ready to reheat the broth for serving.

Note: This broth will keep 3 or 4 days if refrigerated; for a longer period if frozen. It is best to bring the broth to a boil after 4 days and cool it partially before re-storing. This will preserve it for another few days.

* * *

BECHAMEL SAUCE

Makes about 3 cups.

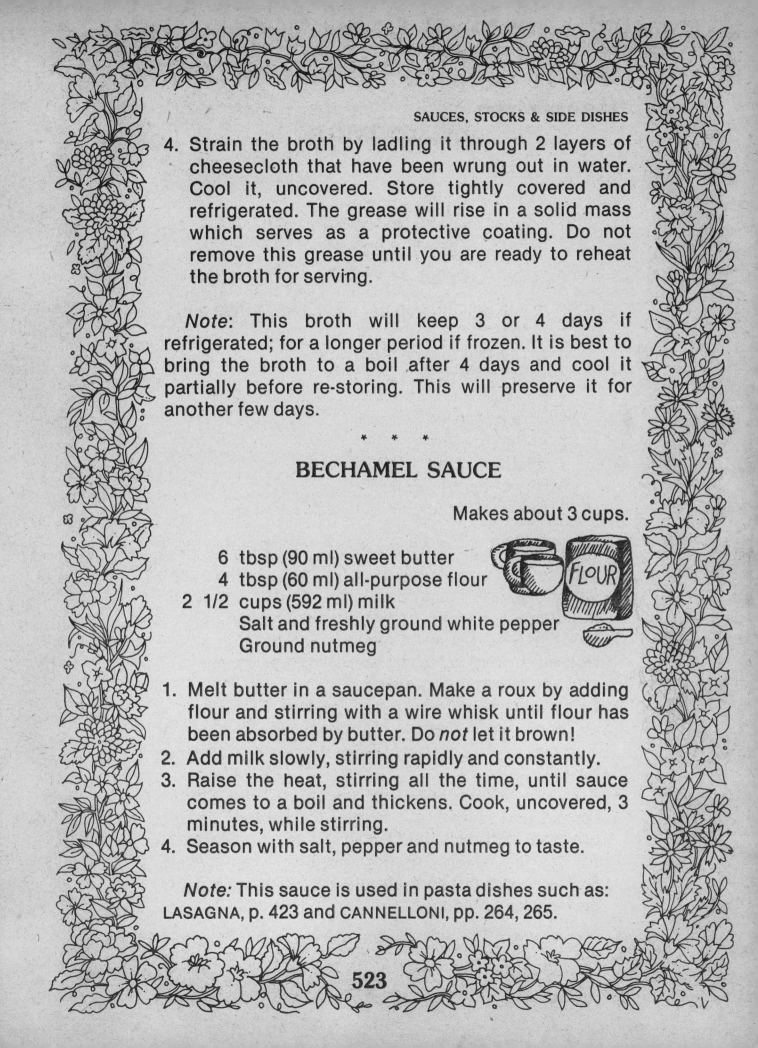

  6 tbsp (90 ml) sweet butter
  4 tbsp (60 ml) all-purpose flour
2 1/2 cups (592 ml) milk
    Salt and freshly ground white pepper
    Ground nutmeg

1. Melt butter in a saucepan. Make a roux by adding flour and stirring with a wire whisk until flour has been absorbed by butter. Do *not* let it brown!
2. Add milk slowly, stirring rapidly and constantly.
3. Raise the heat, stirring all the time, until sauce comes to a boil and thickens. Cook, uncovered, 3 minutes, while stirring.
4. Season with salt, pepper and nutmeg to taste.

Note: This sauce is used in pasta dishes such as: LASAGNA, p. 423 and CANNELLONI, pp. 264, 265.

ORANGE SAUCE

Makes about 2 cups.

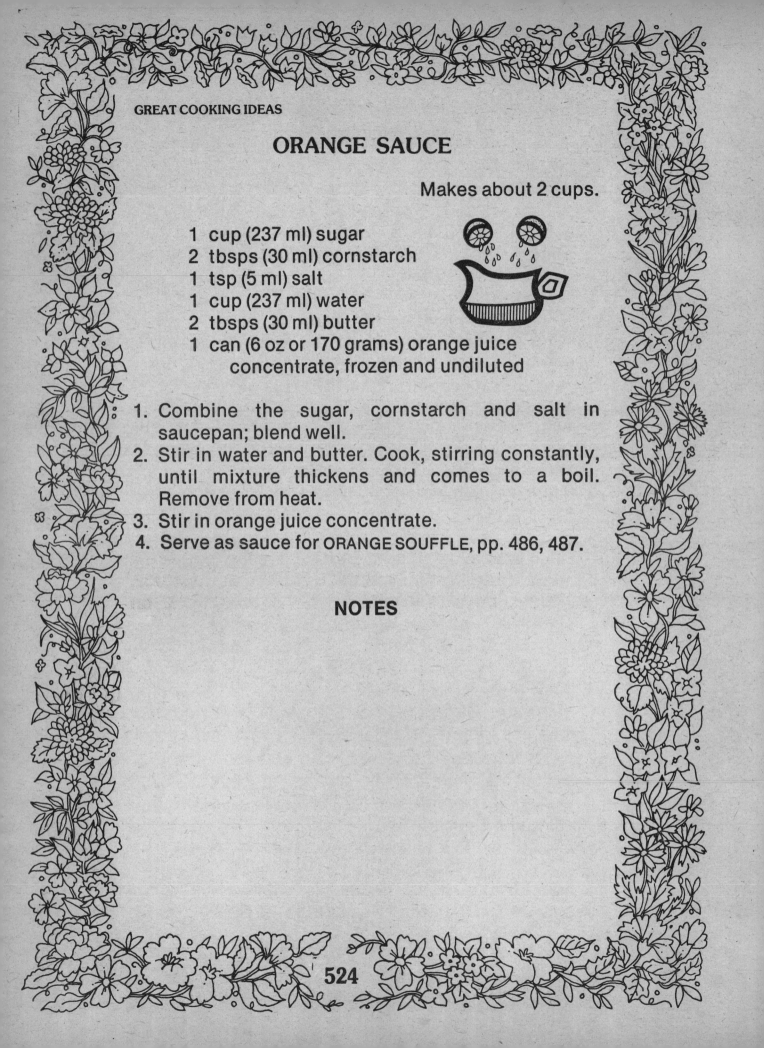

1 cup (237 ml) sugar
2 tbsps (30 ml) cornstarch
1 tsp (5 ml) salt
1 cup (237 ml) water
2 tbsps (30 ml) butter
1 can (6 oz or 170 grams) orange juice
concentrate, frozen and undiluted

1. Combine the sugar, cornstarch and salt in saucepan; blend well.
2. Stir in water and butter. Cook, stirring constantly, until mixture thickens and comes to a boil. Remove from heat.
3. Stir in orange juice concentrate.
4. Serve as sauce for ORANGE SOUFFLE, pp. 486, 487.

NOTES

SNOWY SAUCE

Makes 1 3/4 cups.

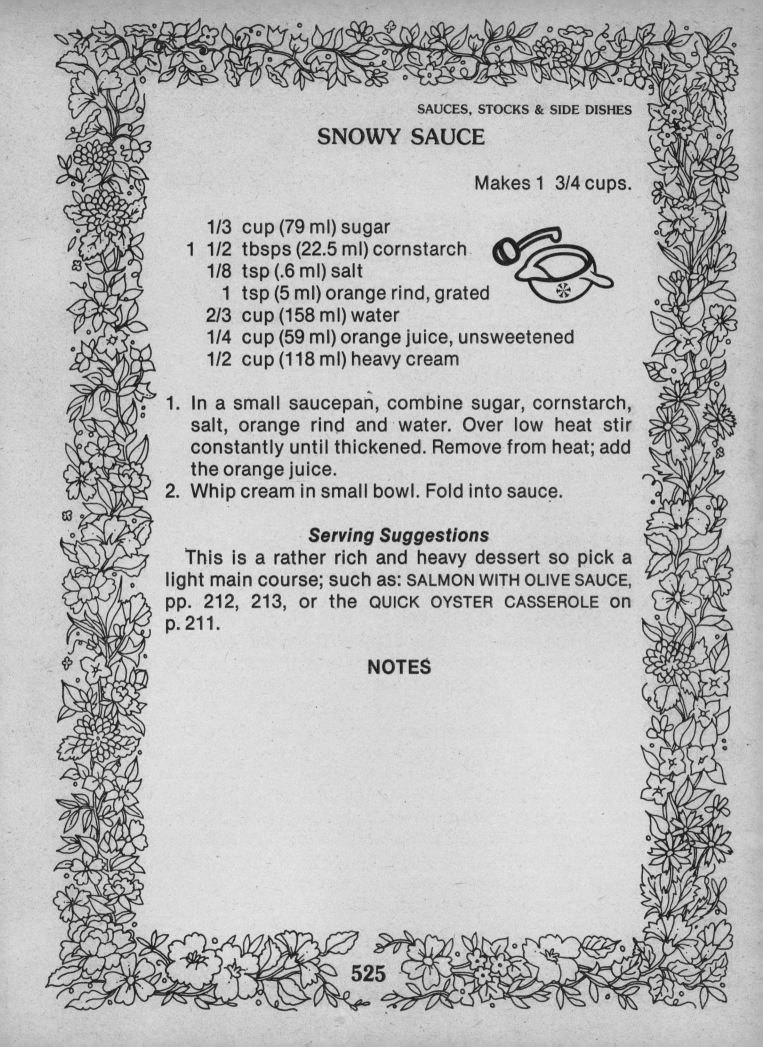

    1/3 cup (79 ml) sugar
1 1/2 tbsps (22.5 ml) cornstarch
    1/8 tsp (.6 ml) salt
      1 tsp (5 ml) orange rind, grated
    2/3 cup (158 ml) water
    1/4 cup (59 ml) orange juice, unsweetened
    1/2 cup (118 ml) heavy cream

1. In a small saucepan, combine sugar, cornstarch, salt, orange rind and water. Over low heat stir constantly until thickened. Remove from heat; add the orange juice.
2. Whip cream in small bowl. Fold into sauce.

Serving Suggestions

This is a rather rich and heavy dessert so pick a light main course; such as: SALMON WITH OLIVE SAUCE, pp. 212, 213, or the QUICK OYSTER CASSEROLE on p. 211.

NOTES

BROWN STOCK

Makes about 2 qts (2 liters).

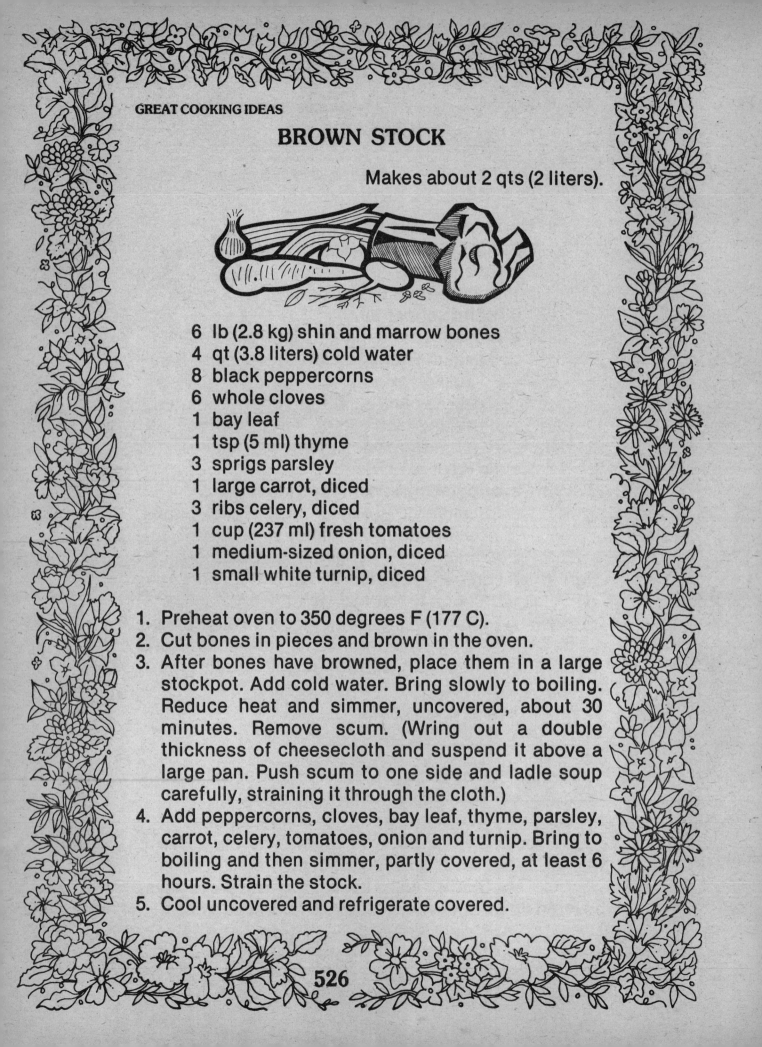

- 6 lb (2.8 kg) shin and marrow bones
- 4 qt (3.8 liters) cold water
- 8 black peppercorns
- 6 whole cloves
- 1 bay leaf
- 1 tsp (5 ml) thyme
- 3 sprigs parsley
- 1 large carrot, diced
- 3 ribs celery, diced
- 1 cup (237 ml) fresh tomatoes
- 1 medium-sized onion, diced
- 1 small white turnip, diced

1. Preheat oven to 350 degrees F (177 C).
2. Cut bones in pieces and brown in the oven.
3. After bones have browned, place them in a large stockpot. Add cold water. Bring slowly to boiling. Reduce heat and simmer, uncovered, about 30 minutes. Remove scum. (Wring out a double thickness of cheesecloth and suspend it above a large pan. Push scum to one side and ladle soup carefully, straining it through the cloth.)
4. Add peppercorns, cloves, bay leaf, thyme, parsley, carrot, celery, tomatoes, onion and turnip. Bring to boiling and then simmer, partly covered, at least 6 hours. Strain the stock.
5. Cool uncovered and refrigerate covered.

SAUCES, STOCKS & SIDE DISHES

FISH STOCK

Makes about 3 cups (710 ml).

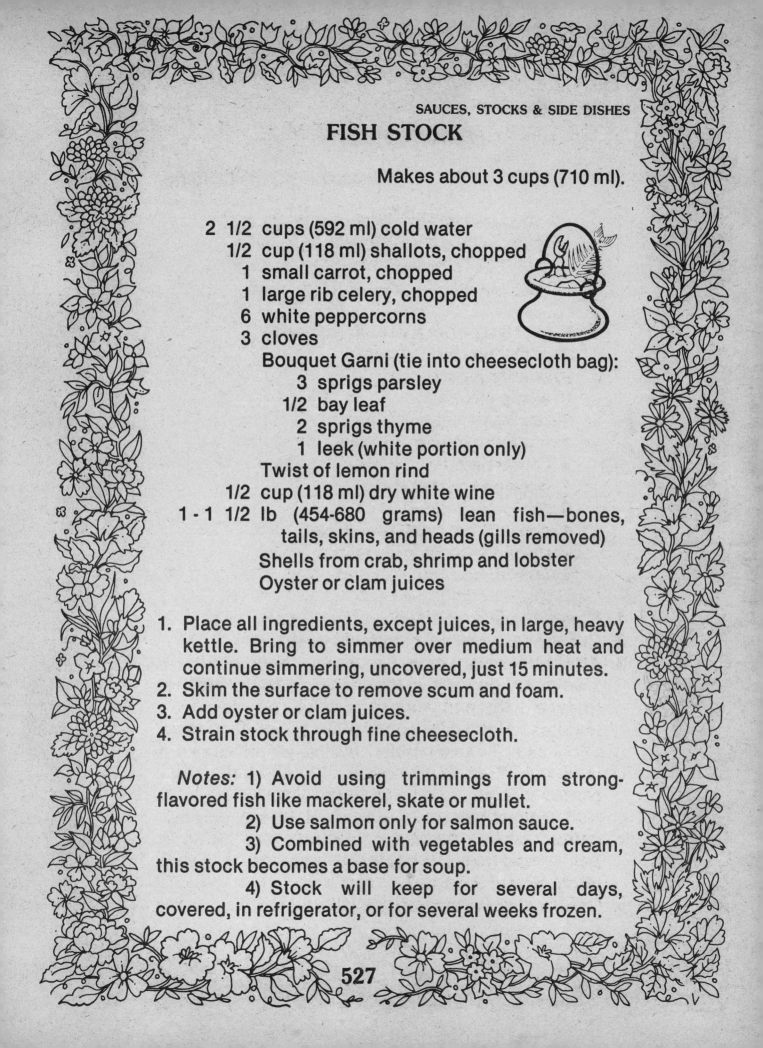

- 2 1/2 cups (592 ml) cold water
- 1/2 cup (118 ml) shallots, chopped
- 1 small carrot, chopped
- 1 large rib celery, chopped
- 6 white peppercorns
- 3 cloves
- Bouquet Garni (tie into cheesecloth bag):
  - 3 sprigs parsley
  - 1/2 bay leaf
  - 2 sprigs thyme
  - 1 leek (white portion only)
- Twist of lemon rind
- 1/2 cup (118 ml) dry white wine
- 1 - 1 1/2 lb (454-680 grams) lean fish—bones, tails, skins, and heads (gills removed)
- Shells from crab, shrimp and lobster
- Oyster or clam juices

1. Place all ingredients, except juices, in large, heavy kettle. Bring to simmer over medium heat and continue simmering, uncovered, just 15 minutes.
2. Skim the surface to remove scum and foam.
3. Add oyster or clam juices.
4. Strain stock through fine cheesecloth.

Notes: 1) Avoid using trimmings from strong-flavored fish like mackerel, skate or mullet.

2) Use salmon only for salmon sauce.

3) Combined with vegetables and cream, this stock becomes a base for soup.

4) Stock will keep for several days, covered, in refrigerator, or for several weeks frozen.

527

POULTRY STOCK MADE FROM LEFTOVERS

Makes 3 - 5 cups (710 ml - 1.2 liters).

1	cooked chicken, duck or turkey carcass
4 - 6	cups (.9 to 1.4 liters) water
1	cup (237 ml) celery with leaves, chopped
1	large onion, sliced
1	large carrot, diced
	Lettuce leaves
1/2	bay leaf
3 - 4	white peppercorns
3	sprigs parsley

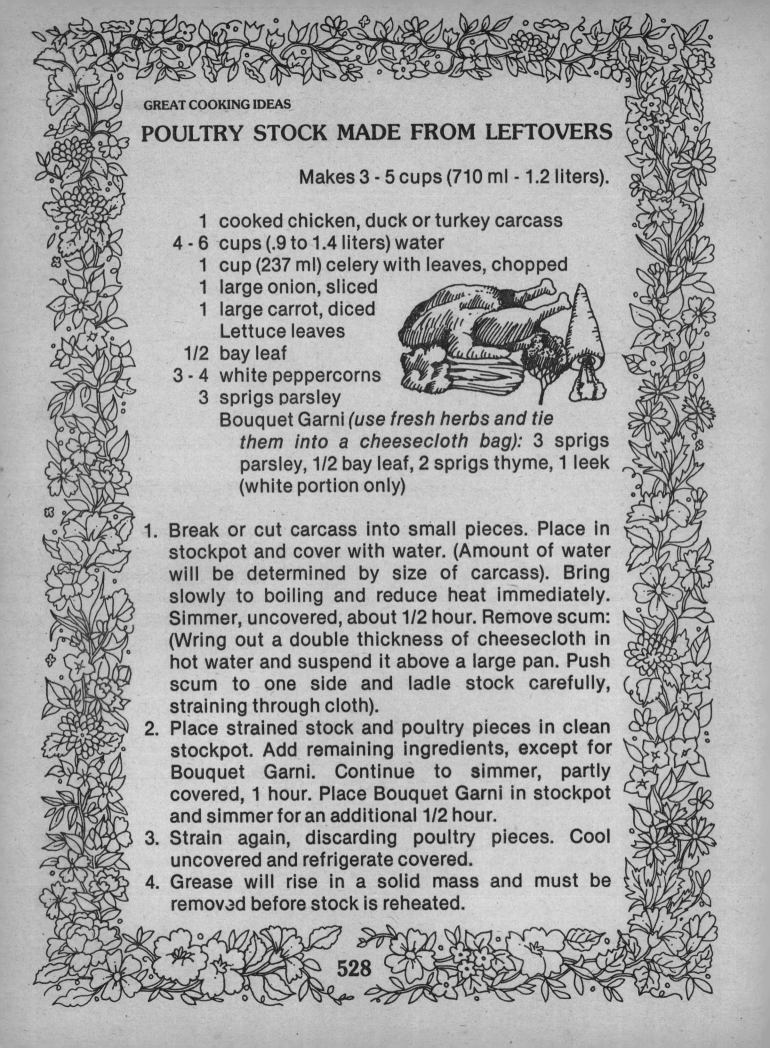

Bouquet Garni *(use fresh herbs and tie them into a cheesecloth bag):* 3 sprigs parsley, 1/2 bay leaf, 2 sprigs thyme, 1 leek (white portion only)

1. Break or cut carcass into small pieces. Place in stockpot and cover with water. (Amount of water will be determined by size of carcass). Bring slowly to boiling and reduce heat immediately. Simmer, uncovered, about 1/2 hour. Remove scum: (Wring out a double thickness of cheesecloth in hot water and suspend it above a large pan. Push scum to one side and ladle stock carefully, straining through cloth).

2. Place strained stock and poultry pieces in clean stockpot. Add remaining ingredients, except for Bouquet Garni. Continue to simmer, partly covered, 1 hour. Place Bouquet Garni in stockpot and simmer for an additional 1/2 hour.

3. Strain again, discarding poultry pieces. Cool uncovered and refrigerate covered.

4. Grease will rise in a solid mass and must be removed before stock is reheated.

VEAL STOCK

Makes about 2 qt (2 liters).

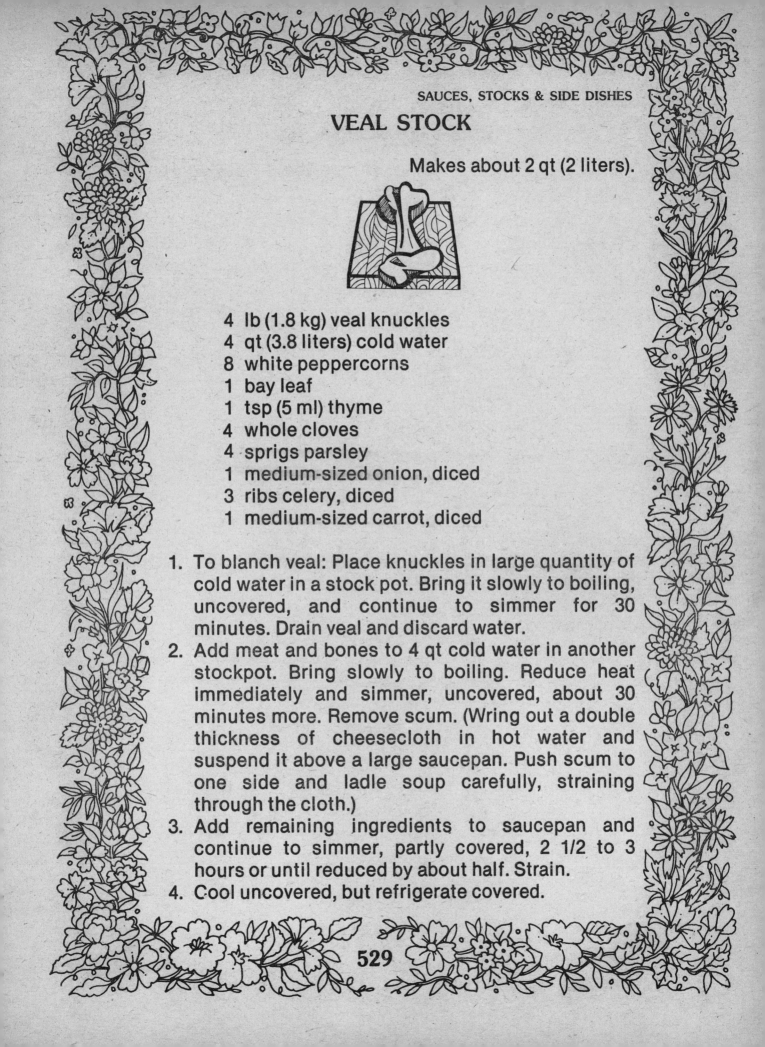

4 lb (1.8 kg) veal knuckles
4 qt (3.8 liters) cold water
8 white peppercorns
1 bay leaf
1 tsp (5 ml) thyme
4 whole cloves
4 sprigs parsley
1 medium-sized onion, diced
3 ribs celery, diced
1 medium-sized carrot, diced

1. To blanch veal: Place knuckles in large quantity of cold water in a stock pot. Bring it slowly to boiling, uncovered, and continue to simmer for 30 minutes. Drain veal and discard water.
2. Add meat and bones to 4 qt cold water in another stockpot. Bring slowly to boiling. Reduce heat immediately and simmer, uncovered, about 30 minutes more. Remove scum. (Wring out a double thickness of cheesecloth in hot water and suspend it above a large saucepan. Push scum to one side and ladle soup carefully, straining through the cloth.)
3. Add remaining ingredients to saucepan and continue to simmer, partly covered, 2 1/2 to 3 hours or until reduced by about half. Strain.
4. Cool uncovered, but refrigerate covered.

VEGETABLE STOCK

Makes about 1 qt (1 liter).

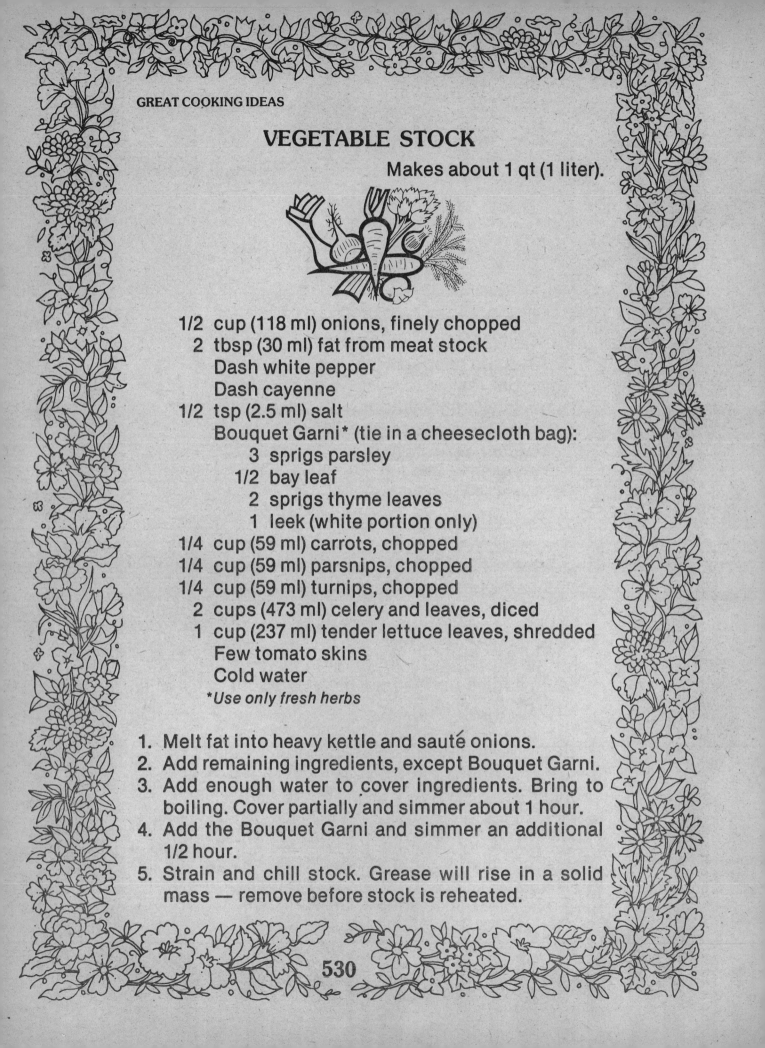

1/2 cup (118 ml) onions, finely chopped
2 tbsp (30 ml) fat from meat stock
Dash white pepper
Dash cayenne
1/2 tsp (2.5 ml) salt
Bouquet Garni* (tie in a cheesecloth bag):
   3 sprigs parsley
  1/2 bay leaf
   2 sprigs thyme leaves
   1 leek (white portion only)
1/4 cup (59 ml) carrots, chopped
1/4 cup (59 ml) parsnips, chopped
1/4 cup (59 ml) turnips, chopped
2 cups (473 ml) celery and leaves, diced
1 cup (237 ml) tender lettuce leaves, shredded
Few tomato skins
Cold water
*Use only fresh herbs

1. Melt fat into heavy kettle and sauté onions.
2. Add remaining ingredients, except Bouquet Garni.
3. Add enough water to cover ingredients. Bring to boiling. Cover partially and simmer about 1 hour.
4. Add the Bouquet Garni and simmer an additional 1/2 hour.
5. Strain and chill stock. Grease will rise in a solid mass — remove before stock is reheated.

DASHI

Makes about 4 cups.

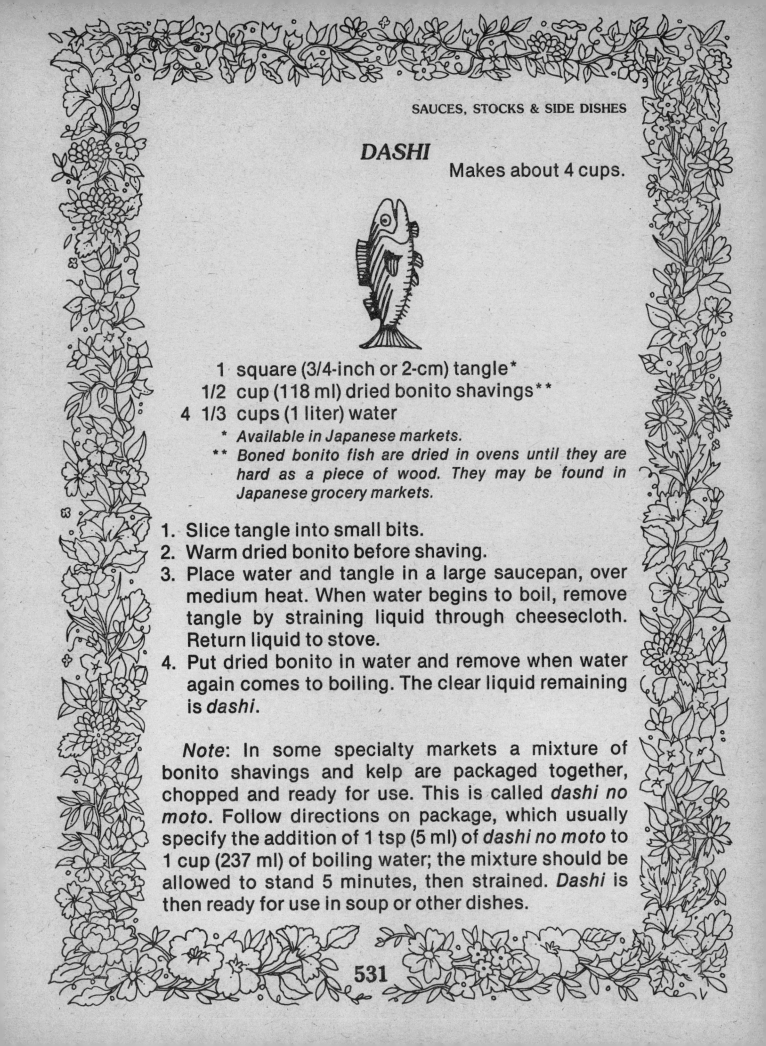

1 square (3/4-inch or 2-cm) tangle*
1/2 cup (118 ml) dried bonito shavings**
4 1/3 cups (1 liter) water

 * *Available in Japanese markets.*
 ** *Boned bonito fish are dried in ovens until they are hard as a piece of wood. They may be found in Japanese grocery markets.*

1. Slice tangle into small bits.
2. Warm dried bonito before shaving.
3. Place water and tangle in a large saucepan, over medium heat. When water begins to boil, remove tangle by straining liquid through cheesecloth. Return liquid to stove.
4. Put dried bonito in water and remove when water again comes to boiling. The clear liquid remaining is *dashi*.

Note: In some specialty markets a mixture of bonito shavings and kelp are packaged together, chopped and ready for use. This is called *dashi no moto*. Follow directions on package, which usually specify the addition of 1 tsp (5 ml) of *dashi no moto* to 1 cup (237 ml) of boiling water; the mixture should be allowed to stand 5 minutes, then strained. *Dashi* is then ready for use in soup or other dishes.

POULTRY GRAVY

Makes about 1 1/2 cups.

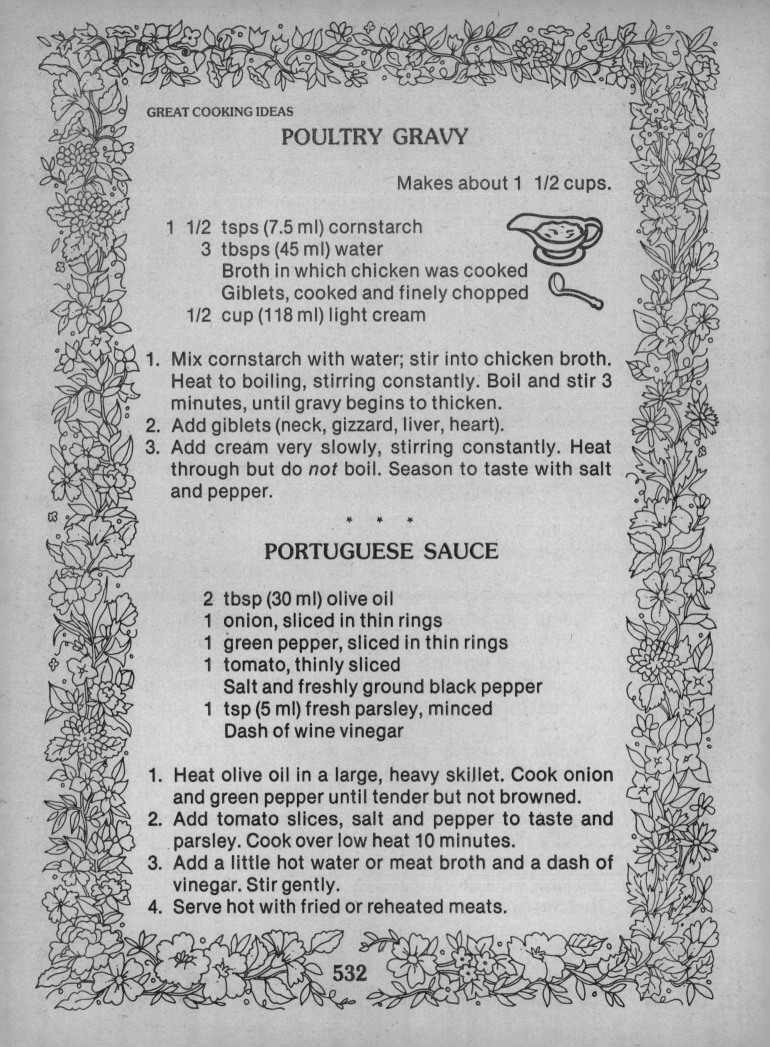

1 1/2 tsps (7.5 ml) cornstarch
3 tbsps (45 ml) water
Broth in which chicken was cooked
Giblets, cooked and finely chopped
1/2 cup (118 ml) light cream

1. Mix cornstarch with water; stir into chicken broth. Heat to boiling, stirring constantly. Boil and stir 3 minutes, until gravy begins to thicken.
2. Add giblets (neck, gizzard, liver, heart).
3. Add cream very slowly, stirring constantly. Heat through but do *not* boil. Season to taste with salt and pepper.

* * *

PORTUGUESE SAUCE

2 tbsp (30 ml) olive oil
1 onion, sliced in thin rings
1 green pepper, sliced in thin rings
1 tomato, thinly sliced
Salt and freshly ground black pepper
1 tsp (5 ml) fresh parsley, minced
Dash of wine vinegar

1. Heat olive oil in a large, heavy skillet. Cook onion and green pepper until tender but not browned.
2. Add tomato slices, salt and pepper to taste and parsley. Cook over low heat 10 minutes.
3. Add a little hot water or meat broth and a dash of vinegar. Stir gently.
4. Serve hot with fried or reheated meats.

BLUE CHEESE DIP

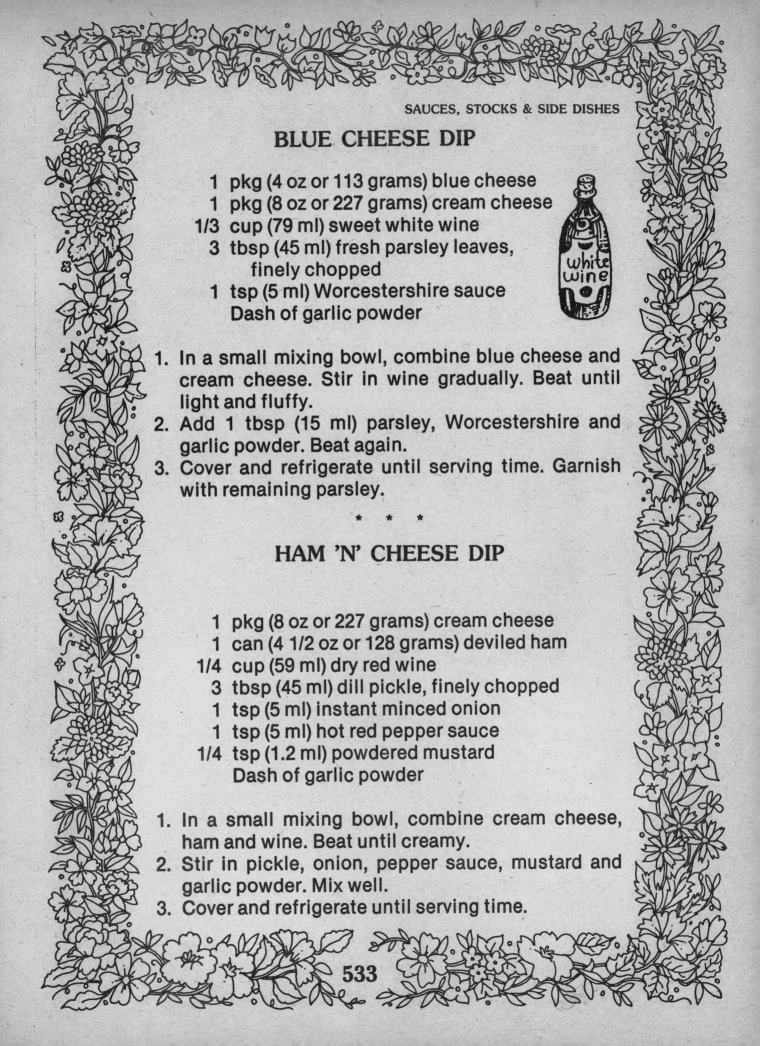

1 pkg (4 oz or 113 grams) blue cheese
1 pkg (8 oz or 227 grams) cream cheese
1/3 cup (79 ml) sweet white wine
3 tbsp (45 ml) fresh parsley leaves,
    finely chopped
1 tsp (5 ml) Worcestershire sauce
Dash of garlic powder

1. In a small mixing bowl, combine blue cheese and cream cheese. Stir in wine gradually. Beat until light and fluffy.
2. Add 1 tbsp (15 ml) parsley, Worcestershire and garlic powder. Beat again.
3. Cover and refrigerate until serving time. Garnish with remaining parsley.

* * *

HAM 'N' CHEESE DIP

1 pkg (8 oz or 227 grams) cream cheese
1 can (4 1/2 oz or 128 grams) deviled ham
1/4 cup (59 ml) dry red wine
3 tbsp (45 ml) dill pickle, finely chopped
1 tsp (5 ml) instant minced onion
1 tsp (5 ml) hot red pepper sauce
1/4 tsp (1.2 ml) powdered mustard
Dash of garlic powder

1. In a small mixing bowl, combine cream cheese, ham and wine. Beat until creamy.
2. Stir in pickle, onion, pepper sauce, mustard and garlic powder. Mix well.
3. Cover and refrigerate until serving time.

EGG DRESSING

Makes about 5 cups.

6 egg yolks
2 tbsp (30 ml) powdered mustard
4 cups (946 ml) olive oil
1 tsp (5 ml) salt
Juice from 2 fresh lemons
1/4 cup (59 ml) white wine vinegar
1/2 tsp (2.5 ml) freshly ground white pepper

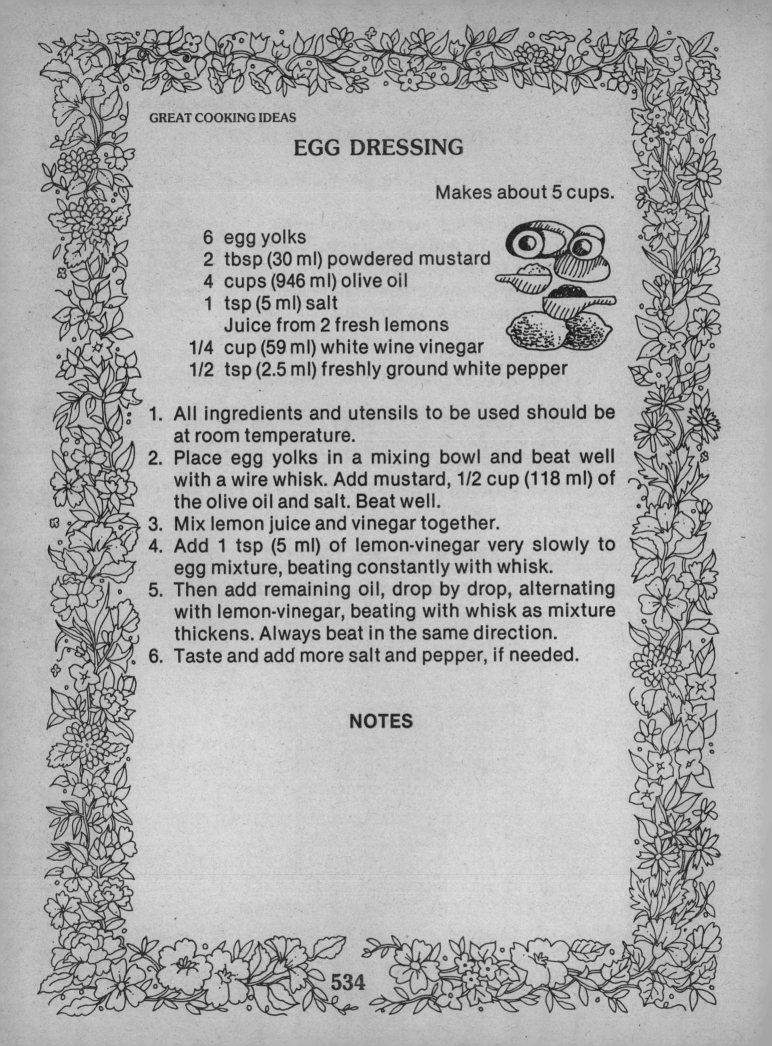

1. All ingredients and utensils to be used should be at room temperature.
2. Place egg yolks in a mixing bowl and beat well with a wire whisk. Add mustard, 1/2 cup (118 ml) of the olive oil and salt. Beat well.
3. Mix lemon juice and vinegar together.
4. Add 1 tsp (5 ml) of lemon-vinegar very slowly to egg mixture, beating constantly with whisk.
5. Then add remaining oil, drop by drop, alternating with lemon-vinegar, beating with whisk as mixture thickens. Always beat in the same direction.
6. Taste and add more salt and pepper, if needed.

NOTES

HOMEMADE CURRY POWDER

Makes 1/2 - 2/3 lb (227 - 284 grams).

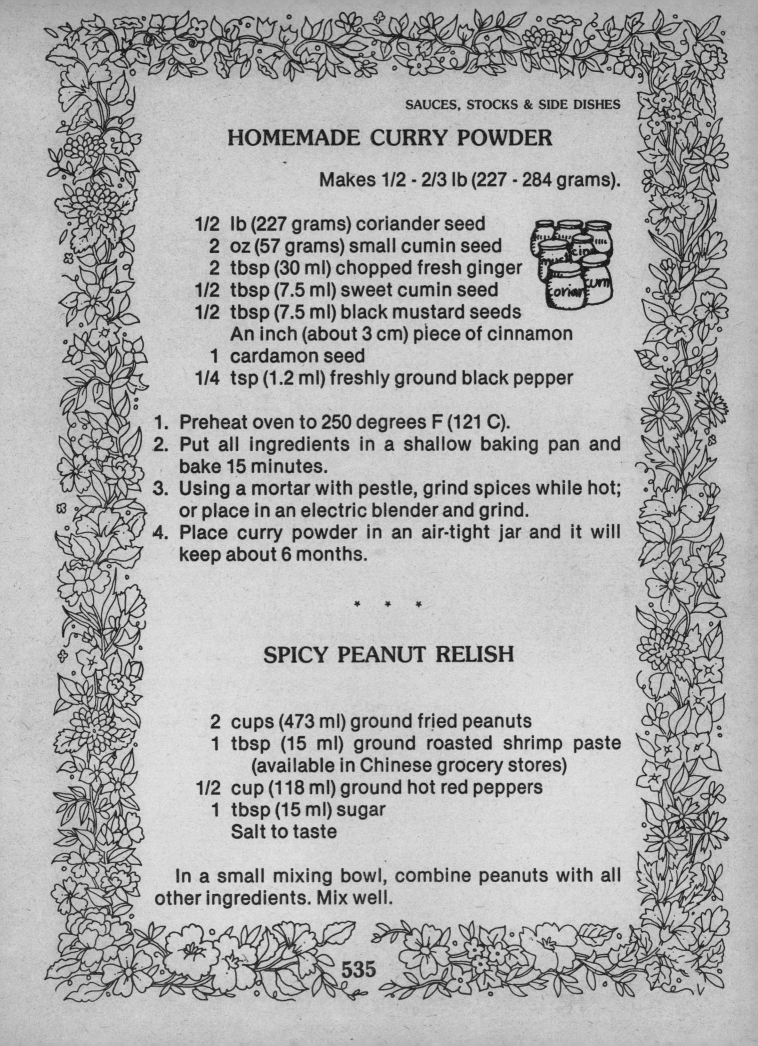

1/2 lb (227 grams) coriander seed
2 oz (57 grams) small cumin seed
2 tbsp (30 ml) chopped fresh ginger
1/2 tbsp (7.5 ml) sweet cumin seed
1/2 tbsp (7.5 ml) black mustard seeds
An inch (about 3 cm) piece of cinnamon
1 cardamon seed
1/4 tsp (1.2 ml) freshly ground black pepper

1. Preheat oven to 250 degrees F (121 C).
2. Put all ingredients in a shallow baking pan and bake 15 minutes.
3. Using a mortar with pestle, grind spices while hot; or place in an electric blender and grind.
4. Place curry powder in an air-tight jar and it will keep about 6 months.

* * *

SPICY PEANUT RELISH

2 cups (473 ml) ground fried peanuts
1 tbsp (15 ml) ground roasted shrimp paste (available in Chinese grocery stores)
1/2 cup (118 ml) ground hot red peppers
1 tbsp (15 ml) sugar
Salt to taste

In a small mixing bowl, combine peanuts with all other ingredients. Mix well.

INDIAN PICKLED LIMES

3/8 cup (89 ml) salt
  6 limes
1/4 cup (59 ml) apple cider vinegar
3/4 tsp (3.7 ml) red pepper, crushed
3/4 tsp (3.7 ml) cumin, ground
3/4 tsp (3.7 ml) garlic powder
1/2 cup (118 ml) sesame oil
  2 tbsp (30 ml) mustard seed
  1 tsp (5 ml) ginger, ground

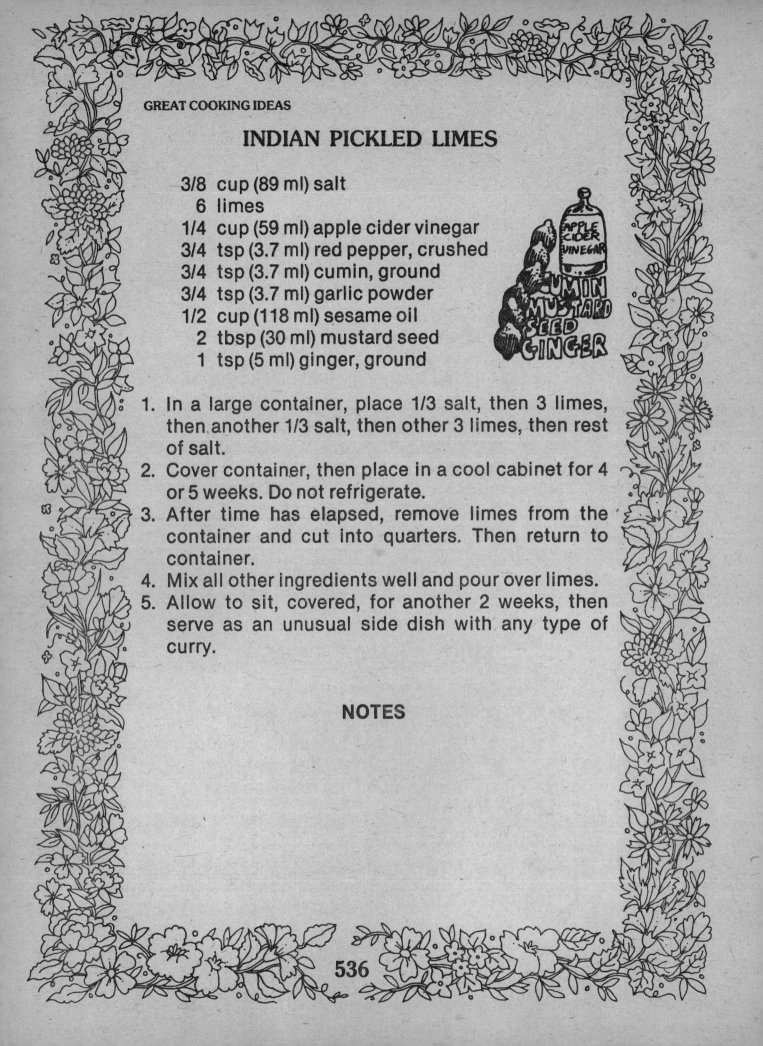

1. In a large container, place 1/3 salt, then 3 limes, then another 1/3 salt, then other 3 limes, then rest of salt.
2. Cover container, then place in a cool cabinet for 4 or 5 weeks. Do not refrigerate.
3. After time has elapsed, remove limes from the container and cut into quarters. Then return to container.
4. Mix all other ingredients well and pour over limes.
5. Allow to sit, covered, for another 2 weeks, then serve as an unusual side dish with any type of curry.

NOTES

MINT CHUTNEY

Makes about 2 cups.

1   cup (237 ml) firmly packed fresh mint leaves
1   cup (237 ml) onion, finely chopped
1   medium-sized tomato, seeded and finely chopped
4   tbsp (60 ml) lemon juice
1/2 tsp (2.5 ml) salt
    Dash hot red pepper sauce

1. Wash mint leaves and chop very fine.
2. Place mint in a medium-sized glass bowl. Add onion, tomato, lemon juice, salt and pepper sauce. Mix well and refrigerate overnight before using.

* * *

TOMATO CHUTNEY

Makes about 2 cups.

3   dried chili peppers
5   cloves garlic
1   1-inch (3-cm) piece ginger root, grated
1   cup (237 ml) red wine vinegar
1   lb (454 grams) tomatoes, peeled and chopped
1   tsp (5 ml) salt
2   cups (473 ml) sugar

1. Grind chili peppers and garlic together. Place in a heavy saucepan.
2. Add ginger root, vinegar, tomatoes, salt and sugar. Simmer over low heat until mixture thickens, 2-3 hours.

RED PEPPER-COCONUT RELISH

Makes 8 servings.

1 cup (237 ml) fresh coconut, grated
1/2 cup (118 ml) hot red peppers, finely chopped
1 tbsp (15 ml) shrimp paste*
1 medium-sized onion, finely chopped
1 tbsp (15 ml) sugar
3 cloves garlic, minced
Salt to taste

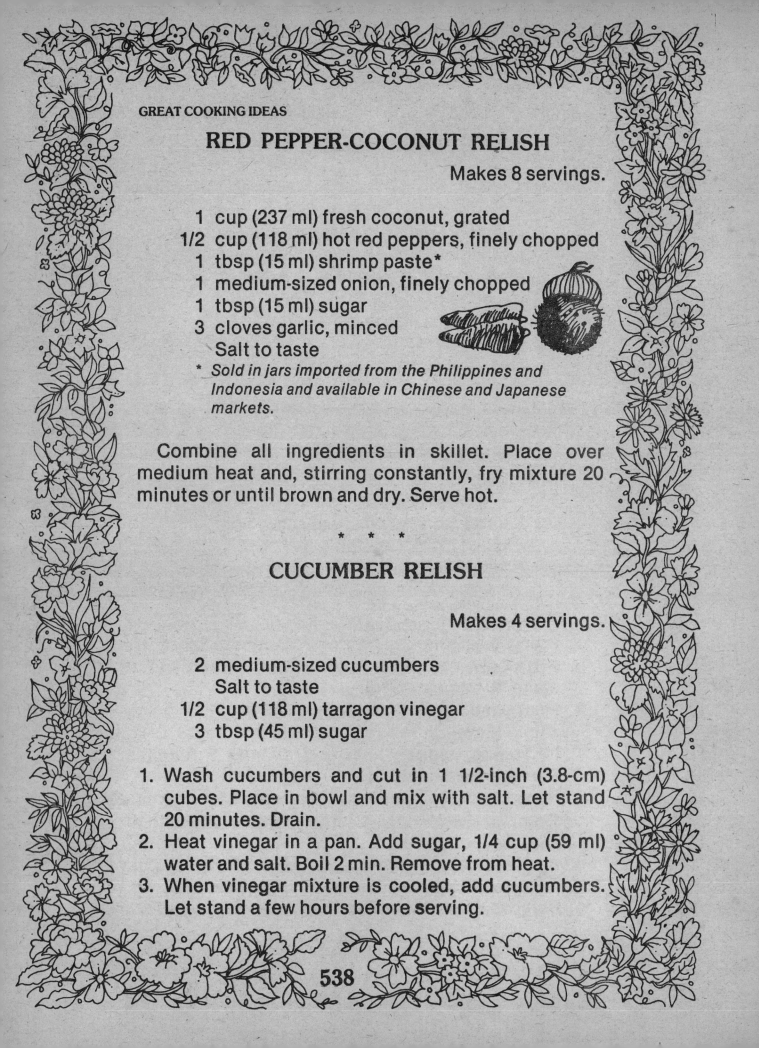

Sold in jars imported from the Philippines and Indonesia and available in Chinese and Japanese markets.

Combine all ingredients in skillet. Place over medium heat and, stirring constantly, fry mixture 20 minutes or until brown and dry. Serve hot.

* * *

CUCUMBER RELISH

Makes 4 servings.

2 medium-sized cucumbers
Salt to taste
1/2 cup (118 ml) tarragon vinegar
3 tbsp (45 ml) sugar

1. Wash cucumbers and cut in 1 1/2-inch (3.8-cm) cubes. Place in bowl and mix with salt. Let stand 20 minutes. Drain.
2. Heat vinegar in a pan. Add sugar, 1/4 cup (59 ml) water and salt. Boil 2 min. Remove from heat.
3. When vinegar mixture is cooled, add cucumbers. Let stand a few hours before serving.

VEGETABLE RELISH WITH NUTS

Makes 8 servings.

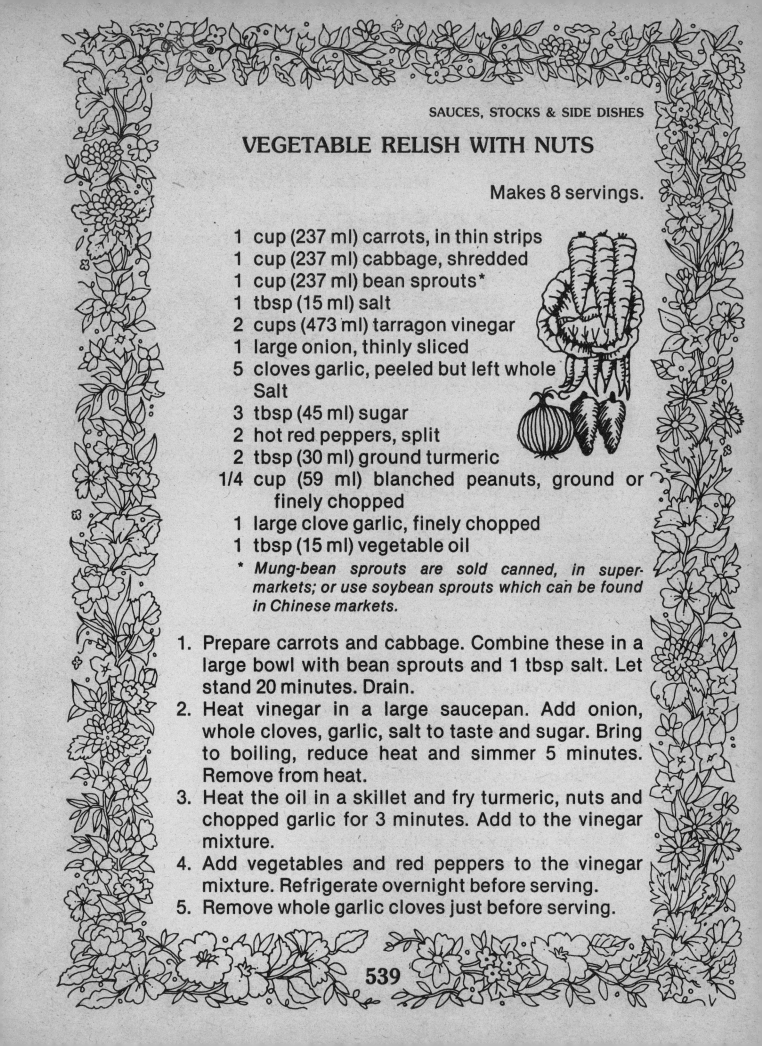

1 cup (237 ml) carrots, in thin strips
1 cup (237 ml) cabbage, shredded
1 cup (237 ml) bean sprouts*
1 tbsp (15 ml) salt
2 cups (473 ml) tarragon vinegar
1 large onion, thinly sliced
5 cloves garlic, peeled but left whole
  Salt
3 tbsp (45 ml) sugar
2 hot red peppers, split
2 tbsp (30 ml) ground turmeric
1/4 cup (59 ml) blanched peanuts, ground or finely chopped
1 large clove garlic, finely chopped
1 tbsp (15 ml) vegetable oil

* *Mung-bean sprouts are sold canned, in supermarkets; or use soybean sprouts which can be found in Chinese markets.*

1. Prepare carrots and cabbage. Combine these in a large bowl with bean sprouts and 1 tbsp salt. Let stand 20 minutes. Drain.
2. Heat vinegar in a large saucepan. Add onion, whole cloves, garlic, salt to taste and sugar. Bring to boiling, reduce heat and simmer 5 minutes. Remove from heat.
3. Heat the oil in a skillet and fry turmeric, nuts and chopped garlic for 3 minutes. Add to the vinegar mixture.
4. Add vegetables and red peppers to the vinegar mixture. Refrigerate overnight before serving.
5. Remove whole garlic cloves just before serving.

THAI CURRY PASTE

Makes about 1/2 cup (118 ml).

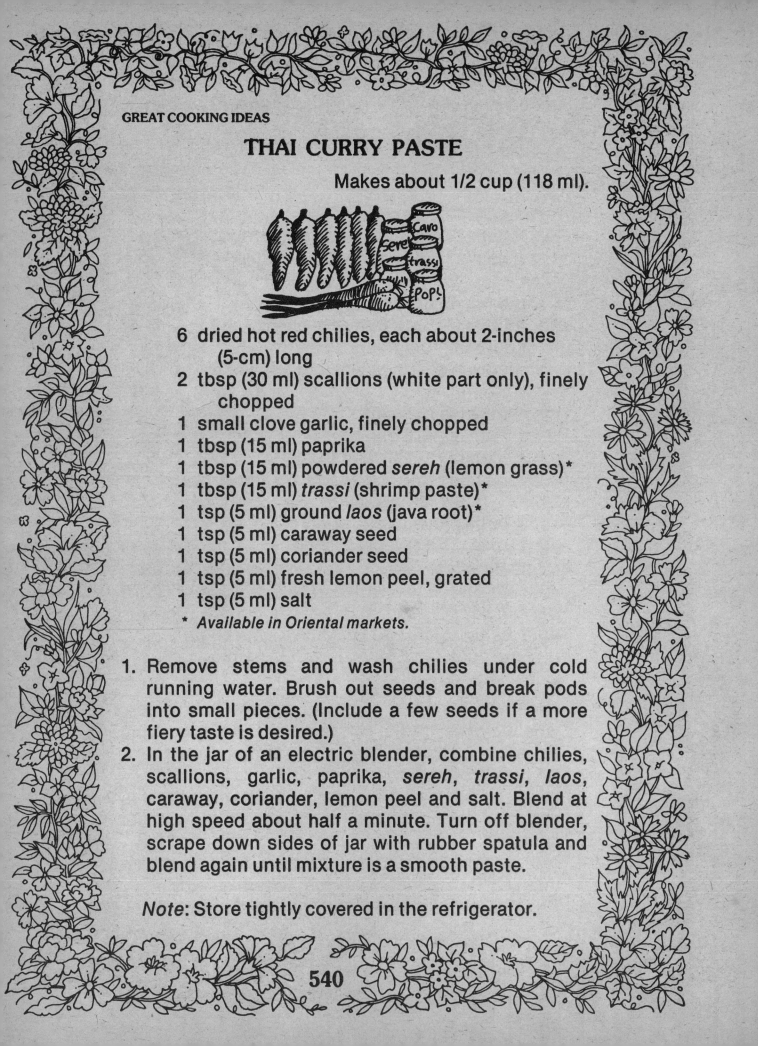

6 dried hot red chilies, each about 2-inches (5-cm) long
2 tbsp (30 ml) scallions (white part only), finely chopped
1 small clove garlic, finely chopped
1 tbsp (15 ml) paprika
1 tbsp (15 ml) powdered *sereh* (lemon grass)*
1 tbsp (15 ml) *trassi* (shrimp paste)*
1 tsp (5 ml) ground *laos* (java root)*
1 tsp (5 ml) caraway seed
1 tsp (5 ml) coriander seed
1 tsp (5 ml) fresh lemon peel, grated
1 tsp (5 ml) salt
 * *Available in Oriental markets.*

1. Remove stems and wash chilies under cold running water. Brush out seeds and break pods into small pieces. (Include a few seeds if a more fiery taste is desired.)
2. In the jar of an electric blender, combine chilies, scallions, garlic, paprika, *sereh*, *trassi*, *laos*, caraway, coriander, lemon peel and salt. Blend at high speed about half a minute. Turn off blender, scrape down sides of jar with rubber spatula and blend again until mixture is a smooth paste.

Note: Store tightly covered in the refrigerator.

TORTILLAS

Makes 12 tortillas.

2 cups (473 ml) masa harina (corn flour)
3/4 tsp (3.7 ml) salt
1 cup (237 ml) water

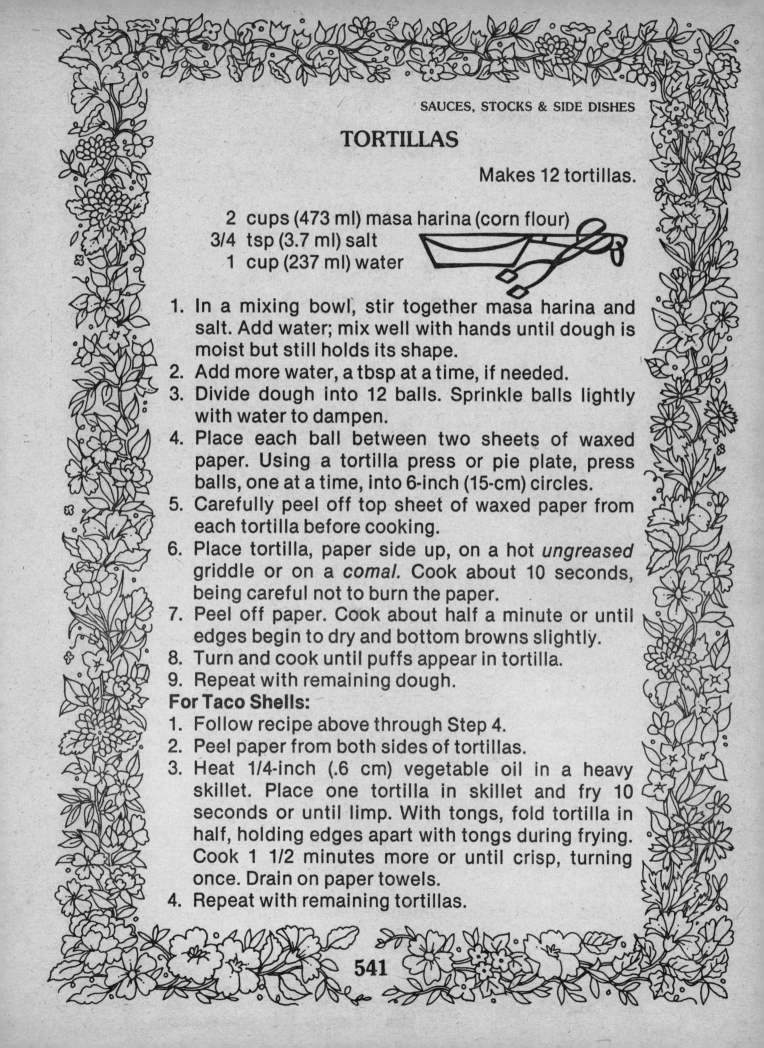

1. In a mixing bowl, stir together masa harina and salt. Add water; mix well with hands until dough is moist but still holds its shape.
2. Add more water, a tbsp at a time, if needed.
3. Divide dough into 12 balls. Sprinkle balls lightly with water to dampen.
4. Place each ball between two sheets of waxed paper. Using a tortilla press or pie plate, press balls, one at a time, into 6-inch (15-cm) circles.
5. Carefully peel off top sheet of waxed paper from each tortilla before cooking.
6. Place tortilla, paper side up, on a hot *ungreased* griddle or on a *comal*. Cook about 10 seconds, being careful not to burn the paper.
7. Peel off paper. Cook about half a minute or until edges begin to dry and bottom browns slightly.
8. Turn and cook until puffs appear in tortilla.
9. Repeat with remaining dough.

For Taco Shells:
1. Follow recipe above through Step 4.
2. Peel paper from both sides of tortillas.
3. Heat 1/4-inch (.6 cm) vegetable oil in a heavy skillet. Place one tortilla in skillet and fry 10 seconds or until limp. With tongs, fold tortilla in half, holding edges apart with tongs during frying. Cook 1 1/2 minutes more or until crisp, turning once. Drain on paper towels.
4. Repeat with remaining tortillas.

TORTILLA CHIPS

TORTILLAS, p. 541 or commercial tortillas
Cooking oil

1. Make tortillas, or use commercial tortillas.
2. Cut tortillas into pie-shaped pieces.
3. Heat oil in a skillet until very hot, but be careful not to let it start smoking. Turn heat down if this happens.
4. When oil is hot, drop pieces of tortillas carefully into skillet and cook until they are golden and start to curl. Turn once. Cooking should take only a minute or so. Chips may be lightly salted as you take them out of the oil to drain, if you so desire.
5. Serve as snacks or with soups or sandwiches.

* * *

TORTILLA TREATS

TORTILLA CHIPS (above)
Cheddar cheese, grated
Olives, sliced

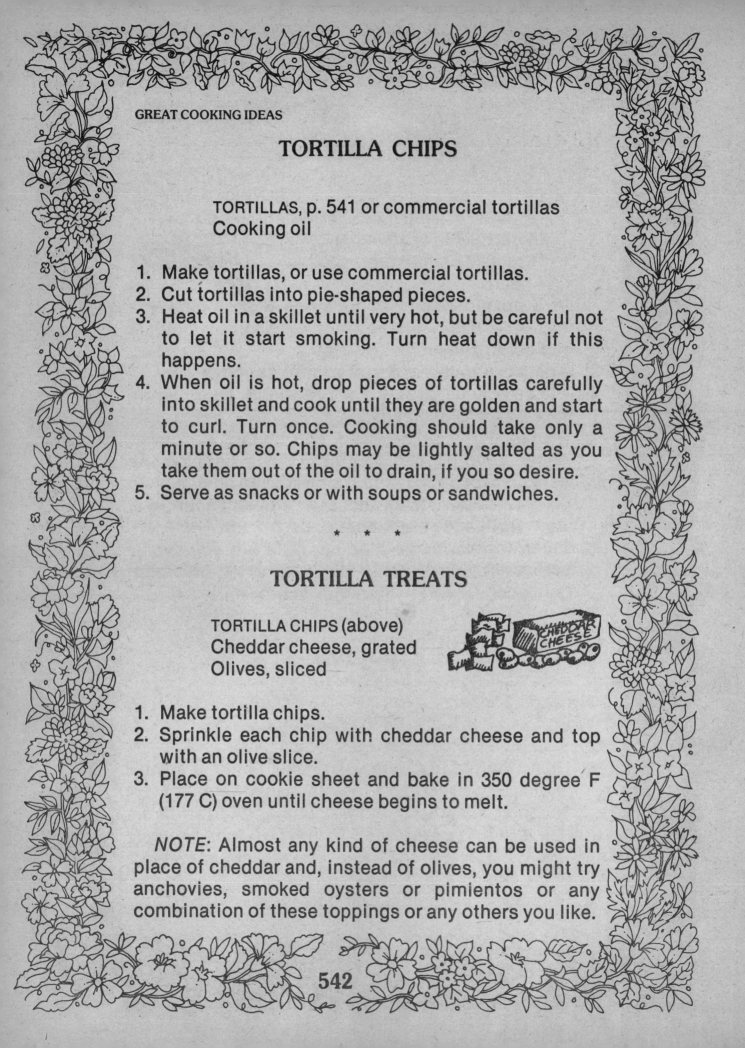

1. Make tortilla chips.
2. Sprinkle each chip with cheddar cheese and top with an olive slice.
3. Place on cookie sheet and bake in 350 degree F (177 C) oven until cheese begins to melt.

NOTE: Almost any kind of cheese can be used in place of cheddar and, instead of olives, you might try anchovies, smoked oysters or pimientos or any combination of these toppings or any others you like.

FRIED NOODLES

Makes 4 servings.

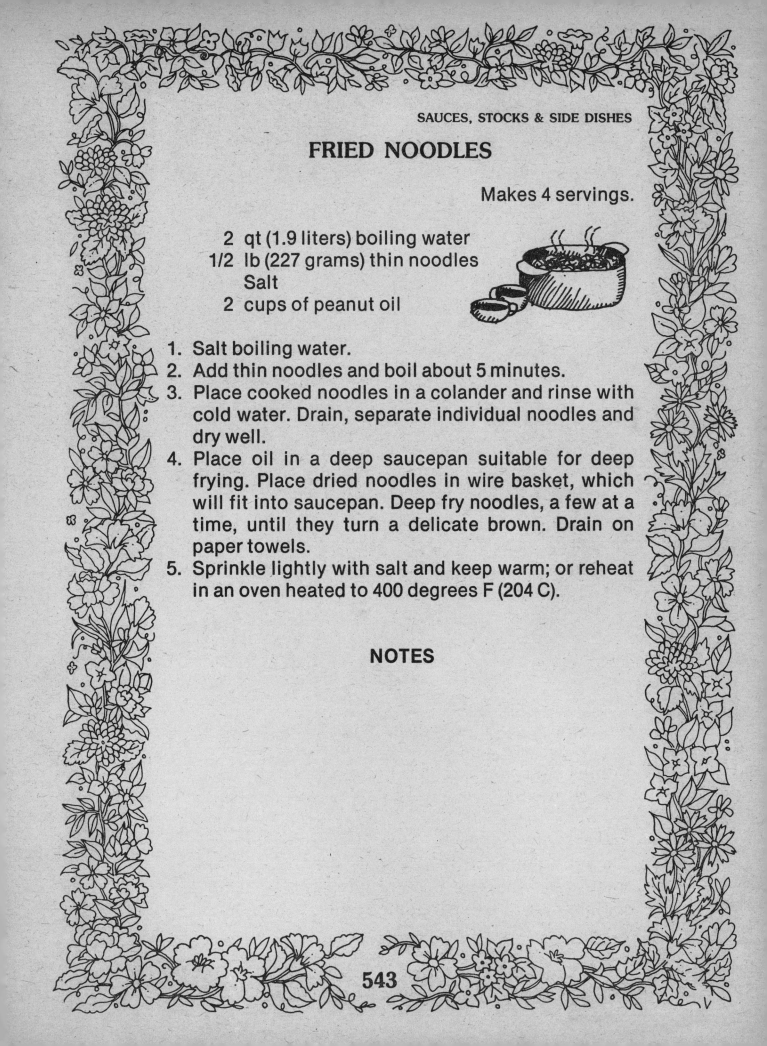

2 qt (1.9 liters) boiling water
1/2 lb (227 grams) thin noodles
Salt
2 cups of peanut oil

1. Salt boiling water.
2. Add thin noodles and boil about 5 minutes.
3. Place cooked noodles in a colander and rinse with cold water. Drain, separate individual noodles and dry well.
4. Place oil in a deep saucepan suitable for deep frying. Place dried noodles in wire basket, which will fit into saucepan. Deep fry noodles, a few at a time, until they turn a delicate brown. Drain on paper towels.
5. Sprinkle lightly with salt and keep warm; or reheat in an oven heated to 400 degrees F (204 C).

NOTES

FRITTER (TEMPURA) BATTER
(for Vegetables, Meat and Fish)

Enough to coat about 2 cups food.

2 eggs
1 1/3 cups (316 ml) all-purpose flour or rice flour
1 tsp (5 ml) salt
1/4 tsp (1.2 ml) freshly ground white pepper
1 tbsp (15 ml) sweet butter, melted
3/4 cup (177 ml) flat beer

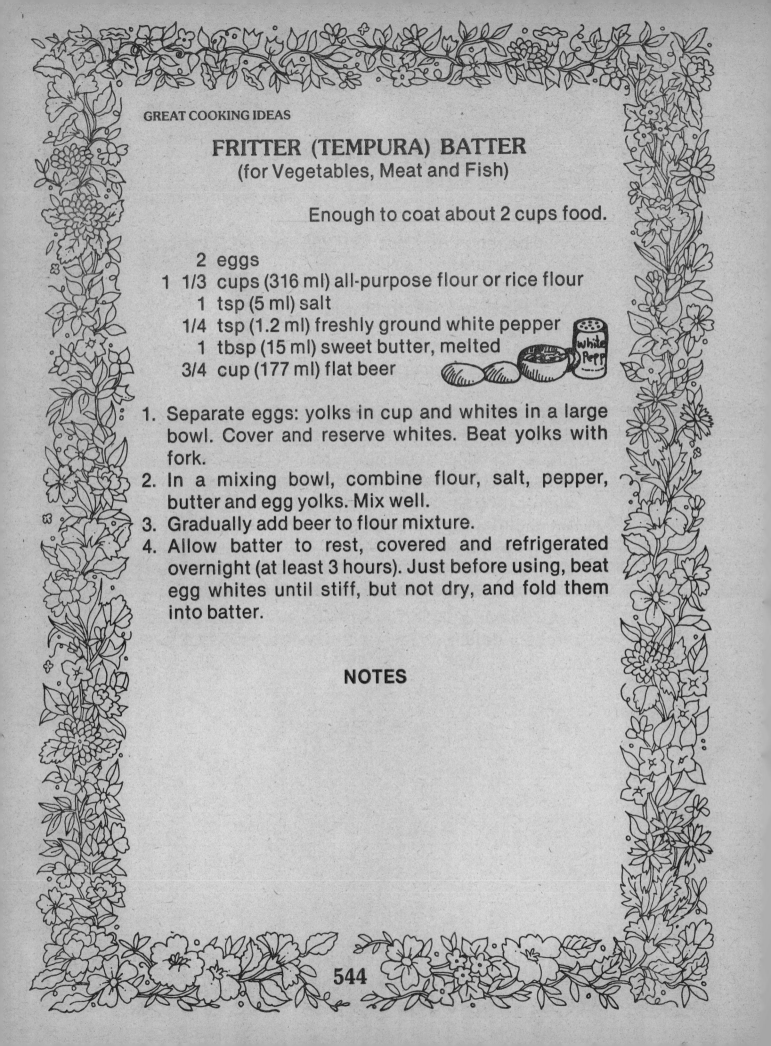

1. Separate eggs: yolks in cup and whites in a large bowl. Cover and reserve whites. Beat yolks with fork.
2. In a mixing bowl, combine flour, salt, pepper, butter and egg yolks. Mix well.
3. Gradually add beer to flour mixture.
4. Allow batter to rest, covered and refrigerated overnight (at least 3 hours). Just before using, beat egg whites until stiff, but not dry, and fold them into batter.

NOTES

FRUIT FRITTERS

Makes 6 servings.

4 bananas or 1 cup (237 ml) canned pineapple chunks
1 cup (237 ml) all-purpose flour
1 tsp (5 ml) baking powder
Salt
Sugar
3 cups (710 ml) vegetable oil

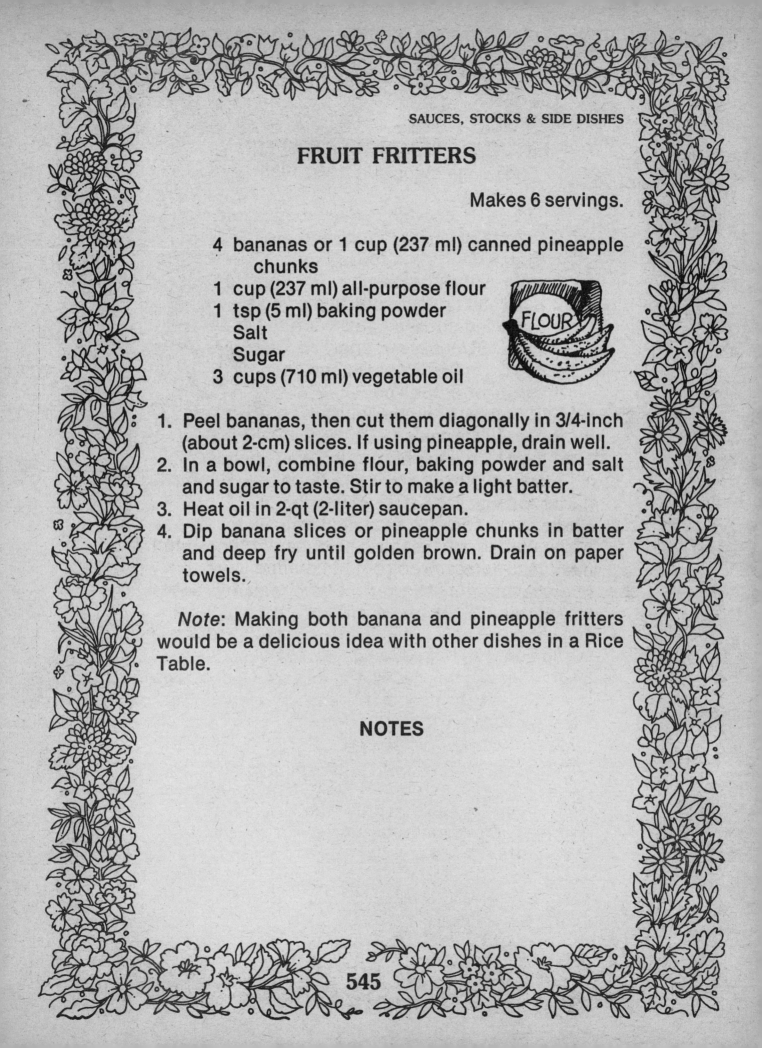

1. Peel bananas, then cut them diagonally in 3/4-inch (about 2-cm) slices. If using pineapple, drain well.
2. In a bowl, combine flour, baking powder and salt and sugar to taste. Stir to make a light batter.
3. Heat oil in 2-qt (2-liter) saucepan.
4. Dip banana slices or pineapple chunks in batter and deep fry until golden brown. Drain on paper towels.

Note: Making both banana and pineapple fritters would be a delicious idea with other dishes in a Rice Table.

NOTES

SPICY CORN FRITTERS

Makes 8 - 12 servings.

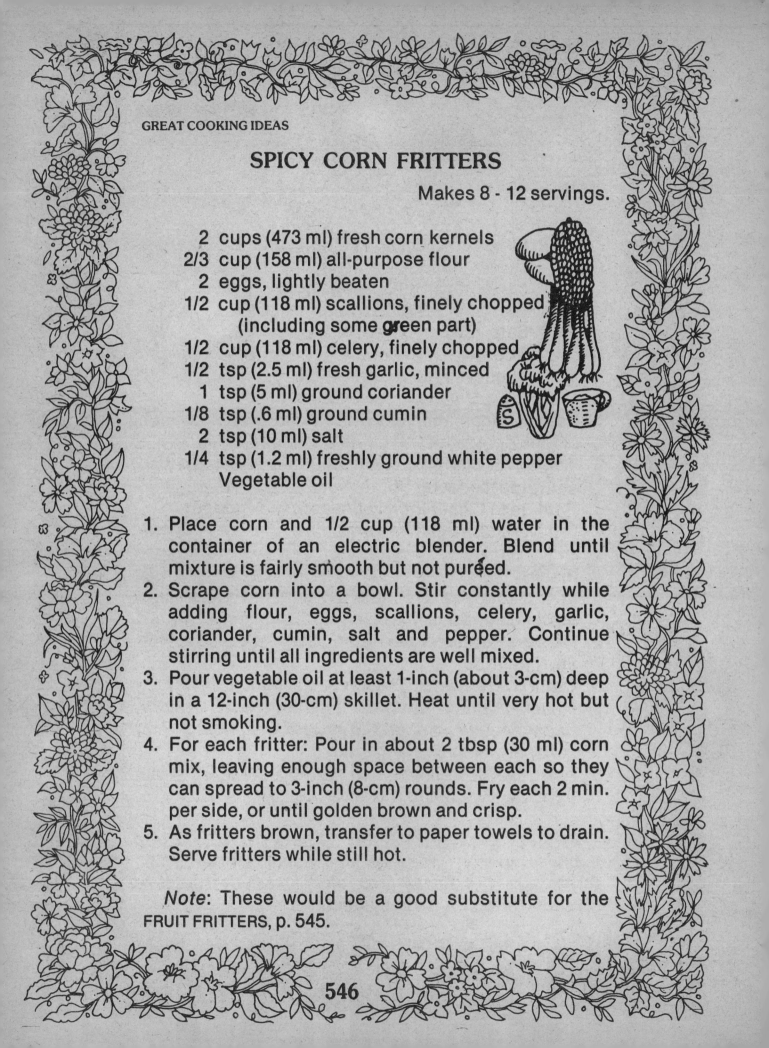

- 2 cups (473 ml) fresh corn kernels
- 2/3 cup (158 ml) all-purpose flour
- 2 eggs, lightly beaten
- 1/2 cup (118 ml) scallions, finely chopped (including some green part)
- 1/2 cup (118 ml) celery, finely chopped
- 1/2 tsp (2.5 ml) fresh garlic, minced
- 1 tsp (5 ml) ground coriander
- 1/8 tsp (.6 ml) ground cumin
- 2 tsp (10 ml) salt
- 1/4 tsp (1.2 ml) freshly ground white pepper
- Vegetable oil

1. Place corn and 1/2 cup (118 ml) water in the container of an electric blender. Blend until mixture is fairly smooth but not puréed.
2. Scrape corn into a bowl. Stir constantly while adding flour, eggs, scallions, celery, garlic, coriander, cumin, salt and pepper. Continue stirring until all ingredients are well mixed.
3. Pour vegetable oil at least 1-inch (about 3-cm) deep in a 12-inch (30-cm) skillet. Heat until very hot but not smoking.
4. For each fritter: Pour in about 2 tbsp (30 ml) corn mix, leaving enough space between each so they can spread to 3-inch (8-cm) rounds. Fry each 2 min. per side, or until golden brown and crisp.
5. As fritters brown, transfer to paper towels to drain. Serve fritters while still hot.

Note: These would be a good substitute for the FRUIT FRITTERS, p. 545.

OYSTER DRESSING

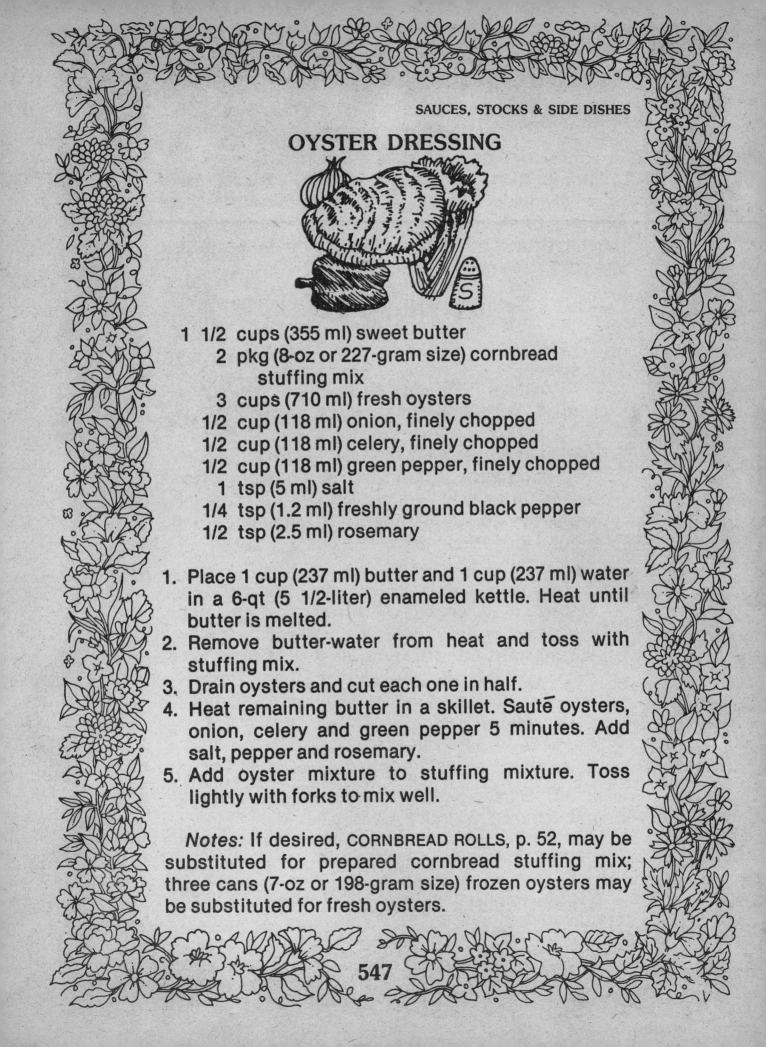

1 1/2 cups (355 ml) sweet butter
2 pkg (8-oz or 227-gram size) cornbread stuffing mix
3 cups (710 ml) fresh oysters
1/2 cup (118 ml) onion, finely chopped
1/2 cup (118 ml) celery, finely chopped
1/2 cup (118 ml) green pepper, finely chopped
1 tsp (5 ml) salt
1/4 tsp (1.2 ml) freshly ground black pepper
1/2 tsp (2.5 ml) rosemary

1. Place 1 cup (237 ml) butter and 1 cup (237 ml) water in a 6-qt (5 1/2-liter) enameled kettle. Heat until butter is melted.
2. Remove butter-water from heat and toss with stuffing mix.
3. Drain oysters and cut each one in half.
4. Heat remaining butter in a skillet. Sauté oysters, onion, celery and green pepper 5 minutes. Add salt, pepper and rosemary.
5. Add oyster mixture to stuffing mixture. Toss lightly with forks to mix well.

Notes: If desired, CORNBREAD ROLLS, p. 52, may be substituted for prepared cornbread stuffing mix; three cans (7-oz or 198-gram size) frozen oysters may be substituted for fresh oysters.

SHRIMP PUFFS

Shrimp puffs, chips or wafers *(krupuk)* were originally made in Indonesia from tapioca flour mixed with fish or shrimp and spices, then steamed, cut in thin slices and dried. Now they are made in the U.S. and sold in Chinese grocery stores.

FRIED SHRIMP PUFFS

Makes 4 servings.

2 cups (473 ml) vegetable oil
1/4 lb (113 grams) shrimp puffs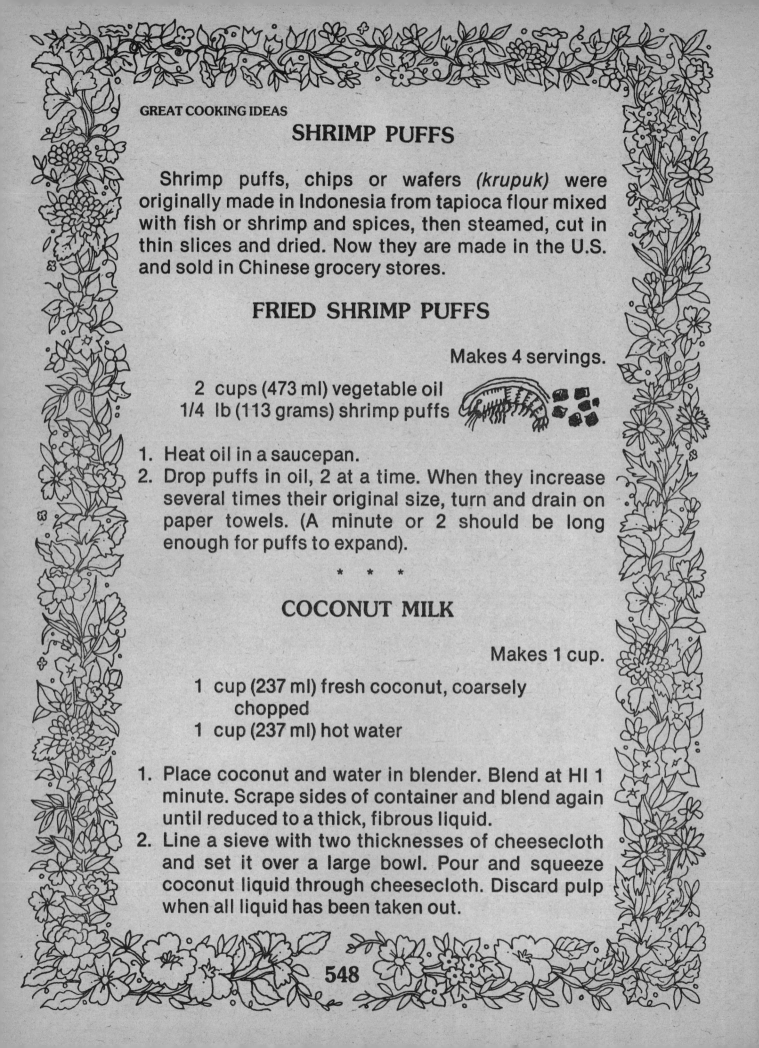

1. Heat oil in a saucepan.
2. Drop puffs in oil, 2 at a time. When they increase several times their original size, turn and drain on paper towels. (A minute or 2 should be long enough for puffs to expand).

* * *

COCONUT MILK

Makes 1 cup.

1 cup (237 ml) fresh coconut, coarsely
    chopped
1 cup (237 ml) hot water

1. Place coconut and water in blender. Blend at HI 1 minute. Scrape sides of container and blend again until reduced to a thick, fibrous liquid.
2. Line a sieve with two thicknesses of cheesecloth and set it over a large bowl. Pour and squeeze coconut liquid through cheesecloth. Discard pulp when all liquid has been taken out.

CURRIED CURDS AND WHEY

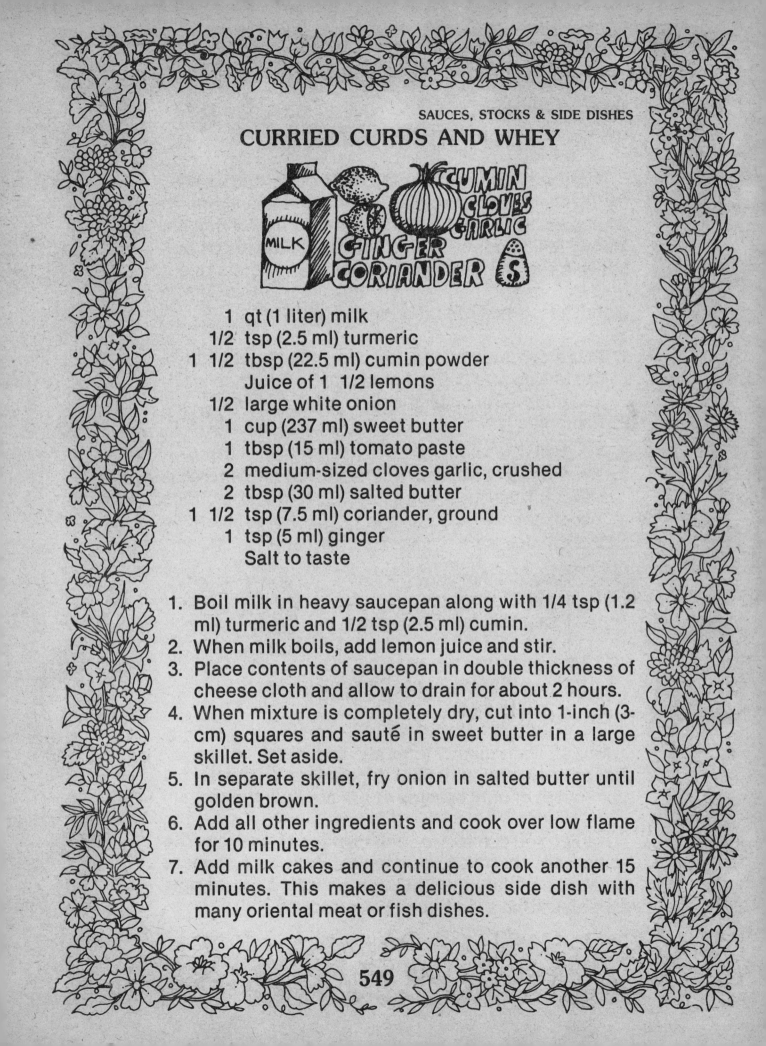

1	qt (1 liter) milk
1/2	tsp (2.5 ml) turmeric
1 1/2	tbsp (22.5 ml) cumin powder
	Juice of 1 1/2 lemons
1/2	large white onion
1	cup (237 ml) sweet butter
1	tbsp (15 ml) tomato paste
2	medium-sized cloves garlic, crushed
2	tbsp (30 ml) salted butter
1 1/2	tsp (7.5 ml) coriander, ground
1	tsp (5 ml) ginger
	Salt to taste

1. Boil milk in heavy saucepan along with 1/4 tsp (1.2 ml) turmeric and 1/2 tsp (2.5 ml) cumin.
2. When milk boils, add lemon juice and stir.
3. Place contents of saucepan in double thickness of cheese cloth and allow to drain for about 2 hours.
4. When mixture is completely dry, cut into 1-inch (3-cm) squares and sauté in sweet butter in a large skillet. Set aside.
5. In separate skillet, fry onion in salted butter until golden brown.
6. Add all other ingredients and cook over low flame for 10 minutes.
7. Add milk cakes and continue to cook another 15 minutes. This makes a delicious side dish with many oriental meat or fish dishes.

HOW TO PREPARE *POI*

If you are curious about the taste of *poi* and want to try it, check the specialty (gourmet) food shops in your area. It is sold bottled, canned and/or frozen. Many "Mainlanders" have romantic ideas about *poi*, but it is definitely an acquired taste. Try to sample it first before you plan a meal integrating this exotic dish. The method of preparing *poi* follows:

1. Place contents of can, bottle or freezer bag in the top of a double boiler. Let steam until soft, smooth and sticky. Stir occasionally.
2. Place in a bowl. Pour enough water on surface of *poi* to prevent crust from forming. Cover.
3. Chill thoroughly and serve cold.

* * *

TOASTED NUTS

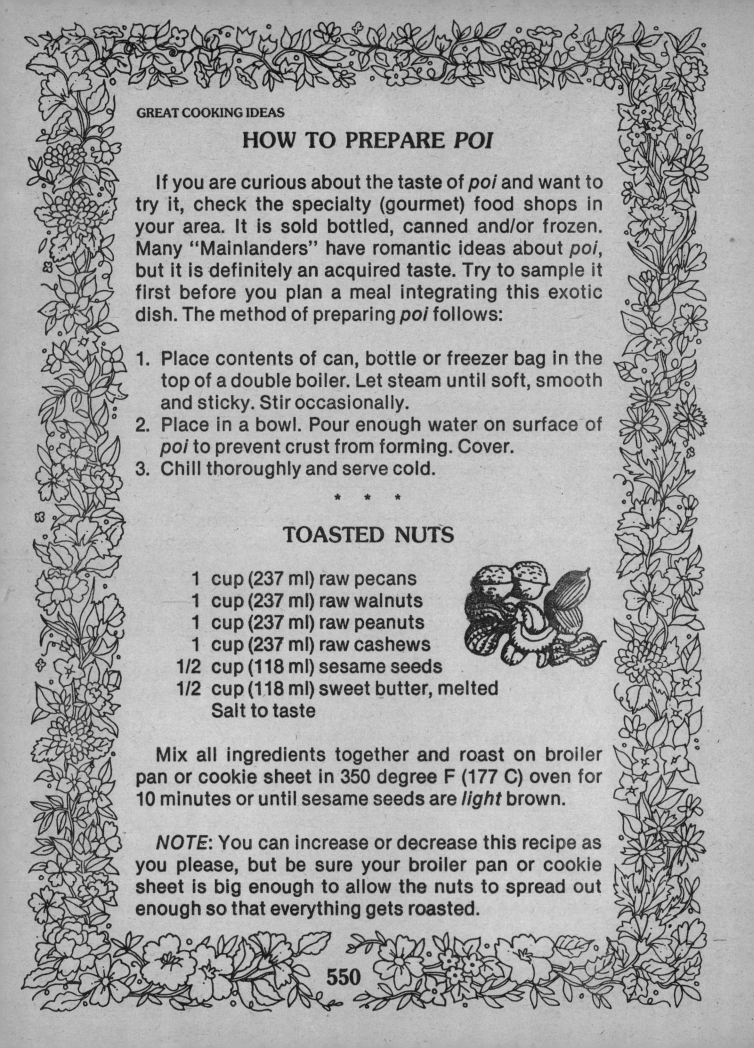

    1 cup (237 ml) raw pecans
    1 cup (237 ml) raw walnuts
    1 cup (237 ml) raw peanuts
    1 cup (237 ml) raw cashews
  1/2 cup (118 ml) sesame seeds
  1/2 cup (118 ml) sweet butter, melted
    Salt to taste

Mix all ingredients together and roast on broiler pan or cookie sheet in 350 degree F (177 C) oven for 10 minutes or until sesame seeds are *light* brown.

NOTE: You can increase or decrease this recipe as you please, but be sure your broiler pan or cookie sheet is big enough to allow the nuts to spread out enough so that everything gets roasted.

GRANOLA

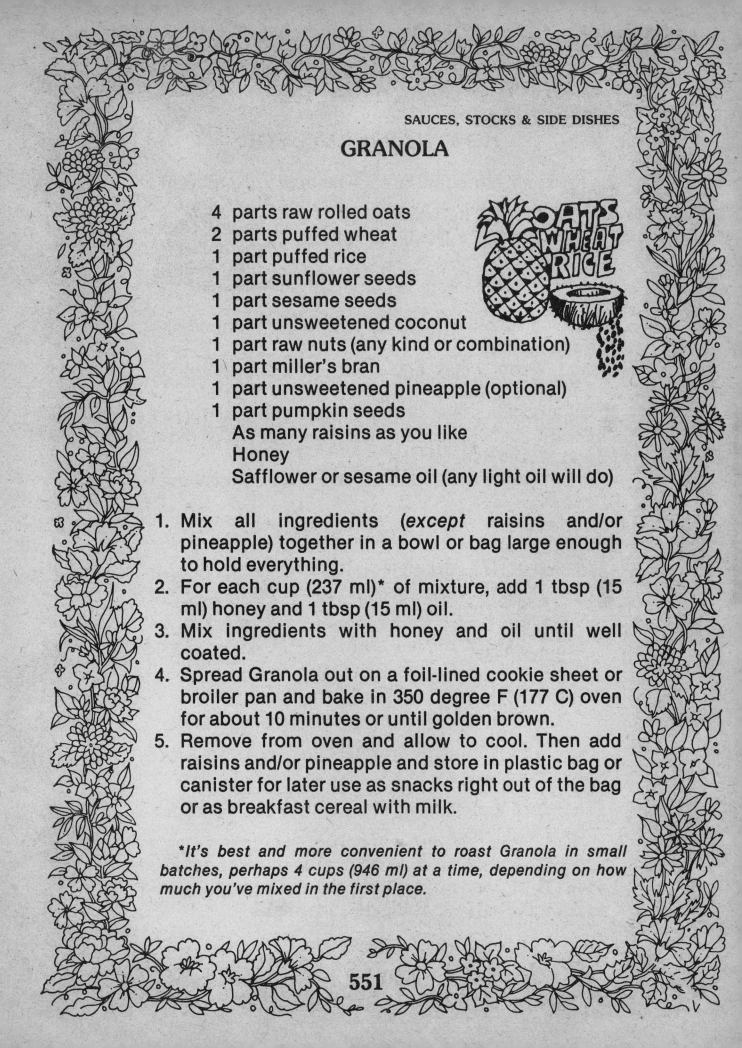

4 parts raw rolled oats
2 parts puffed wheat
1 part puffed rice
1 part sunflower seeds
1 part sesame seeds
1 part unsweetened coconut
1 part raw nuts (any kind or combination)
1 part miller's bran
1 part unsweetened pineapple (optional)
1 part pumpkin seeds
   As many raisins as you like
   Honey
   Safflower or sesame oil (any light oil will do)

1. Mix all ingredients (*except* raisins and/or pineapple) together in a bowl or bag large enough to hold everything.
2. For each cup (237 ml)* of mixture, add 1 tbsp (15 ml) honey and 1 tbsp (15 ml) oil.
3. Mix ingredients with honey and oil until well coated.
4. Spread Granola out on a foil-lined cookie sheet or broiler pan and bake in 350 degree F (177 C) oven for about 10 minutes or until golden brown.
5. Remove from oven and allow to cool. Then add raisins and/or pineapple and store in plastic bag or canister for later use as snacks right out of the bag or as breakfast cereal with milk.

It's best and more convenient to roast Granola in small batches, perhaps 4 cups (946 ml) at a time, depending on how much you've mixed in the first place.

PIZZA

Crust:

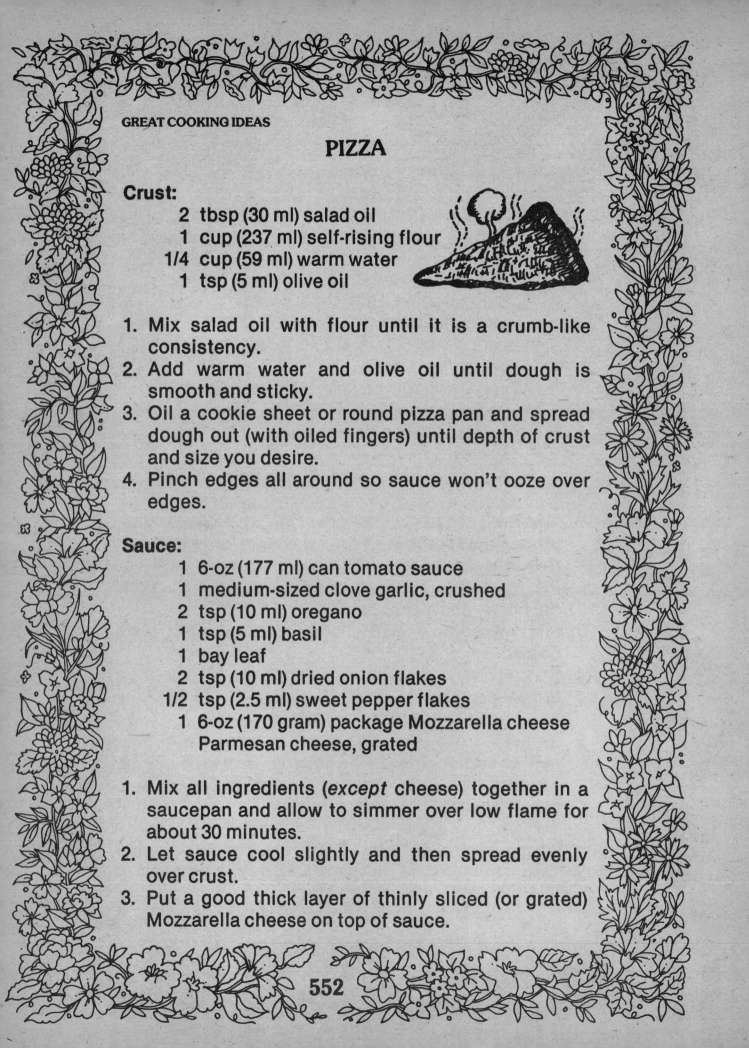

        2 tbsp (30 ml) salad oil
        1 cup (237 ml) self-rising flour
    1/4 cup (59 ml) warm water
        1 tsp (5 ml) olive oil

1. Mix salad oil with flour until it is a crumb-like consistency.
2. Add warm water and olive oil until dough is smooth and sticky.
3. Oil a cookie sheet or round pizza pan and spread dough out (with oiled fingers) until depth of crust and size you desire.
4. Pinch edges all around so sauce won't ooze over edges.

Sauce:

        1 6-oz (177 ml) can tomato sauce
        1 medium-sized clove garlic, crushed
        2 tsp (10 ml) oregano
        1 tsp (5 ml) basil
        1 bay leaf
        2 tsp (10 ml) dried onion flakes
    1/2 tsp (2.5 ml) sweet pepper flakes
        1 6-oz (170 gram) package Mozzarella cheese
           Parmesan cheese, grated

1. Mix all ingredients (*except* cheese) together in a saucepan and allow to simmer over low flame for about 30 minutes.
2. Let sauce cool slightly and then spread evenly over crust.
3. Put a good thick layer of thinly sliced (or grated) Mozzarella cheese on top of sauce.

Toppings:

You can put almost anything on top of a pizza in any combination and in the amount you like. Some suggestions follow:

> Sausage (link or patties), brown lightly first
> Salami
> Pepperoni
> Anchovies
> Ham
> Olives
> Onions
> Banana Peppers
> Mushrooms
> Tomatoes

4. Top everything with a good sprinkling of grated Parmesan cheese and bake in 450 degree F (232 C) oven for 20 minutes or until cheese begins to bubble and crust is light brown.

NOTES

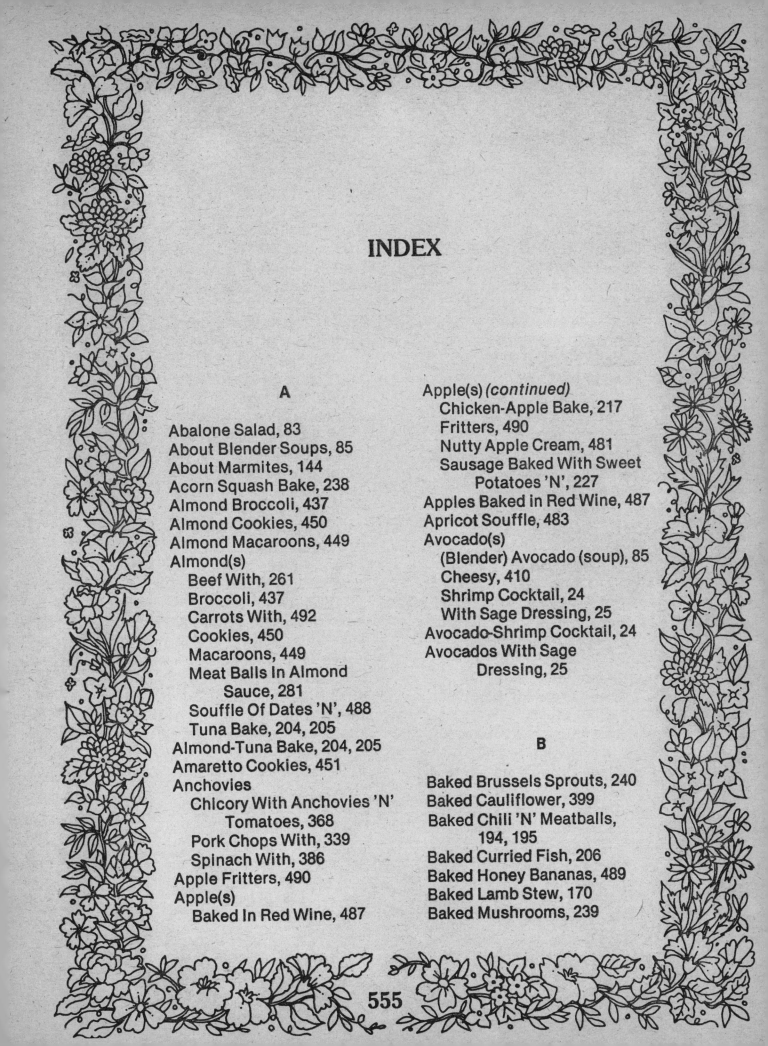

INDEX

Cabbage — Cheese

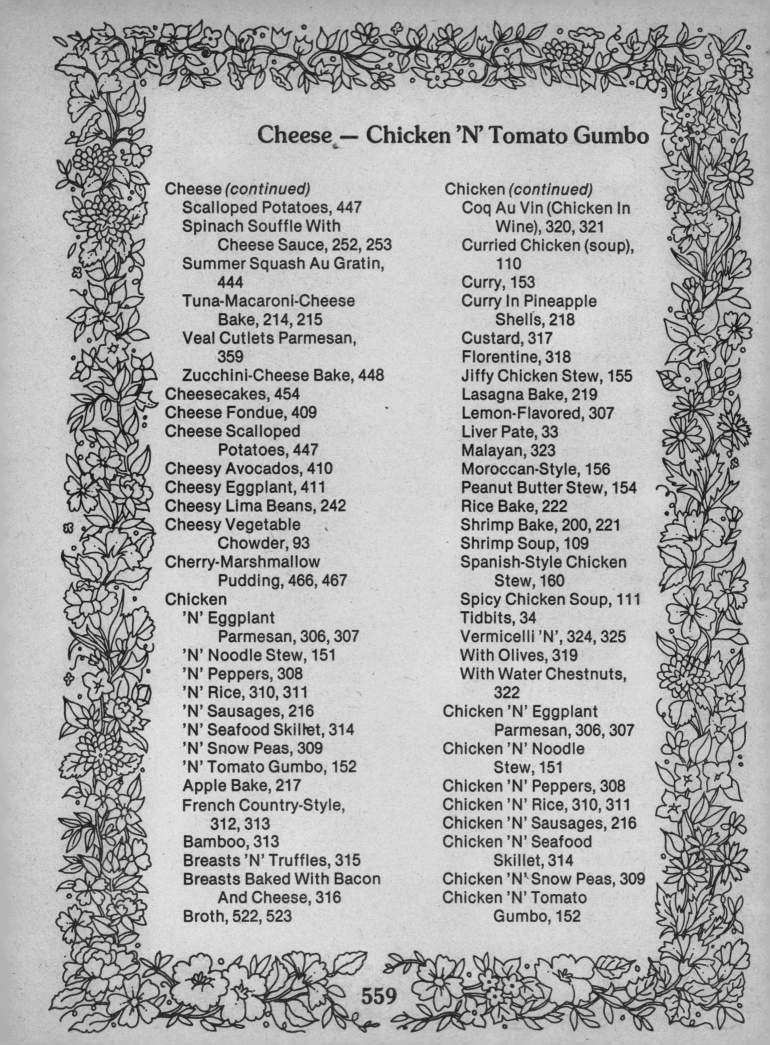

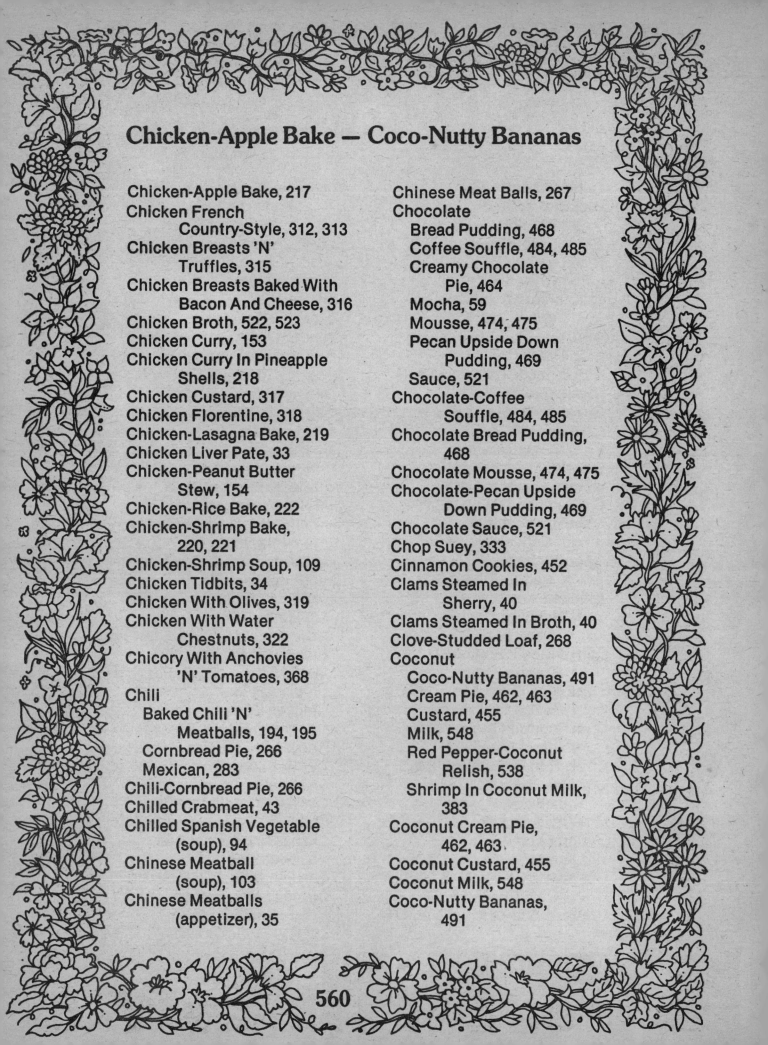

Chicken-Apple Bake — Coco-Nutty Bananas

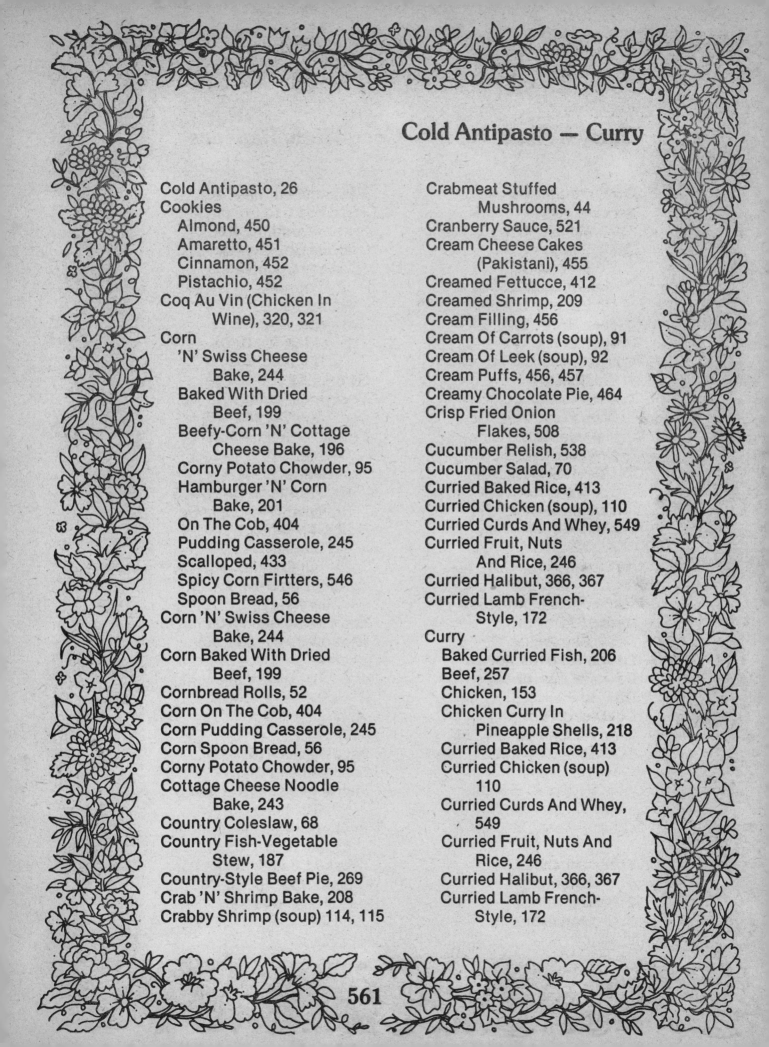

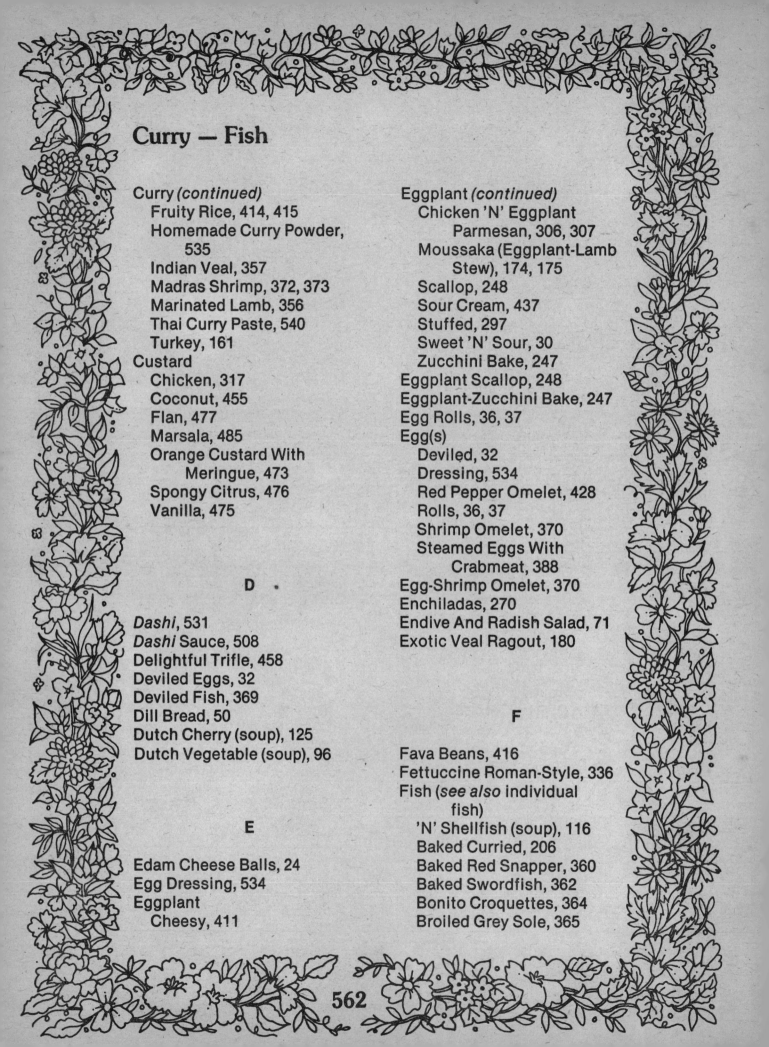

Curry — Fish

562

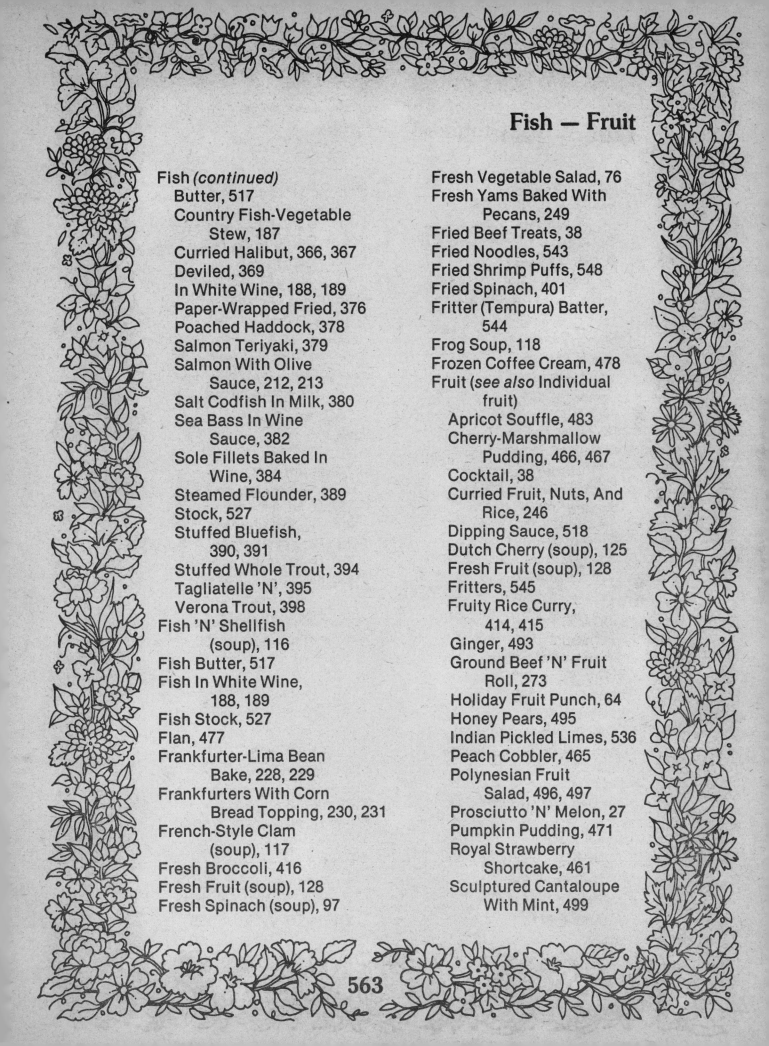

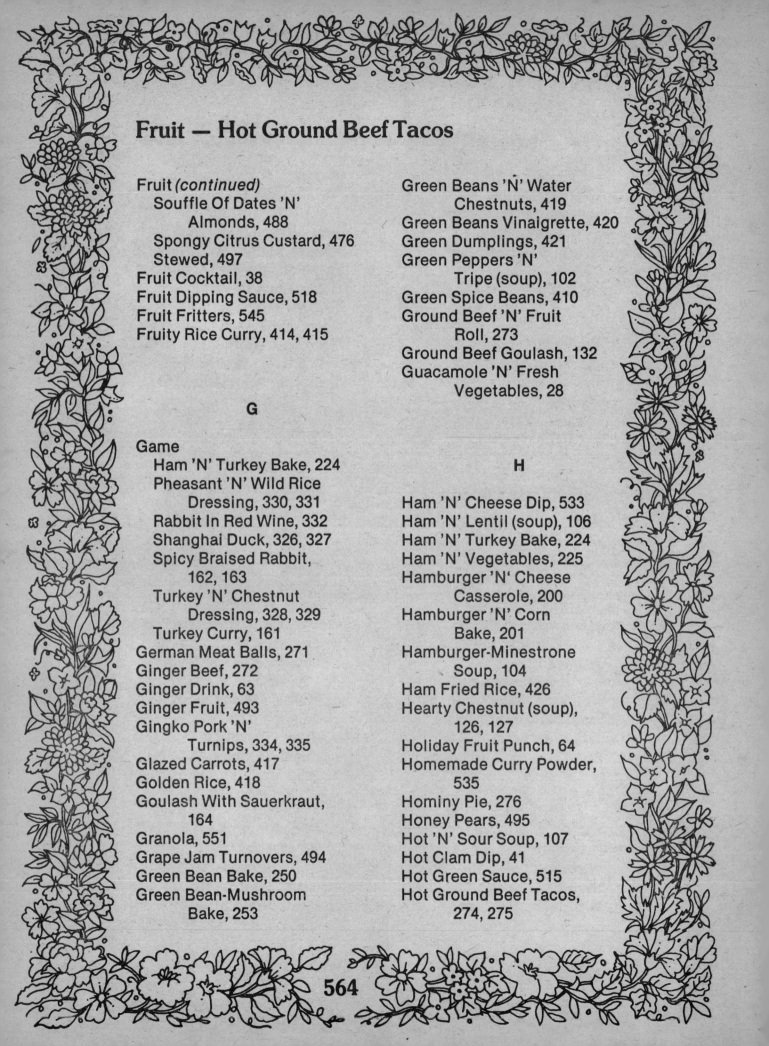

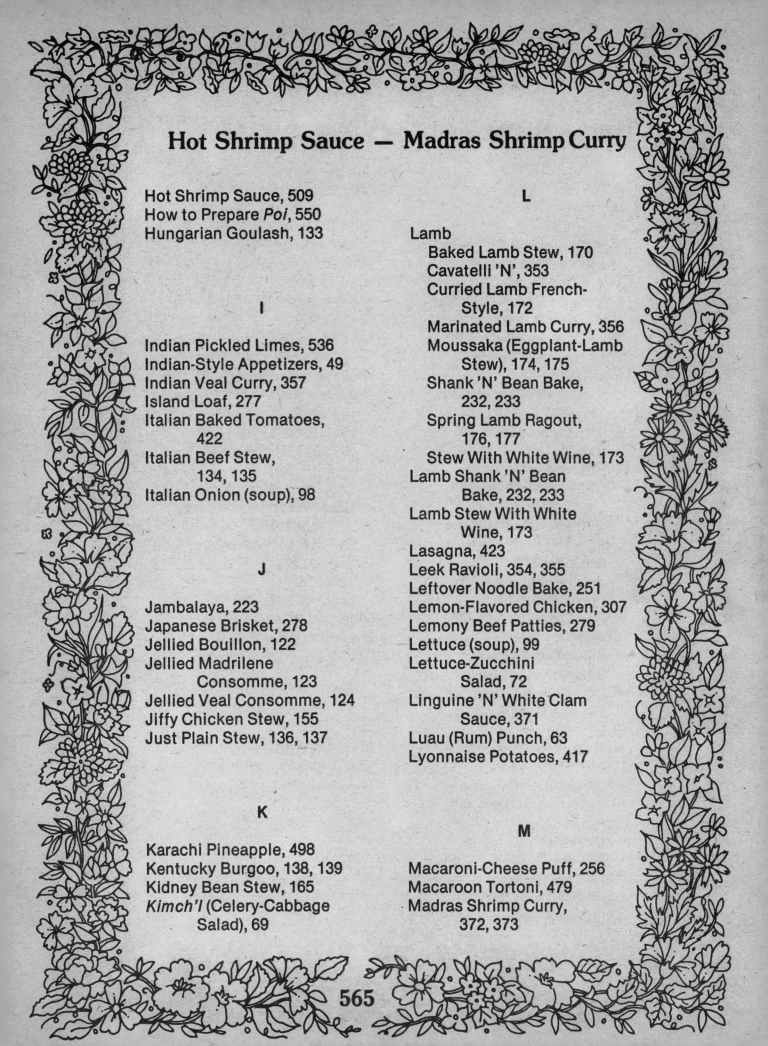

Hot Shrimp Sauce — Madras Shrimp Curry

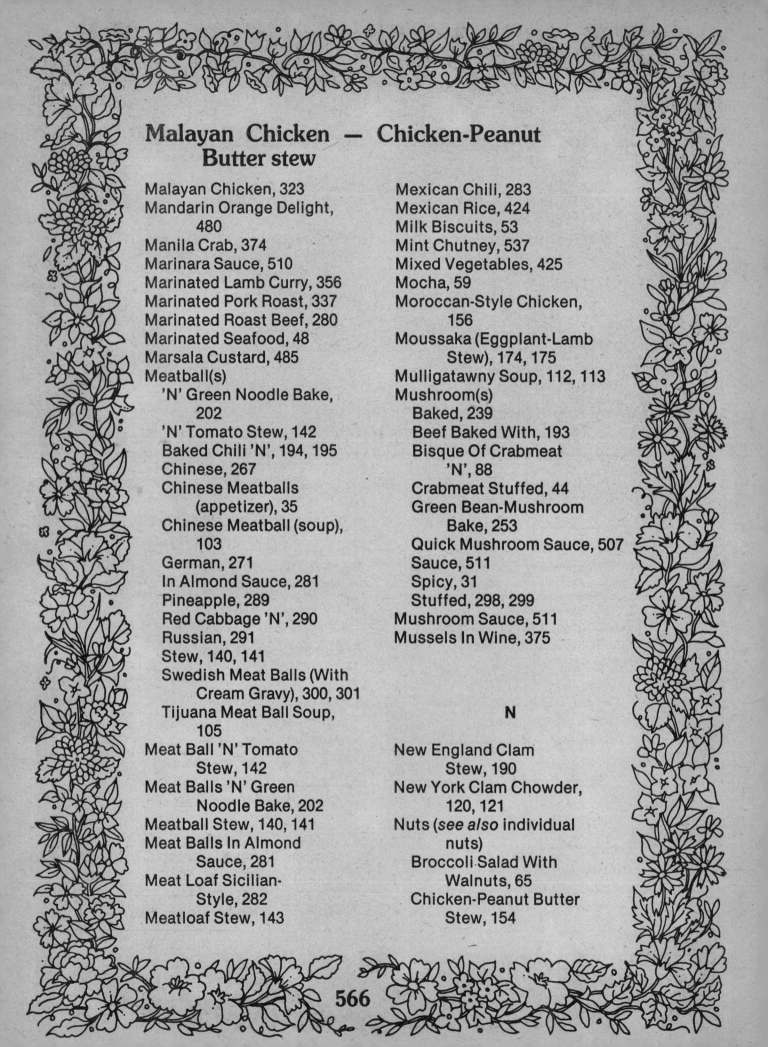

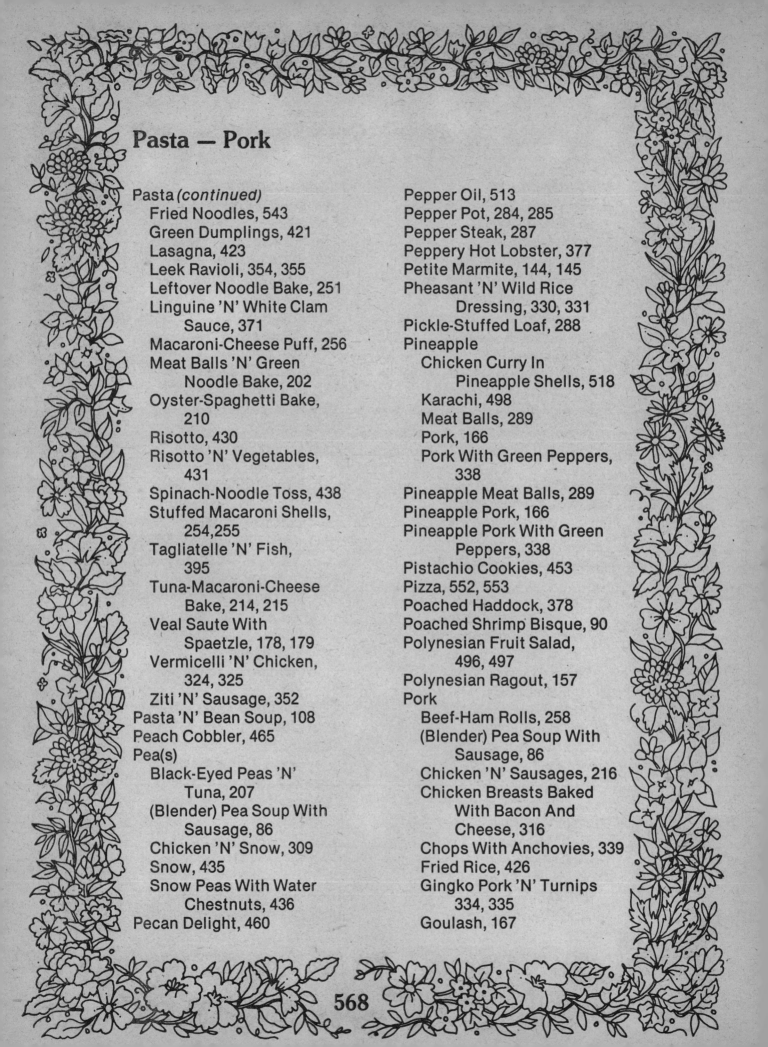

Pasta — Pork

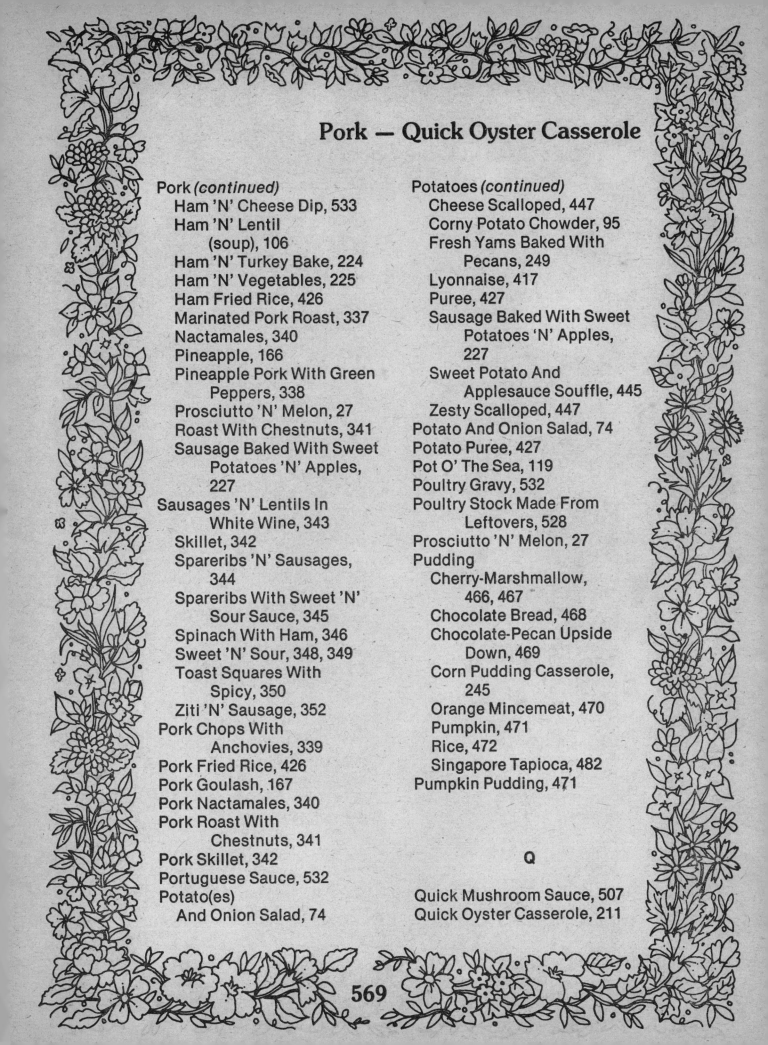

Veal — Zucchini With Oil And Lemon

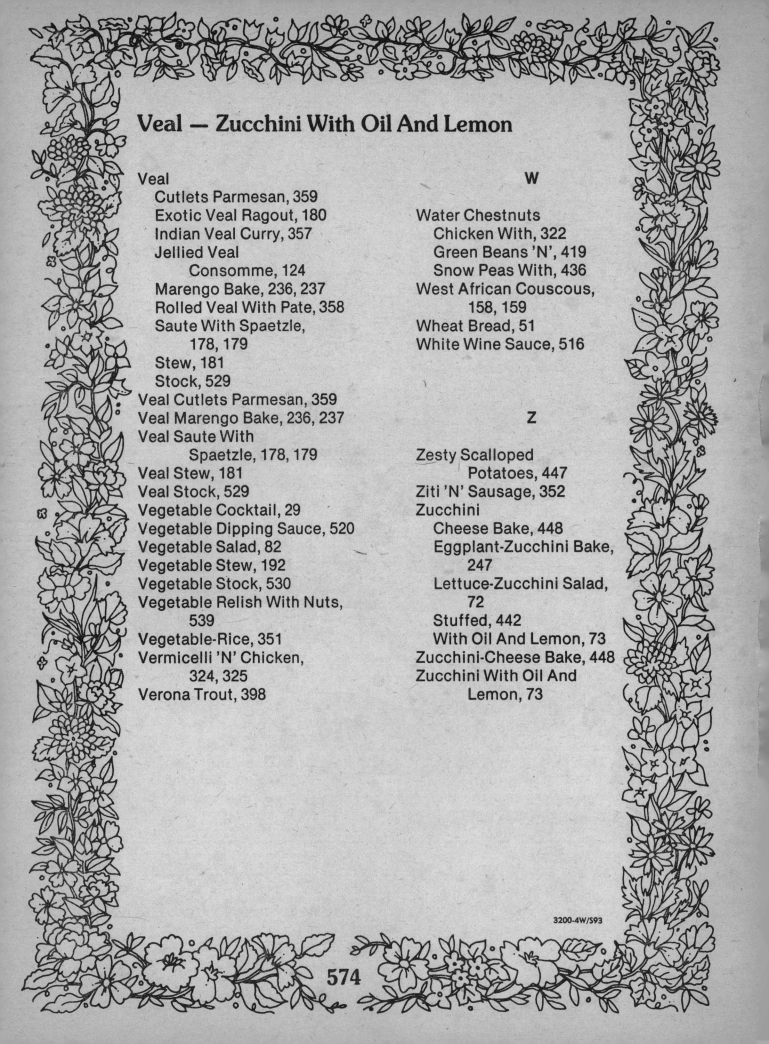

3200-4W/S93